BARRON'S

GRE®

GRADUATE RECORD EXAMINATION

17TH EDITION

Sharon Weiner Green
Former Instructor of English

Ira K. Wolf, Ph.D.
President, PowerPrep, Inc.
Former Professor of Mathematics
Former Director of University Teacher Preparation Program

BARRON'S

® GRE is a registered trademark of Educational Testing Service, which was not involved in the production of and does not endorse this book.

All inquiries should be addressed to:
Barron's Educational Series, Inc.
250 Wireless Boulevard
Hauppauge, New York 11788
www.barronseduc.com

Library of Congress Catalog Card Number 2007011558

ISBN-13: 978-0-7641-3541-5
ISBN-10: 0-7641-3541-4

ISBN-13: 978-0-7641-7949-5 (with CD-ROM)
ISBN-10: 0-7641-7949-7 (with CD-ROM)

Library of Congress Cataloging-in-Publication Data
Green, Sharon, 1939–
     GRE : graduate record examination / Sharon Weiner Green,
Ira K. Wolf.—17th ed.
     p.   cm.
Rev. ed. of: How to prepare for the GRE. 16th ed. 2005
Includes index.
ISBN-13: 978-0-7641-3541-5 (alk. paper)
ISBN-10: 0-7641-3541-4 (alk. paper)
ISBN-13: 978-0-7641-7949-5
ISBN-10: 0-7641-7949-7
     1. Graduate Record Examination—Study guides. I. Wolf,
Ira K. II. Green, Sharon, 1939– How to prepare for the
GRE. III. Title. IV. Title: Graduate record examinaiton.

LB2367.4.G747   2007
378.1'662—dc22   2007011558

Contents

Acknowledgments

The authors gratefully acknowledge the following for permission to reprint reading passages.

Page 27: Wilcomb E. Washburn, *The Indian in America*. Copyright © 1975. Reprinted with permission of HarperCollins Publishers, Inc.

Page 91: Ladislas Segy, "African Sculpture Speaks," Dover Publications, New York 1958. By permission of Helena Segy.

Page 93: From *The Uses of Enchantment*, by Bruno Bettelheim. Copyright © 1975, 1976 by Bruno Bettelheim. Reprinted with the permission of his heirs and their agents, Raines & Raines.

Page 94: Excerpt from *Geoffrey Chaucer* by John Livingston Lowes. Copyright © 1934, renewed 1955, by John Wilbur Lowes. With permission of Houghton Mifflin Co.

Page 98: From *Black Americans in the Roosevelt Era* by John B. Kirby. Copyright 1980, University of Tennessee Press.

Page 104: From *The Madwoman in the Attic* by Sandra M. Gilbert and Susan Gubar, © 1979 by Yale University Press, publisher.

Page 443: Elaine Showalter, *A Literature of Their Own: British Women Novelists from Brontë to Lessing*. Copyright © 1977 by Princeton University Press. Excerpt, pp. 10–12 reprinted with permission of Princeton University Press.

Page 462: From "W.E.B. Du Bois: Protagonist of the Afro-American Protest" by Elliot Rudwick, in *Black Leaders of the Twentieth Century*, edited by John Hope Franklin and August Meier. Copyright 1982, University of Illinois Press.

Page 504: From *Literary Women: The Great Writers* by Ellen Moers. Copyright © 1976, 1977 by Ellen Moers. Used by permission of Doubleday, a division of Bantam Doubleday Dell Publishing Group Inc.

Page 506: From *Eyes on the Prize: Civil Rights Years*, edited by Clayborne Carson et al. Copyright © 1987 by Penguin Books. Blackside, Inc. 1991, with permission.

Page 524: From *The English Novel: Form and Function* by Dorothy Van Ghent. Copyright © 1953. Reprinted with permission of Heinle, a division of Thomson Learning.

Page 525: From *Black History and the Historical Profession, 1915–1980* by August Meier and Elliot Rudwick. Copyright 1986, University of Illinois Press. Used with permission of the University of Illinois Press.

Preface

As prospective graduate students concerned with professional advancement, you know the importance of using good tools and drawing on solid research. In this Seventeenth Edition of *Barron's GRE*, we offer you both.

This revision contains the fruits of our close study of the major changes in the GRE General Tests made public by the Graduate Record Examinations Board. We have scrutinized hundreds of actual GRE questions, traced dozens of GRE reading passages to their sources, analyzed subsets of questions by order of difficulty and question type. We have gone through all the topics in the new analytical writing section, categorizing the actual issues you will encounter on your test and analyzing the argument passages, pinpointing their logical flaws. In the process, we have come up with the following features, which should make this Seventeenth Edition particularly helpful to you:

Typical GRE Questions Analyzed

The Seventeenth Edition takes you step by step through dozens of verbal and mathematical questions that simulate actual GRE questions, showing you how to solve them and how to avoid going wrong.

Testing Tactics

The Seventeenth Edition provides you with dozens of proven, highlighted testing tactics that will help you attack the different types of questions on the GRE.

High-Frequency Word List

The Seventeenth Edition continues to give you an up-to-date 333-word High-Frequency Word List—333 words from *abate* to *zealot* that have been shown by computer analysis to occur and recur on actual published GREs—plus Barron's 3,500-word Master Word List, *the* college-level vocabulary list for over 40 years.

Comprehensive Mathematics Review

The Seventeenth Edition presents you with extensive mathematical review materials that provide a refresher course for students primarily involved in nonscientific disciplines.

GRE-Modeled Tests

The Seventeenth Edition offers you a full-length Diagnostic Test geared to the current GRE, a diagnostic test that will enable you to pinpoint your areas of weakness right away and concentrate your review on subjects in which you need the most work, plus five additional Model Tests, all with answers completely explained, that in format, difficulty, and content echo today's GRE.

Computer GRE Update

The Seventeenth Edition introduces you to the computer-based GRE—and, along with the accompanying CD-ROM (optional), explains everything you need to know about the computer-adaptive GRE.

Analytical Writing Update

The Seventeenth Edition also provides you with an introduction to the GRE analytical writing section, familiarizing you with the range of topics covered and giving you helpful hints on how to write clear, cogent essays in no time at all.

This Seventeenth Edition once more upgrades what has long been a standard text. It reflects the contributions of numerous teachers, editors, and coaches, and the dedication of the staff at Barron's. It also reflects the forensic and rhetorical skills of Lexy Green, Director of Debate at the College Preparatory School, to whom we owe special thanks. We, the authors, are indebted to all these individuals for their ongoing efforts to make this book America's outstanding GRE study guide.

TIMETABLE FOR A TYPICAL COMPUTER-BASED GRADUATE RECORD EXAMINATION

Total Testing Time: 2 hours and 30 minutes

Section	Time Allowed	Description
	variable	*Tutorial*
1	30 minutes	*Verbal Ability* 6 sentence completion questions 7 analogy questions 8 reading comprehension questions 9 antonym questions
2	45 minutes	*Quantitative Ability* 14 quantitative comparison questions 10 discrete quantitative (standard multiple-choice) questions 4 data interpretation questions (tables/graphs)
		10-minute break
3	75 minutes	
	45 minutes	Analytical Writing: 1 essay giving one's perspective on an issue
	30 minutes	Analytical Writing: 1 essay analyzing an argument

PART ONE

Introduction/ Diagnostic Test

1 What You Need to Know About the GRE

- **An Overview of the GRE General Test**
- **Commonly Asked Questions About the GRE**
- **GRE Test Format**
  Verbal Ability
  Quantitative Ability
  Analytical Ability

An Overview of the Computer-Based GRE General Test

The GRE General Test is an examination designed to measure the verbal, quantitative, and analytical writing skills you have developed in the course of your academic career. High GRE scores strongly correlate with the probability of success in graduate school: the higher you score, the more likely you are to complete your graduate degree. For this reason, many graduate and professional schools require applicants to take the GRE General Test, a test now given only on computer. (They may also require you to take a GRE Subject Test in your particular field. Subject Tests currently are available in 14 fields.)

The computer-based GRE General Test you take will have three or four sections. There will always be

- a 30-question verbal section (30 minutes)

- a 28-question quantitative section (45 minutes)

- an analytical writing section composed of two tasks (75 minutes)

In addition, there may be

- an unidentified experimental section, which would be a second verbal or quantitative section

Occasionally there may be

- an identified optional research section

The verbal section measures your ability to use words as tools in reasoning; you are tested not only on the extent of your vocabulary but on your ability to discern the relationships that exist both within written passages and among individual groups of words. The quantitative section measures your ability to use and reason with numbers or mathematical concepts; you are tested not on advanced mathematical theory but on general concepts expected to be part of everyone's academic background. The analytical writing section measures your ability to make rational assessments about unfamiliar, fictitious relationships and to logically present your perspective on an issue.

There are four very important points you should be aware of:

1. In each multiple-choice section, before you can move from one question to the next, you *must* answer the question currently on the screen.

2. Once you have clicked on an answer and confirmed your choice, you *cannot* go back to that question and change your answer choice.

3. Not every question is worth the same number of points; harder questions are worth more than easy ones.

4. The GRE General Test does *not* penalize you for incorrect answers. When you don't know an answer, try to make an educated guess by eliminating clearly incorrect choices; if you can't eliminate any choices, make a wild guess, and move on.

Keep these points in mind as you learn more about what's on the computer-based test, and, in the next chapter, about the tactics and strategies that will help you maximize your test score.

Commonly Asked Questions About the Computer-Based GRE

How Does the GRE Differ from Other Tests?

Most tests college students take are straightforward achievement tests. They attempt to find out how much you have learned, usually in a specific subject, and how well you can apply that information. Without emphasizing memorized data, the GRE General Test attempts to measure verbal, quantitative, and analytical writing skills that you have acquired over the years both in and out of school.

Although the GRE General Test is claimed to measure skills that you have developed over a long period, even a brief period of intensive study can make a great difference in your eventual GRE scores. By thoroughly familiarizing yourself with the process of computer-based testing, the GRE test format, and the various question types, you can enhance your chances of doing well on the test and of being accepted by the graduate school of your choice.

How Can I Learn to Handle the Mechanics of Taking a Computer-Based Test?

By using the CD-ROM that accompanies this book, you will become familiar with everything you need to know. In addition, at the test site before you get to the actual computer-based GRE, you have to work through four tutorials that train you in the mechanics of taking this particular test. They are

- How to Use a Mouse
- How to Select an Answer
- How to Use the Testing Tools
- How to Scroll

You can't skip these tutorials; they're mandatory, even for computer majors. They're also important—every computer program has its idiosyncrasies, and you need to familiarize yourself with how to handle this particular computer setup.

Plan to take your time on these tutorials, and don't worry about how much time you're taking. The 20 to 30 minutes you spend working through the tutorials *before* you begin testing don't count against your time for taking the test. You can even use this free time to organize your scratch paper before you begin the actual timed test. (More on setting up your scratch paper later.)

What Is It Like to Take a Computer-Based GRE?

You sit in a carrel in a computer lab or testing center, facing a computer screen. You may be alone in the room, or other test-takers may be taking tests in nearby carrels. With your mouse, you click on an icon to start your test. A question appears on screen. You answer it, clicking on the oval next to your answer choice. Satisfied with your answer, you click on a box marked Confirm, to indicate you have no second thoughts about your choice. Then, ready to move on, you click on the box marked Next. A new question appears on screen, and you go through the process again.

This is what it is like to take a computerized GRE. At the end of the first section, you are given a one-minute break. After finishing the second section, you have a ten-minute break. The third section may include another one-minute break. (This is the most likely scenario; it's possible you may be instructed to answer a fourth experimental section.)

How Does Taking a Computer-Based Test Differ from Taking a Pencil-and-Paper Test?

On a pencil-and-paper standardized test, within any given section of your test booklet you are free to skip from question to question and to answer questions in any order you choose. If you do better on antonyms than on reading comprehension questions, for example, you can temporarily skip the time-consuming reading passages and go straight to the antonyms. Likewise, if you have second thoughts about a particular answer choice, on a pencil-and-paper test you can go back to the question, erase your original pencil mark, and select a different answer choice. You are also free to write in your test booklet, crossing out incorrect answer choices, underlining key words, and highlighting questions you need to reconsider.

On a computer-based test (CBT), there is no test booklet. Your test questions appear, one at a time, on your computer screen. You must answer the question currently on the screen and confirm that you are sure of your answer choice before you can move on to the next question. Once you have confirmed your answer choice and moved on, you cannot go back and change it.

In addition, on the CBT, questions are not arranged in groups according to question type: two analogy questions may follow two antonyms; they may in turn be followed by a single sentence completion. You cannot predict what type of question will come up next.

Why Do Some People Call the Computer-Based General Test a CAT?

CAT stands for Computer-Adaptive Test. What does this mean?

When you take a pencil-and-paper test, the questions in the test booklet you receive are basically the same as the questions printed in every other booklet distributed to test-takers on that day. When you take a computer-based GRE

General Test, however, the questions you face on screen are likely to differ markedly from those that come up on the screens of the test-takers in the carrels next to you.

Why will your test be different from someone else's test? Because the CBT GRE is a computer-adaptive test. The test adapts to your skill level: it is customized.

How does this work? The computer program begins by assuming you are the "average" GRE candidate, an imaginary figure whose score would place him or her precisely in the middle of the entire test-taking population. The computer program contains a pool of some 1,000 questions organized by content, question type, and level of difficulty. From this pool the computer selects a math question of medium difficulty, a question the average GRE candidate (someone who would wind up in the 50th percentile of test-takers with a Quantitative score of 550) would be likely to get correct. If you answer this question correctly, the computer revises its estimate of your eventual score upward and proceeds to give you a slightly harder question, one that a student scoring 600 should get correct. However, if you answer that question incorrectly, the computer again revises its estimate of your eventual score—*downward* this time, and you are presented with an easier question, one that a student scoring 500 might get correct. Thus, as you answer each question, the computer adapts your test, tailoring it to reflect your previous performance. In the process, it fine-tunes its estimate of your skill level, gradually zeroing in on your eventual score.

Can I Tell How Well I'm Doing on the Test from the Questions the Computer Assigns Me?

Don't even try; it never pays to try to second-guess the computer. There's no point in wasting time and energy wondering whether it's feeding you harder questions or easier ones. Let the computer keep track of how well you're doing—you concentrate on answering questions and pacing yourself.

Should I Guess?

Yes, you must! You are not going to know the correct answer to every question on the GRE. That's a given. But you can't just skip a question. In order to move on to the next question, you first *must* answer the question currently on screen, even if you haven't a clue as to what the correct answer might be. So if the question on screen has you stumped, eliminate any obviously incorrect answer choices, and then guess and don't worry whether you've guessed right or wrong. Your job is to get to the next question you *can* answer. Just remember to use the process of elimination to improve your guessing odds.

How Can I Use the Process of Elimination on a Computer-Based GRE?

Even though the current CBT GRE makes no provision for you to cross out incorrect answer choices on screen, you still can eliminate answers you *know* are wrong before guessing which of the remaining answer choices is correct. This is where your scratch paper comes in. Take a couple of minutes to write out four rough, scratch-paper answer sheets—one for each section. Use these answer sheets as your guessing guides. Before you guess, first cross out any choices on your answer sheet that you are *sure* are wrong. Then choose between the answer choices that are left. You'll increase your chances of coming up with the right answer by making this sort of "educated" guess.

Make use of your scratch paper throughout the test. In the verbal section, jot down key words or phrases from the reading passages. On the mathematics questions, use your scratch paper to draw diagrams and, of course, to do all of your calculations.

1 A B C D E	1 A B C D E
2 A B C D E	2 A B C D E
3 A B C D E	3 A B C D E
4 A B C D E	4 A B C D E
5 A B C D E	5 A B C D E
6 A B C D E	6 A B C D E
7 A B C D E	7 A B C D E
8 A B C D E	8 A B C D E
9 A B C D E	9 A B C D E
10 A B C D E	10 A B C D E
11 A B C D E	11 A B C D E
12 A B C D E	12 A B C D E
13 A B C D E	13 A B C D E
14 A B C D E	14 A B C D E
15 A B C D E	15 A B C D E
16 A B C D E	16 A B C D E
17 A B C D E	17 A B C D E
18 A B C D E	18 A B C D E
19 A B C D E	19 A B C D E
20 A B C D E	20 A B C D E
21 A B C D E	21 A B C D E
22 A B C D E	22 A B C D E
23 A B C D E	23 A B C D E
24 A B C D E	24 A B C D E
25 A B C D E	25 A B C D E
26 A B C D E	26 A B C D E
27 A B C D E	27 A B C D E
28 A B C D E	28 A B C D E
29 A B C D E	29 A B C D E
30 A B C D E	30 A B C D E

How Can I Determine the Unidentified Experimental Section?

You can't. Do not waste time in the exam room trying to identify the experimental section. If you are presented with extra sections, do your best on all of them. Some claim that most often the last section is the experimental section. Others claim that the section with unusual questions is the one that does not count. Ignore the claims: you have no sure way to tell. If you encounter a series of questions that seem strange to you, do your best. Either these are experimental and will not count, in which case you have no reason to worry about them, or they will count, in which case they probably will seem just as strange and trouble-some to your fellow examinees.

When and Where Can I Take the Computer-Based GRE?

You can take the computer-based GRE General Test almost any Monday through Saturday all year round. (Testing centers are closed on Christmas and New Year's Day and other major federal holidays.) Because appoint-ments are scheduled on a first-come, first-served basis, you should be sure to register early to get the date you want, especially if that date falls in the highly popular November through January testing period.

The computer-based GRE is administered at a variety of sites: Sylvan Technology Centers, Educational Testing Service (ETS) field offices, university testing centers, and other academic institutions. Test centers are located in all 50 states, in American Samoa, Guam, Puerto Rico, the U.S. Virgin Islands, and eight provinces of Canada. International test centers also exist: a list of them can be found on-line at *www.gre.org* or in the *GRE Registration and Information Bulletin*.

How Can I Register to Take the GRE?

If you have a credit card or CBT authorization voucher, you can register for the GRE over the phone. This is by far the fastest way. In the United States, American Samoa, Guam, the U.S. Virgin Islands, Puerto Rico, and Canada, contact the Sylvan Candidate Services Call Center at 1-800-GRE-CALL (1-800-473-2255). You can also register by calling your local test center directly. If you plan to take the GRE when abroad, contact the appropriate international Regional Registration Center, also listed on-line at *www.gre.org* as well as in the *Registration and Information Bulletin*.

You can also register by mail to take the GRE. Simply complete the Computer-Based Test Authorization Voucher request located in the center of the *Registration and Information Bulletin*. Then mail the completed form and a check or money order for the appropriate fee (currently $99; $125 for test locations outside the United States and U.S. territories) to Graduate Record Examinations, Educational Testing Service, P.O. Box 6020, Princeton, NJ 08541-6020. You will receive your authorization voucher in two to three weeks and can then call Sylvan Candidate Services to schedule your test date.

Your college counseling office should be able to provide you with a registration form. If a registration form is not available at your school, download one on-line at *www.gre.org* or request one by mail from Graduate Record Examinations, Educational Testing Service, CN 6000, Princeton, NJ 08541-6000.

How and When Are GRE Scores Reported?

The General Test raw score, the number of correct answers, is converted to a score on a scale of 200 to 800. With no correct answers at all, a student would still have a score of 200. With one or two incorrectly answered ques-tions, a student could still have a score of 800. You receive separate scores (from 200 to 800) on the verbal and quanti-tative sections. Your score report will include both your scaled scores and your percentile rank indicating the per-cent of examinees scoring below your scaled scores on the General Test.

Your analytical writing score will be the average of the scores assigned to your essays by two trained readers. These scores are rounded up to the nearest half-point. Your combined analytical writing score can vary from 0 to 6, with 6 the highest score possible.

As soon as you have finished taking the test, the computer will calculate your unofficial scaled scores for the verbal and quantitative sections and display them to you on the screen. Because your essays are sent to trained readers for holistic scoring, you will not receive a score for the analytical writing section on the day of the test. You should receive in the mail an official report containing all three scores approximately three weeks after the test date. (If you have chosen to handwrite your essays, you should allow up to six weeks for the official report to arrive.)

NOTE: Except in the analytical writing sections, every question on the GRE is a multiple-choice question with five choices—except for the quantitative comparisons, which have four choices. In this book, the choices are always labeled A, B, C, D, and E, and these letters are used in the Answer Keys and the explanations. On an actual GRE, these letters never appear on the screen. Rather, each choice is preceded by a blank oval, and you will answer a question by clicking with the mouse on the oval in front of your choice.

GRE Test Format Verbal Ability

The verbal section consists of 30 questions. These fall into four types: antonyms, analogies, sentence completions, and reading comprehension questions. Your academic success will depend on your verbal abilities, especially your ability to understand scholarly prose and to work with specialized and technical vocabulary.

Here is how the 30-question verbal section generally breaks down:

- 8–10 antonym questions
- 6–8 analogy questions
- 5–7 sentence completion questions
- 6–10 reading comprehension questions (based on two to four passages)

Although the amount of time spent on each type of question varies from person to person, in general, antonyms take the least time, then analogies, then sentence completions, and, finally, reading comprehension questions.

Antonym Questions

The antonym questions are the most straightforward vocabulary questions on the test. You are given a word and must choose, from the five choices that follow it, the best antonym (opposite). Some of these words may be totally unfamiliar to you.

A typical antonym question looks like this:

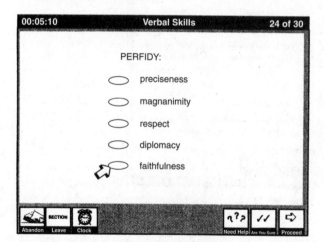

The word *perfidy* contains the root *fid*, meaning faith (as in *fidelity*). *Perfidy* means treachery, the betrayal of faith. Its opposite is *faithfulness*, the last choice given.

Even if you do not know the meaning of *perfidy*, if you know its root, you can guess that its antonym must be either a word meaning faith or loyalty, or a word opposite in meaning to faith, such as treachery or disloyalty. The only answer containing such a word is the final answer choice.

See Chapter 4 for antonym testing tactics and practice exercises that will help you handle these questions, and Chapter 8 for vocabulary and word-part exercises that will help you throughout the verbal section.

Analogy Questions

Like antonyms, analogy questions are vocabulary questions. They test your understanding of the relationships among words and ideas. You are given one pair of words and must choose another pair that is related in the same way. Many relationships are possible. The two terms in the pair can be synonyms; one term can be a cause, the other the effect; one can be a tool, the other the worker who uses the tool.

A typical analogy question looks like this:

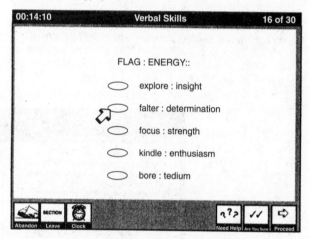

When energy flags, it weakens or grows less. Likewise when determination or resolve falters, it weakens or grows less. The correct answer is the second choice.

See Chapter 5 for analogy question tactics and practice exercises that will help you handle these questions.

Sentence Completion Questions

In the sentence completion questions you are asked to choose the best way to complete a sentence from which one or two words have been omitted. These questions test a combination of reading comprehension skills and vocabulary. You must be able to recognize the logic, style, and tone of the sentence so that you will be able to choose the answer that makes sense in context. You must also be able to recognize differences in usage. The sentences cover a wide variety of topics from a number of academic fields. They do not, however, test specific academic knowledge. You may feel more comfortable if you are familiar with the topic the sentence is discussing, but you should be able to handle any of the sentences using your knowledge of the English language.

Here is a typical sentence completion question.

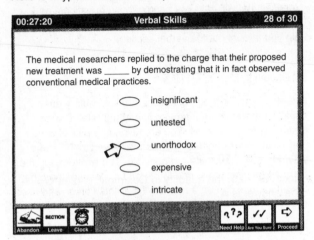

The medical researchers defend their new treatment by saying it follows accepted, conventional practices. What,

therefore, must have been the critics' accusation about the treatment? They must have claimed it was unconventional, violating accepted practices. The missing word is the third choice, *unorthodox*.

See Chapter 6 for sentence completion question tactics and practice exercises that will help you handle these questions.

Reading Comprehension Questions

Reading comprehension questions test your ability to understand and interpret what you read. This is probably the most important ability you will need in graduate school and afterward.

Although the passages may encompass any subject matter, you do not need to know anything about the subject discussed in the passage in order to answer the questions on that passage. The purpose of the questions is to test your reading ability, not your knowledge of history, science, literature, or art.

Here is a typical reading comprehension passage and question.

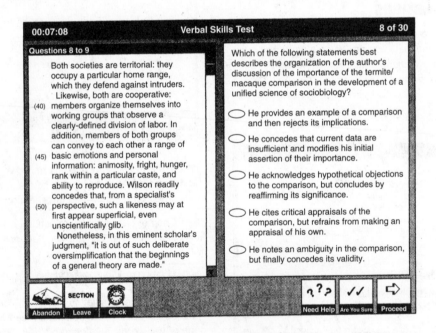

The key lines here are the passage's final sentences. Does the author *acknowledge hypothetical objections* to the comparison? Definitely. Does the author conclude by *reaffirming the significance* of the termite/macaque comparison? Clearly he does: he concludes by quoting Wilson (whom he calls an eminent scholar), in doing so giving implicit support to Wilson's assertion that such oversimplified comparisons can provide the basis for an important general theory. The correct answer is the third choice.

See Chapter 7 for reading comprehension tactics and practice exercises that will help you handle these questions.

Quantitative Ability

The quantitative section consists of 28 questions:

- 14 quantitative comparison questions
- 10 discrete quantitative questions (another name for standard multiple-choice questions)
- 4 data interpretation questions

In order to answer these questions, you need to know arithmetic, some very elementary algebra, and a little geometry. Most of this material you learned in elementary and middle school. You do not need to know any advanced mathematics. The questions are intended to determine if you have a basic knowledge of elementary mathematics, and if you have the ability to reason clearly.

If you haven't done any mathematics in a while, go through the math review in this book before attempting the Model Tests, and certainly before registering to take the GRE. If you feel that your math skills are still pretty good, you can try the Diagnostic Test first, and then read only those sections of the math review relating to those topics that gave you trouble.

Quantitative Comparison Questions

Of the 28 mathematics questions on the GRE, half of them (14) are what is known as quantitative comparisons. It is very likely that you have not seen such a question since you were in high school preparing for the SAT I; if you didn't have to take the SAT I, it is possible that you have never even seen a quantitative comparison. Therefore, read these instructions *very* carefully.

In these questions there are two quantities, one in Column A and one in Column B, and it is your job to compare them. For these problems there are *only four possible answers*:

> The quantity in Column A is greater;
>
> The quantity in Column B is greater;
>
> The two quantities are equal; and
>
> The relationship cannot be determined from the information given.

In this book, these four answer choices will be referred to as A, B, C, and D, respectively. In some of the ques-

tions, information about the quantities being compared is centered above the columns. This information *must* be taken into consideration when comparing the two quantities.

In Chapter 12 you will learn several important strategies for handling quantitative comparisons. For now, let's look at three examples to make sure that you understand the concepts involved.

Column A	Column B
$(3 + 4)^2$	$3^2 + 4^2$

- Evaluate each column: $(3 + 4)^2 = 7^2 = \mathbf{49}$, whereas $3^2 + 4^2 = 9 + 16 = \mathbf{25}$.
- Since $49 > 25$, the quantity in Column A is greater. The answer is **A**.

Column A	Column B
	$a + b = 16$
The average (arithmetic mean) of a and b	8

The quantity in Column A is the average of a and b: $\frac{a + b}{2}$. Since we are told that $a + b = 16$, the quantity in Column A is $\frac{a + b}{2} = \frac{16}{2} = \mathbf{8}$. So, the quantities in Columns A and B are equal. The answer is **C**.

NOTE: We cannot determine the value of either a or b; all we know is that their sum is 16. Perhaps $a = 10$ and $b = 6$, or $a = 0$ and $b = 16$, or $a = -4$ and $b = 20$. *It doesn't matter*. The average of 10 and 6 is 8; the average of 0 and 16 is 8; and the average of -4 and 20 is 8. Since $a + b$ is 16, the average of a and b is 8, *all the time, no matter what*. The answer, therefore, is **C**.

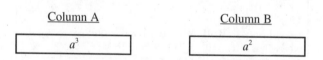

Column A	Column B
a^3	a^2

- If $a = 1$, $a^3 = 1$ and $a^2 = 1$. *In this case*, the quantities in the two columns are equal.
- This means that the answer to this problem *cannot* be A or B. Why?
- The answer can be A (or B) only if the quantity in Column A (or B) is greater *all the time*. But it isn't—not when $a = 1$.
- So, is the answer C? *Maybe*. But for the answer to be C, the quantities would have to be equal *all the time*. Are they?
- No. If $a = 2$, $a^3 = 8$ and $a^2 = 4$, and *in this case* the two quantities are *not equal*.
- The answer, therefore, is **D**.

Discrete Quantitative Questions

Of the 28 mathematics questions on the GRE, 10 are standard multiple-choice questions, what the ETS calls discrete quantitative questions. The way to answer such a question is to do the necessary work, get the solution, and then look at the five choices to find your answer. In Chapter 11 we will discuss other techniques for answering these questions, but for now let's look at two examples.

Edison High School has 840 students, and the ratio of the number of students taking Spanish to the number not taking Spanish is 4:3. How many of the students take Spanish?

(A) 280   (B) 360   (C) 480   (D) 560   (E) 630

To solve this problem requires only that you understand what a ratio is. Ignore the fact that this is a multiple-choice question. *Don't even look at the choices.*

• Let $4x$ and $3x$ be the number of students taking and not taking Spanish, respectively.

• Then $4x + 3x = 840 \Rightarrow 7x = 840 \Rightarrow x = 120$.

• The number of students taking Spanish is $4 \times 120 = 480$.

• Having found the answer to be 480, *now look at the five choices*, see 480 listed as Choice C, click on that choice, and confirm your answer.

Another type of multiple-choice question that appears on the GRE is the Roman numeral-type question. These questions consist of three statements labeled I, II, and III. The five answer choices give various possibilities for which of the statements are true. Here is a typical example.

If x is negative, which of the following *must* be true?

I. $x^3 < x^2$

II. $x + \dfrac{1}{x} < 0$

III. $x = \sqrt{x^2}$

(A) I only   (B) II only   (C) I and II only
(D) II and III only   (E) I, II, and III

To solve this problem, examine each statement independently, and think of it as a true-false question.

• If x is negative, x^3 is negative, and so *must* be less than x^2, which is positive. Statement I is true.

• If x is negative, so is $\dfrac{1}{x}$, and the sum of two negative numbers is negative. Statement II is true.

• The square root of a number is *never* negative, and so could *not possibly* equal x. Statement III is false.

• Only I and II are true. The answer is **C**.

Data Interpretation Questions

Four of the questions in the quantitative section are data interpretation questions. There are always two questions based on one set of data, and later in the section, two more questions based on a second set of data. As you might guess from their name, these questions are based on information provided in graphs, tables, or charts. The questions test your ability to interpret the data that have been provided. You will either have to do a calculation or make an inference from the given data. The various types of questions that could arise will be explored in Chapter 13. Here are two questions based on one set of data.

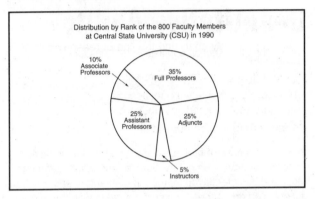

Distribution by Rank of the 800 Faculty Members at Central State University (CSU) in 1990

---

1. In 1990 how many faculty members did not have a professorial rank?

(A) 200   (B) 240   (C) 320   (D) 400   (E) 520

This is a straightforward question that can easily be answered by looking at the chart and doing a small calculation.

• In 1990, 30% of the faculty were not professors (5% were instructors and 25% were adjunct faculty).

• 30% of 800 = .30 × 800 = **240**.

---

2. From 1990 to 2000 the number of faculty members at CSU increased by 20%. If the total number of assistant, associate, and full professors remained the same, and the number of instructors increased by 50%, how many adjunct faculty were there in 2000?

(A) 240   (B) 340   (C) 384   (D) 480   (E) 516

This question is more complicated and requires several calculations.

• Since the number of faculty members increased by 20%, in 2000 there were 960 people on the faculty (20% of 800 = 160, and 800 + 160 = 960).

• In 1990, there were 560 professors.

35% + 10% + 25% = 70% and 70% of 800 = 560

So in 2000, there were also 560 professors.

- In 1990, there were 40 instructors (5% of 800 = 40); since that number increased by 50%, and 50% of 40 is 20, there were 60 instructors in 2000.

- Of the 960 faculty members in 2000, 560 were professors and 60 were instructors. The remaining **340** were adjuncts (960 − 560 − 60 = 340).

Analytical Writing

The analytical writing section consists of two tasks:

- Writing an essay presenting your point of view on an issue of general intellectual concern

- Writing an essay analyzing the line of reasoning in an argument

You are allotted 45 minutes to complete the issue task and 30 minutes to complete the argument analysis task. There is no break between the two tasks. You must finish the first task before you begin the other.

You will find suggestions for tackling both writing tasks in Chapter 9.

The Issue Task

In this task, you are asked to respond to a particular issue, clearly presenting your viewpoint on that issue and supporting your position with reasons and examples. This task is intended to test your ability to write persuasively and effectively.

At the test center, before you begin the timed portion of your issue writing assignment, you first will be shown a set of directions on screen. The directions for the issue task are straightforward. In essence, they say the following:

Give Your Viewpoint on an Issue
45 Minutes

Choose one of the two following topics and compose an essay on that topic. You may not write on any other topic.

Each topic is presented as a one- to two-sentence quotation commenting on an issue of general concern. Your essay may support, refute, or qualify the views expressed in the quotation. Whatever you write, however, must be relevant to the issue under discussion, and you must support your viewpoint with reasons and examples derived from your studies and/or experience.

Before you choose a topic, read both topics carefully. Consider which topic would give you greater scope for writing an effective, well-argued essay.

Faculty members from various institutions will evaluate your essay, judging it on the basis of your skill in the following areas:

- Analysis of the quotation's implications

- Organization and articulation of your ideas

- Use of relevant examples and arguments to support your case

- Handling of the mechanics of standard written English

Once you have decided which topic you prefer, click on the appropriate icon (**Topic 1** or **Topic 2**) to confirm your choice. Do not be hasty confirming your choice of topic. Once you have clicked on a topic, you will not be able to switch to the alternate choice.

To begin the timed portion of this task, click on the icon labeled **Proceed**.

Once you click on **Proceed**, a second screen will appear. This screen contains some general words of advice about how to write an issue essay:

- Think before you write. Plan what you are going to say.

- Work out your ideas in detail.

- Be coherent.

- Leave yourself enough time to revise.

None of this is rocket science. You already know what you are supposed to do. The clock is ticking away, so don't waste your time reading pro forma advice. Just click on the **Dismiss Directions** icon and get to work.

Here are two issue topics modeled on the kinds of topics found in the GRE's "Pool of Issue Topics" available on their web site [*www.gre.org/issuetop.html*]. Please note that these are *not* official GRE issue topics, though they resemble the official topics closely in subject matter and form.

> " 'A mind is a terrible thing to waste.' No society can afford to let its exceptionally bright or talented children go without the training they need to develop their talents fully."

> "The great artists in any medium—painters, poets, choreographers, sculptors—are those who create works of art that the majority of people can comprehend."

The Argument Task

In this task, you are asked to critique the line of reasoning of an argument given in a brief passage, clearly pointing out that argument's strengths and weaknesses and supporting your position with reasons and examples. This task is intended to test both your ability to evaluate the soundness of a position and your ability to get your point across to an academic audience.

Again, before you begin the timed portion of your argument analysis task, you first will be shown a set of directions on screen. The directions for the argument task are straightforward. In essence, they say the following:

Evaluate an Argument
30 Minutes

In 30 minutes, prepare a critical analysis of an argument expressed in a short paragraph. You may not offer an analysis of any other argument.

As you critique the argument, think about the author's underlying assumptions. Ask yourself whether any of them are questionable. Also evaluate any evidence the author brings up. Ask yourself whether it actually supports the author's conclusion.

In your analysis, you may suggest additional kinds of evidence to reinforce the author's argument. You may also suggest methods to refute the argument, or additional data that might be useful to you as you assess the soundness of the argument. *You may **not**, however, present your personal views on the topic.* Your job is to analyze the elements of an argument, not to support or contradict that argument.

Faculty members from various institutions will judge your essay, assessing it on the basis of your skill in the following areas:

• Identification and assessment of the argument's main elements

• Organization and articulation of your thoughts

• Use of relevant examples and arguments to support your case

• Handling of the mechanics of standard written English

Here is an argument topic modeled on the kinds of topics found in the GRE's "Pool of Argument Topics" available on their web site [*www.gre.org/argutop.html*]. Please note that it is *not* an official GRE argument topic, though it resembles the official topics closely in subject matter and form.

The following was written as part of an application for a parade permit made by a special events production company in San Francisco.

A televised Christmas parade held in San Francisco would be a surefire source of profits and publicity for the city. Currently the only nationally televised pre-Christmas parade is the New York Macy's Thanksgiving Day parade in late November; our proposed early December Santa Day parade would both capitalize on the Macy's parade publicity and attract shoppers to San Francisco to take advantage of the pre-Christmas sales. San Franciscans love parades: over 10,000 people attended the St. Patrick's Day parade, while last October's Halloween parade through the Haight-Ashbury district drew at least twice that number. Finally, a recent marketing survey shows that people who come to New York to attend the Thanksgiving Day parade spend over $1,000 that weekend on restaurant meals, hotel rooms, and Christmas shopping.

2 Test-Taking Tactics for the Computer-Based GRE

Before studying the specific tips that will enable you to do your best on this computer-based test or CBT, briefly review the key features of the exam:

- A typical CBT consists of 58 multiple-choice questions in two sections, plus two essay questions.

- The verbal section contains 30 questions: roughly 9 antonyms, 7 analogies, 6 sentence completions, 8 reading comprehension questions. These appear on screen in no set order: 2 sentence completions may be followed on screen by 2 antonyms.

- The mathematics section contains 28 questions: 14 are quantitative comparisons, 10 are standard multiple-choice questions, and 4 are data interpretation questions based on tables or graphs.

- Because the CBT you take will be tailored to your skills, it may vary slightly from the typical test described above.

- In the multiple-choice sections, you receive more credit for getting a hard question right than you do for answering an easy question correctly.

- You cannot skip questions; you must answer the question on screen and confirm that you are satisfied with your answer choice before you can proceed to the next question.

- Once you have confirmed an answer, you cannot go back and change it.

Starting Right Now
Begin to Familiarize Yourself with Computer Skills

Use the CD-ROM that accompanies this book to familiarize yourself with computerized testing.

Using a Mouse

As you probably know, a mouse is a small electronic device that enables you to send signals to your PC. It sits on a mouse pad, its tail (the electric cord that links it to your PC) pointed away from you. As you move the mouse back and forth along the surface of the mouse pad, you see a pointer or arrow moving on the computer screen. There's a "button" on the rear surface of the mouse. Click that button to tell the computer to do something.

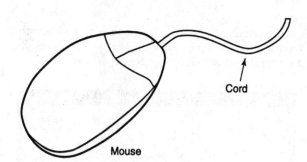

Cord

Mouse

Here is an antonym question as it would appear on a computer screen. Right now the arrow is off to one side.

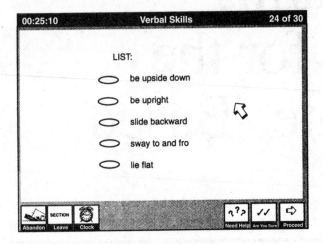

To enter your answer to this question, you must move the mouse until the arrow touches the oval next to your answer choice.

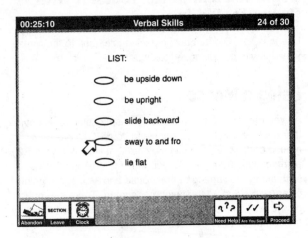

Once the pointer is on the oval, click the button. Note that the oval on which you clicked is now black. This means that the computer has recorded your answer choice.

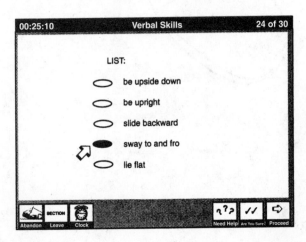

If you decide that you prefer a different answer, simply move the mouse until the arrow is on the appropriate oval. Click the button. The new oval is now black, while the old oval is once more blank.

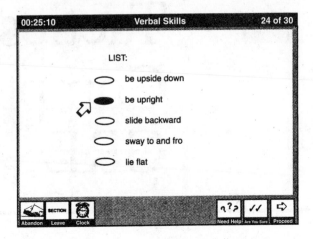

Once you're sure of your answer choice, before you can go on to the next question, you have to use the mouse twice more. First, you have to move the pointer until it's on the box labeled "Next" at the bottom of the screen. Click the button. This signals the computer that you want to move on. Before you can do so, however, you have to confirm that you really want to do that. Up to this moment, you can still change your answer. Once you click on the box labeled "Confirm," however, the screen will change to show the next question. You can never go back to change an answer you have confirmed.

There are six icons at the bottom of a CBT screen, three to the left and three to the right. They read, in order from left to right, as follows:

Quit Test	Exit Section	Time	Help	Confirm Answer	Next

Because ETS currently refuses to allow other publishers to duplicate its testing tools, we have had to create alternative icons for the computer screens that appear on the CD-ROM accompanying this book. Thus, in place of the CBT icon "Next," our screen has the icon "Proceed." Where the CBT tells you to "Confirm" your answer, our screen asks, "Are You Sure?"

Our layout thus reads, from left to right:

Abandon	Leave Section	Clock	Need Help?	Are You Sure?	Proceed

Do not let these minor differences confuse you. The basic layout of the screen is identical, and the functions of the testing tools are the same. Even if our icons don't match the ones on the CBT exactly, you can depend on what we say about the appearance of the test.

Scrolling Through a Text

Occasionally, to answer a question you may have to consider more information than can fit conveniently on a single computer screen. A 500-word reading passage, for example, takes up too much room for one screen; so do certain charts and bar and line graphs.

In such cases, a vertical scroll bar will appear along the right side of that reading passage or chart. It enables you to control what part of the text you see on screen. Click on the scroll bar's down arrow, and it will allow you to move down one line to see the next line of text. Keep on clicking on the down arrow and you'll scroll down even more. Click on the up arrow and you'll scroll back up. You can scroll line by

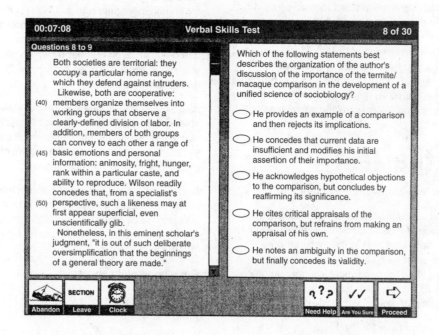

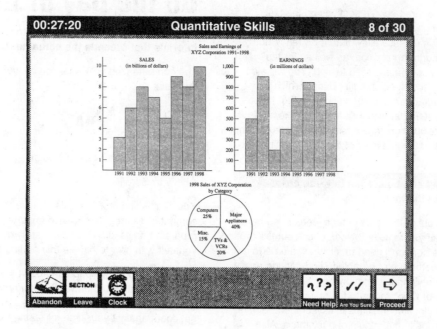

line; you can also scroll a page at a time. If you hold down the mouse button on an arrow, you can scroll through the text quite rapidly.

The small gray status bar at the top of the pane or little window helps you figure out just where you are in the text. When you're at the start of the text, it reads "Begin"; when you're at the end of the text, it reads "End." When you're in the middle and can scroll in either direction, it reads "More Available."

If you're a rapid reader and are unused to word-processing programs and other software programs that incorporate scrolling, you may find the process a bit awkward at first. Practice on the CD-ROM version of this book until you get the hang of it. When you take the CBT, you'll have a chance to work through a tutorial that teaches you how to scroll. However, you'll have an easier time on the test if you come in already comfortable with scrolling techniques.

Before the Test

Schedule the test for your best time of day.

When you sign up to take the test on a specific date, you will be given a choice of time slots. Some people are morning people; others work well in the midafternoon. Consider how your energy and alertness levels vary during the course of a day. Also, consider possible transportation problems, such as rush hour. With these and other relevant factors in mind, select the time slot that works best for you.

Allow yourself enough time for the test.

The GRE Bulletin recommends that you allow $4\frac{1}{2}$ hours for the CBT. There are three scored sections on the test. These sections range in length from 30 minutes to 75 minutes each; you must also allow time for a ten-minute break midway through the session, as well as for the untimed tutorial on computer-based testing. You will also need up to half an hour for signing in, during which time you may be photographed and even fingerprinted! If you sign up to take the GRE at 8:00 A.M., do not make a dentist appointment for 12:00. You can't possibly get there on time, and you'll just spend the last hour of the test worrying about it.

Look over the test site before the day you are scheduled to take the test.

Do a practice run out to the test center a week or so before you take the test. If you're going by car, check out the traffic patterns. See whether you'll need to allow extra time to get to the site, and whether you'll be able to find parking easily. If you'll be using public transportation, figure out how to get from the bus stop or train station to the test center. Some testing centers are located in suites in skyscrapers; others, in storefront locations in the middle of busy malls. Also learn where the restrooms are, and the nearest place to buy a quick snack.

Set out your test kit the night before the test.

Avoid sudden panic on the morning of the test. Before you go to bed, set out everything you will need to take with you in the morning. For the CBT GRE, you need two forms of official I.D., at least one of which must include a current photograph; be sure you have these items in your wallet or purse. If you need to wear special glasses when you work at a computer, set them out. Include also your directions to the site, and your CBT authorization voucher, if you have been given one. [If, however, you register by phone for an imminent date and pay via credit card, the Sylvan Candidate Services Call Center will not send you an authorization voucher; instead, the scheduler will assign you a confirmation number by which you can identify yourself to the test center staff. Have that number with you on the day of the test.]

Also set out the clothes you plan to wear. Choose comfortable, casual clothing. Now is not the time to make a fashion statement; simplicity, not elegance, should be the order of the day. Bring along a sweater, however; you can't do your best if you're shivering from the cold.

Don't bother to set out pencils and scratch paper. The test center will supply you with both. You will not be allowed to take any "testing aids"—calculators, watches with calculator functions, pens, rulers, highlighters, books, handheld PCs—into the testing room.

Get a good night's sleep.

The way to do your best on any test you ever take is to get a good night's sleep so you are well rested and alert.

On the Day of the Test

Take as much time as you need to work through the tutorials that precede the actual test.

The computerized GRE makes you work through four tutorials:

• How to Use a Mouse

• How to Select an Answer

• How to Use the Testing Tools

• How to Scroll

You can't skip these tutorials; they're mandatory, even for computer majors. They're also important; every computer program has its idiosyncrasies, and you need to familiarize yourself with how to handle this particular computer setup.

Proceed at your own pace and don't worry about how much time you're taking. The twenty to thirty minutes you spend working through the tutorials *before* you begin testing will not count against your time for taking the test.

As you work through the tutorials, make sure you know all the test directions thoroughly.

Once the test begins, any time you have to switch screens to look up directions or to get help with scrolling is time you lose from the actual test. The clock keeps on ticking, and, to maximize your score, you've got to keep on thinking and clicking. For this reason, be sure you've memorized the directions for the different question types you'll face on the test.

Before you move on from the tutorial section to the actual test, take a break.

Once you've finished making your rough answer sheet, don't be in a rush to click and start the test. Raise your hand to let the proctor know you need assistance, and, when he or she comes up to your carrel, ask for a restroom break. You'll be escorted out of the computer room and allowed to sign out. You may have spent half an hour or more mastering the material in the tutorials section, and if you're new to working with a mouse, you may be a bit tired or tense. Feel free to wash your face, nibble a quick snack, stretch, or do anything else that will relax you before you move into the test-taking mode. Any time out you take before the test actually starts is "free": it doesn't cost you any of that all important question-answering time.

Once the Test Has Started

Avoid clicking on the boxes at the bottom left of the screen.

As you will learn in the tutorial, there are six boxes at the bottom of the screen, three to the left and three to the right. They read, in order, from left to right: Quit, Exit, Time, Help, Confirm, Next. Avoid the ones to the left, especially the two leftmost ones. If you click on either of those boxes, you're abandoning ship, quitting either the particular section on which you're working or the whole test. There is no point in doing so. Even if you're dissatisfied with your performance and unwilling to have your scores sent to the graduate schools you selected, you still can use this test as a practice session. Don't bail out midway. Wait. After you've completed all four sections of the test, you will get a chance to indicate whether you want to cancel this test or whether you want to receive a score for your work. Make the decision then. Even if you decide to cancel your test, you'll still benefit from having had the chance to see what specific questions the computer selected for you. After all, you've paid more than $100 to take this test. Get your money's worth from the experience.

Avoid clicking on the third lefthand box as well, the "Time" box. This is the "Time" box. If you click on it, the information line at the top of the computer screen will stop showing the amount of time remaining in the section on which you're working. You won't be able to pace yourself effectively,

and you may completely lose track of how much time you have left. Why create problems for yourself? Keep away from those boxes at the bottom left. (If you accidentally click on the "Time" box and hide the time information momentarily, don't panic; just click on the box a second time to turn the time indicator back on again.)

Keep track of the time.

Your job is to answer correctly as many questions as you can within the time allowed for that particular section of the test. Because of the computer-adaptive nature of the test, you can't simply skip time-consuming questions or questions that stump you, and hope to return to them if you have time left over. To move on to the next question, you must enter and confirm an answer for the question currently on your screen. Therefore, whenever you decide it's worth your while to spend time working through a complicated question, you've got to keep one eye on the clock to make sure getting this one answer correct isn't costing you too much time.

Don't get bogged down by any one question.

Now more than ever it is important for you to avoid getting so caught up in figuring out one question that you lose track of the time. Remember, you can't move on to the next question until you've answered the one on screen. If a question is taking too long, guess at the answer and go on to the next question. This is not the time to prove that you can stick to a job no matter how long it takes.

On the other hand, don't rush.

Since your score will depend on how many *correct* answers you give *within a definite period* of time, speed and accuracy both count. Don't fall into the common errors born of haste. Read *all the answer choices*, not just some. Make sure you are answering *the question asked* and not one it may have reminded you of or one you thought was going to be asked. Write down key words like NOT and EXCEPT to make sure that you do not end up trying to answer the exact opposite of the question asked.

Don't be trigger-happy: Think before you click.

Once you get into the swing of things, clicking "Next" to indicate you're ready to go on to the next question and "Confirm" to indicate that you're sure of your answer, watch out that you don't start double-clicking automatically. It's all too easy to fall into a game-playing mode and click twice before you've thought things through. The CBT is *not* a computer game; you don't win any points here by zapping the enemy blindly. Take a moment to reconsider each answer choice. Then move on to the next question, sure that you've given this one your best shot.

Be especially careful answering questions that resemble questions you've seen before.

In the GRE, the test-makers test and retest the same concepts. They follow basic patterns, modifying questions subtly or substantially. Thus, in your CBT, you may come across questions that look very much like ones you have previously seen in published GREs or on *www.gre.com*, the GRE web site. You may even come across some that resemble questions you've just seen on an earlier section of your test. Don't assume that you know the answer to a question because it looks like one you've seen before. Read the question closely. Don't let subtle shifts in wording catch you unaware.

Never rush through the first questions of a section.

Remember, your answers to these initial questions have a greater impact on your score than your answers to the last few questions of the section do.

Always eliminate as many wrong answers as you can.

Deciding between two choices is easier than deciding among five. Even if you have to guess, every answer you eliminate improves your chances of guessing correctly.

Don't waste time second-guessing yourself.

Once you confirm an answer, that's it; you no longer have a chance to change that answer. If, later on in a section, you suddenly realize you got an earlier question wrong, don't sit there kicking yourself. Self-reproach is a waste of time. Remember, the only question you have to worry about is the one now on screen, so concentrate on it.

Similarly, don't try to second-guess the computer. There's no point in wasting time and energy wondering whether it's feeding you harder questions or easier ones. Let the computer keep track of how well you're doing. You concentrate on answering questions and pacing yourself.

Be alert for the five-minute warning.

Toward the end of each section, a brief flash of the clock will indicate that you have only five minutes left. Even if you have clicked "Time" to hide the remaining time display, the time display will come on automatically at this point. Also, instead of showing just the hours and minutes remaining, the display will change to show seconds as well.

Don't miss your five-minute warning signal. As you work through each section, be aware of the clock. When you are running out of time, eliminate any answer choices you can and then guess. At that point, even random guessing those last questions is better than leaving them unanswered.

3

A Diagnostic Test

- ■ **Diagnostic Test**
- ■ **Answer Key**
- ■ **Self-Appraisal**
- ■ **Answer Explanations**

This chapter contains a full-length diagnostic test. The format of the test is identical to the computer-based GRE that you will take, in that it has exactly the same number of verbal and quantitative questions that an actual test has. Within each section, there is also exactly the same breakdown of question types. For example, on the verbal section there are the same number of analogies and antonyms as on a real test; in the quantitative section there are four data interpretation questions and 14 quantitative comparisons. Directions will appear only the first time a given type of question is introduced in each test; after that, only the type of question will appear. What is different, of course, is that this test is not computer adaptive. If you purchased the version of this book that contains a CD-ROM, then later in your preparation, to get a feel for what it is like to take a computerized GRE, do a model test on the CD-ROM.

After taking the test, score your answers and evaluate your results, using the self-rating guides provided. (Be sure also to read the answer explanations for questions you answered incorrectly and questions you answered correctly but found difficult.)

You should now be in a position to approach your review program realistically and allot your time for study. For example, you should know which topics in mathematics require review and drill. You should also know which of your verbal and analytical skills require concentrated study.

Simulate Test Conditions

To best simulate actual test conditions, find a quiet place to work. Have a stop watch or a clock handy so that you can keep perfect track of the time. Go through each section by answering the questions in the order in which they appear. If you don't know the answer to a question, guess (making an educated guess, if possible) and move on. Do not return to a question that you were unsure of, and do not go back to check your work if you have some time left over at the end of a section. (It isn't possible to do that on a real GRE.) Knowing how much time you have for each section and how many questions there are, try to pace yourself so that you use all your time and just finish each section in the time allowed. Do not spend too much time on any one question. Again, if you get stuck, just guess and go on to the next question.

Answer Key—A Diagnostic Test

Section 1

1. Ⓐ Ⓑ Ⓒ Ⓓ Ⓔ
2. Ⓐ Ⓑ Ⓒ Ⓓ Ⓔ
3. Ⓐ Ⓑ Ⓒ Ⓓ Ⓔ
4. Ⓐ Ⓑ Ⓒ Ⓓ Ⓔ
5. Ⓐ Ⓑ Ⓒ Ⓓ Ⓔ
6. Ⓐ Ⓑ Ⓒ Ⓓ Ⓔ
7. Ⓐ Ⓑ Ⓒ Ⓓ Ⓔ
8. Ⓐ Ⓑ Ⓒ Ⓓ Ⓔ
9. Ⓐ Ⓑ Ⓒ Ⓓ Ⓔ
10. Ⓐ Ⓑ Ⓒ Ⓓ Ⓔ

11. Ⓐ Ⓑ Ⓒ Ⓓ Ⓔ
12. Ⓐ Ⓑ Ⓒ Ⓓ Ⓔ
13. Ⓐ Ⓑ Ⓒ Ⓓ Ⓔ
14. Ⓐ Ⓑ Ⓒ Ⓓ Ⓔ
15. Ⓐ Ⓑ Ⓒ Ⓓ Ⓔ
16. Ⓐ Ⓑ Ⓒ Ⓓ Ⓔ
17. Ⓐ Ⓑ Ⓒ Ⓓ Ⓔ
18. Ⓐ Ⓑ Ⓒ Ⓓ Ⓔ
19. Ⓐ Ⓑ Ⓒ Ⓓ Ⓔ
20. Ⓐ Ⓑ Ⓒ Ⓓ Ⓔ

21. Ⓐ Ⓑ Ⓒ Ⓓ Ⓔ
22. Ⓐ Ⓑ Ⓒ Ⓓ Ⓔ
23. Ⓐ Ⓑ Ⓒ Ⓓ Ⓔ
24. Ⓐ Ⓑ Ⓒ Ⓓ Ⓔ
25. Ⓐ Ⓑ Ⓒ Ⓓ Ⓔ
26. Ⓐ Ⓑ Ⓒ Ⓓ Ⓔ
27. Ⓐ Ⓑ Ⓒ Ⓓ Ⓔ
28. Ⓐ Ⓑ Ⓒ Ⓓ Ⓔ
29. Ⓐ Ⓑ Ⓒ Ⓓ Ⓔ
30. Ⓐ Ⓑ Ⓒ Ⓓ Ⓔ

Section 2

1. Ⓐ Ⓑ Ⓒ Ⓓ Ⓔ
2. Ⓐ Ⓑ Ⓒ Ⓓ Ⓔ
3. Ⓐ Ⓑ Ⓒ Ⓓ Ⓔ
4. Ⓐ Ⓑ Ⓒ Ⓓ Ⓔ
5. Ⓐ Ⓑ Ⓒ Ⓓ Ⓔ
6. Ⓐ Ⓑ Ⓒ Ⓓ Ⓔ
7. Ⓐ Ⓑ Ⓒ Ⓓ Ⓔ
8. Ⓐ Ⓑ Ⓒ Ⓓ Ⓔ
9. Ⓐ Ⓑ Ⓒ Ⓓ Ⓔ
10. Ⓐ Ⓑ Ⓒ Ⓓ Ⓔ

11. Ⓐ Ⓑ Ⓒ Ⓓ Ⓔ
12. Ⓐ Ⓑ Ⓒ Ⓓ Ⓔ
13. Ⓐ Ⓑ Ⓒ Ⓓ Ⓔ
14. Ⓐ Ⓑ Ⓒ Ⓓ Ⓔ
15. Ⓐ Ⓑ Ⓒ Ⓓ Ⓔ
16. Ⓐ Ⓑ Ⓒ Ⓓ Ⓔ
17. Ⓐ Ⓑ Ⓒ Ⓓ Ⓔ
18. Ⓐ Ⓑ Ⓒ Ⓓ Ⓔ
19. Ⓐ Ⓑ Ⓒ Ⓓ Ⓔ
20. Ⓐ Ⓑ Ⓒ Ⓓ Ⓔ

21. Ⓐ Ⓑ Ⓒ Ⓓ Ⓔ
22. Ⓐ Ⓑ Ⓒ Ⓓ Ⓔ
23. Ⓐ Ⓑ Ⓒ Ⓓ Ⓔ
24. Ⓐ Ⓑ Ⓒ Ⓓ Ⓔ
25. Ⓐ Ⓑ Ⓒ Ⓓ Ⓔ
26. Ⓐ Ⓑ Ⓒ Ⓓ Ⓔ
27. Ⓐ Ⓑ Ⓒ Ⓓ Ⓔ
28. Ⓐ Ⓑ Ⓒ Ⓓ Ⓔ

Remove answer sheet by cutting on dotted line

DIAGNOSTIC TEST

1

Directions: In each of the following antonym questions, a word printed in capital letters precedes five lettered words or phrases. From these five lettered words or phrases, pick the one most nearly <u>opposite</u> in meaning to the capitalized word.

1. PRODIGAL: self indulgent
    - (A) nomad
    - (B) sycophant
    - (C) gifted child
    - (D) economical person
    - (E) antagonist

2. ARTIFICE:
    - (A) edifice
    - (B) sincerity
    - (C) prejudice
    - (D) creativity
    - (E) affirmation

Directions: Each of the following sentence completion questions contains one or two blanks. These blanks signify that a word or set of words has been left out. Below each sentence are five words or sets of words. For each blank, pick the word or set of words that <u>best</u> reflects the sentence's over-all meaning.

3. The earth is a planet bathed in light; it is therefore _____ that many of the living organisms that have evolved on the earth have _____ the biologically advantageous capacity to trap light energy.
    - (A) anomalous...engendered
    - (B) unsurprising...developed
    - (C) predictable...forfeited
    - (D) problematic...exhibited
    - (E) expectable...relinquished

4. Relatively few politicians willingly forsake center stage, although a touch of _____ on their parts now and again might well increase their popularity with the voting public.
    - (A) garrulity
    - (B) misanthropy
    - (C) self-effacement
    - (D) self-dramatization
    - (E) self-doubt

Directions: Each of the following analogy questions presents a related pair of words linked by a colon. Five lettered pairs of words follow the linked pair. Choose the lettered pair of words whose relationship is <u>most like</u> the relationship expressed in the original linked pair.

5. CIRCUITOUS : ROUTE ::
    - (A) problematic : solution
    - (B) devious : argument
    - (C) elliptical : brevity
    - (D) judicious : selection
    - (E) profound : depth

6. HELPFUL : OFFICIOUS ::
    - (A) dutiful : assiduous
    - (B) effusive : gushing
    - (C) gullible : incredulous
    - (D) enigmatic : dumbfounded
    - (E) deferential : sycophantic

1   1

James's first novels used conventional narrative techniques: explicit characterization, action which related events in distinctly phased sequences,
Line settings firmly outlined and specifically described.
(5) But this method gradually gave way to a subtler, more deliberate, more diffuse style of accumulation of minutely discriminated details whose total significance the reader can grasp only by constant attention and sensitive inference. His later novels
(10) play down scenes of abrupt and prominent action, and do not so much offer a succession of sharp shocks as slow piecemeal additions of perception. The curtain is not suddenly drawn back from shrouded things, but is slowly moved away.
(15)   Such a technique is suited to James's essential subject, which is not human action itself but the states of mind which produce and are produced by human actions and interactions. James was less interested in what characters do, than in the
(20) moral and psychological antecedents, realizations, and consequences which attend their doings. This is why he more often speaks of "cases" than of actions. His stories, therefore, grow more and more lengthy while the actions they relate grow
(25) simpler and less visible; not because they are crammed with adventitious and secondary events, digressive relief, or supernumerary characters, as overstuffed novels of action are; but because he presents in such exhaustive detail every nuance of
(30) his situation. Commonly the interest of a novel is in the variety and excitement of visible actions building up to a climactic event which will settle the outward destinies of characters with storybook promise of permanence. A James novel, however,
(35) possesses its characteristic interest in carrying the reader through a rich analysis of the mental adjustments of characters to the realities of their personal situations as they are slowly revealed to them through exploration and chance discovery.

7. The passage supplies information for answering which of the following questions?

(A) Did James originate the so-called psychological novel?
(B) Is conventional narrative technique strictly chronological in recounting action?
(C) Can novels lacking overtly dramatic incident sustain the reader's interest?
(D) Were James's later novels more acceptable to the general public than his earlier ones?
(E) Is James unique in his predilection for exploring psychological nuances of character?

8. According to the passage, James's later novels differ from his earlier ones in their

(A) preoccupation with specifically described settings
(B) ever-increasing concision and tautness of plot
(C) levels of moral and psychological complexity
(D) development of rising action to a climax
(E) subordination of psychological exploration to dramatic effect

9. The author's attitude toward the novel of action appears to be one of

(A) pointed indignation
(B) detached neutrality
(C) sharp derision
(D) strong partisanship
(E) mild disapprobation

1

1

Antonyms

10. EQUIVOCATE:
    (A) yield
    (B) distinguish
    (C) condescend
    (D) pledge
    (E) denounce

11. OPULENCE:
    (A) transience
    (B) penury
    (C) solitude
    (D) generosity
    (E) transparency

Analogies

12. EPHEMERAL : PERMANENCE ::
    (A) erratic : predictability
    (B) immaculate : cleanliness
    (C) commendable : reputation
    (D) spurious : emulation
    (E) mandatory : obedience

13. NONPLUSSED : BAFFLEMENT ::
    (A) discomfited : embarrassment
    (B) parsimonious : extravagance
    (C) disgruntled : contentment
    (D) despicable : contempt
    (E) surly : harassment

14. OGLE : OBSERVE ::
    (A) haggle : outbid
    (B) clamor : dispute
    (C) discern : perceive
    (D) flaunt : display
    (E) glare : glower

Sentence Completion

15. It may be useful to think of character in fiction as a function of two _____ impulses: the impulse to individualize and the impulse to _____.
    (A) analogous...humanize
    (B) disparate...aggrandize
    (C) divergent...typify
    (D) comparable...delineate
    (E) related...moralize

16. There are any number of theories to explain these events and, since even the experts disagree, it is _____ the rest of us in our role as responsible scholars to _____ dogmatic statements.
    (A) paradoxical for...abstain from
    (B) arrogant of...compensate with
    (C) incumbent on...refrain from
    (D) opportune for...quarrel over
    (E) appropriate for...issue forth

Reading Comprehension

According to the theory of plate tectonics, the lithosphere (earth's relatively hard and solid outer layer consisting of the crust and part of the under-
Line lying mantle) is divided into a few dozen plates
(5) that vary in size and shape; in general, these plates move in relation to one another. They move away from one another at a mid-ocean ridge, a long chain of sub-oceanic mountains that forms a boundary between plates. At a mid-ocean
(10) ridge, new lithospheric material in the form of hot magma pushes up from the earth's interior. The injection of this new lithospheric material from below causes the phenomenon known as sea-floor spreading.
(15)   Given that the earth is not expanding in size to any appreciable degree, how can "new" litho-sphere be created at a mid-ocean ridge? For new lithosphere to come into being in one region, an equal amount of lithospheric material must be
(20) destroyed somewhere else. This destruction takes place at a boundary between plates called a sub-duction zone. At a subduction zone, one plate is pushed down under another into the red-hot mantle, where over a span of millions of years it
(25) is absorbed into the mantle.
In the early 1960's, well before scientists had formulated the theory of plate tectonics, Princeton University professor Harry H. Hess proposed the concept of sea-floor spreading. Hess's original
(30) hypothesis described the creation and spread of ocean floor by means of the upwelling and cool-ing of magma from the earth's interior. Hess, however, did not mention rigid lithospheric plates. The subsequent discovery that the oceanic
(35) crust contains evidence of periodic reversals of the earth's magnetic field helped confirm Hess's hypothesis. According to the explanation formu-lated by Princeton's F. J. Vine and D. H. Matthews, whenever magma wells up under a

1

1

(40) mid-ocean ridge, the ferromagnetic minerals within the magma become magnetized in the direction of the geomagnetic field. As the magma cools and hardens into rock, the direction and the polarity of the geometric field are recorded in the magnetized
(45) volcanic rock. Thus, when reversals of the earth's magnetic field occur, as they do at intervals of from 10,000 to around a million years, they produce a series of magnetic stripes paralleling the axis of the rift. Thus, the oceanic crust is like a
(50) magnetic tape recording, but instead of preserving sounds or visual images, it preserves the history of earth's geomagnetic field. The boundaries between stripes reflect reversals of the magnetic field; these reversals can be dated independently.
(55) Given this information, geologists can deduce the rate of sea-floor spreading from the width of the stripes. (Geologists, however, have yet to solve the mystery of exactly how the earth's magnetic field comes to reverse itself periodically.)

17. According to the passage, a mid-ocean ridge differs from a subduction zone in that

(A) it marks the boundary line between neighboring plates
(B) only the former is located on the ocean floor
(C) it is a site for the emergence of new lithospheric material
(D) the former periodically disrupts the earth's geomagnetic field
(E) it is involved with lithospheric destruction rather than lithospheric creation

18. It can be inferred from the passage that as new lithospheric material is injected from below

(A) the plates become immobilized in a kind of gridlock
(B) it is incorporated into an underwater mountain ridge
(C) the earth's total mass is altered
(D) it reverses its magnetic polarity
(E) the immediately adjacent plates sink

19. According to the passage, lithospheric material at the site of a subduction zone

(A) rises and is polarized
(B) sinks and is reincorporated
(C) slides and is injected
(D) spreads and is absorbed
(E) diverges and is consumed

Antonyms

20. HONE:

(A) broaden
(B) twist
(C) dull
(D) weld
(E) break

21. PHLEGMATIC:

(A) dogmatic
(B) ardent
(C) haphazard
(D) self-assured
(E) abstracted

22. BANALITY:

(A) tentative interpretation
(B) concise summation
(C) accurate delineation
(D) laudatory remark
(E) novel expression

Analogies

23. THIRST : DRIVE ::

(A) inebriety : excess
(B) success : ambition
(C) indifference : passion
(D) taste : gusto
(E) smell : sense

24. SKULDUGGERY : SWINDLER ::

(A) surgery : quack
(B) quandary : craven
(C) chicanery : trickster
(D) forgery : speculator
(E) cutlery : butcher

Sentence Completion

25. According to one optimistic hypothesis, the dense concentration of entrepreneurs and services in the cities would incubate new functions, _____ them, and finally export them to other areas, and so the cities, forever breeding fresh ideas, would _____ themselves repeatedly.

(A) immunize...perpetuate
(B) isolate...revitalize
(C) foster...deplete
(D) spawn...imitate
(E) nurture...renew

26. Man is a _____ animal, and much more so in his mind than in his body: he may like to go alone for a walk, but he hates to stand alone in his _____.

(A) gregarious...opinions
(B) conceited...vanity
(C) singular...uniqueness
(D) solitary...thoughts
(E) nomadic...footsteps

1

1

Antonyms

27. ERUDITE:

(A) unhealthy
(B) ignorant
(C) impolite
(D) indifferent
(E) imprecise

28. EFFRONTERY:

(A) obscurity
(B) indolence
(C) separation
(D) diffidence
(E) fluctuation

Reading Comprehension

The stability that had marked the Iroquois
Confederacy's generally pro-British position was
shattered with the overthrow of James II in 1688,
Line the colonial uprisings that followed in
(5) Massachusetts, New York, and Maryland, and the
commencement of King William's War against
Louis XIV of France. The increasing French
threat to English hegemony in the interior of
North America was signalized by French-led or
(10) French-inspired attacks on the Iroquois and on
outlying colonial settlements in New York and
New England. The high point of the Iroquois
response was the spectacular raid of August 5,
1689, in which the Iroquois virtually wiped out
(15) the French village of Lachine, just outside
Montreal. A counterraid by the French on the
English village of Schenectady in March, 1690,
instilled an appropriate measure of fear among the
English and their Iroquois allies.
(20) The Iroquois position at the end of the war,
which was formalized by treaties made during the
summer of 1701 with the British and the French,
and which was maintained throughout most of the
eighteenth century, was one of "aggressive neu-
(25) trality" between the two competing European
powers. Under the new system the Iroquois initiated a peace policy toward the "far Indians,"
tightened their control over the nearby tribes, and
induced both English and French to support their

(30) neutrality toward the European powers by appropriate gifts and concessions.
By holding the balance of power in the
sparsely settled borderlands between English and
French settlements, and by their willingness to
(35) use their power against one or the other nation if
not appropriately treated, the Iroquois played the
game of European power politics with effectiveness. The system broke down, however, after the
French became convinced that the Iroquois were
(40) compromising the system in favor of the English
and launched a full-scale attempt to establish
French physical and juridical presence in the
Ohio Valley, the heart of the borderlands long
claimed by the Iroquois. As a consequence of the
(45) ensuing Great War for Empire, in which Iroquois
neutrality was dissolved and European influence
moved closer, the play-off system lost its efficacy
and a system of direct bargaining supplanted it.

29. The author's primary purpose in this passage is to

(A) denounce the imperialistic policies of the
French
(B) disprove the charges of barbarism made
against the Indian nations
(C) expose the French government's exploitation
of the Iroquois balance of power
(D) describe and assess the effect of European
military power on the policy of an Indian
nation
(E) show the inability of the Iroquois to engage in
European-style diplomacy

30. With which of the following statements would the
author be LEAST likely to agree?

(A) The Iroquois were able to respond effectively
to French acts of aggression.
(B) James II's removal from the throne caused dissension to break out among the colonies.
(C) The French begrudged the British their alleged
high standing among the Iroquois.
(D) Iroquois negotiations involved playing one
side against the other.
(E) The Iroquois ceased to hold the balance of
power early in the eighteenth century.

2   2

SECTION **2**—QUANTITATIVE ABILITY

Time—45 Minutes
  28 Questions

In this section use scrap paper to solve each problem. Then decide which is the best of the choices given and fill in the corresponding oval on the Answer Sheet.

Directions: In the following type of question, two quantities appear, one in Column A and one in Column B. You must compare them. The correct answer to the question is

A if the quantity in Column A is greater
B if the quantity in Column B is greater
C if the two quantities are equal
D it is impossible to determine which quantity is greater

Notes: Sometimes information about one or both of the quantities is centered above the two columns. If the same symbol appears in both columns, it represents the same thing each time.

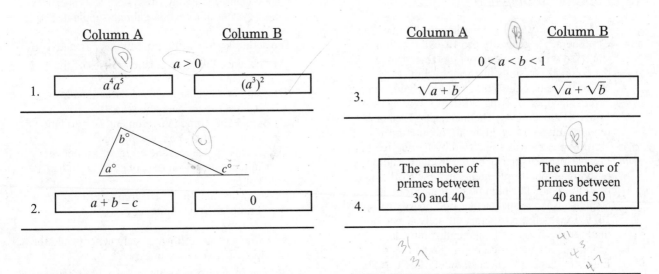

	Column A	Column B
	$a > 0$	
1.	$a^4 a^5$	$(a^3)^2$

	Column A	Column B
2.	$a + b - c$	0

	Column A	Column B
	$0 < a < b < 1$	
3.	$\sqrt{a+b}$	$\sqrt{a} + \sqrt{b}$

	Column A	Column B
4.	The number of primes between 30 and 40	The number of primes between 40 and 50

Directions: In the following questions, choose the best answer from the five choices listed.

5. In the figure at the right, what is the value of $a + b + c$?

   (A) 210   (B) 220
   (C) 240   (D) 270
   (E) 280

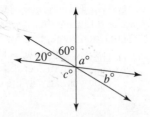

6. Of the 200 seniors at Monroe High School, exactly 40 are in the band, 60 are in the orchestra, and 10 are in both. How many students are in neither the band nor the orchestra?

   (A) 80   (B) 90   (C) 100   (D) 110   (E) 120

7. Twenty children were sharing equally the cost of a present for their teacher. When 4 of the children decided not to contribute, each of the other children had to pay $1.50 more. How much did the present cost, in dollars?

   (A) 50   (B) 80   (C) 100   (D) 120   (E) 150

2 **2**

Column A	Column B
8. 10^{20}	20^{10}

There are 250 people lined up outside a theater. Jack is the 25th person from the front, and Jill is the 125th person from the front.

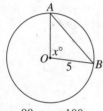

Column A	Column B
9. The number of people between Jack and Jill	100

10. What is the value of n if $4^{10} \times 64^2 = 16^2 \times 4^n$?
   (A) 6   (B) 10   (C) 12   (D) 15   (E) 30

Column A	Column B

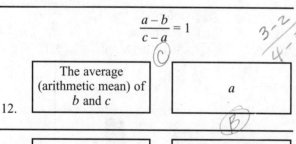

$90 < x < 180$

Column A	Column B
11. The perimeter of $\triangle AOB$	17

$$\frac{a-b}{c-a} = 1$$

Column A	Column B
12. The average (arithmetic mean) of b and c	a

Column A	Column B
13. The area of a square whose sides are 10	The area of a square whose diagonals are 15

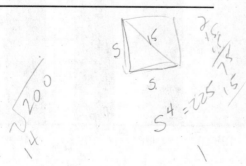

Questions 14–15 refer to the following graphs.

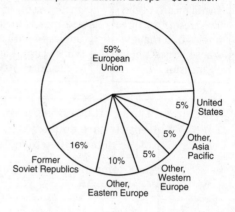

1993
Total Exports to Eastern Europe = $98 Billion

59% European Union

5% United States

5% Other, Asia Pacific

16% Former Soviet Republics

10% Other, Eastern Europe

5% Other, Western Europe

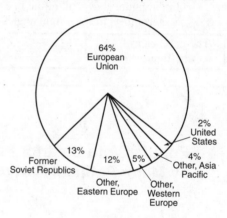

1996
Total Exports to Eastern Europe = $174 Billion

64% European Union

2% United States

4% Other, Asia Pacific

13% Former Soviet Republics

12% Other, Eastern Europe

5% Other, Western Europe

14. Which of the following statements concerning the value of exports to Eastern Europe from other Eastern European countries from 1993 to 1996 is the most accurate?

  (A) They increased by 2%.
  (B) They increased by 12%.
  (C) They increased by 20%.
  (D) They increased by 50%.
  (E) They increased by 100%.

15. France is one of the countries in the European Union. If in 1996 France's exports to Eastern Europe were four times those of the United States, then what percent of the European Union's exports to Eastern Europe came from France that year?

  (A) 5%   (B) 8%   (C) 12.5%
  (D) 20%   (E) 25%

2

2

Column A	Column B
The average (arithmetic mean) of the measures of the three angles of a triangle whose largest angle measures 75°	The average (arithmetic mean) of the measures of the three angles of a triangle whose largest angle measures 105°

16.

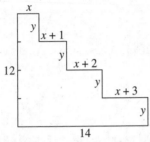

In the figure above, all of the line segments meet to form right angles.

The perimeter of the figure	52

17.

18. Given that $x \neq y$ and that $(x - y)^2 = (x + y)^2$, which of the following must be true?

       I. $x + y = x - y$
       II. $y = 0$
       III. $xy = 0$

   (A) None (B) II only (C) III only
   (D) I and III (E) I, II, and III

19. Let the lengths of the sides of a triangle be represented by $x + 3$, $2x - 3$, and $3x - 5$. If the perimeter of the triangle is 25, what is the length of the shortest side?

   (A) 5 (B) 6 (C) 7 (D) 8 (E) 10

Questions 20–21 refer to the graph below.

20. In which presidential election between 1972 to 1996 inclusive, was the percent of votes received by the winning candidate the lowest?

   (A) 1976 (B) 1980 (C) 1988
   (D) 1992 (E) 1996

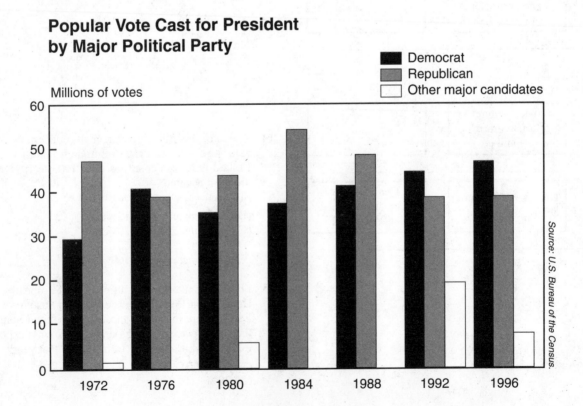

Popular Vote Cast for President by Major Political Party

Democrat
Republican
Other major candidates

Millions of votes

Source: U.S. Bureau of the Census.

2

2

21. In which year between 1972 and 1996 inclusive were the greatest number of votes cast for president?

    (A) 1980   (B) 1984   (C) 1988
    (D) 1992   (E) 1996

22. In 1990, twice as many boys as girls at Adams High School earned varsity letters. From 1990 to 2000 the number of girls earning varsity letters increased by 25% while the number of boys earning varsity letters decreased by 25%. What was the ratio in 2000 of the number of girls to the number of boys who earned varsity letters?

    (A) $\dfrac{5}{3}$ (B) $\dfrac{6}{5}$ (C) $\dfrac{1}{1}$ (D) $\dfrac{5}{6}$ (E) $\dfrac{3}{5}$

Column A	Column B

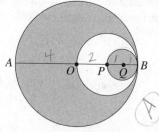

O, P, and Q, which are the centers of the three circles, all lie on diameter AB.

23.

The area of the entire shaded region	4 times the area of the white region

In 1980, Elaine was 8 times as old as Adam, and Judy was 3 times as old as Adam. Elaine is 20 years older than Judy.

24.

Adam's age in 1988	12

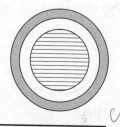

The three circles have the same center. The radii of the circles are 3, 4, and 5.

25.

The area of the shaded region	The area of the striped region

26. A square and an equilateral triangle each have sides of length 5. What is the ratio of the area of the square to the area of the triangle?

    (A) $\dfrac{4}{3}$ (B) $\dfrac{16}{9}$ (C) $\dfrac{\sqrt{3}}{4}$
    (D) $\dfrac{4\sqrt{3}}{3}$ (E) $\dfrac{16\sqrt{3}}{9}$

27. If $x + 2y = a$ and $x - 2y = b$, which of the following expressions is equal to xy?

    (A) ab (B) $\dfrac{a+b}{2}$ (C) $\dfrac{a-b}{2}$
    (D) $\dfrac{a^2-b^2}{4}$ (E) $\dfrac{a^2-b^2}{8}$

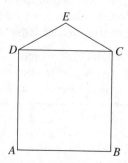

28. In the figure above, the area of square $ABCD$ is 100, the area of triangle DEC is 10, and $EC = ED$. What is the distance from A to E?

    (A) 11   (B) 12   (C) $\sqrt{146}$ (D) 13   (E) $\sqrt{244}$

3   **3**

SECTION 3—ANALYTICAL WRITING

Time—75 Minutes
2 Writing Tasks

Task 1: Issue Exploration
45 Minutes

<u>Directions</u>: In 45 minutes, choose one of the two following topics and compose an essay on that topic. You may not write on any other topic. Write your essay on separate sheets of paper.

Each topic is presented in a one- to two-sentence quotation commenting on an issue of general concern. Your essay may support, refute, or qualify the views expressed in the quotation. Whatever you write, however, must be relevant to the issue under discussion, and you must support your viewpoint with reasons and examples derived from your studies and/or experience.

Before you choose a topic, read both topics carefully. Consider which topic would give you greater scope for writing an effective, well-argued essay.

Faculty members from various institutions will evaluate your essay, judging it on the basis of your skill in the following areas.

• Analysis of the quotation's implications
• Organization and articulation of your ideas
• Use of relevant examples and arguments to support your case
• Handling of the mechanics of standard written English

Once you have decided which topic you prefer, click on the appropriate icon (**Topic 1** or **Topic 2**) to confirm your choice. Do not be hasty confirming your choice of topic. Once you have clicked on a topic, you will not be able to switch to the alternate choice.

Topic 1

"We venerate loyalty—to our schools, employers, institutions, friends—as a virtue. Loyalty, however, can be at least as detrimental an influence as it can be a beneficial one."

Topic 2

"A person who does not thoroughly comprehend the technical side of a craft is incapable of judging it."

3   3

**Task 2: Argument Analysis
30 Minutes**

<u>Directions</u>: In 30 minutes, prepare a critical analysis of an argument expressed in a short paragraph. You may not offer an analysis of any other argument. Write your essay on separate sheets of paper.

As you critique the argument, think about the author's underlying assumptions. Ask yourself whether any of them are questionable. Also evaluate any evidence the author brings up. Ask yourself whether it actually supports the author's conclusion.

In your analysis, you may suggest additional kinds of evidence to reinforce the author's argument. You may also suggest methods to refute the argument, or additional data that might be useful to you as you assess the soundness of the argument. *You may **not**, however, present your personal views on the topic.* Your job is to analyze the elements of an argument, not to support or contradict that argument.

Faculty members from various institutions will judge your essay, assessing it on the basis of your skill in the following areas:

- Identification and assessment of the argument's main elements
- Organization and articulation of your thoughts
- Use of relevant examples and arguments to support your case
- Handling of the mechanics of standard written English

The following appeared in an editorial in the Bayside Sentinel.

"Bayside citizens need to consider raising local taxes if they want to see improvements in the Bayside School District. Test scores, graduation and college admission rates, and a number of other indicators have long made it clear that the Bayside School District is doing a poor job educating our youth. Our schools look run down. Windows are broken, bathrooms unusable, and classroom equipment hopelessly out of date. Yet just across the Bay, in New Harbor, school facilities are up-to-date and in good condition. The difference is money; New Harbor spends twenty-seven percent more per student than Bayside does, and test scores and other indicators of student performance are stronger in New Harbor as well."

Answer Key—Diagnostic Test

Section 1—Verbal Ability

1. **D**	6. **E**	11. **B**	16. **C**	21. **B**	26. **A**
2. **B**	7. **C**	12. **A**	17. **C**	22. **E**	27. **B**
3. **B**	8. **C**	13. **A**	18. **B**	23. **E**	28. **D**
4. **C**	9. **E**	14. **D**	19. **B**	24. **C**	29. **D**
5. **B**	10. **D**	15. **C**	20. **C**	25. **E**	30. **E**

Section 2—Quantitative Ability

Note: The letters in brackets following the Quantitative Ability answers refer to the sections of Chapter 14 in which you can find the information you need to answer the questions. For example, 1. **C** [E] means that the answer to question 1 is C, and that the solution requires information found in Section 14-E: Averages. Also, 20. **A** [13] means that the answer to question 20 is based on information in Chapter 13: Data Interpretation.

1. **D** [A]	6. **D** [O]	11. **A** [J,L]	16. **C** [E,J]	21. **D** [13]	26. **D** [J,K]
2. **C** [J]	7. **D** [G]	12. **C** [E,G]	17. **C** [K]	22. **D** [C,D]	27. **E** [G]
3. **B** [A,B]	8. **A** [A]	13. **B** [K]	18. **C** [F]	23. **A** [L]	28. **D** [J,K]
4. **B** [A]	9. **B** [O]	14. **E** [13]	19. **C** [G]	24. **C** [H]	
5. **B** [I]	10. **C** [A]	15. **C** [13]	20. **D** [13]	25. **C** [L]	

Section 3—Analytical Writing

There are no "correct answers" to this section.

Self-Appraisal

Now that you have completed the Diagnostic Test, evaluate your performance. Identify your strengths and weaknesses, and then plan a practical study program based on what you have discovered.

Use the Answer Key to check your answers. Your raw score for each section is equal to the number of correct answers you had. Once you have determined your raw score for each ability area, use the conversion chart that follows to get your scaled score. Note that this conversion chart is provided to give you a very rough estimate of the GRE score you would achieve if you took the test now without any further preparation. When you take the computer-based GRE, your scaled score will be determined not only by the number of questions you answer correctly, but also by the difficulty level of those questions. The unofficial conversion chart presented here gives you only an approximate idea of how raw scores convert into scaled scores.

Use this Diagnostic Test to identify areas you may be weak in. You may find that you had trouble with a particular question type (for example, you didn't do well on the analogy questions in the verbal section), or with particular subject matter (for example, you didn't do well on any geometry questions, whether they were quantitative comparisons or discrete quantitative). Determining what you need to concentrate on will help you plan an effective study program.

Remember that, in addition to evaluating your scores and identifying weak areas, you should read all the answer explanations for questions you answered incorrectly, questions you guessed on, and questions you answered correctly but found difficult. Reviewing the answer explanations will help you understand concepts and strategies, and may point out shortcuts.

Score Conversion Chart

Raw Score	Scaled Scores	
	Verbal Score	Quantitative Score
30	800	
28	760	800
27	720	770
24	650	700
21	590	630
18	500	560
15	450	500
12	390	430
9	310	350
6	240	270
3	200	200

Answer Explanations

Section 1—Verbal Ability

1. **D.** The opposite of a *prodigal* (spendthrift; extravagant person) is an *economical person*. Beware eye-catchers. Choice C is incorrect. A *prodigal* is not a *prodigy* (wonder; gifted person). Think of "a prodigal squandering his wealth."

2. **B.** The opposite of *artifice* (trickery; guile) is *sincerity*. Think of being "tricked by her skillful artifice."

3. **B.** Given the ubiquity of light, it is *unsurprising* that creatures have *developed* the biologically helpful ability to make use of light energy. Note the use of *therefore* indicating that the omitted portion of the sentence supports or continues a thought developed elsewhere in the sentence.

4. **C.** The politicians do not forsake center stage. However, if they did forsake center stage once in a while, the public might like them better for their *self-effacement* (withdrawal from attention).

5. **B.** By definition, a *route* that is *circuitous* follows an indirect course. Likewise, an *argument* that is *devious* follows an indirect course.   (Defining Characteristic)

6. **E.** To be *officious* (meddlesome) is to be *helpful* in an excessive, offensive manner. To be *sycophantic* (fawning, obsequious) is to be *deferential* (respectful) in an excessive, offensive manner.   (Manner)

7. **C.** The author states that the later novels of James play down prominent action. Thus they lack *overtly dramatic incident*. However, the author goes on to state that James's novels *do* possess interest; they carry the reader through "a rich analysis of the mental adjustments of the characters to the realities of their personal situations." It is this implicitly dramatic psychological revelation that sustains the reader's interest.

   Question A is unanswerable on the basis of the passage. It is evident that James wrote psychological novels; it is nowhere stated that he originated the genre.

   Question B is unanswerable on the basis of the passage. Although conventional narrative technique relates "events in distinctly phased sequences," clearly separating them, it does not necessarily recount action in *strictly* chronological order.

Question D is unanswerable on the basis of the passage. The passage does not deal with the general public's reaction to James. Question E is unanswerable on the basis of the passage. The passage talks of qualities in James as a novelist in terms of their being *characteristic,* not in terms of their making him *unique.*

8. C. While the stories themselves grow simpler, their moral and psychological aspects become increasingly complex. Choice A is incorrect. The passage mentions the specific description of settings as characteristic of James's early, conventional novels, not of his later works.
Choice B is incorrect. In his later novels James grew less concerned with plot and more concerned with psychological revelation.
Choice D is incorrect. The "excitement of visible actions building up to a climactic event" (lines 31–32) is characteristic of the common novel, not of the Jamesian psychological novel.
Choice E is incorrect. The later novels tend instead to subordinate dramatic effect to psychological exploration and revelation.

9. E. The author refers to novels of action as "overstuffed" and describes them as "crammed with *adventitious* events"—events that are not inherent in the situation, but that are added, possibly irrelevantly, to the general story. However, these comments are merely made in passing: the author is not launching an attack against the novel of action. Thus, his attitude is best described as one of *mild disapprobation* or disapproval.
Choice A is incorrect. The author is not *pointedly indignant* or deeply resentful in tone. He is merely making mildly critical remarks in passing.
Choice B is incorrect. The author does make passing comments that disparage the novel of action. He is not wholly *neutral* on the topic.
Choice C is incorrect. While the author does disparage the novel of action, he does not ridicule or *deride* it sharply.
Choice D is incorrect. The author is certainly not a *strong partisan* or advocate of the novel of action.

10. D. The opposite of to *equivocate* (avoid committing oneself in what one says) is to *pledge* (bind or commit oneself solemnly).
Think of politicians "hedging and equivocating."

11. B. The opposite of *opulence* (wealth; affluence) is *penury* or extreme poverty.
Think of "luxurious opulence."

12. A. Something *ephemeral* (fleeting; transient) lacks *permanence.* Something *erratic* (unpredictable) lacks *predictability.*
(Antonym Variant)

13. A. To be *nonplussed* (totally at a loss) is to exhibit *bafflement* (perplexity). To be *discomfited* (abashed; disconcerted) is to exhibit *embarrassment.*
Beware eye-catchers. Choice D is incorrect. To be *despicable* is to be worthy of *contempt*; it is not to *exhibit* contempt.
(Synonym Variant)

14. D. To *ogle* is to *observe* or look at someone provocatively (in an attention-getting manner). To *flaunt* is to *display* or show off something provocatively (in an attention-getting manner).
(Manner)

15. C. You are dealing with either similar or contradictory impulses. If the impulses are similar (that is, *analogous*, *comparable*, or *related*, the second missing word should be a synonym or near-synonym for *individualize*. If the impulses are contradictory (that is, *disparate* or *divergent*), the second missing word should be an antonym or near-antonym for *individualize*. In this case, the latter holds true. The impulses are *divergent*; they are the impulse to individualize and the contradictory impulse to *typify* (treat characters as representatives of a type).

16. C. In a case in which experts disagree, it is *incumbent on* responsible scholars (that is, falls upon them as a scholarly duty or obligation) to *refrain from* making statements that are dogmatic or excessively assertive and arbitrary about the issue.

17. C. The subduction zone is the site of the destruction or consumption of existing lithospheric material. In contrast, the mid-ocean ridge is the site of the creation or emergence of new lithospheric material.
Choice A is incorrect. Both mid-ocean ridges and subduction zones are boundaries between plates.
Choice B is incorrect. Both are located on the ocean floor.
Choice D is incorrect. It is unsupported by the passage.
Choice E is incorrect. The reverse is true.

18. B. Choice B is correct. You are told that the new lithospheric material is injected into a mid-ocean ridge, a suboceanic mountain range. This new material does not disappear; it is added to the material already there. Thus, it is *incorporated into* the existing mid-ocean ridge.

Choice A is incorrect. "In general the plates are in motion with respect to one another." Nothing suggests that they become immobilized; indeed, they are said to diverge from the ridge, sliding as they diverge.

Choice C is incorrect. The passage specifically denies it. ("The size of the earth is essentially constant.")

Choice D is incorrect. It is the earth itself whose magnetic field reverses. Nothing in the passage suggests the new lithospheric material has any such potential.

Choice E is incorrect. At a mid-ocean ridge, the site at which new lithospheric material is injected from below, the plates diverge; they do not sink. (They sink, one plate diving under another, at a subduction zone.)

19. B.   Line 23 states that one plate is pushed under another and is reincorporated or *absorbed* into the mantle.

Choice A is incorrect. Lithospheric material rises at mid-ocean ridges, not at subduction zones.

Choice C is incorrect. New lithospheric material is injected at a mid-ocean ridge.

Choice D is incorrect. The injection of new lithospheric material causes sea-floor spreading around the mid-ocean ridge.

Choice E is incorrect. The lithospheric plates are described as diverging from a mid-ocean ridge, not from a subduction zone.

20. C.   The opposite of to *hone* or sharpen is to *dull* (make blunt).
Think of "honing a razor."

21. B.   The opposite of *phlegmatic* (stolid; undemonstrative) is *ardent* (passionate; eager).
Think of "phlegmatic and uncaring."

22. E.   The opposite of a *banality* (commonplace; trite or overused expression) is a *novel expression*.
Think of "the banality of a greeting card rhyme."

23. E.   *Thirst* is a specific example of a *drive* (state of instinctual need). *Smell* is a specific example of a *sense*.   (Class and Member)

24. C.   *Skulduggery* or dishonest, unscrupulous behavior is the mark of the *swindler*. *Chicanery* or trickery is the mark of the *trickster*.
(Defining Characteristic)

25. E.   After incubating the new functions, the next step would be to *nurture* or foster their growth until they were ready to be sent out

into the world. Their departure, however, would not diminish the cities, for by continuing to breed fresh ideas the cities would *renew* themselves.

Note the metaphoric usage of *incubate* and *breed* that influences the writer's choice of words. Cities do not literally incubate businesses or breed ideas; they only do so figuratively.

26. A.   Man is *gregarious* or sociable. However, he is more in need of mental companionship than of physical companionship. The writer plays on words in his conceit that a man may like to go alone for a walk but hates to stand alone in his *opinions*.

27. B.   The opposite of *erudite* (scholarly; learned) is *ignorant*. Think of "an erudite scholar."

28. D.   The opposite of *effrontery* (shameless boldness) is diffidence (tentativeness; timidity). Think of "shocking effrontery."

29. D.   The opening sentence describes the shattering of the Iroquois leadership's pro-British policy. The remainder of the passage describes how Iroquois policy changed to reflect changes in European military goals.

Choice A is incorrect. The passage is expository, not accusatory.

Choice B is incorrect. Nothing in the passage suggests that such charges were made against the Iroquois.

Choice C is incorrect. It is unsupported by the passage.

Choice E is incorrect. The passage demonstrates the Iroquois were able to play European power politics.

Remember, when asked to find the main idea, be sure to check the opening and summary sentences of each paragraph.

30. E.   Lines 20–31 indicate that in the early 1700s and through most of the eighteenth century the Iroquois *did* hold the balance of power. Therefore, Choice E is the correct answer.

Choice A is incorrect. The raid on Lachine was an effective response to French aggression, as was the Iroquois-enforced policy of aggressive neutrality.

Choice B is incorrect. James II's overthrow was followed by colonial uprisings.

Choice C is incorrect. In response to the Iroquois leaders' supposed favoring of the British (lines 38–44), the French went to war.

Choice D is incorrect. This sums up the policy of aggressive neutrality.

Section 2—Quantitative Ability

Two asterisks (**) indicate an alternative method of solving.

1. **D.** Use the laws of exponents.
   Column A is $a^4 a^5 = a^9$.
   Column B is $(a^3)^2 = a^6$.
   If $a = 1$, the columns are equal; but if $a = 2$, Column A is much greater. Neither column is always greater, and the two columns are not always equal (D).

2. **C.** Since the measure of an exterior angle of a triangle is equal to the sum of the measures of the two opposite interior angles [KEY FACT J2],
   $$c = a + b \Rightarrow a + b - c = 0.$$
   The columns are equal (C).
   **Use TACTIC 13-1: plug in easy-to-use numbers. If $a = 60$ and $b = 70$, then $d = 50 \Rightarrow c = 130$, and $60 + 70 - 130 = 0$.

3. **B.**

	Column A	Column B
	$\sqrt{a + b}$	$\sqrt{a} + \sqrt{b}$
Since the quantities in each column are positive, we can square them [TACTIC 3, Chapter 12].	$a + b$	$a + 2\sqrt{ab} + b$
Subtract $a + b$ from each column	0	$2\sqrt{ab}$

   Since a and b are positive, $2\sqrt{ab}$ is positive. Column B is greater.

4. **B.** There are three primes between 40 and 50: 41, 43, and 47, but only two primes between 30 and 40: 31 and 37. *Note*: remember that other than 2 and 5 *every* prime ends in 1, 3, 7, or 9, so those are the only numbers you need to check.

5. **B.** The unmarked angle opposite the 60° angle also measures 60° [KEY FACT I4], and the sum of the measures of all six angles in the diagram is 360° [KEY FACT I3]. So,
   $$360 = a + b + c + 20 + 60 + 60$$
   $$= a + b + c + 140.$$
   Subtracting 140 from each side, we get that $a + b + c = 220$.

6. **D.** Draw a Venn diagram. Since 10 seniors are in *both* band and orchestra, 30 are in band only and 50 are in orchestra only. Therefore, $10 + 30 + 50 = 90$ seniors are in at least one group, and the remaining 110 are in neither.

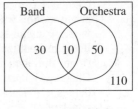

7. **D** Let x be the amount in dollars that each of the 20 children were going to contribute; then $20x$ represents the cost of the present. When 4 children dropped out, the remaining 16 each had to pay $(x + 1.50)$ dollars. So, $16(x + 1.5) = 20x \Rightarrow 16x + 24 = 20x \Rightarrow 24 = 4x \Rightarrow x = 6$, and so the cost of the present was $20 \times 6 = 120$ dollars.
   **Since each of the 16 remaining children had to pay an extra \$1.50, the extra payments totaled $16 \times \$1.50 = \$24$. This is the amount that would have been paid by the 4 children who dropped out, so each of the 4 would have paid \$6. The cost of the gift was $20 \times \$6 = \$120$.

8. **A.**

	Column A	Column B
Rewrite 20^{10}.	10^{20}	$20^{10} = (2 \times 10)^{10}$
Use a law of exponents.	10^{20}	$2^{10} \times 10^{10}$
Divide each column by 10^{10}.	10^{10}	2^{10}

   Column A is *much* greater.

9. **B.** From the 124 people in front of Jill, remove Jack plus the 24 people in front of Jack: $124 - 25 = 99$. Column B is greater.

10. **C.** $4^{10} \times 64^2 = 4^{10} \times (4^3)^2 = 4^{10} \times 4^6 = 4^{16}$.
    Also, $16^2 \times 4^n = (4^2)^2 \times 4^n = 4^4 \times 4^n = 4^{4+n}$.
    So, $4^{16} = 4^{4+n}$ and $16 = 4 + n$. Then $n = 12$.

11. **A.** Since OA and OB are radii, they are each equal to 5. With no restrictions on x, chord AB could be any positive number less than 10 (the length of a diameter). If x were 90, AB would be $\sqrt{50}$; since $x > 90$, $AB > \sqrt{50} > 7$. Therefore, the perimeter of $\triangle AOB$ is greater than $5 + 5 + 7 = 17$. Column A is greater.

12. **C.** $\dfrac{a - b}{c - a} = 1 \Rightarrow a - b = c - a \Rightarrow 2a = b + c \Rightarrow a = \dfrac{b + c}{2}$. The columns are equal (C).
    **Use TACTIC G2. Since you have an equation with three variables, choose values for two of them and find the third. Let $a = 2$ and $b = 1$. Then $\dfrac{2 - 1}{c - 2} = 1 \Rightarrow c = 3$. The average of b and c is 2, which equals a.

13. B. If the side of a square is 10, its diagonal is
$10\sqrt{2} \approx 14$ [KEY FACTS J8 and J9]. So the
square in Column B is larger.
**The area of the square in Column A is
$10^2 = 100$. The area of the square in Column B
is $\frac{1}{2}(15^2) = \frac{1}{2}(225) = 112.5$.

14. E. Exports to Eastern Europe from other Eastern
European countries increased from \$9.8
billion (10% of \$98 billion) to \$20.88 billion
(12% of \$174 billion)—an increase of slightly
more than 100%.

15. C. If France's exports to Eastern Europe were
four times those of the United States, than
France accounted for 8% of the total exports.
Since 8% is $\frac{1}{8}$ of 64%, France accounted for
$\frac{1}{8}$ or 12.5% of the exports from the European
Union.

16. C. The average of the measures of the three
angles of *any* triangle is $180° \div 3 = 60°$. The
columns are equal (C).

17. C. Ignore the x's and the y's. In any "staircase"
the perimeter is just twice the sum of the
height and the length. So the perimeter is
$2(12 + 14) = 2(26) = 52$. The columns are
equal (C).

18. C. Expand both binomial squares:

$(x + y)^2 = (x - y)^2 \Rightarrow$
$x^2 + 2xy + y^2 = x^2 - 2xy + y^2 \Rightarrow$
$2xy = -2xy \Rightarrow 4xy = 0 \Rightarrow xy = 0.$

So III is true. Since $xy = 0$, either $x = 0$ or
$y = 0$ (possibly both), but neither one must be
0. Since $x = 0$ and $y = 1$ is a solution, both I
and II are false. Only statement III is true.

19. C. Set up the equation:
$$(x + 3) + (2x - 3) + (3x - 5) = 25$$
Collect like terms: $6x - 5 = 25$
Add 5 to each side: $6x = 30$
Divide each side by 6: $x = 5$
Plugging in 5 for x, we get that the lengths of
the sides are 8, 7, and 10. The length of the
shortest side is 7.

20. D. In each election with only two candidates, the
candidate who received the greater number of
votes, received more than 50% of them. In
1972 and 1980 the number of votes received
by other major candidates was far less than
and in 1996 that number was approximately
equal to, the difference between the number
of votes received by the Republican and the
Democrat. Therefore, the percent of votes won
by the winner was greater than or approximately equal to 50%. In 1992, however, the
sum of the number of votes received by the
Republican and the other major candidate
greatly exceeded that of the Democratic winner. Consequently, the winner had fewer than
50% of the votes.

21. D. It is easy to see that 1992 was the only year in
which the total number of votes cast for president exceeded 100 million.

22. D. Use TACTIC 3, Chapter 12: pick easy-to-use
numbers. Assume that in 1990 there were 200
boys and 100 girls who earned varsity letters.
Then in 2000, there were 150 boys and 125
girls. So, the ratio of girls to boys was
$125:150 = 5:6$ or $\frac{5}{6}$.

23. A. Pick a simple number for the radius of circle
Q—say, 1. Then the radius of circle P is 2,
and the radius of circle O is 4. The area of the
large shaded region is the area of circle O
minus the area of circle P: $16\pi - 4\pi = 12\pi$.
The small shaded region is just circle Q,
whose area is π. Then, the total shaded area is
$12\pi + \pi = 13\pi$.
The white area is the area of circle P minus
the area of circle Q: $4\pi - \pi = 3\pi$. The area of
the shaded region is more than 4 times the
area of the white region. Column A is greater.

24. C. Let x = Adam's age in 1980. Then, in 1980,
Judy's age was $3x$ and Elaine's age was $8x$.
Since Elaine is 20 years older than Judy,
$8x = 3x + 20 \Rightarrow 5x = 20 \Rightarrow x = 4$. Therefore,
in 1988, Adam was $4 + 8 = 12$. The columns
are equal (C).

25. C. The area of the shaded region is the area of
the large circle, 25π, minus the area of the
middle circle, 16π: $25\pi - 16\pi = 9\pi$. The
striped region is just a circle of radius 3. Its
area is also 9π. The columns are equal (C).

26. **D.** Since you need a ratio, the length of the side is irrelevant. The area of a square is s^2 and the area of an equilateral triangle is $\dfrac{s^2\sqrt{3}}{4}$ [KEY FACT J15]. Then the ratio is

$$s^2 \div \frac{s^2\sqrt{3}}{4} = s^2 \times \frac{4}{s^2\sqrt{3}} = \frac{4}{\sqrt{3}} = \frac{4\sqrt{3}}{3}.$$

Of course, you could have used any number instead of s, and if you forgot the formula for the area of an equilateral triangle, you could have used $A = \dfrac{1}{2}bh$.

27. **E.** The easiest way to solve this is to use TACTIC 2, Chapter 11. Let $x = 2$ and $y = 1$. Then $xy = 2$, $a = 4$ and $b = 0$. Now, plug in 4 for a and 0 for b and see which of the five choices is equal to 2. Only E works:

$$\frac{a^2 - b^2}{8} = \frac{4^2 - 0^2}{8} = \frac{16}{8} = 2.$$

**Here is the correct algebraic solution.
Add the two equations:

$$
\begin{array}{r}
x + 2y = a \\
+\ x - 2y = b \\
\hline
2x = a + b
\end{array}
$$

Divide by 2: $x = \dfrac{a+b}{2}$

Multiply the second equation by –1 and add it to the first:

$$
\begin{array}{r}
x + 2y = a \\
+\ -x + 2y = -b \\
\hline
4y = a - b
\end{array}
$$

Divide by 4: $y = \dfrac{a-b}{4}$

Then $xy = \dfrac{a+b}{2} \cdot \dfrac{a-b}{4} = \dfrac{a^2 - b^2}{8}$.

This is the type of algebra you want to avoid.

28. **D.** Draw in segment $EXY \perp AB$. Then $XY = 10$ since it is the same length as a side of the

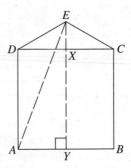

square. EX is the height of $\triangle ECD$, whose base is 10 and whose area is 10, so

$$EX = 2\left[\frac{1}{2}bh = \frac{1}{2}(10)(2) = 10\right], \text{ and } EY = 12.$$

Since $\triangle ECD$ is isosceles, $DX = 5$, so $AY = 5$. Finally, recognize $\triangle AYE$ as a 5-12-13 right triangle, or use the Pythagorean theorem to find the hypotenuse, AE, of the triangle:

$$(AE)^2 = 5^2 + 12^2 = 25 + 144 = 169,$$

so $AE = 13$.

Section 3—Analytical Writing

There are no "correct answers" to this section.

PART TWO

Verbal Ability: Tactics, Review, and Practice

4 Antonym Questions

- Testing Tactics
- Practice Exercises
- Answer Key

These are the antonym directions you will find on the GRE: "Each question below consists of a word printed in capital letters, followed by five lettered words or phrases. Choose the lettered word or phrase that is most nearly *opposite* in meaning to the word in capital letters."

Your task in answering antonym questions is straightforward: You are given a word and must choose, from the five choices that follow it, the best antonym (opposite). Often the first question or two on your verbal section will be an antonym question. Remember, the earliest questions you face on the GRE weigh more heavily than the final ones you answer. Take the time you need to answer these early questions correctly.

Testing Tactics

Think of a Context for the Capitalized Word

Take a quick look at the word in capital letters. If you don't recollect its meaning right away, try to think of a phrase or sentence in which you have heard it used. The context may help you come up with the word's meaning. For example:

> MAGNIFY:
> (A) forgive
> (B) comprehend
> (C) extract
> (D) diminish
> (E) electrify

The term "magnifying glass" should immediately come to mind. A magnifying glass enlarges things. The opposite of enlarging something is to make it smaller or *diminish* it. The answer is Choice D.

Now apply this tactic to a slightly more difficult question.

> ABERRANT:
> (A) exact
> (B) simple
> (C) causative
> (D) ordinary
> (E) pleasant

What phrase comes to your mind? "Aberrant behavior." "Aberrant data." In both cases you should have an impression of something deviating from what is expected, an impression of something unusual or abnormal. Aberrant behavior is odd or extraordinary; *aberrant*, therefore, is an antonym for *ordinary*. The correct answer is Choice D.

Before You Look at the Choices, Think of Antonyms for the Capitalized Word

Suppose your word is *industrious*, hard-working. What opposites come to your mind? You might come up with *lazy, idle, slothful, inactive*—all words that mean lacking industry and energy.

Now look at the choices:

> INDUSTRIOUS:
> (A) stupid
> (B) harsh
> (C) indolent
> (D) complex
> (E) inexpensive

Lazy, idle, and slothful all are synonyms for *indolent*. Your correct answer is Choice C.

This tactic will help you even when you have to deal with unfamiliar words among your answer choices. Suppose you do not know the meaning of the word *indolent*. You know that one antonym for your key word *industrious* is *lazy*. Therefore, you know that you are looking for a word that means the same as *lazy*. At this point you can go through the answer choices eliminating answers that don't work. Does *stupid* mean the same as *lazy*? No, smart people can

be lazy, too. Does *harsh* mean the same as *lazy*? No, harsh means cruel or rough. Does *indolent* mean the same as *lazy*? You don't know; you should check the other choices and then come back. Does *complex* mean the same as *lazy*? No, complex means complicated or intricate. Does *inexpensive* mean the same as *lazy*? No. So what is left? *Indolent*. Once again, your correct answer is Choice C.

See how you do when you apply this tactic to a new question.

> TACITURNITY:
> (A) arrogance
> (B) intolerance
> (C) belligerence
> (D) inconstancy
> (E) loquacity

Taciturnity is the quality of being uncommunicative. In thinking of possible antonyms for *taciturnity*, you may have come up with words like *talkativeness, wordiness,* and *garrulity*, words signifying excessiveness of speech. *Talkativeness, wordiness,* and *garrulity* are all synonyms for *loquacity*. The correct answer is Choice E.

Read All the Choices Before You Decide Which Is Best

On the GRE you are working under time pressure. You may be tempted to mark down the first answer that feels right and ignore the other choices given. Don't do it. Consider each answer. Only in this way can you be sure to distinguish between two possible answers and come up with the best answer for the question.

Words have shades of meaning. In matching a word with its opposite, you must pay attention to these shades of meaning. Try this example to see how this tactic works.

> UNRULY:
> (A) immobile
> (B) engaging
> (C) merciful
> (D) tractable
> (E) indifferent

Suppose you have only a vague sense of the meaning of *unruly*. You associate it with such vaguely negative terms as *wild, disagreeable, bad*. For this reason, you stop short when you come to Choice C. Reasoning that someone wild and disagreeable is *not* compassionate or merciful, you look no further and mark down Choice C.

Choice C, however, is incorrect. True, an unruly person is wild and hard to manage, even rebellious. Someone who lacks rebelliousness, however, is not necessarily merciful. Such a person is easy to manage, compliant, in fact *tractable*. The correct answer is Choice D.

Now try a second example to practice this tactic.

> BANALITY:
> (A) detailed analysis
> (B) unrehearsed statement
> (C) succinct account
> (D) novel expression
> (E) faithful description

A *banality* lacks freshness and originality; something banal is timeworn and trite. Choice B has an immediate appeal: something unrehearsed is by definition spontaneous and at least should seem fresh. However, an unrehearsed statement could be filled with cliches; though spontaneous, it may well be banal or trite. The best antonym for *banality* is Choice D, *novel expression*.

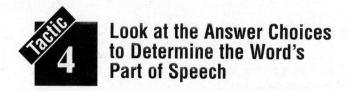

Look at the Answer Choices to Determine the Word's Part of Speech

Look at the capitalized word. What part of speech is it? Words often exist in several forms. You may think of *run* as a verb, for example, but in the phrases, "a run in her stocking," and "hit a home run," *run* is a noun.

The GRE plays on this confusion in testing your verbal ability. When you look at a particular capitalized word, you may not know whether you are dealing with a noun, a verb, or an adjective. *Harbor*, for example, is a very common noun; in "to harbor a fugitive," to give refuge to a runaway, it is a much less common verb.

If you suspect that a capitalized word may have more than one part of speech, don't worry. Just look at the first couple of answer choices and see what part of speech they are. That part of speech will be the capitalized word's part of speech.

In GRE Antonym Questions, **all** *the answer choices have the same part of speech.* You can always tell what that part of speech is by a quick glance at the first answer choice or two.

See how this tactic works in answering a relatively simple question.

POLISH:
(A) ruthlessness
(B) honesty
(C) indolence
(D) gaucheness
(E) complexity

Are you dealing with *polish* the verb or *polish* the noun?

A quick look at the answers assures you that they are all nouns. *Polish* here has nothing to do with rubbing and shining your silverware. The noun *polish* means refinement and culture: The country squire went abroad to acquire polish. Its opposite is *gaucheness* or awkwardness. The correct answer is Choice D.

Now try a second example.

PRECIPITATE:
(A) candid
(B) erratic
(C) cautious
(D) generous
(E) shallow

Is the word in capitals the adjective *precipitate* (hasty, impetuous) or the verb *precipitate* (to expedite or trigger)?

A quick look at the answer choices reveals that it is an adjective. (The *-ic* and *-ous* word endings are common adjective endings.) Thus, its opposite is *cautious* or *deliberate,* Choice C.

Consider Secondary Meanings of the Capitalized Word As Well as Its Primary Meaning

If none of the answer choices seems right to you, take another look at the capitalized word. It may have more than one meaning. The GRE often constructs questions that make use of secondary, less well-known meanings of deceptively familiar words. Take, for example, this typical question.

LIST:
(A) overturn
(B) be upright
(C) lie flat
(D) fall forward
(E) veer from side to side

List here has nothing to do with making lists or enumerating. It has to do with moving. When it *lists* to starboard, a ship simply leans to one side or tilts. The best antonym for this meaning of *list* is Choice B, *be upright*.

Try a second, more difficult question involving a less familiar meaning of a familiar word.

IMPRECISE:
(A) direct
(B) resolute
(C) voluminous
(D) nice
(E) perceptible

Few examinees tested on this question would answer it correctly. Why?

The problem lies not in the capitalized word but in the answer choices. *Imprecise* means inexact, approximate, vague. Thus, its antonym means exact and precise. Not immediately spotting *exact* or *precise* among the answer choices, and looking for a positive term to contrast with *imprecise*, some examinees may settle for Choice A, *direct*.

In doing so, they fail to consider that words have secondary meanings. In this case, *nice* does not mean pleasant or agreeable, as in *enjoying nice weather* or *being nice to your baby brother*. Instead, it means requiring or marked by great accuracy, delicacy, and skill, as in making *a nice distinction* in an argument or hitting *a nice shot* in golf. The correct answer is Choice D.

Break Down Unfamiliar Words into Recognizable Parts

When you come upon a totally unfamiliar word, don't give up. Break it down and see if you recognize any of its parts. Pay particular attention to prefixes—word parts added to the beginning of a word—and to roots, the building blocks of the language.

Look once more at the following question.

> ABERRANT:
> (A) exact
> (B) simple
> (C) causative
> (D) ordinary
> (E) pleasant

Suppose you had never seen *aberrant* before. You have seen dozens of other words beginning with *ab-*: *absent, abnormal, abduct*. Take *abduct*. What do you do when you abduct someone? You kidnap him, or steal him away. *Ab-* means *away*.

What about the root, *err*? To err is to be wrong or to wander, as in wandering from the usual path. Thus, *aberrant* means *wandering away*, straying from what is usual or normal, and its opposite is of course Choice D, *ordinary*.

Now try a second example in which this tactic can prove helpful.

> NEOLOGISM:
> (A) cordial salutation
> (B) brief summary
> (C) lengthy diatribe
> (D) archaic expression
> (E) equivocal remark

Neo- means new. *Log-* means word or speech. A *neologism* must have to do with a new sort of word or speech. Logically, therefore, the opposite of *neologism* must have to do with an *old* sort of word or speech. Only one answer seems possible: Choice D, *archaic expression*. *Archaic* means antiquated or obsolete. Choice D is correct.

Here is a final example, with word parts coming from Greek.

> SYNCHRONOUS:
> (A) not in working order
> (B) without problems
> (C) out of position
> (D) not in phase
> (E) without permission

Syn- means together. *Chron-* means time. Something *synchronous* must have to do with occurring together in time, like the *synchronous* movements of swimmers keeping time with one another. The antonym for *synchronous* thus is Choice D, *not in phase*.

The word part approach can help you interpret new words you encounter. However, apply it cautiously. In many words the roots, prefixes, and suffixes have lost their original meanings. In others, the same root occurs, but with markedly differing effects. It would not do to call a *philanthropist* a *philanderer*, for instance, though both words contain the root for love.

If you find the word part approach appealing, try to spend some time working with the Basic Word Parts List in Chapter 8. Remember, however, there is no substitute for learning the exact meaning of a word as it is used today.

Change Unfamiliar Words from One Part of Speech to Another

Sometimes you may be stumped by a word in one form, yet recognize it easily in another. Take, for example, the word *synchronous* in the previous tactic. To most test-takers, the adjective *synchronous* is far less familiar than is the verb *synchronize*, as in "Synchronize your watches!"

When you confront an unfamiliar word, try replacing its suffix with a different word ending and see whether this change jogs your memory. In the case of the noun *assiduity*, for example, cut off the noun suffix *-ity* and replace it with the adjective suffix *-ous*. You now have the word *assiduous*, as in an assiduous worker. Does that ring a bell? *Assiduous* means hardworking; *assiduity*, therefore, is a synonym for industriousness or diligence.

Practice this tactic as you answer the following question:

DICHOTOMOUS:
(A) apparent
(B) undivided
(C) atypical
(D) indifferent
(E) abstract

Remove the *-ous* ending from *dichotomous*. In its place, substitute *-y*. You have the word *dichotomy*, as in the dichotomy between Good and Evil, or the dichotomy between thought and action. A dichotomy is a division or separation in two parts, often mutually exclusive ones. Something dichotomous, therefore, is divided; its opposite is *undivided*, Choice B.

In Eliminating Answer Choices, Test Words for Their Positive or Negative Connotations

When you are dealing with a partially unfamiliar word, a word that you cannot define or use in a sentence but that you know you have seen previously, try to remember in what sort of context you have seen that word. Did it have positive connotations, or did it have a negative feel? If you are certain the capitalized word has positive connotations, then, since you are looking for its antonym, you *know* the correct answer must have negative ones. Thus, you can eliminate any answer choices that have positive connotations and guess among the answer choices that are negative in tone.

See how this approach applies in the following example.

CHARY:
(A) bold
(B) bright
(C) unsteady
(D) unforgiving
(E) unhappy

You cannot define *chary*. You would hesitate to use it in a sentence of your own. And yet, you are sure the word has a slightly negative feel to it. A person is *chary about* something. You have a sense of someone holding back.

Look at the answer choices. Which of them have negative connotations? *Unsteady? Unforgiving? Unhappy?* Eliminate all three. You have narrowed down your choices to *bold* and *bright*, both words that have a positive feel. You are in an excellent position to guess. As it turns out, *chary* means hesitant or reluctant to proceed. Its opposite is Choice A, *bold*.

Watch Out for Errors Caused by Eye-Catchers

When you look at answer choices, do you find that certain ones seem to leap right off the page? These words are eye-catchers. They look good—but be sure to take a second look.

Try these next antonym questions to see just how an eye-catcher works. First, an easy one.

> UNDERMINE:
> (A) ensnare
> (B) overstrain
> (C) mollify
> (D) terminate
> (E) bolster

What's the opposite of *under*? *Over*. What's the opposite of *undermine*? No, it's not *overstrain*. Be suspicious of answers that come too easily. To *undermine* means to weaken something or cause it to collapse by removing its underlying supports. The opposite of to *undermine* is Choice E, to *bolster* or support.

Here's a more difficult example. See if you can spot the eye-catcher.

> REDOUBTABLE:
> (A) unanticipated
> (B) unambiguous
> (C) unimposing
> (D) inescapable
> (E) immutable

Few test-takers attempting this question would answer it correctly. Why? Once more an early answer choice has been set up to tempt you. In this case, the presence of the familiar word *doubt* in the unfamiliar word *redoubtable* suggests that the word *redoubtable* has something to do with uncertainty. You know that *ambiguous* means uncertain in meaning. Thus, Choice B, *unambiguous*, is particularly appealing here. It is particularly appealing, and it is wrong.

Doubt in *redoubtable* is used in the sense not of uncertainty but of fear. *A redoubtable foe* causes fear; such a person is awesome or imposing. Someone *unimposing* causes no such fear. The correct answer is Choice C.

Practice Exercises

Antonym Exercise A

<u>Directions</u>: In each of the following antonym questions, a word printed in capital letters precedes five lettered words or phrases. From these five lettered words or phrases, pick the one most nearly <u>opposite</u> in meaning to the capitalized word.

Because some of the questions require you to distinguish fine shades of meaning, be sure to consider all the choices before deciding which one is best.

1. MOURNFUL: (A) informal   (B) sympathetic
   (C) private   (D) appropriate   (E) joyous

2. SCAD: (A) parsimony   (B) allocation
   (C) dearth   (D) restraint   (E) provision

3. GRANDIOSE: (A) docile   (B) unlikely to occur
   (C) simple and unimposing   (D) light in weight
   (E) uncommunicative

4. ENTRENCH: (A) defy   (B) oust
   (C) extinguish   (D) squander   (E) intercede

5. LACKLUSTER: (A) superficial
   (B) courteous   (C) vibrant   (D) complex
   (E) abundant

6. CENSURE: (A) augment   (B) eradicate
   (C) enthrall   (D) commend   (E) reform

7. TRANSIENCE: (A) slowness   (B) permanence
   (C) lack of caution   (D) desire for perfection
   (E) original nature

8. DESICCATE: (A) lengthen   (B) hallow
   (C) exonerate   (D) saturate   (E) anesthetize

9. PROTRUSION: (A) deep recess
   (B) strong dislike   (C) growing scarcity
   (D) illusion   (E) chaos

10. ENTICE: (A) repel   (B) authorize   (C) baffle
    (D) misplace   (E) diminish

11. ORTHODOXY: (A) renown   (B) trepidation
    (C) unconventionality   (D) inquisitiveness
    (E) remoteness

12. SUMPTUOUS: (A) dank (B) frequent
(C) partial (D) restrained (E) open

13. DISSOLUTION: (A) retribution
(B) compliance (C) futility (D) persuasion
(E) establishment

14. IRK: (A) pry (B) tinge (C) beguile
(D) convince (E) soothe

15. LIMBER: (A) sturdy (B) orderly
(C) durable (D) stiff (E) gloomy

16. OBLIQUITY: (A) praise
(B) straightforwardness (C) conformity
(D) self-righteousness (E) depreciation

17. SLUR: (A) sensitivity (B) sacrifice
(C) understatement (D) challenge
(E) commendation

18. APOTHEOSIS: (A) departure from tradition
(B) impatience with stupidity
(C) demotion from glory
(D) surrender to impulse
(E) cause for grief

19. ENERVATE: (A) narrate (B) enrage
(C) accomplish (D) invigorate (E) acquiesce

20. PARSIMONIOUS: (A) appropriate
(B) generous (C) complete (D) radiant
(E) ongoing

Antonym Exercise B

<u>Directions:</u> In each of the following antonym questions, a word printed in capital letters precedes five lettered words or phrases. From these five lettered words or phrases, pick the one most nearly <u>opposite</u> in meaning to the capitalized word.

Because some of the questions require you to distinguish fine shades of meaning, be sure to consider all the choices before deciding which one is best.

1. HEDGE:

(A) act on impulse
(B) refuse to represent
(C) state without qualification
(D) make a foolish comment
(E) establish a connection

2. ABROGATE: (A) transgress (B) signify
(C) alleviate (D) question (E) ratify

3. INDUSTRY: (A) cleanliness (B) pragmatism
(C) sloth (D) promptness (E) abasement

4. SPUNK: (A) success (B) timidity
(C) growing awareness (D) lack of intelligence
(E) loss of prestige

5. SAGE: (A) zealot (B) miser (C) braggart
(D) fool (E) tyrant

6. ADMONITION: (A) premonition
(B) hallucination (C) escape (D) commendation
(E) trepidation

7. CHARY: (A) lugubrious (B) brash
(C) indifferent (D) graceful (E) scornful

8. STUPEFY: (A) lie (B) bend (C) enliven
(D) talk nonsense (E) consider thoughtfully

9. COGENT: (A) contemplative (B) unpersuasive
(C) expository (D) stable (E) inconceivable

10. FICKLE: (A) spotless (B) industrious
(C) welcome (D) urgent (E) loyal

11. COMPLY: (A) simplify (B) strive (C) rebel
(D) unite (E) appreciate

12. CREDIT: (A) believe false (B) treat as equal
(C) make more difficult (D) underemphasize
(E) forget

13. STILTED: (A) informal (B) verbose
(C) secretive (D) senseless (E) tentative

14. UNGAINLY: (A) slender (B) graceful
(C) restrained (D) inaccurate (E) unnoticed

15. QUIXOTIC: (A) slow (B) abstemious
(C) pragmatic (D) benevolent (E) grave

16. DISPARITY: (A) timidity (B) complacency
(C) bigotry (D) likeness (E) influence

17. CRITICAL: (A) unimportant (B) uncertain
(C) silent (D) coherent (E) destructive

18. SOBRIETY: (A) influence (B) nonchalance
(C) holiness (D) civility (E) mirth

19. RESTIVENESS: (A) completeness
(B) conviction (C) concern (D) docility
(E) petulance

20. HALLOW: (A) keep silence (B) prove incorrect
(C) accuse openly (D) desecrate (E) instigate

Antonym Exercise C

Directions: In each of the following antonym questions, a word printed in capital letters precedes five lettered words or phrases. From these five lettered words or phrases, pick the one most nearly <u>opposite</u> in meaning to the capitalized word.

Because some of the questions require you to distinguish fine shades of meaning, be sure to consider all the choices before deciding which one is best.

1. HARBINGER: (A) ascetic   (B) miser
    (C) counselor   (D) follower   (E) braggart

2. SPUR: (A) embitter   (B) discourage
    (C) impress   (D) mislead   (E) ignore

3. DISJOINTED: (A) responsible   (B) connected
    (C) implied   (D) useful   (E) imprecise

4. MEALYMOUTHED: (A) hungry   (B) indefinite
    (C) tightlipped   (D) sincere   (E) apathetic

5. PREVARICATE: (A) postulate   (B) emphasize
    (C) support in theory   (D) consider thoughtfully
    (E) state truthfully

6. LUMINARY: (A) impostor   (B) nonentity
    (C) pilgrim   (D) braggart   (E) mutineer

7. TESTY: (A) erroneous   (B) uncommunicative
    (C) even-tempered   (D) quick-witted
    (E) industrious

8. NEFARIOUS: (A) lackadaisical   (B) eccentric
    (C) exemplary   (D) corrigible   (E) hypocritical

9. BEGRUDGE: (A) mourn silently
    (B) grant freely   (C) hunger for
    (D) advance rapidly   (E) fight back

10. BILK: (A) reduce in size   (B) make famous
    (C) roughen   (D) renovate   (E) pay in full

11. COMPOSE: (A) disturb   (B) reveal
    (C) strengthen   (D) isolate   (E) prevent

12. OCCLUDE: (A) determine   (B) transcend
    (C) surround   (D) open   (E) regulate

13. AMBIGUITY: (A) extent   (B) success
    (C) clarity   (D) normality   (E) expression

14. AMELIORATION: (A) prevention
    (B) aggravation   (C) distraction
    (D) indifference   (E) dissuasion

15. CAVIL: (A) discern   (B) disclose
    (C) introduce   (D) flatter   (E) commend

16. SKEPTICAL: (A) theoretical   (B) indifferent
    (C) ready to believe   (D) eager for change
    (E) lost in thought

17. FLEDGLING: (A) experienced person
    (B) shy onlooker   (C) social outcast
    (D) fugitive   (E) adversary

18. CRASS: (A) boastful   (B) temporary
    (C) cheerful   (D) refined   (E) extensive

19. RECALCITRANT: (A) tractable   (B) erratic
    (C) intuitive   (D) vigorous   (E) rambling

20. PROTRACT: (A) defy   (B) supplement
    (C) postpone   (D) shorten   (E) design

Antonym Exercise D

Directions: In each of the following antonym questions, a word printed in capital letters precedes five lettered words or phrases. From these five lettered words or phrases, pick the one most nearly <u>opposite</u> in meaning to the capitalized word.

Because some of the questions require you to distinguish fine shades of meaning, be sure to consider all the choices before deciding which one is best.

1. PRIM: (A) rare   (B) careful   (C) unnecessary
    (D) improper   (E) decisive

2. REPUGNANCE: (A) attraction   (B) lethargy
    (C) blame   (D) virtue   (E) awe

3. NETTLE: (A) disentangle   (B) mollify
    (C) magnify   (D) muffle   (E) recompense

4. REPLETE: (A) unwrinkled   (B) devoid
    (C) vulgar   (D) matchless   (E) unsympathetic

5. UNASSUAGED: (A) presumed   (B) deceptive
    (C) singular   (D) faulty   (E) soothed

6. PALTRY: (A) munificent   (B) improvident
    (C) random   (D) cautious   (E) obsolete

7. CONCLUSIVE: (A) difficult to express
    (B) bringing bad luck   (C) easy to solve
    (D) lacking merit   (E) open to question

8. RESOURCEFULNESS: (A) wealth
    (B) gratitude   (C) melancholy   (D) incompetence
    (E) frustration

9. DISSUADE: (A) extol   (B) exhort
    (C) intensify   (D) complicate   (E) precede

10. SPLENETIC: (A) lackluster   (B) heartless
    (C) diffident   (D) constant   (E) cordial

11. VIRULENCE: (A) pallor (B) orderliness (C) femininity (D) harmlessness (E) cowardice

12. ADHERENT: (A) fugitive (B) dissembler (C) opponent (D) educator (E) witness

13. OSCILLATE: (A) entreat (B) intensify (C) remain fixed (D) expand gradually (E) wither away

14. ASPERITY: (A) gentility (B) superiority (C) kindness (D) clarity (E) vagueness

15. UNSCATHED: (A) honest (B) gathered (C) injured (D) cleansed (E) forgiven

16. FETTER: (A) diminish (B) enervate (C) liberate (D) return (E) cure

17. AUTONOMY: (A) dependence (B) animation (C) renown (D) altruism (E) antipathy

18. SLACK: (A) rough (B) active (C) liberal (D) dependent (E) familiar

19. RECOIL: (A) plunge forward (B) cease firing (C) skirt an issue (D) facilitate (E) surrender

20. ENCUMBER: (A) disburden (B) perform easily (C) challenge boldly (D) observe with care (E) suppress

Antonym Exercise E

Directions: In each of the following antonym questions, a word printed in capital letters precedes five lettered words or phrases. From these five lettered words or phrases, pick the one most nearly opposite in meaning to the capitalized word.

Because some of the questions require you to distinguish fine shades of meaning, be sure to consider all the choices before deciding which one is best.

1. OPACITY: (A) iridescence (B) firmness (C) transparence (D) poverty (E) slum

2. PREDILECTION: (A) postponement (B) afterthought (C) lamentation (D) reoccurrence (E) aversion

3. SEEDY: (A) elegant (B) intricate (C) tranquil (D) irregular (E) slow

4. BOGGLE: (A) disentangle (B) repudiate (C) ascertain (D) remain unruffled (E) lack planning

5. HIDEBOUND: (A) strong-willed (B) open-minded (C) thin-skinned (D) tenderhearted (E) scatterbrained

6. CASTIGATE: (A) diminish (B) imitate (C) compare (D) reward (E) misjudge

7. GAMBOL: (A) dodge (B) masquerade (C) digress (D) plod (E) vex

8. RAUCOUS: (A) orderly (B) absorbent (C) mellifluous (D) contentious (E) buoyant

9. TAPER: (A) emphasize (B) restore (C) split (D) broaden (E) modify

10. HIGH-HANDED: (A) dejected (B) reasonable (C) hard-handed (D) short-handed (E) dynamic

11. DIMINUTION: (A) measurement (B) proximity (C) augmentation (D) orderliness (E) inclination

12. DISTEND: (A) tell the truth (B) respond as expected (C) approximate (D) collect (E) shrink

13. EMBROIL: (A) disengage (B) remonstrate (C) refute thoroughly (D) answer hypothetically (E) consider genuinely

14. VOUCHSAFE: (A) postpone (B) dissemble (C) endanger (D) prohibit (E) justify

15. JETTISON: (A) salvage (B) decelerate (C) muffle (D) distract (E) anchor

16. STOIC: (A) savant (B) herald (C) whiner (D) victor (E) bystander

17. GAMELY: (A) fearfully (B) diligently (C) clumsily (D) gloomily (E) respectfully

18. CRESTFALLEN: (A) haughty (B) impolite (C) frivolous (D) tentative (E) rough

19. DESULTORY: (A) apologetic (B) independent (C) laudatory (D) questionable (E) methodical

20. PULCHRITUDE: (A) antipathy (B) unsightliness (C) inexperience (D) languor (E) rancor

Answer Key

Antonym Exercise A

1. E	6. D	11. C	16. B
2. C	7. B	12. D	17. E
3. C	8. D	13. E	18. C
4. B	9. A	14. E	19. D
5. C	10. A	15. D	20. B

Antonym Exercise B

1. C	6. D	11. C	16. D
2. E	7. B	12. A	17. A
3. C	8. C	13. A	18. E
4. B	9. B	14. B	19. D
5. D	10. E	15. C	20. D

Antonym Exercise C

1. D	6. B	11. A	16. C
2. B	7. C	12. D	17. A
3. B	8. C	13. C	18. D
4. D	9. B	14. B	19. A
5. E	10. E	15. E	20. D

Antonym Exercise D

1. D	6. A	11. D	16. C
2. A	7. E	12. C	17. A
3. B	8. D	13. C	18. B
4. B	9. B	14. C	19. A
5. E	10. E	15. C	20. A

Antonym Exercise E

1. C	6. D	11. C	16. C
2. E	7. D	12. E	17. A
3. A	8. C	13. A	18. A
4. D	9. D	14. D	19. E
5. B	10. B	15. A	20. B

5 Analogy Questions

- ■ **Testing Tactics**
- ■ **Practice Exercises**
- ■ **Answer Key**

Here are the directions for answering analogy questions that you will find on the GRE: "In the following question, a related pair of words or phrases is followed by five lettered pairs of words or phrases. Select the lettered pair that best expresses a relationship similar to that expressed in the original pair."

Analogy questions ask you to determine the relationship between a pair of words and then recognize a similar or parallel relationship between a different pair of words. You are given one pair of words and must choose from the five answer choices another pair that is related in the same way. The relationship between the words in the original pair will always be specific and precise, as will the relationship between the words in the correct answer pair.

Analogies come from a wide variety of fields. You need to know that musicians study in conservatories and ministers in seminaries, that panegyrics praise and elegies lament. You need to be aware of catalysts and conundrums, augers and auguries, and know in which contexts these words are found. You are not, however, dealing with these words in isolation; you are always dealing with them in relationship to other words.

Note how a GRE analogy question is set up. First you have the two capitalized words linked by a symbol. Take a look at a few examples.

FRESCO : WALL

A fresco is related to a wall. **How?** By *definition*, a fresco or mural painting is painted on a wall.

STAMMER : TALK

Stammer is related to talk. **How?** To stammer is to talk haltingly, even inarticulately. It is to talk in a defective or faulty *manner*.

TILE : MOSAIC

Tile is related to mosaic. **How?** A mosaic is made up of tiles. Notice the wording of the last sentence. You could also have said "Tiles are the pieces that make up a mosaic" and maintained the word order of the analogy. Sometimes, however, it is easier to express a relationship if you reverse the order of the words.

Next you come to the five answer choices. See if you can tell which pair best expresses a relationship similar to the relationship of tile to mosaic.

> TILE : MOSAIC ::
> (A) hoop : embroidery
> (B) wick : candle
> (C) whalebone : scrimshaw
> (D) easel : painting
> (E) knot : macrame

The correct answer is Choice E: macrame is made up of knots. Just as the tiles in a mosaic make a pattern, so too the knots in a piece of macrame make a pattern.

Some of the analogy questions on the GRE are as clear-cut as this. Others are more complex. To answer them correctly involves far more than knowing single meanings of individual words: it involves knowing the usual contexts in which they are found, and their connotations as well. Master the tactics that immediately follow. Then proceed to the practice exercises containing both relatively simple and challenging analogies at the chapter's end.

Testing Tactics

Before You Look at the Choices, Try to State the Relationship Between the Capitalized Words in a Clear Sentence

In answering an analogy question, your first problem is to determine the exact relationship between the two capitalized words. *Before you look at the answer pairs*, make up a sentence that illustrates how these capitalized words are related. Then test the possible answers by seeing how well they fit in your sentence.

Try this tactic on the following two questions.

> TORRENT : DROPLET ::
> (A) water : eddy
> (B) swamp : desert
> (C) downpour : puddle
> (D) avalanche : pebble
> (E) hurricane : wreckage

A *torrent* (violent downpour or rushing stream) is made up of *droplets*. An *avalanche* or sudden fall of rocks, snow or earth is made up of *pebbles*. Choice D is correct.

Don't let Choice C fool you: while a downpour, like a torrent, is a violent rain, it is not made up of puddles; rather, it leaves puddles in its aftermath.

> PHILATELY : STAMPS ::
> (A) calligraphy : pens
> (B) cartography : maps
> (C) chronology : events
> (D) numismatics : coins
> (E) geriatrics : ailments

Philately is the study and collecting of *stamps*. *Numismatics* is the study and collecting of *coins*. Choice D is correct.

Note how difficult this question would be if you did not know that philately involved collecting stamps. You might have guessed that philately primarily involves *working with* stamps (as, for example, calligraphy involves working with pens) or even *making* stamps (as cartography involves making maps). Knowing the primary relationship between the capitalized words, however, you can go through the answer choices eliminating any pairs that do not express the same relationship. Thus, you can eliminate Choice A: someone who practices calligraphy may possibly collect pens, but calligraphy's primary, dictionary-defined role is the art of penmanship, the production of beautiful handwriting. Similarly, you can eliminate Choice E: geriatrics certainly involves studying ailments, but the ailments of the elderly, not ailments in general; furthermore, while it studies the ailments of the elderly, it certainly doesn't *collect* any such ailments. You can eliminate Choice C as well: chronology involves arranging events in the order in which they occur. This process of elimination leaves you with two relatively unfamiliar words—*numismatics* and *cartography*—and a fifty percent chance of guessing the answer correctly.

If you are not sure of the answer, *always* rule out answer choices that you *know* cannot be correct, and then guess among the choices that are left.

Remember, you have to do your best to answer the question on your screen before you can move on to the next.

If More Than One Answer Fits the Relationship in Your Sentence, Look for a Narrower Approach

When you try to express the relationship between the two capitalized words in sentence form, occasionally you come up with too simple a sentence, one that fails to include enough details to particularize your analogy. In such cases, more than one answer may fit the relationship, and you will have to analyze the original pair again.

Consider this analogy question.

> PSEUDOPOD : AMOEBA ::
> (A) branch : tree
> (B) minnow : fish
> (C) bristle : hedgehog
> (D) tentacle : octopus
> (E) shell : snail

"A pseudopod is part of an amoeba." You have stated a relationship between the capitalized words in a sentence, but you have not stated a relationship that is precise enough. After all, branches are parts of trees, bristles are parts of hedgehogs, tentacles are parts of octopuses, and shells are parts of snails. You need to focus on some aspect of the relationship between the words in the original pair that corresponds to an aspect of only one of the answer pairs. Go back to the original pair of words for more details. How does an amoeba use a pseudopod? What function does it serve? "An amoeba uses a pseudopod for grasping." Try the answer choices in this new test sentence. "A tree uses a branch for grasping." False. "A hedgehog uses a bristle for grasping." False. "A snail uses its shell for grasping." False. "An octopus uses a tentacle for grasping." Choice D clearly is best.

In answering analogy questions on the GRE, pay special attention to how a dictionary would define the words involved. Do not settle for what "may be" a good relationship. Precision is important in analogies: a pseudopod is not just part of an amoeba, it is the part that the amoeba uses for grasping. Strive to identify the relationship that exists "by definition."

Consider Secondary Meanings of Words As Well as Their Primary Meanings

Frequently, the test-makers attempt to mislead you by using familiar words in relatively uncommon ways. When an apparently familiar word seems incongruous in a particular analogy, consider other definitions of that word.

See how this tactic applies to the following examples.

> PAN : CAMERA ::
> (A) ban : book
> (B) tune : radio
> (C) charge : battery
> (D) filter : lens
> (E) rotate : periscope

Before you can answer this question, you have to know the definition of *pan*. You're not dealing with a frying pan or a gold miner's pan or a dish pan; *pan* here is a verb, not a noun. You can tell because the first word of each answer choice is also a verb. The verb ending *-ate* at the end of *rotate* gives that away.

The verb *pan*, however, has several meanings:

> The miner panned for gold. (The miner washed gravel to separate out the gold.)
>
> The chef panned the carrots. (The chef cooked the carrots in a pan with a small amount of fat or water.)
>
> The critic panned the comedy. (The critic severely criticized the comedy.)

None of these is the meaning you want.

Think how *pan* relates to *camera*. When someone *pans* a *camera*, what happens? The cameraperson rotates the camera on its axis so that he or she can film a panoramic scene (or a moving person or object). Similarly, a submarine crew member *rotates* or revolves a *periscope* on its axis so that he or she can make a panoramic observation. The correct answer is Choice E.

> NEBULOUSNESS : DEFINITION ::
> (A) apathy : zeal
> (B) impetuosity : intuition
> (C) penetration : depth
> (D) rectitude : somberness
> (E) rigidity : homogeneity

What relationship exists between *nebulousness* and *definition*? *Nebulousness* means haziness or indistinctness; a nebulous idea lacks clarity or sharpness. But what does haziness have to do with *definition*? After all, a definition is a statement of the meaning of a word or phrase.

Look closely at the term *definition*. When you define a word, you distinguish its essential characteristics; you make its features clear. *Definition* in fact possesses a secondary meaning: "sharp demarcation of outlines or limits; distinctness of outline or detail." With this meaning in mind, you can state the essential relationship between the capitalized words: *nebulousness* is a lack of *definition*. Analogously, *apathy* (indifference, lethargy) is a lack of *zeal* or enthusiasm. The correct answer is Choice A.

> EMBROIDER : FABRIC ::
> (A) fret : wood
> (B) spin : yarn
> (C) refine : ore
> (D) sculpt : chisel
> (E) glaze : glass

Ostensibly, this is a simple analogy. One embroiders fabric to ornament it, embellishing it with needlework. The relationship between the capitalized words is clear. However, the bulk of the examinees responding to this question would answer it incorrectly. The problem lies not in the original analogy but in the answer pairs.

Consider the answer choices closely. Choices B, C, D, and E are clear enough: one spins yarn, forming it out of threads (or one spins a yarn, fabricating or inventing a story); one refines ore, purifying it; one sculpts with a chisel; one glazes or fills a window with glass. Several of these straightforward choices have something to do with embellishment, but none seems precisely right. But how does one *fret* wood? Certainly not the way one frets a parent! Among the straightforward answer choices, Choice A seems strangely out of place.

When an item in an analogy strikes you as out of place, take a second look. Remember that, if you are a very good test-taker, the computer-adaptive GRE will give you increasingly difficult questions throughout the test. Therefore, if one of the final analogy questions on your screen looks simple, *suspect a trap.* In this case, the trap is a double one. Choice B, *spin : yarn* is an eye-catcher: because embroidery and spinning both are related to cloth, Choice B has an immediate appeal. Choose it and you fall into the test-makers' trap. Choice A, the odd-seeming choice, is the real answer: *fret,* as used here, means to mark decoratively, ornamenting a surface with interlaced designs, as cabinet makers decorate wood with interlaced patterns; fretting wood, thus, is directly analogous to embroidering fabric.

Tactic 4

Watch Out for Errors Caused by Eye-Catchers

When you look at answer choices, do you find that certain ones seem to leap right off the screen? For instance, when you were looking for an analogy similar to EMBROIDER : FABRIC, did the terms related to stitchery catch your eye? These words are eye-catchers. They look good—but not if you take a second glance.

In an analogy you have two capitalized words that relate in a particular way. In creating eye-catchers, the test-makers tempt you with pairs of words that are related, but in a grammatically or logically different way. See how eye-catchers work in the following example.

> MENTOR : GUIDE ::
> (A) medium : advise
> (B) mediator : disagree
> (C) mercenary : demand
> (D) mendicant : beg
> (E) merchant : consume

Just as there are many possible relationships linking word pairs, there are many possible ways an eye-catcher may attract your eye. First, an answer choice may somehow remind you in subject matter of one or both of the terms in the original pair. Thus, Choice A is an eye-catcher: *advise* reminds you of *guide;* both words feel as if they belong in the same set of words, the same *semantic field.* Second, the answer choice may masquerade as a clear-cut, precise, dictionary-perfect analogy and yet not be one. Thus, Choice C is an eye-catcher: while there can be a clear relationship between the adjective *mercenary* and the noun *demand,* there is no such clear relationship between the noun *mercenary* and the verb *demand.* See how this works:

CLEAR ANALOGY (Adjective/Noun)

MERCENARY : DEMAND :: RAVENOUS : APPETITE

A *mercenary demand* is greedy by definition. A *ravenous appetite* is greedy by definition as well.

VAGUE ANALOGY (Noun/Verb)

A *mercenary demands.*

A mercenary (professional soldier) insists or requires? The sentence makes little sense. Mercenaries work for hire; they may or may not make demands. The relationship is vague. Eliminate vague analogies when you find them; their only function is to catch your eye.

You have ruled out Choice C; you are suspicious of Choice A. How do you determine the correct answer? In this case, ask yourself **who is doing what to whom**. A *mentor* (teacher or counselor) by definition *guides* students or proteges. You can eliminate Choices A, B, and E because no necessary, dictionary-supported relationship links the words in these pairs. Mediums represent themselves as channels of communication between the living and the dead; they do not *by definition* advise. Mediators attempt to reconcile disagreeing parties; they do not *by definition* disagree. Merchants buy and sell goods that *others* consume; they do not *by definition* consume. The correct answer is Choice D. Just as a *mentor* by definition *guides,* a *mendicant* or beggar by definition *begs.*

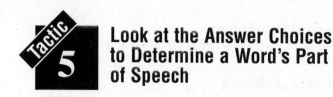

Look at the Answer Choices to Determine a Word's Part of Speech

Look at the capitalized words. What parts of speech are they? Words often have several forms. You may think of *flag* as a noun, for example, but in the phrases "to flag a taxi" and "to flag from exhaustion," *flag* is a verb.

If you suspect that a capitalized word may represent more than one part of speech, don't worry. Grammatical information built into the question can help you recognize analogy types and spot the use of unfamiliar or secondary meanings of words. In GRE analogy questions, the relationship between the parts of speech of the capitalized words and the parts of speech of the answer choices is identical. If your capitalized words are a noun and a verb, each of your answer pairs will be a noun and a verb. If they are an adjective and a noun, each of your answer pairs will be an adjective and a noun. If you can recognize the parts of speech in a single answer pair, you know the parts of speech of every other answer pair and of the original pair as well. See how this tactic works in a somewhat difficult question.

SAP : VITALITY ::
(A) persevere : fortitude
(B) bore : tedium
(C) examine : opinion
(D) drain : resolve
(E) enhance : allure

At first glance, you might think that both *sap* and *vitality* were nouns; *sap*, after all, is a common noun (maple syrup comes from the *sap* of the maple tree), and *vitality* ends in *-ity*, a common noun suffix. However, *persevere* is clearly a verb. Simply from looking at the first answer choice, you know *sap* is a verb, not a noun.

What occurs when someone's vitality is sapped? It decreases and becomes weak. When vitality is sapped, it is undermined. Think of a fortress being undermined by military engineers; "sappers," the British army called them. Only one answer choice conveys this sense of something strong weakening: Choice D. If one's resolve (resolution, determination) is drained, it is depleted or undermined.

Familiarize Yourself with Common Analogy Types

Analogies tend to fall into certain basic types. If you can discover no apparent relationship between the two capitalized words, try establishing a relationship between them based on those types commonly used on this test.

Common Analogy Types

Definition
REFUGE : SHELTER
A *refuge* (place of asylum or sanctuary) by definition *shelters*.

TAXONOMIST : CLASSIFY
A *taxonomist*, a person who specializes in classification, by definition *classifies*.

HAGGLER : BARGAIN
A *haggler*, a person who argues over prices, by definition *bargains*.

Defining Characteristic
TIGER : CARNIVOROUS
A *tiger* is defined as a *carnivorous* or meat-eating animal.

ENTOMOLOGIST : INSECTS
An *entomologist* is defined as a person who studies *insects*.

APIARY : BEE
An *apiary* is defined as a home for *bees*.

Class and Member
AMPHIBIAN : SALAMANDER
A *salamander* is an example of an *amphibian*.

METAPHYSICS : PHILOSOPHY
Metaphysics belongs to (is a branch of) the field of
philosophy.

SONNET : POEM
A *sonnet* is a specific kind of *poem*.

Antonyms

Antonyms are words that are opposite in meaning. Both
words belong to the same part of speech.

CONCERNED : INDIFFERENT
Concerned is the opposite of *indifferent*.

WAX : WANE
Wax, to grow larger, and *wane*, to dwindle, are opposites.

ANARCHY : ORDER
Anarchy is the opposite of *order*.

Antonym Variants

In an Antonym Variant, the words are not strictly antonyms;
their meanings, however, are opposed. Take the adjective
nervous. A strict antonym for the adjective *nervous* would
be the adjective *poised*. However, where an Antonym would
have the adjective *poised*, an Antonym Variant analogy has
the noun *poise*. It looks like this:

NERVOUS : POISE
Nervous means lacking in *poise*.

INIQUITOUS : VIRTUE
Something *iniquitous* (wicked) lacks *virtue*. It is the opposite
of virtuous.

ABSTINENT : GORGE
To be *abstinent* or sparing in eating is the opposite of being
inclined to cram or *gorge*.

Synonyms

Synonyms are words that have the same meaning. Both
words belong to the same part of speech.

MAGNIFICENT : GRANDIOSE
Grandiose means *magnificent*.

RATIOCINATE : THINK
To *ratiocinate* is to *think*.

RECIDIVIST : BACKSLIDER
A *recidivist* or habitual offender is a *backslider*.

Synonym Variants

In a Synonym Variant, the words are not strictly synonyms;
their meanings, however, are opposed. Take the adjective
willful. A strict synonym for the adjective *willful* would be the
adjective *unruly*. However, where a Synonym would have
the adjective *unruly*, a Synonym Variant analogy has the
noun *unruliness*. It looks like this:

WILLFUL : UNRULINESS
Willful means exhibiting *unruliness*.

VERBOSE : WORDINESS
Someone *verbose* is wordy; he or she exhibits *wordiness*.

SOLICITOUS : CONCERN
Someone *solicitous* is concerned; he or she shows
concern.

Degree of Intensity

FOND : DOTING
Fond is less extreme than *doting*.

FLURRY : BLIZZARD
A *flurry* or shower of snow is less extreme than a *blizzard*.

GRASPING : RAPACIOUS
To be *grasping* is less extreme than to be *rapacious*.

Part to Whole

ISLAND : ARCHIPELAGO
Many *islands* make up an *archipelago*.

SHARD : POTTERY
A *shard* is a fragment of *pottery*.

CANTO : POEM
A *canto* is part of a *poem*.

Function

ASYLUM : REFUGE
An *asylum* provides *refuge* or protection.

BALLAST : STABILITY
Ballast provides *stability*.

LULL : STORM
A *lull* temporarily interrupts a *storm*.

Manner

MUMBLE : SPEAK
To *mumble* is to *speak* indistinctly.

STRUT : WALK
To *strut* is to *walk* proudly.

STRAINED : WIT
Wit that is *strained* is forced in manner.

Action and Its Significance

WINCE : PAIN
A *wince* is a sign that one feels *pain*.

BLUSH : DISCOMFITURE
A *blush* signifies *discomfiture* or embarrassment.

PROSTRATION : SUBMISSIVENESS
Prostration (assuming a prostrate position, face to the
ground) is a sign of *submissiveness* or abasement.

Worker and Article Created

POET : SONNET
A *poet* creates a *sonnet*.

ARCHITECT : BLUEPRINT
An *architect* designs a *blueprint*.

MASON : WALL
A *mason* builds a *wall*.

Worker and Tool
PAINTER : BRUSH

A *painter* uses a *brush*.

SICKLE : REAPER

A *reaper* uses a *sickle* to cut the grain.

CARPENTER : VISE

A *carpenter* uses a *vise* to hold the object being worked on.

Worker and Action
ACROBAT : CARTWHEEL

An *acrobat* performs a *cartwheel*.

FINANCIER : INVEST

A *financier invests*.

TENOR : ARIA

A *tenor* sings an *aria*.

Worker and Workplace
MUSICIAN : CONSERVATORY

A *musician* studies at a *conservatory*.

SCULPTOR : ATELIER

A *sculptor* works in an *atelier* or studio.

MINER : QUARRY

A *miner* works in a *quarry* or pit.

Tool and Its Action
DRILL : BORE

A *drill* is a tool used to *bore* holes.

CROWBAR : PRY

A *crowbar* is a tool used to *pry* things apart.

SIEVE : SIFT

A *sieve* is a tool used to strain or *sift*.

Less Common Analogy Types
Cause and Effect
SOPORIFIC : SLEEPINESS

A *soporific* (sleep-inducing medicine or drug) causes *sleepiness*.

Sex
DOE : STAG

A *doe* is a female deer; a *stag*, a male deer.

Age
COLT : STALLION

A *colt* is a young *stallion*.

Time Sequence
CORONATION : REIGN

The *coronation* precedes the *reign*.

Spatial Sequence
ROOF : FOUNDATION

The *roof* is the highest point of a house; the *foundation*, the lowest point.

Symbol and Quality It Represents
DOVE : PEACE

A *dove* is the symbol of *peace*.

Practice Exercises

Analogy Exercise A

Directions: Each of the following analogy questions presents a related pair of words linked by a colon. Five lettered pairs of words follow the linked pair. Choose the lettered pair of words whose relationship is <u>most like</u> the relationship expressed in the original linked pair.

1. MASON : WALL ::   (A) artist : easel
   (B) fisherman : trout   (C) author : book
   (D) congressman : senator   (E) sculptor : mallet

2. FIRE : ASHES ::   (A) accident : delay
   (B) wood : splinters   (C) water : waves
   (D) regret : melancholy   (E) event : memories

3. GOOSE : GANDER ::   (A) duck : drake
   (B) hen : chicken   (C) sheep : flock
   (D) dog : kennel   (E) horse : bridle

4. CARPENTER : SAW ::
   (A) stenographer : typewriter   (B) painter : brush
   (C) lawyer : brief   (D) seamstress : scissors
   (E) runner : sneakers

5. CAPTAIN : SHOAL ::   (A) lawyer : litigation
   (B) pilot : radar   (C) soldier : ambush
   (D) doctor : hospital   (E) corporal : sergeant

6. HORNS : BULL ::   (A) mane : lion
   (B) wattles : turkey   (C) antlers : stag
   (D) hoofs : horse   (E) wings : eagle

7. JUDGE : COURTHOUSE ::   (A) carpenter : bench
   (B) lawyer : brief   (C) architect : blueprint
   (D) physician : infirmary   (E) landlord : studio

8. HELMET : HEAD ::   (A) pedal : foot
   (B) gun : hand   (C) breastplate : chest
   (D) pendant : neck   (E) knapsack : back

9. GULLIBLE : DUPED ::   (A) credible : cheated
   (B) careful : cautioned   (C) malleable : molded
   (D) myopic : misled   (E) articulate : silenced

10. DUNGEON : CONFINEMENT ::
    (A) church : chapel   (B) school : truancy
    (C) asylum : refuge   (D) hospital : mercy
    (E) courthouse : remorse

11. HERMIT : GREGARIOUS ::
    (A) miser : penurious   (B) ascetic : hedonistic
    (C) coward : pusillanimous   (D) scholar : literate
    (E) crab : crustacean

12. MENDACITY : HONESTY ::
    (A) courage : cravenness
    (B) truth : beauty
    (C) courage : fortitude
    (D) unsophistication : ingenuousness
    (E) turpitude : depravity

13. MARATHON : STAMINA ::
    (A) relay : independence
    (B) hurdle : perseverance   (C) sprint : celerity
    (D) jog : weariness   (E) ramble : directness

14. NAIVE : INGENUE ::   (A) ordinary : genius
    (B) venerable : celebrity   (C) urbane : sophisticate
    (D) crafty : artisan   (E) modest : braggart

15. RETOUCH : PHOTOGRAPH ::
    (A) hang : painting   (B) finger : fabric
    (C) retract : statement   (D) compose : melody
    (E) refine : style

16. INDIGENT : WEALTH ::
    (A) contented : happiness
    (B) aristocratic : stature
    (C) smug : complacency
    (D) emaciated : nourishment
    (E) variegated : variety

17. SHALE : GEOLOGIST ::
    (A) catacombs : entomologist   (B) aster : botanist
    (C) obelisk : fireman   (D) love : philologist
    (E) reef : astrologer

18. DIDACTIC : TEACH ::   (A) sophomoric : learn
    (B) satiric : mock   (C) reticent : complain
    (D) chaotic : rule   (E) apologetic : deny

19. HACKNEYED : ORIGINAL ::
    (A) mature : juvenile   (B) trite : morbid
    (C) withdrawn : reserved   (D) evasive : elusive
    (E) derivative : traditional

20. AUGER : CARPENTER ::   (A) studio : sculptor
    (B) awl : cobbler   (C) seam : seamstress
    (D) cement : mason   (E) apron : chef

Analogy Exercise B

Directions: Each of the following analogy questions presents a related pair of words linked by a colon. Five lettered pairs of words follow the linked pair. Choose the lettered pair of words whose relationship is most like the relationship expressed in the original linked pair.

1. MUSTER : CREW ::   (A) convene : committee
   (B) demobilize : troops   (C) dominate : opposition
   (D) cheer : team   (E) dismiss : jury

2. DWELL : DENIZEN ::   (A) shun : outcast
   (B) inherit : heir   (C) squander : miser
   (D) obey : autocrat   (E) patronize : protégé

3. MEANDERING : DIRECTNESS ::
   (A) menacing : ambition
   (B) affable : permissiveness
   (C) digressive : conciseness
   (D) circuitous : rotation
   (E) aboveboard : openness

4. CEMENT : TROWEL ::   (A) lawn : rake
   (B) conflagration : match   (C) paint : brush
   (D) floor : polish   (E) wallpaper : ladder

5. PIGHEADED : YIELD ::
   (A) lionhearted : retreat
   (B) lily-livered : flee
   (C) dogged : pursue
   (D) featherbrained : giggle
   (E) eagle-eyed : discern

6. ALARM : TRIGGER ::   (A) prison : escape
   (B) tunnel : dig   (C) criminal : corner
   (D) fright : allay   (E) trap : spring

7. QUOTATION : QUOTATION MARKS ::
   (A) remark : colon   (B) sentence : period
   (C) aside : parentheses   (D) clause : semicolon
   (E) interjection : exclamation point

8. SIGNATURE : ILLUSTRATION ::
   (A) byline : column   (B) alias : charge
   (C) credit : purchase   (D) note : scale
   (E) reference : recommendation

9. SCALES : JUSTICE :: (A) weights : measures
(B) laws : courts (C) torch : liberty
(D) laurel : peace (E) balance : equity

10. SURPRISE : EXCLAMATION ::
(A) insolence : bow (B) dismay : groan
(C) happiness : grimace (D) deference : nod
(E) contentment : matter

11. APOSTATE : RELIGION ::
(A) potentate : kingdom (B) traitor : country
(C) bureaucrat : government (D) jailer : law
(E) teacher : education

12. FOX : CUNNING :: (A) dog : playful
(B) hyena : amusing (C) beaver : industrious
(D) vixen : cute (E) colt : sturdy

13. PERJURY : OATH :: (A) plagiarism : authority
(B) embezzlement : trust (C) disrespect : age
(D) testimony : court (E) jury : vow

14. EULOGY : BLAME :: (A) elegy : loss
(B) satire : mockery (C) tirade : abuse
(D) simile : likeness (E) benediction : curse

15. PRIDE : LIONS :: (A) gaggle : geese
(B) honor : thieves (C) snarl : wolves
(D) arrogance : kings (E) lair : bears

16. RANGE : MOUNTAINS :: (A) atlas : maps
(B) plain : prairie (C) string : beads
(D) novel : short stories (E) sea : rivers

17. EXCESSIVE : MODERATION ::
(A) extensive : duration
(B) arbitrary : courage
(C) impulsive : reflection
(D) distinguished : reverence
(E) expensive : cost

18. DEADBEAT : PAY :: (A) killjoy : lament
(B) spoilsport : refrain (C) daredevil : risk
(D) diehard : quit (E) turncoat : betray

19. MENDICANT : IMPECUNIOUS ::
(A) critic : quizzical (B) complainer : petulant
(C) physician : noble (D) liar : compulsive
(E) philanthropist : prodigal

20. SNICKER : DISRESPECT ::
(A) whimper : impatience (B) chortle : glee
(C) frown : indifference (D) sneer : detachment
(E) glower : cheerfulness

Analogy Exercise C

<u>Directions:</u> Each of the following analogy questions presents a related pair of words linked by a colon. Five lettered pairs of words follow the linked pair. Choose the lettered pair of words whose relationship is <u>most like</u> the relationship expressed in the original linked pair.

1. MYTH : LEGENDARY :: (A) sermon : lengthy
(B) anecdote : witty (C) fable : didactic
(D) epic : comic (E) allegory : obscure

2. TIRADE : ABUSIVE :: (A) monologue : lengthy
(B) aphorism : boring (C) prologue : conclusive
(D) encomium : laudatory (E) critique : insolent

3. EXPEDITIOUS : SPEED ::
(A) astute : wisdom (B) decorous : impropriety
(C) thoughtful : inanity (D) haggard : sturdiness
(E) portable : frailty

4. ANNOTATE : TEXT ::
(A) enact : law (B) prescribe : medication
(C) caption : photograph (D) abridge : novel
(E) censor : film

5. DRUDGERY : IRKSOME ::
(A) encumbrance : burdensome
(B) journey : wearisome
(C) ambivalence : suspicious
(D) compliance : forced
(E) dissonance : harmonious

6. IMPROMPTU : REHEARSAL ::
(A) practiced : technique (B) makeshift : whim
(C) offhand : premeditation (D) glib : fluency
(E) numerical : calculation

7. ELISION : SYLLABLES ::
(A) contraction : letters (B) thesis : ideas
(C) diagnosis : symptoms (D) almanac : facts
(E) abacus : numbers

8. STICKLER : INSIST :: (A) mumbler : enunciate
(B) trickster : risk (C) haggler : concede
(D) laggard : outlast (E) braggart : boast

9. DETRITUS : GLACIER :: (A) thaw : snowfall
(B) snow : ice cap (C) silt : river
(D) range : mountain (E) foliage : tree

10. DESCRY : DISTANT :: (A) mourn : lost
(B) whisper : muted (C) discern : subtle
(D) destroy : flagrant (E) entrap : hostile

11. HORSE : CORRAL :: (A) oyster : reef
(B) dog : muzzle (C) sheep : flock (D) pig : sty
(E) deer : stag

12. RUBBER : ELASTIC :: (A) paper : brittle
    (B) diamond : hard (C) satin : sheer
    (D) metal : heavy (E) dust : allergic

13. REAM : PAPER :: (A) carton : milk
    (B) statue : marble (C) tablet : clay
    (D) ink : pen (E) cord : wood

14. HOBBLE : WALK :: (A) gallop : run
    (B) stammer : speak (C) stumble : fall
    (D) sniff : smell (E) amble : stroll

15. DETECTIVE : INFORMER ::
    (A) spy : counterspy (B) reporter : source
    (C) author : editor (D) architect : draftsman
    (E) sailor : mutineer

16. SCULPTOR : STONE :: (A) essayist : words
    (B) painter : turpentine (C) composer : symphony
    (D) logger : timber (E) etcher : acid

17. MASTHEAD : NEWSPAPER ::
    (A) footnote : essay (B) credits : film
    (C) spine : book (D) ream : paper
    (E) advertisement : magazine

18. FRAYED : FABRIC :: (A) thawed : ice
    (B) renovated : building (C) frazzled : nerves
    (D) watered : lawn (E) cultivated : manner

19. INDOLENT : WORK :: (A) decisive : act
    (B) gullible : cheat (C) perceptive : observe
    (D) theatrical : perform (E) taciturn : speak

20. INFALLIBLE : ERROR :: (A) irreversible : cure
    (B) invulnerable : emotion (C) impeccable : flaw
    (D) intolerable : defect (E) immovable : choice

Analogy Exercise D

Directions: Each of the following analogy questions presents a related pair of words linked by a colon. Five lettered pairs of words follow the linked pair. Choose the lettered pair of words whose relationship is <u>most like</u> the relationship expressed in the original linked pair.

1. INFRACTION : LAW ::
   (A) interruption : continuity
   (B) renovation : structure
   (C) establishment : order
   (D) enactment : amendment
   (E) punishment : crime

2. LACHRYMOSE : TEARS ::
   (A) effusive : requests (B) ironic : jests
   (C) morose : speeches (D) profound : sighs
   (E) verbose : words

3. MOISTEN : DRENCH :: (A) enclose : confine
   (B) prick : stab (C) disregard : ignore
   (D) scrub : polish (E) heat : chill

4. WITCH : COVEN :: (A) ogre : castle
   (B) seer : prophecy (C) actor : troupe
   (D) fairy : spell (E) doctor : medicine

5. CONTINENT : ISLAND :: (A) ocean : lake
   (B) isthmus : peninsula (C) cape : cove
   (D) river : canal (E) plateau : plain

6. SKINFLINT : STINGY :: (A) daredevil : alert
   (B) braggart : carefree (C) blackguard : protective
   (D) spendthrift : weak (E) diehard : stubborn

7. STORY : BUILDING :: (A) plot : outline
   (B) rung : ladder (C) cable : elevator
   (D) foundation : skyscraper (E) spire : church

8. CANONIZE : SAINT :: (A) train : athlete
   (B) guard : dignitary (C) deify : sinner
   (D) lionize : celebrity (E) humanize : scholar

9. STARE : GLANCE :: (A) participate : observe
   (B) scorn : admire (C) hunt : stalk
   (D) gulp : sip (E) confide : tell

10. PERFORATE : HOLES :: (A) speckle : spots
    (B) evaporate : perfume (C) decorate : rooms
    (D) filter : water (E) repent : sins

11. PUGNACIOUS : BATTLE :: (A) timorous : beg
    (B) loquacious : drink (C) tenacious : persist
    (D) veracious : lie (E) wicked : survive

12. CLEARSIGHTED : PERSPICACITY ::
    (A) daring : temerity (B) reserved : impulsiveness
    (C) transparent : opacity (D) severe : clemency
    (E) lethargic : energy

13. PLEAD : SUPPLIANT :: (A) disperse : rioter
    (B) shun : outcast (C) revere : elder
    (D) beg : philanthropist (E) translate : interpreter

14. EPIGRAM : PITHY :: (A) allegory : lengthy
    (B) saga : heroic (C) anecdote: humorous
    (D) elegy : satiric (E) proverb : modern

15. BOLT : FABRIC :: (A) lock : key
    (B) book : paper (C) roll : film
    (D) needle : thread (E) light : lamp

16. PROOF : ALCOHOL :: (A) cream : milk
    (B) canteen : water (C) tanker : oil
    (D) octane : gasoline (E) pulp : juice

17. INCUBATOR : INFANT ::
    (A) henhouse : chicken (B) greenhouse : plant
    (C) archives : document (D) cooler : wine
    (E) hive : bee

18. CITADEL : DEFENSE ::   (A) chapel : refreshment
(B) gazebo : refuge   (C) marina : contemplation
(D) warehouse : storage   (E) rampart : supervision

19. RANCID : TASTE ::   (A) tepid : temperature
(B) glossy : look   (C) rank : smell
(D) dulcet : sound   (E) savory : odor

20. TRYST : CLANDESTINE ::
(A) reverie : dreamy   (B) acquaintanceship : brief
(C) expectation : hopeless   (D) glance : resentful
(E) journey : leisurely

Analogy Exercise E

Directions: Each of the following analogy questions presents a related pair of words linked by a colon. Five lettered pairs of words follow the linked pair. Choose the lettered pair of words whose relationship is most like the relationship expressed in the original linked pair.

1. WHISPER : SPEAK ::   (A) brush : touch
(B) skip : walk   (C) listen : hear
(D) request : ask   (E) whimper : whine

2. ELUSIVE : CAPTURE ::
(A) persuasive : convince   (B) elastic : stretch
(C) headstrong : control   (D) sensible : decide
(E) gullible : trick

3. LINEAGE : PERSON ::   (A) foliage : tree
(B) derivation : word   (C) adolescence : child
(D) title : book   (E) landscape : portrait

4. IMPANEL : JUROR ::   (A) accuse : defendant
(B) convict : culprit   (C) testify : witness
(D) enroll : student   (E) involve : bystander

5. PECCADILLO : TRIFLING ::
(A) pariah : popular   (B) diagnosis : accurate
(C) notion : farfetched   (D) squabble : petty
(E) pursuit : trivial

6. PHYSIQUE : STURDY ::   (A) intellect : noble
(B) punctuality : tardy   (C) investment : sound
(D) fabric : worn   (E) technique : inept

7. TRAILER : MOTION PICTURE ::
(A) truck : cargo   (B) theater : play
(C) edition : novel   (D) commercial : product
(E) libretto : opera

8. SIGN : ZODIAC ::   (A) poster : billboard
(B) letter : alphabet   (C) prediction : prophecy
(D) signal : beacon   (E) rhyme : almanac

9. LUMINARY : ILLUSTRIOUS ::
(A) zealot : intense   (B) miser : prodigal
(C) atheist : devout   (D) dignitary : conceited
(E) celebrity : wealthy

10. BUFFOON : DIGNITY ::
(A) braggart : modesty   (B) blackguard : strength
(C) laughingstock : ridicule
(D) imposter : identification   (E) gambler : risk

11. ROUT : DEFEAT ::   (A) ovation : applause
(B) triumph : failure   (C) grief : loss
(D) pathway : ruin   (E) memory : oblivion

12. METAPHOR : FIGURATIVE ::
(A) fable : contemporary   (B) adage : paradoxical
(C) precept : instructive   (D) irony : dramatic
(E) epic : literal

13. CALUMNY : ASPERSIONS ::
(A) approbation : praise   (B) slander : mockery
(C) approval : criticism   (D) expectation : threats
(E) satire : lamentations

14. LAST : SHOE ::   (A) cuff : trousers
(B) finale : curtain   (C) pattern : glove
(D) buckle : belt   (E) strap : slip

15. INDOLENT : SLOTH ::   (A) wrathful : ire
(B) arrogant : acuity   (C) covetous : enigma
(D) gluttonous : loyalty   (E) impatient : apathy

16. GROVEL : SERVILITY ::   (A) titter : arrogance
(B) fume : anger   (C) yawn : civility
(D) preen : modesty   (E) snivel : hypocrisy

17. DELICATE : FASTIDIOUS ::
(A) hard-working : diligent
(B) altruistic : mercenary
(C) demonstrative : effusive
(D) deceptive : fallacious
(E) blithe : melancholy

18. RICOCHET : BULLET ::   (A) soar : falcon
(B) aim : crossbow   (C) pierce : dart
(D) carom : ball   (E) catapult : missile

19. JUGGERNAUT : INEXORABLE ::
(A) cosmonaut : worldly   (B) colossus : gigantic
(C) demagogue : liberal   (D) philistine : cultivated
(E) despot : immaculate

20. APOCRYPHAL : AUTHENTICITY ::
(A) nefarious : wickedness
(B) dogmatic : assertiveness
(C) hypocritical : integrity
(D) perspicacious : discernment
(E) deceptive : artifice

Answer Key

Analogy Exercise A

1. C	6. C	11. B	16. D
2. E	7. D	12. A	17. B
3. A	8. C	13. C	18. B
4. D	9. C	14. C	19. A
5. C	10. C	15. E	20. B

Analogy Exercise B

1. A	6. E	11. B	16. C
2. B	7. C	12. C	17. C
3. C	8. A	13. B	18. D
4. C	9. C	14. E	19. B
5. A	10. B	15. A	20. B

Analogy Exercise C

1. C	6. C	11. D	16. A
2. D	7. A	12. B	17. B
3. A	8. E	13. E	18. C
4. C	9. C	14. B	19. E
5. A	10. C	15. B	20. C

Analogy Exercise D

1. A	6. E	11. C	16. D
2. E	7. B	12. A	17. B
3. B	8. D	13. E	18. D
4. C	9. D	14. B	19. C
5. A	10. A	15. C	20. A

Analogy Exercise E

1. A	6. C	11. A	16. B
2. C	7. D	12. C	17. C
3. B	8. B	13. A	18. D
4. D	9. A	14. C	19. B
5. D	10. A	15. A	20. C

6 Sentence Completion Questions

■ **Testing Tactics**
■ **Practice Exercises**
■ **Answer Key**

These are the sentence completion directions you will find on the GRE: "Each sentence below has one or two blanks, each blank indicating that something has been omitted. Beneath the sentence are five lettered words or sets of words. Choose the word or set of words for each blank that <u>best</u> fits the meaning of the sentence as a whole."

GRE sentence completion questions test your ability to use your vocabulary and recognize logical consistency among the elements in a sentence. You need to know more than the dictionary definitions of the words involved. You need to know how the words fit together to make logical and stylistic sense.

Sentence completion questions actually measure one part of reading comprehension. If you can recognize how the different parts of a sentence affect one another, you should do well at choosing the answer that best completes the meaning of the sentence or provides a clear, logical statement of fact. The ability to recognize irony and humor will also stand you in good stead, as will the ability to recognize figurative language and to distinguish between formal and informal levels of speech.

GRE sentence completion questions may come from any of a number of different fields—art, literature, history, philosophy, botany, astronomy, geology, and others. You cannot predict what subject matter the sentences on your test will have. However, even if you are unfamiliar with the subject matter of a particular sentence, you should still be able to analyze that sentence and choose the word that best completes its meaning. It is not the sentence's subject matter that makes hard GRE sentence completion questions hard.

What makes hard sentence completion questions hard?

1. **Vocabulary Level.** Sentences contain words like *intransigence, nonplussed, harbingers.* Answer choices include words like *penchant, abeyance, eclectic.* Questions employ unfamiliar secondary meanings of words—*brook* as a verb, *economy* with the meaning of *restraint.*

2. **Grammatical Complexity.** Sentences combine the entire range of grammatical possibilities—subordinate clauses, relative clauses, prepositional phrases, gerunds, infinitives—in convoluted ways. The more complex the sentence, the more difficult it is for you to spot the key words that can unlock its meaning.

3. **Tone.** Sentences reflect the writer's attitude toward his subject matter. It is simple enough to comprehend material that is presented neutrally. It is far more difficult to comprehend material that is ironic, condescending, playful, somber, or similarly complex in tone.

4. **Style.** Ideas may be expressed in different manners—ornately or sparely, poetically or prosaically, formally or informally, journalistically or academically, originally or imitatively. An author's style depends on such details as word choice, imagery, repetition, rhythm, sentence structure, and length. Many of the most difficult GRE questions hinge on questions of style.

Work through the following tactics and learn the techniques that will help you with vocabulary, grammatical complexity, tone, and style.

Testing Tactics

Before You Look at the Choices, Read the Sentence and Think of a Word That Makes Sense

Your problem is to find the word that best completes the sentence in both thought and style. Before you look at the answer choices, see if you can come up with a word that makes logical sense in the context. Then look at all five choices. If the word you thought of is one of your five choices, select that as your answer. If the word you thought of is not one of your five choices, look for a synonym of that word. Select the synonym as your answer.

This tactic is helpful because it enables you to get a sense of the sentence as a whole without being distracted by any misleading answers among the answer choices. You are free to concentrate on spotting key words or phrases in the body of the sentence and to call on your own "writer's intuition" in arriving at a stylistically apt choice of word.

See how the process works in a typical model question.

> Because experience had convinced her that he was both self-seeking and avaricious, she rejected the likelihood that his donation had been _____.

(A) redundant
(B) frivolous
(C) inexpensive
(D) ephemeral
(E) altruistic

This sentence presents a simple case of cause and effect. The key phrase here is *self-seeking and avaricious*. The woman has found the man to be selfish and greedy. *Therefore*, she refuses to believe he can do something _____. What words immediately come to mind? *Selfless, generous, charitable?* The missing word is, of course, *altruistic*. The woman expects selfishness (*self-seeking*) and greediness (*avaricious*), not altruism (magnanimity). The correct answer is Choice E.

Practice Tactic 1 extensively to develop your intuitive sense of the *mot juste*—the exactly right word. However, do not rely on Tactic 1 alone. On the test, always follow up Tactic 1 with Tactic 2.

Look at All the Possible Answers Before You Make Your Final Choice

Never decide on an answer before you have read all the choices. You are looking for the word that *best* fits the meaning of the sentence as a whole. In order to be sure you have not been hasty in making your decision, substitute all the answer choices for the missing word. Do not spend a lot of time doing so, but do try them all. That way you can satisfy yourself that you have come up with the *best* answer.

See how this tactic helps you deal with another question patterned on examples from the GRE.

> The evil of class and race hatred must be eliminated while it is still in an _____ state; otherwise it may grow to dangerous proportions.

(A) amorphous
(B) overt
(C) uncultivated
(D) embryonic
(E) independent

On the basis of a loose sense of this sentence's meaning, you might be tempted to select Choice A. After all, this sentence basically tells you that you should wipe out hatred before it gets too dangerous. Clearly, if hatred is vague or *amorphous*, it is less formidable than if it is well-defined. However, this reading of the sentence is inadequate: it fails to take into account the sentence's key phrase.

The key phrase here is *grow to dangerous proportions*. The writer fears that class and race hatred may grow large enough to endanger society. He wants us to wipe out this hatred before it is fully grown. Examine each answer choice, eliminating those answers that carry no suggestion that something lacks its full growth. Does *overt* suggest that something isn't fully grown? No, it suggests that something is obvious or evident. Does *uncultivated* suggest that something isn't fully grown?

No, it suggests that something is unrefined or growing without proper care or training. Does *independent* suggest that something isn't fully grown? No, it suggests that something is free and unconstrained. Only one word suggests a lack of full growth: *embryonic* (at a rudimentary, early stage of development). The correct answer is Choice D.

In Double-Blank Sentences, Go Through the Answers, Testing the *First* Word in Each Choice (and Eliminating Those That Don't Fit)

In a sentence completion question with two blanks, read through the entire sentence to get a sense of it as a whole. Then insert the first word of each answer pair in the sentence's first blank. Ask yourself whether this particular word makes sense in this blank. If the initial word of an answer pair makes no sense in the sentence, you can eliminate that answer pair.

(*Note:* Occasionally this tactic will not work. In some questions, for example, the first words of all five answer pairs may be near-synonyms. However, the tactic frequently pays off, as it does in the following example.)

> Critics of the movie version of *The Color Purple* _____ its saccharine, overoptimistic mood as out of keeping with the novel's more _____ tone.
>
> (A) applauded...somber
> (B) condemned...hopeful
> (C) acclaimed...positive
> (D) denounced...sanguine
> (E) decried...acerbic

For a quick, general sense of the opening clause, break it down. What does it say? *Critics _____ the movie's sugary sweet mood.*

How would critics react to something sugary sweet and over-hopeful? They would disapprove. Your first missing word must be a synonym for *disapprove.*

Now eliminate the misfits. Choices A and C fail to meet the test: *applauded* and *acclaimed* signify approval, not disapproval. Choice B, *condemned*, Choice D, *denounced*, and Choice E, *decried*, however, all express disapprobation; they require a second look.

To decide among Choices B, D, and E, consider the second blank. The movie's sugary, overly hopeful mood is out of keeping with the novel's tone: the two moods disagree. Therefore, the novel's tone is *not* hopeful or sickly sweet. It is instead on the bitter or sour side; in a word, *acerbic.* The correct answer is clearly Choice E.

Remember, in double-blank sentences, the right answer must correctly fill **both** blanks. A wrong answer choice often includes one correct and one incorrect answer. ALWAYS test both words.

Watch for Signal Words That Link One Part of the Sentence to Another

Writers use transitions to link their ideas logically. These transitions or signal words are clues that can help you figure out what the sentence actually means.

GRE sentences often contain several signal words, combining them in complex ways.

Cause and Effect Signals

Look for words or phrases explicitly indicating that one thing causes another or logically determines another.

Cause and Effect Signal Words

accordingly	in order to
because	so...that
consequently	therefore
given	thus
hence	when...then
if...then	

Support Signals

Look for words or phrases explicitly indicating that the omitted portion of the sentence **supports** or **continues a thought** developed elsewhere in the sentence. In such cases, a synonym or near-synonym for another word in the sentence may provide the correct answer.

Support Signal Words

additionally	furthermore
also	indeed
and	likewise
as well	moreover
besides	too

Contrast Signals (Explicit)

Look for function words or phrases (conjunctions, sentence adverbs, etc.) that explicitly indicate a **contrast** between one idea and another, setting up a reversal of a thought. In such cases, an antonym or near-antonym for another word in the sentence may provide the correct answer.

Explicit Contrast Signal Words

albeit	nevertheless
although	nonetheless
but	notwithstanding
despite	on the contrary
even though	on the other hand
however	rather than
in contrast	still
in spite of	while
instead of	yet

Contrast Signals (Implicit)

Look for content words whose meaning inherently indicates a contrast. These words can turn a situation on its head. They indicate that something unexpected, possibly even unwanted, has occurred.

Implicit Contrast Signal Words

anomaly	anomalous	anomalously
illogic	illogical	illogically
incongruity	incongruous	incongruously
irony	ironic	ironically
paradox	paradoxical	paradoxically
surprise	surprising	surprisingly
	unexpected	unexpectedly

Note the function of such a contrast signal word in the following question.

> Paradoxically, the more _____ the details this artist chooses, the better able she is to depict her fantastic, other-worldly landscapes.
>
> (A) ethereal
> (B) realistic
> (C) fanciful
> (D) extravagant
> (E) sublime

The artist creates imaginary landscapes that do not seem to belong to this world. We normally would expect the details comprising these landscapes to be as fantastic and supernatural as the landscapes themselves. But the truth of the matter, however, is paradoxical: it contradicts what we expect. The details she chooses are *realistic*, and the more realistic they are, the more fantastic the paintings become. The correct answer is Choice B.

Use Your Knowledge of Word Parts and Parts of Speech to Get at the Meanings of Unfamiliar Words

If a word used by the author is unfamiliar, or if an answer choice is unknown to you, two approaches are helpful.

1. Break the word down into its component parts—prefixes, suffixes, roots—to see whether they provide a clue to its meaning. For example, in the preceding list of Implicit Contrast Signal Words, the word *incongruous* contains three major word parts. *In-* here means not; *con-* means together; *gru-* means to move or come. *Incongruous* behavior, therefore, is behavior that does not go together or agree with someone's usual behavior; it is unexpected.

2. Change the unfamiliar word from one part of speech to another. If the adjective *embryonic* is unfamiliar to you, cut off its adjective suffix *-nic* and recognize the familiar word *embryo*. If the noun *precocity* is

unfamiliar to you, cut off its noun suffix *-ity* and visualize it with different endings. You may come up with the adjective *precocious* (maturing early). If the verb *appropriate* is unfamiliar to you, by adding a word part or two you may come up with the common noun *appropriation* or the still more common noun *misappropriation* (as in the misappropriation of funds).

Note the application of this tactic in the following typical example.

This island is a colony; however, in most matters, it is _____ and receives no orders from the mother country.

(A) synoptic
(B) methodical
(C) heretical
(D) autonomous
(E) disinterested

First, eliminate any answer choices that are obviously incorrect. If a colony receives no orders from its mother country, it is essentially self-governing. It is not necessarily *methodical* or systematic, nor is it by definition *heretical* (unorthodox) or *disinterested* (impartial). Thus, you may rule out Choices B, C, and E.

The two answer choices remaining may be unfamiliar to you. Analyze them, using what you know of related words. Choice A, *synoptic*, is related to the noun *synopsis*, a summary or abridgment. This has nothing to do with how a colony might govern itself. Choice D, *autonomous*, comes from the prefix *auto-* (self) and the root *nom-* (law). An autonomous nation is independent; it rules itself. Thus, the correct answer is *autonomous*, Choice D.

Break Down Complex Sentences into Simpler Components

In analyzing long, complex sentence completion items, you may find it useful to simplify the sentences by breaking them down. Rephrase dependent clauses and long participial phrases, turning them into simple sentences.

See how this tactic helps you to analyze the following sentence.

Museum director Hoving _____ refers to the smuggled Greek urn as the "hot pot," not because there are doubts about its authenticity or even great reservations as to its price, but because its _____ of acquisition is open to question.

(A) informally...costliness
(B) characteristically...date
(C) colloquially...manner
(D) repeatedly...swiftness
(E) cheerfully...mode

What do we know?

1. The urn has been smuggled.

2. Hoving calls it a "hot pot."

3. It is genuine. (There are no doubts about its authenticity.)

4. It did not cost too much. (There are no great reservations as to its price.)

In calling the smuggled urn a "hot pot," Hoving is not necessarily speaking *characteristically* or *repeatedly* or *cheerfully*. He is speaking either *informally* or *colloquially*. (*Hot* here is a slang term meaning stolen or illegally obtained.) The urn's *costliness* is not being questioned. However, because the urn has been smuggled into the country, there clearly are unresolved questions about how it got here, in other words, about its *manner* of acquisition. The correct answer is Choice C.

Note that in sentence completion questions a choice may be complicated by an *unusual word order*, such as

1. *placing the subject after the verb:*
   To the complaints window *strode* the angry *customer.*

2. *placing the subject after an auxiliary of the verb:*
   Only by unending search *could* some few Havana *cigars* be found.

3. *inverting the subject and verb to give the sense of "if":* Were *defeat* to befall him, today's dear friends would be tomorrow's acquaintances, and next week's strangers.

4. *placing a negative word or phrase first, which usually requires at least part of the verb to follow:*
   Never have I encountered so demanding a test!

In all these instances, rephrase the sentence to make it more straightforward. For example:

The angry customer strode to the complaint window.

Some few Havana cigars could be found only by unending search.

If defeat were to befall him, today's dear friends would be tomorrow's acquaintances, and next week's strangers.

I have never encountered so demanding a test!

Tactic 7

If a Sentence Contains a Metaphor, Check to See Whether That Metaphor Controls the Writer's Choice of Words (and Your Answer Choice)

Writers sometimes indulge in extended metaphors, complex analogies that imaginatively identify one object with another.

In the following example, the mind of a prejudiced person is compared to the pupil of an eye in its response to light or illumination.

> The mind of a bigot is like the pupil of the eye: the more light you pour upon it, the more it will _____.
>
> (A) blink
> (B) veer
> (C) stare
> (D) reflect
> (E) contract

The image of light unifies this sentence. In choosing an answer, it is necessary to complete the sentence in such a way as to develop that metaphor fully and accurately. Exactly what takes place when you shine a light into someone's eye? The person may stare back or blink; you may see the light reflected in the person's eye. But what happens to the pupil of the eye? It neither blinks nor reflects. Instead it shrinks in size; it *contracts*. Likewise, exposed to the light of tolerance, the bigot's mind resists illumination. Choice E completes the metaphor; it is the correct answer choice.

Practice Exercises

Sentence Completion Exercise A

Directions: Each of the following sentence completion questions contains one or two blanks. These blanks signify that a word or set of words has been left out. Below each sentence are five words or sets of words. For each blank, pick the word or set of words that best reflects the sentence's overall meaning.

1. Normally an individual thunderstorm lasts about 45 minutes, but under certain conditions the storm may _____, becoming ever more severe, for as long as four hours.

    (A) wane
    (B) moderate
    (C) persist
    (D) vacillate
    (E) disperse

2. Perhaps because something in us instinctively distrusts such displays of natural fluency, some readers approach John Updike's fiction with _____.

    (A) indifference
    (B) suspicion
    (C) veneration
    (D) recklessness
    (E) bewilderment

3. We lost confidence in him because he never _____ the grandiose promises he had made.

    (A) forgot about
    (B) reneged on
    (C) tired of
    (D) delivered on
    (E) retreated from

4. Ms. Sutcliffe's helpful notes on her latest wine discoveries and her no-nonsense warnings to consumers about _____ wines provide _____ guide to the numbing array of wines of Burgundy.

    (A) excellent...a useful
    (B) overrated...an inadequate
    (C) overpriced...a trusty
    (D) unsatisfactory...a spotty
    (E) vintage...an unreliable

5. We were amazed that a man who had been heretofore the most _____ of public speakers could, in a single speech, electrify an audience and bring them cheering to their feet.

    (A) enthralling
    (B) accomplished
    (C) pedestrian
    (D) auspicious
    (E) masterful

6. If you are trying to make a strong impression on your audience, you cannot do so by being understated, tentative, or _____.

    (A) hyperbolic
    (B) restrained
    (C) argumentative
    (D) authoritative
    (E) passionate

7. Despite the mixture's _____ nature, we found that by lowering its temperature in the laboratory we could dramatically reduce its tendency to vaporize.

   (A) resilient
   (B) volatile
   (C) homogeneous
   (D) insipid
   (E) acerbic

8. No other artist rewards the viewer with more sheer pleasure than Miró; he is one of those blessed artists who combine profundity and _____.

   (A) education
   (B) wisdom
   (C) faith
   (D) fun
   (E) depth

9. Some Central Intelligence Agency officers have _____ their previous statements denying any involvement on their part with the Contra aid network and are now revising their earlier testimony.

   (A) justified
   (B) recanted
   (C) repeated
   (D) protracted
   (E) heeded

10. New concerns about growing religious tension in northern India were _____ this week after at least fifty people were killed and hundreds were injured or arrested in rioting between Hindus and Moslems.

    (A) lessened
    (B) invalidated
    (C) restrained
    (D) dispersed
    (E) fueled

11. In a happy, somewhat boisterous celebration of the European discovery of America, the major phase of the Columbus Cinquecentennial got off to _____ start on Friday.

    (A) a slow
    (B) a rousing
    (C) a reluctant
    (D) an indifferent
    (E) a quiet

12. In one shocking instance of _____ research, one of the nation's most influential researchers in the field of genetics reported on experiments that were never carried out and published deliberately _____ scientific papers on his nonexistent work.

    (A) comprehensive...abstract
    (B) theoretical...challenging
    (C) fraudulent...deceptive
    (D) derivative...authoritative
    (E) erroneous...impartial

13. Measurement is, like any other human endeavor, a complex activity, subject to error, not always used _____, and frequently misinterpreted and _____.

    (A) mistakenly...derided
    (B) erratically...analyzed
    (C) systematically...organized
    (D) innovatively...refined
    (E) properly...misunderstood

14. In a revolutionary development in technology, several manufacturers now make biodegradable forms of plastic; some plastic six-pack rings, for example, gradually _____ when exposed to sunlight.

    (A) harden
    (B) stagnate
    (C) inflate
    (D) propagate
    (E) decompose

15. To alleviate the problem of contaminated chicken, the study panel recommends that the federal government shift its inspection emphasis from cursory bird-by-bird visual checks to a more _____ random sampling for bacterial and chemical contamination.

    (A) rigorous
    (B) perfunctory
    (C) symbolic
    (D) discreet
    (E) dubious

16. Her novel published to universal acclaim, her literary gifts acknowledged by the chief figures of the Harlem Renaissance, her reputation as yet _____ by envious slights, Hurston clearly was at the _____ of her career.

    (A) undamaged...ebb
    (B) untarnished...zenith
    (C) untainted...extremity
    (D) blackened...mercy
    (E) unmarred...brink

17. To the dismay of the student body, the class president was _____ berated by the principal at a school assembly.

    (A) ignominiously
    (B) privately
    (C) magnanimously
    (D) fortuitously
    (E) inconspicuously

18. Aimed at curbing European attempts to seize territory in the Americas, the Monroe Doctrine was a warning to _____ foreign powers.

    (A) pertinacious
    (B) credulous
    (C) remote
    (D) overt
    (E) predatory

19. When Frazer's editors at Macmillan tried to
_____ his endless augmentations, he insisted on
a type size so small and a page so packed as to
approach illegibility; and if that proved _____,
thinner paper.

    (A) protract...unwarranted
    (B) expurgate...satisfactory
    (C) reprimand...irrelevant
    (D) restrict...insufficient
    (E) revise...idiosyncratic

20. The authority of voice in Frazer's writing strikes
many readers today as _____ colonialism; his
prose seems as invulnerable and expansive as
something on which the sun was presumed never to
set.

    (A) consonant with
    (B) independent of
    (C) ambivalent toward
    (D) cognizant of
    (E) detrimental to

Sentence Completion Exercise B

Directions: Each of the following sentence completion
questions contains one or two blanks. These blanks
signify that a word or set of words has been left out.
Below each sentence are five words or sets of words.
For each blank, pick the word or set of words that best
reflects the sentence's overall meaning.

1. Baldwin's brilliant *The Fire Next Time* is both so
eloquent in its passion and so searching in its
_____ that it is bound to _____ any reader.

    (A) bitterness...embarrass
    (B) romanticism...appall
    (C) candor...unsettle
    (D) indifference...disappoint
    (E) conception...bore

2. Unlike other examples of _____ verse, Milton's
Lycidas does more than merely mourn the death of
Edward King; it also denounces corruption in the
Church in which King was ordained.

    (A) satiric
    (B) elegiac
    (C) free
    (D) humorous
    (E) didactic

3. Few other plants can grow beneath the canopy of
the sycamore tree, whose leaves and pods produce
a natural herbicide that leaches into the surrounding
soil, _____ other plants that might compete for
water and nutrients.

    (A) inhibiting
    (B) distinguishing
    (C) nourishing
    (D) encouraging
    (E) refreshing

4. Although a few years ago the fundamental facts
about the Milky Way seemed fairly well _____,
now even its mass and its radius have come into
_____.

    (A) determined...resolution
    (B) ignored...danger
    (C) problematic...prominence
    (D) diminished...disrepute
    (E) established...question

5. The officers threatened to take _____ if the
lives of their men were _____ by the conquered
natives.

    (A) liberties...irritated
    (B) measures...enhanced
    (C) pains...destroyed
    (D) reprisals...endangered
    (E) affront...enervated

6. Despite an affected _____ that convinced
casual observers that he was indifferent about his
painting and enjoyed only frivolity, Warhol cared
deeply about his art and labored at it _____.

    (A) nonchalance...diligently
    (B) empathy...methodically
    (C) fervor...secretly
    (D) gloom...intermittently
    (E) hysteria...sporadically

7. Because she had a reputation for _____ we
were surprised and pleased when she greeted us so
_____.

    (A) insolence...irately
    (B) insouciance...cordially
    (C) graciousness...amiably
    (D) arrogance...disdainfully
    (E) querulousness...affably

8. The child was so spoiled by her indulgent parents
that she pouted and became _____ when she
did not receive all of their attention.

    (A) discreet
    (B) suspicious
    (C) elated
    (D) sullen
    (E) tranquil

9. Just as disloyalty is the mark of the renegade,
_____ is the mark of the _____.

    (A) timorousness...hero
    (B) temerity...coward
    (C) avarice...philanthropist
    (D) cowardice...craven
    (E) vanity...flatterer

10. He became quite overbearing and domineering
once he had become accustomed to the _____
shown to soldiers by the natives; he enjoyed his
new sense of power and self-importance.

(A) disrespect
(B) apathy
(C) deference
(D) culpability
(E) enmity

11. The _____ of time had left the castle _____;
    it towered above the village, looking much as it
    must have done in Richard the Lion-Hearted's
    time.

    (A) repairs...destroyed
    (B) remoteness...alone
    (C) lack...defended
    (D) status...lonely
    (E) ravages...untouched

12. One of the most _____ educators in New York,
    Dr. Shalala ignited a controversy in 1984 by calling
    the city public schools a "rotten barrel" in need of
    _____ reform.

    (A) disputatious...little
    (B) outspoken...systemic
    (C) caustic...partial
    (D) indifferent...pretentious
    (E) sycophantic...superficial

13. The newest fiber-optic cables that carry telephone
    calls cross-country are made of glass so _____
    that a piece 100 miles thick is clearer than a
    standard windowpane.

    (A) fragile
    (B) immaculate
    (C) tangible
    (D) transparent
    (E) iridescent

14. The reasoning in this editorial is so _____ that
    we cannot see how anyone can be deceived by it.

    (A) coherent
    (B) astute
    (C) cogent
    (D) specious
    (E) dispassionate

15. The _____ of evidence was on the side of the
    plaintiff since all but one witness testified that his
    story was correct.

    (A) paucity
    (B) propensity
    (C) accuracy
    (D) brunt
    (E) preponderance

16. Glendon provides a dark underside to Frederick
    Jackson Turner's frontier thesis that saw rugged
    individualism as the essence of American society—
    an individualism that she sees as _____ atomism.

    (A) antithetical toward
    (B) skeptical of
    (C) degenerating into

(D) aspiring to
(E) renewed by

17. Chatwin has devoted his life to a kind of Grail
    quest, hoping to prove—by study and direct
    experience with primitive people—that human
    nature is gentle and defensive rather than
    _____, and that man is _____, not a
    predator.

    (A) belligerent...an apostate
    (B) martial...a crusader
    (C) aggressive...a pilgrim
    (D) truculent...a gladiator
    (E) pugnacious...a pawn

18. The texts as we have them were written down
    and edited carefully by Christians proud of their
    ancestors but unable to bear the thought of their
    indulging in heathen practices; thus, all references
    to the ancient religion of the Celts were _____,
    if not _____.

    (A) deleted...expunged
    (B) muddied...suppressed
    (C) labored...denigrated
    (D) aggrieved...overawed
    (E) obscure...ironic

19. Because Inspector Morse could not contain his
    scorn for the police commissioner, he was im-
    prudent enough to make _____ remarks about
    his superior officer.

    (A) ambiguous
    (B) dispassionate
    (C) unfathomable
    (D) interminable
    (E) scathing

20. In Japanese art, profound emotion is frequently
    couched in images of nature, observed with
    _____ conditioned by life in a land of dramatic
    seasonal change, where perils of earthquake and
    typhoon make nature's bounty _____ and its
    processes awesome and beautiful.

    (A) an intimacy...precarious
    (B) a fidelity...munificent
    (C) a skill...excessive
    (D) an indifference...chancy
    (E) a sensitivity...distinctive

Sentence Completion Exercise C

Directions: Each of the following sentence completion
questions contains one or two blanks. These blanks
signify that a word or set of words has been left out.
Below each sentence are five words or sets of words.
For each blank, pick the word or set of words that best
reflects the sentence's overall meaning.

1. A _____ statement is an _____ comparison:
   it does not compare things explicitly, but suggests a
   likeness between them.

(A) sarcastic...unfair
(B) blatant...overt
(C) sanguine...inherent
(D) metaphorical...implied
(E) bellicose...ardent

2. Modern architecture has discarded the_____ trimming on buildings and has concentrated on an almost Greek simplicity of line.

(A) flamboyant
(B) austere
(C) inconspicuous
(D) aesthetic
(E) derivative

3. If you are seeking _____ that will resolve all our ailments, you are undertaking an impossible task.

(A) a precedent
(B) a panacea
(C) an abstraction
(D) a direction
(E) a contrivance

4. I have no _____ motive in offering this advice; I seek no personal advantage or honor.

(A) nominal
(B) altruistic
(C) incongruous
(D) disinterested
(E) ulterior

5. This park has been preserved in all its _____ wildness so that visitors in future years may see how people lived during the eighteenth century.

(A) hedonistic
(B) prospective
(C) esoteric
(D) untrammeled
(E) pristine

6. Though he was theoretically a friend of labor, his voting record in Congress _____ that impression.

(A) implied
(B) created
(C) confirmed
(D) belied
(E) maintained

7. The orator was so _____ that the audience became _____.

(A) soporific...drowsy
(B) inaudible...elated
(C) pompous...bombastic
(D) dramatic...affable
(E) convincing...moribund

8. If you carry this _____ attitude to the conference, you will _____ any supporters you may have at this moment.

(A) belligerent...delight
(B) truculent...alienate
(C) conciliatory...defer
(D) supercilious...attract
(E) ubiquitous...delight

9. The _____ pittance the widow receives from the government cannot keep her from poverty.

(A) magnanimous
(B) indulgent
(C) meticulous
(D) munificent
(E) meager

10. Harriman, Kennan, and Acheson were part of that inner _____ of the American diplomatic establishment whose distinguished legacy _____ U.S. foreign policy.

(A) circle...grieved
(B) sanctum...absorbed
(C) core...dominated
(D) life...biased
(E) coterie...exacerbated

11. The young man was quickly promoted when his employers saw how _____ he was.

(A) indigent
(B) indifferent
(C) assiduous
(D) lethargic
(E) cursory

12. For Miró, art became a _____ ritual; paper and pencils were holy objects to him and he worked as though he were performing a religious rite.

(A) superficial
(B) sacred
(C) banal
(D) cryptic
(E) futile

13. Because it arrives so early in the season, before many other birds, the robin has been called the _____ of spring.

(A) hostage
(B) autocrat
(C) compass
(D) newcomer
(E) harbinger

14. Shy and hypochondriacal, Madison was uncomfortable at public gatherings; his character made him a most _____ lawmaker and practicing politician.

(A) conscientious
(B) unlikely
(C) fervent
(D) gregarious
(E) effective

15. The tapeworm is an example of _____ organism, one that lives within or on another creature, deriving some or all of its nutrients from its host.

    (A) a hospitable
    (B) an exemplary
    (C) a parasitic
    (D) an autonomous
    (E) a protozoan

16. In place of the more general debate about abstract principles of government that most delegates probably expected, the Constitutional Convention put _____ proposals on the table.

    (A) theoretical
    (B) vague
    (C) concrete
    (D) tentative
    (E) redundant

17. Overindulgence _____ character as well as physical stamina.

    (A) strengthens
    (B) stimulates
    (C) debilitates
    (D) maintains
    (E) provides

18. We must try to understand his momentary _____ for he has _____ more strain and anxiety than any among us.

    (A) outcry...described
    (B) senility...understood
    (C) vision...forgotten
    (D) generosity...desired
    (E) aberration...undergone

19. He is _____ opponent; you must respect and fear him at all times.

    (A) a redoubtable
    (B) a disingenuous
    (C) a pugnacious
    (D) an insignificant
    (E) a craven

20. Your _____ tactics may compel me to cancel the contract as the job must be finished on time.

    (A) dilatory
    (B) offensive
    (C) repugnant
    (D) infamous
    (E) confiscatory

Sentence Completion Exercise D

<u>Directions</u>: Each of the following sentence completion questions contains one or two blanks. These blanks signify that a word or set of words has been left out. Below each sentence are five words or sets of words. For each blank, pick the word or set of words that <u>best</u> reflects the sentence's overall meaning.

1. Truculent in defending their individual rights of sovereignty under the Articles of Confederation, the newly formed states _____ constantly.

    (A) apologized   (B) digressed   (C) conferred
         (D) acquiesced   (E) squabbled

2. If the *Titanic* had hit the iceberg head on, its watertight compartments might have saved it from _____, but it swerved to avoid the iceberg, and in the collision so many compartments were opened to the sea that disaster was _____.

    (A) foundering...inevitable
    (B) sinking...escaped
    (C) damage...limited
    (D) buoyancy...unavoidable
    (E) collapse...averted

3. Written in an amiable style, the book provides a comprehensive overview of European wines that should prove inviting to both the virtual _____ and the experienced connoisseur.

    (A) prodigal
    (B) novice
    (C) zealot
    (D) miser
    (E) glutton

4. The members of the religious sect ostracized the _____ who had abandoned their faith.

    (A) coward
    (B) suppliant
    (C) litigant
    (D) recreant
    (E) proselyte

5. I am not attracted by the _____ life of the _____, always wandering through the countryside, begging for charity.

    (A) proud...almsgiver
    (B) noble...philanthropist
    (C) affluent...mendicant
    (D) natural...philosopher
    (E) peripatetic...vagabond

6. Her true feelings _____ themselves in her sarcastic asides; only then was her _____ revealed.

    (A) concealed...sweetness
    (B) manifested...bitterness
    (C) hid...sarcasm
    (D) developed...anxiety
    (E) grieved...charm

7. They fired upon the enemy from behind trees, walls, and any other _____ point they could find.

    (A) conspicuous
    (B) definitive
    (C) vantage
    (D) exposed
    (E) indefensible

8. Because Pauling stubbornly continued to believe in the power of Vitamin C to cure cancer despite much evidence to the contrary, his colleagues felt he had lost his scientific _____.

   (A) tenacity
   (B) experimentation
   (C) daring
   (D) apparatus
   (E) objectivity

9. We need more men of culture and enlightenment; we have too many _____ among us.

   (A) visionaries
   (B) students
   (C) philistines
   (D) pragmatists
   (E) philosophers

10. The sugar dissolved in water _____; finally all that remained was an almost _____ residue on the bottom of the glass.

    (A) quickly...lumpy
    (B) immediately...fragrant
    (C) gradually...imperceptible
    (D) subsequently...glassy
    (E) spectacularly...opaque

11. Alec Guinness has few equals among English-speaking actors, and in his autobiography he reveals himself to be an uncommonly _____ prose stylist as well.

    (A) ambivalent
    (B) infamous
    (C) supercilious
    (D) felicitous
    (E) pedestrian

12. Traffic speed limits are set at a level that achieves some balance between the danger of _____ speed and the desire of most people to travel as quickly as possible.

    (A) marginal
    (B) normal
    (C) prudent
    (D) inadvertent
    (E) excessive

13. Although the economy suffers downturns, it also has strong _____ and self-correcting tendencies.

    (A) unstable
    (B) recidivist
    (C) inauspicious
    (D) recuperative
    (E) self-destructive

14. It is foolish to vent your spleen on _____ object; still, you make _____ enemies that way.

    (A) an inanimate...fewer
    (B) an immobile...bitter

(C) an interesting...curious
(D) an insipid...dull
(E) a humane...more

15. Since Cyrano de Bergerac did not wish to be under an obligation to any man, he refused to be a _____ of Cardinal Richelieu.

    (A) proselytizer
    (B) mentor
    (C) protégé
    (D) benefactor
    (E) predecessor

16. The leader of the group is the passionately committed Crimond, whose _____ politics is inversely proportional to his disciples' _____ political faith.

    (A) retreat from...remote
    (B) penchant for...ardent
    (C) indifference to...jaundiced
    (D) engagement in...lapsed
    (E) disinclination for...problematic

17. After the Japanese attack on Pearl Harbor on December 7, 1941, Japanese-Americans were _____ of being spies for Japan, although there was no _____ to back up this accusation.

    (A) acquitted...buttress
    (B) tired...witness
    (C) reminded...reason
    (D) suspected...evidence
    (E) exonerated...money

18. More than one friendly whale has nudged a boat with such _____ that passengers have been knocked overboard.

    (A) enthusiasm
    (B) lethargy
    (C) hostility
    (D) serenity
    (E) animosity

19. In seeking to rediscover Zora Neale Hurston, it is intriguing to look at the figure she cut in the minds of her contemporaries, the high regard she enjoyed before shifting aesthetic values _____ her to curio status.

    (A) emancipated
    (B) deviated
    (C) exported
    (D) absolved
    (E) relegated

20. We have become so democratic in our habits of thought that we are convinced that truth is determined through _____ of facts.

    (A) a hierarchy
    (B) a transcendance
    (C) a plebiscite
    (D) a repeal
    (E) an ignorance

Sentence Completion Exercise E

Directions: Each of the following sentence completion questions contains one or two blanks. These blanks signify that a word or set of words has been left out. Below each sentence are five words or sets of words. For each blank, pick the word or set of words that best reflects the sentence's overall meaning.

1. Studded starfish are well protected from most _____ and parasites by _____ surface whose studs are actually modified spines.

   (A) dangers...a vulnerable
   (B) predators...an armored
   (C) threats...a fragile
   (D) challenges...an obtuse
   (E) exigencies...a brittle

2. Chaotic in conception but not in _____, Kelly's canvases are as neat as the proverbial pin.

   (A) conceit
   (B) theory
   (C) execution
   (D) origin
   (E) intent

3. After having worked in the soup kitchen feeding the hungry, the volunteer began to see her own good fortune as _____ and her difference from the _____ as chance rather than destiny.

   (A) an omen...homeless
   (B) a fluke...impoverished
   (C) a threat...destitute
   (D) a reward...indigent
   (E) a lie...affluent

4. Some students are _____ and want to take only the courses for which they see immediate value.

   (A) theoretical
   (B) impartial
   (C) pragmatic
   (D) idealistic
   (E) opinionated

5. Unlike the Shakespearean plays that lit up the English stage, the "closet dramas" of the nineteenth century were meant to be _____ rather than _____.

   (A) seen...acted
   (B) read...staged
   (C) quiet...raucous
   (D) sophisticated...urbane
   (E) produced...performed

6. Japan's industrial success is _____ in part to its tradition of group effort and _____, as opposed to the emphasis on personal achievement that is a prominent aspect of other industrial nations.

   (A) responsive...independence
   (B) related...introspection
   (C) equivalent...solidarity
   (D) subordinate...individuality
   (E) attributed...cooperation

7. I was so bored with the verbose and redundant style of Victorian novelists that I welcomed the change to the _____ style of Hemingway.

   (A) prolix
   (B) consistent
   (C) terse
   (D) logistical
   (E) florid

8. As _____ head of the organization, he attended social functions and civic meetings but had no _____ in the formulation of company policy.

   (A) titular...voice
   (B) hypothetical...vote
   (C) former...pride
   (D) nominal...competition
   (E) actual...say

9. His listeners enjoyed his _____ wit but his victims often _____ at its satire.

   (A) lugubrious...suffered
   (B) caustic...laughed
   (C) kindly...smarted
   (D) subtle...smiled
   (E) trenchant...winced

10. The first forty years of life give us the text; the next thirty supply the _____.

    (A) abridgement
    (B) bibliography
    (C) commentary
    (D) epitaph
    (E) title

11. The distinctive qualities of African music were not appreciated or even _____ by Westerners until fairly recently.

    (A) deplored
    (B) revered
    (C) ignored
    (D) neglected
    (E) perceived

12. It is only to the vain that all is vanity; and all is _____ only to those who have never been _____ themselves.

    (A) arrogance...proud of
    (B) deception...sincere with
    (C) cowardice...afraid for
    (D) indolence...bored by
    (E) solitude...left to

13. No act of _____ was more pronounced than his refusal of any rewards for his discovery.

    (A) abeyance
    (B) submission
    (C) egoism
    (D) denunciation
    (E) abnegation

14. Tocqueville decided to swear the oath of loyalty to the new Orleanist king in part _____ (he wanted to keep his position as magistrate), and in part pragmatically (he was convinced that the democratization of politics represented by the new regime was _____).

    (A) expediently...calamitous
    (B) opportunistically...inevitable
    (C) imprudently...circumspect
    (D) selflessly...idealistic
    (E) theoretically...negligible

15. Unlike the gregarious Capote, who was never happier than when he was in the center of a crowd of celebrities, Faulkner, in later years, grew somewhat _____ and shunned company.

    (A) congenial
    (B) decorous
    (C) dispassionate
    (D) reclusive
    (E) ambivalent

16. She is a pragmatist, as _____ to base her future on impractical dreams as she would be to build a castle on shifting sand.

    (A) determined
    (B) disinclined
    (C) quick
    (D) apt
    (E) diligent

17. We are _____ the intellects of the past; or, rather, like children we take it for granted that somebody must supply us with our supper and our _____.

    (A) ungrateful to...ideas
    (B) dependent on...repose
    (C) unfaithful to...needs
    (D) fortunate in...allowance
    (E) generous to...wants

18. During the middle of the eighteenth century, the _____ style in furniture and architecture, marked by scrollwork and excessive decoration, flourished.

    (A) austere
    (B) functional
    (C) medieval
    (D) rococo
    (E) abstract

19. Although eighteenth-century English society as a whole did not encourage learning for its own sake in women, nonetheless it illogically _____ women's sad lack of education.

    (A) palliated
    (B) postulated
    (C) decried
    (D) brooked
    (E) vaunted

20. Faced with these massive changes, the government keeps its own counsel; although generally benevolent, it has always been _____ regime.

    (A) an altruistic
    (B) an unpredictable
    (C) a reticent
    (D) a sanguine
    (E) an indifferent

Answer Key

Sentence Completion Exercise A

1. C	6. B	11. B	16. B
2. B	7. B	12. C	17. A
3. D	8. D	13. E	18. E
4. C	9. B	14. E	19. D
5. C	10. E	15. A	20. A

Sentence Completion Exercise B

1. C	6. A	11. E	16. C
2. B	7. E	12. B	17. C
3. A	8. D	13. D	18. B
4. E	9. D	14. D	19. E
5. D	10. C	15. E	20. A

Sentence Completion Exercise C

1. D	6. D	11. C	16. C
2. A	7. A	12. B	17. C
3. B	8. B	13. E	18. E
4. E	9. E	14. B	19. A
5. E	10. C	15. C	20. A

Sentence Completion Exercise D

1. E	6. B	11. D	16. E
2. A	7. C	12. E	17. D
3. B	8. E	13. D	18. A
4. D	9. C	14. A	19. E
5. E	10. C	15. C	20. C

Sentence Completion Exercise E

1. B	6. E	11. E	16. B
2. C	7. C	12. B	17. A
3. B	8. A	13. E	18. D
4. C	9. E	14. B	19. C
5. B	10. C	15. D	20. C

7 Reading Comprehension Questions

■ **Testing Tactics**
■ **Practice Exercises**
■ **Answer Key**

GRE reading comprehension questions test your ability to understand what you read—both content and technique. Each verbal section on the GRE CAT includes two to four relatively short passages, each passage followed by two to four questions. A passage may deal with the **sciences** (including medicine, botany, zoology, chemistry, physics, geology, astronomy); the **humanities** (including art, literature, music, philosophy, folklore); or the **social sciences** (including history, economics, sociology, government). Some passages are strictly objective, explaining or describing a phenomenon or process neutrally. Others reflect a particular bias or point of view: the author is trying to convince the reader to share his or her opinion about the subject being discussed.

The GRE tends to take its reading passages from *The New York Review of Books*, from prestigious university presses (Harvard, Princeton, Oxford), from scholarly journals. Often the test-makers hit academically "hot" topics—biodiesel fuels, plate tectonics, damage to the ozone layer, Arthurian romance, the status of women's literature—that have aroused controversy over the past several decades. Frequently they edit these passages to make them more demanding both in vocabulary level and in grammatical complexity.

Some of the reading comprehension questions on the GRE are factual, asking you about specific details in the passages. Others ask you to interpret the passages, to make judgments about them. Still others ask you to recognize various techniques used by the authors or possible applications of their ideas to other circumstances. Some questions include lengthy and complex statements, as lengthy and complex as any sentences in the passage. Read the questions closely, as closely as you read the text. Be sure, in answering reading comprehension questions, that you read *all* the answer choices before deciding which is correct.

The reading comprehension questions following each passage are not arranged in order of difficulty. They are arranged to reflect the way the passage's content is organized. A question based on information found at the beginning of the passage generally will come before a question based on information at the passage's end.

Testing Tactics

First Read the Question, Then Read the Passage

In responding to reading comprehension passages on the CAT, you generally will have to consider more material than can fit conveniently on a single screen. You will confront a split screen similar to the one on the next page. On one half of the screen you will see the

question you must answer; on the other you will see a segment of the passage under consideration. You will have to scroll through the passage in order to read the text in its entirety. (For a more comprehensive explanation of scrolling through passages, see Chapter 2.)

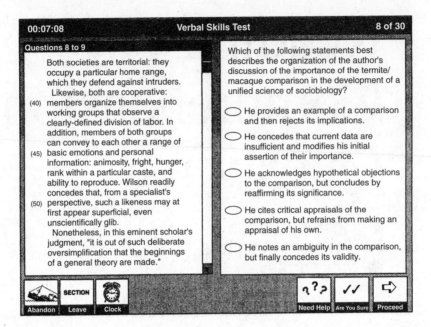

Under these conditions, clearly only one tactic works: first read the question, then read the passage.

1. Read the question carefully, so that you are sure you understand what it is asking. Decide whether it is asking about a specific, readily identifiable detail within the passage, or whether it is asking about the passage as a whole. Note any key words in the question that may help you spot where the answer may be found.

2. Next, turn to the passage. Read as rapidly as you can with understanding, but do not force yourself. Do not worry about the time element. If you worry about not finishing the test, you will begin to take shortcuts and miss the correct answer in your haste.

3. As you read the opening sentences, try to anticipate what the passage will be about. Whom or what is the author talking about? What, in other words, is the *topic* of this passage?

4. As you scroll through the passage, think about what kind of writing this is. What is the author trying to do?

   Is the author trying to *explain* some aspect of the topic?
   Is the author trying to *describe* some aspect of the topic?

Is the author trying to *argue* or debate some aspect of the topic?

What does the author feel about this topic? What audience is the author addressing here? Answering these questions will give you a sense of the passage as a whole.

5. Use your scratch paper intelligently. Take brief notes of important words or phrases in different paragraphs so that you can scroll back to them quickly when you want to verify an answer choice. You may also want to note key words in question stems (words like EXCEPT and LEAST, which the test-makers capitalize for emphasis, and that restrict your answer choice).

6. Your first scrolling through the passage should give you a general impression of the scope of the passage and of the location of its major subdivisions. In order to answer the question properly, **you must go back to the passage to verify your answer choice**. Do not rely on your memory. Above all, do not rely on anything you may have learned from your reading or courses about the topic of this passage. Base your answer on what this passage says, not on what you know from other sources.

Learn to Spot the Major Reading Question Types

Just as it will help you to know the common types of analogies found on the GRE, it will also help you to familiarize yourself with the major types of reading questions on the test.

If you can recognize just what a given question is asking for, you will be better able to tell which reading tactic to apply.

Here are seven categories of reading questions you are likely to face:

1. **Main Idea** Questions that test your ability to find the central thought of a passage or to judge its significance often take one of the following forms:

    The main point of the passage is to...
    The passage is primarily concerned with...
    The author's primary purpose in this passage is to...
    The chief theme of the passage can best be described as...
    Which of the following titles best states the central idea of the passage?
    Which of the following statements best expresses the main idea of the passage?

2. **Finding Specific Details** Questions that test your ability to understand what the author states *explicitly* are often worded:

    According to the author,...
    The author states all of the following EXCEPT...
    According to the passage, which of the following is true of the...
    The passage supplies information that would answer which of the following questions?
    Which of the following statements is (are) best supported by the passage?
    Which of the following is NOT cited in the passage as evidence of...

3. **Drawing Inferences** Questions that test your ability to go beyond the author's explicit statements and see what these statements imply may be worded:

    It can be inferred from the passage that...
    The author implies that...
    The passage suggests that...
    Which of the following statements about...can be inferred from the passage?

4. **Application to Other Situations** Questions that test your ability to recognize how the author's ideas might apply to other situations often are worded:

    With which of the following statements would the author of the passage be most likely to agree?
    With which of the following aphorisms would the author be in strongest agreement?

The author's argument would be most weakened by the discovery of which of the following?
The author's contention would be most clearly strengthened if which of the following were found to be true?
Which of the following examples could best be substituted for the author's example of...
Which of the following statements would be most likely to begin the paragraph immediately following the passage?
The author is most probably addressing which of the following audiences?

5. **Tone/Attitude** Questions that test your ability to sense an author's emotional state often take the form:

    The author's attitude toward the problem can best be described as...
    The author regards that idea that...with...
    The author's tone in the passage is that of a person attempting to...
    Which of the following best describes the author's tone in the passage?

6. **Technique** Questions that test your ability to recognize a passage's method of organization or technique often are worded:

    Which of the following best describes the development of this passage?
    In presenting the argument, the author does all of the following EXCEPT...
    The relationship between the second paragraph and the first paragraph can best be described as...
    In the passage, the author makes the central point primarily by...
    The organization of the passage can best be described as...

7. **Determining the Meaning of Words from Their Context** Questions that test your ability to work out the meaning of unfamiliar words from their context often are worded:

    As it is used in the passage, the term...can best be described as...
    The phrase...is used in the passage to mean that...
    As used by the author, the term...refers to...
    The author uses the phrase...to describe...

When Asked to Find the Main Idea, Be Sure to Check the Opening and Summary Sentences of Each Paragraph

The opening and closing sentences of a paragraph are key sentences for you to read. They can serve as guideposts, pointing out the author's main idea.

When you are asked to determine a passage's main idea, *always* check the opening and summary sen-

tences of each paragraph. Authors typically provide readers with a sentence that expresses a paragraph's main idea succinctly. Although such *topic sentences* may appear anywhere in the paragraph, readers customarily look for them in the opening or closing sentences.

Note that in GRE reading passages topic sentences are sometimes implied rather than stated directly. If you cannot find a topic sentence, ask yourself these questions:

1. Who or what is this passage about?
   (The subject of the passage can be a *person*, *place*, or *thing*. It can be something abstract, such as an *idea*. It can even be a *process*, or something in motion, for which no single-word synonym exists.)

2. What aspect of this subject is the author talking about?

3. What is the author trying to get across about this aspect of the subject?
   (Decide the most important thing that is being said about the subject. Either the subject must be *doing* something, or something is *being done* to it.)

Read the following natural science passage and apply this tactic.

> According to Wilson[1], only when we are able to apply the same parameters and mathematical principles to weighing both troops of rhesus
> *Line* macaques and termite colonies will a unified
> (5) science of sociobiology finally exist. While recognizing that many of his colleagues question such an outcome, Wilson, one of sociobiology's leading proponents, finds himself simultaneously more and more struck by the functional similar-
> (10) ities that characterize both insect and vertebrate societies and less concerned with the structural differences that divide them to such an apparently irreconcilable degree. Thus, he freely compares termites and macaques, pointing out numerous
> (15) likenesses between them. Both societies are territorial: they occupy a particular home range, which they defend against intruders. Likewise, both are cooperative: members organize themselves into working groups that observe a clearly-
> (20) defined division of labor. In addition, members of both groups can convey to each other a range of basic emotions and personal information: animosity, fright, hunger, rank within a particular caste, and ability to reproduce. Wilson readily
> (25) concedes that, from a specialist's perspective, such a likeness may at first appear superficial, even unscientifically glib. Nonetheless, in this eminent scholar's judgment, "it is out of such deliberate oversimplification that the beginnings
> (30) of a general theory are made."

[1]Edwin O. Wilson, Harvard professor and author of *Sociobiology*.

Now look at a typical main idea question on this passage.

Which of the following best summarizes the author's main point?

(A) Facile and simplistic comparisons of animal societies could damage the prospects for the establishment of a unified science of sociobiology.

(B) It is necessary to study both biology and sociology in order to appreciate how animals as different as termites and rhesus macaques can be said to resemble each other.
(C) The majority of animal species arrange themselves in societies whose patterns of group behavior resemble those of human societies.
(D) It is worthwhile noting that animals as dissimilar as termites and rhesus monkeys observe certain analogous and predictable behavior patterns.
(E) An analysis of the ways in which insect and vertebrate societies resemble one another could supply the foundation for a unified science of sociobiology.

Look at the opening and summary sentences of the passage: "only when we are able to apply the same parameters and mathematical principles to weighing both troops of rhesus macaques and termite colonies will a unified science of sociobiology finally exist...it is out of such deliberate oversimplification that the beginnings of a general theory are made." First, is there a person, place, thing, idea, or process that is common to both sentences? Are there any words in the last sentence that repeat something in the first? *A general theory* repeats the idea of *a unified science* of sociobiology. The paragraph's subject seems to be the unified science of sociobiology. Note as well the words pointing to expectations for the future—*will...finally exist, beginnings*. The tone of both sentences appears positive: when certain conditions are met, then, in Wilson's view, a specific result will follow—we will have a unified science or general theory of sociobiology. This result, however, is not guaranteed; it can come about only if the conditions are met.

Now turn to the answer choices. What does Choice A say about a unified science of sociobiology? It states some things could make it less likely, not more likely, to come about. Choice A is incorrect; it contradicts the passage's sense that a unified science of sociobiology is a *likely* outcome. Choices B, C, and D also may be incorrect: not one of them mentions a unified science of sociobiology. On closer inspection, Choice B proves incorrect: it makes an unsupported statement that one needs biological and sociological education to understand the resemblances between insects and vertebrates. Choice C also proves incorrect: it goes far beyond what the passage actually states. Where the passage speaks in terms of termites and rhesus macaques, Choice C speaks in terms of the *majority* of animal species and extends the comparison to include humans as well. Choice D, while factually correct according to the passage, is incorrect because it is too narrow in scope. It ignores the author's main point; it fails to include Wilson's interest in the possibility that a study of such similar patterns of behavior might lead to a general theory of sociobiology. The correct answer is Choice E. It is the only statement that speaks of a unified science of sociobiology as a likely possibility.

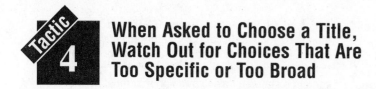

When Asked to Choose a Title, Watch Out for Choices That Are Too Specific or Too Broad

A paragraph has been defined as a group of sentences revolving around a central theme. An appropriate title for a paragraph, therefore, must express this central theme that each of the sentences in the paragraph develops. It should be neither too broad nor too narrow in scope; it should be specific and yet comprehensive enough to include all the essential ideas presented by the sentences. A good title for a passage of two or more paragraphs should express the thoughts of ALL the paragraphs.

When you are trying to select the best title for a passage, watch out for words that come straight out of the passage. They may not always be your best choice.

This second question on the sociobiology passage is a title question. Note how it resembles questions on the passage's purpose or main idea.

> Which of the following is the best title for the passage?
>
> (A) Deceptive Comparisons: Oversimplification in Biological Research
> (B) An Uncanny Likeness: Termites and Rhesus Macaques
> (C) Structural Dissimilarities Between Insects and Vertebrates
> (D) Arguments Against a Science of Sociobiology
> (E) Sociobiology: Intimations of a General Theory

Choice A is incorrect: it is at once too narrow and too broad. It is too narrow in that the passage refers to *oversimplification* only in passing; it does not have over-simplification as its subject. It is too broad in that the passage emphasizes sociobiology, not the whole realm of biological research. It is also misleading; the passage never asserts that the deliberate oversimplification of the comparison between termites and macaques is intended to deceive.

Choice B is incorrect: it is too narrow. True, the author discusses the resemblance between termite and macaque societies; however, this likeness is not his subject. He discusses it to provide an example of the sort of comparison that may lay the groundwork for a potential science of sociobiology.

Choice C is also incorrect because it is not inclusive enough. It fails to mention the potential science of sociobiology. In addition, while the passage refers to *structural differences* between insect and vertebrate societies, it stresses structural similarities, not structural dissimilarities.

Choices D and E both mention the theory of sociobiology. Which is the better title for the piece? Clearly, Choice E: the author is not arguing against the potential science of sociobiology; he is reporting Wilson's opinions concerning the likelihood of sociobiology's emergence as a unified science. Thus, he finds in the termite-macaque comparison *intimations* or hints of an incipient general theory.

When Asked to Determine Questions of Attitude, Mood, or Tone, Look for Words That Convey Emotion, Express Values, or Paint Pictures

In determining the attitude, mood, or tone of an author, examine the specific diction used. Is the author using adjectives to describe the subject? If so, are they words like *fragrant*, *tranquil*, *magnanimous*—words with positive connotations? Or are they words like *fetid*, *ruffled*, *stingy*—words with negative connotations?

When we speak, our tone of voice conveys our mood—frustrated, cheerful, critical, gloomy, angry. When we write, our images and descriptive phrases get our feelings across.

The next model question on the Wilson passage is an attitude question. Note the range of feelings in the answer choices.

> According to the author, Wilson's attitude toward the prospect of a unified theory in sociobiology can best be characterized as which of the following?
>
> (A) Unconditional enthusiasm
> (B) Cautious optimism
> (C) Unbiased objectivity
> (D) Resigned acquiescence
> (E) Strong displeasure

How does Wilson feel about the possibility of a unified theory of sociobiology? The answer choices range from actively negative (*strong displeasure*) to actively positive (*unconditional enthusiasm*), with passively negative (*resigned acquiescence*), neutral (*unbiased objectivity*), and guardedly positive (*cautious optimism*) in between.

Wilson's attitude toward the possibility of a unified theory of sociobiology is implicit in the author's choice of words. It is clear that Wilson views this possibility positively; the whole thrust of his argument is that the current studies of the similarities between insect and vertebrate societies could mark the beginnings of such a unified theory and that the specialist should not dismiss these studies as glib or simpleminded. Note in the second sentence how the author describes Wilson as a leading proponent or champion of sociobiology, someone whose feelings about the field are by definition positive.

Wilson is certainly not unhappy or *strongly displeased* with this potential unified theory, nor is he merely long-suffering or *resigned* to it. Similarly, he is not *unbiased* and *objective* about it; he actively involves himself in arguing the case for sociobiology. Thus, you can eliminate Choices C, D, and E. But how do you decide between the two positive terms, *enthusiasm* and

optimism, Choice A and Choice B? To decide between them, you must look carefully at the adjectives modifying them. Is Wilson's enthusiasm unqualified or *unconditional*? You may think so, but look again. The opening sentence states a basic condition that must be met before there can be a unified science of sociobiology: the same parameters and mathematical principles must be used to analyze insect and vertebrate societies. Though a proponent of sociobiology, Wilson is first and foremost a scientist, one who tests hypotheses and comes to logical conclusions about them. *Unconditional enthusiasm* seems to overstate his attitude.

Choice A appears incorrect. What of Choice B? Is Wilson's optimism *cautious* or guarded? Yes. According to the passage, Wilson is aware that specialists may well find fault with the sociobiologist's conclusions; the passage uses terms that convey values, first the negative "superficial, even unscientifically glib" to suggest the specialist's negative attitude towards sociobiology, then the positive "deliberate" to convey Wilson's own more positive response. The correct answer is Choice B.

When Asked About Specific Details in the Passage, Spot Key Words in the Question and Scan the Passage to Find Them (or Their Synonyms)

Tactic 6

In developing the main idea of a passage, a writer will make statements to support his or her point. To answer questions about such supporting details, you *must* find a word or group of words in the passage supporting your choice of answer. The words "according to the passage" or "according to the author" should focus your attention on what the passage explicitly states. Do not be misled into choosing an answer (even one that makes good sense) if you cannot find it supported by the text.

Detail questions often ask about a particular phrase or line. In such cases, use the following technique:

1. Look for key words (nouns or verbs) in the answer choices.

2. Scroll through the passage, looking for those key words or their synonyms. (This is *scanning*. It is what you do when you look up someone's number in the phone directory.)

3. When you find a key word or its synonym in a sentence, reread that sentence to make sure the test-makers haven't used the original wording to mislead you.

Read the following brief passage and apply this tactic.

What is involved in the process of visual recognition? First, like computer data, visual memories of an object must be stored; then, a

Line mechanism must exist for them to be retrieved.
(5) But how does this process work? The eye triggers the nerves into action. This neural activity constructs a picture in the brain's memory system, an internal image of the object observed. When the eye once again confronts that object, the object is
(10) compared with its internal image; if the two images match, recognition takes place.

Among psychologists, the question as to whether visual recognition is a parallel, single-step operation or a sequential, step-by-step one is
(15) the subject of much debate. Gestalt psychologists contend that objects are perceived as wholes in a parallel operation: the internal image is matched with the retinal impression in one single step. Psychologists of other schools, however, suggest
(20) the opposite, maintaining that the individual features of an object are matched serially with the features of its internal image. Some experiments have demonstrated that the more well-known an object is, the more holistic its internal image
(25) becomes, and the more parallel the process of recognition tends to be. Nonetheless, the bulk of the evidence appears to uphold the serial hypothesis, at least for simple objects that are relatively unfamiliar to the viewer.

Now look at the following question on a specific detail in the passage.

According to the passage, psychologists of the Gestalt school assume which of the following about the process of visual recognition?

    I. The image an object makes on the retina is exactly the same as its internal image.
    II. The mind recognizes a given object as a whole; it has no need to analyze the object's constituent parts individually.
    III. The process of matching an object with its internal image takes place in a single step.

(A) II only
(B) III only
(C) I and III only
(D) II and III only
(E) I, II, and III

You can arrive at the correct answer to this question by elimination.

First, quickly scan the passage looking for the key word *Gestalt*. The sentence mentioning Gestalt psychologists states they maintain that objects are recognized as wholes in a parallel procedure. The sentence immediately preceding defines a parallel procedure as one that takes only one step.

Now examine the statements. Do Gestalt psychologists maintain that an object's retinal image is exactly the same as its internal image? Statement I is unsupported by the passage. Therefore, you can eliminate Choices C and E.

Statement II is supported by the passage: lines 15–17 indicate that Gestalt psychologists believe objects are recognized as wholes. Therefore, you can eliminate Choice B.

Statement III is supported by the passage: lines 17–18 indicate that Gestalt psychologists believe matching is a parallel process that occurs in one step. Therefore, you can eliminate Choice A.

Only Choice D is left. It is the correct answer.

Note how necessary it is to point to specific lines in the passage when you answer questions on specific details.

When Asked to Make Inferences, Base Your Answers on What the Passage Implies, Not What It States Directly

In *Language in Thought and Action*, S. I. Hayakawa defines an inference as "a statement about the unknown made on the basis of the known."

Inference questions require you to use your own judgment. You must not take anything directly stated by the author as an inference. Instead, you must look for clues in the passage that you can use in deriving your own conclusion. You should choose as your answer a statement that is a logical development of the information the author has provided.

Try this relatively easy inference question, based on the previous passage about visual recognition.

One can infer from the passage that, in visual recognition, the process of matching

(A) requires neural inactivity
(B) cannot take place if an attribute of a familiar object has been altered in some way
(C) cannot occur when the observer looks at an object for the very first time
(D) has now been proven to necessitate both serial and parallel processes
(E) can only occur when the brain receives a retinal image as a single unit

Go through the answer choices, eliminating any choices that obviously contradict what the passage states or implies. Remember that in answering inference questions you must go beyond the obvious, beyond what the authors explicitly state, to look for logical implications of what they say.

Choice A is incorrect. Nothing in the passage suggests that the matching process requires or demands neural inactivity. Rather, the entire process of visual recognition, including the matching of images, requires neural *activity*.

Choice D is incorrect. It is clear from the passage that the matching process is not fully understood; nothing yet has been absolutely *proven*. The weight of the evidence *seems* to support the serial hypothesis, but controversy still surrounds the entire question.

Choice E is incorrect. It can be eliminated because it directly contradicts information in the passage stating that recognition most likely is a serial or step-by-step process rather than a parallel one receiving an image as a single unit.

Choices B and C are left. Which is a possible inference? Choice C seems a possible inference. Although the author never says so, it seems logical that you could not match an object if you had never seen it before. After all, if you had never seen the object before, you would have no prior internal image of it and would have nothing with which to match it. What of Choice B? Nothing in the passage mentions altering any attributes or features of a familiar object. Therefore, *on the basis of the passage* you have no way to deduce whether matching would or would not be possible if such a change took place. There is not enough information in the passage to justify Choice B as an inference. The correct answer is Choice C.

Another, more difficult inference question is based on the previous excerpt reviewing Wilson's *Sociobiology*. Review the passage briefly and see how you do with a question that very few of the examinees would have answered correctly.

> According to Wilson, only when we are able to apply the same parameters and mathematical principles to weighing both troops of rhesus
> *Line* macaques and termite colonies will a unified
> (5) science of sociobiology finally exist. While recognizing that many of his colleagues question such an outcome, Wilson, one of sociobiology's leading proponents, finds himself simultaneously more and more struck by the functional similari-
> (10) ties that characterize both insect and vertebrate societies and less concerned with the structural differences that divide them to such an apparently irreconcilable degree. Thus, he freely compares termites and macaques, pointing out numerous
> (15) likenesses between them. Both societies are territorial: they occupy a particular home range, which they defend against intruders. Likewise, both are cooperative: members organize themselves into working groups that observe a clearly-
> (20) defined division of labor. In addition, members of both groups can convey to each other a range of basic emotions and personal information: animosity, fright, hunger, rank within a particular caste, and ability to reproduce. Wilson readily
> (25) concedes that, from a specialist's perspective, such a likeness may at first appear superficial, even unscientifically glib. Nonetheless, in this eminent scholar's judgment, "it is out of such deliberate oversimplification that the beginnings
> (30) of a general theory are made."

In analyzing insect and vertebrate societies, the passage suggests which of the following?

(A) A clearly-defined division of labor is a distinguishing feature of most insect and vertebrate societies.

(B) The caste structures of insect and vertebrate societies share certain likenesses.

(C) Most insect and vertebrate societies utilize cooperative groups to hold and defend their home range.

(D) The system of communication employed by members of insect societies resembles the system that members of vertebrate societies follow.

(E) Major structural differences exist between insect and vertebrate societies.

Why would most examinees answer this question incorrectly? The reason is simple: it is easy to confuse statements made about specific insect and vertebrate societies with statements made about insect and vertebrate societies in general. In this passage, in the fourth sentence, the author switches from talking about Wilson's views of insect and vertebrate societies in general and refers to his comments on termites and macaques in specific.

Go through the answer choices one by one. Does the passage suggest that a clearly-defined division of labor distinguishes *most* insect and vertebrate societies? No. It merely states that, according to Wilson, a clearcut division of labor is a characteristic of termite and rhesus macaque societies. Choice A is incorrect: you cannot justify leaping from a single type of insect (*termites*) and a single type of vertebrate (*rhesus macaques*) to most insects and most vertebrates.

Does the passage suggest that the caste structure of insect societies shares certain likenesses with that of their counterparts in vertebrate societies? No. It merely states that, according to Wilson, termites and macaques both can communicate rank within a particular caste. Choice B is incorrect. You cannot assume that the caste structure of insect societies is similar to the caste structure of vertebrate societies just because termites and rhesus macaques both have some way to communicate caste status or rank.

Does the passage suggest that *most* insect and vertebrate societies form cooperative groups in order to hold and defend their home range or territory? No. It merely states that termites and macaques organize themselves into cooperative groups, and that both species occupy and defend territories. Choice C is incorrect: again, you cannot justify leaping from termites and rhesus macaques to *most* insects and *most* vertebrates.

Does the passage suggest that the system of communication employed by members of insect societies resembles that employed by members of vertebrate societies? No. It merely states that communication among termites and macaques serves similar ends; it says nothing about the specific systems of communication they use, nor about those systems of communication used by other insects and vertebrates. Choice D is incorrect.

The correct answer is Choice E. In the passage, the author states that Wilson has grown less impressed "with the structural differences that divide them (i.e., insect and vertebrate societies) to such an apparently irreconcilable degree." This suggests that, even though Wilson may be unimpressed with them, these differences exist and are *major*.

When Asked to Apply Ideas from the Passage to a New Situation, Put Yourself in the Author's Place

GRE application questions require you to do three things:

1. *Reason*—If X is true, then Y must also be true.

2. *Perceive Feelings*—If the author feels this way about subject A, he probably feels a certain way about subject B.

3. *Sense a Larger Structure*—This passage is part of an argument for a proposal, or part of a description of a process, or part of a critique of a hypothesis.

Like inference questions, application questions require you to go beyond what the author explicitly states. Application questions, however, ask you to go well beyond a simple inference, using clues in the passage to interpret possible reasons for actions and possible outcomes of events. Your concern is to comprehend how the author's ideas might apply to other situations, or be affected by them. To do so, you have to put yourself in the author's place.

Imagine you are the author. What are you arguing for? Given what you have just stated in the passage, what would you want to say next? What might hurt your argument? What might make it stronger? What kind of audience would appreciate what you have to say? Whom are you trying to convince? If you involve yourself personally with the passage, you will be better able to grasp it in its entirety and see its significance.

Answer the following application question based on the previous passage discussing Wilson's *Sociobiology*.

> Which of the following statements would be most likely to begin the paragraph immediately following the passage?
>
> (A) Wilson has raised a problem in ethical philosophy in order to characterize the essence of the discipline of sociobiology.

> (B) It may not be too much to say that sociology and the other social sciences are the last branches of biology waiting to be integrated into neo-Darwinist evolutionary theory.
> (C) Although behavioral biology is traditionally spoken of as if it were a unified subject, it is now emerging as two distinct disciplines centered on neurophysiology and sociobiology, respectively.
> (D) The formulation of a theory of sociobiology constitutes, in Wilson's opinion, one of the great manageable problems of biology for the next twenty or thirty years.
> (E) In the past, the development of sociobiology has been slowed by too close an identification with ethology and behavioral psychology.

As you know from answering the previous main idea and attitude questions, Wilson's point is that students of insect and vertebrate societies may be on the verge of devising a general theory of sociobiology. Like Wilson, the author of the passage appears optimistic about the likelihood of developing this unified science. At the same time, again like Wilson, he is cautious; he too does not wish to overstate the case.

Put yourself in the author's place. What would you be likely to say next? The author has just been describing Wilson's hopeful view of the prospects for putting together a general theory of sociobiology. What would be more natural than for him next to discuss Wilson's opinion of a time frame for formulating this general theory? Choice D, with its confident yet judicious view of the formulation of a theory of sociobiology as "one of the great *manageable* problems of biology for the next twenty or thirty years," seems a logical extension of what the passage has just been saying. While Choices A, B, C, and E all touch on sociobiology in some way, none of them follows as naturally from the passage's immediate argument.

When Asked to Give the Meaning of an Unfamiliar Word, Look for Nearby Context Clues

When a question in the reading comprehension part of an examination asks for the meaning of a word, that meaning can usually be deduced from the word's con-

text. The purpose of this kind of question is to determine how well you can extract meaning from the text, not how extensive your general vocabulary is.

Sometimes the unknown word is a common word used in one of its special or technical meanings. For example:

> He *threw* the pot in an hour. The wheel turned busily and the shape grew quickly as his fingers worked the wet, spinning clay. (*Throw* here means to shape on a potter's wheel.)

At other times, the unknown word may bear a deceptive resemblance to a known word.

> He fell *senseless* to the ground. (He was unconscious. He did not fall foolishly or nonsensically to the ground.)

Just because you know *one* meaning of a word, do not assume that you know its meaning as it is used in a particular passage. You must look within the passage for clues. Often authors will use an unfamiliar word and then immediately define it within the same sentence. The two words or groups of words are juxtaposed—set beside one another—to make their relationship clear. Commas, hyphens, and parentheses may signal this relationship.

1. The *rebec*, a medieval stringed instrument played with a bow, has only three strings.

2. *Paleontologists*—students of fossil remains—explore the earth's history.

3. Most mammals are *quadrupeds* (four-footed animals).

Often an unfamiliar word in one clause of a sentence will be defined or clarified in the sentence's other clause.

1. The early morning dew had frozen, and everything was covered with a thin coat of *rime*.

2. Cowards, we use *euphemisms* when we cannot bear the truth, calling our dead "the dear departed," as if they have just left the room.

Refer once more to the passage on visual recognition to answer the following question.

> What is involved in the process of visual recognition? First, like computer data, visual memories of an object must be stored; then, a
> *Line* mechanism must exist for them to be retrieved.
> *(5)* But how does this process work? The eye triggers

the nerves into action. This neural activity constructs a picture in the brain's memory system, an internal image of the object observed. When the eye once again confronts that object, the object is
(10) compared with its internal image; if the two images match, recognition takes place.

Among psychologists, the question as to whether visual recognition is a parallel, single-step operation or a sequential, step-by-step one is
(15) the subject of much debate. Gestalt psychologists contend that objects are perceived as wholes in a parallel operation: the internal image is matched with the retinal impression in one single step. Psychologists of other schools, however, suggest
(20) the opposite, maintaining that the individual features of an object are matched serially with the features of its internal image. Some experiments have demonstrated that the more well-known an object is, the more holistic its internal image
(25) becomes, and the more parallel the process of recognition tends to be. Nonetheless, the bulk of the evidence appears to uphold the serial hypothesis, at least for simple objects that are relatively unfamiliar to the viewer.

Which of the following phrases could best replace "the more holistic its internal image becomes" (lines 24–25) without significantly changing the sentence's meaning?

(A) the more its internal image increases in detail
(B) the more integrated its internal image grows
(C) the more its internal image decreases in size
(D) the more it reflects its internal image
(E) the more indistinct its internal image appears

What words or phrases in the vicinity of "the more holistic its internal image becomes" give you a clue to the phrase's meaning? The phrase immediately following, "becomes more parallel." If the recognition process becomes more parallel as an object becomes more familiar, then matching takes place in one step in which all the object's features are simultaneously transformed into a single internal representation. Thus, to say that an object's internal image becomes more holistic is to say that it becomes more *integrated* or whole. The correct answer is Choice B.

Familiarize Yourself with the Technical Terms Used to Describe a Passage's Organization

Another aspect of understanding the author's point is understanding how the author organizes what he has to say. You have to understand how the author makes his point, figure out whether he begins with his thesis or main idea or works up to it gradually. Often this means observing how the opening sentence or paragraph relates to the passage as a whole.

Here is a technique question based on the last two sentences of the passage about sociobiology. Those lines are repeated here so that you can easily refer to them.

> Wilson readily concedes that, from a specialist's perspective, such a likeness may at first appear superficial, even unscientifically glib. Nonetheless, in this eminent scholar's judgment, "it is out of such deliberate oversimplification that the beginnings of a general theory are made."

Which of the following statements best describes the organization of the author's discussion of the importance of the termite/macaque comparison in the development of a unified science of sociobiology (lines 24–31)?

(A) He provides an example of a comparison and then rejects its implications.

(B) He concedes that current data are insufficient and modifies his initial assertion of their importance.

(C) He acknowledges hypothetical objections to the comparison, but concludes by re-affirming its significance.

(D) He cites critical appraisals of the comparison, but refrains from making an appraisal of his own.

(E) He notes an ambiguity in the comparison, but finally concedes its validity.

Consider the first clause of each answer choice.

In his comment on how things may seem from the specialist's point of view, does the author *provide an example* of a comparison? No. He refers to a comparison made earlier. Therefore, you can eliminate Choice A.

Does he *concede the insufficiency* of current data? Not quite. He states that some people may quarrel with the comparison because it seems glib to them; he does not grant that they are right or that the data are inadequate. Therefore, you can eliminate Choice B.

Does he *acknowledge hypothetical objections* to the comparison? Definitely. Make a note to come back later to Choice C.

Does he *cite critical appraisals* of the comparison? Possibly. Again, make a note of Choice D.

Does he *note an ambiguity* in the comparison? No. He notes an objection to the comparison; he mentions no ambiguities within it. Therefore, you can eliminate Choice E.

Now consider the second clause of Choices C and D. Does the author *refrain from making an appraisal* of the comparison? No. He calls it a deliberate oversimplification that may bear fruit. Choice D is incorrect. Does the author conclude by *reaffirming the significance* of the termite/macaque comparison? Clearly he does; he quotes Wilson's conclusion that such oversimplified comparisons can provide the basis for an important general theory. The correct answer is Choice C.

Practice Exercises

Reading Comprehension Exercise A

Directions: Each of the following reading comprehension questions are based on the content of the following passage. Read the passage and then determine the best answer choice for each question. Base your choice on what this passage states directly or implies, not on any information you may have gained elsewhere.

One phase of the business cycle is the *expansion phase*. This phase is a twofold one, including recovery and prosperity. During the recovery
Line period there is ever-growing expansion of existing
(5) facilities, and new facilities for production are created. More businesses are created and older ones expanded. Improvements of various kinds are made. There is an ever-increasing optimism about the future of economic growth. Much capi-
(10) tal is invested in machinery or "heavy" industry. More labor is employed. More raw materials are required. As one part of the economy develops, other parts are affected. For example, a great expansion in automobiles results in an expansion
(15) of the steel, glass, and rubber industries. Roads are required; thus the cement and machinery industries are stimulated. Demand for labor and materials results in greater prosperity for workers and suppliers of raw materials, including farmers.
(20) This increases purchasing power and the volume of goods bought and sold. Thus prosperity is diffused among the various segments of the population. This prosperity period may continue to rise and rise without an apparent end. However, a
(25) time comes when this phase reaches a peak and stops spiralling upwards. This is the end of the expansion phase.

1. Which of the following statements is the best example of the optimism mentioned in line 8 of the passage as being part of the expansion phase?

(A) Public funds are designated for the construction of new highways designed to stimulate tourism.

(B) Industrial firms allocate monies for the purchase of machine tools.

(C) The prices of agricultural commodities are increased at the producer level.

(D) Full employment is achieved at all levels of the economy.

(E) As technology advances, innovative businesses replace antiquated firms.

2. It can be inferred from the passage that the author believes that

(A) when consumers lose their confidence in the market, a recession follows

(B) cyclical ends to business expansion are normal

(C) luxury goods such as jewelry are unaffected by industrial expansion

(D) with sound economic policies, prosperity can become a fixed pattern

(E) the creation of new products is essential for prosperity

3. Which of the following statements would be most likely to begin the paragraph immediately following the passage?

(A) Union demands may also have an effect on business cycles.

(B) Some industries are, by their very nature, cyclical, having regular phases of expansion and recession.

(C) Inflation is a factor that must be taken into consideration in any discussion of the expansion phase.

(D) The farmer's role during the expansion phase is of vital importance.

(E) The other phase of the business cycle is called the recession phase.

The history of mammals dates back at least to Triassic time. Development was retarded, how-ever, until the sudden acceleration of evolutional
Line change that occurred in the oldest Paleocene. This
(5) led in Eocene time to increase in average size, larger mental capacity, and special adaptations for different modes of life. In the Oligocene Epoch, there was further improvement, with appearance of some new lines and extinction of others.
(10) Miocene and Pliocene time was marked by culmi-nation of several groups and continued approach toward modern characters. The peak of the career of mammals in variety and average large size was attained in the Miocene.
(15)   The adaptation of mammals to almost all pos-sible modes of life parallels that of the reptiles in Mesozoic time, and except for greater intelligence, the mammals do not seem to have done much bet-ter than corresponding reptilian forms. The bat is
(20) doubtless a better flying animal than the pterosaur, but the dolphin and whale are hardly more fishlike than the ichthyosaur. Many swift-running mam-mals of the plains, like the horse and the antelope, must excel any of the dinosaurs. The tyrannosaur
(25) was a more ponderous and powerful carnivore than any flesh-eating mammal, but the lion or tiger is probably a more efficient and dangerous beast of prey because of a superior brain. The significant point to observe is that different branches of the

(30) mammals gradually fitted themselves for all sorts of life, grazing on the plains and able to run swiftly (horse, deer, bison), living in rivers and swamps (hippopotamus, beaver), dwelling in trees (sloth, monkey), digging underground (mole, rodent),
(35) feeding on flesh in the forest (tiger) and on the plain (wolf), swimming in the sea (dolphin, whale, seal), and flying in the air (bat). Man is able by mechani-cal means to conquer the physical world and to adapt himself to almost any set of conditions.
(40)   This adaptation produces gradual changes of form and structure. It is biologically characteristic of the youthful, plastic stage of a group. Early in its career, an animal assemblage seems to possess capacity for change, which, as the unit becomes
(45) old and fixed, disappears. The generalized types of organisms retain longest the ability to make adjust-ments when required, and it is from them that new, fecund stocks take origin—certainly not from any specialized end products. So, in the mammals, we
(50) witness the birth, plastic spread in many directions, increasing specialization, and in some branches, the extinction, which we have learned from obser-vation of the geologic record of life is a characteris-tic of the evolution of life.

4. Which of the following would be the most appro-priate title for the passage?

(A) From Dinosaur to Man

(B) Adaptation and Extinction

(C) The Superiority of Mammals

(D) The Geologic Life Span

(E) Man, Conqueror of the Physical World

5. It can be inferred from the passage that the chrono-logical order of the geologic periods is

(A) Paleocene, Miocene, Triassic, Mesozoic

(B) Paleocene, Triassic, Mesozoic, Miocene

(C) Miocene, Paleocene, Triassic, Mesozoic

(D) Mesozoic, Oligocene, Paleocene, Miocene

(E) Mesozoic, Paleocene, Eocene, Miocene

6. It can be inferred from the passage that the pterosaur

(A) resembled the bat

(B) was a Mesozoic mammal

(C) was a flying reptile

(D) lived in the sea

(E) evolved during the Miocene period

7. According to the passage, the greatest number of forms of mammalian life is found in the

(A) Triassic period

(B) Eocene period

(C) Oligocene period

(D) Pliocene period

(E) Miocene period

8. Which of the following statements, if true, would weaken the statement made by the author in lines 15–19?

   (A) Tyrannosaur has been found to have a larger brain than was previously thought.
   (B) Mammals will become extinct within the next thousand years.
   (C) Forms of flying ichthyosaurs have recently been discovered.
   (D) The tiger has now been proved to be more powerful than the carnivorous reptiles.
   (E) Computers have been developed that can double human mental capacity.

9. It can be inferred from the passage that the evidence the author uses in discussing the life of past time periods

   (A) was developed by Charles Darwin
   (B) was uncovered by the author
   (C) has been negated by more recent evidence
   (D) was never definitely established
   (E) is based on fossil remains

10. With which of the following proverbial expressions about human existence would the author be most likely to agree?

   (A) It's a cruel world.
   (B) All the world's a stage.
   (C) The more things change, the more they remain the same.
   (D) Footprints in the sands of time.
   (E) A short life, but a merry one.

For me, scientific knowledge is divided into mathematical sciences, natural sciences or sciences dealing with the natural world (physical and
Line biological sciences), and sciences dealing with
(5) mankind (psychology, sociology, all the sciences of cultural achievements, every kind of historical knowledge). Apart from these sciences is philosophy, about which we will talk shortly. In the first place, all this is pure or theoretical knowledge,
(10) sought only for the purpose of understanding, in order to fulfill the need to understand that is intrinsic and consubstantial to man. What distinguishes man from animal is that he knows and needs to know. If man did not know that the
(15) world existed, and that the world was of a certain kind, that he was in the world and that he himself was of a certain kind, he wouldn't be man. The technical aspects of applications of knowledge are equally necessary for man and are of the greatest
(20) importance, because they also contribute to defining him as man and permit him to pursue a life increasingly more truly human.
   But even while enjoying the results of technical progress, he must defend the primacy and
(25) autonomy of pure knowledge. Knowledge sought directly for its practical applications will have immediate and foreseeable success, but not the

kind of important result whose revolutionary scope is in large part unforeseen, except by the
(30) imagination of the Utopians. Let me recall a well-known example. If the Greek mathematicians had not applied themselves to the investigation of conic sections, zealously and without the least suspicion that it might someday be useful, it
(35) would not have been possible centuries later to navigate far from shore. The first men to study the nature of electricity could not imagine that their experiments, carried on because of mere intellectual curiosity, would eventually lead to
(40) modern electrical technology, without which we can scarcely conceive of contemporary life. Pure knowledge is valuable for its own sake, because the human spirit cannot resign itself to ignorance. But, in addition, it is the foundation for practical
(45) results that would not have been reached if this knowledge had not been sought disinterestedly.

11. The author points out that the Greeks who studied conic sections

   (A) invented modern mathematical applications
   (B) were interested in navigation
   (C) were unaware of the value of their studies
   (D) worked with electricity
   (E) were forced to resign themselves to failure

12. The title below that best expresses the ideas of this passage is

   (A) Technical Progress
   (B) A Little Learning Is a Dangerous Thing
   (C) Man's Distinguishing Characteristics
   (D) Learning for Its Own Sake
   (E) The Difference Between Science and Philosophy

13. It can be inferred from the passage that to the author man's need to know is chiefly important in that it

   (A) allows the human race to progress technically
   (B) encompasses both the physical and social sciences
   (C) demonstrates human vulnerability
   (D) defines man's essential humanity
   (E) has increased as our knowledge of the world has grown

When you first saw a piece of African art, it impressed you as a unit; you did not see it as a collection of shapes or forms. This, of course, means
Line that the shapes and volumes within the sculpture
(5) itself were coordinated so successfully that the viewer was affected emotionally.
   It is entirely valid to ask how, from a purely artistic point of view, this unity was achieved. And we must also inquire whether there is a recurrent pat-
(10) tern or rules or a plastic language and vocabulary which is responsible for the powerful communication of emotion which the best African sculpture

achieves. If there is such a pattern or rules, are
these rules applied consciously or instinctively to
(15) obtain so many works of such high artistic quality?

It is obvious from the study of art history that an
intense and unified emotional experience, such as
the Christian credo of the Byzantine or 12th or 13th
century Europe, when expressed in art forms, gave
(20) great unity, coherence, and power to art. But such
an integrated feeling was only the inspirational
element for the artist, only the starting point of the
creative act. The expression of this emotion and its
realization in the work could be done only with dis-
(25) cipline and thorough knowledge of the craft. And
the African sculptor was a highly trained workman.
He started his apprenticeship with a master when a
child, and he learned the tribal styles and the use of
tools and the nature of woods so thoroughly that his
(30) carving became what Boas calls "motor action." He
carved automatically and instinctively.

The African carver followed his rules without
thinking of them; indeed, they never seem to have
been formulated in words. But such rules existed,
(35) for accident and coincidence cannot explain the
common plastic language of African sculpture.
There is too great a consistency from one work to
another. Yet, although the African, with amazing
insight into art, used these rules, I am certain that
(40) he was not conscious of them. This is the great
mystery of such a traditional art: talent, or the ability certain people have, without conscious effort, to
follow the rules which later the analyst can discover only from the work of art which has already
(45) been created.

14. The author is primarily concerned with

(A) discussing how African sculptors achieved
their effects
(B) listing the rules followed in African art
(C) relating African art to the art of 12th or 13th
century Europe
(D) integrating emotion and realization
(E) expressing the beauty of African art

15. According to the passage, one of the outstanding
features of African sculpture is

(A) its esoteric subject matter
(B) the emotional content of the work
(C) the education or training of the artists
(D) its "foreignness" when compared to Western
art
(E) its high degree of conscious control

16. The author uses the phrase "plastic language" in
lines 10 and 36 to refer to African art's

(A) mass reproduction
(B) unrealistic qualities
(C) modernistic orientation
(D) sculptural symbols
(E) repetitive nature

17. The information in the passage suggests that an
African carver might best be compared to a

(A) chef following a recipe
(B) fluent speaker of English who is just beginning
to study French
(C) batter who hits a home run in his or her first
baseball game
(D) concert pianist performing a well-rehearsed
concerto
(E) writer who is grammatically expert but stylistically uncreative

18. Which of the following does the passage imply
about art?

(A) Content is more important than form.
(B) There is no room for untrained artists.
(C) Form is more important than content.
(D) Western artists are too concerned with
technique.
(E) Great art must be consistent.

19. The author's presentation of the material includes
all of the following EXCEPT

(A) comparison
(B) cause and effect
(C) rhetorical questioning
(D) direct quotation
(E) concrete example

20. Which of the following titles best expresses the
content of the passage?

(A) The Apprenticeship of the African Sculptor
(B) The History of African Sculpture
(C) How African Art Achieves Unity
(D) Analyzing African Art
(E) The Unconscious Rules of African Art

Reading Comprehension Exercise B

<u>Directions:</u> Each of the following reading comprehen-
sion questions are based on the content of the following
passage. Read the passage and then determine the best
answer choice for each question. Base your choice on
what this passage <u>states directly</u> or <u>implies</u>, not on any
information you may have gained elsewhere.

Both plants and animals of many sorts show
remarkable changes in form, structure, growth
habits, and even mode of reproduction in becom-
Line ing adapted to different climatic environment,
(5) types of food supply, or mode of living. This
divergence in response to evolution is commonly
expressed by altering the form and function of
some part or parts of the organism, the original
identity of which is clearly discernible. For
(10) example, the creeping foot of the snail is seen in
related marine pteropods to be modified into a
flapping organ useful for swimming, and is

changed into prehensile arms that bear suctorial disks in the squids and other cephalopods. The
(15) limbs of various mammals are modified according to several different modes of life—for swift running (cursorial) as in the horse and antelope, for swinging in trees (arboreal) as in the monkeys, for digging (fossorial) as in the moles and gophers,
(20) for flying (volant) as in the bats, for swimming (aquatic) as in the seals, whales, and dolphins, and for other adaptations. The structures or organs that show main change in connection with this adaptive divergence are commonly identified
(25) readily as homologous, in spite of great alterations. Thus, the finger and wristbones of a bat and whale, for instance, have virtually nothing in common except that they are definitely equivalent elements of the mammalian limb.

1. Which of the following is the most appropriate title for the passage, based on its content?

   (A) Adaptive Divergence
   (B) Evolution
   (C) Unusual Structures
   (D) Changes in Organs
   (E) Our Changing Bodies

2. The author provides information that would answer which of the following questions?

   I. What factors cause change in organisms?
   II. What is the theory of evolution?
   III. How are horses' legs related to seals' flippers?

   (A) I only
   (B) II only
   (C) I and II only
   (D) I and III only
   (E) I, II, and III

3. Which of the following words could best be substituted for "homologous" (line 25) without substantially changing the author's meaning?

   (A) altered
   (B) mammalian
   (C) corresponding
   (D) divergent
   (E) tactile

4. The author's style can best be described as

   (A) humorous
   (B) objective
   (C) patronizing
   (D) esoteric
   (E) archaic

Plato—who may have understood better what forms the mind of man than do some of our contemporaries who want their children exposed only
Line to "real" people and everyday events—knew
(5) what intellectual experiences make for true humanity. He suggested that the future citizens of his ideal republic begin their literary education with the telling of myths, rather than with mere facts or so-called rational teachings. Even
(10) Aristotle, master of pure reason, said: "The friend of wisdom is also a friend of myth."

Modern thinkers who have studied myths and fairy tales from a philosophical or psychological viewpoint arrive at the same conclusion, regard-
(15) less of their original persuasion. Mircea Eliade, for one, describes these stories as "models for human behavior [that], by that very fact, give meaning and value to life." Drawing on anthropological parallels, he and others suggest that
(20) myths and fairy tales were derived from, or give symbolic expression to, initiation rites or *rites of passage*—such as metaphoric death of an old, inadequate self in order to be reborn on a higher plane of existence. He feels that this is why these
(25) tales meet a strongly felt need and are carriers of such deep meaning.

Other investigators with a depth-psychological orientation emphasize the similarities between the fantastic events in myths and fairy tales and those
(30) in adult dreams and daydreams—the fulfillment of wishes, the winning out over all competitors, the destruction of enemies—and conclude that one attraction of this literature is its expression of that which is normally prevented from coming to
(35) awareness.

There are, of course, very significant differences between fairy tales and dreams. For example, in dreams more often than not the wish fulfillment is disguised, while in fairy tales much
(40) of it is openly expressed. To a considerable degree, dreams are the result of inner pressures which have found no relief, of problems which beset a person to which he knows no solution and to which the dream finds none. The fairy tale
(45) does the opposite: it projects the relief of all pressures and not only offers ways to solve problems but promises that a "happy" solution will be found.

We cannot control what goes on in our dreams.
(50) Although our inner censorship influences what we may dream, such control occurs on an unconscious level. The fairy tale, on the other hand, is very much the result of common conscious and unconscious content having been shaped by the
(55) conscious mind, not of one particular person, but the consensus of many in regard to what they view as universal human problems, and what they accept as desirable solutions. If all these elements were not present in a fairy tale, it would not be
(60) retold by generation after generation. Only if a fairy tale met the conscious and unconscious requirements of many people was it repeatedly retold, and listened to with great interest. No dream of a person could arouse such persistent
(65) interest unless it was worked into a myth, as was the story of the pharaoh's dream as interpreted by Joseph in the Bible.

5. It can be inferred from the passage that the author's interest in fairy tales centers chiefly on their

   (A) literary qualities
   (B) historical background
   (C) factual accuracy
   (D) psychological relevance
   (E) ethical weakness

6. According to the passage, fairy tales differ from dreams in which of the following characteristics?

   > I. The communal nature of their creation
   > II. Their convention of a happy ending
   > III. Their enduring general appeal

   (A) I only
   (B) II only
   (C) I and II only
   (D) II and III only
   (E) I, II, and III

7. It can be inferred from the passage that Mircea Eliade is most likely

   (A) a writer of children's literature
   (B) a student of physical anthropology
   (C) a twentieth-century philosopher
   (D) an advocate of practical education
   (E) a contemporary of Plato

8. Which of the following best describes the author's attitude toward fairy tales?

   (A) Reluctant fascination
   (B) Wary skepticism
   (C) Scornful disapprobation
   (D) Indulgent tolerance
   (E) Open approval

9. The author cites Plato and Aristotle primarily in order to

   (A) define the nature of myth
   (B) contrast their opposing points of view
   (C) support the point that myths are valuable
   (D) prove that myths originated in ancient times
   (E) give an example of depth psychology

10. The author mentions all of the following as reasons for reading fairy tales EXCEPT

    (A) emotional catharsis
    (B) behavioral paradigm
    (C) uniqueness of experience
    (D) sublimation of aggression
    (E) symbolic satisfaction

Nothing more unlucky, I sometimes think, could have befallen Chaucer than that he should have been christened "the father of English
Line poetry." For "father" in such a context conveys to
(5) most of us, I fear, a faint suggestion of *vicarious* glory—the derivative celebrity of parents, otherwise obscure, who shine, moon-like, in the reflected luster of their sons. What else than progenitors were the fathers of Plato, or Caesar,
(10) or Shakespeare, or Napoleon? And so to call Chaucer the father of English poetry is often tantamount to dismissing him, not unkindly, as the estimable but archaic ancestor of a brilliant line. But Chaucer—if I may risk the paradox—is him-
(15) self the very thing he begat. He *is* English poetry incarnate, and only two, perhaps, of all his sons outshine his fame. It is with Chaucer himself, then, and not save incidentally with his ancestral eminence that we shall be concerned.
(20)   But five hundred and thirty-three years have passed since Chaucer died. And to overleap five centuries is to find ourselves in another world, a world at once familiar and strange. Its determining concepts are implicit in all that Chaucer, who
(25) was of it, thought and wrote. And, woven as they are into his web, they at once lend to it and gain from it fresh significance. To us they are obsolete; in the *Canterbury Tales*, and the *Troilus*, and the *House of Fame* they are current and alive.
(30) And it is in their habit as they lived, and not as mere curious lore, that I mean to deal with them.
   Let me begin with the very tongue which Chaucer spoke—a speech at once our own and not our own. "You know," he wrote—and for the
(35) moment I rudely modernize lines as liquid in their rhythm as smooth-sliding brandy—"you know that in a thousand years there is change in the forms of speech, and words which were then judged apt and choice now seem to us wondrous
(40) quaint and strange, and yet they spoke them so, and managed as well in love with them as men now do." And to us, after only half a thousand years, those very lines are an embodiment of what they state:

(45)   Ye knowe eek, that in forme of speche is chaunge
       With-inne a thousand yeer, and words tho
       That hadden prys, now wonder nyce and straunge
(50)   Us thinketh hem; and yet they spake hem so,
       And spedde as wel in love as men now do.

   But it is not only Chaucer's speech which has undergone transformation. The change in his world is greater still. And the situation which
(55) confronts us is this. In Chaucer's greatest work we have to do with *timeless creations* upon a *time-determined stage.* And it is one of the inescapable ironies of time that creations of the imagination which are at once of no time and for
(60) all time must nevertheless think and speak and act in terms and in ways which are as transient as they themselves are permanent. Their world—the stage on which they play their parts, and in terms of which they think—has become within a few
(65) lifetimes strange and obsolete, and must be deciphered before it can be read. For the immortal puts on mortality when great conceptions are

clothed in the only garment ever possible—in terms whose import and associations are fixed by
(70) the form and pressure of an inexorably passing time. And that is the situation which we have to face.

11. The author of the passage does all of the following in the discussion of Chaucer and his verse EXCEPT

(A) pose a rhetorical question
(B) cite specific examples
(C) offer a personal opinion
(D) propose a solution
(E) use figurative language

12. The author's attitude toward "mere curious lore" (line 31) can best be described as

(A) skeptical but resigned
(B) admiring and intrigued
(C) dismissive
(D) incredulous
(E) completely detached

13. The author uses the Middle English quotation (lines 45–51) to

(A) refute the contention that Chaucer wrote awkwardly
(B) demonstrate the idiosyncratic spelling common in Chaucer's time
(C) convey the power of reading poetry in its original form
(D) support his hypothesis about the aptness of Chaucer's choice of words
(E) illustrate the degree of linguistic change that has occurred

14. How would the author most likely respond to another critic's use of the term "Father of English Poetry" to describe Chaucer?

(A) The term "Father of English Poetry" is an accurate assessment of an exceptionally distinguished literary figure.
(B) The term implies Chaucer is important not as a great poet in his own right but as the somewhat outdated forerunner of the great poets of today.
(C) The epithet "Father of English Poetry" has been applied to so many poets that it has lost whatever meaning it originally possessed.
(D) "Father of English Poetry" is a sexist term that should be replaced by more inclusive language.
(E) It is appropriate to acknowledge the impact Chaucer had on posterity by revering him as the glorious ancestor of all English poets.

Of the 197 million square miles making up the surface of the globe, 71 percent is covered by the interconnecting bodies of marine water; the
Line Pacific Ocean alone covers half the Earth and
(5) averages nearly 14,000 feet in depth. The *continents*—Eurasia, Africa, North America, South America, Australia, and Antarctica—are the portions of the *continental masses* rising above sea level. The submerged borders of the continental
(10) masses are the *continental shelves*, beyond which lie the deep-sea basins.

The oceans attain their greatest depths not in their central parts, but in certain elongated furrows, or long narrow troughs, called *deeps*. These
(15) profound troughs have a peripheral arrangement, notably around the borders of the Pacific and Indian oceans. The position of the deeps near the continental masses suggests that the deeps, like the highest mountains, are of recent origin, since
(20) otherwise they would have been filled with waste from the lands. This suggestion is strengthened by the fact that the deeps are frequently the sites of world-shaking earthquakes. For example, the "tidal wave" that in April, 1946, caused wide-
(25) spread destruction along Pacific coasts resulted from a strong earthquake on the floor of the Aleutian Deep.

The topography of the ocean floors is none too well known, since in great areas the available
(30) soundings are hundreds or even thousands of miles apart. However, the floor of the Atlantic is becoming fairly well known as a result of special surveys since 1920. A broad, well-defined ridge—the Mid-Atlantic ridge—runs north and
(35) south between Africa and the two Americas, and numerous other major irregularities diversify the Atlantic floor. Closely spaced soundings show that many parts of the oceanic floors are as rugged as mountainous regions of the continents.
(40) Use of the recently perfected method of echo sounding is rapidly enlarging our knowledge of submarine topography. During World War II great strides were made in mapping submarine surfaces, particularly in many parts of the vast
(45) Pacific basin.

The continents stand on the average 2870 feet—slightly more than half a mile—above sea level. North America averages 2300 feet; Europe averages only 1150 feet; and Asia, the highest
(50) of the larger continental subdivisions, averages 3200 feet. The highest point on the globe, Mount Everest in the Himalayas, is 29,000 feet above the sea; and as the greatest known depth in the sea is over 35,000 feet, the maximum *relief* (that is,
(55) the difference in altitude between the lowest and highest points) exceeds 64,000 feet, or exceeds 12 miles. The continental masses and the deep-sea basins are relief features of the first order; the deeps, ridges, and volcanic cones that diversify
(60) the sea floor, as well as the plains, plateaus, and mountains of the continents, are relief features of

the second order. The lands are unendingly subject to a complex of activities summarized in the
term *erosion*, which first sculptures them in great
(65) detail and then tends to reduce them ultimately to
sea level. The modeling of the landscape by
weather, running water, and other agents is apparent to the keenly observant eye and causes thinking people to speculate on what must be the final
(70) result of the ceaseless wearing down of the lands.
Long before there was a science of geology,
Shakespeare wrote "the revolution of the times
makes mountains level."

15. Which of the following would be the most appropriate title for the passage?

(A) Features of the Earth's Surface
(B) Marine Topography
(C) The Causes of Earthquakes
(D) Primary Geologic Considerations
(E) How to Prevent Erosion

16. It can be inferred from the passage that the largest
ocean is the

(A) Atlantic
(B) Pacific
(C) Indian
(D) Antarctic
(E) Arctic

17. The "revolution of the times" as used in the final
sentence means

(A) the passage of years
(B) the current rebellion
(C) the science of geology
(D) the action of the ocean floor
(E) the overthrow of natural forces

18. According to the passage, the peripheral furrows or
deeps are found

(A) only in the Pacific and Indian oceans
(B) near earthquakes
(C) near the shore
(D) in the center of the ocean
(E) to be 14,000 feet in depth in the Pacific

19. The passage contains information that would
answer which of the following questions?

    I. What is the highest point on North America?
    II. Which continental subdivision is, on the
        average, 1150 feet above sea level?
    III. How deep is the deepest part of the ocean?

(A) I only
(B) II only
(C) III only
(D) I and II only
(E) II and III only

20. From this passage, it can be inferred that
earthquakes

(A) occur only in the peripheral furrows
(B) occur more frequently in newly formed land or
sea formations
(C) are a prime cause of soil erosion
(D) will ultimately "make mountains level"
(E) are caused by the weight of the water

Reading Comprehension Exercise C

<u>Directions:</u> Each of the following reading comprehen-
sion questions are based on the content of the following
passage. Read the passage and then determine the best
answer choice for each question. Base your choice on
what this passage <u>states directly</u> or <u>implies</u>, not on any
information you may have gained elsewhere.

      An essay which appeals chiefly to the intellect is
Francis Bacon's "Of Studies." His careful tripartite
division of studies expressed succinctly in apho-
Line ristic prose demands the complete attention of the
(5) mind of the reader. He considers studies as they
should be: for pleasure, for self-improvement, for
business. He considers the evils of excess study:
laziness, affectation, and preciosity. Bacon divides
books into three categories: those to be read in
(10) part, those to be read cursorily, and those to be
read with care. Studies should include reading,
which gives depth; speaking, which adds readiness
of thought; and writing, which trains in precise-
ness. Somewhat mistakenly, the author ascribes
(15) certain virtues to individual fields of study: wisdom to history, wit to poetry, subtlety to mathematics, and depth to natural philosophy. Bacon's
four-hundred-word essay, studded with Latin
phrases and highly compressed in thought, has
(20) intellectual appeal indeed.

1. Which of the following is the most appropriate title
for the passage, based on its content?

(A) Francis Bacon and the Appeal of the Essay
(B) "Of Studies": A Tripartite Division
(C) An Intellectual Exercise: Francis Bacon's "Of
Studies"
(D) The Categorization of Books According to
Bacon
(E) A Method for Reading Books

2. Which of the following words could best be substituted for "aphoristic" (lines 3–4) without substantially changing the author's meaning?

(A) abstruse
(B) pithy
(C) tripartite
(D) proverbial
(E) realistic

3. The passage suggests that the author would be
most likely to agree with which of the following
statements?

(A) "Of Studies" belongs in the category of works
that demand to be read with care.

(B) Scholars' personalities are shaped by the academic discipline in which they are engaged.
(C) It is an affectation to use foreign words in one's writing.
(D) An author can be more persuasive in a long work than in a shorter one.
(E) Studies should be undertaken without thought of personal gain.

Rocks which have solidified directly from molten materials are called igneous rocks. Igneous rocks are commonly referred to as
Line primary rocks because they are the original
(5) source of material found in sedimentaries and metamorphics. Igneous rocks compose the greater part of the earth's crust, but they are generally covered at the surface by a relatively thin layer of sedimentary or metamorphic rocks. Igneous rocks
(10) are distinguished by the following characteristics: (1) they contain no fossils; (2) they have no regular arrangement of layers; and (3) they are nearly always made up of crystals.

Sedimentary rocks are composed largely of
(15) minute fragments derived from the disintegration of existing rocks and in some instances from the remains of animals. As sediments are transported, individual fragments are assorted according to size. Distinct layers of such sediments as gravels,
(20) sand, and clay build up, as they are deposited by water and occasionally wind. These sediments vary in size with the material and the power of the eroding agent. Sedimentary materials are laid down in layers called strata.

(25)   When sediments harden into sedimentary rocks, the names applied to them change to indicate the change in physical state. Thus, small stones and gravel cemented together are known as conglomerates; cemented sand becomes sand-
(30) stone; and hardened clay becomes shale. In addition to these, other sedimentary rocks such as limestone frequently result from the deposition of dissolved material. The ingredient parts are normally precipitated by organic substances, such as
(35) shells of clams or hard skeletons of other marine life.

Both igneous and sedimentary rocks may be changed by pressure, heat, solution, or cementing action. When individual grains from existing
(40) rocks tend to deform and interlock, they are called metamorphic rocks. For example, granite, an igneous rock, may be metamorphosed into a gneiss or a schist. Limestone, a sedimentary rock, when subjected to heat and pressure may become
(45) marble, a metamorphic rock. Shale under pressure becomes slate.

4. The primary purpose of the passage is to
(A) differentiate between and characterize igneous and sedimentary rocks
(B) explain the factors that may cause rocks to change in form
(C) show how the scientific names of rocks reflect the rocks' composition
(D) define and describe several diverse kinds of rocks
(E) explain why rocks are basic parts of the earth's structure

5. All of the following are sedimentary rocks EXCEPT
(A) shale
(B) gravel
(C) sand
(D) limestone
(E) schist

6. The passage would be most likely to appear in a
(A) technical article for geologists
(B) teaching manual accompanying an earth science text
(C) pamphlet promoting conservation of natural resources
(D) newspaper feature explaining how oil is found
(E) nonfiction book explaining where to find the results of sedimentation

7. The relationship between igneous and sedimentary rocks may best be compared to the relationship between
(A) leaves and compost
(B) water and land
(C) DNA and heredity
(D) nucleus and cell wall
(E) sand and clay

8. The passage contains information that would answer which of the following questions?
    I. Which elements form igneous rocks?
    II. What produces sufficient pressure to alter a rock?
    III. Why is marble called a metamorphic rock?
(A) I only
(B) III only
(C) I and II only
(D) II and III only
(E) I, II, and III

9. Which of the following methods is NOT used by the author?
(A) inclusion of concrete examples
(B) classification and discussion
(C) comparison and contrast
(D) observation and hypothesis
(E) cause and effect

10. The author's tone in the passage can best be described as
(A) meditative
(B) objective
(C) ironic
(D) concerned
(E) bombastic

Although vocal cords are lacking in cetaceans, phonation is undoubtedly centered in the larynx.

Line　The toothed whales or odontocetes (sperm whale and porpoises) are much more vociferous than the
(5)　whalebone whales, or mysticetes. In this country observers have recorded only occasional sounds from two species of mysticetes (the humpback and right whale). A Russian cetologist reports hearing sounds from at least five species of whalebone
(10)　whales but gives no details of the circumstances or descriptions of the sounds themselves. Although comparison of the sound-producing apparatus in the two whale groups cannot yet be made, it is interesting to note that the auditory centers of the
(15)　brain are much more highly developed in the odontocetes than in the mysticetes, in fact, to a degree unsurpassed by any other mammalian group.

11.　The passage contains information that would answer which of the following questions?

I.　What are odontocetes and mysticetes?
II.　In which part of the body do whales produce sounds?
III.　In which animals is the auditory center of the brain most developed?

(A) I only
(B) II only
(C) I and II only
(D) II and III only
(E) I, II, and III

12.　The author's attitude toward the observations reported by the Russian cetologist mentioned in lines 8–11 is best described as one of

(A) admiration
(B) indignation
(C) surprise
(D) skepticism
(E) pessimism

13.　It can be inferred from the passage that

(A) animals with more highly developed auditory apparatuses tend to produce more sounds
(B) animals without vocal cords tend to produce as much sound as those with vocal cords
(C) highly intelligent animals tend to produce more sound than less intelligent species
(D) the absence of vocal cords has hindered the adaptation of cetaceans
(E) sound is an important means of communication among whales

---

　　*Like her white friends Eleanor Roosevelt and Aubrey Williams, Mary Bethune believed in the fundamental commitment of the New Deal to
Line　assist the black American's struggle and in the
(5)　need for blacks to assume responsibilities to help win that struggle. Unlike those of her white

liberal associates, however, Bethune's ideas had evolved out of a long experience as a "race leader." Founder of a small black college in
(10)　Florida, she had become widely known by 1935 as an organizer of black women's groups and as a civil and political rights activist. Deeply religious, certain of her own capabilities, she held a relatively uncluttered view of what she felt were the
(15)　New Deal's and her own people's obligations to the cause of racial justice. Unafraid to speak her mind to powerful whites, including the President, or to differing black factions, she combined faith in the ultimate willingness of whites to discard
(20)　their prejudice and bigotry with a strong sense of racial pride and commitment to Negro self-help.

　　More than her liberal white friends, Bethune argued for a strong and direct black voice in initiating and shaping government policy. She pur-
(25)　sued this in her conversations with President Roosevelt, in numerous memoranda to Aubrey Williams, and in her administrative work as head of the National Youth Administration's Office of Negro Affairs. With the assistance of Williams,
(30)　she was successful in having blacks selected to NYA posts at the national, state, and local levels. But she also wanted a black presence throughout the federal government. At the beginning of the war she joined other black leaders in demanding
(35)　appointments to the Selective Service Board and to the Department of the Army; and she was instrumental in 1941 in securing Earl Dickerson's membership on the Fair Employment Practices Committee. By 1944, she was still making
(40)　appeals for black representation in "all public programs, federal, state, and local," and "in policy-making posts as well as rank and file jobs."

　　Though recognizing the weakness in the Roosevelt administration's response to Negro
(45)　needs, Mary Bethune remained in essence a black partisan champion of the New Deal during the 1930s and 1940s. Her strong advocacy of administration policies and programs was predicated on a number of factors: her assessment of the low
(50)　status of black Americans during the Depression; her faith in the willingness of some liberal whites to work for the inclusion of blacks in the government's reform and recovery measures; her conviction that only massive federal aid could elevate
(55)　the Negro economically; and her belief that the thirties and forties were producing a more self-aware and self-assured black population. Like a number of her white friends in government, Bethune assumed that the preservation of democ-
(60)　racy and black people's "full integration into the benefits and the responsibilities" of American life were inextricably tied together. She was convinced that, with the help of a friendly government, a militant, aggressive "New Negro" would
(65)　emerge out of the devastation of depression and war, a "New Negro" who would "save America from itself," who would lead America toward the full realization of its democratic ideas.

14. The author's main purpose in this passage is to

    (A) criticize Mary Bethune for adhering too closely to New Deal policies
    (B) argue that Mary Bethune was too optimistic in her assessment of race relations
    (C) demonstrate Mary Bethune's influence on black progress during the Roosevelt years
    (D) point out the weaknesses of the white liberal approach to black needs
    (E) summarize the attainments of blacks under the auspices of Roosevelt's New Deal

15. It can be inferred from the passage that Aubrey Williams was which of the following?

    I. A man with influence in the National Youth Administration
    II. A white liberal
    III. A man of strong religious convictions

    (A) I only
    (B) II only
    (C) I and II only
    (D) II and III only
    (E) I, II, and III

16. The author mentions Earl Dickerson (line 37) primarily in order to

    (A) cite an instance of Bethune's political impact
    (B) contrast his career with that of Bethune
    (C) introduce the subject of a subsequent paragraph
    (D) provide an example of Bethune's "New Negro"
    (E) show that Dickerson was a leader of his fellow blacks

17. It can be inferred from the passage that Bethune believed the "New Negro" would "save America from itself" (lines 66–67) by

    (A) joining the army and helping America overthrow its Fascist enemies
    (B) helping America accomplish its egalitarian ideals
    (C) voting for administration antipoverty programs
    (D) electing other blacks to government office
    (E) expressing a belief in racial pride

18. The tone of the author's discussion of Bethune is best described as

    (A) deprecatory
    (B) sentimental
    (C) ironic
    (D) objective
    (E) recriminatory

19. The author uses all the following techniques in the passage EXCEPT

    (A) comparison and contrast
    (B) development of an extended analogy
    (C) direct quotation
    (D) general statement and concrete examples
    (E) reiteration of central ideas

20. Which of the following statements about the New Deal does the passage best support?

    (A) It was strongly committed to justice for all races.
    (B) It encouraged black participation in making policy decisions.
    (C) It was actively involved in military strategy.
    (D) It was primarily the province of Eleanor Roosevelt.
    (E) It shaped programs for economic aid and growth.

Reading Comprehension Exercise D

<u>Directions:</u> Each of the following reading comprehension questions are based on the content of the following passage. Read the passage and then determine the best answer choice for each question. Base your choice on what this passage <u>states directly</u> or <u>implies</u>, not on any information you may have gained elsewhere.

"The emancipation of women," James Joyce told one of his friends, "has caused the greatest revolution in our time in the most important
Line relationship there is—that between men and
(5) women." Other modernists agreed: Virginia Woolf, claiming that in about 1910 "human character changed," and, illustrating the new balance between the sexes, urged, "Read the 'Agamemnon,' and see whether...your sympathies
(10) are not almost entirely with Clytemnestra." D.H. Lawrence wrote, "perhaps the deepest fight for 2000 years and more, has been the fight for women's independence."

But if modernist writers considered women's
(15) revolt against men's domination one of their "greatest" and "deepest" themes, only recently—in perhaps the past 15 years—has literary criticism begun to catch up with it. Not that the images of sexual antagonism that abound in modern litera-
(20) ture have gone unremarked; far from it. But what we are able to see in literary works depends on the perspectives we bring to them, and now that women—enough to make a difference—are reforming canons and interpreting literature, the
(25) landscapes of literary history and the features of individual books have begun to change.

1. According to the passage, women are changing literary criticism by

    (A) noting instances of hostility between men and women
    (B) seeing literature from fresh points of view
    (C) studying the works of early twentieth-century writers
    (D) reviewing books written by feminists
    (E) resisting masculine influence

2. The author quotes James Joyce, Virginia Woolf, and D.H. Lawrence primarily in order to show that

   (A) these were feminist writers
   (B) although well-meaning, they were ineffectual
   (C) before the twentieth century, there was little interest in women's literature
   (D) modern literature is dependent on the women's movement
   (E) the interest in feminist issues is not new

3. The author's attitude toward women's reformation of literary canons can best be described as one of

   (A) ambivalence
   (B) antagonism
   (C) indifference
   (D) endorsement
   (E) skepticism

4. Which of the following titles best describes the content of the passage?

   (A) Modernist Writers and the Search for Equality
   (B) The Meaning of Literary Works
   (C) Toward a New Criticism
   (D) Women in Literature, from 1910 On
   (E) Transforming Literature

Ocean water plays an indispensable role in supporting life. The great ocean basins hold about 300 million cubic miles of water. From this vast
Line amount, about 80,000 cubic miles of water are
(5) sucked into the atmosphere each year by evaporation and returned by precipitation and drainage to the ocean. More than 24,000 cubic miles of rain descend annually upon the continents. This vast amount is required to replenish the lakes and
(10) streams, springs and water tables on which all flora and fauna are dependent. Thus, the hydrosphere permits organic existence.

The hydrosphere has strange characteristics because water has properties unlike those of any
(15) other liquid. One anomaly is that water upon freezing expands by about 9 percent, whereas most liquids contract on cooling. For this reason, ice floats on water bodies instead of sinking to the bottom. If the ice sank, the hydrosphere would
(20) soon be frozen solidly, except for a thin layer of surface melt water during the summer season. Thus, all aquatic life would be destroyed and the interchange of warm and cold currents, which moderates climate, would be notably absent.
(25) Another outstanding characteristic of water is that water has a heat capacity which is the highest of all liquids and solids except ammonia. This characteristic enables the oceans to absorb and store vast quantities of heat, thereby often pre-
(30) venting climatic extremes. In addition, water dissolves more substances than any other liquid. It is this characteristic which helps make oceans a great storehouse for minerals which have been washed down from the continents. In several

(35) areas of the world these minerals are being commercially exploited. Solar evaporation of salt is widely practiced, potash is extracted from the Dead Sea, and magnesium is produced from sea water along the American Gulf Coast.

5. The author's main purpose in this passage is to

   (A) describe the properties and uses of water
   (B) illustrate the importance of conserving water
   (C) explain how water is used in commerce and industry
   (D) reveal the extent of the earth's ocean masses
   (E) compare water with other liquids

6. According to the passage, fish can survive in the oceans because

   (A) they do not need oxygen
   (B) ice floats
   (C) evaporation and condensation create a water cycle
   (D) there are currents in the oceans
   (E) water absorbs heat

7. Which of the following characteristics of water does the author mention in the passage?

   I. Water expands when it is frozen.
   II. Water is a good solvent.
   III. Water can absorb heat.

   (A) I only
   (B) II only
   (C) I and II only
   (D) II and III only
   (E) I, II, and III

8. According to the passage, the hydrosphere is NOT

   (A) responsible for all forms of life
   (B) able to modify weather
   (C) a source of natural resources
   (D) in danger of freezing over
   (E) the part of the earth covered by water

9. The author's tone in the passage can best be described as

   (A) dogmatic
   (B) dispassionate
   (C) speculative
   (D) biased
   (E) hortatory

10. The author organizes the passage by

    (A) comparison and contrast
    (B) juxtaposition of true and untrue ideas
    (C) general statements followed by examples
    (D) hypothesis and proof
    (E) definition of key terms

11. Which of the following statements would be most likely to begin the paragraph immediately following the passage?

(A) Water has the ability to erode the land.
(B) Magnesium is widely used in metallurgical processes.
(C) No let us consider the great land masses.
(D) Another remarkable property of ice is its strength.
(E) Droughts and flooding are two types of disasters associated with water.

The opposite of adaptive divergence is an interesting and fairly common expression of evolution. Whereas related groups of organisms take
Line on widely different characters in becoming
(5) adapted to unlike environments in the case of adaptive divergence, we find that unrelated groups of organisms exhibit adaptive convergence when they adopt similar modes of life or become suited for special sorts of environments. For
(10) example, invertebrate marine animals living firmly attached to the sea bottom or to some foreign object tend to develop a subcylindrical or conical form. This is illustrated by coral individuals, by many sponges, and even by the diminutive tubes
(15) of bryozoans. Adaptive convergence in taking this coral-like form is shown by some brachiopods and pelecypods that grew in fixed position. More readily appreciated is the streamlined fitness of most fishes for moving swiftly through water;
(20) they have no neck, the contour of the body is smoothly curved so as to give minimum resistance, and the chief propelling organ is a powerful tail fin. The fact that some fossil reptiles (ichthyosaurs) and modern mammals (whales,
(25) dolphins) are wholly fishlike in form is an expression of adaptive convergence, for these air-breathing reptiles and mammals, which are highly efficient swimmers, are not closely related to fishes. Unrelated or distantly related organisms
(30) that develop similarity of form are sometimes designated as homeomorphs (having the same form).

12. The author mentions ichthyosaurs and dolphins (lines 24 and 25) as examples of
(A) modern mammalian life forms that are aquatic
(B) species of slightly greater mobility than brachiopods
(C) air-breathing reptiles closely related to fish
(D) organisms that have evolved into fishlike forms
(E) invertebrate and vertebrate marine animals

13. According to the passage, adaptive convergence and adaptive divergence are
(A) manifestations of evolutionary patterns
(B) hypotheses unsupported by biological phenomena
(C) ways in which plants and animals adjust to a common environment
(D) demonstrated by brachiopods and pelecypods
(E) compensatory adjustments made in response to unlike environments

14. It can be inferred that in the paragraph immediately preceding this passage the author discussed
(A) marine intelligence
(B) adaptive divergence
(C) air-breathing reptiles
(D) environmental impacts
(E) organisms with similar forms

Nearly two thousand years have passed since a census decreed by Caesar Augustus became part of the greatest story every told. Many things have
Line changed in the intervening years. The hotel indus-
(5) try worries more about overbuilding than overcrowding, and if they had to meet an unexpected influx, few inns would have a manger to accommodate the weary guests. Now it is the census taker that does the traveling in the fond hope that
(10) a highly mobile population will stay put long enough to get a good sampling. Methods of gathering, recording, and evaluating information have presumably been improved a great deal. And where then it was the modest purpose of Rome to
(15) obtain a simple head count as an adequate basis for levying taxes, now batteries of complicated statistical series furnished by governmental agencies and private organizations are eagerly scanned and interpreted by sages and seers to get a clue to
(20) future events. The Bible does not tell us how the Roman census takers made out, and as regards our more immediate concern, the reliability of present-day economic forecasting, there are considerable differences of opinion. They were aired
(25) at the celebration of the 125th anniversary of the American Statistical Association. There was the thought that business forecasting might well be on its way from an art to a science, and some speakers talked about newfangled computers and
(30) high-falutin mathematical systems in terms of excitement and endearment which we, at least in our younger years when these things matter, would have associated more readily with the description of a fair maiden. But others pointed to
(35) the deplorable record of highly esteemed forecasts and forecasters with a batting average below that of the Mets, and the president-elect of the Association cautioned that "high powered statistical methods are usually in order where the facts
(40) are crude and inadequate, the exact contrary of what crude and inadequate statisticians assume." We left this birthday party somewhere between hope and despair and with the conviction, not really newly acquired, that proper statistical
(45) methods applied to ascertainable facts have their merits in economic forecasting as long as neither forecaster nor public is deluded into mistaking the delineation of probabilities and trends for a prediction of certainties of mathematical exactitude.

15. The passage would be most likely to appear in

    (A) a journal of biblical studies
    (B) an introductory college textbook on statistics
    (C) the annual report of the American Statistical Association
    (D) a newspaper review of a recent professional festivity
    (E) the current bulletin of the census bureau

16. According to the passage, taxation in Roman times was based on

    (A) mobility
    (B) wealth
    (C) population
    (D) census takers
    (E) economic predictions

17. The author refers to the Romans primarily in order to

    (A) prove the superiority of modern sampling methods to ancient ones
    (B) provide a historical framework for the passage
    (C) relate an unfamiliar concept to a familiar one
    (D) show that statistical forecasts have not significantly deteriorated
    (E) cite an authority to support the thesis of the passage

18. The author refers to the Mets primarily in order to

    (A) show that sports do not depend on statistics
    (B) provide an example of an unreliable statistic
    (C) contrast verifiable and unverifiable methods of record keeping
    (D) indicate the changes in attitudes from Roman days to the present
    (E) illustrate the failure of statistical predictions

19. On the basis of the passage, it can be inferred that the author would agree with which of the following statements?

    (A) Computers have significantly improved the application of statistics in business.
    (B) Statistics is not, at the present time, a science.
    (C) It is useless to try to predict the economy.
    (D) Most mathematical systems are inexact.
    (E) Statisticians should devote themselves to the study of probability.

20. The author's tone can best be described as

    (A) jocular
    (B) scornful
    (C) pessimistic
    (D) objective
    (E) humanistic

Reading Comprehension Exercise E

Directions: Each of the following reading comprehension questions are based on the content of the following

passage. Read the passage and then determine the best answer choice for each question. Base your choice on what this passage states directly or implies, not on any information you may have gained elsewhere.

Observe the dilemma of the fungus: it is a plant, but it possesses no chlorophyll. While all other plants put the sun's energy to work for them
Line combining the nutrients of ground and air into the
(5) body structure, the chlorophylless fungus must look elsewhere for an energy supply. It finds it in those other plants which, having received their energy free from the sun, relinquish it at some point in their cycle either to animals (like us
(10) humans) or to fungi.
    In this search for energy the fungus has become the earth's major source of rot and decay. Wherever you see mold forming on a piece of bread, or a pile of leaves turning to compost, or a
(15) blown-down tree becoming pulp on the ground, you are watching a fungus eating. Without fungus action the earth would be piled high with the dead plant life of past centuries. In fact, certain plants which contain resins that are toxic to fungi will
(20) last indefinitely; specimens of the redwood, for instance, can still be found resting on the forest floor centuries after having been blown down.

1. Which of the following words best describes the fungus as depicted in the passage?

    (A) Unevolved
    (B) Sporadic
    (C) Enigmatic
    (D) Parasitic
    (E) Toxic

2. The passage states all the following about fungi EXCEPT:

    (A) They are responsible for the decomposition of much plant life.
    (B) They cannot live completely apart from other plants.
    (C) They are vastly different from other plants.
    (D) They are poisonous to resin-producing plants.
    (E) They cannot produce their own store of energy.

3. The author's statement that "you are watching a fungus eating" (line 16) is best described as

    (A) figurative
    (B) ironical
    (C) parenthetical
    (D) erroneous
    (E) contradictory

4. The author is primarily concerned with

    (A) warning people of the dangers of fungi
    (B) writing a humorous essay on fungi
    (C) relating how most plants use solar energy
    (D) describing the actions of fungi
    (E) explaining the long life of some redwoods

The establishment of the Third Reich influenced events in American history by starting a chain of events which culminated in war between
Line Germany and the United States. The complete
(5) destruction of democracy, the persecution of Jews, the war on religion, the cruelty and barbarism of the Nazis, and especially the plans of Germany and her allies, Italy and Japan, for world conquest caused great indignation in this country
(10) and brought on fear of another world war. While speaking out against Hitler's atrocities, the American people generally favored isolationist policies and neutrality. The Neutrality Acts of 1935 and 1936 prohibited trade with any belliger-
(15) ents or loans to them. In 1937 the President was empowered to declare an arms embargo in wars between nations at his discretion.

American opinion began to change somewhat after President Roosevelt's "quarantine the
(20) aggressor" speech at Chicago (1937), in which he severely criticized Hitler's policies. Germany's seizure of Austria and the Munich Pact for the partition of Czechoslovakia (1938) also aroused the American people. The conquest of
(25) Czechoslovakia in March 1939 was another rude awakening to the menace of the Third Reich. In August 1939 came the shock of the Nazi-Soviet Pact and in September the attack on Poland and the outbreak of European war. The United States
(30) attempted to maintain neutrality in spite of sympathy for the democracies arrayed against the Third Reich. The Neutrality Act of 1939 repealed the arms embargo and permitted "cash and carry" exports of arms to belligerent nations. A strong
(35) national defense program was begun. A draft act was passed (1940) to strengthen the military services. A Lend-Lease Act (1941) authorized the President to sell, exchange, or lend materials to any country deemed necessary by him for the
(40) defense of the United States. Help was given to Britain by exchanging certain overage destroyers for the right to establish American bases in British territory in the Western Hemisphere. In August 1941 President Roosevelt and Prime
(45) Minister Churchill met and issued the Atlantic Charter, which proclaimed the kind of a world that should be established after the war. In December 1941 Japan launched an unprovoked attack on the United States at Pearl Harbor.
(50) Immediately thereafter, Germany declared war on the United States.

5. The author is primarily concerned with
   (A) evaluating various legislative efforts to strengthen national defense
   (B) summarizing the events that led up to America's involvement in the war
   (C) criticizing the atrocities perpetrated by the Third Reich
   (D) explaining a basic distinction between American and German policy
   (E) describing the social and psychological effects of war

6. During the years 1933–36, American foreign policy may best be described as being one of
   (A) overt belligerence
   (B) deliberate uninvolvement
   (C) moral indignation
   (D) veiled contempt
   (E) reluctant admiration

7. According to the passage, the United States, while maintaining neutrality, showed its sympathy for the democracies by which of the following actions?
   I. It came to the defense of Poland.
   II. It conscripted recruits for the armed forces.
   III. It supplied weapons to friendly countries.
   (A) I only
   (B) III only
   (C) I and II only
   (D) II and III only
   (E) I, II, and III

8. According to the passage, all of the following events occurred in 1939 EXCEPT
   (A) the invasion of Poland
   (B) the invasion of Czechoslovakia
   (C) the annexation of Austria
   (D) passage of the Neutrality Act
   (E) the beginning of the war in Europe

9. With which of the following statements would the author of the passage be most likely to agree?
   (A) American neutrality during the 1930s was a natural consequence of the course of world events.
   (B) Every nation should be free to determine its own internal policy without interference.
   (C) The United States, through its aggressive actions, invited an attack on its territory.
   (D) Americans were slow to realize the full danger posed by Nazi Germany.
   (E) President Roosevelt showed undue sympathy for Britain.

10. Which of the following best describes the organization of the passage?
    (A) The author presents a thesis and then lists events that support that thesis in chronological order.
    (B) The author presents a thesis and then cites examples that support the thesis as well as evidence that tends to negate it.
    (C) The author summarizes a historical study and then discusses an aspect of the study in detail.
    (D) The author describes historical events and then gives a personal interpretation of them.
    (E) The author cites noted authorities as a means of supporting his or her own opinion.

Not a few of Jane Austen's personal acquaintances might have echoed Sir Samuel Egerton Brydges, who noticed that "she was fair and
Line handsome, slight and elegant, but with cheeks a
(5) little too full," while "never suspect[ing] she was an authoress." For this novelist whose personal obscurity was more complete than that of any other famous writer was always quick to insist either on complete anonymity or on the propriety
(10) of her limited craft, her delight in delineating just "3 or 4 Families in a Country Village." With her self-deprecatory remarks about her inability to join "strong manly, spirited sketches, full of Variety and Glow" with her "little bit (two Inches
(15) wide) of Ivory," Jane Austen perpetuated the belief among her friends that her art was just an accomplishment "by a lady," if anything "rather too light and bright and sparkling." In this respect she resembled one of her favorite contemporaries,
(20) Mary Brunton, who would rather have "glid[ed] through the world unknown" than been "suspected of literary airs—to be shunned, as literary women are, by the more pretending of their own sex, and abhorred, as literary women are, by the
(25) more pretending of the other!—my dear, I would sooner exhibit as a ropedancer."

Yet, decorous though they might first seem, Austen's self-effacing anonymity and her modest description of her miniaturist art also imply a
(30) criticism, even a rejection, of the world at large. For, as Gaston Bachelard explains, the miniature "allows us to be world conscious at slight risk." While the creators of satirically conceived diminutive landscapes seem to see everything as
(35) small because they are themselves so grand, Austen's analogy for her art—her "little bit (two Inches wide) of Ivory"—suggests a fragility that reminds us of the risk and instability outside the fictional space. Besides seeing her art metaphori-
(40) cally, as her critics would too, in relation to female arts severely devalued until quite recently (for painting on ivory was traditionally a "lady-like" occupation), Austen attempted through self-imposed novelistic limitations to define a secure
(45) place, even as she seemed to admit the impossibility of actually inhabiting such a small space with any degree of comfort. And always, for Austen, it is women—because they are too vulnerable in the world at large—who must
(50) acquiesce in their own confinement, no matter how stifling it may be.

11. The passage focuses primarily on

(A) Jane Austen's place in English literature
(B) the literary denigration of female novelists
(C) the implications of Austen's attitude to her work
(D) critical evaluations of the novels of Jane Austen
(E) social rejection of professional women in the 18th and 19th centuries

12. According to the passage, Austen concentrated on a limited range of subjects because

(A) she had a limited degree of experience of fiction
(B) her imagination was incapable of creating other worlds
(C) women in her time were prohibited from writing about significant topics
(D) she wanted to create a safe niche for the exercise of her talents
(E) she did not wish to be acknowledged as an author

13. Which of the following best expresses the relationship of the first sentence to the rest of the passage?

(A) Specific instance followed by generalizations
(B) Assertion followed by analysis
(C) Objective statement followed by personal opinion
(D) Quotation from an authority followed by conflicting views
(E) Challenge followed by debate

The atmosphere is a mixture of several gases. There are about ten chemical elements which remain permanently in gaseous form in the atmo-
Line sphere under all natural conditions. Of these per-
(5) manent gases, oxygen makes up about 21 percent and nitrogen about 78 percent. Several other gases, such as argon, carbon dioxide, hydrogen, neon, krypton, and xenon, comprise the remaining 1 percent of the volume of dry air. The amount
(10) of water vapor, and its variations in amount and distribution, are of extraordinary importance in weather changes. Atmospheric gases hold in suspension great quantities of dust, pollen, smoke, and other impurities which are always present in
(15) considerable, but variable amounts.

The atmosphere has no definite upper limits but gradually thins until it becomes imperceptible. Until recently it was assumed that the air above the first few miles gradually grew thinner and
(20) colder at a constant rate. It was also assumed that upper air had little influence on weather changes. Recent studies of the upper atmosphere, currently being conducted by earth satellites and missile probings, have shown these assumptions to be
(25) incorrect. The atmosphere has three well-defined strata.

The layer of the air next to the earth, which extends upward for about 10 miles, is known as the *troposphere*. On the whole, it makes up about
(30) 75 percent of all the weight of the atmosphere. It is the warmest part of the atmosphere because most of the solar radiation is absorbed by the earth's surface, which warms the air immediately surrounding it. A steady decrease of temperature
(35) with increasing elevation is a most striking characteristic. The upper layers are colder because of their greater distance from the earth's surface

and rapid radiation of heat into space. The temperatures within the troposphere decrease about
(40) 3.5 degrees per 1000-foot increase in altitude.
Within the troposphere, winds and air currents
distribute heat and moisture. Strong winds, called
jet streams, are located at the upper levels of
the troposphere. These jet streams are both
(45) complex and widespread in occurrence. They
normally show a waveshaped pattern and move
from west to east at velocities of 150 mph, but
velocities as high as 400 mph have been noted.
The influences of changing locations and
(50) strengths of jet streams upon weather conditions
and patterns are no doubt considerable. Current
intensive research may eventually reveal their true
significance.

　　　Above the troposphere to a height of about
(55) 50 miles is a zone called the *stratosphere*. The
stratosphere is separated from the troposphere
by a zone of uniform temperatures called the
tropopause. Within the lower portions of the
stratosphere is a layer of ozone gases which filters
(60) out most of the ultraviolet rays from the sun. The
ozone layer varies with air pressure. If this zone
were not there, the full blast of the sun's ultraviolet light would burn our skins, blind our eyes,
and eventually result in our destruction. Within
(65) the stratosphere, the temperature and atmospheric
composition are relatively uniform.

　　　The layer upward of about 50 miles is the
most fascinating but the least known of these
three strata. It is called the *ionosphere* because it
(70) consists of electrically charged particles called
ions, thrown from the sun. The northern lights
(*aurora borealis*) originate within this highly
charged portion of the atmosphere. Its effect upon
weather conditions, if any, is as yet unknown.

14. Which of the following titles best summarizes the
content of the passage?

(A) New Methods for Calculating the Composition
　　of the Atmosphere
(B) New Evidence Concerning the Stratification of
　　the Atmosphere
(C) The Atmosphere: Its Nature and Importance to
　　Our Weather
(D) The Underlying Causes of Atmospheric
　　Turbulence
(E) Stratosphere, Troposphere, Ionosphere: Three
　　Similar Zones

15. The passage supplies information that would
answer which of the following question?

　　I. How do the troposphere and the stratosphere
　　　differ?
　　II. How does the ionosphere affect the weather?
　　III. How do earth satellites study the atmo-
　　　sphere?

(A) I only
(B) III only
(C) I and II only
(D) I and III only
(E) I, II, and III

16. According to the passage, life as we know it exists
on earth because the atmosphere

(A) contains a layer of ozone gases
(B) contains electrically charged particles
(C) is warmest at the bottom
(D) carries the ultraviolet rays of the sun
(E) provides the changes in weather

17. It can be inferred from the passage that a jet plane
will usually have its best average rate of speed on
its run from

(A) New York to San Francisco
(B) Los Angeles to New York
(C) Boston to Miami
(D) Bermuda to New York
(E) London to Washington, D.C.

18. It can be inferred from the passage that at the top
of Jungfrau, which is 12,000 feet above the town
of Interlaken in Switzerland, the temperature is
usually

(A) below freezing
(B) about 42 degrees colder than on the ground
(C) warmer than in Interlaken
(D) affected by the ionosphere
(E) about 75 degrees colder than in Interlaken

19. The passage states that the troposphere is the
warmest part of the atmosphere because it

(A) is closest to the sun
(B) contains electrically charged particles
(C) radiates heat into space
(D) has winds and air current that distribute the
　　heat
(E) is warmed by the earth's heat

20. According to the passage, the atmosphere consists
of all of the following EXCEPT

(A) 21 percent oxygen
(B) a definite amount of water vapor
(C) ten permanent elements
(D) less than 1 percent xenon
(E) considerable waste products

Answer Key

Reading Comprehension Exercise A

1. B	6. C	11. C	16. D
2. B	7. E	12. D	17. D
3. E	8. A	13. D	18. C
4. B	9. E	14. A	19. E
5. E	10. D	15. B	20. E

Reading Comprehension Exercise B

1. A	6. E	11. D	16. B
2. D	7. C	12. C	17. A
3. C	8. E	13. E	18. C
4. B	9. C	14. B	19. E
5. D	10. C	15. A	20. B

Reading Comprehension Exercise C

1. C	6. B	11. C	16. A
2. B	7. A	12. D	17. B
3. A	8. B	13. A	18. D
4. D	9. D	14. C	19. B
5. E	10. B	15. C	20. E

Reading Comprehension Exercise D

1. B	6. B	11. A	16. C
2. E	7. E	12. D	17. B
3. D	8. D	13. A	18. E
4. C	9. B	14. B	19. B
5. A	10. C	15. D	20. A

Reading Comprehension Exercise E

1. D	6. B	11. C	16. A
2. D	7. D	12. D	17. B
3. A	8. C	13. B	18. B
4. D	9. D	14. C	19. E
5. B	10. A	15. A	20. B

8 Reviewing Vocabulary

- **GRE High-Frequency Words**
- **Master Word List**
- **Basic Word Parts**

Now that you have mastered the appropriate strategies for dealing with the four basic types of questions on the Graduate Record Examination that test your verbal ability, you have the opportunity to spend some time refining your vocabulary and acquainting yourself with the fine shades of meaning that words possess. Studies show that, where the average high school graduate recognizes around 50,000 words, the average college graduate recognizes around 70,000. The increase indicates that during your four years of college you have rapidly acquired about 20,000 new words (many of them technical terms from a variety of disciplines), some of which may have connotations and nuances that still escape you.

The best way to develop a powerful vocabulary is to read extensively and well. However, it is possible to fine-tune your vocabulary by exploring unabridged dictionaries, in which usage notes make clear the fine distinctions between related words, and by studying high-level vocabulary lists, such as our 3,500-word Master Word List.

This chapter presents the Master Word List and a Basic Word Parts List, a chart of prefixes, roots, and suffixes that may provide you with clues to the meanings of unfamiliar words. The chapter begins with the GRE High-Frequency Word List, 333 words that have occurred and reoccurred on GREs published in the 1980s and 1990s.

The GRE High-Frequency Word List

How many of the following words do you think you know? Half? Even more? First, check off those words that you recognize. Then, look up all 333 words and their definitions in our Master Word List. Pay particular attention to the following:

1. Words you recognize but cannot use in a sentence or define. You have a feel for these words—you are on the brink of knowing them. Effort you put into mastering these "borderline" words will pay off soon.

2. Words you thought you knew—but didn't. See whether any of them are defined in an unexpected way. If they are, make a special note of them. As you know from the preceding chapters, the GRE often stumps students with questions based on unfamiliar meanings of familiar-looking words.

In the course of your undergraduate career, you have undoubtedly developed your own techniques for building your vocabulary. One familiar technique—flash cards—often is used less than effectively. Students either try to cram too much information onto a flash card or try to cram too many flash cards into a practice session. If you wish to work with flash cards, try following these suggestions.

Writing the Flash Card Be brief—but include all the information you need. On one side write the word. On the other side write a *concise* definition—two or three words at most—for each major meaning of the word you want to learn. Include an antonym, too: the synonym-antonym associations can help you remember both words. To fix the word in your mind, use it in a short phrase. Then write that phrase down.

Memorizing the Flash Card Carry a few of your flash cards with you every day. Look them over whenever you have a spare moment or two. Work in short bursts. Try going through five flash cards at a time, shuffling through them quickly so that you can build up your rapid sight recognition of the words for the test. You want these words and their antonyms to spring to your mind instantaneously.

Test your memory: don't look at the back of the card unless you must. Go through your five cards several times a day. Then, when you have mastered two or three of the cards and have them down pat, set those cards aside and add a couple of new ones to your working pile. That way you will always be working with a limited group, but you won't be wasting time reviewing words you already recognize on sight.

Never try to master a whole stack of flash cards in one long cram session. It won't work.

GRE High-Frequency Words

abate	chicanery	disseminate	gainsay	latent
aberrant	coagulate	dissolution	garrulous	laud
abeyance	coda	dissonance	goad	lethargic
abscond	cogent	distend	gouge	levee
abstemious	commensurate	distill	grandiloquent	levity
admonish	compendium	diverge	gregarious	log
adulterate	complaisant	divest	guileless	loquacious
aesthetic	compliant	document [v.]	gullible	lucid
aggregate	conciliatory	dogmatic	harangue	luminous
alacrity	condone	dormant	homogeneous	magnanimity
alleviate	confound	dupe	hyperbole	malingerer
amalgamate	connoisseur	ebullient	iconoclastic	malleable
ambiguous	contention	eclectic	idolatry	maverick
ambivalence	contentious	efficacy	immutable	mendacious
ameliorate	contrite	effrontery	impair	metamorphosis
anachronism	conundrum	elegy	impassive	meticulous
analogous	converge	elicit	impede	misanthrope
anarchy	convoluted	embellish	impermeable	mitigate
anomalous	craven	empirical	imperturbable	mollify
antipathy	daunt	emulate	impervious	morose
apathy	decorum	endemic	implacable	mundane
appease	default	enervate	implicit	negate
apprise	deference	engender	implode	neophyte
approbation	delineate	enhance	inadvertently	obdurate
appropriate [v.]	denigrate	ephemeral	inchoate	obsequious
arduous	deride	equanimity	incongruity	obviate
artless	derivative	equivocate	inconsequential	occlude
ascetic	desiccate	erudite	incorporate	officious
assiduous	desultory	esoteric	indeterminate	onerous
assuage	deterrent	eulogy	indigence	opprobrium
attenuate	diatribe	euphemism	indolent	oscillate
audacious	dichotomy	exacerbate	inert	ostentatious
austere	diffidence	exculpate	ingenuous	paragon
autonomous	diffuse	exigency	inherent	partisan
aver	digression	extrapolation	innocuous	pathological
banal	dirge	facetious	insensible	paucity
belie	disabuse	facilitate	insinuate	pedantic
beneficent	discerning	fallacious	insipid	penchant
bolster	discordant	fatuous	insularity	penury
bombastic	discredit	fawning	intractable	perennial
boorish	discrepancy	felicitous	intransigence	perfidious
burgeon	discrete	fervor	inundate	perfunctory
burnish	disingenuous	flag [v.]	inured	permeable
buttress	disinterested	fledgling	invective	pervasive
cacophonous	disjointed	flout	irascible	phlegmatic
capricious	dismiss	foment	irresolute	piety
castigation	disparage	forestall	itinerary	placate
catalyst	disparate	frugality	laconic	plasticity
caustic	dissemble	futile	lassitude	platitude

plethora	propitiate	rescind	sporadic	tractable
plummet	propriety	resolution	stigma	transgression
porous	proscribe	resolve	stint [v.]	truculence
pragmatic	pungent	reticent	stipulate	vacillate
preamble	qualified	reverent	stolid	venerate
precarious	quibble	sage [N.]	striated	veracious
precipitate (ADJ.)	quiescent	salubrious	strut [N.]	verbose
precursor	rarefied	sanction	subpoena	viable
presumptuous	recalcitrant	satiate	subside	viscous
prevaricate	recant	saturate	substantiate	vituperative
pristine	recluse	savor	supersede	volatile
probity	recondite	secrete	supposition	warranted
problematic	refractory	shard	tacit	wary
prodigal	refute	skeptic	tangential	welter
profound	relegate	solicitous	tenuous	whimsical
prohibitive	reproach	soporific	tirade	zealot
proliferate	reprobate	specious	torpor	
propensity	repudiate	spectrum	tortuous	

The 3,500-Word Master Word List

The 3,500-Word Master Word List begins on the following page. As a graduate student you should be familiar with the majority of these words. You do not, however, need to memorize every word.

The best way to enlarge your vocabulary is to read extensively in a variety of fields. You can, however, assess the extent of your vocabulary by exploring specialized word lists such as this one.

For those of you who wish to work your way through the word list and feel the need for a plan, we recommend that you follow the procedure described below in order to use the lists and the exercises most profitably:

1. Allot a definite time each day for the study of a list.

2. Devote at least one hour to each list.

3. First go through the list looking at the short, simple-looking words (seven letters at most). Mark those you don't know. In studying, pay particular attention to them.

4. Go through the list again looking at the longer words. Pay particular attention to words with more than one meaning and familiar-looking words with unusual definitions that come as a surprise to you. Many tests make use of these secondary definitions.

5. List unusual words on index cards, which you can shuffle and review from time to time. (Use the flash card technique described earlier in this chapter.)

6. Using the illustrative sentences in the list as models, make up new sentences on your own.

7. Take the test that follows each list at least one day after studying the words. In this way, you will check your ability to remember what you have studied.

8. If you can answer correctly 12 of the 15 questions in the test, you may proceed to the next list; if you cannot answer this number, restudy the list.

9. Keep a record of your guesses and of your success as a guesser.

For each word, the following is provided:

1. The word (printed in heavy type).

2. Its part of speech (abbreviated).

3. A brief definition.

4. A sentence or sentences illustrating the word's use.

5. Whenever appropriate, related words together with their parts of speech.

The word lists are arranged in strict alphabetical order. In each list, words that appear also on the High-Frequency GRE Word List are marked with a square bullet (■).

Master Word List

Word List 1   abase-adroit

abase v. lower; degrade; humiliate. Anna expected to have to curtsy to the King of Siam; when told to cast herself down on the ground before him, however, she refused to *abase* herself. abasement, N.

abash v. embarrass. He was not at all *abashed* by her open admiration.

■ **abate** .v. subside or moderate. Rather than leaving immediately, they waited for the storm to *abate*.

abbreviate v. shorten. Because we were running out of time, the lecturer had to *abbreviate* her speech.

abdicate v. renounce; give up. When Edward VIII *abdicated* the British throne, he surprised the entire world.

■ **aberrant** ADJ. abnormal or deviant. Given the *aberrant* nature of the data, we came to doubt the validity of the entire experiment.

aberration N. abnormality; departure from the norm; mental irregularity or disorder. It remains the consensus among investors on Wall Street that current high oil prices are a temporary *aberration* and that we shall soon see a return to cheap oil.

abet v. assist, usually in doing something wrong; encourage. She was unwilling to *abet* him in the swindle he had planned.

■ **abeyance** N. suspended action. The deal was held in *abeyance* until her arrival.

abhor v. detest; hate. She *abhorred* all forms of bigotry. abhorrence, N.

abject ADJ. wretched; lacking pride. On the streets of New York the homeless live in *abject* poverty, huddling in doorways to find shelter from the wind.

abjure v. renounce upon oath; disavow. Pressure from university authorities caused the young scholar to *abjure* his heretical opinions. abjuration, N.

ablution N. washing. His daily *ablutions* were accompanied by loud noises that he humorously labeled "Opera in the Bath."

abnegation N. renunciation; self-sacrifice. Though Rudolph and Duchess Flavia loved one another, their love was doomed, for she had to wed the king; their act of *abnegation* was necessary to preserve the kingdom.

abolish v. cancel; put an end to. The president of the college refused to *abolish* the physical education requirement. abolition, N.

abominable ADJ. detestable; extremely unpleasant; very bad. Mary liked John until she learned he was also dating Susan; then she called him an *abominable* young man, with *abominable* taste in women.

abominate v. loathe; hate. Moses scolded the idol worshippers in the tribe because he *abominated* the custom.

aboriginal ADJ., N. being the first of its kind in a region; primitive; native. Her studies of the primitive art forms of the *aboriginal* Indians were widely reported in the scientific journals. aborigine, N.

abortive ADJ. unsuccessful; fruitless. Attacked by armed troops, the Chinese students had to abandon their *abortive* attempt to democratize Beijing peacefully. abort, V.

abrasive ADJ. rubbing away; tending to grind down. Just as *abrasive* cleaning powders can wear away a shiny finish, *abrasive* remarks can wear away a listener's patience. abrade, V.

abridge v. condense or shorten. Because the publishers felt the public wanted a shorter version of *War and Peace*, they proceeded to *abridge* the novel.

abrogate v. abolish. The king intended to *abrogate* the decree issued by his predecessor.

abscission N. removal by cutting off, as in surgery; separation. Gas gangrene spreads so swiftly and is so potentially deadly that doctors advise *abscission* of the gangrenous tissue. When a flower or leaf separates naturally from the parent plant, this process is called *abscission* or leaf fall.

■ **abscond** v. depart secretly and hide. The teller who *absconded* with the bonds went uncaptured until someone recognized him from his photograph on *America's Most Wanted*.

absolute ADJ. complete; totally unlimited; certain. Although the King of Siam was an *absolute* monarch, he did not want to behead his unfaithful wife without *absolute* evidence of her infidelity.

absolve v. pardon (an offense). The father confessor *absolved* him of his sins. absolution, N.

abstain v. refrain; withhold from participation. After considering the effect of alcohol on his athletic performance, he decided to *abstain* from drinking while he trained for the race.

■ **abstemious** ADJ. sparing in eating and drinking; temperate. Concerned whether her vegetarian son's *abstemious* diet provided him with sufficient protein, the worried mother pressed food on him.

abstinence N. restraint from eating or drinking. The doctor recommended total *abstinence* from salted foods. abstain, V.

abstract ADJ. theoretical; not concrete; nonrepresentational. To him, hunger was an *abstract* concept; he had never missed a meal.

abstruse ADJ. obscure; profound; difficult to understand. Baffled by the *abstruse* philosophical texts assigned in class, Dave asked Lexy to explain Kant's *Critique of Pure Reason*.

abusive ADJ. coarsely insulting; physically harmful. An *abusive* parent damages a child both mentally and physically.

abut V. border upon; adjoin. Where our estates *abut*, we must build a fence.

abysmal ADJ. bottomless. His arrogance is exceeded only by his *abysmal* ignorance.

abyss N. enormous chasm; vast, bottomless pit. Darth Vader seized the evil emperor and hurled him into the *abyss*.

academic ADJ. related to a school; not practical or directly useful. The dean's talk about reforming *academic* policies was only an *academic* discussion: we knew little, if anything, would change.

accede V. agree. If I *accede* to this demand for blackmail, I am afraid that I will be the victim of future demands.

accelerate V. move faster. In our science class, we learn how falling bodies *accelerate*.

accessible ADJ. easy to approach; obtainable. We asked our guide whether the ruins were *accessible* on foot.

accessory N. additional object; useful but not essential thing. She bought an attractive handbag as an *accessory* for her dress. also ADJ.

acclaim V. applaud; announce with great approval. The sportscasters *acclaimed* every American victory in the Olympics and decried every American defeat. acclamation, N.

acclimate V. adjust to climate or environment; adapt. One of the difficulties of our present air age is the need of travelers to *acclimate* themselves to their new and often strange environments.

acclivity N. sharp upslope of a hill. The car could not go up the *acclivity* in high gear.

accolade N. award of merit. In Hollywood, an "Oscar" is the highest *accolade*.

accommodate V. oblige or help someone; adjust or bring into harmony; adapt. Mitch always did everything possible to *accommodate* his elderly relatives, from driving them to medical appointments to helping them with paperwork. (secondary meaning)

accomplice N. partner in crime. Because he had provided the criminal with the lethal weapon, he was arrested as an *accomplice* in the murder.

accord N. agreement. She was in complete *accord* with the verdict.

accost V. approach and speak first to a person. When the two young men *accosted* me, I was frightened because I thought they were going to attack me.

accoutre V. equip. The fisherman was *accoutred* with the best that the sporting goods store could supply. accoutrement, N.

accretion N. growth; increase. Over the years Bob put on weight; because of this *accretion* of flesh, he went from size M to size XL. accrete, V.

accrue V. come about by addition. You must pay the interest that has *accrued* on your debt as well as the principal sum. accrual, N.

acerbic ADJ. bitter or sour in nature; sharp and cutting. Noted for her *acerbic* wit and gossiping, Alice Roosevelt Longworth had a pillow in her home embroidered with the legend "If you can't say something good about someone, sit right here by me."

acerbity N. bitterness of speech and temper. The meeting of the United Nations Assembly was marked with such *acerbity* that observers held little hope of reaching any useful settlement of the problem.

acetic ADJ. vinegary. The salad had an exceedingly *acetic* flavor.

acidulous ADJ. slightly sour; sharp; caustic. James was unpopular because of his sarcastic and *acidulous* remarks.

acknowledge V. recognize; admit. Although I *acknowledge* that the Beatles' tunes sound pretty dated nowadays, I still prefer them to the gangsta rap songs my brothers play.

acme N. peak; pinnacle; highest point. Welles's success in *Citizen Kane* marked the *acme* of his career as an actor; never again did he achieve such popular acclaim.

acoustics N. science of sound; quality that makes a room easy or hard to hear in. Carnegie Hall is liked by music lovers because of its fine *acoustics*.

acquiesce V. assent; agree passively. Although she appeared to *acquiesce* to her employer's suggestions, I could tell she had reservations about the changes he wanted made. acquiescence, N.; acquiescent, ADJ.

acquittal N. deliverance from a charge. His *acquittal* by the jury surprised those who had thought him guilty. acquit, V.

acrid ADJ. sharp; bitterly pungent. The *acrid* odor of burnt gunpowder filled the room after the pistol had been fired.

acrimonious ADJ. bitter in words or manner. The candidate attacked his opponent in highly *acrimonious* terms. acrimony, N.

acrophobia N. fear of heights. A born salesman, he could convince someone with a bad case of *acrophobia* to sign up for a life membership in a sky-diving club.

actuarial ADJ. calculating; pertaining to insurance statistics. According to recent *actuarial* tables, life expectancy is greater today than it was a century ago.

actuate V. motivate. I fail to understand what *actuated* you to reply to this letter so nastily.

acuity N. sharpness. In time his youthful *acuity* of vision failed him, and he needed glasses.

acumen N. mental keenness. Her business *acumen* helped her to succeed where others had failed.

acute ADJ. quickly perceptive; keen; brief and severe. The *acute* young doctor realized immediately that the gradual deterioration of her patient's once-*acute* hearing was due to a chronic illness, not an *acute* one.

adage   N. wise saying; proverb. There is much truth in the old *adage* about fools and their money.

adamant   ADJ. hard; inflexible. In this movie Bronson played the part of a revenge-driven man, *adamant* in his determination to punish the criminals who destroyed his family. adamancy, N.

adapt   V. alter; modify. Some species of animals have become extinct because they could not *adapt* to a changing environment.

addendum   N. addition; appendix to book. Jane's editor approved her new comparative literature text but thought it would be even better with an *addendum* on recent developments in literary criticism.

addiction   N. compulsive, habitual need. His *addiction* to drugs caused his friends much grief.

addle   V. muddle; drive crazy; become rotten. This idiotic plan is confusing enough to *addle* anyone. addled, ADJ.

address   V. direct a speech to; deal with or discuss. Due to *address* the convention in July, Brown planned to *address* the issue of low-income housing in his speech.

adept   ADJ. expert at. She was *adept* at the fine art of irritating people. also N.

adhere   V. stick fast. I will *adhere* to this opinion until proof that I am wrong is presented. adhesion, N.; adherence, N.

adherent   N. supporter; follower. In the wake of the scandal, the senator's one-time *adherents* quietly deserted him.

adjacent   ADJ. adjoining; neighboring; close by. Philip's best friend Jason lived only four houses down the block, near but not immediately *adjacent*.

adjunct   N. something (generally nonessential or inferior) added on or attached. Although I don't absolutely need a second computer, I plan to buy a laptop to serve as an *adjunct* to my desktop model. also ADJ.

adjuration   N. solemn urging. Her *adjuration* to tell the truth did not change the witnesses' testimony. adjure, v.

adjutant   N. staff officer assisting the commander; assistant. Though Wellington delegated many tasks to his chief *adjutant*, Lord Fitzroy Somerset, Somerset was in no doubt as to who made all major decisions.

■ **admonish**   V. warn; reprove. When her courtiers questioned her religious beliefs, Mary Stuart *admonished* them, declaring that she would worship as she pleased.

adorn   V. decorate. Wall paintings and carved statues *adorned* the temple. adornment, N.

adroit   ADJ. skillful. Her *adroit* handling of the delicate situation pleased her employers.

Test

Word List 1   *Synonyms*

Each of the questions below consists of a word in capital letters, followed by five lettered words or phrases. Choose the lettered word or phrase that is most nearly similar in meaning to the word in capital letters and write the letter of your choice on your answer paper.

1. ABASE (A) incur (B) tax (C) estimate (D) elope (E) humiliate
2. ABERRATION (A) deviation (B) abhorrence (C) dislike (D) absence (E) anecdote
3. ABET (A) conceive (B) wager (C) encourage (D) evade (E) protect
4. ABEYANCE (A) obedience (B) discussion (C) excitement (D) suspended action (E) editorial
5. ABJURE (A) discuss (B) renounce (C) run off secretly (D) perjure (E) project
6. ABLUTION (A) censure (B) forgiveness (C) mutiny (D) survival (E) washing
7. ABNEGATION (A) blackness (B) self-denial (C) selfishness (D) cause (E) effectiveness
8. ABORIGINE (A) first design (B) absolution (C) finale (D) concept (E) primitive inhabitant
9. ABORTIVE (A) unsuccessful (B) consuming (C) financing (D) familiar (E) fruitful
10. ABSTINENCE (A) restrained eating or drinking (B) vulgar display (C) deportment (D) reluctance (E) population
11. ABSTRUSE (A) profound (B) irrespective (C) suspended (D) protesting (E) not thorough
12. ABUT (A) stimulate (B) grasp (C) oppose (D) widen (E) adjoin
13. ABYSMAL (A) bottomless (B) eternal (C) meteoric (D) diabolic (E) internal
14. ACCEDE (A) fail (B) compromise (C) correct (D) consent (E) mollify
15. ACCLIVITY (A) index (B) report (C) upslope of a hill (D) character (E) negotiator

Word List 2   adulation-amend

adulation N. flattery; admiration. The rock star thrived on the *adulation* of his groupies and yes-men. adulate, V.

■ **adulterate** V. make impure by adding inferior or tainted substances. It is a crime to *adulterate* foods without informing the buyer; when consumers learned that Beechnut had *adulterated* its apple juice by mixing the juice with water, they protested vigorously. adulteration, N.

advent N. arrival. Most Americans were unaware of the *advent* of the Nuclear Age until the news of Hiroshima reached them.

adventitious ADJ. accidental; casual. She found this *adventitious* meeting with her friend extremely fortunate.

adversary N. opponent; enemy. Batman struggled to save Gotham City from the machinations of his wicked *adversary*, the Joker.

adverse ADJ. unfavorable; hostile. The recession had a highly *adverse* effect on Father's investment portfolio: he lost so much money that he could no longer afford the butler and the upstairs maid.

adversity N. poverty; misfortune. We must learn to meet *adversity* gracefully.

advert V. refer (to). Since you *advert* to this matter so frequently, you must regard it as important.

advocacy N. support; active pleading on behalf of someone or something. No threats could dissuade Bishop Desmond Tutu from his *advocacy* of the human rights of black South Africans.

advocate V. urge; plead for. The abolitionists *advocated* freedom for the slaves. also N.

aegis N. shield; defense. Under the *aegis* of the Bill of Rights, we enjoy our most treasured freedoms.

aerie N. nest of a large bird of prey (eagle, hawk). The mother eagle swooped down on the rabbit and bore it off to her *aerie* high in the Rocky Mountains.

■ **aesthetic** ADJ. artistic; dealing with or capable of appreciating the beautiful. The beauty of Tiffany's stained glass appealed to Alice's *aesthetic* sense. aesthete, N.

affable ADJ. easily approachable; warmly friendly. Accustomed to cold, aloof supervisors, Nicholas was amazed at how *affable* his new employer was. affability, N.

affected ADJ. artificial; pretended; assumed in order to impress. His *affected* mannerisms—his "Harvard" accent, his air of boredom, his use of obscure foreign words—bugged us: he acted as if he thought he was too good for his old high school friends. affectation, N.

affidavit N. written statement made under oath. The court refused to accept her statement unless she presented it in the form of an *affidavit*.

affiliation N. joining; associating with. His *affiliation* with the political party was of short duration for he soon disagreed with his colleagues.

affinity N. kinship. She felt an *affinity* with all who suffered; their pains were her pains.

affirmation N. positive assertion; confirmation; solemn pledge by one who refuses to take an oath. Despite Tom's *affirmations* of innocence, Aunt Polly still suspected he had eaten the pie.

affix V. attach or add on; fasten. First the registrar had to *affix* his signature to the license; then he had to *affix* his official seal.

affliction N. state of distress; cause of suffering. Even in the midst of her *affliction*, Elizabeth tried to keep up the spirits of those around her.

affluence N. abundance; wealth. Foreigners are amazed by the *affluence* and luxury of the American way of life.

affront N. insult; offense; intentional act of disrespect. When Mrs. Proudie was not seated beside the Archdeacon at the head table, she took it as a personal *affront* and refused to speak to her hosts for a week. also V.

agape ADJ. openmouthed. She stared, *agape*, at the many strange animals in the zoo.

agenda N. items of business at a meeting. We had so much difficulty agreeing upon an *agenda* that there was very little time for the meeting.

agglomeration N. collection; heap. It took weeks to assort the *agglomeration* of miscellaneous items she had collected on her trip.

aggrandize V. increase or intensify; raise in power, wealth, rank or honor. The history of the past quarter century illustrates how a President may *aggrandize* his power to act aggressively in international affairs without considering the wishes of Congress.

■ **aggregate** V. gather; accumulate. Before the Wall Street scandals, dealers in so-called junk bonds managed to *aggregate* great wealth in short periods of time. also ADJ. aggregation, N.

aggressor N. attacker. Before you punish both boys for fighting, see whether you can determine which one was the *aggressor*.

aghast ADJ. horrified; dumbfounded. Miss Manners was *aghast* at the crude behavior of the fraternity brothers at the annual toga party.

agility N. nimbleness. The *agility* of the acrobat amazed and thrilled the audience.

agitate V. stir up; disturb. Her fiery remarks *agitated* the already angry mob.

agnostic N. one who is skeptical of the existence of a god or any ultimate reality. *Agnostics* say we can neither prove nor disprove the existence of God; we simply have no way to know. also ADJ.

agog ADJ. highly excited; intensely curious. We were all *agog* at the news that the celebrated movie star was giving up his career in order to enter a monastery.

agrarian ADJ. pertaining to land or its cultivation. As a result of its recent industrialization, the country is gradually losing its *agrarian* traditions.

■ **alacrity** N. cheerful promptness; eagerness. Phil and Dave were raring to get off to the mountains; they packed up their ski gear and climbed into the van with *alacrity*.

alchemy N. medieval form of speculative thought that aimed to transform base metals (lead or copper) into silver or gold and to discover a means of prolonging life. Although *alchemy* anticipated science in its belief that physical reality was determined by an unvarying set of natural laws, the *alchemist's* experimental method was hardly scientific.

alcove N. nook; recess. Though their apartment lacked a full-scale dining room, an *alcove* adjacent to the living room made an adequate breakfast nook for the young couple.

alias N. an assumed name. John Smith's *alias* was Bob Jones. also ADV.

alienate V. make hostile; separate. Her attempts to *alienate* the two friends failed because they had complete faith in each other.

alimentary ADJ. supplying nourishment. The *alimentary* canal in our bodies is so named because digestion of foods occurs there. When asked for the name of the digestive tract, Sherlock Holmes replied, "*Alimentary*, my dear Watson."

alimony N. payments made to an ex-spouse after divorce. Because Tony had supported Tina through medical school, on their divorce he asked the court to award him $500 a month in *alimony*.

allay V. calm; pacify. The crew tried to *allay* the fears of the passengers by announcing that the fire had been controlled.

allege V. state without proof. Although it is *alleged* that she has worked for the enemy, she denies the *allegation* and, legally, we can take no action against her without proof. allegation, N.

allegiance N. loyalty. Not even a term in prison could shake Lech Walesa's *allegiance* to Solidarity, the Polish trade union he had helped to found.

allegory N. story in which characters are used as symbols; fable. *Pilgrim's Progress* is an *allegory* of the temptations and victories of the human soul. allegorical, ADJ.

■ **alleviate** V. relieve. This should *alleviate* the pain; if it does not, we shall have to use stronger drugs.

alliteration N. repetition of beginning sound in poetry. "The furrow followed free" is an example of *alliteration*.

allocate V. assign. Even though the Red Cross had *allocated* a large sum for the relief of the sufferers of the disaster, many people perished.

alloy N. a mixture as of metals. *Alloys* of gold are used more frequently than the pure metal.

alloy V. mix; make less pure; lessen or moderate. Our delight at the Mets' victory was *alloyed* by our concern

for Al Laites, who injured his pitching arm in the game.

allude V. refer indirectly. Try not to mention divorce in Jack's presence because he will think you are *alluding* to his marital problems with Jill.

allure V. entice; attract. *Allured* by the song of the sirens, the helmsman steered the ship toward the reef. also N.

allusion N. indirect reference. When Amanda said to the ticket scalper, "One hundred bucks? What do you want, a pound of flesh?" she was making an *allusion* to Shakespeare's *Merchant of Venice*.

alluvial ADJ. pertaining to soil deposits left by running water. The farmers found the *alluvial* deposits at the mouth of the river very fertile.

aloof ADJ. apart; reserved. Shy by nature, she remained *aloof* while all the rest conversed.

aloft ADV. upward. The sailor climbed *aloft* into the rigging.

altercation N. noisy quarrel; heated dispute. In that hot-tempered household, no meal ever came to a peaceful conclusion; the inevitable *altercation* sometimes even ended in blows.

altruistic ADJ. unselfishly generous; concerned for others. In providing tutorial assistance and college scholarships for hundreds of economically disadvantaged youths, Eugene Lang performed a truly *altruistic* deed. altruism, N.

■ **amalgamate** V. combine; unite in one body. The unions will attempt to *amalgamate* their groups into one national body.

amass V. collect. The miser's aim is to *amass* and hoard as much gold as possible.

amazon N. female warrior. Ever since the days of Greek mythology we refer to strong and aggressive women as *amazons*.

ambidextrous ADJ. capable of using either hand with equal ease. A switch-hitter in baseball should be naturally *ambidextrous*.

ambience N. environment; atmosphere. She went to the restaurant not for the food but for the *ambience*.

■ **ambiguous** ADJ. unclear or doubtful in meaning. His *ambiguous* instructions misled us; we did not know which road to take. ambiguity, N.

■ **ambivalence** N. the state of having contradictory or conflicting emotional attitudes. Torn between loving her parents one minute and hating them the next, she was confused by the *ambivalence* of her feelings. ambivalent, ADJ.

amble N. moving at an easy pace. When she first mounted the horse, she was afraid to urge the animal to go faster than a gentle *amble*. also V.

ambrosia N. food of the gods. *Ambrosia* was supposed to give immortality to any human who ate it.

ambulatory ADJ. able to walk; not bedridden. Calvin was a highly *ambulatory* patient; not only did he refuse to be confined to bed, but also he insisted on riding his skateboard up and down the halls.

■ **ameliorate** v. improve. Many social workers have attempted to *ameliorate* the conditions of people living in the slums.

amenable ADJ. readily managed or willing to be led; answerable or accountable legally. Although the ambassador was usually *amenable* to friendly suggestions, he balked when we hinted he should pay his parking tickets. As a foreign diplomat, he claimed he was not *amenable* to minor local laws.

amend v. correct; change, generally for the better. Hoping to *amend* his condition, he left Vietnam for the United States.

Test

Word List 2   *Antonyms*

Each of the following questions consists of a word in capital letters, followed by five lettered words or phrases. Choose the lettered word or phrase that is most nearly opposite in meaning to the word in capital letters and write the letter of your choice on your answer paper.

16. ADULATION (A) youth (B) purity (C) brightness (D) defense (E) criticism
17. ADVOCATE (A) define (B) oppose (C) remove (D) inspect (E) discern
18. AFFABLE (A) rude (B) ruddy (C) needy (D) useless (E) conscious
19. AFFECTED (A) weary (B) unfriendly (C) divine (D) unfeigned (E) slow
20. AFFLUENCE (A) poverty (B) fear (C) persuasion (D) consideration (E) neglect
21. AGILITY (A) awkwardness (B) solidity (C) temper (D) harmony (E) warmth
22. ALACRITY (A) slowness (B) plenty (C) filth (D) courtesy (E) despair
23. ALLEVIATE (A) endure (B) worsen (C) enlighten (D) maneuver (E) humiliate
24. ALLURE (A) hinder (B) repel (C) ignore (D) leave (E) wallow
25. ALOOF (A) triangular (B) gregarious (C) comparable (D) honorable (E) savory
26. AMALGAMATE (A) equip (B) separate (C) generate (D) materialize (E) repress
27. AMBIGUOUS (A) salvageable (B) corresponding (C) responsible (D) clear (E) auxiliary
28. AMBLE (A) befriend (B) hasten (C) steal (D) browse (E) prattle
29. AMBULATORY (A) convalescent (B) valedictory (C) bedridden (D) emergency (E) congenital
30. AMELIORATE (A) make slow (B) make sure (C) make young (D) make worse (E) make able

Word List 3   amenities-apothecary

amenities N. convenient features; courtesies. In addition to the customary *amenities* for the business traveler—fax machines, modems, a health club—the hotel offers the services of a butler versed in the social *amenities*.

amiable ADJ. agreeable; lovable; warmly friendly. In *Little Women*, Beth is the *amiable* daughter whose loving disposition endears her to all who know her.

amicable ADJ. politely friendly; not quarrelsome. Beth's sister Jo is the hot-tempered tomboy who has a hard time maintaining *amicable* relationships with those around her. Jo's quarrel with her friend Laurie finally reaches an *amicable* settlement, but not because Jo turns amiable overnight.

amiss ADJ. wrong; faulty. Seeing her frown, he wondered if anything were *amiss*. also ADV.

amity N. friendship. Student exchange programs such as the Experiment in International Living were established to promote international *amity*.

amnesia N. loss of memory. Because she was suffering from *amnesia*, the police could not get the young girl to identify herself.

amnesty N. pardon. When his first child was born, the king granted *amnesty* to all in prison.

amoral ADJ. nonmoral. The *amoral* individual lacks a code of ethics; he cannot tell right from wrong. The immoral person can tell right from wrong; he chooses to do something he knows is wrong.

amorous ADJ. moved by sexual love; loving. "Love them and leave them" was the motto of the *amorous* Don Juan.

amorphous ADJ. formless; lacking shape or definition. As soon as we have decided on our itinerary, we shall send you a copy; right now, our plans are still *amorphous*.

amphibian ADJ. able to live both on land and in water. Frogs are classified as *amphibian*. also N.

amphitheater N. oval building with tiers of seats. The spectators in the *amphitheater* cheered the gladiators.

ample ADJ. abundant. Bond had *ample* opportunity to escape. Why, then, did he let us capture him?

amplify v. broaden or clarify by expanding; intensify; make stronger. Charlie Brown tried to *amplify* his remarks, but he was drowned out by jeers from the audience. Lucy was smarter: she used a loudspeaker to *amplify* her voice.

amputate v. cut off part of body; prune. When the doctors had to *amputate* Ted Kennedy's leg to prevent the spread of cancer, he did not let the loss of his leg keep him from participating in sports.

amok (also amuck) ADV. in a state of rage. The police had to be called in to restrain him after he ran *amok* in the department store.

amulet N. charm; talisman. Around her neck she wore the *amulet* that the witch doctor had given her.

■ **anachronism** N. something or someone misplaced in time. Shakespeare's reference to clocks in *Julius Caesar* is an *anachronism*; no clocks existed in Caesar's time. anachronistic, ADJ.

analgesic ADJ. causing insensitivity to pain. The *analgesic* qualities of this lotion will provide temporary relief.

■ **analogous** ADJ. comparable. She called our attention to the things that had been done in an *analogous* situation and recommended that we do the same.

analogy N. similarity; parallelism. A well-known *analogy* compares the body's immune system with an army whose defending troops are the lymphocytes or white blood cells.

anarchist N. person who seeks to overturn the established government; advocate of abolishing authority. Denying she was an *anarchist*, Katya maintained she wished only to make changes in our government, not to destroy it entirely.

■ **anarchy** N. absence of governing body; state of disorder. The assassination of the leaders led to a period of *anarchy*.

anathema N. solemn curse; someone or something regarded as a curse. The Ayatolla Khomeini heaped *anathema* upon "the Great Satan," that is, the United States. To the Ayatolla, America and the West were *anathema*; he loathed the democratic nations, cursing them in his dying words. anathematize, v.

ancestry N. family descent. David can trace his *ancestry* as far back as the seventeenth century, when one of his *ancestors* was a court trumpeter somewhere in Germany. ancestral, ADJ.

anchor v. secure or fasten firmly; be fixed in place. We set the post in concrete to *anchor* it in place. anchorage, N.

ancillary ADJ. serving as an aid or accessory; auxiliary. In an *ancillary* capacity Doctor Watson was helpful; however, Holmes could not trust the good doctor to solve a perplexing case on his own. also N.

anecdote N. short account of an amusing or interesting event. Rather than make concrete proposals for welfare reform, President Reagan told *anecdotes* about poor people who became wealthy despite their impoverished backgrounds.

anemia N. condition in which blood lacks red corpuscles. The doctor ascribes her tiredness to *anemia*. anemic, ADJ.

anesthetic N. substance that removes sensation with or without loss of consciousness. His monotonous voice acted like an *anesthetic*; his audience was soon asleep. anesthesia, N.

anguish N. acute pain; extreme suffering. Visiting the site of the explosion, the president wept to see the *anguish* of the victims and their families.

angular ADJ. sharp-cornered; stiff in manner. Mr. Spock's features, though *angular*, were curiously attractive, in a Vulcan way.

animadversion N. critical remark. He resented the *animadversions* of his critics, particularly because he realized they were true.

animated ADJ. lively; spirited. Jim Carrey's facial expressions are highly *animated*: when he played Ace Ventura, he was practically rubber-faced.

animosity N. active enmity. He incurred the *animosity* of the ruling class because he advocated limitations of their power.

animus N. hostile feeling or intent. The *animus* of the speaker became obvious to all when he began to indulge in sarcastic and insulting remarks.

annals N. records; history. In the *annals* of this period, we find no mention of democratic movements.

anneal v. reduce brittleness and improve toughness by heating and cooling. After the glass is *annealed*, it will be less subject to chipping and cracking.

annex v. attach; take possession of. Mexico objected to the United States' attempts to *annex* the territory that later became the state of Texas.

annihilate v. destroy. The enemy in its revenge tried to *annihilate* the entire population.

annotate v. comment; make explanatory notes. In the appendix to the novel, the critic sought to *annotate* many of the more esoteric references.

annuity N. yearly allowance. The *annuity* she set up with the insurance company supplements her social security benefits so that she can live very comfortably without working.

annul v. make void. The parents of the eloped couple tried to *annul* the marriage.

anodyne N. drug that relieves pain; opiate. His pain was so great that no *anodyne* could relieve it.

anoint v. consecrate. The prophet Samuel *anointed* David with oil, crowning him king of Israel.

■ **anomalous** ADJ. abnormal; irregular. She was placed in the *anomalous* position of seeming to approve procedures that she despised.

anomaly N. irregularity. A bird that cannot fly is an *anomaly*.

anonymity N. state of being nameless; anonymousness. The donor of the gift asked the college not to mention her by name; the dean readily agreed to respect her *anonymity*. anonymous, ADJ.

antagonism N. hostility; active resistance. Barry showed his *antagonism* toward his new stepmother by ignoring her whenever she tried talking to him. antagonistic, ADJ.

antecede v. precede. The invention of the radiotelegraph *anteceded* the development of television by a quarter of a century.

antecedents N. preceding events or circumstances that influence what comes later; ancestors or early background. Susi Bechhofer's ignorance of her Jewish background had its *antecedents* in the chaos of World War II. Smuggled out of Germany and adopted by a Christian family, she knew nothing of her birth and *antecedents* until she was reunited with her Jewish family in 1989.

antediluvian ADJ. antiquated; extremely ancient. Looking at his great-aunt's antique furniture, which must have been cluttering up her attic since before Noah's flood, the young heir exclaimed, "Heavens! How positively *antediluvian*!"

anthem N. song of praise or patriotism. Let us now all join in singing the national *anthem*.

anthology N. book of literary selections by various authors. This *anthology* of science fiction was compiled by the late Isaac Asimov. anthologize, V.

anthropoid ADJ. manlike. The gorilla is the strongest of the *anthropoid* animals. also N.

anthropologist N. student of the history and science of humankind. *Anthropologists* have discovered several relics of prehistoric humans in this area.

anthropomorphic ADJ. having human form or characteristics. Primitive religions often have deities with *anthropomorphic* characteristics.

antic ADJ. extravagantly odd. Putting on an *antic* disposition, Hamlet acts so odd that the Danish court thinks him mad. also N.

anticlimax N. letdown in thought or emotion. After the fine performance in the first act, the rest of the play was an *anticlimax*. anticlimactic, ADJ.

antidote N. remedy to counteract a poison or disease. When Marge's child accidentally swallowed some cleaning fluid, the local poison control hotline instructed Marge how to administer the *antidote*.

■ **antipathy** N. aversion; dislike. Tom's extreme *antipathy* for disputes keeps him from getting into arguments with his temperamental wife. Noise in any form is *antipathetic* to him. Among his other *antipathies* are honking cars, boom boxes, and heavy metal rock.

antiquated ADJ. obsolete; outdated. Accustomed to editing his papers on word processors, Philip thought typewriters were too *antiquated* for him to use.

antiseptic N. substance that prevents infection. It is advisable to apply an *antiseptic* to any wound, no matter how slight or insignificant. also ADJ.

antithesis N. contrast; direct opposite of or to. This tyranny was the *antithesis* of all that he had hoped for, and he fought it with all his strength. antithetical or antithetic, ADJ.

anvil N. iron block used in hammering out metals. After heating the iron horseshoe in the forge, the blacksmith picked it up with his tongs and set it on the *anvil*.

■ **apathy** N. lack of caring; indifference. A firm believer in democratic government, she could not understand the *apathy* of people who never bothered to vote. apathetic, ADJ.

ape V. imitate or mimic. In the comedy *Young Frankenstein*, when the servant Igor limps off, saying, "Walk this way," the hero *apes* him, hobbling after Igor in an imitation of his walk.

aperture N. opening; hole. She discovered a small *aperture* in the wall, through which the insects had entered the room.

apex N. tip; summit; climax. At the *apex* of his career, the star received offers of leading roles daily; two years later, he was reduced to taking bit parts in B-movies.

aphasia N. loss of speech due to injury or illness. After the automobile accident, the victim had periods of *aphasia* when he could not speak at all or could only mumble incoherently.

aphorism N. pithy maxim or saying. An *aphorism* is usually philosophic or scientific, as compared to an adage, which is usually more homely and concrete. "Absolute power corrupts absolutely" is an *aphorism*. "You can lead a horse to water, but you can't make him drink" is an adage. aphoristic, ADJ.

apiary N. a place where bees are kept. Although he spent many hours daily in the *apiary*, he was very seldom stung by a bee.

aplomb N. poise; assurance. Gwen's *aplomb* in handling potentially embarrassing moments was legendary around the office; when one of her clients broke a piece of her best crystal, she coolly picked up her own goblet and hurled it into the fireplace.

apocalyptic ADJ. prophetic; pertaining to revelations. The crowd jeered at the street preacher's *apocalyptic* predictions of doom. The *Apocalypse* or *Book of Revelations* of Saint John prophesies the end of the world as we know it and foretells marvels and prodigies that signal the coming doom. apocalypse, N.

apocryphal ADJ. spurious; not authentic; invented rather than true. Although many versions exist of the famous story of Emerson's visit to Thoreau in jail, in his writings Thoreau never mentions any such visit by Emerson, and so the tale is most likely *apocryphal*.

apogee N. highest point. When the moon in its orbit is furthest away from the earth, it is at its *apogee*. Discouraged by the apparent deterioration of America's space program, the science columnist wondered whether the golden age of space travel had reached its *apogee* with the Apollo 11 moon landing and would never again achieve such heights.

apolitical ADJ. having an aversion or lack of concern for political affairs. It was hard to remain *apolitical* during the Vietnam War; even people who generally ignored public issues felt they had to take political stands.

apologist N. one who writes in defense of a cause or institution. Rather than act as an *apologist* for the current regime in Beijing and defend its brutal actions, the young diplomat decided to defect to the West.

apostate N. one who abandons his religious faith or political beliefs. Because he switched from one party to another, his former friends shunned him as an *apostate*. An apostle passionately adheres to a belief or cause; an *apostate* passionately renounces or abandons one. apostasy, N.

apothecary N. druggist. In Holland, *apothecaries* still sell spices as well as ointments and pills.

Test

Word List 3   *Antonyms*

Each of the questions below consists of a word in capital letters, followed by five lettered words or phrases. Choose the lettered word or phrase that is most nearly opposite in meaning to the word in capital letters and write the letter of your choice on your answer paper.

31. AMICABLE (A) penetrating (B) compensating (C) unfriendly (D) zigzag (E) inescapable
32. AMORAL (A) unusual (B) unfriendly (C) ethical (D) suave (E) firm
33. AMORPHOUS (A) nauseous (B) obscene (C) providential (D) definite (E) happy
34. AMPLIFY (A) distract (B) infer (C) publicize (D) decrease (E) pioneer
35. ANALOGOUS (A) not comparable (B) not capable (C) not culpable (D) not corporeal (E) not congenial
36. ANATHEMATIZE (A) locate (B) deceive (C) regulate (D) radiate (E) bless

37. ANEMIC (A) pallid (B) cruel (C) red-blooded (D) ventilating (E) hazardous
38. ANIMATED (A) worthy (B) dull (C) humorous (D) lengthy (E) realistic
39. ANIMUS (A) pterodactyl (B) bastion (C) giraffe (D) grimace (E) favor
40. ANOMALY (A) desperation (B) requisition (C) registry (D) regularity (E) radiation
41. ANONYMOUS (A) desperate (B) signed (C) defined (D) expert (E) written
42. ANTEDILUVIAN (A) transported (B) subtle (C) isolated (D) celebrated (E) modern
43. ANTIPATHY (A) profundity (B) objection (C) willingness (D) abstention (E) fondness
44. ANTITHESIS (A) velocity (B) maxim (C) similarity (D) acceleration (E) reaction
45. APHASIA (A) volubility (B) necessity (C) pain (D) crack (E) prayer

Word List 4   apothegm-astigmatism

apothegm   N. pithy, compact saying. Proverbs are *apothegms* that have become familiar sayings.

apotheosis   N. elevation to godhood; an ideal example of something. The Roman empress Livia envied the late emperor Augustus his *apotheosis*; she hoped that on her death she, too, would be exalted to the ranks of the gods. The hero of the novel *Generation X* was the *apotheosis* of a slacker, the quintessential example of a member of his generation.

appall   V. dismay; shock. We were *appalled* by the horrifying conditions in the city's jails.

apparition   N. ghost; phantom. On the castle battlements, an *apparition* materialized and spoke to Hamlet, warning him of his uncle's treachery. In *Ghostbusters*, hordes of *apparitions* materialized, only to be dematerialized by the specialized apparatus wielded by Bill Murray.

■ **appease**   V. pacify or soothe; relieve. Tom and Jody tried to *appease* the crying baby by offering him one toy after another. However, he would not calm down until they *appeased* his hunger by giving him a bottle. appeasement, N.

appellation   N. name; title. Macbeth was startled when the witches greeted him with an incorrect *appellation*. Why did they call him Thane of Cawdor, he wondered, when the holder of that title still lived?

append   V. attach. When you *append* a bibliography to a text, you have created an *appendix*.

application   N. diligent attention. Pleased with how well Tom had whitewashed the fence, Aunt Polly praised him for his *application*. (Tom had *applied* himself to *applying* the paint.) (secondary meaning) apply, V.

apposite   ADJ. appropriate; fitting. She was always able to find the *apposite* phrase, the correct expression for every occasion.

appraise   V. estimate value of. It is difficult to *appraise* old paintings; it is easier to call them priceless. appraisal, N.

appreciate   V. be thankful for; increase in worth; be thoroughly conscious of. Little Orphan Annie truly *appreciated* the stocks Daddy Warbucks gave her, whose value *appreciated* considerably over the years.

apprehend   V. arrest (a criminal); dread; perceive. The police will *apprehend* the culprit and convict him before long.

apprehensive   ADJ. fearful; discerning. His *apprehensive* glances at the people who were walking in the street revealed his nervousness.

■ **apprise**   V. inform. When NASA was *apprised* of the dangerous weather conditions, the head of the space agency decided to postpone the shuttle launch.

■ **approbation**   N. approval. Wanting her parents' regard, she looked for some sign of their *approbation*. Benjamin Franklin, that shrewd observer of mankind, once wrote, "We must not in the course of public life expect immediate *approbation* and immediate grateful acknowledgment of our services."

■ **appropriate**   V. acquire; take possession of for one's own use. The ranch owners *appropriated* the lands that had originally been set aside for the Indians' use.

appurtenances N. subordinate possessions. He bought the estate and all its *appurtenances*.

apropos ADJ. to the point and timely. When Bob spoke out against drunk driving, some of our crowd called him a spoilsport, but the rest of us found his comments extremely *apropos*.

apropos PREP. with reference to; regarding. *Apropos* the waltz, the dance has its faults.

aptitude N. fitness; talent. The American aviator Bessie Coleman grew up in Waxahatchie, Texas, where her mathematical *aptitude* freed her from working in the cotton fields with her twelve brothers and sisters.

aquiline ADJ. curved, hooked. He can be recognized by his *aquiline* nose, curved like the beak of the eagle.

arabesque N. style of decoration involving intertwined plants and abstract curves; ballet position with one leg supporting the weight of the body, while the other leg is extended in back. Because the Koran prohibits the creation of human and animal images, Moorish *arabesques* depict plants but no people. The statue of winged Mercury stands poised on one foot, frozen in an eternal *arabesque*.

arable ADJ. fit for growing crops. The first settlers wrote home glowing reports of the New World, praising its vast acres of *arable* land ready for the plow.

arbiter N. person with power to decide a matter in dispute; judge. As an *arbiter* in labor disputes, she has won the confidence of the workers and the employers.

arbitrary ADJ. unreasonable or capricious; tyrannical. The coach claimed the team lost because the umpire made some *arbitrary* calls.

arbitrate V. act as judge. She was called upon to *arbitrate* the dispute between the union and the management.

arboretum N. place where different varieties of trees and shrubs are studied and exhibited. Walking along the treelined paths of the *arboretum*, Rita noted poplars, firs, and some particularly fine sycamores.

arcade N. a covered passageway, usually lined with shops. The *arcade* was popular with shoppers because it gave them protection from the summer sun and the winter rain.

arcane ADJ. secret; mysterious; known only to the initiated. Secret brotherhoods surround themselves with *arcane* rituals and trappings to mystify outsiders. So do doctors. Consider the *arcane* terminology they use and the impression they try to give that what is *arcane* to us is obvious to them.

archaeology N. study of artifacts and relics of early mankind. The professor of *archaeology* headed an expedition to the Gobi Desert in search of ancient ruins.

archaic ADJ. antiquated. "Methinks," "thee," and "thou" are *archaic* words that are no longer part of our normal vocabulary.

archetype N. prototype; primitive pattern. The Brooklyn Bridge was the *archetype* of the many spans that now connect Manhattan with Long Island and New Jersey.

archipelago N. group of closely located islands. When he looked at the map and saw the *archipelagoes* in the South Seas, he longed to visit them.

archives N. public records; place where public records are kept. These documents should be part of the *archives* so that historians may be able to evaluate them in the future.

ardor N. heat; passion; zeal. Katya's *ardor* was contagious; soon all her fellow demonstrators were busily making posters and handing out flyers, inspired by her *ardent* enthusiasm for the cause. ardent, ADJ.

■ **arduous** ADJ. hard; strenuous. Her *arduous* efforts had sapped her energy.

argot N. slang. In the *argot* of the underworld, she "was taken for a ride."

aria N. operatic solo. At her Metropolitan Opera audition, Marian Anderson sang an *aria* from *Norma*.

arid ADJ. dry; barren. The cactus has adapted to survive in an *arid* environment.

aristocracy N. hereditary nobility; privileged class. Americans have mixed feelings about hereditary *aristocracy*: we say all men are created equal, but we describe particularly outstanding people as natural *aristocrats*.

armada N. fleet of warships. Queen Elizabeth's navy was able to defeat the mighty *armada* that threatened the English coast.

aromatic ADJ. fragrant. Medieval sailing vessels brought *aromatic* herbs from China to Europe.

arraign V. charge in court; indict. After his indictment by the Grand Jury, the accused man was *arraigned* in the County Criminal Court.

array V. marshal; draw up in order. His actions were bound to *array* public sentiment against him. also N.

array V. clothe; adorn. She liked to watch her mother *array* herself in her finest clothes before going out for the evening. also N.

arrears N. being in debt. Because he was in *arrears* with his car payments, the repo men repossessed his Porsche.

arrest V. stop or check; seize or capture (the attention). According to Connolly's "Theory of Permanent Adolescence," the triumphs and disappointments that boys experience at the great British public schools are so intense as to dominate their lives and to *arrest* their development.

arrhythmic ADJ. lacking rhythm or regularity. The doctors feared his *arrhythmic* heartbeat might be the first symptom of an imminent heart attack. arrhythmia, N.

arrogance N. pride; haughtiness. Convinced that Emma thought she was better than anyone else in the class, Ed rebuked her for her *arrogance*.

arroyo N. gully. Until the heavy rains of the past spring, this *arroyo* had been a dry bed.

arsenal N. storage place for military equipment. People are forbidden to smoke in the *arsenal* lest a stray spark set off the munitions stored there.

artful ADJ. cunning; crafty; sly. By using accurate details to suggest a misleading picture of the whole, the *artful* propagandist turns partial truths into more effective instruments of deception than lies.

articulate ADJ. effective; distinct. Her *articulate* presentation of the advertising campaign impressed her employers. also V.

artifact N. object made by human beings, either hand-made or mass-produced. Archaeologists debated the significance of the *artifacts* discovered in the ruins of Asia Minor but came to no conclusion about the culture they represented.

artifice N. deception; trickery. The Trojan War proved to the Greeks that cunning and *artifice* were often more effective than military might.

artisan N. manually skilled worker; craftsman, as opposed to artist. Elderly *artisans* from Italy trained Harlem teenagers to carve the stone figures that would decorate the new wing of the cathedral.

■ **artless** ADJ. without guile; open and honest. Red Riding Hood's *artless* comment, "Grandma, what big eyes you have!" indicates the child's innocent surprise at her "grandmother's" changed appearance.

ascendancy N. controlling influence. President Marcos failed to maintain his *ascendancy* over the Philippines.

ascertain V. find out for certain. Please *ascertain* her present address.

■ **ascetic** ADJ. practicing self-denial; austere. The wealthy, self-indulgent young man felt oddly drawn to the strict, *ascetic* life led by members of some monastic orders. also N. asceticism, N.

ascribe V. refer; attribute; assign. I can *ascribe* no motive for her acts.

aseptic ADJ. preventing infection; having a cleansing effect. Hospitals succeeded in lowering the mortality rate as soon as they introduced *aseptic* conditions.

ashen ADJ. ash-colored; deadly pale. Her face was *ashen* with fear.

asinine ADJ. stupid. Your *asinine* remarks prove that you have not given this problem any serious consideration.

askance ADV. with a sideways or indirect look. Looking *askance* at her questioner, she displayed her scorn.

askew ADV. crookedly; slanted; at an angle. When the clown placed his hat *askew* upon his head, the children in the audience laughed.

asperity N. sharpness (of temper). These remarks, spoken with *asperity*, stung the boys to whom they had been directed.

aspersion N. slanderous remark. Rather than attacking President Cleveland's arguments with logic, his oppo-nent resorted to casting *aspersions* on the president's moral character.

aspirant N. seeker after position or status. Although I am an *aspirant* for public office, I am not willing to accept the dictates of the party bosses. also ADJ.

aspire V. seek to attain; long for. Because he *aspired* to a career in professional sports, Philip enrolled in a graduate program in sports management. aspiration, N.

assail V. assault. He was *assailed* with questions after his lecture.

assay V. analyze; evaluate. When they *assayed* the ore, they found that they had discovered a very rich vein. also N.

assent V. agree; accept. It gives me great pleasure to *assent* to your request. also N.

assert V. state strongly or positively; insist on or demand recognition of (rights, claims, etc.). When Jill *asserted* that nobody else in the junior class had such an early curfew, her parents *asserted* themselves, telling her that if she didn't get home by nine o'clock she would be grounded for the week. assertion, N.

assessment N. estimation; appraisal. I would like to have your *assessment* of the situation in South Africa.

■ **assiduous** ADJ. diligent. It took Rembrandt weeks of *assiduous* labor before he was satisfied with his portrait of his son.

assimilate V. absorb; cause to become homogenous. The manner in which the United States was able to *assimilate* the hordes of immigrants during the nineteenth and early part of the twentieth centuries will always be a source of pride.

■ **assuage** V. ease or lessen (pain); satisfy (hunger); soothe (anger). Jilted by Jane, Dick tried to *assuage* his heartache by indulging in ice cream. One gallon later, he had *assuaged* his appetite but not his grief. assuagement, N.

assumption N. something taken for granted; the taking over or taking possession of. The young princess made the foolish *assumption* that the regent would not object to her *assumption* of power. assume, V.

assurance N. promise or pledge; certainty; self-confidence. When Guthrie gave Guinness his *assurance* that rehearsals were going well, he spoke with such *assurance* that Guinness was convinced. assure, V. assured, ADJ.

asteroid N. small planet. *Asteroids* have become commonplace to the readers of interstellar travel stories in science fiction magazines.

astigmatism N. eye defect that prevents proper focus. As soon as his parents discovered that the boy suffered from *astigmatism*, they took him to the optometrist for corrective glasses.

Test

Word List 4   *Synonyms and Antonyms*

Each of the questions below consists of a word in capital letters, followed by five lettered words or phrases. Choose the lettered word or phrase that is most nearly similar or opposite in meaning to the word in capital letters and write the letter of your choice on your answer paper.

46. APPEASE (A) agitate (B) qualify (C) display (D) predestine (E) interrupt
47. APPOSITE (A) inappropriate (B) diagonal (C) exponential (D) unobtrusive (E) discouraging
48. APPREHEND (A) obviate (B) set free (C) shiver (D) understand (E) contrast
49. APTITUDE (A) sarcasm (B) inversion (C) adulation (D) lack of talent (E) gluttony
50. AQUILINE (A) watery (B) hooked (C) refined (D) antique (E) rodentlike
51. ARCHAIC (A) youthful (B) cautious (C) antiquated (D) placated (E) buttressed

52. ARDOR (A) zeal (B) paint (C) proof (D) group (E) excitement
53. ARRAY (A) swindle (B) lighten (C) strip bare (D) set free (E) cleanse
54. ARROYO (A) crevice (B) gully (C) value (D) food (E) fabric
55. ARTIFICE (A) spite (B) exception (C) anger (D) candor (E) loyalty
56. ARTISAN (A) educator (B) decider (C) sculptor (D) discourser (E) unskilled laborer
57. ASCERTAIN (A) amplify (B) master (C) discover (D) retain (E) explode
58. ASPERITY (A) anguish (B) absence (C) innuendo (D) good temper (E) snake
59. ASSUAGE (A) stuff (B) describe (C) wince (D) worsen (E) introduce
60. ASTEROID (A) Milky Way (B) radiance (C) large planet (D) rising moon (E) setting moon

Word List 5   astral-barb

astral   ADJ. relating to the stars. She was amazed at the number of *astral* bodies the new telescope revealed.

astringent   ADJ. binding; causing contraction; harsh or severe. The *astringent* quality of the unsweetened lemon juice made swallowing difficult. also N.

astronomical   ADJ. enormously large or extensive. The government seemed willing to spend *astronomical* sums on weapons development.

astute   ADJ. wise; shrewd; keen. The painter was an *astute* observer, noticing every tiny detail of her model's appearance and knowing exactly how important each one was.

asunder   ADV. into parts; apart. A fierce quarrel split the partnership *asunder*; the two partners finally sundered their connections because their points of view were poles *asunder*.

asylum   N. place of refuge or shelter; protection. The refugees sought *asylum* from religious persecution in a new land.

asymmetric   ADJ. not identical on both sides of a dividing central line. Because one eyebrow was set markedly higher than the other, William's face had a particularly *asymmetric* appearance. asymmetry, N.

atavism   N. resemblance to remote ancestors rather than to parents; reversion to an earlier type; throwback. In his love for gardening, Martin seemed an *atavism* to his Tuscan ancestors who lavished great care on their small plots of soil. atavistic, ADJ.

atheist   N. one who denies the existence of God. "An *atheist* is a man who has no invisible means of support."

atone   v. make amends for; pay for. He knew no way in which he could *atone* for his brutal crime.

atrocity   N. brutal deed. In time of war, many *atrocities* are committed by invading armies.

atrophy   N. wasting away. Polio victims need physiotherapy to prevent the *atrophy* of affected limbs. also v.

attentive   ADJ. alert and watchful; considerate; thoughtful. Spellbound, the *attentive* audience watched the final game of the tennis match, never taking their eyes from the ball. A cold wind sprang up; Stan's *attentive* daughter slipped a sweater over his shoulders without distracting his attention from the game.

■ **attenuate**   v. make thinner; weaken or lessen (in density, force, degree). The long, dry spell *attenuated* the creek to the merest trickle. When a meteor strikes the ground, the initially intense shock *attenuates* or lessens as it diverges outward.

attest   v. testify; bear witness. Having served as a member of a grand jury, I can *attest* that our system of indicting individuals is in need of improvement.

attribute   N. essential quality. His outstanding *attribute* was his kindness.

attribute   v. ascribe; explain. I *attribute* her success in science to the encouragement she received from her parents.

attrition   N. gradual decrease in numbers; reduction in the work force without firing employees; wearing away of opposition by means of harassment. In the 1960s urban churches suffered from *attrition* as members moved from the cities to the suburbs. Rather than fire staff members, church leaders followed a policy of *attrition*, allowing elderly workers to retire without replacing them.

atypical   ADJ. not normal. The child psychiatrist reassured Mrs. Keaton that playing doctor was not *atypical* behavior for a child of young Alex's age. "Perhaps not," she replied, "but charging for house calls is!"

■ **audacious**   ADJ. daring; bold. Audiences cheered as Luke Skywalker and Princess Leia made their *audacious*, death-defying leap to freedom and escaped Darth Vader's troops. audacity, N.

audit   N. examination of accounts. When the bank examiners arrived to hold their annual *audit*, they discovered the embezzlements of the chief cashier. also v.

augment   V. increase; add to. Armies *augment* their forces by calling up reinforcements; teachers *augment* their salaries by taking odd jobs.

augury   N. omen; prophecy. He interpreted the departure of the birds as an *augury* of evil. augur, v.

august   ADJ. impressive; majestic. Visiting the palace at Versailles, she was impressed by the *august* surroundings in which she found herself.

aureole   N. sun's corona; halo. Many medieval paintings depict saintly characters with *aureoles* around their heads.

auroral   ADJ. pertaining to the aurora borealis. The *auroral* display was particularly spectacular that evening.

auspicious   ADJ. favoring success. With favorable weather conditions, it was an *auspicious* moment to set sail. Thomas, however, had doubts about sailing: a paranoid, he became suspicious whenever conditions seemed *auspicious*.

■ **austere**   ADJ. forbiddingly stern; severely simple and unornamented. The headmaster's *austere* demeanor tended to scare off the more timid students, who never visited his study willingly. The room reflected the man, *austere* and bare, like a monk's cell, with no touches of luxury to moderate its *austerity*.

authenticate   V. prove genuine. An expert was needed to *authenticate* the original Van Gogh painting, distinguishing it from its imitation.

authoritarian   ADJ. subordinating the individual to the state; completely dominating another's will. The leaders of the *authoritarian* regime ordered the suppression of the democratic protest movement. After years of submitting to the will of her *authoritarian* father, Elizabeth Barrett ran away from home with the poet Robert Browning.

authoritative   ADJ. having the weight of authority; peremptory and dictatorial. Impressed by the young researcher's well-documented presentation, we accepted her analysis of the experiment as *authoritative*.

autocratic   ADJ. having absolute, unchecked power; dictatorial. A person accustomed to exercising authority may become *autocratic* if his or her power is unchecked. Dictators by definition are *autocrats*. Bosses who dictate behavior as well as letters can be *autocrats* too. autocracy, N.

automaton   N. mechanism that imitates actions of humans. Long before science fiction readers became aware of robots, writers were creating stories of *automatons* who could outperform humans.

■ **autonomous**   ADJ. self-governing. Although the University of California at Berkeley is just one part of the state university system, in many ways Cal Berkeley is *autonomous*, for it runs several programs that are not subject to outside control. autonomy, N.

autopsy   N. examination of a dead body; postmortem. The medical examiner ordered an *autopsy* to determine the cause of death. also v.

auxiliary   ADJ. offering or providing help; additional or subsidiary. To prepare for the emergency, they built an *auxiliary* power station. also N.

avalanche   N. great mass of falling snow and ice. The park ranger warned the skiers to stay on the main trails, where they would be in no danger of being buried beneath a sudden *avalanche*.

avarice   N. greediness for wealth. Montaigne is correct in maintaining that it is not poverty, but rather abundance, that breeds *avarice*: the more shoes Imelda Marcos had, the more she craved.

avenge   V. take vengeance for something (or on behalf of someone). Hamlet vowed he would *avenge* his father's murder and punish Claudius for his horrible crime.

■ **aver**   V. assert confidently or declare; as used in law, state formally as a fact. The self-proclaimed psychic *averred* that, because he had extrasensory perception on which to base his predictions, he needed no seismographs or other gadgets in order to foretell earthquakes.

averse   ADJ. reluctant; disinclined. The reporter was *averse* to revealing the sources of his information.

aversion   N. firm dislike. Bert had an *aversion* to yuppies; Alex had an *aversion* to punks. Their mutal *aversion* was so great that they refused to speak to one another.

avert   V. prevent; turn away. She *averted* her eyes from the dead cat on the highway.

aviary   N. enclosure for birds. The *aviary* at the zoo held nearly 300 birds.

avid   ADJ. greedy; eager for. He was *avid* for learning and read everything he could get. avidity, N.

avocation   N. secondary or minor occupation. His hobby proved to be so fascinating and profitable that gradually he abandoned his regular occupation and concentrated on his *avocation*.

avow   V. declare openly. Lana *avowed* that she never meant to steal Debbie's boyfriend, but no one believed her *avowal* of innocence.

avuncular   ADJ. like an uncle. *Avuncular* pride did not prevent him from noticing his nephew's shortcomings.

awe   N. solemn wonder. The tourists gazed with *awe* at the tremendous expanse of the Grand Canyon.

awl   N. pointed tool used for piercing. She used an *awl* to punch additional holes in the leather belt she had bought.

awry   ADV. distorted; crooked. He held his head *awry*, giving the impression that he had caught cold in his neck during the night. also ADJ.

axiom   N. self-evident truth requiring no proof. The Declaration of Independence records certain self-evident truths or *axioms*, the first of which is "All men are created equal." To Sherlock Holmes, it was *axiomatic* that the little things were infinitely the most important; he based his theory of detection on this obvious truth.

azure   ADJ. sky blue. *Azure* skies are indicative of good weather.

babble   V. chatter idly. The little girl *babbled* about her doll. also N.

bacchanalian   ADJ. drunken. Emperor Nero attended the *bacchanalian* orgy.

badger   V. pester; annoy. She was forced to change her telephone number because she was *badgered* by obscene phone calls.

badinage   N. teasing conversation. Her friends at work greeted the news of her engagement with cheerful *badinage*.

baffle   V. frustrate; perplex. The new code *baffled* the enemy agents.

bait   V. harass; tease. The school bully *baited* the smaller children, terrorizing them.

baleful   ADJ. threatening; menacing; sinister; foreshadowing evil. The bully's *baleful* glare across the classroom warned Tim to expect trouble after school. Blood-red in color, the planet Mars has long been associated with warfare and slaughter because of its ominous, *baleful* appearance.

balk   V. stop short, as if faced with an obstacle, and refuse to continue. The chief of police *balked* at sending his officers into the riot-torn area.

balk   V. foil. When the warden learned that several inmates were planning to escape, he took steps to *balk* their attempt.

ballast   N. heavy substance used to add stability or weight. The ship was listing badly to one side; it was necessary to shift the *ballast* in the hold to get her back on

an even keel. also v.

balm   N. something that relieves pain. Friendship is the finest *balm* for the pangs of disappointed love.

balmy   ADJ. mild; fragrant. A *balmy* breeze refreshed us after the sultry blast.

■ banal   ADJ. hackneyed; commonplace; trite; lacking originality. The hack writer's worn-out clichés made his comic sketch seem *banal*. He even resorted to the *banality* of having someone slip on a banana peel!

bandy   V. discuss lightly or glibly; exchange (words) heatedly. While the president was happy to *bandy* patriotic generalizations with anyone who would listen to him, he refused to *bandy* words with unfriendly reporters at the press conference.

bane   N. curse; cause of ruin. Lucy's little brother was the *bane* of her existence, scribbling on walls with her lipstick and pouring her shampoo down the drain. While some factions praised technology as the mainspring of social progress, others criticized it as the *bane* of modern man, responsible for the tyranny of the machine and the squalor of urban life.

baneful   ADJ. destructive; causing ruin or death. Anointment seems intended to apply the power of natural and supernatural forces to the sick and thus to ward off the *baneful* influences of diseases and of demons.

bantering   ADJ. good-naturedly ridiculing. They resented his *bantering* remarks because they misinterpreted his teasing as sarcasm.

barb   N. sharp projection from fishhook or other object; openly cutting remark. If you were a politician, which would you prefer, being caught on the *barb* of a fishhook or being subjected to malicious verbal *barbs*? Who can blame the president if he's happier fishing than he is listening to his critics' *barbed* remarks?

Test

Word List 5   *Synonyms*

Each of the questions below consists of a word in capital letters, followed by five lettered words or phrases. Choose the lettered word or phrase that is most nearly similar in meaning to the word in capital letters and write the letter of your choice on your answer paper.

61. ASTUTE (A) sheer (B) noisy (C) astral (D) unusual (E) clever
62. ATROCITY (A) endurance (B) fortitude (C) session (D) heinous act (E) hatred
63. ATROPHY (A) capture (B) waste away (C) govern (D) award prize (E) defeat
64. ATTENUATE (A) appear (B) be absent (C) weaken (D) testify (E) soothe
65. ATYPICAL (A) superfluous (B) fortitude (C) unusual (D) clashing (E) lovely
66. AUDACITY (A) boldness (B) asperity (C) strength (D) stature (E) anchorage

67. AUGMENT (A) make noble (B) anoint (C) increase (D) harvest (E) reach
68. AUXILIARY (A) righteous (B) prospective (C) assistant (D) archaic (E) mandatory
69. AVARICE (A) easiness (B) greed (C) statement (D) invoice (E) power
70. AVERT (A) entertain (B) transform (C) turn away (D) lead toward (E) displease
71. AWRY (A) recommended (B) commiserating (C) startled (D) crooked (E) psychological
72. BALEFUL (A) doubtful (B) virtual (C) deadly (D) conventional (E) virtuous
73. BALMY (A) venturesome (B) dedicated (C) mild (D) fanatic (E) memorable
74. BANAL (A) philosophical (B) trite (C) dramatic (D) heedless (E) discussed
75. BANEFUL (A) intellectual (B) thankful (C) decisive (D) poisonous (E) remorseful

Word List 6   bard-bluff

bard N. poet. The ancient *bard* Homer sang of the fall of Troy.

barefaced ADJ. shameless; bold; unconcealed. Shocked by Huck Finn's *barefaced* lies, Miss Watson prayed the good Lord would give him a sense of his unregenerate wickedness.

baroque ADJ. highly ornate. Accustomed to the severe, angular lines of modern skyscrapers, they found the flamboyance of *baroque* architecture amusing.

barrage N. barrier laid down by artillery fire; overwhelming profusion. The company was forced to retreat through the *barrage* of heavy cannons.

barrister N. counselor-at-law. Galsworthy started as a *barrister*, but, when he found the practice of law boring, turned to writing.

barterer N. trader. The *barterer* exchanged trinkets for the natives' furs.

bask V. luxuriate; take pleasure in warmth. *Basking* on the beach, she relaxed so completely that she fell asleep.

bastion N. stronghold; something seen as a source of protection. The villagers fortified the town hall, hoping this improvised *bastion* could protect them from the guerrilla raids.

bate V. let down; restrain. Until it was time to open the presents, the children had to *bate* their curiosity. bated, ADJ.

bauble N. trinket; trifle. The child was delighted with the *bauble* she had won in the grab bag.

bawdy ADJ. indecent; obscene. Jack took offense at Jill's *bawdy* remarks. What kind of young man did she think he was?

beatific ADJ. showing or producing joy; blissful. When Johnny first saw the new puppy, a *beatific* smile spread across his face. In his novel, Waugh praises Limbo, not Heaven: "Limbo is the place. In Limbo one has natural happiness without the *beatific* vision; no harps; no communal order; but wine and conversation and imperfect, various, humanity."

beatify V. bless or sanctify; proclaim someone dead to be one of the blessed. In 1996 Pope John Paul II traveled to Belgium to *beatify* Joseph De Veuster, better known as Father Damien, who died in 1889 after caring for lepers in Hawaii. How can you tell the pope from a cosmetologist? A cosmetologist beautifies someone living; the Pope *beatifies* someone dead.

beatitude N. blessedness; state of bliss. Growing closer to God each day, the mystic achieved a state of indescribable *beatitude*.

bedizen V. dress with vulgar finery. The witch doctors were *bedizened* in their gaudiest costumes.

bedraggle V. wet thoroughly. We were so *bedraggled* by the severe storm that we had to change into dry clothing. bedraggled, ADJ.

beeline N. direct, quick route. As soon as the movie was over, Jim made a *beeline* for the exit.

befuddle V. confuse thoroughly. His attempts to clarify the situation succeeded only in *befuddling* her further.

beget V. father; produce; give rise to. One good turn may deserve another; it does not necessarily *beget* another.

begrudge V. resent. I *begrudge* every minute I have to spend attending meetings.

beguile V. mislead or delude; cheat; pass time. With flattery and big talk of easy money, the con men *beguiled* Kyle into betting his allowance on the shell game. The men quickly *beguiled* poor Kyle of his money. Broke, he *beguiled* himself during the long hours by playing solitaire.

behemoth N. huge creature; something of monstrous size or power. Sportscasters nicknamed the linebacker "The *Behemoth*."

beholden ADJ. obligated; indebted. Since I do not wish to be *beholden* to anyone, I cannot accept this favor.

behoove V. be necessary or proper for; be incumbent upon. Because the interest of the ruler and the ruled are incompatible, it *behooves* the ruler to trust no one; to be suspicious of sycophants; to permit no one to gain undue power or influence; and, above all, to use guile to unearth plots against the throne.

belabor V. explain or go over excessively or to a ridiculous degree; assail verbally. The debate coach warned her student not to bore the audience by *belaboring* his point.

belated ADJ. delayed. He apologized for his *belated* note of condolence to the widow of his friend and explained that he had just learned of her husband's untimely death.

beleaguer V. besiege or attack; harass. The babysitter was surrounded by a crowd of unmanageable brats who relentlessly *beleaguered* her.

■ **belie** V. contradict; give a false impression. His coarse, hard-bitten exterior *belied* his innate sensitivity.

belittle V. disparage; deprecate. Parents should not *belittle* their children's early attempts at drawing, but should encourage their efforts.

bellicose ADJ. warlike; pugnacious; naturally inclined to fight. Someone who is spoiling for a fight is by definition *bellicose*.

belligerent ADJ. quarrelsome. Whenever he had too much to drink, he became *belligerent* and tried to pick fights with strangers. belligerence, N.

bemoan V. lament; express disapproval of. The widow *bemoaned* the death of her beloved husband. Although critics *bemoaned* the serious flaws in the author's novels, each year his latest book topped the best-seller list.

bemused ADJ. confused; lost in thought; preoccupied. Jill studied the garbled instructions with a *bemused* look on her face.

benediction N. blessing. The appearance of the sun after the many rainy days was like a *benediction*.

benefactor N. gift giver; patron. Scrooge later became Tiny Tim's *benefactor* and gave him gifts.

■ **beneficent** ADJ. kindly; doing good. The overgenerous philanthropist had to curb his *beneficent* impulses before he gave away all his money and left himself with nothing.

beneficial ADJ. helpful; useful. Tiny Tim's cheerful good nature had a *beneficial* influence on Scrooge's once-uncharitable disposition.

beneficiary N. person entitled to benefits or proceeds of an insurance policy or will. In Scrooge's will, he made Tiny Tim his *beneficiary*: everything he left would go to young Tim.

benevolent ADJ. generous; charitable. Mr. Fezziwig was a *benevolent* employer who wished to make Christmas merrier for young Scrooge and his other employees. benevolence, N.

benign ADJ. kindly; favorable; not malignant. Though her *benign* smile and gentle bearing made Miss Marple seem a sweet little old lady, in reality she was a tough-minded, shrewd observer of human nature. benignity, N.

benison N. blessing. Let us pray that the *benison* of peace once more shall prevail among the nations of the world.

bent ADJ.; N. determined; natural talent or inclination. *Bent* on advancing in the business world, the secretary-heroine of *Working Girl* had a true *bent* for high finance.

bequeath V. leave to someone by means of a will; hand down. In his will, Father *bequeathed* his watch to Philip; the *bequest* meant a great deal to the boy. bequest, N.

berate V. scold strongly. He feared she would *berate* him for his forgetfulness.

bereavement N. state of being deprived of something valuable or beloved. His friends gathered to console him upon his sudden *bereavement*.

bereft ADJ. deprived of; lacking. The foolish gambler soon found himself *bereft* of funds.

berserk ADV. frenzied. Angered, he went *berserk* and began to wreck the room.

beseech V. beg; plead with. The workaholic executive's wife *beseeched* him to spend more time with their son.

beset V. harass or trouble; hem in. Many vexing problems *beset* the American public school system. Sleeping Beauty's castle was *beset* on all sides by dense thickets that hid it from view.

besiege V. surround with armed forces; harass (with requests). When the bandits *besieged* the village, the villagers holed up in the town hall and prepared to withstand a long siege. Members of the new administration were *besieged* with job applications from people who had worked on the campaign.

besmirch V. soil, defile. The scandalous remarks in the newspaper *besmirch* the reputations of every member of the society.

bestial ADJ. beastlike; brutal; inhuman. According to legend, the werewolf was able to abandon its human shape and assume a *bestial* form. The Red Cross sought to put an end to the *bestial* treatment of prisoners of war.

bestow V. confer. He wished to *bestow* great honors upon the hero.

betoken V. signify; indicate. The well-equipped docks, tall piles of cargo containers, and numerous vessels being loaded all *betoken* Oakland's importance as a port.

betray V. be unfaithful; reveal (unconsciously or unwillingly). The spy *betrayed* his country by selling military secrets to the enemy. When he was taken in for questioning, the tightness of his lips *betrayed* his fear of incriminating himself. betrayal, N.

betroth V. become engaged to marry. The announcement that they had become *betrothed* surprised their friends who had not suspected any romance. betrothal, N.

bevy N. large group. The movie actor was surrounded by a *bevy* of starlets.

bicameral ADJ. two-chambered, as a legislative body. The United States Congress is a *bicameral* body.

bicker V. quarrel. The children *bickered* morning, noon and night, exasperating their parents.

biennial ADJ. every two years. Seeing no need to meet more frequently, the group held *biennial* meetings instead of annual ones. Plants that bear flowers *biennially* are known as *biennials*.

bifurcated ADJ. divided into two branches; forked. With a *bifurcated* branch and a piece of elastic rubber, he made a crude but effective slingshot.

bigotry N. stubborn intolerance. Brought up in a democratic atmosphere, the student was shocked by the *bigotry* and narrowness expressed by several of his classmates.

bilious ADJ. suffering from a liver complaint; peevishly ill humored. If your tummy's feeling *bilious*, try Carter's Little Liver Pills for fast relief. British linguistic purists regard Americanisms with a *bilious* eye, pouncing on each supposed barbarism viciously.

bilk V. swindle; cheat. The con man specialized in *bilking* insurance companies.

billowing ADJ. swelling out in waves; surging. Standing over the air vent, Marilyn Monroe tried vainly to control her *billowing* skirts.

bivouac N. temporary encampment. While in *bivouac*, we spent the night in our sleeping bags under the stars. also V.

bizarre ADJ. fantastic; violently contrasting. The plot of the novel was too *bizarre* to be believed.

blanch V. bleach; whiten. Although age had *blanched* his hair, he was still vigorous and energetic.

bland ADJ. soothing or mild; agreeable. Jill tried a *bland* ointment for her sunburn. However, when Jack absent-mindedly patted her on the sunburned shoulder, she couldn't maintain her *bland* persona. blandness, N.

blandish V. cajole; coax with flattery. Despite all their sweet-talking, Suzi and Cher were unable to *blandish* the doorman into letting them into the hot new club.

blandishment N. flattery. Despite the salesperson's *blandishments*, the customer did not buy the outfit.

blare N. loud, harsh roar or screech; dazzling blaze of light. I don't know which is worse: the steady *blare* of a boom box deafening your ears or a sudden *blare* of flashbulbs dazzling your eyes. also v.

blasé ADJ. bored with pleasure or dissipation. Although Beth was as thrilled with the idea of a trip to Paris as her classmates were, she tried to act supercool and *blasé*, as if she'd been abroad hundreds of times.

blasphemy N. irreverence; sacrilege; cursing. In my father's house, the Dodgers were the holiest of holies; to cheer for another team was to utter words of *blasphemy*. blasphemous, ADJ.

blatant ADJ. extremely obvious; loudly offensive. Caught in a *blatant* lie, the scoundrel had only one regret: he wished that he had lied more subtly. blatancy, N.

bleak ADJ. cold or cheerless; unlikely to be favorable. The frigid, inhospitable Aleutian Islands are *bleak* military outposts. It's no wonder that soldiers assigned there have a *bleak* attitude toward their posting.

blighted ADJ. suffering from a disease; destroyed. The extent of the *blighted* areas could be seen only when viewed from the air.

blithe ADJ. carefree and unconcerned (perhaps foolishly so); cheerful and gay. Micawber's *blithe* optimism that something would turn up proved unfounded, and he wound up in debtors' prison. Marie Antoinette's famous remark, "Let them eat cake!" epitomizes her *blithe* ignorance of the harsh realities endured by the common people.

bloated ADJ. swollen or puffed as with water or air. Her *bloated* stomach came from drinking so much water.

blowhard N. talkative boaster. After all Sol's talk about his big show business connections led nowhere, Sally decided he was just another *blowhard*.

bludgeon N. club; heavy-headed weapon. Attacked by Dr. Moriarty, Holmes used his walking stick as a *bludgeon* to defend himself. "Watson," he said. "I fear I may have *bludgeoned* Moriarty to death."

bluff ADJ. rough but good-natured. Jack had a *bluff* and hearty manner that belied his actual sensitivity; he never let people know how thin-skinned he really was.

bluff N. pretense (of strength); deception; high cliff. Claire thought Lord Byron's boast that he would swim the Hellespont was just a *bluff*; she was astounded when he dove from the high *bluff* into the waters below.

Test

Word List 6   *Antonyms*

Each of the questions below consists of a word in capital letters, followed by five lettered words or phrases. Choose the lettered word or phrase that is most nearly opposite in meaning to the word in capital letters and write the letter of your choice on your answer paper.

76. BAROQUE (A) polished (B) constant
    (C) transformed (D) simple (E) aglow
77. BEATIFIC (A) glorious (B) dreadful (C) theatrical
    (D) crooked (E) handsome
78. BELITTLE (A) disobey (B) forget (C) magnify
    (D) extol (E) envy
79. BELLICOSE (A) peaceful (B) naval (C) amusing
    (D) piecemeal (E) errant
80. BENIGN (A) tenfold (B) peaceful (C) blessed
    (D) wavering (E) malignant
81. BENISON (A) curse (B) bachelor (C) wedding
    (D) orgy (E) tragedy

82. BERATE (A) grant (B) praise (C) refer
    (D) purchase (E) deny
83. BESTIAL (A) animated (B) noble (C) zoological
    (D) clear (E) dusky
84. BIGOTRY (A) arrogance (B) approval
    (C) mourning (D) promptness (E) tolerance
85. BIZARRE (A) roomy (B) veiled (C) subdued
    (D) triumphant (E) normal
86. BLANCH (A) bleach (B) scatter (C) darken
    (D) analyze (E) subdivide
87. BLAND (A) caustic (B) meager (C) soft
    (D) uncooked (E) helpless
88. BLASÉ (A) fiery (B) clever (C) intriguing
    (D) slim (E) ardent
89. BLEAK (A) pale (B) sudden (C) dry (D) narrow
    (E) cheerful
90. BLITHE (A) spiritual (B) profuse (C) cheerless
    (D) hybrid (E) comfortable

Word List 7   blunder-canter

blunder N. error. The criminal's fatal *blunder* led to his capture. also v.

blurt V. utter impulsively. Before she could stop him, he *blurted* out the news.

bluster V. blow in heavy gusts; threaten emptily; bully. "Let the stormy winds *bluster*," cried Jack, "we'll set sail tonight." Jill let Jack *bluster*: she wasn't going anywhere, no matter what he said. also N.

bode V. foreshadow; portend. The gloomy skies and the sulfurous odors from the mineral springs seemed to *bode* evil to those who settled in the area.

bogus ADJ. counterfiet; not authentic. The police quickly found the distributors of the *bogus* twenty-dollar bills.

bohemian ADJ. unconventional (in an artistic way). Gertrude Stein ran off to Paris to live an eccentric, *bohemian* life with her writer friends. Oakland was not *bohemian*: it was too bourgeois, too middle-class.

boisterous ADJ. violent; rough; noisy. The unruly crowd became even more *boisterous* when he tried to quiet them.

■ **bolster** V. support; reinforce. The debaters amassed file boxes full of evidence to *bolster* their arguments.

bolt N. door bar; fastening pin or screw; length of fabric. The carpenter shut the workshop door, sliding the heavy metal *bolt* into place. He sorted through his toolbox for the nuts and *bolts* and nails required for the job. Before he cut into the *bolt* of canvas, he measured how much fabric he would need.

bolt V. dash or dart off; fasten (a door); gobble down. Jack was set to *bolt* out the front door, but Jill *bolted* the door. "Eat your breakfast," she said, "don't *bolt* your food."

bombardment N. attack (as with missiles). The enemy *bombardment* demolished the town. Members of the opposition party *bombarded* the prime minister with questions about the enemy attack.

■ **bombastic** ADJ. pompous; using inflated language. Puffed up with conceit, the orator spoke in such a *bombastic* manner that we longed to deflate him. bombast, N.

boon N. blessing; benefit. The recent rains that filled our empty reservoirs were a *boon* to the whole community.

■ **boorish** ADJ. rude; insensitive. Though Mr. Potts constantly interrupted his wife, she ignored his *boorish* behavior, for she had lost hope of teaching him courtesy.

bouillon N. clear beef soup. The cup of *bouillon* served by the stewards was welcomed by those who had been chilled by the cold ocean breezes.

bountiful ADJ. abundant; graciously generous. Thanks to the good harvest, we had a *bountiful* supply of food and we could be as *bountiful* as we liked in distributing food to the needy.

bourgeois ADJ. middle class; selfishly materialistic; dully conventional. Technically, anyone who belongs to the middle class is *bourgeois*, but, given the word's connotations, most people resent it if you call them that.

bovine ADJ. cowlike; placid and dull. Nothing excites Esther; even when she won the state lottery, she still preserved her air of *bovine* calm.

bowdlerize V. expurgate. After the film editors had *bowdlerized* the language in the script, the motion picture's rating was changed from "R" to "PG."

boycott V. refrain from buying or using. To put pressure on grape growers to stop using pesticides that harmed the farm workers' health, Cesar Chavez called for consumers to *boycott* grapes. also N.

brackish ADJ. somewhat saline. He found the only wells in the area were *brackish*; drinking the water made him nauseous.

braggadocio N. boasting. He was disliked because his manner was always full of *braggadocio*.

braggart N. boaster. Modest by nature, she was no *braggart*, preferring to let her accomplishments speak for themselves.

brandish V. wave around; flourish. Alarmed, Doctor Watson wildly *brandished* his gun until Holmes told him to put the thing away before he shot himself.

bravado N. swagger; assumed air of defiance. The *bravado* of the young criminal disappeared when he was confronted by the victims of his brutal attack.

brawn N. muscular strength; sturdiness. It takes *brawn* to become a champion weight-lifter. brawny, ADJ.

brazen ADJ. insolent. Her *brazen* contempt for authority angered the officials.

breach N. breaking of contract or duty; fissure or gap. Jill sued Jack for *breach* of promise, claiming he had broken their engagement. The attackers found a *breach* in the enemy's fortifications and penetrated their lines. also V.

breadth N. width; extent. We were impressed by the *breadth* of her knowledge.

brevity N. conciseness. *Brevity* is essential when you send a telegram or cablegram; you are charged for every word.

brindled ADJ. tawny or grayish with streaks or spots. He was disappointed in the litter because the puppies were *brindled*; he had hoped for animals of a uniform color.

bristling ADJ. rising like bristles; showing irritation. The dog stood there, *bristling* with anger.

brittle ADJ. easily broken; difficult. My employer's *brittle* personality made it difficult for me to get along with her.

broach V. introduce; open up. Jack did not even try to *broach* the subject of religion with his in-laws. If you *broach* a touchy subject, the result may be a *breach*.

brocade N. rich, figured fabric. The sofa was covered with expensive *brocade*.

brochure N. pamphlet. This *brochure* of farming was issued by the Department of Agriculture.

brooch N. ornamental clasp. She treasured the *brooch* because it was an heirloom.

brook V. tolerate; endure. The dean would *brook* no interference with his disciplinary actions. (secondary meaning)

browbeat V. bully; intimidate. Billy resisted Ted's attempts to *browbeat* him into handing over his lunch money.

browse V. graze; skim or glance at casually. "How now, brown cow, *browsing* in the green, green grass." I remember lines of verse that I came across while *browsing* through the poetry section of the local bookstore.

brunt N. main impact or shock. Tom Sawyer claimed credit for painting the fence, but the *brunt* of the work fell on others. However, Tom bore the *brunt* of Aunt Polly's complaints when the paint began to peel.

brusque ADJ. blunt; abrupt. She was offended by his *brusque* reply.

buccaneer N. pirate. At Disneyland the Pirates of the Caribbean sing a song about their lives as bloody *buccaneers*.

bucolic ADJ. rustic; pastoral. Filled with browsing cows and bleating sheep, the meadow was a charmingly *bucolic* sight.

buffet N. table with food set out for people to serve themselves; meal at which people help themselves to food that's been set out. (*Buffet* rhymes with *tray*.) Please convey the soufflé on the tray to the *buffet*.

buffet V. slap; batter; knock about. To *buffet* something is to rough it up. (*Buffet* rhymes with *Muffett*.) Was Miss Muffett *buffeted* by the crowd on the way to the buffet tray?

buffoonery N. clowning. In the Ace Ventura movies, Jim Carrey's *buffoonery* was hilarious: like Bozo the Clown, he's a natural *buffoon*.

bugaboo N. bugbear; object of baseless terror. If we become frightened by such *bugaboos*, we are no wiser than the birds who fear scarecrows.

bullion N. gold and silver in the form of bars. Much *bullion* is stored in the vaults at Fort Knox.

bulwark N. earthwork or other strong defense; person who defends. The navy is our principal *bulwark* against invasion.

bungle V. mismanage; blunder. Don't botch this assignment, Bumstead; if you *bungle* the job, you're fired!

buoyant ADJ. able to float; cheerful and optimistic. When the boat capsized, her *buoyant* life jacket kept Jody afloat. Scrambling back on board, she was still in a *buoyant* mood, certain that despite the delay she'd win the race. buoyancy, N.

bureaucracy N. overregulated administrative system marked by red tape. The Internal Revenue Service is the ultimate *bureaucracy*: taxpayers wasted so much paper filling out IRS forms that the IRS *bureaucrats* printed up a new set of rules requiring taxpayers to comply with the Paperwork Reduction Act. bureaucratic, ADJ.

■ **burgeon** V. grow forth; send out buds. In the spring, the plants that *burgeon* are a promise of the beauty that is to come.

burlesque V. give an imitation that ridicules. In *Galaxy Quest*, Alan Rickman *burlesques* Mr. Spock of *Star Trek*, outrageously parodying Spock's unemotional manner and stiff bearing. also N.

■ **burnish** V. make shiny by rubbing; polish. The maid *burnished* the brass fixtures until they reflected the lamplight.

■ **buttress** V. support; prop up. Just as architects *buttress* the walls of cathedrals with flying *buttresses*, debaters *buttress* their arguments with facts. also N.

buxom ADJ. full-bosomed; plump; jolly. High-fashion models usually are slender rather than *buxom*.

cabal N. small group of persons secretly united to promote their own interests. The *cabal* was defeated when its scheme was discovered.

cache N. hiding place. The detectives followed the suspect until he led them to the *cache* where he had stored his loot. also V.

■ **cacophonous** ADJ. discordant; inharmonious. Do the students in the orchestra enjoy the *cacophonous* sounds they make when they're tuning up? I don't know how they can stand the racket. cacophony, N.

cadaver N. corpse. In some states, it is illegal to dissect *cadavers*.

cadaverous ADJ. like a corpse; pale. From his *cadaverous* appearance, we could see how the disease had ravaged him.

cadence N. rhythmic rise and fall (of words or sounds); beat. Marching down the road, the troops sang out, following the *cadence* set by the sergeant.

cadge V. beg; mooch; panhandle. While his car was in the shop, Bob had to *cadge* a ride to work each day. Unwilling to be a complete moocher, however, he offered to pay for the gas.

cajole V. coax; wheedle. Cher tried to *cajole* her father into letting her drive the family car. cajolery, N.

calamity N. disaster; misery. As news of the *calamity* spread, offers of relief poured in to the stricken community.

calculated ADJ. deliberately planned; likely. Lexy's choice of clothes to wear to the debate tournament was carefully *calculated*. Her conventional suit was *calculated* to appeal to the conservative judges.

caldron N. large kettle. "Why, Mr. Crusoe," said the savage heating the giant *caldron*, "we'd love to have you for dinner!"

caliber N. ability; quality. Einstein's cleaning the blackboards again? Albert, quit it! A man of your *caliber* shouldn't have to do such menial tasks.

calligraphy N. beautiful writing; excellent penmanship. As we examine ancient manuscripts, we become impressed with the *calligraphy* of the scribes.

callous ADJ. hardened; unfeeling. He had worked in the hospital for so many years that he was *callous* to the suffering in the wards. callus, N.

callow ADJ. youthful; immature; inexperienced. As a freshman, Jack was sure he was a man of the world; as a sophomore, he made fun of freshmen as *callow* youths. In both cases, his judgment showed just how *callow* he was.

calorific ADJ. heat-producing. Coal is much more *calorific* than green wood.

calumny N. malicious misrepresentation; slander. He could endure his financial failure, but he could not bear the *calumny* that his foes heaped upon him. According to Herodotus, someone *calumniated* is doubly injured, first by the person who utters the *calumny*, and then by the person who believes the slander.

camaraderie N. good-fellowship. What he loved best about his job was the sense of *camaraderie* he and his coworkers shared.

cameo N. shell or jewel carved in relief; star's special appearance in a minor role in a film. Don't bother buying *cameos* from the street peddlers in Rome: the carvings they sell are clumsy jobs. Did you enjoy Bill Murray's *cameo* in *Little Shop of Horrors*? He was onscreen for only a minute, but he cracked me up.

camouflage v. disguise; conceal. In order to rescue Han Solo, Princess Leia *camouflaged* herself in the helmet and cloak of a space bandit. also N.

canard N. false or unfounded story; fabricated report. Rather than becoming upset by the *National Enquirer* story about Tony's supposed infidelity, Tina refused to take the *canard* seriously. To call a lying tale a base *canard* or a vile *canard* is to descend to a cliché.

candor N. frankness; open honesty. Jack can carry *candor* too far: when he told Jill his honest opinion of her, she nearly slapped his face. candid, ADJ.

canine ADJ. related to dogs; doglike. Some days the *canine* population of Berkeley seems almost to outnumber the human population.

canker N. any ulcerous sore; any evil. Poverty is a *canker* in the body politic; it must be cured.

canny ADJ. shrewd; thrifty. The *canny* Scotsman was more than a match for the swindlers.

canon N. collection or authoritative list of books (e.g., by an author, or accepted as scripture). Scholars hotly debated whether the newly discovered sonnet should be accepted as part of the Shakespearean *canon*.

canon N. rule or principle, frequently religious. "One catastrophe, one locality, one day"—these are Aristotle's rules for tragedy, and classic French plays strictly follow them; Shakespeare, however, disregards all these *canons*. A born rebel, Katya was constitutionally incapable of abiding by the *canons* of polite society.

cant N. insincere expressions of piety; jargon of thieves. Shocked by news of the minister's extramarital love affairs, the worshippers dismissed his talk about the sacredness of marriage as mere *cant*. *Cant* is a form of hypocrisy: those who can, pray; those who *cant*, pretend.

cantankerous ADJ. ill-humored; irritable. Constantly complaining about his treatment and refusing to cooperate with the hospital staff, he was a *cantankerous* patient.

cantata N. story set to music, to be sung by a chorus. The choral society sang the new *cantata* composed by its leader.

canter N. slow gallop. Because the racehorse had outdistanced its competition so easily, the reporter wrote that the race was won in a *canter*. also v.

Test

Word List 7 *Synonyms*

Each of the questions below consists of a word in capital letters, followed by five lettered words or phrases. Choose the lettered word or phrase that is most nearly similar in meaning to the word in capital letters and write the letter of your choice on your answer paper.

91. BOISTEROUS (A) conflicting (B) noisy (C) testimonial (D) grateful (E) adolescent
92. BOMBASTIC (A) sensitive (B) pompous (C) rapid (D) sufficient (E) expensive
93. BOORISH (A) brave (B) oafish (C) romantic (D) speedy (E) dry
94. BOUILLON (A) insight (B) chowder (C) gold (D) clear soup (E) stew
95. BRACKISH (A) careful (B) salty (C) chosen (D) tough (E) wet
96. BRAGGADOCIO (A) weaponry (B) boasting (C) skirmish (D) encounter (E) position
97. BRAZEN (A) shameless (B) quick (C) modest (D) pleasant (E) melodramatic
98. BRINDLED (A) equine (B) pathetic (C) hasty (D) spotted (E) mild tasting
99. BROCHURE (A) opening (B) pamphlet (C) censor (D) bureau (E) pin
100. BUCOLIC (A) diseased (B) repulsive (C) rustic (D) twinkling (E) cold
101. BUXOM (A) voluminous (B) indecisive (C) convincing (D) plump (E) bookish
102. CACHE (A) lock (B) hiding place (C) tide (D) automobile (E) grappling hook
103. CACOPHONY (A) discord (B) dance (C) applause (D) type of telephone (E) rooster
104. CALLOW (A) youthful (B) holy (C) mild (D) colored (E) seated
105. CANDID (A) vague (B) outspoken (C) experienced (D) anxious (E) sallow

Word List 8 canto-chameleon

canto N. division of a long poem. Dante's poetic masterpiece *The Divine Comedy* is divided into *cantos*.

canvass v. determine or seek opinions, votes, etc. After *canvassing* the sentiments of his constituents, the congressman was confident that he represented the majority opinion of his district. also N.

capacious ADJ. spacious. In the *capacious* areas of the railroad terminal, thousands of travelers lingered while waiting for their trains.

capacity N. mental or physical ability; role; ability to accommodate. Mike had the *capacity* to handle several jobs at once. In his *capacity* as president of SelecTronics he marketed an electronic dictionary with a *capacity* of 200,000 words.

capillary ADJ. having a very fine bore. The changes in surface tension of liquids in *capillary* vessels is of special interest to physicists. also N.

capitulate V. surrender. The enemy was warned to *capitulate* or face annihilation.

caprice N. whim. She was an unpredictable creature, acting on *caprice*, never taking thought of the consequences.

■ **capricious** ADJ. unpredictable; fickle. The storm was *capricious*: it changed course constantly. Jill was *capricious*, too: she changed boyfriends almost as often as she changed clothes.

caption N. title; chapter heading; text under illustration. The *captions* that accompany *The Far Side* cartoons are almost as funny as the pictures. also V.

captious ADJ. faultfinding. His criticisms were always *captious* and frivolous, never offering constructive suggestions.

carafe N. glass water bottle; decanter. With each dinner, the patron receives a *carafe* of red or white wine.

carapace N. shell covering the back (of a turtle, crab, etc.). At the children's zoo, Richard perched on top of the giant turtle's hard *carapace* as the creature slowly made its way around the enclosure.

carat N. unit of weight for precious stones; measure of fineness of gold. He gave her a diamond that weighed three *carats* and was mounted in an eighteen-*carat* gold band.

carcinogenic ADJ. causing cancer. Many supposedly harmless substances have been revealed to be *carcinogenic*.

cardinal ADJ. chief. If you want to increase your word power, the *cardinal* rule of vocabulary-building is to read.

cardiologist N. doctor specializing in ailments of the heart. When the pediatrician noticed Philip had a slight heart murmur, she referred him to a *cardiologist* for further tests.

careen V. lurch; sway from side to side. The taxicab *careened* wildly as it rounded the corner.

caricature N. distortion; burlesque. The *caricatures* he drew always emphasized personal weaknesses of the people he burlesqued. also V.

carillon N. a set of bells capable of being played. The *carillon* in the bell tower of the Coca-Cola pavilion at the New York World's Fair provided musical entertainment every hour.

carnage N. destruction of life. The film *The Killing Fields* vividly depicts the *carnage* wreaked by Pol Pot's followers in Cambodia.

carnal ADJ. fleshly. Is the public more interested in *carnal* pleasures than in spiritual matters? Compare the number of people who read *Playboy* daily to the number of those who read the Bible every day.

carnivorous ADJ. meat-eating. The lion's a *carnivorous* beast; a hunk of meat makes up his feast. A cow is not a *carnivore*; she likes the taste of grain, not gore.

carousal N. drunken revel. Once the beer-chugging contests started, the drinking got out of control, and the party degenerated into an ugly *carousal*.

carping N. petty criticism; fault-finding. Welcoming constructive criticism, Lexy appreciated her editor's comments, finding them free of *carping*. also ADJ.

carrion N. rotting flesh of a dead body. Buzzards are nature's scavengers; they eat the *carrion* left behind by other predators.

cartographer N. map-maker. Though not a professional *cartographer*, Tolkien was able to construct a map of his fictional world.

cascade N. small waterfall. We were too tired to appreciate the beauty of the many *cascades* because we had to detour around them to avoid being drenched by the torrents *cascading* down.

caste N. one of the hereditary classes in Hindu society; social stratification; prestige. The differences created by *caste* in India must be wiped out if true democracy is to prevail in that country.

■ **castigation** N. punishment; severe criticism. Sensitive even to mild criticism, Woolf could not bear the *castigation* that she found in certain reviews. Ben Jonson was a highly moral playwright: in his plays, his purpose was to *castigate* vice and hypocrisy by exposing them publicly.

casualty N. serious or fatal accident. The number of automotive *casualties* on this holiday weekend was high.

cataclysm N. deluge; upheaval. A *cataclysm* such as the French Revolution affects all countries. cataclysmic, ADJ.

■ **catalyst** N. agent that influences the pace of a chemical reaction while it remains unaffected and unchanged; person or thing that causes action. After a banana is harvested, certain enzymes within its cells continue to act as a *catalyst* for the biochemical processes of ripening, thereby causing the banana eventually to rot. In 1969 the IRA split into two factions: the "officials," who advocated a united socialist Ireland but disavowed terrorist activities, and the "provisionals," who argued that terrorism was a necessary *catalyst* for unification.

catapult N. slingshot; hurling machine. Airplanes are sometimes launched from battleships by *catapults*. also V.

cataract N. great waterfall; eye abnormality. She gazed with awe at the mighty *cataract* known as Niagara Falls.

catastrophe N. calamity; disaster. The 1906 San Francisco earthquake was a *catastrophe* that destroyed most of the city. A similar earthquake striking today could have even more *catastrophic* results.

catcall N. shout of disapproval; boo. Every major league pitcher has off days during which he must learn to ignore *catcalls* and angry hisses from the crowd.

catechism N. book for religious instruction; instruction by question and answer. He taught by engaging his pupils in a *catechism* until they gave him the correct answer.

categorical ADJ. without exceptions; unqualified; absolute. Though the captain claimed he was never, never sick at sea, he finally qualified his *categorical* denial: he was "hardly ever" sick at sea.

catharsis N. purging or cleansing of any passage of the body. Aristotle maintained that tragedy created a *catharsis* by purging the soul of base concepts.

cathartic N. purgative. Some drugs act as laxatives when taken in small doses but act as *cathartics* when taken in much larger doses. also ADJ.

catholic ADJ. universal; wide-ranging liberal. He was extremely *catholic* in his taste and read everything he could find in the library.

caucus N. private meeting of members of a party to select officers or determine policy. At the opening of Congress the members of the Democratic Party held a *caucus* to elect the majority leader of the House and the party whip.

caulk V. to make watertight (by plugging seams). When water from the shower leaked into the basement, we knew it was time to *caulk* the tiles at the edges of the shower stall.

causal ADJ. implying a cause-and-effect relationship. The psychologist maintained there was a *causal* relationship between the nature of one's early childhood experiences and one's adult personality. causality, N.

■ **caustic** ADJ. burning; sarcastically biting. The critic's *caustic* remarks angered the hapless actors who were the subjects of his sarcasm.

cauterize V. burn with hot iron or caustic. In order to prevent infection, the doctor *cauterized* the wound.

cavalcade N. procession; parade. As described by Chaucer, the *cavalcade* of Canterbury pilgrims was a motley group.

cavalier ADJ. casual and offhand; arrogant. Sensitive about having her ideas taken lightly, Marcia felt insulted by Mark's *cavalier* dismissal of her suggestion.

cavil V. make frivolous objections. I respect your sensible criticisms, but I dislike the way you *cavil* about unimportant details. also N.

cede V. yield (title, territory) to; surrender formally. Eventually the descendants of England's Henry II were forced to *cede* their French territories to the King of France. cession, N.

celerity N. speed; rapidity. Hamlet resented his mother's *celerity* in remarrying within a month after his father's death.

celestial ADJ. heavenly. She spoke of the *celestial* joys that awaited virtuous souls in the hereafter.

celibate ADJ. abstaining from sexual intercourse; unmarried. Though the late Havelock Ellis wrote extensively about sexual customs and was considered an expert in such matters, recent studies maintain he was *celibate* throughout his life. celibacy, N.

censor N. overseer of morals; person who eliminates inappropriate matter. Soldiers dislike having their mail read by a *censor* but understand the need for this precaution. also V.

censorious ADJ. critical. *Censorious* people delight in casting blame.

censure V. blame; criticize. The senator was *censured* for behavior inappropriate to a member of Congress. also N.

centaur N. mythical figure, half man and half horse. I was particularly impressed by the statue of the *centaur* in the Roman Hall of the museum.

centigrade ADJ. denoting a widely used temperature scale (basically same as Celsius). On the *centigrade* thermometer, the freezing point of water is zero degrees.

centrifugal ADJ. radiating; departing from the center. Many automatic drying machines remove excess moisture from clothing by *centrifugal* force.

centrifuge N. machine that separates substances by whirling them. At the dairy, we employ a *centrifuge* to separate cream from milk. also V.

centripetal ADJ. tending toward the center. Does *centripetal* force or the force of gravity bring orbiting bodies to the earth's surface?

centurion N. Roman army officer. Because he was in command of a company of one hundred soldiers, he was called a *centurion*.

cerebral ADJ. pertaining to the brain or intellect. The content of philosophical works is *cerebral* in nature and requires much thought.

cerebration N. thought. Mathematics problems sometimes require much *cerebration*.

ceremonious ADJ. marked by formality. Ordinary dress would be inappropriate at so *ceremonious* an affair.

certitude N. certainty. Though there was no *certitude* of his getting the job, Lou thought he had a good chance of being hired.

cessation N. stoppage. The airline's employees threatened a *cessation* of all work if management failed to meet their demands. cease, V.

cession N. yielding (something) to another; ceding. The Battle of Lake Erie, a major U.S. naval victory in the War of 1812, ensured U.S. control over Lake Erie and ruled out any territorial *cession* in the Northwest to Great Britain in the peace settlement.

chafe V. warm by rubbing; make sore (by rubbing). Chilled, he *chafed* his hands before the fire. The collar of his school uniform *chafed* Tom's neck, but not as much the school's strict rules *chafed* his spirit. also N.

chaff N. worthless products of an endeavor. When you separate the wheat from the *chaff*, be sure you throw out the *chaff*.

chaffing ADJ. bantering; joking. Sometimes Chad's flippant, *chaffing* remarks annoy us. Still, Chad's *chaffing* keeps us laughing.

chagrin N. vexation (caused by humiliation or injured pride); disappointment. Embarrassed by his parents' shabby, working-class appearance, Doug felt their visit to his school would bring him nothing but *chagrin*. A person filled with *chagrin* doesn't grin: he's too mortified.

chalice N. goblet; consecrated cup. In a small room adjoining the cathedral, many ornately decorated *chalices* made by the most famous European goldsmiths were on display.

chameleon N. lizard that changes color in different situations. Like the *chameleon*, he assumed the political coloration of every group he met.

Test

Word List 8   *Antonyms*

Each of the questions below consists of a word in capital letters, followed by five lettered words or phrases. Choose the lettered word or phrase that is most nearly opposite in meaning to the word in capital letters and write the letter of your choice on your answer paper.

106. CAPACIOUS (A) warlike (B) cordial (C) curious (D) not spacious (E) not capable

107. CAPRICIOUS (A) satisfied (B) insured (C) photographic (D) scattered (E) steadfast

108. CAPTIOUS (A) tolerant (B) capable (C) frivolous (D) winning (E) recollected

109. CARNAL (A) impressive (B) minute (C) spiritual (D) actual (E) private

110. CARNIVOROUS (A) gloomy (B) tangential (C) productive (D) weak (E) vegetarian

111. CARPING (A) rapid (B) uncritical (C) unintellectual (D) illegal (E) terse

112. CASTIGATION (A) commendation (B) patience (C) generosity (D) understatement (E) honesty

113. CATEGORICAL (A) negative (B) ironic (C) impartial (D) qualified (E) permanent

114. CATHOLIC (A) religious (B) pacific (C) narrow (D) weighty (E) funny

115. CELERITY (A) assurance (B) state (C) acerbity (D) delay (E) infamy

116. CELIBATE (A) investing (B) married (C) retired (D) commodious (E) dubious

117. CENSURE (A) process (B) enclose (C) interest (D) praise (E) penetrate

118. CENTRIFUGAL (A) centripetal (B) ephemeral (C) lasting (D) barometric (E) algebraic

119. CESSATION (A) premium (B) gravity (C) beginning (D) composition (E) apathy

120. CHAFFING (A) achieving (B) serious (C) capitalistic (D) sneezing (E) expensive

Word List 9   champion–colander

champion   v. support militantly. Martin Luther King, Jr., won the Nobel Peace Prize because he *championed* the oppressed in their struggle for equality. also N.

chaotic   ADJ. in utter disorder. He tried to bring order into the *chaotic* state of affairs. chaos, N.

charisma   N. divine gift; great popular charm or appeal. Political commentators have deplored the importance of a candidate's *charisma* in these days of television campaigning.

charlatan   N. quack; pretender to knowledge. When they realized that the Wizard didn't know how to get them back to Kansas, Dorothy and her friends were sure they'd been duped by a *charlatan*.

chary   ADJ. cautious; sparing or restrained about giving. A prudent, thrifty New Englander, DeWitt was as *chary* of investing money in junk bonds as he was *chary* of paying people unnecessary compliments.

chase   v. ornament a metal surface by indenting. With his hammer, he carefully *chased* an intricate design onto the surface of the chalice. (secondary meaning)

chasm   N. abyss. They could not see the bottom of the *chasm*.

chassis   N. framework and working parts of an automobile. Examining the car after the accident, the owner discovered that the body had been ruined but that the *chassis* was unharmed.

chaste   ADJ. pure; virginal; modest. To ensure that his bride would stay *chaste* while he was off to the wars, the crusader had her fitted out with a *chastity* belt. chastity, N.

chasten   v. correct by punishment or scolding; restrain. No matter how much a child deserves to be *chastened* for doing wrong, the maxim "Spare the rod and spoil the child" never justifies physical abuse. Someone sadder but wiser has been *chastened* or subdued by experience.

chastened   ADJ. humbled; subdued; rebuked. After a series of meddlesome and unsuccessful attempts at matchmaking among her friends, a *chastened* Emma finds her destiny in marriage to her protective neighbor George Knightley, long her mentor and friend.

chastise   v. punish or scold; reprimand. Miss Watson liked nothing better than to *chastise* Huck for his alleged offenses.

chauvinist   N. blindly devoted patriot; zealous adherent of a group or cause. A *chauvinist* cannot recognize any faults in his country, no matter how flagrant they may be. Likewise, a male *chauvinist* cannot recognize how biased he is in favor of his own sex, no matter how flagrant that bias may be. chauvinistic, ADJ.

check   v. stop motion; curb or restrain. Thrusting out her arm, Grandma *checked* Bobby's lunge at his sister. "Young man," she said, "you'd better *check* your temper." (secondary meaning)

checkered   ADJ. marked by changes in fortune. During his *checkered* career he had lived in palatial mansions and in dreary boardinghouses.

cherubic   ADJ. angelic; innocent-looking. With her cheerful smile and rosy cheeks, she was a particularly *cherubic* child.

■ **chicanery** N. trickery; deception. Those sneaky lawyers misrepresented what occurred, made up all sorts of implausible alternative scenarios to confuse the jurors, and in general depended on *chicanery* to win the case.

chide V. scold. Grandma began to *chide* Steven for his lying.

chimerical ADJ. fantastically improbable; highly unrealistic; imaginative. As everyone expected, Ted's *chimerical* scheme to make a fortune by raising ermines in his backyard proved a dismal failure. chimera, N.

chisel N. wedgelike tool for cutting. With his hammer and *chisel*, the sculptor chipped away at the block of marble.

chisel V. swindle or cheat; cut with a chisel. That crook *chiseled* me out of a hundred dollars when he sold me that "marble" statue he'd *chiseled* out of some cheap hunk of rock.

chivalrous ADJ. courteous; faithful; brave. *Chivalrous* behavior involves noble words and good deeds.

choleric ADJ. hot-tempered. His flushed, angry face indicated a *choleric* nature.

choreography N. art of representing dances in written symbols; arrangement of dances. Merce Cunningham uses a computer in designing *choreography*: a software program allows him to compose arrangements of possible moves and immediately view them onscreen.

chortle V. chuckle with delight. When she heard that her rival had just been jailed for embezzlement, she *chortled* with joy. She was *not* a nice lady.

chronic ADJ. long established, as a disease. The doctors were finally able to attribute his *chronic* headaches and nausea to traces of formaldehyde gas in his apartment.

chronicle V. report; record (in chronological order). The gossip columnist was paid to *chronicle* the latest escapades of the socially prominent celebrities. also N.

churlish ADJ. boorish; rude. Dismayed by his *churlish* manners at the party, the girls vowed never to invite him again.

ciliated ADJ. having minute hairs. The paramecium is a *ciliated*, one-celled animal.

cipher N. nonentity; worthless person or thing. She claimed her ex-husband was a total *cipher* and wondered why she had ever married him.

cipher N. secret code. Lacking his code book, the spy was unable to decode the message sent to him in *cipher*.

circlet N. small ring; band. This tiny *circlet* is very costly because it is set with precious stones.

circuitous ADJ. roundabout. Because of the traffic congestion on the main highways, she took a *circuitous* route. circuit, N.

circumlocution N. unnecessarily wordy and indirect speech; evasive language. Don't beat about the bush, but just say what you want to say: I'm fed up with listening to your *circumlocutions*.

circumscribe V. limit narrowly; confine or restrict; define. The great lords of state tried to *circumscribe* the queen's power by having her accept a set of conditions that left the decisive voice in all important matters to the privy council.

circumspect ADJ. prudent; cautious. Investigating before acting, she tried always to be *circumspect*.

circumvent V. outwit; baffle. In order to *circumvent* the enemy, we will make two preliminary attacks in other sections before starting our major campaign.

cistern N. reservoir or water tank. The farmers were able to withstand the dry season by using rainwater they had stored in an underground *cistern*.

citadel N. fortress. The *citadel* overlooked the city like a protecting angel.

cite V. quote; commend. She could *cite* passages in the Bible from memory. citation, N.

civil ADJ. having to do with citizens or the state; courteous and polite. Although Internal Revenue Service agents are *civil* servants, they are not always *civil* to suspected tax evaders.

clairvoyant ADJ., N. having foresight; fortuneteller. Cassandra's *clairvoyant* warning was not heeded by the Trojans. clairvoyance, N.

clamber V. climb by crawling. She *clambered* over the wall.

clamor N. noise. The *clamor* of the children at play outside made it impossible for her to take a nap. also V.

clandestine ADJ. secret. After avoiding their chaperon, the lovers had a *clandestine* meeting.

clangor N. loud, resounding noise. The blacksmith was accustomed to the *clangor* of hammers on steel.

clapper N. striker (tongue) of a bell. Wishing to be undisturbed by the bell, Dale wound his scarf around the *clapper* to muffle its striking.

clarion ADJ. shrill, trumpetlike sound. We woke to the *clarion* call of the bugle.

claustrophobia N. fear of being locked in. His fellow classmates laughed at his *claustrophobia* and often threatened to lock him in his room.

clavicle N. collarbone. Even though he wore shoulder pads, the football player broke his *clavicle* during a practice scrimmage.

cleave V. split or sever; cling to; remain faithful to. With her heavy *cleaver*, Julia Child can *cleave* a whole roast duck in two. Soaked through, the soldier tugged at the uniform that *cleaved* annoyingly to his body. He would *cleave* to his post, come rain or shine. cleavage, N. cloven, ADJ.

cleft N. split. Trying for a fresh handhold, the mountain climber grasped the edge of a *cleft* in the sheer rockface. also ADJ.

clemency N. disposition to be lenient; mildness, as of the weather. Why did the defense lawyer look pleased when his case was sent to Judge Bland's chambers? Bland was noted for her *clemency* to first offenders.

cliché N. phrase dulled in meaning by repetition. High school compositions are often marred by such *clichés* as "strong as an ox."

clientele   N. body of customers. The rock club attracted a young, stylish *clientele*.

climactic   ADJ. relating to the highest point. When he reached the *climactic* portions of the book, he could not stop reading. climax, N.

clime   N. region; climate. His doctor advised him to move to a milder *clime*.

clique   N. small, exclusive group. Fitzgerald wished that he belonged to the *clique* of popular athletes and big men on campus who seemed to run Princeton's social life.

cloister   N. monastery or convent. The nuns lived in the *cloister*.

clout   N. great influence (especially political or social). Gatsby wondered whether he had enough *clout* to be admitted to the exclusive club.

cloying   ADJ. distasteful (because excessive); excessively sweet or sentimental. Disliking the *cloying* sweetness of standard wedding cakes, Jody and Tom chose a home-made carrot cake for their reception. cloy, V.

■ **coagulate**   V. thicken; congeal; clot. Even after you remove the pudding from the burner, it will continue to *coagulate* as it stands. coagulant, N.

coalesce   V. combine; fuse. The brooks *coalesce* into one large river. When minor political parties *coalesce*, their *coalescence* may create a major coalition.

coalition   N. partnership; league; union. The Rainbow *Coalition* united people of all races in a common cause.

■ **coda**   N. concluding section of a musical or literary composition; something that rounds out, summarizes, or concludes. The piece concluded with a distinctive *coda* that strikingly brought together various motifs. Several months after Charlie Chaplin's death, his body was briefly kidnapped from a Swiss cemetery by a pair of bungling thieves—a macabre *coda* that Chaplin might have concocted for one of his own two-reelers.

coddle   V. treat gently; pamper. Don't *coddle* the children so much; they need a taste of discipline.

codicil   N. supplement to the body of a will. Miss Havisham kept her lawyers busy drawing up *codicils* to her already complicated will.

codify   V. arrange (laws, rules) as a code; classify. We need to take the varying rules and regulations of the different health agencies and *codify* them into a national health code.

coercion   N. use of force to get someone to obey. The inquisitors used both physical and psychological *coercion* to force Joan of Arc to recant her assertions that her visions were sent by God. coerce, V.

coeval   ADJ. living at the same time as; contemporary. *Coeval* with the dinosaur, the pterodactyl flourished during the Mesozoic era.

cog   N. tooth projecting from a wheel. A bicycle chain moves through a series of *cogs* in order to propel the bike.

■ **cogent**   ADJ. convincing. It was inevitable that David chose to go to Harvard: he had several *cogent* reasons for doing so, including a full-tuition scholarship. Katya argued her case with such *cogency* that the jury had to decide in favor of her client.

cogitate   V. think over. *Cogitate* on this problem; the solution will come.

cognate   ADJ. related linguistically; allied by blood; similar or akin in nature. The English word "mother" is *cognate* to the Latin word "mater," whose influence is visible in the words "maternal" and "maternity." also N.

cognitive   ADJ. having to do with knowing or perceiving related to the mental processes. Though Jack was emotionally immature, his *cognitive* development was admirable; he was very advanced intellectually.

cognizance   N. knowledge. During the election campaign, the two candidates were kept in full *cognizance* of the international situation.

cohabit   V. live together. Many unwed couples who *cohabit* peacefully for years wind up fighting night and day once they marry.

cohere   V. stick together. Solids have a greater tendency to *cohere* than liquids.

cohesion   N. tendency to keep together. A firm believer in the maxim "Divide and conquer," the emperor, by lies and trickery, sought to disrupt the *cohesion* of the free nations.

cohorts   N. armed band. Caesar and his Roman *cohorts* conquered almost all of the known world.

coiffure   N. hairstyle. You can make a statement with your choice of *coiffure*: in the '60's many African-Americans affirmed their racial heritage by wearing their hair in Afros.

coin   V. make coins; invent or fabricate. Mints *coin* good money; counterfeiters *coin* fakes. Slanderers *coin* nasty rumors; writers *coin* words. A neologism is a newly *coined* expression.

coincidence   N. the chance occurrence, at the same time, of two or more seemingly connected events. Was it just a *coincidence* that John and she had met at the market for three days running, or was he deliberately trying to seek her out? coincidental, ADJ.

colander   N. utensil with perforated bottom used for straining. Before serving the spaghetti, place it in a *colander* to drain it.

Test

Word List 9   *Synonyms*

Each of the questions below consists of a word in capital letters, followed by five lettered words or phrases. Choose the lettered word or phrase that is most nearly similar in meaning to the word in capital letters and write the letter of your choice on your answer paper.

121. CHASTE (A) loyal (B) timid (C) curt (D) pure (E) outspoken
122. CHIDE (A) unite (B) fear (C) record (D) skid (E) scold
123. CHIMERICAL (A) developing (B) brief (C) distant (D) economical (E) fantastic
124. CHOLERIC (A) musical (B) episodic (C) hotheaded (D) global (E) seasonal
125. CHURLISH (A) marine (B) economical (C) impolite (D) compact (E) young
126. CILIATED (A) foolish (B) swift (C) early (D) constructed (E) hairy
127. CIRCUITOUS (A) indirect (B) complete (C) obvious (D) aware (E) tortured

128. CITE (A) galvanize (B) visualize (C) locate (D) quote (E) signal
129. CLANDESTINE (A) abortive (B) secret (C) tangible (D) doomed (E) approved
130. CLAUSTROPHOBIA (A) lack of confidence (B) fear of spiders (C) love of books (D) fear of grammar (E) fear of closed places
131. CLEFT (A) split (B) waterfall (C) assembly (D) adherence (E) surplus
132. CLICHÉ (A) increase (B) vehicle (C) morale (D) platitude (E) pique
133. COERCE (A) recover (B) begin (C) force (D) license (E) ignore
134. COGNIZANCE (A) policy (B) knowledge (C) advance (D) omission (E) examination
135. COHERE (A) hold together (B) occur simultaneously (C) recollect (D) materialize (E) understand

Word List 10   collaborate–congenital

collaborate v. work together. Two writers *collaborated* in preparing this book.

collage N. work of art put together from fragments. Scraps of cloth, paper doilies, and old photographs all went into her *collage*.

collate v. examine in order to verify authenticity; arrange in order. They *collated* the newly found manuscripts to determine their age.

collateral N. security given for loan. The sum you wish to borrow is so large that it must be secured by *collateral*.

collation N. a light meal. Tea sandwiches and cookies were offered at the *collation*.

colloquial ADJ. pertaining to conversational or common speech; informal. Some of the new *colloquial* reading passages on standardized tests have a conversational tone intended to make them more appealing to test-takers.

colloquy N. informal discussion. While a colloquium often is a formal seminar or conference, a *colloquy* traditionally is merely a conversational exchange.

collusion N. conspiring in a fraudulent scheme. The swindlers were found guilty of *collusion*.

colossal ADJ. huge. Radio City Music Hall has a *colossal* stage.

colossus N. gigantic statue. The legendary *Colossus* of Rhodes, a bronze statue of the sun god that dominated the harbor of the Greek seaport, was one of the Seven Wonders of the World.

comatose ADJ. in a coma; extremely sleepy. The long-winded orator soon had his audience in a *comatose* state.

combustible ADJ. easily burned. After the recent outbreak of fires in private homes, the fire commissioner ordered that all *combustible* materials be kept in safe containers. also N.

comely ADJ. attractive; agreeable. I would rather have a poor and *comely* wife than a rich and homely one.

comestible N. something fit to be eaten. The roast turkey and other *comestibles*, the wines, and the excellent service made this Thanksgiving dinner particularly memorable.

comeuppance N. rebuke; deserts. After his earlier rudeness, we were delighted to see him get his *comeuppance*.

comity N. courtesy; civility. A spirit of *comity* should exist among nations.

commandeer v. to draft for military purposes; to take for public use. The policeman *commandeered* the first car that approached and ordered the driver to go to the nearest hospital.

commemorative ADJ. remembering; honoring. The new *commemorative* stamp honors the late Martin Luther King, Jr.

■ **commensurate** ADJ. corresponding in extent, degree, amount, etc.; proportionate. By the close of World War II much progress had been made in assigning nurses rank and responsibilities *commensurate* with their training and abilities. Critics in the industry charged that imposing new meat inspection regulations without dismantling the traditional system would raise costs without bringing about a *commensurate* improvement in safety.

commiserate v. feel or express pity or sympathy for. Her friends *commiserated* with the widow.

commodious ADJ. spacious and comfortable. After sleeping in small roadside cabins, they found their hotel suite *commodious*.

communal ADJ. held in common; a group of people. When they were divorced, they had trouble dividing their *communal* property.

compact N. agreement; contract. The signers of the Mayflower *Compact* were establishing a form of government.

compact ADJ. tightly packed; firm; brief. His short, *compact* body was better suited to wrestling than to basketball.

compatible ADJ. harmonious; in harmony with. They were *compatible* neighbors, never quarreling over unimportant matters. compatibility, N.

compelling ADJ. overpowering; irresistible in effect. The prosecutor presented a well-reasoned case, but the defense attorney's *compelling* arguments for leniency won over the jury.

■ **compendium** v. brief, comprehensive summary. This text can serve as a *compendium* of the tremendous amount of new material being developed in this field.

compensatory ADJ. making up for; repaying. Can a *compensatory* education program make up for the inadequate schooling he received in earlier years?

compilation N. listing of statistical information in tabular or book form. The *compilation* of available scholarships serves a very valuable purpose.

compile v. assemble; gather; accumulate. We planned to *compile* a list of the words most frequently used on the GRE.

complacency N. self-satisfaction; smugness. Full of *complacency* about his latest victories, he looked smugly at the row of trophies on his mantelpiece. complacent, ADJ.

■ **complaisant** ADJ. trying to please; overly polite; obliging. Fearing that the king might become enraged if his will were thwarted, the *complaisant* Parliament recognized Henry VIII as king of Ireland. Someone *complaisant* is not smug or complacent; he yields to others because he has an excessive need to please.

complement v. complete; consummate; make perfect. The waiter recommended a glass of port to *complement* the cheese. also N.

complementary ADJ. serving to complete something. John's and Lexy's skills are *complementary*: he's good at following a daily routine, while she's great at improvising and handling emergencies. Together they make a great team.

compliance N. readiness to yield; conformity in fulfilling requirements. Bullheaded Bill was not noted for his easy *compliance* to the demands of others. As an architect, however, Bill recognized that his design for the new school had to be in *compliance* with the local building code.

■ **compliant** ADJ. yielding; conforming to requirements. Because Joel usually gave in and went along with whatever his friends desired, his mother worried that he might be too *compliant*.

complicity N. involvement in a crime; participation. Queen Mary's marriage to Lord Darnley, her suspected *complicity* in his murder, and her hasty marriage to the earl of Bothwell stirred the Protestant lords to revolt. Although Spanish *complicity* in the sinking of the battleship *Maine* was not proved, U.S. public opinion was aroused and war sentiment rose.

component N. element; ingredient. I wish all the *components* of my stereo system were working at the same time.

comport v. bear one's self; behave. He *comported* himself with great dignity.

composure N. mental calmness. Even the latest work crisis failed to shake her *composure*.

compound v. combine; constitute; pay interest; increase. The makers of the popular cold remedy *compounded* a nasal decongestant with an antihistamine. also N.

comprehensive ADJ. thorough; inclusive. This book provides a *comprehensive* review of verbal and math skills for the GRE.

compress v. squeeze or press together; make more compact. Miss Watson *compressed* her lips in disapproval as she noted the bedraggled state of Huck's clothes. On farms, roller-packers are used in dry seasons to *compress* and pack down the soil after plowing.

comprise v. include; consist of. If the District of Columbia were to be granted statehood, the United States of America would *comprise* fifty-one states, not just fifty.

compromise v. adjust or settle by making mutual concessions; endanger the interests or reputation of. Sometimes the presence of a neutral third party can help adversaries *compromise* their differences. Unfortunately, you're not neutral. Therefore, your presence here *compromises* our chances of reaching an agreement. also N.

compunction N. remorse. The judge was especially severe in his sentencing because he felt that the criminal had shown no *compunction* for his heinous crime.

compute v. reckon; calculate. He failed to *compute* the interest, so his bank balance was not accurate.

concatenate v. link as in a chain. It is difficult to understand how these events could *concatenate* as they did without outside assistance.

concave ADJ. hollow. The back-packers found partial shelter from the storm by huddling against the *concave* wall of the cliff.

concede v. admit; yield. Despite all the evidence Monica had assembled, Mark refused to *concede* that she was right.

conceit N. vanity or self-love; whimsical idea; extravagant metaphor. Although Jack was smug and puffed up with *conceit*, he was an entertaining companion, always expressing himself in amusing *conceits* and witty turns of phrase.

concentric ADJ. having a common center. The target was made of *concentric* circles.

conception N. beginning; forming of an idea. At the first *conception* of the work, he was consulted. conceive, v.

concerted ADJ. mutually agreed on; done together. All the Girl Scouts made a *concerted* effort to raise funds for their annual outing. When the movie star appeared, his fans let out a *concerted* sigh.

concession N. an act of yielding. Before they could reach an agreement, both sides had to make certain *concessions*.

■ **conciliatory** ADJ. reconciling; soothing. She was still angry despite his *conciliatory* words. conciliate, V.

concise ADJ. brief and compact. When you define a new word, be *concise*: the shorter the definition, the easier it is to remember.

conclave N. private meeting. He was present at all their *conclaves* as an unofficial observer.

conclusive ADJ. decisive; ending all debate. When the stolen books turned up in John's locker, we finally had *conclusive* evidence of the identity of the mysterious thief.

concoct V. prepare by combining; make up in concert. How did the inventive chef ever *concoct* such a strange dish? concoction, N.

concomitant N. that which accompanies. A decrease of gastric juice secretion may be a congenital abnormality or a *concomitant* of advanced age. The word *hubbub* emphasizes turbulent activity and *concomitant* din: the hubbub of Wall Street traders shouting out buy orders, for example.

concord N. harmony. Watching Tweedledum and Tweedledee battle, Alice wondered why the two brothers could not manage to live in *concord*.

concur V. agree. Did you *concur* with the decision of the court or did you find it unfair?

concurrent ADJ. happening at the same time. In America, the colonists were resisting the demands of the mother country; at the *concurrent* moment in France, the middle class was sowing the seeds of rebellion.

condescend V. bestow courtesies with a superior air. The king *condescended* to grant an audience to the friends of the condemned man. condescension, N.

condign ADJ. appropriate; deserved (almost always, in the sense of deservedly severe, as in *condign* punishment). To be concerned about a possible miscarriage of justice is rational; to brood over a guilty man's just and *condign* punishment makes no sense.

condiment N. food seasoning; spice. Failure is the *condiment* that gives success its flavor. Many *condiments*—cayenne pepper, hot mustard, horseradish, wasabi—are too strong for small children, who prefer a less highly spiced diet.

condole V. express sympathetic sorrow. His friends gathered to *condole* with him over his loss. condolence, N.

■ **condone** V. overlook; forgive; give tacit approval; excuse. Unlike Widow Douglass, who *condoned* Huck's minor offenses, Miss Watson did nothing but scold.

conducive ADJ. helpful; contributive. Rest and proper diet are *conducive* to good health.

conduit N. aqueduct; passageway for fluids. Water was brought to the army in the desert by an improvised *conduit* from the adjoining mountain.

confidant N. trusted friend. He had no *confidants* with whom he could discuss his problems at home.

confine V. shut in; restrict. The terrorists had *confined* their prisoner in a small room. However, they had not chained him to the wall or done anything else to *confine* his movements. confinement, N.

confiscate V. seize; commandeer. The army *confiscated* all available supplies of uranium.

conflagration N. great fire. In the *conflagration* that followed the 1906 earthquake, much of San Francisco was destroyed.

conflate V. meld or fuse; confuse; combine into one. In his painting *White Crucifixion*, which depicts German Jews terrorized by a Nazi mob, Chagall *conflates* Jewish and Christian symbols, portraying the crucified Christ wrapped in a *tallith*, a Jewish prayer shawl. The anthropologist Mahmood Mamdani maintains that terrorism is a unique product of the modern world and should not be *conflated* with Islam.

confluence N. flowing together; crowd. They built the city at the *confluence* of two rivers.

conformity N. harmony; agreement. In *conformity* with our rules and regulations, I am calling a meeting of our organization.

■ **confound** V. confuse; puzzle. No mystery could *confound* Sherlock Holmes for long.

congeal V. freeze; coagulate. His blood *congealed* in his veins as he saw the dread monster rush toward him.

congenial ADJ. pleasant; friendly. My father loved to go out for a meal with *congenial* companions.

congenital ADJ. existing at birth. Doctors are able to cure some *congenital* deformities such as cleft palates by performing operations on infants.

Test

Word List 10   *Synonyms and Antonyms*

Each of the following questions consists of a word in capital letters, followed by five lettered words or phrases. Choose the lettered word or phrase that is most nearly similar or opposite in meaning to the word in capital letters and write the letter of your choice on your answer paper.

136. COLLATION (A) furor (B) emphasis (C) distillery (D) spree (E) lunch
137. COLLOQUIAL (A) burnt (B) polished (C) political (D) gifted (E) problematic
138. COLLOQUY (A) dialect (B) diversion (C) announcement (D) discussion (E) expansion

139. COMATOSE (A) cozy (B) restrained (C) alert (D) dumb (E) grim
140. COMBUSTIBLE (A) flammable (B) industrious (C) waterproof (D) specific (E) plastic
141. COMELY (A) yielding (B) unattractive (C) extremely sleepy (D) equal in extent (E) roving
142. COMMISERATE (A) communicate (B) expand (C) repay (D) diminish (E) sympathize
143. COMMODIOUS (A) numerous (B) yielding (C) leisurely (D) limited (E) expensive
144. COMPLIANT (A) numerous (B) veracious (C) soft (D) adamant (E) livid

145. CONCILIATE (A) defend (B) activate (C) integrate (D) quarrel (E) react
146. CONCOCT (A) thrive (B) wonder (C) intrude (D) drink (E) invent
147. CONDONE (A) build (B) evaluate (C) pierce (D) infuriate (E) overlook
148. CONFISCATE (A) discuss (B) discover (C) seize (D) exist (E) convey
149. CONFORMITY (A) agreement (B) ambition (C) confinement (D) pride (E) restraint
150. CONGENITAL (A) slight (B) obscure (C) thorough (D) existing at birth (E) classified

Word List 11 conglomeration–countermand

conglomeration N. mass of material sticking together. In such a *conglomeration* of miscellaneous statistics, it was impossible to find a single area of analysis.

congruence N. correspondence of parts; harmonious relationship. The student demonstrated the *congruence* of the two triangles by using the hypotenuse-leg theorem.

congruent ADJ. in agreement; corresponding. In formulating a hypothesis, we must keep it *congruent* with what we know of the real world; it cannot disagree with our experience.

conifer N. pine tree; cone-bearing tree. According to geologists, the *conifers* were the first plants to bear flowers.

conjecture V. infer on the basis of insufficient data; surmise; guess. In the absence of any eyewitness reports, we can only *conjecture* what happened in the locked room on the night of the 13th. Would it be a reasonable *conjecture* to decide that the previous sentence is an excerpt from a mystery novel?

conjugal ADJ. pertaining to marriage. Their dreams of *conjugal* bliss were shattered as soon as their temperaments clashed.

conjure V. summon a devil; practice magic; imagine or invent. Sorcerers *conjure* devils to appear. Magicians *conjure* white rabbits out of hats. Political candidates *conjure* up images of reformed cities and a world at peace.

connivance N. pretense of ignorance of something wrong; assistance; permission to offend. With the *connivance* of his friends, he plotted to embarrass the teacher. connive, V.

■ **connoisseur** N. person competent to act as a judge of art, etc.; a lover of an art. Bernard Berenson, the American art critic and *connoisseur* of Italian art, was hired by wealthy art lovers to select paintings for their collections.

connotation N. suggested or implied meaning of an expression. Foreigners frequently are unaware of the *connotations* of the words they use.

connubial ADJ. pertaining to marriage or the matrimonial state. In his telegram, he wished the newlyweds a lifetime of *connubial* bliss.

consanguinity N. kinship. Wanting to be rid of yet another wife, Henry VIII sought a divorce on the grounds of *consanguinity*, claiming their blood relationship was improperly close.

conscientious ADJ. scrupulous; careful. A *conscientious* editor, she checked every definition for its accuracy.

conscript N. draftee; person forced into military service. Did Rambo volunteer to fight in Vietnam, or was he a *conscript*, drafted against his will? also V.

consecrate V. dedicate; sanctify. In 1804, Napoleon forced Pope Pius VII to come to Paris to *consecrate* him as emperor, only to humiliate Pius at the last minute by taking the crown from the pope's hands and crowning himself.

consensus N. general agreement; opinion reached by a group as a whole. Letty Cottin Pogrebin argues that, although the ultra-right would like us to believe that families disintegrate because of secular education and sexual liberation, the *consensus* of Americans is that what tears families apart is unemployment, inflation, and financial worries.

consequential ADJ. pompous; self-important. Convinced of his own importance, the actor strutted about the dressing room with a *consequential* air.

conservatory N. school of the fine arts (especially music or drama). A gifted violinist, Marya was selected to study at the *conservatory*.

consign V. deliver officially; entrust; set apart. The court *consigned* the child to her paternal grandmother's care. consignment, N.

consistency N. absence of contradictions; dependability; uniformity; degree of thickness. Holmes judged puddings and explanations on their *consistency*: he liked his puddings without lumps and his explanations without improbabilities.

console V. lessen sadness or disappointment; give comfort. When her father died, Marius did his best to *console* Cosette. consolation, N.

consolidation N. unification; process of becoming firmer or stronger. The recent *consolidation* of several small airlines into one major company has left observers of the industry wondering whether room still exists for the "little guy" in aviation. consolidate, V.

consonance N. harmony; agreement. Her agitation seemed out of *consonance* with her usual calm. The

1815 so-called "Holy Alliance" of the emperors of Russia and Austria and the king of Prussia accomplished nothing, since it was merely a vague agreement that the sovereigns would conduct themselves in *consonance* with Christian principles.

consort V. associate with. We frequently judge people by the company with whom they *consort*.

consort N. husband or wife. The search for a *consort* for the young Queen Victoria ended happily.

conspiracy N. treacherous plot. Brutus and Cassius joined in the *conspiracy* to kill Julius Caesar.

constituent N. supporter. The congressman received hundreds of letters from angry *constituents* after the Equal Rights Amendment failed to pass.

constraint N. compulsion; repression of feelings. There was a feeling of *constraint* in the room because no one dared to criticize the speaker. constrain, v.

construe V. explain; interpret. If I *construe* your remarks correctly, you disagree with the theory already advanced.

consummate ADJ. wholly without flaw; supremely skilled; complete and utter. Free of her father's autocratic rule, safely married to the man she loved, Elizabeth Barrett Browning felt *consummate* happiness. Da Vinci depicted in his drawings, with scientific precision and *consummate* artistry, subjects ranging from flying machines to intricate anatomical studies of people, animals, and plants. There is no one as boring as Boris; he is a *consummate* bore.

contagion N. infection. Fearing *contagion*, they took drastic steps to prevent the spread of the disease.

contaminate V. pollute. The sewage system of the city so *contaminated* the water that swimming was forbidden.

contempt N. scorn; disdain. The heavyweight boxer looked on ordinary people with *contempt*, scorning them as weaklings who couldn't hurt a fly. We thought it was *contemptible* of him to be *contemptuous* of people for being weak.

contend V. struggle; compete; assert earnestly. In *Revolt of the Black Athlete*, sociologist Harry Edwards *contends* that young black athletes have been exploited by some college recruiters. contention, N.

■ **contention** N. claim; thesis. It is our *contention* that, if you follow our tactics, you will boost your score on the GRE. contend, v.

■ **contentious** ADJ. quarrelsome. Disagreeing violently with the referees' ruling, the coach became so *contentious* that the referees threw him out of the game.

contest V. dispute. The defeated candidate attempted to *contest* the election results.

context N. writings preceding and following the passage quoted. Because these lines are taken out of *context*, they do not convey the message the author intended.

contiguous ADJ. adjacent to; touching upon. The two countries are *contiguous* for a few miles; then they are separated by the gulf.

continence N. self-restraint; sexual chastity. At the convent, Connie vowed to lead a life of *continence*. The question was, could Connie be content with always being *continent*?

contingent ADJ. dependent on; conditional. Cher's father informed her that any increase in her allowance was *contingent* on the quality of her final grades. contingency, N.

contingent N. group that makes up part of a gathering. The New York *contingent* of delegates at the Democratic National Convention was a boisterous, sometimes rowdy lot.

contortions N. twistings; distortions. As the effects of the opiate wore away, the *contortions* of the patient became more violent and demonstrated how much pain she was enduring.

contraband N. illegal trade; smuggling; smuggled goods. The Coast Guard tries to prevent *contraband* in U.S. waters. also ADJ.

contravene V. contradict; oppose: infringe on or transgress. Mr. Barrett did not expect his frail daughter Elizabeth to *contravene* his will by eloping with Robert Browning.

■ **contrite** ADJ. penitent. Her *contrite* tears did not influence the judge when he imposed sentence. contrition, N.

contrived ADJ. forced; artificial; not spontaneous. Feeling ill at ease with his new in-laws, James made a few *contrived* attempts at conversation and then retreated into silence.

controvert V. oppose with arguments; attempt to refute; contradict. The witness's testimony was so clear and her reputation for honesty so well established that the defense attorney decided it was wiser to make no attempt to *controvert* what she said.

contumacious ADJ. disobedient; resisting authority. The *contumacious* mob shouted defiantly at the police. contumacy, N.

contusion N. bruise. Black and blue after her fall, Sue was treated for *contusions* and abrasions.

■ **conundrum** N. riddle; difficult problem. During the long car ride, she invented *conundrums* to entertain the children.

convene V. assemble. Because much needed legislation had to be enacted, the governor ordered the legislature to *convene* in special session by January 15.

convention N. social or moral custom; established practice. Flying in the face of *convention*, George Sand (Amandine Dudevant) shocked her contemporaries by taking lovers and wearing men's clothes.

conventional ADJ. ordinary; typical. His *conventional* upbringing left him wholly unprepared for his wife's eccentric family.

■ **converge** V. approach; tend to meet; come together. African-American men from all over the United States *converged* on Washington to take part in the historic Million Man March. convergence, N.

conversant ADJ. familiar with. In this age of specialization, someone reasonably *conversant* with modern French literature may be wholly unacquainted with the novels of Latin America and Spain.

converse N. opposite. The inevitable *converse* of peace is not war but annihilation.

convert N. one who has adopted a different religion or opinion. On his trip to Japan, though the president spoke at length about the merits of American automobiles, he made few *converts* to his beliefs. also v.

convex ADJ. curving outward. She polished the *convex* lens of her telescope.

conveyance N. vehicle; transfer. During the transit strike, commuters used various kinds of *conveyances*.

conviction N. judgment that someone is guilty of a crime; strongly held belief. Even her *conviction* for murder did not shake Lord Peter's *conviction* that Harriet was innocent of the crime.

convivial ADJ. festive; gay; characterized by joviality. The *convivial* celebrators of the victory sang their college songs.

convoke V. call together. Congress was *convoked* at the outbreak of the emergency. convocation, N.

■ **convoluted** ADJ. coiled around; involved; intricate. His argument was so *convoluted* that few of us could follow it intelligently.

copious ADJ. plentiful. She had *copious* reasons for rejecting the proposal.

coquette N. flirt. Because she refused to give him an answer to his proposal of marriage, he called her a *coquette*. also v.

cordial ADJ. gracious; heartfelt. Our hosts greeted us at the airport with a *cordial* welcome and a hearty hug.

cordon N. extended line of men or fortifications to prevent access or egress. The police *cordon* was so tight that the criminals could not leave the area. also v.

cornice N. projecting molding on building (usually above columns). Because the stones forming the *cornice* had been loosened by the storms, the police closed the building until repairs could be made.

cornucopia N. horn overflowing with fruit and grain; symbol of abundance. The encyclopedia salesman claimed the new edition was a veritable *cornucopia* of information, an inexhaustible source of knowledge for the entire family.

corollary N. consequence; accompaniment. Brotherly love is a complex emotion, with sibling rivalry its natural *corollary*.

corporeal ADJ. bodily; material. The doctor had no patience with spiritual matters: his job was to attend to his patients' *corporeal* problems, not to minister to their souls.

corpulent ADJ. very fat. The *corpulent* man resolved to reduce. corpulence, N.

correlation N. mutual relationship. He sought to determine the *correlation* that existed between ability in algebra and ability to interpret reading exercises. correlate, V., N.

corroborate V. confirm; support. Though Huck was quite willing to *corroborate* Tom's story, Aunt Polly knew better than to believe either of them.

corrode V. destroy by chemical action. The girders supporting the bridge *corroded* so gradually that no one suspected any danger until the bridge suddenly collapsed. corrosion, N.

corrosive ADJ. eating away by chemicals or disease. Stainless steel is able to withstand the effects of *corrosive* chemicals.

corrugated ADJ. wrinkled; ridged. Crack open the rough shell of the walnut and you will find within it a ridged and *corrugated* edible seed or nut.

cosmic ADJ. pertaining to the universe; vast. *Cosmic* rays derive their name from the fact that they bombard the earth's atmosphere from outer space. cosmos, N.

coterie N. group that meets socially; select circle. After his book had been published, he was invited to join the literary *coterie* that lunched daily at the hotel.

countenance V. approve; tolerate. Miss Manners refused to *countenance* such rude behavior on their part.

countenance N. face. When José saw his newborn daughter, a proud smile spread across his *countenance*.

countermand V. cancel; revoke. The general *countermanded* the orders issued in his absence.

Test

Word List 11 *Synonyms*

Each of the questions below consists of a word in capital letters, followed by five lettered words or phrases. Choose the lettered word or phrase that is most nearly similar in meaning to the word in capital letters and write the letter of your choice on your answer paper.

151. CONJECTURE (A) magic (B) guess (C) position (D) form (E) place
152. CONNOISSEUR (A) gourmand (B) lover of art (C) humidor (D) delinquent (E) interpreter
153. CONSANGUINITY (A) kinship (B) friendship (C) bloodletting (D) relief (E) understanding
154. CONSENSUS (A) general agreement (B) project (C) insignificance (D) sheaf (E) crevice
155. CONSTRUE (A) explain (B) promote (C) reserve (D) erect (E) block
156. CONTAMINATE (A) arrest (B) prepare (C) pollute (D) beam (E) inform
157. CONTENTIOUS (A) squealing (B) surprising (C) quarrelsome (D) smug (E) creative
158. CONTINENCE (A) humanity (B) research (C) embryology (D) bodies of land (E) self-restraint
159. CONTRABAND (A) purpose (B) rogue (C) rascality (D) difficulty (E) smuggling

160. CONTRITE (A) smart (B) penitent (C) restful (D) recognized (E) perspiring
161. CONTROVERT (A) turn over (B) contradict (C) mind (D) explain (E) swing
162. CONVENE (A) propose (B) restore (C) question (D) gather (E) motivate

163. CONVERSANT (A) ignorant (B) speaking (C) incorporated (D) familiar (E) pedantic
164. COPIOUS (A) plentiful (B) cheating (C) dishonorable (D) adventurous (E) inspired
165. CORPULENT (A) regenerate (B) obese (C) different (D) hungry (E) bloody

---

Word List 12   counterpart-decelerate

counterpart N. a thing that completes another; things very much alike. Night and day are *counterparts*.

coup N. highly successful action or sudden attack. As the news of his *coup* spread throughout Wall Street, his fellow brokers dropped by to congratulate him.

couple V. join; unite. The Flying Karamazovs *couple* expert juggling and amateur joking in their nightclub act.

courier N. messenger. The publisher sent a special *courier* to pick up the manuscript.

covenant N. agreement. We must comply with the terms of the *covenant*.

covert ADJ. secret; hidden; implied. Investigations of the Central Intelligence Agency and other secret service networks reveal that such *covert* operations can get out of control.

covetous ADJ. avaricious; eagerly desirous of. The poor man wants many things; the *covetous* man, all. During the Civil War, the Confederates cast *covetous* eyes on California, hoping to seize ports for privateers, as well as gold and silver to replenish the South's sagging treasury. covet, V.

cow V. terrorize; intimidate. The little boy was so *cowed* by the hulking bully that he gave up his lunch money without a word of protest.

cower V. shrink quivering, as from fear. The frightened child *cowered* in the corner of the room.

coy ADJ. shy; modest; coquettish. Reluctant to commit herself so early in the game, Kay was *coy* in her answers to Ken's offer.

cozen V. cheat; hoodwink; swindle. He was the kind of individual who would *cozen* his friends in a cheap card game but remain eminently ethical in all his business dealings.

crabbed ADJ. sour; peevish. The children avoided the *crabbed* old man because he scolded them when they made noise.

crass ADJ. very unrefined; grossly insensible. The film critic deplored the *crass* commercialism of movie-makers who abandon artistic standards in order to make a quick buck.

■ **craven** ADJ. cowardly. Lillian's *craven* refusal to join the protest was criticized by her comrades, who had expected her to be brave enough to stand up for her beliefs.

credence N. belief. Do not place any *credence* in his promises.

credo N. creed. Just two months before his death, as he talked about life with some friends, the writer Jack London proclaimed his *credo*: "The proper function of man is to live, not to exist. I shall not waste my days in trying to prolong them. I shall use my time."

credulity N. belief on slight evidence; gullibility; naiveté. Con artists take advantage of the *credulity* of inexperienced investors to swindle them out of their savings. credulous, ADJ.

creed N. system of religious or ethical belief. I have a dream that one day this nation will rise up and live out the true meaning of its *creed*: "We hold these truths to be self-evident that all men are created equal."(Martin Luther King, Jr.)

crescendo N. increase in the volume or intensity, as in a musical passage; climax. The overture suddenly changed from a quiet pastoral theme to a *crescendo* featuring blaring trumpets and clashing cymbals.

crestfallen ADJ. dejected; dispirited. We were surprised at his reaction to the failure of his project; instead of being *crestfallen*, he was busily engaged in planning new activities.

crevice N. crack; fissure. The mountain climbers found footholds in the tiny *crevices* in the mountainside.

cringe V. shrink back, as if in fear. The dog *cringed*, expecting a blow.

criteria N. PL. standards used in judging. What *criteria* did you use when you selected this essay as the prize winner? criterion, SING.

crone N. hag. The toothless *crone* frightened us when she smiled.

crotchety ADJ. eccentric; whimsical. Although he was reputed to be a *crotchety* old gentleman, I found his ideas substantially sound and sensible.

crux N. essential or main point. This is the *crux* of the entire problem: everything centers on its being resolved. crucial, ADJ.

crypt N. secret recess or vault usually used for burial. Until recently only bodies of rulers and leading statesmen were interred in this *crypt*.

cryptic ADJ. mysterious; hidden; secret. Thoroughly baffled by Holmes's *cryptic* remarks, Watson wondered whether Holmes was intentionally concealing his thoughts about the crime.

cubicle   N. small chamber used for sleeping. After her many hours of intensive study in the library, she retired to her *cubicle*.

cuisine   N. style of cooking. French *cuisine* is noted for its use of sauces and wines.

culinary   ADJ. relating to cooking. Many chefs attribute their *culinary* success to the wise use of spices.

cull   V. pick out; reject. Every month the farmer *culls* the nonlaying hens from his flock and sells them to the local butcher. also N.

culmination   N. attainment of highest point. His inauguration as President of the United States marked the *culmination* of his political career.

culpable   ADJ. deserving blame. Corrupt politicians who condone the activities of the gamblers are equally *culpable*.

culvert   N. artificial channel for water. If we build a *culvert* under the road at this point, we will reduce the possibility of the road's being flooded during the rainy season.

cumbersome   ADJ. heavy; hard to manage. She was burdened with *cumbersome* parcels.

cumulative   ADJ. growing by addition. Vocabulary-building is a *cumulative* process: as you go through your flash cards, you will add new words to your vocabulary, one by one.

cupidity   N. greed. The defeated people could not satisfy the *cupidity* of the conquerors, who demanded excessive tribute.

curator   N. superintendent; manager. The members of the board of trustees of the museum expected the new *curator* to plan events and exhibits that would make the museum more popular.

curmudgeon   N. churlish, miserly individual. Although many regarded him as a *curmudgeon*, a few of us were aware of the many kindnesses and acts of charity that he secretly performed.

cursive   ADJ. flowing, running. In normal writing we run our letters together in *cursive* form; in printing, we separate the letters.

cursory   ADJ. casual; hastily done. Because a *cursory* examination of the ruins indicates the possibility of arson, we believe the insurance agency should undertake a more extensive investigation of the fire's cause.

curtail   V. shorten; reduce. When Elton asked Cher for a date, she said she was really sorry she couldn't go out with him, but her dad had ordered her to *curtail* her social life.

cynical   ADJ. skeptical or distrustful of human motives. *Cynical* from birth, Sidney was suspicious whenever anyone gave him a gift "with no strings attached." cynic, N. cynicism, N.

cynosure   N. object of general attention. As soon as the movie star entered the room, she became the *cynosure* of all eyes.

dabble   V. work at in a nonserious fashion; splash around. The amateur painter *dabbled* at art, but seldom produced a finished piece. The children *dabbled* their hands in the bird bath, splashing one another gleefully.

dais   N. raised platform for guests of honor. When she approached the *dais*, she was greeted by cheers from the people who had come to honor her.

dally   V. trifle with; procrastinate. Laertes told Ophelia that Hamlet would only *dally* with her affections.

damp   V. lessen in intensity; diminish; mute. Not even the taunts of his brother, who considered ballet no proper pursuit for a lad, could *damp* Billy Elliot's enthusiasm for dancing.

dank   ADJ. damp. The walls of the dungeon were *dank* and slimy.

dapper   ADJ. neat and trim. In *The Odd Couple*, Tony Randall played Felix Unger, an excessively *dapper* soul who could not stand to have a hair out of place.

dappled   ADJ. spotted. The sunlight filtering through the screens created a *dappled* effect on the wall.

daub   V. smear (as with paint). From the way he *daubed* his paint on the canvas, I could tell he knew nothing of oils. also N.

■ **daunt**   V. intimidate; frighten. "Boast all you like of your prowess. Mere words cannot *daunt* me," the hero answered the villain.

dauntless   ADJ. bold. Despite the dangerous nature of the undertaking, the *dauntless* soldier volunteered for the assignment.

dawdle   V. loiter; waste time. We have to meet a deadline. Don't *dawdle*; just get down to work.

deadlock   N. standstill; stalemate. Because negotiations had reached a *deadlock*, some of the delegates had begun to mutter about breaking off the talks. also V.

deadpan   ADJ. wooden; impassive. We wanted to see how long he could maintain his *deadpan* expression.

dearth   N. scarcity. The *dearth* of skilled labor compelled the employers to open trade schools.

debacle   N. sudden downfall; complete disaster. In the *Airplane* movies, every flight turns into a *debacle*, with passengers and crew members collapsing, engines falling apart, and carry-on baggage popping out of the overhead bins.

debase   V. reduce the quality or value; lower in esteem; degrade. In *The King and I*, Anna refuses to kneel down and prostrate herself before the king; she feels that to do so would *debase* her position, and she will not submit to such *debasement*.

debauch   V. corrupt; seduce from virtue. Did Socrates' teachings lead the young men of Athens to be virtuous citizens, or did they *debauch* the young men, causing them to question the customs of their fathers? Clearly, Socrates' philosophical talks were nothing like the wild *debauchery* of the toga parties in *Animal House*.

debilitate   V. weaken; enfeeble. Michael's severe bout of the flu *debilitated* him so much that he was too tired to go to work for a week.

debonair   ADJ. urbane and suave; amiable; cheerful and carefree. Reporters frequently describe polished and charming leading men—Cary Grant or Pierce Brosnan, for example—as *debonair*.

debris N. rubble. A full year after the earthquake in Mexico City, workers were still carting away the *debris*.

debunk V. expose as false, exaggerated, worthless, etc.; ridicule. Pointing out that he consistently had voted against strengthening antipollution legislation, reporters *debunked* the candidate's claim that he was a fervent environmentalist.

debutante N. young woman making formal entrance into society. As a *debutante*, she was often mentioned in the society columns of the newspapers.

decadence N. decay. The moral *decadence* of the people was reflected in the lewd literature of the period.

decant V. pour off gently. Be sure to *decant* this wine before serving it.

decapitate V. behead. They did not hang Lady Jane Grey; they *decapitated* her. "Off with her head!" cried the Duchess, eager to *decapitate* poor Alice.

decelerate V. slow down. Seeing the emergency blinkers in the road ahead, he *decelerated* quickly.

Test

Word List 12   *Antonyms*

Each of the questions below consists of a word in capital letters, followed by five lettered words or phrases. Choose the lettered word or phrase that is most nearly opposite in meaning to the word in capital letters and write the letter of your choice on your answer paper.

166. COY (A) weak (B) airy (C) brazen (D) old (E) tiresome
167. COZEN (A) amuse (B) treat honestly (C) prate (D) shackle (E) vilify
168. CRAVEN (A) desirous (B) direct (C) bold (D) civilized (E) controlled
169. CRUX (A) affliction (B) spark (C) events (D) trivial point (E) belief
170. CRYPTIC (A) tomblike (B) futile (C) famous (D) candid (E) indifferent
171. CUPIDITY (A) anxiety (B) tragedy (C) generosity (D) entertainment (E) love

172. CURTAIL (A) mutter (B) lengthen (C) express (D) burden (E) shore up
173. CYNICAL (A) trusting (B) effortless (C) conclusive (D) gallant (E) vertical
174. DANK (A) dry (B) guiltless (C) warm (D) babbling (E) reserved
175. DAPPER (A) unintelligent (B) untidy (C) uncertain (D) ungrateful (E) unhealthy
176. DAUNTLESS (A) stolid (B) cowardly (C) irrelevant (D) peculiar (E) particular
177. DEARTH (A) life (B) abundance (C) brightness (D) terror (E) width
178. DEBACLE (A) progress (B) refusal (C) masque (D) cowardice (E) traffic
179. DEBILITATE (A) bedevil (B) repress (C) strengthen (D) animate (E) deaden
180. DEBONAIR (A) awkward (B) windy (C) balmy (D) strong (E) stormy

Word List 13   deciduous-dermatologist

deciduous ADJ. falling off, as of leaves. The oak is a *deciduous* tree.

decimate V. kill, usually one out of ten. We do more to *decimate* our population in automobile accidents than we do in war.

decipher V. decode. I could not *decipher* the doctor's handwriting.

declivity N. downward slope. The children loved to ski down the *declivity*.

décolleté ADJ. having a low-cut neckline. Fashion decrees that evening gowns be *décolleté* this season; bare shoulders are again the vogue.

decomposition N. decay. Despite the body's advanced state of *decomposition*, the police were able to identify the murdered man.

■ **decorum** N. propriety; orderliness and good taste in manners. Even the best-mannered students have trouble behaving with *decorum* on the last day of school. decorous, ADJ.

decoy N. lure or bait. The wild ducks were not fooled by the *decoy*. also V.

decrepitude N. state of collapse caused by illness or old age. I was unprepared for the state of *decrepitude* in which I had found my old friend; he seemed to have aged twenty years in six months.

decry V. express strong disapproval of; disparage. The founder of the Children's Defense Fund, Marian Wright Edelman, strongly *decries* the lack of financial and moral support for children in America today.

deducible ADJ. derived by reasoning. If we accept your premise, your conclusions are easily *deducible*.

deface V. mar; disfigure. If you *deface* a library book you will have to pay a hefty fine.

defame V. harm someone's reputation; malign; slander. If you try to *defame* my good name, my lawyers will see you in court. If rival candidates persist in *defaming* one another, the voters may conclude that all politicians are crooks. defamation, N.

■ **default** N. failure to act. When the visiting team failed to show up for the big game, they lost the game by *default*. When Jack failed to make the payments on his Jaguar, the dealership took back the car because he had *defaulted* on his debt.

defeatist ADJ. resigned to defeat; accepting defeat as a natural outcome. If you maintain your *defeatist* attitude, you will never succeed. also N.

defection N. desertion. The children, who had made him an idol, were hurt most by his *defection* from our cause.

defer V. delay till later; exempt temporarily. In wartime, some young men immediately volunteer to serve; others *defer* making plans until they hear from their draft boards. During the Vietnam War, many young men, hoping to be *deferred*, requested student *deferments*.

defer V. give in respectfully; submit. When it comes to making decisions about purchasing software, we must *defer* to Michael, our computer guru; he has the final word. Michael, however, can *defer* these questions to no one; only he can decide.

■ **deference** N. courteous regard for another's wish. In *deference* to the minister's request, please do not take photographs during the wedding service.

defiance N. refusal to yield; resistance. When John reached the "terrible two's," he responded to every parental request with howls of *defiance*. defy, v. defiant, ADJ.

defile V. pollute; profane. The hoodlums *defiled* the church with their scurrilous writing.

definitive ADJ. most reliable or complete. Carl Sandburg's *Abraham Lincoln* may be regarded as the *definitive* work on the life of the Great Emancipator.

deflect V. turn aside. His life was saved when his cigarette case *deflected* the bullet.

defoliate V. destroy leaves. In Vietnam the army made extensive use of chemical agents to *defoliate* the woodlands.

defray V. provide for the payment of. Her employer offered to *defray* the costs of her postgraduate education.

defrock V. to strip a priest or minister of church authority. We knew the minister had violated church regulations, but we had not realized his offense was serious enough to cause him to be *defrocked*.

deft ADJ. neat; skillful. The *deft* waiter uncorked the champagne without spilling a drop.

defunct ADJ. dead; no longer in use or existence. The lawyers sought to examine the books of the *defunct* corporation.

degenerate V. become worse; deteriorate. As the fight dragged on, the champion's style *degenerated* until he could barely keep on his feet.

degradation N. humiliation; debasement; degeneration. Some secretaries object to fetching the boss a cup of coffee because they resent the *degradation* of being made to perform such lowly tasks. degrade, v.

dehydrate V. remove water from; dry out. Running under a hot sun quickly *dehydrates* the body; joggers avoid *dehydration* by carrying water bottles and drinking from them frequently.

deify V. turn into a god; idolize. Admire the rock star all you want; just don't *deify* him.

deign V. condescend; stoop. The celebrated fashion designer would not *deign* to speak to a mere seamstress; his overburdened assistant had to convey the master's wishes to the lowly workers assembling his great designs.

delete V. erase; strike out. If you *delete* this paragraph, the composition will have more appeal.

deleterious ADJ. harmful. If you believe that smoking is *deleterious* to your health (and the Surgeon General surely does), then quit!

deliberate V. consider; ponder. Offered the new job, she asked for time to *deliberate* before she made her decision.

■ **delineate** V. portray; depict; sketch. Using only a few descriptive phrases, Austen *delineates* the character of Mr. Collins so well that we can predict his every move. delineation, N.

delirium N. mental disorder marked by confusion. In his *delirium*, the drunkard saw pink panthers and talking pigs. Perhaps he wasn't *delirious*: he might just have wandered into a movie house.

delta N. flat plain of mud or sand between branches of a river. His dissertation discussed the effect of intermittent flooding on the fertility of the Nile *delta*.

delude V. deceive. The mistress *deludes* herself into believing that her lover will leave his wife and marry her.

deluge N. flood; rush. When we advertised the position we received a *deluge* of applications. also v.

delusion N. false belief; hallucination. Don suffers from *delusions* of grandeur: he thinks he's a world-famous author when he's published just one paperback book.

delusive ADJ. deceptive; raising vain hopes. Do not raise your hopes on the basis of his *delusive* promises.

delve V. dig; investigate. *Delving* into old books and manuscripts is part of a researcher's job.

demagogue N. person who appeals to people's prejudice; false leader. He was accused of being a *demagogue* because he made promises that aroused futile hopes in his listeners.

demean V. degrade; humiliate. Standing on his dignity, he refused to *demean* himself by replying to the offensive letter. If you truly believed in the dignity of labor, you would not think it would *demean* you to work as a janitor.

demeanor N. behavior; bearing. His sober *demeanor* quieted the noisy revelers.

demented ADJ. insane. Doctor Demento was a radio personality who liked to act as if he were truly *demented*. If you're *demented*, your mental state is out of whack; in other words, you're wacky.

demise N. death. Upon the *demise* of the dictator, a bitter dispute about succession to power developed.

demographic ADJ. related to population balance. In conducting a survey, one should take into account *demographic* trends in the region. demography, N.

demolition N. destruction. One of the major aims of the air force was the complete *demolition* of all means of transportation by the bombing of rail lines and terminals. demolish, v.

demoniac ADJ. fiendish. The Spanish Inquisition devised many *demoniac* means of torture. demon, N.

demotic ADJ. pertaining to the people. He lamented the passing of aristocratic society and maintained that a *demotic* society would lower the nation's standards.

demur N. objection; protest. Michelangelo regularly denied that Leonardo Da Vinci had influenced him, and critics have usually accepted his statements without *demur*.

demur V. object (because of doubts, scruples); hesitate. When offered a post on the board of directors, David *demurred*: he had scruples about taking on the job because he was unsure he could handle it in addition to his other responsibilities.

demure ADJ. grave; serious; coy. She was *demure* and reserved, a nice modest girl whom any young man would be proud to take home to his mother.

■ **denigrate** V. blacken. All attempts to *denigrate* the character of our late president have failed; the people still love him and cherish his memory.

denizen N. inhabitant or resident; regular visitor. In *The Untouchables*, Eliot Ness fights Al Capone and the other *denizens* of Chicago's underworld. Ness's fight against corruption was the talk of all the *denizens* of the local bars.

denotation N. meaning; distinguishing by name. A dictionary will always give us the *denotation* of a word; frequently, it will also give us its connotation.

denouement N. outcome; final development of the plot of a play or other literary work. The play was childishly written; the *denouement* was obvious to sophisticated theatergoers as early as the middle of the first act.

denounce V. condemn; criticize. The reform candidate *denounced* the corrupt city officers for having betrayed the public's trust. denunciation, N.

depict V. portray. In this sensational exposé, the author *depicts* Beatle John Lennon as a drug-crazed neurotic. Do you question the accuracy of this *depiction* of Lennon?

deplete V. reduce; exhaust. We must wait until we *deplete* our present inventory before we order replacements.

deplore V. regret. Although I *deplore* the vulgarity of your language, I defend your right to express yourself freely.

deploy V. spread out [troops] in an extended though shallow battle line. The general ordered the battalion to *deploy* in order to meet the enemy offensive.

depose V. dethrone; remove from office. The army attempted to *depose* the king and set up a military government.

deposition N. testimony under oath. She made her *deposition* in the judge's chamber.

depravity N. extreme corruption; wickedness. The *depravity* of Caligula's behavior eventually sickened even those who had willingly participated in his earlier, comparatively innocent orgies. deprave, V.

deprecate V. express disapproval of; protest against; belittle. A firm believer in old-fashioned courtesy, Miss Post *deprecated* the modern tendency to address new acquaintances by their first names. deprecatory, ADJ.

depreciate V. lessen in value. If you neglect this property, it will *depreciate*.

depredation N. plundering. After the *depredations* of the invaders, the people were penniless.

derange V. make insane; disarrange. Hamlet's cruel rejection *deranged* poor Ophelia; in her madness, she drowned herself.

derelict ADJ. abandoned; negligent. The *derelict* craft was a menace to navigation. Whoever abandoned it in the middle of the harbor was *derelict* in living up to his responsibilities as a boat owner. also N.

■ **deride** V. ridicule; make fun of. The critics *derided* his pretentious dialogue and refused to consider his play seriously. Despite the critics' *derision*, however, audiences were moved by the play, cheering its unabashedly sentimental conclusion. derisive, ADJ.

■ **derivative** ADJ. unoriginal; obtained from another source. Although her early poetry was clearly *derivative* in nature, the critics thought she had promise and eventually would find her own voice.

dermatologist N. one who studies the skin and its diseases. I advise you to consult a *dermatologist* about your acne.

Test

Word List 13   *Synonyms*

Each of the questions below consists of a word in capital letters, followed by five lettered words or phrases. Choose the lettered word or phrase that is most nearly similar in meaning to the word in capital letters and write the letter of your choice on your answer paper.

181. DECIMATE (A) kill (B) disgrace (C) search (D) collide (E) deride

182. DECLIVITY (A) trap (B) quadrangle (C) quarter (D) activity (E) downward slope

183. DÉCOLLETÉ (A) flavored (B) demure (C) flowery (D) low-necked (E) sweet

184. DECOROUS (A) momentary (B) emotional (C) suppressed (D) proper (E) unexpected

185. DECREPITUDE (A) feebleness (B) disease (C) coolness (D) melee (E) crowd

186. DEFAULT (A) failure to act (B) tendency to err (C) desire to remedy (D) debt (E) misunderstanding

187. DEFECTION (A) determination (B) desertion (C) invitation (D) affection (E) reservation

188. DEFILE (A) manicure (B) ride (C) pollute (D) assemble (E) order

189. DEGRADED (A) surprised (B) lowered (C) ascended (D) learned (E) prejudged

190. DELETERIOUS (A) delaying (B) experimental (C) harmful (D) graduating (E) glorious

191. DELUGE (A) confusion (B) deception (C) flood
(D) mountain (E) weapon
192. DENIGRATE (A) refuse (B) blacken (C) terrify
(D) admit (E) review
193. DENOUEMENT (A) action (B) scenery (C) resort
(D) character (E) solution
194. DEPRAVITY (A) wickedness (B) sadness
(C) heaviness (D) tidiness (E) seriousness
195. DERANGED (A) insane (B) systematic
(C) neighborly (D) alphabetical (E) surrounded

Word List 14   derogatory-disgruntle

derogatory ADJ. expressing a low opinion. Because the word *Eskimo* has come under strong attack in recent years for its supposedly *derogatory* connotations, many Americans today either avoid the term or feel uneasy using it.

descry V. catch sight of. In the distance, we could barely *descry* the enemy vessels.

desecrate V. profane; violate the sanctity of. Shattering the altar and trampling the holy objects underfoot, the invaders *desecrated* the sanctuary.

■ **desiccate** V. dry up. A tour of this smokehouse will give you an idea of how the pioneers used to *desiccate* food in order to preserve it.

desolate ADJ. unpopulated; joyless. After six months in the crowded, bustling metropolis, David was so sick of people that he was ready to head for the most *desolate* patch of wilderness he could find.

desolate V. rob of joy; lay waste to; forsake. The bandits *desolated* the countryside, burning farms and carrying off the harvest.

desperado N. reckless outlaw. Butch Cassidy was a bold *desperado* with a price on his head.

despise V. look on with scorn; regard as worthless or distasteful. Mr. Bond, I *despise* spies; I look down on them as mean, *despicable*, honorless men, whom I would wipe from the face of the earth with as little concern as I would scrape dog droppings from the bottom of my shoe.

despoil V. strip of valuables; rob. Seeking plunder, the raiders *despoiled* the village, carrying off any valuables they found.

despondent ADJ. depressed; gloomy. To the distress of his parents, William became seriously *despondent* after he broke up with Jan. despondency, N.

despot N. tyrant; harsh, authoritarian ruler. How could a benevolent king turn overnight into a *despot*? despotism, N.

destitute ADJ. extremely poor. Because they had no health insurance, the father's costly illness left the family *destitute*. destitution, N.

desuetude N. state of disuse. Overshadowed by the newly popular waltzes and cotillions, the English country dances of Jane Austen's time fell into *desuetude* until they were rediscovered during the folk dance revival of the early twentieth century.

■ **desultory** ADJ. aimless; haphazard; digressing at random. In prison Malcolm X set himself the task of reading straight through the dictionary; to him, reading was purposeful, not *desultory*.

detached ADJ. emotionally removed; calm and objective; physically separate. A psychoanalyst must maintain a *detached* point of view and stay uninvolved with her patients' personal lives. To a child growing up in an apartment or a row house, to live in a *detached* house was an unattainable dream. (secondary meaning) detachment, N.

determinate ADJ. having a fixed order of procedure; invariable. At the royal wedding, the procession of the nobles followed a *determinate* order of precedence.

determination N. resolve; measurement or calculation; decision. Nothing could shake his *determination* that his children would get the best education that money could buy. Thanks to my pocket calculator, my *determination* of the answer to the problem took only seconds of my time.

■ **deterrent** N. something that discourages; hindrance. Does the threat of capital punishment serve as a *deterrent* to potential killers? also ADJ.

detonation N. explosion. The *detonation* of the bomb could be heard miles away.

detraction N. slandering; aspersion. Because Susan B. Anthony and Elizabeth Cady Stanton dared to fight for women's rights, their motives, manners, dress, personal appearance, and character were held up to ridicule and *detraction*.

detrimental ADJ. harmful; damaging. The candidate's acceptance of major financial contributions from a well-known racist ultimately proved *detrimental* to his campaign, for he lost the backing of many of his early grassroots supporters. detriment, N.

deviate V. turn away from (a principle, norm); depart; diverge. Richard never *deviated* from his daily routine: every day he set off for work at eight o'clock, had his sack lunch at noon, and headed home at the stroke of five.

devious ADJ. roundabout; erratic; not straightforward. The Joker's plan was so *devious* that it was only with great difficulty we could follow its shifts and dodges.

devise V. think up; invent; plan. How clever he must be to have *devised* such a devious plan! What ingenious inventions might he have *devised* if he had turned his mind to science rather than crime.

devoid ADJ. lacking. You may think Cher's mind is a total void, but she's actually not *devoid* of intelligence. She just sounds like an airhead.

devolve V. be transferred to another; delegate to another; gradually worsen. Because Humpty Dumpty was too shattered by his fall to clean up his own mess, all the work of picking up the pieces *devolved* upon poor Alice.

devotee N. enthusiastic follower. A *devotee* of the opera, she bought season tickets every year.

devout ADJ. pious. The *devout* man prayed daily.

dexterous ADJ. skillful. The magician was so *dexterous* that we could not follow his movements as he performed his tricks.

diabolical ADJ. devilish. "What a fiend I am, to devise such a *diabolical* scheme to destroy Gotham City," chortled the Joker.

diadem N. crown. The king's *diadem* was on display at the museum.

dialectical ADJ. relating to the art of debate; mutual or reciprocal. The debate coach's students grew to develop great forensic and *dialectical* skill. Teaching, however, is inherently a *dialectical* situation: the coach learned at least as much from her students as they learned from her. dialectics, N.

diaphanous ADJ. sheer; transparent. Through the *diaphanous* curtains, the burglar could clearly see the large jewelry box on the dressing table. Sexy nightgowns are *diaphanous*; woolen long johns, fortunately, are not.

■ **diatribe** N. bitter scolding; invective. During the lengthy *diatribe* delivered by his opponent he remained calm and self-controlled.

■ **dichotomy** N. split; branching into two parts (especially contradictory ones). Willie didn't know how to resolve the *dichotomy* between his ambition to go to college and his childhood longing to run away and join the circus. Then he heard about Ringling Brothers Circus College, and he knew he'd found his school.

dictum N. authoritative and weighty statement; saying; maxim. University administrations still follow the old *dictum* "Publish or perish." They don't care how good a teacher you are; if you don't publish enough papers, you're out of a job.

didactic ADJ. teaching; instructional. Pope's lengthy poem *An Essay on Man* is too *didactic* for my taste: I dislike it when poets turn preachy and moralize. didacticism, N.

die N. device for stamping or impressing; mold. In coining pennies, workers at the old mint squeezed sheets of softened copper between two *dies*.

■ **diffidence** N. shyness. You must overcome your *diffidence* if you intend to become a salesperson.

■ **diffuse** ADJ. wordy; rambling; spread out (like a gas). If you pay authors by the word, you tempt them to produce *diffuse* manuscripts rather than brief ones. also v. diffusion, N.

■ **digression** N. wandering away from the subject. Nobody minded when Professor Renoir's lectures wandered away from their official theme; his *digressions* were always more fascinating than the topic of the day. digress, v.

dilapidated ADJ. ruined because of neglect. The *dilapidated* old building needed far more work than just a new coat of paint. dilapidation, N.

dilate V. expand. In the dark, the pupils of your eyes *dilate*.

dilatory ADJ. tending to delay; intentionally delaying. If you are *dilatory* in paying your bills, your credit rating may suffer.

dilemma N. problem; choice of two unsatisfactory alternatives. In this *dilemma*, he knew no one to whom he could turn for advice.

dilettante N. aimless follower of the arts; amateur; dabbler. According to Turgenev, without painstaking work, any writer or artist remains a *dilettante*. In an age of increasing professionalism, the terms *amateur* and *dilettante* have taken on negative connotations they did not originally possess.

diligence N. steadiness of effort; persistent hard work. Her employers were greatly impressed by her *diligence* and offered her a partnership in the firm.

dilute V. make less concentrated; reduce in strength. She preferred her coffee *diluted* with milk.

diminution N. lessening; reduction in size. Old Jack was as sharp at eighty as he had been at fifty; increasing age led to no *diminution* of his mental acuity.

din N. continued loud noise. The *din* of the jackhammers outside the classroom window drowned out the lecturer's voice. also v.

dinghy N. small boat (often ship's boat). In the film *Lifeboat*, an ill-assorted group of passengers from a sunken ocean liner are marooned at sea in a *dinghy*.

dingy ADJ. dull; not fresh; cheerless. Refusing to be depressed by her *dingy* studio apartment, Bea spent the weekend polishing the floors and windows and hanging bright posters on the walls.

dint N. means; effort. By *dint* of much hard work, the volunteers were able to control the raging forest fire.

diorama N. life-size, three-dimensional scene from nature or history. Because they dramatically pose actual stuffed animals against realistic painted landscapes, the *dioramas* at the Museum of Natural History particularly impress high school biology students.

dire ADJ. disastrous. People ignored her *dire* predictions of an approaching depression.

■ **dirge** N. lament with music. The funeral *dirge* stirred us to tears.

■ **disabuse** V. correct a false impression; undeceive. I will attempt to *disabuse* you of your impression of my client's guilt; I know he is innocent.

disaffected ADJ. disloyal. Once the most loyal of Bradley's supporters, Senator Moynihan found himself becoming increasingly *disaffected*.

disapprobation N. disapproval; condemnation. The conservative father viewed his daughter's radical boyfriend with *disapprobation*.

disarray N. a disorderly or untidy state. After the New Year's party, the once orderly house was in total *disarray*.

disavowal N. denial; disclaiming. The novelist André Gide was controversial both for his early support of communism and for his subsequent *disavowal* of it after a visit to the Soviet Union. disavow, v.

disband v. dissolve; disperse. The chess club *disbanded* after its disastrous initial season.

disburse v. pay out. When you *disburse* money on the company's behalf, be sure to get a receipt.

discernible ADJ. distinguishable; perceivable. The ships in the harbor were not *discernible* in the fog.

■ **discerning** ADJ. mentally quick and observant; having insight. Though no genius, the star was sufficiently *discerning* to distinguish her true friends from the countless phonies who flattered her. discern, v. discernment, N.

disclaim v. disown; renounce claim to. If I grant you this privilege, will you *disclaim* all other rights?

disclose v. reveal. Although competitors offered him bribes, he refused to *disclose* any information about his company's forthcoming product. disclosure, N.

discombobulated ADJ. confused; discomposed. The novice square dancer became so *discombobulated* that he wandered into the wrong set.

discomfit v. put to rout; defeat; disconcert. This ruse will *discomfit* the enemy. discomfiture, N. discomfited, ADJ.

disconcert v. confuse; upset; embarrass. The lawyer was *disconcerted* by the evidence produced by her adversary.

disconsolate ADJ. sad. The death of his wife left him *disconsolate*.

discord N. conflict; lack of harmony. Watching Tweedledum battle Tweedledee, Alice wondered what had caused this pointless *discord*.

■ **discordant** ADJ. not harmonious; conflicting. Nothing is quite so *discordant* as the sound of a junior high school orchestra tuning up.

discount v. disregard. Be prepared to *discount* what he has to say about his ex-wife.

discourse N. formal discussion; conversation. The young Plato was drawn to the Agora to hear the philosophical *discourse* of Socrates and his followers. also v.

■ **discredit** v. defame; destroy confidence in; disbelieve. The campaign was highly negative in tone; each candidate tried to *discredit* the other.

■ **discrepancy** N. lack of consistency; difference. The police noticed some *discrepancies* in his description of the crime and did not believe him.

■ **discrete** ADJ. separate; unconnected; consisting of distinct parts. In programmed instruction, the information to be learned is presented in *discrete* units; you must respond correctly to each unit before you may advance to the next. Because human populations have been migrating and intermingling for hundreds of centuries, it is hard to classify humans into *discrete* racial groups. Do not confuse *discrete* (separate) with *discreet* (prudent in speech and actions).

discretion N. prudence in speech, actions; ability to decide responsibly; freedom to act on one's own. Charlotte was the soul of *discretion*: she never would repeat anything told to her in confidence. Because we trusted our architect's judgment, we left many decisions about the house renovation to his *discretion*.

discriminating ADJ. able to see differences; prejudiced. A superb interpreter of Picasso, she was sufficiently *discriminating* to judge the most complex works of modern art. discrimination, N.

discursive ADJ. digressing; rambling. As the lecturer wandered from topic to topic, we wondered what if any point there was to his *discursive* remarks.

disdain v. view with scorn or contempt. In the film *Funny Face*, the bookish heroine *disdained* fashion models for their lack of intellectual interests. also N.

disembark v. go ashore; unload cargo from a ship. Before the passengers could *disembark*, they had to pick up their passports from the ship's purser.

disenfranchise v. deprive of a civil right. The imposition of the poll tax effectively *disenfranchised* poor Southern blacks, who lost their right to vote.

disengage v. uncouple; separate; disconnect. A standard movie routine involves the hero's desperate attempt to *disengage* a railroad car from a moving train.

disfigure v. mar the appearance of; spoil. An ugly frown *disfigured* her normally pleasant face.

disgorge v. surrender something; eject; vomit. Unwilling to *disgorge* the cash he had stolen from the pension fund, the embezzler tried to run away.

disgruntle v. make discontented. The passengers were *disgruntled* by the numerous delays.

Test

Word List 14 *Antonyms*

Each of the questions below consists of a word in capital letters, followed by five lettered words or phrases. Choose the lettered word or phrase that is most nearly opposite in meaning to the word in capital letters and write the letter of your choice on your answer paper.

196. DEROGATORY (A) roguish (B) immediate
(C) opinionated (D) praising (E) conferred
197. DESECRATE (A) desist (B) integrate (C) confuse
(D) intensify (E) consecrate

198. DESPICABLE (A) steering (B) worthy of esteem
(C) inevitable (D) featureless (E) incapable
199. DESTITUTE (A) affluent (B) dazzling (C) stationary
(D) characteristic (E) explanatory
200. DEVOID (A) latent (B) eschewed (C) full of
(D) suspecting (E) evident
201. DEVOUT (A) quiet (B) dual (C) impious
(D) straightforward (E) wrong
202. DIABOLICAL (A) mischievous (B) lavish
(C) seraphic (D) azure (E) redolent

203. DIATRIBE (A) mass (B) range (C) eulogy (D) elegy (E) starvation
204. DIFFIDENCE (A) sharpness (B) boldness (C) malcontent (D) dialogue (E) catalog
205. DILATE (A) procrastinate (B) contract (C) conclude (D) participate (E) divert
206. DILATORY (A) narrowing (B) prompt (C) enlarging (D) portentous (E) sour

207. DIMINUTION (A) expectation (B) context (C) validity (D) appreciation (E) difficulty
208. DIN (A) lightness (B) safety (C) silence (D) hunger (E) promptness
209. DISABUSE (A) crash (B) violate (C) renege (D) control (E) deceive
210. DISCONSOLATE (A) unprejudiced (B) thankful (C) theatrical (D) joyous (E) prominent

Word List 15   dishearten-duplicity

dishearten V. discourage. His failure to pass the bar exam *disheartened* him.

disheveled ADJ. untidy. Your *disheveled* appearance will hurt your chances in this interview.

disinclination N. unwillingness. Some mornings I feel a great *disinclination* to get out of bed.

■ **disingenuous** ADJ. lacking genuine candor; insincere. Now that we know that the mayor and his wife are engaged in a bitter divorce fight, we find their earlier remarks regretting their lack of time together remarkably *disingenuous*.

disinter V. dig up; unearth. They *disinterred* the body and held an autopsy.

■ **disinterested** ADJ. unprejudiced. Given the judge's political ambitions and the lawyers' financial interest in the case, the only *disinterested* person in the courtroom may have been the court reporter.

■ **disjointed** ADJ. lacking coherence; separated at the joints. Unable to think of anything to say about the assigned topic, the unprepared student scribbled a few *disjointed* sentences on his answer sheet.

disjunction N. act or state of separation; disunity. Believing the mind could greatly affect the body's health, the holistic doctor rejected the notion of a necessary *disjunction* of mind and body.

dislodge V. remove (forcibly). Thrusting her fist up under the choking man's lower ribs, Margaret used the Heimlich maneuver to *dislodge* the food caught in his throat.

dismantle V. take apart. When the show closed, they *dismantled* the scenery before storing it.

dismember V. cut into small parts. When the Austrian Empire was *dismembered*, several new countries were established.

■ **dismiss** V. eliminate from consideration; reject. Believing in John's love for her, she *dismissed* the notion that he might be unfaithful. (secondary meaning)

■ **disparage** V. belittle. A doting mother, Emma was more likely to praise her son's crude attempts at art than to *disparage* them.

■ **disparate** ADJ. basically different; unrelated. Unfortunately Tony and Tina have *disparate* notions of marriage: Tony sees it as a carefree extended love affair, while Tina sees it as a solemn commitment to build a family and a home.

disparity N. difference; condition of inequality. Their *disparity* in rank made no difference at all to the prince and Cinderella.

dispassionate ADJ. calm; impartial. Known in the company for his cool judgment, Bill could impartially examine the causes of a problem, giving a *dispassionate* analysis of what had gone wrong, and go on to suggest how to correct the mess.

dispatch N. speediness; prompt execution; message sent with all due speed. Young Napoleon defeated the enemy with all possible *dispatch*; he then sent a *dispatch* to headquarters, informing his commander of the great victory. also V.

dispel V. scatter; drive away; cause to vanish. The bright sunlight eventually *dispelled* the morning mist.

disperse V. scatter. The police fired tear gas into the crowd to *disperse* the protesters. dispersion, N.

dispirited ADJ. lacking in spirit. The coach used all the tricks at his command to buoy up the enthusiasm of his team, which had become *dispirited* at the loss of the star player.

disport V. amuse. The popularity of Florida as a winter resort is constantly increasing; each year, thousands more *disport* themselves at Miami and Palm Beach.

disputatious ADJ. argumentative; fond of arguing. Convinced he knew more than his lawyers, Tony was a *disputatious* client, ready to argue about the best way to conduct the case.

disquietude N. uneasiness; anxiety. When Holmes had been gone for a day, Watson felt only a slight sense of *disquietude*, but after a week with no word, Watson's uneasiness about his missing friend had grown into a deep fear for Holmes's safety. disquiet, V., N.

disquisition N. a formal systematic inquiry; an explanation of the results of a formal inquiry. In his *disquisition*, he outlined the steps he had taken in reaching his conclusions.

dissection N. analysis; cutting apart in order to examine. The *dissection* of frogs in the laboratory is particularly unpleasant to some students.

■ **dissemble** V. disguise; pretend. Even though John tried to *dissemble* his motive for taking modern dance, we all knew he was there not to dance but to meet girls.

■ **disseminate** V. distribute; spread; scatter (like seeds). By their use of the Internet, propagandists have been able to *disseminate* their pet doctrines to new audiences around the globe.

dissent V. disagree. In the recent Supreme Court decision, Justice O'Connor *dissented* from the majority opinion. also N.

dissertation N. formal essay. In order to earn a graduate degree from many of our universities, a candidate is frequently required to prepare a *dissertation* on some scholarly subject.

dissident ADJ. dissenting; rebellious. In the purge that followed the student demonstrations at Tianamen Square, the government hunted down the *dissident* students and their supporters. also N.

dissimulate V. pretend; conceal by feigning. Although the governor tried to *dissimulate* his feelings about the opposing candidate, we all knew he despised his rival.

dissipate V. squander; waste; scatter. He is a fine artist, but I fear he may *dissipate* his gifts if he keeps wasting his time playing Trivial Pursuit.

■ **dissolution** N. disintegration; looseness in morals. The profligacy and *dissolution* of life in Caligula's Rome appall some historians. dissolute, ADJ.

■ **dissonance** N. discord; opposite of harmony. Composer Charles Ives often used *dissonance*—clashing or unresolved chords—for special effects in his musical works. dissonant, ADJ.

dissuade V. persuade not to do; discourage. Since Tom could not *dissuade* Huck from running away from home, he decided to run away with his friend. dissuasion, N.

distant ADJ. reserved or aloof; cold in manner. Her *distant* greeting made me feel unwelcome from the start. (secondary meaning)

■ **distend** V. expand; swell out. I can tell when he is under stress by the way the veins *distend* on his forehead.

■ **distill** V. purify; refine; concentrate. A moonshiner *distills* mash into whiskey; an epigrammatist *distills* thoughts into quips.

distinction N. honor; contrast; discrimination. A holder of the Medal of Honor, George served with great *distinction* in World War II. He made a *distinction*, however, between World War II and Vietnam, which he considered an immoral conflict.

distort V. twist out of shape. It is difficult to believe the newspaper accounts of the riots because of the way some reporters *distort* and exaggerate the actual events. distortion, N.

distrait ADJ. inattentive; distracted, often by anxiety. Jane was so caught up in her wedding plans that her family and friends considered her absent-minded, *distrait*, aloof and generally useless.

distraught ADJ. upset; distracted by anxiety. The *distraught* parents frantically searched the ravine for their lost child.

diurnal ADJ. daily. A farmer cannot neglect his *diurnal* tasks at any time; cows, for example, must be milked regularly.

diva N. operatic singer; prima donna. Although world famous as a *diva*, she did not indulge in fits of temperament.

■ **diverge** V. vary; go in different directions from the same point. The spokes of the wheel *diverge* from the hub.

divergent ADJ. differing; deviating. Since graduating from medical school, the two doctors have followed *divergent* paths, the one going on to become a nationally prominent surgeon, the other dedicating himself to a small family practice in his hometown. divergence, N.

diverse ADJ. differing in some characteristics; various. The professor suggested *diverse* ways of approaching the assignment and recommended that we choose one of them.

diversion N. act of turning aside; pastime. After studying for several hours, he needed a *diversion* from work. divert, V.

diversity N. variety; dissimilitude. When power narrows the area of man's concern, poetry reminds him of the richness and *diversity* of existence. (John Fitzgerald Kennedy)

■ **divest** V. strip; deprive. He was *divested* of his power to act and could no longer govern. divestiture, N.

divine V. perceive intuitively; foresee the future. Nothing infuriated Tom more than Aunt Polly's ability to *divine* when he was not telling the truth.

divulge V. reveal. No lover of gossip, Charlotte would never *divulge* anything that a friend told her in confidence.

docile ADJ. obedient; easily managed. As *docile* as he seems today, that old lion was once a ferocious, snarling beast. docility, N.

docket N. program as for trial; book where such entries are made. The case of *Smith v. Jones* was entered in the *docket* for July 15. also V.

doctrinaire ADJ. unable to compromise about points of doctrine; dogmatic; unyielding. Weng had hoped that the student-led democracy movement might bring about change in China, but the repressive response of the *doctrinaire* hard-liners crushed his dreams of democracy.

doctrine N. teachings in general; particular principle (religious, legal, etc.) taught. He was so committed to the *doctrines* of his faith that he was unable to evaluate them impartially.

■ **document** V. provide written evidence. She kept all the receipts from her business trip in order to *document* her expenses for the firm. also N.

doddering ADJ. shaky; infirm from old age. Lear's cruel daughters treat him as a *doddering* old fool, too aged and infirm to be taken seriously.

doff V. take off. A gentleman used to *doff* his hat to a lady.

dogged ADJ. determined; stubborn. *Les Miserables* tells of Inspector Javert's long, *dogged* pursuit of the criminal Jean Valjean.

doggerel N. poor verse. Although we find occasional snatches of genuine poetry in her work, most of her writing is mere *doggerel.*

■ **dogmatic** ADJ. opinionated; arbitrary; doctrinal. We tried to discourage Doug from being so *dogmatic,* but never could convince him that his opinions might be wrong.

doldrums N. blues; listlessness; slack period. Once the excitement of meeting her deadline was over, she found herself in the *doldrums.*

doleful ADJ. mournful; causing sadness. Eeyore, the lugubrious donkey immortalized by A. A. Milne, looked at his cheerful friend Tigger and sighed a *doleful* sigh.

dolorous ADJ. sorrowful. The conflict between Lancelot's love for Guinevere and his loyalty to King Arthur led to Arthur's "*dolorous* death and departing out of this world."

dolt N. stupid person; dunce. The heroes of *Dumb and Dumber* are, as the title suggests, a classic pair of *dolts.*

domicile N. home. Although his legal *domicile* was in New York City, his work kept him away from his residence for many years. also V.

domineer V. rule over tyrannically. Students prefer teachers who guide, not ones who *domineer.*

don V. put on. When Clark Kent had to *don* his Superman outfit, he changed clothes in a convenient phone booth.

■ **dormant** ADJ. sleeping; lethargic; latent. At fifty her long-*dormant* ambition to write flared up once more; within a year she had completed the first of her great historical novels. dormancy, N.

dormer N. window projecting from roof. In remodeling the attic into a bedroom, we decided that we needed to put in *dormers* to provide sufficient ventilation for the new room.

dorsal ADJ. relating to the back of an animal. A shark may be identified by its *dorsal* fin, which projects above the surface of the ocean.

dossier N. file of documents on a subject. Ordered by J. Edgar Hoover to investigate the senator, the FBI compiled a complete *dossier* on him.

dotage N. senility. In his *dotage,* the old man bored us with long tales of events in his childhood.

dote V. be excessively fond of; show signs of mental decline. Not only grandmothers bore you with stories about their brilliant grandchildren; grandfathers *dote* on the little rascals, too.

dour ADJ. sullen; stubborn. The man was *dour* and taciturn.

douse V. plunge into water; drench; extinguish. They *doused* each other with hoses and water balloons.

dowdy ADJ. slovenly; untidy. She tried to change her *dowdy* image by buying a fashionable new wardrobe.

downcast ADJ. disheartened; sad. Cheerful and optimistic by nature, Beth was never *downcast* despite the difficulties she faced.

drab ADJ. dull; lacking color; cheerless. The Dutch woman's *drab* winter coat contrasted with the distinctive, colorful native costume she wore beneath it.

draconian ADJ. extremely severe. When the principal canceled the senior prom because some seniors had been late to school that week, we thought the *draconian* punishment was far too harsh for such a minor violation of the rules.

dregs N. sediment; worthless residue. David poured the wine carefully to avoid stirring up the *dregs.*

drivel N. nonsense; foolishness. Why do I have to spend my days listening to such idiotic *drivel? Drivel* is related to dribble: think of a dribbling, *driveling* idiot.

droll ADJ. queer and amusing. He was a popular guest because his *droll* anecdotes were always entertaining.

drone N. idle person; male bee. Content to let his wife support him, the would-be writer was in reality nothing but a *drone.*

drone V. talk dully; buzz or murmur like a bee. On a gorgeous day, who wants to be stuck in a classroom listening to the teacher *drone?*

dross N. waste matter; worthless impurities. Many methods have been devised to separate the valuable metal from the *dross.*

drudgery N. menial work. Cinderella's fairy godmother rescued her from a life of *drudgery.*

dubious ADJ. questionable; filled with doubt. Some critics of the GRE contend the test is of *dubious* worth. Tony claimed he could get a perfect score on the test, but Tina was *dubious:* she knew he hadn't cracked a book in three years. dubiety, N.

ductile ADJ. malleable; flexible; pliable. Copper is an extremely *ductile* material: you can stretch it into the thinnest of wires, bend it, even wind it into loops. ductility, N.

dulcet ADJ. sweet sounding. The *dulcet* sounds of the birds at dawn were soon drowned out by the roar of traffic passing our motel.

dumbfound V. astonish. Egbert's perfect score on the GRE *dumbfounded* his classmates, who had always considered him to be utterly dumb.

■ **dupe** N. someone easily fooled. While the gullible Watson often was made a *dupe* by unscrupulous parties, Sherlock Holmes was far more difficult to fool.

duplicity N. double-dealing; hypocrisy. When Tanya learned that Mark had been two-timing her, she was furious at his *duplicity.* duplicitous, ADJ.

Test

Word List 15 *Synonyms and Antonyms*

Each of the questions below consists of a word in capital letters, followed by five lettered words or phrases. Choose the lettered word or phrase that is most nearly similar or opposite in meaning to the word in capital letters and write the letter of your choice on your answer paper.

211. DISINGENUOUS (A) uncomfortable (B) eventual (C) naive (D) complex (E) enthusiastic

212. DISINTERESTED (A) prejudiced (B) horrendous (C) affected (D) arbitrary (E) bored

213. DISJOINTED (A) satisfied (B) carved (C) understood (D) connected (E) evicted

214. DISPARITY (A) resonance (B) elocution (C) relief (D) difference (E) symbolism

215. DISPASSIONATE (A) sensual (B) immoral (C) inhibited (D) impartial (E) scientific

216. DISPIRITED (A) current (B) dented (C) drooping (D) alcoholic (E) dallying

217. DISSIPATE (A) economize (B) clean (C) accept (D) anticipate (E) withdraw

218. DISTEND (A) bloat (B) adjust (C) exist (D) materialize (E) finish

219. DISTRAIT (A) clever (B) industrial (C) absentminded (D) narrow (E) crooked

220. DIVULGE (A) look (B) refuse (C) deride (D) reveal (E) harm

221. DOFF (A) withdraw (B) take off (C) remain (D) control (E) start

222. DOGMATIC (A) benign (B) canine (C) impatient (D) petulant (E) arbitrary

223. DOTAGE (A) senility (B) silence (C) sensitivity (D) interest (E) generosity

224. DOUR (A) sullen (B) ornamental (C) grizzled (D) lacking speech (E) international

225. DROLL (A) rotund (B) amusing (C) fearsome (D) tiny (E) strange

Word List 16 duration-encroachment

duration N. length of time something lasts. Because she wanted the children to make a good impression on the dinner guests, Mother promised them a treat if they'd behave well for the *duration* of the meal.

duress N. forcible restraint, especially unlawfully. The hostages were held under *duress* until the prisoners' demands were met.

dutiful ADJ. respectful; obedient. When Mother told Billy to kiss Great-Aunt Hattie, the boy obediently gave the old woman a *dutiful* peck on her cheek.

dwindle V. shrink; reduce. The food in the lifeboat gradually *dwindled* away to nothing; in the end, they ate the ship's cook.

dynamic ADJ. energetic; vigorously active. The *dynamic* aerobics instructor kept her students on the run; she was a little *dynamo*.

dyspeptic ADJ. suffering from indigestion. All the talk about rich food made him feel *dyspeptic*. dyspepsia, N.

earthy ADJ. unrefined; coarse. His *earthy* remarks often embarrassed the women in his audience.

ebb V. recede; lessen. Sitting on the beach, Mrs. Dalloway watched the tide *ebb*: the waters receded, drawing away from her as she sat there all alone. also N.

■ **ebullient** ADJ. showing excitement; overflowing with enthusiasm. Amy's *ebullient* nature could not be repressed; she was always bubbling over with excitement. ebullience, N.

eccentric ADJ. irregular; odd; whimsical; bizarre. The comet veered dangerously close to the earth in its *eccentric* orbit. People came up with some *eccentric* ideas for dealing with the emergency: one kook suggested tying a knot in the comet's tail!

eccentricity N. oddity; idiosyncrasy. Some of his friends tried to account for his rudeness to strangers as the *eccentricity* of genius.

ecclesiastic ADJ. pertaining to the church. The minister donned his *ecclesiastic* garb and walked to the pulpit. also N.

■ **eclectic** ADJ. selective; composed of elements drawn from disparate sources. His style of interior decoration was *eclectic*: bits and pieces of furnishings from widely divergent periods, strikingly juxtaposed to create a unique decor. eclecticism, N.

eclipse V. darken; extinguish; surpass. The new stock market high *eclipsed* the previous record set in 1985.

ecologist N. person concerned with the interrelationship between living organisms and their environment. The *ecologist* was concerned that the new dam would upset the natural balance of the creatures living in Glen Canyon.

economy N. efficiency or conciseness in using something. Reading the epigrams of Pope, I admire the *economy* of his verse: in few words he conveys worlds of meaning. (secondary meaning)

ecstasy N. rapture; joy; any overpowering emotion. When Allison received her long-hoped-for letter of acceptance from Harvard, she was in *ecstasy*. ecstatic, ADJ.

eddy N. swirling current of water, air, etc. The water in the tide pool was still, except for an occasional *eddy*. also V.

edict N. decree (especially one issued by a sovereign); official command. The emperor issued an *edict* decreeing that everyone should come see him model his magnificent new clothes.

edify V. instruct; correct morally. Although his purpose was to *edify* and not to entertain his audience, many of his listeners were amused and not enlightened.

eerie ADJ. weird. In that *eerie* setting, it was easy to believe in ghosts and other supernatural beings.

efface V. rub out. The coin had been handled so many times that its date had been *effaced*.

effectual ADJ. able to produce a desired effect; valid. Medical researchers are concerned because of the development of drug-resistant strains of bacteria; many once-useful antibiotics are no longer *effectual* in curing bacterial infections.

effeminate ADJ. having womanly traits. "*Effeminate* men intrigue me more than anything in the world. I see them as my alter egos. I feel very drawn to them. I think like a guy, but I'm feminine. So I relate to feminine men." (Madonna)

effervescence N. inner excitement or exuberance; bubbling from fermentation or carbonation. Nothing depressed Sue for long; her natural *effervescence* soon reasserted itself. Soda that loses its *effervescence* goes flat. effervescent, ADJ. effervesce, V.

effete ADJ. lacking vigor; worn out; sterile. Is the Democratic Party still a vital political force, or is it an *effete*, powerless faction, wedded to outmoded liberal policies?

■ **efficacy** N. power to produce desired effect. The *efficacy* of this drug depends on the regularity of the dosage. efficacious, ADJ.

effigy N. dummy. The mob showed its irritation by hanging the judge in *effigy*.

effluvium N. noxious smell. Air pollution has become a serious problem in our major cities; the *effluvium* and the poisons in the air are hazards to life. effluvia, PL.

■ **effrontery** N. impudence; shameless boldness; sheer nerve; presumptuousness. When the boss told Frank she was firing him for laziness and insubordination, he had the *effrontery* to ask her for a letter of recommendation.

effusion N. pouring forth. The critics objected to her literary *effusion* because it was too flowery.

effusive ADJ. pouring forth; gushing. Unmoved by Martha's many compliments on his performance, George dismissed her *effusive* words of praise as the sentimental outpourings of emotional fool.

egoism N. excessive interest in one's self; belief that one should be interested in one's self rather than in others. His *egoism* prevented him from seeing the needs of his colleagues.

egotistical ADJ. excessively self-centered; self-important; conceited. Typical *egotistical* remark: "But enough of this chitchat about you and your little problems. Let's talk about what's really important: me!" egotistic, ADJ. egotism, N.

egregious ADJ. notorious; conspicuously bad or shocking. She was an *egregious* liar; we all knew better than to believe a word she said. Ed's housekeeping was *egregious*: he let his dirty dishes pile up so long that they were stuck together with last week's food.

egress N. exit. Barnum's sign "To the *Egress*" fooled many people who thought they were going to see an animal and instead found themselves in the street.

ejaculation N. exclamation. He could not repress an *ejaculation* of surprise when he heard the news.

elaboration N. addition of details; intricacy. Tell what happened simply, without any *elaboration*. elaborate, V.

elated ADJ. overjoyed; in high spirits. Grinning from ear to ear, Bonnie Blair was clearly *elated* by her fifth Olympic gold medal. elation, N.

■ **elegy** N. poem or song expressing lamentation. On the death of Edward King, Milton composed the *elegy* "Lycidas." elegiacal, ADJ.

■ **elicit** V. draw out by discussion. The detectives tried to *elicit* where he had hidden his loot.

elixir N. cure-all; something invigorating. The news of her chance to go abroad acted on her like an *elixir*.

ellipsis N. omission of words from a text. Sometimes an *ellipsis* can lead to a dangling modifier, as in the sentence "Once dressed, ... you should refrigerate the potato salad."

elliptical ADJ. oval; ambiguous, either purposely or because key words have been left out. An *elliptical* billiard ball wobbles because it is not perfectly round; an *elliptical* remark baffles because it is not perfectly clear.

eloquence N. expressiveness; persuasive speech. The crowds were stirred by Martin Luther King's *eloquence*.

elucidate V. explain; enlighten. He was called upon to *elucidate* the disputed points in his article.

elusive ADJ. evasive; baffling; hard to grasp. No matter how hard Tom tried to lure the trout into taking the bait, the fish was too *elusive* for him to catch. elude, V.

elysian ADJ. relating to paradise; blissful. An afternoon sail on the bay was for her an *elysian* journey.

emaciated ADJ. thin and wasted. A severe illness left him acutely *emaciated*, and he did not recover fully until he had regained most of his lost weight.

emanate V. issue forth. A strong odor of sulfur *emanated* from the spring.

emancipate V. set free. At first, the attempts of the Abolitionists to *emancipate* the slaves were unpopular in New England as well as in the South.

embargo N. ban on commerce or other activity. As a result of the *embargo*, trade with the colonies was at a standstill.

embark V. commence; go on board a boat; begin a journey. In devoting herself to the study of gorillas, Dian Fossey *embarked* on a course of action that was to cost her her life.

embed   v. enclose; place in something. Tales of actual historical figures like King Alfred have become *embedded* in legends.

■ **embellish**   v. adorn; ornament; enhance, as a story. The costume designer *embellished* the leading lady's ball gown with yards and yards of ribbon and lace.

embezzlement   N. stealing. The bank teller confessed his *embezzlement* of the funds.

emboss   v. produce a design in raised relief. The secretary of the corporation uses a special stamp to *emboss* the corporate seal on all official documents.

embrace   v. hug; adopt or espouse; accept readily; encircle; include. Clasping Maid Marian in his arms, Robin Hood *embraced* her lovingly. In joining the outlaws in Sherwood Forest, she had openly *embraced* their cause. also N.

embroider   v. decorate with needlework; ornament with fancy or fictitious details. For her mother's birthday, Beth *embroidered* a lovely design on a handkerchief. When asked what made her late getting home, Jo *embroidered* her account with tales of runaway horses and rescuing people from a ditch. embroidery, N.

embroil   v. throw into confusion; involve in strife; entangle. He became *embroiled* in the heated discussion when he tried to arbitrate the dispute.

embryonic   ADJ. undeveloped; rudimentary. The CEO reminisced about the good old days when the computer industry was still in its *embryonic* stage and start-up companies were being founded in the family garage.

emend   v. correct, usually a text. In editing *Beowulf* for his new scholarly edition, Professor Oliver freely *emended* the manuscript's text whenever it seemed to make no sense.

emendation   N. correction of errors; improvement. Please initial all the *emendations* you have made in this contract.

emetic   N. substance causing vomiting. Ingesting an *emetic* like mustard is useful in some cases of poisoning.

eminent   ADJ. high; lofty. After her appointment to this *eminent* position, she seldom had time for her former friends.

emissary   N. agent; messenger. The Secretary of State was sent as the president's special *emissary* to the conference on disarmament.

emollient   N. soothing or softening remedy. *Emollients* soften the skin by slowing evaporation of water. Beeswax, spermaceti, almond oil, and rosewater were used in ancient Greece, while lanolin or sheep fat was commonly used in medieval Europe. also ADJ.

emolument   N. salary; compensation. In addition to the *emolument* this position offers, you must consider the social prestige it carries with it.

empathy   N. ability to identify with another's feelings, ideas, etc. What made Ann such a fine counselor was her *empathy*, her ability to put herself in her client's place and feel his emotions as if they were her own. empathize, V.

■ **empirical**   ADJ. based on experience. He distrusted hunches and intuitive flashes; he placed his reliance entirely on *empirical* data.

■ **emulate**   v. imitate; rival. In a brief essay, describe a person you admire, someone whose virtues you would like to *emulate*.

enamored   ADJ. in love. Narcissus became *enamored* of his own beauty.

encipher   v. encode; convert a message into code. In one of Bond's first lessons he learned how to *encipher* the messages he sent to Miss Moneypenny so that none of his other lady friends could read them.

enclave   N. territory enclosed within an alien land. The Vatican is an independent *enclave* in Italy.

encomiastic   ADJ. praising; eulogistic. Some critics believe that his *encomiastic* statements about Napoleon were inspired by his desire for material advancement rather than by an honest belief in the Emperor's genius.

encomium   N. high praise; eulogy. Uneasy with the *encomiums* expressed by his supporters, Tolkien felt unworthy of such high praise.

encompass   v. surround or encircle; enclose; include. A moat, or deep water-filled trench, *encompassed* the castle, protecting it from attack. The term *alternative medicine* can *encompass* a wide range of therapies, including chiropractic, homeopathy, acupuncture, herbal medicine, meditation, biofeedback, massage therapy, and various "new age" therapies such as guided imagery and naturopathy.

encroachment   N. gradual intrusion. The *encroachment* of the factories upon the neighborhood lowered the value of the real estate.

Test

Word List 16   *Synonyms*

Each of the questions below consists of a word in capital letters, followed by five lettered words or phrases. Choose the lettered word or phrase that is most nearly similar in meaning to the word in capital letters and write the letter of your choice on your answer paper.

226. DWINDLE (A) blow (B) inhabit (C) spin (D) lessen (E) combine

227. ECSTASY (A) joy (B) speed (C) treasure (D) warmth (E) lack

228. EDIFY (A) mystify (B) suffice (C) improve (D) erect (E) entertain

229. EFFACE (A) countenance (B) encourage (C) recognize (D) blackball (E) rub out

230. EFFIGY (A) requisition (B) organ (C) charge (D) accordion (E) dummy

231. EGREGIOUS (A) pious (B) shocking (C) anxious (D) sociable (E) gloomy

232. EGRESS (A) entrance (B) bird (C) exit (D) double (E) progress

233. ELATED (A) debased (B) respectful (C) drooping (D) gay (E) charitable

234. ELUSIVE (A) deadly (B) eloping (C) evasive (D) simple (E) petrified

235. EMACIATED (A) garrulous (B) primeval (C) vigorous (D) disparate (E) thin

236. EMANCIPATE (A) set free (B) take back (C) make worse (D) embolden (E) run away

237. EMBELLISH (A) doff (B) don (C) abscond (D) adorn (E) equalize

238. EMBROIL (A) cherish (B) overheat (C) entangle (D) assure (E) worry

239. EMENDATION (A) correction (B) interpretation (C) exhumation (D) inquiry (E) fault

240. EMINENT (A) purposeful (B) high (C) delectable (D) curious (E) urgent

Word List 17   encumber-eulogistic

encumber V. burden. Some people *encumber* themselves with too much luggage when they take short trips.

endearment N. fond word or act. Your gifts and *endearments* cannot make me forget your earlier insolence.

■ **endemic** ADJ. prevailing among a specific group of people or in a specific area or country. This disease is *endemic* in this part of the world; more than 80 percent of the population are at one time or another affected by it.

endorse V. approve; support. Everyone waited to see which one of the rival candidates for the city council the mayor would *endorse*. (secondary meaning) endorsement, N.

endue V. provide with some quality; endow. He was *endued* with a lion's courage.

enduring ADJ. lasting; surviving. Keats believed in the *enduring* power of great art, which would outlast its creators' brief lives.

energize V. invigorate; make forceful and active. Rather than exhausting Maggie, dancing *energized* her.

■ **enervate** V. weaken. She was slow to recover from her illness; even a short walk to the window *enervated* her. enervation, N.

enfranchise V. admit to the rights of citizenship (especially the right to vote). Although blacks were *enfranchised* shortly after the Civil War, women did not receive the right to vote until 1920.

engage V. attract; hire; pledge oneself; confront. "Your case has *engaged* my interest, my lord," said Holmes. "You may *engage* my services."

engaging ADJ. charming; attractive. Everyone liked Nancy's pleasant manners and *engaging* personality.

■ **engender** V. cause; produce. To receive praise for real accomplishments *engenders* self-confidence in a child.

engross V. occupy fully. John was so *engrossed* in his studies that he did not hear his mother call.

■ **enhance** V. increase; improve. You can *enhance* your chances of being admitted to the college of your choice by learning to write well; an excellent essay will *enhance* any application.

enigma N. puzzle; mystery. "What do women want?" asked Dr. Sigmund Freud. Their behavior was an *enigma* to him.

enigmatic ADJ. obscure; puzzling. Many have sought to fathom the *enigmatic* smile of the *Mona Lisa*.

enjoin V. command; order; forbid. The owners of the company asked the court to *enjoin* the union from picketing the plant.

enmity N. ill will; hatred. At Camp David President Carter labored to bring an end to the *enmity* that prevented Egypt and Israel from living in peace.

ennui N. boredom. The monotonous routine of hospital life induced a feeling of *ennui* that made her moody and irritable. "This vacation is bor-ing!" complained Heather, tired of being stuck riding in the car with no way to relieve her growing *ennui*.

enormity N. hugeness (in a bad sense). He did not realize the *enormity* of his crime until he saw what suffering he had caused.

enrapture V. please intensely. The audience was *enraptured* by the freshness of the voices and the excellent orchestration.

ensconce V. settle comfortably. Now that their children were *ensconced* safely in the private school, the jet-setting parents decided to leave for Europe.

ensue V. follow as a consequence; result. What a holler would *ensue* if people had to pay the minister as much to marry them as they have to pay a lawyer to get them a divorce. (Claire Trevor)

entail V. require; necessitate; involve. Building a college-level vocabulary will *entail* some work on your part.

enterprising ADJ. full of initiative. By coming up with fresh ways to market the company's products, Mike proved himself to be an *enterprising* businessman.

enthrall V. capture; enslave. From the moment he saw her picture, he was *enthralled* by her beauty.

entice V. lure; attract; tempt. Will Mayor Bloomberg's attempts to *entice* the members of the International Olympic Committee to select New York as the site of the 2012 Olympic Games succeed? Only time will tell.

entity N. real being. As soon as the charter was adopted, the United Nations became an *entity* and had to be considered as a factor in world diplomacy.

entomology N. study of insects. Kent found *entomology* the most annoying part of his biology course; studying insects bugged him.

entrance V. put under a spell; carry away with emotion. Shafts of sunlight on a wall could *entrance* her and leave her spellbound.

entreat V. plead; ask earnestly. She *entreated* her father to let her stay out till midnight.

entree N. entrance; a way in. Because of his wealth and social position, he had *entree* into the most exclusive circles.

entrepreneur N. businessperson; contractor. Opponents of our present tax program argue that it discourages *entrepreneurs* from trying new fields of business activity.

enumerate V. list; mention one by one. Huck hung his head in shame as Miss Watson *enumerated* his many flaws.

enunciate V. utter or speak, especially distinctly. Stop mumbling! How will people understand you if you do not *enunciate* clearly?

environ V. enclose; surround. In medieval days, Paris was *environed* by a wall. environs, N.

eon N. long period of time; an age. It has taken *eons* for our civilization to develop.

epaulet N. ornament worn on the shoulder (of a uniform, etc.). The shoulder loops on Sam Spade's trench coat are the nonmilitary counterparts of the fringed *epaulets* on George Washington's uniform.

■ **ephemeral** ADJ. short-lived; fleeting. The mayfly is an *ephemeral* creature: its adult life lasts little more than a day.

epic N. long heroic poem, novel, or similar work of art. Kurosawa's film *Seven Samurai* is an *epic* portraying the struggle of seven warriors to destroy a band of robbers. also ADJ.

epicure N. connoisseur of food and drink. *Epicures* frequent this restaurant because it features exotic wines and dishes. epicurean, ADJ.

epigram N. witty thought or saying, usually short. Poor Richard's *epigrams* made Benjamin Franklin famous.

epilogue N. short speech at conclusion of dramatic work. The audience was so disappointed in the play that many did not remain to hear the *epilogue*.

episodic ADJ. loosely connected. Though he tried to follow the plot of *Gravity's Rainbow*, John found the novel too *episodic*.

epistemologist N. philosopher who studies the nature of knowledge. "What is more important, a knowledge of nature or the nature of knowledge?" the *epistemologist* asked the naturalist.

epitaph N. inscription in memory of a dead person. In his will, he dictated the *epitaph* he wanted placed on his tombstone.

epithet N. word or phrase characteristically used to describe a person or thing. So many kings of France were named Charles that modern students need *epithets* to tell them apart: Charles the Wise, for example, was someone far different from Charles the Fat.

epitome N. perfect example or embodiment. Singing "I am the very model of a modern Major-General" in *The Pirates of Penzance,* Major-General Stanley proclaimed himself the *epitome* of an officer and a gentleman. epitomize, V.

epoch N. period of time. The glacial *epoch* lasted for thousands of years.

equable ADJ. tranquil; steady; uniform. After the hot summers and cold winters of New England, she found the climate of the West Indies *equable* and pleasant.

■ **equanimity** N. calmness of temperament; composure. Even the inevitable strains of caring for an ailing mother did not disturb Bea's *equanimity*.

equestrian N. rider on horseback. These paths in the park are reserved for *equestrians* and their steeds. also ADJ.

equilibrium N. balance. After the divorce, he needed some time to regain his *equilibrium*.

equine ADJ. resembling a horse. Her long, bony face had an *equine* look to it.

equinox N. period of equal days and nights; the beginning of spring and autumn. The vernal *equinox* is usually marked by heavy rainstorms.

equipoise N. balance; balancing force; equilibrium. The high-wire acrobat used his pole as an *equipoise* to overcome the swaying caused by the wind.

equitable ADJ. fair; impartial. I am seeking an *equitable* solution to this dispute, one that will be fair and acceptable to both sides.

equity N. fairness; justice. Our courts guarantee *equity* to all.

equivocal ADJ. ambiguous; intentionally misleading. Rejecting the candidate's *equivocal* comments on tax reform, the reporters pressed him to state clearly where he stood on the issue. equivocate, V. equivocation, N.

■ **equivocate** V. lie; mislead; attempt to conceal the truth. No matter how bad the news is, give it to us straight. Above all, don't *equivocate*.

erode V. eat away. The limestone was *eroded* by the dripping water until only a thin shell remained. erosion, N.

erotic ADJ. Films with significant *erotic* content are rated R; pornographic films are rated X.

errant ADJ. wandering. Many a charming tale has been written about the knights-*errant* who helped the weak and punished the guilty during the Age of Chivalry.

erratic ADJ. odd; unpredictable. Investors become anxious when the stock market appears *erratic*.

erroneous ADJ. mistaken; wrong. I thought my answer was correct, but it was *erroneous*.

■ **erudite** ADJ. learned; scholarly. Unlike much scholarly writing, Huizinga's prose was entertaining as well as *erudite*, lively as well as learned. erudition, N.

escapade N. prank; flighty conduct. The headmaster could not regard this latest *escapade* as a boyish joke and expelled the young man.

eschew V. avoid. Hoping to present himself to his girlfriend as a totally reformed character, he tried to *eschew* all the vices, especially chewing tobacco and drinking bathtub gin.

■ **esoteric** ADJ. hard to understand; known only to the chosen few. *New Yorker* short stories often include *esoteric* allusions to obscure people and events. The implication is, if you are in the in-crowd, you'll get the reference; if you come from Cleveland, you won't. esoterica, N.

espionage N. spying. In order to maintain its power, the government developed a system of *espionage* that penetrated every household.

espouse V. adopt; support. She was always ready to *espouse* a worthy cause.

essay V. make an attempt at; test. In an effort to enrich the contemporary operatic repertoire, the Santa Fe Opera commissioned three new operas by American composers who had not previously *essayed* the form. Although Lydgate *essayed* courtly verse in Chaucer's manner, his imitations of the master's style rarely succeeded. In 1961 the actor Paul Newman *essayed* the role that perhaps best defined his screen persona, that of pool shark "Fast" Eddie Felson in *The Hustler*.

esteem V. respect; value. Jill *esteemed* Jack's taste in music, but she deplored his taste in clothes. also N.

estimable ADJ. worthy of esteem; admirable. Tennis star Andre Agassi survived a near loss in the semifinals to win the seventh Grand Slam tournament title of his uneven yet *estimable* career.

estranged ADJ. separated; alienated. The *estranged* wife sought a divorce. estrangement, N.

ethereal ADJ. light; heavenly; unusually refined. In Shakespeare's *The Tempest,* the spirit Ariel is an *ethereal* creature, too airy and unearthly for our mortal world.

ethnic ADJ. relating to races. Intolerance between *ethnic* groups is deplorable and usually is based on lack of information.

ethnology N. study of humankind. Sociology is one aspect of the science of *ethnology.*

ethos N. underlying character of a culture, group, etc. Seeing how tenderly Spaniards treated her small daughter made author Barbara Kingsolver aware of how greatly children were valued in the Spanish *ethos.*

etymology N. study of word parts. A knowledge of *etymology* can help you on many English tests: if you know what the roots and prefixes mean, you can determine the meanings of unfamiliar words.

eugenic ADJ. pertaining to the improvement of race. It is easier to apply *eugenic* principles to the raising of racehorses or prize cattle than to the development of human beings.

eulogistic ADJ. praising. To everyone's surprise, the speech was *eulogistic* rather than critical in tone.

Test

Word List 17 *Antonyms*

Each of the questions below consists of a word in capital letters, followed by five lettered words or phrases. Choose the lettered word or phrase that is most nearly opposite in meaning to the word in capital letters and write the letter of your choice on your answer paper.

241. ENERVATE (A) strengthen (B) sputter (C) arrange (D) scrutinize (E) agree

242. ENHANCE (A) degrade (B) doubt (C) scuff (D) gasp (E) avoid

243. ENNUI (A) hate (B) excitement (C) seriousness (D) humility (E) kindness

244. ENUNCIATE (A) pray (B) request (C) deliver (D) wait (E) mumble

245. EPHEMERAL (A) sensuous (B) passing (C) popular (D) distasteful (E) eternal

246. EQUABLE (A) flat (B) decisive (C) stormy (D) dishonest (E) scanty

247. EQUANIMITY (A) agitation (B) stirring (C) volume (D) identity (E) luster

248. EQUILIBRIUM (A) imbalance (B) peace (C) inequity (D) directness (E) urgency

249. EQUITABLE (A) able to leave (B) able to learn (C) unfair (D) preferable (E) rough

250. EQUIVOCAL (A) mistaken (B) quaint (C) azure (D) clear (E) universal

251. ERRATIC (A) unromantic (B) free (C) popular (D) steady (E) unknown

252. ERRONEOUS (A) accurate (B) dignified (C) curious (D) abrupt (E) round

253. ERUDITE (A) professorial (B) stately (C) short (D) unknown (E) ignorant

254. ETHEREAL (A) long-lasting (B) earthy (C) ill (D) critical (E) false

255. EULOGISTIC (A) pretty (B) critical (C) brief (D) stern (E) free

Word List 18   eulogy-faculty

■ **eulogy**   N. expression of praise, often on the occasion of someone's death. Instead of delivering a spoken *eulogy* at Genny's memorial service, Jeff sang a song he had written in her honor. eulogize, V.

■ **euphemism**   N. mild expression in place of an unpleasant one. The expression "he passed away" is a *euphemism* for "he died."

euphony   N. sweet sound. Noted for its *euphony* even when it is spoken, the Italian language is particularly pleasing to the ear when sung. euphonious, ADJ.

euphoria   N. feeling of exaggerated (or unfounded) well-being. "Jill's been on cloud nine ever since Jack asked her out," said Betty, dismissing her friend's *euphoria.*

euthanasia   N. mercy killing. Many people support *euthanasia* for terminally ill patients who wish to die.

evanescent   ADJ. fleeting; vanishing. For a brief moment, the entire skyline was bathed in an orange-red hue in the *evanescent* rays of the sunset.

evasive   ADJ. not frank; eluding. Your *evasive* answers convinced the judge that you were withholding important evidence. evade, V.

evince   V. show clearly. When he tried to answer the questions, he *evinced* his ignorance of the subject matter.

evenhanded   ADJ. impartial; fair. Do men and women receive *evenhanded* treatment from their teachers, or, as recent studies suggest, do teachers pay more attention to male students than to females?

evocative   ADJ. tending to call up (emotions, memories). Scent can be remarkably *evocative.* The aroma of pipe tobacco *evokes* the memory of my father; a whiff of talcum powder calls up images of my daughter as a child.

evoke   V. call forth. He *evoked* much criticism by his hostile manner. evocation, N.

ewe   N. female sheep. The flock of sheep was made up of dozens of *ewes,* together with only a handful of rams.

■ **exacerbate**   V. worsen; embitter. The latest bombing *exacerbated* England's already existing bitterness against the IRA, causing the Prime Minister to break off the peace talks abruptly. exacerbation, N.

exact   V. require or demand, often forcibly; take. In feudal times, landowners *exacted* heavy payments from their peasants in both goods and labor. Asa Philip Randolph proclaimed, "Freedom is never granted; it is won. Justice is never given; it is *exacted.*" The war in Algeria *exacted* a heavy toll in casualties.

exacting   ADJ. extremely demanding. Cleaning the ceiling of the Sistine Chapel was an *exacting* task, one that demanded extremely meticulous care on the part of the restorers. exaction, N.

exalt   V. raise in rank or dignity; praise. The actor Sean Connery was *exalted* to the rank of knighthood by the Queen; he now is known as Sir Sean Connery.

exasperate   V. vex. Johnny often *exasperates* his mother with his pranks.

exceptionable   ADJ. objectionable. Do you find the punk rock band Green Day a highly *exceptionable,* thoroughly distasteful group, or do you think they are exceptionally talented performers?

excerpt   N. selected passage (written or musical). The cinematic equivalent of an *excerpt* from a novel is a clip from a film. also V.

excise   V. cut away; cut out. When you *excise* the dead and dying limbs of a tree, you not only improve its appearance but also enhance its chances of bearing fruit. excision, N.

exclaim   V. cry out suddenly. "Watson! Behind you!" Holmes *exclaimed,* seeing the assassin hurl himself on his friend. exclamation, N. exclamatory, ADJ.

excoriate   V. scold with biting harshness; strip the skin off. Seeing the rips in Bill's new pants, his mother furiously *excoriated* him for ruining his good clothes. The tight, starched collar chafed and *excoriated* his neck, rubbing it raw.

■ **exculpate**   V. clear from blame. She was *exculpated* of the crime when the real criminal confessed.

execrable   ADJ. very bad. The anecdote was in such *execrable* taste that the audience was revolted.

execrate   V. curse; express abhorrence for. The world *execrates* the memory of Hitler and hopes that genocide will never again be the policy of any nation.

execute   V. put into effect; carry out. The choreographer wanted to see how well she could *execute* a pirouette. (secondary meaning) execution, N.

exegesis   N. explanation, especially of biblical passages. The minister based her sermon on her *exegesis* of a difficult passage from the book of Job.

exemplary   ADJ. serving as a model; outstanding. At commencement the dean praised Ellen for her *exemplary* behavior as class president.

exemplify   V. show by example; furnish an example. Three-time winner of the Super Bowl, Joe Montana *exemplifies* the ideal quarterback.

exempt   ADJ. not subject to a duty or obligation. Because of his flat feet, Foster was *exempt* from serving in the armed forces. also V.

exertion   N. effort; expenditure of much physical work. The *exertion* involved in unscrewing the rusty bolt left her exhausted.

exhilarating   ADJ. invigorating and refreshing; cheering. Though some of the hikers found tramping through the snow tiring, Jeffrey found the walk on the cold, crisp day *exhilarating.* His *exhilaration* was so great that, at the hike's end, he wanted to walk another five miles.

exhort   V. urge. The evangelist *exhorted* all the sinners in the audience to repent. exhortation, N.

exhume   v. dig out of the ground; remove from the grave. Could evidence that might identify the serial killer have been buried with his victim? To answer this question, the police asked the authorities for permission to *exhume* the victim's body.

■ **exigency**   N. urgent situation; pressing needs or demands; state of requiring immediate attention. The *exigencies* of war gave impetus and funding to computer research in general and in particular to the development of code-breaking machines. Denmark's Gustav I proved to be a harsh master and an *exigent* lord, known for his heavy taxes and capricious demands.

exiguous   ADJ. small; minute. Grass grew here and there, an *exiguous* outcropping among the rocks.

existential   ADJ. pertaining to existence; pertaining to the philosophy of existentialism. To the *existential* philosopher, human reason is inadequate to explain an irrational, meaningless universe.

exodus   N. departure. The *exodus* from the hot and stuffy city was particularly noticeable on Friday evenings.

exonerate   v. acquit; exculpate. The defense team feverishly sought fresh evidence that might *exonerate* their client.

exorbitant   ADJ. excessive. The people grumbled at his *exorbitant* prices but paid them because he had a monopoly.

exorcise   v. drive out evil spirits. By incantation and prayer, the medicine man sought to *exorcise* the evil spirits that had taken possession of the young warrior.

exotic   ADJ. not native; strange. Because of his *exotic* headdress, he was followed in the streets by small children who laughed at his strange appearance.

expansive   ADJ. outgoing and sociable; broad and extensive; able to increase in size. Mr. Fezziwig was in an *expansive* humor, cheerfully urging his guests to join in the Christmas feast. Looking down on his *expansive* paunch, he sighed: if his belly expanded any further, he'd need an *expansive* waistline for his pants.

expatiate   v. talk at length. At this time, please give us a brief résumé of your work; we shall permit you to *expatiate* later.

expatriate   N. exile; someone who has withdrawn from his native land. Henry James was an American *expatriate* who settled in England.

expedient   ADJ. suitable; practical; politic. A pragmatic politician, she was guided by what was *expedient* rather than by what was ethical. expediency, N.

expedite   v. hasten. Because we are on a tight schedule, we hope you will be able to *expedite* the delivery of our order. The more *expeditious* your response is, the happier we'll be.

expenditure   N. payment or expense; output. When you are operating on an expense account, you must keep receipts for all your *expenditures*. If you don't save your receipts, you won't get repaid without the *expenditure* of a lot of energy arguing with the firm's accountants.

expertise   N. specialized knowledge; expert skill. Although she was knowledgeable in a number of fields, she was hired for her particular *expertise* in computer programming.

expiate   v. make amends for (a sin). Jean Valjean tried to *expiate* his crimes by performing acts of charity.

expletive   N. interjection; profane oath. The sergeant's remarks were filled with *expletives* that offended the new recruits.

explicate   v. explain; interpret; clarify. Harry Levin *explicated* James Joyce's novels with such clarity that even *Finnegan's Wake* seemed comprehensible to his students.

explicit   ADJ. totally clear; definite; outspoken. Don't just hint around that you're dissatisfied: be *explicit* about what's bugging you.

exploit   N. deed or action, particularly a brave deed. Raoul Wallenberg was noted for his *exploits* in rescuing Jews from Hitler's forces.

exploit   v. make use of, sometimes unjustly. Cesar Chavez fought attempts to *exploit* migrant farmworkers in California. exploitation, N.

expository   ADJ. explanatory; serving to explain. The manual that came with my VCR was no masterpiece of *expository* prose: its explanations were so garbled that I couldn't even figure out how to rewind a tape.

expostulation   N. protest; remonstrance. Despite the teacher's scoldings and *expostulations,* the class remained unruly.

exposure   N. risk, particularly of being exposed to disease or to the elements; unmasking; act of laying something open. *Exposure* to sun and wind had dried out her hair and weathered her face. She looked so changed that she no longer feared *exposure* as the notorious Irene Adler, one-time antagonist of Sherlock Holmes.

expropriate   v. take possession of. He questioned the government's right to *expropriate* his land to create a wildlife preserve.

expunge   v. cancel; remove. If you behave, I will *expunge* this notation from your record.

expurgate   v. clean; remove offensive parts of a book. The editors felt that certain passages in the book had to be *expurgated* before it could be used in the classroom.

extant   ADJ. still in existence. Although the book is out of print, some copies are still *extant.* Unfortunately, all of them are in libraries or private collections; none is for sale.

extemporaneous   ADJ. not planned; impromptu. Because her *extemporaneous* remarks were misinterpreted, she decided to write all her speeches in advance.

extenuate   v. weaken; mitigate. It is easier for us to *extenuate* our own shortcomings than those of others.

extirpate   v. root up. The Salem witch trials were a misguided attempt to *extirpate* superstition and heresy.

extol   v. praise; glorify. The president *extolled* the astronauts, calling them the pioneers of the Space Age.

extort v. wring from; get money by threats, etc. The blackmailer *extorted* money from his victim.

extradition N. surrender of prisoner by one state to another. The lawyers opposed the *extradition* of their client on the grounds that for more than five years he had been a model citizen.

extraneous ADJ. not essential; superfluous. No wonder Ted can't think straight! His mind is so cluttered up with *extraneous* trivia, he can't concentrate on the essentials.

■ **extrapolation** N. projection; conjecture. Based on their *extrapolation* from the results of the primaries on Super Tuesday, the networks predicted that George W. Bush would be the Republican candidate for the presidency. extrapolate, v.

extricate v. free; disentangle. Icebreakers were needed to *extricate* the trapped whales from the icy floes that closed them in.

extrinsic ADJ. external; not essential; extraneous. A critically acclaimed *extrinsic* feature of the Chrysler Building is its ornate spire. The judge would not admit the testimony, ruling that it was *extrinsic* to the matter at hand.

extrovert N. person interested mostly in external objects and actions. A good salesperson is usually an *extrovert* who likes to mingle with people.

extrude v. force or push out. Much pressure is required to *extrude* these plastics.

exuberance N. overflowing abundance; joyful enthusiasm; flamboyance; lavishness. I was bowled over by the *exuberance* of Amy's welcome. Cheeks glowing, she was the picture of *exuberant* good health.

exude v. discharge; give forth. We get maple syrup from the sap that the trees *exude* in early spring. exudation, N.

exult v. rejoice. We *exulted* when our team won the victory.

fabricate v. build; lie. If we *fabricate* the buildings in this project out of standardized sections, we can reduce construction costs considerably. Because of Jack's tendency to *fabricate*, Jill had trouble believing a word he said.

facade N. front (of building); superficial or false appearance. The ornate *facade* of the church was often photographed by tourists, who never bothered to walk around the building to view its other sides. Cher's outward show of confidence was just a *facade* she assumed to hide her insecurity.

facet N. small plane surface (of a gem); a side. The stonecutter decided to improve the rough diamond by providing it with several *facets*.

■ **facetious** ADJ. joking (often inappropriately); humorous. I'm serious about this project; I don't need any *facetious*, smart-alecky cracks about do-good little rich girls.

facile ADJ. easily accomplished; ready or fluent; superficial. Words came easily to Jonathan: he was a *facile* speaker and prided himself on being ready to make a speech at a moment's notice. facility, N.

■ **facilitate** v. help bring about; make less difficult. Rest and proper nourishment should *facilitate* the patient's recovery.

facsimile N. copy. Many museums sell *facsimiles* of the works of art on display.

faction N. party; clique; dissension. The quarrels and bickering of the two small *factions* within the club disturbed the majority of the members.

factious ADJ. inclined to form factions; causing dissension. The pollsters' practice of dividing up the map of America into Red and Blue states reinforces *factious* feelings among Americans, who increasingly define themselves as members of one of the two major political parties. Do not confuse *factious* with *fractious* (unruly; unmanageable) or with *factitious* (not natural; not genuine; bogus).

factitious ADJ. artificial; sham. Hollywood actresses often create *factitious* tears by using glycerine.

factotum N. handyman; person who does all kinds of work. Although we had hired him as a messenger, we soon began to use him as a general *factotum* around the office.

faculty N. mental or bodily powers; teaching staff. As he grew old, Professor Twiggly feared he might lose his *faculties* and become unfit to teach. However, while he was in full possession of his *faculties*, the school couldn't kick him off the *faculty*.

Test

Word List 18 *Antonyms*

Each of the questions below consists of a word in capital letters, followed by five lettered words or phrases. Choose the lettered word or phrase that is most nearly opposite in meaning to the word in capital letters and write the letter of your choice on your answer paper.

256. EUPHONIOUS (A) strident (B) lethargic (C) literary (D) significant (E) merry

257. EVASIVE (A) frank (B) correct (C) empty (D) fertile (E) watchful

258. EXASPERATE (A) confide (B) formalize (C) placate (D) betray (E) bargain

259. EXCORIATE (A) scandalize (B) encourage (C) avoid (D) praise (E) vanquish

260. EXCULPATE (A) blame (B) prevail (C) acquire (D) ravish (E) accumulate

261. EXECRABLE (A) innumerable (B) philosophic (C) physical (D) excellent (E) meditative

262. EXECRATE (A) disobey (B) enact (C) perform (D) acclaim (E) fidget

263. EXHUME (A) decipher (B) sadden (C) integrate (D) admit (E) inter

264. EXODUS (A) neglect (B) consent (C) entry (D) gain (E) rebuke

265. EXONERATE (A) forge (B) accuse (C) record (D) doctor (E) reimburse

266. EXORBITANT (A) moderate (B) partisan (C) military (D) barbaric (E) counterfeit

267. EXTEMPORANEOUS (A) rehearsed (B) hybrid (C) humiliating (D) statesmanlike (E) picturesque

268. EXTRANEOUS (A) modern (B) decisive (C) essential (D) effective (E) expressive

269. EXTRINSIC (A) reputable (B) inherent (C) swift (D) ambitious (E) cursory

270. EXTROVERT (A) clown (B) hero (C) ectomorph (D) neurotic (E) introvert

Word List 19　fallacious–flinch

■ **fallacious** ADJ. false; misleading. Paradoxically, *fallacious* reasoning does not always yield erroneous results: even though your logic may be faulty, the answer you get may be correct.

fallacy N. mistaken idea based on flawed reasoning; invalid argument. The challenge that today's social scientists face is to use computers in ways that are most suited to them without falling into the *fallacy* that, by themselves, computers can guide and organize the study of human society.

fallible ADJ. liable to err. Although I am *fallible*, I feel confident that I am right this time.

fallow ADJ. plowed but not sowed; uncultivated. Farmers have learned that it is advisable to permit land to lie *fallow* every few years.

falter V. hesitate. When told to dive off the high board, she did not *falter*, but proceeded at once.

fanaticism N. excessive zeal; extreme devotion to a belief or cause. When Islamic fundamentalists demanded the death of Salman Rushdie because his novel questioned their faith, world opinion condemned them for their *fanaticism*. fanatic, ADJ., N.

fancied ADJ. imagined; unreal. One of the carpal (wrist) bones, the navicular bone was given its name because of its *fancied* resemblance to a boat.

fancier N. breeder or dealer of animals. The dog *fancier* exhibited her prize collie at the annual Kennel Club show.

fancy N. notion; whim; inclination. Martin took a *fancy* to paint his toenails purple. Assuming he would outgrow such a *fanciful* notion, his parents ignored his *fancy* feet. also ADJ.

fanfare N. call by bugles or trumpets; showy display. The exposition was opened with a *fanfare* of trumpets and the firing of cannon.

farce N. broad comedy; mockery. Nothing went right; the entire interview degenerated into a *farce*. farcical, ADJ.

fastidious ADJ. difficult to please; squeamish. Bobby was such a *fastidious* eater that he would eat a sandwich only if his mother first cut off every scrap of crust.

fatalism N. belief that events are determined by forces beyond one's control. With *fatalism*, he accepted the hardships that beset him. fatalistic, ADJ.

fathom V. comprehend; investigate. I find his motives impossible to *fathom*; in fact, I'm totally clueless about what goes on in his mind.

■ **fatuous** ADJ. brainless; inane; foolish, yet smug. Attacking the notion that women should defer to men's supposedly superior intelligence, Germaine Greer wrote that she was sick of pretending that some *fatuous* male's self-important pronouncements were the objects of her undivided attention. Fatheads are by definition *fatuous*.

fauna N. animals of a period or region. The scientist could visualize the *fauna* of the period by examining the skeletal remains and the fossils.

■ **fawning** ADJ. trying to please by behaving obsequiously, flattering, or cringing. In *Pride and Prejudice*, Mr. Collins is the archetypal *fawning* clergyman, wholly dependent for his living on the goodwill of his patron, Lady Catherine, whom he flatters shamelessly. Courtiers *fawn* upon princes; groupies *fawn* upon rock stars.

faze V. disconcert; dismay. No crisis could *faze* the resourceful hotel manager.

feasible ADJ. practical. Is it *feasible* to build a new stadium for the Yankees on New York's West Side? Without additional funding, the project is clearly unrealistic.

febrile ADJ. feverish. In his *febrile* condition, he was subject to nightmares and hallucinations.

feckless ADJ. feeble and ineffective; careless and irresponsible. Richard II proved such a *feckless* ruler that Bolingbroke easily convinced Parliament to elect him king in Richard's place. The film *The Perfect Circle* tells the tale of a *feckless* poet who, unwillingly saddled with two war orphans, discovers a sense of responsibility and community that had eluded him in his own previous family life.

fecundity N. fertility; fruitfulness. The *fecundity* of her mind is illustrated by the many vivid images in her poems. Rabbits are noted for their *fecundity*: in the absence of natural predators, they multiply, well, like rabbits, as the Australians learned to their dismay.

feign v. pretend. Lady Macbeth *feigned* illness in the courtyard although she was actually healthy.

feint N. trick; shift; sham blow. The boxer was fooled by his opponent's *feint* and dropped his guard. also v.

■ **felicitous** ADJ. apt; suitably expressed; well chosen. He was famous for his *felicitous* remarks and was called upon to serve as master-of-ceremonies at many a banquet.

felicity N. happiness; appropriateness (of a remark, choice, etc.). She wrote a note to the newlyweds wishing them great *felicity* in their wedded life.

fell ADJ. cruel; deadly. The newspapers told of the tragic spread of the *fell* disease.

fell v. cut or knock down; bring down (with a missile). Crying "Timber!" Paul Bunyan *felled* the mighty redwood tree. Robin Hood loosed his arrow and *felled* the king's deer.

felon N. person convicted of a grave crime. A convicted *felon* loses the right to vote.

feral ADJ. not domestic; wild. Abandoned by their owners, dogs may revert to their *feral* state, roaming the woods in packs.

ferment N. agitation; commotion. With the breakup of the Soviet Union, much of Eastern Europe was in a state of *ferment*. also v.

ferret v. drive or hunt out of hiding. She *ferreted* out their secret.

fervent ADJ. ardent; hot. She felt that the *fervent* praise was excessive and somewhat undeserved.

fervid ADJ. ardent. Her *fervid* enthusiasm inspired all of us to undertake the dangerous mission.

■ **fervor** N. glowing ardor; intensity of feeling. At the protest rally, the students cheered the strikers and booed the dean with equal *fervor*.

fester v. rankle; produce irritation or resentment. Joe's insult *festered* in Anne's mind for days, and made her too angry to speak to him.

festive ADJ. joyous; celebratory. Their wedding in the park was a *festive* occasion.

fete v. honor at a festival. The returning hero was *feted* at a community supper and dance. also N.

fetid ADJ. malodorous; foul-smelling. When a polecat is alarmed, the scent gland under its tail emits a *fetid* secretion used for territorial marking. Stinky! Does feta cheese smell *fetid* to you?

fetter v. shackle. The prisoner was *fettered* to the wall.

fiasco N. total failure. Our ambitious venture ended in a *fiasco* and we were forced to flee.

fiat N. command; authorization. Although the bill abolishing the allowances and privileges of the former princes was rejected by the upper house, it was put into effect by presidential *fiat*.

fickle ADJ. changeable; faithless. As soon as Romeo saw Juliet, he forgot all about his crush on Rosaline. Was Romeo *fickle*?

fictitious ADJ. imaginary. Although this book purports to be a biography of George Washington, many of the incidents are *fictitious*.

fidelity N. loyalty. Iago wickedly manipulates Othello, arousing his jealousy and causing him to question his wife's *fidelity*.

figment N. invention; imaginary thing. Was he hearing real voices in the night, or were they just a *figment* of his imagination?

figurative ADJ. not literal, but metaphorical; using a figure of speech. "To lose one's marbles" is a *figurative* expression; if you're told Jack has lost his marbles, no one expects you to rush out to buy him a replacement set.

figurine N. small ornamental statuette. In *The Maltese Falcon*, Sam Spade was hired to trace the missing *figurine* of a black bird.

filch v. steal. The boys *filched* apples from the fruit stand.

filial ADJ. pertaining to a son or daughter. Many children forget their *filial* obligations and disregard the wishes of their parents.

filibuster v. block legislation by making long speeches. Even though we disapproved of Senator Foghorn's political goals, we were impressed by his ability to *filibuster* endlessly to keep an issue from coming to a vote.

filigree N. delicate, lacelike metalwork. The pendant with gold *filigree* that she wore round her neck trembled with each breath she took.

filing N. particle removed by a file. As the prisoner *filed* away at the iron bar on the cell window, a small heap of *filings* accumulated on the window sill.

finale N. conclusion. It is not until we reach the *finale* of this play that we can understand the author's message.

finesse N. delicate skill. The *finesse* and adroitness with which the surgeon wielded her scalpel impressed the observers in the operating theater.

finicky ADJ. too particular; fussy. The little girl was *finicky* about her food, leaving anything that wasn't to her taste.

finite ADJ. limited. It is difficult for humanity with its *finite* existence to grasp the infinite.

firebrand N. hothead; troublemaker. The police tried to keep track of all the local *firebrands* when the president came to town.

fissure N. crevice. The mountain climbers secured footholds in tiny *fissures* in the rock.

fitful ADJ. spasmodic; intermittent. After several *fitful* attempts, he decided to postpone the start of the project until he felt more energetic.

flaccid ADJ. flabby. His sedentary life had left him with *flaccid* muscles.

■ **flag** v. droop; grow feeble. When the opposing hockey team scored its third goal only minutes into the first period, the home team's spirits *flagged*. flagging, ADJ.

flagrant ADJ. conspicuously wicked; blatant; outrageous. The governor's appointment of his brother-in-law to the state Supreme Court was a *flagrant* violation of the state laws against nepotism (favoritism based on kinship).

flail v. thresh grain by hand; strike or slap; toss about. In medieval times, warriors *flailed* their foe with a metal ball attached to a handle.

flair N. talent. She has an uncanny *flair* for discovering new artists before the public has become aware of their existence.

flamboyant ADJ. ornate. Modern architecture has discarded the *flamboyant* trimming on buildings and emphasizes simplicity of line.

flaunt v. display ostentatiously. Mae West saw nothing wrong with showing off her considerable physical charms, saying, "Honey, if you've got it, *flaunt* it!"

flay v. strip off skin; plunder; whip; attack with harsh criticism. The reviewer's stinging comments *flayed* the actress's sensitive spirit. How could she go on, after such

a vicious attack?

fleck v. spot. Pollack's coveralls, *flecked* with paint, bore witness to the sloppiness of the spatter school of art.

■ **fledgling** ADJ. inexperienced. The folk dance club set up an apprentice program to allow *fledgling* dance callers a chance to polish their skills. also N.

fleece N. wool coat of a sheep. They shear sheep of their *fleece,* which they then comb into separate strands of wool.

fleece v. rob; plunder. The tricksters *fleeced* him of his inheritance.

flick N. light stroke as with a whip. The horse needed no encouragement; only one *flick* of the whip was all the jockey had to apply to get the animal to run at top speed.

flinch v. hesitate; shrink. She did not *flinch* in the face of danger but fought back bravely.

Test

Word List 19   *Synonyms and Antonyms*

Each of the following questions consists of a word in capital letters, followed by five lettered words or phrases. Choose the lettered word or phrase that is most nearly similar or opposite in meaning to the word in capital letters and write the letter of your choice on your answer paper.

271. FANCIFUL (A) imaginative (B) knowing (C) elaborate (D) quick (E) lusty
272. FATUOUS (A) fatal (B) natal (C) terrible (D) sensible (E) tolerable
273. FEASIBLE (A) theoretical (B) impatient (C) constant (D) present (E) impractical
274. FECUNDITY (A) prophecy (B) futility (C) fruitfulness (D) need (E) dormancy
275. FEIGN (A) deserve (B) condemn (C) condone (D) attend (E) pretend
276. FELL (A) propitious (B) illiterate (C) uppermost (D) futile (E) inherent

277. FERMENT (A) stir up (B) fill (C) ferret (D) mutilate (E) banish
278. FIASCO (A) cameo (B) mansion (C) pollution (D) success (E) gamble
279. FICKLE (A) fallacious (B) tolerant (C) loyal (D) hungry (E) stupid
280. FILCH (A) milk (B) purloin (C) itch (D) cancel (E) resent
281. FINITE (A) bounded (B) established (C) affirmative (D) massive (E) finicky
282. FLAIL (A) succeed (B) harvest (C) mend (D) strike (E) resent
283. FLAIR (A) conflagration (B) inspiration (C) bent (D) egregiousness (E) magnitude
284. FLAMBOYANT (A) old-fashioned (B) restrained (C) impulsive (D) cognizant (E) eloquent
285. FLEDGLING (A) weaving (B) bobbing (C) beginning (D) studying (E) flaying

Word List 20   flippant-gaffe

flippant ADJ. lacking proper seriousness. When Mark told Mona he loved her, she dismissed his earnest declaration with a *flippant* "Oh, you say that to all the girls!" flippancy, N.

flit v. fly; dart lightly; pass swiftly by. Like a bee *flitting* from flower to flower, Rose *flitted* from one boyfriend to the next.

floe N. mass of floating ice. The ship made slow progress as it battered its way through the ice *floes.*

flora N. plants of a region or era. Because she was a botanist, she spent most of her time studying the *flora* of the desert.

florid ADJ. ruddy; reddish; flowery. If you go to Florida and get a sunburn, your complexion will look *florid.* If your postcards about your trip praise it in flowery words, your prose will be *florid,* too.

flotsam N. drifting wreckage. Beachcombers eke out a living by salvaging the *flotsam* and jetsam of the sea.

flounder V. struggle and thrash about; proceed clumsily or falter. Up to his knees in the bog, Floyd *floundered* about, trying to regain his footing. Bewildered by the new software, Flo *floundered* until Jan showed her how to get started.

flourish V. grow well; prosper; make sweeping gestures. The orange trees *flourished* in the sun.

■ **flout** V. reject; mock; show contempt for. The painter Julian Schnabel is known for works that *flout* the conventions of high art, such as paintings on velvet or linoleum. Do not confuse *flout* with *flaunt:* to flaunt something is to show it off; to flout something is to show your scorn for it. Perhaps by *flouting* the conventions of high art, Schnabel was *flaunting* his ability to get away with breaking the rules.

fluctuate V. waver; shift. The water pressure in our shower *fluctuates* wildly; you start rinsing yourself off with a trickle, and two minutes later a blast of water nearly knocks you off your feet. I'll never get used to these *fluctuations.*

fluency N. smoothness of speech. She spoke French with *fluency* and ease.

fluke N. unlikely occurrence; stroke of fortune. When Douglas defeated Tyson for the heavyweight championship, some sportscasters dismissed his victory as a *fluke.*

fluster V. confuse. The teacher's sudden question *flustered* him and he stammered his reply.

fluted ADJ. having vertical parallel grooves (as in a pillar). All that remained of the ancient building were the *fluted* columns.

flux N. flowing; series of changes. While conditions are in such a state of *flux,* I do not wish to commit myself too deeply in this affair.

fodder N. coarse food for cattle, horses, etc. One of Nancy's chores at the ranch was to put fresh supplies of *fodder* in the horses' stalls.

foible N. weakness; slight fault. We can overlook the *foibles* of our friends; no one is perfect.

foil N. contrast. In *Star Wars,* dark, evil Darth Vader is a perfect *foil* for fair-haired, naive Luke Skywalker.

foil V. defeat; frustrate. In the end, Skywalker is able to *foil* Vader's diabolical schemes.

foist V. insert improperly; palm off. I will not permit you to *foist* such ridiculous ideas upon the membership of this group.

foliage N. masses of leaves. Every autumn before the leaves fell he promised himself he would drive through New England to admire the colorful fall *foliage.*

■ **foment** V. stir up; instigate. Cher's archenemy Heather spread some nasty rumors that *fomented* trouble in the club. Do you think Cher's foe meant to *foment* such discord?

foolhardy ADJ. rash. Don't be *foolhardy.* Get the advice of experienced people before undertaking this venture.

fop N. dandy; man excessively preoccupied with his clothes. People who dismissed young Mizrahi as a *fop* for his exaggerated garments felt chagrined when he turned into one of the top fashion designers of his day. foppish, ADJ.

foray N. raid. The company staged a midnight *foray* against the enemy outpost.

forbearance N. patience. Be patient with John. Treat him with *forbearance:* he is still weak from his illness.

ford N. place where a river can be crossed on foot. Rather than risk using the shaky rope bridge, David walked a half-mile downstream until he came to the nearest *ford.* also V.

forebears N. ancestors. Reverence for one's *forebears* (sometimes referred to as ancestor worship) plays an important part in many Oriental cultures.

foreboding N. premonition of evil. Suspecting no conspiracies against him, Caesar gently ridiculed his wife's *forebodings* about the Ides of March.

forensic ADJ. suitable to debate or courts of law. In her best *forensic* manner, the lawyer addressed the jury.

foreshadow V. give an indication beforehand; portend; prefigure. In retrospect, political analysts realized that Yeltsin's defiance of the attempted coup *foreshadowed* his emergence as the dominant figure of the new Russian republic.

foresight N. ability to foresee future happenings; prudence. A wise investor, she had the *foresight* to buy land just before the current real estate boom.

■ **forestall** V. prevent by taking action in advance. By setting up a prenuptial agreement, the prospective bride and groom hoped to *forestall* any potential arguments about money in the event of a divorce.

forgo V. give up; do without. Determined to lose weight for the summer, Ida decided to *forgo* dessert until she could fit into a size eight again.

forlorn ADJ. sad and lonely; wretched. Deserted by her big sisters and her friends, the *forlorn* child sat sadly on the steps awaiting their return.

formality N. ceremonious quality; something done just for form's sake. The president received the visiting heads of state with due *formality:* flags waving, honor guards standing at attention, bands playing anthems at full blast. Signing this petition is a mere *formality;* it does not obligate you in any way.

formidable ADJ. inspiring fear or apprehension; difficult; awe-inspiring. In the film *Meet the Parents,* the hero is understandably nervous around his fiancée's father, a *formidable* CIA agent.

forsake V. desert; abandon; renounce. No one expected Foster to *forsake* his wife and children and run off with another woman.

forswear V. renounce; abandon. The captured knight could escape death only if he agreed to *forswear* Christianity and embrace Islam as the one true faith.

forte   N. strong point or special talent. I am not eager to play this rather serious role, for my *forte* is comedy.

forthright   ADJ. straightforward; direct; frank. I prefer Jill's *forthright* approach to Jack's tendency to beat around the bush. Never afraid to call a spade a spade, she was perhaps too *forthright* to be a successful party politician.

fortitude   N. bravery; courage. He was awarded the medal for his *fortitude* in the battle.

fortuitous   ADJ. accidental; by chance. Though he pretended their encounter was *fortuitous,* he'd actually been hanging around her usual haunts for the past two weeks, hoping she'd turn up.

foster   V. rear; encourage. According to the legend, Romulus and Remus were *fostered* by a she-wolf that raised the abandoned infants as her own. also ADJ.

founder   V. fail completely; sink. After hitting the submerged iceberg, the *Titanic* started taking in water rapidly and soon *foundered.*

founder   N. person who establishes (an organization, business). Among those drowned when the *Titanic* sank was the *founder* of the Abraham & Straus department store chain.

fracas   N. brawl, melee. The military police stopped the *fracas* in the bar and arrested the belligerents.

fractious   ADJ. unruly; disobedient; irritable. Bucking and kicking, the *fractious* horse unseated its rider.

frail   ADJ. weak. The delicate child seemed too *frail* to lift the heavy carton. frailty, N.

franchise   N. right granted by authority; right to vote; license to sell a product in a particular territory. The city issued a *franchise* to the company to operate surface transit lines on the streets for 99 years. For most of American history women lacked the right to vote: not until the early twentieth century was the *franchise* granted to women. Stan owns a Carvel's ice cream *franchise* in Chinatown.

frantic   ADJ. wild. At the time of the collision, many people became *frantic* with fear.

fraudulent   ADJ. cheating; deceitful. The government seeks to prevent *fraudulent* and misleading advertising.

fraught   ADJ. filled or charged with; causing emotional distress. "Parenting, like brain surgery, is now all-consuming, *fraught* with anxiety, worry, and self-doubt. We have allowed what used to be simple and natural to become bewildering and intimidating." (Fred Gosman)

fray   N. brawl. The three musketeers were in the thick of the *fray.*

frenetic   ADJ. frenzied; frantic. The novels of the beat generation reflect a *frenetic,* restless pursuit of new sensation and experience, and a disdain for the conventional measures of economic and social success.

frenzied   ADJ. madly excited. As soon as they smelled smoke, the *frenzied* animals milled about in their cages.

fresco   N. painting on plaster (usually fresh). The cathedral is visited by many tourists who wish to admire the *frescoes* by Giotto.

fret   V. be annoyed or vexed. To *fret* over your poor grades is foolish; instead, decide to work harder in the future.

friction   N. clash in opinion; rubbing against. The activist Saul Alinsky wrote, "Change means movement. Movement means *friction.* Only in the *frictionless* vacuum of a nonexistent abstract world can movement or change occur without that abrasive *friction* of conflict."

frieze   N. ornamental band on a wall. The *frieze* of the church was adorned with sculpture.

frigid   ADJ. intensely cold. Alaska is in the *frigid* zone.

fritter   V. waste. He could not apply himself to any task and *frittered* away his time in idle conversation.

frivolous   ADJ. lacking in seriousness; self-indulgently carefree; relatively unimportant. Though Nancy enjoyed Bill's *frivolous,* lighthearted companionship, she sometimes wondered whether he could ever be serious. frivolity, N.

frolicsome   ADJ. prankish; gay. The *frolicsome* puppy tried to lick the face of its master.

frond   N. fern leaf; palm or banana leaf. After the storm the beach was littered with the *fronds* of palm trees.

froward   ADJ. stubbornly contrary; obstinately disobedient. Miss Watson declared that Huck was a *froward* child, stubborn in his wickedness, and that no good would come of condoning his disobedience.

fructify   V. bear fruit. This peach tree should *fructify* in three years.

■ **frugality**   N. thrift; economy. In economically hard times, anyone who doesn't learn to practice *frugality* risks bankruptcy. frugal, ADJ.

fruition   N. bearing of fruit; fulfillment; realization. After years of scrimping and saving, her dream of owning her own home finally came to *fruition.*

frustrate   V. thwart; defeat. Constant partisan bickering *frustrated* the governor's efforts to persuade the legislature to approve his proposed budget.

fugitive   ADJ. fleeting or transitory; roving. The film brought a few *fugitive* images to her mind, but on the whole it made no lasting impression upon her.

fulcrum   N. support on which a lever rests. If we use this stone as a *fulcrum* and the crowbar as a lever, we may be able to move this boulder.

fulminate   V. denounce thunderously; explode. Known for his "fire and brimstone" sermons, the preacher *fulminated* against sinners and backsliders, consigning them to the flames of hell.

fulsome   ADJ. disgustingly excessive. Disgusted by her fans' *fulsome* admiration, the movie star retreated from the public, crying, "I want to be alone!"

functionary   N. official. As his case was transferred from one *functionary* to another, he began to despair of ever reaching a settlement.

fundamental   V. basic; primary; essential. The committee discussed all sorts of side issues without ever getting down to addressing the *fundamental* problem.

funereal ADJ. sad; solemn. I fail to understand why there is such a *funereal* atmosphere; we have lost a battle, not a war.

furor N. frenzy; great excitement. The story of her embezzlement of the funds created a *furor* on the stock exchange.

furtive ADJ. stealthy; sneaky. Noticing the *furtive* glance the customer gave the diamond bracelet on the counter, the jeweler wondered whether he had a potential shoplifter on his hands.

fusillade N. simultaneous firing or outburst (of missiles, questions, etc.). Tchaikovsky's 1812 *Overture* concludes with a thunderous *fusillade* of cannon fire.

fusion N. union; blending; synthesis. So-called rockabilly music represents a *fusion* of country music and blues that became rock and roll.

■ **futile** ADJ. useless; hopeless; ineffectual. It is *futile* for me to try to get any work done around here while the telephone is ringing every 30 seconds. futility, N.

gadfly N. animal-biting fly; an irritating person. Like a *gadfly*, he irritated all the guests at the hotel; within forty-eight hours, everyone regarded him as an annoying busybody.

gaffe N. social blunder. According to Miss Manners, to call your husband by your lover's name is worse than a mere *gaffe;* it is a tactical mistake.

Test

Word List 20   *Synonyms*

Each of the questions below consists of a word in capital letters, followed by five lettered words or phrases. Choose the lettered word or phrase that is most nearly similar in meaning to the word in capital letters and write the letter of your choice on your answer paper.

286. FLORID (A) ruddy (B) rusty (C) ruined (D) patient (E) poetic

287. FOIL (A) bury (B) frustrate (C) shield (D) desire (E) gain

288. FOMENT (A) spoil (B) instigate (C) interrogate (D) spray (E) maintain

289. FOOLHARDY (A) strong (B) unwise (C) brave (D) futile (E) erudite

290. FOPPISH (A) scanty (B) radical (C) orthodox (D) dandyish (E) magnificent

291. FORAY (A) excursion (B) contest (C) ranger (D) intuition (E) fish

292. FORMIDABLE (A) dangerous (B) outlandish (C) grandiloquent (D) impenetrable (E) venerable

293. FOSTER (A) accelerate (B) fondle (C) become infected (D) raise (E) roll

294. FRANCHISE (A) subway (B) discount (C) license (D) reason (E) fashion

295. FRITTER (A) sour (B) chafe (C) dissipate (D) cancel (E) abuse

296. FRUGALITY (A) foolishness (B) extremity (C) indifference (D) enthusiasm (E) economy

297. FULMINATE (A) fulfill (B) contemplate (C) talk nonsense (D) protest loudly (E) meander

298. FUROR (A) excitement (B) worry (C) flux (D) anteroom (E) lover

299. FURTIVE (A) underhanded (B) coy (C) brilliant (D) quick (E) abortive

300. GADFLY (A) humorist (B) nuisance (C) scholar (D) bum (E) thief

Word List 21   gainsay-gossamer

■ **gainsay** V. deny. She was too honest to *gainsay* the truth of the report.

gait N. manner of walking or running; speed. The lame man walked with an uneven *gait.*

galaxy N. large, isolated system of stars, such as the Milky Way; a collection of brilliant personalities. Science fiction speculates about the possible existence of life in other *galaxies.* The deaths of such famous actors as Bob Hope and Marlon Brando tells us that the *galaxy* of Hollywood superstars is rapidly disappearing.

gale N. windstorm; gust of wind; emotional outburst (laughter, tears). The Weather Channel warned viewers about a rising *gale,* with winds of up to 60 miles per hour.

gall N. bitterness; nerve. The knowledge of his failure filled him with *gall.*

gall V. annoy; chafe. Their taunts *galled* him.

galleon N. large sailing ship. The Spaniards pinned their hopes on the *galleon,* the large warship; the British, on the smaller and faster pinnace.

galvanize V. stimulate by shock; stir up; revitalize. News that the prince was almost at their door *galvanized* the ugly stepsisters into a frenzy of combing and primping.

gambit N. opening in chess in which a piece is sacrificed. The player was afraid to accept his opponent's *gambit* because he feared a trap that as yet he could not see.

gambol V. romp; skip about; leap playfully. Watching the children *gambol* in the park, Betty marveled at their youthful energy and zest. also N.

gamely ADV. in a spirited manner; with courage. Because he had fought *gamely* against a much superior boxer, the crowd gave him a standing ovation when he left the arena.

gamut N. entire range. In a classic put-down of actress Katharine Hepburn, the critic Dorothy Parker wrote that the actress ran the *gamut* of emotions from A to B.

gape V. open widely. The huge pit *gaped* before him; if he stumbled, he would fall in. Slack-jawed in wonder, Huck *gaped* at the huge stalactites hanging from the ceiling of the limestone cavern.

garbled ADJ. mixed up; jumbled; distorted. A favorite party game involves passing a whispered message from one person to another; by the time it reaches the last player, the message has become totally *garbled*. garble, V.

gargantuan ADJ. huge; enormous. The *gargantuan* wrestler was terrified of mice.

gargoyle N. waterspout carved in grotesque figures on a building. The *gargoyles* adorning the Cathedral of Notre Dame in Paris are amusing in their grotesqueness.

garish ADJ. overbright in color; gaudy. She wore a rhinestone necklace with a *garish* red and gold dress trimmed with sequins.

garner V. gather; store up. In her long career as an actress, Katharine Hepburn *garnered* many awards, including the coveted Oscar.

garnish V. decorate. Parsley was used to *garnish* the boiled potato. also N.

■ **garrulous** ADJ. loquacious; wordy; talkative. My Uncle Henry can out-talk any other three people I know. He is the most *garrulous* person in Cayuga County. garrulity, N.

gastronomy N. science of preparing and serving good food. One of the by-products of his trip to Europe was his interest in *gastronomy;* he enjoyed preparing and serving foreign dishes to his friends.

gauche ADJ. clumsy; coarse and uncouth. Compared to the sophisticated young ladies in their elegant gowns, tomboyish Jo felt *gauche* and out of place.

gaudy ADJ. flashy; showy. The newest Trump skyscraper is typically *gaudy*, covered in gilded panels that gleam in the sun.

gaunt ADJ. lean and angular; barren. His once-round face looked surprisingly *gaunt* after he had lost weight.

gavel N. hammerlike tool; mallet. "Sold!" cried the auctioneer, banging her *gavel* on the table to indicate she'd accepted the final bid. also V.

gawk V. stare foolishly; look in open-mouthed awe. The country boy *gawked* at the skyscrapers and neon lights of the big city.

gazette N. official periodical publication. He read the *gazettes* regularly for the announcement of his promotion.

genealogy N. record of descent; lineage. He was proud of his *genealogy* and constantly referred to the achievements of his ancestors.

generality N. vague statement. This report is filled with *generalities;* you must be more specific in your statements.

generate V. cause; produce; create. In his first days in office, President Clinton managed to *generate* a new mood of optimism; we hoped he could also *generate* a few new jobs.

generic ADJ. characteristic of an entire class or species. Sue knew so many computer programmers who spent their spare time playing fantasy games that she began to think that playing Dungeons & Dragons was a *generic* trait.

genesis N. beginning; origin. Tracing the *genesis* of a family is the theme of "Roots."

geniality N. cheerfulness; kindliness; sympathy. This restaurant is famous and popular because of the *geniality* of the proprietor, who tries to make everyone happy. genial, ADJ.

genre N. particular variety of art or literature. Both a short story writer and a poet, Langston Hughes proved himself equally skilled in either *genre*.

genteel ADJ. well-bred; elegant. We are looking for a man with a *genteel* appearance who can inspire confidence by his cultivated manner.

gentility N. those of gentle birth; refinement. Her family was proud of its *gentility* and elegance.

gentry N. people of standing; class of people just below nobility. The local *gentry* did not welcome the visits of the summer tourists and tried to ignore their presence in the community.

genuflect V. bend the knee as in worship. A proud democrat, he refused to *genuflect* to any man.

germane ADJ. pertinent; bearing upon the case at hand. The lawyer objected that the testimony being offered was not *germane* to the case at hand.

germinal ADJ. pertaining to a germ; creative. Such an idea is *germinal;* I am certain that it will influence thinkers and philosophers for many generations.

germinate V. cause to sprout; sprout. After the seeds *germinate* and develop their permanent leaves, the plants may be removed from the cold frames and transplanted to the garden.

gerontocracy N. government ruled by old people. Gulliver visited a *gerontocracy* in which the young people acted as servants to their elders, all the while dreaming of the day they would be old enough to have servants of their own.

gerrymander V. change voting district lines in order to favor a political party. The illogical pattern of the map of this congressional district is proof that the state legislature *gerrymandered* this area in order to favor the majority party. also N.

gestate V. evolve, as in prenatal growth. While this scheme was being *gestated* by the conspirators, they maintained complete silence about their intentions.

gesticulation   N. motion; gesture. Operatic performers are trained to make exaggerated *gesticulations* because of the large auditoriums in which they appear.

ghastly   ADJ. horrible. The murdered man was a *ghastly* sight.

gibberish   N. nonsense; babbling. Did you hear that foolish boy spouting *gibberish* about monsters from outer space?

gibe   V. mock. As you *gibe* at their superstitious beliefs, do you realize that you, too, are guilty of similarly foolish thoughts?

giddy   ADJ. light-hearted; dizzy. He felt his *giddy* youth was past.

gingerly   ADV. very carefully. To separate egg whites, first crack the egg *gingerly*. also ADJ.

girth   N. distance around something; circumference. It took an extra-large cummerbund to fit around Andrew Carnegie's considerable *girth*.

gist   N. essence. She was asked to give the *gist* of the essay in two sentences.

glacial   ADJ. like a glacier; extremely cold. Never a warm person, when offended Hugo could seem positively *glacial*.

glaring   ADJ. highly conspicuous; harshly bright. *Glaring* spelling or grammatical errors in your résumé will unfavorably impress potential employers.

glaze   V. cover with a thin and shiny surface. The freezing rain *glazed* the streets and made driving hazardous. also N.

glean   V. gather leavings. After the crops had been harvested by the machines, the peasants were permitted to *glean* the wheat left in the fields.

glib   ADJ. fluent; facile; slick. Keeping up a steady patter to entertain his customers, the kitchen gadget salesman was a *glib* speaker, never at a loss for a word.

glimmer   V. shine erratically; twinkle. In the darkness of the cavern, the glowworms hanging from the cavern roof *glimmered* like distant stars.

gloat   V. express evil satisfaction; view malevolently. As you *gloat* over your ill-gotten wealth, do you think of the many victims you have defrauded?

gloss over   V. explain away. No matter how hard he tried to talk around the issue, President Bush could not *gloss over* the fact that he had raised taxes after all.

glossary   N. brief explanation of words used in the text. I have found the *glossary* in this book very useful; it has eliminated many trips to the dictionary.

glossy   ADJ. smooth and shining. I want this photograph printed on *glossy* paper, not matte.

glower   V. scowl. The angry boy *glowered* at his father.

glut   V. overstock; fill to excess. The many manufacturers *glutted* the market and could not find purchasers for the many articles they had produced. also N.

glutinous   ADJ. sticky; viscous. Molasses is a *glutinous* substance.

glutton   N. someone who eats too much. When Mother saw that Bobby had eaten all the cookies, she called him a little *glutton*. gluttonous, ADJ.

gnarled   ADJ. twisted. The *gnarled* oak tree had been a landmark for years and was mentioned in several deeds.

gnome   N. dwarf; underground spirit. In medieval mythology, *gnomes* were the special guardians and inhabitants of subterranean mines.

■ **goad**   V. urge on. She was *goaded* by her friends until she yielded to their wishes. also N.

gorge   N. narrow canyon; steep, rocky cleft. Terrified of heights, George could not bring himself to peer down into the *gorge* to see the rapids below.

gorge   V. stuff oneself. The gluttonous guest *gorged* himself with food as though he had not eaten for days.

gory   ADJ. bloody. The audience shuddered as they listened to the details of the *gory* massacre. gore, N.

gossamer   ADJ. sheer; like cobwebs. Nylon can be woven into *gossamer* or thick fabrics. also N.

Test

Word List 21   *Synonyms*

Each of the questions below consists of a word in capital letters, followed by five lettered words or phrases. Choose the lettered word or phrase that is most nearly similar in meaning to the word in capital letters and write the letter of your choice on your answer paper.

301. GALLEON (A) liquid measure (B) ship (C) armada (D) company (E) printer's proof

302. GARISH (A) sordid (B) flashy (C) prominent (D) lusty (E) thoughtful

303. GARNER (A) prevent (B) assist (C) collect (D) compute (E) consult

304. GARNISH (A) paint (B) garner (C) adorn (D) abuse (E) banish

305. GARRULITY (A) credulity (B) senility (C) loquaciousness (D) speciousness (E) artistry

306. GARRULOUS (A) arid (B) hasty (C) sociable (D) quaint (E) talkative

307. GAUCHE (A) rigid (B) swift (C) awkward (D) taciturn (E) needy

308. GAUDY (A) holy (B) showy (C) sentimental (D) mild (E) whimsical

309. GAUNT (A) victorious (B) tiny (C) stylish
(D) haggard (E) nervous

310. GENUFLECT (A) falsify (B) trick (C) project
(D) bend the knee (E) pronounce correctly

311. GERMANE (A) bacteriological (B) Middle
European (C) prominent (D) warlike (E) relevant

312. GERMINAL (A) creative (B) excused (C) sterilized
(D) primitive (E) strategic

313. GIST (A) chaff (B) summary (C) expostulation
(D) expiation (E) chore

314. GLIB (A) slippery (B) fashionable (C) antiquated
(D) articulate (E) anticlimactic

315. GNOME (A) fury (B) giant (C) dwarf (D) native
(E) alien

Word List 22   gouge-hiatus

gouge   v. tear out. In that fight, all the rules were forgotten; the adversaries bit, kicked, and tried to *gouge* each other's eyes out.

■ **gouge**   v. overcharge. During the World Series, ticket scalpers tried to *gouge* the public, asking astronomical prices even for bleacher seats.

gourmand   N. epicure; person who takes excessive pleasure in food and drink. *Gourmands* lack self-restraint; if they enjoy a particular cuisine, they eat far too much of it.

gourmet   N. connoisseur of food and drink. The *gourmet* stated that this was the best onion soup she had ever tasted.

graduated   ADJ. arranged by degrees (of height, difficulty, etc.). Margaret loved her *graduated* set of Russian hollow wooden dolls; she spent hours happily putting the smaller dolls into their larger counterparts.

granary   N. storehouse for grain. We have reason to be thankful, for our crops were good and our *granaries* are full.

grandeur   N. impressiveness; stateliness; majesty. No matter how often he hiked through the mountains, David never failed to be struck by the *grandeur* of the Sierra Nevada range.

■ **grandiloquent**   ADJ. pompous; bombastic; using high-sounding language. The politician could never speak simply; she was always *grandiloquent*.

grandiose   ADJ. pretentious; high-flown; ridiculously exaggerated; impressive. The aged matinee idol still had *grandiose* notions of his supposed importance in the theatrical world.

granulate   v. form into grains. Sugar that has been *granulated* dissolves more readily than lump sugar. granule, N.

graphic   ADJ. pertaining to the art of delineating; vividly described. I was particularly impressed by the *graphic* presentation of the storm.

grapple   v. wrestle; come to grips with. He *grappled* with the burglar and overpowered him.

grate   v. make a harsh noise; have an unpleasant effect; shred. The screams of the quarreling children *grated* on her nerves.

gratify   v. please. Lori's parents were *gratified* by her successful performance on the GRE.

gratis   ADV. free. The company offered to give one package *gratis* to every purchaser of one of their products. also ADJ.

gratuitous   ADJ. given freely; unwarranted; uncalled for. Quit making *gratuitous* comments about my driving; no one asked you for your opinion.

gratuity   N. tip. Many service employees rely more on *gratuities* than on salaries for their livelihood.

gravity   N. seriousness. We could tell we were in serious trouble from the *gravity* of her expression. grave, ADJ.

■ **gregarious**   ADJ. sociable. Typically, party-throwers are *gregarious*; hermits are not.

grievance   N. cause of complaint. When her supervisor ignored her complaint, she took her *grievance* to the union.

grill   v. question severely. In violation of the Miranda law, the police *grilled* the suspect for several hours before reading him his rights. (secondary meaning)

grimace   N. a facial distortion to show feeling such as pain, disgust, etc. Even though he remained silent, his *grimace* indicated his displeasure. also v.

grisly   ADJ. ghastly. She shuddered at the *grisly* sight.

grotesque   ADJ. fantastic; comically hideous. On Halloween people enjoy wearing *grotesque* costumes.

grotto   N. small cavern. The Blue *Grotto* in Capri can be entered only by small boats rowed by natives through a natural opening in the rocks.

grouse   v. complain; fuss. Students traditionally *grouse* about the abysmal quality of "mystery meat" and similar dormitory food.

grovel   v. crawl or creep on ground; remain prostrate. Even though we have been defeated, we do not have to *grovel* before our conquerors.

grudging   ADJ. unwilling; reluctant; stingy. We received only *grudging* support from the mayor despite his earlier promises of aid.

gruel   N. thin, liquid porridge. Our daily allotment of *gruel* made the meal not only monotonous but also unpalatable.

grueling   ADJ. exhausting. The marathon is a *grueling* race.

gruesome   ADJ. grisly; horrible. His face was the stuff of nightmares: all the children in the audience screamed when Freddy Kruger's *gruesome* countenance was flashed on the screen.

gruff   ADJ. rough-mannered. Although he was blunt and *gruff* with most people, he was always gentle with children.

guffaw   N. boisterous laughter. The loud *guffaws* that came from the closed room indicated that the members of the committee had not yet settled down to serious business. also V.

guile   N. deceit; duplicity; wiliness; cunning. Iago uses considerable *guile* to trick Othello into believing that Desdemona has been unfaithful.

■ **guileless**   ADJ. without deceit. He is naive, simple, and *guileless;* he cannot be guilty of fraud.

guise   N. appearance; costume. In the *guise* of a plumber, the detective investigated the murder case.

gull   V. trick; hoodwink. Confident no one could *gull* him, Paul prided himself on his skeptical disposition.

■ **gullible**   ADJ. easily deceived. *Gullible* people have only themselves to blame if they fall for con artists repeatedly. As the saying goes, "Fool me once, shame on you. Fool me twice, shame on me."

gustatory   ADJ. affecting the sense of taste. The Thai restaurant offered an unusual *gustatory* experience for those used to a bland cuisine.

gusto   N. enjoyment; enthusiasm. He accepted the assignment with such *gusto* that I feel he would have been satisfied with a smaller salary.

gusty   ADJ. windy. The *gusty* weather made sailing precarious.

guy   N. cable or chain attached to something that needs to be braced or steadied. If the *guys* holding up the mast on that derrick snap, the mast will topple.

gyroscope   N. apparatus used to maintain balance, ascertain direction, etc. By using a rotating *gyroscope,* they were able to stabilize the vessel, counteracting the rolling movements of the sea.

habituate   V. accustom or familiarize; addict. Macbeth gradually *habituated* himself to murder, shedding his scruples as he grew accustomed to his bloody deeds.

hackles   N. hairs on back and neck, especially of a dog. The dog's *hackles* rose and he began to growl as the sound of footsteps grew louder.

hackneyed   ADJ. commonplace; trite. When the reviewer criticized the movie for its *hackneyed* plot, we agreed; we had seen similar stories hundreds of times before.

haggard   ADJ. wasted away; gaunt. After his long illness, he was pale and *haggard.*

haggle   V. argue about prices. I prefer to shop in a store that has a one-price policy because, whenever I *haggle* with a shopkeeper, I am never certain that I paid a fair price for the articles I purchased.

halcyon   ADJ. calm; peaceful. In those *halcyon* days, people were not worried about sneak attacks and bombings.

hale   ADJ. healthy. After a brief illness, he was soon *hale.*

hallowed   ADJ. blessed; consecrated. Although the dead girl's parents had never been active churchgoers, they insisted that their daughter be buried in *hallowed* ground.

hallucination   N. delusion. I think you were frightened by a *hallucination* that you created in your own mind.

halting   ADJ. hesitant; faltering. Novice extemporaneous speakers often talk in a *halting* fashion as they grope for the right words.

hamper   V. obstruct. The new mother hadn't realized how much the effort of caring for an infant would *hamper* her ability to keep an immaculate house.

hap   N. chance; luck. In his poem *Hap,* Thomas Hardy objects to the part chance plays in our lives. also V.

haphazard   ADJ. random; by chance. His *haphazard* reading left him unacquainted with many classic books.

hapless   ADJ. unfortunate. This *hapless* creature had never known a moment's pleasure.

■ **harangue**   N. long, passionate, and vehement speech. In her lengthy *harangue,* the principal berated the offenders. also V.

harass   V. annoy by repeated attacks. When he could not pay his bills as quickly as he had promised, he was *harassed* by his creditors.

harbinger   N. forerunner. The crocus is an early *harbinger* of spring.

harbor   V. provide a refuge for; hide. The church *harbored* illegal aliens who were political refugees. also N.

hardy   ADJ. sturdy; robust; able to stand inclement weather. We asked the gardening expert to recommend particularly *hardy* plants that could withstand our harsh New England winters.

harping   N. tiresome dwelling on a subject. After he had reminded me several times about what he had done for me I told him to stop his *harping* on my indebtedness to him. harp, V.

harrowing   ADJ. agonizing; distressing; traumatic. At first Terry Anderson did not wish to discuss his *harrowing* months of captivity as a political hostage. harrow, V.

harry   V. harass, annoy, torment; raid. The guerrilla band *harried* the enemy nightly.

hatch   N. deck opening; lid covering a deck opening. The latch on the *hatch* failed to catch, so the *hatch* remained unlatched.

haughtiness   N. pride; arrogance. When she realized that Darcy believed himself too good to dance with his inferiors, Elizabeth took great offense at his *haughtiness.*

haven   N. place of safety; refuge. For Ricardo, the school library became his *haven,* a place to which he could retreat during chaotic times.

hazardous   ADJ. dangerous. Your occupation is too *hazardous* for insurance companies to consider your application.

hazy   ADJ. slightly obscure. In *hazy* weather, you cannot see the top of this mountain.

headlong ADJ. hasty; rash. The slave seized the unexpected chance to make a *headlong* dash across the border to freedom.

headstrong ADJ. stubborn; willful; unyielding. Because she refused to marry the man her parents had chosen for her, everyone scolded Minna and called her a foolish, *headstrong* girl.

heckler N. person who verbally harasses others. The *heckler* kept interrupting the speaker with rude remarks. heckle, V.

hedonist N. one who believes that pleasure is the sole aim in life. A thoroughgoing *hedonist,* he considered only his own pleasure and ignored any claims others had on his money or time. hedonism, N.

heedless ADJ. not noticing; disregarding. She drove on, *heedless* of the warnings that the road was dangerous. heed, V.

hegemony N. dominance, especially of one nation over others. As one Eastern European nation after another declared its independence, commentators marveled at the sudden breakdown of the once monolithic Soviet *hegemony.*

heinous ADJ. atrocious; hatefully bad. Hitler's *heinous* crimes will never be forgotten.

herbivorous ADJ. grain-eating. Some *herbivorous* animals have two stomachs for digesting their food.

heresy N. opinion contrary to popular belief; opinion contrary to accepted religion. Galileo's assertion that the earth moved around the sun directly contradicted the religious teachings of his day; as a result, he was tried for *heresy.* heretic, N. heretical, ADJ.

hermetic ADJ. sealed by fusion so as to be airtight. After you sterilize the bandages, place them in a container and seal it with a *hermetic* seal to protect them from contamination by airborne bacteria.

hermetic ADJ. obscure and mysterious; occult. It is strange to consider that modern chemistry originated in the *hermetic* teachings of the ancient alchemists. (secondary meaning)

hermitage N. home of a hermit. Even in his remote *hermitage* he could not escape completely from the world.

herpetologist N. one who studies reptiles. As a boy, Indiana Jones had a traumatic experience involving snakes; sensibly enough, he studied to be an archaeologist, not a *herpetologist.*

heterodox ADJ. unorthodox; unconventional. To those who upheld the belief that the earth did not move, Galileo's theory that the earth circled the sun was disturbingly *heterodox.*

heterogeneous ADJ. dissimilar; mixed. This year's entering class is a remarkably *heterogeneous* body: it includes students from 40 different states and 26 foreign countries, some the children of billionaires, others the offspring of welfare families. heterogeneity, N.

hew V. cut to pieces with ax or sword. The cavalry rushed into the melee and *hewed* the enemy with their swords, N.

heyday N. time of greatest success; prime. In their *heyday,* the San Francisco Forty-Niners won the Super Bowl two years running.

hiatus N. gap; pause. Except for a brief two-year *hiatus,* during which she enrolled in the Peace Corps, Ms. Clements has devoted herself to her medical career.

Test

Word List 22   *Antonyms*

Each of the following questions consists of a word in capital letters, followed by five lettered words or phrases. Choose the lettered word or phrase that is most nearly opposite in meaning to the word in capital letters and write the letter of your choice on your answer paper.

316. GRANDIOSE (A) false (B) ideal (C) proud (D) simple (E) functional

317. GRATUITOUS (A) warranted (B) frank (C) ingenuous (D) frugal (E) pithy

318. GREGARIOUS (A) antisocial (B) anticipatory (C) glorious (D) horrendous (E) similar

319. GRISLY (A) suggestive (B) doubtful (C) untidy (D) pleasant (E) bearish

320. GULLIBLE (A) incredulous (B) fickle (C) tantamount (D) easy (E) stylish

321. GUSTO (A) noise (B) panic (C) atmosphere (D) gloom (E) distaste

322. GUSTY (A) calm (B) noisy (C) fragrant (D) routine (E) gloomy

323. HACKNEYED (A) carried (B) original (C) banned (D) timely (E) oratorical

324. HAGGARD (A) shrewish (B) inspired (C) plump (D) maidenly (E) vast

325. HALCYON (A) wasteful (B) prior (C) subsequent (D) puerile (E) martial

326. HAPHAZARD (A) safe (B) indifferent (C) deliberate (D) tense (E) conspiring

327. HAPLESS (A) cheerful (B) consistent (C) fortunate (D) considerate (E) shapely

328. HEED (A) ignore (B) hope (C) overtake (D) nurture (E) depart

329. HERETIC (A) sophist (B) believer (C) interpreter (D) pacifist (E) owner

330. HETEROGENEOUS (A) orthodox (B) pagan (C) unlikely (D) similar (E) banished

Word List 23   hibernal-imbue

hibernal   ADJ. wintry. Bears prepare for their long *hibernal* sleep by overeating.

hibernate   V. sleep throughout the winter. Bears are one of the many species of animals that *hibernate*. hibernation, N.

hierarchy   N. arrangement by rank or standing; authoritarian body divided into ranks. To be low man on the totem pole is to have an inferior place in the *hierarchy*. hierarchical, ADJ.

hieroglyphic   N. picture writing. The discovery of the Rosetta Stone enabled scholars to read the ancient Egyptian *hieroglyphics*.

hilarity   N. boisterous mirth. This *hilarity* is improper on this solemn day of mourning. hilarious, ADJ.

hindmost   ADJ. furthest behind. The coward could always be found in the *hindmost* lines whenever a battle was being waged.

hindrance   N. block; obstacle. Stalled cars along the highway are a *hindrance* to traffic that tow trucks should remove without delay. hinder, V.

hinterlands   N. back country. They seldom had visitors, living as they did way out in the *hinterlands*.

hireling   N. one who serves for hire (usually used contemptuously). In a matter of such importance, I do not wish to deal with *hirelings;* I must meet with the chief.

hirsute   ADJ. hairy. He was a *hirsute* individual with a heavy black beard.

histrionic   ADJ. theatrical. He was proud of his *histrionic* ability and wanted to play the role of Hamlet. histrionics, N.

hoard   V. stockpile; accumulate for future use. Whenever there are rumors of a food shortage, people are tempted to *hoard* food. also N.

hoary   ADJ. white with age. The man was *hoary* and wrinkled when he was 70.

hoax   N. trick; practical joke. Embarrassed by the *hoax*, she reddened and left the room. also V.

holocaust   N. destruction by fire. Citizens of San Francisco remember that the destruction of the city was caused not by the earthquake but by the *holocaust* that followed.

holster   N. pistol case. Even when he was not in uniform, he carried a *holster* and pistol under his arm.

homage   N. honor; tribute. In her speech she tried to pay *homage* to a great man.

homeostasis   N. tendency of a system to maintain relative stability. A breakdown of the body's immune system severely undermines the body's ability to maintain *homeostasis*.

homespun   ADJ. domestic; made at home. *Homespun* wit, like *homespun* cloth, was often coarse and plain.

homily   N. sermon; serious warning. His speeches were always *homilies*, advising his listeners to repent and reform. homiletic, ADJ.

■ **homogeneous**   ADJ. of the same kind. Because the student body at Elite Prep was so *homogeneous*, Sara and James decided to send their daughter to a school that offered greater cultural diversity. homogeneity, N.

hone   V. sharpen. To make shaving easier, he *honed* his razor with great care.

hoodwink   V. deceive; delude. Having been *hoodwinked* once by the fast-talking salesman, he was extremely cautious when he went to purchase a used car.

horde   N. crowd. Just before Christmas the stores are filled with *hordes* of shoppers.

hortatory   ADJ. encouraging; exhortive. The crowd listened to his *hortatory* statements with ever-growing excitement; finally they rushed from the hall to carry out his suggestions.

horticultural   ADJ. pertaining to cultivation of gardens. When he bought his house, he began to look for flowers and decorative shrubs, and began to read books dealing with *horticultural* matters.

hostility   N. unfriendliness; hatred. A child who has been the sole object of his parents' affection often feels *hostility* toward a new baby in the family, resenting the newcomer who has taken his place. hostile, ADJ.

hovel   N. shack; small, wretched house. She wondered how poor people could stand living in such a *hovel*.

hover   V. hang about; wait nearby. The police helicopter *hovered* above the accident.

hubbub   N. confused uproar. The marketplace was a scene of *hubbub* and excitement; in all the noise, we could not distinguish particular voices.

hubris   N. arrogance; excessive self-conceit. Filled with *hubris*, Lear refused to heed his friends' warnings.

hue   N. color; aspect. The aviary contained birds of every possible *hue*.

hue and cry   N. outcry. When her purse was snatched, she raised such a *hue and cry* that the thief was captured.

humane   ADJ. marked by kindness or consideration. It is ironic that the *Humane* Society sometimes must show its compassion toward mistreated animals by killing them to end their misery.

humdrum   ADJ. dull; monotonous. After her years of adventure, she could not settle down to a *humdrum* existence.

humid   ADJ. damp. She could not stand the *humid* climate and moved to a drier area.

humility   N. humbleness of spirit. He spoke with a *humility* and lack of pride that impressed his listeners.

hummock   N. small hill. The ascent of the *hummock* is not difficult and the view from the hilltop is ample reward for the effort.

humus N. substance formed by decaying vegetable matter. In order to improve his garden, he spread *humus* over his lawn and flower beds.

hurtle V. crash; rush. The runaway train *hurtled* toward disaster.

husband V. use sparingly; conserve; save. Marathon runners must *husband* their energy so that they can keep going for the entire distance.

husbandry N. frugality; thrift; agriculture. He accumulated his small fortune by diligence and *husbandry*. husband, V.

hybrid N. mongrel; mixed breed. Mendel's formula explains the appearance of *hybrids* and pure species in breeding. also ADJ.

hydrophobia N. fear of water; rabies. A dog that bites a human being must be observed for symptoms of *hydrophobia.*

■ **hyperbole** N. exaggeration; overstatement. As far as I'm concerned, Apple's claims about the new computer are pure *hyperbole*: no machine is that good! hyperbolic, ADJ.

hypercritical ADJ. excessively exacting. You are *hypercritical* in your demands for perfection; we all make mistakes.

hypochondriac N. person unduly worried about his health; worrier without cause about illness. The doctor prescribed chocolate pills for her patient who was a *hypochondriac.*

hypocritical ADJ. pretending to be virtuous; deceiving. Because he believed Eddie to be interested only in his own advancement, Greg resented Eddie's *hypocritical* protestations of friendship. hypocrisy, N.

hypothetical ADJ. based on assumptions or hypotheses; supposed. Suppose you are accepted by Harvard, Stanford, and Yale. Which graduate school will you choose to attend? Remember, this is only a *hypothetical* situation. hypothesis, N.

ichthyology N. study of fish. Jacques Cousteau's programs about sea life have advanced the cause of *ichthyology.*

icon N. religious image; idol. The *icons* on the walls of the church were painted in the 13th century.

■ **iconoclastic** ADJ. attacking cherished traditions. Deeply *iconoclastic*, Jean Genet deliberately set out to shock conventional theatergoers with his radical plays. iconoclasm, N.

ideology N. system of ideas characteristic of a group or culture. For people who had grown up believing in the Communist *ideology,* it was hard to adjust to capitalism.

idiom N. expression whose meaning as a whole differs from the meanings of its individual words; distinctive style. The phrase "to lose one's marbles" is an *idiom:* if I say that Joe has lost his marbles, I'm not asking you to find them for him. I'm telling you *idiomatically* that he's crazy.

idiosyncrasy N. individual trait, usually odd in nature; eccentricity. One of Richard Nixon's little *idiosyncrasies* was his liking for ketchup on cottage cheese. One of Hannibal Lecter's little *idiosyncrasies* was his liking for human flesh. idiosyncratic, ADJ.

■ **idolatry** N. worship of idols; excessive admiration. Such *idolatry* of singers of country music is typical of the excessive enthusiasm of youth.

idyllic ADJ. charmingly carefree; simple. Far from the city, she led an *idyllic* existence in her rural retreat.

igneous ADJ. produced by fire; volcanic. Lava, pumice, and other *igneous* rocks are found in great abundance around Mount Vesuvius near Naples.

ignite V. kindle; light. When Desi crooned, "Baby, light my fire," literal-minded Lucy looked around for some paper to *ignite.*

ignoble ADJ. unworthy; not noble. A true knight, Sir Galahad never stooped to perform an *ignoble* deed.

ignominy N. deep disgrace; shame or dishonor. To lose the Ping-Pong match to a trained chimpanzee! How could Rollo endure the *ignominy* of his defeat? ignominious, ADJ.

illicit ADJ. illegal. The defense attorney claimed that the police had entrapped his client; that is, they had elicited the *illicit* action of which they now accused him.

illimitable ADJ. infinite. Human beings, having explored the far corners of the earth, are now reaching out into *illimitable* space.

illuminate V. brighten; clear up or make understandable; enlighten. Just as a lamp can *illuminate* a dark room, a perceptive comment can *illuminate* a knotty problem.

illusion N. misleading vision. It is easy to create an optical *illusion* in which lines of equal length appear different.

illusive ADJ. deceiving. This is only a mirage; let us not be fooled by its *illusive* effect.

illusory ADJ. deceptive; not real. Unfortunately, the costs of running the lemonade stand were so high that Tom's profits proved *illusory.*

imbalance N. lack of balance or symmetry; disproportion. To correct racial *imbalance* in the schools, school boards have bused black children into white neighborhoods and white children into black ones.

imbecility N. weakness of mind. I am amazed at the *imbecility* of the readers of these trashy magazines.

imbibe V. drink in. The dry soil *imbibed* the rain quickly.

imbroglio N. complicated situation; painful or complex misunderstanding; entanglement; confused mass (as of papers). The humor of Shakespearean comedies often depends on cases of mistaken identity that involve the perplexed protagonists in one comic *imbroglio* after another. embroil, V.

imbue V. saturate, fill. His visits to the famous Gothic cathedrals *imbued* him with feelings of awe and reverence.

Test

Word List 23   *Antonyms*

Each of the questions below consists of a word in capital letters, followed by five lettered words or phrases. Choose the lettered word or phrase that is most nearly opposite in meaning to the word in capital letters and write the letter of your choice on your answer paper.

331. HIBERNAL (A) musical (B) summerlike (C) local
     (D) seasonal (E) discordant

332. HILARITY (A) gloom (B) heartiness (C) weakness
     (D) casualty (E) paucity

333. HIRSUTE (A) scaly (B) bald (C) erudite (D) quiet
     (E) long

334. HORTATORY (A) inquiring (B) denying (C) killing
     (D) frantic (E) dissuading

335. HOVER (A) commence (B) soothe (C) leave
     (D) transform (E) solidify

336. HUBBUB (A) calm (B) fury (C) capital (D) axle
     (E) wax

337. HUMMOCK (A) unmusical (B) scorn
     (C) wakefulness (D) vale (E) vestment

338. HUSBANDRY (A) sportsmanship (B) dishonesty
     (C) wastefulness (D) friction (E) cowardice

339. HYBRID (A) productive (B) special (C) purebred
     (D) oafish (E) genial

340. HYPERBOLE (A) velocity (B) climax (C) curve
     (D) understatement (E) expansion

341. HYPERCRITICAL (A) tolerant (B) false (C) extreme
     (D) inarticulate (E) cautious

342. HYPOCRITICAL (A) sincere (B) narrow-minded
     (C) shameful (D) amiable (E) modest

343. HYPOTHETICAL (A) rational (B) fantastic
     (C) wizened (D) opposed (E) axiomatic

344. IGNOBLE (A) produced by fire (B) worthy
     (C) given to questioning (D) huge (E) known

345. ILLUSIVE (A) not deceptive (B) not certain
     (C) not obvious (D) not coherent (E) not brilliant

Word List 24   immaculate-incessant

immaculate   ADJ. spotless; flawless; absolutely clean. Ken and Jessica were wonderful tenants who left the apartment in *immaculate* condition when they moved out.

imminent   ADJ. near at hand; impending. Rosa was such a last-minute worker that she could never start writing a paper till the deadline was *imminent.*

immobility   N. state of being immovable. Modern armies cannot afford the luxury of *immobility,* as they are vulnerable to attack while standing still.

immolate   V. offer as a sacrifice. The tribal king offered to *immolate* his daughter to quiet the angry gods.

immune   ADJ. resistant to; free or exempt from. Fortunately, Florence had contracted chicken pox as a child and was *immune* to it when her baby came down with spots. immunity, N.

immure   V. imprison; shut up in confinement. For the two weeks before the examination, the student *immured* himself in his room and concentrated upon his studies.

■ **immutable**   ADJ. unchangeable. All things change over time; nothing is *immutable.*

■ **impair**   V. injure; hurt. Drinking alcohol can *impair* your ability to drive safely; if you're going to drink, don't drive.

impale   V. pierce. He was *impaled* by the spear hurled by his adversary.

impalpable   ADJ. imperceptible; intangible. The ash is so fine that it is *impalpable* to the touch but it can be seen as a fine layer covering the window ledge.

impartial   ADJ. not biased; fair. Knowing she could not be *impartial* about her own child, Jo refused to judge any match in which Billy was competing. impartiality, N.

impassable   ADJ. not able to be traveled or crossed. A giant redwood had fallen across the highway, blocking all four lanes: the road was *impassable.*

impasse   N. predicament from which there is no escape. In this *impasse,* all turned to prayer as their last hope.

■ **impassive**   ADJ. without feeling; imperturbable; stoical. Refusing to let the enemy see how deeply shaken he was by his capture, the prisoner kept his face *impassive.*

impeach   V. charge with crime in office; indict. The angry congressman wanted to *impeach* the president for his misdeeds.

impeccable   ADJ. faultless. The uncrowned queen of the fashion industry, Diana was acclaimed for her *impeccable* taste.

impecunious   ADJ. without money. Though Scrooge claimed he was too *impecunious* to give alms, he easily could have afforded to be charitable.

■ **impede**   V. hinder; block. The special prosecutor determined that the Attorney General, though inept, had not intentionally set out to *impede* the progress of the investigation.

impediment   N. hindrance; stumbling-block. She had a speech *impediment* that prevented her from speaking clearly.

impel V. drive or force onward. A strong feeling of urgency *impelled* her; if she failed to finish the project right then, she knew that she would never get it done.

impending ADJ. nearing; approaching. The entire country was saddened by the news of his *impending* death.

impenetrable ADJ. not able to be pierced or entered; beyond understanding. How could the murderer have gotten into the locked room? To Watson, the mystery, like the room, was *impenetrable*.

impenitent ADJ. not repentant. We could see by his brazen attitude that he was *impenitent*.

imperative ADJ. absolutely necessary; critically important. It is *imperative* that you be extremely agreeable to Great-Aunt Maud when she comes to tea: otherwise she may not leave you that million dollars in her will. also N.

imperceptible ADJ. unnoticeable; undetectable. Fortunately, the stain on the blouse was *imperceptible* after the garment had gone through the wash.

imperial ADJ. like an emperor; related to an empire. When hotel owner Leona Helmsley appeared in ads as Queen Leona standing guard over the Palace Hotel, her critics mocked her *imperial* fancies.

imperious ADJ. domineering; haughty. Jane rather liked a man to be masterful, but Mr. Rochester seemed so bent on getting his own way that he was actually *imperious*! imperiousness, N.

■ **impermeable** ADJ. impervious; not permitting passage through its substance. This new material is *impermeable* to liquids.

impertinent ADJ. insolent; rude. His neighbors' *impertinent* curiosity about his lack of dates angered Ted. It was downright rude of them to ask him such personal questions. impertinence, N.

■ **imperturbable** ADJ. calm; placid. Wellington remained *imperturbable* and in full command of the situation in spite of the hysteria and panic all around him. imperturbability, N.

■ **impervious** ADJ. impenetrable; incapable of being damaged or distressed. The carpet salesman told Simone that his most expensive brand of floor covering was warranted to be *impervious* to ordinary wear and tear. Having read so many negative reviews of his acting, the movie star had learned to ignore them, and was now *impervious* to criticism.

impetuous ADJ. violent; hasty; rash. "Leap before you look" was the motto suggested by one particularly *impetuous* young man.

impetus N. moving force; incentive; stimulus. A new federal highway program would create jobs and give added *impetus* to our economic recovery.

impiety N. irreverence; lack of respect for God. When members of the youth group draped the church in toilet paper one Halloween, the minister reprimanded them for their *impiety*. impious, ADJ.

impinge V. infringe; touch; collide with. How could they be married without *impinging* on one another's freedom?

impious ADJ. irreverent. The congregation was offended by her *impious* remarks.

■ **implacable** ADJ. incapable of being pacified. Madame Defarge was the *implacable* enemy of the Evremonde family.

implausible ADJ. unlikely; unbelievable. Though her alibi seemed *implausible*, it in fact turned out to be true.

implement V. put into effect; supply with tools. The mayor was unwilling to *implement* the plan until she was sure it had the governor's backing. also N.

implicate V. incriminate; show to be involved. Here's the deal: if you agree to take the witness stand and *implicate* your partners in crime, the prosecution will recommend that the judge go easy in sentencing you.

implication N. something hinted at or suggested. When Miss Watson said she hadn't seen her purse since the last time Jim was in the house, the *implication* was that she suspected Jim had taken it.

■ **implicit** ADJ. understood but not stated. Jack never told Jill he adored her; he believed his love was *implicit* in his deeds.

■ **implode** V. burst inward. If you break a vacuum tube, the glass tube *implodes*. implosion, N.

implore V. beg. He *implored* her to give him a second chance.

imply V. suggest a meaning not expressed; signify. When Aunt Millie said, "My! That's a big piece of pie, young man!" was she *implying* that Bobby was being a glutton in helping himself to such a huge piece?

impolitic ADJ. not wise. I think it is *impolitic* to raise this issue at the present time because the public is too angry.

imponderable ADJ. weightless. I can evaluate the data gathered in this study; the *imponderable* items are not so easily analyzed.

import N. significance. I feel that you have not grasped the full *import* of the message sent to us by the enemy.

importunate ADJ. urging; demanding. He tried to hide from his *importunate* creditors until his allowance arrived.

importune V. beg persistently. Democratic and Republican phone solicitors *importuned* her for contributions so frequently that she decided to give nothing to either party.

imposture N. assuming a false identity; masquerade. She was imprisoned for her *imposture* of a doctor.

impotent ADJ. weak; ineffective. Although he wished to break the nicotine habit, he found himself *impotent* in resisting the craving for a cigarette.

imprecation N. curse. Roused from bed at what he considered an ungodly hour, Roy muttered *imprecations* under his breath.

impregnable ADJ. invulnerable. Until the development of the airplane as a military weapon, the fort was considered *impregnable*.

impromptu ADJ. without previous preparation; off the cuff; on the spur of the moment. The judges were amazed that she could make such a thorough, well-supported presentation in an *impromptu* speech.

impropriety N. improperness; unsuitableness. Because of the *impropriety* of the punk rocker's slashed T-shirt and jeans, the management refused to admit him to the hotel's very formal dining room.

improvident ADJ. thriftless. He was constantly being warned to mend his *improvident* ways and begin to "save for a rainy day." improvidence, N.

improvise V. compose on the spur of the moment. She would sit at the piano and *improvise* for hours on themes from Bach and Handel.

imprudent ADJ. lacking caution; injudicious. It is *imprudent* to exercise vigorously and become overheated when you are unwell.

impudence N. impertinence; insolence. Kissed on the cheek by a perfect stranger, Lady Catherine exclaimed, "Of all the nerve! Young man, I should have you horse-whipped for your *impudence.*"

impugn V. dispute or contradict (often in an insulting way); challenge; gainsay. Our treasurer was furious when the finance committee's report *impugned* the accuracy of his financial records and recommended that he take bonehead math.

impuissance N. powerlessness; feebleness. The lame duck president was frustrated by his shift from enormous power to relative *impuissance.*

impunity N. freedom from punishment or harm. A 98-pound weakling can't attack a beachfront bully with *impunity:* the poor, puny guy is sure to get mashed.

impute V. attribute; ascribe. If I wished to *impute* blame to the officers in charge of this program, I would state my feelings definitely and immediately.

■ **inadvertently** ADV. unintentionally; by oversight; carelessly. Judy's great fear was that she might *inadvertently* omit a question on the exam and mismark her whole answer sheet.

inalienable ADJ. not to be taken away; nontransferable. The Declaration of Independence mentions the *inalienable* rights that all of us possess.

inane ADJ. silly; senseless. There's no point in what you're saying. Why are you bothering to make such *inane* remarks? inanity, N.

inanimate ADJ. lifeless. She was asked to identify the still and *inanimate* body.

inarticulate ADJ. speechless; producing indistinct speech. She became *inarticulate* with rage and uttered sounds without meaning.

inaugurate V. begin formally; install in office. The candidate promised that he would *inaugurate* a new nation-wide health care plan as soon as he was *inaugurated* as president. inauguration, N.

incandescent ADJ. strikingly bright; shining with intense heat. If you leave on an *incandescent* light bulb, it quickly grows too hot to touch.

incantation N. singing or chanting of magic spells; magical formula. Uttering *incantations* to make the brew more potent, the witch doctor stirred the liquid in the caldron.

incapacitate V. disable. During the winter, many people were *incapacitated* by respiratory ailments.

incarcerate V. imprison. The civil rights workers were willing to be arrested and even *incarcerated* if by their imprisonment they could serve the cause.

incarnate ADJ. endowed with flesh; personified. Your attitude is so fiendish that you must be a devil *incarnate.*

incarnation N. act of assuming a human body and human nature. The *incarnation* of Jesus Christ is a basic tenet of Christian theology.

incendiary N. arsonist. The fire spread in such an unusual manner that the fire department chiefs were certain that it had been set by an *incendiary.* also ADJ.

incense V. enrage; infuriate. Cruelty to defenseless animals *incensed* Kit: the very idea brought tears of anger to her eyes.

incentive N. spur; motive. Mike's strong desire to outshine his big sister was all the *incentive* he needed to do well in school.

inception N. start; beginning. She was involved with the project from its *inception.*

incessant ADJ. uninterrupted; unceasing. In a famous TV commercial, the frogs' *incessant* croaking goes on and on until eventually it turns into a single word: "Bud-weis-er."

Test

Word List 24   *Synonyms and Antonyms*

Each of the questions below consists of a word in capital letters, followed by five lettered words or phrases. Choose the lettered word or phrase that is most nearly similar or opposite in meaning to the word in capital letters and write the letter of your choice on your answer paper.

346. IMMOLATE (A) debate (B) scour (C) sacrifice (D) sanctify (E) ratify

347. IMMUTABLE (A) silent (B) changeable (C) articulate (D) loyal (E) varied

348. IMPAIR (A) separate (B) make amends (C) make worse (D) falsify (E) cancel

349. IMPALPABLE (A) obvious (B) combined (C) high (D) connecting (E) lost

350. IMPASSIVE (A) active (B) demonstrative (C) perfect (D) anxious (E) irritated

351. IMPECCABLE (A) unmentionable (B) quotable (C) blinding (D) faulty (E) hampering

352. IMPECUNIOUS (A) affluent (B) afflicted (C) affectionate (D) affable (E) afraid

353. IMPERVIOUS (A) impenetrable (B) perplexing (C) chaotic (D) cool (E) perfect

354. IMPETUOUS (A) rash (B) inane (C) just (D) flagrant (E) redolent

355. IMPOLITIC (A) campaigning (B) advisable (C) aggressive (D) legal (E) fortunate

356. IMPORTUNE (A) export (B) plead (C) exhibit (D) account (E) visit

357. IMPROMPTU (A) prompted (B) appropriate (C) rehearsed (D) foolish (E) vast

358. INALIENABLE (A) inherent (B) repugnant (C) closed to immigration (D) full (E) accountable

359. INANE (A) passive (B) wise (C) intoxicated (D) mellow (E) silent

360. INCARCERATE (A) inhibit (B) acquit (C) account (D) imprison (E) force

---

Word List 25   inchoate-infraction

■ **inchoate** ADJ. recently begun; rudimentary; elementary. Before the Creation, the world was an *inchoate* mass.

incidence N. rate of occurrence; particular occurrence. Health professionals expressed great concern over the high *incidence* of infant mortality in major urban areas.

incidental ADJ. not essential; minor. The scholarship covered his major expenses at college and some of his *incidental* expenses as well.

incipient ADJ. beginning; in an early stage. I will go to sleep early for I want to break an *incipient* cold.

incisive ADJ. cutting; sharp. Her *incisive* remarks made us see the fallacy in our plans. incision, N.

incite V. arouse to action; goad; motivate; induce to exist. In a fiery speech, Mario *incited* his fellow students to go out on strike to protest the university's anti-affirmative-action stand.

inclement ADJ. stormy; unkind. In *inclement* weather, I like to curl up on the sofa with a good book and listen to the storm blowing outside.

incline N. slope; slant. The architect recommended that the nursing home's ramp be rebuilt because its *incline* was too steep for wheelchairs.

inclined ADJ. tending or leaning toward; bent. Though I am *inclined* to be skeptical, the witness's manner *inclines* me to believe his story. incline, V.

inclusive ADJ. tending to include all. The comedian turned down the invitation to join the Players' Club, saying any club that would let him in was too *inclusive* for him.

incognito ADV. with identity concealed; using an assumed name. The monarch enjoyed traveling through the town *incognito* and mingling with the populace. also ADJ.

incoherent ADJ. unintelligible; muddled; illogical. The excited fan blushed and stammered, her words becoming almost *incoherent* in the thrill of meeting her favorite rock star face to face. incoherence, N.

incommodious ADJ. not spacious; inconvenient. In their *incommodious* quarters, they had to improvise for closet space.

incompatible ADJ. inharmonious. The married couple argued incessantly and finally decided to separate because they were *incompatible*. incompatibility, N.

■ **incongruity** N. lack of harmony; absurdity. The *incongruity* of his wearing sneakers with formal attire amused the observers. incongruous, ADJ.

■ **inconsequential** ADJ. insignificant; unimportant. Brushing off Ali's apologies for having broken the wine glass, Tamara said, "Don't worry about it; it's *inconsequential.*"

inconsistency N. state of being self-contradictory; lack of uniformity or steadiness. How are lawyers different from agricultural inspectors? Where lawyers check *inconsistencies* in witnesses' statements, agricultural inspectors check *inconsistencies* in Grade A eggs. inconsistent, ADJ.

incontinent ADJ. lacking self-restraint; licentious. His *incontinent* behavior off stage so shocked many people that they refused to attend the plays and movies in which he appeared.

incontrovertible ADJ. indisputable; not open to question. Unless you find the evidence against my client absolutely *incontrovertible,* you must declare her not guilty of this charge.

■ **incorporate** V. introduce something into a larger whole; combine; unite. Breaking with precedent, President Truman ordered the military to *incorporate* blacks into every branch of the armed services. also ADJ.

incorporeal ADJ. lacking a material body; insubstantial. Although Casper the friendly ghost is an *incorporeal* being, he and his fellow ghosts make quite an impact on the physical world.

incorrigible ADJ. uncorrectable. Though Widow Douglass hoped to reform Huck, Miss Watson pronounced him *incorrigible* and said he would come to no good end.

incredulity N. tendency to disbelief. Your *incredulity* in the face of all the evidence is hard to understand.

incredulous ADJ. withholding belief; skeptical. When Jack claimed he hadn't eaten the jelly doughnut, Jill took an *incredulous* look at his smeared face and laughed.

increment N. increase. The new contract calls for a ten percent *increment* in salary for each employee for the next two years.

incriminate V. accuse; serve as evidence against. The witness's testimony against the racketeers *incriminates* some high public officials as well.

incrustation N. hard coating or crust. In dry dock, we scraped off the *incrustation* of dirt and barnacles that covered the hull of the ship.

incubate V. hatch. Inasmuch as our supply of electricity is cut off, we shall have to rely on the hens to *incubate* these eggs.

incubus N. burden; mental care; nightmare. The *incubus* of financial worry helped bring on her nervous breakdown.

inculcate V. teach. In an effort to *inculcate* religious devotion, the officials ordered that the school day begin with the singing of a hymn.

incumbent ADJ. obligatory; currently holding an office. It is *incumbent* upon all *incumbent* elected officials to keep accurate records of expenses incurred in office. also N.

incur V. bring upon oneself. His parents refused to pay any future debts he might *incur*.

incursion N. temporary invasion. The nightly *incursions* and hit-and-run raids of our neighbors across the border tried the patience of the country to the point where we decided to retaliate in force.

indefatigable ADJ. tireless. Although the effort of taking out the garbage exhausted Wayne for the entire morning, when it came to partying, he was *indefatigable*.

indelible ADJ. not able to be erased. The *indelible* ink left a permanent mark on my shirt. Young Bill Clinton's meeting with President Kennedy made an *indelible* impression on the youth.

indemnify V. make secure against loss; compensate for loss. The city will *indemnify* all home owners whose property is spoiled by this project.

indentation N. notch; deep recess. You can tell one tree from another by noting the differences in the *indentations* along the edges of the leaves. indent, V.

indenture V. bind as servant or apprentice to master. Many immigrants could come to America only after they had *indentured* themselves for several years. also N.

■ **indeterminate** ADJ. uncertain; not clearly fixed; indefinite. That interest rates shall rise appears certain; when they will do so, however, remains *indeterminate*.

indicative ADJ. suggestive; implying. A lack of appetite may be *indicative* of a major mental or physical disorder.

indices N. PL. signs; indications. Many college admissions officers believe that SAT scores and high school grades are the best *indices* of a student's potential to succeed in college. index, N. SING.

indict V. charge. The district attorney didn't want to *indict* the suspect until she was sure she had a strong enough case to convince a jury. indictment, N.

indifferent ADJ. unmoved or unconcerned by; mediocre. Because Ann felt no desire to marry, she was *indifferent* to Carl's constant proposals. Not only was she *indifferent* to him personally, but she felt that, given his general inanity, he would make an *indifferent* husband.

■ **indigence** N. poverty. Neither the economists nor the political scientists have found a way to wipe out the inequities of wealth and eliminate *indigence* from our society. indigent, ADJ., N.

indigenous ADJ. native. Cigarettes are made of tobacco, a plant *indigenous* to the New World.

indigent ADJ. poor; destitute. Someone who is truly *indigent* can't even afford to buy a pack of cigarettes. [Don't mix up *indigent* and *indigenous*. See preceding entry.]

also N.

indignation N. anger at an injustice. She felt *indignation* at the ill-treatment of the helpless animals.

indignity N. offensive or insulting treatment. Although he seemed to accept cheerfully the *indignities* heaped upon him, he was inwardly very angry.

indiscriminate ADJ. choosing at random; confused. She disapproved of her son's *indiscriminate* television viewing and decided to restrict him to educational programs.

indisputable ADJ. too certain to be disputed. In the face of these *indisputable* statements, I withdraw my complaint.

indissoluble ADJ. permanent. The *indissoluble* bonds of marriage are all too often being dissolved.

indite V. write; compose. Cyrano *indited* many letters for Christian.

■ **indolent** ADJ. lazy. Couch potatoes lead an *indolent* life lying back in their Lazyboy recliners watching TV. indolence, N.

indomitable ADJ. unconquerable; unyielding. Focusing on her game despite all her personal problems, tennis champion Steffi Graf displayed an *indomitable* will to win.

indubitable ADJ. unable to be doubted; unquestionable. Auditioning for the chorus line, Molly was an *indubitable* hit: the director fired the leading lady and hired Molly in her place!

induce V. persuade; bring about. After the quarrel, Tina said nothing could *induce* her to talk to Tony again. inducement, N.

inductive ADJ. pertaining to induction or proceeding from the specific to the general. The discovery of the planet Pluto is an excellent example of the results that can be obtained from *inductive* reasoning.

indulgent ADJ. humoring; yielding; lenient. Jay's mom was excessively *indulgent*: she bought him every computer game on the market. In fact, she *indulged* Jay so much, she spoiled him rotten.

industrious ADJ. diligent; hard-working. Look busy when the boss walks by your desk; it never hurts to appear *industrious*. industry, N.

inebriated ADJ. habitually intoxicated; drunk. Abe was *inebriated* more often than he was sober. Because of his *inebriety*, he was discharged from his job as a bus driver.

ineffable ADJ. unutterable; cannot be expressed in speech. Such *ineffable* joy must be experienced; it cannot be described.

ineffectual ADJ. not effective; weak. Because the candidate failed to get across her message to the public, her campaign was *ineffectual*.

ineluctable ADJ. irresistible; not to be escaped. He felt that his fate was *ineluctable* and refused to make any attempt to improve his lot.

inept ADJ. lacking skill; unsuited; incompetent. The *inept* glovemaker was all thumbs. ineptness, N.

inequity N. unfairness. In demanding equal pay for equal work, women protest the basic *inequity* of a system that allots greater financial rewards to men. inequitable, ADJ.

inerrancy N. infallibility. Jane refused to believe in the pope's *inerrancy,* reasoning: "All human beings are capable of error. The pope is a human being. Therefore, the pope is capable of error."

■ **inert** ADJ. inactive; lacking power to move. "Get up, you lazybones," Tina cried to Tony, who lay in bed *inert.* inertia, N.

inevitable ADJ. unavoidable. Though death and taxes are both supposedly *inevitable,* some people avoid paying taxes for years.

inexorable ADJ. relentless; unyielding; implacable. After listening to the pleas for clemency, the judge was *inexorable* and gave the convicted man the maximum punishment allowed by law.

infallible ADJ. unerring. We must remember that none of us is *infallible;* we all make mistakes.

infamous ADJ. notoriously bad. Charles Manson and Jeffrey Dahmer are two examples of *infamous* killers.

infantile ADJ. childish; infantlike. When will he outgrow such *infantile* behavior?

infer V. deduce; conclude. From the students' glazed looks, it was easy for me to *infer* that they were bored out of their minds. inference, N.

infernal ADJ. pertaining to hell; devilish. Batman was baffled: he could think of no way to hinder the Joker's *infernal* scheme to destroy the city.

infidel N. unbeliever. The Saracens made war against the *infidels.*

infiltrate V. pass into or through; penetrate (an organization) sneakily. In order to *infiltrate* enemy lines at night without being seen, the scouts darkened their faces and wore black coveralls. infiltrator, N.

infinitesimal ADJ. very small. In the twentieth century, physicists have made their greatest discoveries about the characteristics of *infinitesimal* objects like the atom and its parts.

infirmity N. weakness. Her greatest *infirmity* was lack of willpower.

inflated ADJ. exaggerated; pompous; enlarged (with air or gas). His claims about the new product were *inflated;* it did not work as well as he had promised.

influx N. flowing into. The *influx* of refugees into the country has taxed the relief agencies severely.

infraction N. violation (of a rule or regulation); breach. When basketball star Dennis Rodman butted heads with the referee, he committed a clear *infraction* of NBA rules.

Test

Word List 25   *Synonyms*

Each of the questions below consists of a word in capital letters, followed by five lettered words or phrases. Choose the lettered word or phrase that is most nearly similar in meaning to the word in capital letters and write the letter of your choice on your answer paper.

361. INCLEMENT (A) unfavorable (B) abandoned (C) kindly (D) selfish (E) active

362. INCOMPATIBLE (A) capable (B) reasonable (C) faulty (D) indifferent (E) alienated

363. INCONSEQUENTIAL (A) disorderly (B) insignificant (C) subsequent (D) insufficient (E) preceding

364. INCONTINENT (A) insular (B) complaisant (C) crass (D) wanton (E) false

365. INCORRIGIBLE (A) narrow (B) straight (C) inconceivable (D) unreliable (E) unreformable

366. INCRIMINATE (A) exacerbate (B) involve (C) intimidate (D) lacerate (E) prevaricate

367. INCULCATE (A) exculpate (B) educate (C) exonerate (D) prepare (E) embarrass

368. INDIGENT (A) lazy (B) pusillanimous (C) penurious (D) affluent (E) contrary

369. INDIGNITY (A) pomposity (B) bombast (C) obeisance (D) insult (E) message

370. INDOLENCE (A) sloth (B) poverty (C) latitude (D) aptitude (E) anger

371. INDUBITABLY (A) flagrantly (B) doubtfully (C) carefully (D) carelessly (E) certainly

372. INEBRIETY (A) revelation (B) drunkenness (C) felony (D) starvation (E) gluttony

373. INEPT (A) outward (B) spiritual (C) foolish (D) clumsy (E) abundant

374. INFALLIBLE (A) final (B) unbelievable (C) perfect (D) inaccurate (E) inquisitive

375. INFIRMITY (A) disability (B) age (C) inoculation (D) hospital (E) unity

Word List 26   infringe-invert

infringe   v. violate; encroach. I think your machine *infringes* on my patent and I intend to sue.

ingenious   ADJ. clever; resourceful. Kit admired the *ingenious* way that her computer keyboard opened up to reveal the built-in CD-ROM below. ingenuity, N.

■ **ingenuous**   ADJ. naive and trusting; young; unsophisticated. The woodsman did not realize how *ingenuous* Little Red Riding Hood was until he heard that she had gone off for a walk in the woods with the Big Bad Wolf. ingenue, N.

ingrained   ADJ. deeply established; firmly rooted. Try as they would, the missionaries were unable to uproot the *ingrained* superstitions of the natives.

ingrate   N. ungrateful person. That *ingrate* Bob sneered at the tie I gave him.

ingratiate   v. become popular with. He tried to *ingratiate* himself into her parents' good graces.

■ **inherent**   ADJ. firmly established by nature or habit. Katya's *inherent* love of justice caused her to champion anyone she considered to be treated unfairly by society.

inhibit   v. restrain; retard or prevent. Only two things *inhibited* him from taking a punch at Mike Tyson: Tyson's left hook, and Tyson's right jab. The protective undercoating on my car *inhibits* the formation of rust. inhibition, N.

inimical   ADJ. unfriendly; hostile; harmful; detrimental. I've always been friendly to Martha. Why is she so *inimical* to me?

inimitable   ADJ. matchless; not able to be imitated. We admire Auden for his *inimitable* use of language; he is one of a kind.

iniquitous   ADJ. wicked; immoral; unrighteous. Whether or not King Richard III was responsible for the murder of the two young princes in the Tower, it was an *iniquitous* deed. iniquity, N.

initiate   v. begin; originate; receive into a group. The college is about to *initiate* a program for reducing math anxiety among students.

injurious   ADJ. harmful. Smoking cigarettes can be *injurious* to your health.

inkling   N. hint. This came as a complete surprise to me as I did not have the slightest *inkling* of your plans.

innate   ADJ. inborn. Mozart's parents soon recognized young Wolfgang's *innate* talent for music.

■ **innocuous**   ADJ. harmless. An occasional glass of wine with dinner is relatively *innocuous* and should have no ill effect on most people.

innovation   N. change; introduction of something new. Although Richard liked to keep up with all the latest technological *innovations*, he didn't always abandon tried and true techniques in favor of something new. innovate, v. innovative, ADJ.

innuendo   N. hint; insinuation. I can defend myself against direct accusations; *innuendos* and oblique attacks on my character are what trouble me.

inopportune   ADJ. untimely; poorly chosen. A rock concert is an *inopportune* setting for a quiet conversation.

inordinate   ADJ. unrestrained; excessive. She had an *inordinate* fondness for candy, eating two or three boxes in a single day.

inquisitor   N. questioner (especially harsh); investigator. Fearing being grilled ruthlessly by the secret police, Marsha faced her *inquisitors* with trepidation.

insalubrious   ADJ. unwholesome; not healthful. The mosquito-ridden swamp was an *insalubrious* place, a breeding ground for malarial contagion.

insatiable   ADJ. not easily satisfied; unquenchable; greedy. The young writer's thirst for knowledge was *insatiable;* she was always in the library.

inscrutable   ADJ. impenetrable; not readily understood; mysterious. Experienced poker players try to keep their expressions *inscrutable,* hiding their reactions to the cards behind a so-called poker face.

insensate   ADJ. without feeling. She lay there as *insensate* as a log.

■ **insensible**   ADJ. unconscious; unresponsive. Sherry and I are very different; at times when I would be covered with embarrassment, she seems *insensible* to shame.

insidious   ADJ. treacherous; stealthy; sly. The fifth column is *insidious* because it works secretly within our territory for our defeat.

insightful   ADJ. discerning; perceptive. Sol thought he was very *insightful* about human behavior, but actually he was clueless as to why people acted the way they did.

■ **insinuate**   v. hint; imply; creep in. When you said I looked robust, did you mean to *insinuate* that I'm getting fat?

■ **insipid**   ADJ. lacking in flavor; dull. Flat prose and flat ginger ale are equally *insipid:* both lack sparkle.

insolence   N. impudent disrespect; haughtiness. How dare you treat me so rudely! The manager will hear of your *insolence*. insolent, ADJ.

insolvent   ADJ. bankrupt; lacking money to pay. When rumors that he was *insolvent* reached his creditors, they began to press him for payment of the money due them. insolvency, N.

insomnia   N. wakefulness; inability to sleep. She refused to join us in a midnight cup of coffee because she claimed it gave her *insomnia*.

insouciant   ADJ. indifferent; without concern or care. Your *insouciant* attitude at such a critical moment indicates that you do not understand the gravity of the situation.

instigate   v. urge; start; provoke. Delighting in making mischief, Sir Toby sets out to *instigate* a quarrel between Sir Andrew and Cesario.

insubordination   N. disobedience; rebelliousness. At the slightest hint of *insubordination* from the sailors on the *Bounty*, Captain Bligh had them flogged; finally, they mutinied. insubordinate, ADJ.

insubstantial ADJ. lacking substance; insignificant; frail. His hopes for a career in acting proved *insubstantial;* no one would cast him, even in an *insubstantial* role.

■ **insularity** N. narrow-mindedness; isolation. The *insularity* of the islanders manifested itself in their suspicion of anything foreign. insular, ADJ.

insuperable ADJ. insurmountable; unbeatable. Though the odds against their survival seemed *insuperable,* the Apollo 13 astronauts reached earth safely.

insurgent ADJ. rebellious. Because the *insurgent* forces had occupied the capital and had gained control of the railway lines, several of the war correspondents covering the uprising predicted a rebel victory. also N. insurgency, N.

insurmountable ADJ. overwhelming; unbeatable; insuperable. Facing almost *insurmountable* obstacles, the members of the underground maintained their courage and will to resist.

insurrection N. rebellion; uprising. In retrospect, given how badly the British treated the American colonists, the eventual *insurrection* seems inevitable.

intangible ADJ. not able to be perceived by touch; vague. Though the financial benefits of his Oxford post were meager, Lewis was drawn to it by its *intangible* rewards: prestige, intellectual freedom, the fellowship of his peers.

integral ADJ. complete; necessary for completeness. Physical education is an *integral* part of our curriculum; a sound mind and a sound body are complementary.

integrate V. make whole; combine; make into one unit. She tried to *integrate* all their activities into one program.

integrity N. uprightness; wholeness. Lincoln, whose personal *integrity* has inspired millions, fought a civil war to maintain the *integrity* of the republic, that these United States might remain undivided for all time.

intellect N. higher mental powers. He thought college would develop his *intellect*.

intelligentsia N. intellectuals; members of the educated elite [often used derogatorily]. She preferred discussions about sports and politics to the literary conversations of the *intelligentsia*.

inter V. bury. They are going to *inter* the body tomorrow at Broadlawn Cemetry. interment, N.

interdict V. prohibit; forbid. Civilized nations must *interdict* the use of nuclear weapons if we expect our society to live.

interim N. meantime. The company will not consider our proposal until next week; in the *interim,* let us proceed as we have in the past.

interloper N. intruder. The merchant thought of his competitors as *interlopers* who were stealing away his trade.

interminable ADJ. endless. Although his speech lasted for only twenty minutes, it seemed *interminable* to his bored audience.

intermittent ADJ. periodic; on and off. The outdoor wedding reception had to be moved indoors to avoid the *intermittent* showers that fell on and off all afternoon.

internecine ADJ. mutually destructive. The rising death toll on both sides indicates the *internecine* nature of this conflict.

interpolate V. insert between. She talked so much that I could not *interpolate* a single remark.

interregnum N. period between two reigns. Henry VIII desperately sought a male heir because he feared the civil strife that might occur if any prolonged *interregnum* succeeded his death.

interrogate V. question closely; cross-examine. Knowing that the Nazis would *interrogate* him about his background, the secret agent invented a cover story that would help him meet their questions.

intervene V. come between. When two close friends get into a fight, be careful if you try to *intervene;* they may join forces and gang up on you. intervention, N.

intimate V. hint. She *intimated* rather than stated her preferences.

intimidate V. frighten. I'll learn karate and then those big bullies won't be able to *intimidate* me anymore. intimidation, N.

■ **intractable** ADJ. unruly; stubborn; unyielding. Charlie Brown's friend Pigpen was *intractable:* he absolutely refused to take a bath.

■ **intransigence** N. refusal of any compromise; stubbornness. The negotiating team had not expected such *intransigence* from the striking workers, who rejected any hint of a compromise. intransigent, ADJ.

intrepid ADJ. fearless. For her *intrepid* conduct nursing the wounded during the war, Florence Nightingale was honored by Queen Victoria.

intrinsic ADJ. essential; inherent; built-in. Although my grandmother's china has little *intrinsic* value, I shall always cherish it for the memories it evokes.

introspective ADJ. looking within oneself. Though young Francis of Assisi led a wild and worldly life, even he had *introspective* moments during which he examined his soul. introspection, N.

introvert N. one who is introspective; inclined to think more about oneself. In his poetry, he reveals that he is an *introvert* by his intense interest in his own problems.

intrude V. trespass; enter as an uninvited person. She hesitated to *intrude* on their conversation.

intuition N. immediate insight; power of knowing without reasoning. Even though Tony denied that anything was wrong, Tina trusted her *intuition* that something was bothering him. intuitive, ADJ. intuit, V.

■ **inundate** V. overwhelm; flood; submerge. This semester I am *inundated* with work: you should see the piles of paperwork flooding my desk. Until the great dam was built, the waters of the Nile used to *inundate* the river valley every year.

■ **inured** ADJ. accustomed; hardened. She became *inured* to the Alaskan cold.

invalidate V. weaken; destroy. The relatives who received little or nothing sought to *invalidate* the will by claiming that the deceased had not been in his right mind when he signed the document.

■ **invective** N. abuse. He had expected criticism but not the *invective* that greeted his proposal.

inveigh V. denounce; utter censure or invective. He *inveighed* against the demagoguery of the previous speaker and urged that the audience reject his philosophy as dangerous.

inveigle V. lead astray; wheedle. She was *inveigled* into joining the club after an initial reluctance.

inverse ADJ. opposite. There is an *inverse* ratio between the strength of light and its distance.

invert V. turn upside down or inside out. When he *inverted* his body in a hand stand, he felt the blood rush to his head.

Test

Word List 26 *Synonyms*

Each of the questions below consists of a word in capital letters, followed by five lettered words or phrases. Choose the lettered word or phrase that is most nearly similar in meaning to the word in capital letters and write the letter of your choice on your answer paper.

376. INGENUOUS (A) clever (B) stimulating (C) naive (D) worried (E) cautious

377. INIMICAL (A) antagonistic (B) anonymous (C) fanciful (D) accurate (E) atypical

378. INNOCUOUS (A) not capable (B) not dangerous (C) not eager (D) not frank (E) not peaceful

379. INSINUATE (A) resist (B) suggest (C) report (D) rectify (E) lecture

380. INSIPID (A) witty (B) flat (C) wily (D) talkative (E) lucid

381. INTEGRATE (A) tolerate (B) unite (C) flow (D) copy (E) assume

382. INTER (A) bury (B) amuse (C) relate (D) frequent (E) abandon

383. INTERDICT (A) acclaim (B) dispute (C) prohibit (D) decide (E) fret

384. INTERMITTENT (A) heavy (B) fleet (C) occasional (D) fearless (E) responding

385. INTRACTABLE (A) culpable (B) flexible (C) unruly (D) efficient (E) base

386. INTRANSIGENCE (A) lack of training (B) stubbornness (C) novelty (D) timidity (E) cupidity

387. INTREPID (A) cold (B) hot (C) understood (D) callow (E) courageous

388. INTRINSIC (A) extrinsic (B) abnormal (C) above (D) abandoned (E) basic

389. INUNDATE (A) abuse (B) deny (C) swallow (D) treat (E) flood

390. INVEIGH (A) speak violently (B) orate (C) disturb (D) apply (E) whisper

Word List 27 inveterate-laggard

inveterate ADJ. deep-rooted; habitual. She is an *inveterate* smoker and cannot break the habit.

invidious ADJ. designed to create ill will or envy. We disregarded her *invidious* remarks because we realized how jealous she was.

invincible ADJ. unconquerable. Superman is *invincible*.

inviolable ADJ. secure from corruption, attack, or violation; unassailable. Batman considered his oath to keep the people of Gotham City safe *inviolable:* nothing on earth could make him break this promise. inviolability, N.

invocation N. prayer for help; calling upon as a reference or support. The service of Morning Prayer opens with an *invocation* during which we ask God to hear our prayers.

invoke V. call upon; ask for. She *invoked* her advisor's aid in filling out her financial aid forms.

invulnerable ADJ. incapable of injury. Achilles was *invulnerable* except in his heel.

iota N. very small quantity. She hadn't an *iota* of common sense.

■ **irascible** ADJ. irritable; easily angered. Miss Minchin's *irascible* temper intimidated the younger schoolgirls, who feared she'd burst into a rage at any moment.

irate ADJ. angry. When John's mother found out that he had overdrawn his checking account for the third month in a row, she was so *irate* that she could scarcely speak to him.

iridescent ADJ. exhibiting rainbowlike colors. She admired the *iridescent* hues of the oil that floated on the surface of the water. iridescence, N.

irksome ADJ. annoying; tedious. He found working on the assembly line *irksome* because of the monotony of the operation he had to perform. irk, V.

ironic ADJ. occurring in an unexpected and contrary manner. It is *ironic* that his success came when he least wanted it.

irony N. hidden sarcasm or satire; use of words that seem to mean the opposite of what they actually mean. Gradually his listeners began to realize that the excessive praise he was lavishing on his opponent was actually *irony;* he was, in fact, ridiculing the poor fool.

irreconcilable ADJ. incompatible; not able to be resolved. Because the separated couple were *irreconcilable,* the marriage counselor recommended a divorce.

irrefutable ADJ. indisputable; incontrovertible; undeniable. No matter how hard I tried to find a good comeback for her argument, I couldn't think of one: her logic was *irrefutable.*

irrelevant ADJ. not applicable; unrelated. No matter how *irrelevant* the patient's mumblings may seem, they give us some indications of what is on his mind. irrelevancy, N.

irremediable ADJ. incurable; uncorrectable. The error she made was *irremediable;* she could see no way to rectify it.

irreparable ADJ. not able to be corrected or repaired. Your apology cannot atone for the *irreparable* damage you have done to her reputation.

irrepressible ADJ. unable to be restrained or held back. My friend Kitty's curiosity was *irrepressible:* she poked her nose into everybody's business and just laughed when I warned her that curiosity killed the cat.

irreproachable ADJ. blameless; impeccable. Homer's conduct at the office party was *irreproachable;* even Marge had nothing bad to say about how he behaved.

■ **irresolute** ADJ. uncertain how to act; weak. Once you have made your decision, don't waver; a leader should never appear *irresolute.*

irretrievable ADJ. impossible to recover or regain; irreparable. The left fielder tried to retrieve the ball, but it flew over the fence, bounced off a wall, and fell into the sewer: it was *irretrievable.*

irreverence N. lack of proper respect. Some people in the audience were amused by the *irreverence* of the comedian's jokes about the pope; others felt offended by his lack of respect for their faith. irreverent, ADJ.

irrevocable ADJ. unalterable; irreversible. As Sue dropped the "Dear John" letter into the mailbox, she suddenly had second thoughts and wanted to take it back, but she could not: her action was *irrevocable.*

isotope N. varying form of an element. The study of the *isotopes* of uranium led to the development of the nuclear bomb.

isthmus N. narrow neck of land connecting two larger bodies of land. In a magnificent feat of engineering, Goethals and his men cut through the *isthmus* of Panama in constructing the Panama Canal.

itinerant ADJ. wandering; traveling. He was an *itinerant* peddler and traveled through Pennsylvania and Virginia selling his wares. also N.

■ **itinerary** N. plan of a trip. Disliking sudden changes in plans when she traveled abroad, Ethel refused to make any alterations in her *itinerary.*

jabber V. chatter rapidly or unintelligibly. Why does the fellow insist on *jabbering* away in French when I can't understand a word he says?

jaded ADJ. fatigued; surfeited. He looked for exotic foods to stimulate his *jaded* appetite.

jargon N. language used by a special group; technical terminology; gibberish. The computer salesmen at the store used a *jargon* of their own that we simply couldn't follow; we had no idea what they were jabbering about.

jaundiced ADJ. prejudiced (envious, hostile, or resentful); yellowed. Because Sue disliked Carolyn, she looked at Carolyn's paintings with a *jaundiced* eye, calling them formless smears. Newborn infants afflicted with *jaundice* look slightly yellow: they have *jaundiced* skin.

jaunt N. trip; short journey. He took a quick *jaunt* to Atlantic City.

jaunty ADJ. lighthearted; animated; easy and carefree. In *Singing in the Rain,* Gene Kelly sang and danced his way through the lighthearted title number in a properly *jaunty* style.

jeopardize V. endanger; imperil; put at risk. You can't give me a D in chemistry: you'll *jeopardize* my chances of being admitted to M.I.T. jeopardy, N.

jettison V. throw overboard. In order to enable the ship to ride safely through the storm, the captain had to *jettison* much of his cargo.

jibe V. agree; be in harmony with. Moe says Curly started the fight; Curly insists it was Moe. Their stories just don't *jibe.*

jingoist N. extremely aggressive and militant patriot; warlike chauvinist. Always bellowing "America first!" the congressman was such a *jingoist* you could almost hear the sabers rattling as he marched down the halls. jingoism, N.

jocose ADJ. given to joking. The salesman was so *jocose* that many of his customers suggested that he become a stand-up comic.

jocular ADJ. said or done in jest. Although Bill knew the boss hated jokes, he couldn't resist making one *jocular* remark; his *jocularity* cost him the job.

jocund ADJ. merry. Santa Claus is always cheerful and *jocund.*

jollity N. gaiety; cheerfulness. The festive Christmas dinner was a merry one, and old and young alike joined in the general *jollity.*

jostle V. shove; bump. In the subway he was *jostled* by the crowds.

jovial ADJ. good-natured; merry. A frown seemed out of place on his invariably *jovial* face.

jubilation N. rejoicing. There was great *jubilation* when the armistice was announced.

judicious ADJ. sound in judgment; wise. At a key moment in his life, he made a *judicious* investment that was the foundation of his later wealth.

juggernaut N. irresistible crushing force. Nothing could survive in the path of the *juggernaut.*

juncture N. crisis; joining point. At this critical *juncture*, let us think carefully before determining the course we shall follow.

junket N. trip, especially one taken for pleasure by an official at public expense. Though she maintained she had gone abroad to collect firsthand data on the Common Market, the opposition claimed that her trip was merely a political *junket*.

junta N. group of persons joined in political intrigue; cabal. As soon as he learned of its existence, the dictator ordered the execution of all of the members of the *junta*.

jurisprudence N. science of law. She was more a student of *jurisprudence* than a practitioner of the law.

justification N. good or just reason; defense; excuse. The jury found him guilty of the more serious charge because they could see no possible *justification* for his actions.

juxtapose V. place side by side. Comparison will be easier if you *juxtapose* the two objects.

kaleidoscope N. tube in which patterns made by the reflection in mirrors of colored pieces of glass, etc., produce interesting symmetrical effects. People found a new source of entertainment while peering through the *kaleidoscope;* they found the ever-changing patterns fascinating.

ken N. range of knowledge. I cannot answer your question since this matter is beyond my *ken*.

kernel N. central or vital part; whole seed (as of corn). "Watson, buried within this tissue of lies there is a *kernel* of truth; when I find it, the mystery will be solved."

killjoy N. grouch; spoilsport. At breakfast we had all been enjoying our bacon and eggs until that *killjoy* John started talking about how bad animal fats and cholesterol were for our health.

kindle V. start a fire; inspire. One of the first things Ben learned in the Boy Scouts was how to *kindle* a fire by rubbing two dry sticks together. Her teacher's praise for her poetry *kindled* a spark of hope inside Maya.

kindred ADJ. related; similar in nature or character. Tom Sawyer and Huck Finn were two *kindred* spirits. also N.

kinetic ADJ. producing motion. Designers of the electric automobile find that their greatest obstacle lies in the development of light and efficient storage batteries, the source of the *kinetic* energy needed to propel the vehicle.

kismet N. fate. *Kismet* is the Arabic word for "fate."

kleptomaniac N. person who has a compulsive desire to steal. They discovered that the wealthy customer was a *kleptomaniac* when they caught her stealing some cheap trinkets.

knave N. untrustworthy person; rogue; scoundrel. Any politician nicknamed Tricky Dick clearly has the reputation of a *knave*. knavery, N.

knead V. mix; work dough. Her hands grew strong from *kneading* bread.

knell N. tolling of a bell, especially to indicate a funeral, disaster, etc.; sound of the funeral bell. "The curfew tolls the *knell* of parting day." also V.

knit V. contract into wrinkles; grow together. Whenever David worries, his brow *knits* in a frown. When he broke his leg, he sat around the house all day waiting for the bones to *knit*.

knoll N. little, round hill. Robert Louis Stevenson's grave is on a *knoll* in Samoa; to reach the grave site, you must climb uphill and walk a short distance along a marked path.

knotty ADJ. intricate; difficult; tangled. What to Watson had been a *knotty* problem to Sherlock Holmes was simplicity itself.

kudos N. honor; glory; praise. The singer complacently received *kudos* on his performance from his entourage.

labile ADJ. likely to change; unstable. Because the hormonal changes they undergo affect their spirits, adolescents may become emotionally *labile* and experience sudden shifts of mood. lability, N.

laborious ADJ. demanding much work or care; tedious. In putting together his dictionary of the English language, Doctor Johnson undertook a *laborious* task.

labyrinth N. maze. Hiding from Indian Joe, Tom and Becky soon lost themselves in the *labyrinth* of secret underground caves.

laceration N. torn, ragged wound. The stock-car driver needed stitches to close the *lacerations* he received in the car crash. lacerate, V.

lachrymose ADJ. producing tears. His voice has a *lachrymose* quality that is more appropriate at a funeral than a class reunion.

lackadaisical ADJ. lacking purpose or zest; halfhearted; languid. Because Gatsby had his mind more on his love life than on his finances, he did a very *lackadaisical* job of managing his money.

lackluster ADJ. dull. We were disappointed by the *lackluster* performance.

■ **laconic** ADJ. brief and to the point. Many of the characters portrayed by Clint Eastwood are *laconic* types: strong men of few words.

laggard ADJ. slow; sluggish. The sailor had been taught not to be *laggard* in carrying out orders. lag, N., V.

Test

Word List 27   *Antonyms*

Each of the questions below consists of a word in capital letters, followed by five lettered words or phrases. Choose the lettered word or phrase that is most nearly opposite in meaning to the word in capital letters and write the letter of your choice on your answer paper.

391. IRKSOME (A) interesting (B) lazy (C) tireless (D) devious (E) excessive

392. IRRELEVANT (A) lacking piety (B) fragile (C) congruent (D) pertinent (E) varied

393. IRREPARABLE (A) legible (B) correctable (C) proverbial (D) concise (E) legal

394. IRREVERENT (A) related (B) mischievous (C) respective (D) pious (E) violent

395. JADED (A) upright (B) stimulated (C) aspiring (D) applied (E) void

396. JAUNDICED (A) whitened (B) inflamed (C) quickened (D) aged (E) unbiased

397. JAUNTY (A) youthful (B) ruddy (C) strong (D) untraveled (E) sedate

398. JEOPARDY (A) patience (B) courage (C) safety (D) willingness (E) liberty

399. JETTISON (A) salvage (B) submerge (C) descend (D) decelerate (E) repent

400. JOCULAR (A) arterial (B) bloodless (C) verbose (D) serious (E) blind

401. JUDICIOUS (A) punitive (B) unwise (C) criminal (D) licit (E) temporary

402. KINDLE (A) dislike (B) quench (C) gather (D) sparkle (E) estrange

403. LACHRYMOSE (A) cheering (B) smooth (C) passionate (D) curt (E) tense

404. LACKADAISICAL (A) monthly (B) possessing time (C) ambitious (D) pusillanimous (E) intelligent

405. LACONIC (A) milky (B) verbose (C) wicked (D) flagrant (E) derelict

Word List 28   lagoon-loquacious

lagoon N. shallow body of water near a sea; lake. They enjoyed their swim in the calm *lagoon*.

laity N. laypersons; persons not connected with the clergy. The *laity* does not always understand the clergy's problems.

lambaste V. beat; thrash verbally or physically. It was painful to watch the champion *lambaste* his opponent, tearing into him mercilessly.

lament V. grieve; express sorrow. Even advocates of the war *lamented* the loss of so many lives in combat. lamentation, N.

lampoon V. ridicule. This article *lampoons* the pretensions of some movie moguls. also N.

lancet N. small surgical tool for making incisions. With the sharp tip of her *lancet,* Doctor Wheeler cut into the abscess, opening it to let it drain.

languid ADJ. weary; sluggish; listless. Her siege of illness left her *languid* and pallid.

languish V. lose animation or strength. Left at Miss Minchin's school for girls while her father went off to war, Sarah Crewe refused to *languish;* instead, she hid her grief and actively befriended her less fortunate classmates.

languor N. lassitude; depression. His friends tried to overcome the *languor* into which he had fallen by taking him to parties and to the theater.

lank ADJ. long and thin. *Lank,* gaunt, Abraham Lincoln was a striking figure.

lap V. take in food or drink with one's tongue; splash gently. The kitten neatly *lapped* up her milk. The waves softly *lapped* against the pier.

larceny N. theft. Because of the prisoner's record, the district attorney refused to reduce the charge from grand *larceny* to petty *larceny.*

larder N. pantry; place where food is kept. The first thing Bill did on returning home from school was to check what snacks his mother had in the *larder.*

largess N. generous gift. Lady Bountiful distributed *largess* to the poor.

lascivious ADJ. lustful. Because they might arouse *lascivious* impulses in their readers, the lewd books were banned by the clergy.

■ **lassitude** N. languor; weariness. After a massage and a long soak in the hot tub, I surrendered to my growing *lassitude* and lay down for a nap.

■ **latent** ADJ. potential but undeveloped; dormant; hidden. Polaroid pictures are popular at parties because you can see the *latent* photographic image gradually appear before your eyes. latency, N.

lateral ADJ. coming from the side. In order to get good plant growth, the gardener must pinch off all *lateral* shoots.

latitude N. freedom from narrow limitations. I think you have permitted your son too much *latitude* in this matter.

■ **laud** V. praise. The NFL *lauded* Boomer Esiason's efforts to raise money to combat cystic fibrosis. also N. laudable, laudatory, ADJ.

lavish ADJ. liberal; wasteful. The actor's *lavish* gifts pleased her. also V.

lax ADJ. careless. We dislike restaurants where the service is *lax* and inattentive.

leaven V. cause to rise or grow lighter; enliven. As bread dough is *leavened,* it puffs up, expanding in volume.

lechery N. gross lewdness; lustfulness. In his youth he led a life of *lechery* and debauchery; he did not mend his ways until middle age. lecherous, ADJ.

lectern N. reading desk. The chaplain delivered his sermon from a hastily improvised *lectern.*

leery ADJ. suspicious; cautious. Don't eat the sushi at this restaurant; I'm a bit *leery* about how fresh it is.

leeway N. room to move; margin. When you set a deadline, allow a little *leeway.*

legacy N. a gift made by a will. Part of my *legacy* from my parents is an album of family photographs.

legend N. explanatory list of symbols on a map. The *legend* at the bottom of the map made it clear which symbols stood for rest areas along the highway and which stood for public camp sites. (secondary meaning)

legerdemain N. sleight of hand. The magician demonstrated his renowned *legerdemain.*

leniency N. mildness; permissiveness. Considering the gravity of the offense, we were surprised by the *leniency* of the sentence. lenient, ADJ.

leonine ADJ. like a lion. He was *leonine* in his rage.

lethal ADJ. deadly. It is unwise to leave *lethal* weapons where children may find them.

■ **lethargic** ADJ. drowsy; dull. In class, she tried to stay alert and listen to the professor, but the stuffy room made her *lethargic*; she felt as if she was about to nod off. lethargy, N.

■ **levee** N. earthen or stone embankment to prevent flooding. As the river rose and threatened to overflow the *levee,* emergency workers rushed to reinforce the walls with sandbags.

levitate V. float in the air (especially by magical means). As the magician passed his hands over the recumbent body of his assistant, she appeared to rise and *levitate* about three feet above the table.

■ **levity** N. lack of seriousness or steadiness; frivolity. Stop giggling and wriggling around in the pew: such *levity* is improper in church.

levy V. impose (a fine); collect (a payment). Crying "No taxation without representation!" the colonists demonstrated against England's power to *levy* taxes. also N.

lewd ADJ. lustful. They found his *lewd* stories objectionable.

lexicographer N. compiler of a dictionary. The new dictionary is the work of many *lexicographers* who spent years compiling and editing the work.

lexicon N. dictionary. I cannot find this word in any *lexicon* in the library.

liability N. drawback; debts. Her lack of an extensive vocabulary was a *liability* that she was able to overcome.

liaison N. contact that keeps parties in communication; go-between; secret love affair. As the *liaison* between the American and British forces during World War II, the colonel had to ease tensions between the leaders of the two armies. Romeo's romantic *liaison* with Juliet ended in tragedy. also ADJ.

libel N. defamatory statement; act of writing something that smears a person's character. If Batman wrote that the Joker was a dirty, rotten, mass-murdering criminal, could the Joker sue Batman for *libel?* libelous, ADJ.

libertine N. debauched person, roué. Although she was aware of his reputation as a *libertine,* she felt she could reform him and help him abandon his dissolute way of life.

libidinous ADJ. lustful. They objected to his *libidinous* behavior.

libido N. emotional urges behind human activity. The psychiatrist maintained that suppression of the *libido* often resulted in maladjustment and neuroses.

libretto N. text of an opera. The composer of an opera's music is remembered more frequently than the author of its *libretto.*

licentious ADJ. amoral; lewd and lascivious; unrestrained. Unscrupulously seducing the daughter of his host, Don Juan felt no qualms about the immorality of his *licentious* behavior.

lien N. legal claim on a property. There was a delay before Ralph could take possession of his late uncle's home; apparently, another claimant had a *lien* upon the estate.

ligneous ADJ. like wood. Petrified wood may be *ligneous* in appearance, but it is stonelike in composition.

lilliputian ADJ. extremely small. Tiny and delicate, the model was built on a *lilliputian* scale. also N.

limber ADJ. flexible. Hours of ballet classes kept him *limber.*

limbo N. region near heaven or hell where certain souls are kept; a prison (slang). Among the divisions of Hell are Purgatory and *Limbo.*

limn V. draw; outline; describe. Paradoxically, the more realistic the details this artist chooses, the better able she is to *limn* her fantastic, other-worldly landscapes.

limpid ADJ. clear. A *limpid* stream ran through his property.

lineage N. descent; ancestry. He traced his *lineage* back to *Mayflower* days.

lineaments N. features, especially of the face. She quickly sketched the *lineaments* of his face.

linger V. loiter or dawdle; continue or persist. Hoping to see Juliet pass by, Romeo *lingered* outside the Capulet house for hours. Though Mother made stuffed cabbage on Monday, the smell *lingered* around the house for days.

linguistic ADJ. pertaining to language. The modern tourist will encounter very little *linguistic* difficulty as English has become an almost universal language.

lionize V. treat as a celebrity. She enjoyed being *lionized* and adored by the public.

liquidate v. settle accounts; clear up. He was able to *liquidate* all his debts in a short period of time.

list v. tilt; lean over. That flagpole should be absolutely vertical; instead, it *lists* to one side. (secondary meaning) also N.

listless ADJ. lacking in spirit or energy. We had expected her to be full of enthusiasm and were surprised by her *listless* attitude.

litany N. supplicatory prayer. On this solemn day, the congregation responded to the prayers of the priest during the *litany* with fervor and intensity.

lithe ADJ. flexible; supple. Her figure was *lithe* and willowy.

litigation N. lawsuit. Try to settle this amicably; I do not want to start *litigation*. litigant, N.

litotes N. understatement for emphasis. To say, "He little realizes," when we mean that he does not realize at all, is an example of the kind of understatement we call *litotes*.

livid ADJ. lead-colored; black and blue; ashen; enraged. His face was so *livid* with rage that we were afraid that he might have an attack of apoplexy.

loath ADJ. reluctant; disinclined. Romeo and Juliet were both *loath* for him to go.

loathe v. detest. Booing and hissing, the audience showed how much they *loathed* the villain. loathsome, ADJ.

lode N. metal-bearing vein. If this *lode* that we have discovered extends for any distance, we have found a fortune.

lofty ADJ. very high. Though Barbara Jordan's fellow students used to tease her about her *lofty* ambitions, she rose to hold one of the highest positions in the land.

■ **log** N. record of a voyage or flight; record of day-to-day activities. "Flogged two seamen today for insubordination," wrote Captain Bligh in the *Bounty's log*. To see how much work I've accomplished recently, just take a look at the number of new files listed on my computer *log*. also v.

loiter v. hang around; linger. The policeman told him not to *loiter* in the alley.

loll v. lounge about. They *lolled* around in their chairs watching television.

longevity N. long life. When he reached ninety, the old man was proud of his *longevity*.

loom v. appear or take shape (usually in an enlarged or distorted form). The shadow of the gallows *loomed* threateningly above the small boy.

lope v. gallop slowly. As the horses *loped* along, we had an opportunity to admire the ever-changing scenery.

■ **loquacious** ADJ. talkative. Though our daughter barely says a word to us these days, put a phone in her hand and see how *loquacious* she can be: our phone bills are out of sight! loquacity, N.

Test

Word List 28   *Antonyms*

Each of the following questions consists of a word in capital letters, followed by five lettered words or phrases. Choose the lettered word or phrase that is most nearly opposite in meaning to the word in capital letters and write the letter of your choice on your answer paper.

406. LAMPOON (A) darken (B) praise (C) abandon (D) sail (E) fly

407. LANGUOR (A) vitality (B) length (C) embarrassment (D) wine (E) avarice

408. LATENT (A) trim (B) forbidding (C) execrable (D) early (E) obvious

409. LAVISH (A) hostile (B) unwashed (C) timely (D) decent (E) frugal

410. LAUDATORY (A) dirtying (B) disclaiming (C) defamatory (D) inflammatory (E) debased

411. LAX (A) salty (B) strict (C) shrill (D) boring (E) cowardly

412. LECHERY (A) trust (B) compulsion (C) zeal (D) addiction (E) purity

413. LETHARGIC (A) convalescent (B) beautiful (C) enervating (D) invigorating (E) interrogating

414. LEVITY (A) bridge (B) dam (C) praise (D) blame (E) solemnity

415. LILLIPUTIAN (A) destructive (B) proper (C) gigantic (D) elegant (E) barren

416. LIMPID (A) erect (B) turbid (C) tangential (D) timid (E) weary

417. LITHE (A) stiff (B) limpid (C) facetious (D) insipid (E) vast

418. LIVID (A) alive (B) mundane (C) positive (D) undiscolored (E) vast

419. LOATH (A) loose (B) evident (C) deliberate (D) eager (E) tiny

420. LOQUACIOUS (A) taciturn (B) sentimental (C) soporific (D) soothing (E) sedate

Word List 29   lout–maul

lout   N. clumsy person. The delivery boy is an awkward *lout*. loutish, ADJ.

low   V. moo. From the hilltop, they could see the herd like ants in the distance; they could barely hear the cattle *low*.

■ **lucid**   ADJ. easily understood; clear; intelligible. Lexy makes an excellent teacher: her explanations of technical points are *lucid* enough for a child to grasp. lucidity, N.

lucrative   ADJ. profitable. He turned his hobby into a *lucrative* profession.

lucre   N. money. Preferring *lucre* to undying fame, he wrote stories of popular appeal.

ludicrous   ADJ. laughable; trifling. Let us be serious; this is not a *ludicrous* issue.

lugubrious   ADJ. mournful. The *lugubrious* howling of the dogs added to our sadness.

lull   N. moment of calm. Not wanting to get wet, they waited under the awning for a *lull* in the rain.

lumber   V. move heavily or clumsily. Still somewhat torpid after its long hibernation, the bear *lumbered* through the woods.

lumen   N. unit of light energy (one candle's worth). In buying light bulbs, she checked not only their power, as measured in watts, but their brightness, as measured in *lumens*.

luminary   N. celebrity; dignitary. A leading light of the American stage, Ethel Barrymore was a theatrical *luminary* whose name lives on.

■ **luminous**   ADJ. shining; issuing light. The sun is a *luminous* body.

lunar   ADJ. pertaining to the moon. *Lunar* craters can be plainly seen with the aid of a small telescope.

lunge   V. make a quick forward dive or reach; thrust. The wide receiver *lunged* forward to grab the football. With his sword, Dartagnan *lunged* at his adversary. also N.

lurid   ADJ. wild; sensational; graphic; gruesome. Do the *lurid* cover stories in the *Enquirer* actually influence people to buy that trashy tabloid?

lurk   V. stealthily lie in waiting; slink; exist unperceived. "Who knows what evils *lurk* in the hearts of men? The Shadow knows."

luscious   ADJ. pleasing to taste or smell. The ripe peach was *luscious*.

luster   N. shine; gloss. The soft *luster* of the silk in the dim light was pleasing.

lustrous   ADJ. shining. Her large and *lustrous* eyes gave a touch of beauty to an otherwise drab face.

luxuriant   ADJ. abundant; rich and splendid; fertile. Lady Godiva was completely covered by her *luxuriant* hair.

macabre   ADJ. gruesome; grisly. The city morgue is a *macabre* spot for the uninitiated.

mace   N. ceremonial staff; clublike medieval weapon. The Grand Marshal of the parade raised his *mace* to signal that it was time for the procession to begin.

macerate   V. soften by soaking in liquid; waste away. The strawberries had been soaking in the champagne for so long that they had begun to *macerate*: they literally fell apart at the touch of a spoon.

Machiavellian   ADJ. crafty; double-dealing. I do not think he will be a good ambassador because he is not accustomed to the *Machiavellian* maneuverings of foreign diplomats.

machinations   N. evil schemes or plots. Fortunately, Batman saw through the wily *machinations* of the Riddler and saved Gotham City from destruction by the forces of evil.

maculated   ADJ. spotted; stained. Instead of writing that Gorbachev had a birthmark on his forehead, the pompous young poet sang of the former premier's *maculated* brow.

madrigal   N. pastoral song. Her program of folk songs included several *madrigals* that she sang to the accompaniment of a lute.

maelstrom   N. whirlpool. The canoe was tossed about in the *maelstrom*.

magisterial   ADJ. authoritative; imperious. The learned doctor laid down the law to his patient in a *magisterial* tone of voice.

■ **magnanimity**   N. generosity. Noted for his *magnanimity*, philanthropist Eugene Lang donated millions to charity. magnanimous, ADJ.

magnate   N. person of prominence or influence. Growing up in Pittsburgh, Annie Dillard was surrounded by the mansions of the great steel and coal *magnates* who set their mark on that city.

magniloquent   ADJ. boastful, pompous. In their stories of the trial, the reporters ridiculed the *magniloquent* speeches of the defense attorney.

magnitude   N. greatness; extent. It is difficult to comprehend the *magnitude* of his crime.

maim   V. mutilate; injure. The hospital could not take care of all who had been mangled or *maimed* in the railroad accident.

maladroit   ADJ. clumsy; bungling. "Oh! My stupid tongue!" exclaimed Jane, embarrassed at having said anything so *maladroit*.

malady   N. illness. A mysterious *malady* swept the country, filling doctors' offices with feverish, purple-spotted patients.

malaise   N. uneasiness; vague feeling of ill health. Feeling slightly queasy before going onstage, Carol realized that this touch of *malaise* was merely stage fright.

malapropism   N. comic misuse of a word. When Mrs. Malaprop criticizes Lydia for being "as headstrong as an allegory on the banks of the Nile," she confuses "allegory" and "alligator" in a typical *malapropism*.

malcontent   N. person dissatisfied with existing state of affairs. He was one of the few *malcontents* in Congress;

he constantly voiced his objections to the presidential program. also ADJ.

malediction   N. curse. When the magic mirror revealed that Snow White was still alive, the wicked queen cried out in rage and uttered dreadful *maledictions.*

malefactor   N. evildoer; criminal. Mighty Mouse will save the day, hunting down *malefactors* and rescuing innocent mice from peril.

malevolent   ADJ. wishing evil. Iago is a *malevolent* villain who takes pleasure in ruining Othello. malevolence, N.

malfeasance   N. wrongdoing. The authorities did not discover the campaign manager's *malfeasance* until after he had spent most of the money he had embezzled.

malicious   ADJ. hateful; spiteful. Jealous of Cinderella's beauty, her *malicious* stepsisters expressed their spite by forcing her to do menial tasks. malice, N.

malign   V. speak evil of; bad-mouth; defame. Putting her hands over her ears, Rose refused to listen to Betty *malign* her friend Susan.

malignant   ADJ. injurious; tending to cause death; aggressively malevolent. Though many tumors are benign, some are *malignant,* growing out of control and endangering the life of the patient. malignancy, N.

■ **malingerer**   N. one who feigns illness to escape duty. The captain ordered the sergeant to punish all *malingerers* and force them to work. malinger, V.

■ **malleable**   ADJ. capable of being shaped by pounding; impressionable. Gold is a *malleable* metal, easily shaped into bracelets and rings. Fagin hoped Oliver was a *malleable* lad, easily shaped into a thief.

malodorous   ADJ. foul-smelling. The compost heap was most *malodorous* in summer.

mammal   N. vertebrate animal whose female suckles its young. Many people regard the whale as a fish and do not realize that it is a *mammal.*

mammoth   ADJ. gigantic; enormous. To try to memorize every word on this vocabulary list would be a *mammoth* undertaking; take on projects that are more manageable in size.

manacle   V. restrain; handcuff. The police immediately *manacled* the prisoner so he could not escape. also N.

mandate   N. order; charge. In his inaugural address, the president stated that he had a *mandate* from the people to seek an end to social evils such as poverty and poor housing. also V.

mandatory   ADJ. obligatory. These instructions are *mandatory;* any violation will be severely punished.

mangy   ADJ. shabby; wretched. We finally threw out the *mangy* rug that the dog had destroyed.

maniacal   ADJ. raging mad; insane. Though Mr. Rochester had locked his mad wife in the attic, he could still hear her *maniacal* laughter echoing throughout the house. maniac, N.

manifest   ADJ. evident; visible; obvious. Digby's embarrassment when he met Madonna was *manifest:* his ears turned bright pink, he kept scuffing one shoe in the dirt, and he couldn't look her in the eye.

manifestation   N. outward demonstration; indication. Mozart's early attraction to the harpsichord was the first *manifestation* of his pronounced musical bent.

manifesto   N. declaration; statement of policy. The *Communist Manifesto* by Marx and Engels proclaimed the principles of modern communism.

manifold   ADJ. numerous; varied. I cannot begin to tell you how much I appreciate your *manifold* kindnesses.

manipulate   V. operate with one's hands; control or play upon (people, forces, etc.) artfully. Jim Henson understood how to *manipulate* the Muppets. Madonna understands how to *manipulate* publicity (and men).

mannered   ADJ. affected; not natural. Attempting to copy the style of his wealthy neighbors, Gatsby adopted a *mannered,* artificial way of speech.

manumit   V. emancipate; free from bondage. Enlightened slave owners were willing to *manumit* their slaves and thus put an end to the evil of slavery in the country.

marital   ADJ. pertaining to marriage. After the publication of his book on *marital* affairs, he was often consulted by married people on the verge of divorce.

maritime   ADJ. bordering on the sea; nautical. The *Maritime* Provinces depend on the sea for their wealth.

marked   ADJ. noticeable; targeted for vengeance. He walked with a *marked* limp, a souvenir of an old IRA attack. As British ambassador, he knew he was a *marked* man.

marred   ADJ. damaged; disfigured. She had to refinish the *marred* surface of the table. mar, V.

marshal   V. put in order. At a debate tournament, extemporaneous speakers have only a minute or two to *marshal* their thoughts before addressing their audience.

marsupial   N. one of a family of mammals that nurse their offspring in a pouch. The most common *marsupial* in North America is the opossum.

martial   ADJ. warlike. The sound of *martial* music inspired the young cadet with dreams of military glory.

martinet   N. No talking at meals! No mingling with the servants! Miss Minchin was a *martinet* who insisted that the schoolgirls in her charge observe each regulation to the letter.

martyr   N. one who voluntarily suffers death for his or her religion or cause; great sufferer. By burning her at the stake, the English made Joan of Arc a *martyr* for her faith. Mother played the *martyr* by staying home to clean the house while the rest of the family went off to the beach.

masochist   N. person who enjoys his own pain. The *masochist* begs, "Hit me." The sadist smiles and says, "I won't."

masticate   V. chew. We must *masticate* our food carefully and slowly in order to avoid digestive disorders.

materialism   N. preoccupation with physical comforts and things. By its nature, *materialism* is opposed to idealism, for where the *materialist* emphasizes the needs of the body, the idealist emphasizes the needs of the soul.

maternal   ADJ. motherly. Many animals display *maternal* instincts only while their offspring are young and helpless. maternity, N.

matriarch N. woman who rules a family or larger social group. The *matriarch* ruled her gypsy tribe with a firm hand.

matriculate V. enroll (in college or graduate school). Incoming students formally *matriculate* at our college in a special ceremony during which they sign the official register of students.

matrix N. point of origin; array of numbers or algebraic symbols; mold or die. Some historians claim the Nile Valley was the *matrix* of Western civilization.

maudlin ADJ. effusively sentimental. Whenever a particularly *maudlin* tearjerker was playing at the movies, Marvin would embarrass himself by weeping copiously.

maul V. handle roughly. The rock star was *mauled* by his overexcited fans.

Test

Word List 29   *Synonyms and Antonyms*

Each of the questions below consists of a word in capital letters, followed by five lettered words or phrases. Choose the lettered word or phrase that is most nearly similar to or opposite of the word in capital letters and write the letter of your choice on your answer paper.

421. LUGUBRIOUS (A) frantic (B) cheerful (C) burdensome (D) oily (E) militant

422. LURID (A) dull (B) duplicate (C) heavy (D) painstaking (E) intelligent

423. MACABRE (A) musical (B) frightening (C) chewed (D) wicked (E) exceptional

424. MAGNILOQUENT (A) loquacious (B) bombastic (C) rudimentary (D) qualitative (E) minimizing

425. MAGNITUDE (A) realization (B) fascination (C) enormity (D) gratitude (E) interference

426. MALADROIT (A) malicious (B) starving (C) thirsty (D) tactless (E) artistic

427. MALEDICTION (A) misfortune (B) hap (C) fruition (D) correct pronunciation (E) benediction

428. MALEFACTOR (A) quail (B) lawbreaker (C) beneficiary (D) banker (E) female agent

429. MALEVOLENT (A) kindly (B) vacuous (C) ambivalent (D) volatile (E) primitive

430. MALIGN (A) intersperse (B) vary (C) emphasize (D) frighten (E) eulogize

431. MALLEABLE (A) brittle (B) blatant (C) brilliant (D) brownish (E) basking

432. MANIACAL (A) demoniac (B) saturated (C) sane (D) sanitary (E) handcuffed

433. MANIFEST (A) limited (B) obscure (C) faulty (D) varied (E) vital

434. MANUMIT (A) print (B) impress (C) enslave (D) endeavor (E) fail

435. MARTIAL (A) bellicose (B) celibate (C) divorced (D) quiescent (E) planetary

Word List 30   mausoleum-misnomer

mausoleum N. monumental tomb. His body was placed in the family *mausoleum.*

mauve ADJ. pale purple. The *mauve* tint in the lilac bush was another indication that spring had finally arrived.

■ **maverick** N. rebel; nonconformist. To the masculine literary establishment, George Sand with her insistence on wearing trousers and smoking cigars was clearly a *maverick* who fought her proper womanly role.

mawkish ADJ. mushy and gushy; icky-sticky sentimental; maudlin. Whenever Gigi and her boyfriend would sigh and get all lovey-dovey, her little brother would shout, "Yuck!" protesting their *mawkish* behavior.

maxim N. proverb; a truth pithily stated. Aesop's fables illustrate moral *maxims.*

mayhem N. injury to body. The riot was marked not only by *mayhem,* with its attendant loss of life and limb, but also by arson and pillage.

meager ADJ. scanty; inadequate. Still hungry after his *meager* serving of porridge, Oliver Twist asked for a second helping.

mealymouthed ADJ. indirect in speech; hypocritical; evasive. Rather than tell Jill directly what he disliked, Jack made a few *mealymouthed* comments and tried to change the subject.

meander V. wind or turn in its course. Needing to stay close to a source of water, he followed every twist and turn of the stream as it *meandered* through the countryside.

meddlesome ADJ. interfering. He felt his marriage was suffering because of his *meddlesome* mother-in-law.

mediate V. settle a dispute through the services of an outsider. King Solomon was asked to *mediate* a dispute between two women, each of whom claimed to be the mother of the same child.

mediocre ADJ. ordinary; commonplace. We were disappointed because he gave a rather *mediocre* performance in this role.

meditation N. reflection; thought. She reached her decision only after much *meditation.*

medium N. element that is a creature's natural environment; nutrient setting in which microorganisms are cultivated. We watched the dolphins sporting in the sea and marveled at their grace in their proper *medium.* The bacteriologist carefully observed the microorganisms' rapid growth in the culture *medium.*

medium N. appropriate occupation or means of expression; channel of communication; compromise. Film was Anna's *medium:* she expressed herself through her cinematography. However, she never watched television, claiming she despised the *medium.* For Anna, it was all or nothing: she could never strike a happy *medium.*

medley N. mixture. To avoid boring dancers by playing any one tune for too long, bands may combine three or four tunes into a *medley.*

meek ADJ. submissive; patient and long-suffering. Mr. Barrett never expected his *meek* daughter would dare to defy him by eloping with her suitor.

megalomania N. mania for doing grandiose things. Developers who spend millions trying to build the world's tallest skyscraper suffer from *megalomania.*

melancholy ADJ. gloomy; morose; blue. To Eugene, stuck in his small town, a train whistle was a *melancholy* sound, for it made him think of all the places he would never get to see.

melee N. fight. The captain tried to ascertain the cause of the *melee* that had broken out among the crew members.

mellifluous ADJ. sweetly or smoothly flowing; melodious. Italian is a *mellifluous* language, especially suited to being sung.

memento N. token; reminder. Take this book as a *memento* of your visit.

memorialize V. commemorate. Let us *memorialize* his great contribution by dedicating this library in his honor.

menagerie N. collection of wild animals. Whenever the children run wild around the house, Mom shouts, "Calm down! I'm not running a *menagerie!*"

■ **mendacious** ADJ. lying; habitually dishonest. Distrusting Huck from the start, Miss Watson assumed he was *mendacious* and refused to believe a word he said. mendacity, N.

mendicant N. beggar. "O noble sir, give alms to the poor," cried Aladdin, playing the *mendicant.* mendicancy, N.

menial ADJ. suitable for servants; lowly; mean. Her wicked stepmother forced Cinderella to do *menial* tasks around the house while her ugly stepsisters lolled around painting their toenails. also N.

mentor N. counselor; teacher. During this very trying period, she could not have had a better *mentor,* for the teacher was sympathetic and understanding.

mercantile ADJ. concerning trade. I am more interested in the opportunities available in the *mercantile* field than I am in those in the legal profession.

mercenary ADJ. motivated solely by money or gain. "I'm not in this war because I get my kicks waving flags," said the *mercenary* soldier. "I'm in it for the dough." also N.

mercurial ADJ. capricious; changing; fickle. Quick as quicksilver to change, he was *mercurial* in nature and therefore unreliable.

meretricious ADJ. flashy; tawdry. Her jewels were inexpensive but not *meretricious.*

merger N. combination (of two business corporations). When the firm's president married the director of financial planning, the office joke was that it wasn't a marriage, it was a *merger.*

mesmerize V. hypnotize. The incessant drone seemed to *mesmerize* him and place him in a trance.

metallurgical ADJ. pertaining to the art of removing metals from ores. During the course of his *metallurgical* research, the scientist developed a steel alloy of tremendous strength.

■ **metamorphosis** N. change of form. The *metamorphosis* of caterpillar to butterfly is typical of many such changes in animal life. metamorphose, V.

metaphor N. implied comparison. "He soared like an eagle" is an example of a simile; "He is an eagle in flight," a *metaphor.*

metaphysical ADJ. pertaining to speculative philosophy. The modern poets have gone back to the fanciful poems of the *metaphysical* poets of the seventeenth century for many of their images. metaphysics, N.

mete V. measure; distribute. He tried to be impartial in his efforts to *mete* out justice.

meteoric ADJ. swift; momentarily brilliant. We all wondered at his *meteoric* rise to fame.

methodical ADJ. systematic. An accountant must be *methodical* and maintain order among his financial records.

■ **meticulous** ADJ. excessively careful; painstaking; scrupulous. Martha Stewart was a *meticulous* housekeeper, fussing about each and every detail that went into making up her perfect home.

metropolis N. large city. Every evening this terminal is filled with the thousands of commuters who are going from this *metropolis* to their homes in the suburbs.

mettle N. courage; spirit. When challenged by the other horses in the race, the thoroughbred proved its *mettle* by its determination to hold the lead. mettlesome, ADJ.

miasma N. swamp gas; heavy, vaporous atmosphere, often emanating from decaying matter; pervasive corrupting influence. The smog hung over Victorian London like a dark cloud; noisome, reeking of decay, it was a visible *miasma.*

microcosm N. small world; the world in miniature. The village community that Jane Austen depicts serves as a *microcosm* of English society in her time, for in this small world we see all the social classes meeting and mingling.

migrant ADJ. changing its habitat; wandering. These *migrant* birds return every spring. also N.

migratory ADJ. wandering. The return of the *migratory* birds to the northern sections of this country is a harbinger of spring.

milieu N. environment; means of expression. Surrounded by smooth preppies and arty bohemians, the country boy from Smalltown, USA, felt out of his *milieu*. Although he has produced excellent oil paintings and lithographs, his proper *milieu* is watercolor.

militant ADJ. combative; bellicose. Although at this time he was advocating a policy of neutrality, one could usually find him adopting a more *militant* attitude. also N.

militate V. work against. Your record of lateness and absence will *militate* against your chances of promotion.

millennium N. thousand-year period; period of happiness and prosperity. I do not expect the *millennium* to come during my lifetime.

mimicry N. imitation. Her gift for *mimicry* was so great that her friends said that she should be in the theater.

minatory ADJ. menacing; threatening. Jabbing a *minatory* forefinger at Dorothy, the Wicked Witch cried, "I'll get you, and your little dog, too!"

mincing ADJ. affectedly dainty. Yum-Yum walked across the stage with *mincing* steps.

minion N. a servile dependent. He was always accompanied by several of his *minions* because he enjoyed their subservience and flattery.

minuscule ADJ. extremely small. Why should I involve myself with a project with so *minuscule* a chance for success?

minute ADJ. extremely small. The twins resembled one another closely; only *minute* differences set them apart.

minutiae N. petty details. She would have liked to ignore the *minutiae* of daily living.

mirage N. unreal reflection; optical illusion. The lost prospector was fooled by a *mirage* in the desert.

mire V. entangle; stick in swampy ground. Their rear wheels became *mired* in mud. also N.

mirth N. merriment; laughter. Sober Malvolio found Sir Toby's *mirth* improper.

misadventure N. mischance; ill luck. The young explorer met death by *misadventure*.

■ **misanthrope** N. one who hates mankind. In *Gulliver's Travels*, Swift portrays human beings as vile, degraded beasts; for this reason, various critics consider him a *misanthrope*. misanthropic, ADJ.

misapprehension N. error; misunderstanding. To avoid *misapprehension*, I am going to ask all of you to repeat the instructions I have given.

miscellany N. mixture of writings on various subjects. This is an interesting *miscellany* of nineteenth-century prose and poetry.

mischance N. ill luck. By *mischance*, he lost his week's salary.

misconstrue V. interpret incorrectly; misjudge. She took the passage seriously rather than humorously because she *misconstrued* the author's ironic tone.

miscreant N. wretch; villain. His kindness to the *miscreant* amazed all of us who had expected to hear severe punishment pronounced.

misdemeanor N. minor crime. The culprit pleaded guilty to a *misdemeanor* rather than face trial for a felony.

miserly ADJ. stingy; mean. Transformed by his vision on Christmas Eve, mean old Scrooge ceased being *miserly* and became a generous, kind old man. miser, N.

misgivings N. doubts. Hamlet described his *misgivings* to Horatio but decided to fence with Laertes despite his foreboding of evil.

mishap N. accident. With a little care you could have avoided this *mishap*.

misnomer N. wrong name; incorrect designation. His tyrannical conduct proved to all that his nickname, King Eric the Just, was a *misnomer*.

Test

Word List 30   *Synonyms*

Each of the questions below consists of a word in capital letters, followed by five lettered words or phrases. Choose the lettered word or phrase that is most nearly similar in meaning to the word in capital letters and write the letter of your choice on your answer paper.

436. MAWKISH (A) sentimental (B) true (C) certain (D) devious (E) carefree

437. MEDIOCRE (A) average (B) bitter (C) medieval (D) industrial (E) agricultural

438. MELEE (A) heat (B) brawl (C) attempt (D) weapon (E) choice

439. MELLIFLUOUS (A) porous (B) honeycombed (C) strong (D) smooth (E) viscous

440. MENIAL (A) intellectual (B) clairvoyant (C) servile (D) arrogant (E) laudatory

441. MENTOR (A) guide (B) genius (C) talker (D) philosopher (E) stylist

442. MESMERIZE (A) remember (B) hypnotize (C) delay (D) bore (E) analyze

443. METICULOUS (A) steadfast (B) recent (C) quaint (D) painstaking (E) overt

444. MIASMA (A) dream (B) noxious fumes (C) scenario (D) quantity (E) total

445. MILITANT (A) combative (B) dramatic (C) religious (D) quaint (E) paternal

446. MINION (A) monster (B) quorum (C) majority (D) host (E) dependent

447. MIRAGE (A) dessert (B) illusion (C) water (D) mirror (E) statement

448. MISANTHROPE (A) benefactor (B) philanderer (C) man-hater (D) aesthete (E) epicure

449. MISCHANCE (A) gamble (B) ordinance (C) aperture (D) anecdote (E) adversity

450. MISDEMEANOR (A) felony (B) peccadillo (C) indignity (D) fiat (E) illiteracy

---

Word List 31   misogamy-nascent

misogamy N. hatred of marriage. He remained a bachelor not because of *misogamy* but because of ill fate: his fiancee died before the wedding.

misogynist N. hater of women. She accused him of being a *misogynist* because he had been a bachelor all his life.

missile N. object to be thrown or projected. After carefully folding his book report into a paper airplane, Beavis threw the *missile* across the classroom at Butthead. Rocket scientists are building guided *missiles;* Beavis and Butthead can barely make unguided ones.

missive N. letter. The ambassador received a *missive* from the Secretary of State.

mite N. very small object or creature; small coin. Gnats are annoying *mites* that sting.

■ **mitigate** V. lessen in intensity; moderate; appease. Because solar energy has the power to reduce greenhouse gases and provide increased energy efficiency, conversion to the use of solar energy may help *mitigate* global warming.

mnemonic ADJ. pertaining to memory. She used *mnemonic* tricks to master new words.

mobile ADJ. movable; not fixed. The *mobile* blood bank operated by the Red Cross visited our neighborhood today. mobility, N.

mock V. ridicule; imitate, often in derision. It is unkind to *mock* anyone; it is stupid to *mock* anyone significantly bigger than you. mockery, N.

mode N. prevailing style; manner; way of doing something. The rock star had to have her hair done in the latest *mode:* frizzed, with occasional moussed spikes for variety. Henry plans to adopt a simpler *mode* of life: he is going to become a mushroom hunter and live off the land.

modicum N. limited quantity. Although his story is based on a *modicum* of truth, most of the events he describes are fictitious.

modish ADJ. fashionable. She always discarded all garments that were no longer *modish*.

modulate V. tone down in intensity; regulate; change from one key to another. Always singing at the top of her lungs, the budding Brunhilde never learned to *modulate* her voice. modulation, N.

mogul N. powerful person. The oil *moguls* made great profits when the price of gasoline rose.

molecule N. the smallest particle (one or more atoms) of a substance that has all the properties of that substance.

In chemistry, we study how atoms and *molecules* react to form new substances.

■ **mollify** V. soothe. The airline customer service representative tried to *mollify* the angry passenger by offering her a seat in first class.

mollycoddle V. pamper; indulge excessively. Don't *mollycoddle* the boy, Maud! You'll spoil him.

molt V. shed or cast off hair or feathers. When Molly's canary *molted,* he shed feathers all over the house.

molten ADJ. melted. The city of Pompeii was destroyed by volcanic ash rather than by *molten* lava flowing from Mount Vesuvius.

momentous ADJ. very important. When Marie and Pierre Curie discovered radium, they had no idea of the *momentous* impact their discovery would have upon society.

momentum N. quantity of motion of a moving body; impetus. The car lost *momentum* as it tried to ascend the steep hill.

monarchy N. government under a single ruler. Though England today is a *monarchy,* there is some question whether it will be one in 20 years, given the present discontent at the prospect of Prince Charles as king.

monastic ADJ. related to monks or monasteries; removed from worldly concerns. Withdrawing from the world, Thomas Merton joined a contemplative religious order and adopted the *monastic* life.

monetary ADJ. pertaining to money. Jane held the family purse strings: she made all *monetary* decisions affecting the household.

monochromatic ADJ. having only one color. Most people who are color blind actually can distinguish several colors; some, however, have a truly *monochromatic* view of a world all in shades of gray.

monolithic ADJ. solidly uniform; unyielding. Knowing the importance of appearing resolute, the patriots sought to present a *monolithic* front.

monotheism N. belief in one God. Abraham was the first to proclaim his belief in *monotheism*.

monotony N. sameness leading to boredom. What could be more deadly dull than the *monotony* of punching numbers into a computer hour after hour? monotonous, ADJ.

monumental ADJ. massive. Writing a dictionary is a *monumental* task.

moodiness N. fits of depression or gloom. We could not discover the cause of her recurrent *moodiness*.

moratorium N. legal delay of payment. If we declare a *moratorium* and delay collection of debts for six months, I am sure the farmers will be able to meet their bills.

morbid ADJ. given to unwholesome thought; moody; characteristic of disease. People who come to disaster sites just to peer at the grisly wreckage are indulging their *morbid* curiosity. morbidity, N.

mordant ADJ. biting; sarcastic; stinging. Actors feared the critic's *mordant* pen.

mores N. conventions; moral standards; customs. In America, Benazir Bhutto dressed as Western women did; in Pakistan, however, she followed the *mores* of her people, dressing in traditional veil and robes.

moribund ADJ. dying. Hearst took a *moribund,* failing weekly newspaper and transformed it into one of the liveliest, most profitable daily papers around.

■ **morose** ADJ. ill-humored; sullen; melancholy. Forced to take early retirement, Bill acted *morose* for months; then, all of a sudden, he shook off his gloom and was his usual cheerful self.

mortician N. undertaker. The *mortician* prepared the corpse for burial.

mortify V. humiliate; punish the flesh. She was so *mortified* by her blunder that she ran to her room in tears.

mosaic N. picture made of small, colorful inlaid tiles. The mayor compared the city to a beautiful *mosaic* made up of people of every race and religion on earth. also ADJ.

mote N. small speck. The tiniest *mote* in the eye is very painful.

motif N. theme. This simple *motif* runs throughout the score.

motility N. ability to move spontaneously. Certain organisms exhibit remarkable *motility; motile* spores, for example, may travel for miles before coming to rest. motile, ADJ.

motley ADJ. multicolored; mixed. The jester wore a *motley* tunic, red and green and blue and gold all patched together haphazardly. Captain Ahab had gathered a *motley* crew to sail the vessel: old sea dogs and runaway boys, pillars of the church and drunkards, even a tattooed islander who terrified the rest of the crew.

mottled ADJ. blotched in coloring; spotted. When old Falstaff blushed, his face became *mottled,* all pink and purple and red.

mountebank N. charlatan; boastful pretender. The patent medicine man was a *mountebank.*

muddle V. confuse; mix up. Her thoughts were *muddled* and chaotic. also N.

muggy ADJ. warm and damp. August in New York City is often *muggy.*

mulct V. defraud a person of something. The lawyer was accused of trying to *mulct* the boy of his legacy.

multifarious ADJ. varied; greatly diversified. A career woman and mother, she was constantly busy with the *multifarious* activities of her daily life.

multiform ADJ. having many forms. Snowflakes are *multiform* but always hexagonal.

multilingual ADJ. having many languages. Because they are bordered by so many countries, the Swiss people are *multilingual.*

multiplicity N. state of being numerous. She was appalled by the *multiplicity* of details she had to complete before setting out on her mission.

■ **mundane** ADJ. worldly as opposed to spiritual; everyday. Uninterested in philosophical or spiritual discussions, Tom talked only of *mundane* matters such as the daily weather forecast or the latest basketball results.

munificent ADJ. very generous. Shamelessly fawning over a particularly generous donor, the dean kept referring to her as "our *munificent* benefactor." munificence, N.

mural N. wall painting. The walls of the Chicano Community Center are covered with *murals* painted in the style of Diego Rivera, the great Mexican artist.

murky ADJ. dark and gloomy; thick with fog; vague. The *murky* depths of the swamp were so dark that you couldn't tell the vines and branches from the snakes. murkiness, N.

muse V. ponder. For a moment he *mused* about the beauty of the scene, but his thoughts soon changed as he recalled his own personal problems. also N.

musky ADJ. having the odor of musk. She left a trace of *musky* perfume behind her.

muster V. gather; assemble. Washington *mustered* his forces at Trenton.

musty ADJ. stale; spoiled by age. The attic was dark and *musty.*

mutability N. ability to change in form; fickleness. Going from rags to riches, and then back to rags again, the bankrupt financier was a victim of the *mutability* of fortune. mutable, ADJ.

muted ADJ. silent; muffled; toned down. Thanks to the thick, sound-absorbing walls of the cathedral, only *muted* traffic noise reached the worshippers within. mute, V., N.

mutilate V. maim. The torturer threatened to *mutilate* his victim.

mutinous ADJ. unruly; rebellious. The captain had to use force to quiet his *mutinous* crew. mutiny, N.

myopic ADJ. nearsighted; lacking foresight. Stumbling into doors despite the coke-bottle lenses on his glasses, the nearsighted Mr. Magoo is markedly *myopic.* In playing all summer long and failing to store up food for winter, the grasshopper in Aesop's fable was *myopic* as well. myopia, N.

myriad N. very large number. *Myriads* of mosquitoes from the swamps invaded our village every twilight. also ADJ.

nadir N. lowest point. Although few people realized it, the Dow-Jones averages had reached their *nadir* and would soon begin an upward surge.

naiveté N. quality of being unsophisticated; simplicity; artlessness; gullibility. Touched by the *naiveté* of sweet, convent-trained Cosette, Marius pledges himself to protect her innocence. naive, ADJ.

narcissist N. conceited person. A *narcissist* is his own best friend.

narrative ADJ. related to telling a story. A born teller of tales, Olsen used her impressive *narrative* skills to advantage in her story "I Stand Here Ironing." also N. narration, N.

nascent ADJ. incipient; coming into being. If we could identify these revolutionary movements in their *nascent* state, we would be able to eliminate serious trouble in later years.

Test

Word List 31   *Synonyms*

Each of the questions below consists of a word in capital letters, followed by five lettered words or phrases. Choose the lettered word or phrase that is most nearly similar in meaning to the word in capital letters and write the letter of your choice on your answer paper.

451. MODISH (A) sentimental (B) stylish (C) vacillating (D) contrary (E) adorned

452. MOLLIFY (A) avenge (B) attenuate (C) attribute (D) mortify (E) appease

453. MONETARY (A) boring (B) fascinating (C) fiscal (D) stationary (E) scrupulous

454. MORATORIUM (A) burial (B) gathering (C) delay (D) refusal (E) suspicion

455. MORDANT (A) dying (B) trenchant (C) fabricating (D) controlling (E) avenging

456. MORIBUND (A) dying (B) appropriate (C) leather bound (D) answering (E) undertaking

457. MOTLEY (A) active (B) disguised (C) variegated (D) somber (E) sick

458. MUGGY (A) attacking (B) fascinating (C) humid (D) characteristic (E) gelid

459. MULCT (A) swindle (B) hold (C) record (D) print (E) fertilize

460. MULTILINGUAL (A) variegated (B) polyglot (C) multilateral (D) polyandrous (E) multiplied

461. MUNDANE (A) global (B) futile (C) spatial (D) heretic (E) worldly

462. MUNIFICENT (A) grandiose (B) puny (C) philanthropic (D) poor (E) gracious

463. MUSTY (A) flat (B) necessary (C) indifferent (D) nonchalant (E) vivid

464. MYOPIC (A) visionary (B) nearsighted (C) moral (D) glassy (E) blind

465. NASCENT (A) incipient (B) ignorant (C) loyal (D) treacherous (E) unnamed

Word List 32   natation-obsidian

natation N. swimming. The Red Cross emphasizes the need for courses in *natation*.

natty ADJ. neatly or smartly dressed. Priding himself on being a *natty* dresser, the gangster Bugsy Siegel collected a wardrobe of imported suits and ties.

nauseate V. cause to become sick; fill with disgust. The foul smells began to *nauseate* her.

nautical ADJ. pertaining to ships or navigation. The Maritime Museum contains models of clipper ships, logbooks, anchors, and many other items of a *nautical* nature.

navigable ADJ. wide and deep enough to allow ships to pass through; able to be steered. So much sand had built up at the bottom of the canal that the waterway was barely *navigable*.

nebulous ADJ. vague; hazy; cloudy. Phil and Dave tried to come up with a clear, intelligible business plan, not some hazy, *nebulous* proposal.

necromancy N. black magic; dealings with the dead. The evil sorcerer performed feats of *necromancy,* calling on the spirits of the dead to tell the future. necromancer, N.

nefarious ADJ. very wicked. The villain's crimes, though various, were one and all *nefarious*.

■ **negate** V. cancel out; nullify; deny. A sudden surge of adrenalin can *negate* the effects of fatigue: there's nothing like a good shock to wake you up. negation, N.

negligence N. neglect; failure to take reasonable care. Tommy failed to put back the cover on the well after he fetched his pail of water; because of his *negligence,* Kitty fell in. negligent, ADJ.

negligible ADJ. so small, trifling, or unimportant as to be easily disregarded. Because the damage to his car had been *negligible,* Michael decided he wouldn't bother to report the matter to his insurance company.

nemesis N. someone seeking revenge. Abandoned at sea in a small boat, the vengeful Captain Bligh vowed to be the *nemesis* of Fletcher Christian and his fellow mutineers.

neologism N. new or newly coined word or phrase. As we invent new techniques and professions, we must also invent *neologisms* such as "microcomputer" and "astronaut" to describe them.

■ **neophyte** N. recent convert; beginner. This mountain slope contains slides that will challenge experts as well as *neophytes.*

nepotism N. favoritism (to a relative). John left his position with the company because he felt that advancement was based on *nepotism* rather than ability.

nether ADJ. lower. Tradition locates hell in the *nether* regions.

nettle V. annoy; vex. Do not let her *nettle* you with her sarcastic remarks.

nexus N. connection. I fail to see the *nexus* that binds these two widely separated events.

nib N. beak; pen point. The *nibs* of fountain pens often become clotted and corroded.

nicety N. precision; minute distinction. I cannot distinguish between such *niceties* of reasoning. nice, ADJ. (secondary meaning)

niggardly ADJ. meanly stingy; parsimonious. The *niggardly* pittance the widow receives from the government cannot keep her from poverty.

niggle V. spend too much time on minor points; carp. Let's not *niggle* over details. niggling, ADJ.

nihilist N. one who considers traditional beliefs to be groundless and existence meaningless; absolute skeptic; revolutionary terrorist. In his final days, Hitler revealed himself a power-mad *nihilist,* ready to annihilate all of Western Europe, even to destroy Germany itself, in order that his will might prevail. The root of the word *nihilist* is *nihil,* Latin for "nothing." nihilism, N.

nip V. stop something's growth or development; snip off; bite; make numb with cold. The twins were plotting mischief, but Mother intervened and *nipped* their plan in the bud. The gardener *nipped* off a lovely rose and gave it to me. Last week a guard dog *nipped* the postman in the leg; this week the extreme chill *nipped* his fingers till he could barely hold the mail.

nirvana N. in Buddhist teachings, the ideal state in which the individual loses himself in the attainment of an impersonal beatitude. Despite his desire to achieve *nirvana,* the young Buddhist found that even the buzzing of a fly could distract him from his meditation.

nocturnal ADJ. done at night. Mr. Jones obtained a watchdog to prevent the *nocturnal* raids on his chicken coops.

noisome ADJ. foul-smelling; unwholesome. The *noisome* atmosphere downwind of the oil refinery not only stank but also damaged the lungs of everyone living in the area.

nomadic ADJ. wandering. Several *nomadic* tribes of Indians would hunt in this area each year. nomad, N.

nomenclature N. terminology; system of names. Sharon found Latin word parts useful in translating medical *nomenclature:* when her son had to have a bilateral myringotomy, she figured out that he needed a hole in each of his eardrums to end his earaches.

nominal ADJ. in name only; trifling. He offered to drive her to the airport for only a *nominal* fee.

nonchalance N. indifference; lack of concern; composure. Cool, calm, and collected under fire, James Bond shows remarkable *nonchalance* in the face of danger. nonchalant, ADJ.

noncommittal ADJ. neutral; unpledged; undecided. We were annoyed by his *noncommittal* reply for we had been led to expect definite assurances of his approval.

nondescript ADJ. undistinctive; ordinary. The private detective was a short, *nondescript* fellow with no outstanding features, the sort of person one would never notice in a crowd.

nonentity N. person of no importance; nonexistence. Because the two older princes dismissed their youngest brother as a *nonentity,* they did not realize that he was quietly plotting to seize the throne.

nonplus V. bring to a halt by confusion; perplex. Jack's uncharacteristic rudeness *nonplussed* Jill, leaving her uncertain how to react.

nostalgia N. homesickness; longing for the past. My grandfather seldom spoke of life in the old country; he had little patience with *nostalgia.* nostalgic, ADJ.

nostrum N. questionable medicine. No quack selling *nostrums* is going to cheat me.

notable ADJ. conspicuous; important; distinguished. Normally *notable* for his calm in the kitchen, today the head cook was shaking, for the *notable* chef Julia Child was coming to dinner. also N.

notoriety N. disrepute; ill fame. To the starlet, any publicity was good publicity: if she couldn't have a good reputation, she'd settle for *notoriety.* notorious, ADJ.

novelty N. something new; newness. The computer is no longer a *novelty* around the office. novel, ADJ.

novice N. beginner. Even a *novice* at working with computers can install *Barron's Computer Study Program for the GRE* by following the easy steps outlined in the user's manual.

noxious ADJ. harmful. We must trace the source of these *noxious* gases before they asphyxiate us.

nuance N. shade of difference in meaning or color; subtle distinction. Jody gazed at the Monet landscape for an hour, appreciating every subtle *nuance* of color in the painting.

nubile ADJ. marriageable. Mrs. Bennet, in *Pride and Prejudice* by Jane Austen, was worried about finding suitable husbands for her five *nubile* daughters.

nugatory ADJ. futile; worthless. This agreement is *nugatory* for no court will enforce it.

nullify V. to make invalid. Once the contract was *nullified,* it no longer had any legal force.

numismatist N. person who collects coins. The *numismatist* had a splendid collection of antique coins.

nuptial ADJ. related to marriage. Reluctant to be married in a traditional setting, they decided to hold their *nuptial* ceremony at the carousel in Golden Gate Park. nuptials, N. PL.

nurture V. nourish; educate; foster. The Head Start program attempts to *nurture* prekindergarten children so that they will do well when they enter public school. also N.

nutrient N. nourishing substance. As a budding nutritionist, Kim has learned to design diets that contain foods rich in important basic *nutrients*. also ADJ.

oaf N. stupid, awkward person. "Watch what you're doing, you clumsy *oaf!*" Bill shouted at the waiter who had drenched him with iced coffee.

■ **obdurate** ADJ. stubborn. He was *obdurate* in his refusal to listen to our complaints.

obeisance N. bow. She made an *obeisance* as the king and queen entered the room.

obelisk N. tall column tapering and ending in a pyramid. Cleopatra's Needle is an *obelisk* in New York City's Central Park.

obese ADJ. excessively fat. It is advisable that *obese* people try to lose weight. obesity, N.

obfuscate V. confuse; muddle; cause confusion; make needlessly complex. Was the president's spokesman trying to clarify the Whitewater mystery, or was he trying to *obfuscate* the issue so the voters would never figure out what went on?

obituary N. death notice. I first learned of her death when I read the *obituary* in the newspaper. also ADJ.

objective ADJ. not influenced by emotions; fair. Even though he was her son, she tried to be *objective* about his behavior.

objective N. goal; aim. A degree in medicine was her ultimate *objective*.

obligatory ADJ. binding; required. It is *obligatory* that books borrowed from the library be returned within two weeks.

oblique ADJ. indirect; slanting (deviating from the perpendicular or from a straight line). Casting a quick, *oblique* glance at the reviewing stand, the sergeant ordered the company to march "*Oblique* Right."

obliterate V. destroy completely. The tidal wave *obliterated* several island villages.

oblivion N. obscurity; forgetfulness. After a decade of popularity, Hurston's works had fallen into *oblivion;* no one bothered to read them any more.

oblivious ADJ. inattentive or unmindful; wholly absorbed. Deep in her book, Nancy was *oblivious* to the noisy squabbles of her brother and his friends.

obloquy N. slander; disgrace; infamy. I resent the *obloquy* that you are casting upon my reputation.

obnoxious ADJ. offensive. I find your behavior *obnoxious;* please mend your ways.

obscure ADJ. dark; vague; unclear. Even after I read the poem a fourth time, its meaning was still *obscure*. obscurity, N.

obscure V. darken; make unclear. At times he seemed purposely to *obscure* his meaning, preferring mystery to clarity.

■ **obsequious** ADJ. slavishly attentive; servile; sycophantic. Helen valued people who behaved as if they respected themselves; nothing irritated her more than an excessively *obsequious* waiter or a fawning salesclerk.

obsequy N. funeral ceremony. Hundreds paid their last respects at his *obsequies*.

obsessive ADJ. related to thinking about something constantly; preoccupying. Ballet, which had been a hobby, began to dominate his life: his love of dancing became *obsessive*. obsession, N.

obsidian N. black volcanic rock. The deposits of *obsidian* on the mountain slopes were an indication that the volcano had erupted in ancient times.

Test

Word List 32   *Antonyms*

Each of the questions below consists of a word in capital letters, followed by five lettered words or phrases. Choose the lettered word or phrase that is most nearly opposite in meaning to the word in capital letters and write the letter of your choice on your answer paper.

466. NEBULOUS (A) starry (B) clear (C) cold (D) fundamental (E) porous

467. NEFARIOUS (A) various (B) lacking (C) benign (D) pompous (E) futile

468. NEGATION (A) postulation (B) hypothecation (C) affirmation (D) violation (E) anticipation

469. NEOPHYTE (A) veteran (B) satellite (C) desperado (D) handwriting (E) violence

470. NIGGARDLY (A) protected (B) biased (C) prodigal (D) bankrupt (E) placated

471. NOCTURNAL (A) harsh (B) marauding (C) patrolling (D) daily (E) fallow

472. NOISOME (A) quiet (B) dismayed (C) fragrant (D) sleepy (E) inquisitive

473. NOTORIOUS (A) fashionable (B) renowned (C) inactive (D) intrepid (E) invincible

474. OBDURATE (A) yielding (B) fleeting (C) finite (D) fascinating (E) permanent

475. OBESE (A) skillful (B) cadaverous (C) clever (D) unpredictable (E) lucid

476. OBJECTIVE (A) indecisive (B) apathetic (C) markedly inferior (D) emotionally involved (E) authoritative

477. OBLIGATORY (A) demanding (B) optional (C) facile (D) friendly (E) divorced

478. OBLOQUY (A) praise (B) rectangle (C) circle (D) dialogue (E) cure

479. OBSEQUIOUS (A) successful (B) democratic (C) supercilious (D) ambitious (E) lamentable

480. OBSESSION (A) whim (B) loss (C) phobia (D) delusion (E) feud

---

Word List 33   obsolete–overweening

obsolete ADJ. outmoded. "Hip" is an *obsolete* expression; it went out with love beads and tie-dye shirts.

obstetrician N. physician specializing in delivery of babies. Unlike midwives, who care for women giving birth at home, *obstetricians* generally work in a hospital setting.

obstinate ADJ. stubborn; hard to control or treat. We tried to persuade him to give up smoking, but he was *obstinate* and refused to change. Blackberry stickers are the most *obstinate* weeds I know: once established in a yard, they're extremely hard to root out. obstinacy, N.

obstreperous ADJ. boisterous; noisy. What do you do when an *obstreperous* horde of drunken policemen carouses through your hotel, crashing into potted plants and singing vulgar songs?

obtrude V. push (oneself or one's ideas) forward or intrude; butt in; stick out or extrude. Because Fanny was reluctant to *obtrude* her opinions about child-raising upon her daughter-in-law, she kept a close watch on her tongue. obtrusive, ADJ. obtrusion, N.

obtuse ADJ. blunt; stupid. What can you do with somebody who's so *obtuse* that he can't even tell that you're insulting him?

■ **obviate** V. make unnecessary; get rid of. I hope this contribution will *obviate* any need for further collections of funds.

Occident N. the West. It will take time for the *Occident* to understand the ways and customs of the Orient.

■ **occlude** V. shut; close. A blood clot *occluded* an artery to the heart. occlusion, N.

occult ADJ. mysterious; secret; supernatural. The *occult* rites of the organization were revealed only to members. also N.

oculist N. physician who specializes in treatment of the eyes. In many states, an *oculist* is the only one who may apply medicinal drops to the eyes for the purpose of examining them.

odious ADJ. hateful; vile. Cinderella's ugly stepsisters had the *odious* habit of popping their zits in public.

odium N. detestation; hatefulness; disrepute. Prince Charming could not express the *odium* he felt toward Cinderella's stepsisters because of their mistreatment of poor Cinderella.

odoriferous ADJ. giving off an odor. The *odoriferous* spices stimulated her jaded appetite.

odorous ADJ. having an odor. This variety of hybrid tea rose is more *odorous* than the one you have in your garden.

odyssey N. long, eventful journey. The refugee's journey from Cambodia was a terrifying *odyssey*.

offensive ADJ. attacking; insulting; distasteful. Getting into street brawls is no minor offense for professional boxers, who are required by law to restrict their *offensive* impulses to the ring.

offhand ADJ. casual; done without prior thought. Expecting to be treated with due propriety by her hosts, Great-Aunt Maud was offended by their *offhand* manner.

■ **officious** ADJ. meddlesome; excessively pushy in offering one's services. After her long flight, Jill just wanted to nap, but the *officious* bellboy was intent on showing her all the special features of the deluxe suite.

ogle V. look at amorously; make eyes at. At the coffee house, Walter was too shy to *ogle* the pretty girls openly; instead, he peeked out at them from behind a rubber plant.

olfactory ADJ. concerning the sense of smell. A wine taster must have a discriminating palate and a keen *olfactory* sense, for a good wine appeals both to the taste buds and to the nose.

oligarchy N. government by a privileged few. One small clique ran the student council: what had been intended as a democratic governing body had turned into an *oligarchy*.

ominous ADJ. threatening. Those clouds are *ominous;* they suggest that a severe storm is on the way.

omnipotent ADJ. all-powerful. The monarch regarded himself as *omnipotent* and responsible to no one for his acts.

omnipresent ADJ. universally present; ubiquitous. On Christmas Eve, Santa Claus is *omnipresent*.

omniscient ADJ. all-knowing. I do not pretend to be *omniscient,* but I am positive about this fact.

omnivorous ADJ. eating both plant and animal food; devouring everything. Some animals, including humans, are *omnivorous* and eat both meat and vegetables; others are either carnivorous or herbivorous.

■ **onerous** ADJ. burdensome. She asked for an assistant because her work load was too *onerous*.

onomatopoeia N. words formed in imitation of natural sounds. Words like "rustle" and "gargle" are illustrations of *onomatopoeia*.

onslaught N. vicious assault. We suffered many casualties during the unexpected *onslaught* of the enemy troops.

onus N. burden; responsibility. The emperor was spared the *onus* of signing the surrender papers; instead, he relegated the assignment to his generals.

opalescent ADJ. iridescent; lustrous. The oil slick on the water had an *opalescent,* rainbowlike sheen. opalescence, N.

opaque ADJ. dark; not transparent. The *opaque* window shade kept the sunlight out of the room. opacity, N.

opiate N. medicine to induce sleep or deaden pain; something that relieves emotions or causes inaction. To say that religion is the *opiate* of the people is to condemn religion as a drug that keeps the people quiet and submissive to those in power.

opportune ADJ. timely; well-chosen. Cher looked at her father struggling to balance his checkbook; clearly this would not be an *opportune* moment to ask him for an increase in her allowance.

opportunist N. individual who sacrifices principles for expediency by taking advantage of circumstances. Forget about ethics! He's such an *opportunist* that he'll vote in favor of any deal that will give him a break.

■ **opprobrium** N. infamy; vilification. He refused to defend himself against the slander and *opprobrium* hurled against him by the newspapers; he preferred to rely on his record.

optician N. maker and seller of eyeglasses. The patient took the prescription given him by his oculist to the *optician.*

optimist N. person who looks on the bright side. The pessimist says the glass is half-empty; the *optimist* says it is half-full.

optimum ADJ. most favorable. If you wait for the *optimum* moment to act, you may never begin your project. also N.

optional ADJ. not compulsory; left to one's choice. I was impressed by the range of *optional* accessories for my microcomputer that were available. option, N.

optometrist N. one who fits glasses to remedy visual defects. Although an *optometrist* is qualified to treat many eye disorders, she may not use medicines or surgery in her examinations.

opulence N. extreme wealth; luxuriousness; abundance. The glitter and *opulence* of the ballroom took Cinderella's breath away. opulent, ADJ.

opus N. work. Although many critics hailed his Fifth Symphony, he did not regard it as his major *opus.*

oracular ADJ. prophetic; uttered as if with divine authority; mysterious or ambiguous. Like many others who sought divine guidance from the *oracle* at Delphi, Oedipus could not understand the enigmatic *oracular* warning he received. oracle, N.

orator N. public speaker. The abolitionist Frederick Douglass was a brilliant *orator* whose speeches brought home to his audience the evils of slavery.

oratorio N. dramatic poem set to music. The Glee Club decided to present an *oratorio* during their recital.

ordain V. decree or command; grant holy orders; predestine. The king *ordained* that no foreigner should be allowed to enter the city. The Bishop of Michigan *ordained* David a deacon in the Episcopal Church. The young lovers felt that fate had *ordained* their meeting.

ordeal N. severe trial or affliction. June was so painfully shy that it was an *ordeal* for her to speak up when the teacher called on her in class.

ordinance N. decree. Passing a red light is a violation of a city *ordinance.*

ordination N. ceremony conferring holy orders. The candidate for *ordination* had to meet with the bishop and the diocesan officers before being judged ready to be *ordained* a deacon. ordain, V.

orgy N. wild, drunken revelry; unrestrained indulgence. The Roman emperor's *orgies* were far wilder than the toga party in the movie *Animal House.* When her income tax refund check finally arrived, Sally indulged in an *orgy* of shopping.

orient V. get one's bearings; adjust. Philip spent his first day in Denver *orienting* himself to the city.

orientation N. act of finding oneself in society. Freshman *orientation* provides the incoming students with an opportunity to learn about their new environment and their place in it.

orifice N. mouthlike opening; small opening. The Howe Caverns were discovered when someone observed that a cold wind was issuing from an *orifice* in the hillside.

ornate ADJ. excessively or elaborately decorated. With its elaborately carved, convoluted lines, furniture of the Baroque period was highly *ornate.*

ornithologist N. scientific student of birds. Audubon's drawings of American bird life have been of interest not only to *ornithologists* but also to the general public.

orthodox ADJ. traditional; conservative in belief. Faced with a problem, she preferred to take an *orthodox* approach rather than shock anyone. orthodoxy, N.

orthography N. correct spelling. Many of us find English *orthography* difficult to master because so many of our words are not written phonetically.

■ **oscillate** V. vibrate pendulumlike; waver. It is interesting to note how public opinion *oscillates* between the extremes of optimism and pessimism.

osseous ADJ. made of bone; bony. The hollow "soft spot" found at the top of the infant's skull gradually closes as new *osseous* tissue fills in the gap.

ossify V. change or harden into bone. When he called his opponent a "bonehead," he implied that his adversary's brain had *ossified* and that he was not capable of clear thinking.

ostensible ADJ. apparent; professed; pretended. Although the *ostensible* purpose of this expedition is to discover new lands, we are really interested in finding new markets for our products.

■ **ostentatious** ADJ. showy; pretentious; trying to attract attention. Trump's latest casino in Atlantic City is the most *ostentatious* gambling palace in the East: it easily out-glitters its competitors. ostentation, N.

ostracize V. exclude from public favor; ban. As soon as the newspapers carried the story of his connection with the criminals, his friends began to *ostracize* him. ostracism, N.

oust   v. expel; drive out. The world wondered if Aquino would be able to *oust* Marcos from office.

outlandish   ADJ. bizarre; peculiar; unconventional. The eccentric professor who engages in markedly *outlandish* behavior is a stock figure in novels with an academic setting.

outmoded   ADJ. no longer stylish; old-fashioned. Unconcerned about keeping in style, Lenore was perfectly happy to wear *outmoded* clothes as long as they were clean and unfrayed.

outskirts   N. fringes; outer borders. Living on the *outskirts* of Boston, Sarah sometimes felt as if she were cut off from the cultural heart of the city.

outspoken   ADJ. candid; blunt. The candidate was too *outspoken* to be a successful politician; he had not yet learned to weigh his words carefully.

outstrip   v. surpass; outdo. Jesse Owens easily *outstripped* his competitors to win the gold medal at the Olympic Games.

outwit   v. outsmart; trick. By disguising himself as an old woman, Holmes was able to *outwit* his pursuers and escape capture.

ovation   N. enthusiastic applause. When Placido Domingo came on stage in the first act of *La Bohème,* he was greeted by a tremendous *ovation.*

overbearing   ADJ. bossy; arrogant; decisively important. Certain of her own importance and of the unimportance of everyone else, Lady Bracknell was intolerably *overbearing* in manner. "In choosing a husband," she said, "good birth is of *overbearing* importance; compared to that, neither wealth nor talent signifies."

overt   ADJ. open to view. According to the United States Constitution, a person must commit an *overt* act before he may be tried for treason.

overweening   ADJ. presumptuous; arrogant. His *overweening* pride in his accomplishments was not justified.

Test

Word List 33   *Antonyms*

Each of the questions below consists of a word in capital letters, followed by five lettered words or phrases. Choose the lettered word or phrase that is most nearly opposite in meaning to the word in capital letters and write the letter of your choice on your answer paper.

481. OBSOLETE (A) heated (B) desolate (C) renovated (D) frightful (E) automatic

482. OBSTREPEROUS (A) turbid (B) quiet (C) remote (D) lucid (E) active

483. OBTUSE (A) sheer (B) transparent (C) tranquil (D) timid (E) shrewd

484. ODIOUS (A) fragrant (B) redolent (C) fetid (D) delightful (E) puny

485. ODIUM (A) noise (B) liking (C) dominant (D) hasty (E) atrium

486. OMNIPOTENT (A) weak (B) democratic (C) despotic (D) passionate (E) late

487. OMNISCIENT (A) sophisticated (B) ignorant (C) essential (D) trivial (E) isolated

488. OPIATE (A) distress (B) sleep (C) stimulant (D) laziness (E) despair

489. OPPORTUNE (A) occasional (B) fragrant (C) fragile (D) awkward (E) neglected

490. OPPORTUNIST (A) man of destiny (B) man of principle (C) changeling (D) adversary (E) colleague

491. OPPROBRIUM (A) delineation (B) aptitude (C) majesty (D) freedom (E) praise

492. OPTIMUM (A) pessimistic (B) knowledgeable (C) worst (D) minimum (E) chosen

493. OPULENCE (A) pessimism (B) patriotism (C) potency (D) passion (E) poverty

494. OSTENTATIOUS (A) inactive (B) unassuming (C) impolite (D) illicit (E) irrational

495. OVERWEENING (A) humble (B) impotent (C) avid (D) acrimonious (E) exaggerated

Word List 34   overwrought-peccadillo

overwrought   ADJ. extremely agitated; hysterical. When Kate heard the news of the sudden tragedy, she became too *overwrought* to work and had to leave the office early.

ovoid   ADJ. egg-shaped. At Easter she had to cut out hundreds of brightly colored *ovoid* shapes.

pachyderm   N. thick-skinned animal. The elephant is probably the best-known *pachyderm.*

pacifist   N. one opposed to force; antimilitarist. During the war, *pacifists*, though they refused to bear arms, served in the front lines as ambulance drivers and medical corpsmen. also ADJ. pacifism, N.

pacify   V. soothe; make calm or quiet; subdue. Dentists criticize the practice of giving fussy children sweets to *pacify* them.

paean   N. song of praise or joy. *Paeans* celebrating the victory filled the air.

painstaking   ADJ. showing hard work; taking great care. The new high-frequency word list is the result of *painstaking* efforts on the part of our research staff.

palatable   ADJ. agreeable; pleasing to the taste. Neither Jack's underbaked opinions nor his overcooked casseroles were *palatable* to me.

palate   N. roof of the mouth; sense of taste. When you sound out the letter "d," your tongue curves up to touch the edge of your *palate*. When Alice was sick, her mother made special meals to tempt her *palate*.

palatial   ADJ. magnificent. He proudly showed us through his *palatial* home.

paleontology   N. study of prehistoric life. The professor of *paleontology* had a superb collection of fossils.

palette   N. board on which a painter mixes pigments. At the present time, art supply stores are selling a paper *palette* that may be discarded after use.

palimpsest   N. parchment used for second time after original writing has been erased. Using chemical reagents, scientists have been able to restore the original writings on many *palimpsests.*

pall   V. grow tiresome. The study of word lists can eventually *pall* and put one to sleep.

pallet   N. small, poor bed. The weary traveler went to sleep on his straw *pallet.*

palliate   V. ease pain; make less severe or offensive. If we cannot cure this disease at present, we can, at least, try to *palliate* the symptoms. palliation, N.

pallid   ADJ. pale; wan. Because his occupation required that he work at night and sleep during the day, he had an exceptionally *pallid* complexion.

palpable   ADJ. tangible; easily perceptible. I cannot understand how you could overlook such a *palpable* blunder.

palpitate   V. throb; flutter. As she became excited, her heart began to *palpitate* more and more erratically.

paltry   ADJ. insignificant; petty; trifling. "One hundred dollars for a genuine imitation Rolex watch! Lady, this is a *paltry* sum to pay for such a high-class piece of jewelry."

pan   V. criticize harshly. Hoping for a rave review of his new show, the playwright was miserable when the critics *panned* it unanimously.

panacea   N. cure-all; remedy for all diseases. There is no easy *panacea* that will solve our complicated international situation.

panache   N. flair; flamboyance. Many performers imitate Noel Coward, but few have his *panache* and sense of style.

pandemic   ADJ. widespread; affecting the majority of people. They feared the AIDS epidemic would soon reach *pandemic* proportions.

pandemonium   N. wild tumult. When the ships collided in the harbor, *pandemonium* broke out among the passengers.

pander   V. cater to the low desires of others. The reviewer accused the makers of *Lethal Weapon* of *pandering* to the masses' taste for violence.

panegyric   N. formal praise. Blushing at all the praise heaped upon him by the speakers, the modest hero said, "I don't deserve such *panegyrics.*"

panoramic   ADJ. denoting an unobstructed and comprehensive view. On a clear day, from the top of the Empire State Building you can get a *panoramic* view of New York City and neighboring stretches of New Jersey and Long Island. panorama, N.

pantomime   N. acting without dialogue. Because he worked in *pantomime,* the clown could be understood wherever he appeared. also V.

papyrus   N. ancient paper made from stem of papyrus plant. The ancient Egyptians were among the first to write on *papyrus.*

parable   N. short, simple story teaching a moral. Let us apply to our own conduct the lesson that this *parable* teaches.

paradigm   N. model; example; pattern. Pavlov's experiment in which he trains a dog to salivate on hearing a bell is a *paradigm* of the conditioned-response experiment in behavioral psychology. paradigmatic, ADJ.

paradox   N. something apparently contradictory in nature; statement that looks false but is actually correct. Richard presents a bit of a *paradox*, for he is a card-carrying member of both the National Rifle Association and the relatively pacifist American Civil Liberties Union. paradoxical, ADJ.

■ **paragon**   N. model of perfection. Her fellow students disliked Lavinia because Miss Minchin always pointed her out as a *paragon* of virtue.

parallelism N. state of being parallel; similarity. Although the twins were separated at birth and grew up in different adoptive families, a striking *parallelism* exists between their lives.

parameter N. limit; independent variable. We need to define the *parameters* of the problem.

paramount ADJ. foremost in importance; supreme. Proper nutrition and hygiene are of *paramount* importance in adolescent development and growth.

paramour N. illicit lover. She sought a divorce on the grounds that her husband had a *paramour* in another town.

paranoia N. psychosis marked by delusions of grandeur or persecution. Suffering from *paranoia,* he claimed everyone was out to get him. Ironically, his claim was accurate; even *paranoids* have enemies. paranoid, paranoiac, N. and ADJ.

paraphernalia N. equipment; odds and ends. Her desk was cluttered with paper, pen, ink, dictionary and other *paraphernalia* of the writing craft.

paraphrase V. restate a passage in one's own words while retaining thought of author. In 250 words or less, *paraphrase* this article. also N.

parasite N. animal or plant living on another; toady; sycophant. The tapeworm is an example of the kind of *parasite* that may infest the human body.

parched ADJ. extremely dry; very thirsty. The *parched* desert landscape seemed hostile to life.

pariah N. social outcast. If everyone ostracized singer Mariah Carey, would she then be Mariah the *pariah*?

parity N. equality; close resemblance. I find your analogy inaccurate because I do not see the *parity* between the two illustrations.

parlance N. language; idiom. All this legal *parlance* confuses me; I need an interpreter.

parley N. conference. The peace *parley* has not produced the anticipated truce. also V.

parochial ADJ. narrow in outlook; provincial; related to parishes. Although Jane Austen writes novels set in small rural communities, her concerns are universal, not *parochial*.

parody N. humorous imitation; spoof; takeoff; travesty. The show *Forbidden Broadway* presents *parodies* spoofing the year's new productions playing on Broadway. also V.

paroxysm N. fit or attack of pain, laughter, rage. When he heard of his son's misdeeds, he was seized by a *paroxysm* of rage.

parquet N. floor made of wood strips inlaid in a mosaic-like pattern. In laying the floor, the carpenters combined redwood and oak in an elegant *parquet*.

parry V. ward off a blow; deflect. Unwilling to injure his opponent in such a pointless clash, Dartagnan simply tried to *parry* his rival's thrusts. What fun it was to watch Katherine Hepburn and Spencer Tracy *parry* each other's verbal thrusts in their classic screwball comedies! also N.

parsimony N. stinginess; excessive frugality. Silas Marner's *parsimony* did not allow him to indulge in any luxuries. parsimonious, ADJ.

partial ADJ. incomplete; having a liking for something. In this issue we have published only a *partial* list of contributors because we lack space to acknowledge everyone. I am extremely *partial* to chocolate eclairs. partiality, N.

partiality N. inclination; bias. As a judge, not only must I be unbiased, but I must also avoid any evidence of *partiality* when I award the prize.

■ **partisan** ADJ. one-sided; prejudiced; committed to a party. Rather than joining forces to solve our nation's problems, the Democrats and Republicans spend their time on *partisan* struggles. also N.

partition V. divide into parts. Before their second daughter was born, Jason and Lizzie decided each child needed a room of her own, and so they *partitioned* a large bedroom into two small but separate rooms. also N.

passé ADJ. old-fashioned; past the prime. Her style is *passé* and reminiscent of the Victorian era.

passive ADJ. not active; acted upon. Mahatma Gandhi urged his followers to pursue a program of *passive* resistance as he felt that it was more effective than violence and acts of terrorism.

pastiche N. imitation of another's style in musical composition or in writing. We cannot even say that her music is a *pastiche* of this or that composer; it is, rather, reminiscent of many musicians.

pastoral ADJ. rural. In these stories of *pastoral* life, we find an understanding of the daily tasks of country folk.

patent ADJ. open for the public to read; obvious. It was *patent* to everyone that the witness spoke the truth.

pathetic ADJ. causing sadness, compassion, pity; touching. Everyone in the auditorium was weeping by the time she finished her *pathetic* tale about the orphaned boy.

■ **pathological** ADJ. pertaining to disease. As we study the *pathological* aspects of this disease, we must not overlook the psychological elements.

pathos N. tender sorrow; pity; quality in art or literature that produces these feelings. The quiet tone of *pathos* that ran through the novel never degenerated into the maudlin or the overly sentimental.

patina N. green crust on old bronze works; tone slowly taken by varnished painting. Judging by the *patina* on this bronze statue, we can conclude that this is the work of a medieval artist.

patois N. local or provincial dialect. His years of study of the language at the university did not enable him to understand the *patois* of the natives.

patriarch N. father and ruler of a family or tribe. In many primitive tribes, the leader and lawmaker was the *patriarch*.

patrician ADJ. noble; aristocratic. We greatly admired her well-bred, *patrician* elegance. also N.

patronize v. support; act superior toward; be a customer of. Penniless artists hope to find some wealthy art lover who will *patronize* them. If some condescending wine steward *patronized* me because he saw I knew nothing about fine wine, I'd refuse to *patronize* his restaurant.

■ **paucity** N. scarcity. They closed the restaurant because the *paucity* of customers made it uneconomical to operate.

pauper N. very poor person. Though Widow Brown was living on a reduced income, she was by no means a *pauper*.

peccadillo N. slight offense. Whenever Huck swiped a cookie from the jar, Miss Watson reacted as if he were guilty of armed robbery, not of some mere *peccadillo*.

Test

Word List 34 *Synonyms and Antonyms*

Each of the following questions consists of a word in capital letters, followed by five lettered words or phrases. Choose the lettered word or phrase that is most nearly similar or opposite in meaning to the word in capital letters and write the letter of your choice on your answer paper.

496. PAEAN (A) serf (B) pealing (C) lien (D) lament (E) folly

497. PALLET (A) bed (B) pigment board (C) bench (D) spectrum (E) quality

498. PALLIATE (A) smoke (B) quicken (C) substitute (D) alleviate (E) sadden

499. PANDEMONIUM (A) calm (B) frustration (C) efficiency (D) impishness (E) sophistication

500. PANEGYRIC (A) medication (B) panacea (C) rotation (D) vacillation (E) praise

501. PARABLE (A) equality (B) allegory (C) frenzy (D) folly (E) cuticle

502. PARADOX (A) exaggeration (B) contradiction (C) hyperbole (D) invective (E) poetic device

503. PARAMOUR (A) illicit lover (B) majority (C) importance (D) hatred (E) clandestine affair

504. PARANOIA (A) fracture (B) statement (C) quantity (D) benefaction (E) sanity

505. PARIAH (A) village (B) suburb (C) outcast (D) disease (E) benefactor

506. PARITY (A) duplicate (B) miniature (C) golf tee (D) similarity (E) event

507. PARSIMONIOUS (A) grammatical (B) syntactical (C) effective (D) extravagant (E) esoteric

508. PARTIALITY (A) completion (B) equality (C) bias (D) divorce (E) reflection

509. PASSÉ (A) scornful (B) rural (C) out-of-date (D) silly (E) barbaric

510. PASTICHE (A) imitation (B) glue (C) present (D) greeting (E) family

Word List 35 pecuniary-philanderer

pecuniary ADJ. pertaining to money. Seldom earning enough to cover their expenses, folk-dance teachers work because they love dancing, not because they expect any *pecuniary* reward.

pedagogue N. teacher. He could never be a stuffy *pedagogue;* his classes were always lively and filled with humor.

pedagogy N. teaching; art of education. Though Maria Montessori gained fame for her innovations in *pedagogy*, it took years before her teaching techniques became common practice in American schools.

pedant N. scholar who overemphasizes book learning or technicalities. Her insistence that the book be memorized marked the teacher as a *pedant* rather than a scholar.

■ **pedantic** ADJ. showing off learning; bookish. Leavening her decisions with humorous, down-to-earth

anecdotes, Judge Judy was not at all the *pedantic* legal scholar. pedantry, N.

pedestrian ADJ. ordinary; unimaginative. Unintentionally boring, he wrote page after page of *pedestrian* prose.

pediatrician N. physician specializing in children's diseases. The family doctor advised the parents to consult a *pediatrician* about their child's ailment.

peerless ADJ. having no equal; incomparable. The reigning operatic tenor of his generation, to his admirers Luciano Pavarotti was *peerless*: no one could compare with him.

pejorative ADJ. negative in connotation; having a belittling effect. Instead of criticizing Clinton's policies, the Republicans made *pejorative* remarks about his character.

pell-mell ADV. in confusion; disorderly. The excited students dashed *pell-mell* into the stadium to celebrate the victory.

pellucid ADJ. transparent; limpid; easy to understand. After reading these stodgy philosophers, I find his *pellucid* style very enjoyable.

penance N. self-imposed punishment for sin. The Ancient Mariner said, "I have *penance* done and *penance* more will do," to atone for the sin of killing the albatross.

■ **penchant** N. strong inclination; liking. Dave has a *penchant* for taking risks: one semester he went steady with three girls, two of whom were stars on the school karate team.

pendant ADJ. hanging down from something. Her *pendant* earrings glistened in the light.

pendant N. ornament (hanging from a necklace, etc.). The grateful team presented the coach with a silver chain and *pendant* engraved with the school's motto.

pendulous ADJ. hanging; suspended. The *pendulous* chandeliers swayed in the breeze as if they were about to fall from the ceiling.

penitent ADJ. repentant. When he realized the enormity of his crime, he became remorseful and *penitent*. also N.

pensive ADJ. dreamily thoughtful; thoughtful with a hint of sadness; contemplative. The *pensive* lover gazed at the portrait of his beloved and sighed deeply.

penumbra N. partial shadow (in an eclipse). During an eclipse, we can see an area of total darkness and a lighter area, which is the *penumbra*.

■ **penury** N. severe poverty; stinginess. When his pension fund failed, George feared he would end his days in *penury*. He became such a penny-pincher that he turned into a closefisted, *penurious* miser.

peon N. landless agricultural worker; bond servant. The land reformers sought to liberate the *peons* and establish them as independent farmers. peonage, N.

perceptive ADJ. insightful; aware; wise. Although Maud was a generally *perceptive* critic, she had her blind spots: she could never see flaws in the work of her friends.

percussion ADJ. striking one object against another sharply. The drum is a *percussion* instrument. also N.

perdition N. damnation; complete ruin. Praying for salvation, young Daedalus feared he was damned to eternal *perdition*.

peregrination N. journey. Auntie Mame was a world traveler whose *peregrinations* took her from Tijuana to Timbuktu.

peremptory ADJ. demanding and leaving no choice. From Jack's *peremptory* knock on the door, Jill could tell he would not give up until she let him in.

■ **perennial** N. something long-lasting. These plants are hardy *perennials* and will bloom for many years. also ADJ.

■ **perfidious** ADJ. treacherous; disloyal. When Caesar realized that Brutus had betrayed him, he reproached his *perfidious* friend. perfidy, N.

perforate V. pierce; put a hole through. Before you can open the aspirin bottle, you must first *perforate* the plastic safety seal that covers the cap.

■ **perfunctory** ADJ. superficial; not thorough; lacking interest, care, or enthusiasm. The auditor's *perfunctory* inspection of the books overlooked many errors.

perigee N. point of moon's orbit when it is nearest the earth. The rocket which was designed to take photographs of the moon was launched as the moon approached its *perigee*.

perimeter N. outer boundary. To find the *perimeter* of any quadrilateral, we add the lengths of the four sides.

peripatetic ADJ. walking about; moving. The *peripatetic* school of philosophy derives its name from the fact that Aristotle walked with his pupils while discussing philosophy with them.

peripheral ADJ. marginal; outer. We lived, not in central London, but in one of those *peripheral* suburbs that spring up on the outskirts of a great city.

periphery N. edge, especially of a round surface. He sensed that there was something just beyond the *periphery* of his vision.

perjury N. false testimony while under oath. Rather than lie under oath and perhaps be indicted for *perjury*, the witness chose to take the Fifth Amendment, refusing to answer any questions on the grounds that he might incriminate himself.

■ **permeable** ADJ. penetrable; porous; allowing liquids or gas to pass through. If your jogging clothes weren't made out of *permeable* fabric, you'd drown in your own sweat (figuratively speaking). permeate, V.

pernicious ADJ. very destructive. The Athenians argued that Socrates's teachings had a *pernicious* effect on young and susceptible minds; therefore, they condemned him to death.

peroration N. conclusion of an oration. The *peroration* was largely hortatory and brought the audience to its feet clamoring for action at its close.

perpetrate V. commit an offense. Only an insane person could *perpetrate* such a horrible crime.

perpetual ADJ. everlasting. Ponce de Leon hoped to find the legendary fountain of *perpetual* youth.

perpetuate V. make something last; preserve from extinction. Some critics attack *The Adventures of Huckleberry Finn* because they believe Twain's book *perpetuates* a false image of blacks in this country. perpetuity, N.

perquisite N. any gain above stipulated salary. The *perquisites* attached to this job make it even more attractive than the salary indicates.

personable ADJ. attractive. The individual I am seeking to fill this position must be *personable* since he or she will be representing us before the public.

perspicacious ADJ. having insight; penetrating; astute. The brilliant lawyer was known for his *perspicacious* deductions.

perspicuity N. clearness of expression; freedom from ambiguity. One of the outstanding features of this book is the *perspicuity* of its author; her meaning is always clear.

perspicuous ADJ. plainly expressed. Her *perspicuous* comments eliminated all possibility of misinterpretation.

pert ADJ. impertinent; forward. I think your *pert* and impudent remarks call for an apology.

pertinacious ADJ. stubborn; persistent. She is bound to succeed because her *pertinacious* nature will not permit her to quit.

pertinent ADJ. suitable; to the point. The lawyer wanted to know all the *pertinent* details.

perturb V. disturb greatly. The thought that electricity might be leaking out of the empty light-bulb sockets *perturbed* my aunt so much that at night she crept about the house screwing fresh bulbs in the vacant spots. perturbation, N.

peruse V. read with care. After the conflagration that burned down her house, Joan closely *perused* her home insurance policy to discover exactly what benefits her coverage provided. perusal, N.

■ **pervasive** ADJ. spread throughout. Despite airing them for several hours, she could not rid her clothes of the *pervasive* odor of mothballs that clung to them. pervade, V.

perverse ADJ. stubbornly wrongheaded; wicked and unacceptable. When Jack was in a *perverse* mood, he would do the opposite of whatever Jill asked him. When Hannibal Lecter was in a *perverse* mood, he ate the flesh of his victims. perversity, N.

perversion N. corruption; turning from right to wrong. Inasmuch as he had no motive for his crimes, we could not understand his *perversion*.

pessimism N. belief that life is basically bad or evil; gloominess. Considering how well you have done in the course so far, you have no real reason for such *pessimism* about your final grade. pessimistic, ADJ.

pestilential ADJ. causing plague; baneful. People were afraid to explore the *pestilential* swamp. pestilence, N.

pestle N. tool for mashing or grinding substances in a hard bowl. From the way in which the elderly pharmacist pounded the drug with his *pestle,* young George could tell that his employer was agitated about something.

petrify V. turn to stone. His sudden and unexpected appearance seemed to *petrify* her.

petty ADJ. trivial; unimportant; very small. She had no major complaints to make about his work, only a few *petty* quibbles that were almost too minor to state.

petulant ADJ. touchy; peevish. If you'd had hardly any sleep for three nights and people kept on phoning and waking you up, you'd sound *petulant*, too. petulance, N.

pharisaical ADJ. pertaining to the Pharisees, who paid scrupulous attention to tradition; self-righteous; hypocritical. Walter Lippmann has pointed out that moralists who do not attempt to explain the moral code they advocate are often regarded as *pharisaical* and ignored.

phenomena N, PL. observable facts; subjects of scientific investigation. We kept careful records of the *phenomena* we noted in the course of these experiments. phenomenon, SING.

philanderer N. faithless lover; flirt. Swearing he had never so much as looked at another woman, Jack assured Jill he was no *philanderer*.

Test

Word List 35   *Antonyms*

Each of the questions below consists of a word in capital letters, followed by five lettered words or phrases. Choose the lettered word or phrase that is most nearly opposite in meaning to the word in capital letters and write the letter of your choice on your answer paper.

511. PEJORATIVE (A) positive (B) legal (C) determining (D) delighting (E) declaiming

512. PELLUCID (A) logistical (B) philandering (C) incomprehensible (D) vagrant (E) warranted

513. PENCHANT (A) distance (B) imminence (C) dislike (D) attitude (E) void

514. PENURIOUS (A) imprisoned (B) captivated (C) generous (D) vacant (E) abolished

515. PERFUNCTORY (A) official (B) thorough (C) insipid (D) vicarious (E) distinctive

516. PERIGEE (A) eclipse (B) planet (C) apogee (D) refugee (E) danger

517. PERIPATETIC (A) worldly (B) stationary (C) disarming (D) seeking (E) inherent

518. PERMEABLE (A) perishable (B) effective (C) plodding (D) impenetrable (E) lasting

519. PERNICIOUS (A) practical (B) comparative (C) harmless (D) tangible (E) detailed

520. PERPETUAL (A) momentary (B) standard (C) serious (D) industrial (E) interpretive

521. PERSPICUITY (A) grace (B) feature (C) review (D) difficulty (E) vagueness

522. PERT (A) polite (B) perishable (C) moral (D) deliberate (E) stubborn

523. PERTINACIOUS (A) vengeful (B) consumptive (C) superficial (D) skilled (E) advertised

524. PERTINENT (A) understood (B) living (C) discontented (D) puzzling (E) irrelevant

525. PETULANT (A) angry (B) moral (C) declining (D) underhanded (E) uncomplaining

Word List 36   philanthropist-precedent

philanthropist   N. lover of mankind; doer of good. In his role as *philanthropist* and public benefactor, John D. Rockefeller, Sr., donated millions to charity; as an individual, however, he was a tight-fisted old man.

philatelist   N. stamp-collector. When she heard the value of the Penny Black stamp, Phyllis was inspired to become a *philatelist.*

philistine   N. narrow-minded person, uncultured and exclusively interested in material gain. We need more men and women of culture and enlightenment; we have too many *philistines* among us.

philology   N. study of language. The professor of *philology* advocated the use of Esperanto as an international language.

■ **phlegmatic**   ADJ. calm; not easily disturbed. The nurse was a cheerful but *phlegmatic* person, unexcited in the face of sudden emergencies.

phobia   N. morbid fear. Her fear of flying was more than mere nervousness; it was a real *phobia.*

phoenix   N. symbol of immortality or rebirth. Like the legendary *phoenix* rising from its ashes, the city of San Francisco rose again after its destruction during the 1906 earthquake.

phylum   N. major classification, second to kingdom, of plants and animals; division. In sorting out her hundreds of packets of seeds, Katya decided to file them by *phylum.*

physiognomy   N. face. He prided himself on his ability to analyze a person's character by studying his *physiognomy.*

physiological   ADJ. pertaining to the science of the function of living organisms. To understand this disease fully, we must examine not only its *physiological* aspects but also its psychological elements.

piebald   ADJ. of different colors; mottled; spotted. You should be able to identify Polka Dot in this race; he is the only *piebald* horse running.

piecemeal   ADV. one part at a time; gradually. Tolstoy's *War and Peace* is too huge to finish in one sitting; I'll have to read it *piecemeal.*

pied   ADJ. variegated; multicolored. The *Pied* Piper of Hamelin got his name from the multicolored clothing he wore.

■ **piety**   N. devoutness; reverence for God. Living her life in prayer and good works, Mother Teresa exemplified the true spirit of *piety.* pious, ADJ.

pigment   N. coloring matter. Van Gogh mixed various *pigments* with linseed oil to create his paints.

pillage   V. plunder. The enemy *pillaged* the quiet village and left it in ruins. also N.

pillory   V. punish by placing in a wooden frame; subject to criticism and ridicule. Even though he was mocked and *pilloried,* he maintained that he was correct in his beliefs. also N.

pine   V. languish, decline; long for; yearn. Though she tried to be happy living with Clara in the city, Heidi *pined* for the mountains and for her gruff but loving grandfather.

pinion   V. restrain. They *pinioned* his arms against his body but left his legs free so that he could move about. also N.

pinnacle   N. peak. We could see the morning sunlight illuminate the *pinnacle* while the rest of the mountain lay in shadow.

pious   ADJ. devout; religious. The challenge for church people today is how to be *pious* in the best sense, that is, to be devout without becoming hypocritical or sanctimonious. piety, N.

piquant   ADJ. pleasantly tart-tasting; stimulating. The *piquant* sauce added to our enjoyment of the meal. piquancy, N.

pique   N. irritation; resentment. She showed her *pique* at her loss by refusing to appear with the other contestants at the end of the competition.

pique   V. provoke or arouse; annoy. "I know something *you* don't know," said Lucy, trying to *pique* Ethel's interest.

piscatorial   ADJ. pertaining to fishing. He spent many happy hours at the lake in his *piscatorial* activities.

pitfall   N. hidden danger; concealed trap. The preacher warned his flock to beware the *pitfall* of excessive pride, for pride brought on the angels' fall.

pith   N. core or marrow; essence; substance. In preparing a pineapple for the table, first slice it in half and remove the woody central *pith.*

pithy   ADJ. concise; meaningful; substantial; meaty. While other girls might have gone on and on about how uncool Elton was, Cher summed it up in one *pithy* remark: "He's bogus!"

pittance   N. a small allowance or wage. He could not live on the *pittance* he received as a pension and had to look for an additional source of revenue.

pivotal   ADJ. central; critical. De Klerk's decision to set Nelson Mandela free was *pivotal;* without Mandela's release, there was no possibility that the African National Congress would entertain talks with the South African government.

■ **placate**   V. pacify; conciliate. The store manager tried to *placate* the angry customer, offering to replace the damaged merchandise or to give back her money.

placebo   N. harmless substance prescribed as a dummy pill. In a controlled experiment, fifty volunteers were given erythromycin tablets; the control group received only *placebos.*

placid   ADJ. peaceful; calm. After his vacation in this *placid* section, he felt soothed and rested.

plagiarize   V. steal another's ideas and pass them off as one's own. The teacher could tell that the student had *plagiarized* parts of his essay; she recognized whole paragraphs straight from *Barron's Book Notes.* plagiarism, N.

plaintive   ADJ. mournful. The dove has a *plaintive* and melancholy call.

plait V. braid; intertwine. The maypole dancers *plaited* bright green ribbons in their hair. also N.

■ **plasticity** N. ability to be molded. When clay dries out, it loses its *plasticity* and becomes less malleable.

■ **platitude** N. trite remark; commonplace statement. In giving advice to his son, old Polonius expressed himself only in *platitudes*; every word out of his mouth was a truism.

platonic ADJ. purely spiritual; theoretical; without sensual desire. Accused of impropriety in his dealings with female students, the professor maintained he had only a *platonic* interest in the women involved.

plaudit N. enthusiastic approval; round of applause. The theatrical company reprinted the *plaudits* of the critics in its advertisements. plauditory, ADJ.

plausible ADJ. having a show of truth but open to doubt; specious. Your mother made you stay home from school because she needed you to program the VCR? I'm sorry, you'll have to come up with a more *plausible* excuse than that.

plebeian ADJ. common; pertaining to the common people. His speeches were aimed at the *plebeian* minds and emotions; they disgusted the more refined.

plenary ADJ. complete; full. The union leader was given *plenary* power to negotiate a new contract with the employers.

plenitude N. abundance; completeness. Looking in the pantry, we admired the *plenitude* of fruits and pickles we had preserved during the summer.

■ **plethora** N. excess; overabundance. She offered a *plethora* of excuses for her shortcomings.

pliable ADJ. flexible; yielding; adaptable. In remodeling the bathroom, we replaced all the old, rigid lead pipes with new, *pliable* copper tubing.

pliant ADJ. flexible; easily influenced. Pinocchio's disposition was *pliant*; he was like putty in his tempters' hands.

plight N. condition, state (especially a bad state or condition); predicament. Loggers, unmoved by the *plight* of the spotted owl, plan to keep on felling trees whether or not they ruin the bird's habitat.

pluck N. courage. Even the adversaries of young Indiana Jones were impressed by the boy's *pluck* in trying to rescue the archeological treasure they had stolen.

plumage N. feathers of a bird. Bird watchers identify different species of birds by their characteristic songs and distinctive *plumage*.

plumb V. examine critically in order to understand; measure depth (by sounding). Try as he would, Watson could never fully *plumb* the depths of Holmes's thought processes.

plumb ADJ. vertical. Before hanging wallpaper it is advisable to drop a *plumb* line from the ceiling as a guide. also N.

■ **plummet** V. fall sharply. Stock prices *plummeted* as Wall Street reacted to the rise in interest rates.

plutocracy N. society ruled by the wealthy. From the way the government caters to the rich, you might think our society is a *plutocracy* rather than a democracy.

podiatrist N. doctor who treats ailments of the feet. He consulted a *podiatrist* about his fallen arches.

podium N. pedestal; raised platform. The audience applauded as the conductor made her way to the *podium*.

poignancy N. quality of being deeply moving; keenness of emotion. Watching the tearful reunion of the long-separated mother and child, the social worker was touched by the *poignancy* of the scene. poignant, ADJ.

polarize V. split into opposite extremes or camps. The abortion issue has *polarized* the country into pro-choice and anti-abortion camps.

polemic N. controversy; argument in support of point of view. Her essays were, for the main part, *polemics* for the party's policy.

polemical ADJ. aggressive in verbal attack; disputatious. Lexy was a master of *polemical* rhetoric; she should have worn a T-shirt with the slogan "Born to Debate."

politic ADJ. expedient; prudent; well devised. Even though he was disappointed, he did not think it *politic* to refuse this offer.

polity N. form of government of nation or state. Our *polity* should be devoted to the concept that the government should strive for the good of all citizens.

polygamist N. one who has more than one spouse at a time. He was arrested as a *polygamist* when his two wives filed complaints about him.

polyglot ADJ. speaking several languages. New York City is a *polyglot* community because of the thousands of immigrants who settle there.

pomposity N. self-important behavior; acting like a stuffed shirt. Although the commencement speaker had some good things to say, we had to laugh at his *pomposity* and general air of parading his own dignity. pompous, ADJ.

ponderous ADJ. weighty; unwieldy. His humor lacked the light touch; his jokes were always *ponderous*.

pontifical ADJ. pertaining to a bishop or pope; pompous or pretentious. From the very beginning of his ministry it was clear from his *pontifical* pronouncements that John was destined for a high *pontifical* office.

pore V. study industriously; ponder; scrutinize. Determined to become a physician, Beth spends hours *poring* over her anatomy text.

■ **porous** ADJ. full of pores; like a sieve. Dancers like to wear *porous* clothing because it allows the ready passage of water and air.

portend V. foretell; presage. The king did not know what these omens might *portend* and asked his soothsayers to interpret them.

portent N. sign; omen; forewarning. He regarded the black cloud as a *portent* of evil.

portly ADJ. stout; corpulent. The salesclerk tactfully referred to the overweight customer as *portly* rather than fat.

poseur N. person who pretends to be sophisticated, elegant, etc., to impress others. Some thought Dali was a brilliant painter; others dismissed him as a *poseur*.

posterity N. descendants; future generations. We hope to leave a better world to *posterity*.

posthumous ADJ. after death (as of child born after father's death or book published after author's death). The critics ignored his works during his lifetime; it was only after the *posthumous* publication of his last novel that they recognized his great talent.

postulate N. self-evident truth. We must accept these statements as *postulates* before pursuing our discussions any further. also V.

posture V. assume an affected pose; act artificially. No matter how much Arnold boasted or *postured,* I could not believe he was as important as he pretended to be.

potable ADJ. suitable for drinking. The recent drought in the Middle Atlantic States has emphasized the need for extensive research in ways of making sea water *potable.* also N.

potent ADJ. powerful; persuasive; greatly influential. Looking at the expiration date on the cough syrup bottle, we wondered whether the medication would still be *potent.* potency, N.

potentate N. monarch; sovereign. The *potentate* spent more time at Monte Carlo than he did at home on his throne.

potential ADJ. expressing possibility; latent. This juvenile delinquent is a *potential* murderer. also N.

potion N. dose (of liquid). Tristan and Isolde drink a love *potion* in the first act of the opera.

potpourri N. heterogeneous mixture; medley. The folk singer offered a *potpourri* of songs from many lands.

poultice N. soothing application applied to sore and inflamed portions of the body. She was advised to apply a flaxseed *poultice* to the inflammation.

practicable ADJ. feasible. The board of directors decided that the plan was *practicable* and agreed to undertake the project.

practical ADJ. based on experience; useful. He was a *practical* man, opposed to theory.

■ **pragmatic** ADJ. practical (as opposed to idealistic); concerned with the practical worth or impact of something. This coming trip to France should provide me with a *pragmatic* test of the value of my conversational French class.

pragmatist N. practical person. No *pragmatist* enjoys becoming involved in a game that he can never win.

prate V. speak foolishly; boast idly. Let us not *prate* about our qualities; rather, let our virtues speak for themselves.

prattle V. babble. Baby John *prattled* on and on about the cats and his ball and the Cookie Monster. also N.

■ **preamble** N. introductory statement. In the *Preamble* to the Constitution, the purpose of the document is set forth.

■ **precarious** ADJ. uncertain; risky. Saying the stock was currently overpriced and would be a *precarious* investment, the broker advised her client against purchasing it.

precedent N. something preceding in time that may be used as an authority or guide for future action; an earlier occurrence. The law professor asked Jill to state which famous case served as a *precedent* for the court's decision in *Brown II.* precede, V.

precedent ADJ. preceding in time, rank, etc. Our discussions, *precedent* to this event, certainly did not give you any reason to believe that we would adopt your proposal.

Test

Word List 36   *Synonyms*

Each of the questions below consists of a word in capital letters, followed by five lettered words or phrases. Choose the lettered word or phrase that is most nearly similar in meaning to the word in capital letters and write the letter of your choice on your answer paper.

526. PHLEGMATIC (A) calm (B) cryptic (C) practical
  (D) salivary (E) dishonest

527. PHYSIOGNOMY (A) posture (B) head
  (C) physique (D) face (E) size

528. PIEBALD (A) motley (B) coltish (C) hairless
  (D) thoroughbred (E) delicious

529. PILLAGE (A) hoard (B) plunder (C) versify
  (D) denigrate (E) confide

530. PINION (A) express (B) report (C) reveal
  (D) submit (E) restrain

531. PINNACLE (A) foothills (B) card game (C) pass
  (D) taunt (E) peak

532. PIOUS (A) historic (B) devout (C) multiple
  (D) fortunate (E) authoritative

533. PIQUE (A) pyramid (B) revolt (C) resentment
  (D) struggle (E) inventory

534. PLACATE (A) determine (B) transmit (C) pacify
  (D) allow (E) define

535. PLAGIARISM (A) theft of funds (B) theft of ideas
  (C) belief in God (D) arson (E) ethical theory

536. PLAINTIVE (A) mournful (B) senseless
  (C) persistent (D) rural (E) evasive

537. PLATITUDE (A) fatness (B) bravery (C) dimension (D) trite remark (E) strong belief

538. POLEMIC (A) blackness (B) lighting (C) magnetism (D) controversy (E) grimace

539. PONDEROUS (A) contemplative (B) moist (C) rambling (D) bulky (E) erect

540. PRECARIOUS (A) priceless (B) premature (C) primitive (D) hazardous (E) unwelcome

Word List 37   precept-propitiate

precept N. practical rule guiding conduct. "Love thy neighbor as thyself" is a worthwhile *precept*.

precipice N. cliff; dangerous position. Suddenly Indiana Jones found himself dangling from the edge of a *precipice*.

precipitant N. something that causes a substance in a chemical solution to separate out in solid form. Solvents by definition dissolve; *precipitants*, however, cause solids to *precipitate* or form. precipitate, V.

■ **precipitate** ADJ. rash; premature; hasty; sudden. Though I was angry enough to resign on the spot, I had enough sense to keep myself from quitting a job in such a *precipitate* fashion.

precipitate V. throw headlong; hasten. The removal of American political support appeared to have *precipitated* the downfall of the Marcos regime.

precipitous ADJ. steep; overhasty. This hill is difficult to climb because it is so *precipitous;* one slip, and our descent will be *precipitous* as well.

précis N. concise summing up of main points. Before making her presentation at the conference, Ellen wrote a neat *précis* of the major elements she would cover.

precise ADJ. exact. If you don't give me *precise* directions and a map, I'll never find your place.

preclude V. make impossible; eliminate. The fact that the band was already booked to play in Hollywood on New Year's Eve *precluded* their accepting the offer of a New Year's Eve gig in London.

precocious ADJ. advanced in development. Listening to the grown-up way the child discussed serious topics, we couldn't help remarking how *precocious* she was. precocity, N.

■ **precursor** N. forerunner. Though Gray and Burns share many traits with the Romantic poets who followed them, most critics consider them *precursors* of the Romantic Movement, not true Romantics.

predator N. creature that seizes and devours another animal; person who robs or exploits others. Not just cats, but a wide variety of *predators*—owls, hawks, weasels, foxes—catch mice for dinner. A carnivore is by definition *predatory*, for he *preys* on weaker creatures. predation, N.

predecessor N. former occupant of a post. I hope I can live up to the fine example set by my late *predecessor* in this office.

predetermine V. predestine; settle or decide beforehand; influence markedly. Romeo and Juliet believed that Fate had *predetermined* their meeting. Bea gathered estimates from caterers, florists, and stationers so that she could *predetermine* the costs of holding a catered buffet. Philip's love of athletics *predetermined* his choice of a career in sports marketing.

predicament N. tricky or dangerous situation; dilemma. Tied to the railroad tracks by the villain, Pauline strained against her bonds. How would she escape from this terrible *predicament*?

predilection N. partiality; preference. Although the artist used various media from time to time, she had a *predilection* for watercolors.

predispose V. give an inclination toward; make susceptible to. Oleg's love of dressing up his big sister's Barbie doll may have *predisposed* him to become a fashion designer. Genetic influences apparently *predispose* people to certain forms of cancer. predisposition, N.

preeminent ADJ. outstanding; superior. The king traveled to Boston because he wanted the *preeminent* surgeon in the field to perform the operation.

preempt V. head off; forestall by acting first; appropriate for oneself; supplant. Hoping to *preempt* any attempts by the opposition to make educational reform a hot political issue, the candidate set out her own plan to revitalize the public schools. preemptive, ADJ.

preen V. make oneself tidy in appearance; feel self-satisfaction. As Kitty *preened* before the mirror, carefully smoothing her shining hair, she couldn't help *preening* herself on her good looks.

prefatory ADJ. introductory. The chairman made a few *prefatory* remarks before he called on the first speaker.

prehensile ADJ. capable of grasping or holding. Monkeys use not only their arms and legs but also their *prehensile* tails in traveling through the trees.

prelate N. church dignitary. The archbishop of Moscow and other high-ranking *prelates* visited the Russian Orthodox seminary.

prelude N. introduction; forerunner. I am afraid that this border raid is the *prelude* to more serious attacks.

premeditate V. plan in advance. She had *premeditated* the murder for months, reading about common poisons and buying weed killer that contained arsenic.

premise N. assumption; postulate. On the *premise* that there's no fool like an old fool, P. T. Barnum hired a 90-year-old clown for his circus.

premonition N. forewarning. We ignored these *premonitions* of disaster because they appeared to be based on childish fears.

premonitory ADJ. serving to warn. You should have visited a doctor as soon as you felt these *premonitory* chest pains.

preponderance N. superiority of power, quantity, etc. The rebels sought to overcome the *preponderance* of strength of the government forces by engaging in guerrilla tactics. preponderate, V. preponderant, ADJ.

preposterous ADJ. absurd; ridiculous. When the candidate tried to downplay his youthful experiments with marijuana by saying he hadn't inhaled, we all thought, "What a *preposterous* excuse!"

prerogative N. privilege; unquestionable right. The President cannot levy taxes; that is the *prerogative* of the legislative branch of government.

presage V. foretell. The vultures flying overhead *presaged* the discovery of the corpse in the desert.

prescience N. ability to foretell the future. Given the current wave of Japan-bashing, it does not take *prescience* for me to foresee problems in our future trade relations with Japan.

presentiment N. feeling something will happen; anticipatory fear; premonition. Saying goodbye at the airport, Jack had a sudden *presentiment* that this was the last time he would see Jill.

prestige N. impression produced by achievements or reputation. Many students want to go to Harvard University, not for the education offered, but for the *prestige* of Harvard's name. prestigious, ADJ.

■ **presumptuous** ADJ. arrogant; taking liberties. It seems *presumptuous* for one so relatively new to the field to challenge the conclusions of its leading experts. presumption, N.

pretentious ADJ. ostentatious; pompous; making unjustified claims; overambitious. The other prize winner isn't wearing her medal; isn't it a bit *pretentious* of you to wear yours?

preternatural ADJ. beyond that which is normal in nature. John's mother's total ability to tell when he was lying struck him as almost *preternatural*.

pretext N. excuse. She looked for a good *pretext* to get out of paying a visit to her aunt.

prevail V. induce; triumph over. He tried to *prevail* on her to type his essay for him.

prevalent ADJ. widespread; generally accepted. A radical committed to social change, Reed had no patience with the conservative views *prevalent* in the America of his day.

■ **prevaricate** V. lie. Some people believe that to *prevaricate* in a good cause is justifiable and regard the statement as a "white lie."

prey N. target of a hunt; victim. In *Stalking the Wild Asparagus*, Euell Gibbons has as his *prey* not wild beasts but wild plants. also V.

prim ADJ. very precise and formal; exceedingly proper. Many people commented on the contrast between the *prim* attire of the young lady and the inappropriate clothing worn by her escort.

primogeniture N. seniority by birth. By virtue of *primogeniture*, in some cultures the first-born child has many privileges denied his brothers and sisters.

primordial ADJ. existing at the beginning (of time); rudimentary. The Neanderthal Man is one of our *primordial* ancestors.

primp V. groom oneself with care; adorn oneself. The groom stood by idly while his nervous bride-to-be *primped* one last time before the mirror.

■ **pristine** ADJ. characteristic of earlier times; primitive, unspoiled. This area has been preserved in all its *pristine* wildness.

privation N. hardship; want. In his youth, he knew hunger and *privation*.

privy ADJ. secret; hidden; not public. We do not care for *privy* chamber government.

probe V. explore with tools. The surgeon *probed* the wound for foreign matter before suturing it. also N.

■ **probity** N. uprightness; incorruptibility. Everyone took his *probity* for granted; his defalcations, therefore, shocked us all.

■ **problematic** ADJ. doubtful; unsettled; questionable; perplexing. Given the way building costs have exceeded estimates for the job, whether the arena will ever be completed is *problematic*.

proclivity N. inclination; natural tendency. Watching the two-year-old voluntarily put away his toys, I was amazed by his *proclivity* for neatness.

procrastinate V. postpone; delay or put off. Looking at four years of receipts and checks he still had to sort through, Bob was truly sorry he had *procrastinated* for so long and had not finished filing his taxes long ago.

procurement N. obtaining. The personnel department handles the *procurement* of new employees.

prod V. poke; stir up; urge. If you *prod* him hard enough, he'll eventually clean his room.

■ **prodigal** ADJ. wasteful; reckless with money. Don't be so *prodigal* spending my money; when you've earned some money, you can waste as much of it as you want! also N.

prodigious ADJ. marvelous; enormous. Watching the champion weight lifter heave the weighty barbell to shoulder height and then boost it overhead, we marveled at his *prodigious* strength.

prodigy N. highly gifted child; marvel. Menuhin was a *prodigy*, performing wonders on his violin when he was barely eight years old.

profane V. violate; desecrate; treat unworthily. The members of the mysterious Far Eastern cult sought to kill the British explorer because he had *profaned* the sanctity of their holy goblet by using it as an ashtray. also ADJ.

profligate ADJ. dissipated; wasteful; wildly immoral. Although surrounded by wild and *profligate* companions, she managed to retain some sense of decency. also N. profligacy, N.

■ **profound** ADJ. deep; not superficial; complete. Freud's remarkable insights into human behavior caused his fellow scientists to honor him as a *profound* thinker. profundity, N.

profusion N. overabundance; lavish expenditure; excess. Freddy was so overwhelmed by the *profusion* of choices on the menu that he knocked over his wine glass and soaked his host. He made *profuse* apologies to his host, the waiter, the busboy, the people at the next table, and the man in the men's room giving out paper towels.

progenitor N. ancestor. The Roth family, whose *progenitors* emigrated from Germany early in the nineteenth century, settled in Peru, Illinois.

progeny N. children; offspring. He was proud of his *progeny* but regarded George as the most promising of all his children.

prognosis N. forecasted course of a disease; prediction. If the doctor's *prognosis* is correct, the patient will be in a coma for at least twenty-four hours.

prognosticate V. predict. I *prognosticate* disaster unless we change our wasteful ways.

■ **prohibitive** ADJ. tending to prevent the purchase or use of something; inclined to prevent or forbid. Susie wanted to buy a new Volvo but had to settle for a used Dodge because the new car's price was *prohibitive*. prohibition, N.

projectile N. missile. Man has always hurled *projectiles* at his enemy whether in the form of stones or of highly explosive shells.

proletarian N. member of the working class; blue collar guy. "Workers of the world, unite! You have nothing to lose but your chains" is addressed to *proletarians*, not preppies. also ADJ. proletariat, N.

■ **proliferate** V. grow rapidly; spread; multiply. Times of economic hardship inevitably encourage countless get-rich-quick schemes to *proliferate*. proliferation, N.

prolific ADJ. abundantly fruitful. She was a *prolific* writer who produced as many as three books a year.

prolixity N. tedious wordiness; verbosity. A writer who suffers from *prolixity* tells his readers everything they *never* wanted to know about his subject (or were too bored to ask). prolix, ADJ.

prologue N. introduction (to a poem or play). In the *prologue* to *Romeo and Juliet*, Shakespeare introduces the audience to the feud between the Montagues and the Capulets.

prolong V. extend; draw out; lengthen. In their determination to discover ways to *prolong* human life, doctors fail to take into account that longer lives are not always happier ones.

prominent ADJ. conspicuous; notable; protruding. Have you ever noticed that Prince Charles's *prominent* ears make him resemble the big-eared character in *Mad* comics?

promiscuous ADJ. mixed indiscriminately; haphazard; irregular, particularly sexually. In the opera *La Bohème*, we get a picture of the *promiscuous* life led by the young artists of Paris. promiscuity, N.

promontory N. headland. They erected a lighthouse on the *promontory* to warn approaching ships of their nearness to the shore.

promote V. help to flourish; advance in rank; publicize. Founder of the Children's Defense Fund, Marian Wright Edelman ceaselessly *promotes* the welfare of young people everywhere.

prompt V. cause; provoke; provide a cue for an actor. Whatever *prompted* you to ask for such a big piece of cake when you're on a diet?

promulgate V. proclaim a doctrine or law; make known by official publication. When Moses came down from the mountaintop prepared to *promulgate* God's commandments, he was appalled to discover his followers worshipping a golden calf.

prone ADJ. inclined to; prostrate. She was *prone* to sudden fits of anger during which she would lie *prone* on the floor, screaming and kicking her heels.

propagate V. multiply; spread. Since bacteria *propagate* more quickly in unsanitary environments, it is important to keep hospital rooms clean.

propellant N. substance that propels or drives forward. The development of our missile program has forced our scientists to seek more powerful *propellants*. also ADJ.

■ **propensity** N. natural inclination. Convinced of his own talent, Sol has an unfortunate *propensity* to belittle the talents of others.

prophetic ADJ. having to do with predicting the future. In interpreting Pharaoh's *prophetic* dream, Joseph said that the seven fat cows eaten by the seven lean cows represented seven years of plenty followed by seven years of famine. prophecy, N.

prophylactic ADJ. used to prevent disease. Despite all *prophylactic* measures introduced by the authorities, the epidemic raged until cool weather set in. prophylaxis, N.

propinquity N. nearness; kinship. Their relationship could not be explained as being based on mere *propinquity*. They were more than relatives; they were true friends.

■ **propitiate** V. appease. The natives offered sacrifices to *propitiate* the gods.

Test

Word List 37   *Antonyms*

Each of the following questions consists of a word in capital letters, followed by five lettered words or phrases. Choose the lettered word or phrase that is most nearly opposite in meaning to the word in capital letters and write the letter of your choice on your answer paper.

541. PRECIPITATE (A) dull (B) anticipatory (C) cautious (D) considerate (E) welcome

542. PREFATORY (A) outstanding (B) magnificent (C) conclusive (D) intelligent (E) predatory

543. PRELUDE (A) intermezzo (B) diva (C) aria (D) aftermath (E) duplication

544. PRESUMPTION (A) assertion (B) activation (C) motivation (D) proposition (E) humility

545. PRETENTIOUS (A) ominous (B) calm (C) unassuming (D) futile (E) volatile

546. PRIM (A) informal (B) prior (C) exterior (D) private (E) cautious

547. PRISTINE (A) cultivated (B) condemned (C) irreligious (D) cautious (E) critical

548. PROBITY (A) regret (B) assumption (C) corruptibility (D) extent (E) upswing

549. PRODIGAL (A) large (B) thrifty (C) consistent (D) compatible (E) remote

550. PRODIGIOUS (A) infinitesimal (B) indignant (C) indifferent (D) indisposed (E) insufficient

551. PROFANE (A) sanctify (B) desecrate (C) define (D) manifest (E) urge

552. PROLIFIC (A) unworkable (B) backward (C) barren (D) controversial (E) unfocused

553. PROLIX (A) stupid (B) indifferent (C) redundant (D) livid (E) pithy

554. PROPHYLACTIC (A) causing growth (B) causing disease (C) antagonistic (D) brushing (E) favorable

555. PROPINQUITY (A) remoteness (B) uniqueness (C) health (D) virtue (E) simplicity

Word List 38   propitious–quarry

propitious ADJ. favorable; fortunate; advantageous. Chloe consulted her horoscope to see whether Tuesday would be a *propitious* day to dump her boyfriend.

proponent N. supporter; backer; opposite of *opponent*. In the Senate, *proponents* of the universal health care measure lobbied to gain additional support for the controversial legislation.

propound V. put forth for analysis. In your discussion, you have *propounded* several questions; let us consider each one separately.

■ **propriety** N. fitness; correct conduct. Miss Manners counsels her readers so that they may behave with *propriety* in any social situation and not embarrass themselves.

propulsive ADJ. driving forward. The jet plane has a greater *propulsive* power than the engine-driven plane.

prosaic ADJ. dull and unimaginative; matter-of-fact; factual. Though the ad writers had come up with a highly creative campaign to publicize the company's newest product, the head office rejected it for a more *prosaic*, down-to-earth approach.

proscenium N. part of stage in front of curtain. In the theater-in-the-round there can be no *proscenium* or *proscenium* arch. also ADJ.

■ **proscribe** V. ostracize; banish; outlaw. Antony, Octavius, and Lepidus *proscribed* all those who had conspired against Julius Caesar.

proselytize V. induce someone to convert to a religion or belief. In these interfaith meetings, there must be no attempt to *proselytize;* we must respect all points of view.

prosody N. the art of versification. This book on *prosody* contains a rhyming dictionary as well as samples of the various verse forms.

prosperity N. good fortune; financial success; physical well-being. Promising to stay together "for richer, for poorer," the newlyweds vowed to be true to one another in *prosperity* and hardship alike.

prostrate V. stretch out full on ground. He *prostrated* himself before the idol. also ADJ.

protean ADJ. versatile; able to take on many forms. A remarkably *protean* actor, Alec Guinness could take on any role.

protégé N. person receiving protection and support from a patron. Born with an independent spirit, Cyrano de Bergerac refused to be a *protégé* of Cardinal Richelieu.

protocol N. diplomatic etiquette. We must run this state dinner according to *protocol* if we are to avoid offending any of our guests.

prototype N. original work used as a model by others. The crude typewriter on display in this museum is the *prototype* of the elaborate machines in use today.

protract V. prolong. Seeking to delay the union members' vote, the management team tried to *protract* the negotiations endlessly, but the union representatives saw through their strategy.

protrude V. stick out. His fingers *protruded* from the holes in his gloves.

protuberance N. protrusion; bulge. A ganglionic cyst is a fluid-filled tumor (generally benign) that develops near a joint membrane or tendon sheath, and that bulges beneath the skin, forming a *protuberance*.

provenance N. origin or source of something. I am not interested in its *provenance;* I am more concerned with its usefulness than with its source.

provender   N. dry food; fodder. I am not afraid of a severe winter because I have stored a large quantity of *provender* for the cattle.

provident   ADJ. displaying foresight; thrifty; preparing for emergencies. In his usual *provident* manner, he had insured himself against this type of loss.

provincial   ADJ. pertaining to a province; limited in outlook; unsophisticated. As *provincial* governor, Sir Henry administered the Queen's law in his remote corner of Canada. Caught up in local problems, out of touch with London news, he became sadly *provincial*.

provisional   ADJ. tentative. Kim's acceptance as an American Express cardholder was *provisional*: before issuing her a card, American Express wanted to check her employment record and credit history.

proviso   N. stipulation. I am ready to accept your proposal with the *proviso* that you meet your obligations within the next two weeks.

provocative   ADJ. arousing anger or interest; annoying. In a typically *provocative* act, the bully kicked sand into the weaker man's face. provoke, V. provocation, N.

prowess   N. extraordinary ability; military bravery. Performing triple axels and double lutzes at the age of six, the young figure skater was world famous for her *prowess* on the ice.

proximity   N. nearness. Blind people sometimes develop a compensatory ability to sense the *proximity* of objects around them.

proxy   N. authorized agent. Please act as my *proxy* and vote for this slate of candidates in my absence.

prude   N. excessively modest or proper person. The X-rated film was definitely not for *prudes*.

prudent   ADJ. cautious; careful. A miser hoards money not because he is *prudent* but because he is greedy. prudence, N.

prune   V. cut away; trim. With the help of her editor, she was able to *prune* her manuscript into publishable form.

prurient   ADJ. having or causing lustful thoughts and desires. Aroused by his *prurient* impulses, the dirty old man leered at the sweet young thing and offered to give her a sample of his "prowess"; his *prurience* appalled her.

pry   V. inquire impertinently; use leverage to raise or open something. Though Nora claimed she didn't mean to *pry*, everyone knew she was just plain nosy. With a crowbar Long John Silver *pried* up the lid of the treasure chest.

pseudonym   N. pen name. Samuel Clemens' *pseudonym* was Mark Twain.

psyche   N. soul; mind. It is difficult to delve into the *psyche* of a human being.

psychiatrist   N. a doctor who treats mental diseases. A *psychiatrist* often needs long conferences with his patient before a diagnosis can be made.

psychopathic   ADJ. pertaining to mental derangement. The *psychopathic* patient suffers more frequently from a disorder of the nervous system than from a diseased brain.

psychosis   N. mental disorder. We must endeavor to find an outlet for the patient's repressed desires if we hope to combat this *psychosis*. psychotic, ADJ.

pterodactyl   N. extinct flying reptile. The remains of *pterodactyls* indicate that these flying reptiles had a wingspan of as much as twenty feet.

puerile   ADJ. childish. His *puerile* pranks sometimes offended his more mature friends.

pugilist   N. boxer. The famous *pugilist* Cassius Clay changed his name to Muhammed Ali.

pugnacity   N. combativeness; disposition to fight. "Put up your dukes!" he cried, making a fist to show his *pugnacity*. pugnacious, ADJ.

puissant   ADJ. powerful; strong; potent. We must keep his friendship for he will make a *puissant* ally.

pulchritude   N. beauty; comeliness. I do not envy the judges who have to select this year's Miss America from this collection of female *pulchritude*.

pulmonary   ADJ. pertaining to the lungs. In his researches on *pulmonary* diseases, he discovered many facts about the lungs of animals and human beings.

pulsate   V. throb. We could see the blood vessels in his temple *pulsate* as he became more angry.

pulverize   V. crush or grind into very small particles. Before sprinkling the dried herbs into the stew, Michael first *pulverized* them into a fine powder.

pummel   V. beat or pound with fists. Swinging wildly, Pammy *pummeled* her brother around the head and shoulders.

punctilious   ADJ. stressing niceties of conduct or form; minutely attentive (perhaps too much so) to fine points. Percy is *punctilious* about observing the rules of etiquette whenever Miss Manners invites him to stay. punctiliousness, N.

pundit   N. authority on a subject; learned person; expert. Some authors who write about the GRE as if they are *pundits* actually know very little about the test.

■ **pungent**   ADJ. stinging; sharp in taste or smell; caustic. The *pungent* odor of ripe Limburger cheese appealed to Simone but made Stanley gag. pungency, N.

punitive   ADJ. punishing. He asked for *punitive* measures against the offender.

puny   ADJ. insignificant; tiny; weak. Our *puny* efforts to stop the flood were futile.

purchase   N. firm grasp or footing. The mountaineer struggled to get a proper *purchase* on the slippery rock.

purgatory   N. place of spiritual expiation. In this *purgatory*, he could expect no help from his comrades.

purge   V. remove or get rid of something unwanted; free from blame or guilt; cleanse or purify. The Communist government *purged* the party to get rid of members suspected of capitalist sympathies, sending those believed to be disloyal to labor camps in Siberia. also N.

purport N. intention; meaning. If the *purport* of your speech was to arouse the rabble, you succeeded admirably. also V.

purported ADJ. alleged; claimed; reputed or rumored. The *purported* Satanists sacrificing live roosters in the park turned out to be a party of Shriners holding a chicken barbecue.

purse V. pucker; contract into wrinkles. Miss Watson *pursed* her lips to show her disapproval of Huck's bedraggled appearance.

purveyor N. furnisher of foodstuffs; caterer. As *purveyor* of rare wines and viands, he traveled through France and Italy every year in search of new products to sell.

pusillanimous ADJ. cowardly; fainthearted. You should be ashamed of your *pusillanimous* conduct during this dispute. pusillanimity, N.

putative ADJ. supposed; reputed. Although there are some doubts, the *putative* author of this work is Massinger.

putrid ADJ. foul; rotten; decayed. When the doctor removed the bandages, the *putrid* smell indicated that the wound had turned gangrenous. putrescence, putrefaction, N.

pylon N. marking post to guide aviators; steel tower supporting cables or telephone lines. Amelia Earhart carefully banked her airplane as she followed the line of *pylons* set up to mark the course of the Great Plane Race.

pyromaniac N. person with an insane desire to set things on fire. The detectives searched the area for the *pyromaniac* who had set these costly fires.

quack N. charlatan; impostor. Do not be misled by the exorbitant claims of this *quack;* he cannot cure you.

quadruped N. four-footed animal. Most mammals are *quadrupeds.*

quaff V. drink with relish. As we *quaffed* our ale, we listened to the gay songs of the students in the tavern.

quagmire N. soft, wet, boggy land; complex or dangerous situation from which it is difficult to free oneself. Up to her knees in mud, Myra wondered how on earth she was going to extricate herself from this *quagmire.*

quail V. cower; lose heart. He was afraid that he would *quail* in the face of danger.

quaint ADJ. odd; old-fashioned; picturesque. Her *quaint* clothes and old-fashioned language marked her as an eccentric.

■ **qualified** ADJ. limited; restricted. Unable to give the candidate full support, the mayor gave him only a *qualified* endorsement. (secondary meaning)

qualms N. misgivings; uneasy fears, especially about matters of conscience. I have no *qualms* about giving this assignment to Helen; I know she will handle it admirably.

quandary N. dilemma. When both Harvard and Stanford accepted Laura, she was in a *quandary* as to which school she should attend.

quarantine N. isolation of a person, place, or ship to prevent spread of infection. We will have to place this house under *quarantine* until we determine the exact nature of the disease. also V.

quarry N. victim; object of a hunt. The police closed in on their *quarry.*

quarry V. dig into. They *quarried* blocks of marble out of the hillside.

Test

Word List 38   *Antonyms*

Each of the questions below consists of a word in capital letters, followed by five lettered words or phrases. Choose the lettered word or phrase that is most nearly opposite in meaning to the word in capital letters and write the letter of your choice on your answer paper.

556. PROPITIOUS (A) rich (B) induced (C) promoted (D) indicative (E) unfavorable

557. PROSAIC (A) pacified (B) reprieved (C) pensive (D) imaginative (E) rhetorical

558. PROTEAN (A) amateur (B) catholic (C) unchanging (D) rapid (E) unfavorable

559. PROTRACT (A) make circular (B) shorten (C) further (D) retrace (E) involve

560. PROVIDENT (A) unholy (B) rash (C) miserable (D) disabled (E) remote

561. PROVINCIAL (A) wealthy (B) crass (C) literary (D) aural (E) sophisticated

562. PSYCHOTIC (A) dangerous (B) clairvoyant (C) criminal (D) soulful (E) sane

563. PUERILE (A) fragrant (B) adult (C) lonely (D) feminine (E) masterly

564. PUGNACIOUS (A) pacific (B) feline (C) mature (D) angular (E) inactive

565. PUISSANT (A) pouring (B) fashionable (C) articulate (D) healthy (E) weak

566. PULCHRITUDE (A) ugliness (B) notoriety (C) bestiality (D) masculinity (E) servitude

567. PUNCTILIOUS (A) happy (B) active (C) vivid (D) careless (E) futile

568. PUNITIVE (A) large (B) humorous (C) rewarding (D) restive (E) languishing

569. PUSILLANIMOUS (A) poverty-stricken (B) chained (C) posthumous (D) courageous (E) strident

570. PUTATIVE (A) colonial (B) quarrelsome (C) undisputed (D) powerful (E) unremarkable

Word List 39   quash-recurrent

quash V. subdue; crush; squash. The authorities acted quickly to *quash* the student rebellion, sending in tanks to cow the demonstrators.

quay N. dock; landing place. Because of the captain's carelessness, the ship crashed into the *quay*.

queasy ADJ. easily nauseated; squeamish. Remember that great chase movie, the one with the carsick passenger? That's right: *Queasy Rider*!

quell V. extinguish; put down; quiet. Miss Minchin's demeanor was so stern and forbidding that she could *quell* any unrest among her students with one intimidating glance.

quench V. douse or extinguish; assuage or satisfy. What's the favorite song of the Fire Department? "Baby, *Quench* My Fire!" After Bob ate the heavily salted popcorn, he had to drink a pitcherful of water to *quench* his thirst.

querulous ADJ. fretful; whining. Even the most agreeable toddlers can begin to act *querulous* if they miss their nap.

query N. inquiry; question. In her column "Ask Beth," the columnist invites young readers to send their *queries* about life and love to her. also v.

queue N. line. They stood patiently in the *queue* outside the movie theatre.

■ **quibble** N. minor objection or complaint. Aside from a few hundred teensy-weensy *quibbles* about the set, the script, the actors, the director, the costumes, the lighting, and the props, the hypercritical critic loved the play. also v.

■ **quiescent** ADJ. at rest; dormant; temporarily inactive. After the devastating eruption, fear of Mount Etna was great; people did not return to cultivate its rich hillside lands until the volcano had been *quiescent* for a full two years. quiescence, N.

quietude N. tranquillity. He was impressed by the air of *quietude* and peace that pervaded the valley.

quintessence N. purest and highest embodiment. Noel Coward displayed the *quintessence* of wit.

quip N. taunt. You are unpopular because you are too free with your *quips* and sarcastic comments. also v.

quirk N. startling twist; caprice, By a *quirk* of fate, he found himself working for the man whom he had discharged years before.

quisling N. traitor who aids invaders. In his conquest of Europe, Hitler was aided by the *quislings* who betrayed their own people and served in the puppet governments established by the Nazis.

quiver N. case for arrows. Robin Hood reached back and plucked one last arrow from his *quiver*. (secondary meaning)

quiver V. tremble; shake. The bird dog's nose twitched and his whiskers *quivered* as he strained eagerly against the leash. also N.

quixotic ADJ. idealistic but impractical. Constantly coming up with *quixotic*, unworkable schemes to save the world, Simon has his heart in the right place, but his head is somewhere off in the clouds.

quizzical ADJ. teasing; bantering; mocking; curious. When the skinny teenager tripped over his own feet stepping into the bullpen, Coach raised one *quizzical* eyebrow, shook his head, and said, "Okay, kid. You're here; let's see what you've got."

quorum N. number of members necessary to conduct a meeting. The senator asked for a roll call to determine whether a *quorum* was present.

quotidian ADJ. daily; commonplace; customary. To Philip, each new day of his internship was filled with excitement; he could not dismiss his rounds as merely *quotidian* routine.

rabid ADJ. like a fanatic; furious. He was a *rabid* follower of the Dodgers and watched them play whenever he could go to the ballpark.

raconteur N. story-teller. My father was a gifted *raconteur* with an unlimited supply of anecdotes.

ragamuffin N. person wearing tattered clothes. He felt sorry for the *ragamuffin* who was begging for food and gave him money to buy a meal.

rail V. scold; rant. You may *rail* at him all you want; you will never change him.

raiment N. clothing. "How can I go to the ball?" asked Cinderella. "I have no *raiment* fit to wear."

rakish ADJ. stylish; sporty. He wore his hat at a *rakish* and jaunty angle.

rally V. call up or summon (forces, vital powers, etc.); revive or recuperate. Washington quickly *rallied* his troops to fight off the British attack. The patient had been sinking throughout the night, but at dawn she *rallied* and made a complete recovery. also N.

ramble V. wander aimlessly (physically or mentally). Listening to the teacher *ramble*, Judy wondered whether he'd ever get to his point. also N.

ramification N. branching out; subdivision. We must examine all the *ramifications* of this problem.

ramify V. divide into branches or subdivisions. When the plant begins to *ramify*, it is advisable to nip off most of the new branches.

ramp N. slope; inclined plane. The house was built with *ramps* instead of stairs in order to enable the man in the wheelchair to move easily from room to room and floor to floor.

rampant ADJ. growing in profusion; unrestrained. The *rampant* weeds in the garden choked the asters and marigolds until the flowers died. rampancy, N.

rampart N. defensive mound of earth. "From the *ramparts* we watched" as the fighting continued.

ramshackle ADJ. rickety; falling apart. The boys propped up the *ramshackle* clubhouse with a couple of boards.

rancid ADJ. having the odor of stale fat. A *rancid* odor filled the ship's galley and nauseated the crew.

rancor N. bitterness; hatred. Thirty years after the war, she could not let go of the past but was still consumed with *rancor* against the foe. rancorous, ADJ.

random ADJ. without definite purpose, plan, or aim; haphazard. Although the sponsor of the raffle claimed all winners were chosen at *random,* people had their suspicions when the grand prize went to the sponsor's brother-in-law.

rankle V. irritate; fester. The memory of having been jilted *rankled* him for years.

rant V. rave; talk excitedly; scold; make a grandiloquent speech. When he heard that I'd totaled the family car, Dad began to *rant* at me like a complete madman.

rapacious ADJ. excessively grasping; plundering. Hawks and other *rapacious* birds prey on a variety of small animals.

rapport N. emotional closeness; harmony. In team teaching, it is important that all teachers in the group have good *rapport* with one another.

rapt ADJ. absorbed; enchanted. Caught up in the wonder of the storyteller's tale, the *rapt* listeners sat motionless, hanging on his every word.

■ **rarefied** ADJ. made less dense [of a gas]. The mountain climbers had difficulty breathing in the *rarefied* atmosphere. rarefy, V. rarefaction, N.

raspy ADJ. grating; harsh. The sergeant's *raspy* voice grated on the recruits' ears.

ratify V. approve formally; confirm; verify. Party leaders doubted that they had enough votes in both houses of Congress to *ratify* the constitutional amendment.

ratiocination N. reasoning; act of drawing conclusions from premises. While Watson was a man of average intelligence, Holmes was a genius, whose gift for *ratiocination* made him a superb detective.

rationale N. fundamental reason or justification; grounds for an action. Her need for a vehicle large enough to accommodate five children and a Saint Bernard was Judy's *rationale* for buying a minivan.

rationalize V. give a plausible reason for an action in place of a true, less admirable one; offer an excuse. When David refused gabby Gabrielle a ride to the dance because, he said, he had no room in the car, he was *rationalizing*; actually, he couldn't stand being cooped up in a car with anyone who talked as much as she did. rationalization, N.

raucous ADJ. harsh and shrill; disorderly and boisterous. The *raucous* crowd of New Year's Eve revelers grew progressively noisier as midnight drew near.

ravage V. plunder; despoil. The marauding army *ravaged* the countryside.

rave N. overwhelmingly favorable review. Though critic John Simon seldom has a good word to say about contemporary plays, his review of *All in the Timing* was a total *rave.*

ravel V. fall apart into tangles; unravel or untwist; entangle. A single thread pulled loose, and the entire scarf started to *ravel.*

ravenous ADJ. extremely hungry. The *ravenous* dog upset several garbage pails in its search for food.

ravine N. narrow valley with steep sides. Steeper than a gully, less precipitous than a canyon, a *ravine* is, like them, the product of years of erosion.

raze V. destroy completely. Spelling matters: to raise a building is to put it up; to *raze* a building is to tear it down.

reactionary ADJ. opposing progress; politically ultraconservative. Opposing the use of English in worship services, *reactionary* forces in the church fought to reinstate the mass in Latin. also N.

realm N. kingdom; field or sphere. In the animal *realm*, the lion is the king of beasts.

reaper N. one who harvests grain. Death, the Grim *Reaper,* cuts down mortal men and women, just as a farmer cuts down the ripened grain.

rebate N. discount. We offer a *rebate* of ten percent to those who pay cash.

rebuff V. snub; beat back. She *rebuffed* his invitation so smoothly that he did not realize he had been snubbed. also N.

rebuke V. scold harshly; criticize severely. No matter how sharply Miss Watson *rebuked* Huck for his misconduct, he never talked back but just stood there like a stump. also N.

rebus N. puzzle in which pictures stand for words. A coven of witches beside a tree is a possible *rebus* for the town Coventry.

rebuttal N. refutation; response with contrary evidence. The defense lawyer confidently listened to the prosecutor sum up his case, sure that she could answer his arguments in her *rebuttal.*

■ **recalcitrant** ADJ. obstinately stubborn; determined to resist authority; unruly. Which animal do you think is more *recalcitrant*, a pig or a mule?

■ **recant** V. disclaim or disavow; retract a previous statement; openly confess error. Hoping to make Joan of Arc *recant* her sworn testimony, her English captors tried to convince her that her visions had been sent to her by the Devil.

recapitulate V. summarize. Let us *recapitulate* what has been said thus far before going ahead.

recast V. reconstruct (a sentence, story, etc.); fashion again. Let me *recast* this sentence in terms your feeble brain can grasp: in words of one syllable, you are a fool.

receptive ADJ. quick or willing to receive ideas, suggestions, etc. Adventure-loving Huck Finn proved a *receptive* audience for Tom's tales of buried treasure and piracy.

recession N. withdrawal; retreat; time of low economic activity. The slow *recession* of the flood waters created problems for the crews working to restore power to the area.

recidivism N. habitual return to crime. Prison reformers in the United States are disturbed by the high rate of *recidi-*

vism; the number of persons serving second and third terms indicates the failure of the prisons to rehabilitate the inmates.

recipient N. receiver. Although he had been the *recipient* of many favors, he was not grateful to his benefactor.

reciprocal ADJ. mutual; exchangeable; interacting. The two nations signed a *reciprocal* trade agreement.

reciprocate V. repay in kind. If they attack us, we shall be compelled to *reciprocate* and bomb their territory. reciprocity, N.

■ **recluse** N. hermit; loner. Disappointed in love, Miss Emily became a *recluse*; she shut herself away in her empty mansion and refused to see another living soul. reclusive, ADJ.

reconcile V. correct inconsistencies; become friendly after a quarrel. Every time we try to *reconcile* our checkbook with the bank statement, we quarrel. However, despite these monthly lovers' quarrels, we always manage to *reconcile.*

■ **recondite** ADJ. abstruse; profound; secret. He read many *recondite* books in order to obtain the material for his scholarly thesis.

reconnaissance N. survey of enemy by soldiers; reconnoitering. If you encounter any enemy soldiers during your *reconnaissance,* capture them for questioning.

recount V. narrate or tell; count over again. About to *recount* the latest adventure of Sherlock Holmes, Watson lost track of exactly how many cases Holmes had solved and refused to begin his tale until he'd *recounted* them one by one.

recourse N. resorting to help when in trouble. The boy's only *recourse* was to appeal to his father for aid.

recrimination N. countercharges. Loud and angry *recriminations* were her answer to his accusations.

rectify V. set right; correct. You had better send a check to *rectify* your account before American Express cancels your credit card.

rectitude N. uprightness; moral virtue; correctness of judgment. The Eagle Scout was a model of *rectitude*; smugness was the only flaw he needed to correct.

recumbent ADJ. reclining; lying down completely or in part. The command "AT EASE" does not permit you to take a *recumbent* position.

recuperate V. recover. The doctors were worried because the patient did not *recuperate* as rapidly as they had expected.

recurrent ADJ. occurring again and again. These *recurrent* attacks disturbed us and we consulted a physician.

Test

Word List 39   *Synonyms and Antonyms*

Each of the questions below consists of a word in capital letters, followed by five lettered words or phrases. Choose the lettered word or phrase that is most nearly similar or opposite in meaning to the word in capital letters and write the letter of your choice on your answer paper.

571. QUEASY (A) toxic (B) easily upset (C) chronic (D) choleric (E) false

572. QUELL (A) boast (B) incite (C) reverse (D) wet (E) answer

573. QUIXOTIC (A) rapid (B) exotic (C) longing (D) timid (E) idealistic

574. RAGAMUFFIN (A) dandy (B) miser (C) exotic dance (D) light snack (E) baker

575. RAUCOUS (A) mellifluous (B) uncooked (C) realistic (D) veracious (E) anticipating

576. RAVAGE (A) rankle (B) revive (C) plunder (D) pillory (E) age

577. RAZE (A) shave (B) heckle (C) finish (D) tear down (E) write

578. REACTIONARY (A) conservative (B) retrograde (C) dramatist (D) militant (E) chemical

579. REBATE (A) relinquish (B) settle (C) discount (D) cancel (E) elicit

580. RECALCITRANT (A) grievous (B) secretive (C) cowardly (D) thoughtful (E) cooperative

581. RECLUSE (A) learned scholar (B) mocker (C) social person (D) careful worker (E) daredevil

582. RECONDITE (A) unfriendly (B) easily comprehensible (C) closely juxtaposed (D) broadminded (E) sardonic

583. RECTIFY (A) remedy (B) avenge (C) create (D) assemble (E) attribute

584. RECUPERATE (A) reenact (B) engage (C) recapitulate (D) recover (E) encounter

585. RECURRENT (A) happening repeatedly (B) flowing backward (C) healing quickly (D) eventful (E) timely

Word List 40   redolent-requite

redolent ADJ. fragrant; odorous; suggestive of an odor. Even though it is February, the air is *redolent* of spring.

redoubtable ADJ. formidable; causing fear. During the Cold War period, neighboring countries tried not to offend the Russians because they could be *redoubtable* foes.

redress N. remedy; compensation. Do you mean to tell me that I can get no *redress* for my injuries? also V.

redundant ADJ. superfluous; repetitious; excessively wordy. The bottle of wine I brought to Bob's party was certainly *redundant*: how was I to know Bob owned a winery? In your essay, you repeat several points unnecessarily; try to avoid *redundancy* in the future.

reek V. emit (odor). The room *reeked* with stale tobacco smoke. also N.

refectory N. dining hall. In this huge *refectory*, we can feed the entire student body at one sitting.

refraction N. bending of a ray of light. When you look at a stick inserted in water, it looks bent because of the *refraction* of the light by the water.

■ **refractory** ADJ. stubborn; unmanageable. The *refractory* horse was eliminated from the race when he refused to obey the jockey.

refrain V. abstain from; resist. N. chorus. Whenever he heard a song with a lively chorus, Sol could never *refrain* from joining in on the *refrain*.

refulgent ADJ. brightly shining; gleaming. The squire polished the knight's armor until it gleamed in the light like the *refulgent* moon.

refurbish V. renovate; make bright by polishing. The flood left a deposit of mud on everything; it was necessary to *refurbish* our belongings.

■ **refute** V. disprove. The defense called several respectable witnesses who were able to *refute* the lying testimony of the prosecution's sole witness. refutation, N.

regal ADJ. royal. Prince Albert had a *regal* manner.

regale V. entertain. John *regaled* us with tales of his adventures in Africa.

regatta N. boat or yacht race. Many boating enthusiasts followed the *regatta* in their own yachts.

regeneration N. spiritual rebirth. Modern penologists strive for the *regeneration* of the prisoners.

regicide N. murder of a king or queen. The beheading of Mary Queen of Scots was an act of *regicide*.

regime N. method or system of government. When a Frenchman mentions the Old *Regime*, he refers to the government existing before the revolution.

regimen N. prescribed diet and habits. I doubt whether the results warrant our living under such a strict *regimen*.

rehabilitate V. restore to proper condition. We must *rehabilitate* those whom we send to prison.

reimburse V. repay. Let me know what you have spent and I will *reimburse* you.

reiterate V. repeat. She *reiterated* the warning to make sure everyone understood it.

rejoinder N. retort; comeback; reply. When someone has been rude to me, I find it particularly satisfying to come up with a quick *rejoinder*.

rejuvenate V. make young again. The charlatan claimed that his elixir would *rejuvenate* the aged and weary.

■ **relegate** V. banish to an inferior position; delegate; assign. After Ralph dropped his second tray of drinks that week, the manager swiftly *relegated* him to a minor post cleaning up behind the bar.

relent V. give in. When her stern father would not *relent* and allow her to marry Robert Browning, Elizabeth Barrett eloped with her suitor. relentless, ADJ.

relevant ADJ. pertinent; referring to the case in hand. Teri was impressed by how *relevant* Virginia Woolf's remarks were to her as a woman writer; it was as if Woolf had been writing with Teri's situation in mind. relevance, N. relevancy, N.

relic N. surviving remnant; memento. Egypt's Department of Antiquities prohibits tourists from taking mummies and other ancient *relics* out of the country. Mike keeps his photos of his trip to Egypt in a box with other *relics* of his travels.

relinquish V. give up something with reluctance; yield. Once you get used to fringe benefits like expense-account meals and a company car, it's very hard to *relinquish* them.

relish V. savor; enjoy. Watching Peter enthusiastically chow down, I thought, "Now there's a man who *relishes* a good dinner!" also N.

remediable ADJ. reparable. Let us be grateful that the damage is *remediable*.

reminiscence N. recollection. Her *reminiscences* of her experiences are so fascinating that she ought to write a book.

remiss ADJ. negligent. When the prisoner escaped, the guard was accused of being *remiss* in his duty.

remission N. temporary moderation of disease symptoms; cancellation of a debt; forgiveness or pardon. Though Senator Tsongas had been treated for cancer, his symptoms were in *remission*, and he was considered fit to handle the strains of a presidential race.

remnant N. remainder. I suggest that you wait until the store places the *remnants* of these goods on sale.

remonstrance N. protest; objection. The authorities were deaf to the pastor's *remonstrances* about the lack of police protection in the area. remonstrate, V.

remorse N. guilt; self-reproach. The murderer felt no *remorse* for his crime.

remunerative ADJ. compensating; rewarding. I find my new work so *remunerative* that I may not return to my previous employment. remuneration, N.

rend   v. split; tear apart. In his grief, he tried to *rend* his garments. rent, N.

render   v. deliver; provide; represent. He *rendered* aid to the needy and indigent.

rendezvous   N. meeting place. The two fleets met at the *rendezvous* at the appointed time. also v.

rendition   N. translation; artistic interpretation of a song, etc. The audience cheered enthusiastically as she completed her *rendition* of the aria.

renegade   N. deserter; traitor. Because he had abandoned his post and joined forces with the Indians, his fellow officers considered the hero of *Dances with Wolves* a *renegade*. also ADJ.

renege   v. deny; go back on. He *reneged* on paying off his debt.

renounce   v. abandon; disown; repudiate. Even though she knew she would be burned at the stake as a witch, Joan of Arc refused to *renounce* her belief that her voices came from God. renunciation, N.

renovate   v. restore to good condition; renew. They claim that they can *renovate* worn shoes so that they look like new ones.

renown   N. fame. For many years an unheralded researcher, Barbara McClintock gained international *renown* when she won the Nobel Prize in Physiology and Medicine. renowned, ADJ.

rent   N. rip; split. Kit did an excellent job of mending the *rent* in the lining of her coat. rend, v.

reparable   ADJ. capable of being repaired. Fortunately, the damages we suffered in the accident were *reparable* and our car looks brand new.

reparation   N. amends; compensation. At the peace conference, the defeated country promised to pay *reparations* to the victors.

repartee   N. clever reply. He was famous for his witty *repartee* and his sarcasm.

repast   N. meal; feast; banquet. The caterers prepared a delicious *repast* for Fred and Judy's wedding day.

repeal   v. revoke; annul. What would the effect on our society be if we decriminalized drug use by *repealing* the laws against the possession and sale of narcotics?

repel   v. drive away; disgust. At first, the Beast's ferocious appearance *repelled* Beauty, but she came to love the tender heart hidden behind that beastly exterior.

repellent   ADJ. driving away; unattractive. Mosquitoes find the odor so *repellent* that they leave any spot where this liquid has been sprayed. also N.

repercussion   N. rebound; reverberation; reaction. I am afraid that this event will have serious *repercussions*.

repertoire   N. list of works of music, drama, etc., a performer is prepared to present. The opera company decided to include *Madame Butterfly* in its *repertoire* for the following season.

repine   v. fret; complain. There is no sense *repining* over the work you have left undone.

replenish   v. fill up again. Before she could take another backpacking trip, Carla had to *replenish* her stock of freeze-dried foods.

replete   ADJ. filled to the brim or to the point of being stuffed; abundantly supplied. The movie star's memoir was *replete* with juicy details about the love life of half of Hollywood.

replica   N. copy. Are you going to hang this *replica* of the Declaration of Independence in the classroom or in the auditorium?

replicate   v. reproduce; duplicate. Because he had always wanted a palace, Donald decided to *replicate* the Taj Mahal in miniature on his estate.

repository   N. storehouse. Libraries are *repositories* of the world's best thoughts.

reprehensible   ADJ. deserving blame. Shocked by the viciousness of the bombing, politicians of every party uniformly condemned the terrorists' *reprehensible* deed.

repress   v. restrain; crush; oppress. Anne's parents tried to curb her impetuosity without *repressing* her boundless high spirits.

reprieve   N. temporary stay. During the twenty-four-hour *reprieve*, the lawyers sought to make the stay of execution permanent. also v.

reprimand   N. strong rebuke; formal reproof; scolding. Every time Ermengarde made a mistake in class, she was terrified that she would receive a harsh *reprimand* from Miss Minchin.

reprisal   N. retaliation. I am confident that we are ready for any *reprisals* the enemy may undertake.

reprise   N. musical repetition; repeat performance; recurrent action. We enjoyed the soprano's solo in Act I so much that we were delighted by its *reprise* in the finale. At Waterloo, it was not the effect of any one skirmish that exhausted Colonel Audley; rather, it was the cumulative effect of the constant *reprises* that left him spent.

■ **reproach**   v. express disapproval or disappointment. He never could do anything wrong without imagining how the look on his mother's face would *reproach* him afterwards. also N. reproachful, ADJ.

■ **reprobate**   N. person hardened in sin, devoid of a sense of decency. I cannot understand why he has so many admirers if he is the *reprobate* you say he is.

reprobation   N. severe disapproval. The students showed their *reprobation* of his act by refusing to talk with him.

reprove   v. censure; rebuke. Though Aunt Bea at times would *reprove* Opie for inattention in church, she believed he was at heart a God-fearing lad. reproof, N.

■ **repudiate**   v. disown; disavow. On separating from Tony, Tina announced that she would *repudiate* all debts incurred by her soon-to-be ex-husband.

repugnance   N. loathing. She looked at the snake with *repugnance*.

repulsion   N. distaste; act of driving back. Hating bloodshed, she viewed war with *repulsion*. Even defensive battles distressed her, for the *repulsion* of enemy forces is never accomplished bloodlessly. repulse, v.

reputable   ADJ. respectable. If you want to buy antiques, look for a *reputable* dealer; far too many dealers today pass off fakes as genuine antiques.

reputed   ADJ. supposed. He is the *reputed* father of the child. repute, V. repute, N.

requiem   N. mass for the dead; dirge. They played Mozart's *Requiem* at the funeral.

requisite   N. necessary requirement. Many colleges state that a student must offer three years of a language as a *requisite* for admission.

requite   V. repay; revenge. The wretch *requited* his benefactors by betraying them.

Test

Word List 40   *Synonyms*

Each of the questions below consists of a word in capital letters, followed by five lettered words or phrases. Choose the lettered word or phrase that is most nearly similar in meaning to the word in capital letters and write the letter of your choice on your answer paper.

586. REFRACTORY (A) articulate (B) sinkable
     (C) vaunted (D) useless (E) unmanageable

587. REGAL (A) oppressive (B) royal (C) major
     (D) basic (E) entertaining

588. REITERATE (A) gainsay (B) revive (C) revenge
     (D) repeat (E) return

589. RELISH (A) desire (B) nibble (C) savor
     (D) vindicate (E) avail

590. REMISS (A) lax (B) lost (C) foolish (D) violating
     (E) ambitious

591. REMONSTRATE (A) display (B) restate (C) protest
     (D) resign (E) reiterate

592. REPARTEE (A) witty retort (B) willful departure
     (C) spectator (D) monologue (E) sacrifice

593. REPELLENT (A) propulsive (B) unattractive
     (C) porous (D) stiff (E) elastic

594. REPERCUSSION (A) reaction (B) restitution
     (C) resistance (D) magnificence (E) acceptance

595. REPLENISH (A) polish (B) repeat (C) reinstate
     (D) refill (E) refuse

596. REPLICA (A) museum piece (B) famous site
     (C) battle emblem (D) facsimile (E) replacement

597. REPRISAL (A) reevaluation (B) assessment
     (C) loss (D) retaliation (E) nonsense

598. REPROVE (A) prevail (B) rebuke (C) ascertain
     (D) prove false (E) draw back

599. REPUDIATE (A) besmirch (B) appropriate
     (C) annoy (D) reject (E) avow

600. REPUGNANCE (A) belligerence (B) tenacity
     (C) renewal (D) pity (E) loathing

Word List 41   rescind-sacrosanct

■ rescind   V. cancel. Because of the public outcry against the new taxes, the senator proposed a bill to *rescind* the unpopular financial measure.

resentment   N. indignation; bitterness; displeasure. Not wanting to appear a sore loser, Bill tried to hide his *resentment* of Barry's success.

reserve   N. self-control; formal but distant manner. Although some girls were attracted by Mark's *reserve*, Judy was put off by it, for she felt his aloofness indicated a lack of openness. reserved, ADJ.

residue   N. remainder; balance. In his will, he requested that after payment of debts, taxes, and funeral expenses, the *residue* be given to his wife.

resignation   N. patient submissiveness; statement that one is quitting a job. If Bob Cratchit had not accepted Scrooge's bullying with timid *resignation,* he might have gotten up the nerve to hand in his *resignation*. resigned, ADJ.

resilient   ADJ. elastic; having the power of springing back. Highly *resilient,* steel makes excellent bedsprings. resilience, N.

■ resolution   N. determination. Nothing could shake his *resolution* to succeed despite all difficulties. resolute, ADJ.

■ resolve   N. determination; firmness of purpose. How dare you question my *resolve* to take up sky-diving! Of course I haven't changed my mind! also V.

resolve   V. decide; settle; solve. Holmes *resolved* to travel to Bohemia to resolve the dispute between Irene Adler and the King.

resonant   ADJ. echoing; resounding; deep and full in sound. The deep, *resonant* voice of the actor James Earl Jones makes him particularly effective when he appears on stage.

respiration   N. breathing; exhalation. The doctor found that the patient's years of smoking had adversely affected both his lung capacity and his rate of *respiration*.

respite   N. interval of relief; time for rest; delay in punishment. For David, the two weeks vacationing in New Zealand were a delightful *respite* from the pressures of his job.

resplendent ADJ. dazzling; glorious; brilliant. While all the adults were commenting how glorious the emperor looked in his *resplendent* new clothes, one little boy was heard to say, "But he's naked!"

responsiveness N. state of reacting readily to appeals, orders, etc. The audience cheered and applauded, delighting the performers by its *responsiveness*.

restitution N. reparation; indemnification. He offered to make *restitution* for the window broken by his son.

restive ADJ. restlessly impatient; obstinately resisting control. Waiting impatiently in line to see Santa Claus, even the best-behaved children grow *restive* and start to fidget.

restraint N. moderation or self-control; controlling force; restriction. Show some *restraint,* young lady! Three desserts is quite enough!

resumption N. taking up again; recommencement. During the summer break, Don had not realized how much he missed university life: at the *resumption* of classes, however, he felt marked excitement and pleasure. resume, V.

resurge V. rise again; flow to and fro. It was startling to see the spirit of nationalism *resurge* as the Soviet Union disintegrated into a loose federation of ethnic and national groups. resurgence, N. resurgent, ADJ.

resuscitate V. revive. The lifeguard tried to *resuscitate* the drowned child by applying artificial respiration.

retain V. keep; employ. Fighting to *retain* his seat in Congress, Senator Foghorn *retained* a new manager to head his reelection campaign.

retaliation V. repayment in kind (usually for bad treatment). Because everyone knew the Princeton band had stolen Brown's mascot, the whole Princeton student body expected some sort of *retaliation* from Brown. retaliate, V.

retentive ADJ. holding; having a good memory. The pupil did not need to spend much time in study as he had a *retentive* mind.

■ **reticent** ADJ. reserved; uncommunicative; inclined to silence. Fearing his competitors might get advance word about his plans from talkative staff members, Hughes preferred *reticent* employees to loquacious ones. reticence, N.

retinue N. following; attendants. The queen's *retinue* followed her down the aisle.

retiring ADJ. modest; shy. Given Susan's *retiring* personality, no one expected her to take up public speaking; surprisingly enough, she became a star of the school debate team.

retort N. quick, sharp reply. Even when it was advisable for her to keep her mouth shut, she was always ready with a *retort*. also V.

retract V. withdraw; take back. When I saw how Fred and his fraternity brothers had trashed the frat house, I decided to *retract* my offer to let them use our summer cottage for the weekend. retraction, N.

retrench V. cut down; economize. If they were to be able to send their children to college, they would have to *retrench*.

retribution N. vengeance; compensation; punishment for offenses. The evangelist maintained that an angry deity would exact *retribution* from the sinners.

retrieve V. recover; find and bring in. The dog was intelligent and quickly learned to *retrieve* the game killed by the hunter. retrieval, N.

retroactive ADJ. taking effect before its enactment (as a law) or imposition (as a tax). Because the new pension law was *retroactive* to the first of the year, even though Martha had retired in February she was eligible for the pension.

retrograde V. go backwards; degenerate. Instead of advancing, our civilization seems to have *retrograded* in ethics and culture. also ADJ.

retrospective ADJ. looking back on the past. The Museum of Graphic Arts is holding a *retrospective* showing of the paintings of Michael Whelan over the past two decades. also N. retrospection, N.

revelry N. boisterous merrymaking. New Year's Eve is a night of *revelry*.

reverberate V. echo; resound. The entire valley *reverberated* with the sound of the church bells.

■ **reverent** ADJ. respectful; worshipful. Though I bow my head in church and recite the prayers, sometimes I don't feel properly *reverent*. revere, V. reverence, N.

reverie N. daydream; musing. She was awakened from her *reverie* by the teacher's question.

revert V. relapse; backslide; turn back to. Most of the time Andy seemed sensitive and mature, but occasionally he would *revert* to his smart-alecky, macho, adolescent self. reversion, N.

revile V. attack with abusive language; vilify. Though most of his contemporaries *reviled* Captain Kidd as a notorious, bloody-handed pirate, some of his fellow merchant-captains believed him innocent of his alleged crimes.

revoke V. cancel; retract. Repeat offenders who continue to drive under the influence of alcohol face having their driver's licenses permanently *revoked*. revocation, N.

revulsion N. sudden violent change of feeling; negative reaction. Many people in this country who admired dictatorships underwent a *revulsion* when they realized what Hitler and Mussolini were trying to do.

rhapsodize V. to speak or write in an exaggeratedly enthusiastic manner. She greatly enjoyed her Hawaiian vacation and *rhapsodized* about it for weeks.

rhetoric N. art of effective communication; insincere or grandiloquent language. All writers, by necessity, must be skilled in *rhetoric*. rhetorical, ADJ.

ribald ADJ. wanton; profane. He sang a *ribald* song that offended many of the more prudish listeners. ribaldry, N.

riddle V. pierce with holes; permeate or spread throughout. With his machine gun, Tracy *riddled* the car with bullets till it looked like a slice of Swiss cheese. During the proofreaders' strike, the newspaper was *riddled* with typos.

rider N. amendment or clause added to a legislative bill. Senator Foghorn said he would support Senator Filibuster's tax reform bill only if Filibuster agreed to add an antipollution *rider* to the bill.

rife ADJ. abundant; current. In the face of the many rumors of scandal, which are *rife* at the moment, it is best to remain silent.

rift N. opening; break. The plane was lost in the stormy sky until the pilot saw the city through a *rift* in the clouds.

rig V. fix or manipulate. The ward boss was able to *rig* the election by bribing people to stuff the ballot boxes with ballots marked in his candidate's favor.

rigid ADJ. stiff and unyielding; strict; hard and unbending. By living with a man to whom she was not married, George Eliot broke Victorian society's most *rigid* rule of respectable behavior.

rigor N. severity. Many settlers could not stand the *rigors* of the New England winters.

rile V. vex; irritate; muddy. Red had a hair-trigger temper: he was an easy man to *rile*.

riveting ADJ. absorbing; engrossing. The reviewer described Byatt's novel *Possession* as a *riveting* tale: absorbed in the story, she had finished it in a single evening.

rivulet N. small stream. As the rains continued, the trickle of water running down the hillside grew into a *rivulet* that threatened to wash away a portion of the slope.

robust ADJ. vigorous; strong. After pumping iron and taking karate for six months, the little old lady was far more *robust* in health and could break a plank with her fist.

rococo ADJ. ornate; highly decorated. The *rococo* style in furniture and architecture, marked by scrollwork and excessive decoration, flourished during the middle of the eighteenth century.

roil V. to make liquids murky by stirring up sediment; to disturb. Be careful when you pour not to *roil* the wine; if you stir up the sediment you'll destroy the flavor.

roseate ADJ. rosy; optimistic. I am afraid you will have to alter your *roseate* views in the light of the distressing news that has just arrived.

roster N. list. They print the *roster* of players in the season's program.

rostrum N. platform for speech-making; pulpit. The crowd murmured angrily and indicated that they did not care to listen to the speaker who was approaching the *rostrum*.

rote N. repetition. He recited the passage by *rote* and gave no indication he understood what he was saying. also ADJ.

rotunda N. circular building or hall covered with a dome. His body lay in state in the *rotunda* of the Capitol.

rotundity N. roundness; sonorousness of speech. Washington Irving emphasized the *rotundity* of the governor by describing his height and circumference.

rousing ADJ. lively; stirring. "And now, let's have a *rousing* welcome for TV's own Rosie O'Donnell, who'll lead us in a *rousing* rendition of 'The Star-Spangled Banner.'"

rout V. stampede; drive out. The reinforcements were able to *rout* the enemy. also N.

rubble N. fragments. Ten years after World War II, some of the *rubble* left by enemy bombings could still be seen.

rubric N. title or heading (in red print); directions for religious ceremony; protocol. In ordaining the new priests, the bishop carefully observed all the *rubrics* for the ordination service.

ruddy ADJ. reddish; healthy-looking. Santa Claus's *ruddy* cheeks nicely complement Rudolph the Reindeer's bright red nose.

rudimentary ADJ. not developed; elementary; crude. Although my grandmother's English vocabulary was limited to a few *rudimentary* phrases, she always could make herself understood.

rue V. regret; lament; mourn. Tina *rued* the night she met Tony and wondered how she ever fell for such a jerk. also N. rueful, ADJ.

ruffian N. bully; scoundrel. The *ruffians* threw stones at the police.

ruminate V. chew over and over (mentally or, like cows, physically); mull over; ponder. Unable to digest quickly the baffling events of the day, Reuben *ruminated* about them till four in the morning.

rummage V. ransack; thoroughly search. When we *rummaged* through the trunks in the attic, we found many souvenirs of our childhood days. also N.

runic ADJ. mysterious; set down in an ancient alphabet. Tolkien's use of Old English words and inscriptions in the *runic* alphabet give *The Lord of the Rings* its atmosphere of antiquity.

ruse N. trick; stratagem. You will not be able to fool your friends with such an obvious *ruse*.

rustic ADJ. pertaining to country people; uncouth. The backwoodsman looked out of place in his *rustic* attire.

rusticate V. banish to the country; dwell in the country. I like city life so much that I can never understand how people can *rusticate* in the suburbs.

ruthless ADJ. pitiless; cruel. Captain Hook was a dangerous, *ruthless* villain who would stop at nothing to destroy Peter Pan.

saboteur N. one who commits sabotage; destroyer of property. Members of the Resistance acted as *saboteurs*, blowing up train lines to prevent supplies from reaching the Nazi army.

saccharine ADJ. cloyingly sweet. She tried to ingratiate herself, speaking sweetly and smiling a *saccharine* smile.

sacrilegious ADJ. desecrating; profane. His stealing of the altar cloth was a very *sacrilegious* act.

sacrosanct ADJ. most sacred; inviolable. The brash insurance salesman invaded the *sacrosanct* privacy of the office of the president of the company.

Test

Word List 41   *Antonyms*

Each of the questions below consists of a word in capital letters, followed by five lettered words or phrases. Choose the lettered word or phrase that is most nearly opposite in meaning to the word in capital letters and write the letter of your choice on your answer paper.

601. RESILIENT (A) pungent (B) foolish (C) worthy (D) insolent (E) unyielding

602. RESTIVE (A) buoyant (B) placid (C) remorseful (D) resistant (E) retiring

603. RETENTIVE (A) forgetful (B) accepting (C) repetitive (D) avoiding (E) fascinating

604. RETICENCE (A) fatigue (B) fashion (C) treachery (D) loquaciousness (E) magnanimity

605. RETROGRADE (A) progressing (B) inclining (C) evaluating (D) concentrating (E) directing

606. REVERE (A) advance (B) dishonor (C) age (D) precede (E) wake

607. RIFE (A) direct (B) scant (C) peaceful (D) grim (E) mature

608. ROBUST (A) weak (B) violent (C) vicious (D) villainous (E) hungry

609. ROTUNDITY (A) promenade (B) nave (C) grotesqueness (D) slimness (E) impropriety

610. RUBBLE (A) artificial facade (B) unbroken stone (C) pale complexion (D) strong defense (E) glib answer

611. RUDDY (A) robust (B) witty (C) wan (D) exotic (E) creative

612. RUDIMENTARY (A) pale (B) polite (C) asinine (D) developed (E) quiescent

613. RUEFUL (A) trite (B) content (C) capable (D) capital (E) zealous

614. RUSTIC (A) urban (B) slow (C) corroded (D) mercenary (E) civilian

615. RUTHLESS (A) merciful (B) majestic (C) mighty (D) militant (E) maximum

Word List 42   sadistic-sepulcher

sadistic ADJ. inclined to cruelty. If we are to improve conditions in this prison, we must first get rid of the *sadistic* warden. sadism, N.

saga N. Scandinavian myth; any legend. This is a *saga* of the sea and the men who risk their lives on it.

sagacious ADJ. perceptive; shrewd; having insight. My father was a *sagacious* judge of character: he could spot a phony a mile away. sagacity, N.

■ **sage** N. person celebrated for wisdom. Hearing tales of a mysterious Master of All Knowledge who lived in the hills of Tibet, Sandy was possessed with a burning desire to consult the legendary *sage*. also ADJ.

salacious ADJ. lascivious; lustful. Chaucer's monk is not pious but *salacious*, a teller of lewd tales and ribald jests.

salient ADJ. prominent. One of the *salient* features of that newspaper is its excellent editorial page.

saline ADJ. salty. The slightly *saline* taste of this mineral water is pleasant.

sallow ADJ. yellowish; sickly in color. We were disturbed by her *sallow* complexion, which was due to jaundice.

■ **salubrious** ADJ. healthful. Many people with hay fever move to more *salubrious* sections of the country during the months of August and September.

salutary ADJ. tending to improve; beneficial; wholesome. The punishment had a *salutary* effect on the boy, as he became a model student.

salvage V. rescue from loss. All attempts to *salvage* the wrecked ship failed. also N.

sanctimonious ADJ. displaying ostentatious or hypocritical devoutness. You do not have to be so *sanctimonious* to prove that you are devout.

■ **sanction** V. approve; ratify. Nothing will convince me to *sanction* the engagement of my daughter to such a worthless young man.

sanctuary N. refuge; shelter; shrine; holy place. The tiny attic was Helen's *sanctuary* to which she fled when she had to get away from her bickering parents and brothers.

sanguinary ADJ. bloody. The battle of Iwo Jima was unexpectedly *sanguinary*, with many casualties.

sanguine ADJ. cheerful; hopeful. Let us not be too *sanguine* about the outcome; something could go wrong.

sap V. diminish; undermine. The element kryptonite had an unhealthy effect on Superman: it *sapped* his strength.

sarcasm N. scornful remark; stinging rebuke. Though Ralph pretended to ignore the mocking comments of his supposed friends, their *sarcasm* wounded him deeply. sarcastic, ADJ.

sardonic ADJ. disdainful; sarcastic; cynical. The *sardonic* humor of nightclub comedians who satirize or ridicule patrons in the audience strikes some people as amusing and others as rude.

sartorial ADJ. pertaining to tailors. He was as famous for the *sartorial* splendor of his attire as he was for his acting.

sate V. satisfy to the full; cloy. Its hunger *sated*, the lion dozed.

satellite   N. small body revolving around a larger one. During the first few years of the Space Age, hundreds of *satellites* were launched by Russia and the United States.

■ **satiate**   V. satisfy fully. Having stuffed themselves with goodies until they were *satiated*, the guests were so full they were ready for a nap. satiety, N.

satire   N. form of literature in which irony, sarcasm, and ridicule are employed to attack vice and folly. *Gulliver's Travels*, which is regarded by many as a tale for children, is actually a bitter *satire* attacking human folly.

satirical   ADJ. mocking. The humor of cartoonist Gary Trudeau often is *satirical;* through the comments of the Doonesbury characters, Trudeau ridicules political corruption and folly.

■ **saturate**   V. soak thoroughly. Thorough watering is the key to lawn care: you must *saturate* your new lawn well to encourage its growth.

saturnine   ADJ. gloomy. Do not be misled by his *saturnine* countenance; he is not as gloomy as he looks.

satyr   N. half-human, half-bestial being in the court of Dionysus, portrayed as wanton and cunning. He was like a *satyr* in his lustful conduct.

saunter   V. stroll slowly. As we *sauntered* through the park, we stopped frequently to admire the spring flowers.

savant   N. scholar. Our faculty includes many world-famous *savants*.

■ **savor**   V. enjoy; have a distinctive flavor, smell, or quality. Relishing his triumph, Costner especially *savored* the chagrin of the critics who had predicted his failure.

savory   ADJ. tasty; pleasing, attractive, or agreeable. Julia Child's recipes enable amateur chefs to create *savory* delicacies for their guests.

scabbard   N. case for a sword blade; sheath. The drill master told the recruit to wipe the blood from his sword before slipping it back into the *scabbard*.

scad   N. a great quantity. Refusing Dave's offer to lend him a shirt, Phil replied, "No, thanks; I've got *scads* of clothes."

scaffold   N. temporary platform for workers; bracing framework; platform for execution. Before painting the house, the workers put up a *scaffold* to allow them to work on the second story.

scale   V. climb up; ascend. To locate a book on the top shelf of the stacks, Lee had to *scale* an exceptionally rickety ladder.

scanty   ADJ. meager; insufficient. Thinking his helping of food was *scanty*, Oliver Twist asked for more.

scapegoat   N. someone who bears the blame for others. After the Challenger disaster, NASA searched for *scapegoats* on whom they could cast the blame.

scavenge   V. hunt through discarded materials for usable items; search, especially for food. If you need car parts that the dealers no longer stock, try *scavenging* for odd bits and pieces at the auto wreckers' yards. scavenger, N.

scenario   N. plot outline; screenplay; opera libretto. Scaramouche startled the other actors in the commedia troupe when he suddenly departed from their customary *scenario* and began to improvise.

schematic   ADJ. relating to an outline or diagram; using a system of symbols. In working out the solution to an analytical logic question, you may find it helpful to construct a simple *schematic* diagram illustrating the relationships between the items of information given in the question. schema, N.

schism   N. division; split. Let us not widen the *schism* by further bickering.

scintilla   N. shred; least bit. You have not produced a *scintilla* of evidence to support your argument.

scintillate   V. sparkle; flash. I enjoy her dinner parties because the food is excellent and the conversation *scintillates*.

scoff   V. mock; ridicule. He *scoffed* at dentists until he had his first toothache.

scotch   V. stamp out; thwart; hinder. Heather tried to *scotch* the rumor that she had stolen her best friend's fiancé.

scourge   N. lash; whip; severe punishment. They feared the plague and regarded it as a deadly *scourge*. also V.

scruple   V. fret about; hesitate, for ethical reasons. Fearing that her husband had become involved in an affair, she did not *scruple* to read his diary. also N.

scrupulous   ADJ. conscientious; extremely thorough. Though Alfred is *scrupulous* in fulfilling his duties at work, he is less conscientious about his obligations to his family and friends.

scrutinize   V. examine closely and critically. Searching for flaws, the sergeant *scrutinized* every detail of the private's uniform.

scuffle   V. struggle confusedly; move off in a confused hurry. The twins briefly *scuffled*, wrestling to see which of them would get the toy. When their big brother yelled, "Let go of my Gameboy!" they *scuffled* off down the hall.

scurrilous   ADJ. obscene; indecent. Your *scurrilous* remarks are especially offensive because they are untrue.

scurry   V. move briskly. The White Rabbit had to *scurry* to get to his appointment on time.

scurvy   ADJ. despicable; contemptible. Peter Pan sneered at Captain Hook and his *scurvy* crew.

scuttle   V. sink. The sailors decided to *scuttle* their vessel rather than surrender it to the enemy.

seamy   ADJ. sordid; unwholesome. In *The Godfather*, Michael Corleone is unwilling to expose his wife and children to the *seamy* side of his life as the son of a Mafia don.

sear   V. char or burn; brand. Accidentally brushing against the hot grill, she *seared* her hand badly.

seasoned   ADJ. experienced. Though pleased with her new batch of rookies, the basketball coach wished she had a few more *seasoned* players on the team.

secession N. withdrawal. The *secession* of the Southern states provided Lincoln with his first major problem after his inauguration. secede, V.

seclusion N. isolation; solitude. One moment she loved crowds; the next, she sought *seclusion*.

■ **secrete** V. hide away or cache; produce and release a substance into an organism. The pack rat *secretes* odds and ends in its nest; the pancreas *secretes* insulin in the islets of Langerhans.

sect N. separate religious body; faction. As university chaplain, she sought to address universal religious issues and not limit herself to the concerns of any one *sect*. sectarian, ADJ.

secular ADJ. worldly; not pertaining to church matters; temporal. The church leaders decided not to interfere in *secular* matters.

sedate ADJ. composed; grave. The parents were worried because they felt their son was too quiet and *sedate*.

sedentary ADJ. requiring sitting. Sitting all day at the computer, Sharon grew to resent the *sedentary* nature of her job.

sedition N. resistance to authority; insubordination. Her words, though not treasonous in themselves, were calculated to arouse thoughts of *sedition*.

sedulous ADJ. diligent. The young woman was so *sedulous* that she received a commendation for her hard work. sedulity, N.

seedy ADJ. run-down; decrepit; disreputable. I would rather stay in dormitory lodgings in a decent youth hostel than have a room of my own in a *seedy* downtown hotel.

seemly ADJ. proper; appropriate. Lady Bracknell did not think it was *seemly* for Ernest to lack a proper family: no baby abandoned on a doorstep could grow up to marry *her* daughter.

seep V. ooze; trickle. During the rainstorm, water *seeped* through the crack in the basement wall and damaged the floor boards. seepage, N.

seethe V. be disturbed; boil. The nation was *seething* with discontent as the noblemen continued their arrogant ways.

seine N. net for catching fish. When the shad run during the spring, you may see fishermen with *seines* along the banks of our coastal rivers.

seismic ADJ. pertaining to earthquakes. The Richter scale is a measurement of *seismic* disturbances.

semblance N. outward appearance; guise. Although this book has a *semblance* of wisdom and scholarship, a careful examination will reveal many errors and omissions.

seminal ADJ. germinal; influencing future developments; related to seed or semen. Although Freud has generally been regarded as a *seminal* thinker who shaped the course of psychology, his psychoanalytic methods have come under attack recently.

seminary N. school for training future ministers; secondary school, especially for young women. Sure of his priestly vocation, Terrence planned to pursue his theological training at the local Roman Catholic *seminary*.

senility N. old age; feeblemindedness of old age. Most of the decisions are being made by the junior members of the company because of the *senility* of the president. senile, ADJ.

sensitization N. process of being made sensitive or acutely responsive to an external agent or substance. The paint fumes triggered a bad allergic response in Vicky; even now, her extreme *sensitization* to these chemicals causes her to faint whenever she is around wet paint.

sensual ADJ. devoted to the pleasures of the senses; carnal; voluptuous. I cannot understand what caused him to drop his *sensual* way of life and become so ascetic.

sensuous ADJ. pertaining to the physical senses; operating through the senses. She was stimulated by the sights, sounds, and smells about her; she was enjoying her *sensuous* experience.

sententious ADJ. terse; concise; aphoristic. After reading so many redundant speeches, I find his *sententious* style particularly pleasing.

sentient ADJ. capable of sensation; aware; sensitive. In the science fiction story, the hero had to discover a way to prove that the rocklike extraterrestrial creature was actually a *sentient*, intelligent creature. sentience, N.

sentinel N. sentry; lookout. Though camped in enemy territory, Bledsoe ignored the elementary precaution of posting *sentinels* around the encampment.

septic ADJ. putrid; producing putrefaction. The hospital was in such a filthy state that we were afraid that many of the patients would suffer from *septic* poisoning. sepsis, N.

sepulcher N. tomb. Annabel Lee was buried in a *sepulcher* by the sea.

Test

Word List 42   *Antonyms*

Each of the following questions consists of a word in capital letters, followed by five lettered words or phrases. Choose the lettered word or phrase that is most nearly opposite in meaning to the word in capital letters and write the letter of your choice on your answer paper.

616. SADISTIC (A) happy (B) quaint (C) kindhearted (D) vacant (E) fortunate

617. SAGACIOUS (A) foolish (B) bitter (C) voracious (D) veracious (E) fallacious

618. SALLOW (A) salacious (B) ruddy (C) colorless
(D) permitted (E) minimum

619. SALUBRIOUS (A) salty (B) bloody (C) miasmic
(D) maudlin (E) wanted

620. SALVAGE (A) remove (B) outfit (C) burn (D) lose
(E) confuse

621. SANCTIMONIOUS (A) hypothetical (B) paltry
(C) mercenary (D) pious (E) grateful

622. SANGUINE (A) choleric (B) sickening
(C) warranted (D) irritated (E) pessimistic

623. SATIETY (A) emptiness (B) warmth (C) erectness
(D) ignorance (E) straightness

624. SCANTY (A) collected (B) remote (C) invisible
(D) plentiful (E) straight

625. SCURRILOUS (A) savage (B) scabby (C) decent
(D) volatile (E) major

626. SECULAR (A) vivid (B) clerical (C) punitive
(D) positive (E) varying

627. SEDENTARY (A) vicarious (B) loyal (C) accidental
(D) active (E) afraid

628. SEDULOUS (A) indolent (B) guileless
(C) vindictive (D) upright (E) incorrect

629. SENILITY (A) virility (B) loquaciousness
(C) forgetfulness (D) youth (E) majority

630. SENTENTIOUS (A) paragraphed (B) positive
(C) posthumous (D) pacific (E) wordy

Word List 43　　sequester–somatic

sequester V. isolate; retire from public life; segregate; seclude. To prevent the jurors from hearing news broadcasts about the case, the judge decided to *sequester* the jury.

sere ADJ. parched; dry. After the unseasonably dry winter the Berkeley hills looked dusty and *sere*.

serendipity N. gift for finding valuable or desirable things by accident; accidental good fortune or luck. Many scientific discoveries are a matter of *serendipity*: Newton was not sitting there thinking about gravity when the apple dropped on his head.

serenity N. calmness, placidity. The *serenity* of the sleepy town was shattered by a tremendous explosion.

serpentine ADJ. winding; twisting. The car swerved at every curve in the *serpentine* road.

serrated ADJ. having a sawtoothed edge. The beech tree is one of many plants that have *serrated* leaves.

servile ADJ. slavish; cringing. Constantly fawning on his employer, humble Uriah Heep was a *servile* creature. servility, N.

servitude N. slavery; compulsory labor. Born a slave, Douglass resented his life of *servitude* and plotted to escape to the North.

sever V. cut; separate. Dr. Guillotin invented a machine that could neatly *sever* an aristocratic head from its equally aristocratic body. Unfortunately, he couldn't collect any *severance* pay.

severity N. harshness; intensity; sternness; austerity. The *severity* of Jane's migraine attack was so great that she took to her bed for a week. severe, ADJ.

sextant N. navigation tool used to determine a ship's latitude and longitude. Given a clear night, with the aid of his *sextant* and compass he could keep the ship safely on course.

shackle V. chain; fetter. The criminal's ankles were *shackled* to prevent his escape. also N.

sham V. pretend. She *shammed* sickness to get out of going to school. also N.

shambles N. wreck; mess. After the hurricane, the Carolina coast was a *shambles*. After the New Year's Eve party, the host's apartment was a *shambles*.

■ **shard** N. fragment, generally of pottery. The archaeologist assigned several students the task of reassembling earthenware vessels from the *shards* he had brought back from the expedition.

shaving N. very thin piece, usually of wood. As the carpenter pared away the edge of the board with his plane, a small pile of *shavings* began to accumulate on the floor.

sheaf N. bundle of stalks of grain; any bundle of things tied together. The lawyer picked up a *sheaf* of papers as she rose to question the witness.

sheathe V. place into a case. As soon as he recognized the approaching men, he *sheathed* his dagger and hailed them as friends.

sherbet N. flavored dessert ice. I prefer raspberry *sherbet* to ice cream since it is less fattening.

shimmer V. glimmer intermittently. The moonlight *shimmered* on the water as the moon broke through the clouds for a moment. also N.

shirk V. avoid (responsibility, work, etc.); malinger. Brian has a strong sense of duty; he would never *shirk* any responsibility.

shoddy ADJ. sham; not genuine; inferior. You will never get the public to buy such *shoddy* material.

shrew N. scolding woman. No one wanted to marry Shakespeare's Kate because she was a *shrew*.

shrewd ADJ. clever; astute. A *shrewd* investor, she took clever advantage of the fluctuations of the stock market.

shun V. keep away from. Cherishing his solitude, the recluse *shunned* the company of other human beings.

shunt V. turn aside; divert; sidetrack. If the switchman failed to *shunt* the Silver Streak onto a side track, the train would plow right into Union Station.

shyster N. lawyer using questionable methods. On *L.A. Law,* respectable attorney Brackman was horrified to learn that his newly discovered half brother was a cheap *shyster.*

sibling N. brother or sister. We may not enjoy being *siblings,* but we cannot forget that we still belong to the same family.

sibylline ADJ. prophetic; oracular. Until their destruction by fire in 83 B.C., the *sibylline* books were often consulted by the Romans.

sidereal ADJ. relating to the stars. Although hampered by optical and mechanical flaws, the orbiting *Hubble* space telescope has relayed extraordinary images of distant *sidereal* bodies.

silt N. sediment deposited by running water. The harbor channel must be dredged annually to remove the *silt.*

simian ADJ. monkeylike. Lemurs are nocturnal mammals and have many *simian* characteristics, although they are less intelligent than monkeys.

simile N. comparison of one thing with another, using the word *like* or *as.* "My love is like a red, red rose" is a *simile.*

simper V. smirk; smile affectedly. Complimented on her appearance, Stella self-consciously *simpered.*

simplistic ADJ. oversimplified. Though Jack's solution dealt adequately with one aspect of the problem, it was *simplistic* in failing to consider various complicating factors that might arise.

simulate V. feign. She *simulated* insanity in order to avoid punishment for her crime.

sinecure N. well-paid position with little responsibility. My job is no *sinecure;* I work long hours and have much responsibility.

sinewy ADJ. tough; strong and firm. The steak was too *sinewy* to chew.

singular ADJ. unique; extraordinary; odd. Though the young man tried to understand Father William's *singular* behavior, he still found it odd that the old man incessantly stood on his head.

sinister ADJ. evil. We must defeat the *sinister* forces that seek our downfall.

sinuous ADJ. winding; bending in and out; not morally honest. The snake moved in a *sinuous* manner.

■ **skeptic** N. doubter; person who suspends judgment until having examined the evidence supporting a point of view. I am a *skeptic* about the new health plan; I want some proof that it can work. skeptical, ADJ. skepticism, N.

skiff N. small, light sailboat or rowboat. Tom dreamed of owning an ocean-going yacht but had to settle for a *skiff* he could sail in the bay.

skimp V. provide scantily; live very economically. They were forced to *skimp* on necessities in order to make their limited supplies last the winter.

skinflint N. stingy person; miser. Scrooge was an ungenerous old *skinflint* until he reformed his ways and became a notable philanthropist.

skirmish N. minor fight. Custer's troops expected they might run into a *skirmish* or two on maneuvers; they did not expect to face a major battle. also V.

skittish ADJ. lively; frisky. She is as *skittish* as a kitten playing with a piece of string.

skulduggery N. dishonest behavior. The investigation into municipal corruption turned up new instances of *skulduggery* daily.

skulk V. move furtively and secretly. He *skulked* through the less fashionable sections of the city in order to avoid meeting any of his former friends.

slacken V. slow up; loosen. As they passed the finish line, the runners *slackened* their pace.

slag N. residue from smelting metal; dross; waste matter. The blast furnace had a special opening at the bottom to allow the workers to remove the worthless *slag.*

slake V. quench; sate. When we reached the oasis, we were able to *slake* our thirst.

slander N. defamation; utterance of false and malicious statements. Considering the negative comments politicians make about each other, it's a wonder that more of them aren't sued for *slander.* also V. slanderous, ADJ.

slapdash ADJ. haphazard; careless; sloppy. From the number of typos and misspellings I've found in it, it's clear that Mario proofread the report in a remarkably *slapdash* fashion.

sleazy ADJ. flimsy; unsubstantial. This is a *sleazy* fabric; it will not wear well.

sleeper N. something originally of little value or importance that in time becomes very valuable. Unnoticed by the critics at its publication, the eventual Pulitzer Prize winner was a classic *sleeper.*

sleight N. dexterity. The magician amazed the audience with his *sleight* of hand.

slew N. large quantity or number. Although Ellen had checked off a number of items on her "To Do" list, she still had a whole *slew* of errands left.

slight N. insult to one's dignity; snub. Hypersensitive and ready to take offense at any discourtesy, Bertha was always on the lookout for real or imaginary *slights.* also V.

slipshod ADJ. untidy or slovenly; shabby. As a master craftsman, the carpenter prided himself on never doing *slipshod* work.

slither V. slip or slide. During the recent ice storm, many people *slithered* down this hill as they walked to the station.

sloth N. slow-moving tree-dwelling mammal. Note how well the somewhat greenish coat of the *sloth* enables it to blend in with its arboreal surroundings. (secondary meaning)

slothful ADJ. lazy. The British word "layabout" is a splendid descriptive term for someone *slothful:* What did the lazy bum do? He lay about the house all day. sloth, N.

slough V. cast off. Each spring, the snake *sloughs* off its skin. also N.

slovenly ADJ. untidy; careless in work habits. Unshaven, sitting around in his bathrobe all afternoon, Gus didn't care about the *slovenly* appearance he presented. sloven, N.

sluggard N. lazy person. "You are a *sluggard*, a drone, a parasite," the angry father shouted at his lazy son.

sluggish ADJ. slow; lazy; lethargic. After two nights without sleep, she felt *sluggish* and incapable of exertion.

sluice N. artificial channel for directing or controlling the flow of water. In times of drought, this *sluice* enables farmers to obtain water for irrigation.

slur N. insult to one's character or reputation; slander. Polls revealed that the front-runner's standing had been damaged by the *slurs* and innuendoes circulated by his opponent's staff. (secondary meaning) also V.

slur V. speak indistinctly; mumble. When Sol has too much to drink, he starts to *slur* his words: "Washamatter? Cansh you undershtand what I shay?"

smattering N. slight knowledge. I don't know whether it is better to be ignorant of a subject or to have a mere *smattering* of information about it.

smelt V. melt or blend ores, changing their chemical composition. The furnaceman *smelts* tin with copper to create a special alloy used in making bells.

smirk N. conceited smile. Wipe that *smirk* off your face! also V.

smolder V. burn without flame; be liable to break out at any moment. The rags *smoldered* for hours before they burst into flame.

snicker N. half-stifled laugh. The boy could not suppress a *snicker* when the teacher sat on the tack. also V.

snivel V. run at the nose; snuffle; whine. Don't you come *sniveling* to me complaining about your big brother.

sobriety N. moderation (especially regarding indulgence in alcohol); seriousness. Neither falling-down drunks nor stand-up comics are noted for *sobriety*. sober, ADJ.

sodden ADJ. soaked; dull, as if from drink. He set his *sodden* overcoat near the radiator to dry.

sojourn N. temporary stay. After his *sojourn* in Florida, he began to long for the colder climate of his native New England home.

solace N. comfort in trouble. I hope you will find *solace* in the thought that all of us share your loss.

solder V. repair or make whole by using a metal alloy. The plumber fixed the leak in the pipes by *soldering* a couple of joints from which water had been oozing.

solecism N. construction that is flagrantly incorrect grammatically. I must give this paper a failing mark because it contains many *solecisms*.

solemnity N. seriousness; gravity. The minister was concerned that nothing should disturb the *solemnity* of the marriage service.

solicit V. request earnestly; seek. Knowing she needed to have a solid majority for the budget to pass, the mayor telephoned all the members of the city council to *solicit* their votes.

■ **solicitous** ADJ. worried, concerned. The employer was very *solicitous* about the health of her employees as replacements were difficult to get. solicitude, N.

soliloquy N. talking to oneself. The *soliloquy* is a device used by the dramatist to reveal a character's innermost thoughts and emotions.

solitude N. state of being alone; seclusion. Much depends on how much you like your own company. What to one person seems fearful isolation to another is blessed *solitude*. solitary, ADJ.

solstice N. point at which the sun is farthest from the equator. The winter *solstice* usually occurs on December 21.

soluble ADJ. able to be dissolved; able to be worked out. Sugar is *soluble* in water; put a sugar cube in water and it will quickly dissolve. Because the test-maker had left out some necessary data, the problem was not *soluble*.

solvent ADJ. able to pay all debts. By dint of very frugal living, he was finally able to become *solvent* and avoid bankruptcy proceedings. solvency, N.

solvent N. substance that dissolves another. Dip a cube of sugar into a cup of water; note how the water acts as a *solvent*, causing the cube to break down.

somatic ADJ. pertaining to the body; physical. Why do you ignore the spiritual aspects and emphasize only the corporeal and the *somatic* ones?

Test

Word List 43   *Synonyms and Antonyms*

Each of the following questions consists of a word in capital letters, followed by five lettered words or phrases. Choose the lettered word or phrase that is most nearly similar or opposite in meaning to the word in capital letters and write the letter of your choice on your answer paper.

631. SEQUESTER (A) request (B) preclude (C) seclude (D) witness (E) evolve

632. SERRATED (A) riddled (B) diagonal (C) sawtoothed (D) grooved (E) linear

633. SERVILE (A) moral (B) puerile (C) futile (D) foul (E) haughty

634. SHODDY (A) superior (B) barefoot (C) sunlit (D) querulous (E) garrulous

635. SINGULAR (A) silent (B) angular (C) ordinary (D) desirable (E) garrulous

636. SINISTER (A) unwed (B) ministerial (C) good (D) returned (E) splintered

637. SKITTISH (A) tractable (B) inquiring (C) dramatic (D) vain (E) frisky

638. SLEAZY (A) fanciful (B) creeping (C) substantial (D) uneasy (E) warranted

639. SLOTH (A) penitence (B) filth (C) futility (D) poverty (E) industry

640. SLOUGH (A) toughen (B) trap (C) violate (D) cast off (E) depart quickly

641. SLOVENLY (A) half-baked (B) loved (C) inappropriate (D) tidy (E) rapid

642. SOBRIETY (A) inebriety (B) aptitude (C) scholasticism (D) monotony (E) aversion

643. SOLECISM (A) praise (B) embarrassment (C) concise phrase (D) inaccurate count (E) correct expression

644. SOLSTICE (A) equinox (B) sunrise (C) pigsty (D) interstices (E) iniquity

645. SOLVENT (A) enigmatic (B) bankrupt (C) fiducial (D) puzzling (E) gilded

Word List 44   somber-sublime

somber ADJ. gloomy; depressing. From the doctor's grim expression, I could tell he had *somber* news.

somnambulist N. sleepwalker. The most famous *somnambulist* in literature is Lady Macbeth; her monologue in the sleepwalking scene is one of the highlights of Shakespeare's play.

somnolent ADJ. half asleep. The heavy meal and the overheated room made us all *somnolent* and indifferent to the speaker. somnolence, N.

sonorous ADJ. resonant. His *sonorous* voice resounded through the hall.

sophist N. teacher of philosophy; quibbler; employer of fallacious reasoning. You are using all the devices of a *sophist* in trying to prove your case; your argument is specious.

sophisticated ADJ. worldly wise and urbane; complex. When Sophy makes wisecracks, she thinks she sounds *sophisticated*, but instead she sounds sophomoric. The IBM laptop with the butterfly keyboard and the built-in FAX modem is a pretty *sophisticated* machine. sophistication, N.

sophistry N. seemingly plausible but fallacious reasoning. Instead of advancing valid arguments, he tried to overwhelm his audience with a flood of *sophistries*.

sophomoric ADJ. immature; half-baked, like a sophomore. Even if you're only a freshman, it's no compliment to be told your humor is *sophomoric*. The humor in *Dumb and Dumber* is *sophomoric* at best.

■ **soporific** ADJ. sleep-causing; marked by sleepiness. Professor Pringle's lectures were so *soporific* that even he fell asleep in class. also N.

sordid ADJ. filthy; base; vile. The social worker was angered by the *sordid* housing provided for the homeless.

spangle N. small metallic piece sewn to clothing for ornamentation. The thousands of *spangles* on her dress sparkled in the glare of the stage lights.

sparse ADJ. not thick; thinly scattered; scanty. No matter how carefully Albert combed his hair to make it appear as full as possible, it still looked *sparse*.

spartan ADJ. lacking luxury and comfort; sternly disciplined. Looking over the bare, unheated room with its hard cot, he wondered what he was doing in such *spartan* quarters. Only his *spartan* sense of duty kept him at his post.

spasmodic ADJ. fitful; periodic. The *spasmodic* coughing in the auditorium annoyed the performers.

spat N. squabble; minor dispute. What had started out as a mere *spat* escalated into a full-blown argument.

spate N. sudden flood. I am worried about the possibility of a *spate* if the rains do not diminish soon.

spatial ADJ. relating to space. Certain exercises test your sense of *spatial* relations by asking you to identify two views of an object seen from different points in space.

spatula N. broad-bladed instrument used for spreading or mixing. The manufacturers of this frying pan recommend the use of a rubber *spatula* to avoid scratching the specially treated surface.

spawn V. lay eggs. Fish ladders had to be built in the dams to assist the salmon returning to *spawn* in their native streams. also N.

■ **specious** ADJ. seemingly reasonable but incorrect; misleading (often intentionally). To claim that, because houses and birds both have wings, both can fly is extremely *specious* reasoning.

spectral ADJ. ghostly. We were frightened by the *spectral* glow that filled the room.

■ **spectrum** N. colored band produced when a beam of light passes through a prism. The visible portion of the *spectrum* includes red at one end and violet at the other.

spendthrift N. someone who wastes money. Easy access to credit encourages people to turn into *spendthrifts* who shop till they drop.

sphinx-like ADJ. enigmatic; mysterious. The Mona Lisa's *sphinx-like* expression has puzzled art lovers for centuries.

splice V. fasten together; unite. Before you *splice* two strips of tape together, be sure to line them up evenly. also N.

spontaneity N. lack of premeditation; naturalness; freedom from constraint. The cast overrehearsed the play so much that the eventual performance lacked any *spontaneity*. spontaneous, ADJ.

spoonerism N. accidental transposition of sounds in successive words. When the radio announcer introduced the President as Hoobert Herver, he was guilty of a *spoonerism*.

■ **sporadic** ADJ. occurring irregularly. Although you can still hear *sporadic* outbursts of laughter and singing outside, the big Halloween parade has passed; the party's over till next year.

sportive ADJ. playful. Such a *sportive* attitude is surprising in a person as serious as you usually are.

spruce ADJ. neat and trim. Every button buttoned, tie firmly in place, young Alex Keaton looked *spruce* and tidy for his job interview at the bank. also V.

spry ADJ. vigorously active; nimble. She was eighty years old, yet still *spry* and alert.

spurious ADJ. false; counterfeit; forged; illogical. The hero of Jonathan Gash's mystery novels is an antique dealer who gives the reader advice on how to tell *spurious* antiques from the real thing.

spurn V. reject; scorn. The heroine *spurned* the villain's advances.

squabble N. minor quarrel; bickering. Children invariably get involved in petty *squabbles;* wise parents know when to interfere and when to let the children work things out on their own.

squalor N. filth; degradation; dirty, neglected state. Rusted, broken-down cars in the yard, trash piled on the porch, tar paper peeling from the roof—the shack was the picture of *squalor*. squalid, ADJ.

squander V. waste. If you *squander* your allowance on candy and comic books, you won't have any money left to buy the new box of crayons you want.

squat ADJ. stocky; short and thick. Tolkien's hobbits are somewhat *squat,* sturdy little creatures, fond of good ale, good music, and good food.

staccato ADJ. played in an abrupt manner; marked by abrupt, sharp sound. His *staccato* speech reminded one of the sound of a machine gun.

stagnant ADJ. motionless; stale; dull. Mosquitoes commonly breed in ponds of *stagnant* water. Mike's career was *stagnant*; it wasn't going anywhere, and neither was he! stagnate, V.

staid ADJ. sober; sedate. Her conduct during the funeral ceremony was *staid* and solemn.

stalemate N. deadlock. Negotiations between the union and the employers have reached a *stalemate;* neither side is willing to budge from previously stated positions.

stalwart ADJ. strong, brawny; steadfast. His consistent support of the party has proved that he is a *stalwart* and loyal member. also N.

stamina N. strength; staying power. I doubt that she has the *stamina* to run the full distance of the marathon race.

stanch V. check flow of blood. It is imperative that we *stanch* the gushing wound before we attend to the other injuries.

stanza N. division of a poem. Do you know the last *stanza* of "The Star-Spangled Banner"?

static ADJ. unchanging; lacking development. Why do you watch chess on TV? I like watching a game with action, not something *static* where nothing seems to be going on. stasis, N.

statute N. law enacted by the legislature. The *statute* of limitations sets limits on how long you have to take legal action in specific cases.

statutory ADJ. created by statute or legislative action. The judicial courts review and try *statutory* crimes.

steadfast ADJ. loyal; unswerving. Penelope was *steadfast* in her affections, faithfully waiting for Ulysses to return from his wanderings.

stealth N. slyness; sneakiness; secretiveness. Fearing detection by the sentries on duty, the scout inched his way toward the enemy camp with great *stealth*.

steep V. soak; saturate. Be sure to *steep* the fabric in the dye bath for the full time prescribed.

stellar ADJ. pertaining to the stars. He was the *stellar* attraction of the entire performance.

stem V. check the flow. The paramedic used a tourniquet to *stem* the bleeding from the slashed artery.

stem from V. arise from. Milton's problems in school *stemmed from* his poor study habits.

stentorian ADJ. extremely loud. The town crier had a *stentorian* voice.

stereotype N. fixed and unvarying representation; standardized mental picture, often reflecting prejudice. Critics object to the character of Jim in *The Adventures of Huckleberry Finn* because he seems to reflect the *stereotype* of the happy, ignorant slave. also V.

stickler N. perfectionist; person who insists things be exactly right. The Internal Revenue Service agent was a *stickler* for accuracy; no approximations or rough estimates would satisfy him.

stifle V. suppress; extinguish; inhibit. Halfway through the boring lecture, Laura gave up trying to *stifle* her yawns.

■ **stigma** N. token of disgrace; brand. I do not attach any *stigma* to the fact that you were accused of this crime; the fact that you were acquitted clears you completely. stigmatize, N.

stilted ADJ. bombastic; stiffly pompous. His *stilted* rhetoric did not impress the college audience; they were immune to bombastic utterances.

■ **stint** V. be thrifty; set limits. "Spare no expense," the bride's father said, refusing to *stint* on the wedding arrangements.

stint N. supply; allotted amount; assigned portion of work. She performed her daily *stint* cheerfully and willingly.

stipend N. pay for services. There is a nominal *stipend* for this position.

stipple V. paint or draw with dots. Seurat carefully *stippled* dabs of pure color on the canvas, juxtaposing dots of blue and yellow that the viewer's eye would interpret as green.

■ **stipulate** V. make express conditions, specify. Before agreeing to reduce American military forces in Europe, the president *stipulated* that NATO teams be allowed to inspect Russian bases.

stock ADJ. typical; standard; kept regularly in supply. Victorian melodramas portrayed *stock* characters—the rich but wicked villain, the sweet young ingenue, the poor but honest young man—in exaggerated situations. Although the stationery store kept only *stock* sizes of paper on hand, the staff would special-order any items not regularly in *stock*.

stockade N. wooden enclosure or pen; fixed line of posts used as defensive barrier. The Indians are coming! Quick! Round up the horses and drive them into the *stockade*.

stodgy ADJ. stuffy; boringly conservative. For a young person, Winston seems remarkably *stodgy:* you'd expect someone his age to have a little more life.

stoic ADJ. impassive; unmoved by joy or grief. I wasn't particularly *stoic* when I had my flu shot; I squealed like a stuck pig. also N. stoicism, N.

stoke V. stir up a fire; feed plentifully. As a Scout, Marisa learned how to light a fire, how to *stoke* it if it started to die down, and how to extinguish it completely.

■ **stolid** ADJ. dull; impassive. The earthquake shattered Stuart's usual *stolid* demeanor; trembling, he crouched on the no longer stable ground. stolidity, N.

stratagem N. clever trick; deceptive scheme. What a gem of a *stratagem*! Watson, I have the perfect plan to trick Moriarty into revealing himself.

stratified ADJ. divided into classes; arranged into strata. As the economic gap between the rich and the poor increased, Roman society grew increasingly *stratified*. stratify, V.

stratum N. layer of earth's surface; layer of society. Unless we alleviate conditions in the lowest *stratum* of our society, we may expect grumbling and revolt. strata, PL.

strew V. spread randomly; sprinkle; scatter. Preceding the bride to the altar, the flower girl will *strew* rose petals along the aisle.

■ **striated** ADJ. marked with parallel bands; grooved. The glacier left many *striated* rocks. striate, V.

stricture N. critical comments; severe and adverse criticism. His *strictures* on the author's style are prejudiced and unwarranted.

strident ADJ. loud and harsh; insistent. We could barely hear the speaker over the *strident* cries of the hecklers. stridency, N.

stringent ADJ. binding; rigid. I think these regulations are too *stringent*.

■ **strut** N. pompous walk. His *strut* as he marched about the parade ground revealed him for what he was: a pompous buffoon. also V.

■ **strut** N. supporting bar. The engineer calculated that the *strut* supporting the rafter needed to be reinforced.

studied ADJ. unspontaneous; deliberate; thoughtful. Given Jill's previous slights, Jack felt that the omission of his name from the guest list was a *studied* insult.

stultify V. cause to appear or become stupid or inconsistent; frustrate or hinder. His long hours in the blacking factory left young Dickens numb and incurious, as if the menial labor had *stultified* his mind.

stupefy V. make numb; stun; amaze. Disapproving of drugs in general, Laura refused to take sleeping pills or any other medicine that might *stupefy* her.

stupor N. state of apathy; daze; lack of awareness. In his *stupor,* the addict was unaware of the events taking place around him.

stygian ADJ. gloomy; hellish; deathly. Shielding the flickering candle from any threatening draft, Tom and Becky descended into the *stygian* darkness of the underground cavern. *Stygian* derives from *Styx,* the chief river in the subterranean land of the dead.

stymie V. present an obstacle; stump. The detective was *stymied* by the contradictory evidence in the robbery investigation.

suavity N. urbanity; polish. He is particularly good in roles that require *suavity* and sophistication. suave, ADJ.

subaltern N. subordinate. The captain treated his *subalterns* as though they were children rather than commissioned officers.

subdued ADJ. less intense; quieter. Bob liked the *subdued* lighting at the restaurant because he thought it was romantic. I just thought the place was dimly lit.

subjective ADJ. occurring or taking place within the mind; unreal. Your analysis is highly *subjective;* you have permitted your emotions and your opinions to color your thinking.

subjugate V. conquer; bring under control. It is not our aim to *subjugate* our foe; we are interested only in establishing peaceful relations.

sublimate V. refine; purify. We must strive to *sublimate* these desires and emotions into worthwhile activities.

sublime ADJ. exalted; noble and uplifting; utter. Lucy was in awe of Desi's *sublime* musicianship, while he was in awe of her *sublime* naiveté.

Test

Word List 44 *Synonyms and Antonyms*

Each of the following questions consists of a word in capital letters, followed by five lettered words or phrases. Choose the lettered word or phrase that is most nearly similar or opposite in meaning to the word in capital letters and write the letter of your choice on your answer paper.

646. SONOROUS (A) resonant (B) reassuring (C) repetitive (D) resinous (E) sisterly

647. SOPHOMORIC (A) unprecedented (B) mature (C) insipid (D) intellectual (E) illusionary

648. SOPORIFIC (A) dining (B) caustic (C) memorial (D) awakening (E) springing

649. SPASMODIC (A) intermittent (B) fit (C) inaccurate (D) violent (E) physical

650. SPORADIC (A) seedy (B) latent (C) vivid (D) inconsequential (E) occasional

651. SPORTIVE (A) competing (B) playful (C) indignant (D) foppish (E) fundamental

652. SPURIOUS (A) genuine (B) angry (C) mitigated (D) interrogated (E) glorious

653. SQUANDER (A) fortify (B) depart (C) roam (D) preserve (E) forfeit

654. STACCATO (A) musical (B) long (C) legato (D) sneezing (E) pounded

655. STAMINA (A) patience (B) pistils (C) weakness (D) fascination (E) patina

656. STEREOTYPED (A) original (B) antique (C) modeled (D) repetitious (E) continued

657. STILTED (A) candid (B) pompous (C) modish (D) acute (E) inarticulate

658. STRINGENT (A) binding (B) reserved (C) utilized (D) lambent (E) indigent

659. SUAVITY (A) ingeniousness (B) indifference (C) urbanity (D) constancy (E) paucity

660. SUBLIME (A) unconscious (B) respected (C) exalted (D) sneaky (E) replaced

Word List 45   subliminal–tantamount

subliminal   ADJ. below the threshold. We may not be aware of the *subliminal* influences that affect our thinking.

submissive   ADJ. yielding; timid. When he refused to permit Elizabeth to marry her poet, Mr. Barrett expected her to be properly *submissive*; instead, she eloped with the guy!

subordinate   ADJ. occupying a lower rank; inferior; submissive. Bishop Proudie's wife expected the *subordinate* clergy to behave with great deference to the wife of their superior. also N.

suborn   V. persuade to act unlawfully (especially to commit perjury). In *The Godfather,* the mobsters used bribery and threats to *suborn* the witnesses against Don Michael Corleone.

■ **subpoena**   N. writ summoning a witness to appear. The prosecutor's office was ready to serve a *subpoena* on the reluctant witness. also V.

subsequent   ADJ. following; later. In *subsequent* lessons, we shall take up more difficult problems.

subservient   ADJ. behaving like a slave; servile; obsequious. She was proud and dignified; she refused to be *subservient* to anyone. subservience, N.

■ **subside**   V. settle down; descend; grow quiet. The doctor assured us that the fever would eventually *subside*.

subsidiary   ADJ. subordinate; secondary. This information may be used as *subsidiary* evidence but is not sufficient by itself to prove your argument. also N.

subsidy   N. direct financial aid by government, etc. Without this *subsidy,* American ship operators would not be able to compete in world markets.

subsistence   N. existence; means of support; livelihood. In those days of inflated prices, my salary provided a mere *subsistence*.

substantial   ADJ. ample; solid; essential or fundamental. The generous scholarship represented a *substantial* sum of money. If you don't eat a more *substantial* dinner, you'll be hungry later on.

■ **substantiate**   V. establish by evidence; verify; support. These endorsements from satisfied customers *substantiate* our claim that Barron's *How to Prepare for the GRE* is the best GRE-prep book on the market.

substantive   ADJ. essential; pertaining to the substance. Although the delegates were aware of the importance of the problem, they could not agree on the *substantive* issues.

subsume   V. include; encompass. Does the general theory of relativity contradict Newtonian physics, or is Newton's law of gravity *subsumed* into Einstein's larger scheme?

subterfuge   N. pretense; evasion. As soon as we realized that you had won our support by a *subterfuge,* we withdrew our endorsement of your candidacy.

subtlety   N. perceptiveness; ingenuity; delicacy. Never obvious, she expressed herself with such *subtlety* that her remarks went right over the heads of most of her audience. subtle, ADJ.

subversive   ADJ. tending to overthrow; destructive. At first glance, the notion that Styrofoam cups may actually be more ecologically sound than paper cups strikes most environmentalists as *subversive*.

succinct   ADJ. brief; terse; compact. Don't bore your audience with excess verbiage: be *succinct*.

succor   V. aid; assist; comfort. If you believe that con man has come here to *succor* you in your hour of need, you're even a bigger sucker than I thought. also N.

succulent   ADJ. juicy; full of richness. To some people, Florida citrus fruits are more *succulent* than those from California. also N.

succumb V. yield; give in; die. I *succumb* to temptation whenever it comes my way.

suffragist N. advocate of voting rights (for women). In recognition of her efforts to win the vote for women, Congress authorized coining a silver dollar honoring the *suffragist* Susan B. Anthony.

suffuse V. spread over. A blush *suffused* her cheeks when we teased her about her love affair.

sully V. tarnish; soil. He felt that it was beneath his dignity to *sully* his hands in such menial labor.

sultry ADJ. sweltering. He could not adjust himself to the *sultry* climate of the tropics.

summation N. act of finding the total; summary. In his *summation,* the lawyer emphasized the testimony given by the two witnesses.

sumptuous ADJ. lavish; rich. I cannot recall when I have had such a *sumptuous* Thanksgiving feast.

sunder V. separate; part. Northern and southern Ireland are politically and religiously *sundered.*

sundry ADJ. various; several. My suspicions were aroused when I read *sundry* items in the newspapers about your behavior.

superannuated ADJ. retired or disqualified because of age. Don't call me *superannuated;* I can still perform a good day's work!

supercilious ADJ. arrogant; condescending; patronizing. The *supercilious* headwaiter sneered at customers who he thought did not fit the image of a restaurant catering to an ultrafashionable crowd.

supererogatory ADJ. superfluous; more than needed or demanded. We have more than enough witnesses to corroborate your statement; to present any more would be *supererogatory.*

superficial ADJ. trivial; shallow. Since your report gave only a *superficial* analysis of the problem, I cannot give you more than a passing grade.

superfluous ADJ. excessive; overabundant, unnecessary. Please try not to include so many *superfluous* details in your report; just give me the bare facts. superfluity, N.

superimpose V. place over something else. Your attempt to *superimpose* another agency in this field will merely increase the bureaucratic nature of our government.

supernumerary N. person or thing in excess of what is necessary; extra. His first appearance on the stage was as a *supernumerary* in a Shakespearean tragedy.

■ **supersede** V. cause to be set aside; replace; make obsolete. Bulk mailing postal regulation 326D *supersedes* bulk mailing postal regulation 326C. If, in bundling your bulk mailing, you follow regulation 326C, your bulk mailing will be returned. supersession, N.

supine ADJ. lying on back. The defeated pugilist lay *supine* on the canvas.

supplant V. replace; usurp. Did the other woman actually *supplant* Princess Diana in Prince Charles's affections, or did Charles never love Diana at all? Bolingbroke, later to be known as King Henry IV, fought to *supplant* his cousin, Richard III, as King of England.

supple ADJ. flexible; pliant. Years of yoga exercises made Grace's body *supple.*

suppliant ADJ. entreating; beseeching. Unable to resist the dog's *suppliant* whimpering, he gave it some food. also N.

supplicate V. petition humbly; pray to grant a favor. We *supplicate* Your Majesty to grant him amnesty.

■ **supposition** N. hypothesis; surmise. I based my decision to confide in him on the *supposition* that he would be discreet. suppose, V.

supposititious ADJ. assumed; counterfeit; hypothetical. I find no similarity between your *supposititious* illustration and the problem we are facing.

suppress V. stifle; overwhelm; subdue; inhibit. Too polite to laugh in anyone's face, Roy did his best to *suppress* his amusement at Ed's inane remark.

surfeit V. satiate; stuff; indulge to excess in anything. Every Thanksgiving we are *surfeited* with an overabundance of holiday treats. also N.

surly ADJ. rude; cross. Because of his *surly* attitude, many people avoided his company.

surmise V. guess. I *surmise* that he will be late for this meeting. also N.

surmount V. overcome. I know you can *surmount* any difficulties that may stand in the way of your getting an education.

surpass V. exceed. Her SAT scores *surpassed* our expectations.

surreptitious ADJ. secret; furtive; sneaky; hidden. Hoping to discover where his mom had hidden the Christmas presents, Timmy took a *surreptitious* peek into the master bedroom closet.

surrogate N. substitute. For a fatherless child, a male teacher may become a father *surrogate.*

surveillance N. watching; guarding. The FBI kept the house under constant *surveillance* in the hope of capturing all the criminals at one time.

susceptible ADJ. impressionable; easily influenced; having little resistance, as to a disease; receptive to. Said the patent medicine man to his very *susceptible* customer: "Buy this new miracle drug, and you will no longer be *susceptible* to the common cold." susceptibility, N.

sustain V. experience; support; nourish. He *sustained* such a severe injury that the doctors feared he would be unable to work to *sustain* his growing family.

sustenance N. means of support, food, nourishment. In the tropics, the natives find *sustenance* easy to obtain because of all the fruit trees.

suture N. stitches sewn to hold the cut edges of a wound or incision; material used in sewing. We will remove the *sutures* as soon as the wound heals. also V.

swarthy ADJ. dark; dusky. Despite the stereotype, not all Italians are *swarthy;* many are fair and blond.

swathe v. wrap around; bandage. When I visited him in the hospital, I found him *swathed* in bandages.

swelter v. be oppressed by heat. I am going to buy an air conditioning unit for my apartment as I do not intend to *swelter* through another hot and humid summer.

swerve v. deviate; turn aside sharply. The car *swerved* wildly as the driver struggled to regain control of the wheel.

swill v. drink greedily. Singing "Yo, ho, ho, and a bottle of rum," Long John Silver and his fellow pirates *swilled* their grog.

swindler n. cheat. She was gullible and trusting, an easy victim for the first *swindler* who came along.

sybarite n. lover of luxury. Rich people are not always *sybarites;* some of them have little taste for a life of luxury.

sycophant n. servile flatterer; bootlicker; yes man. Fed up with the toadies and brownnosers who made up his entourage, the star cried, "Get out, all of you! I'm sick of *sycophants*!" sycophantic, ADJ.

syllogism n. logical formula consisting of a major premise, a minor premise and a conclusion; deceptive or specious argument. There must be a fallacy in this *syllogism*; I cannot accept its conclusion.

sylvan ADJ. pertaining to the woods; rustic. His paintings of nymphs in *sylvan* backgrounds were criticized as oversentimental.

symbiosis n. interdependent relationship (between groups, species), often mutually beneficial. Both the crocodile bird and the crocodile derive benefit from their *symbiosis;* pecking away at food particles embedded in the crocodile's teeth, the bird derives nourishment; the crocodile, meanwhile, derives proper dental hygiene. symbiotic, ADJ.

symmetry n. arrangement of parts so that balance is obtained; congruity. By definition, something lopsided lacks *symmetry*. symmetrical, ADJ.

synchronous ADJ. similarly timed; simultaneous with. We have many examples of scientists in different parts of the world who have made *synchronous* discoveries.

synoptic ADJ. providing a general overview; summary. The professor turned to the latest issue of *Dissertation Abstracts* for a *synoptic* account of what was new in the field. synopsis, N.

synthesis N. combining parts into a whole. Now that we have succeeded in isolating this drug, our next problem is to plan its *synthesis* in the laboratory. syntheses, PL., synthesize, V.

synthetic ADJ. artificial; resulting from synthesis. During the twentieth century, many *synthetic* products have replaced their natural counterparts. also N.

■ **tacit** ADJ. understood; not put into words. We have a *tacit* agreement based on only a handshake.

taciturn ADJ. habitually silent; talking little. The stereotypical cowboy is a *taciturn* soul, answering lengthy questions with a "Yep" or "Nope."

tactile ADJ. pertaining to the organs or sense of touch. His callused hands had lost their *tactile* sensitivity.

taint v. contaminate; cause to lose purity; modify with a trace of something bad. One speck of dirt on your utensils may contain enough germs to *taint* an entire batch of preserves. also N.

talisman N. charm. She wore the *talisman* to ward off evil.

talon N. claw of bird. The falconer wore a leather gauntlet to avoid being clawed by the hawk's *talons*.

■ **tangential** ADJ. peripheral; only slightly connected; digressing. Despite Clark's attempts to distract her with *tangential* remarks, Lois kept on coming back to her main question: Why couldn't he come out to dinner with Superman and her?

tangible ADJ. able to be touched; real; palpable. Although Tom did not own a house, he had several *tangible* assets—a car, a television, a PC—that he could sell if he needed cash.

tanner N. person who turns animal hides into leather. Using a solution of tanbark, the *tanner* treated the cowhide, transforming it into supple leather.

tantalize v. tease; torture with disappointment. Tom loved to *tantalize* his younger brother with candy; he knew the boy was forbidden to have it.

tantamount ADJ. equivalent in effect or value. Because so few Southern blacks could afford to pay the poll tax, the imposition of this tax on prospective voters was *tantamount* to disenfranchisement for black voters.

Test

Word List 45   *Synonyms and Antonyms*

Each of the following questions consists of a word in capital letters, followed by five lettered words or phrases. Choose the lettered word or phrase that is most nearly similar or opposite in meaning to the word in capital letters and write the letter of your choice on your answer paper.

661. SUBLIMINAL (A) radiant (B) indifferent (C) obvious (D) domestic (E) horizontal

662. SUPERANNUATED (A) senile (B) experienced (C) retired (D) attenuated (E) accepted

663. SUPERCILIOUS (A) haughty (B) highbrow (C) angry (D) inane (E) philosophic

664. SUPERFICIAL (A) abnormal (B) portentous (C) shallow (D) angry (E) tiny

665. SUPERNUMERARY (A) miser (B) extra (C) associate (D) astronomer (E) inferiority

666. SUPPLIANT (A) intolerant (B) swallowing
(C) beseeching (D) finishing (E) flexible

667. SURFEIT (A) belittle (B) cloy (C) drop (D) estimate
(E) claim

668. SURREPTITIOUS (A) secret (B) snakelike
(C) nightly (D) abstract (E) furnished

669. SUTURE (A) stitch (B) reflection (C) knitting
(D) tailor (E) past

670. SWATHED (A) wrapped around (B) waved
(C) gambled (D) rapt (E) mystified

671. SYCOPHANTIC (A) quiet (B) reclusive
(C) servilely flattering (D) frolicsome
(E) eagerly awaiting

672. SYNTHETIC (A) simplified (B) doubled (C) tuneful
(D) artificial (E) fiscal

673. TACIT (A) spoken (B) allowed (C) neutral
(D) impertinent (E) unwanted

674. TALISMAN (A) chief (B) juror (C) medicine man
(D) amulet (E) gift

675. TANTALIZE (A) tease (B) wax (C) warrant
(D) authorize (E) summarize

Word List 46   tantrum-tome

tantrum N. fit of petulance; caprice. The child learned that he could have almost anything if he went into *tantrums*.

taper N. candle. She lit the *taper* on the windowsill.

tarantula N. venomous spider. We need an antitoxin to counteract the bite of the *tarantula*.

tarry V. delay; dawdle. We can't *tarry* if we want to get to the airport on time.

tatty ADJ. worn and shabby; bedraggled. Cinderella's stepsisters sneered at her in her frayed apron and *tatty* old gown.

taut ADJ. tight; ready. The captain maintained that he ran a *taut* ship.

tautological ADJ. needlessly repetitious. In the sentence "It was visible to the eye," the phrase "to the eye" is *tautological*. tautology, N.

tawdry ADJ. cheap and gaudy. He won a few *tawdry* trinkets at Coney Island.

taxonomist N. specialist in classifying (animals, etc.). Dental patterns often enable the *taxonomist* to distinguish members of one rodent species from those of another.

tedium N. boredom; weariness. We hope this new Game Boy will help you overcome the *tedium* of your stay in the hospital. tedious, ADJ.

teetotalism N. practice of abstaining totally from alcoholic drinks. Though the doctor warned Bert to cut down his booze intake, she didn't insist that he practice *teetotalism*. teetotaler, N.

temerity N. boldness; rashness. Do you have the *temerity* to argue with me?

temper V. moderate; tone down or restrain; toughen (steel). Not even her supervisor's grumpiness could *temper* Nancy's enthusiasm for her new job.

temperament N. characteristic frame of mind; disposition; emotional excess. Although the twins look alike, they differ markedly in *temperament*: Tod is calm, but Rod is excitable.

temperate ADJ. restrained; self-controlled; moderate in respect to temperature. Try to be *temperate* in your eating this holiday season; if you control your appetite, you won't gain too much weight. Goldilocks found San Francisco's *temperate* climate neither too hot nor too cold but just right.

tempestuous ADJ. stormy; impassioned; violent. Racket-throwing tennis star John McEnroe was famed for his displays of *tempestuous* temperament.

tempo N. speed of music. I find the band's *tempo* too slow for such a lively dance.

temporal ADJ. not lasting forever; limited by time; secular. At one time in our history, *temporal* rulers assumed that they had been given their thrones by divine right.

temporize V. act evasively to gain time; avoid committing oneself. Ordered by King John to drive Robin Hood out of Sherwood Forest, the sheriff *temporized*, hoping to put off any confrontation with the outlaw band.

tenacious ADJ. holding fast. I had to struggle to break his *tenacious* hold on my arm.

tenacity N. firmness; persistence. Jean Valjean could not believe the *tenacity* of Inspector Javert. Here all Valjean had done was to steal a loaf of bread, and the inspector had pursued him doggedly for 20 years!

tendentious ADJ. having an aim; biased; designed to further a cause. The editorials in this periodical are *tendentious* rather than truth-seeking.

tender V. offer; extend. Although no formal charges had been made against him, in the wake of the recent scandal the mayor felt he should *tender* his resignation.

tenet N. doctrine; dogma. The agnostic did not accept the *tenets* of their faith.

tensile ADJ. capable of being stretched. Mountain climbers must know the *tensile* strength of their ropes.

tentative ADJ. hesitant; not fully worked out or developed; experimental; not definite or positive. Unsure of his welcome at the Christmas party, Scrooge took a *tentative* step into his nephew's drawing room.

■ **tenuous** ADJ. thin; rare; slim. The allegiance of our allies is held by such *tenuous* ties that we have little hope they will remain loyal.

tenure N. holding of an office; time during which such an office is held. A special recall election put an end to Gray Davis's *tenure* in office as governor of California.

tepid ADJ. lukewarm. To avoid scalding the baby, make sure the bath water is *tepid*, not hot.

termination N. end. Though the time for *termination* of the project was near, we still had a lot of work to finish before we shut up shop. terminate, V.

terminology N. terms used in a science or art. The special *terminology* developed by some authorities in the field has done more to confuse laypersons than to enlighten them.

terminus N. last stop of railroad. After we reached the railroad *terminus*, we continued our journey into the wilderness on saddle horses.

terrestrial ADJ. on or relating to the earth. We have been able to explore the *terrestrial* regions much more thoroughly than the aquatic or celestial regions.

terse ADJ. concise; abrupt; pithy. There is a fine line between speech that is *terse* and to the point and speech that is too abrupt.

tertiary ADJ. third. He is so thorough that he analyzes *tertiary* causes where other writers are content with primary and secondary reasons.

tesselated ADJ. inlaid; mosaic. I recall seeing a table with a *tesselated* top of bits of stone and glass in a very interesting pattern.

testator N. maker of a will. The attorney called in his secretary and his partner to witness the signature of the *testator*.

testy ADJ. irritable; short-tempered. My advice is to avoid discussing this problem with her today as she is rather *testy* and may shout at you. testiness, N.

tether V. tie with a rope. Before we went to sleep, we *tethered* the horses to prevent their wandering off during the night.

thematic ADJ. relating to a unifying motif or idea. Those who think of *Moby Dick* as a simple adventure story about whaling miss its underlying *thematic* import.

theocracy N. government run by religious leaders. Though some Pilgrims aboard the Mayflower favored the establishment of a *theocracy* in New England, many of their fellow voyagers preferred a nonreligious form of government.

theoretical ADJ. not practical or applied; hypothetical. Bob was better at applied engineering and computer programming than he was at *theoretical* physics and math. While I can still think of some *theoretical* objections to your plan, you've convinced me of its basic soundness.

therapeutic ADJ. curative. Now better known for its racetrack, Saratoga Springs first gained attention for the *therapeutic* qualities of its famous "healing waters."

thermal ADJ. pertaining to heat. The natives discovered that the hot springs gave excellent *thermal* baths and began to develop their community as a health resort. also N.

thespian ADJ. pertaining to drama. Her success in the school play convinced her she was destined for a *thespian* career. also N.

thrall N. slave; bondage. The captured soldier was held in *thrall* by the conquering army.

threadbare ADJ. worn through till the threads show; shabby and poor. The poorly paid adjunct professor hid the *threadbare* spots on his jacket by sewing leather patches on his sleeves.

thrifty ADJ. careful about money; economical. A *thrifty* shopper compares prices before making major purchases.

thrive V. prosper; flourish. Despite the impact of the recession on the restaurant trade, Philip's cafe *thrived*.

throes N. violent anguish. The *throes* of despair can be as devastating as the spasms accompanying physical pain.

throng N. crowd. *Throngs* of shoppers jammed the aisles. also V.

throttle V. strangle. The criminal tried to *throttle* the old man with his bare hands.

thwart V. baffle; frustrate. He felt that everyone was trying to *thwart* his plans and prevent his success.

tightwad N. excessively frugal person; miser. Jill called Jack a *tightwad* because he never picked up the check.

tiller N. handle used to move boat's rudder (to steer). Fearing the wind might shift suddenly and capsize the skiff, Tom kept one hand on the *tiller* at all times.

timbre N. quality of a musical tone produced by a musical instrument. We identify the instrument producing a musical sound by its *timbre*.

timidity N. lack of self-confidence or courage. If you are to succeed as a salesperson, you must first lose your *timidity* and fear of failure.

timorous ADJ. fearful; demonstrating fear. Her *timorous* manner betrayed the anxiety she felt at the moment.

tipple V. drink (alcoholic beverages) frequently. He found that his most enjoyable evenings occurred when he *tippled* with his friends at the local pub. N.

■ **tirade** N. extended scolding; denunciation; harangue. Every time the boss holds a meeting, he goes into a lengthy *tirade*, scolding us for everything from tardiness to padding our expenses.

titanic ADJ. gigantic. *Titanic* waves beat against the majestic S.S. *Titanic*, driving it against the concealed iceberg. titan, N.

tithe N. tax of one-tenth. Because he was an agnostic, he refused to pay his *tithes* to the clergy. also V.

titillate V. tickle. I am here not to *titillate* my audience but to enlighten it.

title N. right or claim to possession; mark of rank; name (of a book, film, etc.). Though the penniless Duke of Ragwort no longer held *title* to the family estate, he still retained his *title* as head of one of England's oldest families.

titter N. nervous laugh. Her aunt's constant *titter* nearly drove her mad. also V.

titular ADJ. having the title of an office without the obligations. Although he was the *titular* head of the company, the real decisions were made by his general manager.

toady N. servile flatterer; yes man. Never tell the boss anything he doesn't wish to hear: he doesn't want an independent adviser, he just wants a *toady*. also V.

toga N. Roman outer robe. Marc Antony pointed to the slashes in Caesar's *toga*.

tome N. large volume. She spent much time in the libraries poring over ancient *tomes*.

Test

Word List 46   *Synonyms*

Each of the questions below consists of a word in capital letters, followed by five lettered words or phrases. Choose the lettered word or phrase that is most nearly similar in meaning to the word in capital letters and write the letter of your choice on your answer paper.

676. TARRY (A) polish (B) restrain (C) surpass
(D) linger (E) disturb

677. TAUTOLOGY (A) memory (B) repetition (C) tension
(D) simile (E) lack of logic

678. TAWDRY (A) orderly (B) meretricious
(C) reclaimed (D) filtered (E) proper

679. TEMERITY (A) timidity (B) resourcefulness
(C) boldness (D) tremulousness (E) caution

680. TEMPORAL (A) priestly (B) scholarly (C) secular
(D) sleepy (E) sporadic

681. TENACIOUS (A) fast running (B) intentional
(C) obnoxious (D) holding fast (E) collecting

682. TENACITY (A) splendor (B) perseverance
(C) tendency (D) ingratitude (E) decimation

683. TENDENTIOUS (A) biased (B) likely (C) absurd
(D) festive (E) literary

684. TENTATIVE (A) prevalent (B) portable (C) mocking
(D) wry (E) experimental

685. TENUOUS (A) vital (B) thin (C) careful
(D) dangerous (E) necessary

686. TEPID (A) boiling (B) lukewarm (C) freezing
(D) gaseous (E) cold

687. TERSE (A) brief in speech (B) bold in manner
(C) under strain (D) without honor (E) beyond fear

688. TESSELATED (A) striped (B) made of mosaics
(C) piebald (D) uniform (E) trimmed

689. THESPIAN (A) foreigner (B) skeptic
(C) daydreamer (D) magician (E) actor

690. TITILLATE (A) hasten (B) fasten (C) stimulate
(D) incorporate (E) enlarge

Word List 47   tonsure-ubiquitous

tonsure N. shaving of the head, especially by person entering religious orders. His *tonsure,* even more than his monastic garb, indicated that he was a member of the religious order.

topography N. physical features of a region. Before the generals gave the order to attack, they ordered a complete study of the *topography* of the region.

■ **torpor** N. lethargy; sluggishness; dormancy. Throughout the winter, nothing aroused the bear from his *torpor*: he would not emerge from hibernation until spring. torpid, ADJ.

torque N. twisting force; force producing rotation. With her wrench she applied sufficient *torque* to the nut to loosen it.

torrent N. rushing stream; flood. Day after day of heavy rain saturated the hillside until the water ran downhill in *torrents*. torrential, ADJ.

torrid ADJ. passionate; hot or scorching. The novels published by Harlequin Romances feature *torrid* love affairs, some set in *torrid* climates.

torso N. trunk of statue with head and limbs missing; human trunk. This *torso*, found in the ruins of Pompeii, is now on exhibition in the museum in Naples.

■ **tortuous** ADJ. winding; full of curves. Because this road is so *tortuous*, it is unwise to go faster than twenty miles an hour on it.

totter V. move unsteadily; sway, as if about to fall. On unsteady feet, the drunk *tottered* down the hill to the nearest bar.

touchstone N. stone used to test the fineness of gold alloys; criterion. What *touchstone* can be used to measure the character of a person?

touchy ADJ. sensitive; irascible. Do not discuss his acne with Archy; he is very *touchy* about it.

tout V. publicize; praise excessively. I lost confidence in my broker after he *touted* some junk bonds that turned out to be a bad investment.

toxic ADJ. poisonous. We must seek an antidote for whatever *toxic* substance he has eaten. toxicity, N.

tract N. pamphlet; a region of indefinite size. The King granted William Penn a *tract* of land in the New World.

■ **tractable** ADJ. docile; easily managed. Although Susan seemed a *tractable* young woman, she had a stubborn streak of independence that occasionally led her to defy the powers-that-be when she felt they were in the wrong. tractability, N.

traduce V. expose to slander. His opponents tried to *traduce* the candidate's reputation by spreading rumors about his past.

trajectory N. path taken by a projectile. The police tried to locate the spot from which the assassin had fired the fatal shot by tracing the *trajectory* of the bullet.

tranquillity N. calmness; peace. After the commotion and excitement of the city, I appreciate the *tranquillity* of these fields and forests.

transcendent ADJ. surpassing; exceeding ordinary limits; superior. Standing on the hillside watching the sunset through the Golden Gate was a *transcendent* experience for Lise: the sight was so beautiful it surpassed her wildest dreams. transcend, V. transcendency, N.

transcribe V. copy. When you *transcribe* your notes, please send a copy to Mr. Smith and keep the original for our files. transcription, N.

transfigure V. transform outwardly, usually for the better; change in form or aspect. Elizabeth Barrett's love for Robert Browning *transfigured* her poetry as well as transforming her life. Bely's poetic novel, *Peterburg*, is a travel fantasy set within a city that is both real and *transfigured* into a myth.

■ **transgression** N. violation of a law; sin. Although Widow Douglass was willing to overlook Huck's minor *transgressions*, Miss Watson refused to forgive and forget.

transient ADJ. momentary; temporary; staying for a short time. Lexy's joy at finding the perfect Christmas gift for Phil was *transient*; she still had to find presents for the cousins and Uncle Bob. Located near the airport, this hotel caters to the largely *transient* trade. also N.

transition N. going from one state of action to another. During the period of *transition* from oil heat to gas heat, the furnace will have to be shut off.

transitory ADJ. impermanent; fleeting. Fame is *transitory*: today's rising star is all too soon tomorrow's washed-up has-been. transitoriness, N.

translucent ADJ. partly transparent. We could not recognize the people in the next room because of the *translucent* curtains that separated us.

transmute V. change; convert to something different. He was unable to *transmute* his dreams into actualities.

transparent ADJ. easily detected; permitting light to pass through freely. John's pride in his son is *transparent*; no one who sees the two of them together can miss it. transparency, N.

transpire V. be revealed; happen. When Austen writes the sentence "It had just *transpired* that he had left gaming debts behind him," her meaning is not that the debts had just been incurred, but that the shocking news had just leaked out.

transport N. strong emotion. Margo was a creature of extremes, at one moment in *transports* of joy over a vivid sunset, at another moment in *transports* of grief over a dying bird. also V.

trappings N. outward decorations; ornaments. He loved the *trappings* of success: the limousines, the stock options, the company jet.

traumatic ADJ. pertaining to an injury caused by violence. In his nightmares, he kept on recalling the *traumatic* experience of being wounded in battle. trauma, N.

travail N. painful physical or mental labor; drudgery; torment. Like every other recent law school graduate she knew, Shelby hated the seemingly endless *travail* of cramming for the bar exam.

traverse V. go through or across. When you *traverse* this field, be careful of the bull.

travesty N. harshly distorted imitation; parody; debased likeness. Phillips's translation of *Don Quixote* is so inadequate and clumsy that it seems a *travesty* of the original.

treatise N. article treating a subject systematically and thoroughly. He is preparing a *treatise* on the Elizabethan playwrights for his graduate degree.

trek N. travel; journey. The tribe made their *trek* further north that summer in search of game. also V.

tremor N. trembling; slight quiver. She had a nervous *tremor* in her right hand.

tremulous ADJ. trembling; wavering. She was *tremulous* more from excitement than from fear.

trenchant ADJ. forceful and vigorous; cutting. With his *trenchant* wit, reviewer Frank Rich cut straight to the heart of the matter, panning a truly dreadful play.

trepidation N. fear; nervous apprehension. As she entered the office of the dean of admissions, Sharon felt some *trepidation* about how she would do in her interview.

tribulation N. distress; suffering. After all the trials and *tribulations* we have gone through, we need this rest.

tribunal N. court of justice. The decision of the *tribunal* was final and the prisoner was sentenced to death.

tribute N. tax levied by a ruler; mark of respect. The colonists refused to pay *tribute* to a foreign despot.

trident N. three-pronged spear. Neptune is usually depicted as rising from the sea, carrying his *trident* on his shoulder.

trifling ADJ. trivial; unimportant. Why bother going to see a doctor for such a *trifling*, everyday cold? trifle, N.

trigger V. set off. John is touchy today; say one word wrong and you'll *trigger* an explosion.

trilogy N. group of three works. Having read the first two volumes of Philip Pullman's *trilogy*, Alison could hardly wait to read volume three.

trinket N. knickknack; bauble. Whenever she traveled abroad, Ethel would pick up costume jewelry and other *trinkets* as souvenirs.

trite ADJ. hackneyed; commonplace. The *trite* and predictable situations in many television programs turn off many viewers, who, in turn, turn off their sets.

trivia N. trifles; unimportant matters. Too many magazines ignore newsworthy subjects and feature *trivia*.

troth N. pledge of good faith especially in betrothal. He gave her his *troth* and vowed to cherish her always.

trough N. container for feeding farm animals; lowest point (of a wave, business cycle, etc.). The hungry pigs struggled to get at the fresh swill in the *trough.* The surfer rode her board, coasting along in the *trough* between two waves.

■ **truculence** N. aggressiveness; ferocity. Tynan's reviews were noted for their caustic attacks and general tone of *truculence.* truculent, ADJ.

truism N. self-evident truth. Many a *truism* is summed up in a proverb; for example, "Marry in haste, repent at leisure."

truncate V. cut the top off. The top of the cone that has been *truncated* in a plane parallel to its base is a circle.

tryst N. meeting. The lovers kept their *tryst* even though they realized their danger. also V.

tumid ADJ. swollen; pompous; bombastic. I especially dislike his *tumid* style; I prefer writing that is less swollen and bombastic.

tumult N. commotion; riot; noise. She could not make herself heard over the *tumult* of the mob.

tundra N. rolling, treeless plain in Siberia and arctic North America. Despite the cold, many geologists are trying to discover valuable mineral deposits in the *tundra.*

turbid ADJ. muddy; having the sediment disturbed. The water was *turbid* after the children had waded through it.

turbulence N. state of violent agitation. Warned of approaching *turbulence* in the atmosphere, the pilot told the passengers to fasten their seat belts.

tureen N. deep dish for serving soup. The waiters brought the soup to the tables in silver *tureens.*

turgid ADJ. swollen; distended. The *turgid* river threatened to overflow the levees and flood the countryside.

turmoil N. great commotion and confusion. Lydia running off with a soldier! Mother fainting at the news! The Bennet household was in *turmoil.*

turncoat N. traitor. The British considered Benedict Arnold a loyalist; the Americans considered him a *turncoat.*

turpitude N. depravity. A visitor may be denied admittance to this country if she has been guilty of moral *turpitude.*

tutelage N. guardianship; training. Under the *tutelage* of such masters of the instrument, she made rapid progress as a virtuoso.

tutelary ADJ. protective; pertaining to a guardianship. I am acting in my *tutelary* capacity when I refuse to grant you permission to leave the campus.

tycoon N. wealthy leader. John D. Rockefeller was a prominent *tycoon.*

typhoon N. tropical hurricane or cyclone. If you liked *Twister,* you'll love *Typhoon*!

tyranny N. oppression; cruel government. Frederick Douglass fought against the *tyranny* of slavery throughout his entire life.

tyro N. beginner; novice. For a mere *tyro,* you have produced some marvelous results.

ubiquitous ADJ. being everywhere; omnipresent. That Christmas "The Little Drummer Boy" seemed *ubiquitous*: Justin heard the tune everywhere he went. ubiquity, N.

Test

Word List 47   *Antonyms*

Each of the questions below consists of a word in capital letters, followed by five lettered words or phrases. Choose the lettered word or phrase that is most nearly opposite in meaning to the word in capital letters and write the letter of your choice on your answer paper.

691. TRACTABLE (A) unmanageable (B) irreligious (C) mortal (D) incapable (E) unreal

692. TRADUCE (A) exhume (B) increase (C) purchase (D) extol (E) donate

693. TRANQUILLITY (A) lack of sleep (B) lack of calm (C) emptiness (D) renewal (E) closeness

694. TRANSIENT (A) carried (B) close (C) permanent (D) removed (E) certain

695. TREMULOUS (A) steady (B) obese (C) young (D) healthy (E) unkempt

696. TRENCHANT (A) lacking bite (B) imperious (C) inessential (D) unafraid (E) narrow-minded

697. TREPIDATION (A) slowness (B) amputation (C) fearlessness (D) adroitness (E) death

698. TRITE (A) correct (B) original (C) distinguished (D) premature (E) certain

699. TRUCULENT (A) juicy (B) overflowing (C) peaceful (D) determined (E) false

700. TUMULT (A) scarcity (B) defeat (C) coolness (D) density (E) serenity

701. TURBID (A) clear (B) improbable (C) invariable (D) honest (E) turgid

702. TURBULENCE (A) reaction (B) approach (C) impropriety (D) calm (E) hostility

703. TURGID (A) rancid (B) shrunken (C) cool (D) explosive (E) painful

704. TURPITUDE (A) amplitude (B) heat (C) wealth (D) virtue (E) quiet

705. TYRO (A) infant (B) rubber (C) personnel (D) idiot (E) expert

Word List 48   ulterior-vehement

ulterior ADJ. situated beyond; unstated and often questionable. You must have an *ulterior* motive for your behavior, since there is no obvious reason for it.

ultimate ADJ. final; not susceptible to further analysis. Scientists are searching for the *ultimate* truths.

ultimatum N. last demand; warning. Since they have ignored our *ultimatum,* our only recourse is to declare war.

umbrage N. resentment; anger; sense of injury or insult. She took *umbrage* at his remarks and stormed away in a huff.

unaccountable ADJ. inexplicable; unreasonable or mysterious. I have taken an *unaccountable* dislike to my doctor: "I do not love thee, Doctor Fell. The reason why, I cannot tell."

unanimity N. complete agreement. We were surprised by the *unanimity* with which our proposals were accepted by the different groups. unanimous, ADJ.

unassailable ADJ. not subject to question; not open to attack. Penelope's virtue was *unassailable*; while she waited for her husband to come back from the war, no other guy had a chance.

unassuaged ADJ. unsatisfied; not soothed. Her anger is *unassuaged* by your apology.

unassuming ADJ. modest. He is so *unassuming* that some people fail to realize how great a man he really is.

unbridled ADJ. violent. She had a sudden fit of *unbridled* rage.

uncanny ADJ. strange; mysterious. You have the *uncanny* knack of reading my innermost thoughts.

unconscionable ADJ. unscrupulous; excessive. She found the loan shark's demands *unconscionable* and impossible to meet.

uncouth ADJ. outlandish; clumsy; boorish. Most biographers portray Lincoln as an *uncouth* and ungainly young man.

unction N. the act of anointing with oil. The anointing with oil of a person near death is called extreme *unction.*

unctuous ADJ. oily; bland; insincerely suave. Uriah Heep disguised his nefarious actions by *unctuous* protestations of his "'umility."

underlying ADJ. fundamental; lying below. The *underlying* cause of the student riot was not the strict curfew rule but the moldy cafeteria food. Miss Marple seems a sweet little old lady at first, but an iron will *underlies* that soft and fluffy facade.

undermine V. weaken; sap. The recent corruption scandals have *undermined* many people's faith in the city government.

underscore V. emphasize. Addressing the jogging class, Kim *underscored* the importance to runners of good nutrition.

undulating ADJ. moving with a wavelike motion. The Hilo Hula Festival featured an *undulating* sea of grass skirts.

unearth V. dig up. When they *unearthed* the city, the archeologists found many relics of an ancient civilization.

unearthly ADJ. not earthly; weird. There is an *unearthly* atmosphere in her work that amazes the casual observer.

unequivocal ADJ. plain; obvious. My answer to your proposal is an *unequivocal* and absolute "No."

unerringly ADV. infallibly. My teacher *unerringly* pounced on the one typographical error in my essay.

unexceptionable ADJ. not offering any basis for criticism; entirely acceptable. Objecting to Jack's lack of a respectable family background, Lady Bracknell declared that Cecily could marry only a man of *unexceptionable* lineage and character.

unfaltering ADJ. steadfast. She approached the guillotine with *unfaltering* steps.

unfeigned ADJ. genuine; real. She turned so pale that I am sure her surprise was *unfeigned.*

unfettered ADJ. liberated; freed from chains. Chained to the wall for months on end, the hostage despaired that he would ever be *unfettered.* unfetter, V.

unfledged ADJ. immature. It is hard for an *unfledged* writer to find a sympathetic publisher.

unfrock V. to strip a priest or minister of church authority. To disbar a lawyer, to *unfrock* a priest, to suspend a doctor's license to practice—these are extreme steps that the authorities should take only after careful consideration.

ungainly ADJ. awkward; clumsy; unwieldy. "If you want to know whether Nick's an *ungainly* dancer, check out my bruised feet," said Nora. Anyone who has ever tried to carry a bass fiddle knows it's an *ungainly* instrument.

unguent N. ointment. Apply this *unguent* to the sore muscles before retiring.

uniformity N. sameness; monotony. At *Persons* magazine, we strive for *uniformity* of style; as a result, all our writers wind up sounding exactly alike. uniform, ADJ.

unilateral ADJ. one-sided. This legislation is *unilateral* since it binds only one party in the controversy.

unimpeachable ADJ. blameless and exemplary. Her conduct in office was *unimpeachable* and her record is spotless.

uninhibited ADJ. unrepressed. The congregation was shocked by her *uninhibited* laughter during the sermon.

unintimidating ADJ. unfrightening. Though Phil had expected to feel overawed when he met Joe Montana, he found the world-famous quarterback friendly and *unintimidating.*

unique ADJ. without an equal; single in kind. You have the *unique* distinction of being the first student whom I have had to fail in this course.

unison N. unity of pitch; complete accord. The choir sang in *unison.*

universal ADJ. characterizing or affecting all; present everywhere. At first, no one shared Christopher's opinions; his theory that the world was round was met with *universal* disdain.

unkempt ADJ. disheveled; uncared for in appearance. Jeremy hated his neighbor's *unkempt* lawn: he thought its neglected appearance had a detrimental effect on neighborhood property values.

unmitigated ADJ. unrelieved or immoderate; absolute. After four days of *unmitigated* heat, I was ready to collapse from heat prostration. The congresswoman's husband was an *unmitigated* jerk: not only did he abandon her, but also he took her campaign funds!

unobtrusive ADJ. inconspicuous; not blatant. Reluctant to attract notice, the governess took a chair in a far corner of the room and tried to be as *unobtrusive* as possible.

unpalatable ADJ. distasteful; disagreeable. "I refuse to swallow your conclusion," she said, finding his logic *unpalatable*.

unprecedented ADJ. novel; unparalleled. For a first novel, Margaret Mitchell's book *Gone with the Wind* was an *unprecedented* success.

unprepossessing ADJ. unattractive. During adolescence many attractive young people somehow acquire the false notion that their appearance is *unprepossessing*.

unravel V. disentangle; solve. With equal ease Miss Marple *unraveled* tangled balls of yarn and baffling murder mysteries.

unrequited ADJ. not reciprocated. Suffering the pangs of *unrequited* love, Olivia rebukes Cesario for his hardheartedness.

unruly ADJ. disobedient; lawless. The only way to curb this *unruly* mob is to use tear gas.

unsavory ADJ. distasteful; morally offensive. People with *unsavory* reputations should not be allowed to work with young children.

unscathed ADJ. unharmed. They prayed he would come back from the war *unscathed*.

unseemly ADJ. unbecoming; indecent; in poor taste. When Seymour put whoopee cushions on all the seats in the funeral parlor, his conduct was most *unseemly*.

unsightly ADJ. ugly. Although James was an experienced emergency room nurse, he occasionally became queasy when faced with a particularly *unsightly* injury.

unsullied ADJ. untarnished. I am happy that my reputation is *unsullied*.

untenable ADJ. indefensible; not able to be maintained. Wayne is so contrary that, the more *untenable* a position is, the harder he'll try to defend it.

untoward ADJ. unfortunate or unlucky; adverse; unexpected. Trying to sneak out of the house, Huck had a most *untoward* encounter with Miss Watson, who thwarted his escape.

untrammeled ADJ. without limits or restrictions; unrestrained. The first principle of a free society is an *untrammeled* flow of words in an open forum. The free-spirited young radical led an unconventional life, *untrammeled* by rigid norms of ideological orthodoxy.

unwarranted ADJ. unjustified; groundless; undeserved. Your assumption that I would accept your proposal is *unwarranted*, sir; I do not want to marry you at all. We could not understand Martin's *unwarranted* rudeness to his mother's guests.

unwieldy ADJ. awkward; cumbersome; unmanageable. The large carton was so *unwieldy* that the movers had trouble getting it up the stairs.

unwitting ADJ. unintentional; not knowing. She was the *unwitting* tool of the swindlers.

unwonted ADJ. unaccustomed. He hesitated to assume the *unwonted* role of master of ceremonies at the dinner.

upbraid V. severely scold; reprimand. Not only did Miss Minchin *upbraid* Ermengarde for her disobedience, but also she hung her up by her braids from a coatrack in the classroom.

uproarious ADJ. marked by commotion; extremely funny; very noisy. The *uproarious* comedy hit *Ace Ventura: Pet Detective* starred Jim Carrey, whose comic mugging provoked gales of *uproarious* laughter from audiences coast to coast.

upshot N. outcome. The *upshot* of the rematch was that the former champion proved that he still possessed all the skills of his youth.

urbane ADJ. suave; refined; elegant. The courtier was *urbane* and sophisticated. urbanity, N.

urchin N. mischievous child (usually a boy). Get out! This store is no place for grubby *urchins!*

ursine ADJ. bearlike; pertaining to a bear. Because of its *ursine* appearance, the great panda has been identified with the bears; actually, it is closely related to the raccoon.

usurp V. seize another's power or rank. The revolution ended when the victorious rebel general succeeded in his attempt to *usurp* the throne. usurpation, N.

usury N. lending money at illegal rates of interest. The loan shark was found guilty of *usury*.

utopia N. ideal place, state, or society. Fed up with this imperfect universe, Don would have liked to run off to Shangri-la or some other imaginary *utopia*. utopian, ADJ.

uxorious ADJ. excessively devoted to one's wife. His friends laughed at him because he was so *uxorious* and submissive to his wife's desires.

■ **vacillate** V. waver; fluctuate. Uncertain which suitor she ought to marry, the princess *vacillated*, saying now one, now the other. vacillation, N.

vacuous ADJ. empty; lacking in ideas; stupid. The candidate's *vacuous* remarks annoyed the audience, who had hoped to hear more than empty platitudes. vacuity, N.

vagabond N. wanderer; tramp. In summer, college students wander the roads of Europe like carefree *vagabonds*. also ADJ.

vagary N. caprice; whim. She followed every *vagary* of fashion.

vagrant ADJ. stray; random. He tried to study, but could not collect his *vagrant* thoughts.

vagrant N. homeless wanderer. Because he was a stranger in town with no visible means of support, Martin feared he would be jailed as a *vagrant*. vagrancy, N.

vainglorious ADJ. boastful; excessively conceited. She was a *vainglorious* and arrogant individual.

valedictory ADJ. pertaining to farewell. I found the *valedictory* address too long; leave-taking should be brief. also N.

valid ADJ. logically convincing; sound; legally acceptable. You're going to have to come up with a better argument if you want to convince me that your reasoning is *valid*.

validate V. confirm; ratify. I will not publish my findings until I *validate* my results.

valor N. bravery. He received the Medal of Honor for his *valor* in battle.

vampire N. ghostly being that sucks the blood of the living. Children were afraid to go to sleep at night because of the many legends of *vampires*.

vanguard N. forerunners; advance forces. We are the *vanguard* of a tremendous army that is following us.

vantage N. position giving an advantage. They fired upon the enemy from behind trees, walls and any other point of *vantage* they could find.

vapid ADJ. dull and unimaginative; insipid and flavorless. "*Bor*-ing!" said Cher, as she suffered through yet another *vapid* lecture about Dead White Male Poets.

vaporize V. turn into vapor (steam, gas, fog, etc.). "Zap!" went Super Mario's atomic ray gun as he *vaporized* another deadly foe.

variegated ADJ. many-colored. Without her glasses, Gretchen saw the fields of tulips as a *variegated* blur.

vassal N. in feudalism, one who held land of a superior lord. The lord demanded that his *vassals* contribute more to his military campaign.

vaunted ADJ. boasted; bragged; highly publicized. This much *vaunted* project proved a disappointment when it collapsed.

veer V. change in direction. After what seemed an eternity, the wind *veered* to the east and the storm abated.

vegetate V. live in a monotonous way. I do not understand how you can *vegetate* in this quiet village after the adventurous life you have led.

vehement ADJ. forceful; intensely emotional; with marked vigor. Alfred became so *vehement* in describing what was wrong with the Internal Revenue Service that he began jumping up and down and gesticulating wildly. vehemence, N.

Test

Word List 48 *Antonyms*

Each of the questions below consists of a word in capital letters, followed by five lettered words or phrases. Choose the lettered word or phrase that is most nearly opposite in meaning to the word in capital letters and write the letter of your choice on your answer paper.

706. UNEARTH (A) conceal (B) gnaw (C) clean (D) fling (E) react

707. UNFEIGNED (A) pretended (B) fashionable (C) wary (D) switched (E) colonial

708. UNGAINLY (A) ignorant (B) graceful (C) detailed (D) dancing (E) pedantic

709. UNIMPEACHABLE (A) fruitful (B) rampaging (C) faulty (D) pensive (E) thorough

710. UNKEMPT (A) bombed (B) washed (C) neat (D) showy (E) tawdry

711. UNRULY (A) chatting (B) obedient (C) definite (D) lined (E) curious

712. UNSEEMLY (A) effortless (B) proper (C) conducive (D) pointed (E) informative

713. UNSULLIED (A) tarnished (B) countless (C) soggy (D) papered (E) homicidal

714. UNTENABLE (A) supportable (B) tender (C) sheepish (D) tremulous (E) adequate

715. UNWITTING (A) clever (B) intense (C) sensitive (D) freezing (E) intentional

716. VACILLATION (A) remorse (B) relief (C) respect (D) steadfastness (E) inoculation

717. VALEDICTORY (A) sad (B) collegiate (C) derivative (D) salutatory (E) promising

718. VALOR (A) admonition (B) injustice (C) cowardice (D) generosity (E) repression

719. VANGUARD (A) regiment (B) rear (C) echelon (D) protection (E) loyalty

720. VAUNTED (A) unvanquished (B) fell (C) belittled (D) exacting (E) believed

Word List 49   velocity-vogue

velocity   N. speed. The train went by at considerable *velocity*.

venal   ADJ. capable of being bribed. The *venal* policeman accepted the bribe offered him by the speeding motorist whom he had stopped.

vendetta   N. blood feud. The rival mobs engaged in a bitter *vendetta*.

vendor   N. seller. The fruit *vendor* sold her wares from a stall on the sidewalk.

veneer   N. thin layer; cover. Casual acquaintances were deceived by his *veneer* of sophistication and failed to recognize his fundamental shallowness.

venerable   ADJ. deserving high respect. We do not mean to be disrespectful when we refuse to follow the advice of our *venerable* leader.

■ **venerate**   V. revere. In Tibet today, the common people still *venerate* their traditional spiritual leader, the Dalai Lama.

venial   ADJ. forgivable; trivial. When Jean Valjean stole a loaf of bread to feed his starving sister, he committed a *venial* offense.

venison   N. the meat of a deer. The hunters dined on *venison*.

venom   N. poison; hatred. Bitten on his ankle by a *venomous* snake, the cowboy contortionist curled up like a pretzel and sucked the *venom* out of the wound.

vent   N. small opening; outlet. The wine did not flow because the air *vent* in the barrel was clogged.

vent   V. express; utter. He *vented* his wrath on his class.

ventral   ADJ. abdominal. We shall now examine the *ventral* plates of this serpent, not the dorsal side.

ventriloquist   N. someone who can make his or her voice seem to come from another person or thing. This *ventriloquist* does an act in which she has a conversation with a wooden dummy.

venture   V. risk; dare; undertake a risk. Fearing to distress the actors, the timorous reviewer never *ventured* to criticize a performance in harsh terms. also N.

venturesome   ADJ. bold. A group of *venturesome* women were the first to scale Mt. Annapurna.

venue   N. location. The attorney asked for a change of *venue;* he thought his client would do better if the trial were held in a less conservative county.

■ **veracious**   ADJ. truthful. I can recommend him for this position because I have always found him *veracious* and reliable. veracity, N.

veracity   N. truthfulness. Trying to prove Hill a liar, Senator Spector repeatedly questioned her *veracity*. veracious, ADJ.

verbalize   V. put into words. I know you don't like to talk about these things, but please try to *verbalize* your feelings.

verbatim   ADV. word for word. He repeated the message *verbatim*. also ADJ.

verbiage   N. pompous array of words. After we had waded through all the *verbiage*, we discovered that the writer had said very little.

■ **verbose**   ADJ. wordy. We had to make some major cuts in Senator Foghorn's speech because it was far too *verbose*. verbosity, N.

verdant   ADJ. green; lush in vegetation. Monet's paintings of the *verdant* meadows were symphonies in green.

verdigris   N. green coating on copper that has been exposed to the weather. Despite all attempts to protect the statue from the elements, it became coated with *verdigris*.

verge   N. border; edge. Madame Curie knew she was on the *verge* of discovering the secrets of radioactive elements. also V.

verisimilar   ADJ. probable or likely; having the appearance of truth. Something *verisimilar* is very similar to the truth, or at least seems to be.

verisimilitude   N. appearance of truth; likelihood. Critics praised her for the *verisimilitude* of her performance as Lady Macbeth. She was completely believable.

veritable   ADJ. actual; being truly so; not false or imaginary. At his computer, Pavel is a *veritable* wizard, creating graphic effects that seem magical to programmers less skilled than he.

verity   N. quality of being true; lasting truth or principle. Do you question the *verity* of Kato Kaelin's testimony about what he heard the night Nicole Brown Simpson was slain? To the skeptic, everything was relative: there were no eternal *verities* in which one could believe.

vernacular   N. living language; natural style. Cut out those old-fashioned "thee's" and "thou's" and write in the *vernacular*. also ADJ.

vernal   ADJ. pertaining to spring. We may expect *vernal* showers all during the month of April.

versatile   ADJ. having many talents; capable of working in many fields. She was a *versatile* athlete, earning varsity letters in basketball, hockey, and track. versatility, N.

vertex   N. summit. Let us drop a perpendicular line from the *vertex* of the triangle to the base. vertices, PL.

vertigo   N. severe dizziness. When you test potential plane pilots for susceptibility to spells of *vertigo*, be sure to hand out airsick bags.

verve   N. enthusiasm; liveliness. She approached her studies with such *verve* that it was impossible for her to do poorly.

vestige   N. trace; remains. We discovered *vestiges* of early Indian life in the cave.

vex   N. annoy; distress. Please try not to *vex* your mother; she is doing the best she can.

■ **viable** ADJ. practical or workable; capable of maintaining life. The plan to build a new baseball stadium, though missing a few details, is *viable* and stands a good chance of winning popular support.

viand N. food. There was a variety of *viands* at the feast.

vicarious ADJ. acting as a substitute; done by a deputy. Many people get a *vicarious* thrill at the movies by imagining they are the characters on the screen.

vicissitude N. change of fortune. Humbled by life's *vicissitudes,* the last emperor of China worked as a lowly gardener in the palace over which he had once ruled.

victuals N. food. I am very happy to be able to provide you with these *victuals;* I know you are hungry.

vie V. contend; compete. Politicians *vie* with one another, competing for donations and votes.

vigilant ADJ. watchfully awake; alert to spot danger. From the battlement, the *vigilant* sentry kept his eyes open for any sign of enemy troops approaching. vigilance, N.

vigor N. active strength. Although he was over seventy years old, Jack had the *vigor* of a man in his prime. vigorous, ADJ.

vignette N. picture; short literary sketch. The *New Yorker* published her latest *vignette.*

vilify V. slander. Waging a highly negative campaign, the candidate attempted to *vilify* his opponent's reputation. vilification, N.

vindicate V. clear from blame; exonerate; justify or support. The lawyer's goal was to *vindicate* her client and prove him innocent on all charges. The critics' extremely favorable reviews *vindicate* my opinion that *The Madness of King George* is a brilliant movie.

vindictive ADJ. out for revenge; malicious. Divorce sometimes brings out a *vindictive* streak in people; when Tony told Tina he was getting a divorce, she poured green Jell-O into his aquarium and turned his tropical fish into dessert.

vintner N. winemaker; seller of wine. The poet wondered what the *vintners* could buy that would be half as precious as the wine they sold.

viper N. poisonous snake. The habitat of the horned *viper,* a particularly venomous snake, is in sandy regions like the Sahara or the Sinai peninsula.

virile ADJ. manly. I do not accept the premise that a man is *virile* only when he is belligerent.

virtual ADJ. in essence; for practical purposes. She is a *virtual* financial wizard when it comes to money matters.

virtue N. goodness; moral excellence; good quality. A *virtue* carried to extremes can turn into something resembling vice; humility, for example, can degenerate into servility and spinelessness.

virtuoso N. highly skilled artist. The child prodigy Yehudi Menuhin grew into a *virtuoso* whose *virtuosity* on the violin thrilled millions. virtuosity, N.

virulent ADJ. extremely poisonous; hostile; bitter. Laid up with a *virulent* case of measles, Vera blamed her doctors because her recovery took so long. In fact, she became quite *virulent* on the subject of the quality of modern medical care. virulence, N.

virus N. disease communicator. The doctors are looking for a specific medicine to control this *virus.*

visage N. face; appearance. The stern *visage* of the judge indicated that she had decided to impose a severe penalty.

visceral ADJ. felt in one's inner organs. She disliked the *visceral* sensations she had whenever she rode the roller coaster.

viscid ADJ. adhesive; gluey. The trunk of the maple tree was *viscid* with sap.

■ **viscous** ADJ. sticky, gluey. Melted tar is a *viscous* substance. viscosity, N.

vise N. tool for holding work in place. Before filing its edges, the keysmith took the blank key and fixed it firmly between the jaws of a *vise.*

visionary ADJ. produced by imagination; fanciful; mystical. She was given to *visionary* schemes that never materialized. also N.

vital ADJ. vibrant and lively; critical; living; breathing. The *vital,* highly energetic first aid instructor stressed that it was *vital* in examining accident victims to note their *vital* signs.

vitiate V. spoil the effect of; make inoperative. Fraud will *vitiate* the contract.

vitreous ADJ. pertaining to or resembling glass. Although this plastic has many *vitreous* qualities such as transparency, it is unbreakable.

vitriolic ADJ. corrosive; sarcastic. Such *vitriolic* criticism is uncalled for.

■ **vituperative** ADJ. abusive; scolding. He became more *vituperative* as he realized that we were not going to grant him his wish.

vivacious ADJ. lively or animated; sprightly. She had always been *vivacious* and sparkling.

vivisection N. act of dissecting living animals. The Society for the Prevention of Cruelty to Animals opposed *vivisection* and deplored the practice of using animals in scientific experiments.

vixen N. female fox; ill-tempered woman. Aware that she was right once again, he lost his temper and called her a shrew and a *vixen.*

vociferous ADJ. clamorous; noisy. The crowd grew *vociferous* in its anger and threatened to take the law into its own hands.

vogue N. popular fashion. Jeans became the *vogue* on many college campuses.

Test

Word List 49   *Synonyms and Antonyms*

Each of the questions below consists of a word in capital letters, followed by five lettered words or phrases. Choose the lettered word or phrase that is most nearly similar or opposite in meaning to the word in capital letters and write the letter of your choice on your answer paper.

721. VENAL (A) springlike (B) honest (C) angry (D) indifferent (E) going

722. VENERATE (A) revere (B) age (C) reject (D) reverberate (E) degenerate

723. VENIAL (A) unforgivable (B) unforgettable (C) unmistaken (D) fearful (E) fragrant

724. VERACIOUS (A) worried (B) slight (C) alert (D) truthful (E) instrumental

725. VERDANT (A) poetic (B) green (C) red (D) autumnal (E) frequent

726. VERITY (A) sanctity (B) reverence (C) falsehood (D) rarity (E) household

727. VESTIGE (A) trek (B) trail (C) trace (D) trial (E) tract

728. VIABLE (A) moribund (B) salable (C) useful (D) foolish (E) inadequate

729. VIAND (A) wand (B) gown (C) food (D) orchestra (E) frock

730. VICARIOUS (A) substitutional (B) aggressive (C) sporadic (D) reverent (E) internal

731. VIGILANCE (A) bivouac (B) guide (C) watchfulness (D) mob rule (E) posse

732. VILIFY (A) erect (B) eulogize (C) better (D) magnify (E) horrify

733. VINDICTIVE (A) revengeful (B) fearful (C) divided (D) literal (E) convincing

734. VIRULENT (A) sensuous (B) malignant (C) masculine (D) conforming (E) approaching

735. VISAGE (A) doubt (B) personality (C) hermitage (D) face (E) armor

Word List 50   volatile-zephyr

■ **volatile** ADJ. changeable; explosive; evaporating rapidly. The political climate today is extremely *volatile*: no one can predict what the electorate will do next. Maria Callas's temper was extremely *volatile*: the only thing you could predict was that she would blow up. Acetone is an extremely *volatile* liquid: it evaporates instantly. volatility, N.

volition N. act of making a conscious choice. She selected this dress of her own *volition*.

voluble ADJ. fluent; glib; talkative. An excessively *voluble* speaker suffers from logorrhea: he continually runs off at the mouth! volubility, N.

voluminous ADJ. bulky; large. A caftan is a *voluminous* garment; the average person wearing one looks as if he or she is draped in a small tent.

voracious ADJ. ravenous. The wolf is a *voracious* animal, its hunger never satisfied.

vortex N. whirlwind; whirlpool; center of turbulence; predicament into which one is inexorably plunged. Sucked into the *vortex* of the tornado, Dorothy and Toto were carried from Kansas to Oz.

vouchsafe V. grant condescendingly; guarantee. I can safely *vouchsafe* you fair return on your investment.

voyeur N. Peeping Tom. Jill called Jack a *voyeur* when she caught him aiming his binoculars at a bedroom window of the house next door.

vulnerable ADJ. susceptible to wounds. His opponents could not harm Achilles, who was *vulnerable* only in his heel. vulnerability, N.

vulpine ADJ. like a fox; crafty. She disliked his sly ways, but granted him a certain *vulpine* intelligence.

waffle V. speak equivocally about an issue. When asked directly about the governor's involvement in the savings and loan scandal, the press secretary *waffled*, talking all around the issue.

waft V. moved gently by wind or waves. Daydreaming, he gazed at the leaves that *wafted* past his window.

waggish ADJ. mischievous; humorous; tricky. He was a prankster who, unfortunately, often overlooked the damage he could cause with his *waggish* tricks. wag, N.

waif N. homeless child or animal. Although he already had eight cats, he could not resist adopting yet another feline *waif*.

waive V. give up temporarily; yield. I will *waive* my rights in this matter in order to expedite our reaching a proper decision.

wake N. trail of ship or other object through water; path of something that has gone before. The *wake* of the swan gliding through the water glistened in the moonlight. Reporters and photographers converged on South Carolina in the *wake* of the hurricane that devastated much of the eastern seaboard.

wallow V. roll in; indulge in; become helpless. The hippopotamus loves to *wallow* in the mud.

wan ADJ. having a pale or sickly color; pallid. Suckling asked, "Why so pale and *wan*, fond lover?"

wanderlust N. strong longing to travel. Don't set your heart on a traveling man. He's got too much *wanderlust* to settle down.

wane V. decrease in size or strength; draw gradually to an end. To *wane* is the opposite of to wax or increase in size. When lit, does a wax candle *wane*?

wangle V. wiggle out; fake. She tried to *wangle* an invitation to the party.

wanton ADJ. unrestrained; willfully malicious; unchaste. Pointing to the stack of bills, Sheldon criticized Sarah for her *wanton* expenditures. In response, Sara accused Sheldon of making an unfounded, *wanton* attack.

warble V. sing; babble. Every morning the birds *warbled* outside her window. also N.

■ **warranted** ADJ. justified; authorized. Before the judge issues the injunction, you must convince her this action is *warranted*.

warranty N. guarantee; assurance by seller. The purchaser of this automobile is protected by the manufacturer's *warranty* that he will replace any defective part for five years or 50,000 miles.

warren N. tunnels in which rabbits live; crowded conditions in which people live. The tenement was a veritable *warren*, packed with people too poor to live elsewhere.

■ **wary** ADJ. very cautious. The spies grew *wary* as they approached the sentry.

wastrel N. profligate. He was denounced as a *wastrel* who had dissipated his inheritance.

wax V. increase; grow. With proper handling, her fortunes *waxed* and she became rich.

waylay V. ambush; lie in wait. They agreed to *waylay* their victim as he passed through the dark alley going home.

wean V. accustom a baby not to nurse; give up a cherished activity. He decided he would *wean* himself away from eating junk food and stick to fruits and vegetables.

weather V. endure the effects of weather or other forces. He *weathered* the changes in his personal life with difficulty, as he had no one in whom to confide.

welt N. mark from a beating or whipping. The evidence of child abuse was very clear; Jennifer's small body was covered with *welts* and bruises.

■ **welter** N. turmoil; bewildering jumble. The existing *welter* of overlapping federal and state proclaims cries out for immediate reform.

welter V. wallow. At the height of the battle, the casualties were so numerous that the victims *weltered* in their blood while waiting for medical attention.

wheedle V. cajole; coax; deceive by flattery. She knows she can *wheedle* almost anything she wants from her father.

whelp N. young wolf, dog, tiger, etc. This collie *whelp* won't do for breeding, but he'd make a fine pet.

whet V. sharpen; stimulate. The odors from the kitchen are *whetting* my appetite; I will be ravenous by the time the meal is served.

whiff N. puff or gust (of air, scent, etc.); hint. The slightest *whiff* of Old Spice cologne brought memories of George to her mind.

■ **whimsical** N. capricious; fanciful. In *Mrs. Doubtfire*, the hero is a playful, *whimsical* man who takes a notion to dress up as a woman so that he can look after his children, who are in the custody of his ex-wife. whimsy, N.

whinny V. neigh like a horse. When he laughed through his nose, it sounded as if he *whinnied*.

whit N. smallest speck; shred; tiny bit. There's not one *whit* of truth in your allegations.

whittle V. pare; cut off bits. As a present for Aunt Polly, Tom *whittled* some clothespins out of a chunk of wood.

whorl N. ring of leaves around stem; ring. Identification by fingerprints is based on the difference in shape and number of the *whorls* on the fingers.

willful ADJ. intentional; headstrong. Donald had planned to kill his wife for months; clearly, her death was a case of deliberate, *willful* murder, not a crime of passion committed by a hasty, *willful* youth unable to foresee the consequences of his deeds.

wily ADJ. cunning; artful. She is as *wily* as a fox in avoiding trouble.

wince V. shrink back; flinch. The screech of the chalk on the blackboard made her *wince*.

windfall N. fallen fruit; unexpected lucky event. This huge tax refund is quite a *windfall*.

winnow V. sift; separate good parts from bad. This test will *winnow* out the students who study from those who don't bother.

winsome ADJ. agreeable; gracious; engaging. By her *winsome* manner, she made herself liked by everyone who met her.

wispy ADJ. thin; slight; barely discernible. Worried about preserving his few *wispy* tufts of hair, Walter carefully massaged his scalp and applied hair restorer every night.

wistful ADJ. vaguely longing; sadly pensive. With a last *wistful* glance at the happy couples dancing in the hall, Sue headed back to her room to study for her exam.

withdrawn ADJ. introverted; remote. Rebuffed by his colleagues, the initially outgoing young researcher became increasingly *withdrawn*.

wither V. shrivel; decay. Cut flowers are beautiful for a day, but all too soon they *wither*.

withhold V. refuse to give; hold back. The tenants decided to *withhold* a portion of the rent until the landlord kept his promise to renovate the building.

withstand V. stand up against; successfully resist. If you can *withstand* all the peer pressure in high school to cut classes and goof off, you should survive college in fine shape.

witless ADJ. foolish; idiotic. If Beavis is a half-wit, then Butthead is totally *witless*.

witticism N. witty saying; wisecrack. I don't mean any criticism, but your last supposed *witticism* really hurt my feelings.

wizardry N. sorcery; magic. Merlin amazed the knights with his *wizardry*.

wizened ADJ. withered; shriveled. The *wizened* old man in the home for the aged was still active and energetic.

woe N. deep, inconsolable grief; affliction; suffering. Pale and wan with grief, Wanda was bowed down beneath the burden of her *woes*.

wont N. custom; habitual procedure. As was her *wont*, she jogged two miles every morning before going to work.

worldly ADJ. engrossed in matters of this earth; not spiritual. You must leave your *worldly* goods behind you when you go to meet your Maker.

wrangle V. quarrel; obtain through arguing; herd cattle. They *wrangled* over their inheritance.

wrath N. anger; fury. She turned to him, full of *wrath*, and said, "What makes you think I'll accept lower pay for this job than you get?"

wreak V. inflict. I am afraid he will *wreak* his vengeance on the innocent as well as the guilty.

wrench V. pull; strain; twist. She *wrenched* free of her attacker and landed a powerful kick to his kneecap.

wrest V. pull away; take by violence. With only ten seconds left to play, our team *wrested* victory from their grasp.

writ N. written command issued by a court. The hero of Leonard's novel is a process server who invents unorthodox ways of serving *writs* on reluctant parties.

writhe V. twist in coils; contort in pain. In *Dances with Snakes*, the snake dancer wriggled sinuously as her boa constrictor *writhed* around her torso.

wry ADJ. twisted; with a humorous twist. We enjoy Dorothy Parker's verse for its *wry* wit.

xenophobia N. fear or hatred of foreigners. When the refugee arrived in America, he was unprepared for the *xenophobia* he found there.

yen N. longing; urge. She had a *yen* to get away and live on her own for a while.

yeoman N. man owning small estate; middle-class farmer. It was not the aristocrat but the *yeoman* who determined the nation's policies.

yield N. amount produced; crop; income on investment. An experienced farmer can estimate the annual *yield* of his acres with surprising accuracy. also V.

yield V. give in; surrender. The wounded knight refused to *yield* to his foe.

yoke V. join together, unite. I don't wish to be *yoked* to him in marriage, as if we were cattle pulling a plow. also N.

yokel N. country bumpkin. Although her older sisters both had married farmers, Rita rejected the notion of marrying some uncultivated *yokel*.

yore N. time past. She dreamed of the elegant homes of *yore*, but gave no thought to their inelegant plumbing.

zany ADJ. crazy; comic. I can watch the Marx brothers' *zany* antics for hours.

zeal N. eager enthusiasm. Wang's *zeal* was contagious; soon all his fellow students were busily making posters, inspired by his ardent enthusiasm for the cause. zealous, ADJ.

■ **zealot** N. fanatic; person who shows excessive zeal. Though Glenn was devout, he was no *zealot*; he never tried to force his religious beliefs on his friends.

zenith N. point directly overhead in the sky; summit. When the sun was at its *zenith*, the glare was not as strong as at sunrise and sunset.

zephyr N. gentle breeze; west wind. When these *zephyrs* blow, it is good to be in an open boat under a full sail.

Test

Word List 50   *Synonyms*

Each of the following questions consists of a word in capital letters, followed by five lettered words or phrases. Choose the lettered word or phrase that is most nearly similar in meaning to the word in capital letters and write the letter of your choice on your answer paper.

736. VOLUBLE (A) worthwhile (B) serious (C) terminal (D) loquacious (E) circular

737. VORACIOUS (A) ravenous (B) spacious (C) truthful (D) pacific (E) tenacious

738. VOUCHSAFE (A) borrow (B) grant (C) punish (D) desire (E) qualify

739. WAIF (A) soldier (B) urchin (C) surrender (D) breeze (E) spouse

740. WANTON (A) needy (B) passive (C) rumored (D) oriental (E) unchaste

741. WARRANTY (A) threat (B) guarantee (C) order for arrest (D) issue (E) fund

742. WASTREL (A) refuse (B) spendthrift (C) mortal (D) tolerance (E) song

743. WAYLAY (A) ambush (B) journey (C) rest (D) road map (E) song

744. WELTER (A) heat (B) greeting (C) recovery (D) universe (E) tumult

745. WHINNY (A) complain (B) hurry (C) request (D) neigh (E) gallop

746. WINDFALL (A) unexpected gain (B) widespread destruction (C) calm (D) autumn (E) wait

747. WINSOME (A) victorious (B) gracious (C) married (D) permanent (E) pained

748. WIZENED (A) magical (B) clever (C) shriveled (D) swift (E) active

749. YEOMAN (A) masses (B) middle-class farmer (C) proletarian (D) indigent person (E) man of rank

750. ZEALOT (A) beginner (B) patron (C) fanatic (D) murderer (E) leper

Answer Key

Test—Word List 1

1. E	6. E	11. A
2. A	7. B	12. E
3. C	8. E	13. A
4. D	9. A	14. D
5. B	10. A	15. C

Test—Word List 2

16. E	21. A	26. B
17. B	22. A	27. D
18. A	23. B	28. B
19. D	24. B	29. C
20. A	25. B	30. D

Test—Word List 3

31. C	36. E	41. B
32. C	37. C	42. E
33. D	38. B	43. E
34. D	39. E	44. C
35. A	40. D	45. A

Test—Word List 4

46. A	51. C	56. E
47. A	52. A	57. C
48. B	53. C	58. D
49. D	54. B	59. D
50. B	55. D	60. C

Test—Word List 5

61. E	66. A	71. D
62. D	67. C	72. C
63. B	68. C	73. C
64. C	69. B	74. B
65. C	70. C	75. D

Test—Word List 6

76. D	81. A	86. C
77. B	82. B	87. A
78. D	83. B	88. E
79. A	84. E	89. E
80. E	85. E	90. C

Test—Word List 7

91. B	96. B	101. D
92. B	97. A	102. B
93. B	98. D	103. A
94. D	99. B	104. A
95. B	100. C	105. B

Test—Word List 8

106. D	111. B	116. B
107. E	112. A	117. D
108. A	113. D	118. A
109. C	114. C	119. C
110. E	115. D	120. B

Test—Word List 9

121. D	126. E	131. A
122. E	127. A	132. D
123. E	128. D	133. C
124. C	129. B	134. B
125. C	130. E	135. A

Test—Word List 10

136. E	141. B	146. E
137. B	142. E	147. E
138. D	143. D	148. C
139. C	144. D	149. A
140. A	145. D	150. D

Test—Word List 11

151. B	156. C	161. B
152. B	157. C	162. D
153. A	158. E	163. D
154. A	159. E	164. A
155. A	160. B	165. B

Test—Word List 12

166. C	171. C	176. B
167. B	172. B	177. B
168. C	173. A	178. A
169. D	174. A	179. C
170. D	175. B	180. A

Test—Word List 13

181. A	186. A	191. C
182. E	187. B	192. B
183. D	188. C	193. E
184. D	189. B	194. A
185. A	190. C	195. A

Test—Word List 14

196. D	201. C	206. B
197. E	202. C	207. D
198. B	203. C	208. C
199. A	204. B	209. E
200. C	205. B	210. D

Test—Word List 15

211. C	216. C	221. B
212. A	217. A	222. E
213. D	218. A	223. A
214. D	219. C	224. A
215. D	220. D	225. B

Test—Word List 16

226. D	231. B	236. A
227. A	232. C	237. D
228. C	233. D	238. C
229. E	234. C	239. A
230. E	235. E	240. B

Test—Word List 17

241. A	246. C	251. D
242. A	247. A	252. A
243. B	248. A	253. E
244. E	249. C	254. B
245. E	250. D	255. B

Test—Word List 18

256. A	261. D	266. A
257. A	262. D	267. A
258. C	263. E	268. C
259. D	264. C	269. B
260. A	265. B	270. E

Test—Word List 19

271. A	276. A	281. A
272. D	277. A	282. D
273. E	278. D	283. C
274. C	279. C	284. B
275. E	280. B	285. C

Test—Word List 20

286. A	291. A	296. E
287. B	292. A	297. D
288. B	293. D	298. A
289. B	294. C	299. A
290. D	295. C	300. B

Test—Word List 21

301. B	306. E	311. E
302. B	307. C	312. A
303. C	308. B	313. B
304. C	309. D	314. D
305. C	310. D	315. C

Test—Word List 22

316. D	321. E	326. C
317. A	322. A	327. C
318. A	323. B	328. A
319. D	324. C	329. B
320. A	325. E	330. D

Test—Word List 23

331. B	336. A	341. A
332. A	337. D	342. A
333. B	338. C	343. E
334. E	339. C	344. B
335. C	340. D	345. A

Test—Word List 24

346. C	351. D	356. B
347. B	352. A	357. C
348. C	353. A	358. A
349. A	354. A	359. B
350. B	355. B	360. D

Test—Word List 25

361. A	366. B	371. E
362. E	367. B	372. B
363. B	368. C	373. D
364. D	369. D	374. C
365. E	370. A	375. A

Test—Word List 26

376. C	381. B	386. B
377. A	382. A	387. E
378. B	383. C	388. E
379. B	384. C	389. E
380. B	385. C	390. A

Test—Word List 27

391. A	396. E	401. B
392. D	397. E	402. B
393. B	398. C	403. A
394. D	399. A	404. C
395. B	400. D	405. B

Test—Word List 28

406. B	411. B	416. B
407. A	412. E	417. A
408. E	413. D	418. D
409. E	414. E	419. D
410. C	415. C	420. A

Test—Word List 29

421. B	426. D	431. A
422. A	427. E	432. C
423. B	428. B	433. B
424. B	429. A	434. C
425. C	430. E	435. A

Test—Word List 30

436. A	441. A	446. E
437. A	442. B	447. B
438. B	443. D	448. C
439. D	444. B	449. E
440. C	445. A	450. B

Test—Word List 31

451. B	456. A	461. E
452. E	457. C	462. C
453. C	458. C	463. A
454. C	459. A	464. B
455. B	460. B	465. A

Test—Word List 32

466. B	471. D	476. D
467. C	472. C	477. B
468. C	473. B	478. A
469. A	474. A	479. C
470. C	475. B	480. A

Test—Word List 33

481. C	486. A	491. E
482. B	487. B	492. C
483. E	488. C	493. E
484. D	489. D	494. B
485. B	490. B	495. A

Test—Word List 34

496. D	501. B	506. D
497. A	502. B	507. D
498. D	503. A	508. C
499. A	504. E	509. C
500. E	505. C	510. A

Test—Word List 35

511. A	516. C	521. E
512. C	517. B	522. A
513. C	518. D	523. C
514. C	519. C	524. E
515. B	520. A	525. E

Test—Word List 36

526. A	531. E	536. A
527. D	532. B	537. D
528. A	533. C	538. D
529. B	534. C	539. D
530. E	535. B	540. D

Test—Word List 37

541. C	546. A	551. A
542. C	547. A	552. C
543. D	548. C	553. E
544. E	549. B	554. B
545. C	550. A	555. A

Test—Word List 38

556. E	561. E	566. A
557. D	562. E	567. D
558. C	563. B	568. C
559. B	564. A	569. D
560. B	565. E	570. C

Test—Word List 39

571. B	576. C	581. C
572. B	577. D	582. B
573. E	578. B	583. A
574. A	579. C	584. D
575. A	580. E	585. A

Test—Word List 40

586. E	591. C	596. D
587. B	592. A	597. D
588. D	593. B	598. B
589. C	594. A	599. D
590. A	595. D	600. E

Test—Word List 41

601. E	606. B	611. C
602. B	607. B	612. D
603. A	608. A	613. B
604. D	609. D	614. A
605. A	610. B	615. A

Test—Word List 42

616. C	621. D	626. B
617. A	622. E	627. D
618. B	623. A	628. A
619. C	624. D	629. D
620. D	625. C	630. E

Test—Word List 43

631. C	636. C	641. D
632. C	637. E	642. A
633. E	638. C	643. E
634. A	639. E	644. A
635. C	640. D	645. B

Test—Word List 44

646. A	651. B	656. A
647. B	652. A	657. B
648. D	653. D	658. A
649. A	654. C	659. C
650. E	655. C	660. C

Test—Word List 45

661. C	666. C	671. C
662. C	667. B	672. D
663. A	668. A	673. A
664. C	669. A	674. D
665. B	670. A	675. A

Test—Word List 46

676. D	681. D	686. B
677. B	682. B	687. A
678. B	683. A	688. B
679. C	684. E	689. E
680. C	685. B	690. C

Test—Word List 47

691. A	696. A	701. A
692. D	697. C	702. D
693. B	698. B	703. B
694. C	699. C	704. D
695. A	700. E	705. E

Test—Word List 48

706. A	711. B	716. D
707. A	712. B	717. D
708. B	713. A	718. C
709. C	714. A	719. B
710. C	715. E	720. C

Test—Word List 49

721. B	726. C	731. C
722. A	727. C	732. B
723. A	728. A	733. A
724. D	729. C	734. B
725. B	730. A	735. D

Test—Word List 50

736. D	741. B	746. A
737. A	742. B	747. B
738. B	743. A	748. C
739. B	744. E	749. B
740. E	745. D	750. C

Basic Word Parts

Words are made up of word parts: prefixes, suffixes and roots. A knowledge of these word parts and their meanings can help you determine the meanings of unfamiliar words.

Common Prefixes

A *prefix* is a syllable that precedes the root or stem and changes or refines its meaning.

Prefix	Meaning	Illustration
ab, abs	from, away from	*abduct* lead away, kidnap *abjure* renounce
ad, ac, af, ag, an, ap, ar, as, at	to, forward	*adit* entrance *accord* agreement, harmony *affliction* cause of distress *aggregation* collection *annexation* addition *appease* bring toward peace *arraignment* indictment *assumption* arrogance, taking for granted *attendance* presence, the persons present
ambi	both	*ambiguous* of double meaning *ambivalent* having two conflicting emotions
an, a	without	*anarchy* lack of government *amoral* without moral sense
ante	before	*antecedent* preceding event or word *antediluvian* ancient (before the flood)
anti	against, opposite	*antipathy* hatred *antithetical* exactly opposite
arch	chief, first	*archetype* original *archbishop* chief bishop
be	over, thoroughly	*bedaub* smear over *befuddle* confuse thoroughly
bi	two	*bicameral* composed of two houses (Congress) *biennial* every two years
cata	down	*catastrophe* disaster *cataract* waterfall *catapult* hurl (throw down)
circum	around	*circumnavigate* sail around (the globe) *circumspect* cautious (looking around) *circumscribe* limit (place a circle around)
com, co, col, con, cor	with, together	*combine* merge with *coeditor* joint editor *collateral* subordinate, connected *conference* meeting *corroborate* confirm

Prefix	Meaning	Illustration
contra, contro	against	*contravene* conflict with *controversy* dispute
de	down, away	*debase* lower in value *decadence* deterioration
demi	partly, half	*demigod* partly divine being
di	two	*dichotomy* division into two parts *dilemma* choice between two bad alternatives
dia	across	*diagonal* across a figure *diameter* distance across a circle
dis, dif	not, apart	*discord* lack of harmony *differ* disagree (carry apart)
dys	faulty, bad	*dyslexia* faulty ability to read *dyspepsia* indigestion
ex, e	out	*expel* drive out *eject* throw out
extra, extro	beyond, outside	*extracurricular* beyond the curriculum *extraterritorial* beyond a nation's bounds *extrovert* person interested chiefly in external objects and actions
hyper	above; excessively	*hyperbole* exaggeration *hyperventilate* breathe at an excessive rate
hypo	beneath; lower	*hypoglycemia* low blood sugar
in, il, im, ir	not	*inefficient* not efficient *inarticulate* not clear or distinct *illegible* not readable *impeccable* not capable of sinning; flawless *irrevocable* not able to be called back
in, il, im, ir	in, on, upon	*invite* call in *illustration* something that makes clear *impression* effect upon mind or feelings *irradiate* shine upon
inter	between, among	*intervene* come between *international* between nations *interjection* a statement thrown in
intra, intro	within	*intramural* within a school *introvert* person who turns within himself
macro	large, long	*macrobiotic* tending to prolong life *macrocosm* the great world (the entire universe)
mega	great, million	*megalomania* delusions of grandeur *megaton* explosive force of a million tons of TNT
meta	involving change	*metamorphosis* change of form
micro	small	*microcosm* miniature universe *microscopic* extremely small

Prefix	Meaning	Illustration
mis	bad, improper	*misdemeanor* minor crime; bad conduct *mischance* unfortunate accident
mis	hatred	*misanthrope* person who hates mankind *misogynist* woman-hater
mono	one	*monarchy* government by one ruler *monotheism* belief in one god
multi	many	*multifarious* having many parts *multitudinous* numerous
neo	new	*neologism* newly coined word *neophyte* beginner; novice
non	not	*noncommittal* undecided
ob, oc, of, op	against	*obloquy* infamy; disgrace *occlude* close; block out *offend* insult *opponent* someone who struggles against; foe
olig	few	*oligarchy* government by a few
pan	all, every	*panacea* cure-all *panorama* unobstructed view in all directions
para	beyond, related	*parallel* similar *paraphrase* restate; translate
per	through, completely	*permeable* allowing passage through *pervade* spread throughout
peri	around, near	*perimeter* outer boundary *periphery* edge
poly	many	*polyglot* speaking several languages
post	after	*posthumous* after death
pre	before	*preamble* introductory statement *premonition* forewarning
prim	first	*primordial* existing at the dawn of time *primogeniture* state of being the first born
pro	forward, in favor of	*propulsive* driving forward *proponent* supporter
proto	first	*prototype* first of its kind
pseudo	false	*pseudonym* pen name
re	again, back	*reiterate* repeat *reimburse* pay back
retro	backward	*retrospect* looking back *retroactive* effective as of a past date
se	away, aside	*secede* withdraw *seclude* shut away
semi	half, partly	*semiconscious* partly conscious

Prefix	Meaning	Illustration
sub, suc, suf, sug, sup, sus	under, less	*subjugate* bring under control *succumb* yield; cease to resist *suffuse* spread through *suggest* hint *suppress* put down by force *suspend* delay; temporarily cease
super, sur	over, above	*supernatural* above natural things *surtax* additional tax
syn, sym, syl, sys	with, together	*synchronize* time together *sympathize* pity; identify with *syllogism* explanation of how ideas relate *system* network
tele	far	*telegraphic* communicated over a distance
trans	across	*transport* carry across
ultra	beyond, excessive	*ultracritical* exceedingly critical
un	not	*unkempt* not combed; disheveled
under	below	*underling* someone inferior
uni	one	*unison* oneness of pitch; complete accord
vice	in place of	*viceroy* governor acting in place of a king
with	away, against	*withstand* stand up against; resist

Common Roots and Stems

Roots are basic words which have been carried over into English. *Stems* are variations of roots brought about by changes in declension or conjugation.

Root or Stem	Meaning	Illustration
ac, acr	sharp	*acrimonious* bitter; caustic *acerbity* bitterness of temper *acidulate* make somewhat acid or sour
aev, ev	age, era	*primeval* of the age *coeval* of the same age or era *medieval* or *mediaeval* of the Middle Ages
ag, act	to do	*act* deed *agent* doer
agog	leader	*demagogue* false leader of people *pedagogue* teacher (leader of children)
agri, agrari	field	*agrarian* one who works in the field *agriculture* cultivation of fields *peregrination* wandering (through fields)

Root or Stem	Meaning	Illustration
ali	another	*alias* assumed (another) name *alienate* estrange (turn away from another)
alt	high	*altitude* height *altimeter* instrument for measuring height
alter	other	*altruistic* unselfish, considering others *alter ego* a second self
am	love	*amorous* loving, especially sexually *amity* friendship *amicable* friendly
anim	mind, soul	*animadvert* cast criticism upon *unanimous* of one mind *magnanimity* greatness of mind or spirit
ann, enn	year	*annuity* yearly remittance *biennial* every two years *perennial* present all year; persisting for several years
anthrop	human beings	*anthropology* study of human beings *misanthrope* hater of humankind *philanthropy* love of humankind; charity
apt	fit	*aptitude* skill *adapt* make suitable or fit
aqua	water	*aqueduct* passageway for conducting water *aquatic* living in water *aqua fortis* nitric acid (strong water)
arch	ruler, first	*archaeology* study of antiquities (study of first things) *monarch* sole ruler *anarchy* lack of government
aster	star	*astronomy* study of the stars *asterisk* starlike type character (*) *disaster* catastrophe (contrary star)
aud, audit	to hear	*audible* able to be heard *auditorium* place where people may be heard *audience* hearers
auto	self	*autocracy* rule by one person (self) *automobile* vehicle that moves by itself *autobiography* story of one's own life
belli	war	*bellicose* inclined to fight *belligerent* inclined to wage war *rebellious* resisting authority
ben, bon	good	*benefactor* one who does good deeds *benevolence* charity (wishing good) *bonus* something extra above regular pay
biblio	book	*bibliography* list of books *bibliophile* lover of books *Bible* The Book

Root or Stem	Meaning	Illustration
bio	life	*biography* writing about a person's life *biology* study of living things *biochemist* student of the chemistry of living things
breve	short	*brevity* briefness *abbreviate* shorten *breviloquent* marked by brevity of speech
cad, cas	to fall	*decadent* deteriorating *cadence* intonation, musical movement *cascade* waterfall
cap, capt, cept, cip	to take	*capture* seize *participate* take part *precept* wise saying (originally a command)
capit, capt	head	*decapitate* remove (cut off) someone's head *captain* chief
carn	flesh	*carnivorous* flesh-eating *carnage* destruction of life *carnal* fleshly
ced, cess	to yield, to go	*recede* go back, withdraw *antecedent* that which goes before *process* go forward
celer	swift	*celerity* swiftness *decelerate* reduce swiftness *accelerate* increase swiftness
cent	one hundred	*century* one hundred years *centennial* one-hundredth anniversary *centipede* many-footed, wingless animal
chron	time	*chronology* timetable of events *anachronism* a thing out of time sequence *chronicle* register events in order of time
cid, cis	to cut, to kill	*incision* a cut (surgical) *homicide* killing of a human being *fratricide* killing of a brother
cit, citat	to call, to start	*incite* stir up, start up *excite* stir up *recitation* a recalling (or repeating) aloud
civi	citizen	*civilization* society of citizens, culture *civilian* member of community *civil* courteous
clam, clamat	to cry out	*clamorous* loud *declamation* speech *acclamation* shouted approval
claud, claus, clos, clud	to close	*claustrophobia* fear of close places *enclose* close in *conclude* finish

Root or Stem	Meaning	Illustration
cognosc, cognit	to learn	*agnostic* lacking knowledge, skeptical *incognito* traveling under assumed name *cognition* knowledge
compl	to fill	*complete* filled out *complement* that which completes something *comply* fulfill
cord	heart	*accord* agreement (from the heart) *cordial* friendly *discord* lack of harmony
corpor	body	*incorporate* organize into a body *corporeal* pertaining to the body, fleshly *corpse* dead body
cred, credit	to believe	*incredulous* not believing, skeptical *credulity* gullibility *credence* belief
cur	to care	*curator* person who has the care of something *sinecure* position without responsibility *secure* safe
curr, curs	to run	*excursion* journey *cursory* brief *precursor* forerunner
da, dat	to give	*data* facts, statistics *mandate* command *date* given time
deb, debit	to owe	*debt* something owed *indebtedness* debt *debenture* bond
dem	people	*democracy* rule of the people *demagogue* (false) leader of the people *epidemic* widespread (among the people)
derm	skin	*epidermis* skin *pachyderm* thick-skinned quadruped *dermatology* study of skin and its disorders
di, diurn	day	*diary* a daily record of activities, feelings, etc. *diurnal* pertaining to daytime
dic, dict	to say	*abdicate* renounce *diction* speech *verdict* statement of jury
doc, doct	to teach	*docile* obedient; easily taught *document* something that provides evidence *doctor* learned person (originally, teacher)
domin	to rule	*dominate* have power over *domain* land under rule *dominant* prevailing

Root or Stem	Meaning	Illustration
duc, duct	to lead	*viaduct* arched roadway *aqueduct* artificial waterway
dynam	power, strength	*dynamic* powerful *dynamite* powerful explosive *dynamo* engine making electric power
ego	I	*egoist* person who is self-centered *egotist* selfish person *egocentric* revolving about self
erg, urg	work	*energy* power *ergatocracy* rule of the workers *metallurgy* science and technology of metals
err	to wander	*error* mistake *erratic* not reliable, wandering *knight-errant* wandering knight
eu	good, well, beautiful	*eupeptic* having good digestion *eulogize* praise *euphemism* pleasant way of saying something blunt
fac, fic, fec, fect	to make, to do	*factory* place where things are made *fiction* manufactured story *affect* cause to change
fall, fals	to deceive	*fallacious* misleading *infallible* not prone to error, perfect *falsify* lie
fer, lat	to bring, to bear	*transfer* bring from one place to another *translate* bring from one language to another *conifer* bearing cones, as pine trees
fid	belief, faith	*infidel* nonbeliever, heathen *confidence* assurance, belief
fin	end, limit	*confine* keep within limits *finite* having definite limits
flect, flex	to bend	*flexible* able to bend *deflect* bend away, turn aside
fort	luck, chance	*fortuitous* accidental, occurring by chance *fortunate* lucky
fort	strong	*fortitude* strength, firmness of mind *fortification* strengthening *fortress* stronghold
frag, fract	to break	*fragile* easily broken *infraction* breaking of a rule *fractious* unruly, tending to break rules
fug	to flee	*fugitive* someone who flees *refuge* shelter, home for someone fleeing
fus	to pour	*effusive* gushing, pouring out *diffuse* widespread (poured in many directions)

Root or Stem	Meaning	Illustration
gam	marriage	*monogamy* marriage to one person *bigamy* marriage to two people at the same time *polygamy* having many wives or husbands at the same time
gen, gener	class, race	*genus* group of animals or plants with similar traits *generic* characteristic of a class *gender* class organized by sex
grad, gress	to go, to step	*digress* go astray (from the main point) *regress* go backward *gradual* step by step, by degrees
graph, gram	writing	*epigram* pithy statement *telegram* instantaneous message over great distance *stenography* shorthand (writing narrowly)
greg	flock, herd	*gregarious* tending to group together as in a herd *aggregate* group, total *egregious* conspicuously bad; shocking
helio	sun	*heliotrope* flower that faces the sun *heliograph* instrument that uses the sun's rays to send signals
it, itiner	journey, road	*exit* way out *itinerary* plan of journey
jac, jact, jec	to throw	*projectile* missile; something thrown forward *trajectory* path taken by thrown object *ejaculatory* casting or throwing out
jur, jurat	to swear	*perjure* testify falsely *jury* group of men and women sworn to seek the truth *adjuration* solemn urging
labor, laborat	to work	*laboratory* place where work is done *collaborate* work together with others *laborious* difficult
leg, lect, lig	to choose, to read	*election* choice *legible* able to be read *eligible* able to be selected
leg	law	*legislature* law-making body *legitimate* lawful *legal* lawful
liber, libr	book	*library* collection of books *libretto* the "book" of a musical play *libel* slander (originally found in a little book)
liber	free	*liberation* the fact of setting free *liberal* generous (giving freely); tolerant
log	word, study	*entomology* study of insects *etymology* study of word parts and derivations *monologue* speech by one person

Root or Stem	Meaning	Illustration
loqu, locut	to talk	*soliloquy* speech by one individual *loquacious* talkative *elocution* speech
luc	light	*elucidate* enlighten *lucid* clear *translucent* allowing some light to pass through
magn	great	*magnify* enlarge *magnanimity* generosity, greatness of soul *magnitude* greatness, extent
mal	bad	*malevolent* wishing evil *malediction* curse *malefactor* evil-doer
man	hand	*manufacture* create (make by hand) *manuscript* written by hand *emancipate* free (let go from the hand)
mar	sea	*maritime* connected with seafaring *submarine* undersea craft *mariner* seafarer
mater, matr	mother	*maternal* pertaining to motherhood *matriarch* female ruler of a family, group, or state *matrilineal* descended on the mother's side
mit, miss	to send	*missile* projectile *dismiss* send away *transmit* send across
mob, mot, mov	to move	*mobilize* cause to move *motility* ability to move *immovable* not able to be moved
mon, monit	to warn	*admonish* warn *premonition* foreboding *monitor* watcher (warner)
mori, mort	to die	*mortuary* funeral parlor *moribund* dying *immortal* not dying
morph	shape, form	*amorphous* formless, lacking shape *metamorphosis* change of shape *anthropomorphic* in human shape
mut	to change	*immutable* not able to be changed *mutate* undergo a great change *mutability* changeableness, inconstancy
nat	born	*innate* from birth *prenatal* before birth *nativity* birth
nav	ship	*navigate* sail a ship *circumnavigate* sail around the world *naval* pertaining to ships

Root or Stem	Meaning	Illustration
neg	to deny	*negation* denial *renege* deny, go back on one's word *renegade* turncoat, traitor
nomen	name	*nomenclature* act of naming, terminology *nominal* in name only (as opposed to actual) *cognomen* surname, distinguishing nickname
nov	new	*novice* beginner *renovate* make new again *novelty* newness
omni	all	*omniscient* all knowing *omnipotent* all powerful *omnivorous* eating everything
oper	to work	*operate* work *cooperation* working together
pac	peace	*pacify* make peaceful *pacific* peaceful *pacifist* person opposed to war
pass	to feel	*dispassionate* free of emotion *impassioned* emotion-filled *impassive* showing no feeling
pater, patr	father	*patriotism* love of one's country (fatherland) *patriarch* male ruler of a family, group, or state *paternity* fatherhood
path	disease, feeling	*pathology* study of diseased tissue *apathetic* lacking feeling; indifferent *antipathy* hostile feeling
ped, pod	foot	*impediment* stumbling-block; hindrance *tripod* three-footed stand *quadruped* four-footed animal
ped	child	*pedagogue* teacher of children *pediatrician* children's doctor
pel, puls	to drive	*compulsion* a forcing to do *repel* drive back *expel* drive out, banish
pet, petit	to seek	*petition* request *appetite* craving, desire *compete* vie with others
phil	love	*philanthropist* benefactor, lover of humanity *Anglophile* lover of everything English *philanderer* one involved in brief love affairs
pon, posit	to place	*postpone* place after *positive* definite, unquestioned (definitely placed)
port, portat	to carry	*portable* able to be carried *transport* carry across

Root or Stem	Meaning	Illustration
poten	able, powerful	*omnipotent* all-powerful
psych	mind	*psychology* study of the mind
put, putat	to trim, to calculate	*computation* calculation *amputate* cut off
quer, ques, quir, quis	to ask	*inquiry* investigation *inquisitive* questioning *query* question
reg, rect	to rule	*regent* ruler *insurrection* rebellion; overthrow of a ruler
rid, ris	to laugh	*derision* scorn *ridiculous* deserving to be laughed at
rog, rogat	to ask	*interrogate* question
rupt	to break	*interrupt* break into *rupture* a break
sacr	holy	*sacrilegious* impious, violating something holy *sacrament* religious act
sci	to know	*omniscient* knowing all *conscious* aware
scop	to watch, to see	*periscope* device for seeing around corners *microscope* device for seeing small objects
scrib, script	to write	*transcribe* make a written copy *script* written text
sect	cut	*dissect* cut apart *bisect* cut into two pieces
sed, sess	to sit	*sedentary* inactive (sitting)
sent, sens	to think, to feel	*resent* show indignation *sensitive* showing feeling
sequi, secut, seque	to follow	*consecutive* following in order *sequence* arrangement *sequel* that which follows *nonsequitur* something that does not follow logically
solv, solut	to loosen	*absolve* free from blame *dissolute* morally lax
somn	sleep	*insomnia* inability to sleep
soph	wisdom	*philosopher* lover of wisdom
spec, spect, spic	to look at	*spectator* observer *circumspect* cautious (looking around) *despicable* detestable (deserving to be looked down on) *perspicacity* clearsightedness
spir	to breathe	*respiratory* pertaining to breathing *spirited* full of life (breathe)
string, strict	bind	*stringent* strict *stricture* limit, something that restrains

Root or Stem	Meaning	Illustration
stru, struct	to build	*constructive* helping to build *construe* analyze (how something is built)
tang, tact, ting	to touch	*tangent* touching *contact* touching with, meeting *contingent* depending upon
tempor	time	*contemporary* at same time
ten, tent	to hold	*tenable* able to be held *retentive* holding; having a good memory
term	end	*interminable* endless *terminate* end
terr	land	*terrestrial* pertaining to earth *subterranean* underground
therm	heat	*thermostat* instrument that regulates heat
tors, tort	to twist	*distort* twist out of true shape or meaning *torsion* act of twisting
tract	to drag, to pull	*distract* pull (one's attention) away *intractable* stubborn, unable to be dragged
trud, trus	to push, to shove	*intrude* push one's way in *protrusion* something sticking out
urb	city	*urban* pertaining to a city
vac	empty	*vacuous* lacking content, empty-headed *evacuate* compel to empty an area
vad, vas	to go	*invade* enter in a hostile fashion *evasive* not frank; eluding
veni, vent, ven	to come	*intervene* come between *prevent* stop *convention* meeting
ver	true	*veracious* truthful *verisimilitude* appearance of truth
verb	word	*verbose* wordy
vers, vert	to turn	*vertigo* turning dizzy *revert* turn back (to an earlier state) *diversion* something causing one to turn aside
via	way	*deviation* departure from the way *viaduct* roadway (arched)
vid, vis	to see	*vision* sight *evidence* things seen
vinc, vict, vanq	to conquer	*invincible* unconquerable *victory* winning *vanquish* defeat
viv, vit	alive	*vivacious* full of life *vitality* liveliness

Root or Stem	Meaning	Illustration
voc, vocat	to call	*avocation* calling, minor occupation *provocation* calling or rousing the anger of
vol	wish	*malevolent* wishing someone ill *voluntary* of one's own will
volv, volut	to roll	*revolve* roll around *convolution* coiled state

Common Suffixes

A *suffix* is a syllable that is added to a word. Occasionally, it changes the meaning of the word; more frequently, it serves to change the grammatical form of the word (noun to adjective, adjective to noun, noun to verb).

Suffix	Meaning	Illustration
able, ible	capable of (adjective suffix)	*portable* able to be carried *legible* able to be read
ac, ic	like, pertaining to (adjective suffix)	*cardiac* pertaining to the heart *aquatic* pertaining to the water
acious, icious	full of (adjective suffix)	*audacious* full of daring *avaricious* full of greed
al	pertaining to (adjective or noun suffix)	*maniacal* insane *portal* doorway *logical* pertaining to logic
ant, ent	full of (adjective or noun suffix)	*eloquent* pertaining to fluid, effective speech *suppliant* pleader (person full of requests) *verdant* green
ary	like, connected with (adjective or noun suffix)	*dictionary* book connected with words *honorary* with honor *luminary* celestial body
ate	to make (verb suffix)	*consecrate* to make holy *enervate* to make weary *mitigate* to make less severe
ation	that which is (noun suffix)	*exasperation* irritation *irritation* annoyance
cy	state of being (noun suffix)	*democracy* government ruled by the people *obstinacy* stubbornness
eer, er, or	person who (noun suffix)	*mutineer* person who rebels *lecher* person who lusts *censor* person who deletes improper remarks
escent	becoming (adjective suffix)	*evanescent* tending to vanish *pubescent* arriving at puberty

Suffix	Meaning	Illustration
fic	making, doing (adjective suffix)	*terrific* arousing great fear *soporific* causing sleep
fy	to make (verb suffix)	*magnify* enlarge *petrify* turn to stone
iferous	producing, bearing (adjective suffix)	*pestiferous* carrying disease *vociferous* bearing a loud voice
il, ile	pertaining to, capable of (adjective suffix)	*puerile* pertaining to a boy or child *civil* polite
ism	doctrine, belief (noun suffix)	*monotheism* belief in one god *fanaticism* excessive zeal; extreme belief
ist	dealer, doer (noun suffix)	*realist* one who is realistic *artist* one who deals with art
ity	state of being (noun suffix)	*credulity* state of being unduly willing to believe *sagacity* wisdom
ive	like (adjective suffix)	*quantitative* concerned with quantity *effusive* gushing
ize, ise	to make (verb suffix)	*harmonize* make harmonious *enfranchise* make free or set free
oid	resembling, like (adjective suffix)	*ovoid* like an egg *anthropoid* resembling a human being *spheroid* resembling a sphere
ose	full of (adjective suffix)	*verbose* full of words
osis	condition (noun suffix)	*psychosis* diseased mental condition *hypnosis* condition of induced sleep
ous	full of (adjective suffix)	*nauseous* full of nausea *ludicrous* foolish
tude	state of (noun suffix)	*fortitude* state of strength *certitude* state of sureness

PART THREE

ANALYTICAL WRITING: TACTICS, STRATEGIES, AND PRACTICE

Introduction to Part Three

What sort of test is this new analytical writing test? First and foremost, it is *not* a multiple-choice test. It is a *performance* test—you have to write two analytical essays in an hour and fifteen minutes.

The new analytical writing section of the GRE is the longest of the three sections in terms of time allotted. This section is organized in two parts. In Part 1, "Present Your Perspective on an Issue," you have 45 minutes to write an essay expressing your point of view on a particular issue. You will be given your choice of two quotations, each of which states an opinion about an issue; you will probably write a better essay if you go for the quotation that "grabs" you, whose topic seems more appealing to you.

Your job is to take a stand and to support it, drawing on your own experiences and on your readings to come up with examples that reinforce your argument. It does not matter what stand you take; there is no "correct" position, no one true answer. Many different approaches can work. You can agree completely with the quotation's point of view or you can dispute it absolutely. You can disagree with some aspects of the quote, but agree with others. What matters is how you present your case.

Part 2 of the analytical writing section asks you to perform a different but complementary task. In Part 2,

"Analyze an Argument," you have 30 minutes to write an essay critiquing the logical soundness of an argument. You will be given one short passage in which an author makes a claim and backs it up, giving reasons that may well be flawed. You get no choice of passages to analyze; you must work with whatever passage comes up on your screen.

This time your job is *not* to advocate a particular point of view. This is not the moment for you to agree or disagree with the author; it is the moment for you to weigh the validity of the author's reasoning. Your approach is analytical and expository, not argumentative or persuasive. It is your task to examine carefully what the author offers as evidence. You will find it helpful to note what the author claims explicitly, and also to note what she or he assumes (not necessarily justifiably!).

If you study the tactics and work through the practice exercises in the following chapter, and take full advantage of the study materials on the GRE's web site, *www.gre.org*, you will be well prepared for the analytical writing section of the GRE and should feel confident in your ability to write high-scoring essays.

9 Analytical Writing

- ■ **Scoring Guidelines**
- ■ **Essay-Writing: The 5-Step Approach**
- ■ **Tactics**
- ■ **Practice Exercises**

Scoring Guidelines

Two readers will judge your GRE analytical essays, awarding each essay a grade ranging from 0 to 6, with 6 the highest possible score. The powers-that-be then calculate your analytical writing score by taking the average of your four grades, rounding up the result to the nearest half-point. If one reader awarded your issues essay a 5 and your argument essay a 4, while the other reader gave both your essays 4's, you'd come out with a score of 4.25, rounded up to 4.5.

You probably have a sense of what score you need to be accepted by the graduate school of your choice. If you're seeking admission to Harvard's Ph.D. program in history, you're clearly aiming for a 5.5 or 6. If you're aiming for a graduate program in a field that favors number-crunching over essay-writing—mathematics or electrical engineering, for instance—you clearly don't need to aim so high. But however high a score you're seeking, you want to come out of the essay-writing section looking good. And to do that, you have to know what the GRE readers are looking for.

What are the GRE readers looking for? In essence, fluency, organization, and a command of technical English. These are the skills they assess.

Fluency

Fluency is smoothness and ease in communicating. In this case, it is your ability to set down a given number of words on paper within a limited period of time. If you freeze on essay examinations, writing only a sentence or two when whole paragraphs are called for, then you need to practice letting your words and ideas *flow*.

Literary fluency, however, involves more than just the number of words you type. The readers tend to award their highest grades to test-takers who use language well, those who employ a variety of sentence types and demonstrate a command of vocabulary. If you invariably use short, simple sentences, you need to practice constructing more complex ones. If you have a limited vocabulary, you need to expand it, working with our Master Word List (page 110) and other tools to learn the precise meaning of each new word you employ.

Organization

Organization is coherent arrangement. In this case, it is your ability to arrange your thoughts in order, following a clear game plan. In *The Elements of Style,* William Strunk describes certain elementary principles of composition. The paragraph is the basic unit of composition; the beginning of each new paragraph serves to alert readers that they are coming to a new step in the development of the subject. One paragraph leads to the next, drawing readers on to the essay's conclusion.

Organization involves your ability to reason and to marshal evidence to support your viewpoint. If you jump from subject to subject within a single paragraph, if you leave out critical elements, if you misorder your points or never manage to state exactly what you mean, then you need to practice outlining your position briefly before you express it in essay form.

Technical English

Technical English is the part of English that most students hate—grammar, spelling, punctuation, word usage. In this case, it is your ability to produce grammatically correct sentences in standard written English. If your English compositions used to come back to you with the abbreviations "frag" or "agr" or "sp" scribbled all over the margins, then you need to practice reading through your papers to catch any technical mistakes.

There are literally hundreds of handbooks available that will help you handle the mechanics of writing essays. Strunk and White's manual, *The Elements of Style,* provides clear, concise advice, as does William Zinsser's *On Writing Well.* Other good reference tools are *The Harbrace College Handbook,* Edward Johnson's *Handbook of Good English,* and, for the complete grammarphobe, Patricia O'Conner's aptly named *Woe Is I.*

NOTE: Unless you are someone who can't type two words in a row without making a spelling error, do not worry about spelling and punctuation mistakes. The GRE readers generally ignore them. However, if you make so many errors that it becomes difficult for the readers to make sense of what you have written, they will lower your score accordingly.

Essay-Writing: The 5-Step Approach

How to Handle the Issue-Writing Task

You have 45 minutes to complete the issue-writing task. To earn a top score, you need to produce a smooth, 400–700-word essay with solid content, coherent organization, and few, if any, mechanical errors.

Each issue topic is presented as a 1–2 sentence statement commenting on a subject of general concern. This statement makes a claim. Your essay may support, refute, or qualify the views expressed in the statement. Whatever you write, however, must be relevant to the issue under discussion, and you must support your viewpoint with data—reasons and examples derived from your studies, experience, and reading.

GRE readers will evaluate your essay, grading it on the basis of your effectiveness in the following areas:

• Analysis of the statement's implications.

• Organization and articulation of your ideas.

• Use of relevant examples and arguments to support your case.

• Handling of the mechanics of standard written English.

Here is a 5-step plan you can use in writing your issue essay. Suggested times are approximate.

Step One: Begin with Brainstorming (2 minutes).

You do not lack ideas. What you may lack is a direct means of getting in touch with the ideas you already have. One useful technique to "prime the pump" and encourage fluency is *clustering.* Clustering is a method of brainstorming in which you start with a key word or short phrase and let that word or phrase act as a stimulus, triggering all sorts of associations that you jot down. In just a minute or two, you can come up with dozens of associations, some of which you may later be able to incorporate into your essay. (For a thought-provoking discussion of clustering and other brainstorming techniques, see *Writing the Natural Way* by Gabriele Rico.)

Let the issue statement or prompt trigger your brainstorming. As soon as you've clicked on your chosen topic, grab your pencil and sum up the claim the author is making. If, for example, the issue prompt is "Historians and other social scientists are as useful to society as are biochemists and engineers because society's ills cannot be cured by technological progress alone," your quick summation might be "Historians are as useful as scientists." Once you're clear about the author's point, start scribbling. Write down as many reasons that support or weaken the author's claim as you possibly can. Be sure to write both reasons *for* and reasons *against.* Don't worry right now if any of these reasons strike you as flimsy or implausible or clichéd; you can always cut them later or find ways to strengthen them, if you need to. Just note them down on your scratch paper, together with examples supporting both sides of the issue. Stay loose; this is your time for free associations, not self-censorship.

Step Two: Organize Your Outline (3 minutes).

According to British rhetorical theorist and philosopher Stephen Toulmin, a sound argument requires three elements: CLAIM, GROUNDS (or data), and WARRANT. Your claim is your thesis; it is an overall statement of the argument you hope to prove. The grounds for your argument are your evidence. Grounds for an argument can include statistics, examples, and even anecdotes. The warrant is the connection between the claim and the grounds. It is an explanation of how the grounds justify the claim.

CLAIM (thesis): Historians and other social scientists are as useful to society as are biochemists and engineers because society's ills cannot be cured by technological progress alone.

Once you have settled on your claim, look to your brainstorming for the arguments that support it. Each of these arguments requires its own claim, grounds, and warrant.

1. CLAIM: War is not prevented by technological progress.
   GROUNDS: Invention of gunpowder, nuclear weapons.
   WARRANT: Technological progress is driven by war; in fact, technology tends to make war more destructive.

2. CLAIM: Historians and social scientists can prevent, or at least discourage, war through their understanding of why wars have occurred in the past.
   GROUNDS: Treaty of Versailles, Marshall Plan.
   WARRANT: An understanding of history can allow us to design policies that encourage peace.

3. CLAIM: Technological progress does not prevent poverty.

GROUNDS: Industrial Revolution, sweatshops.
WARRANT: Technology changes the distribution of wealth, increasing extreme poverty as it increases wealth for some.

4. CLAIM: Historians and social scientists can prevent poverty through economic policy.
    GROUNDS: New Deal, Social Security.
    WARRANT: Social programs prevent poverty.

Though not a necessary component of the argument, RESERVATIONS can strengthen a claim. A reservation is a rebuttal to the claim that is introduced and granted by the writer. Reservations strengthen arguments in several ways: First, they moderate the writer's claim, thereby decreasing the level of proof required. Second, reservations make the writer appear more reliable by demonstrating that she is open-minded, and that her position is not extreme. Third, reservations allow the writer to defuse criticism before it is made. When you include a reservation in your argument, be sure to take the opportunity to weigh it against your other claims.

5. RESERVATION: Biochemists and engineers do contribute to society.
    WEIGHING: Though technological progress can increase the food supply and cure disease, we will always need historians and social scientists to show us how to use technology without causing more harm than good.

Step Three: Write the Body of Your Essay (20 minutes).

You already know your general line of reasoning, the direction you want your argument to take. You need to spend the bulk of your time writing the body of your essay. As rapidly as you can, type up your points, writing two to three sentences to flesh out each reason or example in your outline. Do not worry if time pressure doesn't allow you to deal with every point you dreamed up. Start with a reason or example that you can easily put into words, preferably your best, most compelling reason or example. Given the 45-minute time limit you're working under, you want to be sure to cover your best points right away, before you run out of time. During the revision period, you can always rearrange your paragraphs, putting the strongest paragraph immediately before the conclusion, so that your essay builds to a solid climax.

Step Four: Now Write Your Opening and Summary Paragraphs (10 minutes).

It may seem strange to write your introductory paragraph after you have written the body of your essay, but it is a useful technique. Many writers launch into writing the introduction, only to find, once they have finished the essay, that their conclusion is unrelated to, or even contradicts, what they had written in the introduction. By writing the introduction *after* you have composed the bulk of the essay, you will avoid having to rewrite the introduction to support the conclusion that you *actually* reached, rather than the conclusion that you *expected* to reach.

This is one area in which the technology of the new GRE will greatly assist you. If the GRE were a hard copy (paper) exam, you would need to save space on your page to insert your introduction, guessing exactly how much room you would need. Instead, because the GRE is computerized, you can simply go back to the top of the page and begin writing the introduction.

What then should your introduction include? Your introductory paragraph should both introduce the topic on which you are writing and clearly indicate your thesis or point. While in some situations it is strategic (or simply more graceful) to reveal your thesis fully only in the conclusion, the GRE is *not* one of those situations. Clarity is key; you do not want to risk leaving your readers uncertain of your line of reasoning, or under the impression that you have strayed from the point.

For a top score, your introductory paragraph should also provide some context for the argument. The GRE readers appear to favor introductions that place the topic in an historical or social context, rather than simply discussing it in a contextual vacuum. The two introductory paragraphs below demonstrate the difference between these two types of introduction.

Introduction with Context

> Western society tends to glorify the individual over the group. Our social and political philosophy, based on John Stuart Mill's faith that progress is fostered by competition within the marketplace of ideas, encourages people, as the Apple computer commercial says, to "think different." This cult of the individual overemphasizes the importance of being different and fails to recognize that a healthy person will be both a conformist and an individualist. Ironically, self-conscious dedication to nonconformity will ultimately result in extreme slavishness to custom.

Introduction without Context

> A healthy individual is neither a conformist, nor an individualist; he is *both* a conformist and an individualist. Balancing conformity and individualism allows people to follow their interests and passions without wasting time on issues that do not interest them, while a self-conscious dedication to nonconformity ultimately results in an extreme slavishness to custom.

One last note on introductions: While you may have been taught in school that a paragraph must comprise at least three sentences, the GRE readers are not concerned about the length of your introductory paragraph. In fact, they appear willing to grant the highest score to essays whose introduction is only one sentence long.

This does not mean that they favor essays with single-sentence introductions, only that they do not discriminate against them. If your introduction makes your thesis clear, it has done its job.

Your conclusion should, however, be longer than one sentence. It should restate your thesis and summarize the arguments that you make in its support. You should mention your supporting arguments in the same order in which they appear in the body of the essay. This technique underscores the organization of your essay, giving it a predictable and orderly appearance.

Step Five: Reread and Revise (10 minutes).

Expert writers often test their work by reading it aloud. In the exam room, you cannot read out loud. However, when you read your essay silently, take your time and listen with your inner ear to how it sounds. Read to get a sense of your essay's logic and rhythm. Does one sentence flow smoothly into the next? Would they flow more smoothly if you were to add a transition word or phrase (*therefore*, *however*, *nevertheless*, *in contrast*, *similarly*)? Do the sentences follow a logical order? Is any key idea or example missing? Does any sentence seem out of place? How would things sound if you cut out that awkward sentence or inserted that transition word?

Take a minute to act on your response to hearing your essay. If it sounded to you as if a transition word was needed, insert it. If it sounded as if a sentence should be cut, delete it. If it sounded as if a sentence was out of place, move it. Trust your inner ear, but do not attempt to do too much. Have faith in your basic outline for the essay. You have neither the need nor the time to revise everything.

Now think of yourself as an editor, not an auditor. Just as you need to have an ear for problems of logic and language, you also need to have an eye for errors that damage your text. Take a minute to look over your essay for problems in spelling and grammar. From your English classes you should know which words and grammatical constructions have given you trouble in the past. See whether you can spot any of these words or constructions in your essay. Correct any really glaring errors that you find. Do not worry if you fail to catch every mechanical error or awkward phrase. The readers understand that 45 minutes doesn't give you enough time to produce polished, gemlike prose. They won't penalize you for an occasional mechanical glitch.

How to Handle the Argument-Analysis Task

You have 30 minutes to complete the argument-analysis task. To earn a top score, you need to produce a smooth, 300–400 word critique with solid content, coherent organization, and few, if any, mechanical errors.

As you critique the argument, think about the writer's underlying assumptions. Ask yourself whether any of them are questionable. Also evaluate any data or evidence the writer brings up. Ask yourself whether this evidence actually supports the writer's conclusion.

In your analysis, you may suggest additional kinds of evidence to reinforce the writer's argument. You may also suggest methods to refute the argument, or additional data that might be useful to you as you assess the soundness of the argument. *You may **not**, however, present your personal views on the topic.* Your job is to analyze the elements of an argument, not to support or contradict that argument.

GRE readers will evaluate your essay, grading it on the basis of your effectiveness in the following areas:

- Identification and assessment of the argument's main elements.

- Organization and articulation of your thoughts.

- Use of relevant examples and arguments to support your analysis.

- Handling of the mechanics of standard written English.

Again, follow a 5-step approach in dealing with the argument-analysis task.

Step One: Identify the Claims (2 minutes).

Before you can identify the flaws in an argument essay prompt, you must have a clear understanding of the claims it makes. After reading the prompt once for general understanding, examine it more carefully, one sentence at a time. As you do this, use your scratch paper to write a list of the claims made in the prompt. List the claims in the order in which they are made. GRE argument prompts typically contain at least three flaws in the author's reasoning or use of evidence.

Here is an example of the notes you might take if you were writing on the topic below.

> **Discuss how effective you find the reasoning in this argument.**

The following appeared in an article in the Real Estate section of the Springfield Bugle.

Springfield is a great place to live. Every year, hundreds of former city dwellers move to Springfield, spurning the sophisticated cultural offerings of the urban setting for Springfield's more relaxed atmosphere. Despite the attractions of big city life, Springfield's new citizens choose their home for its rural setting and small town atmosphere. If Springfield wants to continue to attract these newcomers, it must adopt aggressive planning regulations to keep out chain stores, fast food establishments, bars, and other businesses more appropriate to an urban setting.

Overall Point: Springfield must control the growth of certain types of businesses in order for it to remain attractive to newcomers.

Claim One: People come to Springfield to get away from sophisticated city culture, and to have a relaxed atmosphere.

Claim Two: People come to Springfield for its rural, small-town atmosphere.

Claim Three: Keeping chain stores, bars, and fast food restaurants out of Springfield will maintain its attractiveness to newcomers.

Step Two: Question the Claims (3 minutes).

Once you have identified the claims made in the prompt, you need to assess the strength of those claims. In most cases, their shortcomings will be apparent to you. If, however, you are having trouble figuring out the flaws in a given claim, try applying a few handy questions to it.

1. GROUNDS. Is there any **evidence** to support the claim? The first two claims in the prompt above are assertions. Though the author might have survey data to support her claim that newcomers move to Springfield to escape urban culture and enjoy a more relaxed, rural, small-town atmosphere, she presents no such data in her argument.

2. WARRANT. Does the evidence provided support the claim?

   Could **other factors** cause the effect about which the author is writing? In the situation described in the prompt above, there are many possible reasons to choose to move to Springfield. The author gives no reason for readers to believe that she has correctly identified the cause of Springfield's popularity.

   Does the author assert a general rule based on an overly **small sample**? For example, if the author of the Springfield argument based her claims about why newcomers generally move to Springfield on the comments of a single new neighbor, her claims would lack adequate support. They would be unwarranted.

   Does the author compare **comparable groups**? If, for example, the author of the Springfield argument attempted to support her claims about why newcomers move to Springfield with surveys of residents who moved to Springfield twenty years ago, she would have no basis to make claims about people who have moved to Springfield more recently.

Step Three: Write the Body of Your Critique, Following the Order of the Claims Made in the Prompt (15 minutes).

Organization is an important part of writing a clear and coherent essay. The simplest and best approach is to discuss the claims made in the prompt in the order in which they are presented. There is no reason to try any-

thing tricky or fancy. The test-makers have given you an order. Use it. Using the structure of the prompt will save you time. It will also discourage you from writing a discursive essay that wanders unpredictably from one idea to another. High scores go to test-takers who write clear and well-reasoned essays. Creativity in this context is more likely to confuse your readers than to earn you extra points.

As we recommended in the previous section on the issue essay, spend the bulk of your time writing the body of your critique. Get those ideas onto the screen, allotting two to three sentences to each claim to flesh it out.

Step Four: Then Add Your Introductory and Summary Paragraphs (5 minutes).

While following the structure of the prompt is a handy way to organize the body of your critique, you still need to write an introduction and conclusion to your essay. Your introductory paragraph should provide a general overview of the criticisms you have made in the body of your essay. Do not give too much detail in the introduction; it is where you introduce, rather than explain, your analysis. *Present your points in the introduction in the same order in which they appear in the body of the essay.* By doing so, you will give your reader a clear idea of where you are going and what you intend to demonstrate. *In your conclusion, briefly restate the main points you have made in the body of your critique, and suggest one or two ways the author could have made his or her argument more persuasive.*

Step Five: Reread and Revise (5 minutes).

Once again, our recommendation is: First listen, then look. Begin by reading your essay silently, listening with your inner ear to how it sounds. Ask yourself whether one sentence flows smoothly into the next, and whether any transition words might help the flow. Consider whether any key idea or example might be missing or any sentence seems out of place. Do not make any major changes. Just tweak things slightly to improve your essay's sound and sense.

Now cast an eye over your essay, looking for mechanical errors. You know the sorts of grammatical constructions and spelling words that create problems for you. See whether you can spot any of them in your essay. Correct any errors that jump out at you.

Here is an example of an argument critique that follows the organization of the prompt:

Discuss how effective you find the reasoning in this argument.

The following appeared in an article in the Real Estate section of the Springfield Bugle.

Springfield is a great place to live. Every year, hundreds of former city dwellers move to Springfield, spurning the sophisticated cultural offerings of the urban setting for Springfield's more relaxed atmosphere. Despite the attractions of big city life, Springfield's new citizens choose their home for its rural setting and small town atmosphere. If Springfield wants to continue to attract these newcomers, it must adopt aggressive planning regulations to keep out chain stores, fast food establishments, bars, and other businesses more appropriate to an urban setting.

Response to the Argument

Springfield may well be a great place to live, but the author of this article makes a number of unsubstantiated assumptions about the attributes that make Springfield an attractive home. Based on these assumptions, the author makes a bold proposal regarding zoning and city planning. Though this proposal is intended to maintain the positive attributes that bring new residents to Springfield, it may fail to achieve this goal or even have the perverse effect of worsening the quality of life in the town.

The author's first mistake is to assume that she knows why hundreds of former city dwellers move to Springfield each year. She claims that in moving to Springfield, people are rejecting the culture of the city in favor of Springfield's more relaxed suburban lifestyle. This is a classic case of confusing correlation with causation. While Springfield may in fact be more relaxed than the city, and while the city may have more sophisticated culture than Springfield, it does not follow that those who move from the city to Springfield are choosing relaxation over sophistication. Perhaps they are moving to Springfield for entirely different reasons. High urban property values, with their concomitant high urban property taxes, may be driving potential homeowners to less expensive suburban areas. People may also be moving to Springfield for better schools or a lower crime rate.

The claim that people move to Springfield for its small-town atmosphere and rural setting is similarly unsubstantiated. Yes, Springfield is a small, rural suburb. It does not follow, however, that this is why new residents move to Springfield. They could be moving to Springfield for any of the reasons mentioned above, or for any number of other reasons.

The conclusion that Springfield must keep out businesses that are common in urban areas if it is to remain an attractive community is unsupported. If new residents are really being drawn to Springfield by something other than the ways in which it is different from a big city, there is no reason to believe that keeping Springfield from growing city-like will make it more attractive. In fact, if people move to Springfield in spite of its lack of big-city amenities and because of its lower cost (or some other factor), the addition of big-city businesses may make Springfield more attractive to newcomers.

Ironically, if the author is correct that Springfield's relaxed, small-town feel is what attracts new residents, making Springfield attractive to former city dwellers may, in the long run, destroy Springfield's positive attributes. After all, for how long can Springfield maintain this small-town atmosphere, if hundreds of newcomers are encouraged to move there each year? Ultimately, the author of this article appears to seek the impossible—a quiet small town with sustained, robust population growth.

Despite the flaws in this author's argument, she may be correct in her assessment of why newcomers move to Springfield. She could strengthen her argument by documenting its most important premise with data. If, for example, she provided survey results from newcomers, indicating that they did indeed come to Springfield to escape urban culture and to enjoy a more relaxed, rural, small-town atmosphere, her argument would be far more persuasive. Were this the case, her call for more restrictive zoning might be justified.

Tactics

Preparing for the Writing Test

Take Advantage of the GRE's Free Study Aids

When you sign up to take the GRE General Test, you will eventually be sent *PowerPrep*, a CD-ROM containing test preparation software for the General Test and Writing Assessment. (The GRE's new analytical writing section is the same as the former Writing Assessment test, which you previously had to take separately. Don't worry about the name change; it has no significance.)

However, you do not have to wait for your copy of *PowerPrep* to come in the mail. You can download it immediately from the GRE web site, *www.gre.org*.

PowerPrep is helpful because it uses the same GRE word processing software that you will have to use to write your essays when you take your computer-based test. It is a very basic word processor that lets you perform very basic tasks. You can insert text, delete text, and move text around using a cut-and-paste function. You can also undo an action you've just performed.

Familiarize yourself with this word processing software so that, on the test date, you'll be comfortable using it. This software simulates actual testing conditions and presents actual essay topics. Practice writing your essays while you keep one eye on the clock. You need to develop a sense of how much time to allow for thinking over your essay and how much time to set aside for the actual writing.

A Word of Warning

Attention, Mac users: *PowerPrep* is compatible only with IBMs or PCs. If you own an Apple MacIntosh computer, you'll have to gain access to a PC to run *PowerPrep*. Do it, even if it means making an extra trip to the campus computer lab or the nearest public library.

Practice Taking Shortcuts to Maximize Your Typing Efficiency

Slow and steady is not the way to go, at least not when you're taking the analytical writing test on the GRE. Fast typists have a decided advantage here. Unfortunately, you cannot turn yourself into a typing whiz overnight. However, you can use your time right now to practice some shortcuts to help you on the day of the test.

First, using the GRE's own word processing program (which comes when you download *PowerPrep*), you can practice using the cut-and-paste function to copy phrases that you want to repeat in your essay. In an argument essay, for example, you might want to reuse such phrases as "the author makes the following assumption" or "another flaw in the author's argument is that...." In an issues essay, if you are running out of time and still haven't written your opening and summary paragraphs (which we advise you to compose *after* you've written the body of your text), you can write just your concluding paragraph, cutting and pasting it to both the beginning and end of the essay. Then, in a few seconds, you can change the wording of that initial paragraph so that it works as an introduction, not as a conclusion. How does that cliché about essay-writing go? "Tell them what you're going to tell them, tell them it, then tell them what you've told them." It's easy to do so, using cut-and-paste.

One thing to note: The GRE word processor currently lacks a copy function. To copy a chunk of text, you must first cut it and then directly paste it back in its original spot; next, you must move the cursor to the place where you want to reproduce the text and paste it there. The process may feel cumbersome at first, but by practicing with the word processor you will quickly build up speed copying using cut-and-paste.

Second, you can also practice abbreviating multiword names or titles. Consider the following argument topic or prompt:

> **Discuss how effective you find the reasoning in this argument.**

The parent of a Collegiate High student included these remarks in a letter to the education page of the Oakville Bugle.

If you look closely at Oakville's two leading private high schools—Collegiate Preparatory High School and Exover Academy—you must conclude that Collegiate is unmistakably superior to the Academy. Collegiate has a staff of 35 teachers, many of them with doctorates. In contrast, Exover has a staff of 22, several holding only a bachelor's degree. Moreover, Collegiate's average class size is 12, compared to Exover's average class size of 20; Collegiate's students receive much more individual attention than their peers do at the Academy. Students graduating from Collegiate High also are accepted by better universities than Exover graduates are: 40% of last year's Collegiate senior class went on to Ivy League colleges, compared to only 15% of Exover's senior class. Thus, if you want your children to get individual attention from their high school teachers and would like them to get in to good colleges, you should send them to Collegiate Prep.

In critiquing this argument, you can follow the letter writer's example and refer to Exover Academy and Collegiate Preparatory High School simply as Exover and Collegiate. You can also refer to Collegiate by its initials. Be sure, however, to identify the institution fully when you first mention it, inserting its initials in parentheses: Collegiate Preparatory High School (CPHS). Then your readers will know what you mean by future references to CPHS. Similarly, instead of typing out "for example," you can substitute the abbreviation "e.g."

Acquaint Yourself with the Actual Essay Topics You Will Face

The GRE has posted its entire selection of potential essay topics on its web site. The pool of issue topics can be found at *www.gre.org/issuetop.html.* The pool of argument topics can be found at *www.gre.org/argutop.html.* There is no point in trying to memorize these topics or in trying to write an essay for each one. There are well over 200 items in the pool of issue topics alone. There is, however, a real point to exploring these potential topics and to noting their common themes.

We suggest that you print out both topic pools so that you can go through their contents at leisure. When you do so, you will see that the issue topics fall naturally into groups with common themes. Some of these themes involve contrasts:

- Tradition versus innovation and modernization.

- Competition versus cooperation.

- Present social needs versus future social needs.

- Conformity versus individualism.

- Imagination versus knowledge.

- Pragmatism versus idealism.

Many of the issue topics pose a simple question:

- What makes an effective leader?

- What are education's proper goals?

- How does technology affect our society?

- Why should we study history (or art, literature)?

- What is government's proper role (in education, art, wilderness preservation, and so on)?

- How do we define progress?

Others ask you to question conventional wisdom:

- Is loyalty *always* a virtue?

- Is "moderation in all things" *truly* good advice?

- Does conformity *always* have a negative impact?

Go over these recurrent questions and themes. They relate to all the areas of the college curriculum: political science, sociology, anthropology, economics, history, law, philosophy, psychology, the physical sciences, the fine arts, literature, even media studies. Whether or not you have any special knowledge of a suggested topic's subject area, you most likely have opinions about it. You probably have class notes on it as well.

If you have old notebooks from your general education courses, skim through them to refresh your memory of classroom discussions of typical GRE issues. In the course of flipping through these old notes, you're very likely to come across examples that you might want to note for possible use in writing the issue essay.

Writing the Issue Essay

Break Down the Topic Statement into Separate Areas to Consider

Here is an example of an issue topic, modeled on actual topics found in the GRE pool.

> "The end does justify the means,
> if the end is truly meritorious."

Break down the statements into its component elements. Look for key words and phrases. First, consider ***ends*** or goals. These can be divided into personal goals—taking a trip to a foreign country, for example, or providing for one's family—and societal goals—preserving endangered species, for example, or protecting the health of the elderly.

Next, consider what ***means*** you might use to reach these goals. If you have to spend your savings and take a leave of absence from college to travel abroad, thereby postponing or potentially jeopardizing your eventual graduation, then perhaps your goal is insufficiently meritorious to justify the means. If, however, your goal is not simply to take a pleasure trip but to use the time abroad working in a refugee camp, the worthiness of the cause you are serving might well outweigh the expense and the risk of your not graduating. Similarly, while most people would agree that preserving an endangered species is a worthwhile societal goal, the cost to society of doing so can occasionally outweigh the benefits: think about the societal cost in ruined crops and lost income to Klamath Basin farmers when the government cut off water to their farms in an effort to preserve endangered coho salmon and sucker fish, an action later criticized as unnecessary by the National Academy of Sciences.

Finally, consider the phrase **truly meritorious**. The author is begging the question, qualifying his assertion to make it appear incontrovertible. But what makes an action meritorious? Even more, what makes an action *truly* meritorious? How do you measure merit? Whose standards do you use?

Breaking down the topic statement into its components helps start you thinking analytically about the subject. It's a good way to begin composing your issue essay.

Adopt a Balanced Approach

Consider your readers. Who are they? Academics, junior members of college faculties. What are they looking for? They are looking for articulate and persuasive arguments expressed in scholarly, well-reasoned prose. In other words, they are looking for the sort of essay they might write themselves.

How do you go about writing for an academic audience? First, avoid extremes. You want to come across as a mature, evenhanded writer, someone who can take a strong stand on an issue, but who can see others' positions as well. Restrain yourself: don't get so carried away by the "rightness" of your argument that you wind up sounding fanatical or shrill. Second, be sure to acknowledge that other viewpoints exist. Cite them; you'll win points for scholarly objectivity.

Draw examples to support your position from "the great world" and from the academic realm. In writing about teaching methods, for example, you'll win more points citing current newspaper articles about magnet schools or relevant passages from John Dewey and Maria Montessori than telling anecdotes about your favorite gym teacher in junior high school. While it is certainly acceptable for you to offer an occasional example from personal experience, for the most part your object is to show the readers the *breadth* of your knowledge (without showing off by quoting the most obscure sources you can find!).

One additional point: Do not try to second-guess your readers. Yes, they want you to come up with a scholarly, convincing essay. But there is no "one true answer" that they are looking for. You can argue for the position. You can argue against the position. You can strike a middle ground, arguing both for and against the position, hedging your bet. The readers don't care what position you adopt. Don't waste your time trying to psych them out.

Make Use of Transitions or Signal Words to Point the Way

Assume that typical GRE readers must read hundreds of issue essays in a day. You want to make the readers' job as easy as possible, so that when they come to your essay they breathe a sigh of relief, saying, "Ah! Someone who knows how to write!"

One way to make the readers' job easy is to lead them by the hand from one idea to the next, using signal words to point the way. The GRE readers like it when test-takers use signal words (transitions); in their analyses of sample essays scoring a 5 or 6, they particularly mention the writers' use of transitions as a good thing.

Here are a few helpful transitions. Practice using them precisely: you earn no points for sticking them in at random!

Support Signal Words

Use the following words or abbreviations to signal the reader that you are going to support your claim with an illustration or example:

e.g., (short for Latin *exempli gratia*, for the sake of an example)
for example
for instance
let me illustrate
such as

Use these words to signal the reader that you are about to add an additional reason or example to support your claim:

additionally
also

furthermore
in addition
likewise
moreover

Contrast Signal Words

Use the following words to signal a switch of direction in your argument.

although
but
despite
even though
except
however
in contrast
in spite of
instead of
nevertheless
not
on the contrary
on the other hand
rather than

still
unlike
yet

Cause and Effect Signal Words

Use the following words to signal the next step in your line of reasoning or the conclusion of your argument.

accordingly
consequently
for this reason
hence
in conclusion
in short
in summary
so . . . that
therefore
thus
when . . . then

See Tactic 10 for a discussion of how signal words can be helpful to you in the second of your two writing tasks, the argument critique.

Writing the Argument Critique

Learn to Spot Common Logical Fallacies

You may remember studying a list of logical fallacies during your undergraduate education. It probably included Latin terms such as "post hoc ergo propter hoc" and "argumentum ad hominem." Fortunately, you do not need to memorize these terms to perform well on the GRE argument essay. The GRE's essay readers are not concerned with whether you know the name of a given logical fallacy; they are more concerned with whether you can recognize and explain fallacies as they occur in simulated real-world situations. Labeling a claim a "post hoc" fallacy will not win you a 6 (the top score) unless you can *explain* the flaw in the argument. And a straightforward logical explanation of the argument's flaw can get you a 6, whether or not you use the fancy Latin terminology.

This does not mean, however, that brushing up on the common logical fallacies is a waste of your time. A decent understanding of the ways in which arguments can be wrong will help you write a better essay by enabling you to identify more flaws in the assigned argument (GRE argument statements generally include more than one logical error), and by giving you a clearer understanding of the nature of those flaws. Our advice is, therefore, to review the common logical fallacies without spending too much time trying to memorize their names.

Here are two examples of arguments, or prompts, similar to those in the GRE pool. Read them. The discussion following will point out what common logical fallacies they embody.

> **Discuss how effective you find the reasoning in this argument.**

Argument 1

The school board of the Shadow Valley Unified School District included these remarks in a letter sent to the families of all students attending school in the district.

Over the past few years, an increase in disciplinary problems and a high drop out rate have plagued District schools. The Ash Lake School District to our north adopted a mandatory uniform policy three years ago. Since that time, suspensions and expulsions in Ash Lake have fallen by 40 percent, while the mean grade point average of Ash Lake students has risen from 2.3 (C+) to 2.7 (B−). In order to improve the discipline and academic performance of Shadow Valley students, we have adopted a mandatory uniform policy effective on the first day of the new school year.

Discuss how effective you find the reasoning in this argument.

Argument 2

The following is excerpted from a letter to the editor in the Chillington Gazette.

The recent residential property tax increase to improve park maintenance in Chillington is a waste of money. There is no need to improve Chillington's parks because the people of Chillington do not enjoy outdoor recreation. I live across the street from Green Park in South Chillington, and I've noticed that there is never anyone in the park. Park use did not increase in Warm Springs last year when they implemented a similar tax. There is no reason to improve parks that will not be used.

Common Logical Fallacies

Causal Fallacies

The classic fallacy of causation is often known by a Latin phrase, "post hoc ergo propter hoc," or its nickname, "the post hoc fallacy." The Latin phrase translates to, "after this, therefore because of this." The post hoc fallacy confuses correlation with causation, assuming that when one event follows another, the second event must have been caused by the first. It is as if you were to say that because your birthday precedes your husband's by one month, your birth must have caused him to be born. The Shadow Valley School District argument presents an excellent example of a post hoc fallacy. The author of this argument assumes that because "suspensions and expulsions in Ash Lake have fallen by 40 percent, while the mean grade point average of Ash Lake students has risen from 2.3 (C+) to 2.7 (B−)" since Ash Lake's adoption of a mandatory uniform policy, the uniform policy has caused the improved student performance. Despite this correlation, it is possible that other factors are responsible for Ash Lake's progress. Perhaps the school uniform policy coincided with a significant decrease in average class size, or the arrival of a new superintendent of schools. Or perhaps the recent improvements were brought about by an increase in federal aid for at-risk students. School uniforms may have been a partial cause of Ash Lake's improvements, or they may have played no role at all. Without further information, no reliable conclusion can be reached.

Inductive Fallacies

Fallacies of induction involve the drawing of general rules from specific examples. They are among the most common fallacies found in the GRE argument essay topics. To induce a general rule correctly from specific examples, it is crucial that the specific examples be representative of the larger group. All too often, this is not the case.

The **hasty generalization** (too small sample) is the most common inductive fallacy. A hasty generalization is a general conclusion that is based on too small a sample set. If, for example, you wanted to learn the most popular flavor of ice cream in Italy, you would need to interview a substantial number of Italians. Drawing a conclusion based on the taste of the three Italian tourists you met last week would not be justified. The *Chillington Gazette* argument provides another good example of the hasty generalization. The author of this argument concludes that "the people of Chillington do not enjoy outdoor recreation," but he draws this general conclusion from the lack of visitors to the park across the street from his home. Readers are never told just how many parks there are in Chillington. There could be dozens of parks, all possibly overflowing with happy visitors, despite the unpopularity of the one park viewed by the author.

Small sample size is a problem because it increases the risk of drawing a general conclusion from an **unrepresentative sample**. If, for example, you wanted to learn who was most likely to be elected president of the United States, you could not draw a reliable conclusion based on the preferences of the citizens of a single city, or even a single state. The views of the citizens of Salt Lake City are not necessarily the views of the citizens of the nation as a whole, nor are the views of Californians representative of those of the entire nation. This is why pollsters go to such great lengths to ensure that they interview a representative sample of the entire population.

Unrepresentative samples do not, however, always result from too small a sample. The *Chillington Gazette* argument concludes that the citizens of Chillington will not use improved parks because "Park use did not increase in Warm Springs last year when they implemented a similar tax." The author gives no reason to believe, however, that the two towns' situations are similar. Perhaps park use did not increase in Warm Springs because its parks were already extremely popular, unlike those of Chillington. Or perhaps Warm Springs is an industrial city with little housing, while Chillington is a bedroom community with a large number of school-aged children. Should we conclude that the experiences of one city will be mirrored by the other?

(To learn more about common logical fallacies, consult standard works on rhetoric and critical reasoning. Two currently popular texts are James Herrick's *Argumentation* and T. Edward Damer's *Attacking Faulty Reasoning*.)

Remember That Your Purpose Is to Analyze, *Not* to Persuade

You are not asked to agree or disagree with the argument in the prompt. Do not be distracted by your feelings on the subject of the prompt, and do not give in to the temptation to write your own argument. Be especially vigilant against this temptation if the topic is on a subject that you know very well. If, for example, the prompt argues that class size reduction is a poor idea because it did not improve test scores in one city, do not answer this argument with data you happen to know about another city in which test scores improved after class sizes were reduced. Instead, point out that one city is not a large enough sample on which to base a general conclusion. Go on to identify other factors that could have caused test scores to remain the same, despite lower class size. (Perhaps test scores in the sample city were already nearly as high as they could go, or the student population in that city was changing at the time class sizes were reduced.) Remember, the readers are not interested in how much you *know* about the subject of the prompt; they want to know how well you *think*.

Examine the Argument for Unstated Assumptions and Missing Information

An argument is based upon certain assumptions made by its author. If an argument's basic premises are sound, the argument is strengthened. If the argument's basic premises are flawed, the argument is weakened.

Pinpoint what the argument assumes but never states. Then consider the validity of these unstated assumptions. For example, the Shadow Valley argument assumes that the populations of Shadow Valley and Ash Lake are analogous. Is this unstated assumption warranted? Not necessarily. The two towns might well have distinctly dissimilar populations—one might be a working-class suburb with high unemployment, while the other might be a suburb populated by wealthy professionals. If that were so, there would be no reason to believe that the same factors would cause poor student performance in both towns.

Ask yourself what additional evidence would strengthen or weaken the claim. Generally, GRE argument prompts are flawed but could be true under some circumstances. Only rarely will you find an argument that is absolutely untrue. Instead, you will find plausible arguments for which support (grounds and warrant) is lacking.

Put yourself in the place of the argument's author. If you were trying to prove this argument, what evidence would you need? What missing data should you assemble to support your claim? Use your concluding paragraph to list this evidence and explain how its presence would solve the shortcomings that you identified earlier in your essay.

Pay Particular Attention to Signal Words in the Argument

In analyzing arguments, be on the lookout for transitions or signal words that can clarify the structure of the argument. These words are like road signs, pointing out the direction the author wants you to take, showing you the connection between one logical step and the next. When you spot such a word linking elements in the author's argument, ask yourself whether this connection is logically watertight. Does A unquestionably lead to B? These signal words can indicate vulnerable areas in the argument, points you can attack.

In particular, be alert for:

Cause and Effect Signal Words

The following words often signal the conclusion of an argument.

accordingly
consequently
for this reason
hence
in conclusion

in short
in summary
so
therefore
thus

Contrast Signal Words

The following words often signal a reversal of thought within an argument.

although
but
despite
even though
except
however
in contrast
instead
nevertheless
not
on the contrary
on the other hand
rather than
still
unlike
yet

Notice that in the following argument several of these words are present: *despite*, *not*, and *consequently*. Each of these words plays an important role in the argument.

> **Discuss how effective you find the reasoning in this argument.**

Argument 3

The following is from a letter to the state Department of Education.

Despite the fact that the River City School District increased the average size by more than 15% in all grades two years ago, this year's average SAT scores for the junior class were the highest ever. This shows that class size is not a good determinant of student performance. Consequently, other school districts should follow River City's lead and save money by increasing the size of their classes.

Think about each link in the chain of reasoning signaled by the three transition words. These words should act like a red flag, alerting you that danger (flawed logic) may lie ahead. Did the average SAT score for the junior class increase *despite* the increase in class size? Maybe. Then again, maybe not; the average score for that year's junior class may have increased because that year's juniors were unusually bright. Do this year's extra-high SAT scores show that class size is *not* a good determinant of student performance? Not necessarily. Many factors could have contributed to the junior class's high scores. Finally, consider the implications of *consequently*. Even if class size were not a good determinant of student performance, does it necessarily follow *as a consequence* that school districts should increase the size of their classes? In the words of the old song, "It ain't necessarily so."

Practice Exercises

Practice for the Issue Task

1. Brainstorm for 5 minutes, jotting down any words and phrases that are triggered by one of the following questions:

   • What should the goals of higher education be?

   • Why should we study history?

   • How does technology affect our society?

   • What is the proper role of art?

   • Which poses the greater threat to society, individualism or conformity?

   • Which is more socially valuable, preserving tradition or promoting innovation?

   • Is it better to be a specialist or a generalist?

   • Can a politician be both honest and effective?

2. In a brief paragraph, define one of the following words:

   • Freedom

   • Originality

   • Honesty

   • Progress

3. To improve your ear for language, read aloud short selections of good prose: editorials from *The New York Times* or *The Christian Science Monitor*, as well as columns or brief essays by prose stylists like Annie Dillard, M. F. K. Fisher, or E. B. White. Listen for the ways in which these authors vary their sentence structure. Note the precision with which they choose their words. The more good prose you hear, the better able you'll be to improve your writing style.

4. Selecting three or four issue topics from the GRE's published pool of topics (*www.gre.org/issuetop.html*), break down the topic statements in terms of Toulmin's three elements: claim, grounds, and warrant. Ask yourself the following questions. What claims are made in each topic statement? What grounds or data are given to support each of these claims? Is the claim warranted or unwarranted? Why? In what way do the grounds logically justify the claim?

5. Choosing another issue topic from the GRE's published pool of topics, write an essay giving your viewpoint concerning the particular issue raised. Set no time limit; take as long as you want to complete this task, then choose a second issue topic from the pool. *In only 45 minutes*, write an essay presenting your perspective on this second issue.

   Compare your two essays. Ask yourself how working under time pressure affected your second essay. Did its major problems stem from a lack of fluency? A lack of organization? A lack of familiarity with the subject matter under discussion? A lack of knowledge of the mechanics of formal written English? Depending on what problems you spot, review the appropriate sections of this chapter, as well as any style manuals or other texts we suggest.

Practice for the Argument Task

1. Choosing a sample of argument topics from the GRE's published pool of topics (*www.gre.org/argutop.html*), practice applying the list of logical fallacies to the published prompts. See how many fallacies you can find for each argument. If you have time, write practice essays for some of these arguments. If you are short of time, or would simply like to move more quickly, get together with a friend and explain the fallacies you have found in the argument essay prompts. This will be especially rewarding if you can work with a friend who is also preparing to take the GRE.

2. Write an "original" argument topic, modeling it on one of the argument prompts in the GRE's published pool. Your job is to change the details of the situation (names, figures, and so on) without changing the types of logical fallacies involved. By doing this, you will learn to spot the same old fallacies whenever they crop up in a new guise.

3. Choosing an argument prompt from the GRE's published pool of topics (*www.gre.org/argutop.html*), write an essay critiquing the particular argument expressed. Set no time limit; take as long as you want to complete this task, then choose a second argument prompt from the pool. *In only 30 minutes*, write an essay critiquing this second argument.

   Compare your two critiques. Ask yourself how working under time pressure affected your second critique. Would more familiarity with the common logical fallacies have helped you? Depending on what problems you spot, review the appropriate sections of this chapter, as well as any other materials we suggest.

PART FOUR

QUANTITATIVE
ABILITY: TACTICS,
STRATEGIES,
PRACTICE, AND
REVIEW

Introduction to Part Four

PART FOUR consists of five chapters. Chapter 10 presents several important strategies that can be used on any mathematics questions that appear on the GRE. In Chapters 11, 12, and 13 you will find tactics that are specific to one of the three different types of questions: discrete quantitative questions, quantitative comparison questions, and data interpretation questions, respectively. Chapter 14 contains a complete review of all the mathematics you need to know in order to do well on the GRE, as well as hundreds of sample problems patterned on actual test questions.

Five Types of Tactics

Five different types of tactics are discussed in this book.

1. In Chapters 1 and 2, you learned many basic tactics used by all good test-takers, such as read each question carefully, pace yourself, don't get bogged down on any one question, and never waste time reading the directions. You also learned the specific tactics required to excel on a computer-adaptive test. These tactics apply to both the verbal and quantitative sections of the GRE.

2. In Chapters 4, 5, 6, and 7 you learned the important tactics needed for handling each of the four types of verbal questions.

3. In Chapter 9 you learned the strategies for planning and writing the two essays that constitute the analytical writing section of the GRE.

4. In Chapters 10–13 you will find all of the tactics that apply to the quantitative sections of the GRE. Chapter 10 contains those techniques that can be applied to all types of mathematics questions; Chapters 11, 12, and 13 present specific strategies to deal with each of the three kinds of quantitative questions found on the GRE: discrete quantitative questions, quantitative comparison questions, and data interpretation questions.

5. In Chapter 14 you will learn or review all of the mathematics that is needed for the GRE, and you will master the specific tactics and key facts that apply to each of the different mathematical topics.

Using these tactics will enable you to answer more quickly many questions that you already know how to do. But the greatest value of these tactics is that they will allow you to correctly answer or make educated guesses on problems that *you do not know how to do.*

An Important Symbol

Throughout the rest of this book, the symbol "$\Rightarrow$" is used to indicate that one step in the solution of a problem follows *immediately* from the preceding one, and no explanation is necessary. You should read

$$3x = 12 \Rightarrow x = 4$$

as $\quad\quad 3x = 12$ *implies that* $x = 4$

or $\quad\quad 3x = 12$, *which implies that* $x = 4$

or $\quad\quad$ *since* $3x = 12$, *then* $x = 4$.

Here is a sample solution to the following problem using $\Rightarrow$:

What is the value of $2x^2 - 5$ when $x = -4$?

$$x = -4 \Rightarrow x^2 = (-4)^2 = 16 \Rightarrow$$

$$2x^2 = 2(16) = 32 \Rightarrow$$

$$2x^2 - 5 = 32 - 5 = \mathbf{27}$$

When the reason for a step is not obvious, $\Rightarrow$ is not used: rather, an explanation is given, often including a reference to a KEY FACT from Chapter 14. In many solutions, some steps are explained, while others are linked by the $\Rightarrow$ symbol, as in the following example.

In the diagram at the right, if $w = 10$, what is the value of z?

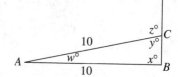

- By KEY FACT J1, $w + x + y = 180$.

- Since $\triangle ABC$ is isosceles, $x = y$ (KEY FACT J5).

- Therefore, $w + 2y = 180 \Rightarrow 10 + 2y = 180 \Rightarrow 2y = 170 \Rightarrow y = 85$.

- Finally, since $y + z = 180$ (KEY FACT I3), $85 + z = 180 \Rightarrow z = \mathbf{95}$.

10 General Math Strategies

- ■ **Tactics**
- ■ **Practice Exercises**
- ■ **Answer Key and Explanations**

In Chapters 11 and 12, you will learn tactics that are specifically applicable to multiple-choice questions and quantitative comparison questions, respectively. In this chapter you will learn several important general math strategies that can be used on both of these types of questions.

The directions that appear on the screen at the beginning of the quantitative section include the following cautionary information:

> Figures that accompany questions are intended to provide information useful in answering the questions.

> However, unless a note states that a figure is drawn to scale, you should solve these problems NOT by estimating sizes by sight or measurement, but by using your knowledge of mathematics.

Despite the fact that they are telling you that you cannot totally rely on *their* diagrams, if you learn how to draw diagrams accurately, *you can trust the ones you draw*. Knowing the best ways of handling diagrams on the GRE is critically important. Consequently, the first five tactics all deal with diagrams.

TACTIC 1. Draw a diagram.

TACTIC 2. Trust a diagram that has been drawn to scale.

TACTIC 3. Exaggerate or change a diagram.

TACTIC 4. Add a line to a diagram.

TACTIC 5. Subtract to find shaded regions.

To implement these tactics, you need to be able to draw line segments and angles accurately, and you need to be able to look at segments and angles and accurately estimate their measures. Let's look at three variations of the same problem.

1. If the diagonal of a rectangle is twice as long as the shorter side, what is the degree measure of the angle it makes with the longer side?

2. In the rectangle at the right, what is the value of *x*?

3. In the rectangle at the right, what is the value of *x*?

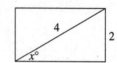

For the moment, let's ignore the correct mathematical way of solving this problem. In the diagram in (3), the side labeled 2 appears to be half as long as the diagonal, which is labeled 4; consequently, you should assume that the diagram has been drawn to scale, and you should see that *x* is about 30, *certainly* between 25 and 35. In (1) you aren't given a diagram, and in (2) the diagram is useless because you can see that it has not been drawn to scale (the side labeled 2 is nearly as long as the diagonal, which is labeled 4). However, if while taking the GRE, you see a question such as (1) or (2), you should be able to quickly draw on your scrap paper a diagram that looks just like the one in (3), and then look at *your* diagram and see that the measure of *x* is just about 30. If the answer choices for these questions were

(A) 15   (B) 30   (C) 45   (D) 60   (E) 75

you would, of course, choose **30, B**. If the choices were

(A) 20   (B) 25   (C) 30   (D) 35   (E) 40

you might not be quite as confident, but you should still choose **30**, here **C**.

When you take the GRE, even though you are not allowed to have rulers or protractors, you should be able to draw your diagrams very accurately. For example, in (1) above, you should draw a horizontal line, and then, either freehand or by tracing the corner of a piece of scrap paper, draw a right angle on the line. The vertical line segment will be the width of the rectangle; label it 2.

289

Mark off that distance twice on a piece of scrap paper and use that to draw the diagonal.

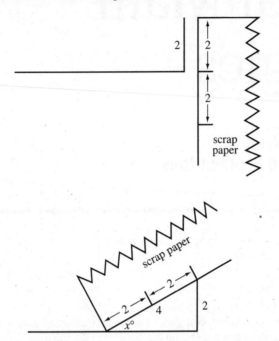

You should now have a diagram that is similar to that in (3), and you should be able to see that *x* is about 30.

By the way, *x* is *exactly* 30. A right triangle in which one leg is half the hypotenuse must be a 30-60-90 triangle, and that leg is opposite the 30° angle [see KEY FACT J11].

Having drawn an accurate diagram, are you still unsure as to how you should know that the value of *x* is 30 just by looking at the diagram? You will now learn not only how to look at *any* angle and know its measure within 5 or 10 degrees, but how to draw any angle that accurately.

You should easily recognize a 90° angle and can probably draw one freehand; but you can always just trace the corner of a piece of scrap paper. To draw a 45° angle, just bisect a 90° angle. Again, you can probably do this freehand. If not, or to be even more accurate, draw a right angle, mark off the same distance on each side, draw a square, and then draw in the diagonal.

To draw other acute angles, just divide the two 45° angles in the above diagram with as many lines as necessary.

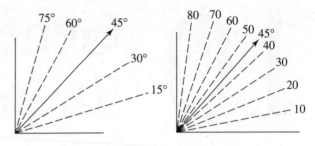

Finally, to draw an obtuse angle, add an acute angle to a right angle.

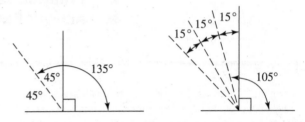

Now, to estimate the measure of a given angle, just draw in some lines.

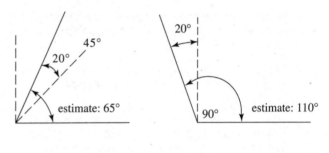

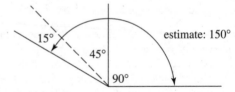

To test yourself, find the measure of each angle shown. The answers are found below.

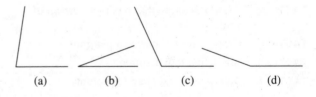

Testing Tactics

Draw a Diagram

On *any* geometry question for which a figure is not provided, draw one (as accurately as possible) on your scrap paper—*never attempt a geometry problem without first drawing a diagram*.

Example 1.

What is the area of a rectangle whose length is twice its width and whose perimeter is equal to that of a square whose area is 1?

(A) 1 (B) 6 (C) $\frac{2}{3}$ (D) $\frac{4}{3}$ (E) $\frac{8}{9}$

SOLUTION. Don't even think of answering this question until you have drawn a square and a rectangle and labeled each of them: each side of the square is 1, and if the width of the rectangle is w, its length (ℓ) is $2w$.

```
   1
 ┌─────┐
1│     │1   P = 4        ┌────2w────┐
 │     │               w│          │w   P = 6w
 └─────┘                └────2w────┘
   1
```

Now, write the required equation and solve it:

$$6w = 4 \Rightarrow w = \frac{4}{6} = \frac{2}{3} \Rightarrow 2w = \frac{4}{3}$$

The area of the rectangle = $\ell w = \left(\frac{4}{3}\right)\left(\frac{2}{3}\right) = \frac{8}{9}$, **E.**

Example 2.

Betty drove 8 miles west, 6 miles north, 3 miles east, and 6 more miles north. How many miles was Betty from her starting place?

(A) 13 (B) 17 (C) 19 (D) 21 (E) 23

SOLUTION. Draw a diagram. Now, extend line segment *ED* until it intersects *AB* at *F*. Then, *AFE* is a right triangle, whose legs are 5 and 12 and, therefore, whose hypotenuse is **13, A.**

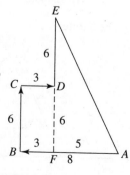

Example 3.

What is the difference in the degree measures of the angles formed by the hour hand and the minute hand of a clock at 12:35 and 12:36?

(A) 1° (B) 5° (C) 5.5° (D) 6° (E) 30°

SOLUTION. Draw a simple picture of a clock. The hour hand makes a complete revolution, 360°, once every 12 hours. So, in 1 hour it goes through 360° ÷ 12 = 30°, and in one minute it advances through 30° ÷ 60 = 0.5°. The minute hand moves through 30° every 5 minutes or 6° per minute. So, in the minute from 12:35 to 12:36 (or any other minute), the *difference* between the hands increased by 6° − 0.5° = **5.5°, C.**

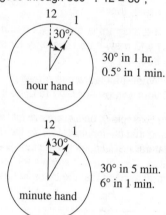

30° in 1 hr.
0.5° in 1 min.

30° in 5 min.
6° in 1 min.

NOTE: It was not necessary, and would have been more time-consuming, to determine the angle between the hands at either 12:35 or 12:36. (See TACTIC 6: Don't do more than you have to.)

Drawings should not be limited to geometry questions; there are many other questions on which drawings will help.

Example 4.

A jar contains 10 red marbles and 30 green ones. How many red marbles must be added to the jar so that 60% of the marbles will be red?

(A) 25 (B) 30 (C) 35 (D) 40 (E) 60

SOLUTION. First, draw a diagram and label it. From the diagram it is clear that there are now $40 + x$ marbles in the jar, of which $10 + x$ are red. Since we want the fraction of red marbles to be 60%, we have

$$\frac{10 + x}{40 + x} = 60\% = \frac{3}{5}.$$

x	Red
30	Green
10	Red

Cross-multiplying, we get:

$$50 + 5x = 120 + 3x \Rightarrow 2x = 70 \Rightarrow x = \mathbf{35}, \mathbf{C}.$$

Of course, you could have set up the equation and solved it without the diagram, but the diagram makes the solution easier and you are less likely to make a careless mistake.

Trust a Diagram That Has Been Drawn to Scale

Whenever diagrams have been drawn to scale, they can be trusted. This means that you can look at the diagram and use your eyes to accurately estimate the sizes of angles and line segments. For example, in the first problem discussed at the beginning of this chapter, you could "see" that the measure of the angle was about 30°.

To take advantage of this situation:

- If a diagram is given that appears to be drawn to scale, trust it.

- If a diagram is given that has not been drawn to scale, try to draw it to scale on your scrap paper, and then trust it.

- When no diagram is provided, and you draw one on your scrap paper, try to draw it to scale.

In Example 5, below, we are told that *ABCD* is a square and that diagonal *BD* is 3. In the diagram provided, quadrilateral *ABCD* does indeed look like a square, and *BD* = 3 does not contradict any other information. We can, therefore, assume that the diagram has been drawn to scale.

Example 5.

In the figure at the right, diagonal *BD* of square *ABCD* is 3. What is the perimeter of the square?

(A) 4.5 (B) 12 (C) $3\sqrt{2}$
(D) $6\sqrt{2}$ (E) $12\sqrt{2}$

SOLUTION. Since this diagram has been drawn to scale, you can trust it. The sides of the square appear to be about two thirds as long as the diagonal, so assume that each side is 2. Then the perimeter is 8. Which of the choices is approximately 8? Certainly not A or B. Since $\sqrt{2} \approx 1.4$, Choices C, D, and E are approximately 4.2, 8.4, and 12.6, respectively. Clearly, the answer must be **D**.

Direct mathematical solution. Let *s* be a side of the square. Then since $\triangle BCD$ is a 45-45-90 right triangle,

$$s = \frac{3}{\sqrt{2}} = \frac{3\sqrt{2}}{2}, \text{ and the perimeter of the square is}$$

$$4s = 4\left(\frac{3\sqrt{2}}{2}\right) = 6\sqrt{2}.$$

Remember the goal of this book is to help you get credit for *all* the problems you know how to do, and, by using the

TACTICS, to get credit for *many* that you don't know how to do. Example 5 is typical. Many students would miss this question. *You*, however, can now answer it correctly, even though you may not remember how to solve it directly.

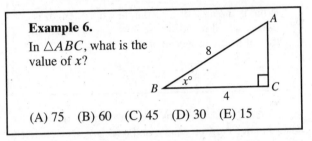

Example 6.

In $\triangle ABC$, what is the value of *x*?

(A) 75 (B) 60 (C) 45 (D) 30 (E) 15

SOLUTION. If you don't see the correct mathematical solution, you should use TACTIC 2 and trust the diagram; but to do that you must be careful that when you copy it onto your scrap paper you *fix it*. What's wrong with the way it is drawn now? *AB* = 8 and *BC* = 4, but in the figure, *AB* and *BC* are almost the same length. Redraw it so that *AB* is *twice* as long as *BC*. Now, just look: *x* is about **60, B**.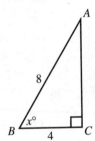

In fact, *x* is exactly 60. If the hypotenuse of a right triangle is twice the length of one of the legs, then it's a 30-60-90 triangle, and the angle formed by the hypotenuse and that leg is 60° (see Section 14-J).

TACTIC 2 is equally effective on quantitative comparison questions that have diagrams. See page 9 for directions on how to solve quantitative comparison questions.

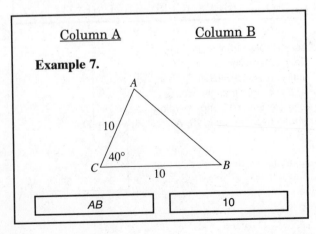

Column A	Column B
Example 7.	
AB	10

SOLUTION. There are two things wrong with the given diagram: ∠C is labeled 40°, but looks much more like 60° or 70°, and AC and BC are each labeled 10, but BC is drawn much longer. When you copy the diagram onto your scrap paper, be sure to correct these two mistakes: draw a triangle that has a 40° angle and two sides of the same length.

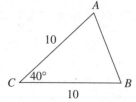

Now, it's clear: AB < 10. The answer is **B**.

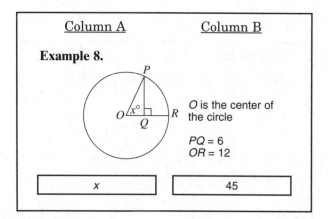

SOLUTION. In the diagram at the left, the value of x is at least 60, so if the diagram has been drawn to scale, the answer must be **A**. If, on the other hand, the diagram has not been drawn to scale, we can't trust it. Which is it? The diagram is *not* OK—PQ is drawn almost as long as OR, even though OR is twice as long. Correct the diagram:

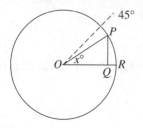

Now you can see that x is less than 45. The answer is **B**.

Exaggerate or Otherwise Change a Diagram

Sometimes it is appropriate to take a diagram that appears to be drawn to scale and intentionally exaggerate it. Why would we do this? Consider the following example.

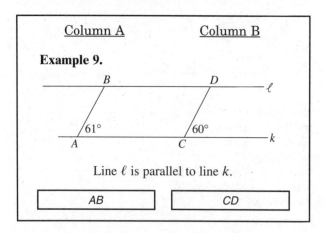

SOLUTION. In the diagram, which appears to be drawn correctly, AB and CD look as though they are the same length. However, there *might* be an imperceptible difference due to the fact that angle C is slightly smaller than angle A. So exaggerate the diagram:

redraw it, making angle C *much* smaller than angle A. Now, it's clear: CD is longer. The answer is **B**.

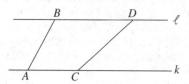

When you copy a diagram onto your scrap paper, you can change anything you like as long as your diagram is consistent with all the given data.

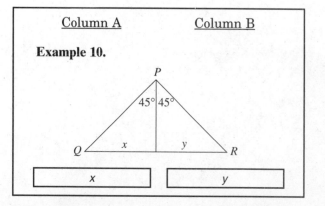

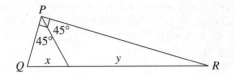

SOLUTION. You may redraw this diagram any way you like, as long as the two angles that are marked 45° remain 45°. If *PQ* and *PR* are equal, as they appear to be in the given diagram, then *x* would equal *y*. Since the given information doesn't state that *PQ* = *PR*, draw a diagram in which *PR* and *QR* are clearly unequal. In the diagram at the right, *PR* is much longer than *PQ*, and *x* and *y* are clearly unequal. The answer is **D**.

Add a Line to a Diagram

Occasionally, after staring at a diagram, you still have no idea how to solve the problem to which it applies. It looks as though not enough information has been given. When this happens, it often helps to draw another line in the diagram.

Example 11.

In the figure at the right, *Q* is a point on the circle whose center is *O* and whose radius is *r*, and *OPQR* is a rectangle. What is the length of diagonal *PR*?

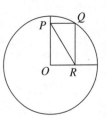

(A) *r*   (B) r^2 (C) $\dfrac{r^2}{\pi}$ (D) $\dfrac{r\sqrt{2}}{\pi}$

(E) It cannot be determined from the information given.

SOLUTION. If after staring at the diagram and thinking about rectangles, circles, and the Pythagorean theorem, you're still lost, don't give up. Ask yourself, "Can I add another line to this diagram?" As soon as you think to draw in *OQ*, the other diagonal, the problem becomes easy: the two diagonals are equal and, since *OQ* is a radius, it is equal to *r*, **A**.

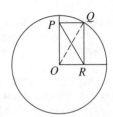

Example 12.

What is the area of quadrilateral *ABCD*?

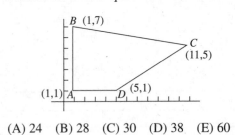

(A) 24   (B) 28   (C) 30   (D) 38   (E) 60

SOLUTION. Since the quadrilateral is irregular, there isn't a formula to find the area. However, if you draw in *AC*, you will divide *ABCD* into two triangles, each of whose areas can be determined. If you then draw in the height of each triangle, you see that the area of △*ACD* is $\frac{1}{2}$(4)(4) = 8, and the area of △*BAC* is $\frac{1}{2}$(6)(10) = 30, so the area of *ABCD* is 30 + 8 = **38**, **D**.

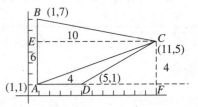

Note that this problem could also have been solved by drawing in lines to create rectangle *ABEF*, and subtracting the areas of △*BEC* and △*CFD* from the area of the rectangle.

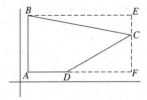

Tactic 5

Subtract to Find Shaded Regions

Whenever part of a figure is shaded, the straightforward way to find the area of the shaded portion is to find the area of the entire figure and subtract from it the area of the unshaded region. Of course, if you are asked for the area of the unshaded region, you can, instead, subtract the shaded area from the total area. Occasionally, you may see an easy way to calculate the shaded area directly, but usually you should subtract.

Example 13.

In the figure below, *ABCD* is a rectangle, and *BE* and *CF* are arcs of circles centered at *A* and *D*. What is the area of the striped region?

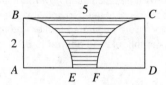

(A) $10 - \pi$ (B) $2(5 - \pi)$ (C) $2(5 - 2\pi)$
(D) $6 + 2\pi$ (E) $5(2 - \pi)$

SOLUTION. The entire region is a 2×5 rectangle whose area is 10. Since the white region consists of two quarter-circles of radius 2, the total white area is that of a semicircle of radius 2: $\frac{1}{2}\pi(2)^2 = 2\pi$. Therefore, the area of the striped region is $10 - 2\pi = \mathbf{2(5 - \pi)}$, **B**.

Example 14.

In the figure at the right, square *ABCD* is inscribed in circle *O*. If the perimeter of *ABCD* is 24, what is the area of the shaded region?

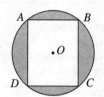

(A) $18\pi - 36$ (B) $18\pi - 24$ (C) $12\pi - 36$
(D) $9\pi - 36$ (E) $9\pi - 24$

SOLUTION. Since the perimeter of square *ABCD* is 24, each of its sides is 6, and its area is $6^2 = 36$. Since diagonal *AC* is the hypotenuse of isosceles right triangle *ABC*, $AC = 6\sqrt{2}$. But *AC* is also a diameter of circle *O*, so the radius of the circle is $3\sqrt{2}$, and its area is $\pi(3\sqrt{2})^2 = 18\pi$. Finally, the area of the shaded region is $\mathbf{18\pi - 36}$, **A**.

Tactic 6

Don't Do More Than You Have To

Very often a problem can be solved in more than one way. You should always try to do it in the easiest way possible. Consider the following examples.

Example 15.

If $5(3x - 7) = 20$, what is $3x - 8$?

(A) $\frac{11}{3}$ (B) 0   (C) 3   (D) 14   (E) 19

It is not difficult to solve for *x*:

$$5(3x - 7) = 20 \Rightarrow 15x - 35 = 20 \Rightarrow 15x = 55 \Rightarrow$$
$$x = \frac{55}{15} = \frac{11}{3}.$$

But it's too much work. Besides, once you find that $x = \frac{11}{3}$, you still have to multiply to get 3*x*: $3\left(\frac{11}{3}\right) = 11$, and then subtract to get $3x - 8$: $11 - 8 = \mathbf{3}$.

SOLUTION. The key is to recognize that you don't need to find *x*. Finding $3x - 7$ is easy (just divide the original equation by 5), and $3x - 8$ is just 1 less:

$$5(3x - 7) = 20 \Rightarrow 3x - 7 = 4 \Rightarrow 3x - 8 = \mathbf{3}, \mathbf{C}.$$

Example 16.

If $7x + 3y = 17$ and $3x + 7y = 19$, what is the average (arithmetic mean) of x and y?

(A) $\dfrac{31}{20}$　(B) $\dfrac{41}{20}$　(C) 1.8　(D) 3.6　(E) 36

The obvious way to do this is to first find x and y by solving the two equations simultaneously and then to take their average. If you know how to do this, try it now, before reading further. If you worked carefully, you should have found that $x = \dfrac{31}{20}$ and $y = \dfrac{41}{20}$, and their average is

$\dfrac{\frac{31}{20} + \frac{41}{20}}{2} = \dfrac{9}{5}$. This is not too difficult, but it is quite

time-consuming, and questions on the GRE never require you to do that much work. Look for a shortcut. Is there a way to find the average without first finding x and y? Absolutely! Here's the best way to do this.

SOLUTION. Add the two equations:

$$\begin{array}{r} 7x + 3y = 17 \\ +\ 3x + 7y = 19 \\ \hline 10x + 10y = 36 \end{array}$$

Divide each side by 10:　　　　$x + y = 3.6$

Calculate the average:　　$\dfrac{x+y}{2} = \dfrac{3.6}{2} = \mathbf{1.8}$

The answer is **C**.

Column A	Column B

Example 17.

Benjamin worked from 9:47 A.M. until 12:11 P.M.

Jeremy worked from 9:11 A.M. until 12:47 P.M.

The number of minutes Benjamin worked	The number of minutes Jeremy worked

---

Do not spend any time calculating how many minutes either of them worked. You only need to know which column is greater, and since Jeremy started earlier and finished later, he clearly worked longer. The answer is **B**.

Pay Attention to Units

Often the answer to a question must be in units different from the data given in the question. As you read the question, write on your scratch paper exactly what you are being asked and circle it or put an asterisk next to it. Do they want hours or minutes or seconds, dollars or cents, feet or inches, meters or centimeters? On multiple-choice questions, an answer using the wrong units is almost always one of the choices.

Example 18.

Driving at 48 miles per hour, how many minutes will it take to drive 32 miles?

(A) $\dfrac{2}{3}$　(B) $\dfrac{3}{2}$　(C) 40　(D) 45　(E) 2400

SOLUTION. This is a relatively easy question. Just be

attentive. Divide the distance, 32, by the rate, 48: $\dfrac{32}{48} = \dfrac{2}{3}$,

so it will take $\dfrac{2}{3}$ of an *hour* to drive 32 miles. Choice A is $\dfrac{2}{3}$,

but that is not the correct answer, because you are asked how many *minutes* it will take. To convert hours to minutes,

multiply by 60: it will take $\dfrac{2}{3}(60) = \mathbf{40}$ minutes, **C**.

Note that you could have been asked how many *seconds* it would take, in which case the answer would be 40(60) = 2400, Choice E.

Example 19.

At Nat's Nuts a $2\frac{1}{4}$-pound bag of pistachio nuts costs $6.00. At this rate, what is the cost in cents of a bag weighing 9 ounces?

(A) 1.5　(B) 24　(C) 150　(D) 1350　(E) 2400

SOLUTION. This is a relatively simple ratio, but make sure you get the units right. To do this you need to know that there are 100 cents in a dollar and 16 ounces in a pound.

$\dfrac{\text{price}}{\text{weight}} : \dfrac{6 \text{ dollars}}{2.25 \text{ pounds}} = \dfrac{600 \text{ cents}}{36 \text{ ounces}} = \dfrac{x \text{ cents}}{9 \text{ ounces}}$. Now

cross-multiply and solve: $36x = 5400 \Rightarrow x = \mathbf{150}$, **C**.

Systematically Make Lists

When a question asks "how many," often the best strategy is to make a list of all the possibilities. If you do this it is important that you make the list in a *systematic* fashion so that you don't inadvertently leave something out. Usually, this means listing the possibilities in numerical or alphabetical order. Often, shortly after starting the list, you can see a pattern developing and you can figure out how many more entries there will be without writing them all down. Even if the question does not specifically ask "how many," you may need to count something to answer it; in this case, as well, the best plan may be to write out a list.

Example 20.
A palindrome is a number, such as 93539, that reads the same forward and backward. How many palindromes are there between 100 and 1,000?

(A) 10   (B) 81   (C) 90   (D) 100   (E) 200

SOLUTION. First, write down the numbers that begin and end in 1:

101, 111, 121, 131, 141, 151, 161, 171, 181, 191

Next write the numbers that begin and end in a 2:

202, 212, 222, 232, 242, 252, 262, 272, 282, 292

By now you should see the pattern: there are 10 numbers beginning with 1, 10 beginning with 2, and there will be 10 beginning with 3, 4, ..., 9 for a total of $9 \times 10 = 90$ palindromes, **C**.

Example 21.
The product of three positive integers is 300. If one of them is 5, what is the least possible value of the sum of the other two?

(A) 16   (B) 17   (C) 19   (D) 23   (E) 32

SOLUTION. Since one of the integers is 5, the product of the other two is 60. Systematically, list all possible pairs, (a, b), of positive integers whose product is 60 and check their sums. First let $a = 1$, then 2, and so on.

a	b	a + b
1	60	61
2	30	32
3	20	23
4	15	19
5	12	17
6	10	16

The answer is **16, A**.

Practice Exercises

General Math Strategies

1. At Leo's Lumberyard, an 8-foot long wooden pole costs $3.00. At this rate, what is the cost, in cents, of a pole that is 16 inches long?

   (A) 0.5   (B) 48   (C) 50   (D) 64   (E) 96

2. In the figure below, vertex Q of square $OPQR$ is on a circle with center O. If the area of the square is 8, what is the area of the circle?

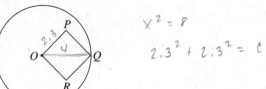

   (A) 8π (B) $8\pi\sqrt{2}$ (C) 16π (D) 32π (E) 64π

3. In 1999, Diana read 10 English books and 7 French books. In 2000, she read twice as many French books as English books. If 60% of the books that she read during the two years were French, how many books did she read in 2000?

   (A) 16   (B) 26   (C) 32   (D) 39   (E) 48

4. In the figure below, if the radius of circle O is 10, what is the length of diagonal AC of rectangle $OABC$?

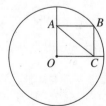

   (A) $\sqrt{2}$ (B) $\sqrt{10}$ (C) $5\sqrt{2}$ (D) 10   (E) $10\sqrt{2}$

5. In writing all of the integers from 1 to 300, how many times is the digit 1 used?

   (A) 60   (B) 120   (C) 150   (D) 160   (E) 180

6. In the figure at the right, $ABCD$ is a square and AED is an equilateral triangle. If $AB = 2$, what is the area of the shaded region?

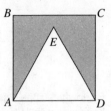

(A) $\sqrt{3}$ (B) 2   (C) 3   (D) $4 - 2\sqrt{3}$ (E) $4 - \sqrt{3}$

7. If $5x + 13 = 31$, what is the value of $\sqrt{5x + 31}$?

(A) $\sqrt{13}$ (B) $\sqrt{\dfrac{173}{5}}$ (C) 7   (D) 13   (E) 169

8. If $a + 2b = 14$ and $5a + 4b = 16$, what is the average (arithmetic mean) of a and b?

(A) 1.5   (B) 2   (C) 2.5   (D) 3   (E) 3.5

9. In the figure below, equilateral triangle ABC is inscribed in circle O, whose radius is 4. Altitude BD is extended until it intersects the circle at E. What is the length of DE?

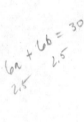

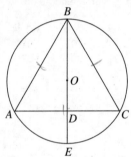

(A) 1   (B) $\sqrt{3}$ (C) 2   (D) $2\sqrt{3}$ (E) $4\sqrt{3}$

10. In the figure below, three circles of radius 1 are tangent to one another. What is the area of the shaded region between them?

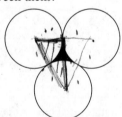

(A) $\dfrac{\pi}{2} - \sqrt{3}$ (B) 1.5   (C) $\pi - \sqrt{3}$

(D) $\sqrt{3} - \dfrac{\pi}{2}$ (E) $2 - \dfrac{\pi}{2}$

Column A	Column B

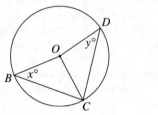

11. | $a + b$ | $c + d$ |

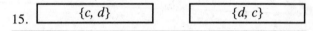

In circle O, $BC > CD$

12. | x | y |

13. | The number of odd positive factors of 30 | The number of even positive factors of 30 |

Questions 14–15 refer to the following definition.

$\{a, b\}$ represents the remainder when a is divided by b.

14. | $\{10^3, 3\}$ | $\{10^5, 5\}$ |

c and d are positive integers with $c < d$.

15. | $\{c, d\}$ | $\{d, c\}$ |

Answer Key

1. **C**	3. **E**	5. **D**	7. **C**	9. **C**	11. **B**	13. **C**	15. **A**
2. **C**	4. **D**	6. **E**	8. **C**	10. **D**	12. **B**	14. **A**	

Answer Explanations

Two asterisks (**) indicate an alternative method of solving.

1. **C.** This is a relatively simple ratio problem, but use TACTIC 7 and make sure you get the units right. To do this you need to know that there are 100 cents in a dollar and 12 inches in a foot.

$$\frac{price}{weight}: \frac{3\ dollars}{8\ feet} = \frac{300\ cents}{96\ inches} = \frac{x\ cents}{16\ inches}.$$

Now cross-multiply and solve: $96x = 4800 \Rightarrow x = 50$.

2. **C.** Use TACTICS 2 and 4. On your scrap paper, extend line segments OP and OR.

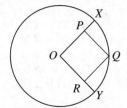

Square $OPQR$, whose area is 8, takes up most of quarter-circle OXY. So the area of the quarter-circle is certainly between 11 and 13. The area of the whole circle is 4 times as great: between 44 and 52. Check the five choices: they are approximately 25, 36, 50, 100, 200. The answer is clearly C.
**Another way to use TACTIC 4 is to draw in line segment OQ.

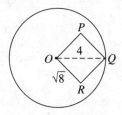

Since the area of the square is 8, each side is $\sqrt{8}$, and diagonal OQ is $\sqrt{8} \times \sqrt{2} = \sqrt{16} = 4$. But OQ is also a radius, so the area of the circle is 16π.

3. **E.** Use TACTIC 1: draw a picture representing a pile of books or a bookshelf.

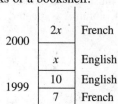

2000	2x	French
	x	English
1999	10	English
	7	French

Eng.	Fr.	Eng.	Fr.
10	7	x	2x
1999		2000	

In the two years the number of French books Diana read was $7 + 2x$ and the total number of books was $17 + 3x$. Then 60% or $\frac{3}{5} = \frac{7 + 2x}{17 + 3x}$. To solve, cross-multiply:

$$35 + 10x = 51 + 9x \Rightarrow x = 16.$$

In 2000, Diana read 16 English books and 32 French books, a total of 48 books.

4. **D.** Use TACTIC 2. Trust the diagram: AC, which is clearly longer than OC, is approximately as long as radius OE.

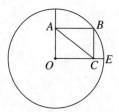

Therefore, AC must be about 10. Check the choices. They are approximately 1.4, 3.1, 7, 10, and 14. The answer must be 10.
**The answer *is* 10. Use TACTIC 4: copy the diagram on your scrap paper and draw in diagonal OB.

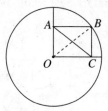

Since the two diagonals of a rectangle are equal, and diagonal OB is a radius, $OA = OB = 10$.

5. **D.** Use TACTIC 8. Systematically list the numbers that contain the digit 1, writing as many as you need to see the pattern. Between 1 and 99 the digit 1 is used 10 times as the units digit (1, 11, 21, ... , 91) and 10 times as the tens digit (10, 11, 12, ... , 19) for a total of 20 times. From 200 to 299, there are 20 more (the same 20 preceded by a 2). From 100 to 199 there are 20 more plus 100 numbers where the digit 1 is used in the hundreds place. So the total is $20 + 20 + 20 + 100 = 160$.

6. **E.** Use TACTIC 5: subtract to find the shaded area. The area of the square is 4. The area of the equilateral triangle (see Section 14-J) is $\frac{2^2\sqrt{3}}{4} = \frac{4\sqrt{3}}{4} = \sqrt{3}$. So the area of the shaded region is $4 - \sqrt{3}$.

7. **C.** Use TACTIC 6: don't do more than you have to. In particular, don't solve for x.
$$5x + 13 = 31 \Rightarrow 5x = 18 \Rightarrow 5x + 31 = 18 + 31 = 49 \Rightarrow \sqrt{5x + 31} = \sqrt{49} = 7.$$

8. C. Use TACTIC 6: don't do more than is necessary. You do not need to solve this system of equations; we don't need to know the values of *a* and *b*, only their average. Adding the two equations, we get $6a + 6b = 30 \Rightarrow a + b = 5 \Rightarrow \dfrac{a+b}{2} = \dfrac{5}{2} = 2.5$.

9. C. Use TACTIC 5: to get *DE*, subtract *OD* from radius *OE*, which is 4. Draw *AO* (TACTIC 4). Since △*AOD* is a 30-60-90 right triangle, *OD* is 2 (one half of *OA*). So, *DE* = 4 − 2 = 2.

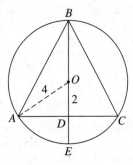

10. D. Use TACTIC 4 and add some lines: connect the centers of the three circles to form an equilateral triangle whose sides are 2.

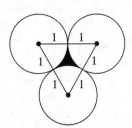

Now use TACTIC 5 and find the shaded area by subtracting the area of the three sectors from the area of the triangle. The area of the triangle is $\dfrac{2^2 \sqrt{3}}{4} = \sqrt{3}$ (see Section 14-J). Each sector is one sixth of a circle of radius 1. Together they form one half of such a circle, so their total area is $\dfrac{1}{2}\pi(1)^2 = \dfrac{\pi}{2}$. Finally, subtract: the shaded area is $\sqrt{3} - \dfrac{\pi}{2}$.

11. B. If you don't see how to do this, use TACTIC 2: trust the diagram. Estimate the measure of each angle: for example, *a* = 45, *b* = 70, *c* = 30, and *d* = 120. So *c* + *d* (150) is considerably greater than *a* + *b* (115). Choose B.

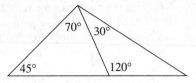

**In fact, *d* by itself is equal to *a* + *b* (an exterior angle of a triangle is equal to the sum of the opposite two interior angles). So *c* + *d* > *a* + *b*.

12. B. From the figure, it appears that *x* and *y* are equal, or nearly so. However, the given information states that *BC* > *CD*, but this is not clear from the diagram. Use TACTIC 3: when you draw the figure on your scrap paper, exaggerate it. Draw it with *BC* much greater than *CD*. Now it is clear that *y* is greater.

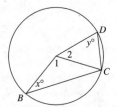

**Since *BC* > *CD*, central angle 1 is greater than central angle 2, which means that *x* < *y*.

13. C. Use TACTIC 8. Systematically list all the factors of 30, either individually or in pairs: 1, 30; 2, 15; 3, 10; 5, 6. Of the 8 factors, 4 are even and 4 are odd.

14. A. Column A: When 10^3 (1000) is divided by 3, the quotient is 333 and the remainder is 1. Column B: 10^5 is divisible by 5, so the remainder is 0. Column A is greater.

15. A. Column A: since *c* < *d*, the quotient when *c* is divided by *d* is 0, and the remainder is *c*. Column B: when *d* is divided by *c* the remainder must be less than *c*. So Column A is greater.

11 Discrete Quantitative Questions

- ■ Tactics
- ■ Practice Exercises
- ■ Answer Key and Explanations

Of the 28 questions in the quantitative section, 10 are called discrete quantitative questions, which is just a fancy name for standard multiple-choice questions, similar to those that you have encountered on many other standardized tests, such as the PSAT and SAT I.

In this chapter you will learn all of the important strategies to help you answer multiple-choice questions on the GRE. However, as invaluable as these tactics are, use them only when you need them. *If you know how to do a problem and are confident that you can do it accurately and reasonably quickly, JUST DO IT!*

Before the first discrete quantitative question appears on the screen, you will see the following instructions:

Select the best of the answer choices given.

This one-sentence set of directions is quite simple. Unfortunately, it is also quite useless. First of all, it is misleading. It is never the case that two of the answers are bad and three are good, and you then need to choose the *best* answer from among the three good ones. Every quantitative multiple-choice question has

exactly one correct answer and four incorrect ones. Second, the implication is that you should just *solve each problem* and *then* look at the five choices to see which one is best (i.e., correct). As you will learn in this chapter, that is not always the best strategy.

Helpful Hint

When you take the GRE, dismiss the instructions for these questions instantly — do not spend even one second reading them — and certainly never accept their offer of clicking on "HELP" to return to them during the test.

As we have done throughout this book, we will continue to label the five answer choices A, B, C, D, and E and to refer to them as such. Of course, when you take the the GRE, these letters will not appear—there will simply be a blank oval in front of each of the answer choices. When we refer to Choice C—as we do, for example, in TACTIC 1 below—we are simply referring to the third answer choice among the five presented.

Testing Tactics

Test the Choices, Starting with C

TACTIC 1, often called **backsolving**, is useful when you are asked to solve for an unknown and you understand what needs to be done to answer the question, but you want to avoid doing the algebra. The idea is simple: test the various choices to see which one is correct.

NOTE: On the GRE the answers to virtually all numerical multiple-choice questions are listed in either increasing or decreasing order. Consequently, C is the middle value, and *in applying TACTIC 1, you should always start with C.* For example, assume that choices A, B, C,

D, and E are given in increasing order. Try C. If it works, you've found the answer. If C doesn't work, you should know whether you need to test a larger number or a smaller one, and that permits you to eliminate two more choices. If C is too small, you need a larger number, and so A and B are out; if C is too large, eliminate D and E, which are even larger.

Examples 1 and 2 illustrate the proper use of TACTIC 1.

Example 1.

If the average (arithmetic mean) of 5, 6, 7, and w is 10, what is the value of w?

(A) 8 (B) 13 (C) 18 (D) 22 (E) 28

SOLUTION. Use TACTIC 1. Test Choice C: $w = 18$.

• Is the average of 5, 6, 7, and 18 equal to 10?

• No: $\dfrac{5 + 6 + 7 + 18}{4} = \dfrac{36}{4} = 9$, which is *too small*.

• Eliminate C, and, since for the average to be 10, w must be *greater* than 18, eliminate A and B, as well.

• Try D: $w = 22$. Is the average of 5, 6, 7, and 22 equal to 10?

• Yes: $\dfrac{5 + 6 + 7 + 22}{4} = \dfrac{40}{4} = 10$. The answer is **D**.

Every problem that can be solved using TACTIC 1 can be solved directly, usually in less time. So we stress: *if you are confident that you can solve a problem quickly and accurately, just do so.*

Here are two direct methods for solving Example 1, each of which is faster than backsolving. (See Section 14-E on averages.) If you know either method you should use it, and save TACTIC 1 for those problems which you can't easily solve directly.

Direct Solution 1. If the average of four numbers is 10, their sum is 40. So,

$$5 + 6 + 7 + w = 40 \Rightarrow 18 + w = 40 \Rightarrow w = \mathbf{22.}$$

Direct Solution 2. Since 5 is *5 less than* 10, 6 is *4 less than* 10, and 7 is *3 less than* 10, to compensate, w must be *5 + 4 + 3 = 12 more* than 10. So, $w = 10 + 12 = \mathbf{22.}$

Example 2.

Judy is now twice as old as Adam, but 6 years ago, she was 5 times as old as he was. How old is Judy now?

(A) 10 (B) 16 (C) 20 (D) 24 (E) 32

SOLUTION. Use TACTIC 1: backsolve starting with C. If Judy is now 20, Adam is 10, and 6 years ago, they

would have been 14 and 4. Since Judy would have been less than 5 times as old as Adam, eliminate C, D, and E, and try a smaller value. If Judy is now 16, Adam is 8; 6 years ago, they would have been 10 and 2. That's it; 10 *is* 5 times 2. The answer is **B**.

(See Section 14-H on word problems for the correct algebraic solution.)

Some tactics allow you to eliminate a few choices so you can make an educated guess. On those problems where it can be used, TACTIC 1 *always* gets you the right answer. The only reason not to use it on a particular problem is that you can *easily* solve the problem directly.

Helpful Hint

Don't start with C if some of the other choices are much easier to work with. If you start with B and it is too small, you may only get to eliminate two choices (A and B), instead of three, but it will save time if plugging in Choice C would be messy.

Example 3.

If $3x = 2(5 - 2x)$, then $x =$

(A) $-\dfrac{10}{7}$ (B) 0 (C) $\dfrac{3}{7}$ (D) 1 (E) $\dfrac{10}{7}$

SOLUTION. Since plugging in 0 is so much easier than plugging in $\dfrac{3}{7}$, start with B: then the left-hand side of the equation is 0 and the right-hand side is 10. The left-hand side is much too small. Eliminate A and B and try something bigger—D, of course; it will be much easier to deal with 1 than with $\dfrac{3}{7}$ or $\dfrac{10}{7}$. Now the left-hand side is 3 and the right-hand side is 6. We're closer, but not there. The answer must be **E**. Notice that we got the right answer without ever plugging in one of those unpleasant fractions. Are you uncomfortable choosing E without checking it? Don't be. If you *know* that the answer is greater than 1, and only one choice is greater than 1, that choice has to be right.

Again, we emphasize that, no matter what the choices are, you backsolve *only* if you can't easily do the algebra. Most students would probably do this problem directly:

$$3x = 2(5 - 2x) \Rightarrow 3x = 10 - 4x \Rightarrow 7x = 10 \Rightarrow x = \dfrac{10}{7}$$

and save backsolving for a harder problem. You have to determine which method is best for you.

$$3x = 10 - 4x$$
$$7x = 10$$
$$x = \dfrac{10}{7}$$

Tactic 2

Replace Variables with Numbers

Mastery of TACTIC 2 is critical for anyone developing good test-taking skills. This tactic can be used whenever the five choices involve the variables in the question. There are three steps:

1. Replace each letter with an easy-to-use number.

2. Solve the problem using those numbers.

3. Evaluate each of the five choices with the numbers you picked to see which choice is equal to the answer you obtained.

Examples 4 and 5 illustrate the proper use of TACTIC 2.

Example 4.

If a is equal to the sum of b and c, which of the following is equal to the difference of b and c?

(A) $a - b - c$ (B) $a - b + c$ (C) $a - c$
     (D) $a - 2c$ (E) $a - b - 2c$

SOLUTION.

• Pick three easy-to-use numbers which satisfy $a = b + c$: for example, $a = 5$, $b = 3$, $c = 2$.

• Then, solve the problem with these numbers: the difference of b and c is $3 - 2 = 1$.

• Finally, check each of the five choices to see which one is equal to 1:

(A) Does $a - b - c = 1$?   NO. $5 - 3 - 2 = 0$

(B) Does $a - b + c = 1$?   NO. $5 - 3 + 2 = 4$

(C) Does $a - c = 1$?   NO. $5 - 2 = 3$

(D) Does $a - 2c = 1$?   YES! $5 - 2(2) = 5 - 4 = 1$

(E) Does $a - b - 2c = 1$? NO. $5 - 3 - 2(2) = 2 - 4 = -2$

• The answer is **D**.

Example 5.

If the sum of five consecutive even integers is t, then, in terms of t, what is the greatest of these integers?

(A) $\dfrac{t - 20}{5}$ (B) $\dfrac{t - 10}{5}$ (C) $\dfrac{t}{5}$ (D) $\dfrac{t + 10}{5}$

(E) $\dfrac{t + 20}{5}$

SOLUTION.

• Pick five easy-to-use consecutive even integers: say, 2, 4, 6, 8, 10. Then t, their sum, is 30.

• Solve the problem with these numbers: the greatest of these integers is 10.

• When $t = 30$, the five choices are $\dfrac{10}{5}, \dfrac{20}{5}, \dfrac{30}{5}, \dfrac{40}{5}, \dfrac{50}{5}$.

• Only $\dfrac{50}{5}$, Choice **E**, is equal to 10.

Of course, Examples 4 and 5 can be solved without using TACTIC 3 *if your algebra skills are good*. Here are the solutions.

Solution 4. $a = b + c \Rightarrow b = a - c \Rightarrow$
$b - c = (a - c) - c = a - 2c$.

Solution 5. Let n, $n + 2$, $n + 4$, $n + 6$, and $n + 8$ be five consecutive even integers, and let t be their sum. Then,

$$t = n + (n + 2) + (n + 4) + (n + 6) + (n + 8) = 5n + 20$$

So, $n = \dfrac{t - 20}{5} \Rightarrow n + 8 = \dfrac{t - 20}{5} + 8 =$

$$\dfrac{t - 20}{5} + \dfrac{40}{5} = \dfrac{t + 20}{5}.$$

The important point is that if you can't do the algebra, you can still use TACTIC 2 and *always* get the right answer. Of course, you should use TACTIC 2 even if you can do the algebra, if you think that by using this tactic you will solve the problem faster or will be less likely to make a mistake. This is a good example of what we mean when we say that with the proper use of these tactics, you can correctly answer many questions for which you may not know the correct mathematical solution.

Examples 6 and 7 are somewhat different. You are asked to reason through word problems involving only variables. Most students find problems like these mind-boggling. Here, the use of TACTIC 2 is essential. Without it, Example 6 is difficult and Example 7 is nearly impossible. This is not an easy tactic to master, but with practice you will catch on.

Helpful Hint

Replace the letters with numbers that are easy to use, not necessarily ones that make sense. *It is perfectly OK to ignore reality*. A school can have 5 students, apples can cost 10 dollars each, trains can go 5 miles per hour or 1000 miles per hour—it doesn't matter.

Example 6.

If a school cafeteria needs c cans of soup each week for each student, and if there are s students in the school, for how many weeks will x cans of soup last?

(A) csx (B) $\dfrac{xs}{c}$ (C) $\dfrac{s}{cx}$ (D) $\dfrac{x}{cs}$ (E) $\dfrac{cx}{s}$

SOLUTION.

• Replace c, s, and x with three easy-to-use numbers. If a school cafeteria needs 2 cans of soup each week for each student, and if there are 5 students in the school, how many weeks will 20 cans of soup last?

• Since the cafeteria needs $2 \times 5 = 10$ cans of soup per week, 20 cans will last 2 weeks.

• Which of the choices equals 2 when $c = 2$, $s = 5$, and $x = 20$?

• $csx = 200$; $\dfrac{xs}{c} = 50$; $\dfrac{s}{cx} = \dfrac{1}{8}$; $\dfrac{x}{cs} = 2$; and $\dfrac{cx}{s} = 8$.

The answer is $\dfrac{x}{cs}$, **D**.

NOTE: You do not need to get the exact value of each choice. As soon as you see that a choice does not equal the value you are looking for, stop—eliminate that choice and move on. For example, in the preceding problem, it is clear that csx is much greater than 2, so eliminate it immediately; you do not need to multiply it out to determine that the value is 200.

CAUTION: In this type of problem it is *not* a good idea to replace any of the variables by 1. Since multiplying and dividing by 1 give the same result, you would not be able to distinguish between $\dfrac{cx}{s}$ and $\dfrac{x}{cs}$, both of which are equal to 4 when $c = 1$, $s = 5$, and $x = 20$. It is also not a good idea to use the same number for different variables: $\dfrac{cx}{s}$ and $\dfrac{xs}{c}$ are each equal to x when c and s are equal.

Example 7.

A vendor sell h hot dogs and s sodas. If a hot dog costs twice as much as a soda, and if the vendor takes in a total of d dollars, how many <u>cents</u> does a soda cost?

(A) $\dfrac{100d}{s + 2h}$ (B) $\dfrac{s + 2h}{100d}$ (C) $\dfrac{d(s + 2h)}{100}$

(D) $100d(s + 2h)$ (E) $\dfrac{d}{100(s + 2h)}$

SOLUTION.

• Replace h, s, and d with three easy-to-use numbers. Suppose a soda costs 50¢ and a hot dog $1.00. Then, if he sold 2 sodas and 3 hot dogs, he took in 4 dollars.

• Which of the choices equals 50 when $s = 2$, $h = 3$, and $d = 4$?

• Only $\dfrac{100d}{s + 2h}$ (**A**): $\dfrac{100(4)}{2 + 2(3)} = \dfrac{400}{8} = 50$.

Now, practice TACTIC 3 on the following problems.

Example 8.

Yann will be x years old y years from now. How old was he z years ago?

(A) $x + y + z$ (B) $x + y - z$ (C) $x - y - z$
(D) $y - x - z$ (E) $z - y - x$

Example 9.

Stan drove for h hours at a constant rate of r miles per hour. How many miles did he go during the final 20 minutes of his drive?

(A) $20r$ (B) $\dfrac{hr}{3}$ (C) $3rh$ (D) $\dfrac{hr}{20}$ (E) $\dfrac{r}{3}$

Solution 8. Assume that Yann will be 10 in 2 years. How old was he 3 years ago? If he will be 10 in 2 years, he is 8 now and 3 years ago he was 5. Which of the choices equals 5 when $x = 10$, $y = 2$, and $z = 3$? Only $x - y - z$, **C**.

Solution 9. If Stan drove at 60 miles per hour for 2 hours, how far did he go in the last 20 minutes? Since 20 minutes is $\dfrac{1}{3}$ of an hour, he went 20 ($\dfrac{1}{3}$ of 60) miles. Only $\dfrac{r}{3}$ is 20 when $r = 60$ and $h = 2$. Notice that h is irrelevant. Whether he had been driving for 2 hours or 20 hours, the distance he covered in the last 20 minutes would be the same.

Choose an Appropriate Number

TACTIC 3 is similar to TACTIC 2, in that we pick convenient numbers. However, here no variable is given in the problem. TACTIC 3 is especially useful in problems involving fractions, ratios, and percents.

Helpful Hint

In problems involving fractions, the best number to use is the least common denominator of all the fractions. In problems involving percents, the easiest number to use is 100. (See Sections 14-B and 14-C.)

Example 10.

At Madison High School each student studies exactly one foreign language. Three-fifths of the students take Spanish, and one-fourth of the remaining students take German. If all of the others take French, what <u>percent</u> of the students take French?

(A) 10   (B) 15   (C) 20   (D) 25   (E) 30

SOLUTION. The least common denominator of $\frac{3}{5}$ and $\frac{1}{4}$ is 20, so assume that there are 20 students at

Madison High. (Remember the numbers don't have to be realistic.) The number of students taking Spanish is $12 \left(\frac{3}{5} \text{ of } 20\right)$. Of the remaining 8 students, 2 of them $\left(\frac{1}{4} \text{ of } 8\right)$ take German. The other 6 take French. Finally, 6 is **30%** of 20. The answer is **E**.

Example 11.

From 1994 to 1995 the sales of a book decreased by 80%. If the sales in 1996 were the same as in 1994, by what percent did they increase from 1995 to 1996?

(A) 80%   (B) 100%   (C) 120%
(D) 400%   (E) 500%

SOLUTION. Since this problem involves percents, assume that 100 copies of the book were sold in 1994 (and 1996). Sales dropped by 80 (80% of 100) to 20 in 1995 and then increased by 80, from 20 back to 100, in 1996. The percent increase was

$$\frac{\text{the actual increase}}{\text{the original amount}} \times 100\% = \frac{80}{20} \times 100\% = \textbf{400\%, D.}$$

Eliminate Absurd Choices and Guess

When you have no idea how to solve a problem, you are forced to guess since you can't get to the next question until you answer and confirm the one on the screen; but first eliminate all the absurd choices. Then guess from among the remaining ones.

During the course of a GRE, you will probably find at least a few multiple-choice questions that you have no idea how to solve. Since you can't omit them, you have to guess. But take a moment to look at the answer choices. Often two or three of them are absurd. Eliminate those and then guess one of the others. Occasionally, four of the choices are absurd. When this occurs, your answer is no longer a guess.

What makes a choice absurd? Lots of things. Even if you don't know how to solve a problem you may realize that

• the answer must be positive, but some of the choices are negative;

• the answer must be even, but some of the choices are odd;

• the answer must be less than 100, but some choices exceed 100;

• a ratio must be less than 1, but some choices are greater than 1.

Let's look at several examples. In a few of them the information given is intentionally insufficient to solve the problem; but you will still be able to determine that some of the answers are absurd. In each case the "solution" will indicate which choices you should have eliminated. At that point you would simply guess. Remember, on the GRE when you have to guess, don't agonize. Just guess and move on.

Example 12.

A region inside a semicircle of radius r is shaded and you are asked for its area.

(A) $\frac{1}{4}\pi r^2$ (B) $\frac{1}{3}\pi r^2$ (C) $\frac{1}{2}\pi r^2$

(D) $\frac{2}{3}\pi r^2$ (E) πr^2

SOLUTION. You may have no idea how to find the area of the shaded region, but you should know that since the area of a circle is πr^2, the area of a semicircle is $\frac{1}{2}\pi r^2$. Therefore, the area of the shaded region must be *less* than $\frac{1}{2}\pi r^2$, so eliminate C, D, and E. On an actual GRE problem, you may be able to make an educated guess between A and B. If so, terrific; if not, just choose one or the other.

Example 13.

The average (arithmetic mean) of 5, 10, 15, and z is 20. What is z?

(A) 0   (B) 20   (C) 25   (D) 45   (E) 50

SOLUTION. If the average of four numbers is 20, and three of them are less than 20, the other one must be greater than 20. Eliminate A and B and guess. If you further realize that since 5 and 10 are a *lot less* than 20, z will probably be a *lot more* than 20; eliminate C, as well.

Example 14.

If 25% of 260 equals 6.5% of a, what is a?

(A) 10   (B) 65   (C) 100   (D) 130   (E) 1000

SOLUTION. Since 6.5% of a equals 25% of 260, which is surely greater than 6.5% of 260, a must be greater than 260. Eliminate A, B, C, and D. The answer *must* be **E**!

Example 14 illustrates an important point. *Even if you know how to solve a problem*, if you immediately see that four of the five choices are absurd, just pick the fifth choice and move on.

Example 15.

A jackpot of $39,000 is to be divided in some ratio among three people. What is the value of the largest share?

(A) $23,400   (B) $19,500   (C) $11,700
   (D) $7800   (E) $3900

SOLUTION. If the prize were divided equally, each of the three shares would be worth $13,000. If it is divided unequally, the largest share is surely worth *more than*

$13,000. Eliminate C, D, and E. In an actual question, you would be told what the ratio is, and that might enable you to eliminate A or B. If not, you just guess.

Example 16.

In a certain club, the ratio of the number of boys to girls is 5:3. What percent of the members of the club are girls?

(A) 37.5%   (B) 50%   (C) 60%   (D) 62.5%
   (E) 80%

SOLUTION. Since there are 5 boys for every 3 girls, there are fewer girls than boys. Therefore, *fewer than half* (50%) of the members are girls. Eliminate B, C, D, and E. The answer is **A**.

Example 17.

In the figure at the right, four semicircles are drawn, each one centered at the midpoint of one of the sides of square *ABCD*. Each of the four shaded "petals" is the intersection of two of the semicircles. If $AB = 4$, what is the total area of the shaded region?

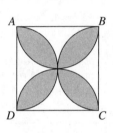

(A) 8π (B) $32 - 8\pi$ (C) $16 - 8\pi$ (D) $8\pi - 32$
   (E) $8\pi - 16$

SOLUTION. Since the diagram is drawn to scale, you may trust it in making your estimate (TACTIC 2, Chapter 10).

• Since the shaded area *appears* to take up a little more than half of the square, it does.

• The area of the square is 16, and so the area of the shaded region must be *about* 9.

• Check each choice. Since π is slightly more than 3 ($\pi \approx 3.14$), 8π is somewhat greater than 24, approximately 25.

• (A) $8\pi \approx 25$. More than the area of the whole square: way too big.

• (B) $32 - 8\pi \approx 32 - 25 = 7$. Too small (but close enough to consider if nothing is closer).

• (C) $16 - 8\pi$ is negative. Clearly impossible!

• (D) $8\pi - 32$ is also negative.

• (E) $\mathbf{8\pi - 16} \approx 25 - 16 = 9$. Finally! The answer is **E**.

NOTE: Three of the choices are absurd: A is more than the area of the entire square and C and D are negative; they can be eliminated immediately. No matter what your estimate was, at worst you had to guess between two choices.

Now use TACTIC 5 on each of the following problems. Even if you know how to solve them, don't. Practice this technique and see how many choices you can eliminate *without* actually solving.

Example 18.

In the figure at the right, diagonal EG of square $EFGH$ is $\frac{1}{2}$ of diagonal AC of the square $ABCD$. What is the ratio of the area of the shaded region to the area of $ABCD$?

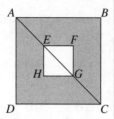

(A) $\sqrt{2}{:}1$ (B) 3:4   (C) $\sqrt{2}{:}2$
     (D) 1:2   (E) $1{:}2\sqrt{2}$

Example 19.

Shari receives a commission of 25¢ for every $20.00 worth of merchandise she sells. What percent is her commission?

(A) $1\frac{1}{4}\%$ (B) $2\frac{1}{2}\%$ (C) 5%
     (D) 25%   (E) 125%

Example 20.

From 1980 to 1990, Lior's weight increased by 25%. If his weight was k kilograms in 1990, what was it in 1980?

(A) $1.75k$ (B) $1.25k$ (C) $1.20k$
     (D) $.80k$ (E) $.75k$

Example 21.

The average of 10 numbers is –10. If the sum of 6 of them is 100, what is the average of the other 4?

(A) –100   (B) –50   (C) 0   (D) 50   (E) 100

Solution 18. Obviously, the shaded region is smaller than square $ABCD$, so the ratio must be less than 1. Eliminate A. Also, from the diagram, it is clear that the shaded region is more than half of square $ABCD$, so the ratio is greater than 0.5. Eliminate D and E. Since 3:4 = .75 and $\sqrt{2}{:}2 \approx .71$, B and C are too close to tell which is correct just by looking; so guess. The answer is **B**.

Solution 19. Clearly, a commission of 25¢ on $20 is quite small. Eliminate D and E and guess one of the small percents. If you realize that 1% of $20 is 20¢, then you know the answer is a little more than 1%, and you should guess A (maybe B, but definitely not C). The answer is **A**.

Solution 20. Since Lior's weight increased, his weight in 1980 was *less than k*. Eliminate A, B, and C and guess. The answer is **D**.

Solution 21. Since the average of all 10 numbers is negative, so is their sum. But the sum of the first 6 is positive, so the sum (and the average) of the others must be negative. Eliminate C, D, and E. **B** is correct.

Practice Exercises

Discrete Quantitative Questions

1. Evan has 4 times as many books as David and 5 times as many as Jason. If Jason has more than 40 books, what is the least number of books that Evan could have?

   (A) 200   (B) 205   (C) 210   (D) 220   (E) 240

2. Judy plans to visit the National Gallery once each month in 2001 except in July and August when she plans to go three times each. A single admission costs $3.50, a pass valid for unlimited visits in any 3-month period can be purchased for $18, and an annual pass costs $60.00. What is the least amount, in dollars, that Judy can spend for her intended number of visits?

   (A) 72   (B) 60   (C) 56   (D) 49.5   (E) 48

3. Alison is now three times as old as Jeremy, but 5 years ago, she was 5 times as old as he was. How old is Alison now?

   (A) 10   (B) 12   (C) 24   (D) 30   (E) 36

4. What is the largest prime factor of 255?

   (A) 5   (B) 15   (C) 17   (D) 51   (E) 255

5. If c is the product of a and b, which of the following is the quotient of a and b?

   (A) $\dfrac{b^2}{c}$ (B) $\dfrac{c}{b^2}$ (C) $\dfrac{b}{c^2}$ (D) $\dfrac{c^2}{b}$ (E) b^2c

6. If w widgets cost c cents, how many widgets can you get for d dollars?

   (A) $\dfrac{100dw}{c}$ (B) $\dfrac{dw}{100c}$ (C) $100cdw$
        (D) $\dfrac{dw}{c}$ (E) cdw

7. If 120% of a is equal to 80% of b, which of the following is equal to $a + b$?

   (A) 1.5a (B) 2a (C) 2.5a (D) 3a (E) 5a

8. In the figure at the right, $WXYZ$ is a square whose sides are 12. AB, CD, EF, and GH are each 8, and are the diameters of the four semicircles. What is the area of the shaded region?

   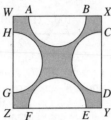

   (A) $144 - 128\pi$ (B) $144 - 64\pi$ (C) $144 - 32\pi$
   (D) $144 - 16\pi$ (E) 16π

9. If x and y are integers such that $x^3 = y^2$, which of the following could <u>not</u> be the value of y?

   (A) –1   (B) 1   (C) 8   (D) 16   (E) 27

10. What is a divided by a% of a?

    (A) $\dfrac{a}{100}$ (B) $\dfrac{100}{a}$ (C) $\dfrac{a^2}{100}$ (D) $\dfrac{100}{a^2}$
    (E) $100a$

11. If an object is moving at a speed of 36 kilometers per hour, how many meters does it travel in one second?

    (A) 10   (B) 36   (C) 100   (D) 360   (E) 1000

12. On a certain French-American committee, $\dfrac{2}{3}$ of the members are men, and $\dfrac{3}{8}$ of the men are Americans. If $\dfrac{3}{5}$ of the committee members are French, what fraction of the members are American women?

    (A) $\dfrac{3}{20}$ (B) $\dfrac{11}{60}$ (C) $\dfrac{1}{4}$ (D) $\dfrac{2}{5}$ (E) $\dfrac{5}{12}$

13. For what value of x is $8^{2x-4} = 16^x$?

    (A) 2   (B) 3   (C) 4   (D) 6   (E) 8

14. If $12a + 3b = 1$ and $7b - 2a = 9$, what is the average (arithmetic mean) of a and b?

    (A) 0.1   (B) 0.5   (C) 1   (D) 2.5   (E) 5

15. If x% of y is 10, what is y?

    (A) $\dfrac{10}{x}$ (B) $\dfrac{100}{x}$ (C) $\dfrac{1000}{x}$ (D) $\dfrac{x}{100}$ (E) $\dfrac{x}{10}$

Answer Key

1. **D**	3. **D**	5. **B**	7. **C**	9. **D**	11. **A**	13. **D**	15. **C**
2. **D**	4. **C**	6. **A**	8. **C**	10. **B**	12. **A**	14. **B**	

Answer Explanations

Two asterisks (**) indicate an alternative method of solving.

1. **D.**   Test the answer choices starting with the smallest value. If Evan had 200 books, Jason would have 40. But Jason has more than 40, so 200 is too small. Trying 205 and 210, we see that neither is a multiple of 4, so David wouldn't have a whole number of books. Finally, 220 works. (So does 240, but we shouldn't even test it since we want the least value.)
   **Since Jason has at least 41 books, Evan has at least $41 \times 5 = 205$. But Evan's total must be a multiple of 4 and 5, hence of 20. The smallest multiple of 20 greater than 205 is 220.

2. **D.**   Judy intends to go to the Gallery 16 times during the year. Buying a single admission each time would cost $16 \times \$3.50 = \$56$, which is less than the annual pass. If she

bought a 3-month pass for June, July, and August, she would pay $18 plus $31.50 for 9 single admissions ($9 \times \$3.50$), for a total expense of $49.50, which is the least expensive option.

3. **D.**   Use TACTIC 1: backsolve starting with C. If Alison is now 24, Jeremy is 8, and 5 years ago, they would have been 19 and 3, which is more than 5 times as much. Eliminate A, B, and C, and try a bigger value. If Alison is now 30, Jeremy is 10, and 5 years ago, they would have been 25 and 5. That's it; 25 is 5 times 5. **If Jeremy is now x, Alison is $3x$, and 5 years ago they were $x - 5$ and $3x - 5$, respectively. Now, solve:

   $$3x - 5 = 5(x - 5) \Rightarrow 3x - 5 = 5x - 25 \Rightarrow$$
   $$2x = 20 \Rightarrow x = 10 \Rightarrow 3x = 30.$$

4. **C.**   Test the choices starting with C: 255 *is* divisible by 17 ($255 = 17 \times 15$), so this is a possible answer. Does 255 have a larger prime factor? Neither Choice D nor E is prime, so the answer must be Choice C.

5. **B.** Use TACTIC 2. Pick simple values for a, b, and c. Let $a = 3$, $b = 2$, and $c = 6$. Then $a \div b = 3/2$. Without these values of a, b, and c, only B is equal to 3/2.
   ** $c - ab \Rightarrow a = c/b \Rightarrow a \div b = c/b \div b = c/b \cdot 1/b = c/b^2$.

6. **A.** Use TACTIC 2. If 2 widgets cost 10 cents, then widgets cost 5 cents each, and for 3 dollars, you can get 60. Which of the choices equals 60 when $w = 2$, $c = 10$, and $d = 3$? Only A.
   ** $\dfrac{\text{widgets}}{\text{cents}} = \dfrac{w}{c} = \dfrac{x}{100d} \Rightarrow x = \dfrac{100dw}{c}$.

7. **C.** Since 120% of 80 = 80% of 120, let $a = 80$ and $b = 120$. Then $a + b = 200$, and $200 \div 80 = 2.5$.

8. **C.** If you don't know how to solve this, you must use TACTIC 4 and guess after eliminating the absurd choices. Which choices are absurd? Certainly, A and B, both of which are negative. Also, since Choice D is about 94, which is much more than half the area of the square, it is much too big. Guess between Choice C (about 43) and Choice E (about 50). If you remember that the way to find shaded areas is to subtract, guess C.
   **The area of the square is $12^2 = 144$. The area of each semicircle is 8π, one-half the area of a circle of radius 4. So together the areas of the semicircles is 32π.

9. **D.** Test each choice until you find the correct answer. Could $y = -1$? Is there an integer x such that $x^3 = (-1)^2 = 1$? Yes, $x = 1$. Similarly, if $y = 1$, $x = 1$. Could $y = 8$? Is there an integer x such that $x^3 = (8)^2 = 64$? Yes, $x = 4$. Could $y = 16$? Is there an integer x such that $x^3 = 16^2 = 256$? No, $6^3 = 216$, which is too small; and $7^3 = 343$, which is too big. The answer is D.

10. **B.** $a \div (a\% \text{ of } a) = a \div \left(\dfrac{a}{100} \times a \right) =$
    $$a \div \left(\dfrac{a^2}{100} \right) = a \times \dfrac{100}{a^2} = \dfrac{100}{a}.$$
    **Use TACTICS 2 and 3: replace a by a number, and use 100 since the problem involves percents. $100 \div (100\% \text{ of } 100) = 100 \div 100 = 1$. Test each choice; which one equals 1 when $a = 100$. Both A and B: $\dfrac{100}{100} = 1$. Eliminate Choices C, D, and E, and test A and B with another value for a. $50 \div (50\% \text{ of } 50) = 50 \div (25) = 2$. Now, only B works $\left(\dfrac{100}{50} = 2, \text{ whereas } \dfrac{50}{100} = \dfrac{1}{2} \right)$.

11. **A.** Set up a ratio:
    $$\dfrac{\text{distance}}{\text{time}} = \dfrac{36 \text{ kilometers}}{1 \text{ hour}} = \dfrac{36{,}000 \text{ meters}}{60 \text{ minutes}} =$$
    $$\dfrac{36{,}000 \text{ meters}}{3600 \text{ seconds}} = 10 \text{ meters/second}.$$
    **Use TACTIC 1: Test choices starting with C:
    100 meters/second = 6000 meters/minute = 360,000 meters/hour = 360 kilometers/hour.
    Not only is that too big, it is too big by a factor of 10. The answer is 10.

12. **A.** Use TACTIC 3. The LCM of all the denominators is 120, so assume that the committee has 120 members. Then there are $\dfrac{2}{3} \times 120 = 80$ men and 40 women. Of the 80 men 30 $\left(\dfrac{3}{8} \times 80 \right)$ are American. Since there are 72 $\left(\dfrac{3}{5} \times 120 \right)$ French members, there are $120 - 72 = 48$ Americans, of whom 30 are men, so the other 18 are women. Finally, the fraction of American women is $\dfrac{18}{120} = \dfrac{3}{20}$. This is illustrated in the Venn diagram below.

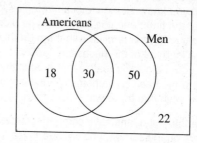

13. **D.** Use the laws of exponents to simplify the equation, and then solve it: $8^{2x-4} = 16^x \Rightarrow (2^3)^{2x-4} = (2^4)^x \Rightarrow 3(2x - 4) = 4x \Rightarrow 6x - 12 = 4x \Rightarrow 2x = 12 \Rightarrow x = 6$.

14. **B.** Add the two equations:
    $$10a + 10b = 10 \Rightarrow a + b = 1 \Rightarrow \dfrac{a + b}{2} = \dfrac{1}{2}.$$
    Do not waste time solving for a and b.

15. **C.** Pick easy-to-use numbers. Since 100% of 10 is 10, let $x = 100$ and $y = 10$. When $x = 100$, Choices C and E are each 10. Eliminate Choices A, B, and D, and try some other numbers: 50% of 20 is 10. Of Choices C and E, only C = 20 when $x = 50$.

12 Quantitative Comparison Questions

■ Tactics
■ Practice Exercises
■ Answer Key and Explanations

One half of the 28 questions on the quantitative section of the GRE are quantitative comparisons. It is very likely that the only time you ever encountered questions of this type before was when you were preparing for the PSAT or SAT I, in your junior or senior year of high school. Therefore, it may be at least four years since you last answered a quantitative comparison question. Even if you knew all the various strategies for answering them at the time, and it is likely that you didn't, you are probably no longer familiar with them. In this chapter you will learn all of the necessary tactics. If you master them, you will quickly realize that quantitative comparisons are the easiest mathematics questions on the GRE and will wish that there were more than 14 of them.

Before the first quantitative comparison question appears on the screen, you will see these instructions.

<u>Directions:</u> This question consists of two quantities, one in Column A and one in Column B. You are to compare the two quantities and decide whether

    the quantity in Column A is greater;
    the quantity in Column B is greater;
    the two quantities are equal;
    the relationship cannot be determined from the information given.

<u>Common information:</u> Information concerning one or both of the quantities to be compared is centered above the two columns. A symbol that appears in both columns represents the same thing in Column A as it does in Column B.

Before learning the different strategies for solving this type of question, let's clarify these instructions. In quantitative comparison questions there are two quantities, one in Column A and one in Column B, and it is your job to compare them.

You should click on the oval in front of	if
The quantity in Column A is greater.	The quantity in Column A is greater *all the time, no matter what.*
The quantity in Column B is greater.	The quantity in Column B is greater *all the time, no matter what.*
The two quantities are equal.	The two quantities are equal *all the time, no matter what.*
The relationship cannot be determined from the information given.	*The answer is not one of the first three choices.*

This means, for example, that *if you can find a single instance* when the quantity in Column A is greater than the quantity in Column B, then you can immediately eliminate two choices: the answer cannot be "The quantity in Column B is greater," and the answer cannot be "The two quantities are equal." In order for the answer to be "The quantity in Column B is greater," the quantity in Column B would have to be greater *all the time*; but you know of one instance when it isn't. Similarly, since the quantities are not equal *all the time*, the answer can't be "The two quantities are equal." The correct answer, therefore, is either "The quantity in Column A is greater" or "The relationship cannot be determined from the information given." If it turns out that the quantity in Column A *is* greater all the time, then that is the answer; if, however, you can find a single instance where the quantity in Column A is not greater, the answer is "The relationship cannot be determined from the information given."

By applying the tactics that you will learn in this chapter, you will probably be able to determine which of the choices is correct; if, however, after eliminating two of the choices, you still cannot determine which answer is correct, quickly guess between the two remaining choices and move on.

Helpful Hint

Right now, memorize the instructions for answering quantitative comparison questions. *When you take the GRE, dismiss the instructions for these questions immediately— do not spend even one second reading the directions (or looking at the sample problems.)*

Before learning the most important tactics for handling quantitative comparison questions, let's look at two examples to illustrate the preceding instructions.

Column A	Column B

Example 1.

$$1 < x < 3$$

x^2	$2x$

○ The quantity in Column A is greater.
○ The quantity in Column B is greater.
○ The two quantities are equal.
○ The relationship cannot be determined from the information given.

SOLUTION. In each column, x represents the same thing—a number between 1 and 3. If x is 2, then x^2 and $2x$ are each 4, and *in this case* the two quantities are equal. We can, therefore, eliminate the first two choices: neither Column A nor Column B is greater *all the time*. However, in order for the correct answer to be "The two quantities are equal," the columns would have to be

equal *all the time*. Are they? Note that although 2 is the only *integer* between 1 and 3, it is not the only *number* between 2 and 3: x could be 1.1 or 2.5 or any of infinitely many other numbers. And in those cases the quantities are not equal (For example, $2.5^2 = 6.25$, whereas $2(2.5) = 5$). The columns are *not* always equal, and so the correct answer is the fourth choice: "The relationship cannot be determined from the information given."

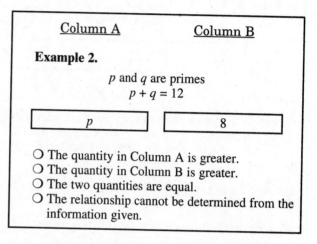

Column A	Column B

Example 2.

p and q are primes
$$p + q = 12$$

p	8

○ The quantity in Column A is greater.
○ The quantity in Column B is greater.
○ The two quantities are equal.
○ The relationship cannot be determined from the information given.

SOLUTION. Since 5 and 7 are the only primes whose sum is 12, p could be 5 or 7. In either case, p is less than 8, and so the quantity in Column B is greater, *all the time*. Note that although $1 + 11 = 12$, p cannot be 11, because 1 is not a prime [See Section 14-A].

NOTE: To simplify the discussion, throughout the rest of this chapter, in the explanations of the answers to all sample questions and the Model Tests, the four answer choices will be referred to as A, B, C, and D, respectively. For example, we will write

The correct answer is **B**.

rather than

The correct answer is "The quantity in Column B is greater."

Testing Tactics

Replace Variables with Numbers

Many problems that are hard to analyze because they contain variables become easy to solve when the variables are replaced by simple numbers.

TACTIC 1 is the most important tactic in this chapter. Using it properly will earn you more points on the quantitative comparison questions of the GRE than you can gain by applying any of the others. *Be sure to master it!*

Most quantitative comparison questions contain variables. When those variables are replaced by simple numbers such as 0 or 1, the quantities in the two columns become much easier to compare.

The reason that TACTIC 1 is so important is that it *guarantees* that on any quantitative comparison question that involve variables, you will be able to immediately eliminate two of the four choices, and very often a third choice as well, leaving you with at least a 50% chance of guessing correctly, and often a certainty. Try the following example, and then read the explanation very carefully.

Column A	Column B
Example 3.	
$a < b < c < d$	
ab	cd

SOLUTION.

- Replace a, b, c, and d with easy-to-use numbers which satisfy the condition $a < b < c < d$: for example, $a = 1$, $b = 3$, $c = 6$, $d = 10$. [See the guidelines that follow to learn why 1, 2, 3, 4 is not the best choice.]

- Evaluate the two columns: $ab = (1)(3) = 3$, and $cd = (6)(10) = 60$.

- So *in this case*, the quantity in Column B is greater.

- Does that mean that B is the correct answer? Not necessarily. The quantity in Column B *is* greater this time, but will it be greater **every single time, no matter what**?

- What it does mean is that neither A nor C could possibly be the correct answer: Column A can't be greater **every single time**, **no matter what** because it isn't greater *this* time; and the quantities aren't equal **every single time, no matter what** because they aren't equal *this* time.

So in the few seconds that it took you to plug in 1, 3, 6, and 10 for a, b, c, and d, you were able to eliminate two of the four choices. You now know that the correct answer is either B or D, and if you could do nothing else, you would now guess with a 50% chance of being correct.

But, of course, *you will do something else*. You will try some other numbers. But *which* numbers? Since the first numbers you chose were positive, try some negative numbers this time.

- Let $a = -5$, $b = -3$, $c = -2$, and $d = -1$.

- Evaluate: $ab = (-5)(-3) = 15$ and $cd = (-2)(-1) = 2$.

- So *in this case*, the quantity in Column A is greater.

- Column B is *not* greater all the time. B is *not* the correct answer.

- The correct answer is **D**: The relationship cannot be determined from the information given.

NOTES:

1. If for your second substitution you had chosen 3, 7, 8, 10 or 2, 10, 20, 35 or *any* four positive numbers, Column B would have been bigger. No matter how many substitutions you made, Column B would have been bigger each time, and you would have incorrectly concluded that B was the answer. In fact, if the given condition had been $0 < a < b < c < d$, then B *would have been* the correct answer.

2. Therefore, knowing which numbers to plug in when you are using TACTIC 1 is critical. As long as you comply with the conditions written above the columns, you have complete freedom in choosing the numbers. Some choices, however, are much better than others.

Here are some guidelines for deciding which numbers to use when applying TACTIC 1.

1. **The very best numbers to use first are: 1, 0, and −1.**

2. **Often, fractions between 0 and 1 are useful.**

3. **Occasionally, "large" numbers such as 10 or 100 can be used.**

4. **If there is more than one letter, it is permissible to replace each with the same number.**

5. **Do not impose any conditions not specifically stated.** In particular, do not assume that variables must be integers. For example, 3 is not the only number that satisfies $2 < x < 4$ (2.1, 3.95, and π all work). The expression $a < b < c < d$ does not mean that a, b, c, d are *integers*, let alone *consecutive* integers (which is why we didn't choose 1, 2, 3, and 4 in Example 3), nor does it mean that any or all of them are *positive*.

When you replace the variables in a quantitative comparison question with numbers, remember:

If the value in Column A is ever greater:	eliminate B and C — the answer must be A or D.
If the value in Column B is ever greater:	eliminate A and C — the answer must be B or D.
If the two columns are ever equal:	eliminate A and B — the answer must be C or D.

You have learned that, no matter how hard a quantitative comparison is, as soon as you replace the variables, two choices can *immediately* be eliminated; and if you can't decide between the other two, just guess. This guarantees that in addition to correctly answering all the questions that you know how to solve, you will be able to answer correctly at least half, and probably many more, of the questions that you don't know how to do.

Practice applying TACTIC 1 on these examples.

	Column A	Column B
	Example 4.	
	$m > 0$ and $m \neq 1$	
	m^2	m^3
	Example 5.	
	$13y$	$15y$
	Example 6.	
	$w + 11$	$w - 11$
	Example 7.	
	The perimeter of a rectangle whose area is 18	The perimeter of a rectangle whose area is 28
	Example 8.	
	$a = \dfrac{2}{3}t \quad b = \dfrac{5}{6}t \quad c = \dfrac{3}{5}b$	
	$3a$	$4c$

	Column A	Column B	Compare	Eliminate
Let $w = 1$	$1 + 11 = 12$	$1 - 11 = -10$	A is greater	B and C
Let $w = 0$	$0 + 11 = 11$	$0 - 11 = -11$	A is greater	
Let $w = -1$	$-1 + 11 = 10$	$-1 - 11 = -12$	A is greater	

Guess **A**. We let w be a positive number, a negative number, and 0. Each time, Column A was greater. That's not proof, but it justifies an educated guess. [The answer *is* A. Clearly, $11 > -11$ and if we add w to each side, we get: $w + 11 > w - 11$.]

SOLUTION 7. What's this question doing here? How can we use TACTIC 1? Where are the variables that we're supposed to replace? Well, in each column there are rectangles, and the variables are their lengths and widths.

Column A	Column B	Compare	Eliminate
Choose a rectangle whose area is 18:	Choose a rectangle whose area is 28:		
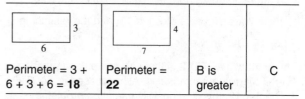			
The perimeter here is	The perimeter here is	Columns A and B are equal	
$9 + 2 + 9 + 2 = \mathbf{22}$	$7 + 4 + 7 + 4 = \mathbf{22}$		A and B

Keep Column B, but take a different rectangle of area 18 in Column A:

Perimeter = $3 + 6 + 3 + 6 = \mathbf{18}$	Perimeter = 22	B is greater	C

The answer is **D**.

SOLUTION 4. Use TACTIC 1. Replace m with numbers satisfying $m > 0$ and $m \neq 1$.

	Column A	Column B	Compare	Eliminate
Let $m = 2$	$2^2 = 4$	$2^3 = 8$	B is greater	A and C
Let $m = \dfrac{1}{2}$	$\left(\dfrac{1}{2}\right)^2 = \dfrac{1}{4}$	$\left(\dfrac{1}{2}\right)^3 = \dfrac{1}{8}$	A is greater	B

The answer is **D**.

SOLUTION 5. Use TACTIC 1. There are no restrictions on y, so use the best numbers: 1, 0, −1.

	Column A	Column B	Compare	Eliminate
Let $y = 1$	$13(1) = 13$	$15(1) = 15$	B is greater	A and C
Let $y = 0$	$13(0) = 0$	$15(0) = 0$	They're equal	B

The answer is **D**.

SOLUTION 6. Use TACTIC 1. There are no restrictions on w, so use the best numbers: 1, 0, −1.

SOLUTION 8. Use TACTIC 1. First, try the easiest number: let $t = 0$. Then a, b, and c are each 0, and *in this case*, the columns are equal—they're both 0. Eliminate A and B. Now, try another number for t. The obvious choice is 1, but then a, b, and c will all be fractions. To avoid this, let $t = 6$. Then, $a = \dfrac{2}{3}(6) = 4$, $b = \dfrac{5}{6}(6) = 5$, and $c = \dfrac{3}{5}(5) = 3$. This time, $3a = 3(4) = \mathbf{12}$ and $4b = 4(3) = \mathbf{12}$. *Again, the two columns are equal.* Choose **C**.

NOTE: You should consider answering this question directly (i.e., without plugging in numbers), *only if you are very comfortable with both fractions and elementary algebra.* Here's the solution:

$$c = \frac{3}{5}b = \frac{3}{5}\left(\frac{5}{6}t\right) = \frac{1}{2}t$$

Therefore, $2c = t$, and $4c = 2t$. Since $a = \frac{2}{3}t$, $3a = 2t$. So, $4c = 3a$. The answer is **C**.

Choose an Appropriate Number

This is just like TACTIC 1. We are replacing a variable with a number, but the variable isn't mentioned in the problem.

Column A	Column B

Example 9.

Every band member is either 15, 16, or 17 years old. One third of the band members are 16, and twice as many band members are 16 as 15.

The number of 17-year-old band members	The total number of 15- and 16-year-old band members

If the first sentence of Example 9 had been "There are *n* students in the school band, all of whom are 15, 16, or 17 years old," the problem would have been identical to this one. Using TACTIC 1, you could have replaced *n* with an easy-to-use number, such as 6, and solved:

$\frac{1}{3}(6) = 2$ are 16 years old; 1 is 15, and the remaining 3 are 17. The answer is **C**.

The point of TACTIC 2 is that you can plug in numbers even if there are no variables. As discussed in TACTIC 3, chapter 12, this is especially useful on problems involving percents, in which case 100 is a good number, and problems involving fractions, in which case the LCD of the fractions is a good choice. However, the use of TACTIC 2 is not limited to these situations. Try using TACTIC 2 on the following three problems.

Column A	Column B

Example 10.

The perimeter of a square and the circumference of a circle are equal.

The area of the circle	The area of the square

Example 11.

Jen, Ken, and Len divided a cash prize.

Jen took 50% of the money and spent $\frac{3}{5}$ of what she took.

Ken took 40% of the money and spent $\frac{3}{4}$ of what he took.

The amount that Jen spent	The amount that Ken spent

Example 12.

Eliane types twice as fast as Delphine. Delphine charges 50% more per page than Eliane.

Amount Eliane earns in 9 hours	Amount Delphine earns in 12 hours

SOLUTION 10. First use TACTIC 1, chapter 10: draw a diagram.

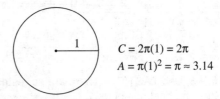

$$C = 2\pi(1) = 2\pi$$
$$A = \pi(1)^2 = \pi \approx 3.14$$

Then use TACTIC 2: choose an easy-to-use number. Let the radius of the circle be 1. Then its area is π. Let *s* be the side of the square:

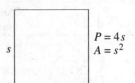

$$P = 4s$$
$$A = s^2$$

$$4s = 2\pi \approx 6 \Rightarrow s \approx 1.5 \Rightarrow$$
$$\text{area of the square} \approx (1.5)^2 = 2.25$$

The answer is **A**.

SOLUTION 11. Use TACTIC 2. Assume the prize was $100. Then Jen took $50 and spent $\frac{3}{5}$($50) = $30. Ken took $40 and spent $\frac{3}{4}$($40) = $30. The answer is **C**.

SOLUTION 12. Use TACTIC 2. Choose appropriate numbers. Assume Delphine can type 1 page per hour

and Eliane can type 2. Assume Eliane charges $1.00 per page and Delphine charges $1.50. Then in 9 hours, Eliane types 18 pages, earning **$18.00**. In 12 hours, Delphine types 12 pages, earning 12 × $1.50 = **$18.00**. The answer is **C**.

Make the Problem Easier: Do the Same Thing to Each Column

A quantitative comparison question can be treated as an equation or an inequality. Either:

Column A < Column B, or
Column A = Column B, or
Column A > Column B

In solving an equation or an inequality, you can always add the same quantity to each side or subtract the same quantity from each side. Similarly, in solving a quantitative comparison, you can always add the same quantity to each column or subtract the same quantity from each column. You can also multiply or divide each side of an equation or inequality by the same quantity, *but in the case of inequalities you can do this only if the quantity is positive*. Since you don't know whether the columns are equal or unequal, you cannot multiply or divide by a variable *unless you know that it is positive*. If the quantities in each column are positive you may square them or take their square roots.

To illustrate the proper use of TACTIC 3, we will give alternate solutions to three of the examples which we already solved using TACTIC 1.

SOLUTION 4. Divide each column by m^2 (that's OK—m^2 is positive):

Column A	Column B
$\frac{m^2}{m^2} = 1$	$\frac{m^3}{m^2} = m$

This is a much easier comparison. Which is greater, m or 1? We don't know. We know $m > 0$ and $m \neq 1$, but it could be greater than 1 or less than 1. The answer is **D**.

SOLUTION 5. Subtract $13y$ from each column: $13y - 13y = 0$ $15y - 13y = 2y$

Since there are no restrictions on y, $2y$ could be greater than, less than, or equal to 0. The answer is **D**.

SOLUTION 6. Subtract w from each column:

Column A	Column B
$w + 11$	$w - 11$
$-\ w$	$-\ w$
$\overline{11}$	$\overline{-11}$

Clearly, 11 is greater than −11. Column **A** is greater.

Here are five more examples on which to practice TACTIC 3.

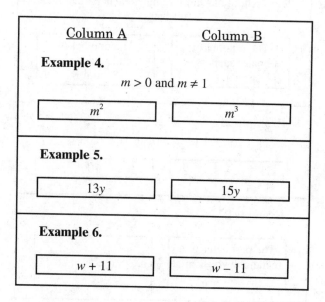

Column A	Column B
Example 4.	
$m > 0$ and $m \neq 1$	
m^2	m^3
Example 5.	
$13y$	$15y$
Example 6.	
$w + 11$	$w - 11$

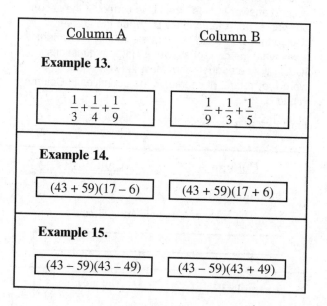

Column A	Column B
Example 13.	
$\frac{1}{3}+\frac{1}{4}+\frac{1}{9}$	$\frac{1}{9}+\frac{1}{3}+\frac{1}{5}$
Example 14.	
$(43+59)(17-6)$	$(43+59)(17+6)$
Example 15.	
$(43-59)(43-49)$	$(43-59)(43+49)$

Column A	Column B
Example 16.	
a is a negative number	
a^2	$-a^2$
Example 17.	
$\dfrac{\sqrt{20}}{2}$	$\dfrac{5}{\sqrt{5}}$

	Column A	Column B

SOLUTION 13.
Subtract $\frac{1}{3}$ and $\frac{1}{9}$
from each column:

$\cancel{\frac{1}{3}} + \frac{1}{4} + \cancel{\frac{1}{9}}$ $\cancel{\frac{1}{9}} + \cancel{\frac{1}{3}} + \frac{1}{5}$

Since $\frac{1}{4} > \frac{1}{5}$, the answer is **A**.

SOLUTION 14.
Divide each
column by
$(43 + 59)$: $\cancel{(43 + 59)}(17 - 6)$ $\cancel{(43 + 59)}(17 + 6)$

Clearly, $(17 + 6) > (17 - 6)$. The answer is **B**.

SOLUTION 15. CAUTION: $(43 - 59)$ is negative, and you *may not* divide the columns by a negative number. The easiest alternative: Column A, being the product of 2 negative numbers, is positive, whereas Column B is negative. Column **A** is greater.

SOLUTION 16.
Add a^2 to each
column: $a^2 + a^2 = 2a^2$ $-a^2 + a^2 = 0$

Since a is negative, $2a^2$ is positive. The answer is **A**.

SOLUTION 17.
Square each
column: $\left(\dfrac{\sqrt{20}}{2}\right)^2 = \dfrac{20}{4} = 5$ $\left(\dfrac{5}{\sqrt{5}}\right)^2 = \dfrac{25}{5} = 5$

The answer is **C**.

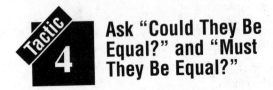

Tactic 4 — Ask "Could They Be Equal?" and "Must They Be Equal?"

TACTIC 4 has many applications, but is most useful when one of the columns contains a variable and the other contains a number. In this situation ask yourself, "Could they be equal?" If the answer is "yes," eliminate A and B, and then ask, "Must they be equal?" If the second answer is "yes," then C is correct; if the second answer is "no," then choose D. When the answer to "Could they be equal?" is "no," we usually know right away what the correct answer is. In both questions, "Could they be equal" and "Must they be equal," the word *they* refers, of course, to the quantities in Columns A and B.

Let's look at a few examples.

Column A	Column B
Example 18.	
The sides of a triangle are 3, 4, and x	
x	5
Example 19.	
$56 < 5c < 64$	
c	12

Column A	Column B
Example 20.	
School A has 100 teachers and School B has 200 teachers.	
Each school has more female teachers than male teachers.	
The number of female teachers at School A	The number of female teachers at School B
Example 21.	
$(m + 1)(m + 2)(m + 3) = 720$	
$m + 2$	10
Example 22.	
The perimeter of a rectangle whose area is 21	20

SOLUTION 18. Could they be equal? Could $x = 5$? Of course. That's the all-important 3-4-5 right triangle. Eliminate A and B. Must they be equal? Must $x = 5$? If you're not sure, try drawing an acute or an obtuse triangle. The answer is No. Actually, x can be any number satisfying: $1 < x < 7$. (See KEY FACT J12, the triangle inequality, and the figure below.) The answer is **D**.

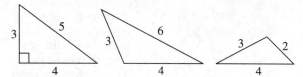

SOLUTION 19. Could they be equal? Could $c = 12$? If $c = 12$, then $5c = 60$, so, yes, they could be equal. Eliminate A and B. Must they be equal? Must $c = 12$? Could c be more or less than 12? BE CAREFUL: $5 \times 11 = 55$, which is too small; and $5 \times 13 = 65$, which is too big. Therefore, the only *integer* that c could be is 12; but c doesn't have to be an integer. The *only* restriction is that $56 < 5c < 64$. If $5c$ were 58 or 61.6 or 63, then c would not be 12. The answer is **D**.

SOLUTION 20. Could they be equal? Could the number of female teachers be the same in both schools? No. More than half (i.e., more than 100) of School B's 200 teachers are female, but School A has only 100 teachers in all. The answer is **B**.

SOLUTION 21. Could they be equal? Could $m + 2 = 10$? No, if $m + 2 = 10$, then $m + 1 = 9$ and $m + 3 = 11$, and $9 \times 10 \times 11 = 990$, which is too big. The answer is *not* C, and since $m + 2$ clearly has to be smaller than 10, the answer is **B**.

SOLUTION 22. Could they be equal? Could a rectangle whose area is 21 have a perimeter of 20? Yes, if its length is 7 and its width is 3: $7 + 3 + 7 + 3 = 20$. Eliminate A and B. Must they be equal? If you're *sure* that there is no other rectangle with an area of 21, then choose C; if you're *not* sure, guess between C and D; if you *know* there are other rectangles of area 21, choose D.

There are other possibilities—lots of them; here are a 7×3 rectangle and a few other rectangles whose areas are 21:

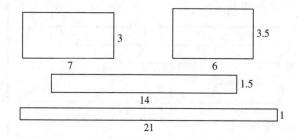

Don't Calculate: Compare°

Avoid unnecessary calculations. You don't have to determine the exact values of the quantities in Columns A and B; you just have to compare them.

TACTIC 5 is the special application of TACTIC 7, Chapter 10 (Don't do more than you have to) to quantitative comparison questions. The proper use of TACTIC 5 allows you to solve many quantitative comparisons without doing tedious calculations, thereby saving you valuable test time that you can use on other questions. *Before you start calculating,* stop, look at the columns, and ask yourself, "Can I easily and quickly determine which quantity is greater without doing *any* arithmetic?" Consider Examples 23 and 24, which look very similar, but really aren't.

Column A	Column B
Example 23.	
37×43	30×53

Column A	Column B
Example 24.	
37×43	39×47

Example 23 is very easy. Just multiply: $37 \times 43 = 1591$ and $30 \times 53 = 1590$. The answer is **A**.

Example 24 is even easier. *Don't* multiply. In far less time than it takes to do the multiplications, you can see that $37 < 39$ and $43 < 47$, so clearly $37 \times 43 < 39 \times 47$. The answer is **B**. *You don't get any extra credit for taking the time to determine the value of each product!*

Remember: do not start calculating immediately. Always take a second or two to glance at each column. In Example 23 it's not at all clear which product is larger, so you have to multiply. In Example 24, however, no calculations are necessary.

These are problems on which poor test-takers do a lot of arithmetic and good test-takers think! Practicing TACTIC 5 will help you become a good test-taker.

Now, test your understanding of TACTIC 5 by solving these problems.

Column A	Column B
Example 25.	
The number of years from 1776 to 1929	The number of years from 1767 to 1992
Example 26.	
$45^2 + 25^2$	$(45 + 25)^2$
Example 27.	
$45(35 + 65)$	$45 \times 35 + 45 \times 65$
Example 28.	

Example 28.
Marianne earned a 75 on each of her first three math tests and an 80 on her fourth and fifth tests.

Marianne's average after 4 tests	Marianne's average after 5 tests

SOLUTIONS 25–28

Performing the Indicated Calculations	Using TACTIC 5 to Avoid Doing the Calculations
25. Column A: $1929 - 1776 = 153$ Column B: $1992 - 1767 = 225$ The answer is **B**.	25. The subtraction is easy enough, but why do it? The dates in Column **B** start earlier and end later. Clearly, they span more years. You don't need to know how many years. The answer is **B**.
26. Column A: $45^2 + 25^2 =$ $2025 + 625 = 2650$ Column B: $(45 + 25)^2$ $= 70^2 = 4900$ The answer is **B**.	26. For *any positive numbers a and b*: $(a + b)^2 > a^2 + b^2$. You should do the calculations only if you don't know this fact. The answer is **B**.
27. Column A: $45(35 + 65) =$ $45(100) = 4500$ Column B: $45 \times 35 + 45 \times 65 =$ $1575 + 2925 = 4500$ The answer is **C**.	27. This is just the distributive property (KEY FACT A20), which states that, for *any* numbers a, b, c: $a(b + c) = ab + ac$. The answer is **C**.
28. Column A: $\dfrac{75 + 75 + 75 + 80}{4} =$ $\dfrac{305}{4} = 76.25$ Column B: $\dfrac{75 + 75 + 75 + 80 + 80}{5} =$ $\dfrac{385}{5} = 77$ The answer is **B**.	28. Remember, you want to know which average is higher, *not* what the averages are. After 4 tests Marianne's average is clearly less than 80, so an 80 on the fifth test had to *raise* her average (KEY FACT E4). The answer is **B**.

CAUTION: TACTIC 5 is important, but *don't spend a lot of time looking for ways to avoid a simple calculation.*

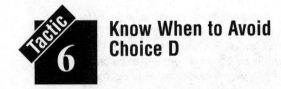

Know When to Avoid Choice D

If the quantities in Columns A and B are both fixed numbers, the answer cannot be D.

Notice that D was not the correct answer to any of the six examples discussed under TACTIC 5. Those problems had no variables. The quantities in each column were all specific numbers. In each of the next four examples, the quantities in Columns A and B are also fixed numbers. In each case, either the two numbers are equal or one is greater than the other. It can *always* be determined, and so D *cannot be the correct answer to any of these problems*. If, while taking the GRE, you find a problem of this type that you can't solve, just guess: A, B, or C. Now try these four examples.

Column A	Column B

Example 29.

The number of seconds in one day	The number of days in one century

Example 30.

The area of a square whose sides are 4	Twice the area of an equilateral triangle whose sides are 4

Example 31.

Three fair coins are flipped.

The probability of getting one head	The probability of getting two heads

Example 32.

The time it takes to drive 40 miles at 35 mph	The time it takes to drive 35 miles at 40 mph

Here's the important point to remember: don't choose D because *you* can't determine which quantity is bigger; choose D only if *nobody* could determine it. *You* may or may not know how to compute the number of seconds in a day, the area of an equilateral triangle, or a certain probability, but *these calculations can be made*.

SOLUTIONS 29–32

Direct Calculation	**Solution Using Various TACTICS**
29. Recall the facts you need and calculate. 60 seconds = 1 minute, 60 minutes = 1 hour, 24 hours = 1 day, 365 days = 1 year, and 100 years = 1 century. Column A: 60 × 60 × 24 = 86,400 Column B: 365 × 100 = 36,500 Even if we throw in some days for leap years, the answer is clearly **A**.	29. The point of TACTIC 6 is that even if you have no idea how to calculate the number of seconds in a day, you can eliminate two choices. The answer *cannot* be D, and it would be an incredible coincidence if these two quantities were actually equal, so don't choose C. *Guess* between A and B.

Direct Calculation	**Solution Using Various TACTICS**
30. Calculate both areas. (See KEY FACT J15 for the easy way to find the area of an equilateral triangle.) Column A: $A = s^2 = 4^2 = 16$ Column B: $A = \dfrac{s^2\sqrt{3}}{4} = \dfrac{4^2\sqrt{3}}{4} =$ $4\sqrt{3}$; and *twice* A is $8\sqrt{3}$. Since $\sqrt{3} \approx$ 1.7, $8\sqrt{3} \approx 13.6$. The answer is **A**.	30. Use TACTIC 5: don't calculate—draw a diagram and then compare. Since the height of the triangle is less than 4, its area is less than $\dfrac{1}{2}(4)(4) = 8$, and twice its area is less than 16, the area of the square. The answer is **A**. (If you don't see that, and just have to guess in order to move on, be sure not to guess D.)
31. When a coin is flipped 3 times, there are 8 possible outcomes: HHH, HHT, HTH, HTT, THH, THT, TTH, and TTT. Of these, 3 have one head and 3 have two heads. Each probability is $\dfrac{3}{8}$. The answer is **C**.	31. Don't forget TACTIC 5. Even if you know how, you don't *have to* calculate the probabilities. When 3 coins are flipped, getting two heads means getting one tail. Therefore, the probability of two heads equals the probability of one tail, which by symmetry equals the probability of one head. The answer is **C**. (If you don't remember anything about probability, TACTIC 5 at least allows you to eliminate D before you guess.)
32. Since $d = rt$, $t = \dfrac{d}{r}$ [see Sect. 14-H]. Column A: $\dfrac{40}{35}$ hours—more than 1 hour. Column B: $\dfrac{35}{40}$ hours—less than 1 hour. The answer is **A**.	32. You *do* need to know these formulas, but *not* for this problem. At 35 mph it takes *more than an hour* to drive 40 miles. At 40 mph it takes *less than an hour* to drive 35 miles. Choose **A**.

Practice Exercises

Quantitative Comparison Questions

Column A	Column B

1. $197 + 398 + 586$ | $203 + 405 + 607$

$x > 0$

2. $10x$ | $\dfrac{10}{x}$

---

3. The time that it takes to type 7 pages at a rate of 6 pages per hour | The time that it takes to type 6 pages at a rate of 7 pages per hour

---

$cd < 0$

4. $(c + d)^2$ | $c^2 + d^2$

---

a, b, and c are the measures of the angles of isosceles triangle ABC

x, y, and z are the measures of the angles of right triangle XYZ

5. The average of a, b, and c | The average of x, y, and z

$b < 0$

6. $6b$ | b^6

---

7. The area of a circle whose radius is 17 | The area of a circle whose diameter is 35

Line k goes through $(1,1)$ and $(5,2)$.
Line m is perpendicular to k.

8. The slope of line k | The slope of line m

---

x is a positive integer

9. The number of multiples of 6 between 100 and $x + 100$ | The number of multiples of 9 between 100 and $x + 100$

Column A	Column B

$x + y = 5$
$y - x = -5$

10. y | 0

---

11. $\dfrac{7}{8}$ | $\left(\dfrac{7}{8}\right)^5$

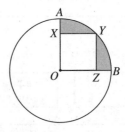

O is the center of the circle of radius 6.
$OXYZ$ is a square.

12. The area of the shaded region | 12

The number of square inches in the surface area of a cube is equal to the number of cubic inches in its volume.

13. The length of an edge of the cube | 6 inches

$1 < x < 4$

14. πx | x^2

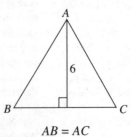

$AB = AC$

15. The area of $\triangle ABC$ | 3

Answer Key

1. **B**	6. **B**	11. **A**
2. **D**	7. **B**	12. **B**
3. **A**	8. **A**	13. **C**
4. **B**	9. **D**	14. **D**
5. **C**	10. **C**	15. **D**

Answer Explanations

The direct mathematical solution to a problem is almost always the preferable one, so it is given first. It is often followed by one or more alternate solutions, indicated by a double asterisk, based on the various tactics discussed in this chapter. Occasionally, a solution based on one of the tactics is much easier than the straightforward one. In that case, it is given first.

1. **B.** This can easily be solved in less than a minute by adding, but in only 5 seconds by thinking! Use TACTIC 5: don't calculate; compare. Each of the three numbers in Column B is greater than the corresponding number in Column A.

2. **D.** Use TACTIC 1. When $x = 1$, the columns are equal; when $x = 2$, they aren't.
   **Use TACTIC 3

	Column A	Column B
	$10x$	$\dfrac{10}{x}$
Multiply each column by x (this is OK since $x > 0$):	$10x^2$	10
Divide each column by 10:	x^2	1

   This is a much easier comparison. x^2 *could* equal 1, but doesn't have to. The answer is Choice D.

3. **A.** You can easily calculate each of the times—by dividing 7 by 6 in Column A, and 6 by 7 in Column B. However, it is easier to just observe that the time in Column A is more than one hour, whereas the time in Column B is less than one hour.

4. **B.** Use TACTIC 3

	Column A	Column B
Expand Column A:	$(c + d)^2 =$	
	$c^2 + 2cd + d^2$	$c^2 + d^2$
Subtract $c^2 + d^2$ from each column:	$2cd$	0

   Since it is given that $cd < 0$, so is $2cd$.
   **If you can't expand $(c + d)^2$, use TACTIC 1. Replace c and d with numbers satisfying $cd < 0$.

	Column A	Column B	Compare	Eliminate
Let $c = 1$ and $d = -1$	$(1 + -1)^2 =$ 0	$1^2 + (-1)^2 =$ $1 + 1 = 2$	B is greater	A and C
Let $c = 3$ and $d = -5$	$(3 + -5)^2 =$ $(-2)^2 = 4$	$3^2 + (-5)^2 =$ $9 + 25 = 34$	B is greater	

Both times Column B was greater: choose B.

5. **C.** The average of 3 numbers is their sum divided by 3. Since in *any* triangle the sum of the measures of the 3 angles is 180° [KEY FACT J1], the average in each column is equal to $180 \div 3 = 60$.
   **Use TACTIC 1. Pick values for the measures of the angles. For example, in isosceles $\triangle ABC$ choose 70, 70, 40; in right $\triangle XYZ$, choose 30, 60, 90. Each average is 60. Choose C.

6. **B.** Since $b < 0$, $6b$ is negative, whereas b^6 is positive.
   **Use TACTIC 1. Replace b with numbers satisfying $b < 0$.

	Column A	Column B	Compare	Eliminate
Let $b = -1$	$6(-1) = -6$	$(-1)^6 = 1$	B is greater	A and C
Let $b = -2$	$6(-2) = -12$	$(-2)^6 = 64$	B is greater	

Both times Column B was greater: choose B.

7. **B.** Again, use TACTIC 5: don't calculate the two areas; compare them. The circle in Column A has a radius of 17, and so its diameter is 34. Since the circle in Column B has a larger diameter, its area is greater.

8. **A.** Again, use TACTIC 5: don't calculate either slope. Quickly, make a rough sketch of line k, going through $(1,1)$ and $(5,2)$, and draw line m perpendicular to it.

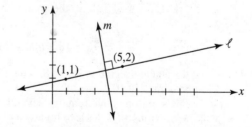

Line k has a positive slope (it slopes upward), whereas line m has a negative slope (it slopes downward). Column A is greater. [Note: the slope of k is $\dfrac{1}{4}$ and the slope of m is -4.

See Section 14-N for all the facts you need to know about slopes.]
**If you don't know this fact about slopes, use TACTIC 6. The answer cannot be Choice D, and if two lines intersect, their slopes cannot be equal, so eliminate Choice C. Guess Choices A or B.

9. D.   Every sixth integer is a multiple of 6 and every ninth integer is a multiple of 9, so in a large interval there will be many more multiples of 6. But in a very small interval, there might be none or possibly just one of each. **Use TACTIC 1. Let $x = 1$. Between 100 and 101 there are *no* multiples of 6 and *no* multiples of 9. Eliminate Choices A and B. Choose a large number for x: 100, for example. Between 100 and 200 there are many more multiples of 6 than there are multiples of 9. Eliminate Choice C.

10. C.   Add the equations.

$$x + y = 5$$
$$\underline{+\ y - x = -5}$$
$$2y = 0$$

Since $2y = 0$, $y = 0$.
**Use TACTIC 4. Could $y = 0$? In each equation, if $y = 0$, then $x = -5$. So, y can equal 0. Eliminate Choices A and B, and either guess between Choices C and D or try to continue. Must $y = 0$? Yes, when you have two linear equations in two variables, there is only one solution, so nothing else is possible.

11. A.   The arithmetic is annoying and time-consuming, but not difficult. However, you can avoid the arithmetic, if you know KEY FACT A24:

If $0 < x < 1$ and $n > 1$, then $x^n < x$.

Since $\dfrac{7}{8} < 1$, then $\left(\dfrac{7}{8}\right)^5 < \dfrac{7}{8}$.

12. B.   The area of the shaded region is the area of quarter-circle AOB minus the area of the square. Since $r = OA = 6$, the area of the quarter-circle is $\dfrac{1}{4}\pi r^2 = \dfrac{1}{4}36\pi = 9\pi$. OY, the diagonal of the square, is 6 (since it is a radius of the circle), so OZ, the side of the square, is $\dfrac{6}{\sqrt{2}}$ [KEY FACT J8]. So the area of the square is $\left(\dfrac{6}{\sqrt{2}}\right)^2 = \dfrac{36}{2} = 18$. Finally, the area of the shaded region is $9\pi - 18$, which is approximately 10.
**The solution above requires several steps. [See Sections 14-J, K, L to review any of the facts used.] If you can't reason through this, you still should be able to answer this question correctly. Use TACTIC 6. The shaded region has a definite area, which is either 12, more than 12, or less than 12. Eliminate D. Also, the area of a curved region almost always involves π, so assume the area isn't exactly 12. Eliminate Choice C. You can now *guess* between Choices A and B, but if you trust the diagram and know a little bit you can improve

your guess. If you know that the area of the circle is 36π, so that the quarter-circle is 9π or about 28, you can estimate the shaded region. It's well less than half of the quarter-circle, so less than 14 and probably less than 12. Guess Choice B.

13. C.   Use TACTIC 4. Could the edge be 6? Test it. If each edge is 6, the area of each face is $6 \times 6 = 36$, and since a cube has 6 faces, the total surface area is $6 \times 36 = 216$. The volume is $6^3 = 216$. So the columns could be equal. Eliminate Choices A and B. If you have a sense that this is the only cube with this property, choose C. In fact, if you had no idea how to do this, you might use TACTIC 6, assume that there is only one way, eliminate Choice D, and then guess C. The direct solution is simple enough if you know the formulas. The area is $6e^2$ and the volume is e^3: $6e^2 = e^3 \Rightarrow 6 = e$.

14. D.   There are several ways to do this. Use TACTIC 1: plug in a number for x. If $x = 2$, Column A is 2π, which is slightly more than 6, and Column B is $2^2 = 4$. Column A is greater: eliminate Choices B and C. Must Column A be greater? If the only other number you try is $x = 3$, you'll think so, because $3^2 = 9$, but $3\pi > 9$. But remember, x does not have to be an integer: $3.9^2 > 15$, whereas $3.9\pi < 4\pi$, which is a little over 12.
**Use TACTIC 4. Could $\pi x = x^2$? Yes, if $x = \pi$. Must $x = \pi$? No.
**Use TACTIC 3. Divide each side by x: Now Column A is π and Column B is x. Which is bigger, π or x? We cannot tell.

15. D.   Use TACTIC 4. Could the area of $\triangle ABC = 3$? Since the height is 6, the area would be 3 only if the base were 1: $\dfrac{1}{2}(1)(6) = 3$. Could $BC = 1$? Sure (see the figure). Must the base be 1? Of course not.

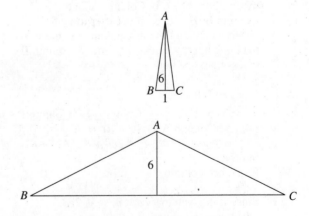

13 Data Interpretation Questions

- ■ **Tactics**
- ■ **Practice Exercises**
- ■ **Answer Key and Explanations**

Four of the 28 questions in the quantitative section are data interpretation questions. As their name suggests, these questions are always based on the information that is presented in some form of a graph or a chart. Occasionally, the data are presented in a chart or table, but much more often, they are presented graphically. The most common types of graphs are

- line graphs   • bar graphs   • circle graphs

Data interpretation questions always appear in two sets of two questions each. For example, questions 14 and 15 might refer to a particular set of graphs or charts, and then later there will be two more questions, say numbers 22 and 23, which refer to a completely different set of graphs and charts.

When the first data interpretation question appears, one or more graphs will be on the left-hand side of the screen, and the question will be on the right-hand side. It is possible that you will have to scroll down in order to see all of the data. After you confirm your answer to the first question, the second question will replace it on the right-hand side of the screen; the graphs, of course, will still be on the left-hand side for you to refer to.

The tactics discussed in this chapter can be applied to any type of data, no matter how they are displayed. In the practice exercises at the end of the chapter, there are data interpretation questions based on every type of graph that could appear on the GRE. Carefully, read through the answer explanations for each exercise, so that you learn the best way to handle each type of graph.

Infrequently, an easy data interpretation question will require only that you read the graph and find a numerical fact that is displayed. Usually, however, you will have to do some calculation on the data that you are analyzing. In harder questions, you may be given hypothetical situations and asked to make inferences based on the information provided in the given graphs.

Testing Tactics

The four questions that follow will be used to illustrate the tactics that you should use in answering data interpretation questions. Remember, however, that on the GRE there will always be exactly two questions that refer to a particular graph or set of graphs.

Questions 1–4 refer to the following graphs.

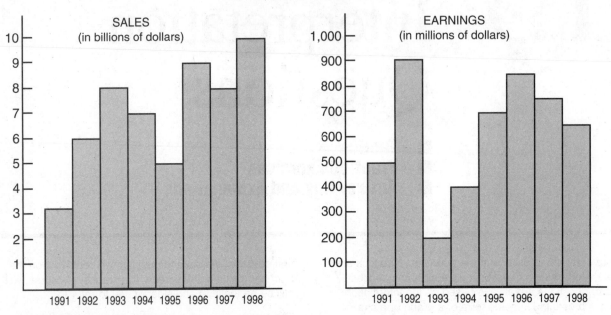

**Sales and Earnings of
XYZ Corporation 1991–1998**

**1998 Sales of XYZ Corporation
by Category**

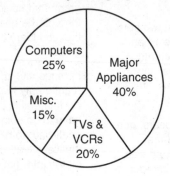

1. What is the average (arithmetic mean) in billions of
   dollars of the sales of XYZ Corporation for the
   period 1991–1998?

   (A) 5.5   (B) 6.0   (C) 7.0   (D) 8.0   (E) 8.5

2. For which year was the percentage increase in
   earnings from the previous year the greatest?

   (A) 1992   (B) 1993   (C) 1994
       (D) 1995   (E) 1996

3. Which of the following statements can be deduced
   from the data in the given charts and circle graph?

   I. Sales of major appliances in 1998 exceeded
      total sales in 1991.
   II. Earnings for the year in which earnings were
      greatest were more than sales for the year in
      which sales were lowest.

III. If in 1998, the sales of major appliances had
     been 10% less, and the sales of computers
     had been 10% greater, the sales of major
     appliances would have been less than the
     sales of computers.

(A) None   (B) I only   (C) III only
    (D) I and III only   (E) I, II, and III

4. What was the ratio of earnings to sales in 1993?

   (A) $\frac{1}{40}$ (B) $\frac{1}{25}$ (C) $\frac{1}{4}$ (D) $\frac{25}{1}$ (E) $\frac{40}{1}$

First Read the Titles

When the first data interpretation question appears on the screen, do not even read it! Before you attempt to answer a data interpretation question, take 15 or 30 seconds to study the graphs. Try to get a general idea about the information that is being displayed.

Observe that the bar graphs on which questions 1–4 are based present two different sets of data. The bar graph

on the left-hand side provides information about the sales of XYZ Corporation, and the right-hand graph provides information about the corporation's earnings. Also, note that whereas sales are given in billions of dollars, earnings are given in millions of dollars. Finally, the circle graph gives a breakdown by category of the sales of XYZ Corporation for one particular year.

Don't Confuse Percents and Numbers

Many students make mistakes on data interpretation questions because they don't distinguish between absolute numbers and percents. Although few students would look at the circle graph shown and think that XYZ Corporation sold 25 computers in 1998, many would mistakenly think that it sold 15% more major appliances than computers.

The problem is particularly serious when the questions involve percent increases or percent decreases. In question 2 you are not asked for the year in which the increase in earnings from the previous year was the greatest. You are asked for the year in which the per-

cent increase in earnings was the greatest. A quick glance at the right-hand graph reveals that the greatest increase occurred from 1991 to 1992 when earnings jumped by $400 million. However, when we solve this problem in the discussion of TACTIC 3, you will see that Choice A is not the correct answer.

NOTE: Since many data interpretation questions involve percents, you should carefully study Section 15-C, and be sure that you know all of the tactics for solving percent problems. In particular, always try to use the number 100 or 1000, since it is so easy to mentally calculate percents of powers of 10.

Whenever Possible, Estimate

Since you are not allowed to have a calculator when you take the GRE, you will not be expected to do complicated or lengthy calculations. Often, thinking and using some common sense can save you considerable time. For example, it may seem that in order to get the correct answer to question 2, you have to calculate five different percents. In fact, you only need to do one calculation, and that one you can do in your head!

Just looking at the Earnings bar graph, it is clear that the only possible answers are 1992, 1994, and 1995,

the three years in which there was a significant increase in earnings from the year before. From 1993 to 1994 expenditures doubled, from $200 million to $400 million—an increase of 100%. From 1991 to 1992 expenditures increased by $400 million (from $500 million to $900 million), but that is less than a 100% increase (we don't care how much less). From 1994 to 1995 expenditures increased by $300 million (from $400 million to $700 million); but again, this is less than a 100% increase. The answer is **C**.

Tactic 4 — Do Each Calculation Separately

As in all Roman numeral questions, question 3 requires you to determine which of three separate statements is true. The key is to work with the statements individually.

To determine whether or not statement I is true, look at both the Sales bar graph and the circle graph. In 1998, total sales were $10 billion, and sales of major appliances accounted for 40% of the total: 40% of $10 billion = $4 billion. This exceeds the $3 billion total sales figure for 1991, so statement I is true.

In 1992, the year in which earnings were greatest, earnings were $900 million. In 1991, the year in which sales were lowest, sales were $3 billion, which is much greater than $900 million. Statement II is false.

In 1998, sales of major appliances were $4 billion. If they had been 10% less, they would have been $3.6 billion. That year, sales of computers were $2.5 billion (25% of $10 billion). If computer sales had increased by 10%, sales would have been $2.75 billion. Statement III is false.

The answer is **B**: only statement I is true.

Tactic 5 — Use Only the Information Given

You must base your answer to each question only on the information in the given charts and graphs. It is unlikely that you have any preconceived notion as to the sales of XYZ Corporation, but you might think that you know the population of the United States for a particular year or the percent of women currently in the workplace.

If your knowledge contradicts any of the data presented in the graphs, ignore what you know. First of all, you may be mistaken; but more important, the data may refer to a different, unspecified location or year. In any event, *always* base your answers on the given data.

Tactic 6 — Always Use the Proper Units

In answering question 4, observe that earnings are given in millions, while sales are in billions. If you answer too quickly, you might say that in 1993 earnings were 200 and sales were 8, and conclude that the desired ratio is $\frac{200}{8} = \frac{25}{1}$. You will avoid this mistake if you keep track of units: earnings were 200 *million* dollars, whereas sales were 8 *billion* dollars. The correct ratio is

$$\frac{200,000,000}{8,000,000,000} = \frac{2}{80} = \frac{1}{40}.$$

The answer is **A**.

Tactic 7 — Be Sure That Your Answer Is Reasonable

Before confirming your answer, take a second to be sure that it is reasonable. For example, in question 4,

Choices D and E are unreasonable. From the logic of the situation, you should realize that earnings can't exceed sales. The desired ratio, therefore, must be less than 1. If you use the wrong units (see TACTIC 6, above), your initial thought would be to choose D. By testing your answer for reasonableness, you will realize that you made a mistake.

Remember that if you don't know how to solve a problem, you must guess in order to move on. Before guess-

ing, however, check to see if one or more of the choices are unreasonable. If so, eliminate them. For example, if you forget how to calculate a percent increase, you would have to guess at question 2. But before guessing wildly, you should at least eliminate Choice B, since from 1992 to 1993 earnings decreased.

Try to Visualize the Answer

Because graphs and tables present data in a form that enables you to readily see relationships and to make quick comparisons, you can often avoid doing any calculations. Whenever possible, use your eye instead of your computational skills.

For example, to answer question 1, rather than reading the sales figures in the bar graph on the left for each of the eight years, adding them, and then dividing by 8,

visualize the situation. Where could you draw a horizontal line across the graph so that there would be the same amount of gray area above the line as white area below it? Imagine a horizontal line drawn through the 7 on the vertical axis. The portions of the bars above the line for 1993 and 1996–1998 are just about exactly the same size as the white areas below the line for 1991, 1992, and 1994. The answer is **C**.

Practice Exercises

Data Interpretation Questions

On the GRE there will always be exactly two questions based on any set of graphs. Accordingly, in all the model tests in this book, there are two pairs of data

interpretation questions, each pair referring to a different set of graphs. However, to illustrate the variety of questions that can be asked, in this exercise set, for some of the graphs there is only one question and for some there are three questions.

Questions 1–2 refer to the following graphs.

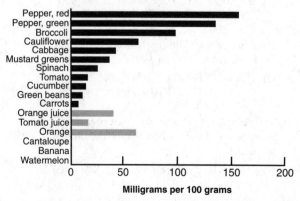

Vitamin C Content of Foods

Source: U.S. Department of Agriculture.

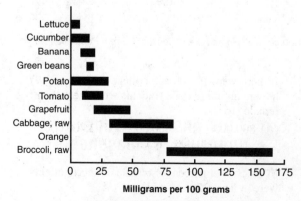

Source: U.S. Department of Agriculture.

1. What is the ratio of the amount of Vitamin C in 500 grams of orange to the amount of Vitamin C in 500 grams of orange juice?

    (A) 4:7   (B) 1:1   (C) 7:4   (D) 2:1   (E) 4:1

2. How many grams of tomato would you have to eat to be certain of getting more vitamin C than you would get by eating 100 grams of raw broccoli?

    (A) 300   (B) 500   (C) 750   (D) 1200   (E) 1650

Questions 3–5 refer to the following graphs.

College Enrollment, by Age and Sex: 1975 and 1995

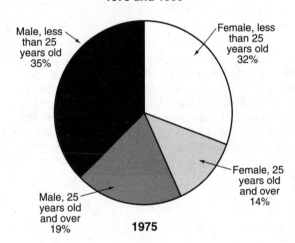

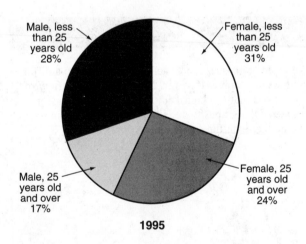

Source: U.S. Bureau of the Census, Current Population Survey.

3. If there were 10,000,000 college students in 1975, how many more male students were there than female students?

    (A) 800,000   (B) 1,600,000   (C) 2,400,000
    (D) 4,600,000   (E) 5,400,000

4. In 1975 what percent of female college students were at least 25 years old?

    (A) 14%   (B) 30%   (C) 45%
    (D) 69%   (E) 76%

5. If the total number of students enrolled in college was 40% higher in 1995 than in 1975, what is the ratio of the number of male students in 1995 to the number of male students in 1975?

    (A) 5:6   (B) 6:7   (C) 7:6   (D) 6:5   (E) 7:5

Questions 6–8 refer to the following graph.

Motor Vehicle Theft in the U.S. Percent Change from 1994 to 1998

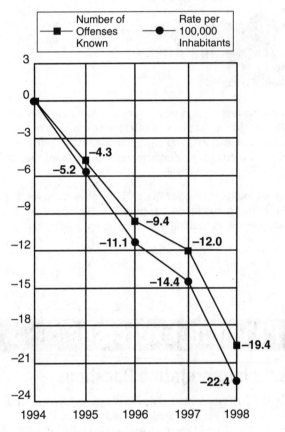

Source: U.S. Department of Justice, Federal Bureau of Investigation.

6. If 1,000,000 vehicles were stolen in 1994, how many were stolen in 1996?

    (A) 889,000   (B) 906,000   (C) 940,000
    (D) 1,094,000   (E) 1,100,000

7. By what percent did the number of vehicles stolen decrease from 1997 to 1998?

    (A) 7.4%   (B) 8.0%   (C) 8.4%
    (D) 12.0%   (E) 19.4%

8. To the nearest percent, by what percent did the population of the United States increase from 1994 to 1998?

    (A) 1%   (B) 2%   (C) 3%   (D) 4%   (E) 5%

Questions 9–10 refer to the following graph.

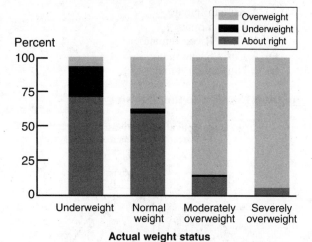

Perceptions of Body Weight Status

Perceived compared with actual weight status of adult females.

Source: U.S. Department of Agriculture.

9. What percent of underweight adult females perceive themselves to be underweight?

   (A) 5%   (B) 22%   (C) 38%   (D) 50%   (E) 70%

10. The members of which of the four groups had the least accurate perception of their body weight?

    (A) Underweight

(B) Normal weight
(C) Moderately overweight
(D) Severely overweight
(E) It cannot be determined from the information given in the graph.

Questions 11–12 refer to the tables at the bottom of the page.

Residents of New York City pay both New York State and New York City tax.

Residents of New York State who live and work outside of New York City pay only New York State tax.

11. In 1979 how much tax would a resident of New York State who lived and worked outside New York City have paid on a taxable income of $16,100?

    (A) $34   (B) $110   (C) $352
      (D) $970   (E) $1322

12. In 1979, how much more total tax would a resident of New York City who had a taxable income of $36,500 pay, compared to a resident of New York City who had a taxable income of $36,000?

    (A) $21.50   (B) $43   (C) $70
      (D) $91.50   (E) $183

Tax Rate Schedules for 1979

New York State

Taxable Income					
over	but not over			Amount of Tax	
$ 0	$1,000		2%	of taxable income	
1,000	3,000	$20 plus	3%	of excess over	$1,000
3,000	5,000	80 plus	4%	of excess over	3,000
5,000	7,000	160 plus	5%	of excess over	5,000
7,000	9,000	260 plus	6%	of excess over	7,000
9,000	11,000	380 plus	7%	of excess over	9,000
11,000	13,000	520 plus	8%	of excess over	11,000
13,000	15,000	680 plus	9%	of excess over	13,000
15,000	17,000	860 plus	10%	of excess over	15,000
17,000	19,000	1,060 plus	11%	of excess over	17,000
19,000	21,000	1,280 plus	12%	of excess over	19,000
21,000	23,000	1,520 plus	13%	of excess over	21,000
23,000		1,780 plus	14%	of excess over	23,000

City of New York

Taxable Income					
over	but not over			Amount of Tax	
$ 0	$1,000		0.9%	of taxable income	
1,000	3,000	$ 9 plus	1.4%	of excess over	$1,000
3,000	5,000	37 plus	1.8%	of excess over	3,000
5,000	7,000	73 plus	2.0%	of excess over	5,000
7,000	9,000	113 plus	2.3%	of excess over	7,000
9,000	11,000	159 plus	2.5%	of excess over	9,000
11,000	13,000	209 plus	2.7%	of excess over	11,000
13,000	15,000	263 plus	2.9%	of excess over	13,000
15,000	17,000	321 plus	3.1%	of excess over	15,000
17,000	19,000	383 plus	3.3%	of excess over	17,000
19,000	21,000	449 plus	3.5%	of excess over	19,000
21,000	23,000	519 plus	3.8%	of excess over	21,000
23,000	25,000	595 plus	4.0%	of excess over	23,000
25,000		675 plus	4.3%	of excess over	25,000

Questions 13–14 refer to the following tables.

Years of Life Expectancy at Birth
(Life expectancy in years)

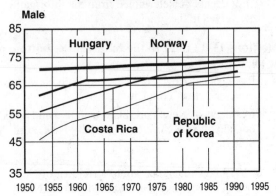

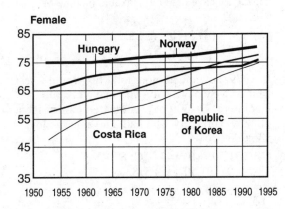

Source: U.S. Bureau of the Census,
Center for International Research.

13. For how many of the countries listed in the graphs
is it true that the life expectancy of a female born
in 1955 was higher than the life expectancy of a
male born in 1990?

   (A) None   (B) 1   (C) 2   (D) 3   (E) 4

14. By sex and nationality, who had the greatest
increase in life expectancy between 1955 and
1990?

   (A) A Korean female
   (B) A Korean male
   (C) A Costa Rican female
   (D) A Costa Rican male
   (E) A Norwegian female

Question 15 refers to the following graph.

Bias-Motivated Offenses 1998
Percent Distribution

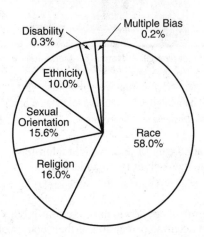

Source: U.S. Department of Justice,
Federal Bureau of Investigation.

15. If in 1998 there were 10,000 bias-motivated
offenses based on ethnicity, how many more
offenses were based on religion than on sexual
orientation?

   (A) 4   (B) 40   (C) 400   (D) 4000   (E) 40,000

Answer Key

1. C	6. B	11. D
2. E	7. C	12. D
3. A	8. D	13. B
4. B	9. B	14. A
5. C	10. A	15. C

Answer Explanations

1. **C.** According to the graph on the left, there are
   approximately 70 milligrams of vitamin C in
   100 grams of orange and 40 milligrams in the
   same amount of orange juice. This is a ratio of

70:40 = 7:4. Since the question refers to the
same amount of orange and orange juice (500
grams), the ratio is unchanged.

2. **E.** From the graph on the right, you can see that
   by eating 100 grams of raw broccoli, you
   could receive as much as 165 milligrams of
   vitamin C. Since 100 grams of tomato could
   have as little as 10 milligrams of vitamin C,
   you would have to eat 1650 grams of tomato to
   be sure of getting 165 milligrams of vitamin C.

3. **A.** From the top graph, we see that in 1975, 54%
   (35% + 19%) of all college students were
   male, and the other 46% were female. So there

were 5,400,000 males and 4,600,000 females—a difference of 800,000.

4. **B.** In 1975, of every 100 college students, 46 were female—32 of whom were less than 25 years old, and 14 of whom were 25 years old and over. So, 14 of every 46 female students were at least 25 years old. Finally, $\frac{14}{46} = .30 = 30\%$.

5. **C.** From the two graphs, we see that in 1975 54% (35% + 19%) of all college students were male, whereas in 1995 the corresponding figure was 45% (28% + 17%). For simplicity, assume that there were 100 college students in 1975, 54 of whom were male. Then in 1995, there were 140 college students, 63 of whom were male (45% of 140 = 63). So the ratio of the number of male students in 1995 to the number of male students in 1975 is 63:54 = 7:6.

6. **B.** From 1994 to 1996 there was a 9.4% decrease in the number of vehicles stolen. Since 9.4% of 1,000,000 = 94,000, the number of vehicles stolen in 1996 was 1,000,000 − 94,000 = 906,000. If you can't solve problems such as this, you have to guess. But since the number of stolen vehicles is clearly decreasing, be sure to eliminate Choices D and E first.

7. **C.** For simplicity, assume that 1000 vehicles were stolen in 1994. By 1997, the number had decreased by 12.0% to 880 (12% of 1000 = 120, and 1000 − 120 = 880); by 1998, the number had decreased 19.4% to 806 (19.4% of 1000 = 194 and 1000 − 194 = 806). So from 1997 to 1998, the number of vehicles stolen decreased by 74 from 880 to 806. This represents a decrease of

$$\frac{74}{880} = .084 = 8.4\%.$$

8. **D.** Simplify the situation by assuming that in 1994 the population was 100,000 and there were 1000 vehicles stolen. As in the solution to question 7, in 1998 the number of stolen vehicles was 806. At the same time, the number of thefts per 100,000 inhabitants decreased 22.4% from 1000 to 776. So if there were 776 vehicles stolen for every 100,000 inhabitants, and 806 cars were stolen, the number of inhabitants must have increased. To know by how much, solve the proportion: $\frac{776}{100,000} = \frac{806}{x}$. Cross-multiply: 776x = 80,600,000.

Divide by 776: x = 103,800. So for every 100,000 inhabitants in 1994, there were 103,800 in 1998, an increase of 3.8%.

9. **B.** The bar representing underweight adult females who perceive themselves to be underweight extends from about 70% to about 95%, a range of approximately 25%. Choice B is closest.

10. **A.** Almost all overweight females correctly considered themselves to be overweight; and more than half of all females of normal weight correctly considered themselves "about right." But nearly 70% of underweight adult females inaccurately considered themselves "about right."

11. **D.** Referring only to the New York State table, we see that the amount of tax on a taxable income between $15,000 and $17,000 was $860 plus 10% of the excess over $15,000. Therefore, the tax on $16,100 is $860 plus 10% of $1,100 = $860 + $110 = $970.

12. **D.** According to the tables, each additional dollar of taxable income over $25,000 was subject to a New York State tax of 14% and a New York City tax of 4.3%, for a total tax of 18.3%. Therefore, an additional $500 in taxable income would have incurred an additional tax of 0.183 × 500 = $91.50.

13. **B.** In Norway, the life expectancy of a female born in 1955 was 75 years, which is greater than the life expectancy of a male born in 1990. In Hungary, the life expectancy of a female born in 1955 was 66 years, whereas the life expectancy of a male born in 1990 was greater than 67. In the other two countries, the life expectancy of a female born in 1955 was less than 65 years, and the life expectancy of a male born in 1990 was greater than 65.

14. **A.** The life expectancy of a Korean female born in 1955 was about 51 and in 1990 it was about 74, an increase of 23 years. This is greater than any other nationality and sex.

15. **C.** Since there were 10,000 bias-motivated offenses based on ethnicity, and that represents 10% of the total, there were 100,000 bias-motivated offenses in total. Of these, 16,000 (16% of 100,000) were based on religion, and 15,600 (15.6% of 100,000) were based on sexual orientation. The difference is 400.

14 Mathematics Review

- **Arithmetic**
- **Algebra**
- **Geometry**
- **Counting and Probability**

The mathematics questions on the GRE General Test require a working knowledge of mathematical principles, including an understanding of the fundamentals of algebra, plane geometry, and arithmetic, as well as the ability to translate problems into formulas and to interpret graphs. The following review covers these areas thoroughly and will prove helpful.

This chapter is divided into 15 sections, labeled 14-A through 14-O. For each question on the Diagnostic Test and the five Model Tests, the Answer Key indicates which section of Chapter 14 you should consult if you need help on a particular topic.

How much time you initially devote to reviewing mathematics should depend on your math skills. If you have always been a good math student and you have taken some math in college and remember most of your high school math, you can skip the instructional parts of this chapter for now. If while doing the model tests in PART FIVE or on the accompanying CD-ROM, you find that you keep making mistakes on certain types of problems (averages, percents, circles, solid geometry, word problems, for example), or they take you too long, you should then study the appropriate sections here. Even if your math skills are excellent, and you don't need the review, you should complete the sample questions in those sections; they are an excellent source of additional GRE questions. If you know that your math skills are not very good and you have not done much math since high school, then it is advisable to review all of this material, including working out the problems, *before* tackling the model tests.

No matter how good you are in math, *you should carefully read and do the problems* in Chapters 10, 11, 12, and 13. For many of these problems, two solutions are given: the most direct mathematical solution and a second solution using one or more of the special tactics taught in these chapters.

ARITHMETIC

To do well on the GRE, you need to feel comfortable with most topics of basic arithmetic. In the first five sections of Chapter 14, we will review the basic arithmetic operations, signed numbers, fractions, decimals, ratios, percents, and averages. Since the GRE uses these concepts to test your reasoning skills, not your ability to perform tedious calculations, we will concentrate on the concepts and not on arithmetic drill. The solutions to more than one-third of the mathematics questions on the GRE depend on your knowing the key facts in these sections. Be sure to review them all.

14-A. BASIC ARITHMETIC CONCEPTS

Let's start by reviewing the most important sets of numbers and their properties. On the GRE the word *number* always means *real number*, a number that can be represented by a point on the number line.

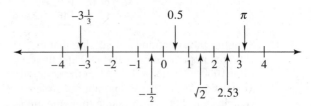

Signed Numbers

The numbers to the right of 0 on the number line are called **positive** and those to the left of 0 are called **negative**. Negative numbers must be written with a *negative sign* (–2); positive numbers can be written with a *plus sign* (+2) but are usually written without a sign (2). All numbers can be called **signed numbers**.

KEY FACT A1:

For any number *a*, exactly one of the following is true:

• *a* is negative	• *a* = 0	• *a* is positive

The ***absolute value*** of a number *a*, denoted |*a*|, is the distance between *a* and 0 on the number line. Since 3 is 3 units to the right of 0 on the number line and –3 is 3 units to the left of 0, both have an absolute value of 3:

- |3| = 3
- |–3| = 3

Two unequal numbers that have the same absolute value are called ***opposites***. So, 3 is the opposite of –3 and –3 is the opposite of 3.

KEY FACT A2:

The only number that is equal to its opposite is 0.

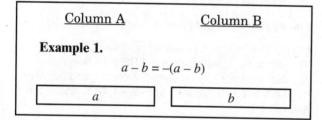

Column A   Column B

Example 1.

$$a - b = -(a - b)$$

| *a* | *b* |

SOLUTION. Since –(*a* – *b*) is the opposite of *a* – *b*, *a* – *b* = 0, and so *a* = *b*. The answer is **C**.

In arithmetic we are basically concerned with the addition, subtraction, multiplication, and division of numbers. The third column of the following table gives the terms for the results of these operations.

Operation	Symbol	Result	Example	
Addition	+	**Sum**	16 is the sum of 12 and 4	16 = 12 + 4
Subtraction	–	**Difference**	8 is the difference of 12 and 4	8 = 12 – 4
Multiplication*	×	**Product**	48 is the product of 12 and 4	48 = 12 × 4
Division	÷	**Quotient**	3 is the quotient of 12 and 4	3 = 12 ÷ 4

*Multiplication can be indicated also by a dot, parentheses, or the juxtaposition of symbols without any sign: $2^2 \cdot 2^4$, 3(4), 3(*x* + 2), 3*a*, 4*abc*.

Given any two numbers *a* and *b*, we can *always* find their sum, difference, product, and quotient, except that we may *never divide by zero*.

- 0 ÷ 7 = 0
- 7 ÷ 0 is meaningless

Example 2.

What is the sum of the product and quotient of 8 and 8?

(A) 16   (B) 17   (C) 63   (D) 64   (E) 65

SOLUTION: Product: 8 × 8 = 64. Quotient: 8 ÷ 8 = 1. Sum: 64 + 1 = **65 (E)**.

KEY FACT A3:

- **The product of 0 and any number is 0. For any number *a*: *a* × 0 = 0.**

- **Conversely, if the product of two numbers is 0, *at least one* of them must be 0:**
$$ab = 0 \Rightarrow a = 0 \text{ or } b = 0.$$

Column A   Column B

Example 3.

| The product of the integers from –7 to 2 | The product of the integers from –2 to 7 |

SOLUTION. *Do not multiply.* Each column is the product of 10 numbers, one of which is 0. So, by KEY FACT A3, each product is 0. The columns are equal (**C**).

KEY FACT A4:

The product and quotient of two positive numbers or two negative numbers are positive; the product and quotient of a positive number and a negative number are negative.

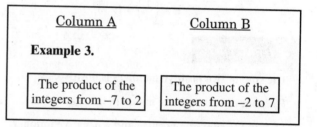

6 × 3 = 18   6 × (–3) = –18   (–6) × 3 = –18   (–6) × (–3) = 18
6 ÷ 3 = 2   6 ÷ (–3) = –2   (–6) ÷ 3 = –2   (–6) ÷ (–3) = 2

To determine whether a product of more than two numbers is positive or negative, count the number of negative factors.

KEY FACT A5:

- **The product of an *even* number of negative factors is positive.**

- **The product of an *odd* number of negative factors is negative.**

Column A | Column B

Example 4.

| $(-1)(2)(-3)(4)(-5)$ | $(1)(-2)(3)(-4)(5)$ |

SOLUTION. *Don't waste time multiplying.* The product in Column A is negative since it has 3 negative factors, whereas the product in Column B is positive since it has 2 negative factors. The answer is **B**.

KEY FACT A6:

- The *reciprocal* of any nonzero number a is $\dfrac{1}{a}$.

- The product of any number and its reciprocal is 1:

$$a \times \left(\frac{1}{a}\right) = 1.$$

KEY FACT A7:

- The sum of two positive numbers is positive.

- The sum of two negative numbers is negative.

- To find the sum of a positive and a negative number, find the difference of their absolute values and use the sign of the number with the larger absolute value.

$$6 + 2 = 8 \qquad (-6) + (-2) = -8$$

To calculate either $6 + (-2)$ or $(-6) + 2$, take the *difference*, $6 - 2 = 4$, and use the sign of the number whose absolute value is 6. So,

$$6 + (-2) = 4 \qquad (-6) + 2 = -4$$

KEY FACT A8:

The sum of any number and its opposite is 0:
$$a + (-a) = 0.$$

Many of the properties of arithmetic depend on the relationship between subtraction and addition and between division and multiplication.

KEY FACT A9:

- Subtracting a number is the same as adding its opposite.

- Dividing by a number is the same as multiplying by its reciprocal.

$$a - b = a + (-b) \qquad a + b = a \times \left(\frac{1}{b}\right)$$

Many problems involving subtraction and division can be simplified by changing them to addition and multiplication problems, respectively.

KEY FACT A10:

To subtract signed numbers, change the problem to an addition problem, by changing the sign of what is being subtracted, and use KEY FACT A7.

$$2 - 6 = 2 + (-6) = -4 \qquad 2 - (-6) = 2 + (6) = 8$$

$$(-2) - (-6) = (-2) + (6) = 4 \qquad (-2) - 6 = (-2) + (-6) = -8$$

In each case, the minus sign was changed to a plus sign, and either the 6 was changed to –6 or the –6 was changed to 6.

Integers

The *integers* are $\{..., -4, -3, -2, -1, 0, 1, 2, 3, 4, ...\}$.

The *positive integers* are $\{1, 2, 3, 4, 5, ...\}$.

The *negative integers* are $\{..., -5, -4, -3, -2, -1\}$.

NOTE: The integer 0 is neither positive nor negative. Therefore, if a question on the GRE asks how many positive numbers have a certain property, and the only numbers with that property are –2, –1, 0, 1, and 2, the answer is **2**.

Consecutive integers are two or more integers written in sequence in which each integer is 1 more than the preceding integer. For example:

$$22, 23 \quad 6, 7, 8, 9 \quad -2, -1, 0, 1 \quad n, n+1, n+2, n+3$$

Example 5.

If the sum of three consecutive integers is less than 75, what is the greatest possible value of the smallest one?

(A) 23　(B) 24　(C) 25　(D) 26　(E) 27

SOLUTION. Let the numbers be n, $n + 1$, and $n + 2$. Then,

$$n + (n + 1) + (n + 2) = 3n + 3 \Rightarrow$$
$$3n + 3 < 75 \Rightarrow 3n < 72 \Rightarrow n < 24.$$

So, the most n can be is **23 (A)**.

CAUTION: Never assume that *number* means *integer*: 3 is not the only number between 2 and 4; there are infinitely many, including 2.5, 3.99, $\dfrac{10}{3}$, π, and $\sqrt{10}$.

Example 6.

If $2 < x < 4$ and $3 < y < 7$, what is the largest integer value of $x + y$?

(A) 7　(B) 8　(C) 9　(D) 10　(E) 11

SOLUTION. If x and y are integers, the largest value is $3 + 6 = 9$. However, although $x + y$ is to be an integer, neither x nor y must be. If $x = 3.8$ and $y = 6.2$, then $x + y = \mathbf{10}$ (**D**).

The sum, difference, and product of two integers are *always* integers; the quotient of two integers may be an integer, but it is not necessarily one. The quotient $23 \div 10$ can be expressed as $\frac{23}{10}$ or $2\frac{3}{10}$ or 2.3. If the quotient is to be an integer, we can also say that the quotient is 2 and there is a **remainder** of 3. It depends upon our point of view. For example, if 23 dollars is to be divided among 10 people, each one will get $2.30 (2.3 dollars); but if 23 books are to be divided among 10 people, each one will get 2 books and there will be 3 left over (the remainder).

Example 7.

How many positive integers less than 100 have a remainder of 3 when divided by 7?

SOLUTION. To leave a remainder of 3 when divided by 7, an integer must be 3 more than a multiple of 7. For example, when 73 is divided by 7, the quotient is 10 and the remainder is 3: $73 = 10 \times 7 + 3$. So, just take the multiples of 7 and add 3. (*Don't forget that 0 is a multiple of 7.*)

$\underline{0} \times 7 + 3 = 3; \quad \underline{1} \times 7 + 3 = 10; \quad \underline{2} \times 7 + 3 = 17;$
$\dots; \quad \underline{13} \times 7 + 3 = 94$

A total of **14** numbers.

If a and b are integers, the following four terms are synonymous:

a is a **divisor** of b	a is a **factor** of b
b is **divisible** by a	b is a **multiple** of a

They all mean that when b is divided by a there is no remainder (or, more precisely, the remainder is 0). For example:

3 is a divisor of 12	3 is a factor of 12
12 is divisible by 3	12 is a multiple of 3

KEY FACT A11:

Every integer has a finite set of factors (or divisors) and an infinite set of multiples.

The factors of 12: $-12, -6, -4, -3, -2, -1, 1, 2, 3, 4,$ 6, 12

The multiples of 12: $\dots, -48, -36, -24, -12, 0, 12, 24,$ 36, 48, $\dots$

The only positive divisor of 1 is 1. All other positive integers have at least 2 positive divisors: 1 and itself, and possibly many more. For example, 6 is divisible by 1 and 6, as well as 2 and 3, whereas 7 is divisible only by 1 and 7. Positive integers, such as 7, that have exactly

2 positive divisors are called **prime numbers** or **primes**. The first few primes are

$$2, 3, 5, 7, 11, 13, 17, 19, 23.$$

Memorize this list—it will come in handy. Note that 1 is not a prime.

KEY FACT A12:

Every integer greater than 1 that is not a prime can be written as a product of primes.

To find the prime factorization of any integer, find any two factors; if they're both primes, you are done; if not, factor them. Continue until each factor has been written in terms of primes. A useful method is to make a *factor tree*.

For example, here are the prime factorizations of 108 and 240:

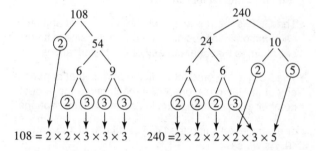

$108 = 2 \times 2 \times 3 \times 3 \times 3 \qquad 240 = 2 \times 2 \times 2 \times 2 \times 3 \times 5$

Example 8.

For any positive integer a, let $\lceil a \rfloor$ denote the smallest prime factor of a. Which of the following is equal to $\lceil 35 \rfloor$?
(A) $\lceil 10 \rfloor$ (B) $\lceil 15 \rfloor$ (C) $\lceil 45 \rfloor$ (D) $\lceil 55 \rfloor$
(E) $\lceil 75 \rfloor$

SOLUTION. Check the first few primes; 35 is not divisible by 2 or 3, but is divisible by 5, so 5 is the *smallest* prime factor of 35: $\lceil 35 \rfloor = 5$. Now check the five choices: $\lceil 10 \rfloor = 2$, and $\lceil 15 \rfloor$, $\lceil 45 \rfloor$, and $\lceil 75 \rfloor$ are all equal to 3. Only $\lceil \mathbf{55} \rfloor = 5$. The answer is **D**.

The **least common multiple** (**LCM**) of two or more integers is the smallest positive integer that is a multiple of each of them. For example, the LCM of 6 and 10 is 30. Infinitely many positive integers are multiples of both 6 and 10, including 60, 90, 180, 600, 6000, and 66,000,000, but 30 is the smallest one. The **greatest common factor** (**GCF**) or **greatest common divisor** (**GCD**) of two or more integers is the largest integer that is a factor of each of them. For example, the only positive integers that are factors of both 6 and 10 are 1 and 2, so the GCF of 6 and 10 is 2. For small numbers, you can often find their GCF and LCM by inspection. For larger numbers, KEY FACTS A13 and A14 are useful.

KEY FACT A13:

The product of the GCF and LCM of two numbers is equal to the product of the two numbers.

Helpful Hint

It is usually easier to find the GCF than the LCM. For example, you might see immediately that the GCF of 36 and 48 is 12. You could then use KEY FACT A12 to find the LCM: since GCF × LCM = 36 × 48, then

$$\text{LCM} = \frac{\overset{3}{\cancel{36}} \times 48}{\underset{1}{\cancel{12}}} = 3 \times 48 = 144.$$

KEY FACT A14:

To find the GCF or LCM of two or more integers, first get their prime factorizations.

• The GCF is the product of all the primes that appear in each factorization, using each prime the smallest number of times it appears in any of the factorizations.

• The LCM is the product of all the primes that appear in any of the factorizations, using each prime the largest number of times it appears in any of the factorizations.

For example, let's find the GCF and LCM of 108 and 240. As we saw:

$108 = 2 \times 2 \times 3 \times 3 \times 3$ and $240 = 2 \times 2 \times 2 \times 2 \times 3 \times 5$.

• **GCF.** The primes that appear in both factorizations are 2 and 3: 2 appears twice in the factorization of 108 and 4 times in the factorization of 240, so we take it twice; 3 appears 3 times in the factorization of 108, but only once in the factorization of 240, so we take it just once. The GCF = $2 \times 2 \times 3 = \textbf{12}$.

• **LCM.** Take one of the factorizations and add to it any primes from the other that are not yet listed. So, start with $2 \times 2 \times 3 \times 3 \times 3$ (108) and look at the primes from 240: there are four 2s; we already wrote two 2s, so we need two more; there is a 3 but we already have that; there is a 5, which we need. So, the LCM = $(2 \times 2 \times 3 \times 3 \times 3) \times (2 \times 2 \times 5) = 108 \times 20 = \textbf{2160}$.

Example 9.

What is the smallest number that is divisible by both 34 and 35?

SOLUTION. We are being asked for the LCM of 34 and 35. By KEY FACT A12, LCM = $\dfrac{34 \times 35}{\text{GCF}}$. But the GCF is 1 since no number greater than 1 divides evenly into both 34 and 35. So, the LCM is $34 \times 35 = \textbf{1190}$.

The **even numbers** are all the multiples of 2:
$$\{..., -4, -2, 0, 2, 4, 6, ...\}$$

The **odd numbers** are the integers not divisible by 2:
$$\{..., -5, -3, -1, 1, 3, 5, ...\}$$

NOTE: • The terms *odd* and *even* apply only to integers.
• Every integer (positive, negative, or 0) is either odd or even.
• 0 is an even integer; it is a multiple of 2. $(0 = 0 \times 2)$
• 0 is a multiple of *every* integer. $(0 = 0 \times n)$
• 2 is the only even prime number.

KEY FACT A15:

The tables below summarize three important facts:

1. **If two integers are both even or both odd, their sum and difference are even.**

2. **If one integer is even and the other odd, their sum and difference are odd.**

3. **The product of two integers is even unless both of them are odd.**

+ and −	even	odd		×	even	odd
even	even	odd		even	even	even
odd	odd	even		odd	even	odd

Exponents and Roots

Repeated addition of the same number is indicated by multiplication:

$$17 + 17 + 17 + 17 + 17 + 17 + 17 = 7 \times 17$$

Repeated multiplication of the same number is indicated by an exponent:

$$17 \times 17 \times 17 \times 17 \times 17 \times 17 \times 17 = 17^7$$

In the expression 17^7, 17 is called the **base** and 7 is the **exponent**.

At some time, you may have seen expressions such as 2^{-4}, $2^{\frac{1}{2}}$, or even $2^{\sqrt{2}}$. On the GRE, although the base, b, can be any number, the only exponents you will see will be positive integers.

KEY FACT A16:

For any number b: $b^1 = b$, and $b^n = b \times b \times ... \times b$, where b is used as a factor n times.

(i) $2^5 \times 2^3 = (2 \times 2 \times 2 \times 2 \times 2) \times (2 \times 2 \times 2) = 2^8 = \textbf{2}^{\textbf{5+3}}$

(ii) $\dfrac{2^5}{2^3} = \dfrac{2 \times 2 \times 2 \times 2 \times 2}{2 \times 2 \times 2} = 2 \times 2 = 2^2 = \textbf{2}^{\textbf{5−3}}$

(iii) $(2^2)^3 = (2 \times 2)^3 = (2 \times 2) \times (2 \times 2) \times (2 \times 2) = 2^6 = \textbf{2}^{\textbf{2×3}}$

(iv) $2^3 \times 7^3 = (2 \times 2 \times 2) \times (7 \times 7 \times 7) = (2 \times 7)(2 \times 7)(2 \times 7) = \textbf{(2} \times \textbf{7)}^{\textbf{3}}$

These four examples illustrate the following important laws of exponents given in KEY FACT A17.

KEY FACT A17:

For any numbers b and c and positive integers m and n:

(i) $b^m b^n = b^{m+n}$ (ii) $\dfrac{b^m}{b^n} = b^{m-n}$ (iii) $(b^m)^n = b^{mn}$

(iv) $b^m c^m = (bc)^m$

> CAUTION: In (i) and (ii) the bases are the same and in (iv) the exponents are the same. None of these rules applies to expressions such as $7^5 \times 5^7$, in which both the bases and the exponents are different.

Example 10.

If $2^x = 32$, what is x^2?

(A) 5   (B) 10   (C) 25   (D) 100   (E) 1024

SOLUTION. To solve $2^x = 32$, just count (and keep track of) how many 2s you need to multiply to get 32: $2 \times 2 \times 2 \times 2 \times 2 = 32$, so $x = 5$ and $x^2 = $ **25 (C)**.

Example 11.

If $3^a \times 3^b = 3^{100}$, what is the average (arithmetic mean) of a and b?

SOLUTION. Since $3^a \times 3^b = 3^{a+b}$, we see that

$$a + b = 100 \Rightarrow \frac{a+b}{2} = \mathbf{50}.$$

The next KEY FACT is an immediate consequence of KEY FACTS A4 and A5.

KEY FACT A18:

For any positive integer n:

- $0^n = 0$

- if a is positive, then a^n is positive

- if a is negative and n is even, then a^n is positive

- if a is negative and n is odd, then a^n is negative.

<u>Column A</u>	<u>Column B</u>
Example 12.	
$(-13)^{10}$	$(-13)^{25}$

SOLUTION. Column A is positive and Column B is negative. So Column **A** is greater.

Squares and Square Roots

The exponent that appears most often on the GRE is 2. It is used to form the square of a number, as in πr^2 (the area of a circle), $a^2 + b^2 = c^2$ (the Pythagorean theorem), or $x^2 - y^2$ (the difference of two squares). Therefore, it is helpful to recognize the **perfect squares**, numbers that are the squares of integers. The squares of the integers from 0 to 15 are as follows:

x	0	1	2	3	4	5	6	7
x^2	0	1	4	9	16	25	36	49

x	8	9	10	11	12	13	14	15
x^2	64	81	100	121	144	169	196	225

There are two numbers that satisfy the equation $x^2 = 9$: $x = 3$ and $x = -3$. The positive one, 3, is called the (**principal**) **square root** of 9 and is denoted by the symbol $\sqrt{9}$. Clearly, each perfect square has a square root: $\sqrt{0} = 0$, $\sqrt{36} = 6$, $\sqrt{81} = 9$, and $\sqrt{144} = 12$. But, it is an important fact that *every* positive number has a square root.

KEY FACT A19:

For any positive number a, there is a positive number b that satisfies the equation $b^2 = a$. That number is called the square root of a and we write $b = \sqrt{a}$.

So, for any positive number a: $(\sqrt{a})^2 = \sqrt{a} \times \sqrt{a} = a$.

The only difference between $\sqrt{9}$ and $\sqrt{10}$ is that the first square root is an integer, while the second one isn't. Since 10 is a little more than 9, we should expect that $\sqrt{10}$ is a little more than $\sqrt{9} = 3$. In fact, $(3.1)^2 = 9.61$, which is close to 10, and $(3.16)^2 = 9.9856$, which is very close to 10. So, $\sqrt{10} \approx 3.16$. On the GRE you will *never* have to evaluate such a square root; if the solution to a problem involves a square root, that square root will be among the answer choices.

Example 13.

What is the circumference of a circle whose area is 10π?

(A) 5π (B) 10π (C) $\pi\sqrt{10}$ (D) $2\pi\sqrt{10}$
(E) $\pi\sqrt{20}$

SOLUTION. Since the area of a circle is given by the formula $A = \pi r^2$, we have

$$\pi r^2 = 10\pi \Rightarrow r^2 = 10 \Rightarrow r = \sqrt{10}.$$

The circumference is given by the formula $C = 2\pi r$, so $C = \mathbf{2\pi\sqrt{10}}$ **(D)**. (See Section 14-L on circles.)

KEY FACT A20:

For any positive numbers **a** and **b**:

$$\bullet \ \sqrt{ab} = \sqrt{a} \times \sqrt{b} \qquad \bullet \ \sqrt{\dfrac{a}{b}} = \dfrac{\sqrt{a}}{\sqrt{b}}$$

CAUTION: $\sqrt{a+b} \neq \sqrt{a} + \sqrt{b}$. For example:

$$5 = \sqrt{25} = \sqrt{9+16} \neq \sqrt{9} + \sqrt{16} = 3 + 4 = 7.$$

CAUTION: Although it is always true that $(\sqrt{a})^2 = a$, $\sqrt{a^2} = a$ is true *only if a* is positive:

$$\sqrt{(-5)^2} = \sqrt{25} = 5, \ not \ -5.$$

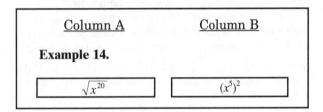

Column A	Column B
Example 14.	
$\sqrt{x^{20}}$	$(x^5)^2$

SOLUTION. Column A: Since $x^{10}x^{10} = x^{20}$, $\sqrt{x^{20}} = x^{10}$.

Column B: $(x^5)^2 = x^{10}$. The columns are equal **(C)**.

PEMDAS

When a calculation requires performing more than one operation, it is important to carry them out in the correct order. For decades students have memorized the sentence "Please Excuse My Dear Aunt Sally," or just the first letters, PEMDAS, to remember the proper order of operations. The letters stand for:

• Parentheses: first do whatever appears in parentheses, following PEMDAS within the parentheses if necessary.

• Exponents: next evaluate all terms with exponents.

• Multiplication and Division: then do all multiplications and divisions *in order from left to right—do not* multiply first and then divide.

• Addition and Subtraction: finally, do all additions and subtractions *in order from left to right—do not add* first and then subtract.

Here are some worked-out examples.

1. $12 + 3 \times 2 = 12 + 6 = 18$ [Multiply before you add.]
   $(12 + 3) \times 2 = 15 \times 2 = 30$ [First add in the parentheses.]

2. $12 \div 3 \times 2 = 4 \times 2 = 8$ [Just go from left to right.]
   $12 \div (3 \times 2) = 12 \div 6 = 2$ [First multiply inside the parentheses.]

3. $5 \times 2^3 = 5 \times 8 = 40$ [Do exponents first.]
   $(5 \times 2)^3 = 10^3 = 1000$ [First multiply inside the parentheses.]

4. $4 + 4 \div (2 + 6) = 4 + 4 \div 8 = 4 + .5 = 4.5$
   [First add in the parentheses, then divide, and finally add.]

5. $100 - 2^2(3 + 4 \times 5) = 100 - 2^2(23) = 100 - 4(23) = 100 - 92 = 8$
   [First evaluate what's inside the parentheses (using PEMDAS); then take the exponent; then multiply; and finally subtract.]

There is an important situation when you shouldn't start with what's in the parentheses. Consider the following two examples.

(i) What is the value of $7(100 - 1)$?

   Using PEMDAS, you would write $7(100 - 1) = 7(99)$, and then multiply: $7 \times 99 = 693$. But you can do this even quicker in your head if you think of it this way: $7(100 - 1) = 700 - 7 = 693$.

(ii) What is the value of $(77 + 49) \div 7$?

   If you followed the rules of PEMDAS, you would first add, $77 + 49 = 126$, and then divide, $126 \div 7 = 18$. This is definitely more difficult and time-consuming than mentally doing $\dfrac{77}{7} + \dfrac{49}{7} = 11 + 7 = 18$.

Both of these examples illustrate the very important distributive law.

KEY FACT A21:

The distributive law

For any real numbers **a**, **b**, and **c**:

$$\bullet \ a(b + c) = ab + ac \qquad \bullet \ a(b - c) = ab - ac$$

and if $a \neq 0$

$$\bullet \ \frac{b + c}{a} = \frac{b}{a} + \frac{c}{a} \qquad \bullet \ \frac{b - c}{a} = \frac{b}{a} - \frac{c}{a}$$

Helpful Hint

Many students who use the distributive law with multiplication forget about it with division. Don't you do that.

Column A	Column B
Example 15.	
$5(a - 7)$	$5a - 7$
Example 16.	
$\dfrac{50 + x}{5}$	$10 + x$

SOLUTION 15. By the distributive law, Column $A = 5a - 35$. The result of subtracting 35 from a number is *always less* than the result of subtracting 7 from that number. Column **B** is greater.

SOLUTION 16.

	Column A	Column B
By the distributive law:	$10 + \dfrac{x}{5}$	$10 + x$
Subtract 10 from each column:	$\dfrac{x}{5}$	x

The columns are equal if $x = 0$, but not if $x = 1$.

The answer is **D**.

Example 17.

If $a = 9 \times 8321$ and $b = 9 \times 7321$, what is the value of $a - b$?

SOLUTION. Remember, you will *never* have to do tedious multiplications on the GRE, so there must be an easier way to solve this. If you think, you can do it in your head. Remember the distributive law—in far less time than it takes to write the equation on your scrap paper, you should realize that
$$a - b = 9(8321) - 9(7321) =$$
$$9(8321 - 7321) = 9(1000) = \mathbf{9000}.$$

Inequalities

The number a is **greater than** the number b, denoted $a > b$, if a is to the right of b on the number line. Similarly, a is **less than** b, denoted $a < b$, if a is to the left of b on the number line. Therefore, if a is positive, $a > 0$, and if a is negative, $a < 0$. Clearly, if $a > b$, then $b < a$.

The following KEY FACT gives an important alternate way to describe greater than and less than.

KEY FACT A22:

• For any numbers a and b:
   $a > b$ means that $a - b$ is positive.

• For any numbers a and b:
   $a < b$ means that $a - b$ is negative.

KEY FACT A23:

• For any numbers a and b, exactly one of the following is true:

   $a > b$ or $a = b$ or $a < b$.

The symbol $\geq$ means **greater than or equal to** and the symbol $\leq$ means **less than or equal to**. The statement "$x \geq 5$" means that x can be 5 or any number greater than 5; the statement "$x \leq 5$" means that x can be 5 or any number less than 5. The statement "$2 < x < 5$" is an abbreviation for the statement "$2 < x$ and $x < 5$." It means that x is a number between 2 and 5 (greater than 2 and less than 5).

Inequalities are very important on the GRE, especially on the quantitative comparison questions where you have to determine which of two quantities is the greater one. KEY FACTS A24 and A25 give some important facts about inequalities.

If the result of performing an arithmetic operation on an inequality is a new inequality in the same direction, we say that the inequality has been **preserved**. If the result of performing an arithmetic operation on an inequality is a new inequality in the opposite direction, we say that the inequality has been **reversed**.

KEY FACT A24:

• **Adding a number to an inequality or subtracting a number from an inequality preserves it.**

   If $a < b$, then $a + c < b + c$ and $a - c < b - c$.
   $3 < 7 \Rightarrow 3 + 100 < 7 + 100$ $(103 < 107)$
   $3 < 7 \Rightarrow 3 - 100 < 7 - 100$ $(-97 < -93)$

• **Adding inequalities in the same direction preserves them.**

   If $a < b$ and $c < d$, then $a + c < b + d$.
   $3 < 7$ and $5 < 10 \Rightarrow 3 + 5 < 7 + 10$ $(8 < 17)$

• **Multiplying or dividing an inequality by a positive number preserves it.**

   If $a < b$, and c is positive, then $ac < bc$ and $\dfrac{a}{c} < \dfrac{b}{c}$.
   $3 < 7 \Rightarrow 3 \times 100 < 7 \times 100$ $(300 < 700)$
   $3 < 7 \Rightarrow 3 \div 100 < 7 \div 100$ $\left(\dfrac{3}{100} < \dfrac{7}{100}\right)$

• **Multiplying or dividing an inequality by a negative number reverses it.**

   If $a < b$, and c is negative, then $ac > bc$ and $\dfrac{a}{c} > \dfrac{b}{c}$.
   $3 < 7 \Rightarrow 3 \times (-100) > 7 \times (-100)$ $(-300 > -700)$
   $3 < 7 \Rightarrow 3 \div (-100) > 7 \div (-100)$ $\left(-\dfrac{3}{100} > -\dfrac{7}{100}\right)$

• **Taking negatives reverses an inequality.**

   If $a < b$, then $-a > -b$ and if $a > b$, then $-a < -b$.
   $3 < 7 \Rightarrow -3 > -7$ and $7 > 3 \Rightarrow -7 < -3$

• **If two numbers are each positive or negative, then taking reciprocals reverses an inequality.**

   If a and b are both positive or both negative and $a < b$,
   then $\dfrac{1}{a} > \dfrac{1}{b}$.

   $3 < 7 \Rightarrow \dfrac{1}{3} > \dfrac{1}{7}$ $-7 < -3 \Rightarrow -\dfrac{1}{7} > -\dfrac{1}{3}$

Helpful Hint

Be sure you understand KEY FACT A24; it is very useful. Also, review the important properties listed in KEY FACTS A25 and A26. These properties come up often on the GRE.

KEY FACT A25:

Important inequalities for numbers between 0 and 1.

- If $0 < x < 1$, and a is positive, then $xa < a$. For example: $.85 \times 19 < 19$.

- If $0 < x < 1$, and m and n are integers with $m > n$, then $x^m < x^n < x$.

$$\text{For example, } \left(\frac{1}{2}\right)^5 < \left(\frac{1}{2}\right)^2 < \frac{1}{2}.$$

- If $0 < x < 1$, then $\sqrt{x} > x$. For example, $\sqrt{\frac{3}{4}} > \frac{3}{4}$.

- If $0 < x < 1$, then $\frac{1}{x} > x$. In fact, $\frac{1}{x} > 1$.

$$\text{For example, } \frac{1}{0.2} > 1 > 0.2.$$

KEY FACT A26:

Properties of Zero

- 0 is the only number that is neither positive nor negative.

- 0 is smaller than every positive number and greater than every negative number.

- 0 is an even integer.

- 0 is a multiple of every integer.

- For every number a: $a + 0 = a$ and $a - 0 = a$.

- For every number a: $a \times 0 = 0$.

- For every positive integer n: $0^n = 0$.

- For every number a (including 0): $a \div 0$ and $\frac{a}{0}$ are **meaningless symbols**. (They are **undefined**.)

- For every number a other than 0: $0 \div a = \frac{0}{a} = 0$.

- 0 is the only number that is equal to its opposite: $0 = -0$.

- If the product of two or more numbers is 0, at least one of them is 0.

KEY FACT A27:

Properties of 1

- For any number a: $1 \times a = a$ and $\frac{a}{1} = a$.

- For any integer n: $1^n = 1$.

- 1 is a divisor of every integer.

- 1 is the smallest positive integer.

- 1 is an odd integer.

- 1 is **not** a prime.

PRACTICE EXERCISES—BASIC ARITHMETIC

Multiple-Choice Questions

1. For how many positive integers, a, is it true that $a^2 \le 2a$?
   (A) None   (B) 1   (C) 2   (D) 4   (E) More than 4

2. If $0 < a < b < 1$, which of the following are true?
   I. $a - b$ is negative
   II. $\frac{1}{ab}$ is positive
   III. $\frac{1}{b} - \frac{1}{a}$ is positive

   (A) I only   (B) II only   (C) III only
   (D) I and II only   (E) I, II, and III

3. If the product of 4 consecutive integers is equal to one of them, what is the largest possible value of one of the integers?
   (A) 0   (B) 3   (C) 4   (D) 6   (E) 24

4. At 3:00 A.M. the temperature was 13° below zero. By noon it had risen to 32°. What was the average hourly increase in temperature?
   (A) $\left(\frac{19}{9}\right)^\circ$ (B) $\left(\frac{19}{6}\right)^\circ$ (C) 5°   (D) 7.5°
   (E) 45°

5. If a and b are negative, and c is positive, which of the following statements are true?
   I. $a - b < a - c$
   II. If $a < b$, then $\frac{a}{c} < \frac{b}{c}$
   III. $\frac{1}{b} < \frac{1}{c}$

   (A) I only   (B) II only   (C) III only
   (D) II and III only   (E) I, II, and III

6. If $-7 \le x \le 7$ and $0 \le y \le 12$, what is the greatest possible value of $y - x$?
   (A) −19   (B) 5   (C) 7   (D) 17   (E) 19

7. If $(7^a)(7^b) = \dfrac{7^c}{7^d}$, what is d in terms of a, b, and c?

   (A) $\dfrac{c}{ab}$ (B) $c - a - b$ (C) $a + b - c$ (D) $c - ab$

   (E) $\dfrac{c}{a + b}$

8. If each of ★ and ❖ can be replaced by $+$, $-$, or $\times$, how many different values are there for the expression $2 ★ 2 ❖ 2$?

   (A) 4   (B) 5   (C) 6   (D) 7   (E) 9

9. A number is "terrific" if it is a multiple of 2 or 3. How many terrific numbers are there between -11 and 11?

   (A) 6   (B) 7   (C) 11   (D) 15   (E) 17

Questions 10 and 11 refer to the following definition. For any positive integer n, $\tau(n)$ represents the number of positive divisors of n.

10. Which of the following are true?

    I. $\tau(5) = \tau(7)$
    II. $\tau(5) \cdot \tau(7) = \tau(35)$
    III. $\tau(5) + \tau(7) = \tau(12)$

    (A) I only   (B) II only   (C) I and II only
        (D) I and III only   (E) I, II, and III

11. What is the value of $\tau(\tau(\tau(12)))$?

    (A) 1   (B) 2   (C) 3   (D) 4   (E) 6

12. If p and q are primes greater than 2, which of the following must be true?

    I. $p + q$ is even
    II. pq is odd
    III. $p^2 - q^2$ is even

    (A) I only   (B) II only   (C) I and II only
        (D) I and III only   (E) I, II, and III

13. If $0 < x < 1$, which of the following lists the numbers in increasing order?

    (A) $\sqrt{x}, x, x^2$ (B) $x^2, x, \sqrt{x}$ (C) $x^2, \sqrt{x}, x$

    (D) $x, x^2, \sqrt{x}$ (E) $x, \sqrt{x}, x^2$

14. Which of the following is equal to $(7^8 \times 7^9)^{10}$?

    (A) 7^{27} (B) 7^{82} (C) 7^{170} (D) 49^{170} (E) 49^{720}

15. If $x \; ⊘ \; y$ represents the number of integers greater than x and less than y, what is the value of $-\pi \; ⊘ \; \sqrt{2}$?

    (A) 2   (B) 3   (C) 4   (D) 5   (E) 6

Quantitative Comparison Questions

	Column A	Column B
16.	The product of the odd integers between -8 and 8	The product of the even integers between -9 and 9

a and b are nonzero integers

17.	$a + b$	ab

18.	The remainder when a positive integer is divided by 7	7

19.	$24 \div 6 \times 4$	12

20.	$\dfrac{2x - 17}{2}$	$x - 17$

n is an integer greater than 1 that leaves a remainder of 1 when it is divided by 2, 3, 4, 5, and 6

21.	n	60

22.	The number of primes that are divisible by 2	The number of primes that are divisible by 3

n is a positive integer

23.	The number of different prime factors of n	The number of different prime factors of n^2

24.	The number of even positive factors of 30	The number of odd positive factors of 30

n is a positive integer

25.	$(-10)^n$	$(-10)^{n+1}$

Answer Key

1. **C**	6. **E**	11. **C**	16. **A**	21. **A**
2. **D**	7. **B**	12. **E**	17. **D**	22. **C**
3. **B**	8. **A**	13. **B**	18. **B**	23. **C**
4. **C**	9. **D**	14. **C**	19. **A**	24. **C**
5. **D**	10. **C**	15. **D**	20. **A**	25. **D**

Answer Explanations

1. **C.** Since a is positive, we can divide both sides of the given inequality by a:
$$a^2 \le 2a \Rightarrow a \le 2 \Rightarrow a = 1 \text{ or } 2.$$

2. **D.** Since $a < b$, $a - b$ is negative (I is true). Since a and b are positive, so is their product, ab; and the reciprocal of a positive number is positive (II is true).
$\dfrac{1}{b} - \dfrac{1}{a} = \dfrac{a-b}{ab}$, and have just seen that the numerator is negative and the denominator positive; so the value of the fraction is negative (III is false).

3. **B.** If all four integers were negative, their product would be positive, and so could not equal one of them. If all of the integers were positive, their product would be much greater than any of them (even $1 \times 2 \times 3 \times 4 = 24$). So, the integers must include 0, in which case their product *is* 0. The largest set of four consecutive integers that includes 0 is 0, 1, 2, 3.

4. **C.** In the 9 hours from 3:00 to 12:00, the temperature rose $32 - (-13) = 32 + 13 = 45$ degrees. So, the average hourly increase was $45° \div 9 = 5°$.

5. **D.** Since b is negative and c is positive,
$$b < c \Rightarrow -b > -c \Rightarrow a - b > a - c$$
(I is false). Since c is positive, dividing by c preserves the inequality. (II is true.) Since b is negative, $\dfrac{1}{b}$ is negative, and so is less than $\dfrac{1}{c}$, which is positive (III is true).

6. **E.** To make $y - x$ as large as possible, let y be as big as possible (12), and subtract the smallest amount possible ($x = -7$): $12 - (-7) = 19$.

7. **B.** $(7^a)(7^b) = 7^{a+b}$, and $\dfrac{7^c}{7^d} = 7^{c-d}$. Therefore,
$$a + b = c - d \Rightarrow a + b + d = c \Rightarrow d = c - a - b$$

8. **A.** Just list the 9 possible outcomes of replacing ★ and ❖ by +, −, and ×, and see that there are 4 different values: −2, 2, 6, 8.

$2 + 2 + 2 = 6$	$2 - 2 - 2 = -2$	$2 \times 2 \times 2 = 8$
$2 + 2 - 2 = 2$	$2 - 2 \times 2 = -2$	$2 \times 2 + 2 = 6$
$2 + 2 \times 2 = 6$	$2 - 2 + 2 = 2$	$2 \times 2 - 2 = 2$

9. **D.** There are 15 "terrific" numbers: 2, 3, 4, 6, 8, 9, 10, their opposites, and 0.

10. **C.** Since 5 and 7 have two positive factors each, $\tau(5) = \tau(7)$. (I is true.)
Since 35 has 4 divisors (1, 5, 7, and 35) and $\tau(5) \cdot \tau(7) = 2 \times 2 = 4$. (II is true.)
Since the positive divisors of 12 are 1, 2, 3, 4, 6, and 12, $\tau(12)$ is 6, which is *not* equal to $2 + 2$. (III is false.)

11. **C.** $\tau(\tau(\tau(12))) = \tau(\tau(6)) = \tau(4) = 3$

12. **E.** All primes greater than 2 are odd, so p and q are odd, and $p + q$ is even (I is true). The product of two odd numbers is odd (II is true). Since p and q are odd, so are their squares, and so the difference of the squares is even (III is true).

13. **B.** For any number, x, between 0 and 1:
$$x^2 < x \text{ and } x < \sqrt{x}.$$

14. **C.** First, multiply inside the parentheses: $7^8 \times 7^9 = 7^{17}$; then, raise to the 10th power: $(7^{17})^{10} = 7^{170}$.

15. **D.** There are 5 integers (1, 0, −1, −2, −3) that are greater than −3.14 ($-\pi$) and less than 1.41 ($\sqrt{2}$).

16. **A.** Since the product in Column A has 4 negative factors (−7, −5, −3, −1), it is positive. The product in Column B also has 4 negative factors, but be careful—it also has the factor 0, and so Column B is 0.

17. **D.** If a and b are each 1, then $a + b = 2$, and $ab = 1$; so, Column A is greater. But, if a and b are each 3, $a + b = 6$, and $ab = 9$, and Column B is greater.

18. **B.** The remainder is *always* less than the divisor.

19. **A.** According to PEMDAS, you divide and multiply from left to right (do *not* do the multiplication first): $24 \div 6 \times 4 = 4 \times 4 = 16$.

20. **A.** By the distributive law,
$\dfrac{2x - 17}{2} = \dfrac{2x}{2} - \dfrac{17}{2} = x - 8.5$, which is greater than $x - 17$ (the larger the number you subtract, the smaller the difference.)

21. **A.** The LCM of 2, 3, 4, 5, 6 is 60; and all multiples of 60 are divisible by each of them. So, n could be 61 or 1 more than any multiple of 60.

22. **C.** The only prime divisible by 2 is 2, and the only prime divisible by 3 is 3. The number in each column is 1.

23. **C.** If you make a factor tree for n^2, the first branches would be n and n. Now, when you factor each n, you get exactly the same prime factors. (See the example below.)

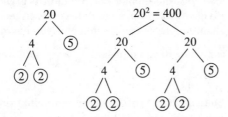

24. **C.** Just list the factors of 30: 1, 2, 3, 5, 6, 10, 15, 30. Four of them are odd and four are even.

25. **D.** If n is even, then $n + 1$ is odd, and consequently $(-10)^n$ is positive, whereas $(-10)^{n+1}$ is negative. If n is odd, exactly the opposite is true.

14-B. FRACTIONS AND DECIMALS

Several questions on the GRE involve fractions or decimals. The 23 KEY FACTS in this section cover all of the important facts you need to know for the GRE.

When a whole is *divided* into n equal parts, each part is called *one nth* of the whole, written $\frac{1}{n}$. For example, if a pizza is cut (*divided*) into 8 equal slices, each slice is one eighth $\left(\frac{1}{8}\right)$ of the pizza; a day is *divided* into 24 equal hours, so an hour is one twenty-fourth $\left(\frac{1}{24}\right)$ of a day; and an inch is one twelfth $\left(\frac{1}{12}\right)$ of a foot.

- If Donna slept for 5 hours, she slept for five twenty-fourths $\left(\frac{5}{24}\right)$ of a day.

- If Taryn bought 8 slices of pizza, she bought eight eighths $\left(\frac{8}{8}\right)$ of a pie.

- If Aviva's shelf is 30 inches long, it measures thirty twelfths $\left(\frac{30}{12}\right)$ of a foot.

Numbers such as $\frac{5}{24}$, $\frac{8}{8}$, and $\frac{30}{12}$, in which one integer is written over a second integer, are called *fractions*. The center line is called the fraction bar. The number above the bar is called the *numerator*, and the number below the bar is called the *denominator*.

> CAUTION: The denominator of a fraction can *never* be 0.

- A fraction, such as $\frac{5}{24}$, in which the numerator is less than the denominator, is called a *proper fraction*. Its value is less than 1.

- A fraction, such as $\frac{30}{12}$, in which the numerator is more than the denominator, is called an *improper fraction*. Its value is greater than 1.

- A fraction, such as $\frac{8}{8}$, in which the numerator and denominator are the same, is also *improper*, but it is equal to 1.

It is useful to think of the fraction bar as a symbol for division. If three pizzas are divided equally among eight people, each person gets $\frac{3}{8}$ of a pizza. If you actually divide 3 by 8, you get that $\frac{3}{8} = .375$.

KEY FACT B1:

Every fraction, proper or improper, can be expressed in decimal form (or as a whole number) by dividing the numerator by the denominator.

$$\frac{3}{10} = 0.3 \qquad \frac{3}{4} = 0.75 \qquad \frac{5}{8} = 0.625 \qquad \frac{3}{16} = 0.1875$$

$$\frac{8}{8} = 1 \qquad \frac{11}{8} = 1.375 \qquad \frac{48}{16} = 3 \qquad \frac{100}{8} = 12.5$$

Note that any number beginning with a decimal point can be written with a 0 to the left of the decimal point. In fact, some calculators will express 3 ÷ 8 as .375, whereas others will print 0.375.

Unlike the examples above, when most fractions are converted to decimals, the division does not terminate after 2 or 3 or 4 decimal places; rather it goes on forever with some set of digits repeating itself.

$$\frac{2}{3} = 0.666666... \qquad \frac{3}{11} = 0.272727... \qquad \frac{5}{12} = 0.416666...$$

$$\frac{17}{15} = 1.133333...$$

However, *on the GRE, you do not need to be concerned with this*. On both multiple-choice and quantitative comparison questions, all numbers written as decimals terminate.

Comparing Fractions and Decimals

KEY FACT B2:

To compare two decimals, follow these rules.

- Whichever number has the greater number to the left of the decimal point is greater: since 11 > 9, 11.001 > 9.896 and since 1 > 0, 1.234 > 0.8. (Recall that if a decimal is written without a number to the left of the decimal point, you may assume that a 0 is there. So, 1.234 > .8.)

- If the numbers to the left of the decimal point are equal (or if there are no numbers to the left of the decimal point), proceed as follows:

  (1) If the numbers do not have the same number of digits to the right of the decimal point, add zeros to the end of the shorter one.
  (2) Now, compare the numbers *ignoring* the decimal point.

For example, to compare 1.83 and 1.823, add a 0 to the end of 1.83, forming 1.830. Now compare them, *thinking of them as whole numbers*: since, 1830 > 1823, then 1.830 > 1.823.

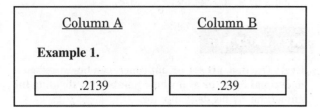

	Column A	Column B
Example 1.		
	.2139	.239

SOLUTION. Do not think that Column A is greater because 2139 > 239. Be sure to add a 0 to the end of .239 (forming .2390) before comparing. Now, since 2390 > 2139, Column **B** is greater.

KEY FACT B3:

There are two methods of comparing fractions:

1. Convert them to decimals (by dividing), and use KEY FACT B2.

2. Cross-multiply.

For example, to compare $\frac{1}{3}$ and $\frac{3}{8}$, we have two choices.

1. Write $\frac{1}{3}$ = .3333... and $\frac{3}{8}$ = .375. Since .375 > .333, then $\frac{3}{8} > \frac{1}{3}$.

2. Cross-multiply:

   $\frac{1}{3} \diagup\!\!\!\!\diagdown \frac{3}{8}$ Since $3 \times 3 > 8 \times 1$, then $\frac{3}{8} > \frac{1}{3}$.

KEY FACT B4:

When comparing fractions, there are three situations in which it is easier just to look at the fractions, and not use either method in KEY FACT B3.

1. If the fractions have the same denominator, the fraction with the larger numerator is greater. Just as $9 is more than $7, and 9 books are more than 7 books, 9 tenths are more than 7 tenths: $\frac{9}{10} > \frac{7}{10}$.

2. If the fractions have the same numerator, the fraction with the smaller denominator is greater. If you divide a cake into 5 equal pieces, each piece is larger than the pieces you would get if you had divided the cake into 10 equal pieces: $\frac{1}{5} > \frac{1}{10}$, and similarly $\frac{3}{5} > \frac{3}{10}$.

3. Sometimes the fractions are so familiar or easy to work with, you just know the answer. For example, $\frac{3}{4} > \frac{1}{5}$ and $\frac{11}{20} > \frac{1}{2}$ $\left(\text{since } \frac{10}{20} = \frac{1}{2} \right)$.

KEY FACT B5:

KEY FACTS B2, B3, and B4 apply to *positive* decimals and fractions.

- Clearly, any positive number is greater than any negative number:

$$\frac{1}{2} > -\frac{1}{5} \quad \text{and} \quad 0.123 > -2.56$$

- For negative decimals and fractions, use KEY FACT A24, which states that if $a > b$, then $-a < -b$:

$$\frac{1}{2} > \frac{1}{5} \Rightarrow -\frac{1}{2} < -\frac{1}{5} \quad \text{and} \quad .83 > .829 \Rightarrow -.83 < -.829$$

> **Example 2.**
> Which of the following lists the fractions $\frac{2}{3}, \frac{5}{8},$ and $\frac{13}{20}$ in order from least to greatest?
>
> (A) $\frac{2}{3}, \frac{5}{8}, \frac{13}{20}$ (B) $\frac{5}{8}, \frac{2}{3}, \frac{13}{20}$
>
> (C) $\frac{5}{8}, \frac{13}{20}, \frac{2}{3}$ (D) $\frac{13}{20}, \frac{5}{8}, \frac{2}{3}$
>
> (E) $\frac{13}{20}, \frac{2}{3}, \frac{5}{8}$

SOLUTION. Quickly, convert each to a decimal, writing down the first few decimal places: $\frac{2}{3}$ = .666,

$\dfrac{5}{8}$ = .625, and $\dfrac{13}{20}$ = .65. It is now easy to order the decimals: .625 < .650 < .666. The answer is **C**.

Alternative solution. Cross-multiply.

• Since $8 \times 2 > 3 \times 5$, then $\dfrac{2}{3} > \dfrac{5}{8}$.

• Since $8 \times 13 > 20 \times 5$, then $\dfrac{13}{20} > \dfrac{5}{8}$.

• Since $20 \times 2 > 3 \times 13$, then $\dfrac{2}{3} > \dfrac{13}{20}$.

Column A	Column B
Example 3.	
$0 < x < y$	
$\dfrac{1}{x} - \dfrac{1}{y}$	0

SOLUTION. By KEY FACT B4, $x < y \Rightarrow \dfrac{1}{x} > \dfrac{1}{y}$, and so by KEY FACT A22, $\dfrac{1}{x} - \dfrac{1}{y}$ is positive. Column **A** is greater.

Equivalent Fractions

If Bill and Al shared a pizza, and Bill ate $\dfrac{1}{2}$ the pizza and Al ate $\dfrac{4}{8}$ of it, they had exactly the same amount.

We express this idea by saying that $\dfrac{1}{2}$ and $\dfrac{4}{8}$ are **equivalent fractions**: they have the exact same value.

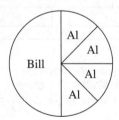

NOTE: If you multiply both the numerator and denominator of $\dfrac{1}{2}$ by 4 you get $\dfrac{4}{8}$; and if you divide both the numerator and denominator of $\dfrac{4}{8}$ by 4 you get $\dfrac{1}{2}$. This illustrates the next KEY FACT.

KEY FACT B6:

Two fractions are equivalent if multiplying or dividing both the numerator and denominator of the first one *by the same number* gives the second one.

Consider the following two cases.

1. When the numerator and denominator of $\dfrac{3}{8}$ are each multiplied by 15, the products are $3 \times 15 = 45$ and $8 \times 15 = 120$. Therefore, $\dfrac{3}{8}$ and $\dfrac{45}{120}$ and are equivalent fractions.

2. Since 2 must be multiplied by 14 to get 28, but 3 must be multiplied by 15 to get 45, then $\dfrac{2}{3}$ and $\dfrac{28}{45}$ are not equivalent fractions.

KEY FACT B7:

To determine if two fractions are equivalent, cross-multiply. The fractions are equivalent if and only if the two products are equal.

For example, since $120 \times 3 = 8 \times 45$, then $\dfrac{3}{8}$ and $\dfrac{45}{120}$ are equivalent.

Since $45 \times 2 \neq 3 \times 28$, then $\dfrac{2}{3}$ and $\dfrac{28}{45}$ are not equivalent fractions.

A fraction is in **lowest terms** if no positive integer greater than 1 is a factor of both the numerator and denominator. For example, $\dfrac{9}{20}$ is in lowest terms, since no integer greater than 1 is a factor of both 9 and 20; but $\dfrac{9}{24}$ is not in lowest terms, since 3 is a factor of both 9 and 24.

KEY FACT B8:

Every fraction can be *reduced* to lowest terms by dividing the numerator and the denominator by their greatest common factor (GCF). If the GCF is 1, the fraction is already in lowest terms.

> **Example 4.**
> For any positive integer n: $n!$ means the product of all the integers from 1 to n. What is the value of $\dfrac{6!}{8!}$?
>
> (A) $\dfrac{1}{56}$　(B) $\dfrac{1}{48}$　(C) $\dfrac{1}{8}$　(D) $\dfrac{1}{4}$　(E) $\dfrac{3}{4}$

SOLUTION. Clearly, you do not want to calculate 6! ($1 \cdot 2 \cdot 3 \cdot 4 \cdot 5 \cdot 6 = 720$) and 8! ($1 \cdot 2 \cdot 3 \cdot 4 \cdot 5 \cdot 6 \cdot 7 \cdot 8 = 40{,}320$) and then have to reduce $\dfrac{720}{40{,}320}$. Here's the easy solution:

$$\dfrac{6!}{8!} = \dfrac{\cancel{6 \times 5 \times 4 \times 3 \times 2 \times 1}^{\,1}}{8 \times 7 \times \cancel{6 \times 5 \times 4 \times 3 \times 2 \times 1}_{\,1}} = \dfrac{1}{8 \times 7} = \dfrac{1}{56}$$

Arithmetic Operations with Decimals

KEY FACT B9:

To add or subtract decimal numbers, make sure that the decimal points are lined up, and then add or subtract normally, ignoring the decimal points. Finally, place a decimal point in the answer immediately below the other decimal points.

For example, 3.2 + 7 + 1.125 = 11.325 and 3.456 − 1.28 = 2.176

$$\begin{array}{r} 3.2 \\ 7. \\ +1.125 \\ \hline 11.325 \end{array} \qquad \begin{array}{r} 3.456 \\ -1.28 \\ \hline 2.176 \end{array}$$

KEY FACT B10:

To multiply decimal numbers, multiply normally, ignoring the decimal points. Then count the total number of digits to the right of the decimal points in both factors, and place a decimal point in the product that many places from the right.

For example, 2.6 × 3.14 = 8.164

$$\begin{array}{r} 3.14 \text{ (two decimal places)} \\ \times 2.6 \text{ (one decimal place)} \\ \hline 1884 \\ 628 \\ \hline 8.164 \text{ (three decimal places)} \end{array}$$

KEY FACT B11:

To divide decimal numbers, count the number of digits to the right of the decimal point in the divisor, and move the decimal point in both the divisor and the dividend that many places to the right (adding zeros if necessary). Now, divide normally and if there is a decimal point in the dividend, place a decimal place in the quotient directly above the one in the dividend.

For example, 35 ÷ 1.25 = 28 and .035 ÷ 1.25 = .028

$$1.25\overline{)35} \qquad\qquad 1.25\overline{).035}$$

$$\begin{array}{r} 28 \\ =125\overline{)3500} \\ 250\downarrow \\ \hline 1000 \\ 1000 \\ \hline 0 \end{array} \qquad \begin{array}{r} .028 \\ =125\overline{)03.500} \\ 2\,50\downarrow \\ \hline 1\,000 \\ 1\,000 \\ \hline 0 \end{array}$$

Multiplying and dividing by powers of 10 is particularly easy and can be accomplished just by moving the decimal point.

KEY FACT B12:

To multiply any decimal or whole number by a power of 10, move the decimal point as many places to the right as there are 0s in the power of 10, filling in with 0s, if necessary.

$$1.35 \times 10 = 13.5 \qquad 1.35 \times 100 = 135$$

$$1.35 \times 1000 = 1350$$

$$23 \times 10 = 230 \qquad 23 \times 100 = 2300$$

$$23 \times 1{,}000{,}000 = 23{,}000{,}000$$

KEY FACT B13:

To divide any decimal or whole number by a power of 10, move the decimal point as many places to the left as there are 0s in the power of 10, filling in with 0s, if necessary.

$$67.8 \div 10 = 6.78 \qquad 67.8 \div 100 = 0.678$$

$$67.8 \div 1000 = 0.0678$$

$$14 \div 10 = 1.4 \qquad 14 \div 100 = 0.14$$

$$14 \div 1{,}000{,}000 = 0.000014$$

Column A	Column B
Example 5.	
3.75×10^4	$37{,}500{,}000 \div 10^3$

SOLUTION. In Column A, move the decimal point 4 places to the right: **37,500**. In Column B, move the decimal point 3 places to the left: **37,500**. The answer is **C**.

Arithmetic Operations with Fractions

KEY FACT B14:

To multiply two fractions, multiply their numerators and multiply their denominators: $\dfrac{3}{5} \times \dfrac{4}{7} = \dfrac{3 \times 4}{5 \times 7} = \dfrac{12}{35}$

KEY FACT B15:

To multiply a fraction by any other number, write that number as a fraction whose denominator is 1:

$$\frac{3}{5} \times 7 = \frac{3}{5} \times \frac{7}{1} = \frac{21}{5} \qquad \frac{3}{4} \times \pi = \frac{3}{4} \times \frac{\pi}{1} = \frac{3\pi}{4}$$

Before multiplying fractions, reduce. You may reduce by dividing any numerator and any denominator by a common factor.

Example 6.

Express the product, $\frac{3}{4} \times \frac{8}{9} \times \frac{15}{16}$, in lowest terms.

SOLUTION. If you multiply the numerators and denominators you get $\frac{360}{576}$, which is a nuisance to reduce. It is better to use TACTIC B1 and reduce first:

$$\frac{\overset{1}{\cancel{3}}}{4} \times \frac{\overset{1}{\cancel{8}}}{\underset{3}{\cancel{9}}} \times \frac{\overset{5}{\cancel{15}}}{\underset{2}{\cancel{16}}} = \frac{1 \times 1 \times 5}{4 \times 1 \times 2} = \frac{5}{8}$$

When a problem requires you to find a fraction of a number, multiply.

Example 7.

If $\frac{4}{7}$ of the 350 sophomores at Monroe High School are girls, and $\frac{7}{8}$ of them play on a team, how many sophomore girls do <u>not</u> play on a team?

SOLUTION. There are $\frac{4}{7} \times 350 = 200$ sophomore girls.

Of these, $\frac{7}{8} \times 200 = 175$ play on a team. So,

$200 - 175 = \textbf{25}$ do not play on a team.

The ***reciprocal*** of any nonzero number x is that number y such that $xy = 1$. Since $x\left(\frac{1}{x}\right) = 1$, then $\frac{1}{x}$ is the reciprocal of x. Similarly, the reciprocal of the fraction $\frac{a}{b}$ is the fraction $\frac{b}{a}$, since $\frac{a}{b} \cdot \frac{b}{a} = 1$.

KEY FACT B16:

To divide any number by a fraction, multiply that number by the reciprocal of the fraction.

$$20 \div \frac{2}{3} = \frac{20}{1} \times \frac{3}{2} = 30 \qquad \frac{3}{5} \div \frac{2}{3} = \frac{3}{5} \times \frac{3}{2} = \frac{9}{10}$$

$$\sqrt{2} \div \frac{2}{3} = \frac{\sqrt{2}}{1} \times \frac{3}{2} = \frac{3\sqrt{2}}{2}$$

Example 8.

In the meat department of a supermarket, 100 pounds of chopped meat was divided into packages, each of which weighed $\frac{4}{7}$ of a pound. How many packages were there?

SOLUTION. $100 \div \frac{4}{7} = \frac{100}{1} \times \frac{7}{4} = \textbf{175}$

KEY FACT B17:

- **To add or subtract fractions with the same denominator, add or subtract the numerators and keep the denominator:**

$$\frac{4}{9} + \frac{1}{9} = \frac{5}{9} \quad \text{and} \quad \frac{4}{9} - \frac{1}{9} = \frac{3}{9} = \frac{1}{3}$$

- **To add or subtract fractions with different denominators, first rewrite the fractions as equivalent fractions with the same denominators:**

$$\frac{1}{6} + \frac{3}{4} = \frac{2}{12} + \frac{9}{12} = \frac{11}{12}$$

NOTE: The *easiest* common denominator to find is the product of the denominators ($6 \times 4 = 24$, in this example), but the best denominator to use is the ***least common denominator,*** which is the least common multiple (LCM) of the denominators (12, in this case). Using the least common denominator minimizes the amount of reducing that is necessary to express the answer in lowest terms.

KEY FACT B18:

If $\frac{a}{b}$ is the fraction of a whole that satisfies some property, then $1 - \frac{a}{b}$ is the fraction of that whole that does not satisfy it.

Example 9.

In a jar, $\frac{1}{2}$ of the marbles are red, $\frac{1}{4}$ are white, and $\frac{1}{5}$ are blue. What fraction of the marbles are neither red, white, nor blue?

SOLUTION. The red, white, and blue marbles constitute

$$\frac{1}{2} + \frac{1}{4} + \frac{1}{5} = \frac{10}{20} + \frac{5}{20} + \frac{4}{20} = \frac{19}{20}$$

of the total, so

$$1 - \frac{19}{20} = \frac{20}{20} - \frac{19}{20} = \frac{1}{\mathbf{20}}$$

of the marbles are neither red, white, nor blue.

Example 10.

Lindsay ate $\frac{1}{3}$ of a cake and Emily ate $\frac{1}{4}$ of it. What fraction of the cake was still uneaten?

Example 11.

Lindsay ate $\frac{1}{3}$ of a cake and Emily ate $\frac{1}{4}$ of what was left. What fraction of the cake was still uneaten?

CAUTION: Be sure to read questions carefully. In Example 10, Emily ate $\frac{1}{4}$ of the cake. In Example 11, however, she only ate $\frac{1}{4}$ of the $\frac{2}{3}$ that was left after Lindsay had her piece: she ate $\frac{1}{4} \times \frac{2}{3} = \frac{1}{6}$ of the cake.

SOLUTION 10: $\frac{1}{3} + \frac{1}{4} = \frac{4}{12} + \frac{3}{12} = \frac{7}{12}$ of the cake was eaten, and $1 - \frac{7}{12} = \frac{\mathbf{5}}{\mathbf{12}}$ was uneaten.

SOLUTION 11: $\frac{1}{3} + \frac{1}{6} = \frac{2}{6} + \frac{1}{6} = \frac{1}{2}$ of the cake was eaten, and the other $\frac{\mathbf{1}}{\mathbf{2}}$ was uneaten.

Arithmetic Operations with Mixed Numbers

A *mixed number* is a number such as $3\frac{1}{2}$, which consists of an integer followed by a fraction. It is an abbreviation for the *sum* of the number and the fraction; so, $3\frac{1}{2}$ is an abbreviation for $3 + \frac{1}{2}$. Every mixed number can be written as an improper fraction, and every improper fraction can be written as a mixed number:

$$3\frac{1}{2} = 3 + \frac{1}{2} = \frac{3}{1} + \frac{1}{2} = \frac{6}{2} + \frac{1}{2} = \frac{7}{2}$$

and $\quad \frac{7}{2} = \frac{6}{2} + \frac{1}{2} = 3 + \frac{1}{2} = 3\frac{1}{2}$

KEY FACT B19:

1. To write a mixed number $\left(3\frac{1}{2}\right)$ as an improper fraction, multiply the whole number (3) by the denominator (2), add the numerator (1), and write the sum over the denominator (2): $\dfrac{3 \times 2 + 1}{2} = \dfrac{7}{2}$.

2. To write an improper fraction $\left(\dfrac{7}{2}\right)$ as a mixed number, divide the numerator by the denominator; the quotient (3) is the whole number and the remainder (1) is placed over the denominator to form the fractional part $\left(\dfrac{1}{2}\right)$: $3\frac{1}{2}$.

KEY FACT B20:

To add mixed numbers, add the integers and add the fractions:

$$5\frac{1}{4} + 3\frac{2}{3} = (5 + 3) + \left(\frac{1}{4} + \frac{2}{3}\right) = 8 + \left(\frac{3}{12} + \frac{8}{12}\right) =$$

$$8 + \frac{11}{12} = 8\frac{11}{12}$$

KEY FACT B21:

To subtract mixed numbers, subtract the integers and the fractions. However, if the fraction in the second number is greater than the fraction in the first number, you first have to borrow 1 from the integer part. For example, since $\frac{2}{3} > \frac{1}{4}$, we can't subtract $5\frac{1}{4} - 3\frac{2}{3}$ until we borrow 1 from the 5:

$$5\frac{1}{4} = 5 + \frac{1}{4} = (4 + 1) + \frac{1}{4} = 4 + \left(1 + \frac{1}{4}\right) = 4 + \frac{5}{4}$$

Now, you have

$$5\frac{1}{4} - 3\frac{2}{3} = 4\frac{5}{4} - 3\frac{2}{3} = (4 - 3) + \left(\frac{5}{4} - \frac{2}{3}\right) =$$

$$1 + \left(\frac{15}{12} - \frac{8}{12}\right) = 1\frac{7}{12}.$$

KEY FACT B22:

To multiply or divide mixed numbers, change them to improper fractions:

$$1\frac{2}{3} \times 3\frac{1}{4} = \frac{5}{3} \times \frac{13}{4} = \frac{65}{12} = 5\frac{5}{12}.$$

CAUTION: Be aware that $3 \times 5\frac{1}{2}$ is *not* $15\frac{1}{2}$; rather:

$$3 \times 5\frac{1}{2} = 3\left(5 + \frac{1}{2}\right) = 15 + \frac{3}{2} =$$

$$15 + 1\frac{1}{2} = 16\frac{1}{2}.$$

Complex Fractions

A *complex fraction* is a fraction, such as $\dfrac{1+\frac{1}{6}}{2-\frac{3}{4}}$, which

has one or more fractions in its numerator or denominator or both.

KEY FACT B23:

There are two ways to simplify a complex fraction:

- Multiply *every* term in the numerator and denominator by the least common multiple of all the denominators that appear in the fraction.

- Simplify the numerator and the denominator, and then divide.

To simplify $\dfrac{1+\frac{1}{6}}{2-\frac{3}{4}}$, multiply each term by 12, the LCM of

6 and 4:

$$\frac{12(1) + 12\left(\frac{1}{6}\right)}{12(2) - 12\left(\frac{3}{4}\right)} = \frac{12 + 2}{24 - 9} = \frac{14}{15},$$

or write

$$\frac{1+\frac{1}{6}}{2-\frac{3}{4}} = \frac{\frac{7}{6}}{\frac{5}{4}} = \frac{7}{6} \times \frac{4}{5} = \frac{14}{15}.$$

PRACTICE EXERCISES—FRACTIONS AND DECIMALS

Multiple-Choice Questions

1. A biology class has 12 boys and 18 girls. What fraction of the class are boys?

   (A) $\frac{2}{5}$ (B) $\frac{3}{5}$ (C) $\frac{2}{3}$ (D) $\frac{3}{4}$ (E) $\frac{3}{2}$

2. For how many integers, a, between 30 and 40 is it true that $\frac{5}{a}$, $\frac{8}{a}$, and $\frac{13}{a}$ are all in lowest terms?

   (A) 1 (B) 2 (C) 3 (D) 4 (E) 5

3. What fractional part of a week is 98 hours?

   (A) $\frac{7}{24}$ (B) $\frac{24}{98}$ (C) $\frac{1}{2}$ (D) $\frac{4}{7}$ (E) $\frac{7}{12}$

4. What is the value of the product $\frac{5}{5} \times \frac{5}{10} \times \frac{5}{15} \times \frac{5}{20} \times \frac{5}{25}$?

   (A) $\frac{1}{120}$ (B) $\frac{1}{60}$ (C) $\frac{1}{30}$ (D) $\frac{5}{30}$ (E) $\frac{1}{2}$

5. If $\frac{3}{11}$ of a number is 22, what is $\frac{6}{11}$ of that number?

   (A) 6 (B) 11 (C) 12 (D) 33 (E) 44

6. Jason won some goldfish at the state fair. During the first week, $\frac{1}{5}$ of them died, and during the second week, $\frac{3}{8}$ of those still alive at the end of the first week died. What fraction of the original goldfish were still alive after two weeks?

   (A) $\frac{3}{10}$ (B) $\frac{17}{40}$ (C) $\frac{1}{2}$ (D) $\frac{23}{40}$ (E) $\frac{7}{10}$

7. $\frac{5}{8}$ of 24 is equal to $\frac{15}{7}$ of what number?

   (A) 7 (B) 8 (C) 15 (D) $\frac{7}{225}$ (E) $\frac{225}{7}$

8. If $7a = 3$ and $3b = 7$, what is the value of $\frac{a}{b}$?

   (A) $\frac{9}{49}$ (B) $\frac{3}{7}$ (C) 1 (D) $\frac{7}{3}$ (E) $\frac{49}{9}$

9. What is the value of $\dfrac{\frac{7}{9} \times \frac{7}{9}}{\frac{7}{9} + \frac{7}{9} + \frac{7}{9}}$?

   (A) $\frac{7}{27}$ (B) $\frac{2}{3}$ (C) $\frac{7}{9}$ (D) $\frac{9}{7}$ (E) $\frac{3}{2}$

10. Which of the following are greater than x when $x = \dfrac{9}{11}$?

   I. $\dfrac{1}{x}$

   II. $\dfrac{x+1}{x}$

   III. $\dfrac{x+1}{x-1}$

   (A) I only   (B) I and II only   (C) I and III only
   (D) II and III only   (E) I, II, and III

11. One day at Lincoln High School, $\dfrac{1}{12}$ of the

   students were absent, and $\dfrac{1}{5}$ of those present went
   on a field trip. If the number of students staying in
   school that day was 704, how many students are
   enrolled at Lincoln High?

   (A) 840   (B) 960   (C) 1080   (D) 1600
   (E) 3520

12. If $a = 0.87$, which of the following are less than a?

   I. $\sqrt{a}$

   II. a^2

   III. $\dfrac{1}{a}$

   (A) None   (B) I only   (C) II only   (D) III only
   (E) II and III only

13. For what value of x is
   $\dfrac{(34.56)(7.89)}{x} = (.3456)(78.9)$?

   (A) .001   (B) .01   (C) .1   (D) 10   (E) 100

14. If $A = \{1, 2, 3\}$, $B = \{2, 3, 4\}$, and C is the set consisting of all the fractions whose numerators are in A and whose denominators are in B, what is the product of all of the numbers in C?

   (A) $\dfrac{1}{64}$ (B) $\dfrac{1}{48}$ (C) $\dfrac{1}{24}$ (D) $\dfrac{1}{12}$ (E) $\dfrac{1}{2}$

15. For the final step in a calculation, Ezra accidentally divided by 1000 instead of multiplying by 1000. What should he do to his incorrect answer to correct it?

   (A) Multiply it by 1000.
   (B) Multiply it by 100,000.
   (C) Multiply it by 1,000,000.
   (D) Square it.
   (E) Double it.

Quantitative Comparison Questions

Column A	Column B

16.

$\dfrac{5}{13}$ of 47	$\dfrac{47}{13}$ of 5

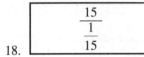
$$x = -\dfrac{2}{3} \text{ and } y = \dfrac{3}{5}$$

17.

xy	$\dfrac{x}{y}$

18.

$\dfrac{15}{\frac{1}{15}}$	1

Judy needed 8 pounds of chicken. At the supermarket, the only packages available weighed $\dfrac{3}{4}$ of a pound each.

19.

The number of packages Judy needed to buy	11

20.

$\dfrac{11}{12}$ of $\dfrac{13}{14}$	$\dfrac{14}{15}$

$$a \nabla b = \dfrac{a}{b} + \dfrac{b}{a}$$

21.

$3 \nabla 4$	$\dfrac{1}{2} \nabla \dfrac{2}{3}$

22.

$\dfrac{100}{2^{100}}$	$\dfrac{100}{3^{100}}$

23.

$\left(-\dfrac{1}{2}\right)\left(-\dfrac{3}{4}\right)\left(-\dfrac{5}{6}\right)\left(-\dfrac{7}{8}\right)$	$\left(-\dfrac{3}{7}\right)\left(-\dfrac{5}{9}\right)\left(-\dfrac{7}{11}\right)$

$$a = \dfrac{1}{2} \text{ and } b = \dfrac{1}{3}$$

24.

$\dfrac{a}{b}$	$\dfrac{b}{a}$

25.

$\left(\dfrac{3}{11}\right)^2$	$\sqrt{\dfrac{3}{11}}$

Answer Key

1. **A**	6. **C**	11. **B**	16. **C**	21. **C**
2. **C**	7. **A**	12. **C**	17. **A**	22. **A**
3. **E**	8. **A**	13. **D**	18. **A**	23. **A**
4. **A**	9. **A**	14. **A**	19. **C**	24. **A**
5. **E**	10. **B**	15. **C**	20. **B**	25. **B**

Answer Explanations

1. **A.** The class has 30 students, of whom 12 are boys. So, the boys make up $\frac{12}{30} = \frac{2}{5}$ of the class.

2. **C.** If a is even, then $\frac{8}{a}$ is *not* in lowest terms, since both a and 8 are divisible by 2. Therefore, the only possibilities are 31, 33, 35, 37, and 39; but $\frac{5}{35} = \frac{1}{7}$ and $\frac{13}{39} = \frac{1}{3}$, so only 3 integers—31, 33, and 37—satisfy the given condition.

3. **E.** There are 24 hours in a day and 7 days in a week, so there are $24 \times 7 = 168$ hours in a week: $\frac{98}{168} = \frac{7}{12}$.

4. **A.** Reduce each fraction and multiply:
$$1 \times \frac{1}{2} \times \frac{1}{3} \times \frac{1}{4} \times \frac{1}{5} = \frac{1}{120}.$$

5. **E.** Don't bother writing an equation for this one; just think. We know that $\frac{3}{11}$ of the number is 22, and $\frac{6}{11}$ of a number is twice as much as $\frac{3}{11}$ of it: $2 \times 22 = 44$.

6. **C.** The *algebra* way is to let x = the number of goldfish Jason won. During the first week $\frac{1}{5}x$ died, so $\frac{4}{5}x$ were still alive. During week two, $\frac{3}{8}$ of them died and $\frac{5}{8}$ of them survived:
$$\left(\frac{5}{8}\right)\left(\frac{4}{5}x\right) = \frac{1}{2}x.$$

On the GRE, the best way is to assume that the original number of goldfish was 40, the LCM of the denominators (see TACTIC 3, Chapter 12).

Then, 8 died the first week $\left(\frac{1}{5}$ of $40\right)$, and 12 of the 32 survivors $\left(\frac{3}{8}$ of $32\right)$ died the second

week. In all, $8 + 12 = 20$ died; the other 20 $\left(\frac{1}{2}$ the original number$\right)$ were still alive.

7. **A.** If x is the number, then $\frac{15}{7}x = \frac{5}{8} \times 24^{3} = 15$.

So, $\frac{15}{7}x = 15$, which means (dividing by 15) that $\frac{1}{7}x = 1$, and so $x = 7$.

8. **A.** $7a = 3$ and $3b = 7 \Rightarrow a = \frac{3}{7}$ and $b = \frac{7}{3} \Rightarrow$
$$\frac{a}{b} = \frac{3}{7} \div \frac{7}{3} = \frac{3}{7} \times \frac{3}{7} = \frac{9}{49}.$$

9. **A.** Don't start by doing the arithmetic. This is just
$$\frac{(a)(a)}{a + a + a} = \frac{(a)(a)}{3a} = \frac{a}{3}.$$

Now, replacing a with $\frac{7}{9}$ gives
$$\frac{7}{9} \div 3 = \frac{7}{9} \times \frac{1}{3} = \frac{7}{27}.$$

10. **B.** The reciprocal of a positive number less than 1 is greater than 1 (I is true). $\frac{x+1}{x} = 1 + \frac{1}{x}$, which is greater than 1 (II is true). Since $\frac{9}{11} + 1$ is positive and $\frac{9}{11} - 1$ is negative, when $x = \frac{9}{11}$, $\frac{x+1}{x-1} < 0$ and, therefore, less than x (III is false).

11. **B.** If s is the number of students enrolled, $\frac{1}{12}s$ is the number who were absent, and $\frac{11}{12}s$ is the number who were present. Since $\frac{1}{5}$ of them went on a field trip, $\frac{4}{5}$ of them stayed in school. Therefore,
$$704 = \frac{4}{5} \times \frac{11}{12}s = \frac{11}{15}s \Rightarrow$$
$$s = 704 \div \frac{11}{15} = 704 \times \frac{15}{11} = 960.$$

12. **C.** Since $a < 1$, $\sqrt{a} > a$ (I is false).
Since $a < 1$, $a^2 < a$ (II is true).
The reciprocal of a positive number less than 1 is greater than 1 (III is false).

13. **D.** There are two easy ways to do this. The first is to see that $(34.56)(7.89)$ has 4 decimal places, whereas $(.3456)(78.9)$ has 5, so the numerator has to be divided by 10. The second is to round off and calculate mentally: since $30 \times 8 = 240$, and $.3 \times 80 = 24$, we must divide by 10.

14. **A.** Nine fractions are formed:
$$\frac{1}{2}, \frac{1}{3}, \frac{1}{4}, \frac{2}{2}, \frac{2}{3}, \frac{2}{4}, \frac{3}{2}, \frac{3}{3}, \frac{3}{4}.$$

Note that although some of these fractions are equivalent, we do have nine distinct fractions. When you multiply, the three 2s and the three 3s in the numerators cancel with the three 2s and three 3s in the denominators. So, the numerator is 1 and the denominator is $4 \times 4 \times 4 = 64$.

15. **C.** Multiplying Ezra's incorrect answer by 1000 would undo the final division he made. At that point he should have multiplied by 1000. So, to correct his error, he should multiply again by 1000. In all, Ezra should multiply his incorrect answer by $1000 \times 1000 = 1,000,000$.

16. **C.** Each column equals $\dfrac{5 \times 47}{13}$.

17. **A.** Column A: $-\dfrac{2}{3} \times \dfrac{3}{5} = -\dfrac{2}{5}$.

Column B: $-\dfrac{2}{3} \div \dfrac{3}{5} = -\dfrac{2}{3} \times \dfrac{5}{3} = -\dfrac{10}{9}$.

Finally, $\dfrac{10}{9} > \dfrac{2}{5} \Rightarrow -\dfrac{10}{9} < -\dfrac{2}{5}$.

18. **A.** Column A: $\dfrac{15}{\frac{1}{15}} = 15 \times 15 = 225$.

19. **C.** $8 \div \dfrac{3}{4} = 8 \times \dfrac{4}{3} = \dfrac{32}{3} = 10\dfrac{2}{3}$. Since 10 packages wouldn't be enough, she had to buy 11. (10 packages would weigh only $7\dfrac{1}{2}$ pounds.)

20. **B.** You don't need to multiply on this one: since $\dfrac{11}{12} < 1$, $\dfrac{11}{12}$ of $\dfrac{13}{14}$ is less than $\dfrac{13}{14}$, which is already less than $\dfrac{14}{15}$.

21. **C.** Column B is the sum of 2 complex fractions:
$$\frac{\frac{1}{2}}{\frac{2}{3}} + \frac{\frac{2}{3}}{\frac{1}{2}}.$$

Simplifying each complex fraction, by multiplying numerator and denominator by 6, or treating these as the quotient of 2 fractions, we get $\dfrac{3}{4} + \dfrac{4}{3}$, which is exactly the value of Column A.

22. **A.** When two fractions have the same numerator, the one with the smaller denominator is bigger, and $2^{100} < 3^{100}$.

23. **A.** Since Column A is the product of 4 negative numbers, it is positive, and so is greater than Column B, which, being the product of 3 negative numbers, is negative.

24. **A.** Column A: $\dfrac{1}{2} \div \dfrac{1}{3} = \dfrac{1}{2} \times \dfrac{3}{1} = \dfrac{3}{2}$. Since Column B is the reciprocal of Column A, Column B $= \dfrac{2}{3}$.

25. **B.** If $0 < x < 1$, then $x^2 < x < \sqrt{x}$. In this question, $x = \dfrac{3}{11}$.

14-C. PERCENTS

The word *percent* means hundredth. We use the symbol "%" to express the word "percent." For example, "17 percent" means "17 hundredths," and can be written with a % symbol, as a fraction, or as a decimal:
$$17\% = \frac{17}{100} = 0.17.$$

KEY FACT C1:

- **To convert a percent to a decimal, drop the % symbol and move the decimal point two places to the left, adding 0s if necessary. (Remember that we assume that there is a decimal point to the right of any whole number.)**

- **To convert a percent to a fraction, drop the % symbol, write the number over 100, and reduce.**

$$25\% = 0.25 = \frac{25}{100} = \frac{1}{4} \qquad 100\% = 1.00 = \frac{100}{100}$$

$$12.5\% = 0.125 = \frac{12.5}{100} = \frac{125}{1000} = \frac{1}{8}$$

$$1\% = 0.01 = \frac{1}{100} \qquad \frac{1}{2}\% = 0.5\% = 0.005 = \frac{.5}{100} = \frac{1}{200}$$

$$250\% = 2.50 = \frac{250}{100} = \frac{5}{2}$$

KEY FACT C2:

- **To convert a decimal to a percent, move the decimal point two places to the right, adding 0s if necessary, and add the % symbol.**

- **To convert a fraction to a percent, first convert the fraction to a decimal, then convert the decimal to a percent, as indicated above.**

$0.375 = 37.5\%$ $0.3 = 30\%$ $1.25 = 125\%$ $10 = 1000\%$

$\frac{3}{4} = 0.75 = 75\%$ $\frac{1}{3} = 0.33333\ldots = 33.333\ldots\% = 33\frac{1}{3}\%$

$\frac{1}{5} = 0.2 = 20\%$

You should be familiar with the following basic conversions:

$\frac{1}{2} = 50\%$	$\frac{1}{10} = 10\%$	$\frac{6}{10} = \frac{3}{5} = 60\%$
$\frac{1}{3} = 33\frac{1}{3}\%$	$\frac{2}{10} = \frac{1}{5} = 20\%$	$\frac{7}{10} = 70\%$
$\frac{2}{3} = 66\frac{2}{3}\%$	$\frac{3}{10} = 30\%$	$\frac{8}{10} = \frac{4}{5} = 80\%$
$\frac{1}{4} = 25\%$	$\frac{4}{10} = \frac{2}{5} = 40\%$	$\frac{9}{10} = 90\%$
$\frac{3}{4} = 75\%$	$\frac{5}{10} = \frac{1}{2} = 50\%$	$\frac{10}{10} = 1 = 100\%$

Knowing the above conversions can help solve many problems more quickly. For example, the fastest way to find 25% of 32 is not to multiply 32 by 0.25; rather, it is to know that $25\% = \frac{1}{4}$, and that $\frac{1}{4}$ of 32 is 8.

Many questions involving percents can actually be answered more quickly in your head than by using paper and pencil. Since $10\% = \frac{1}{10}$, to take 10% of a number, just divide by 10 by moving the decimal point one place to the left: 10% of 60 is 6. Also, since 5% is half of 10%, then 5% of 60 is 3 (half of 6); and since 30% is 3 times 10%, then 30% of 60 is 18 (3 × 6).

Practice doing this, because improving your ability to do mental math will add valuable points to your score on the GRE.

Solving Percent Problems

Consider the following three questions:

   (i) What is 45% of 200?
   (ii) 90 is 45% of what number?
   (iii) 90 is what percent of 200?

The arithmetic needed to answer each of these questions is very easy, but unless you set a question up properly, you won't know whether you should multiply or divide. In each case, there is one unknown, which we will call x. Now just translate each sentence, replacing "is" by "=" and the unknown by x.

   (i) $x = 45\%$ of $200 \Rightarrow x = .45 \times 200 = 90$
   (ii) $90 = 45\%$ of $x \Rightarrow 90 = .45x \Rightarrow x = 90 \div .45 = 200$
   (iii) $90 = x\%$ of $200 \Rightarrow 90 = \frac{x}{100}(200) \Rightarrow 90 = 2x \Rightarrow x = 45$

Example 1.

Charlie gave 20% of his baseball cards to Kenne and 15% to Paulie. If he still had 520 cards, how many did he have originally?

(A) 555   (B) 700   (C) 800   (D) 888   (E) 1000

SOLUTION. Originally, Charlie had 100% of the cards (all of them). Since he gave away 35% of them, he has $100\% - 35\% = 65\%$ of them left. So, 520 is 65% of what number?

$$520 = .65x \Rightarrow x = 520 \div .65 = \textbf{800 (C)}.$$

Example 2.

After Ruth gave 110 baseball cards to Alison and 75 to Susanna, she still had 315 left. What percent of her cards did Ruth give away?

(A) 25%   (B) $33\frac{1}{3}\%$ (C) 37%   (D) 40%
(E) 50%

SOLUTION. Ruth gave away a total of 185 cards and had 315 left. Therefore, she started with $185 + 315 = 500$ cards. So, 185 is what percent of 500?

$$185 = \frac{x}{100}(500) \Rightarrow 5x = 185 \Rightarrow x = 185 \div 5 = \textbf{37}$$

Ruth gave away 37% of her cards, **(C)**.

Since percent means hundredth, the easiest number to use in any percent problem is 100:

$$a\% \text{ of } 100 = \frac{a}{100} \times 100 = a.$$

KEY FACT C3:

For any positive number a: $a\%$ of 100 is a.

For example: 91.2% of 100 is 91.2; 300% of 100 is 300; and $\frac{1}{2}\%$ of 100 is $\frac{1}{2}$.

In any problem involving percents, use the number 100 (It doesn't matter whether or not 100 is a realistic number—a country can have a population of 100; an apple can cost $100; a man can run 100 miles per hour.)

Example 3.

In 1985 the populations of town A and town B were the same. From 1985 to 1995 the population of town A increased by 60% while the population of town B decreased by 60%. In 1995, the population of town B was what percent of the population of town A?

(A) 25%　(B) 36%　(C) 40%　(D) 60%
　　　(E) 120%

SOLUTION. *On the GRE, do not waste time with a nice algebraic solution.* Simply, assume that in 1985 the population of each town was 100. Then, since 60% of 100 is 60, in 1995, the populations were 100 + 60 = 160 and 100 − 60 = 40. So, in 1995, town B's population was $\frac{40}{160} = \frac{1}{4}$ = **25**% of town A's (**A**).

Since a% of b is $\frac{a}{100} \times b = \frac{ab}{100}$, and b% of a is

$\frac{b}{100} \times a = \frac{ba}{100}$, we have the result shown in KEY FACT C4.

KEY FACT C4:

For any positive numbers a and b: a% of $b = b$% of a.

KEY FACT C4 often comes up on the GRE in quantitative comparison questions: Which is greater, 13% of 87 or 87% of 13? Don't multiply—they're equal.

Percent Increase and Decrease

KEY FACT C5:

• The *percent increase* of a quantity is
$$\frac{\text{actual increase}}{\text{original amount}} \times 100\%.$$

• The *percent decrease* of a quantity is
$$\frac{\text{actual decrease}}{\text{original amount}} \times 100\%.$$

For example:

• If the price of a lamp goes from $80 to $100, the actual increase is $20, and the percent increase is
$\frac{20}{80} \times 100\% = \frac{1}{4} \times 100\% = 25\%.$

• If a $100 lamp is on sale for $80, the actual decrease in price is $20, and the percent decrease is
$\frac{20}{100} \times 100\% = 20\%.$

Notice that the percent increase in going from 80 to 100 is not the same as the percent decrease in going from 100 to 80.

KEY FACT C6:

If $a < b$, the percent increase in going from a to b is *always* greater than the percent decrease in going from b to a.

KEY FACT C7:

• To increase a number by k%, multiply it by $(1 + k\%)$.

• To decrease a number by k%, multiply it by $(1 − k\%)$.

For example:

• The value of a $1600 investment after a 25% increase is $1600(1 + 25%) = $1600(1.25) = $2000.

• If the investment then loses 25% of its value, it is worth $2000(1 − 25%) = $2000(.75) = $1500.

Note that, after a 25% increase followed by a 25% decrease, the value is $1500, $100 *less* than the original amount.

KEY FACT C8:

An increase of k% followed by a decrease of k% is equal to a decrease of k% followed by an increase of k%, and is *always* less than the original value. The original value is never regained.

Column A	Column B

Example 4.

Store B always sells CDs at 60% off the list price. Store A sells its CDs at 40% off the list price, but often runs a special sale during which it reduces its prices by 20%.

The price of a CD when it is on sale at store A	The price of the same CD at store B

SOLUTION. Assume the list price of the CD is $100. Store B always sells the CD for $40 ($60 off the list price). Store A normally sells the CD for $60 ($40 off the list price), but on sale reduces its price by 20%. Since 20% of 60 is 12, the sale price is $48 ($60 − $12). The price is greater at Store A.

Notice that a decrease of 40% followed by a decrease of 20% is not the same as a single decrease of 60%; it is less. In fact, a decrease of 40% followed by a decrease of 30% wouldn't even be as much as a single decrease of 60%.

KEY FACT C9:

- A decrease of $a\%$ followed by a decrease of $b\%$ *always* results in a smaller decrease than a single decrease of $(a + b)\%$.

- An increase of $a\%$ followed by an increase of $b\%$ *always* results in a larger increase than a single increase of $(a + b)\%$.

- An increase (or decrease) of $a\%$ followed by another increase (or decrease) of $a\%$ is *never* the same as a single increase (or decrease) of $2a\%$.

Column A	Column B

Example 5.

Sally and Heidi were both hired in January at the same salary. Sally got two 40% raises, one in July and another in November. Heidi got one 90% raise in October.

Sally's salary at the end of the year	Heidi's salary at the end of the year

---

SOLUTION. Since this is a percent problem, assume their salaries were $100. Column A: Sally's salary rose to 100(1.40) = 140, and then to 140(1.40) = $196. Column B: Heidi's salary rose to 100(1.90) = $190. Column **A** is greater.

Example 6.

In January, the value of a stock increased by 25%, and in February, it decreased by 20%. How did the value of the stock at the end of February compare with its value at the beginning of January?

(A) It was less.
(B) It was the same.
(C) It was 5% greater.
(D) It was more than 5% greater.
(E) It cannot be determined from the information given.

SOLUTION. Assume that at the beginning of January the stock was worth $100. Then at the end of January it was worth $125. Since 20% of 125 is 25, during February its value decreased from $125 to $100. The answer is **B**.

KEY FACT C10:

- If a number is the result of increasing another number by $k\%$, to find the original number, divide by $(1 + k\%)$.

- If a number is the result of decreasing another number by $k\%$, to find the original number, divide it by $(1 - k\%)$.

For example, if the population of a town in 1990 was 3000, and this represents an increase of 20% since 1980, to find the population in 1980, divide 3000 by $(1 + 20\%)$: 3000 ÷ 1.20 = 2500.

Example 7.

From 1989 to 1990, the number of applicants to a college increased 15% to 5060. How many applicants were there in 1989?

(A) 759   (B) 4301   (C) 4400   (D) 5819
   (E) 5953

SOLUTION. The number of applicants in 1989 was 5060 ÷ 1.15 = **4400 (C)**.

CAUTION. Percents over 100%, which come up most often on questions involving percent increases, are often confusing for students. First of all, be sure you understand that 100% of a number is that number, 200% of a number is 2 times the number, and 1000% of a number is 10 times the number. If the value of an investment goes from $1000 to $5000, it is now worth 5 times, or 500%, as much as it was originally; but there has only been a *400%* increase in value:

$$\frac{\text{actual increase}}{\text{original amount}} \times 100\% = \frac{4000}{1000} \times 100\% = 4 \times 100\% = 400\%.$$

Example 8.

The population of a country doubled every 10 years from 1960 to 1990. What was the percent increase in population during this time?

(A) 200%   (B) 300%   (C) 700%   (D) 800%
   (E) 1000%

SOLUTION. The population doubled three times (once from 1960 to 1970, again from 1970 to 1980, and a third time from 1980 to 1990). Assume that the population was originally 100. Then it increased from 100 to 200 to 400 to 800. So the population in 1990 was 8 times the population in 1960, but this was an increase of 700 people, or **700**% **(C)**.

PRACTICE EXERCISES—PERCENTS

Multiple-Choice Questions

1. If 25 students took an exam and 4 of them failed, what percent of them passed?

   (A) 4%   (B) 21%   (C) 42%   (D) 84%   (E) 96%

2. Amanda bought a $60 sweater on sale at 5% off. How much did she pay, including 5% sales tax?

   (A) $54.15   (B) $57.00   (C) $57.75   (D) $59.85   (E) $60.00

3. What is 10% of 20% of 30%?

   (A) 0.006%   (B) 0.6%   (C) 6%   (D) 60%   (E) 6000%

4. If c is a positive number, 500% of c is what percent of $500c$?

   (A) 0.01   (B) 0.1   (C) 1   (D) 10   (E) 100

5. What percent of 50 is b?

   (A) $\dfrac{b}{50}$ (B) $\dfrac{b}{2}$ (C) $\dfrac{50}{b}$ (D) $\dfrac{2}{b}$ (E) $2b$

6. 8 is $\dfrac{1}{3}$% of what number?

   (A) .24   (B) 2.4   (C) 24   (D) 240   (E) 2400

7. During his second week on the job, Mario earned $110. This represented a 25% increase over his earnings of the previous week. How much did he earn during his first week of work?

   (A) $82.50   (B) $85.00   (C) $88.00   (D) $137.50   (E) $146.67

8. At Bernie's Bargain Basement everything is sold for 20% less than the price marked. If Bernie buys radios for $80, what price should he mark them if he wants to make a 20% profit on his cost?

   (A) $96   (B) $100   (C) $112   (D) $120   (E) $125

9. Mrs. Fisher was planning on depositing a certain amount of money each month into a vacation fund. She then decided not to make any contributions during June and July. To make the same annual contribution that she had originally planned, by what percent should she increase her monthly deposits?

   (A) $16\dfrac{2}{3}$%   (B) 20%   (C) 25%   (D) $33\dfrac{1}{3}$%

   (E) It cannot be determined from the information given.

10. If 1 micron = 10,000 angstroms, then 100 angstroms is what percent of 10 microns?

    (A) 0.0001%   (B) 0.001%   (C) 0.01%   (D) 0.1%   (E) 1%

11. The price of a loaf of bread was increased by 20%. How many loaves can be purchased for the amount of money that used to buy 300 loaves?

    (A) 240   (B) 250   (C) 280   (D) 320   (E) 360

12. There are twice as many girls as boys in an English class. If 30% of the girls and 45% of the boys have already handed in their book reports, what percent of the students have not yet handed in their reports?

    (A) 25%   (B) 35%   (C) 50%   (D) 65%   (E) 75%

13. An art dealer bought a Ming vase for $1000 and later sold it for $10,000. By what percent did the value of the vase increase?

    (A) 10%   (B) 90%   (C) 100%   (D) 900%   (E) 1000%

14. During a sale a clerk was putting a new price tag on each item. On one jacket, he accidentally raised the price by 15% instead of lowering the price by 15%. As a result the price on the tag was $45 too high. What was the original price of the jacket?

    (A) $60   (B) $75   (C) $90   (D) $105   (E) $150

15. On a test consisting of 80 questions, Eve answered 75% of the first 60 questions correctly. What percent of the other 20 questions does she need to answer correctly for her grade on the entire exam to be 80%?

    (A) 85%   (B) 87.5%   (C) 90%   (D) 95%   (E) 100%

Quantitative Comparison Questions

	Column A	Column B
16.	400% of 3	300% of 4

n% of 25 is 50

	Column A	Column B
17.	50% of n	75

	Column A	Column B
18.	The price of a television when it is on sale at 25% off	The price of that television when it's on sale at $25 off

Column A	Column B

The price of cellular phone 1 is 20% more than the price of cellular phone 2.

19.

The price of cellular phone 1 when it is on sale at 20% off	The price of cellular phone 2

20.

$\frac{2}{3}$% of $\frac{3}{4}$	$\frac{3}{4}$% of $\frac{2}{3}$

21.

a% of $\frac{1}{b}$	b% of $\frac{1}{a}$

Bank A pays 5% interest on its savings accounts.
Bank B pays 4% interest on its savings accounts.

22.

Percent by which bank B would have to raise its interest rate to match bank A	20%

Column A	Column B

A solution that is 20% sugar is made sweeter by doubling the amount of sugar.

23.

The percent of sugar in the new solution	40%

b is an integer greater than 1,
and b equals n% of b^2

24.

n	50

After Ali gave Lior 50% of her money,
she had 20% as much as he did.

25.

75% of the amount Lior had originally	150% of the amount Ali had originally

Answer Key

1. **D**	6. **E**	11. **B**	16. **C**	21. **D**
2. **D**	7. **C**	12. **D**	17. **A**	22. **A**
3. **B**	8. **D**	13. **D**	18. **D**	23. **B**
4. **C**	9. **B**	14. **E**	19. **B**	24. **D**
5. **E**	10. **D**	15. **D**	20. **C**	25. **C**

Answer Explanations

1. **D.** If 4 students failed, then the other $25 - 4 = 21$ students passed, and $\frac{21}{25} = \frac{84}{100} = .84 = 84\%$.

2. **D.** Since 5% of 60 is 3, Amanda saved $3, and thus paid $57 for the sweater. She then had to pay 5% sales tax on the $57: $.05 \times 57 = 2.85$, so the total cost was $57 + \$2.85 = \$59.85$.

3. **B.** 10% of 20% of 30% = $.10 \times .20 \times .30 = .006 = .6\%$.

4. **C.** 500% of $c = 5c$, which is 1% of $500c$.

5. **E.** $b = \frac{x}{\cancel{100}_{2}}(\cancel{50}^{1}) \Rightarrow b = \frac{x}{2} \Rightarrow x = 2b$.

6. **E.** $8 = \frac{\frac{1}{3}}{100}x = \frac{1}{300}x \Rightarrow x = 8 \times 300 = 2400$.

7. **C.** To find Mario's earnings during his first week, divide his earnings from the second week by 1.25: $110 \div 1.25 = 88$.

8. **D.** Since 20% of 80 is 16, Bernie wants to get $96 for each radio he sells. What price should the radios be marked so that after a 20% discount, the customer will pay $96? If x represents the marked price, then
$.80x = 96 \Rightarrow x = 96 \div .80 = 120.$

9. **B.** Assume that Mrs. Fisher was going to contribute $100 each month, for an annual total of

$1200. Having decided not to contribute for 2 months, the $1200 will have to be paid in 10 monthly deposits of $120 each. This is an increase of $20, and a percent increase of

$$\frac{\text{actual increase}}{\text{original amount}} = \frac{20}{100} = 20\%.$$

10. D.   1 micron = 10,000 angstroms $\Rightarrow$ 10 microns = 100,000 angstroms; dividing both sides by 1000, we get

$$100 \text{ angstroms} = \frac{1}{1000} \text{ (10 microns)};$$

and $\dfrac{1}{1000} = .001 = 0.1\%.$

11. B.   Assume that a loaf of bread used to cost $1 and that now it costs $1.20 (20% more). Then 300 loaves of bread used to cost $300. How many loaves costing $1.20 each can be bought for $300? $300 \div 1.20 = 250.$

12. D.   Assume that there are 100 boys and 200 girls in the class. Then, 45 boys (45% of 100) and 60 girls (30% of 200), have handed in their reports. So 105 of the 300 students have handed them in, and $300 - 105 = 195$ have not handed them in. What percent of 300 is 195?
$$\frac{195}{300} = .65 = 65\%.$$

13. D.   The increase in the value of the vase was $9,000. So the percent increase is
$$\frac{\text{actual increase}}{\text{original cost}} = \frac{9000}{1000} = 9 = 900\%.$$

14. E.   If p represents the original price, the jacket was priced at $1.15p$ instead of $.85p$. Since this was a $45 difference,
$$45 = 1.15p - .85p = .30p \Rightarrow$$
$$p = 45 \div .30 = \$150.$$

15. D.   To earn a grade of 80% on the entire exam, Eve needs to correctly answer 64 questions (80% of 80). So far, she has answered 45 questions correctly (75% of 60). Therefore, on the last 20 questions she needs $64 - 45 = 19$ correct answers; and $\dfrac{19}{20} = 95\%.$

16. C.   Column A: 400% of 3 = $4 \times 3 = 12.$
Column B: 300% of 4 = $3 \times 4 = 12.$

17. A.   Since $n\%$ of 25 is 50, then 25% of n is also 50, and 50% of n is twice as much: 100. If you don't see that, just solve for n:

$$\frac{n}{100} \times 25 = 50 \Rightarrow \frac{n}{4} = 50 \Rightarrow n = 200 \Rightarrow$$

50% of $n = 100.$

18. D.   A 25% discount on a $10 television is much less than $25, whereas a 25% discount on a $1000 television is much more than $25. (They would be equal only if the regular price of the television were $100.)

19. B.   Assume that the price of cellular phone 2 is $100; then the price of cellular phone 1 is $120, and on sale at 20% off it costs $24 less: $96.

20. C.   For *any* numbers a and b: $a\%$ of b is equal to $b\%$ of a.

21. D.

Column A	Column B
$a\%$ of $\dfrac{1}{b}$	$b\%$ of $\dfrac{1}{a}$
$\dfrac{a}{100} \times \dfrac{1}{b} = \dfrac{a}{100b}$	$\dfrac{b}{100} \times \dfrac{1}{a} = \dfrac{b}{100a}$

Multiply by 100: $\dfrac{a}{b}$ $\dfrac{b}{a}$

The columns are equal if a and b are equal, and unequal otherwise.

22. A.   Bank B would have to increase its rate from 4% to 5%, an actual increase of 1%. This represents a percent increase of
$$\frac{1\%}{4\%} \times 100\% = 25\%.$$

23. B.   Assume a vat contains 100 ounces of a solution, of which 20% or 20 ounces is sugar (the remaining 80 ounces being water). If the amount of sugar is doubled, there would be 40 ounces of sugar and 80 ounces of water. The sugar will then comprise
$$\frac{40}{120} = \frac{1}{3} = 33\frac{1}{3} \% \text{ of the solution.}$$

24. D.   If $b = 2$, then $b^2 = 4$, and 2 is 50% of 4; in this case, the columns are equal. If $b = 4$, $b^2 = 16$, and 4 is not 50% of 16; in this case, the columns are not equal.

25. C.   Avoid the algebra and just assume Ali started with $100. After giving Lior $50, she had $50 left, which was 20% or one-fifth of what he had. So, Lior had $5 \times \$50 = \$250$, which means that originally he had $200.

Column A: 75% of $200 = $150.

Column B: 150% of $100 = $150.

The columns are equal.

14-D. RATIOS AND PROPORTIONS

A *ratio* is a fraction that compares two quantities that are measured in the same units. The first quantity is the numerator and the second quantity is the denominator.

For example, if there are 4 boys and 16 girls on the debate team, we say that the ratio of the number of boys to the number of girls on the team is 4 to 16, or $\frac{4}{16}$. This is often written 4:16. Since a ratio is just a fraction, it can be reduced or converted to a decimal or a percent. The following are all different ways to express the same ratio:

$$4 \text{ to } 16 \quad 4:16 \quad \frac{4}{16} \qquad 2 \text{ to } 8 \quad 2:8 \quad \frac{2}{8}$$

$$1 \text{ to } 4 \quad 1:4 \quad \frac{1}{4} \qquad\qquad 0.25 \quad 25\%$$

> CAUTION: Saying that the ratio of boys to girls on the team is 1:4 does *not* mean that $\frac{1}{4}$ of the team members are boys. It means that for each boy on the team there are 4 girls; so for every 5 members of the team, there are 4 girls and 1 boy. Boys, therefore, make up $\frac{1}{5}$ of the team, and girls $\frac{4}{5}$.

KEY FACT D1:

If a set of objects is divided into two groups in the ratio of ***a:b***, then the first group contains $\frac{a}{a+b}$ of the objects and the second group contains $\frac{b}{a+b}$ of the objects.

Example 1.

Last year, the ratio of the number of tennis matches that Central College's women's team won to the number of matches they lost was 7:3. What percent of their matches did the team win?

SOLUTION. The team won $\frac{7}{7+3} = \frac{7}{10} = \textbf{70\%}$ of their matches.

Example 2.

If 45% of the students at a college are male, what is the ratio of male students to female students?

Reminder: In problems involving percents the best number to use is 100.

SOLUTION. Assume that there are 100 students. Then 45 of them are male, and 100 − 45 = 55 of them are female. So, the ratio of males to females is $= \frac{45}{55} = \frac{9}{11}$.

If we know how many boys and girls there are in a club, then, clearly, we know not only the ratio of boys to girls, but several other ratios too. For example, if the club has 7 boys and 3 girls: the ratio of boys to girls is $\frac{7}{3}$, the ratio of girls to boys is $\frac{3}{7}$, the ratio of boys to members is $\frac{7}{10}$, the ratio of members to girls is $\frac{10}{3}$, and so on.

However, if we know a ratio, we *cannot* determine how many objects there are. For example, if a jar contains only red and blue marbles, and if the ratio of red marbles to blue marbles is 3:5, there *may* be 3 red marbles and 5 blue marbles, but *not necessarily*. There may be 300 red marbles and 500 blue ones, since the ratio 300:500 reduces to 3:5. In the same way, all of the following are possibilities for the distribution of marbles.

Red	6	12	33	51	150	3000	**3x**
Blue	10	20	55	85	250	5000	**5x**

The important thing to observe is that the number of red marbles can be *any* multiple of 3, as long as the number of blue marbles is the *same* multiple of 5.

KEY FACT D2:

If two numbers are in the ratio of ***a:b***, then for some number ***x***, the first number is ***ax*** and the second number is ***bx***. If the ratio is in lowest terms, and if the quantities must be integers, then ***x*** is also an integer.

Tactic

D1

In any ratio problem, write the letter *x* after each number and use some given information to solve for *x*.

Example 3.

If the ratio of men to women in a particular dormitory is 5:3, which of the following could not be the number of residents in the dormitory?

(A) 24   (B) 40   (C) 96   (D) 150   (E) 224

SOLUTION. If 5*x* and 3*x* are the number of men and women in the dormitory, respectively, then the number of residents in the dormitory is 5*x* + 3*x* = 8*x*. So, the number of students must be a multiple of 8. Of the five choices, only **150 (D)** is not divisible by 8.

Note: Assume that the ratio of the number of pounds of cole slaw to the number of pounds of potato salad consumed in the dormitory's cafeteria was 5:3. Then, it is possible that a total of exactly 150 pounds was eaten:

93.75 pounds of cole slaw and 56.25 pounds of potato salad. In Example 3, 150 wasn't possible because there had to be a *whole* number of men and women.

Example 4.

The measures of the two acute angles in a right triangle are in the ratio of 5:13. What is the measure of the larger angle?

(A) 25°   (B) 45°   (C) 60°   (D) 65°   (E) 75°

SOLUTION: Let the measure of the smaller angle be $5x$ and the measure of the larger angle be $13x$. Since the sum of the measures of the 2 acute angles of a right triangle is 90° (KEY FACT J1),

$$5x + 13x = 90 \Rightarrow 18x = 90 \Rightarrow x = 5.$$

Therefore, the measure of the larger angle is $13 \times 5 =$ **65° (D)**.

Ratios can be extended to 3 or 4 or more terms. For example, we can say that the ratio of freshmen to sophomores to juniors to seniors in a college marching band is 6:8:5:8, which means that for every 6 freshmen in the band there are 8 sophomores, 5 juniors, and 8 seniors.

NOTE: TACTIC D1 applies to extended ratios, as well.

Example 5.

The concession stand at Cinema City sells popcorn in three sizes: large, super, and jumbo. One day, Cinema City sold 240 bags of popcorn, and the ratio of large to super to jumbo was 8:17:15. How many super bags of popcorn were sold that day?

(A) 48   (B) 90   (C) 102   (D) 108   (E) 120

SOLUTION: Let $8x$, $17x$, and $15x$ be the number of large, super, and jumbo bags of popcorn sold, respectively. Then

$$8x + 17x + 15x = 240 \Rightarrow 40x = 240 \Rightarrow x = 6.$$

The number of super bags sold was $17 \times 6 =$ **102 (D)**.

KEY FACT D3:

KEY FACT D1 applies to extended ratios, as well. If a set of objects is divided into 3 groups in the ratio $a{:}b{:}c$**, then the first group contains** $\dfrac{a}{a+b+c}$ **of the objects, the second** $\dfrac{b}{a+b+c}$**, and the third** $\dfrac{c}{a+b+c}$**.**

Example 6.

If the ratio of large to super to jumbo bags of popcorn sold at Cinema City was 8:17:15, what percent of the bags sold were super?

(A) 20%   (B) 25%   (C) $33\frac{1}{3}$%   (D) 37.5%

(E) 42.5%

SOLUTION. Super bags made up

$$\frac{17}{8+17+15} = \frac{17}{40} = \textbf{42.5\%}\ \text{of the total (E)}.$$

A jar contains a number of red (R), white (W), and blue (B) marbles. Suppose that R:W = 2:3 and W:B = 3:5. Then, for every 2 red marbles, there are 3 white ones, and for those 3 white ones, there are 5 blue ones. So, R:B = 2:5, and we can form the extended ratio R:W:B = 2:3:5.

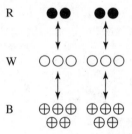

If the ratios were R:W = 2:3 and W:B = 4:5, however, we wouldn't be able to combine them as easily. From the diagram below, you see that for every 8 reds there are 15 blues, so R:B = 8:15.

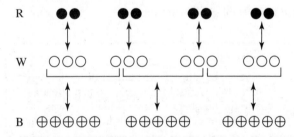

To see this without drawing a picture, we write the ratios as fractions: $\dfrac{R}{W} = \dfrac{2}{3}$ and $\dfrac{W}{B} = \dfrac{4}{5}$. Then, we multiply the fractions:

$$\frac{R}{\cancel{W}} \times \frac{\cancel{W}}{B} = \frac{2}{3} \times \frac{4}{5} = \frac{8}{15}, \quad \text{so} \quad \frac{R}{B} = \frac{8}{15}.$$

Not only does this give us R:B = 8:15, but also, if we multiply both W numbers, $3 \times 4 = 12$, we can write the extended ratio: R:W:B = 8:12:15.

Column A   Column B

Example 7.

Jar A and jar B each have 70 marbles,
all of which are red, white, or blue.
In jar A, R:W = 2:3 and W:B = 3:5.
In jar B, R:W = 2:3 and W:B = 4:5.

The number of white marbles in jar A	The number of white marbles in jar B

SOLUTION. From the discussion immediately preceding
this example, in jar A the extended ratio R:W:B is 2:3:5,
which implies that the white marbles constitute

$\dfrac{3}{2+3+5} = \dfrac{3}{10}$ of the total: $\dfrac{3}{10} \times 70 = \mathbf{21}$.

In jar B the extended ratio R:W:B is 8:12:15, so the

white marbles are $\dfrac{12}{8+12+15} = \dfrac{12}{35}$ of the total:

$\dfrac{12}{35} \times 70 = \mathbf{24}$. The answer is **B**.

A **proportion** is an equation that states that two
ratios are equivalent. Since ratios are just fractions, any

equation such as $\dfrac{4}{6} = \dfrac{10}{15}$ in which each side is a single

fraction is a proportion. Usually the proportions you
encounter on the GRE involve one or more variables.

Solve proportions by cross-multiplying: if $\dfrac{a}{b} = \dfrac{c}{d}$, then
$ad = bc$.

Setting up a proportion is a common way of solving a
problem on the GRE.

Example 8.

If $\dfrac{3}{7} = \dfrac{x}{84}$, what is the value of x?

(A) 12   (B) 24   (C) 36   (D) 42   (E) 48

SOLUTION. Cross-multiply:

$3(84) = 7x \Rightarrow 252 = 7x \Rightarrow x = \mathbf{36}$ **(C)**.

Example 9.

If $\dfrac{x+2}{17} = \dfrac{x}{16}$, what is the value of $\dfrac{x+6}{19}$?

(A) $\dfrac{1}{2}$ (B) 1   (C) $\dfrac{3}{2}$ (D) 2   (E) 3

SOLUTION. Cross-multiply:

$16(x + 2) = 17x \Rightarrow 16x + 32 = 17x \Rightarrow x = 32.$

So, $\dfrac{x+6}{19} = \dfrac{32+6}{19} = \dfrac{38}{19} = \mathbf{2}$ **(D)**.

Example 10.

A state law requires that on any field trip the
ratio of the number of chaperones to the number
of students must be at least 1:12. If 100 students
are going on a field trip, what is the minimum
number of chaperones required?

(A) 6   (B) 8   (C) $8\dfrac{1}{3}$ (D) 9   (E) 12

SOLUTION: Let x represent the number of chaperones
required, and set up a proportion:
$\dfrac{\text{number of chaperones}}{\text{number of students}} = \dfrac{1}{12} = \dfrac{x}{100}$. Cross-multiply:

$100 = 12x \Rightarrow x = 8\dfrac{1}{3}$. This, of course, is *not* the

answer since, clearly, the number of chaperones must
be a whole number. Since x is greater than 8, 8 chaperones would not be enough. The answer is **9** **(D)**.

A **rate** is a fraction that compares two quantities measured in different units. The word "per" often appears in
rate problems: miles per hour, dollars per week, cents
per ounce, students per classroom, and so on.

Set up rate problems just like ratio problems. Solve the
proportions by cross-multiplying.

Example 11.

Brigitte solved 24 math problems in 15 minutes.
At this rate, how many problems can she solve in
40 minutes?

(A) 25   (B) 40   (C) 48   (D) 60   (E) 64

SOLUTION. Handle this rate problem exactly like a ratio
problem. Set up a proportion and cross-multiply:

$\dfrac{\text{problems}}{\text{minutes}} = \dfrac{24}{15} = \dfrac{x}{40} \Rightarrow 15x = 40 \times 24 = 960 \Rightarrow x = \mathbf{64}$ **(E)**.

When the denominator in the given rate is 1 unit
(1 minute, 1 mile, 1 dollar), the problem can be solved
by a single division or multiplication. Consider Examples
12 and 13.

Example 12.

If Stefano types at the rate of 35 words per minute, how long will it take him to type 987 words?

Example 13.

If Mario types at the rate of 35 words per minute, how many words can he type in 85 minutes?

SOLUTION 12. Set up a proportion and cross-multiply:

$$\frac{\text{words typed}}{\text{minutes}} = \frac{35}{1} = \frac{987}{x} \Rightarrow 35x = 987 \Rightarrow$$

$$x = \frac{987}{35} = \textbf{28.2 minutes.}$$

SOLUTION 13. Set up a proportion and cross-multiply:

$$\frac{\text{words typed}}{\text{minutes}} = \frac{35}{1} = \frac{x}{85} \Rightarrow x = 35 \times 85 = \textbf{2975 words.}$$

Notice that in Example 12, all we did was divide 987 by 35, and in Example 13, we multiplied 35 by 85. If you realize that, you don't have to introduce x and set up a proportion. You must know, however, whether to multiply or divide. If you're not absolutely positive which is correct, write the proportion; then you can't go wrong.

CAUTION: In rate problems it is essential that the units in both fractions be the same.

Example 14.

If 3 apples cost 50¢, how many apples can you buy for $20?

(A) 20   (B) 60   (C) 120   (D) 600   (E) 2000

SOLUTION. We have to set up a proportion, but it is *not*
$\frac{3}{50} = \frac{x}{20}$. In the first fraction, the denominator represents *cents*, whereas in the second fraction, the denominator represents *dollars*. The units must be the same. We can change 50 cents to 0.5 dollar or we can change 20 dollars to 2000 cents:

$$\frac{3}{50} = \frac{x}{2000} \Rightarrow 50x = 6000 \Rightarrow x = \textbf{120 apples (C).}$$

On the GRE, some rate problems involve only variables. They are handled in exactly the same way.

Example 15.

If a apples cost c cents, how many apples can be bought for d dollars?

(A) $100acd$ (B) $\dfrac{100d}{ac}$ (C) $\dfrac{ad}{100c}$ (D) $\dfrac{c}{100ad}$

(E) $\dfrac{100ad}{c}$

SOLUTION. First change d dollars to $100d$ cents, and set up a proportion: $\dfrac{\text{apples}}{\text{cents}} = \dfrac{a}{c} = \dfrac{x}{100d}$. Now cross-multiply:

$$100ad = cx \Rightarrow x = \frac{100ad}{c} \textbf{ (E).}$$

Most students find problems such as Example 15 very difficult. If you get stuck on such a problem, use TACTIC 2, Chapter 11, which gives another strategy for handling these problems.

Notice that in rate problems, as one quantity increases or decreases, so does the other. If you are driving at 45 miles per hour, the more hours you drive, the further you go; if you drive fewer miles, it takes less time. If chopped meat cost $3.00 per pound, the less you spend, the fewer pounds you get; the more meat you buy, the more it costs.

In some problems, however, as one quantity increases, the other decreases. These *cannot* be solved by setting up a proportion. Consider the following two examples, which look similar but must be handled differently.

Example 16.

A hospital needs 150 pills to treat 6 patients for a week. How many pills does it need to treat 10 patients for a week?

Example 17.

A hospital has enough pills on hand to treat 10 patients for 14 days. How long will the pills last if there are 35 patients?

SOLUTION 16. Example 16 is a standard rate problem. The more patients there are, the more pills are needed. The *ratio* or *quotient* remains constant:

$$\frac{150}{6} = \frac{x}{10} \Rightarrow 6x = 1500 \Rightarrow x = \textbf{250.}$$

SOLUTION 17. In Example 17, the situation is different. With more patients, the supply of pills will last for a shorter period of time; if there were fewer patients, the supply would last longer. It is not the ratio that remains constant, it is the *product*.

There are enough pills to last for $10 \times 14 = 140$ patient-days:

$$\frac{140 \text{ patient-days}}{10 \text{ patients}} = 14 \text{ days}$$

$$\frac{140 \text{ patient-days}}{35 \text{ patients}} = \textbf{4 days}$$

$$\frac{140 \text{ patient-days}}{70 \text{ patients}} = 2 \text{ days}$$

$$\frac{140 \text{ patient-days}}{1 \text{ patient}} = 140 \text{ days}$$

There are many mathematical situations in which one quantity increases as another decreases, but their product is not constant. Those types of problems, however, do not appear on the GRE.

D4

If one quantity increases as a second quantity decreases, multiply them; their product will be a constant.

Example 18.

If 15 workers can pave a certain number of driveways in 24 days, how many days will 40 workers take, working at the same rate, to do the same job?

(A) 6   (B) 9   (C) 15   (D) 24   (E) 40

SOLUTION. Clearly, the more workers there are, the less time it will take, so use TACTIC D4: multiply. The job takes $15 \times 24 = 360$ worker-days:

$$\frac{360 \text{ worker-days}}{40 \text{ workers}} = \textbf{9 days (B)}.$$

Note that it doesn't matter how many driveways have to be paved, as long as the 15 workers and the 40 workers are doing the same job. Even if the question had said, "15 workers can pave 18 driveways in 24 days," the number 18 would not have entered into the solution. This number would be important only if the second group of workers was going to pave a different number of driveways.

Example 19.

If 15 workers can pave 18 driveways in 24 days, how many days would it take 40 workers to pave 22 driveways?

(A) 6   (B) 9   (C) 11   (D) 15   (E) 18

SOLUTION. This question is similar to Example 18, except that now the jobs that the two groups of workers are doing is different. The solution, however, starts out exactly the same way. Just as in Example 18, 40 workers can do in 9 days the *same* job that 15 workers can do in 24 days. Since that job is to pave 18 driveways, 40 workers can pave $18 \div 9 = 2$ driveways every day. So, it will take **11** days to pave 22 driveways (**C**).

PRACTICE EXERCISES—RATIOS AND PROPORTIONS

Multiple-Choice Questions

1. If $\frac{3}{4}$ of the employees in a supermarket are not college graduates, what is the ratio of the number of college graduates to those who are not college graduates?

   (A) 1:3   (B) 3:7   (C) 3:4   (D) 4:3   (E) 3:1

2. If $\frac{a}{9} = \frac{10}{2a}$, what is the value of a^2?

   (A) $3\sqrt{6}$ (B) $3\sqrt{5}$ (C) $9\sqrt{6}$ (D) 45   (E) 90

3. If all the members of a team are juniors or seniors, and if the ratio of juniors to seniors on the team is 3:5, what percent of the team members are seniors?

   (A) 37.5%   (B) 40%   (C) 60%   (D) 62.5%
   (E) It cannot be determined from the information given.

4. Scott can read 50 pages per hour. At this rate, how many pages can he read in 50 minutes?

   (A) 25   (B) $41\frac{2}{3}$ (C) $45\frac{1}{2}$ (D) 48   (E) 60

5. If 80% of the applicants to a program were rejected, what is the ratio of the number accepted to the number rejected?

   (A) $\frac{1}{5}$ (B) $\frac{1}{4}$ (C) $\frac{2}{5}$ (D) $\frac{4}{5}$ (E) $\frac{4}{1}$

6. The measures of the three angles in a triangle are in the ratio of 1:1:2. Which of the following must be true?

   I. The triangle is isosceles.
   II. The triangle is a right triangle.
   III. The triangle is equilateral.

   (A) None   (B) I only   (C) II only
         (D) I and II only   (E) I and III only

7. What is the ratio of the circumference of a circle to its radius?

   (A) 1   (B) $\frac{\pi}{2}$ (C) $\sqrt{\pi}$ (D) π (E) 2π

8. The ratio of the number of freshmen to sophomores to juniors to seniors on a college basketball team is 4:7:6:8. What percent of the team are sophomores?

   (A) 16%   (B) 24%   (C) 25%   (D) 28%
         (E) 32%

9. At Central State College the ratio of the number of students taking Spanish to the number taking French is 7:2. If 140 students are taking French, how many are taking Spanish?

    (A) 40   (B) 140   (C) 360   (D) 490   (E) 630

10. If $a:b = 3:5$ and $a:c = 5:7$, what is the value of $b:c$?

    (A) 3:7   (B) 21:35   (C) 21:25   (D) 25:21
    (E) 7:3

11. If x is a positive number and $\dfrac{x}{3} = \dfrac{12}{x}$, then $x =$

    (A) 3   (B) 4   (C) 6   (D) 12   (E) 36

12. In the diagram below, $b:a = 7:2$. What is $b - a$?

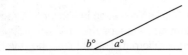

    (A) 20   (B) 70   (C) 100   (D) 110   (E) 160

13. A snail can move i inches in m minutes. At this rate, how many feet can it move in h hours?

    (A) $\dfrac{5hi}{m}$ (B) $\dfrac{60hi}{m}$ (C) $\dfrac{hi}{12m}$ (D) $\dfrac{5m}{hi}$
    (E) $5him$

14. Gilda can grade t tests in $\dfrac{1}{x}$ hours. At this rate, how many tests can she grade in x hours?

    (A) tx (B) tx^2 (C) $\dfrac{1}{t}$ (D) $\dfrac{x}{t}$ (E) $\dfrac{1}{tx}$

15. A club had 3 boys and 5 girls. During a membership drive the same number of boys and girls joined the club. How many members does the club have now if the ratio of boys to girls is 3:4?

    (A) 12   (B) 14   (C) 16   (D) 21   (E) 28

16. If $\dfrac{3x-1}{25} = \dfrac{x+5}{11}$, what is the value of x?

    (A) $\dfrac{3}{4}$ (B) 3   (C) 7   (D) 17   (E) 136

17. If 4 boys can shovel a driveway in 2 hours, how many minutes will it take 5 boys to do the job?

    (A) 60   (B) 72   (C) 96   (D) 120   (E) 150

18. If 500 pounds of mush will feed 20 pigs for a week, for how many days will 200 pounds of mush feed 14 pigs?

    (A) 4   (B) 5   (C) 6   (D) 7   (E) 8

Quantitative Comparison Questions

	Column A	Column B

The ratio of red to blue marbles in a jar was 3:5. The same number of red and blue marbles were added to the jar.

19.

The ratio of red to blue marbles now	3:5

Three associates agreed to split the $3000 profit of an investment in the ratio of 2:5:8.

20.

The difference between the largest and the smallest share	$1200

The ratio of the number of boys to girls in the chess club is 5:2.
The ratio of the number of boys to girls in the glee club is 11:4.

21.

The number of boys in the chess club	The number of boys in the glee club

Sally invited the same number of boys and girls to her party. Everyone who was invited came, but 5 additional boys showed up. This caused the ratio of girls to boys at the party to be 4:5.

22.

The number of people she invited to her party	40

A large jar is full of marbles. When a single marble is drawn at random from the jar, the probability that it is red is $\dfrac{3}{7}$.

23.

The ratio of the number of red marbles to non-red marbles in the jar	$\dfrac{1}{2}$

$3a = 2b$ and $3b = 5c$

24.

The ratio of a to c	1

The radius of circle II is 3 times the radius of circle I

25.

$\dfrac{\text{area of circle II}}{\text{area of circle I}}$	3π

Answer Key

1. **A**	6. **D**	11. **C**	16. **D**	21. **D**
2. **D**	7. **E**	12. **C**	17. **C**	22. **C**
3. **D**	8. **D**	13. **A**	18. **A**	23. **A**
4. **B**	9. **D**	14. **B**	19. **A**	24. **A**
5. **B**	10. **D**	15. **B**	20. **C**	25. **B**

Answer Explanations

1. **A.** Of every 4 employees, 3 are not college graduates, and 1 is a college graduate. So the ratio of graduates to nongraduates is 1:3.

2. **D.** Cross-multiplying, we get:
$$2a^2 = 90 \Rightarrow a^2 = 45.$$

3. **D.** Out of every 8 team members, 3 are juniors and 5 are seniors. Seniors, therefore, make up $\frac{5}{8}$ = 62.5% of the team.

4. **B.** Set up a proportion:
$$\frac{50 \text{ pages}}{1 \text{ hour}} = \frac{50 \text{ pages}}{60 \text{ minutes}} = \frac{x \text{ pages}}{50 \text{ minutes}}, \text{ and}$$
cross-multiply: $50 \times 50 = 60x \Rightarrow$
$$2500 = 60x \Rightarrow x = 41\frac{2}{3}.$$

5. **B.** If 80% were rejected, 20% were accepted, and the ratio of accepted to rejected is 20:80 = 1:4.

6. **D.** It is worth remembering that if the ratio of the measures of the angles of a triangle is 1:1:2, the angles are 45-45-90 (see Section 14-J). Otherwise, the first step is to write
$$x + x + 2x = 180 \Rightarrow 4x = 180 \Rightarrow x = 45.$$
Since two of the angles have the same measure, the triangle is isosceles, and since one of the angles measures 90°, it is a right triangle. I and II are true, and, of course, III is false.

7. **E.** By definition, π is the ratio of the circumference to the diameter of a circle (see Section 14-L). Therefore, $\pi = \dfrac{C}{d} = \dfrac{C}{2r} \Rightarrow 2\pi = \dfrac{C}{r}$.

8. **D.** The *fraction* of the team that is sophomores is $\dfrac{7}{4+7+6+8} = \dfrac{7}{25}$, and $\dfrac{7}{25} \times 100\% = 28\%$.

9. **D.** Let the number of students taking Spanish be $7x$, and the number taking French be $2x$. Then,
$$2x = 140 \Rightarrow x = 70 \Rightarrow 7x = 490.$$

10. **D.** Since $\dfrac{a}{b} = \dfrac{3}{5}$, $\dfrac{b}{a} = \dfrac{5}{3}$. So,
$$b{:}c = \frac{b}{c} = \frac{b}{\overset{1}{\cancel{A}}} \times \frac{\cancel{A}}{c} = \frac{5}{3} \times \frac{5}{7} = \frac{25}{21} = 25{:}21.$$

Alternatively, we could write equivalent ratios with the same value for a:
$$a{:}b = 3{:}5 = 15{:}25 \text{ and } a{:}c = 5{:}7 = 15{:}21.$$
So, when $a = 15$, $b = 25$, and $c = 21$.

11. **C.** To solve a proportion, cross-multiply:
$$\frac{x}{3} = \frac{12}{x} \Rightarrow x^2 = 36 \Rightarrow x = 6.$$

12. **C.** Let $b = 7x$ and $a = 2x$. Then,
$$7x + 2x = 180 \Rightarrow 9x = 180 \Rightarrow x = 20 \Rightarrow$$
$$b = 140 \text{ and } a = 40 \Rightarrow b - a = 140 - 40 = 100.$$

13. **A.** Set up the proportion, keeping track of units:
$$\frac{x \text{ feet}}{h \text{ hours}} = \frac{\overset{1}{\cancel{12}}x \text{ inches}}{\underset{5}{\cancel{60}}h \text{ minutes}} = \frac{i \text{ inches}}{m \text{ minutes}} \Rightarrow$$
$$\frac{x}{5h} = \frac{i}{m} \Rightarrow x = \frac{5hi}{m}.$$

14. **B.** Gilda grades at the rate of $\dfrac{t \text{ tests}}{\frac{1}{x} \text{ hours}} = \dfrac{tx \text{ tests}}{1 \text{ hour}}$.

Since she can grade tx tests each hour, in x hours she can grade $x(tx) = tx^2$ tests.

15. **B.** Suppose that x boys and x girls joined the club. Then, the new ratio of boys to girls would be $(3 + x){:}(5 + x)$, which we are told is 3:4. So,
$$\frac{3+x}{5+x} = \frac{3}{4} \Rightarrow 4(3 + x) = 3(5 + x) \Rightarrow$$
$$12 + 4x = 15 + 3x \Rightarrow x = 3.$$
Therefore, 3 boys and 3 girls joined the other 3 boys and 5 girls: a total of 14.

16. **D.** Cross-multiplying, we get:
$$11(3x - 1) = 25(x + 5) \Rightarrow$$
$$33x - 11 = 25x + 125 \Rightarrow 8x = 136 \Rightarrow x = 17.$$

17. **C.** Since 4 boys can shovel the driveway in 2 hours, or $2 \times 60 = 120$ minutes, the job takes $4 \times 120 = 480$ boy-minutes; and so 5 boys would need $\dfrac{480 \text{ boy-minutes}}{5 \text{ boys}} = 96$ minutes.

18. A. Since 500 pounds will last for 20 pig-weeks = 140 pig-days, 200 pounds will last for

$\frac{2}{5} \times 140$ pig-days = 56 pig-days, and

$\frac{56 \text{ pig-days}}{14 \text{ pigs}} = 4$ days.

19. A. Assume that to start there were $3x$ red marbles and $5x$ blue ones and that y of each color were added.

	Column A	Column B
	$\frac{3x + y}{5x + y}$	$\frac{3}{5}$
Cross-multiply:	$5(3x + y)$	$3(5x + y)$
Distribute:	$15x + 5y$	$15x + 3y$
Subtract $15x$:	$5y$	$3y$

Since y is positive, Column A is greater.

20. C. The shares are $2x$, $5x$, and $8x$, and their sum is 3000:

$$2x + 5x + 8x = 3000 \Rightarrow 15x = 3000 \Rightarrow$$
$$x = 200, \text{ and so } 8x - 2x = 6x = 1200.$$

21. D. Ratios alone can't answer the question, "How many?" There could be 5 boys in the chess club or 500. We can't tell.

22. C. Assume that Sally invited x boys and x girls. When she wound up with x girls and $x + 5$ boys, the girl:boy ratio was 4:5. So,

$$\frac{x}{x + 5} = \frac{4}{5} \Rightarrow 5x = 4x + 20 \Rightarrow x = 20$$

Sally invited 40 people (20 boys and 20 girls).

23. A. If the probability of drawing a red marble is $\frac{3}{7}$, 3 out of every 7 marbles are red, and 4 out of every 7 are non-red. So the ratio red:non-red = 3:4, which is greater than $\frac{1}{2}$.

24. A. Multiplying the first equation by 3 and the second by 2 to get the same coefficient of b, we have:

$$9a = 6b \text{ and } 6b = 10c \Rightarrow 9a = 10c \Rightarrow \frac{a}{c} = \frac{10}{9}.$$

25. B. Assume the radius of circle I is 1 and the radius of circle II is 3. Then the areas are π and 9π, respectively. So, the area of circle II is 9 times the area of circle I, and $3\pi > 9$.

14-E. AVERAGES

The ***average*** of a set of n numbers is the sum of those numbers divided by n.

$$\text{average} = \frac{\text{sum of the } n \text{ numbers}}{n} \text{ or simply}$$

$$A = \frac{\text{sum}}{n}.$$

If the weights of three children are 80, 90, and 76 pounds, respectively, to calculate the average weight of the children, you would add the three weights and divide by 3:

$$\frac{80 + 90 + 76}{3} = \frac{246}{3} = 82$$

The technical name for this type of average is "arithmetic mean," and on the GRE those words always appear in parentheses—for example, "What is the average (arithmetic mean) of 80, 90, and 76?"

Usually, on the GRE, you are not asked to find an average; rather, you are given the average of a set of numbers and asked for some other information. The key to solving all of these problems is to first find the sum of the numbers. Since $A = \frac{\text{sum}}{n}$, multiplying both sides by n yields the equation: sum = nA.

If you know the average, A, of a set of n numbers, multiply A by n to get their sum.

Example 1.

One day a supermarket received a delivery of 25 frozen turkeys. If the average (arithmetic mean) weight of a turkey was 14.2 pounds, what was the total weight, in pounds, of all the turkeys?

SOLUTION. Use TACTIC E1: $25 \times 14.2 = $ **355**.

NOTE: We do not know how much any individual turkey weighed nor how many turkeys weighed more or less than 14.2 pounds. All we know is their total weight.

Example 2.

Sheila took five chemistry tests during the semester and the average (arithmetic mean) of her test scores was 85. If her average after the first three tests was 83, what was the average of her fourth and fifth tests?

(A) 83 (B) 85 (C) 87 (D) 88 (E) 90

SOLUTION.

- Use TACTIC E1: On her five tests, Sheila earned $5 \times 85 = 425$ points.

- Use TACTIC E1 again: On her first three tests she earned $3 \times 83 = 249$ points.

- Subtract: On her last two tests Sheila earned $425 - 249 = 176$ points.

- Calculate her average on her last two tests:
  $$\frac{176}{2} = \textbf{88 (D)}.$$

NOTE: *We cannot determine Sheila's grade on even one of the tests.*

KEY FACT E1:

- **If all the numbers in a set are the same, then that number is the average.**

- **If the numbers in a set are not all the same, then the average must be greater than the smallest number and less than the largest number. Equivalently, at least one of the numbers is less than the average and at least one is greater.**

If Jessica's test grades are 85, 85, 85, and 85, her average is 85. If Gary's test grades are 76, 83, 88, and 88, his average must be greater than 76 and less than 88. What can we conclude if, after taking five tests, Kristen's average is 90? We know that she earned exactly $5 \times 90 = 450$ points, and that either she got a 90 on every test or at least one grade was less than 90 and at least one was over 90. Here are a few of the thousands of possibilities for Kristen's grades:

      (a) 90, 90, 90, 90, 90   (b) 80, 90, 90, 90, 100
      (c) 83, 84, 87, 97, 99   (d) 77, 88, 93, 95, 97
      (e) 50, 100, 100, 100, 100

In (b), 80, the one grade below 90, is *10 points below*, and 100, the one grade above 90, is *10 points above*. In (c), 83 is 7 points below 90, 84 is 6 points below 90, and 87 is 3 points below 90, for a total of $7 + 6 + 3 = 16$ *points below 90*; 97 is 7 points above 90, and 99 is 9 points above 90, for a total of $7 + 9 = 16$ *points above 90*.

These differences from the average are called *deviations*, and the situation in these examples is not a coincidence.

KEY FACT E2:

The total deviation below the average is equal to the total deviation above the average.

Example 3.

If the average (arithmetic mean) of 25, 31, and x is 37, what is the value of x?

(A) 31   (B) 37   (C) 43   (D) 55   (E) 56

SOLUTION 1. Use KEY FACT E2. Since 25 is 12 less than 37 and 31 is 6 less than 37, the total deviation below the average is $12 + 6 = 18$. Therefore, the total deviation above must also be 18. So, $x = 37 + 18 = \textbf{55 (D)}$.

SOLUTION 2. Use TACTIC E1. Since the average of the three numbers is 37, the sum of the 3 numbers is $3 \times 37 = 111$. Then,

$$25 + 31 + x = 111 \Rightarrow 56 + x = 111 \Rightarrow x = \textbf{55}.$$

KEY FACT E3:

Assume that the average of a set of numbers is A. If a number x is added to the set and a new average is calculated, then the new average will be less than, equal to, or greater than A, depending on whether x is less than, equal to, or greater than A, respectively.

Column A	Column B
Example 4.	
The average (arithmetic mean) of the integers from 0 to 12	The average (arithmetic mean) of the integers from 1 to 12

Helpful Hint

Remember TACTIC 5 from Chapter 12. We don't have to *calculate* the averages, we just have to *compare* them.

SOLUTION 1. Column B is the average of the integers from 1 to 12, which is surely greater than 1. In Column A we are taking the average of those same 12 numbers and 0. Since the extra number, 0, is less than the Column B average, the Column A average must be *lower* [KEY FACT E3]. The answer is **B**.

SOLUTION 2. Clearly the sum of the 13 integers from 0 to 12 is the same as the sum of the 12 integers from 1 to 12. Since that sum is positive, dividing by 13 yields a smaller quotient than dividing by 12 [KEY FACT B4].

Although in solving Example 4 we didn't calculate the averages, we could have:

$$0 + 1 + 2 + 3 + 4 + 5 + \textbf{6} + 7 + 8 + 9 + 10 + 11 + 12 = 78$$
$$\text{and } \frac{78}{13} = 6.$$

$$1 + 2 + 3 + 4 + 5 + \textbf{6 + 7} + 8 + 9 + 10 + 11 + 12 = 78$$
$$\text{and } \frac{78}{12} = 6.5.$$

Notice that the average of the 13 *consecutive* integers 0, 1,...,12 is the *middle integer*, **6**, and the average of the 12 *consecutive* integers 1, 2,...,12 is the *average of the two middle integers*, **6** and **7**. This is a special case of KEY FACT E4.

KEY FACT E4:

Whenever *n* numbers form an arithmetic sequence (one in which the difference between any two consecutive terms is the same): (i) if *n* is odd, the average of the numbers is the middle term in the sequence and (ii) if *n* is even, the average of the numbers is the average of the two middle terms.

For example, in the arithmetic sequence 6, 9, 12, 15, 18, the average is the middle number, **12**; in the sequence 10, 20, 30, 40, 50, 60, the average is **35**, the average of the two middle numbers—30 and 40.

> ### Example 5.
> On Thursday, 20 of the 25 students in a chemistry class took a test and their average was 80. On Friday, the other 5 students took the test, and their average was 90. What was the average (arithmetic mean) for the entire class?
> (A) 80   (B) 82   (C) 84   (D) 85   (E) 88

SOLUTION. The class average is calculated by dividing the sum of all 25 test grades by 25.

- The first 20 students
  earned a total of: $20 \times 80 = 1600$ points
- The other 5 students
  earned a total of: $5 \times 90 = 450$ points
- Add: altogether the
  class earned: $1600 + 450 = 2050$ points
- Calculate the class
  average: $\dfrac{2050}{25} = $ **82 (B)**.

Notice that the answer to Example 5 is *not* 85, which is the average of 80 and 90. This is because the averages of 80 and 90 were earned by different numbers of students, and so the two averages had to be given different weights in the calculation. For this reason, this is called a ***weighted average***.

KEY FACT E5:

To calculate the weighted average of a set of numbers, multiply each number in the set by the number of times it appears, add all the products, and divide by the total number of numbers in the set.

So, the solution to Example 5 should look like this:

$$\frac{20(80) + 5(90)}{25} = \frac{1600 + 450}{25} = \frac{2050}{25} = 82$$

> **Helpful Hint**
> Without doing any calculations, you should immediately realize that since the grade of 80 is being given more weight than the grade of 90, the average will be closer to 80 than to 90—certainly *less than 85*.

Problems involving *average speed* will be discussed in Section 15-H, but we mention them briefly here because they are closely related to problems on weighted averages.

> ### Example 6.
> For the first 3 hours of his trip, Justin drove at 50 miles per hour. Then, due to construction delays, he drove at only 40 miles per hour for the next 2 hours. What was his average speed, in miles per hour, for the entire trip?
> (A) 40   (B) 43   (C) 46   (D) 48   (E) 50

SOLUTION. This is just a weighted average:

$$\frac{3(50) + 2(40)}{5} = \frac{150 + 80}{5} = \frac{230}{5} = \textbf{46}.$$

Note that in the fractions above, the numerator is the total distance traveled and the denominator the total time the trip took. This is *always* the way to find an average speed. Consider the following slight variation on Example 6.

> ### Example 6a.
> For the first 100 miles of his trip, Justin drove at 50 miles per hour, and then due to construction delays, he drove at only 40 miles per hour for the next 120 miles. What was his average speed, in miles per hour, for the entire trip?

SOLUTION. This is not a *weighted* average. Here we immediately know the total distance traveled, 220 miles. To get the total time the trip took, we find the time for each portion and add: the first 100 miles took $100 \div 50 = 2$ hours, and the next 120 miles took $120 \div 40 = 3$ hours. So the average speed was $\dfrac{220}{5} = $ **44** miles per hour.

Notice that in Example 6 since Justin spent more time traveling at 50 miles per hour than at 40 miles per hour, his average speed was closer to 50; in Example 6a, he spent more time driving at 40 miles per hour than at 50 miles per hour, so his average speed was closer to 40.

Two other terms that are associated with averages are ***median*** and ***mode***. In a set of *n* numbers that are arranged in increasing order, the ***median*** is the middle number (if *n* is odd), or the average of the two middle numbers (if *n* is even). The **mode** is the number in the set that occurs most often.

Example 7.

During a 10-day period, Jorge received the following number of phone calls each day: 2, 3, 9, 3, 5, 7, 7, 10, 7, 6. What is the average (arithmetic mean) of the median and mode of this set of data?

(A) 6   (B) 6.25   (C) 6.5   (D) 6.75   (E) 7

SOLUTION. The first step is to write the data in increasing order: 2, 3, 3, 5, 6, 7, 7, 7, 9, 10.

• The median is 6.5, the average of the middle two numbers.

• The mode is 7, the number that appears more times than any other.

• The average of the median and the mode is
$$\frac{6.5 + 7}{2} = \textbf{6.75 (D)}.$$

PRACTICE EXERCISES—AVERAGES

Multiple-Choice Questions

1. Michael's average (arithmetic mean) on 4 tests is 80. What does he need on his fifth test to raise his average to 84?

   (A) 82   (B) 84   (C) 92   (D) 96   (E) 100

2. Maryline's average (arithmetic mean) on 4 tests is 80. Assuming she can earn no more than 100 on any test, what is the least she can earn on her fifth test and still have a chance for an 85 average after seven tests?

   (A) 60   (B) 70   (C) 75   (D) 80   (E) 85

3. Sandrine's average (arithmetic mean) on 4 tests is 80. Which of the following <u>cannot</u> be the number of tests on which she earned exactly 80 points?

   (A) 0   (B) 1   (C) 2   (D) 3   (E) 4

4. What is the average (arithmetic mean) of the positive integers from 1 to 100, inclusive?

   (A) 49   (B) 49.5   (C) 50   (D) 50.5   (E) 51

5. If $10a + 10b = 35$, what is the average (arithmetic mean) of a and b?

   (A) 1.75   (B) 3.5   (C) 7   (D) 10   (E) 17.5

6. If $x + y = 6$, $y + z = 7$, and $z + x = 9$, what is the average (arithmetic mean) of x, y, and z?

   (A) $\frac{11}{3}$ (B) $\frac{11}{2}$ (C) $\frac{22}{3}$ (D) 11   (E) 22

7. If $a + b = 3(c + d)$, which of the following is the average (arithmetic mean) of a, b, c, and d?

   (A) $\frac{c + d}{4}$ (B) $\frac{3(c + d)}{8}$ (C) $\frac{c + d}{2}$ (D) $\frac{3(c + d)}{4}$
   (E) $c + d$

8. If the average (arithmetic mean) of 5, 6, 7, and w is 8, what is the value of w?

   (A) 8   (B) 12   (C) 14   (D) 16   (E) 24

9. What is the average (arithmetic mean) of the measures of the five angles in a pentagon?

   (A) 36°   (B) 72°   (C) 90°   (D) 108°   (E) 144°

10. In the diagram below, lines ℓ and m are *not* parallel.

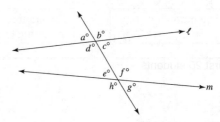

    If A represents the average (arithmetic mean) of the degree measures of all eight angles, which of the following is true?

    (A) $A = 45$ (B) $45 < A < 90$ (C) $A = 90$
       (D) $90 < A < 180$ (E) $A = 180$

11. What is the average (arithmetic mean) of 2^{10} and 2^{20}?

    (A) 2^{15} (B) $2^5 + 2^{10}$ (C) $2^9 + 2^{19}$ (D) 2^{29} (E) 30

12. Let M be the median and m the mode of the following set of numbers: 10, 70, 20, 40, 70, 90. What is the average (arithmetic mean) of M and m?

    (A) 50   (B) 55   (C) 60   (D) 62.5   (E) 65

Quantitative Comparison Questions

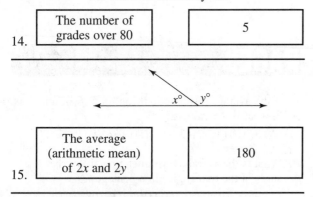

Column A	Column B
13. The average (arithmetic mean) of the measures of the three angles of an equilateral triangle	The average (arithmetic mean) of the measures of the three angles of a right triangle

10 students took a test and the average grade was 80.
No one scored exactly 80.

Column A	Column B
14. The number of grades over 80	5

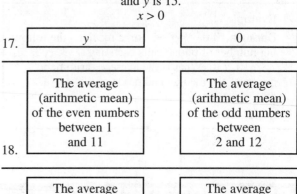

Column A	Column B
15. The average (arithmetic mean) of $2x$ and $2y$	180

There are the same number of boys and girls in a club.
The average weight of the boys is 150 pounds.
The average weight of the girls is 110 pounds.

16. The number of boys weighing over 150	The number of girls weighing over 110

Column A   Column B

The average (arithmetic mean) of 22, 38, x,
and y is 15.
$x > 0$

Column A	Column B
17. y	0

Column A	Column B
18. The average (arithmetic mean) of the even numbers between 1 and 11	The average (arithmetic mean) of the odd numbers between 2 and 12

Column A	Column B
19. The average (arithmetic mean) of 17, 217, 417	The average (arithmetic mean) of 0, 17, 217, 417

$y > 0$

Column A	Column B
20. The average (arithmetic mean) of x and y	The average (arithmetic mean) of x, y, and $2y$

Answer Key

1. E	6. A	11. C	16. D
2. C	7. E	12. D	17. B
3. D	8. C	13. C	18. B
4. D	9. D	14. D	19. A
5. A	10. C	15. C	20. D

Answer Explanations

1. E.   Use TACTIC E1. For Michael's average on five tests to be an 84, he needs a total of $5 \times 84 = 420$ points. So far, he has earned $4 \times 80 = 320$ points. Therefore, he needs 100 points more.
Alternative solution. Use KEY FACT E2. Assume Michael's first 4 tests were all 80s. His total deviation below 84 is $4 \times 4 = 16$. So, his total deviation above 84 must also be 16. He needs $84 + 16 = 100$.

2. C.   Use TACTIC E1. So far, Maryline has earned 320 points. She can survive a low grade on test five if she gets the maximum possible on both the sixth and seventh tests. So, assume she gets two 100s. Then her total for tests 1, 2, 3, 4, 6, and 7 would be 520. For her seven-test average to be 85, she needs a total of $7 \times 85 = 595$ points. Therefore, she needs at least $595 - 520 = 75$ points.
Alternative solution. Use KEY FACT E2. Assume Maryline's first four tests were all

80s. Then her total deviation below 85 would be $4 \times 5 = 20$. Her maximum possible deviation above 85 (assuming 100s on tests 6 and 7) is $15 + 15 = 30$. So, on test 5 she can deviate at most 10 more points below 85: $85 - 10 = 75$.

3. **D.** Since Sandrine's 4-test average is 80, she earned a total of $4 \times 80 = 320$ points. Could Sandrine have earned a total of 320 points with:

0 grades of 80?	Easily; for example, 20, 100, 100, 100 or 60, 70, 90, 100.
1 grade of 80?	Lots of ways; 80, 40, 100, 100, for instance.
2 grades of 80?	Yes; 80, 80, 60, 100.
4 grades of 80?	Sure: 80, 80, 80, 80.
3 grades of 80?	NO! $80 + 80 + 80 + x = 320 \Rightarrow x = 80$, as well.

4. **D.** Clearly, the sequence of integers from 1 to 100 has 100 terms, and so by KEY FACT E4, we know that the average of all the numbers is the average of the two middle ones: 50 and 51. The average, therefore, is 50.5.

5. **A.** Since $10a + 10b = 35$, dividing both sides of the equation by 10, we get that $a + b = 3.5$. Therefore, the average of a and b is $3.5 \div 2 = 1.75$.

6. **A.** Whenever a question involves three equations, add them:

$$\begin{array}{r} x + y = 6 \\ y + z = 7 \\ + \quad z + x = 9 \\ \hline 2x + 2y + 2z = 22 \end{array}$$

Divide by 2: $x + y + z = 11$

The average of x, y, and z is $\dfrac{x+y+z}{3} = \dfrac{11}{3}$.

7. **E.** Calculate the average:

$$\frac{a+b+c+d}{4} = \frac{3(c+d)+c+d}{4} = \frac{3c+3d+c+d}{4} = \frac{4c+4d}{4} = c + d$$

8. **C.** Use TACTIC E1: the sum of the 4 numbers is 4 times their average:

$$5 + 6 + 7 + w = 4 \times 8 = 32 \Rightarrow$$
$$18 + w = 32 \Rightarrow w = 14.$$

Alternative solution. Use KEY FACT E2: 5 is 3 below 8, 6 is 2 below 8, and 7 is 1 below 8, for a total deviation of $3 + 2 + 1 = 6$ below the average of 8. To compensate, w must be 6 more than 8: $6 + 8 = 14$.

9. **D.** The average of the measures of the five angles is the sum of their measures divided by 5. The sum is $(5 - 2) \times 180 = 3 \times 180 = 540$ (see Section 14-K). So, the average is $540 \div 5 = 108$.

10. **C.** Since $a + b + c + d = 360$, and $e + f + g + h = 360$ (see Section 14-I), the sum of the measures of all 8 angles is $360 + 360 = 720$, and their average is $720 \div 8 = 90$.

11. **C.** The average of 2^{10} and 2^{20} is

$$\frac{2^{10} + 2^{20}}{2} = \frac{2^{10}}{2} + \frac{2^{20}}{2} = 2^9 + 2^{19}.$$

12. **D.** Arrange the numbers in increasing order: 10, 20, 40, 70, 70, 90. M, the median, is the average of the middle two numbers: $\dfrac{40+70}{2} = 55$; the mode, m, is 70, the number that appears most frequently. The average of M and m, therefore, is the average of 55 and 70, which is 62.5.

13. **C.** In *any* triangle, the sum of the measures of the three angles is $180°$, and the average of their measures is $180 \div 3 = 60$.

14. **D.** From KEY FACT E1, we know only that *at least one grade was above 80*. In fact, there may have been only one (9 grades of 79 and 1 grade of 89, for example). But there could have been five or even nine (for example, 9 grades of 85 and 1 grade of 35).
Alternative solution. The ten students scored exactly 800 points. Ask, "Could they be equal?" Could there be exactly five grades above 80? Sure, five grades of 100 for 500 points and five grades of 60 for 300 points. Must they be equal? No, eight grades of 100 and two grades of 0 also total 800.

15. **C.** The average of $2x$ and $2y$ is $\dfrac{2x+2y}{2} = x + y$, which equals 180.

16. **D.** It is possible that no boy weighs over 150 (if every single boy weighs exactly 150); on the other hand, it is possible that almost every boy weighs over 150. The same is true for the girls.

17. **B.** Use TACTIC E1:

$$22 + 38 + x + y = 4(15) = 60 \Rightarrow$$
$$60 + x + y = 60 \Rightarrow x + y = 0.$$

Since it is given that x is positive, y must be negative.

18. **B.** Don't calculate the averages. Each number in Column A (2, 4, 6, 8, 10) is less than the corresponding number in Column B (3, 5, 7, 9, 11), and so the Column A average must be less than the Column B average.
Alternative solution. Observe that the numbers in each column form an arithmetic sequence, so by KEY FACT E4 the averages are just the middle numbers (6 and 7).

19. **A.** You don't have to calculate the averages. The average of the set of numbers in Column A is clearly positive, and by KEY FACT E3, adding 0 to that set must lower the average.

20. **D.** Use KEY FACT E3: if $x < y$, then the average of x and y is less than y, and surely less than $2y$. So, $2y$ has to raise the average. On the other hand, if x is much larger than y, then $2y$ would lower the average.

ALGEBRA

For the GRE you need to know only a small portion of the algebra normally taught in a high school elementary algebra course and none of the material taught in an intermediate or advanced algebra course. Sections 14-F, 14-G, and 14-H review only those topics that you absolutely need for the GRE.

14-F. POLYNOMIALS

Even though the terms *monomial, binomial, trinomial,* and *polynomial* are not used on the GRE, you must be able to work with simple polynomials, and the use of these terms will make it easier for us to discuss the important concepts.

A *monomial* is any number or variable or product of numbers and variables. Each of the following is a monomial:

$$3 \quad -4 \quad x \quad y \quad 3x \quad -4xyz \quad 5x^3 \quad 1.5xy^2 \quad a^3b^4$$

The number that appears in front of the variables in a monomial is called the *coefficient*. The coefficient of $5x^3$ is 5. If there is no number, the coefficient is 1 or –1, because x means $1x$ and $-ab^2$ means $-1ab^2$.

On the GRE, you could be asked to evaluate a monomial for specific values of the variables.

Example 1.
What is the value of $-3a^2b$ when $a = -4$ and $b = 0.5$?

(A) –72   (B) –24   (C) 24   (D) 48   (E) 72

SOLUTION. Rewrite the expression, replacing the letters a and b with the numbers –4 and 0.5, respectively. Make sure to write each number in parentheses. Then evaluate: $-3(-4)^2(0.5) = -3(16)(0.5) = \mathbf{-24}$ **(B)**.

> CAUTION: Be sure you follow PEMDAS (see Section 14-A): handle exponents before the other operations. In Example 1, you *cannot* multiply –4 by –3, get 12, and then square the 12; you must first square –4.

A *polynomial* is a monomial or the sum of two or more monomials. Each monomial that makes up the polynomial is called a *term* of the polynomial. Each of the following is a polynomial:

$$2x^2 \quad 2x^2 + 3 \quad 3x^2 - 7 \quad x^2 + 5x - 1$$
$$a^2b + b^2a \quad x^2 - y^2 \quad w^2 - 2w + 1$$

The first polynomial in the above list is a monomial; the second, third, fifth, and sixth polynomials are called *binomials*, because each has two terms; the fourth and seventh polynomials are called *trinomials*, because each has three terms. Two terms are called *like terms* if they have exactly the same variables and exponents; they can differ only in their coefficients: $5a^2b$ and $-3a^2b$ are like terms, whereas a^2b and b^2a are not.

The polynomial $3x^2 + 4x + 5x + 2x^2 + x - 7$ has 6 terms, but some of them are like terms and can be combined:

$$3x^2 + 2x^2 = 5x^2 \quad \text{and} \quad 4x + 5x + x = 10x.$$

So, the original polynomial is equivalent to the trinomial $5x^2 + 10x - 7$.

KEY FACT F1:

The only terms of a polynomial that can be combined are like terms.

Helpful Hint
To add, subtract, multiply, and divide polynomials, use the usual laws of arithmetic. To avoid careless errors, before performing any arithmetic operations, write each polynomial in parentheses.

KEY FACT F2:

To add two polynomials, put a plus sign between them, erase the parentheses, and combine like terms.

Example 2.
What is the sum of $5x^2 + 10x - 7$ and $3x^2 - 4x + 2$?

SOLUTION. $(5x^2 + 10x - 7) + (3x^2 - 4x + 2)$
$= 5x^2 + 10x - 7 + 3x^2 - 4x + 2$
$= (5x^2 + 3x^2) + (10x - 4x) + (-7 + 2)$
$= \mathbf{8x^2 + 6x - 5}$.

KEY FACT F3:

To subtract two polynomials, change the minus sign between them to a plus sign and change the sign of every term in the second parentheses. Then just use KEY FACT F2 to add them: erase the parentheses and then combine like terms.

CAUTION: Make sure you get the order right in a subtraction problem.

Example 3.
Subtract $3x^2 - 4x + 2$ from $5x^2 + 10x - 7$.

SOLUTION. Be careful. Start with the second polynomial and subtract the first:

$$(5x^2 + 10x - 7) - (3x^2 - 4x + 2)$$
$$= (5x^2 + 10x - 7) + (-3x^2 + 4x - 2)$$
$$= \mathbf{2x^2 + 14x - 9}.$$

Example 4.
What is the average (arithmetic mean) of $5x^2 + 10x - 7$, $3x^2 - 4x + 2$, and $4x^2 + 2$?

SOLUTION. As in any average problem, add and divide:

$$(5x^2 + 10x - 7) + (3x^2 - 4x + 2) + (4x^2 + 2) =$$
$$12x^2 + 6x - 3,$$

and by the distributive law (KEY FACT A21),

$$\frac{12x^2 + 6x - 3}{3} = \mathbf{4x^2 + 2x - 1}.$$

KEY FACT F4:

To multiply monomials, first multiply their coefficients, and then multiply their variables (letter by letter), by adding the exponents (see Section 12A).

Example 5.
What is the product of $3xy^2z^3$ and $-2x^2y^2$?

SOLUTION. $(3xy^2z^3)(-2x^2y^2) =$
$3(-2)(x)(x^2)(y^2)(y^2)(z^3) = \mathbf{-6x^3y^4z^3}$.

All other polynomials are multiplied by using the distributive law.

[handwritten note: when x exponents → add the exponents]

KEY FACT F5:

To multiply a monomial by a polynomial, just multiply each term of the polynomial by the monomial.

Example 6.
What is the product of $2a$ and $3a^2 - 6ab + b^2$?

SOLUTION. $2a(3a^2 - 6ab + b^2) = \mathbf{6a^3 - 12a^2b + 2ab^2}$.

On the GRE, the only other polynomials that you could be asked to multiply are two binomials.

KEY FACT F6:

To multiply two binomials, use the so-called FOIL method, which is really nothing more than the distributive law: Multiply each term in the first parentheses by each term in the second parentheses and simplify by combining terms, if possible.

$(2x - 7)(3x + 2) = (2x)(3x) + (2x)(2) + (-7)(3x) + (-7)(2) =$
First terms   Outer terms   Inner terms   Last terms
$6x^2 + 4x - 21x - 14 = 6x^2 - 17x - 14$

Example 7.
What is the value of $(x - 2)(x + 3) - (x - 4)(x + 5)$?

SOLUTION. First, multiply both pairs of binomials:

$(x - 2)(x + 3) = x^2 + 3x - 2x - 6 = x^2 + x - 6$

$(x - 4)(x + 5) = x^2 + 5x - 4x - 20 = x^2 + x - 20$

Now, subtract:
$(x^2 + x - 6) - (x^2 + x - 20) =$

$x^2 + x - 6 - x^2 - x + 20 = \mathbf{14}$.

KEY FACT F7:

The three most important binomial products on the GRE are these:

• $(x - y)(x + y) = x^2 + xy - yx - y^2 = x^2 - y^2$

• $(x - y)^2 = (x - y)(x - y) = x^2 - xy - yx + y^2 = x^2 - 2xy + y^2$

• $(x + y)^2 = (x + y)(x + y) = x^2 + xy + yx + y^2 = x^2 + 2xy + y^2$

Helpful Hint
If you memorize these, you won't have to multiply them out each time you need them.

Example 8.

If $a - b = 7$ and $a + b = 13$, what is the value of $a^2 - b^2$?

(A) –120   (B) 20   (C) 91   (D) 120   (E) 218

SOLUTION. In Section 14-G, we will review how to solve such a pair of equations; but even if you know how, *you should not do it here*. You do not need to know the values of a and b to answer this question. The moment you see $a^2 - b^2$, you should think $(a - b)(a + b)$. Then:

$$a^2 - b^2 = (a - b)(a + b) = (7)(13) = 91 \ (\textbf{C}).$$

Example 9.

If $x^2 + y^2 = 36$ and $(x + y)^2 = 64$, what is the value of xy?

(A) 14   (B) 28   (C) 100   (D) 128   (E) 2304

SOLUTION.

$$64 = (x + y)^2 = x^2 + 2xy + y^2 = x^2 + y^2 + 2xy = 36 + 2xy.$$

Therefore, $2xy = 64 - 36 = 28 \Rightarrow xy = 14 \ (\textbf{A})$.

On the GRE, the only division of polynomials you might have to do is to divide a polynomial by a monomial. You will *not* have to do long division of polynomials.

KEY FACT F8:

To divide a polynomial by a monomial, use the distributive law. Then simplify each term by reducing the fraction formed by the coefficients to lowest terms and applying the laws of exponents.

Example 10.

What is the quotient when $32a^2b + 12ab^3c$ is divided by $8ab$?

SOLUTION. By the distributive law,

$$\frac{32a^2b + 12ab^3c}{8ab} = \frac{32a^2b}{8ab} + \frac{12ab^3c}{8ab}.$$

Now reduce each fraction: $4a + \dfrac{3}{2}b^2c$.

On the GRE, the most important way to use the three formulas in KEY FACT F7 is to recognize them in reverse. In other words, whenever you see $x^2 - y^2$, you should realize that it can be rewritten as $(x - y)(x + y)$. This process, which is the reverse of multiplication, is called *factoring*.

Column A   **Column B**

Example 11.

| The value of $x^2 + 4x + 4$ when $x = 95.9$ | The value of $x^2 - 4x + 4$ when $x = 99.5$ |

SOLUTION. Obviously, you don't want to plug in 95.9 and 99.5 (remember that the GRE *never* requires you to do tedious arithmetic). Recognize that $x^2 + 4x + 4$ is equal to $(x + 2)^2$ and that $x^2 - 4x + 4$ is equal to $(x - 2)^2$. So, Column A is just $(95.9 + 2)^2 = 97.9^2$, whereas Column B is $(99.5 - 2)^2 = 97.5^2$. Column **A** is greater.

Example 12.

What is the value of $(1,000,001)^2 - (999,999)^2$?

SOLUTION. Do not even consider squaring 999,999. You know that there has to be an easier way to do this. In fact, if you stop to think, you can get the right answer in a few seconds. This is just $a^2 - b^2$ where $a = 1,000,001$ and $b = 999,999$, so change it to $(a - b)(a + b)$:

$$(1,000,001)^2 - (999,999)^2$$
$$= (1,000,001 - 999,999)(1,000,001 + 999,999)$$
$$= (2)(2,000,000) = \textbf{4,000,000}.$$

Although the coefficients of any of the terms in a polynomial can be fractions, as in $\frac{2}{3}x^2 - \frac{1}{2}x$, the variable itself cannot be in the denominator. An expression such as $\frac{3 + x}{x^2}$, which does have a variable in the denominator is called an *algebraic fraction*. Fortunately, you should have no trouble with algebraic fractions, since they are handled just like regular fractions. The rules that you reviewed in Section 14-B for adding, subtracting, multiplying, and dividing fractions apply to algebraic fractions, as well.

Example 13.

What is the sum of the reciprocals of x^2 and y^2?

SOLUTION. To add $\frac{1}{x^2} + \frac{1}{y^2}$, you need a common denominator, which is x^2y^2.

Multiply the numerator and denominator of $\frac{1}{x^2}$ by y^2 and the numerator and denominator of $\frac{1}{y^2}$ by x^2, and then add:

$$\frac{1}{x^2} + \frac{1}{y^2} = \frac{y^2}{x^2y^2} + \frac{x^2}{x^2y^2} = \frac{x^2 + y^2}{x^2y^2}.$$

Often, the way to simplify algebraic fractions is to factor the numerator or the denominator or both. Consider the following example, which is harder than anything you will see on the GRE, but still quite manageable.

Example 14.

What is the value of $\dfrac{4x^3 - x}{(2x+1)(6x-3)}$ when $x = 9999$?

SOLUTION. Don't use FOIL to multiply the denominator. That's going the wrong way. We want to simplify this fraction by factoring everything we can. First factor an x out of the numerator and notice that what's left is the difference of two squares, which can be factored. Then factor out the 3 in the second factor in the denominator:

$$\frac{4x^3 - x}{(2x+1)(6x-3)} = \frac{x(4x^2 - 1)}{(2x+1)3(2x-1)} =$$

$$\frac{x\cancel{(2x-1)}\cancel{(2x+1)}}{3\cancel{(2x+1)}\cancel{(2x-1)}} = \frac{x}{3}.$$

So, instead of plugging 9999 into the original expression, plug it into $\dfrac{x}{3}$: $9999 \div 3 = \mathbf{3333}$.

PRACTICE EXERCISES—POLYNOMIALS

Multiple-Choice Questions

1. What is the value of $\dfrac{a^2 - b^2}{a - b}$ when $a = 117$ and $b = 118$?
   (A) –1   (B) 1   (C) 117.5   (D) 175   (E) 235

2. If $a^2 - b^2 = 21$ and $a^2 + b^2 = 29$, which of the following could be the value of ab?
   I.   –10
   II. $5\sqrt{2}$
   III. 10

   (A) I only   (B) II only   (C) III only
       (D) I and III only   (E) II and III only

3. What is the average (arithmetic mean) of $x^2 + 2x - 3$, $3x^2 - 2x - 3$, and $30 - 4x^2$?
   (A) $\dfrac{8x^2 + 4x + 24}{3}$ (B) $\dfrac{8x^2 + 24}{3}$ (C) $\dfrac{24 - 4x}{3}$
   (D) –12   (E) 8

4. What is the value of $x^2 + 12x + 36$ when $x = 994$?
   (A) 11,928   (B) 98,836   (C) 100,000
       (D) 988,036   (E) 1,000,000

5. If $c^2 + d^2 = 4$ and $(c - d)^2 = 2$, what is the value of cd?
   (A) 1   (B) $\sqrt{2}$ (C) 2   (D) 3   (E) 4

6. What is the value of $(2x + 3)(x + 6) - (2x - 5)(x + 10)$?
   (A) 32   (B) 16   (C) 68
       (D) $4x^2 + 30x + 68$ (E) $4x^2 + 30x - 32$

7. If $\dfrac{1}{a} + \dfrac{1}{b} = \dfrac{1}{c}$ and $ab = c$, what is the average of a and b?
   (A) 0   (B) $\dfrac{1}{2}$ (C) 1   (D) $\dfrac{c}{2}$ (E) $\dfrac{a+b}{2c}$

8. If $x^2 - y^2 = 28$ and $x - y = 8$, what is the average of x and y?
   (A) 1.75   (B) 3.5   (C) 7   (D) 8   (E) 10

9. Which of the following is equal to
   $$\left(\frac{1}{a} + a\right)^2 - \left(\frac{1}{a} - a\right)^2 ?$$
   (A) 0   (B) 4   (C) $\dfrac{1}{a^2} - a^2$ (D) $\dfrac{2}{a^2} - 2a^2$
   (E) $\dfrac{1}{a^2} - 4 - a^2$

10. If $\left(\dfrac{1}{a} + a\right)^2 = 100$, what is the value of $\dfrac{1}{a^2} + a^2$?
    (A) 10   (B) 64   (C) 98   (D) 100   (E) 102

Quantitative Comparison Questions

Column A	Column B
$n < 0$	
11. $-2n^2$	$(-2n)^2$
$d < c$	
12. $(c - d)(c + d)$	$(c - d)(c - d)$
$x = -3$ and $y = 2$	
13. $-x^2y^3$	0
14. $(r + s)(r - s)$	$r(s + r) - s(r + s)$
15. $\dfrac{5x^2 - 20}{x - 2}$	$4x + 8$

Answer Key

1. **E**	6. **C**	11. **B**
2. **D**	7. **B**	12. **D**
3. **E**	8. **A**	13. **B**
4. **E**	9. **B**	14. **C**
5. **A**	10. **C**	15. **D**

Answer Explanations

1. **E.** $\dfrac{a^2 - b^2}{a - b} = \dfrac{(a - b)(a + b)}{a - b} = a + b =$
   $117 + 118 = 235$.

2. **D.** Adding the two equations, we get that
   $2a^2 = 50 \Rightarrow a^2 = 25 \Rightarrow b^2 = 4$. So, $a = 5$ or -5
   and $b = 2$ or -2. The only possibilities for
   their product are 10 and -10. (Only I and III
   are true.)

3. **E.** To find the average, take the sum of the three
   polynomials and then divide by 3. Their sum is
   $(x^2 + 2x - 3) + (3x^2 - 2x - 3) + (30 - 4x^2) = 24$,
   and $24 \div 3 = 8$.

4. **E.** You can avoid messy, time-consuming arithmetic if you recognize that $x^2 + 12x + 36 =$
   $(x + 6)^2$. The value is $(994 + 6)^2 = 1000^2 =$
   $1{,}000{,}000$.

5. **A.** Start by squaring $c - d$:
   $$2 = (c - d)^2 = c^2 - 2cd + d^2 = c^2 + d^2 - 2cd = $$
   $$4 - 2cd.$$
   So, $2 = 4 - 2cd \Rightarrow 2cd = 2 \Rightarrow cd = 1$.

6. **C.** First multiply out both pairs of binomials:
   $$(2x + 3)(x + 6) = 2x^2 + 15x + 18$$
   and $(2x - 5)(x + 10) = 2x^2 + 15x - 50$.
   Now subtract:
   $$(2x^2 + 15x + 18) - (2x^2 + 15x - 50) =$$
   $$18 - (-50) = 68.$$

7. **B.** $\dfrac{1}{c} = \dfrac{1}{a} + \dfrac{1}{b} = \dfrac{a + b}{ab} = \dfrac{a + b}{c} \Rightarrow$

   $1 = a + b \Rightarrow \dfrac{a + b}{2} = \dfrac{1}{2}$.

8. **A.** $x^2 - y^2 = (x - y)(x + y) \Rightarrow 28 = 8(x + y) \Rightarrow$
   $x + y = 28 \div 8 = 3.5$. Finally, the average of
   x and y is $\dfrac{x + y}{2} = \dfrac{3.5}{2} = 1.75$.

9. **B.** Expand each square: $\left(\dfrac{1}{a} + a\right)^2 =$

   $\dfrac{1}{a^2} + 2\left(\dfrac{1}{a}\right)(a) + a^2 = \dfrac{1}{a^2} + 2 + a^2$.

   Similarly, $\left(\dfrac{1}{a} - a\right)^2 = \dfrac{1}{a^2} - 2 + a^2$.

   Subtract: $\left(\dfrac{1}{a^2} + 2 + a^2\right) - \left(\dfrac{1}{a^2} - 2 + a^2\right) = 4$.

10. **C.** $100 = \left(\dfrac{1}{a} + a\right)^2 = \dfrac{1}{a^2} + 2 + a^2 \Rightarrow \dfrac{1}{a^2} + a^2 = 98$.

11. **B.** Since n is negative, n^2 is positive, and so $-2n^2$
    is negative. Therefore, Column A is negative,
    whereas Column B is positive.

	Column A	Column B

12. **D.** $c > d \Rightarrow c - d$ is
    positive, so divide
    each side by $c - d$: $c + d$ $c - d$
    Subtract c from each
    column: d $-d$

    If $d = 0$ the columns are equal; if $d = 1$, they
    aren't.

13. **B.** Column A: $-(-3)^2 2^3 = -(9)(8) = -72$.

14. **C.** Column B: $r(s + r) - s(r + s) =$
    $rs + r^2 - sr - s^2 = r^2 - s^2$.
    Column A: $(r + s)(r - s) = r^2 - s^2$.

15. **D.** Column A: $\dfrac{5x^2 - 20}{x - 2} = \dfrac{5(x^2 - 4)}{x - 2} =$

    $\dfrac{5(x - 2)(x + 2)}{x - 2} = 5(x + 2)$.

    Column B: $4x + 8 = 4(x + 2)$. If $x = -2$, both
    columns are 0; for any other value of x the
    columns are unequal.

14-G. SOLVING EQUATIONS AND INEQUALITIES

The basic principle that you must adhere to in solving any *equation* is that you can manipulate it in any way, as long as *you do the same thing to both sides*. For example, you may always add the same number to each side; subtract the same number from each side; multiply or divide each side by the same number (except 0); square each side; take the square root of each side (if the quantities are positive); or take the reciprocal of each side. These comments apply to inequalities, as well, except you must be very careful, because some procedures, such as multiplying or dividing by a negative number and taking reciprocals, reverse inequalities (see Section 14-A).

Most of the equations and inequalities that you will have to solve on the GRE have only one variable and no exponents. The following simple six-step method can be used on all of them.

Example 1.

If $\frac{1}{2}x + 3(x - 2) = 2(x + 1) + 1$, what is the value of x?

SOLUTION. Follow the steps outlined in the following table.

Step	What to Do	Example 1
1	Get rid of fractions and decimals by multiplying both sides by the Lowest Common Denominator (LCD).	Multiply each term by 2: $x + 6(x - 2) = 4(x + 1) + 2$.
2	Get rid of all parentheses by using the distributive law.	$x + 6x - 12 = 4x + 4 + 2$.
3	Combine like terms on each side.	$7x - 12 = 4x + 6$.
4	By adding or subtracting, get all the variables on one side.	Subtract $4x$ from each side: $3x - 12 = 6$.
5	By adding or subtracting, get all the plain numbers on the other side.	Add 12 to each side: $3x = 18$.
6	Divide both sides by the coefficient of the variable.*	Divide both sides by 3: $x = \mathbf{6}$.

*Note: If you start with an inequality and in Step 6 you divide by a negative number, remember to reverse the inequality (see KEY FACT A24).

Example 1 is actually harder than any equation on the GRE, because it required all six steps. On the GRE that

never happens. Think of the six steps as a list of questions that must be answered. Ask if each step is necessary. If it isn't, move on to the next one; if it is, do it.

Let's look at Example 2, which does not require all six steps.

Example 2.

For what real number n is it true that $3(n - 20) = n$?

(A) –10   (B) 0   (C) 10   (D) 20   (E) 30

SOLUTION. Do whichever of the six steps are necessary.

Step	Question	Yes/No	What to Do
1	Are there any fractions or decimals?	No	
2	Are there any parentheses?	Yes	Get rid of them: $3n - 60 = n$.
3	Are there any like terms to combine?	No	
4	Are there variables on both sides?	Yes	Subtract n from each side: $2n - 60 = 0$.
5	Is there a plain number on the same side as the variable?	Yes	Add 60 to each side: $2n = 60$.
6	Does the variable have a coefficient?	Yes	Divide both sides by 2: $n = \mathbf{30}$.

Tactic
G1

Memorize the six steps *in order* and use this method whenever you have to solve this type of equation or inequality.

Example 3.

Three brothers divided a prize as follows. The oldest received $\frac{2}{5}$ of it, the middle brother received $\frac{1}{3}$ of it, and the youngest received the remaining $120. What was the value of the prize?

SOLUTION: If x represents the value of the prize, then

$$\frac{2}{5}x + \frac{1}{3}x + 120 = x.$$

Solve this equation using the six-step method.

Step	Question	Yes/No	What to Do
1	Are there any fractions or decimals?	Yes	To get rid of them, multiply by 15. $15\left(\frac{2}{5}x\right) + 15\left(\frac{1}{3}x\right) +$ $15(120) = 15(x)$ $6x + 5x + 1800 = 15x$
2	Are there any parentheses?	No	
3	Are there any like terms to combine?	Yes	Combine them: $11x + 1800 = 15x$.
4	Are there variables on both sides?	Yes	Subtract $11x$ from each side: $1800 = 4x$.
5	Is there a plain number on the same side as the variable?	No	
6	Does the variable have a coefficient?	Yes	Divide both sides by 4: $x = \mathbf{450}$.

Sometimes on the GRE, you are given an equation with several variables and asked to solve for one of them in terms of the others.

When you have to solve for one variable in terms of the others, treat all of the others as if they were numbers, and apply the six-step method.

> **Example 4.**
> If $a = 3b - c$, what is the value of b in terms of a and c?

SOLUTION. To solve for b, treat a and c as numbers and use the six-step method with b as the variable.

Step	Question	Yes/No	What to Do
1	Are there any fractions or decimals?	No	
2	Are there any parentheses?	No	
3	Are there any like terms to combine?	No	
4	Are there variables on both sides?	No	Remember: the only variable is b.
5	Is there a plain number on the same side as the variable?	Yes	Remember: we're considering c as a number, and it is on the same side as b, the variable. Add c to both sides: $a + c = 3b$.
6	Does the variable have a coefficient?	Yes	Divide both sides by 3: $b = \dfrac{a + c}{3}$.

Sometimes when solving equations, you may see a shortcut. For example, to solve $7(w - 3) = 42$, it saves time to start by dividing both sides by 7, getting $w - 3 = 6$, rather than by using the distributive law to eliminate the parentheses. Similarly, if you have to solve a proportion such as $\dfrac{x}{7} = \dfrac{3}{5}$, it is easier to cross-multiply, getting $5x = 21$, than to multiply both sides by 35 to get rid of the fractions (although that's exactly what cross-multiplying accomplishes). Other shortcuts will be illustrated in the problems at the end of the section. If you spot such a shortcut, use it; but if you don't, be assured that the six-step method *always* works.

Helpful Hint

In applying the six-step method, you shouldn't actually write out the table, as we did in Examples 1–4, since it would be too time consuming. Instead, use the method as a guideline and mentally go through each step, doing whichever ones are required.

> **Example 5.**
> If $x - 4 = 11$, what is the value of $x - 8$?
> (A) –15 (B) –7 (C) –1 (D) 7 (E) 15

SOLUTION. Going immediately to Step 5, add 4 to each side: $x = 15$. But this is *not* the answer. You need the value not of x, but of $x - 8$: $15 - 8 = \mathbf{7}$ (**D**).

As in Example 5, on the GRE you are often asked to solve for something other than the simple variable. In

Example 5, we could have been asked for the value of x^2 or $x + 4$ or $(x - 4)^2$, and so on.

G3

As you read each question on the GRE, on your scrap paper write down whatever you are looking for, and circle it. This way you will always be sure that you are answering the question that is asked.

Helpful Hint

Very often, solving the equation is *not* the quickest way to answer the question. Consider the following example.

Example 6.

If $2x - 5 = 98$, what is the value of $2x + 5$?

SOLUTION. The first thing you should do is write $2x + 5$ on your paper and circle it. The fact that you are asked for the value of something other than x should alert you to look at the question carefully to see if there is a shortcut.

• The best approach here is to observe that $2x + 5$ is 10 more than $2x - 5$, so the answer is **108** (10 more than 98).

• Next best would be to do only one step of the six-step method, add 5 to both sides: $2x = 103$. Now, add 5 to both sides: $2x + 5 = 103 + 5 = 108$.

• The *worst* method would be to divide $2x = 103$ by 2, get $x = 51.5$, and then use that to calculate $2x + 5$.

Example 7.

If w is an integer, and the average (arithmetic mean) of 3, 4, and w is less than 10, what is the greatest possible value of w ?

(A) 9   (B) 10   (C) 17   (D) 22   (E) 23

SOLUTION. Set up the inequality: $\dfrac{3 + 4 + w}{3} < 10$. Do Step 1 (get rid of fractions by multiplying by 3): $3 + 4 + w < 30$. Do Step 3 (combine like terms): $7 + w < 30$. Finally, do Step 5 (subtract 7 from each side): $w < 23$. Since w is an integer, the most it can be is **22**.

The six-step method also works when there are variables in denominators.

Example 8.

For what value of x is $\dfrac{4}{x} + \dfrac{3}{5} = \dfrac{10}{x}$?

(A) 5   (B) 10   (C) 20   (D) 30   (E) 50

SOLUTION. Multiply each side by the LCD, $5x$:

$$5x\left(\frac{4}{x}\right) + 5x\left(\frac{3}{5}\right) = 5x\left(\frac{10}{x}\right) \Rightarrow 20 + 3x = 50.$$

Now solve normally: $20 + 3x = 50 \Rightarrow 3x = 30 \Rightarrow x = \mathbf{10}$ **(B)**.

Example 9. If x is positive, and $y = 5x^2 + 3$, which of the following is an expression for x in terms of y?

(A) $\sqrt{\dfrac{y}{5} - 3}$ (B) $\sqrt{\dfrac{y - 3}{5}}$ (C) $\dfrac{\sqrt{y - 3}}{5}$

(D) $\dfrac{\sqrt{y} - 3}{5}$ (E) $\dfrac{\sqrt{y} - \sqrt{3}}{5}$

SOLUTION. The six-step method works when there are no exponents. However, we can treat x^2 as a single variable, and use the method as far as possible:

$$y = 5x^2 + 3 \Rightarrow y - 3 = 5x^2 \Rightarrow \frac{y - 3}{5} = x^2.$$

Now take the square root of each side; since x is positive, the only solution is $x = \sqrt{\dfrac{y - 3}{5}}$ **(B)**.

CAUTION: Doing the same thing to each *side* of an equation does *not* mean doing the same thing to each *term* of the equation. Study Examples 10 and 11 carefully.

Example 10.

If $\dfrac{1}{a} = \dfrac{1}{b} + \dfrac{1}{c}$, what is a in terms of b and c?

NOTE: You *cannot* just take the reciprocal of each term; the answer is *not* $a = b + c$. Here are two solutions.

SOLUTION 1. First add the fractions on the right hand side: $\dfrac{1}{a} = \dfrac{1}{b} + \dfrac{1}{c} = \dfrac{b + c}{bc}$.

Now, take the reciprocal of each *side*: $a = \dfrac{bc}{b + c}$.

SOLUTION 2. Use the six-step method. Multiply each term by abc, the LCD: $abc\left(\dfrac{1}{a}\right) = abc\left(\dfrac{1}{b}\right) + abc\left(\dfrac{1}{c}\right) \Rightarrow$ $bc = ac + ab = a(c + b) \Rightarrow a = \dfrac{bc}{c + b}$.

Example 11.

If $a > 0$ and $a^2 + b^2 = c^2$, what is a in terms of b and c?

SOLUTION. $a^2 + b^2 = c^2 \Rightarrow a^2 = c^2 - b^2$. Be careful: you *cannot* now take the square root of each *term* and write, $a = c - b$. Rather, you must take the square root of each *side*: $a = \sqrt{a^2} = \sqrt{c^2 - b^2}$.

There are a few other types of equations that you could have to solve on the GRE. Fortunately, they are quite easy. You probably will not have to solve a quadratic equation. However, if you do, you will *not* need the quadratic formula, and you will not have to factor a trinomial. Here are two examples.

Example 12.

If x is a positive number and $x^2 + 64 = 100$, what is the value of x?

(A) 6   (B) 12   (C) 13   (D) 14   (E) 36

SOLUTION. When there is an x^2-term, but no x-term, we just have to take the square root:

$$x^2 + 64 = 100 \Rightarrow x^2 = 36 \Rightarrow x = \sqrt{36} = \mathbf{6}\ \mathbf{(A)}.$$

Example 13.

What is the largest value of x that satisfies the equation $2x^2 - 3x = 0$?

(A) 0   (B) 1.5   (C) 2   (D) 2.5   (E) 3

SOLUTION: When an equation has an x^2-term and an x-term but no constant term, the way to solve it is to factor out the x and to use the fact that if the product of two numbers is 0, one of them must be 0 (KEY FACT A3):

$$2x^2 - 3x = 0 \Rightarrow x(2x - 3) = 0$$
$$x = 0 \text{ or } 2x - 3 = 0$$
$$x = 0 \text{ or } 2x = 3$$
$$x = 0 \text{ or } x = 1.5.$$

The largest value is **1.5 (B)**.

In another type of equation that occasionally appears on the GRE, the variable is in the exponent. These equations are particularly easy and are basically solved by inspection.

Example 14.

If $2^{x+3} = 32$, what is the value of 3^{x+2}?

(A) 5   (B) 9   (C) 27   (D) 81   (E) 125

SOLUTION. How many 2s do you have to multiply together to get 32? If you don't know that it's 5, just multiply and keep track. Count the 2s on your fingers as

you say to yourself, "2 times 2 is 4, times 2 is 8, times 2 is 16, times 2 is 32." Then

$$2^{x+3} = 32 = 2^5 \Rightarrow x + 3 = 5 \Rightarrow x = 2.$$

Therefore, $x + 2 = 4$, and $3^{x+2} = 3^4 = 3 \times 3 \times 3 \times 3 = $ **81 (D)**.

Occasionally, both sides of an equation have variables in the exponents. In that case, it is necessary to write both exponentials with the same base.

Example 15. If $4^{w+3} = 8^{w-1}$, what is the value of w?

(A) 0   (B) 1   (C) 2   (D) 3   (E) 9

SOLUTION. Since it is necessary to have the same base on each side of the equation, write $4 = 2^2$ and $8 = 2^3$. Then

$$4^{w+3} = (2^2)^{w+3} = 2^{2(w+3)} = 2^{2w+6} \text{ and}$$
$$8^{w-1} = (2^3)^{w-1} = 2^{3(w-1)} = 2^{3w-3}.$$

So, $2^{2w+6} = 2^{3w-3} \Rightarrow 2w + 6 = 3w - 3 \Rightarrow w = \mathbf{9}\ \mathbf{(E)}$.

Systems of Linear Equations

The equations $x + y = 10$ and $x - y = 2$ each have lots of solutions (infinitely many, in fact). Some of them are given in the tables below.

$x + y = 10$						
x	5	6	4	1	1.2	10	20
y	5	4	6	9	8.8	0	−10
$x + y$	10	10	10	10	10	10	10

$x - y = 2$						
x	5	6	2	0	2.5	19	40
y	3	4	0	−2	.5	17	38
$x - y$	2	2	2	2	2	2	2

However, only one pair of numbers, **x = 6** and **y = 4**, satisfy both equations simultaneously: $6 + 4 = 10$ and $6 - 4 = 2$. This then is the only solution of the **system of equations**: $\begin{cases} x + y = 10 \\ x - y = 2 \end{cases}$.

A system of equations is a set of two or more equations involving two or more variables. To solve such a system, you must find values for each of the variables that will make each equation true. In an algebra course you learn several ways to solve systems of equations. On the GRE, the most useful way to solve them is to add or subtract (usually add) the equations. After demonstrating this method, we will show in Example 19 one other way to handle some systems of equations.

To solve a system of equations, add or subtract them. If there are more than two equations, add them.

Column A   Column B

Example 16.

$$x + y = 10$$
$$x - y = 2$$

| x | y |

SOLUTION. Add the two equations:

$$x + y = 10$$
$$+ \; x - y = \; 2$$
$$\overline{2x \qquad = 12}$$
$$x = \; 6$$

Replacing x with 6 in $x + y = 10$ yields $y = 4$. So, Column **A** is greater.

Helpful Hint

On the GRE, most problems involving systems of equations do *not* require you to solve the system. They usually ask for something other than the values of each variable. Read the questions very carefully, circle what you need, and do no more than is required.

Example 17.

If $3a + 5b = 10$ and $5a + 3b = 30$, what is the average (arithmetic mean) of a and b?

(A) 2.5   (B) 4   (C) 5   (D) 20
    (E) It cannot be determined from the information given.

SOLUTION. Add the two equations:
$$3a + 5b = 10$$
$$+ \; 5a + 3b = 30$$
$$\overline{8a + 8b = 40}$$

Divide both sides by 8: $a + b = 5$

The average of a and b is: $\dfrac{a+b}{2} = \dfrac{5}{2} = \mathbf{2.5\ (A)}$

Note: It is not only unnecessary to first solve for a and b ($a = 7.5$ and $b = -2.5$.), but, because that procedure is so much more time-consuming, it would be foolish to do so.

Column A   Column B

Example 18.

$$7a - 3b = 200$$
$$7a + 3b = 100$$

| a | b |

SOLUTION. Don't actually solve the system. Add the equations: $14a = 300 \Rightarrow 7a = 150$. So, replacing $7a$ with 150 in the second equation, we get $150 + 3b = 100$; so $3b$, and hence b, must be negative, whereas a is positive. Therefore, $a > b$, and Column **A** is greater.

Helpful Hint

Remember TACTIC 5, Chapter 12. On quantitative comparison questions, you don't need to know the value of the quantity in each column; you only need to know which one is greater.

Occasionally on the GRE, it is as easy, or easier, to solve the system by substitution.

If one of the equations in a system of equations consists of a single variable equal to some expression, substitute that expression for the variable in the other equation.

Column A   Column B

Example 19.

$$x + y = 10$$
$$y = x - 2$$

| x | y |

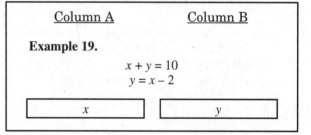

SOLUTION. Since the second equation states that a single variable (y), is equal to some expression ($x - 2$), substitute that expression for y in the first equation: $x + y = 10$ becomes $x + (x - 2) = 10$. Then, $2x - 2 = 10$, $2x = 12$, and $x = 6$. As always, to find the value of the other variable (y), plug the value of x into one of the two original equations: $y = 6 - 2 = 4$. Column **A** is greater.

PRACTICE EXERCISES—EQUATIONS/INEQUALITIES

Multiple-Choice Questions

1. If $4x + 12 = 36$, what is the value of $x + 3$?
   (A) 3   (B) 6   (C) 9   (D) 12   (E) 18

2. If $7x + 10 = 44$, what is the value of $7x - 10$?
   (A) $-6\frac{6}{7}$ (B) $4\frac{6}{7}$ (C) $14\frac{6}{7}$ (D) 24
   (E) 34

3. If $4x + 13 = 7 - 2x$, what is the value of x?
   (A) $-\frac{10}{3}$ (B) -3 (C) -1 (D) 1   (E) $\frac{10}{3}$

4. If $x - 4 = 9$, what is the value of $x^2 - 4$?
   (A) 21   (B) 77   (C) 81   (D) 165   (E) 169

5. If $ax - b = c - dx$, what is the value of x in terms of a, b, c, and d?
   (A) $\frac{b+c}{a+d}$ (B) $\frac{c-b}{a-d}$ (C) $\frac{b+c-d}{a}$
   (D) $\frac{c-b}{a+d}$ (E) $\frac{c}{b} - \frac{d}{a}$

6. If $\frac{1}{3}x + \frac{1}{6}x + \frac{1}{9}x = 33$, what is the value of x?
   (A) 3   (B) 18   (C) 27   (D) 54   (E) 72

7. If $3x - 4 = 11$, what is the value of $(3x - 4)^2$?
   (A) 22   (B) 36   (C) 116   (D) 121   (E) 256

8. If $64^{12} = 2^{a-3}$, what is the value of a?
   (A) 9   (B) 15   (C) 69   (D) 72   (E) 75

9. If the average (arithmetic mean) of $3a$ and $4b$ is less than 50, and a is twice b, what is the largest possible integer value of a?
   (A) 9   (B) 10   (C) 11   (D) 19   (E) 20

10. If $\frac{1}{a-b} = 5$, then $a =$
   (A) $b + 5$ (B) $b - 5$ (C) $b + \frac{1}{5}$ (D) $b - \frac{1}{5}$
   (E) $\frac{1 - 5b}{5}$

11. If $x = 3a + 7$ and $y = 9a^2$, what is y in terms of x?
   (A) $(x - 7)^2$ (B) $3(x - 7)^2$ (C) $\frac{(x-7)^2}{3}$
   (D) $\frac{(x+7)^2}{3}$ (E) $(x + 7)^2$

12. If $4y - 3x = 5$, what is the smallest integer value of x for which $y > 100$?
   (A) 130   (B) 131   (C) 132   (D) 395   (E) 396

Quantitative Comparison Questions

	Column A	Column B

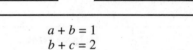

$a + b = 13$
$a - b = 13$

13. b 13

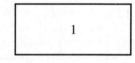

$\dfrac{2^{a-1}}{2^{b+1}} = 8$

14. a b

$4x^2 = 3x$

15. x 1

$a + b = 1$
$b + c = 2$
$c + a = 3$

16.   The average (arithmetic mean) of a, b, and c 1

$3x - 4y = 5$
$y = 2x$

17. x y

$\dfrac{x}{2} - 2 > \dfrac{x}{3}$

18. x 12

$3r - 5s = 17$
$2r - 6s = 7$

19.   The average (arithmetic mean) of r and s 10

$\dfrac{1}{c} = 1 + \dfrac{1}{d}$
c and d are positive

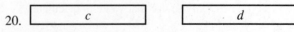

20. c d

Answer Key

1. **C**	6. **D**	11. **A**	16. **C**
2. **D**	7. **D**	12. **C**	17. **A**
3. **C**	8. **E**	13. **B**	18. **A**
4. **D**	9. **D**	14. **A**	19. **B**
5. **A**	10. **C**	15. **B**	20. **B**

Answer Explanations

1. **C.** The easiest method is to recognize that $x + 3$ is $\frac{1}{4}$ of $4x + 12$ and, therefore, equals $\frac{1}{4}$ of 36, which is 9. If you don't see that, solve normally: $4x + 12 = 36 \Rightarrow 4x = 24 \Rightarrow x = 6 \Rightarrow x + 3 = 9$.

2. **D.** Subtracting 20 from each side of $7x + 10 = 44$ gives $7x - 10 = 24$. If you don't see that, subtract 10 from each side, getting $7x = 34$. Then subtract 10 to get $7x - 10 = 24$. The worst alternative is to divide both sides of $7x = 34$ by 7 to get $x = \frac{34}{7}$; then you have to multiply by 7 to get back to 34, and then subtract 10.

3. **C.** Add $2x$ to each side: $6x + 13 = 7$. Subtract 13 from each side: $6x = -6$. Divide by 6: $x = -1$.

4. **D.** $x - 4 = 9 \Rightarrow x = 13 \Rightarrow x^2 = 169 \Rightarrow x^2 - 4 = 165$.

5. **A.** Treat a, b, c, and d as constants, and use the six-step method to solve for x:

$$ax - b = c - dx \Rightarrow ax - b + dx = c \Rightarrow$$
$$ax + dx = c + b \Rightarrow x(a + d) = b + c \Rightarrow$$
$$x = \frac{b+c}{a+d}.$$

6. **D.** Multiply both sides by 18, the LCD:

$$18\left(\frac{1}{3}x + \frac{1}{6}x + \frac{1}{9}x\right) = 18(33) \Rightarrow$$
$$6x + 3x + 2x = 594 \Rightarrow 11x = 594 \Rightarrow x = 54.$$

It's actually easier not to multiply out 18×33; leave it in that form, and then divide by 11: $\dfrac{18 \times \cancel{33}^{\,3}}{\cancel{11}_{\,1}} = 3 \times 18 = 54$.

7. **D.** Be alert. Since you are given the value of $3x - 4$, and want the value of $(3x - 4)^2$, just square both sides: $11^2 = 121$. If you don't see that, you'll waste time solving $3x - 4 = 11$ ($x = 5$), only to use that value to calculate that $3x - 4$ is equal to 11, which you already knew.

8. **E.** $2^{a-3} = 64^{12} = (2^6)^{12} = 2^{72} \Rightarrow a - 3 = 72 \Rightarrow a = 75$.

9. **D.** Since $a = 2b$, $2a = 4b$. Therefore, the average of $3a$ and $4b$ is the average of $3a$ and $2a$, which is $2.5a$. Therefore, $2.5a < 50 \Rightarrow a < 20$. So the largest *integer* value of a is 19.

10. **C.** Taking the reciprocal of each side, we get $a - b = \frac{1}{5}$. So $a = b + \frac{1}{5}$.

11. **A.** $x = 3a + 7 \Rightarrow x - 7 = 3a \Rightarrow a = \frac{x-7}{3}$. Therefore,

$$y = 9a^2 = 9\left(\frac{x-7}{3}\right)^2 = 9\frac{(x-7)^2}{3^2} = (x-7)^2.$$

12. **C.** First, solve for y in terms of x:

$$4y - 3x = 5 \Rightarrow 4y = 5 + 3x \Rightarrow y = \frac{5+3x}{4}.$$

Then, since $y > 100$:

$$\frac{5+3x}{4} > 100 \Rightarrow 5 + 3x > 400 \Rightarrow$$
$$3x > 395 \Rightarrow x > 131.666.$$

The smallest integer value of x is 132.

13. **B.** Adding the two equations, we get that $2a = 26$. Therefore, $a = 13$ and $b = 0$.

14. **A.** Express each side of $\dfrac{2^{a-1}}{2^{b+1}} = 8$ as a power of 2:

$$8 = 2^3 \quad \text{and} \quad \frac{2^{a-1}}{2^{b+1}} = 2^{(a-1)-(b+1)} = 2^{a-b-2}.$$

Therefore, $a - b - 2 = 3 \Rightarrow a = b + 5$, and so a is greater.

15. **B.** $4x^2 = 3x \Rightarrow 4x^2 - 3x = 0 \Rightarrow x(4x - 3) = 0 \Rightarrow$

$$x = 0 \quad \text{or} \quad 4x - 3 = 0 \Rightarrow$$
$$x = 0 \quad \text{or} \quad 4x = 3 \Rightarrow$$
$$x = 0 \quad \text{or} \quad x = \frac{3}{4}.$$

There are two possible values of x, both of which are less than 1.

16. C. When we add all three equations, we get
$2a + 2b + 2c = 6 \Rightarrow a + b + c = 3 \Rightarrow$
$\dfrac{a+b+c}{3} = 1.$

17. A. Use substitution. Replace y in the first equation with $2x$: $3x - 4(2x) = 5 \Rightarrow 3x - 8x = 5 \Rightarrow -5x = 5 \Rightarrow x = -1 \Rightarrow y = -2.$

18. A. Multiply both sides by 6, the LCD:
$6\left(\dfrac{x}{2} - 2\right) > 6\left(\dfrac{x}{3}\right) \Rightarrow 3x - 12 > 2x \Rightarrow$
$-12 > -x \Rightarrow x > 12.$

19. B. The first thing to try is to add the equations. That yields $5r - 11s = 24$, which does not appear to be useful. So now try to subtract the equations. That yields $r + s = 10$. So the average of r and s is $\dfrac{r+s}{2} = \dfrac{10}{2} = 5.$

20. B. Multiply both sides by cd, the LCD of the fractions:

$$cd\left(\dfrac{1}{c}\right) = cd\left(1 + \dfrac{1}{d}\right) \Rightarrow$$

$$d = cd + c = c(d + 1) \Rightarrow c = \dfrac{d}{d+1}$$

Since d is positive, $d + 1 > 1 \Rightarrow \dfrac{d}{d+1} < d.$
So $c < d.$

14-H. WORD PROBLEMS

On a typical GRE you will see several word problems, covering almost every math topic for which you are responsible. In this chapter you have already seen word problems on consecutive integers in Section A; fractions and percents in Sections B and C; ratios and rates in Section D; and averages in Section E. Later in this chapter you will see word problems involving probability, circles, triangles, and other geometric figures. A few of these problems can be solved with just arithmetic, but most of them require basic algebra.

To solve word problems algebraically, you must treat algebra as a foreign language and learn to translate "word for word" from English into algebra, just as you would from English into French or Spanish or any other language. When translating into algebra, we use some letter (often x) to represent the unknown quantity we are trying to determine. It is this translation process that causes difficulty for some students. Once translated, solving is easy using the techniques we have already reviewed. Consider the following pairs of typical GRE questions. The first ones in each pair (1a and 2a) would be considered easy, whereas the second ones (1b and 2b) would be considered harder.

Example 1a.

What is 4% of 4% of 40,000?

Example 1b.

In a lottery, 4% of the tickets printed can be redeemed for prizes, and 4% of those tickets have values in excess of $100. If the state prints 40,000 tickets, how many of them can be redeemed for more than $100?

Example 2a.

If $x + 7 = 2(x - 8)$, what is the value of x?

Example 2b.

In 7 years Erin will be twice as old as she was 8 years ago. How old is Erin now?

Once you translate the words into arithmetic expressions or algebraic equations, Examples 1a and 1b and 2a and 2b are identical. The problem that many students have is doing the translation. It really isn't very difficult, and we'll show you how. First, though, look over the following English to algebra "dictionary."

English Words	Mathematical Meaning	Symbol
Is, was, will be, had, has, will have, is equal to, is the same as	Equals	=
Plus, more than, sum, increased by, added to, exceeds, received, got, older than, farther than, greater than	Addition	+
Minus, fewer, less than, difference, decreased by, subtracted from, younger than, gave, lost	Subtraction	−
Times, of, product, multiplied by	Multiplication	×
Divided by, quotient, per, for	Division	$\div$, $\dfrac{a}{b}$
More than, greater than	Inequality	>
At least	Inequality	≥
Fewer than, less than	Inequality	<
At most	Inequality	≤
What, how many, etc.	Unknown quantity	x (or some some other variable)

Let's use our dictionary to translate some phrases and sentences.

1. The <u>sum</u> of 5 and some number <u>is</u> 13. $5 + x = 13$
2. John <u>was</u> 2 years <u>younger than</u> Sam. $J = S - 2$
3. Bill has <u>at most</u> $100. $B \leq 100$
4. The <u>product</u> of 2 and a number <u>exceeds</u> that number by 5 (is 5 more than). $2N = N + 5$

In translating statements, you first must decide what quantity the variable will represent. Often it's obvious. Other times there is more than one possibility.

Let's translate and solve the two questions from the beginning of this section, and then we'll look at a few new ones.

Example 1b.

In a lottery, 4% of the tickets printed can be redeemed for prizes, and 4% of those tickets have values in excess of $100. If the state prints 40,000 tickets, how many of them can be redeemed for more than $100?

SOLUTION. Let x = the number of tickets worth more than $100. Then

$$x = 4\% \text{ of } 4\% \text{ of } 40,000 = .04 \times .04 \times 40,000 = \textbf{64},$$

which is also the solution to Example 1a.

Example 2b.

In 7 years Erin will be twice as old as she was 8 years ago. How old is Erin now?

SOLUTION. Let x = Erin's age now. Then 8 years ago she was $x - 8$, and 7 years from now she will be $x + 7$. So,

$$x + 7 = 2(x - 8) \Rightarrow x + 7 = 2x - 16 \Rightarrow 7 = x - 16 \Rightarrow x = \textbf{23},$$

which is also the solution to Example 2a.

Most algebraic word problems on the GRE are not too difficult, and if you can do the algebra, that's usually the best way. But if, after studying this section, you still get stuck on a question during the test, don't despair. Use the tactics that you learned in Chapter 11, especially TACTIC 1—backsolving.

Helpful Hint

In all word problems on the GRE, remember to write down and circle what you are looking for. Don't answer the wrong question!

Age Problems

Helpful Hint

In problems involving ages, remember that "years ago" means you need to subtract, and "years from now" means you need to add.

Example 3.

In 1980, Judy was 3 times as old as Adam, but in 1984 she was only twice as old as he was. How old was Adam in 1990?

(A) 4   (B) 8   (C) 12   (D) 14   (E) 16

Helpful Hint

It is often very useful to organize the data from a word problem in a table.

SOLUTION. Let x be Adam's age in 1980 and fill in the table below.

Year	Judy	Adam
1980	$3x$	x
1984	$3x + 4$	$x + 4$

Now translate: Judy's age in 1984 was twice Adam's age in 1984: $3x + 4 = 2(x + 4)$

$$3x + 4 = 2x + 8 \Rightarrow x + 4 = 8 \Rightarrow x = 4$$

So, Adam was 4 in 1980. However, 4 is *not* the answer to this question. Did you remember to circle what you're looking for? The question *could have* asked for Adam's age in 1980 (Choice A) or 1984 (Choice B) or Judy's age in any year whatsoever (Choice C is 1980 and Choice E is 1984); but it didn't. It asked for *Adam's age in 1990*. Since he was 4 in 1980, then 10 years later, in 1990, he was **14 (D)**.

Distance Problems

Distance problems all depend on three variations of the same formula:

$$\textbf{distance} = \textbf{rate} \times \textbf{time} \qquad \textbf{rate} = \frac{\textbf{distance}}{\textbf{time}}$$

$$\textbf{time} = \frac{\textbf{distance}}{\textbf{rate}}$$

These are usually abbreviated, $d = rt$, $r = \dfrac{d}{t}$, and $t = \dfrac{d}{r}$.

Example 4.

How much longer, in *seconds,* is required to drive 1 mile at 40 miles per hour than at 60 miles per hour?

SOLUTION. The time to drive 1 mile at 40 miles per hour is given by

$$t = \frac{1}{40} \text{ hour} = \frac{1}{40} \times \overset{3}{\cancel{60}} \text{ minutes} = 1\frac{1}{2} \text{ minutes.}$$

The time to drive 1 mile at 60 miles per hour is given by

$$t = \frac{1}{60} \text{ hour} = 1 \text{ minute.}$$

The difference is $\frac{1}{2}$ minute = **30 seconds.**

Note that this solution used the time formula given, but required only arithmetic, not algebra. Example 5 requires an algebraic solution.

Example 5.

Avi drove from his home to college at 60 miles per hour. Returning over the same route, there was a lot of traffic, and he was only able to drive at 40 miles per hour. If the return trip took 1 hour longer, how many miles did he drive each way?
(A) 2   (B) 3   (C) 5   (D) 120   (E) 240

SOLUTION. Let x = the number of hours Avi took going to college and make a table.

	rate	time	distance
Going	60	x	$60x$
Returning	40	$x + 1$	$40(x + 1)$

Since he drove the same distance going and returning,

$$60x = 40(x + 1) \Rightarrow 60x = 40x + 40 \Rightarrow 20x = 40 \Rightarrow x = 2.$$

Now be sure to answer the correct question. When $x = 2$, Choices A, B, and C are the time in hours that it took going, returning, and round-trip; Choices D and E are the distances each way and round-trip. You could have been asked for any of the five. If you circled what you're looking for, you won't make a careless mistake. Avi drove **120** miles each way, and so the correct answer is **D**.

The d in $d = rt$ stands for "distance," but it could really be any type of work that is performed at a certain rate, r, for a certain amount of time, t. Example 5 need not be about distance. Instead of driving 120 miles at 60 miles per hour for 2 hours, Avi could have read 120 pages at a rate of 60 pages per hour for 2 hours; or planted 120 flowers at the rate of 60 flowers per hour for 2 hours; or typed 120 words at a rate of 60 words per minute for 2 minutes.

Examples 6 and 7 illustrate two additional word problems of the type that you might find on the GRE.

Example 6.

Lindsay is trying to collect all the cards in a special commemorative set of baseball cards. She currently has exactly $\frac{1}{4}$ of the cards in that set. When she gets 10 more cards, she will then have $\frac{1}{3}$ of the cards. How many cards are in the set?
(A) 30   (B) 60   (C) 120   (D) 180   (E) 240

SOLUTION. Let x be the number cards in the set. First, translate this problem from English into algebra: $\frac{1}{4}x + 10 = \frac{1}{3}x$. Now, use the six-step method of Section 14-G to solve the equation. Multiply by 12 to get, $3x + 120 = 4x$, and then subtract $3x$ from each side: $x = $ **120 (D).**

Example 7.

Jen, Ken, and Len have a total of $390. Jen has 5 times as much as Len, and Ken has $\frac{3}{4}$ as much as Jen. How much money does Ken have?
(A) $40   (B) $78   (C) $150   (D) $195
   (E) $200

Helpful Hint

You often have a choice as to what to let the variable represent. Don't necessarily let it represent what you're looking for; rather, choose what will make the problem easiest to solve.

Suppose, for example, that in this problem you let x represent the amount of money that Ken has. Then since Ken has $\frac{3}{4}$ as much as Jen, Jen has $\frac{4}{3}$ as much as Ken: $\frac{4}{3}x$; and Jen would have $\frac{1}{5}$ of that: $\left(\frac{1}{5}\right)\left(\frac{4}{3}x\right)$. It is much easier here to let x represent the amount of money Len has.

SOLUTION. Let x represent the amount of money Len has. Then $5x$ is the amount that Jen has, and $\frac{3}{4}(5x)$ is the amount that Ken has. Since the total amount of money is $390,

$$x + 5x + \frac{15}{4}x = 390.$$

Multiply by 4 to get rid of the fraction:

$$4x + 20x + 15x = 1560.$$

Combine like terms and then divide:

$$39x = 1560 \Rightarrow x = 40.$$

So Len has $40, Jen has $5 \times 40 = 200, and Ken has $\frac{3}{4}(200) = $ **$150 (C).**

PRACTICE EXERCISES—WORD PROBLEMS

Multiple-Choice Questions

1. Howard has three times as much money as Ronald. If Howard gives Ronald $50, Ronald will then have three times as much money as Howard. How much money do the two of them have together?

   (A) $75   (B) $100   (C) $125   (D) $150
   (E) $200

2. In the afternoon, Beth read 100 pages at the rate of 60 pages per hour; in the evening, when she was tired, she read another 100 pages at the rate of 40 pages per hour. What was her average rate of reading for the day?

   (A) 45   (B) 48   (C) 50   (D) 52   (E) 55

3. If the sum of five consecutive integers is S, what is the largest of those integers in terms of S?

   (A) $\dfrac{S-10}{5}$ (B) $\dfrac{S+4}{4}$ (C) $\dfrac{S+5}{4}$ (D) $\dfrac{S-5}{2}$

   (E) $\dfrac{S+10}{5}$

4. The number of shells in Judy's collection is 80% of the number in Justin's collection. If Justin has 80 more shells than Judy, how many shells do they have altogether?

   (A) 180   (B) 320   (C) 400   (D) 720   (E) 800

5. A jar contains only red, white, and blue marbles. The number of red marbles is $\dfrac{4}{5}$ the number of white ones, and the number of white ones is $\dfrac{3}{4}$ the number of blue ones. If there are 470 marbles in all, how many of them are blue?

   (A) 120   (B) 135   (C) 150   (D) 184   (E) 200

6. As a fund-raiser, the school band was selling two types of candy: lollipops for 40 cents each and chocolate bars for 75 cents each. On Monday, they sold 150 candies and raised 74 dollars. How many lollipops did they sell?

   (A) 75   (B) 90   (C) 96   (D) 110   (E) 120

7. What is the greater of two numbers whose product is 900, if the sum of the two numbers exceeds their difference by 30?

   (A) 15   (B) 60   (C) 75   (D) 90   (E) 100

8. On a certain project the only grades awarded were 80 and 100. If 10 students completed the project and the average of their grades was 94, how many earned 100?

   (A) 2   (B) 3   (C) 5   (D) 7   (E) 8

9. If $\dfrac{1}{2}x$ years ago Adam was 12, and $\dfrac{1}{2}x$ years from now he will be $2x$ years old, how old will he be $3x$ years from now?

   (A) 18   (B) 24   (C) 30   (D) 54
       (E) It cannot be determined from the information given.

10. Since 1950, when Barry was discharged from the army, he has gained 2 pounds every year. In 1980 he was 40% heavier than in 1950. What percent of his 1995 weight was his 1980 weight?

    (A) 80   (B) 85   (C) 87.5   (D) 90   (E) 95

Quantitative Comparison Questions

Column A	Column B

Lindsay is twice as old as she was 10 years ago. Kimberly is half as old as she will be in 10 years.

11. Lindsay's age now | Kimberly's age now

Boris spent $\dfrac{1}{4}$ of his take-home pay on Saturday and $\dfrac{1}{3}$ of what was left on Sunday. The rest he put in his savings account.

12. The amount of his take-home pay that he spent | The amount of his take-home pay that he saved

In 8 years, Tiffany will be 3 times as old as she is now.

13. The number of years until Tiffany will be 6 times as old as she is now | 16

Rachel put exactly 50 cents worth of postage on an envelope using only 4-cent stamps and 7-cent stamps.

14. The number of 4-cent stamps she used | The number of 7-cent stamps she used

Car A and Car B leave from the same spot at the same time.
Car A travels due north at 40 mph.
Car B travels due east at 30 mph.

15. Distance from Car A to Car B 9 hours after they left | 450 miles

Answer Key

1. **B**	6. **D**	11. **A**
2. **B**	7. **B**	12. **C**
3. **E**	8. **D**	13. **A**
4. **D**	9. **D**	14. **D**
5. **E**	10. **C**	15. **C**

Answer Explanations

1. **B.**

	Ronald	Howard
At the beginning	x	$3x$
After the gift	$x + 50$	$3x - 50$

After the gift, Ronald will have 3 times as much money as Howard:

$$x + 50 = 3(3x - 50) \Rightarrow x + 50 = 9x - 150 \Rightarrow$$
$$8x = 200 \Rightarrow x = 25.$$

So Ronald has $25 and Howard has $75, for a total of $100.

2. **B.** Beth's average rate of reading is determined by dividing the total number of pages she read (200) by the total amount of time she spent reading. In the afternoon she read for $\dfrac{100}{60} = \dfrac{5}{3}$ hours, and in the evening for $\dfrac{100}{40} = \dfrac{5}{2}$ hours, for a total time of $\dfrac{5}{3} + \dfrac{5}{2} = \dfrac{10}{6} + \dfrac{15}{6} = \dfrac{25}{6}$ hours. So, her average rate was
$$200 \div \dfrac{25}{6} = 200 \times \dfrac{6}{25} = 48 \text{ pages per hour.}$$

3. **E.** Let the 5 consecutive integers be $n, n + 1, n + 2, n + 3, n + 4$. Then,

$$S = n + n + 1 + n + 2 + n + 3 + n + 4 =$$
$$5n + 10 \Rightarrow 5n = S - 10 \Rightarrow n = \dfrac{S - 10}{5}.$$

Choice A, therefore, is the *smallest* of the integers; the *largest* is

$$n + 4 = \dfrac{S - 10}{5} + 4 = \dfrac{S - 10}{5} + \dfrac{20}{5} = \dfrac{S + 10}{5}.$$

4. **D.** If x is the number of shells in Justin's collection, then Judy has $.80x$. Since Justin has 80 more shells than Judy,
$$x = .80x + 80 \Rightarrow .20x = 80 \Rightarrow$$
$$x = 80 \div .20 = 400.$$
So Justin has 400 and Judy has 320: a total of 720.

5. **E.** If b is the number of blue marbles, then there are $\dfrac{3}{4}b$ white ones, and $\dfrac{4}{5}\left(\dfrac{3}{4}b\right) = \dfrac{3}{5}b$ red ones. Therefore,

$$470 = b + \dfrac{3}{4}b + \dfrac{3}{5}b = b\left(1 + \dfrac{3}{4} + \dfrac{3}{5}\right) = \dfrac{47}{20}b.$$

So, $b = 470 \div \dfrac{47}{20} = \overset{10}{\cancel{470}} \times \dfrac{20}{\underset{1}{\cancel{47}}} = 200.$

6. **D.** Let x represent the number of chocolate bars sold; then $150 - x$ is the number of lollipops sold. We must use the same units, so we could write 75 cents as .75 dollars or 74 dollars as 7400 cents. Let's avoid the decimals: x chocolates sold for $75x$ cents and $(150 - x)$ lollipops sold for $40(150 - x)$ cents. So,
$$7400 = 75x + 40(150 - x) =$$
$$75x + 6000 - 40x = 6000 + 35x \Rightarrow$$
$$1400 = 35x \Rightarrow x = 40 \text{ and } 150 - 40 = 110.$$

7. **B.** If x represents the greater and y the smaller of the two numbers, then $(x + y) = 30 + (x - y) \Rightarrow y = 30 - y \Rightarrow 2y = 30 \Rightarrow y = 15$; and since $xy = 900$, $x = 900 \div 15 = 60$.

8. **D.** If x represents the number of students earning 100, then $10 - x$ is the number of students earning 80. So

$$94 = \dfrac{100x + 80(10 - x)}{10} \Rightarrow$$
$$94 = \dfrac{100x + 800 - 80x}{10} = \dfrac{20x + 800}{10} \Rightarrow$$
$$94 \times 10 = 940 = 20x + 800 \Rightarrow$$
$$140 = 20x \Rightarrow x = 7.$$

9. **D.** Since $\dfrac{1}{2}x$ years ago, Adam was 12, he is now $12 + \dfrac{1}{2}x$. So $\dfrac{1}{2}x$ years from now, he will be $12 + \dfrac{1}{2}x + \dfrac{1}{2}x = 12 + x$. But, we are told that at that time he will be $2x$ years old. So, $12 + x = 2x \Rightarrow x = 12$. Thus, he is now $12 + 6 = 18$, and $3x$ or 36 years from now he will be $18 + 36 = 54$.

10. **C.** Let x be Barry's weight in 1950. By 1980, he had gained 60 pounds (2 pounds per year for 30 years) and was 40% heavier: $60 = .40x \Rightarrow$ $x = 60 \div .4 = 150$. So in 1980, he weighed 210. Fifteen years later, in 1995, he weighed 240: $\dfrac{210}{240} = \dfrac{7}{8} = 87.5\%$.

11. **A.** You can do the simple algebra, but you should realize that Lindsay is as old now as Kimberly will be in 10 years. If x represents Lindsay's age now, $x = 2(x - 10) \Rightarrow x = 2x - 20 \Rightarrow$ $x = 20$. Similarly, Kimberly is now 10 and will be 20 in 10 years.

12. **C.** Let x represent the amount of Boris's take-home pay. On Saturday, he spent $\dfrac{1}{4}x$ and still had $\dfrac{3}{4}x$; but on Sunday, he spent $\dfrac{1}{3}$ of that: $\dfrac{1}{3}\left(\dfrac{3}{4}x\right) = \dfrac{1}{4}x$. So he spent $\dfrac{1}{4}$ of his take-home pay each day. He spent $\dfrac{1}{2}$ and saved $\dfrac{1}{2}$.

13. **A.** If x represents Tiffany's age now, then $x + 8$ is her age in 8 years, and so $x + 8 = 3x \Rightarrow$ $8 = 2x \Rightarrow x = 4$. Tiffany will be 6 times as old 20 years from now, when she will be 24.

14. **D.** If x and y represent the number of 4-cent stamps and 7-cent stamps that Rachel used, respectively, then $4x + 7y = 50$. There are infinitely many solutions to this equation, but there are only 2 solutions in which x and y are both positive integers: $y = 2$ and $x = 9$ or $y = 6$ and $x = 2$.

15. **C.** Draw a diagram. In 9 hours Car A drove 360 miles north and Car B drove 270 miles east. These are the legs of a right triangle, whose hypotenuse is the distance between them. You can use the Pythagorean theorem if you don't recognize that this is just a 3-4-5 right triangle: the legs are 90×3 and 90×4, and the hypotenuse is $90 \times 5 = 450$.

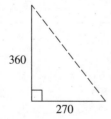

GEOMETRY

Although about 30% of the math questions on the GRE have to do with geometry, there are only a relatively small number of facts you need to know—far less than you would learn in a geometry course—and, of course, there are no proofs. In the next six sections we will review all of the geometry that you need to know to do well on the GRE. We will present the material exactly as it appears on the GRE, using the same vocabulary and notation, which might be slightly different from the terminology you learned in your high school math classes. In particular, the word "congruent" and the symbol "≅" are not used—angles or line segments that have the same measure are considered "equal." The numerous multiple-choice and quantitative comparison examples will show you exactly how these topics are treated on the GRE.

14-I. LINES AND ANGLES

An **angle** is formed by the intersection of two line segments, rays, or lines. The point of intersection is called the **vertex**. On the GRE, angles are always measured in degrees.

KEY FACT I1:

Angles are classified according to their degree measures.

- **An acute angle measures less than 90°.**
- **A right angle measures 90°.**
- **An obtuse angle measures more than 90° but less than 180°.**
- **A straight angle measures 180°.**

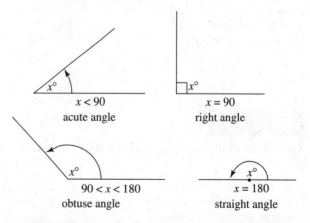

NOTE: The small square in the second angle in the figure above is *always* used to mean that the angle is a right angle. On the GRE, if an angle has a square in it, it must measure exactly 90°, *whether or not you think that the figure has been drawn to scale.*

KEY FACT I2:

If two or more angles form a straight angle, the sum of their measures is 180°.

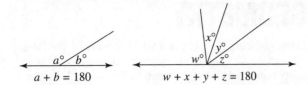

$a + b = 180$ $w + x + y + z = 180$

Example 1.

In the figure below, R, S, and T are all on line ℓ. What is the average of a, b, c, d, and e?

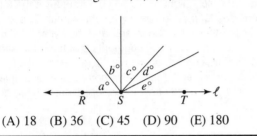

(A) 18   (B) 36   (C) 45   (D) 90   (E) 180

SOLUTION. Since $\angle RST$ is a straight angle, by KEY FACT 12, the sum of a, b, c, d, and e is 180, and so their average is $\dfrac{180}{5}$ = **36 (B)**.

In the figure at the right, since $a + b + c + d = 180$ and $e + f + g = 180$, $a + b + c + d + e + f + g = 180 + 180 = 360$.

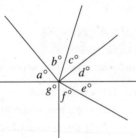

It is also true that $u + v + w + x + y + z = 360$, even though none of the angles forms a straight angle.

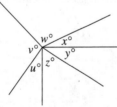

KEY FACT 13:

The sum of all the measures of all the angles around a point is 360°.

Note: This fact is particularly important when the point is the center of a circle, as we shall see in Section 14-L.

$a + b + c + d = 360$

When two lines intersect, four angles are formed. The two angles in each pair of opposite angles are called **vertical angles**.

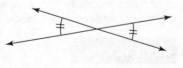

KEY FACT 14:

Vertical angles have equal measures.

Example 2.

In the figure at the right, what is the value of x?

(A) 6   (B) 8
(C) 10   (D) 20
(E) 40

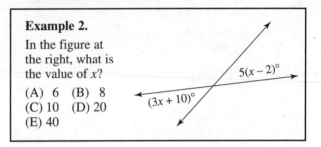

SOLUTION. Since the measures of vertical angles are equal,

$$3x + 10 = 5(x - 2) \Rightarrow 3x + 10 = 5x - 10 \Rightarrow$$
$$3x + 20 = 5x \Rightarrow 20 = 2x \Rightarrow x = \textbf{10 (C)}.$$

KEY FACT 15:

If one of the angles formed by the intersection of two lines (or line segments) is a right angle, then all four angles are right angles.

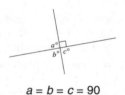

$a = b = c = 90$

Two lines that intersect to form right angles are called **perpendicular.**

In the figures below, line ℓ divides $\angle ABC$ into two equal parts, and line k divides line segment DE into two equal parts. Line ℓ is said to **bisect** the angle, and line k **bisects** the line segment. Point M is called the **midpoint** of segment DE.

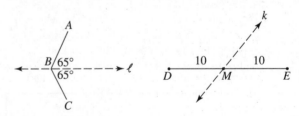

Example 3.

In the figure at the right, lines k, ℓ, and m intersect at O. If line m bisects $\angle AOB$, what is the value of x?

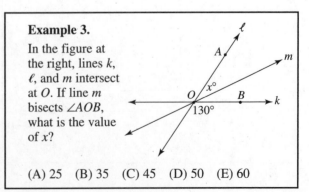

(A) 25   (B) 35   (C) 45   (D) 50   (E) 60

SOLUTION. m∠AOB + 130 = 180 ⇒ m∠AOB = 50; and since *m* bisects ∠AOB, x = **25 (A)**.

Two lines that never intersect are said to be **parallel**. Consequently, parallel lines form no angles. However, if a third line, called a **transversal**, intersects a pair of parallel lines, eight angles are formed, and the relationships among these angles are very important.

KEY FACT 16:

If a pair of parallel lines is cut by a transversal that is perpendicular to the parallel lines, all eight angles are right angles.

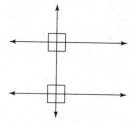

KEY FACT 17:

If a pair of parallel lines is cut by a transversal that is not perpendicular to the parallel lines,

- Four of the angles are acute and four are obtuse;
- The four acute angles are equal: *a = c = e = g*;
- The four obtuse angles are equal: *b = d = f = h*;
- The sum of any acute angle and any obtuse angle is 180°: for example, *d* + *e* = 180, *c* + *f* = 180, *b* + *g* = 180, ...

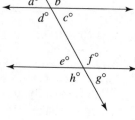

KEY FACT 18:

If a pair of lines that are not parallel is cut by a transversal, **none** of the properties listed in KEY FACT 17 is true.

You must know KEY FACT 17—virtually every GRE has at least one question based on it. However, you do *not* need to know the special terms you learned in high school for these pairs of angles; those terms are not used on the GRE.

Example 4.

In the figure below, *AB* is parallel to *CD*. What is the value of *x*?

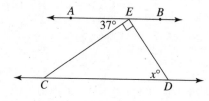

(A) 37　(B) 45　(C) 53　(D) 63　(E) 143

SOLUTION. Let *y* be the measure of ∠BED. Then by KEY FACT 12:

$$37 + 90 + y = 180 \Rightarrow 127 + y = 180 \Rightarrow y = 53.$$

Since *AB* is parallel to *CD*, by KEY FACT 17, x = y ⇒ x = **53 (C)**.

Example 5.

In the figure below, lines ℓ and *k* are parallel. What is the value of *a* + *b*?

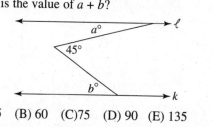

(A) 45　(B) 60　(C)75　(D) 90　(E) 135

SOLUTION. It is impossible to determine the value of either *a* or *b*. We can, however, find the value of *a* + *b*. We draw a line through the vertex of the angle parallel to ℓ and *k*. Then, looking at the top two lines, we see that *a* = *x*, and looking at the bottom two lines, we see that *b* = *y*. So, *a* + *b* = *x* + *y* = **45 (A)**.

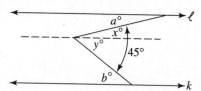

Alternative solution. Draw a different line and use a Key Fact from Section 14-J on triangles. Extend one of the line segments to form a triangle. Since ℓ and *k* are parallel, the measure of the third angle in the triangle equals *a*. Now, use the fact that the sum of the measures of the three angles in a triangle is 180° or, even easier, that the given 45° angle is an external angle of the triangle, and so is equal to the sum of *a* and *b*.

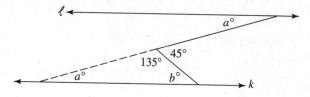

PRACTICE EXERCISES—LINES AND ANGLES

Multiple-Choice Questions

1. In the figure below, what is the average (arithmetic mean) of the measures of the five angles?

(A) 36   (B) 45   (C) 60   (D) 72   (E) 90

2. In the figure below, what is the value of $\dfrac{b+a}{b-a}$?

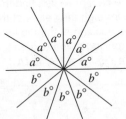

(A) 1   (B) 10   (C) 11   (D) 30   (E) 36

3. In the figure below, what is the value of b?

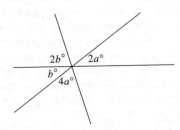

(A) 9   (B) 18   (C) 27   (D) 36   (E) 45

4. In the figure below, what is the value of x if $y:x = 3:2$?

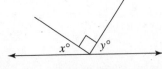

(A) 18   (B) 27   (C) 36   (D) 45   (E) 54

5. What is the measure of the angle formed by the minute and hour hands of a clock at 1:50?
   (A) 90°   (B) 95°   (C) 105°   (D) 115°   (E) 120°

6. Concerning the figure below, if $a = b$, which of the following statements must be true?

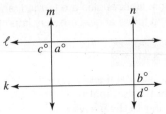

   I. $c = d$
   II. ℓ and k are parallel
   III. m and ℓ are perpendicular

   (A) none   (B) I only   (C) I and II only
   (D) I and III only   (E) I, II, and III

7. In the figure below, $a:b = 3:5$ and $c:b = 2:1$. What is the measure of the largest angle?

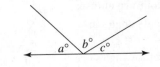

   (A) 30   (B) 45   (C) 50   (D) 90   (E) 100

8. A, B, and C are points on a line with B between A and C. Let M and N be the midpoints of AB and BC, respectively. If $AB:BC = 3:1$, what is $MN:BC$?
   (A) 1:2   (B) 2:3   (C) 1:1   (D) 3:2   (E) 2:1

9. In the figure below, lines k and ℓ are parallel. What is the value of $y - x$?

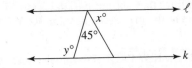

   (A) 15   (B) 30   (C) 45   (D) 60   (E) 75

10. In the figure below, line m bisects $\angle AOC$ and line ℓ bisects $\angle AOB$. What is the measure of $\angle DOE$?

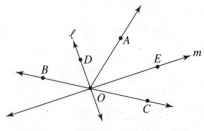

   (A) 75   (B) 90   (C) 100   (D) 105   (E) 120

Quantitative Comparison Questions

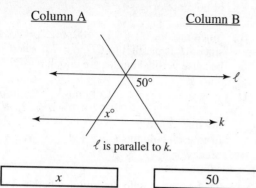

Column A   Column B

ℓ is parallel to *k*.

11. | x | | 50 |

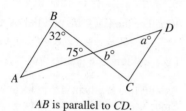

AB is parallel to *CD*.

12. | a | | b |

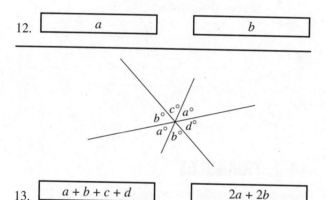

13. | $a + b + c + d$ | | $2a + 2b$ |

Column A   Column B

14. | $a + b + c + d$ | | $e + f + g + h$ |

k and *ℓ* are parallel.

15. | z | | $x + y$ |

Answer Key

1. **D**	6. **B**	11. **D**
2. **C**	7. **E**	12. **B**
3. **D**	8. **E**	13. **D**
4. **C**	9. **C**	14. **C**
5. **D**	10. **B**	15. **C**

Answer Explanations

1. **D.** The markings in the five angles are irrelevant. The sum of the measures of the five angles is 360°, and 360 ÷ 5 = 72. If you calculated the measure of each angle you should have gotten 36, 54, 72, 90, and 108; but you would have wasted time.

2. **C.** From the diagram, we see that $6a = 180$, which implies that $a = 30$, and that $5b = 180$, which implies that $b = 36$. So, $\dfrac{b+a}{b-a} = \dfrac{36+30}{36-30} = \dfrac{66}{6} = 11$.

3. **D.** Since vertical angles are equal, the two unmarked angles are $2b$ and $4a$. Since the sum of all six angles is 360°,

$$360 = 4a + 2b + 2a + 4a + 2b + b = 10a + 5b.$$

However, since vertical angles are equal, $b = 2a \Rightarrow 5b = 10a$. Hence,

$$360 = 10a + 5b = 10a + 10a = 20a \Rightarrow$$
$$a = 18 \Rightarrow b = 36.$$

4. C. Since $x + y + 90 = 180$, $x + y = 90$. Also, since $y{:}x = 3{:}2$, $y = 3t$ and $x = 2t$. Therefore,

$$3t + 2t = 90 \Rightarrow 5t = 90 \Rightarrow$$
$$t = 18 \Rightarrow x = 2(18) = 36.$$

5. D. For problems such as this, always draw a diagram. The measure of each of the 12 central angles from one number to the next on the clock is 30°. At 1:50 the minute hand is pointing at 10, and the hour hand has gone

$$\frac{50}{60} = \frac{5}{6} \text{ of the way}$$

from 1 to 2. So from 10 to 1 on the clock is 90°, and from 1 to the hour hand is $\frac{5}{6}(30°) = 25°$, for a total of $90° + 25° = 115°$.

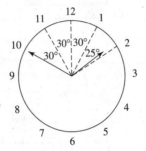

6. B. No conclusions can be made about the lines; they could form any angles whatsoever. (II and III are both false.) I is true:

$$c = 180 - a = 180 - b = d.$$

7. E. Since $a{:}b = 3{:}5$, then $a = 3x$ and $b = 5x$; and since $c{:}b = c{:}5x = 2{:}1$, $c = 10x$. Then,

$$3x + 5x + 10x = 180 \Rightarrow 18x = 180 \Rightarrow$$
$$x = 10 \Rightarrow c = 10x = 100.$$

8. E. If a diagram is not provided on a geometry question, draw one on your scrap paper. From the figure below, you can see that $MN{:}BC = 2{:}1$.

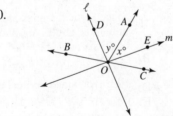

9. C. Since the lines are parallel, the angle marked y and the sum of the angles marked x and 45 are equal: $y = x + 45 \Rightarrow y - x = 45$.

10. B. Let $x = \frac{1}{2}m\angle AOC$, and $y = \frac{1}{2}m\angle AOB$. Then,

$$x + y = \frac{1}{2}m\angle AOC + \frac{1}{2}m\angle AOB =$$
$$\frac{1}{2}(180) = 90.$$

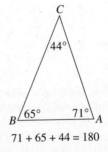

11. D. No conclusion can be made: x could equal 50 or be more or less.

12. B. Since $m\angle A + 32 + 75 = 180$, $m\angle A = 73$; and since AB is parallel to CD, $a = 73$, whereas, because vertical angles are equal, $b = 75$.

13. D.

	Column A	Column B
	$a + b + c + d$	$2a + 2b$
Subtract a and b from each column:	$c + d$	$a + b$
Since $b = d$, subtract them:	c	a

There is no way to determine whether a is less than, greater than, or equal to c.

14. C. Whether the lines are parallel or not,

$$a + b = c + d = e + f = g + h = 180.$$

Each column is equal to 360.

15. C. Extend line segment AB to form a transversal. Since $w + z = 180$ and $w + (x + y) = 180$, it follows that $z = x + y$.

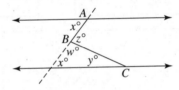

14-J. TRIANGLES

More geometry questions on the GRE pertain to triangles than to any other topic. To answer them, there are several important facts that you need to know about the angles and sides of triangles. The KEY FACTS in this section are extremely useful. Read them carefully, a few times if necessary, and *make sure you learn them all*.

KEY FACT J1:

In any triangle, the sum of the measures of the three angles is 180°: $x + y + z = 180$.

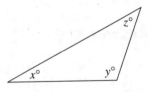

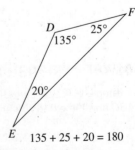

(a)   (b)

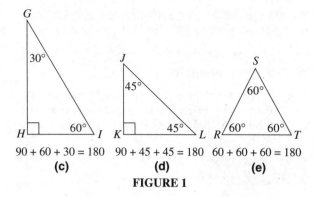

$$90 + 60 + 30 = 180 \qquad 90 + 45 + 45 = 180 \qquad 60 + 60 + 60 = 180$$
(c) **(d)** **(e)**
FIGURE 1

Figure 1 (a–e) illustrates KEY FACT J1 for five different triangles, which will be discussed below.

Example 1.

In the figure below, what is the value of x?

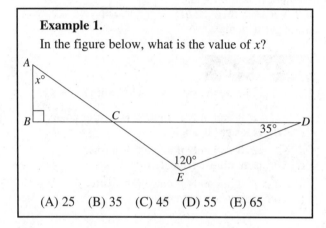

(A) 25 (B) 35 (C) 45 (D) 55 (E) 65

SOLUTION. Use KEY FACT J1 twice: first, for $\triangle CDE$ and then for $\triangle ABC$.

- m$\angle DCE$ + 120 + 35 = 180 $\Rightarrow$ m$\angle DCE$ + 155 = 180 $\Rightarrow$ m$\angle DCE$ = 25.

- Since vertical angles are equal, m$\angle ACB$ = 25 (see KEY FACT I6).

- x + 90 + 25 = 180 $\Rightarrow$ x + 115 = 180 $\Rightarrow$ x = **65 (E)**.

Example 2.

In the figure at the right, what is the value of a?

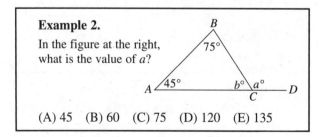

(A) 45 (B) 60 (C) 75 (D) 120 (E) 135

SOLUTION. First find the value of b:

$$180 = 45 + 75 + b = 120 + b \Rightarrow b = 60.$$

Then, $a + b = 180 \Rightarrow a = 180 - b = 180 - 60 = $ **120 (D)**.

In Example 2, $\angle BCD$, which is formed by one side of $\triangle ABC$ and the extension of another side, is called an **exterior angle**. Note that to find a we did not have to first find b; we could have just added the other two angles: $a = 75 + 45 = 120$. This is a useful fact to remember.

KEY FACT J2:

The measure of an exterior angle of a triangle is equal to the sum of the measures of the two opposite interior angles.

KEY FACT J3:

In any triangle:

- the longest side is opposite the largest angle;
- the shortest side is opposite the smallest angle;
- sides with the same length are opposite angles with the same measure.

CAUTION: In KEY FACT J3 the condition "in any triangle" is crucial. If the angles are not in the same triangle, none of the conclusions hold. For example, in the figures below, *AB* and *DE* are *not* equal even though they are each opposite a 90° angle, and *QS* is not the longest side in the figure, even though it is opposite the largest angle in the figure.

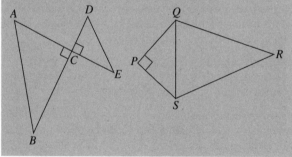

Consider triangles *ABC*, *JKL*, and *RST* in Figure 1.

- In $\triangle ABC$: *BC* is the longest side since it is opposite angle *A*, the largest angle (71°). Similarly, *AB* is the shortest side since it is opposite angle *C*, the smallest angle (54°). So *AB* < *AC* < *BC*.

- In $\triangle JKL$: angles *J* and *L* have the same measure (45°), so *JK* = *KL*.

- In $\triangle RST$: since all three angles have the same measure (60°), all three sides have the same length: *RS* = *ST* = *TR*.

Example 3.

Which of the following statements concerning the length of side *YZ* is true?

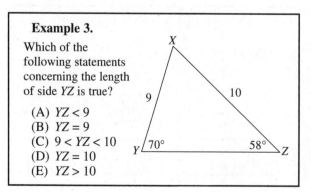

(A) *YZ* < 9
(B) *YZ* = 9
(C) 9 < *YZ* < 10
(D) *YZ* = 10
(E) *YZ* > 10

SOLUTION.

• By KEY FACT J1, $m\angle X + 70 + 58 = 180 \Rightarrow m\angle X = 52$.
• So, X is the smallest angle.
• Therefore, by KEY FACT J3, YZ is the shortest side. So

$$YZ < 9 \text{ (\textbf{A})}.$$

Classification of Triangles

Name	Lengths of the Sides	Measures of the Angles	Examples from Figure 1
scalene	all 3 different	all 3 different	ABC, DEF, GHI
isosceles	2 the same	2 the same	JKL
equilateral	all 3 the same	all 3 the same	RST

Acute triangles are triangles such as *ABC* and *RST*, in which all three angles are acute. An acute triangle could be scalene, isosceles, or equilateral.

Obtuse triangles are triangles such as *DEF*, in which one angle is obtuse and two are acute. An obtuse triangle could be scalene or isosceles.

Right triangles are triangles such as *GHI* and *JKL*, which have one right angle and two acute ones. A right triangle could be scalene or isosceles. The side opposite the 90° angle is called the **hypotenuse**, and by KEY FACT J3, it is the longest side. The other two sides are called the **legs**.

If x and y are the measures of the acute angles of a right triangle, then by KEY FACT J1,

$$90 + x + y = 180 \Rightarrow x + y = 90.$$

KEY FACT J4:

In any right triangle, the sum of the measures of the two acute angles is 90°.

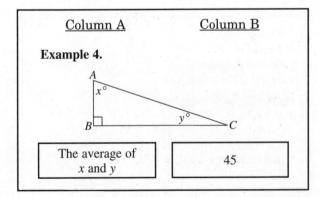

Column A	Column B

Example 4.

The average of x and y	45

Solution. Since the diagram indicates that $\triangle ABC$ is a right triangle, then, by KEY FACT J1, $x + y = 90$. So

$$\text{the average of } x \text{ and } y = \frac{x+y}{2} = \frac{90}{2} = 45.$$

The columns are equal (**C**).

The most important facts concerning right triangles are the **Pythagorean theorem** and its converse, which are given in KEY FACT J5 and repeated as the first line of KEY FACT J6.

KEY FACT J5:

Let a, b, and c be the sides of $\triangle ABC$, with $a \le b \le c$. If $\triangle ABC$ is a right triangle, $a^2 + b^2 = c^2$; and if $a^2 + b^2 = c^2$, then $\triangle ABC$ is a right triangle.

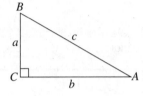

KEY FACT J6:

Let a, b, and c be the sides of $\triangle ABC$, with $a \le b \le c$.

• $a^2 + b^2 = c^2$ if and only if angle C is a right angle. ($\triangle ABC$ is a right triangle.)
• $a^2 + b^2 < c^2$ if and only if angle C is obtuse. ($\triangle ABC$ is an obtuse triangle.)
• $a^2 + b^2 > c^2$ if and only if angle C is acute. ($\triangle ABC$ is an acute triangle.)

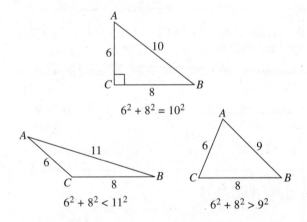

Example 5.

Which of the following are *not* the sides of a right triangle?

(A) 3, 4, 5   (B) 1, 1, $\sqrt{2}$ (C) 1, $\sqrt{3}$, 2

(D) $\sqrt{3}, \sqrt{4}, \sqrt{5}$ (E) 30, 40, 50

SOLUTION. Just check each choice.

A: $3^2 + 4^2 = 9 + 16 = 25 = 5^2$ These *are* the sides of a right triangle.

B: $1^2 + 1^2 = 1 + 1 = 2 = (\sqrt{2})^2$ These *are* the sides of a right triangle.

C: $1^2 + (\sqrt{3})^2 = 1 + 3 = 4 = 2^2$

These *are* the sides of a right triangle.

D: $(\sqrt{3})^2 + (\sqrt{4})^2 = 3 + 4 = 7 \neq (\sqrt{5})^2$

These *are not* the sides of a right triangle.

E: $30^2 + 40^2 = 900 + 1600 = 2500 = 50^2$

These *are* the sides of a right triangle.

The answer is **D**.

Below are the right triangles that appear most often on the GRE. You should recognize them immediately whenever they come up in questions. Carefully study each one, and memorize KEY FACTS J7–J11.

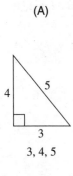

(A)

3, 4, 5

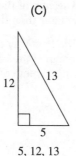

(B)

3x, 4x, 5x

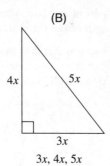

(C)

5, 12, 13

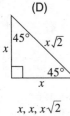

(D)

x, x, x√2

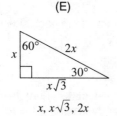

(E)

x, x√3, 2x

On the GRE, the most common right triangles whose sides are integers are the 3-4-5 triangle (A) and its multiples (B).

KEY FACT J7:

For any positive number x, there is a right triangle whose sides are $3x$, $4x$, $5x$.

For example:

$x = 1$ 3, 4, 5 $x = 5$ 15, 20, 25

$x = 2$ 6, 8, 10 $x = 10$ 30, 40, 50

$x = 3$ 9, 12, 15 $x = 50$ 150, 200, 250

$x = 4$ 12, 16, 20 $x = 100$ 300, 400, 500

NOTE: KEY FACT J7 applies even if x is not an integer. For example:

$x = .5$ 1.5, 2, 2.5 $x = \pi$ 3π, 4π, 5π

The only other right triangle with integer sides that you should recognize immediately is the one whose sides are 5, 12, 13, (C).

Let x = length of each leg, and h = length of the hypotenuse, of an isosceles right triangle (D). By the Pythagorean theorem (KEY FACT J5), $x^2 + x^2 = h^2$.

So, $2x^2 = h^2$, and $h = \sqrt{2x^2} = x\sqrt{2}$.

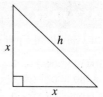

KEY FACT J8:

In a 45-45-90 right triangle, the sides are x, x, and $x\sqrt{2}$. So,

- **by multiplying the length of a leg by $\sqrt{2}$, you get the hypotenuse.**
- **by dividing the hypotenuse by $\sqrt{2}$, you get the length of each leg.**

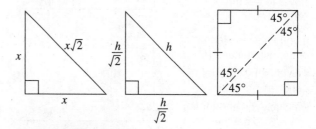

KEY FACT J9:

The diagonal of a square divides the square into two isosceles right triangles.

The last important right triangle is the one whose angles measure 30°, 60°, and 90°. (E)

KEY FACT J10:

An altitude divides an equilateral triangle into two 30-60-90 right triangles.

Let $2x$ be the length of each side of equilateral $\triangle ABC$ in which altitude AD is drawn. Then $\triangle ABD$ is a 30-60-90 right triangle, and its sides are x, $2x$, and h.

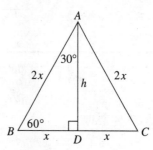

By the Pythagorean theorem,

$$x^2 + h^2 = (2x)^2 = 4x^2.$$

So $h^2 = 3x^2$, and $h = \sqrt{3x^2} = x\sqrt{3}$.

KEY FACT J11:

In a 30-60-90 right triangle the sides are x, $x\sqrt{3}$, and $2x$.

If you know the length of the shorter leg (x),

- multiply it by $\sqrt{3}$ to get the longer leg, and

- multiply it by 2 to get the hypotenuse.

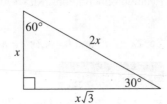

If you know the length of the longer leg (a),

- divide it by $\sqrt{3}$ to get the shorter leg, and

- multiply the shorter leg by 2 to get the hypotenuse.

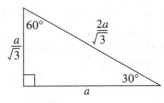

If you know the length of the hypotenuse (h),

- divide it by 2 to get the shorter leg, and

- multiply the shorter leg by $\sqrt{3}$ to get the longer leg.

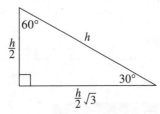

Example 6.

What is the area of a square whose diagonal is 10?

(A) 20   (B) 40   (C) 50   (D) 100   (E) 200

SOLUTION. Draw a diagonal in a square of side s, creating a 45-45-90 right triangle. By KEY FACT J8:

$s = \dfrac{10}{\sqrt{2}}$ and $A = s^2 = \left(\dfrac{10}{\sqrt{2}}\right)^2 =$

$\dfrac{100}{2} = 50$. The answer is **C**.

Example 7.

In the diagram at the right, if $BC = \sqrt{6}$, what is the value of CD?

(A) $2\sqrt{2}$ (B) $4\sqrt{2}$
(C) $2\sqrt{3}$ (D) $2\sqrt{6}$
(E) 4

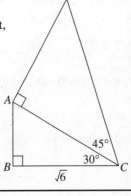

SOLUTION. Since $\triangle ABC$ and $\triangle DAC$ are 30-60-90 and 45-45-90 right triangles, respectively, use KEY FACTS J11 and J8.

- Divide the longer leg, BC, by $\sqrt{3}$ to get the shorter leg, AB: $\dfrac{\sqrt{6}}{\sqrt{3}} = \sqrt{2}$.

- Multiply AB by 2 to get the hypotenuse: $AC = 2\sqrt{2}$.

- Since AC is also a leg of isosceles right $\triangle DAC$, to get hypotenuse CD, multiply AC by $\sqrt{2}$:

$$CD = 2\sqrt{2} \times \sqrt{2} = 2 \times 2 = 4\ \textbf{(E)}.$$

KEY FACT J12:

Triangle Inequality

The sum of the lengths of any two sides of a triangle is greater than the length of the third side.

The best way to remember this is to see that $x + y$, the length of the path from A to C through B, is greater than z, the length of the direct path from A to C.

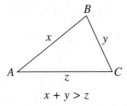

$$x + y > z$$

NOTE: If you subtract x from each side of $x + y > z$, you see that $z - x < y$.

KEY FACT J13:

The difference of the lengths of any two sides of a triangle is less than the length of the third side.

Example 8.

If the lengths of two of the sides of a triangle are 6 and 7, which of the following could be the length of the third side?

 I. 1
 II. 5
 III. 15

(A) None   (B) I only   (C) II only
    (D) I and II only   (E) I, II, and III

SOLUTION. Use KEY FACTS J12 and J13.

- The third side must be *less* than $6 + 7 = 13$. (III is false.)

- The third side must be *greater* than $7 - 6 = 1$. (I is false.)

- *Any* number between 1 and 13 could be the length of the third side. (I is true.)

The answer is **C**.

The following diagram illustrates several triangles, two of whose sides have lengths of 6 and 7.

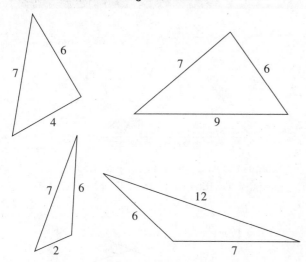

On the GRE, two other terms that appear regularly in triangle problems are **perimeter** and **area** (see Section 14-K).

Example 9.

In the figure at the right, what is the perimeter of △ABC?

(A) $20 + 10\sqrt{2}$

(B) $20 + 10\sqrt{3}$

(C) 25

(D) 30

(E) 40

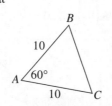

SOLUTION. First, use KEY FACTS J3 and J1 to find the measures of the angles.

- Since $AB = AC$, m∠B = m∠C. Represent each of them by x.

- Then, $x + x + 60 = 180 \Rightarrow 2x = 120 \Rightarrow x = 60$.

- Since the measure of each angle of △ABC is 60, the triangle is equilateral.

- So $BC = 10$, and the perimeter is $10 + 10 + 10 = $ **30 (D)**.

KEY FACT J14:

The area of a triangle is given by $A = \dfrac{1}{2}bh$, where b is the base and h is the height.

NOTE:

(1) *Any* side of the triangle can be taken as the **base**.

(2) The **height** or **altitude** is a line segment drawn to the base or, if necessary, to an extension of the base from the opposite vertex.

---

(3) In a right triangle, either leg can be the base and the other the height.

(4) The height may be outside the triangle. [See the figure at right.]

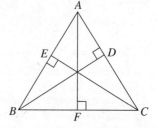

In the figure at the right:

- If AC is the base, BD is the height.

- If AB is the base, CE is the height.

- If BC is the base, AF is the height.

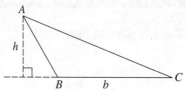

Example 10.

What is the area of an equilateral triangle whose sides are 10?

(A) 30   (B) $25\sqrt{3}$ (C) 50   (D) $50\sqrt{3}$ (E) 100

$\dfrac{1}{5}$

SOLUTION: Draw an equilateral triangle and one of its altitudes.

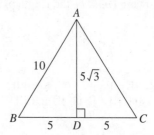

- By KEY FACT J10, △ABD is a 30-60-90 right triangle.

- By KEY FACT J11, $BD = 5$ and $AD = 5\sqrt{3}$.

- The area of △ABC $= \dfrac{1}{2}(10)(5\sqrt{3}) = $ **$25\sqrt{3}$ (B)**.

Replacing 10 by s in Example 10 yields a very useful result.

KEY FACT J15:

If A represents the area of an equilateral triangle with side s, then $A = \dfrac{s^2\sqrt{3}}{4}$.

PRACTICE EXERCISES—TRIANGLES

Multiple-Choice Questions

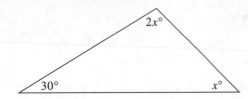

1. In the triangle above, what is the value of x?

   (A) 20   (B) 30   (C) 40   (D) 50   (E) 60

2. If the difference between the measures of the two smaller angles of a right triangle is $8°$, what is the measure, in degrees, of the smallest angle?

   (A) 37   (B) 41   (C) 42   (D) 49   (E) 53

3. What is the area of an equilateral triangle whose altitude is 6?

   (A) 18   (B) $12\sqrt{3}$ (C) $18\sqrt{3}$ (D) 36

   (E) $24\sqrt{3}$

4. Two sides of a right triangle are 12 and 13. Which of the following *could be* the length of the third side?

   I. 5
   II. 11
   III. $\sqrt{313}$

   (A) I only   (B) II only   (C) I and II
       (D) I and III   (E) I, II, and III

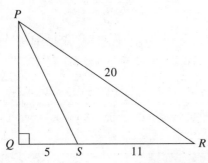

5. What is the value of PS in the triangle above?

   (A) $5\sqrt{2}$ (B) 10   (C) 11   (D) 13   (E) $12\sqrt{2}$

6. If the measures of the angles of a triangle are in the ratio of 1:2:3, and if the length of the smallest side of the triangle is 10, what is the length of the longest side?

   (A) $10\sqrt{2}$ (B) $10\sqrt{3}$ (C) 15   (D) 20   (E) 30

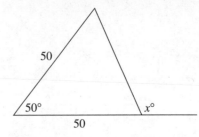

7. What is the value of x in the figure above?

   (A) 80   (B) 100   (C) 115   (D) 120   (E) 130

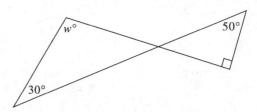

8. In the figure above, what is the value of w?

   (A) 100   (B) 110   (C) 120   (D) 130   (E) 140

Questions 9–10 refer to the following figure.

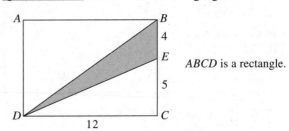

ABCD is a rectangle.

9. What is the area of $\triangle BED$?

   (A) 12   (B) 24   (C) 36   (D) 48   (E) 60

10. What is the perimeter of $\triangle BED$?

   (A) $19 + 5\sqrt{2}$ (B) 28   (C) $17 + \sqrt{185}$
       (D) 32   (E) 36

Questions 11–12 refer to the following figure.

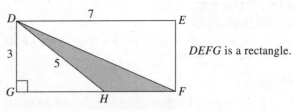

DEFG is a rectangle.

11. What is the area of $\triangle DFH$?

   (A) 3   (B) 4.5   (C) 6   (D) 7.5   (E) 10

12. What is the perimeter of $\triangle DFH$?

   (A) $8 + \sqrt{41}$ (B) $8 + \sqrt{58}$ (C) 16   (D) 17
       (E) 18

Questions 13–14 refer to the following figure.

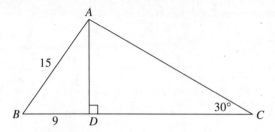

13. What is the perimeter of △ABC?
    (A) 48   (B) 48 + 12√2   (C) 48 + 12√3
       (D) 60   (E) 60 + 6√3

14. What is the area of △ABC?
    (A) 108   (B) 54 + 72√2   (C) 54 + 72√3
    (D) 198   (E) 216

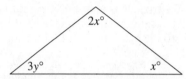

15. Which of the following expresses a true relationship between x and y in the figure above?
    (A) y = 60 – x   (B) y = x   (C) x + y = 90
       (D) y = 180 – 3x   (E) x = 90 – 3y

Quantitative Comparison Questions

Column A   Column B

The lengths of two sides of a triangle are 7 and 11.

16. The length of the third side | 4

17. The ratio of the diagonal to a side of a square | √2

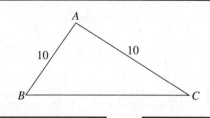

18. The perimeter of △ABC | 30

Column A   Column B

Questions 19–20 refer to the following figure.

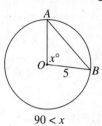

90 < x

19. The length of AB | 7

20. The perimeter of △AOB | 20

21. The area of an equilateral triangle whose sides are 10 | The area of an equilateral triangle whose altitude is 10

Questions 22–23 refer to the following figure in which the horizontal and vertical lines divide square ABCD into 16 smaller squares.

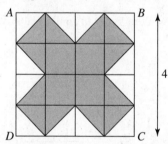

22. The perimeter of the shaded region | The perimeter of the square

23. The area of the shaded region | The area of the white region

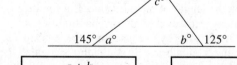

24. a + b | c

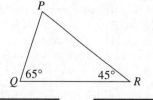

25. PR | QR

Answer Key

1. **D**	6. **D**	11. **B**	16. **A**	21. **B**
2. **B**	7. **C**	12. **B**	17. **C**	22. **A**
3. **B**	8. **B**	13. **C**	18. **D**	23. **A**
4. **D**	9. **B**	14. **C**	19. **A**	24. **C**
5. **D**	10. **D**	15. **A**	20. **B**	25. **B**

Answer Explanations

1. **D.** $x + 2x + 30 = 180 \Rightarrow 3x + 30 = 180 \Rightarrow$
   $3x = 150 \Rightarrow x = 50.$

2. **B.** Draw a diagram and label it.

   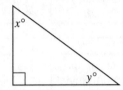

   Then write the equations: $x + y = 90$ and
   $x - y = 8.$
   Add the equations:

   $$
   \begin{array}{r}
   x + y = 90 \\
   + x - y = \ \ 8 \\
   \hline
   2x = 98
   \end{array}
   $$

   So $x = 49$ and $y = 90 - 49 = 41.$

3. **B.** Draw altitude AD in equilateral $\triangle ABC$.

   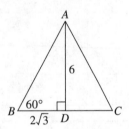

   By KEY FACT J11, $BD = \dfrac{6}{\sqrt{3}} = \dfrac{6\sqrt{3}}{3} = 2\sqrt{3}$,
   and BD is one half the base. So, the area is
   $2\sqrt{3} \times 6 = 12\sqrt{3}.$

4. **D.** If the triangle were not required to be a right
   triangle, by KEY FACTS J11 and J12 *any*
   number greater than 1 and less than 25 could
   be the length of the third side. But for a right
   triangle, there are only *two* possibilities:
   • If 13 is the hypotenuse, then the legs are 12
   and 5. (I is true.) (If you didn't recognize the
   5-12-13 triangle, use the Pythagorean theorem: $12^2 + x^2 = 13^2$, and solve.)
   • If 12 and 13 are the two legs, then use the
   Pythagorean theorem to find the hypotenuse:
   $12^2 + 13^2 = c^2 \Rightarrow c^2 = 144 + 169 = 313 \Rightarrow$
   $c = \sqrt{313}$. (III is true.)
   An 11-12-13 triangle is not a *right* triangle. So
   II is false.

5. **D.** Use the Pythagorean theorem twice, unless
   you recognize the common right triangles in
   this figure (*which you should*). Since $PR = 20$
   and $QR = 16$, $\triangle PQR$ is a 3x-4x-5x right trian-

gle with $x = 4$. So $PQ = 12$, and $\triangle PQS$ is a
right triangle whose legs are 5 and 12. The
hypotenuse, PS, therefore, is 13.

6. **D.** If the measures of the angles are in the ratio of
   1:2:3,

   $$x + 2x + 3x = 180 \Rightarrow 6x = 180 \Rightarrow x = 30.$$

   So the triangle is a 30-60-90 right triangle,
   and the sides are a, $2a$, and $a\sqrt{3}$. Since
   $a = 10$, then $2a$, the length of the longest side,
   is 20.

7. **C.** Label the other angles in the triangle.

   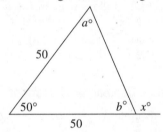

   $$50 + a + b = 180 \Rightarrow a + b = 130,$$

   and since the triangle is isosceles, $a = b$.
   Therefore, a and b are each 65, and
   $x = 180 - 65 = 115.$

8. **B.** Here, $50 + 90 + a = 180 \Rightarrow a = 40$, and
   since vertical angles are equal, $b = 40$. Then,
   $40 + 30 + w = 180 \Rightarrow w = 110.$

   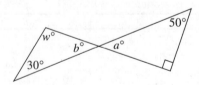

9. **B.** You *could* calculate the area of the rectangle
   and subtract the area of the two white right triangles, but you shouldn't. It is easier to
   solve this problem if you realize that the
   shaded area is a triangle whose base is 4 and
   whose height is 12. The area is $\dfrac{1}{2}(4)(12) = 24.$

10. **D.** Since both BD and ED are the hypotenuses of
    right triangles, their lengths can be calculated
    by the Pythagorean theorem, but these are tri-
    angles you should recognize: the sides of
    $\triangle DCE$ are 5-12-13, and those of $\triangle BAD$ are 9-
    12-15 (3x-4x-5x, with $x = 3$). So the perimeter
    of $\triangle BED$ is $4 + 13 + 15 = 32.$

11. **B.** Since $\triangle DGH$ is a right triangle whose hypotenuse is 5 and one of whose legs is 3, the other leg, GH, is 4. Since $GF = DE$ is 7, HF is 3. Now, $\triangle DFH$ has a base of 3 (HF) and a height of 3 (DG), and its area is $\frac{1}{2}(3)(3) = 4.5$.

12. **B.** In $\triangle DFH$, we already have that $DH = 5$ and $HF = 3$; we need only find DF, which is the hypotenuse of $\triangle DEF$. By the Pythagorean theorem,
$$(DF)^2 = 3^2 + 7^2 = 9 + 49 = 58 \Rightarrow DF = \sqrt{58}.$$
So the perimeter is
$$3 + 5 + \sqrt{58} = 8 + \sqrt{58}.$$

13. **C.** $\triangle ABD$ is a right triangle whose hypotenuse is 15 and one of whose legs is 9, so this is a $3x$-$4x$-$5x$ triangle with $x = 3$; so $AD = 12$. Now $\triangle ADC$ is a 30-60-90 triangle, whose shorter leg is 12. Hypotenuse AC is 24, and leg CD is $12\sqrt{3}$. So the perimeter is
$$24 + 15 + 9 + 12\sqrt{3} = 48 + 12\sqrt{3}.$$

14. **C.** From the solution to 13, we have the base $(9 + 12\sqrt{3})$ and the height (12) of $\triangle ABC$. Then, the area is $\frac{1}{2}(12)(9 + 12\sqrt{3}) = 54 + 72\sqrt{3}$.

15. **A.** $x + 2x + 3y = 180 \Rightarrow 3x + 3y = 180 \Rightarrow x + y = 60 \Rightarrow y = 60 - x$.

16. **A.** Any side of a triangle must be greater than the difference of the other two sides (KEY FACT J13), so the third side is greater than $11 - 7 = 4$.

17. **C.** Draw a diagram. A diagonal of a square is the hypotenuse of each of the two 45-45-90 right triangles formed. The ratio of the hypotenuse to a leg in such a triangle is $\sqrt{2}$:1, so the columns are equal.

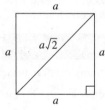

18. **D.** BC can be any positive number less than 20 (by KEY FACTS J12 and J13, $BC > 10 - 10 = 0$ and $BC < 10 + 10 = 20$). So the perimeter can be *any* number greater than 20 and less than 40.

19. **A.** Since OA and OB are radii, they are each equal to 5. With no restrictions on x, AB could be any positive number less than 10, and the bigger x is, the bigger AB is. If x were 90, AB would be $5\sqrt{2}$, but we are told that $x > 90$, so $AB > 5\sqrt{2} > 7$.

20. **B.** Since AB must be less than 10, the perimeter is *less* than 20.

21. **B.** Don't calculate either area. The length of a side of an equilateral triangle is *greater* than the length of an altitude. So the triangle in Column B is larger (its sides are greater than 10).

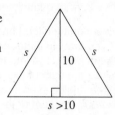

22. **A.** Column A: The perimeter of the shaded region consists of 12 line segments, each of which is the hypotenuse of a 45-45-90 right triangle whose legs are 1. So each line segment is $\sqrt{2}$, and the perimeter is $12\sqrt{2}$.
Column B: The perimeter of the square is 16. To compare $12\sqrt{2}$ and 16, square them:
$$(12\sqrt{2})^2 = 144 \times 2 = 288; \ 16^2 = 256.$$

23. **A.** The white region consists of 12 right triangles, each of which has an area of $\frac{1}{2}$, for a total area of 6. Since the area of the large square is 16, the area of the shaded region is $16 - 6 = 10$.

24. **C.** Since $a = 180 - 145 = 35$ and $b = 180 - 125 = 55$, $a + b = 35 + 55 = 90$. Therefore, $180 = a + b + c = 90 + c \Rightarrow c = 90$.

25. **B.** Since $65 + 45 = 110$, $\text{m}\angle P = 70$. Since $\angle P$ is the largest angle, QR, the side opposite it, is the largest side.

14-K. QUADRILATERALS AND OTHER POLYGONS

A *polygon* is a closed geometric figure made up of line segments. The line segments are called *sides* and the endpoints of the line segments are called *vertices* (each one is called a *vertex*). Line segments inside the polygon drawn from one vertex to another are called *diagonals*. The simplest polygons, which have three sides, are the triangles, which you just studied in Section J. A polygon with four sides is called a *quadrilateral*. The only other terms you should be familiar with are *pentagon*, *hexagon*, *octagon*, and *decagon*, which are the names for polygons with five, six, eight, and ten sides, respectively.

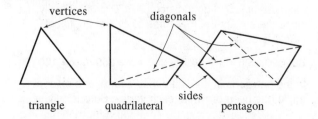

In this section we will present a few facts about polygons and quadrilaterals in general, but the emphasis will be on reviewing the key facts you need to know about four special quadrilaterals.

Every quadrilateral has two diagonals. If you draw in either one, you will divide the quadrilateral into two triangles. Since the sum of the measures of the three angles in each of the triangles is 180°, the sum of the measures of the angles in the quadrilateral is 360°.

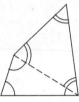

KEY FACT K1:

In any quadrilateral, the sum of the measures of the four angles is 360°.

In exactly the same way, any polygon can be divided into triangles by drawing in all of the diagonals emanating from one vertex.

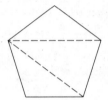 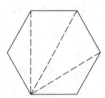

Notice that the pentagon is divided into three triangles, and the hexagon is divided into four triangles. In general, an *n*-sided polygon is divided into (*n* − 2) triangles, which leads to KEY FACT K2.

KEY FACT K2:

The sum of the measures of the *n* angles in a polygon with *n* sides is (*n* − 2) × 180°.

Example 1.

In the figure below, what is the value of *x*?

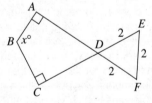

(A) 60   (B) 90   (C) 100   (D) 120   (E) 150

SOLUTION. Since △*DEF* is equilateral, all of its angles measure 60°; also, since the two angles at vertex *D* are vertical angles, their measures are equal. Therefore, the measure of ∠*D* in quadrilateral *ABCD* is 60°. Finally, since the sum of the measures of all four angles of *ABCD* is 360°,

$$60 + 90 + 90 + x = 360 \Rightarrow 240 + x = 360 \Rightarrow x = \textbf{120 (D)}.$$

In the polygons in the figure that follows, one exterior angle has been drawn at each vertex. Surprisingly, if

you add the measures of all of the exterior angles in any of the polygons, the sums are equal.

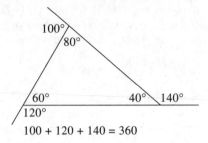

$$100 + 120 + 140 = 360$$

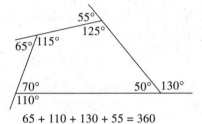

$$65 + 110 + 130 + 55 = 360$$

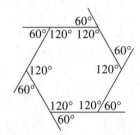

$$60 + 60 + 60 + 60 + 60 + 60 = 360$$

KEY FACT K3:

In any polygon, the sum of the exterior angles, taking one at each vertex, is 360°.

A *regular polygon* is a polygon in which all of the sides are the same length and each angle has the same measure. KEY FACT K4 follows immediately from this definition and from KEY FACTS K2 and K3.

KEY FACT K4:

In any regular polygon the measure of each interior angle is $\dfrac{(n-2) \times 180°}{n}$ and the measure of each exterior angle is $\dfrac{360°}{n}$.

Example 2.

What is the measure of each interior angle in a regular decagon?

(A) 36   (B) 72   (C) 108   (D) 144   (E) 180

SOLUTION 1. The measure of each of the 10 interior angles is

$$\frac{(10-2) \times 180}{10} = \frac{8 \times 180}{10} = \frac{1440}{10} = \textbf{144 (D)}.$$

SOLUTION 2. The measure of each of the 10 exterior angles is 36 (360 ÷ 10). Therefore, the measure of each interior angle is 180 − 36 = **144**.

A *parallelogram* is a quadrilateral in which both pairs of opposite sides are parallel.

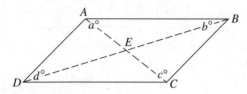

KEY FACT K5:

Parallelograms have the following properties:

• **Opposite sides are equal: *AB* = *CD* and *AD* = *BC*.**

• **Opposite angles are equal: *a* = *c* and *b* = *d*.**

• **Consecutive angles add up to 180°:**
  ***a* + *b* = 180, *b* + *c* = 180, *c* + *d* = 180, and *a* + *d* = 180.**

• **The two diagonals bisect each other:**
  ***AE* = *EC* and *BE* = *ED*.**

• **A diagonal divides the parallelogram into two triangles that have the exact same size and shape. (The triangles are congruent.)**

<u>Column A</u>   <u>Column B</u>

Example 3.

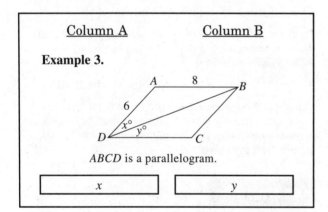

ABCD is a parallelogram.

| *x* | *y* |

SOLUTION. In △*ABD* the larger angle is opposite the larger side (KEY FACT J2); so *x* > m∠*ABD*. However, since *AB* and *CD* are parallel sides cut by transversal *BD*, *y* = m∠*ABD*. Therefore, *x* > *y*. Column **A** is greater.

A *rectangle* is a parallelogram in which all four angles are right angles. Two adjacent sides of a rectangle are usually called the *length* (ℓ) and the *width* (*w*). Note in the right-hand figure that the length is not necessarily greater than the width.

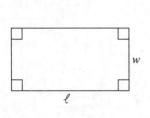

KEY FACT K6:

Since a rectangle is a parallelogram, all of the properties listed in KEY FACT K5 hold for rectangles. In addition:

• **The measure of each angle in a rectangle is 90°.**

• **The diagonals of a rectangle have the same length: *AC* = *BD*.**

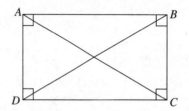

A *square* is a rectangle in which all four sides have the same length.

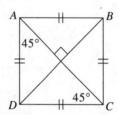

KEY FACT K7:

Since a square is a rectangle, all of the properties listed in KEY FACTS K5 and K6 hold for squares. In addition:

• **All four sides have the same length.**

• **Each diagonal divides the square into two 45-45-90 right triangles.**

• **The diagonals are perpendicular to each other: *AC* ⊥ *BD*.**

Example 4.

What is the length of each side of a square if its diagonals are 10?

(A) 5   (B) 7   (C) 5√2   (D) 10√2   (E) 10√3

SOLUTION. Draw a diagram. In square *ABCD*, diagonal *AC* is the hypotenuse of a 45-45-90 right triangle, and side *AB* is a leg of that triangle. By KEY FACT J7,

$$AB = \frac{AC}{\sqrt{2}} = \frac{10}{\sqrt{2}} \times \frac{\sqrt{2}}{\sqrt{2}} = \frac{10\sqrt{2}}{2} = 5\sqrt{2}.$$

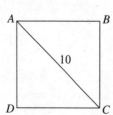

A ***trapezoid*** is a quadrilateral in which one pair of sides is parallel and the other pair of sides is not parallel. The parallel sides are called the ***bases*** of the trapezoid. The two bases are never equal. In general, the two non-parallel sides are not equal; if they are the trapezoid is called an ***isosceles trapezoid***.

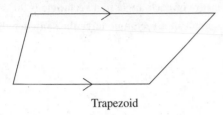

Trapezoid

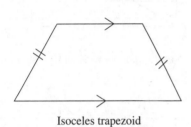

Isoceles trapezoid

The ***perimeter*** (P) of any polygon is the sum of the lengths of all of its sides.

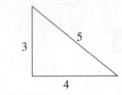

$$P = 3 + 4 + 5 = 12$$

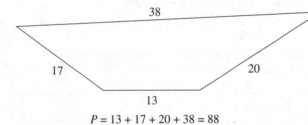

$$P = 13 + 17 + 20 + 38 = 88$$

In a rectangle, $P = 2(\ell + w)$; in a square, $P = 4s$.

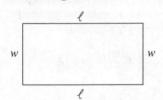

$$P = \ell + w + \ell + w = 2(\ell + w) \qquad P = s + s + s + s = 4s$$

Example 5.

The length of a rectangle is 7 more than its width. If the perimeter of the rectangle is the same as the perimeter of a square of side 8.5, what is the length of a diagonal of the rectangle?

(A) 12   (B) 13   (C) 17   (D) 34   (E) 169

SOLUTION. Don't do anything until you have drawn a diagram.

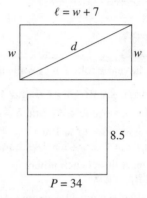

Since the perimeter of the square = $4 \times 8.5 = 34$, the perimeter of the rectangle is also 34: $2(\ell + w) = 34 \Rightarrow \ell + w = 17$. Replacing ℓ by $w + 7$, we get:

$$w + 7 + w = 17 \Rightarrow 2w + 7 = 17 \Rightarrow 2w = 10 \Rightarrow w = 5$$

Then $\ell = 5 + 7 = 12$. Finally, realize that the diagonal is the hypotenuse of a 5-12-13 triangle, or use the Pythagorean theorem:

$$d^2 = 5^2 + 12^2 = 25 + 144 = 169 \Rightarrow d = \mathbf{13} \ (\mathbf{B}).$$

In Section 14-J we reviewed the formula for the area of a triangle. The only other figures for which you need to know area formulas are the parallelogram, rectangle, square, and trapezoid.

Here are the area formulas you need to know:

• For a parallelogram: $A = bh$.

• For a rectangle: $A = \ell w$.

• For a square: $A = s^2$ or $A = \dfrac{1}{2}d^2$.

• For a trapezoid: $A = \dfrac{1}{2}(b_1 + b_2)\,h$.

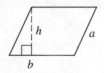

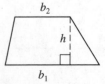

Example 6.

In the figure below, the area of parallelogram *ABCD* is 40. What is the area of rectangle *AFCE*?

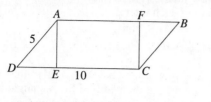

(A) 20 (B) 24 (C) 28 (D) 32 (E) 36

SOLUTION. Since the base, *CD*, is 10 and the area is 40, the height, *AE*, must be 4. Then △*AED* must be a 3-4-5 right triangle with *DE* = 3, which implies that *EC* = 7. So the area of the rectangle is 7 × 4 = **28 (C)**.

Two rectangles with the same perimeter can have different areas, and two rectangles with the same area can have different perimeters. These facts are a common source of questions on the GRE.

RECTANGLES WHOSE PERIMETERS ARE 100

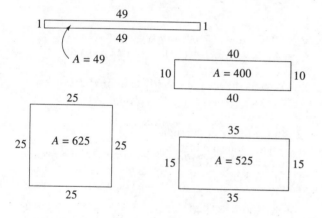

RECTANGLES WHOSE AREAS ARE 100

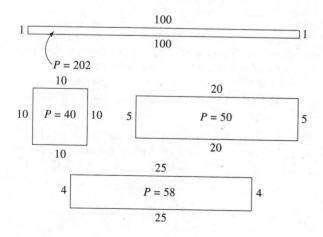

For a given perimeter, the rectangle with the largest area is a square. For a given area, the rectangle with the smallest perimeter is a square.

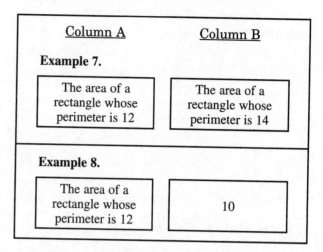

| Column A | Column B |

SOLUTION 7. Draw any rectangles whose perimeters are 12 and 14 and compute their areas. As drawn below, Column A = 8 and Column B = 12.

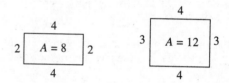

This time Column B is greater. Is it always? Draw a different rectangle whose perimeter is 14.

The one drawn here has an area of 6. Now Column B isn't greater. The answer is **D**.

SOLUTION 8. There are many rectangles of different areas whose perimeters are 12. But the largest area is 9, when the rectangle is a 3 × 3 square. Column **B** is greater.

PRACTICE EXERCISES—QUADRILATERALS

Multiple-Choice Questions

1. If the length of a rectangle is 4 times its width, and if its area is 144, what is its perimeter?

   (A) 6 (B) 24 (C) 30 (D) 60 (E) 96

Questions 2–3 refer to the diagram below in which the diagonals of square *ABCD* intersect at *E*.

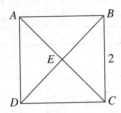

2. What is the area of △*DEC*?

   (A) $\frac{1}{2}$ (B) 1 (C) $\sqrt{2}$ (D) 2 (E) $2\sqrt{2}$

3. What is the perimeter of △*DEC*?

   (A) $1 + \sqrt{2}$ (B) $2 + \sqrt{2}$ (C) 4 (D) $2 + 2\sqrt{2}$
   (E) 6

4. If the angles of a five-sided polygon are in the ratio of 2:3:3:5:5, what is the measure of the smallest angle?

   (A) 20 (B) 40 (C) 60 (D) 80 (E) 90

5. If in the figures below, the area of rectangle *ABCD* is 100, what is the area of rectangle *EFGH*?

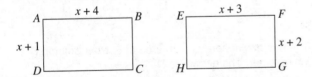

   (A) 98 (B) 100 (C) 102 (D) 104 (E) 106

Questions 6–7 refer to a rectangle in which the length of each diagonal is 12, and one of the angles formed by the diagonal and a side measures 30°.

6. What is the area of the rectangle?

   (A) 18 (B) 72 (C) $18\sqrt{3}$ (D) $36\sqrt{3}$
   (E) $36\sqrt{2}$

7. What is the perimeter of the rectangle?

   (A) 18 (B) 24 (C) $12 + 12\sqrt{3}$ (D) $18 + 6\sqrt{3}$
   (E) $24\sqrt{2}$

8. How many sides does a polygon have if the measure of each interior angle is 8 times the measure of each exterior angle?

   (A) 8 (B) 9 (C) 10 (D) 12 (E) 18

9. The length of a rectangle is 5 more than the side of a square, and the width of the rectangle is 5 less than the side of the square. If the area of the square is 45, what is the area of the rectangle?

   (A) 20 (B) 25 (C) 45 (D) 50 (E) 70

Questions 10–11 refer to the following figure, in which *M*, *N*, *O*, and *P* are the midpoints of the sides of rectangle *ABCD*.

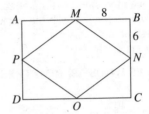

10. What is the perimeter of quadrilateral *MNOP*?

    (A) 24 (B) 32 (C) 40 (D) 48 (E) 60

11. What is the area of quadrilateral *MNOP*?

    (A) 48 (B) 60 (C) 72 (D) 96 (E) 108

12. In the figure at the right, what is the sum of the measures of all of the marked angles?

    (A) 360 (B) 540
    (C) 720 (D) 900
    (E) 1080

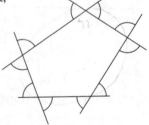

13. In quadrilateral *WXYZ*, the measure of angle *Z* is 10 more than twice the average of the measures of the other three angles. What is the measure of angle *Z*?

    (A) 100 (B) 105 (C) 120 (D) 135 (E) 150

Questions 14–15 refer to the following figure, in which *M* and *N* are the midpoints of two of the sides of square *ABCD*.

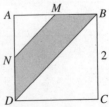

14. What is the perimeter of the shaded region?

    (A) 3   (B) $2 + 3\sqrt{2}$ (C) $3 + 2\sqrt{2}$ (D) 5   (E) 8

15. What is the area of the shaded region?

    (A) 1.5   (B) 1.75   (C) 3   (D) $2\sqrt{2}$ (E) $3\sqrt{2}$

Quantitative Comparison Questions

Column A	Column B

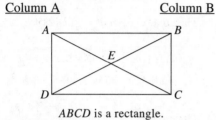

ABCD is a rectangle.

16. | The area of $\triangle AED$ | The area of $\triangle EDC$ |

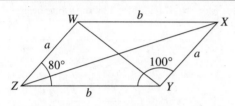

WXYZ is a parallelogram.

17. | Diagonal WY | Diagonal XZ |

Column A	Column B

18. | The perimeter of a 30-60-90 right triangle whose shorter leg is $2x$ | The perimeter of an octagon, each of whose sides is x |

19. | The perimeter of a rectangle whose area is 50 | 28 |

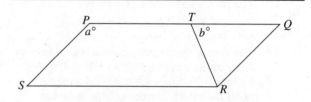

In parallelogram $PQRS$, TR bisects $\angle QRS$.

20. | a | $2b$ |

Answer Key

1. **D**	6. **D**	11. **D**	16. **C**
2. **B**	7. **C**	12. **C**	17. **B**
3. **D**	8. **E**	13. **E**	18. **A**
4. **C**	9. **A**	14. **B**	19. **A**
5. **C**	10. **C**	15. **A**	20. **C**

Answer Explanations

1. **D.**   Draw a diagram and label it.

    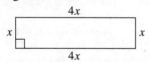

    Since the area is 144, then
    $$144 = 4x^2 \Rightarrow x^2 = 36 \Rightarrow x = 6.$$
    So the width is 6, the length is 24, and the perimeter is 60.

2. **B.**   The area of the square is $2^2 = 4$, and each triangle is one-fourth of the square. So the area of $\triangle DEC$ is 1.

3. **D.** $\triangle DEC$ is a 45-45-90 right triangle whose hypotenuse, DC, is 2. Therefore, each of the legs is $\dfrac{2}{\sqrt{2}} = \sqrt{2}$. So the perimeter is $2 + 2\sqrt{2}$.

4. **C.**   The sum of the angles of a five-sided polygon is $(5 - 2) \times 180 = 3 \times 180 = 540$. Therefore,
    $$540 = 2x + 3x + 3x + 5x + 5x = 18x \Rightarrow$$
    $$x = 540 \div 18 = 30.$$
    The measure of the smallest angle is $2x = 2 \times 30 = 60$.

5. **C.**   The area of rectangle $ABCD = (x + 1)(x + 4) = x^2 + 5x + 4$. The area of rectangle $EFGH = (x + 2)(x + 3) = x^2 + 5x + 6$, which is exactly 2 more than the area of rectangle $ABCD$: $100 + 2 = 102$.

6. D. Draw a picture and label it. Since $\triangle BCD$ is a 30-60-90 right triangle, BC is 6 (half the hypotenuse) and CD is $6\sqrt{3}$. So the area is $\ell w = 6(6\sqrt{3}) = 36\sqrt{3}$.

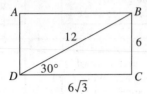

7. C. The perimeter of the rectangle is
$$2(\ell + w) = 2(6 + 6\sqrt{3}) = 12 + 12\sqrt{3}.$$

8. E. The sum of the degree measures of an interior and exterior angle is 180, so $180 = 8x + x = 9x \Rightarrow x = 20$. Since the sum of the measures of all the exterior angles is 360, there are $360 \div 20 = 18$ angles and 18 sides.

9. A. Let x represent the side of the square. Then the dimensions of the rectangle are $(x + 5)$ and $(x - 5)$, and its area is $(x + 5)(x - 5) = x^2 - 25$. Since the area of the square is 45,
$$x^2 = 45 \Rightarrow x^2 - 25 = 45 - 25 = 20.$$

10. C. Each triangle surrounding quadrilateral $MNOP$ is a 6-8-10 right triangle. So each side of the quadrilateral is 10, and its perimeter is 40.

11. D. The area of each of the triangles is $\frac{1}{2}(6)(8) = 24$, so together the four triangles have an area of 96. The area of the rectangle is $16 \times 12 = 192$. Therefore, the area of quadrilateral $MNOP$ is $192 - 96 = 96$.
Note: Joining the midpoints of the four sides of any quadrilateral creates a parallelogram whose area is one-half the area of the original quadrilateral.

12. C. Each of the 10 marked angles is an exterior angle of the pentagon. If we take one angle at each vertex, the sum of those five angles is 360; the sum of the other five is also 360: $360 + 360 = 720$.

13. E. Let W, X, Y, and Z represent the measures of the four angles. Since $W + X + Y + Z = 360$, $W + X + Y = 360 - Z$. Also,
$$Z = 10 + 2\left(\frac{W + X + Y}{3}\right) = 10 + 2\left(\frac{360 - Z}{3}\right).$$

So $Z = 10 + \frac{2}{3}(360) - \frac{2}{3}Z = 10 + 240 - \frac{2}{3}Z$
$$\Rightarrow \frac{5}{3}Z = 250 \Rightarrow Z = 150.$$

14. B. Since M and N are midpoints of sides of length 2, AM, MB, AN, and ND are all 1. $MN = \sqrt{2}$, since it's the hypotenuse of an isosceles right triangle whose legs are 1; and $BD = 2\sqrt{2}$, since it's the hypotenuse of an isosceles right triangle whose legs are 2. So the perimeter of the shaded region is
$$1 + \sqrt{2} + 1 + 2\sqrt{2} = 2 + 3\sqrt{2}.$$

15. A. The area of $\triangle ABD = \frac{1}{2}(2)(2) = 2$, and the area of $\triangle AMN$ is $\frac{1}{2}(1)(1) = 0.5$. So the area of the shaded region is $2 - 0.5 = 1.5$.

16. C. The area of $\triangle AED$ is $\frac{1}{2}w\left(\frac{\ell}{2}\right) = \frac{\ell w}{4}$. The area of $\triangle EDC$ is $\frac{1}{2}\ell\left(\frac{w}{2}\right) = \frac{\ell w}{4}$. Note: Each of the four small triangles has the same area.

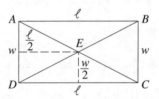

17. B. By KEY FACT J5, since $\angle Z$ is acute and $\angle Y$ is obtuse, $(WY)^2 < a^2 + b^2$, whereas $(XZ)^2 > a^2 + b^2$.

18. A. Since an octagon has eight sides, Column B is $8x$.
Column A: By KEY FACT J10, the hypotenuse of the triangle is $4x$, and the longer leg is $2x\sqrt{3}$. So the perimeter is $2x + 4x + 2x\sqrt{3}$. Since $\sqrt{3} > 1$, then
$$2x + 4x + 2x\sqrt{3} > 2x + 4x + 2x = 8x.$$

19. A. The perimeter of a rectangle of area 50 can be as large as we like, but the least it can be is when the rectangle is a square. In that case, each side is $\sqrt{50}$, which is greater than 7, and so the perimeter is greater than 28.

20. C. TR is a transversal cutting the parallel sides PQ and RS. So $b = x$ and $2b = 2x$. But since the opposite angles of a parallelogram are equal, $a = 2x$. So $a = 2b$.

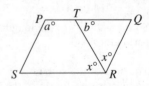

14-L. CIRCLES

A *circle* consists of all the points that are the same distance from one fixed point called the **center**. That distance is called the **radius** of the circle. The figure below is a circle of radius 1 unit whose center is at the point O. A, B, C, D, and E, which are each 1 unit from O, are all points on circle O. The word *radius* is also used to represent any of the line segments joining the center and a point on the circle. The plural of **radius** is **radii**. In circle O, below, OA, OB, OC, OD, and OE are all radii. If a circle has radius r, each of the radii is r units long.

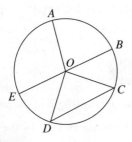

KEY FACT L1:

Any triangle, such as △COD in the figure above, formed by connecting the endpoints of two radii, is isosceles.

Example 1.

If P and Q are points on circle O, what is the value of x?

(A) 35 (B) 45 (C) 55
  (D) 65 (E) 70

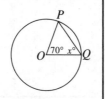

SOLUTION. Since △POQ is isosceles, angles P and Q have the same measure. Then, 70 + x + x = 180 ⇒ 2x = 110 ⇒ x = **55 (C)**.

A line segment, such as CD in circle O at the beginning of this section, both of whose endpoints are on a circle is called a **chord**. A chord such as BE, which passes through the center of the circle, is called a **diameter**. Since BE is the sum of two radii, OB and OE, it is twice as long as a radius.

KEY FACT L2:

If *d* is the diameter and *r* the radius of a circle, *d* = 2r.

KEY FACT L3:

A diameter is the longest chord that can be drawn in a circle.

Column A	Column B

Example 2.

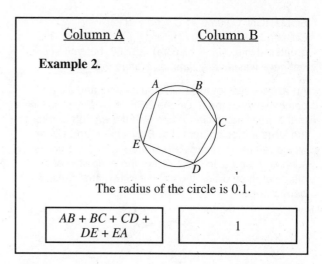

The radius of the circle is 0.1.

AB + BC + CD + DE + EA	1

SOLUTION. Since the radius of the circle is 0.1, the diameter is 0.2. Therefore, the length of each of the five line segments is less than 0.2, and the sum of their lengths is less than 5 × 0.2 = 1. The answer is **B**.

The total length around a circle, from A to B to C to D to E and back to A, is called the **circumference** of the circle. In every circle the ratio of the circumference to the diameter is exactly the same and is denoted by the symbol π (the Greek letter "pi").

KEY FACT L4:

- $\pi = \dfrac{\text{circumference}}{\text{diameter}} = \dfrac{C}{d}$
- $C = \pi d$
- $C = 2\pi r$

KEY FACT L5:

The value of π is approximately 3.14.

On GRE questions that involve circles, you are expected to leave your answer in terms of π. So *never* multiply by 3.14. If you are ever stuck on a problem whose answers involve π, try to estimate the answer, and then use 3 as an approximation of π to test the answers. For example, assume that you think that an answer is about 50, and the answer choices are 4π, 6π, 12π, 16π, and 24π. Since π is slightly greater than 3, these choices are a little greater than 12, 18, 36, 48, and 72. The answer must be 16π. (To the nearest hundredth, 16π is actually 50.27, but approximating it by 48 was close enough.)

Column A	Column B

Example 3.

The circumference of a circle whose diameter is 12	The perimeter of a square whose side is 12

SOLUTION. Column A: $C = \pi d = \pi(\mathbf{12})$.
Column B: $P = 4s = \mathbf{4(12)}$. Since $4 > \pi$, Column **B** is greater. (Note: $12\pi \approx 12(3.14) = 37.68$, but *you should not have wasted any time calculating this*.)

An **arc** consists of two points on a circle and all the points between them. On the GRE, *arc AB* always refers to the small arc joining *A* and *B*. If we wanted to refer to the large arc going from *A* to *B* through *P* and *Q*, we would refer to it as arc *APB* or arc *AQB*. If two points, such as *P* and *Q* in circle *O*, are the endpoints of a diameter, they divide the circle into two arcs called **semicircles**.

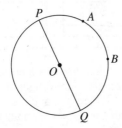

An angle whose vertex is at the center of a circle is called a **central angle**.

KEY FACT L6:

The degree measure of a complete circle is 360°.

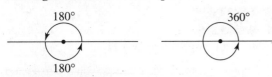

KEY FACT L7:

The degree measure of an arc equals the degree measure of the central angle that intercepts it.

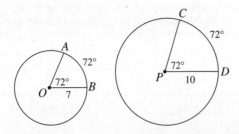

CAUTION: Degree measure is *not* a measure of length. In the circles above, arc *AB* and arc *CD* each measure 72°, even though arc *CD* is much longer.

How long *is* arc *CD*? Since the radius of Circle *P* is 10, its diameter is 20, and its circumference is 20π. Since there are 360° in a circle, arc *CD* is $\frac{72}{360}$, or $\frac{1}{5}$, of the circumference: $\frac{1}{5}(20\pi) = 4\pi$.

KEY FACT L8:

The formula for the area of a circle of radius *r* is $A = \pi r^2$.

The area of Circle *P*, in KEY FACT L7, is $\pi(10)^2 = 100\pi$ square units. The area of sector *CPD* is $\frac{1}{5}$ of the area of the circle: $\frac{1}{5}(100\pi) = 20\pi$.

KEY FACT L9:

If an arc measures $x°$, the length of the arc is $\dfrac{x}{360}(2\pi r)$, and the area of the sector formed by the arc and 2 radii is $\dfrac{x}{360}(\pi r^2)$.

Examples 4 and 5 refer to the circle below.

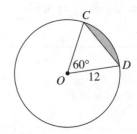

Example 4.
What is the area of the shaded region?
(A) $144\pi - 144\sqrt{3}$ (B) $144\pi - 36\sqrt{3}$
   (C) $144 - 72\sqrt{3}$ (D) $24\pi - 36\sqrt{3}$
      (E) $24\pi - 72\sqrt{3}$

Example 5.
What is the perimeter of the shaded region?
(A) $12 + 4\pi$ (B) $12 + 12\pi$ (C) $12 + 24\pi$
   (D) $12\sqrt{2} + 4\pi$ (E) $12\sqrt{2} + 24\pi$

SOLUTION 4. The area of the shaded region is equal to the area of sector *COD* minus the area of $\triangle COD$. The area of the circle is $\pi(12)^2 = 144\pi$.

Since $\dfrac{60}{360} = \dfrac{1}{6}$, the area of sector *COD* is $\dfrac{1}{6}(144\pi) =$

24π. Since $m\angle O = 60°$, $m\angle C + \angle D = 120°$; but $\triangle COD$ is isosceles, so $m\angle C = m\angle D$. Therefore, they each measure 60°, and the triangle is equilateral. By KEY FACT J15, area of $\triangle COD = \dfrac{12^2\sqrt{3}}{4} = \dfrac{144\sqrt{3}}{4} = 36\sqrt{3}$,

so the area of the shaded region is **$24\pi - 36\sqrt{3}$ (D)**.

SOLUTION 5. Since $\triangle COD$ is equilateral, $CD = 12$. Since the circumference of the circle $= 2\pi(12) = 24\pi$, arc $CD = \dfrac{1}{6}(24\pi) = 4\pi$. So the perimeter is **$12 + 4\pi$ (A)**.

Suppose that in Example 5 you see that $CD = 12$, but you don't remember how to find the length of arc CD. From the diagram, it is clear that it is slightly longer than CD, say 13. So you know that the perimeter is *about* 25. Now, approximate the value of each of the choices and see which one is closest to 25. Only Choice A is even close.

A line and a circle or two circles are **tangent** if they have only one point of intersection. A circle is **inscribed** in a triangle or square if it is tangent to each side. A polygon is **inscribed** in a circle if each vertex is on the circle.

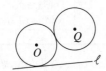

Line ℓ is tangent to circle O.
Circles O and Q are tangent.

The circle is inscribed in the square.

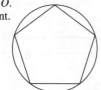

The pentagon is inscribed in the circle.

KEY FACT L10:

If a line is tangent to a circle, a radius (or diameter) drawn to the point where the tangent touches the circle is perpendicular to the tangent line.

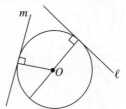

Lines ℓ and m are tangent to circle O.

Example 6.

A is the center of a circle whose radius is 8, and B is the center of a circle whose diameter is 8. If these two circles are tangent to one another, what is the area of the circle whose diameter is AB?

(A) 12π (B) 36π (C) 64π (D) 144π
(E) 256π

SOLUTION. Draw a diagram. Since the diameter, AB, of the dotted circle is 12, its radius is 6 and the area is $\pi(6)^2 = \textbf{36}\boldsymbol{\pi}$ **(B)**.

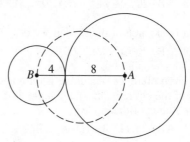

PRACTICE EXERCISES—CIRCLES

Multiple-Choice Questions

1. What is the circumference of a circle whose area is 100π?

   (A) 10   (B) 20   (C) 10π (D) 20π (E) 25π

2. What is the area of a circle whose circumference is π?

   (A) $\dfrac{\pi}{4}$ (B) $\dfrac{\pi}{2}$ (C) π (D) 2π (E) 4π

3. What is the area of a circle that is inscribed in a square of area 2?

   (A) $\dfrac{\pi}{4}$ (B) $\dfrac{\pi}{2}$ (C) π (D) $\pi\sqrt{2}$ (E) 2π

4. A square of area 2 is inscribed in a circle. What is the area of the circle?

   (A) $\dfrac{\pi}{4}$ (B) $\dfrac{\pi}{2}$ (C) π (D) $\pi\sqrt{2}$ (E) 2π

5. A 5 × 12 rectangle is inscribed in a circle. What is the radius of the circle?

    (A) 6.5 (B) 7 (C) 8.5 (D) 13 (E) 17

6. If in the figure below, the area of the shaded sector is 85% of the area of the entire circle, what is the value of w?

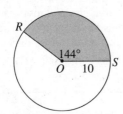

    (A) 15 (B) 30 (C) 45 (D) 54 (E) 60

Questions 7–8 refer to the following figure.

7. What is the length of arc RS?

    (A) 8 (B) 20 (C) 8π (D) 20π (E) 40π

8. What is the area of the shaded sector?

    (A) 8 (B) 20 (C) 8π (D) 20π (E) 40π

9. The circumference of a circle is $a\pi$ units, and the area of the circle is $b\pi$ square units. If $a = b$, what is the radius of the circle?

    (A) 1 (B) 2 (C) 3 (D) π (E) 2π

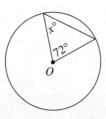

10. In the figure above, what is the value of x?

    (A) 30 (B) 36 (C) 45 (D) 54 (E) 60

11. If A is the area and C the circumference of a circle, which of the following is an expression for A in terms of C?

    (A) $\dfrac{C^2}{4\pi}$ (B) $\dfrac{C^2}{4\pi^2}$ (C) $2C$ (D) $2C^2\sqrt{\pi}$

    (E) $\dfrac{C^2\sqrt{\pi}}{4}$

12. What is the area of a circle whose radius is the diagonal of a square whose area is 4?

    (A) 2π (B) $2\pi\sqrt{2}$ (C) 4π (D) 8π (E) 16π

Quantitative Comparison Questions

	Column A	Column B

13. | The perimeter of the pentagon | The circumference of the circle |

The circumference of a circle is C inches. The area of the same circle is A square inches.

14. | $\dfrac{C}{A}$ | $\dfrac{A}{C}$ |

15. | The area of a circle of radius 2 | The area of a semi-circle of radius 3 |

C is the circumference of a circle of radius r

16. | $\dfrac{C}{r}$ | 6 |

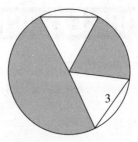

17. | The area of sector A | The area of sector B |

Each of the triangles is equilateral.

18. | The area of the shaded region | 6π |

<u>Column A</u>   <u>Column B</u>

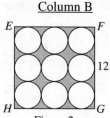

Figure 1

Figure 2

ABCD and EFGH are squares, and all the circles are tangent to one another and to the sides of the squares.

19.

| The area of the shaded region in Figure 1 | The area of the shaded region in Figure 2 |

<u>Column A</u>   <u>Column B</u>

A square and a circle have equal areas.

20.

| The perimeter of the square | The circumference of the circle |

Answer Key

1. **D**	6. **D**	11. **A**	16. **A**
2. **A**	7. **C**	12. **D**	17. **B**
3. **B**	8. **E**	13. **B**	18. **C**
4. **C**	9. **B**	14. **D**	19. **C**
5. **A**	10. **D**	15. **B**	20. **A**

Answer Explanations

1. **D.** $A = \pi r^2 = 100\pi \Rightarrow r^2 = 100 \Rightarrow r = 10 \Rightarrow$
   $C = 2\pi r = 2\pi(10) = 20\pi$.

2. **A.** $C = 2\pi r = \pi \Rightarrow 2r = 1 \Rightarrow r = \dfrac{1}{2} \Rightarrow$

   $A = \pi r^2 = \pi\left(\dfrac{1}{2}\right)^2 = \dfrac{1}{4}\pi = \dfrac{\pi}{4}$.

3. **B.** Draw a diagram.

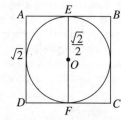

Since the area of square ABCD is 2, $AD = \sqrt{2}$. Then diameter $EF = \sqrt{2}$ and radius $OE = \dfrac{\sqrt{2}}{2}$. Then the area of the circle =

$\pi\left(\dfrac{\sqrt{2}}{2}\right)^2 = \dfrac{2}{4}\pi = \dfrac{\pi}{2}$.

4. **C.** Draw a diagram.

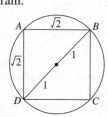

Since the area of square ABCD is 2, $AD = \sqrt{2}$. Then, since $\triangle ABD$ is an isosceles right triangle, diagonal $BD = \sqrt{2} \times \sqrt{2} = 2$. But BD is also a diameter of the circle. So the diameter is 2 and the radius is 1. Therefore, the area is $\pi(1)^2 = \pi$.

5. **A.** Draw a diagram.

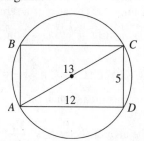

By the Pythagorean theorem (or by recognizing a 5-12-13 triangle), we see that diagonal AC is 13. But AC is also a diameter of the circle, so the diameter is 13 and the radius is 6.5.

6. D.   Since the shaded area is 85% of the circle, the white area is 15% of the circle. So, w is 15% of 360°: $0.15 \times 360 = 54$.

7. C.   The length of arc RS is $\dfrac{144}{360}$ of the circumference:
$$\left(\frac{144}{360}\right)2\pi(10) = \left(\frac{2}{5}\right)20\pi = 8\pi.$$

8. E.   The area of the shaded sector is $\left(\dfrac{144}{360}\right)$ of the area of the circle:
$$\left(\frac{144}{360}\right)\pi(10)^2 = \left(\frac{2}{5}\right)100\pi = 40\pi.$$

9. B.   Since $C = a\pi = b\pi = A$, we have
$$2\pi r = \pi r^2 \Rightarrow 2r = r^2 \Rightarrow r = 2.$$

10. D.   Since two of the sides are radii of the circles, the triangle is isosceles. So the unmarked angle is also x:
$$180 = 72 + 2x \Rightarrow 2x = 108 \Rightarrow x = 54.$$

11. A. $C = 2\pi r \Rightarrow r = \dfrac{C}{2\pi} \Rightarrow$
$$A = \pi\left(\frac{C}{2\pi}\right)^2 = \pi\left(\frac{C^2}{4\pi^2}\right) = \frac{C^2}{4\pi}.$$

12. D.   If the area of the square is 4, each side is 2, and the length of a diagonal is $2\sqrt{2}$. The area of a circle whose radius is $2\sqrt{2}$ is
$$\pi(2\sqrt{2})^2 = 8\pi.$$

13. B.   There's nothing to calculate here. Each arc of the circle is clearly longer than the corresponding chord, which is a side of the pentagon. So the circumference, which is the sum of all the arcs, is greater than the perimeter, which is the sum of all the chords.

14. D.   Column A: $\dfrac{C}{A} = \dfrac{2\pi r}{\pi r^2} = \dfrac{2}{r}$.
Column B: $\dfrac{A}{C} = \dfrac{r}{2}$.
If $r = 2$, the columns are equal; otherwise, they're not.

15. B.   Column A: $A = \pi(2)^2 = 4\pi$.
Column B: The area of a semicircle of radius 3 is $\dfrac{1}{2}\pi(3)^2 = \dfrac{1}{2}(9\pi) = 4.5\pi$.

16. A.   By KEY FACT L4, $\pi = \dfrac{C}{d} = \dfrac{C}{2r} \Rightarrow \dfrac{C}{r} = 2\pi$, which is greater than 6.

17. B.   The area of sector A is $\dfrac{40}{360}(16\pi) = \dfrac{16\pi}{9}$. The area of sector B is $\dfrac{20}{360}(64\pi) = \dfrac{64\pi}{18} = \dfrac{32\pi}{9}$.

So sector B is twice as big as sector A.

18. C.   Since the triangles are equilateral, the two white central angles each measure 60°, and their sum is 120°. So the white area is $\dfrac{120}{360} = \dfrac{1}{3}$ of the circle, and the shaded area is $\dfrac{2}{3}$ of the circle. The area of the circle is $\pi(3)^2 = 9\pi$, so the shaded area is $\dfrac{2}{3}(9\pi) = 6\pi$.

19. C.   In Figure 1, since the radius of each circle is 3, the area of each circle is 9π, and the total area of the 4 circles is 36π. In Figure 2, the radius of each circle is 2, and so the area of each circle is 4π, and the total area of the 9 circles is 36π. In the two figures, the white areas are equal, as are the shaded areas.

20. A.   Let A represent the area of the square and the circle.
Column A: $A = s^2 \Rightarrow s = \sqrt{A} \Rightarrow P = 4\sqrt{A}$.
Column B: $A = \pi r^2 \Rightarrow r = \sqrt{\dfrac{A}{\pi}} \Rightarrow$
$$C = 2\pi\left(\frac{\sqrt{A}}{\sqrt{\pi}}\right) = 2\sqrt{\pi}\sqrt{A}.$$
Since $\pi < 4$, $\sqrt{\pi} < 2 \Rightarrow 2\sqrt{\pi} < 4$.

14-M. SOLID GEOMETRY

There are very few solid geometry questions on the GRE, and they cover only a few elementary topics. Basically, all you need to know are the formulas for the volume and surface areas of rectangular solids (including cubes) and cylinders.

A **rectangular solid** or **box** is a solid formed by six rectangles, called **faces**. The sides of the rectangles are called **edges**. As shown in the diagram below, the edges are called the **length**, **width**, and **height**. A **cube** is a rectangular solid in which the length, width, and height are equal; so all the edges are the same length.

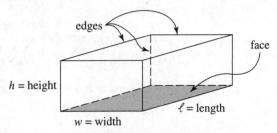

RECTANGULAR SOLID

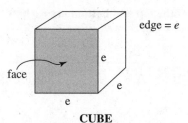

CUBE

The **volume** of a solid is the amount of space it takes up and is measured in **cubic units**. One cubic unit is the amount of space occupied by a cube all of whose edges are one unit long. In the figure above, if each edge of the cube is 1 inch long, then the area of each face is 1 square inch, and the volume of the cube is 1 cubic inch.

KEY FACT M1:

• The formula for the volume of a rectangular solid is
$V = \ell wh$.

• The formula for the volume of a cube is
$V = e \cdot e \cdot e = e^3$.

Example 1.

The base of a rectangular tank is 12 feet long and 8 feet wide; the height of the tank is 30 inches. If water is pouring into the tank at the rate of 2 cubic feet per second, how many <u>minutes</u> will be required to fill the tank?

(A) 1   (B) 2   (C) 10   (D) 120   (E) 240

SOLUTION. Draw a diagram. In order to express all of the dimensions of the tank in the same units, convert 30 inches to 2.5 feet. Then the volume of the tank is $12 \times 8 \times 2.5 = 240$ cubic feet. At 2 cubic feet per second, it will take $240 \div 2 = 120$ seconds = **2** minutes to fill the tank (**B**).

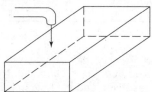

The **surface area** of a rectangular solid is the sum of the areas of the six faces. Since the top and bottom faces are equal, the front and back faces are equal, and the left and right faces are equal, we can calculate the area of one from each pair and then double the sum. In a cube, each of the six faces has the same area.

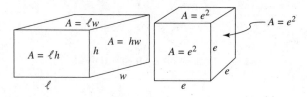

KEY FACT M2:

• The formula for the surface area of a rectangular solid is $A = 2(\ell w + \ell h + wh)$.

• The formula for the surface area of a cube is $A = 6e^2$.

Example 2.

The volume of a cube is v cubic *yards*, and its surface area is a square *feet*. If $v = a$, what is the length in *inches* of each edge?

(A) 12   (B) 36   (C) 144   (D) 648   (E) 1944

SOLUTION. Draw a diagram. If e is the length of the edge in yards, $3e$ is the length in feet, and $36e$ the length in inches. Therefore, $v = e^3$ and $a = 6(3e)^2 = 6(9e^2) = 54e^2$. Since $v = a$, $e^3 = 54e^2 \Rightarrow e = 54$, so the length is $36(54) = $ **1944** inches (**E**).

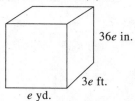

A **diagonal** of a box is a line segment joining a vertex on the top of the box to the opposite vertex on the bottom. A box has 4 diagonals, all the same length. In the box below they are line segments AG, BH, CE, and DF.

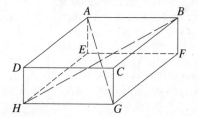

KEY FACT M3:

A diagonal of a box is the longest line segment that can be drawn between two points on the box.

KEY FACT M4:

If the dimensions of a box are ℓ, w, and h, and if d is the length of a diagonal, then $d^2 = \ell^2 + w^2 + h^2$.

For example, in the box below:

$$d^2 = 3^2 + 4^2 + 12^2 = 9 + 16 + 144 = 169 \Rightarrow d = 13.$$

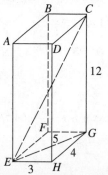

This formula is really just an extended Pythagorean theorem. *EG* is the diagonal of rectangular base *EFGH*. Since the sides of the base are 3 and 4, *EG* is 5. Now, △*CGE* is a right triangle whose legs are 12 and 5, so diagonal *CE* is 13.

Example 3.

What is the length of a diagonal of a cube whose edges are 1?

(A) 1   (B) 2   (C) 3   (D) $\sqrt{2}$ (E) $\sqrt{3}$

SOLUTION. Use the formula:

$$d^2 = 1^2 + 1^2 + 1^2 = 3 \Rightarrow d = \sqrt{3} \text{ (E)}.$$

Without the formula you would draw a diagram and label it. Since the base is a 1 × 1 square, its diagonal is $\sqrt{2}$. Then the diagonal of the cube is the hypotenuse of a right triangle whose legs are 1 and $\sqrt{2}$, so

$$d^2 = 1^2 + (\sqrt{2})^2 = 1 + 2 = 3, \text{ and } d = \sqrt{3}.$$

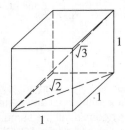

A *cylinder* is similar to a rectangular solid except that the base is a circle instead of a rectangle. The volume of a cylinder is the area of its circular base (πr^2) times its height (*h*). The surface area of a cylinder depends on whether you are envisioning a tube, such as a straw, without a top or bottom, or a can, which has both a top and a bottom.

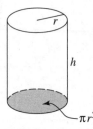

KEY FACT M5:

• The formula for the volume, *V*, of a cylinder whose circular base has radius *r* and whose height is *h* is
$V = \pi r^2 h$.

• The surface area, *A*, of the side of the cylinder is the circumference of the circular base times the height:
$A = 2\pi rh$.

• The area of the top and bottom are each πr^2, so the total area of a can is $2\pi rh + 2\pi r^2$.

Column A	Column B

Example 4.

The radius of cylinder II equals the height of cylinder I.
The height of cylinder II equals the radius of cylinder I.

The volume of cylinder I	The volume of cylinder II

SOLUTION. Let *r* and *h* be the radius and height, respectively, of cylinder I. Then

Column A	Column B
$\pi r^2 h$	$\pi h^2 r$

Divide each column by πrh:

Column A	Column B
r	*h*

Either *r* or *h* could be greater, or the two could be equal. The answer is **D**.

These are the only formulas you need to know. Any other solid geometry questions that might appear on the GRE would require you to visualize a situation and reason it out, rather than to apply a formula.

Example 5.

How many small cubes are needed to construct the tower in the figure at the right?

(A) 25   (B) 28
(C) 35   (D) 44
(E) 67

SOLUTION. You need to "see" the answer. The top level consists of 1 cube, the second and third levels consist of 9 cubes each, and the bottom layer consists of 25 cubes. The total is 1 + 9 + 9 + 25 = **44 (D)**.

PRACTICE EXERCISES—SOLID GEOMETRY

Multiple-Choice Questions

1. The sum of the lengths of all the edges of a cube is 6 centimeters. What is the volume, in cubic centimeters, of the cube?

   (A) $\frac{1}{8}$ (B) $\frac{1}{4}$ (C) $\frac{1}{2}$ (D) 1   (E) 8

2. What is the volume of a cube whose surface area is 150?

   (A) 25   (B) 100   (C) 125   (D) 1000   (E) 15,625

3. What is the surface area of a cube whose volume is 64?

   (A) 16   (B) 64   (C) 96   (D) 128   (E) 384

4. What is the number of cubic inches in one cubic foot?

   (A) 12   (B) 24   (C) 144   (D) 684   (E) 1728

5. A solid metal cube of edge 3 feet is placed in a rectangular tank whose length, width, and height are 3, 4, and 5 feet, respectively. What is the volume, in cubic feet, of water that the tank can now hold?

   (A) 20   (B) 27   (C) 33   (D) 48   (E) 60

6. The height, h, of a cylinder is equal to the edge of a cube. If the cylinder and cube have the same volume, what is the radius of the cylinder?

   (A) $\frac{h}{\sqrt{\pi}}$ (B) $h\sqrt{\pi}$ (C) $\frac{\sqrt{\pi}}{h}$ (D) $\frac{h^2}{\pi}$ (E) πh^2

7. A rectangular tank has a base that is 10 centimeters by 5 centimeters and a height of 20 centimeters. If the tank is half full of water, by how many centimeters will the water level rise if 325 cubic centimeters of water are poured into the tank?

   (A) 3.25   (B) 6.5   (C) 16.25   (D) 32.5   (E) 65

8. A 5-foot-long cylindrical pipe has an inner diameter of 6 feet and an outer diameter of 8 feet. If the total surface area (inside and out, including the ends) is $k\pi$, what is the value of k?

   (A) 7   (B) 40   (C) 48   (D) 70   (E) 84

9. If the height of a cylinder is 4 times its circumference, what is the volume of the cylinder in terms of its circumference, C?

   (A) $\frac{C^3}{\pi}$ (B) $\frac{2C^3}{\pi}$ (C) $\frac{2C^2}{\pi^2}$ (D) $\frac{\pi C^2}{4}$

   (E) $4\pi C^3$

10. Three identical balls fit snugly into a cylindrical can: the radius of the spheres equals the radius of the can, and the balls just touch the bottom and the top of the can. If the formula for the volume of a sphere is $V = \frac{4}{3}\pi r^3$, what fraction of the volume of the can is taken up by the balls?

    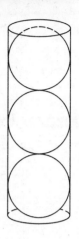

    (A) $\frac{1}{6}$ (B) $\frac{1}{3}$ (C) $\frac{1}{2}$ (D) $\frac{2}{3}$

    (E) $\frac{3}{4}$

Quantitative Comparison Questions

Column A	Column B

Jack and Jill each roll a sheet of 9×12 paper to form a cylinder.
Jack tapes the two 9-inch edges together.
Jill tapes the two 12-inch edges together.

11.

The volume of Jack's cylinder	The volume of Jill's cylinder

12.

The volume of a cube whose edges are 6	The volume of a box whose dimensions are 5, 6, and 7

A is the surface area of a rectangular box in square units.
V is the volume of the same box in cubic units.

13.

A	V

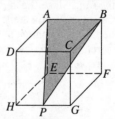

P is a point on edge GH of cube $ABCDEFGH$.
Each edge of the cube is 1.

14.

The area of $\triangle ABP$	1

15.

The volume of a sphere whose radius is 1	The volume of a cube whose edge is 1

Answer Key

1. **A**	6. **A**	11. **A**
2. **C**	7. **B**	12. **A**
3. **C**	8. **E**	13. **D**
4. **E**	9. **A**	14. **B**
5. **C**	10. **D**	15. **A**

Answer Explanations

1. **A.** Since a cube has 12 edges, we have

   $12e = 6 \Rightarrow e = \dfrac{1}{2}$. Therefore,

   $$V = e^3 = \left(\frac{1}{2}\right)^3 = \frac{1}{8}.$$

2. **C.** Since the surface area is 150, each of the 6 faces is a square whose area is $150 \div 6 = 25$. So the edges are all 5, and the volume is $5^3 = 125$.

3. **C.** Since the volume of the cube is 64, we have $e^3 = 64 \Rightarrow e = 4$. The surface area is $6e^2 = 6 \times 16 = 96$.

4. **E.** The volume of a cube whose edges are 1 foot can be expressed in either of two ways:

   $$(1 \text{ foot})^3 = 1 \text{ cubic foot or}$$
   $$(12 \text{ inches})^3 = 1728 \text{ cubic inches.}$$

5. **C.** The volume of the tank is $3 \times 4 \times 5 = 60$ cubic units, but the solid cube is taking up $3^3 = 27$ cubic units. Therefore, the tank can hold $60 - 27 = 33$ cubic units of water.

6. **A.** Since the volumes are equal, $\pi r^2 h = e^3 = h^3$. Therefore,

   $$\pi r^2 = h^2 \Rightarrow r^2 = \frac{h^2}{\pi} \Rightarrow r = \frac{h}{\sqrt{\pi}}.$$

7. **B.** Draw a diagram. Since the area of the base is $5 \times 10 = 50$ square centimeters, each 1 centimeter of depth has a volume of 50 cubic centimeters. Therefore, 325 cubic centimeters will raise the water level $325 \div 50 = 6.5$ centimeters.

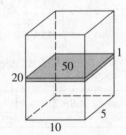

(Note that we didn't use the fact that the tank was half full, except to be sure that the tank didn't overflow. Since the tank was half full, the water was 10 centimeters deep, and the water level could rise by 6.5 centimeters. Had the tank been three-fourths full, the water would have been 15 centimeters deep and the extra water would have caused the level to rise 5 centimeters, filling the tank; the rest of the water would have spilled out.)

8. **E.** Draw a diagram and label it. Since the surface of a cylinder is given by $A = 2\pi r h$, the area of the exterior is $2\pi(4)(5) = 40\pi$, and the area of the interior is $2\pi(3)(5) = 30\pi$. The area of *each* shaded end is the area of the outer circle minus the area of the inner circle: $16\pi - 9\pi = 7\pi$, so total surface area =

   $$40\pi + 30\pi + 7\pi + 7\pi = 84\pi \Rightarrow k = 84.$$

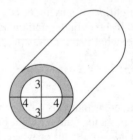

9. **A.** Since $V = \pi r^2 h$, we need to express r and h in terms of C. It is given that $h = 4C$; and since

   $C = 2\pi r$, then $r = \dfrac{C}{2\pi}$. Therefore,

   $$V = \pi\left(\frac{C}{2\pi}\right)^2(4C) = \pi\left(\frac{C^2}{4\pi^2}\right)(4C) = \frac{C^3}{\pi}.$$

10. **D.** To avoid using r, assume that the radii of the spheres and the can are 1. Then the volume of

    each ball is $\dfrac{4}{3}\pi(1)^3 = \dfrac{4}{3}\pi$, and the total

    volume of the 3 balls is $3\left(\dfrac{4}{3}\pi\right) = 4\pi$. Since

    the height of the can is 6 (the diameter of each

sphere is 2), the volume of the can is

$\pi(1)^2(6) = 6\pi$. So the balls take up $\dfrac{4\pi}{6\pi} = \dfrac{2}{3}$ of the can.

11. A. Drawing a diagram makes it easier to visualize the problem. The volume of a cylinder is $\pi r^2 h$. In each case, we know the height but have to determine the radius in order to calculate the volume.

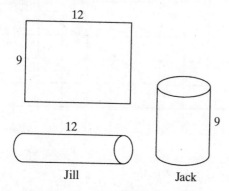

12
9

12
Jill

9
Jack

Jack's cylinder has a circumference of 12:

$$2\pi r = 12 \Rightarrow r = \frac{12}{2\pi} = \frac{6}{\pi} \Rightarrow$$

$$V = \pi\left(\frac{6}{\pi}\right)^2(9) = \pi\left(\frac{36}{\pi^2}\right)(9) = \frac{324}{\pi}.$$

Jill's cylinder has a circumference of 9:

$$2\pi r = 9 \Rightarrow r = \frac{9}{2\pi} \Rightarrow$$

$$V = \pi\left(\frac{9}{2\pi}\right)^2(12) = \pi\left(\frac{81}{4\pi^2}\right)(12) = \frac{243}{\pi}.$$

12. A. Column A: $V = 6^3 = 216$.
Column B: $V = 5 \times 6 \times 7 = 210$.

13. D. There is no relationship between the two columns. If the box is a cube of edge 1, $A = 6$ and $V = 1$. If the box is a cube of edge 10, $A = 600$ and $V = 1000$.

14. B. The base, AB, of $\triangle ABP$ is 1. Since the diagonal is the longest line segment in the cube, the height, h, of the triangle is definitely less than the diagonal, which is $\sqrt{1^2 + 1^2 + 1^2} = \sqrt{3}$. So the area of the triangle is less than $\dfrac{1}{2}(1)\sqrt{3} \approx .87$, which is less than 1. (You could also have just calculated the area: $h = BG = \sqrt{2}$, so the area is $\dfrac{1}{2}\sqrt{2} \approx .71$.)

15. A. You probably don't know how to find the volume of a sphere; fortunately, you don't

need to. You should be able to visualize that the sphere is *much* bigger than the cube. (In fact, it is more than 4 times the size.)

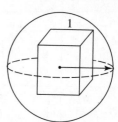

1

14-N. COORDINATE GEOMETRY

The GRE has very few questions on coordinate geometry. Most often they deal with the coordinates of points and occasionally with the slope of a line. You will *never* have to draw a graph; nor will you have to provide the equation for a given graph.

The coordinate plane is formed by two perpendicular number lines called the **x-axis** and **y-axis**, which intersect at the **origin**. The axes divide the plane into four **quadrants**, labeled I, II, III, and IV.

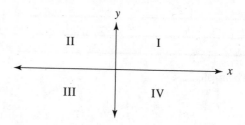

Each point in the plane is assigned two numbers, an **x-coordinate** and a **y-coordinate**, which are written as an ordered pair, (**x, y**).

• Points to the right of the y-axis have positive x-coordinates, and those to the left have negative x-coordinates.

• Points above the x-axis have positive y-coordinates, and those below it have negative y-coordinates.

• If a point is on the x-axis, its y-coordinate is 0.

• If a point is on the y-axis, its x-coordinate is 0.

For example, point A in the following figure is labeled (2, 3), since it is 2 units to the right of the y-axis and 3 units above the x-axis. Similarly, B(–3, –5) is in Quadrant III, 3 units to the left of the y-axis and 5 units below the x-axis.

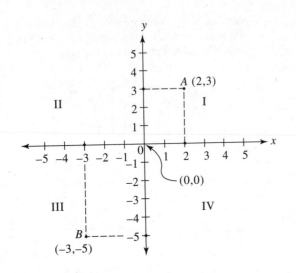

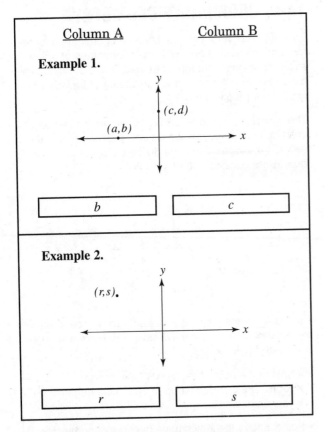

Column A   Column B

Example 1.

b		c

Example 2.

r		s

SOLUTION 1. Since (a, b) lies on the x-axis, $b = 0$. Since (c, d) lies on the y-axis, $c = 0$. The answer is **C**.

SOLUTION 2. Since (r, s) is in Quadrant II, r is negative and s is positive. The answer is **B**.

Often a question requires you to calculate the distance between two points. This is easiest when the points lie on the same horizontal or vertical line.

KEY FACT N1:

• All the points on a horizontal line have the same **y**-coordinate. To find the distance between them, subtract their **x**-coordinates.

• All the points on a vertical line have the same **x**-coordinate. To find the distance between them, subtract their **y**-coordinates.

Helpful Hint

If the points have been plotted on a graph, you can find the distance between them by counting boxes.

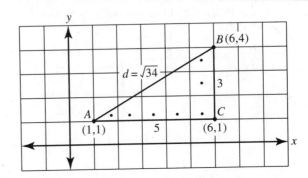

The distance from A to C is $6 - 1 = 5$. The distance from B to C is $4 - 1 = 3$.

It is a little more difficult to find the distance between two points that are not on the same horizontal or vertical line. In this case, use the Pythagorean theorem. For example, in the figure above, if d represents the distance from A to B, $d^2 = 5^2 + 3^2 = 25 + 9 = 34 \Rightarrow d = \sqrt{34}$.

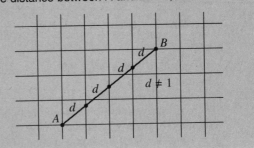

CAUTION: You *cannot* count boxes unless the points are on the same horizontal or vertical line. The distance between A and B is 5, not 4.

KEY FACT N2:

The distance, d, between two points, $A(x_1, y_1)$ and $B(x_2, y_2)$, can be calculated using the distance formula:
$$d = \sqrt{(x_2 - x_1)^2 + (y_2 - y_1)^2}.$$

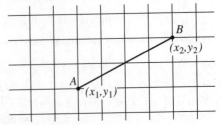

Helpful Hint

The "distance formula" is nothing more than the Pythagorean theorem. If you ever forget the formula, and you need the distance between two points that do not lie on the same horizontal or vertical line, do as follows: create a right triangle by drawing a horizontal line through one of the points and a vertical line through the other, and then use the Pythagorean theorem.

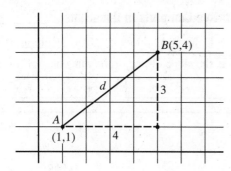

Examples 3–4 refer to the triangle in the following figure.

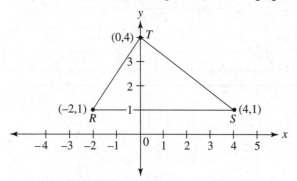

Example 3.

What is the area of $\triangle RST$?

(A) 6   (B) 9   (C) 12   (D) 15   (E) 18

SOLUTION. $R(-2, 1)$ and $S(4, 1)$ lie on the same horizontal line, so $RS = 4 - (-2) = 6$. Let that be the base of the triangle. Then the height is the distance along the vertical line from T to RS: $4 - 1 = 3$. The area is $\frac{1}{2}(6)(3) = $ **9 (B)**.

Example 4.

What is the perimeter of $\triangle RST$?

(A) 13   (B) 14   (C) 16   (D) $11 + \sqrt{13}$
   (E) $11 + \sqrt{61}$

SOLUTION. The perimeter is $RS + ST + RT$. From the solution to Example 3, you know that $RS = 6$. Also, $ST = 5$, since it is the hypotenuse of a 3-4-5 right triangle. To calculate RT, either use the distance formula:

$$\sqrt{(-2-0)^2 + (1-4)^2} = \sqrt{(-2)^2 + (-3)^2} = \sqrt{4+9} = \sqrt{13}$$

or the Pythagorean theorem:

$$RT^2 = 2^2 + 3^2 = 4 + 9 = 13 \Rightarrow RT = \sqrt{13}.$$

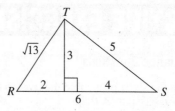

So the perimeter is: $6 + 5 + \sqrt{13} = $ **$11 + \sqrt{13}$ (D)**.

The **slope** of a line is a number that indicates how steep the line is.

KEY FACT N3:

• Vertical lines **do not have slopes**.
• To find the slope of any other line proceed as follows:
   1. Choose any two points $A(x_1, y_1)$ and $B(x_2, y_2)$ on the line.
   2. Take the differences of the y-coordinates, $y_2 - y_1$, and the x-coordinates, $x_2 - x_1$.
   3. Divide: slope $= \dfrac{y_2 - y_1}{x_2 - x_1}$.

We will illustrate the next KEY FACT by using this formula to calculate the slopes of RS, RT, and ST from Example 3: $R(-2, 1)$, $S(4, 1)$, $T(0, 4)$.

KEY FACT N4:

• The slope of any horizontal line is 0:
   slope of $RS = \dfrac{1-1}{4-(-2)} = \dfrac{0}{6} = 0$
• The slope of any line that goes up as you move from left to right is positive: slope of $RT = \dfrac{4-1}{0-(-2)} = \dfrac{3}{2}$
• The slope of any line that goes down as you move from left to right is negative: slope of $ST = \dfrac{1-4}{4-0} = \dfrac{-3}{4} = -\dfrac{3}{4}$

Column A	Column B
Example 5.	
Line ℓ passes through $(1, 2)$ and $(3, 5)$ Line m is perpendicular to ℓ	
The slope of ℓ	The slope of m

SOLUTION. First, make a quick sketch. Do not use the formula to calculate the slope of ℓ. Simply notice that ℓ slopes upward, so its slope is positive, whereas m slopes downward, so its slope is negative. Column **A** is greater.

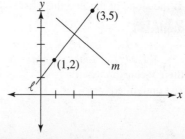

PRACTICE EXERCISES—COORDINATE GEOMETRY

Multiple-Choice Questions

1. What is the slope of the line that passes through points (0, –2) and (3, 0)?

   (A) $-\dfrac{3}{2}$ (B) $-\dfrac{2}{3}$ (C) 0   (D) $\dfrac{2}{3}$ (E) $\dfrac{3}{2}$

2. If the coordinates of $\triangle RST$ are $R(0, 0)$, $S(7, 0)$, and $T(2, 5)$, what is the sum of the slopes of the three sides of the triangle?

   (A) –1.5   (B) 0   (C) 1.5   (D) 2.5   (E) 3.5

3. If $A(-1, 1)$ and $B(3, -1)$ are the endpoints of one side of square $ABCD$, what is the area of the square?

   (A) 12   (B) 16   (C) 20   (D) 25   (E) 36

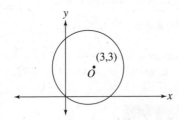

4. If the area of circle O above is $k\pi$, what is the value of k?

   (A) 3   (B) 6   (C) 9   (D) 18   (E) 27

5. If $P(2, 1)$ and $Q(8, 1)$ are two of the vertices of a rectangle, which of the following could *not* be another of the vertices?

   (A) (2, 8)   (B) (8, 2)   (C) (2, –8)
   (D) (–2, 8)   (E) (8, 8)

6. A circle whose center is at (6, 8) passes through the origin. Which of the following points is *not* on the circle?

   (A) (12, 0)   (B) (6, –2)   (C) (16, 8)
   (D) (–2, 12)   (E) (–4, 8)

Questions 7–8 concern parallelogram $JKLM$, whose coordinates are $J(-5, 2)$, $K(-2, 6)$, $L(5, 6)$, $M(2, 2)$.

7. What is the area of parallelogram $JKLM$?

   (A) 35   (B) 28   (C) 24   (D) 20   (E) 12

8. What is the perimeter of parallelogram $JKLM$?

   (A) 35   (B) 28   (C) 24   (D) 20   (E) 12

9. What is the slope of the line that passes through (a, b) and $\left(\dfrac{1}{a}, b\right)$?

   (A) 0   (B) $\dfrac{1}{b}$ (C) $\dfrac{1 - a^2}{a}$ (D) $\dfrac{a^2 - 1}{a}$
   (E) undefined

10. If $c \neq 0$ and the slope of the line passing through $(-c, c)$ and $(3c, a)$ is 1, which of the following is an expression for a in terms of c?

    (A) –3c   (B) $-\dfrac{c}{3}$ (C) 2c   (D) 3c   (E) 5c

Quantitative Comparison Questions

Column A	Column B

m is the slope of one of the diagonals of a square.

11.
m^2	1

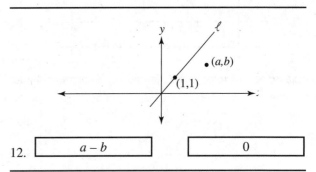

12.
$a - b$	0

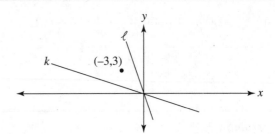

13.
The slope of line k	The slope of line ℓ

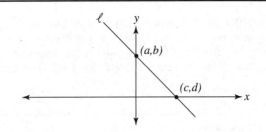

The slope of line ℓ is –0.8.

14.
c	b

The distance from $(b, 5)$ to $(c, -3)$ is 10.
$b < c$

15.
$c - b$	6

Answer Key

1. **D**	6. **D**	11. **D**
2. **C**	7. **B**	12. **A**
3. **C**	8. **C**	13. **A**
4. **D**	9. **A**	14. **A**
5. **D**	10. **E**	15. **C**

Answer Explanations

1. D. If you sketch the line, you see immediately that the slope of the line is positive. Without even knowing the slope formula, therefore, you can eliminate Choices A, B, and C. To determine the actual slope, use the formula:
$$\frac{y_2 - y_1}{x_2 - x_1} = \frac{0 - (-2)}{3 - 0} = \frac{2}{3}.$$

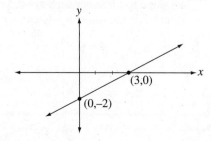

2. C. Sketch the triangle, and then calculate the slopes.

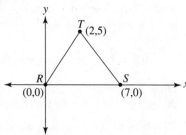

   Since *RS* is horizontal, its slope is 0.

   The slope of $RT = \dfrac{5 - 0}{2 - 0} = 2.5.$

   The slope of $ST = \dfrac{5 - 0}{2 - 7} = \dfrac{5}{-5} = -1.$

   Now add: $0 + 2.5 + (-1) = 1.5$

3. C. Draw a diagram and label it. The area of square *ABCD* is s^2, where $s = AB =$ length of a side. By the Pythagorean theorem:
$$s^2 = 2^2 + 4^2 = 4 + 16 = 20.$$

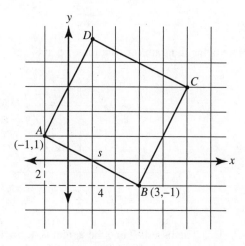

4. D. Since the line segment joining (3, 3) and (0, 0) is a radius of the circle, $r^2 = 3^2 + 3^2 = 18$. Therefore, area $= \pi r^2 = 18\pi \Rightarrow k = 18$. Note that you do not actually have to find that the value of r is $3\sqrt{2}$.

5. D. Draw a diagram. Any point whose *x*-coordinate is 2 or 8 could be another vertex. Of the choices, only (–2, 8) is *not* possible.

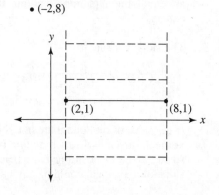

6. D. Draw a diagram. The radius of the circle is 10 (since it's the hypotenuse of a 6-8-10 right triangle). Which of the choices are 10 units from (6, 8)? First, check the easy ones: (–4, 8) and (16, 8) are 10 units to the left and right of (6, 8), and (6, –2) is 10 units below. What

remains is to check (12, 0), which works, and (–2, 12), which doesn't.

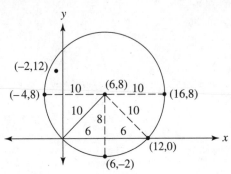

Here is the diagram for solutions 7 and 8.

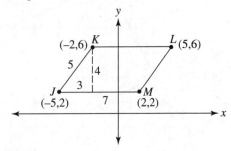

7. **B.** The base is 7 and the height is 4. So, the area is $7 \times 4 = 28$.

8. **C.** Sides JM and KL are each 7, and sides JK and LM are each the hypotenuse of a 3-4-5 right triangle, so they are 5. The perimeter is $2(7 + 5) = 24$.

9. **A.** The formula for the slope is $\dfrac{y_2 - y_1}{x_2 - x_1}$, but before using it, look. Since the y-coordinates are equal, the numerator, and thus the fraction, equals 0.

10. **E.** The slope is equal to
$$\frac{y_2 - y_1}{x_2 - x_1} = \frac{a - c}{3c - (-c)} = \frac{a - c}{4c} = 1 \Rightarrow$$
$$a - c = 4c \Rightarrow a = 5c.$$

11. **D.** If the sides of the square are horizontal and vertical, then m is 1 or –1, and m^2 is 1. But the square could be positioned any place, and the slope of a diagonal could be any number.

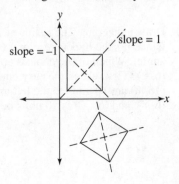

12. **A.** Line ℓ, which goes through (0, 0) and (1, 1), also goes through (a, a), and since (a, b) is below (a, a), $b < a$. Therefore, $a - b$ is positive.

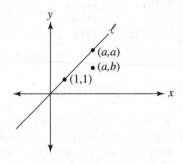

13. **A.** The line going through (–3, 3) and (0, 0) has slope –1. Since ℓ is steeper, its slope is a number such as –2 or –3; since k is less steep, its slope is a number such as –0.5 or –0.3. Therefore, the slope of k is greater.

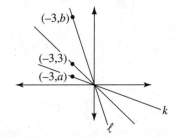

14. **A.** Since (a, b) is on the y-axis, $a = 0$; and since (c, d) is on the x-axis, $d = 0$. Then by the slope formula,
$$-0.8 = \frac{0 - b}{c - 0} = -\frac{b}{c} \Rightarrow b = .8c \Rightarrow b < c.$$

15. **C.** Draw a diagram. Since the distance between the two points is 10, by the distance formula:
$$10 = \sqrt{(c - b)^2 + (-3 - 5)^2} = \sqrt{(c - b)^2 + (-8)^2} = \sqrt{(c - b)^2 + 64}.$$

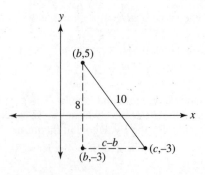

Squaring both sides gives
$$100 = (c - b)^2 + 64 \Rightarrow (c - b)^2 = 36 \Rightarrow$$
$$c - b = 6.$$

14-O. COUNTING AND PROBABILITY

Some questions on the GRE begin, "How many ... ." In these problems you are being asked to count something: how many apples can she buy, how many dollars did he spend, how many pages did she read, how many numbers satisfy a certain property, or how many ways are there to complete a particular task. Sometimes these problems can be handled by simple arithmetic. Other times it helps to use TACTIC 8 from Chapter 10 and systematically make a list. Occasionally it helps to know the counting principle and other strategies that we will review in this section.

COUNTING

Using Arithmetic to Count

The following three examples require only arithmetic. But be careful; they are not the same.

Example 1.

Brian bought some apples. If he entered the store with $113 and left with $109, how much did the apples cost?

Example 2.

Scott was selling tickets for the school play. One day he sold tickets numbered 109 through 113. How many tickets did he sell that day?

Example 3.

Brian is the 109th person in a line and Scott is the 113th person. How many people are there between Brian and Scott?

SOLUTIONS 1–3.

- It may seem that each of these examples requires a simple subtraction: 113 − 109 = 4. In Example 1, Brian did spend **$4** on apples; in Example 2, however, Scott sold **5** tickets; and in Example 3, only **3** people are on line between Brian and Scott!

- Assume that Brian went into the store with 113 one-dollar bills, numbered 1 through 113; he spent the 4 dollars numbered 113, 112, 111, and 110, and still had the dollars numbered 1 through 109; Scott sold the 5 tickets numbered 109, 110, 111, 112, and 113; and between Brian and Scott the 110th, 111th, and 112th persons—3 people—were on line.

In Example 1, you just needed to subtract: 113 − 109 = 4. In Example 2, you need to subtract *and then add 1*: 113 − 109 + 1 = 4 + 1 = 5. And in Example 3, you need to subtract and then *subtract 1 more*: 113 − 109 − 1 = 3. Although Example 1 is too easy for the GRE, questions such as Examples 2 and 3 do appear, because they're not as obvious and they require that little extra thought. *When do you have to add or subtract 1?*

The issue is whether or not the first and last numbers are included. In Example 1, Brian spent dollar number 113, but he still had dollar number 109 when he left the store. In Example 2, Scott sold both ticket number 109 and ticket 113. In Example 3, neither Scott (the 113th person) nor Brian (the 109th person) was to be counted.

KEY FACT O1:

To count how many integers there are between two integers, follow these rules:

- **If exactly one of the endpoints is included, subtract.**
- **If both endpoints are included, subtract and add 1.**
- **If neither endpoint is included, subtract and subtract 1 more.**

Example 4.

From 1:09 to 1:13, Adam read pages 109 through 113 in his English book. What was his rate of reading, in pages per minute?

(A) $\frac{3}{5}$ (B) $\frac{3}{4}$ (C) $\frac{4}{5}$ (D) 1   (E) $\frac{5}{4}$

SOLUTION. Since Adam read both pages 109 and 113, he read 113 − 109 + 1 = 5 pages. He started reading during the minute that started at 1:09 (and ended at 1:10). Since he stopped reading at 1:13, he did not read during the minute that began at 1:13 (and ended at 1:14). So he read for 1:13 − 1:09 = 4 minutes. He read at the rate of $\frac{5}{4}$ pages per minute.

Systematically Making a List

Tactic O1

When a question asks "How many...?" and the numbers in the problem are small, just systematically list all of the possibilities.

Proper use of TACTIC O1 eliminates the risk of making an error in arithmetic. In Example 4, rather than even thinking about whether or not to add 1 or subtract 1 after subtracting the number of pages, you could have just quickly jotted down the numbers of the pages Adam read (109, 110, 111, 112, 113), and then counted them.

Example 5.

Ariel has 4 paintings in the basement. She is going to bring up 2 of them and hang 1 in her den and 1 in her bedroom. In how many ways can she choose which paintings go in each room?

(A) 4   (B) 6   (C) 12   (D) 16   (E) 24

SOLUTION. Label the paintings 1, 2, 3, and 4, write B for bedroom and D for den, and make a list.

B-D	B-D	B-D	B-D
1-2	2-2	3-1	4-1
1-3	2-3	3-2	4-2
1-4	2-4	3-4	4-3

There are **12** ways to choose (**C**).

In Example 5, making a list was feasible, but if Ariel had 10 paintings and needed to hang 4 of them, it would be impossible to list all the different ways of hanging them. In such cases, we need the *counting principle*.

The Counting Principle

KEY FACT O2:

If two jobs need to be completed and there are *m* ways to do the first job and *n* ways to do the second job, then there are *m* × *n* ways to do one job followed by the other. This principle can be extended to any number of jobs.

In Example 5, the first job was to pick 1 of the 4 paintings and hang it in the bedroom. That could be done in 4 ways. The second job was to pick a second painting to hang in the den. That job could be accomplished by choosing any of the remaining 3 paintings. So there are 4 × 3 = **12** ways to hang 2 of the paintings.

Now, assume that there are 10 paintings to be hung in 4 rooms. The first job is to choose one of the 10 paintings for the bedroom. The second job is to choose one of the 9 remaining paintings to hang in the den. The third job is to choose one of the 8 remaining paintings for the living room. Finally, the fourth job is to pick one of the 7 remaining paintings for the dining room. These 4 jobs can be completed in 10 × 9 × 8 × 7 = **5040** ways.

Example 6.

How many integers are there between 100 and 1000 all of whose digits are odd?

SOLUTION. We're looking for three-digit numbers, such as 135, 711, 353, and 999, in which all three digits are odd. Note that we are *not* required to use three different digits. Although you certainly wouldn't want to list all of them, you could count them by listing some of them and seeing if a pattern develops. In the 100s there are 5 numbers that begin with 11: 111, 113, 115, 117, 119. Similarly, there are 5 numbers that begin with 13: 131, 133, 135, 137, 139; 5 that begin with 15; 5 that begin with 17; and 5 that begin with 19, for a total of 5 × 5 = 25 in the 100s. In the same way there are 25 in the 300s, 25 in the 500s, 25 in the 700s, and 25 in the 900s, for a grand total of 5 × 25 = **125**. You can actually do this in less time than it takes to read this paragraph.

The best way to solve Example 6, however, is to use the counting principle. Think of writing a three-digit number as three jobs that need to be done. The first job is to select one of the five odd digits and use it as the digit in the hundreds place. The second job is to select one of the five odd digits to be the digit that goes in the tens place. Finally, the third job is to select one of the five odd digits to be the digit in the units place. Each of these jobs can be done in 5 ways. So the total number of ways is 5 × 5 × 5 = **125**.

Example 7.

How many different arrangements are there of the letters *A*, *B*, *C*, and *D*?

(A) 4   (B) 6   (C) 8   (D) 12   (E) 24

Since from the choices given, we know that the answer is a relatively small number, we could just use TACTIC O1 and systematically list them: *ABCD*, *ABDC*, *ACBD*, ... However, this method would not be suitable if you had to arrange as few as 5 or 6 letters and would be practically impossible if you had to arrange 10 or 20 letters.

SOLUTION. Think of the act of arranging the four letters as four jobs that need to be done, and use the counting principle. The first job is to choose one of the four letters to write in the first position; there are 4 ways to complete that job. The second job is to choose one of the remaining three letters to write in the second position; there are 3 ways to complete that job. The third job is to choose one of the two remaining letters to write in the third position; there are 2 ways to complete that job. Finally, the fourth job is to choose the only remaining letter and to write it: 4 × 3 × 2 × 1 = **24**.

Venn Diagrams

A **Venn diagram** is a figure with two or three overlapping circles, usually enclosed in a rectangle, which is used to solve certain counting problems. To illustrate this, assume that a school has 100 seniors. The following Venn diagram, which divides the rectangle into four regions, shows the distribution of those students in the band and the orchestra.

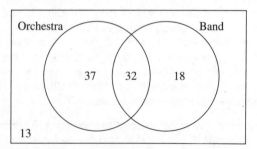

The 32 written in the part of the diagram where the two circles overlap represents the 32 seniors who are in both band and orchestra. The 18 written in the circle on the right represents the 18 seniors who are in band but not in orchestra, while the 37 written in the left circle represents the 37 seniors who are in orchestra but not in band. Finally, the 13 written in the rectangle outside of the circles represents the 13 seniors who are in neither band nor orchestra. The numbers in all four regions must add up to the total number of seniors: $32 + 18 + 37 + 13 = 100$. Note that there are 50 seniors in the band—32 who are also in the orchestra and 18 who are not in the orchestra. Similarly, there are $32 + 37 = 69$ seniors in the orchestra. Be careful: the 50 names on the band roster and the 69 names on the orchestra roster add up to 119 names—more than the number of seniors. That's because 32 names are on both lists and so have been counted twice. The number of seniors who are in band or orchestra is only $119 - 32 = 87$. Those 87 together with the 13 seniors who are in neither make up the total of 100.

On the GRE, Venn diagrams are used in two ways. It is possible to be given a Venn diagram and asked a question about it, as in Example 7. More often, you will come across a problem, such as Example 8, that you will be able to solve more easily if you think to draw a Venn diagram.

Example 7.

If the integers from 1 through 15 are each placed in the diagram at the right, which regions are empty?

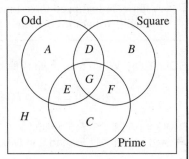

(A) D only (B) F only (C) G only
(D) F and G only (E) D and G only

SOLUTION. The easiest way is just to put each of the numbers from 1 through 15 in the appropriate region.

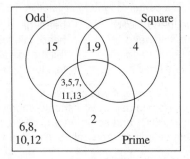

The empty regions are **F and G only (D)**.

Example 8.

Of the 410 students at H. S. Truman High School, 240 study Spanish and 180 study French. If 25 students study neither language, how many study both?

(A) 25 (B) 35 (C) 60 (D) 170 (E) 230

SOLUTION. Draw a Venn diagram. Let x represent the number of students who study both languages, and write x in the part of the diagram where the two circles overlap. Then the number who study only Spanish is $240 - x$, and the number who study only French is $180 - x$. The number who study at least one of the languages is $410 - 25 = 385$, so we have

$$385 = (240 - x) + x + (180 - x) = 420 - x \Rightarrow$$
$$x = 420 - 385 = \mathbf{35} \text{ students who study both (\textbf{B}).}$$

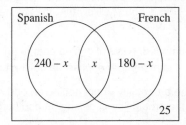

Note: No problem *requires* the use of a Venn diagram. On some problems you might even find it easier not to use one. In Example 8, you could have reasoned that if there were 410 students in the school and 25 didn't study either language, then there were $410 - 25 = 385$ students who studied at least one language. There are 240 names on the Spanish class lists and 180 on the French class lists, a total of $240 + 180 = 420$ names. But those 420 names belong to only 385 students. It must be that $420 - 385 = 35$ names were repeated. In other words, 35 students are in both French and Spanish classes.

PROBABILITY

The **probability** that an **event** will occur is a number between 0 and 1, usually written as a fraction, which indicates how likely it is that the event will happen. For example, if you spin the spinner below, there are 4 possible outcomes. It is equally likely that the spinner will stop in any of the 4 regions. There is 1 chance in 4 that it will stop in the region marked 2. So we say that the probability of spinning a 2 is one-fourth and write $P(2) = \dfrac{1}{4}$. Since 2 is the only even number on the spinner we could also say $P(\text{even}) = \dfrac{1}{4}$. There are 3 chances in 4 that the spinner will land in a region with an odd number in it, so $P(\text{odd}) = \dfrac{3}{4}$.

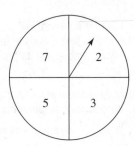

KEY FACT O3:

If E is any event, the probability that E will occur is given by $P(E) = \dfrac{\text{number of favorable outcomes}}{\text{total number of possible outcomes}}$, assuming that the possible outcomes are all equally likely.

In the preceding example, each of the 4 regions is the same size, so it is equally likely that the spinner will land on the 2, 3, 5, or 7. Therefore,

$$P(\text{odd}) = \frac{\text{number of ways of getting an odd number}}{\text{total number of possible outcomes}} = \frac{3}{4}.$$

Note that the probability of *not* getting an odd number is 1 minus the probability of getting an odd number: $1 - \dfrac{3}{4} = \dfrac{1}{4}$. Let's look at some other probabilities associated with spinning this spinner once.

$P(\text{number} > 10) =$
$$\frac{\text{number of ways of getting a number} > 10}{\text{total number of possible outcomes}} = \frac{0}{4} = 0.$$

$P(\text{prime number}) =$
$$\frac{\text{number of ways of getting a prime number}}{\text{total number of possible outcomes}} = \frac{4}{4} = 1.$$

$P(\text{number} < 4) =$
$$\frac{\text{number of ways of getting a number} < 4}{\text{total number of possible outcomes}} = \frac{2}{4} = \frac{1}{2}.$$

KEY FACT O4:

Let E be an event, and $P(E)$ the probability it will occur.

- If E is **impossible** (such as getting a number greater than 10), **$P(E) = 0$**.

- If it is **certain** that E will occur (such as getting a prime number), **$P(E) = 1$**.

- In all cases **$0 \le P(E) \le 1$**.

- The probability that event E will not occur is **$1 - P(E)$**.

- If 2 or more events constitute all the outcomes, the sum of their probabilities is 1.

  [For example, $P(\text{even}) + P(\text{odd}) = \dfrac{1}{4} + \dfrac{3}{4} = 1$.]

- The more likely it is that an event will occur, the higher its probability (the closer to 1 it is); the less likely it is that an event will occur, the lower its probability (the closer to 0 it is).

Even though probability is defined as a fraction, we can write probabilities as decimals or percents, as well. Instead of writing $P(E) = \dfrac{1}{2}$, we can write $P(E) = .50$ or $P(E) = 50\%$.

Example 9.

An integer between 100 and 999, inclusive, is chosen at random. What is the probability that all the digits of the number are odd?

SOLUTION. By KEY FACT O1, since both endpoints are included, there are $999 - 100 + 1 = 900$ integers between 100 and 999. In Example 6, we saw that there are 125 three-digit numbers all of whose digits are odd. So the probability is

$$\frac{\text{number of favorable outcomes}}{\text{total number of possible outcomes}} = \frac{125}{900} = \frac{5}{36}.$$

KEY FACT O5:

If an experiment is done two (or more) times, the probability that first one event will occur and then a second event will occur is the product of the probabilities.

Example 10.

A fair coin is flipped three times. What is the probability that the coin lands heads each time?

SOLUTION. When a fair coin is flipped:

$$P(\text{head}) = \frac{1}{2} \text{ and } P(\text{tail}) = \frac{1}{2}.$$

By KEY FACT O5, $P(3 \text{ heads}) =$
$P(\text{head 1st time}) \times P(\text{head 2nd time}) \times P(\text{head 3rd time})$

$$= \frac{1}{2} \times \frac{1}{2} \times \frac{1}{2} = \frac{1}{8}.$$

Another way to handle problems such as Example 10 is to make a list of all the possible outcomes. For example, if a coin is tossed three times, the possible outcomes are

head, head, head	head, head, tail
head, tail, head	head, tail, tail
tail, head, head	tail, head, tail
tail, tail, head	tail, tail, tail

On the GRE, of course, if you choose to list the outcomes on your scrap paper, you should abbreviate and just write HHH, HHT, and so on. In any event, there are eight possible outcomes, and only one of them (HHH) is favorable. So the probability is $\dfrac{1}{8}$.

Column A	Column B

Example 11.

Three fair coins are flipped.

The probability of getting more heads than tails	The probability of getting more tails than heads

SOLUTION. From the list of the 8 possible outcomes mentioned, you can see that in 4 of them (HHH, HHT, HTH, THH) there are more heads than tails, and that in 4 of them (TTT, TTH, THT, HTT) there are more tails than heads. Each probability is $\frac{4}{8}$. The answer is **C**.

In Example 11, it wasn't even necessary to calculate the two probabilities. Since heads and tails are equally likely, when several coins are flipped, it is just as likely to have more heads as it is to have more tails. This is typical of quantitative comparison questions on probability; you usually can tell which of the two probabilities is greater without having to calculate either one. This is another instance where TACTIC 5 from Chapter 13 (don't calculate, compare) is useful.

Column A	Column B

Example 12.

The numbers from 1 to 1000 are each written on a slip of paper and placed in a box. Then 1 slip is removed.

The probability that the number drawn is a multiple of 5	The probability that the number drawn is a multiple of 7

SOLUTION. Since there are many more multiples of 5 than there are of 7, it is more likely that a multiple of 5 will be drawn. Column **A** is greater.

PRACTICE EXERCISES—COUNTING AND PROBABILITY

Multiple-Choice Questions

1. Alyssa completed exercises 6–20 on her math review sheet in 30 minutes. At this rate, how long, in minutes, will it take her to complete exercises 29–57?
   (A) 56   (B) 57   (C) 58   (D) 60   (E) 65

2. A diner serves a lunch special, consisting of soup or salad, a sandwich, coffee or tea, and a dessert. If the menu lists 3 soups, 2 salads, 7 sandwiches, and 8 desserts, how many different lunches can you choose? (*Note*: Two lunches are different if they differ in any aspect.)
   (A) 22   (B) 280   (C) 336   (D) 560   (E) 672

3. Dwight Eisenhower was born on October 14, 1890 and died on March 28, 1969. What was his age, in years, at the time of his death?
   (A) 77   (B) 78   (C) 79   (D) 80   (E) 81

4. How many four-digit numbers have only even digits?
   (A) 96   (B) 128   (C) 256   (D) 500   (E) 625

5. There are 27 students on the college debate team. What is the probability that at least 3 of them have their birthdays in the same month?
   (A) 0   (B) $\frac{3}{27}$ (C) $\frac{3}{12}$ (D) $\frac{1}{2}$ (E) 1

6. There are 100 people on a line. Aviva is the 37th person and Naomi is the 67th person. If a person on line is chosen at random, what is the probability that the person is standing between Aviva and Naomi?
   (A) $\frac{1}{100}$ (B) $\frac{29}{100}$ (C) $\frac{3}{10}$ (D) $\frac{31}{100}$ (E) $\frac{1}{2}$

7. Let A be the set of primes less than 6, and B be the set of positive odd numbers less than 6. How many different sums of the form $a + b$ are possible, if a is in A and b is in B?
   (A) 6   (B) 7   (C) 8   (D) 9   (E) 10

8. A jar has 5 marbles, 1 of each of the colors red, white, blue, green, and yellow. If 4 marbles are removed from the jar, what is the probability that the yellow one was removed?
   (A) $\frac{1}{20}$ (B) $\frac{1}{5}$ (C) $\frac{1}{4}$ (D) $\frac{4}{5}$ (E) $\frac{5}{4}$

9. Josh works on the second floor of a building. There are 10 doors to the building and 8 staircases from the first to the second floor. Josh decided that each day he would enter by one door and leave by a different one, and go up one staircase and down another. How many days could Josh do this before he had to repeat a path he had previously taken?
   (A) 80   (B) 640   (C) 800   (D) 5040   (E) 6400

10. A jar contains 20 marbles: 4 red, 6 white, and 10 blue. If you remove marbles one at a time, randomly, what is the minimum number that must be removed to be certain that you have at least 2 marbles of each color?
    (A) 6   (B) 10   (C) 12   (D) 16   (E) 18

11. At the audition for the school play, n people tried out. If k people went before Judy, who went before Liz, and m people went after Liz, how many people tried out between Judy and Liz?
    (A) $n - m - k - 2$ (B) $n - m - k - 1$
    (C) $n - m - k$ (D) $n - m - k + 1$
    (E) $n - m - k + 2$

12. In a group of 100 students, more students are on the fencing team than are members of the French club. If 70 are in the club and 20 are neither on the team nor in the club, what is the minimum number of students who could be both on the team and in the club?

    (A) 10   (B) 49   (C) 50   (D) 60   (E) 61

13. In a singles tennis tournament that has 125 entrants, a player is eliminated whenever he loses a match. How many matches are played in the entire tournament?

    (A) 62   (B) 63   (C) 124   (D) 125   (E) 246

Questions 14–15 refer to the following diagram. *A* is the set of positive integers less than 20; *B* is the set of positive integers that contain the digit 7; and *C* is the set of primes.

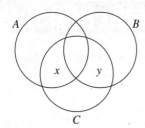

14. How many numbers are in the region labeled *x*?
    (A) 4   (B) 5   (C) 6   (D) 7   (E) 8

15. What is the sum of all the numbers less than 50 that are in the region labeled *y*?
    (A) 24   (B) 37   (C) 47   (D) 84   (E) 108

Quantitative Comparison Questions

	Column A	Column B
16.	The probability of getting no heads when a fair coin is flipped 7 times	The probability of getting 7 heads when a fair coin is flipped 7 times

A jar contains 4 marbles: 2 red and 2 white. 2 marbles are chosen at random.

	Column A	Column B
17.	The probability that the marbles chosen are the same color	The probability that the marbles chosen are different colors
18.	The number of ways to assign a number from 1 to 5 to each of 4 people	The number of ways to assign a number from 1 to 5 to each of 5 people
19.	The probability that 2 people chosen at random were born on the same day of the week	The probability that 2 people chosen at random were born in the same month
20.	The probability that a number chosen at random from the primes between 100 and 199 is odd.	.99

Answer Key

1. **C**	6. **B**	11. **A**	16. **C**
2. **D**	7. **B**	12. **E**	17. **B**
3. **B**	8. **D**	13. **C**	18. **C**
4. **D**	9. **D**	14. **C**	19. **A**
5. **E**	10. **E**	15. **D**	20. **A**

Answer Explanations

1. **C.** Alyssa completed $20 - 6 + 1 = 15$ exercises in 30 minutes, which is a rate of 1 exercise every 2 minutes. Therefore, to complete $57 - 29 + 1 = 29$ exercises would take her 58 minutes.

2. **D.** You can choose your soup or salad in any of 5 ways, your beverage in any of 2 ways, your sandwich in 7 ways, and your dessert in 8 ways. The counting principle says to multiply: $5 \times 2 \times 7 \times 8 = 560$. (Note that if you got soup

and a salad, then instead of 5 choices for the first course there would have been $2 \times 3 = 6$ choices for the first two courses.)

3. B. His last birthday was in October 1968, when he turned 78: $1968 - 1890 = 78$

4. D. The easiest way to solve this problem is to use the counting principle. The first digit can be chosen in any of 4 ways (2, 4, 6, 8), whereas the second, third, and fourth digits can be chosen in any of 5 ways (0, 2, 4, 6, 8). Therefore, the total number of four-digit numbers all of whose digits are even is $4 \times 5 \times 5 \times 5 = 500$.

5. E. If there were no month in which at least 3 students had a birthday, then each month would have the birthdays of at most 2 students. But that's not possible. Even if there were 2 birthdays in January, 2 in February, ..., and 2 in December, that would account for only 24 students. It is guaranteed that with more than 24 students, at least one month will have 3 or more birthdays. The probability is 1.

6. B. There are $67 - 37 - 1 = 29$ people between Aviva and Naomi, so, the probability that one of them is chosen is $\dfrac{29}{100}$.

7. B. $A = \{2, 3, 5\}$ and $B = \{1, 3, 5\}$. Any of the 3 numbers in A could be added to any of the 3 numbers in B, so there are 9 sums that could be formed. However, there could be some duplication. List the sums systematically; first add 1 to each number in A, then 3, and then 5: 3, 4, 6; 5, 6, 10; 7, 8, 10. There are 7 different sums.

8. D. It is equally likely that any one of the 5 marbles will be the one that is not removed. So, the probability that the yellow one is left is $\dfrac{1}{5}$ and the probability that it is removed is $\dfrac{4}{5}$.

9. D. This is the counting principle at work. Each day Josh has four jobs to do: choose 1 of the 10 doors to enter and 1 of the 9 other doors to exit; choose 1 of the 8 staircases to go up and 1 of the other 7 to come down. This can be done in $10 \times 9 \times 8 \times 7 = 5040$ ways. So on each of 5040 days Josh could choose a different path.

10. E. In a problem like this the easiest thing to do is to see what could go wrong in your attempt to get 2 marbles of each color. If you were really unlucky, you might remove 10 blue ones in a row, followed by all 6 white ones. At that point you would have 16 marbles, and you

still wouldn't have even 1 red one. The next 2 marbles, however, must both be red. The answer is 18.

11. A. It may help to draw a line and label it:

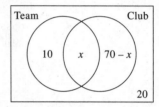

Since k people went before Judy, she was number $k + 1$ to try out; and since m people went after Liz, she was number $n - m$ to try out. So the number of people to try out between them was

$$(n - m) - (k + 1) - 1 = n - m - k - 2.$$

12. E. Draw a Venn diagram, letting x be the number of students who are on the team and in the club. Of the 100 students, 70 are in the club, so 30 are not in the club. Of these 30, 20 are also not on the team, so 10 are on the team but not in the club.

Team | Club
10 x $70 - x$
20

Since more students are on the team than in the club, $10 + x > 70 \Rightarrow x > 60$. Since x must be an integer, the least it can be is 61.

13. C. You could try to break it down by saying that first 124 of the 125 players would be paired off and play 62 matches. The 62 losers would be eliminated and there would still be 63 people left, the 62 winners and the 1 person who didn't play yet. Then continue until only 1 person was left. This is too time-consuming. An easier way is to observe that the winner never loses and the other 124 players each lose once. Since each match has exactly one loser, there must be 124 matches.

14. C. The region labeled x contains all of the primes less than 20 that do *not* contain the digit 7. They are 2, 3, 5, 11, 13, 19.

15. D. Region y consists of primes that contain the digit 7 and that are greater than 20. There are two of them that are less than 50: 37 and 47. Their sum is 84.

16. C. Don't calculate the probabilities. The probability of no heads is equal to the probability of no tails; but no tails means all heads.

17. B. The simplest solution is to notice that whatever color the first marble is, there is only 1

more marble of that color, but there are 2 of the other color, so it is twice as likely that the marbles will be of different colors.

18. C.   By the counting principle, Column A is 5·4·3·2 and Column B is 5·4·3·2·1. Clearly, the columns are equal.

19. A.   Column A: the probability is $\frac{1}{7}$.

Column B: the probability is $\frac{1}{12}$.

20. A.   Every prime between 100 and 199 is odd (the only even prime is 2). So the probability in Column A is 1, which is greater than .99.

PART FIVE

Model Tests

15 Model Tests

■ **5 Full-Length Model Tests**
■ **Answer Keys**
■ **Answer Explanations**

This chapter is designed to give you further experience in what to expect on the verbal, quantitative, and analytical writing sections of the Graduate Record Examination General Test. These tests should serve as a basis for analysis, which for some may signal the need for further drill before taking the actual test, and for others, may indicate that preparation for this part of the test is adequate. For the best results, take these tests only after reviewing your weak areas, found as a result of completing our Diagnostic Test.

Remember that the actual GRE Test you take will be computer adaptive. Therefore, we strongly recommend that, if you purchased this book with a CD-ROM, in addition to completing these five model tests, you take a computer-based model test using the CD-ROM. Note that although the model tests in the book cannot be adaptive, each section has the exact same format as the test you will be taking. In each of the five model tests in this book, the order of the sections is verbal, quantitative, and analytical writing. On the actual computerized GRE that you take, the computerized sections can appear in any order.

To best simulate actual test conditions, find a quiet place to work. Have a stopwatch or a clock handy so that you can keep perfect track of the time. Go through each section by answering the questions in the order in which they appear. If you don't know the answer to a question, guess, making an educated guess, if possible, and move on. Do not return to a question that you were unsure of, and do not go back to check your work if you have some time left over at the end of a section. (It isn't possible to do that on a real GRE.) Practice pacing yourself so that you use all your time and just finish each section in the time allowed. Do not spend too much time on any one question. If you get stuck, just guess and go on to the next question.

After you have devoted the specified time allowed for each section of a model examination, refer to the correct answers furnished, determine your raw score, judge your progress, and plan further study. You should then carefully study the explanations for the correct answers of those questions that gave you difficulty. If you find that a particular topic needs further review, refer to the earlier part of the book where this topic is treated before attempting to take the next model test. If you follow this procedure, by the time you complete the last test in this chapter you will feel confident about your success.

Answer Sheet—Model Test 1

Section 1

1. Ⓐ Ⓑ Ⓒ Ⓓ Ⓔ
2. Ⓐ Ⓑ Ⓒ Ⓓ Ⓔ
3. Ⓐ Ⓑ Ⓒ Ⓓ Ⓔ
4. Ⓐ Ⓑ Ⓒ Ⓓ Ⓔ
5. Ⓐ Ⓑ Ⓒ Ⓓ Ⓔ
6. Ⓐ Ⓑ Ⓒ Ⓓ Ⓔ
7. Ⓐ Ⓑ Ⓒ Ⓓ Ⓔ
8. Ⓐ Ⓑ Ⓒ Ⓓ Ⓔ
9. Ⓐ Ⓑ Ⓒ Ⓓ Ⓔ
10. Ⓐ Ⓑ Ⓒ Ⓓ Ⓔ

11. Ⓐ Ⓑ Ⓒ Ⓓ Ⓔ
12. Ⓐ Ⓑ Ⓒ Ⓓ Ⓔ
13. Ⓐ Ⓑ Ⓒ Ⓓ Ⓔ
14. Ⓐ Ⓑ Ⓒ Ⓓ Ⓔ
15. Ⓐ Ⓑ Ⓒ Ⓓ Ⓔ
16. Ⓐ Ⓑ Ⓒ Ⓓ Ⓔ
17. Ⓐ Ⓑ Ⓒ Ⓓ Ⓔ
18. Ⓐ Ⓑ Ⓒ Ⓓ Ⓔ
19. Ⓐ Ⓑ Ⓒ Ⓓ Ⓔ
20. Ⓐ Ⓑ Ⓒ Ⓓ Ⓔ

21. Ⓐ Ⓑ Ⓒ Ⓓ Ⓔ
22. Ⓐ Ⓑ Ⓒ Ⓓ Ⓔ
23. Ⓐ Ⓑ Ⓒ Ⓓ Ⓔ
24. Ⓐ Ⓑ Ⓒ Ⓓ Ⓔ
25. Ⓐ Ⓑ Ⓒ Ⓓ Ⓔ
26. Ⓐ Ⓑ Ⓒ Ⓓ Ⓔ
27. Ⓐ Ⓑ Ⓒ Ⓓ Ⓔ
28. Ⓐ Ⓑ Ⓒ Ⓓ Ⓔ
29. Ⓐ Ⓑ Ⓒ Ⓓ Ⓔ
30. Ⓐ Ⓑ Ⓒ Ⓓ Ⓔ

Section 2

1. Ⓐ Ⓑ Ⓒ Ⓓ Ⓔ
2. Ⓐ Ⓑ Ⓒ Ⓓ Ⓔ
3. Ⓐ Ⓑ Ⓒ Ⓓ Ⓔ
4. Ⓐ Ⓑ Ⓒ Ⓓ Ⓔ
5. Ⓐ Ⓑ Ⓒ Ⓓ Ⓔ
6. Ⓐ Ⓑ Ⓒ Ⓓ Ⓔ
7. Ⓐ Ⓑ Ⓒ Ⓓ Ⓔ
8. Ⓐ Ⓑ Ⓒ Ⓓ Ⓔ
9. Ⓐ Ⓑ Ⓒ Ⓓ Ⓔ
10. Ⓐ Ⓑ Ⓒ Ⓓ Ⓔ

11. Ⓐ Ⓑ Ⓒ Ⓓ Ⓔ
12. Ⓐ Ⓑ Ⓒ Ⓓ Ⓔ
13. Ⓐ Ⓑ Ⓒ Ⓓ Ⓔ
14. Ⓐ Ⓑ Ⓒ Ⓓ Ⓔ
15. Ⓐ Ⓑ Ⓒ Ⓓ Ⓔ
16. Ⓐ Ⓑ Ⓒ Ⓓ Ⓔ
17. Ⓐ Ⓑ Ⓒ Ⓓ Ⓔ
18. Ⓐ Ⓑ Ⓒ Ⓓ Ⓔ
19. Ⓐ Ⓑ Ⓒ Ⓓ Ⓔ
20. Ⓐ Ⓑ Ⓒ Ⓓ Ⓔ

21. Ⓐ Ⓑ Ⓒ Ⓓ Ⓔ
22. Ⓐ Ⓑ Ⓒ Ⓓ Ⓔ
23. Ⓐ Ⓑ Ⓒ Ⓓ Ⓔ
24. Ⓐ Ⓑ Ⓒ Ⓓ Ⓔ
25. Ⓐ Ⓑ Ⓒ Ⓓ Ⓔ
26. Ⓐ Ⓑ Ⓒ Ⓓ Ⓔ
27. Ⓐ Ⓑ Ⓒ Ⓓ Ⓔ
28. Ⓐ Ⓑ Ⓒ Ⓓ Ⓔ

MODEL TEST 1

1

SECTION 1—VERBAL ABILITY

Time—30 Minutes
30 Questions

Select the best answer to the following questions, then fill in the appropriate space on your Answer Sheet.

<u>Directions</u>: In each of the following antonym questions, a word printed in capital letters precedes five lettered words or phrases. From these five lettered words or phrases, pick the one most nearly <u>opposite</u> in meaning to the capitalized word.

1. ESTRANGE:
   (A) reconcile
   (B) feign
   (C) perplex
   (D) arbitrate
   (E) commiserate

2. PROVIDENT:
   (A) manifest
   (B) prodigal
   (C) thankful
   (D) tidy
   (E) transient

<u>Directions</u>: Each of the following sentence completion questions contains one or two blanks. These blanks signify that a word or set of words has been left out. Below each sentence are five words or sets of words. For each blank, pick the word or set of words that <u>best</u> reflects the sentence's overall meaning.

3. Like the theory of evolution, the big-bang model of the universe's formation has undergone modification and _____, but it has _____ all serious challenges.
   (A) alteration...confirmed
   (B) refinement...resisted
   (C) transformation...ignored
   (D) evaluation...acknowledged
   (E) refutation...misdirected

4. A university training enables a graduate to see things as they are, to go right to the point, to disentangle a _____ of thought.
   (A) line
   (B) strand
   (C) mass
   (D) plethora
   (E) skein

<u>Directions</u>: Each of the following analogy questions presents a related pair of words linked by a colon. Five lettered pairs of words follow the linked pair. Choose the lettered pair of words whose relationship is <u>most like</u> the relationship expressed in the original linked pair.

5. SONG : CYCLE ::
   (A) waltz : dance
   (B) tune : arrangement
   (C) sonnet : sequence
   (D) agenda : meeting
   (E) cadenza : aria

6. OBDURATE : FLEXIBILITY ::
   (A) accurate : perception
   (B) turbid : roughness
   (C) principled : fallibility
   (D) diaphanous : transparency
   (E) adamant : submissiveness

1

1

> Directions: Each of the following reading comprehension questions is based on the content of the following passage. Read the passage and then determine the best answer choice for each question. Base your choice on what this passage *states directly* or *implies*, not on any information you may have gained elsewhere.

(This passage was written prior to 1950)

In the long run a government will always
encroach upon freedom to the extent to which it
has the power to do so; this is almost a natural
Line law of politics, since, whatever the intentions of
(5) the men who exercise political power, the sheer
momentum of government leads to a constant
pressure upon the liberties of the citizen. But in
many countries society has responded by throw-
ing up its own defenses in the shape of social
(10) classes or organized corporations which, enjoying
economic power and popular support, have been
able to set limits to the scope of action of the
executive. Such, for example, in England was the
origin of all our liberties—won from government
(15) by the stand first of the feudal nobility, then of
churches and political parties, and latterly of trade
unions, commercial organizations, and the societies for promoting various causes. Even in
European lands which were arbitrarily ruled, the
(20) powers of the monarchy, though absolute in
theory, were in their exercise checked in a similar
fashion. Indeed, the fascist dictatorships of today
are the first truly tyrannical governments which
western Europe has known for centuries, and they
(25) have been rendered possible only because on
coming to power they destroyed all forms of
social organization which were in any way rivals
to the state.

7. According to the passage, the natural relationship
between government and individual liberty is
one of

(A) marked indifference
(B) secret collusion
(C) inherent opposition
(D) moderate complicity
(E) fundamental interdependence

8. Fascist dictatorships differ from monarchies of
recent times in

(A) setting limits to their scope of action
(B) effecting results by sheer momentum
(C) rivaling the state in power
(D) exerting constant pressure on liberties
(E) eradicating people's organizations

9. The passage suggests which of the following about
fascist dictatorships?

(A) They represent a more efficient form of the
executive.
(B) Their rise to power came about through an
accident of history.
(C) They mark a regression to earlier despotic
forms of government.
(D) Despite superficial dissimilarities, they are in
essence like absolute monarchies.
(E) They maintain their dominance by rechannel-
ing opposing forces in new directions.

Sentence Completion

10. We have in America a _____ speech that is
neither American, Oxford English, nor colloquial
English, but _____ of all three.

(A) motley...an enhancement
(B) hybrid...a combination
(C) nasal...a blend
(D) mangled...a medley
(E) formal...a patchwork

11. Rather than portraying Joseph II as a radical
reformer whose reign was strikingly enlightened,
the play *Amadeus* depicts him as _____
thinker, too wedded to orthodox theories of musical
composition to appreciate an artist of Mozart's
genius.

(A) a revolutionary
(B) an idiosyncratic
(C) a politic
(D) a doctrinaire
(E) an iconoclastic

1

1

Antonyms

12. CAPITULATE:

    (A) initiate
    (B) defame
    (C) exonerate
    (D) resist
    (E) escalate

13. INDIGENOUS:

    (A) affluent
    (B) parochial
    (C) alien
    (D) serene
    (E) inimical

Analogies

14. SCURRY : MOVE ::

    (A) chant : sing
    (B) chatter : talk
    (C) carry : lift
    (D) sleep : drowse
    (E) limp : walk

15. CHAMELEON : HERPETOLOGIST ::

    (A) fungi : ecologist
    (B) salmon : ichthyologist
    (C) mongoose : ornithologist
    (D) oriole : virologist
    (E) aphid : etymologist

Reading Comprehension

As the works of dozens of women writers have been rescued from what E. P. Thompson calls "the enormous condescension of posterity," and
Line considered in relation to each other, the lost conti-
(5) nent of the female tradition has risen like Atlantis from the sea of English literature. It is now becoming clear that, contrary to Mill's theory, women have had a literature of their own all along. The woman novelist, according to Vineta
(10) Colby, was "really neither single nor anomalous," but she was also more than a "register and spokesman for her age." She was part of a tradition that had its origins before her age, and has carried on through our own.
(15)   Many literary historians have begun to reinterpret and revise the study of women writers. Ellen Moers sees women's literature as an international movement, "apart from, but hardly subordinate to the mainstream: an undercurrent, rapid and
(20) powerful. This 'movement' began in the late

eighteenth century, was multinational, and produced some of the greatest literary works of two centuries, as well as most of the lucrative potboilers." Patricia Meyer Spacks, in *The Female*
(25) *Imagination*, finds that "for readily discernible historical reasons women have characteristically concerned themselves with matters more or less peripheral to male concerns, or at least slightly skewed from them. The differences between tra-
(30) ditional female preoccupations and roles and male ones make a difference in female writing." Many other critics are beginning to agree that when we look at women writers collectively we can see an imaginative continuum, the recurrence of certain
(35) patterns, themes, problems, and images from generation to generation.

16. In the second paragraph of the passage the author's attitude toward the literary critics cited can best be described as one of

    (A) irony
    (B) ambivalence
    (C) disparagement
    (D) receptiveness
    (E) awe

17. The passage supplies information for answering which of the following questions?

    (A) Does the author believe the female literary tradition to be richer in depth than its masculine counterpart?
    (B) Are women psychological as well as sociological chameleons?
    (C) Does Moers share Mill's concern over the ephemeral nature of female literary renown?
    (D) What patterns, themes, images, and problems recur sufficiently in the work of women writers to belong to the female imaginative continuum?
    (E) Did Mill acknowledge the existence of a separate female literary tradition?

18. In the first paragraph, the author makes use of all the following techniques EXCEPT

    (A) extended metaphor
    (B) enumeration and classification
    (C) classical allusion
    (D) direct quotation
    (E) comparison and contrast

1   1

Antonyms

19. CHAGRIN:
    (A) frown
    (B) disguise
    (C) make indifferent
    (D) make aware
    (E) please

20. DISINGENUOUS:
    (A) naive
    (B) accurate
    (C) hostile
    (D) witty
    (E) polite

Sentence Completion

21. When those whom he had injured accused him of being a _____, he retorted curtly that he had never been a quack.
    (A) libertine
    (B) sycophant
    (C) charlatan
    (D) plagiarist
    (E) reprobate

22. There is an essential _____ in human gestures, and when someone raises the palms of his hands together, we do not know whether it is to bury himself in prayer or to throw himself into the sea.
    (A) economy
    (B) dignity
    (C) insincerity
    (D) reverence
    (E) ambiguity

Analogies

23. ASCETIC : SELF-DENIAL ::
    (A) nomad : dissipation
    (B) miser : affluence
    (C) zealot : fanaticism
    (D) renegade : loyalty
    (E) athlete : stamina

24. CAMOUFLAGE : DISCERN ::
    (A) encipher : comprehend
    (B) adorn : admire
    (C) magnify : observe
    (D) renovate : construct
    (E) embroider : unravel

25. SEER : PROPHECY ::
    (A) mentor : reward
    (B) sage : wisdom
    (C) pilgrim : diligence
    (D) diplomat : flattery
    (E) virtuoso : penance

Reading Comprehension

The physics of elementary particles is notorious for the fancifulness of its terminology, abounding as it does in names such as "quark," "flavor,"
Line "strangeness" and "charm." One term, however,
(5) even to the nonscientist seems most apt: "gluon." Physicists conjecture that the gluon is the "glue" connecting quarks into hadrons or strongly interacting particles (protons, neutrons, pions, etc.). Initially, physicists envisaged the gluon's adhe-
(10) sive strength to be so powerful that a quark could not be extracted from a hadron no matter how great the force brought to bear on it. Furthermore, the gluon itself also seemed to be permanently bound: just as no force seemed strong enough to
(15) pry apart the quarks, none appeared strong enough to squeeze out a single drop of the glue that bound them. Today, however, some physicists hypothesize the existence of pure glue: gluons without quarks, or gluonium, as they call it.

26. The author refers to charms and quarks (lines 3–4) primarily in order to
    (A) demonstrate the similarity between these particles and the gluon
    (B) make a distinction between apposite and inapposite terminology
    (C) offer an objection to suggestions of similar frivolous names
    (D) provide illustrations of idiosyncratic nomenclature in contemporary physics
    (E) cite preliminary experimental evidence supporting the existence of gluons

27. The tone of the author's discussion of the neologisms coined by physicists is one of
    (A) scientific detachment
    (B) moderate indignation
    (C) marked derision
    (D) amused approbation
    (E) qualified skepticism

1   **1**

Antonyms

28. SPURIOUS:

    (A) cautious
    (B) fantastic
    (C) modest
    (D) genuine
    (E) pertinent

29. TANTAMOUNT:

    (A) not negotiable
    (B) not equivalent
    (C) not ambitious
    (D) not evident
    (E) not relevant

Sentence Completion

30. It has been Virginia Woolf's peculiar destiny to be declared annoyingly feminine by male critics at the same time that she has been _____ by women interested in the sexual revolution as not really eligible to be _____ their ranks.

    (A) lauded...enlisted in
    (B) emulated...counted among
    (C) neglected...helpful to
    (D) dismissed...drafted into
    (E) excoriated...discharged from

2   2

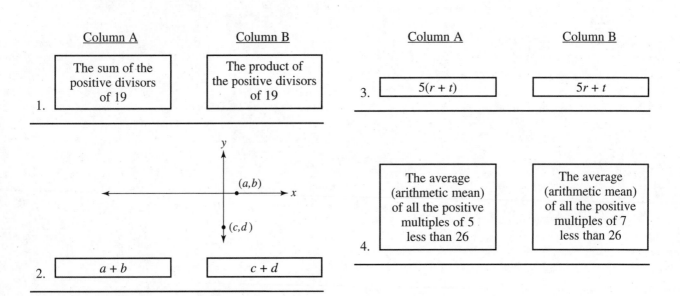

	Column A	Column B
1.	The sum of the positive divisors of 19	The product of the positive divisors of 19

| 2. | $a + b$ | $c + d$ |

	Column A	Column B
3.	$5(r + t)$	$5r + t$
4.	The average (arithmetic mean) of all the positive multiples of 5 less than 26	The average (arithmetic mean) of all the positive multiples of 7 less than 26

Directions: In the following questions, choose the best answer from the five choices listed.

5. If it is now June, what month will it be 400 months from now?

(A) January   (B) April   (C) June
(D) October   (E) December

6. If $\frac{5}{9}$ of the members of the school chorus are boys, what is the ratio of girls to boys in the chorus?

(A) $\frac{4}{9}$ (B) $\frac{4}{5}$ (C) $\frac{5}{4}$ (D) $\frac{9}{4}$

(E) It cannot be determined from the information given.

7. What is the volume of a cube whose total surface area is 54?

(A) 9   (B) 27   (C) 54   (D) 81   (E) 729

2

2

Column A	Column B
8. $(a + b)(a - b)$	$a(b + a) - b(a + b)$

Dalia put exactly 75 cents worth of postage on an envelope using only 5-cent stamps and 7-cent stamps.

The number of 5-cent stamps she used	The number of 7-cent stamps she used

9.

10. If A is 25 kilometers east of B, which is 12 kilometers south of C, which is 9 kilometers west of D, how far is it, in kilometers, from A to D?

    (A) 20   (B) $5\sqrt{34}$ (C) $5\sqrt{41}$
    (D) $10\sqrt{13}$ (E) 71

Column A	Column B

A wooden cube whose edges are 4 inches is painted red.
The cube is then cut into 64 small cubes whose edges are 1 inch.

The number of small cubes that have exactly three red faces	The number of small cubes that have no red faces

11.

Column A	Column B

c and d are positive
$$\frac{1}{c} = 1 + \frac{1}{d}$$

12. c	d

A number is a *palindrome* if it reads exactly the same from right to left as it does from left to right. For example, 959 and 24742 are palindromes.

The probability that a three-digit number chosen at random is a palindrome	$\dfrac{1}{10}$

13.

2

2

Total enrollment in higher education institutions, by control and type of institution: Fall 1972–95

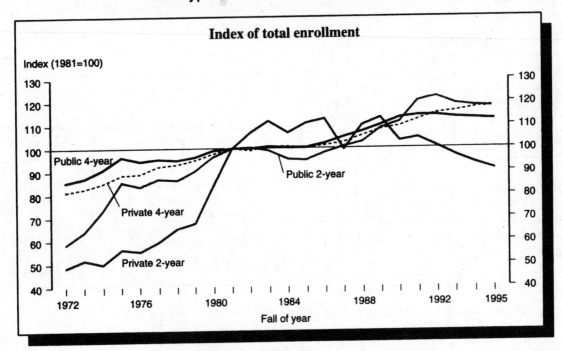

Index of total enrollment

Index (1981=100)

Public 4-year

Public 2-year

Private 4-year

Private 2-year

Fall of year

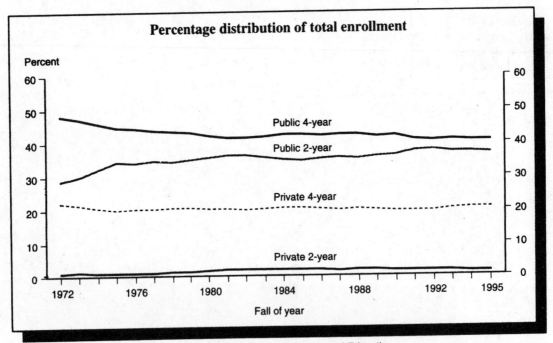

Percentage distribution of total enrollment

Percent

Public 4-year

Public 2-year

Private 4-year

Private 2-year

Fall of year

SOURCE: U.S. Department of Education.

2

2

14. In 1995 the number of students enrolled in public institutions of higher education was approximately how many times the number of students enrolled in private institutions of higher education?

(A) 2   (B) 2.5   (C) 3   (D) 3.5   (E) 4

15. If the total enrollment in institutions of higher education in 1972 was 5,000,000, approximately how many students were enrolled in private 4-year institutions in 1995?

(A) 1,000,000   (B) 1,100,000   (C) 1,250,000
(D) 1,500,000   (E) 1,650,000

Column A	Column B

Jack and Jill each bought the same TV set using a 10% off coupon. Jack's cashier took 10% off the price and then added 8.5% sales tax. Jill's cashier first added the tax and then took 10% off the total price.

16.
The amount Jack paid	The amount Jill paid

$$\begin{array}{r} ABA \\ \times\, A \\ \hline DCD \end{array}$$

In the multiplication problem above, each letter represents a different digit.

17.
B	5

---

18. If the lengths of two of the sides of a triangle are 9 and 10, which of the following could be the length of the third side?

I. 1
II. 11
III. 21

(A) None   (B) I only   (C) II only
(D) I and II only   (E) I, II, and III

19. If x is a positive integer, which of the following CANNOT be an integer?

(A) $\sqrt{x-1}$ (B) $\sqrt{x^2-1}$ (C) $\dfrac{1}{x}$

(D) $\dfrac{x+2}{x+1}$ (E) $\dfrac{7}{x+1}$

2   2

Percentage of students who reported spending time on homework and watching television

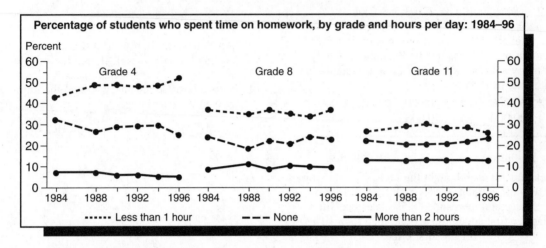

Percentage of students who spent time on homework, by grade and hours per day: 1984–96

Grade 4   Grade 8   Grade 11

······ Less than 1 hour   — — None   —— More than 2 hours

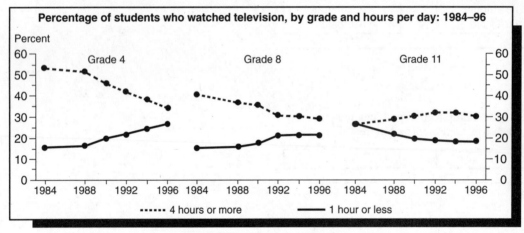

Percentage of students who watched television, by grade and hours per day: 1984–96

Grade 4   Grade 8   Grade 11

······ 4 hours or more   —— 1 hour or less

SOURCE: U.S. Department of Education.

20. In 1996, what percent of fourth-graders did between 1 and 2 hours of homework per day?

(A) 5%   (B) 15%   (C) 25%
(D) 40%   (E) 55%

21. If in 1984 there were 2,000,000 eleventh-graders, and if between 1984 and 1996 the number of eleventh-graders increased by 10%, then approximately how many more eleventh-graders watched 1 hour or less of television in 1996 than in 1984?

(A) 25,000   (B) 50,000   (C) 75,000
(D) 100,000   (E) 150,000

2   **2**

22. Which of the following expresses the area of a circle in terms of C, its circumference?

(A) $\dfrac{C^2}{4\pi}$ (B) $\dfrac{C^2}{2\pi}$ (C) $\dfrac{\sqrt{C}}{2\pi}$ (D) $\dfrac{C\pi}{4}$ (E) $\dfrac{C}{4\pi}$

Column A	Column B

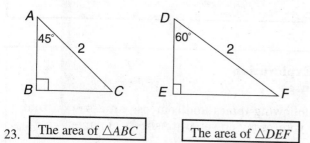

23. | The area of $\triangle ABC$ | The area of $\triangle DEF$ |

A is the sum of the integers from 1 to 50, and B is the sum of the integers from 51 to 100.

24. | $B - A$ | 2500 |

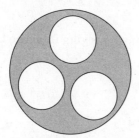

Each small circle has radius r, and the large circle has radius R.
The areas of the shaded region and the white region are equal.

25. | $\dfrac{R}{r}$ | 2 |

26. If p pencils cost c cents, how many can be bought for d dollars?

(A) cdp (B) $100\,cdp$ (C) $\dfrac{dp}{100c}$

(D) $\dfrac{100\,cd}{p}$ (E) $\dfrac{100\,dp}{c}$

27. Because her test turned out to be more difficult than she intended it to be, a teacher decided to adjust the grades by deducting only half the number of points a student missed. For example, if a student missed 10 points, she received a 95 instead of a 90. Before the grades were adjusted the class average was A. What was the average after the adjustment?

(A) $50 + \dfrac{A}{2}$ (B) $\dfrac{1}{2}(100 - A)$ (C) $100 - \dfrac{A}{2}$

(D) $\dfrac{50 + A}{2}$ (E) $A + 25$

28. If a square and an equilateral triangle have equal perimeters, what is the ratio of the area of the triangle to the area of the square?

(A) $\dfrac{4\sqrt{3}}{9}$ (B) $\dfrac{3}{4}$ (C) $\dfrac{1}{1}$ (D) $\dfrac{4}{3}$

(E) It cannot be determined from the information given.

3   3

SECTION 3—ANALYTICAL WRITING

Time—75 Minutes
2 Writing Tasks

Task 1: Issue Exploration
45 Minutes

<u>Directions</u>: In 45 minutes, choose one of the two following topics and compose an essay on that topic. You may not write on any other topic. Write your essay on separate sheets of paper.

Each topic is presented in a one- to two-sentence quotation commenting on an issue of general concern. Your essay may support, refute, or qualify the views expressed in the quotation. Whatever you write, however, must be relevant to the issue under discussion, and you must support your viewpoint with reasons and examples derived from your studies and/or experience.

Before you choose a topic, read both topics carefully. Consider which topic would give you greater scope for writing an effective, well-argued essay.

Faculty members from various institutions will evaluate your essay, judging it on the basis of your skill in the following areas.

- Analysis of the quotation's implications
- Organization and articulation of your ideas
- Use of relevant examples and arguments to support your case
- Handling of the mechanics of standard written English

Once you have decided which topic you prefer, click on the appropriate icon (**Topic 1** or **Topic 2**) to confirm your choice. Do not be hasty confirming your choice of topic. Once you have clicked on a topic, you will not be able to switch to the alternate choice.

Topic 1

"Young people frequently fall into the trap of assuming that the difficulties they face today are greater and more troublesome than those faced by previous generations. As they gain experience and maturity, however, they eventually become aware of the falsity of this assumption."

Topic 2

"Question authority. Only by questioning accepted wisdom can we advance our understanding of the world."

3

3

**Task 2: Argument Analysis
30 Minutes**

<u>Directions</u>: In 30 minutes, prepare a critical analysis of an argument expressed in a short para-
graph. You may not offer an analysis of any other argument. Write your essay on separate sheets
of paper.

As you critique the argument, think about the author's underlying assumptions. Ask yourself
whether any of them are questionable. Also evaluate any evidence the author brings up. Ask yourself whether it actually supports the author's conclusion.

In your analysis, you may suggest additional kinds of evidence to reinforce the author's argument.
You may also suggest methods to refute the argument, or additional data that might be useful to
you as you assess the soundness of the argument. *You may **not**, however, present your personal
views on the topic.* Your job is to analyze the elements of an argument, not to support or contradict
that argument.

Faculty members from various institutions will judge your essay, assessing it on the basis of your
skill in the following areas:

- Identification and assessment of the argument's main elements
- Organization and articulation of your thoughts
- Use of relevant examples and arguments to support your case
- Handling of the mechanics of standard written English

The following appeared in a petition presented by Classen University students to the school's
administration.

The purpose of higher education is to prepare students for the future, but Classen students are at
a serious disadvantage in the competition for post-college employment due to the University's burdensome breadth requirements. Classen's job placement rate is substantially lower than placement
rates of many top-ranked schools. Classen students would be more attractive to employers if they
had more time to take advanced courses in their specialty, rather than being required to spend
fifteen percent of their time at Classen taking courses outside of their subject area. We demand,
therefore, that the University abandon or drastically cut back on its breadth requirements.

Answer Key

Section 1—Verbal Ability

1. A	6. E	11. D	16. D	21. C	26. D
2. B	7. C	12. D	17. E	22. E	27. D
3. B	8. E	13. C	18. B	23. C	28. D
4. E	9. C	14. B	19. E	24. A	29. B
5. C	10. B	15. B	20. A	25. B	30. D

Section 2—Quantitative Ability

NOTE: The letters in brackets following the Quantitative Ability answers refer to the sections of Chapter 14 in which you can find the information you need to answer the questions. For example, 1. C [E] means that the answer to question 1 is C, and that the solution requires information found in Section 14-E: Averages. Also, 20. A [13] means that the answer to question 20 is based on information in Chapter 13: Data Interpretation.

1. A [A]	6. B [B,D]	11. C [M]	16. C [C]	21. E [13]	26. E [D]
2. A [N]	7. B [M]	12. B [B]	17. B [A]	22. A [L]	27. A [E,H]
3. D [A]	8. C [F]	13. C [O]	18. C [J]	23. A [J]	28. A [J,K]
4. A [A,E]	9. D [O]	14. D [13]	19. D [A]	24. C [A]	
5. D [A]	10. A [J]	15. E [13]	20. B [13]	25. A [L]	

Section 3—Analytical Writing

There are no "correct answers" to this section.

Answer Explanations

Section 1—Verbal Ability

1. **A.** The opposite of to *estrange* or to alienate is to *reconcile*.
   Think of "estranged couples" in a divorce.

2. **B.** The opposite of *provident* or frugal is *prodigal* or extravagant.
   Think of the fable of the prodigal grasshopper and the provident ant.

3. **B.** The author concedes that the big-bang theory has been changed somewhat: it has undergone *refinement* or polishing. However, he denies that its validity has been threatened seriously by any rival theories: it has *resisted* or defied all challenges.
   The use of the support signal *and* indicates that the first missing word is similar in meaning to "modification." The use of the contrast signal *but* indicates that the second missing word is contrary in meaning to "undergone modification."

4. **E.** One would have to disentangle a *skein* or coiled and twisted bundle of yarn.
   Note how the presence of the verb *disentangle*, which may be used both figuratively and literally, influences the writer's choice of words. In this case, while *line* and *strand* are possible choices, neither word possesses the connotations of twistings and tangled contortions that make *skein* the most suitable choice.

5. **C.** A *song* is part of a *cycle* or series of songs. A *sonnet* is part of a *sequence* or series of sonnets.   (Group and Member)

6. **E.** Someone *obdurate* (unyielding, inflexible) is lacking in *flexibility*. Someone *adamant* (unshakable in opposition) is lacking in *submissiveness*.   (Antonym Variant)

7. **C.** The author says that the tendency for a government to encroach upon individual liberty to the extent to which it has the power to do so is "almost a natural law" of politics. Thus, government and individual liberty are *inherently* by their very natures in *opposition* to one another.

8. E. The final sentence states that the fascist dicta-torships "destroyed (*eradicated*) all forms of social organization that were in any way rivals to the state."

9. C. If the fascist dictatorships "are the first truly tyrannical governments which western Europe has known for centuries," then it can be inferred that centuries ago there were tyranni-cal or *despotic* governments in western Europe. Thus, the fascist governments repre-sent a *regression* or reversion to an earlier form of government.

10. B. Speech that is *hybrid* (made up of several elements) by definition combines these ele-ments. The technical term *hybrid* best suits this context because it is a neutral term devoid of negative connotations (which *motley* and *mangled* possess).

11. D. A man too wedded to *orthodox* theories or doctrines can best be described as *doctrinaire* or dogmatic.

12. D. The opposite of to *capitulate* or yield is to *resist*.
Think of "capitulating without a fight."

13. C. The opposite of *indigenous* or native is *alien* or foreign.
Beware eye-catchers. Choice A is incorrect. Do not confuse *indigenous* or native with *indigent* or poor.

14. B. To *scurry* is to *move* in a brisk and rapid manner. To *chatter* is to *talk* in a brisk and rapid manner.   (Manner)

15. B. A *chameleon*, a kind of lizard, is studied by a *herpetologist* (scientist who studies reptiles and amphibians). A *salmon*, a kind of fish, is studied by an *ichthyologist*.
                                      (Defining Characteristic)

16. D. The author opens the paragraph by stating that many literary critics have begun reinterpreting the study of women's literature. She then goes on to cite individual comments that support her assertion. Clearly, she is *receptive* or open to the ideas of these writers, for they and she share a common sense of the need to reinter-pret their common field.
Choices A and B are incorrect. The author cites the literary critics straightforwardly, presenting their statements as evidence sup-porting her thesis.
Choice C is incorrect. The author does not *disparage* or belittle these critics. By quoting them respectfully she implicitly acknowledges their competence.

Choice E is incorrect. The author quotes the critics as acknowledged experts in the field. However, she is quite ready to disagree with their conclusions (as she disagrees with Moers' view of women's literature as an inter-national movement). Clearly, she does not look on these critics with *awe*.

17. E. Question E is answerable on the basis of the passage. According to lines 6–8, Mill dis-believed in the idea that women "have had a literature of their own all along."

18. B. The writer neither lists (*enumerates*) nor sorts (*classifies*) anything in the opening paragraph.
Choice A is incorrect. The writer likens the female tradition to a lost continent and devel-ops the metaphor by describing the continent "rising ... from the sea of English literature."
Choice C is incorrect. The author refers or *alludes* to the classical legend of Atlantis.
Choice D is incorrect. The author quotes Colby and Thompson.
Choice E is incorrect. The author contrasts the revised view of women's literature with Mill's view.

19. E. The opposite of to *chagrin* (disappoint) is to *please*.
Beware eye-catchers. Choice A is incorrect. *Chagrin* is unrelated to *grin*.
Think of "being chagrined by a defeat."

20. A. The opposite of *disingenuous* or guileful (giving a false impression of naiveté) is *naive* or unsophisticated.
Think of a "disingenuous appearance of candor."

21. C. *Charlatan* is another term for a *quack* or pretender to medical knowledge.

22. E. The statement that "we do not know" whether a gesture indicates devotion or despair sug-gests that gestures are by their nature *ambigu-ous* or unclear.

23. C. By definition, an *ascetic* (one who practices severe self-discipline) is characterized by *self-denial*. A *zealot* (extreme enthusiast) is characterized by *fanaticism*.
Beware eye-catchers. A *miser* may hoard wealth, but he is not necessarily characterized by *affluence*. Even poor persons may be misers.   (Defining Characteristic)

24. A. To *camouflage* something is to make it diffi-cult to *discern* or perceive. To *encipher* or encode something is to make it difficult to *comprehend*.   (Function)

25. B.   A *seer* or prophet is by definition someone gifted in *prophecy*. A *sage* or wise person is by definition someone gifted in *wisdom*.
                                    (Defining Characteristic)

26. D.   The author provides them as examples of what he means by the "fanciful ... terminology" or *idiosyncratic nomenclature* in modern particle physics.

27. D.   Since the author considers the gluon to be *aptly* named, he clearly views this particular neologism or newly coined term with *approbation*. However, he tempers his approval with *amusement*, for he finds the terms fanciful (capricious, whimsical) as well as apt.

28. D.   The opposite of *spurious* (false or fraudulent) is *genuine*.
         Think of forgers selling "a spurious work of art."

29. B.   The opposite of *tantamount* or equivalent in value is *not equivalent*.
         Context Clue: "Failure to publish is tantamount to suppression."

30. D.   The incongruity here is that one group finds Woolf too feminine for their tastes while another finds her not feminine (or perhaps feminist) enough for theirs.
         Note that the word *peculiar* signals that Woolf's destiny is an unexpected one.

Section 2—Quantitative Ability

Two asterisks (**) indicate an alternative method of solving.

1. A.   The only positive divisors of 19 are 1 and 19.
        Column A: $1 + 19 = 20$.
        Column B: $1 \times 19 = 19$.

2. A.   Since (a, b) is on the positive portion of the x-axis, a is positive and $b = 0$; so $a + b$ is positive. Also, since (c, d) is on the negative portion of the y-axis, c is negative and $d = 0$; so $c + d$ is negative. Column A is greater.

3. D.   By the distributive law, Column A is $5r + 5t$. Subtract $5r$ from each column, and compare $5t$ and t. They are equal if $t = 0$ and unequal otherwise. Neither column is always greater, and the two columns are not always equal (D).

4. A.   Column A: there are 5 positive multiples of 5 less than 26: 5, 10, 15, 20, 25; their average is 15, the middle one [KEY FACT E5].

Column B: there are 3 positive multiples of 7 less than 26: 7, 14, 21; their average is 14. Column A is greater.

5. D.   Since $400 = 12 \times 33 + 4$, 100 months is 4 months more than 33 years. 33 years from June it will again be June, and 4 months later it will be October. [See Section 14-P]
        **Look for a pattern. Since there are 12 months in a year, after every 12 months it will again be June; i.e., it will be June after 12, 24, 36, 48,..., 120,..., 360 months. So, 396 (33×12) months from now, it will again be June. Count 4 more months to October.

6. B.   Use TACTIC 3 in Chapter 11: pick an easy-to-use number. Since $\frac{5}{9}$ of the members are boys, assume there are 9 members, 5 of whom are boys. Then the other 4 are girls, and the ratio of girls to boys is 4 to 5, or $\frac{4}{5}$.

7. B.   Since the surface area of the cube is 54, the area of each of the six faces is a square. $54 \div 6 = 9$. Then each edge is 3, and the volume is $3^3 = 27$.

8. C.   Column A: $(a + b)(a - b) = a^2 - b^2$.
        Column B: $a(b + a) - b(a + b) = ab + a^2 - ba - b^2 = a^2 - b^2$.

9. D.   If x and y represent the number of 5-cent stamps and 7-cent stamps, respectively, that Dalia used, then $5x + 7y = 75$. There are infinitely many solutions to this equation, but there are only two solutions in which x and y are both positive integers: $y = 10$ and $x = 1$ or $y = 5$ and $x = 8$. Neither column is always greater, and the two columns are not always equal (D).

10. A. Use TACTIC 1 in Chapter 10: draw a diagram. In the figure below, form rectangle $BCDE$ by drawing $DE \perp AB$. Then, $BE = 9$, $AE = 16$, and $DE = 12$. Finally, $DA = 20$, because right triangle AED is a 3-4-5 triangle in which each side is multiplied by 4. If you don't realize that, use the Pythagorean theorem to get DA:
        $$(DA)^2 = (AE)^2 + (DE)^2 = 256 + 144 = 400 \Rightarrow$$
        $$DA = 20.$$

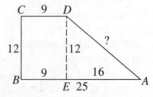

11. **C.** Draw a diagram, and on each small cube write the number of red faces it has. The cubes with three red faces are the eight corners. The cubes with no red faces are the "inside" ones that can't be seen. If you cut off the top and bottom rows, the front and back rows, and the left and right rows, you are left with a small 2-inch cube, none of whose faces is red. That 2-inch cube is made up of eight 1-inch cubes. The columns are equal (C).

12. **B.** Since $\frac{1}{c} = 1 + \frac{1}{d}$, then $1 = \frac{1}{c} - \frac{1}{d} = \frac{d-c}{cd}$. Therefore, $d - c = cd$, which is positive. Then, $d - c$ is positive, and so $d > c$. Column B is greater.

13. **C.** The simplest solution is to realize that there is one palindrome between 100 and 109 (101), one between 390 and 399 (393), one between 880 and 889 (888), and in general, one out of every 10 numbers. So the probability is $\frac{1}{10}$.

The answer is (C).
**The more direct solution is to count the number of palindromes. Either systematically make a list and notice that there are 10 of them between 100 and 199, and 10 in each of the hundreds from the 100s to the 900s, for a total of 90; or use the counting principle: the first digit can be chosen in any of 9 ways, the second in any of 10 ways, and the third, since it must match the first, can be chosen in only 1 way ($9 \times 10 \times 1 = 90$). Since there are 900 three-digit numbers, the probability is $\frac{90}{900} = \frac{1}{10}$.

14. **D.** From the bottom graph, we can estimate the percentage distribution of total enrollment to be:

Public 4-year	41%	Private 4-year	21%
Public 2-year	37%	Private 2-year	1%
Total public	78%	Total private	22%

$78 \div 22 \approx 3.5$, so there were 3.5 times as many students enrolled in public institutions as private ones.

15. **E.** In 1972, enrollment in private 4-year institutions was approximately 1,100,000 (22% of the total enrollment of 5,000,000). By 1995, the index for private 4-year institutions had increased from 80 to 120, a 50% increase. Therefore, the number of private 4-year students enrolled in 1995 was approximately 1,650,000 (50% more than the 1,100,000 students enrolled in 1972).

16. **C.** Let P = the price of the TV set. Then Jack paid $1.085(.90P)$, whereas Jill paid $.90(1.085P)$. The columns are equal (C). **Use TACTIC 2, Chapter 12, and choose a convenient number: assume the TV cost $100. Jack paid $90 plus $7.65 tax (8.5% of $90) for a total of $97.65. Jill's cashier rang up $100 plus $8.50 tax and then deducted $10.85 (10% of $108.50) for a final cost of $97.65.

17. **B.** Since A times ABA is a three-digit number, A has to be less than 4; but 1 times ABA is ABA, so $A \neq 1$. Therefore, $A = 2$ or $A = 3$.

$2B2$		$3B3$
$\times\ 2$	or	$\times\ 3$
$4C4$		$9C9$

Since there is no carrying, either $2 \times B = C$, a one-digit number, and $B < 5$, or $3 \times B = C$, and $B < 3$. In either case, column B is greater.

18. **C.** By the triangle inequality (KEY FACTS J12 and J13),
• The third side must be *less* than $9 + 10 = 19$. (III is false.)
• The third side must be *greater* than $10 - 9 = 1$. (I is false.)
• *Any* number between 1 and 19 could be the length of the third side. (II is true.)
The answer is C.

19. **D.** Check each choice. (A) If $x = 5$, $\sqrt{x-1} = 2$. (B) This one is more difficult; the only possibility if $x = 1$, in which case $\sqrt{x^2 - 1} = 0$. If you don't see that immediately, keep Choice B under consideration, and test the rest. (C) If $x = 1$, $\frac{1}{x} = 1$. (D) For positive x, $\frac{x+2}{x+1}$ is always greater than 1 but less than 2; $\frac{x+2}{x+1}$ cannot be an integer—that's it. If you didn't reason that out, check Choice E. $\frac{7}{x+1}$ is an integer if $x = 6$. You should have eliminated at least Choices, A, C, and E.

20. **B.** From the top graph, we see that among fourth-graders in 1996:

25% did no homework;
55% did less than 1 hour;
 5% did more than 2 hours.

This accounts for 85% of the fourth-graders; the other 15% did between 1 and 2 hours of homework per day.

21. **E.** In 1984, approximately 540,000 eleventh-graders watched television 1 hour or less per day (27% of 2,000,000). By 1996, the number of eleventh-graders had increased by 10%

to 2,200,000, but the percent of them who watched television 1 hour or less per day decreased to about 18%: 18% of 2,200,000 is 396,000. This is a decrease of 144,000, or approximately 150,000.

22. **A.** Since $C = 2\pi r$, then $r = \dfrac{C}{2\pi}$, and

area of circle $= \pi r^2 = \pi\left(\dfrac{C}{2\pi}\right)^2 = \pi\left(\dfrac{C^2}{4\pi^2}\right) = \dfrac{C^2}{4\pi}$

23. **A.** Column A: Since the hypotenuse is 2, the length of each leg is $\dfrac{2}{\sqrt{2}} = \sqrt{2}$, and the area is $\dfrac{1}{2}(\sqrt{2})(\sqrt{2}) = \dfrac{1}{2}(2) = 1.$

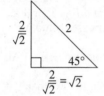 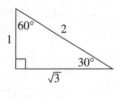

Column B: Since the hypotenuse is 2, the shorter leg is 1, the longer leg is $\sqrt{3}$, and the area is

$\dfrac{1}{2}(1)(\sqrt{3}) = \dfrac{\sqrt{3}}{2}$, which is less than 1 because $\sqrt{3}$ is less than 2.

Column A is greater.

24. **C.** $B - A =$
$(51+52+53+...+99+100) - (1+2+3+...+49+50)$
$= (51-1)+(52-2)+(53-3)+...+(99-49)+(100-50)$
$= 50 + 50 + 50 +...+ 50 + 50 = 50 \times 50 = 2500.$

**If you know the formula, $\dfrac{n(n+1)}{2}$, for adding up the first n positive integers, you can use it: $A = \dfrac{50(51)}{2} = 25(51) = 1275$. B is the sum of the integers from 1 to 100 minus the sum of the integers from 1 to 50:

$B = \dfrac{100(101)}{2} - 1275 = 50(101) - 1275 =$

$5050 - 1275 = 3875.$

Finally, $B - A = 3875 - 1275 = 2500.$
The columns are equal (C).

25. **A.** Since the area of each small circle is πr^2, the area of the white region is $3\pi r^2$. Also, since the area of the large circle is πR^2, the shaded area is $\pi R^2 - 3\pi r^2 = \pi(R^2 - 3r^2)$. Since the areas of the white region and the shaded region are equal:

$3\pi r^2 = \pi(R^2 - 3r^2) \Rightarrow 3r^2 = R^2 - 3r^2 \Rightarrow$

$R^2 = 6r^2 \Rightarrow \dfrac{R^2}{r^2} = 6 \Rightarrow \dfrac{R}{r} = \sqrt{6}$

which is greater than 2. Column A is greater.

26. **E.** Since p pencils cost c cents, each pencil costs $\dfrac{c}{p}$ cents. By dividing the number of cents we have by $\dfrac{c}{p}$, we find out how many pencils we can buy. Since d dollars equals $100d$ cents, we divide $100d$ by $\dfrac{c}{p}$, which is equivalent to multiplying $100d$ by $\dfrac{p}{c}$: $100d\left(\dfrac{p}{c}\right) = \dfrac{100dp}{c}$.
You will probably prefer the alternate solution below.
**Use TACTIC 2, Chapter 12. Assume 2 pencils cost 10 cents. So, pencils cost 5 cents each or 20 for one dollar. So, for 3 dollars, we can buy 60 pencils. Which of the choices equals 60 when $p = 2$, $c = 10$, and $d = 3$? Only $\dfrac{100dp}{c}$.

27. **A.** If a student earned a grade of g, she missed $(100 - g)$ points. In adjusting the grades, the teacher decided to deduct only half that number: $\dfrac{100 - g}{2}$. So the student's new grade was

$100 - \left(\dfrac{100 - g}{2}\right) = 100 - 50 + \dfrac{g}{2} = 50 + \dfrac{g}{2}.$

Since this was done to each student's grade, the effect on the average was exactly the same. The new average was $50 + \dfrac{A}{2}$.

28. **A.** Use TACTIC 3, Chapter 11. Choose an appropriate number for the common perimeter. Any number will work; but since a triangle has 3 sides and a square has 4 sides, 12 is a good choice. Then, each side of the square is 3, and the area is $3^2 = 9$. Each side of the equilateral triangle is 4, and the area is $\dfrac{4^2\sqrt{3}}{9} = 4\sqrt{3}$.

(KEY FACT J15). The ratio is $\dfrac{4\sqrt{3}}{9}$.

Section 3—Analytical Writing

There are no "correct answers" to this section.

Answer Sheet—Model Test 2

Section 1

1. Ⓐ Ⓑ Ⓒ Ⓓ Ⓔ
2. Ⓐ Ⓑ Ⓒ Ⓓ Ⓔ
3. Ⓐ Ⓑ Ⓒ Ⓓ Ⓔ
4. Ⓐ Ⓑ Ⓒ Ⓓ Ⓔ
5. Ⓐ Ⓑ Ⓒ Ⓓ Ⓔ
6. Ⓐ Ⓑ Ⓒ Ⓓ Ⓔ
7. Ⓐ Ⓑ Ⓒ Ⓓ Ⓔ
8. Ⓐ Ⓑ Ⓒ Ⓓ Ⓔ
9. Ⓐ Ⓑ Ⓒ Ⓓ Ⓔ
10. Ⓐ Ⓑ Ⓒ Ⓓ Ⓔ

11. Ⓐ Ⓑ Ⓒ Ⓓ Ⓔ
12. Ⓐ Ⓑ Ⓒ Ⓓ Ⓔ
13. Ⓐ Ⓑ Ⓒ Ⓓ Ⓔ
14. Ⓐ Ⓑ Ⓒ Ⓓ Ⓔ
15. Ⓐ Ⓑ Ⓒ Ⓓ Ⓔ
16. Ⓐ Ⓑ Ⓒ Ⓓ Ⓔ
17. Ⓐ Ⓑ Ⓒ Ⓓ Ⓔ
18. Ⓐ Ⓑ Ⓒ Ⓓ Ⓔ
19. Ⓐ Ⓑ Ⓒ Ⓓ Ⓔ
20. Ⓐ Ⓑ Ⓒ Ⓓ Ⓔ

21. Ⓐ Ⓑ Ⓒ Ⓓ Ⓔ
22. Ⓐ Ⓑ Ⓒ Ⓓ Ⓔ
23. Ⓐ Ⓑ Ⓒ Ⓓ Ⓔ
24. Ⓐ Ⓑ Ⓒ Ⓓ Ⓔ
25. Ⓐ Ⓑ Ⓒ Ⓓ Ⓔ
26. Ⓐ Ⓑ Ⓒ Ⓓ Ⓔ
27. Ⓐ Ⓑ Ⓒ Ⓓ Ⓔ
28. Ⓐ Ⓑ Ⓒ Ⓓ Ⓔ
29. Ⓐ Ⓑ Ⓒ Ⓓ Ⓔ
30. Ⓐ Ⓑ Ⓒ Ⓓ Ⓔ

Section 2

1. Ⓐ Ⓑ Ⓒ Ⓓ Ⓔ
2. Ⓐ Ⓑ Ⓒ Ⓓ Ⓔ
3. Ⓐ Ⓑ Ⓒ Ⓓ Ⓔ
4. Ⓐ Ⓑ Ⓒ Ⓓ Ⓔ
5. Ⓐ Ⓑ Ⓒ Ⓓ Ⓔ
6. Ⓐ Ⓑ Ⓒ Ⓓ Ⓔ
7. Ⓐ Ⓑ Ⓒ Ⓓ Ⓔ
8. Ⓐ Ⓑ Ⓒ Ⓓ Ⓔ
9. Ⓐ Ⓑ Ⓒ Ⓓ Ⓔ
10. Ⓐ Ⓑ Ⓒ Ⓓ Ⓔ

11. Ⓐ Ⓑ Ⓒ Ⓓ Ⓔ
12. Ⓐ Ⓑ Ⓒ Ⓓ Ⓔ
13. Ⓐ Ⓑ Ⓒ Ⓓ Ⓔ
14. Ⓐ Ⓑ Ⓒ Ⓓ Ⓔ
15. Ⓐ Ⓑ Ⓒ Ⓓ Ⓔ
16. Ⓐ Ⓑ Ⓒ Ⓓ Ⓔ
17. Ⓐ Ⓑ Ⓒ Ⓓ Ⓔ
18. Ⓐ Ⓑ Ⓒ Ⓓ Ⓔ
19. Ⓐ Ⓑ Ⓒ Ⓓ Ⓔ
20. Ⓐ Ⓑ Ⓒ Ⓓ Ⓔ

21. Ⓐ Ⓑ Ⓒ Ⓓ Ⓔ
22. Ⓐ Ⓑ Ⓒ Ⓓ Ⓔ
23. Ⓐ Ⓑ Ⓒ Ⓓ Ⓔ
24. Ⓐ Ⓑ Ⓒ Ⓓ Ⓔ
25. Ⓐ Ⓑ Ⓒ Ⓓ Ⓔ
26. Ⓐ Ⓑ Ⓒ Ⓓ Ⓔ
27. Ⓐ Ⓑ Ⓒ Ⓓ Ⓔ
28. Ⓐ Ⓑ Ⓒ Ⓓ Ⓔ

MODEL TEST 2

SECTION 1—VERBAL ABILITY

Time—30 Minutes
30 Questions

Select the best answer to the following questions, then fill in the appropriate space on your Answer Sheet.

Directions: In each of the following antonym questions, a word printed in capital letters precedes five lettered words or phrases. From these five lettered words or phrases, pick the one most nearly opposite in meaning to the capitalized word.

1. ELATED:
   (A) crestfallen
   (B) inebriated
   (C) punctual
   (D) insulted
   (E) lamented

2. RETICENCE:
   (A) irascibility
   (B) loquaciousness
   (C) quiescence
   (D) patience
   (E) surrender

Directions: Each of the following sentence completion questions contains one or two blanks. These blanks signify that a word or set of words has been left out. Below each sentence are five words or sets of words. For each blank, pick the word or set of words that best reflects the sentence's overall meaning.

3. You may wonder how the expert on fossil remains is able to trace descent through teeth, which seem _____ pegs upon which to hang whole ancestries.
   (A) novel
   (B) reliable
   (C) specious
   (D) inadequate
   (E) academic

4. An essential purpose of the criminal justice system is to enable purgation to take place; that is, to provide a _____ by which a community expresses its collective _____ the transgression of the criminal.
   (A) catharsis...outrage at
   (B) disclaimer...forgiveness of
   (C) means...empathy with
   (D) procedure...distaste for
   (E) document...disapprobation of

Directions: Each of the following analogy questions presents a related pair of words linked by a colon. Five lettered pairs of words follow the linked pair. Choose the lettered pair of words whose relationship is most like the relationship expressed in the original linked pair.

5. VINDICTIVE : MERCY ::
   (A) avaricious : greed
   (B) insightful : hope
   (C) modest : dignity
   (D) skeptical : trustfulness
   (E) pathetic : sympathy

6. RUFFLE : COMPOSURE ::
   (A) flounce : turmoil
   (B) flourish : prosperity
   (C) provoke : discussion
   (D) adjust : balance
   (E) upset : equilibrium

Directions: Each of the following reading comprehension questions is based on the content of the following passage. Read the passage and then determine the best answer choice for each question. Base your choice on what this passage *states directly* or *implies*, not on any information you may have gained elsewhere.

Given the persistent and intransigent nature of the American race system, which proved quite impervious to black attacks, Du Bois in his
Line speeches and writings moved from one proposed
(5) solution to another, and the salience of various parts of his philosophy changed as his perceptions of the needs and strategies of black America shifted over time. Aloof and autonomous in his personality, Du Bois did not hesitate to depart
(10) markedly from whatever was the current mainstream of black thinking when he perceived that the conventional wisdom being enunciated by black spokesmen was proving inadequate to the task of advancing the race. His willingness to
(15) seek different solutions often placed him well in advance of his contemporaries, and this, combined with a strong-willed, even arrogant personality made his career as a black leader essentially a series of stormy conflicts.
(20)   Thus Du Bois first achieved his role as a major black leader in the controversy that arose over the program of Booker T. Washington, the most prominent and influential black leader at the opening of the twentieth century. Amidst the
(25) wave of lynchings, disfranchisement, and segregation laws, Washington, seeking the good will of powerful whites, taught blacks not to protest against discrimination, but to elevate themselves through industrial education, hard work, and prop-
(30) erty accumulation; then, they would ultimately obtain recognition of their citizenship rights. At first Du Bois agreed with this gradualist strategy, but in 1903 with the publication of his most influential book, *Souls of Black Folk,* he became the
(35) chief leader of the onslaught against Washington that polarized the black community into two wings—the "conservative" supporters of Washington and his "radical" critics.

7. Which of the following statements about W. E. B. Du Bois does the passage best support?

(A) He sacrificed the proven strategies of earlier black leaders to his craving for political novelty.
(B) Preferring conflict to harmony, he followed a disruptive course that alienated him from the bulk of his followers.
(C) He proved unable to change with the times in mounting fresh attacks against white racism.

(D) He relied on the fundamental benevolence of the white population for the eventual success of his movement.
(E) Once an adherent of Washington's policies, he ultimately lost patience with them for their inefficacy.

8. It can be inferred that Booker T. Washington in comparison with W. E. B. Du Bois could be described as all of the following EXCEPT

(A) submissive to the majority
(B) concerned with financial success
(C) versatile in adopting strategies
(D) traditional in preaching industry
(E) respectful of authority

9. The author's attitude toward Du Bois' departure from conventional black policies can best be described as

(A) skeptical
(B) derisive
(C) shocked
(D) approving
(E) resigned

Antonyms

10. REVILE:
(A) compose
(B) awake
(C) deaden
(D) praise
(E) secrete

11. PROPITIOUS:
(A) adjacent
(B) clandestine
(C) contentious
(D) unfavorable
(E) coy

1

1

Analogies

12. OFFHAND : PREMEDITATION ::
    (A) upright : integrity
    (B) aboveboard : guile
    (C) cutthroat : competition
    (D) backward : direction
    (E) underlying : foundation

13. LARVAL : INSECT ::
    (A) serpentine : snake
    (B) floral : plant
    (C) amphibian : reptile
    (D) embryonic : mammal
    (E) alate : bird

Sentence Completion

14. When facts are _____ and data hard to come by, even scientists occasionally throw aside the professional pretense of _____ and tear into each other with shameless appeals to authority and arguments that are unabashedly ad hominem.
    (A) elusive...objectivity
    (B) established...courtesy
    (C) demonstrable...neutrality
    (D) ineluctable...cooperation
    (E) hypothetical...scholarship

15. In the tradition of scholarly _____, the poet and scholar A.E. Housman once assailed a German rival for relying on manuscripts "as a drunkard relies on lampposts, for _____ rather than illumination."
    (A) animosity...current
    (B) discourse...stability
    (C) erudition...shadow
    (D) invective...support
    (E) competition...assistance

Reading Comprehension

At night, schools of prey and predators are almost always spectacularly illuminated by the bioluminescence produced by the microscopic
Line and larger plankton. The reason for the ubiquitous
(5) production of light by the microorganisms of the sea remains obscure, and suggested explanations are controversial. It has been suggested that light is a kind of inadvertent by-product of life in transparent organisms. It has also been hypothesized
(10) that the emission of light on disturbance is advantageous to the plankton in making the predators of the plankton conspicuous to *their* predators! Unquestionably, it does act this way. Indeed, some fisheries base the detection of their prey on

(15) the bioluminescence that the fish excite. It is difficult, however, to defend the thesis that this effect was the direct factor in the original development of bioluminescence, since the effect was of no advantage to the individual microorganism
(20) that first developed it. Perhaps the luminescence of a microorganism also discourages attack by light-avoiding predators and is of initial survival benefit to the individual. As it then becomes general in the population, the effect of revealing
(25) plankton predators to their predators would also become important.

16. The primary topic of the passage is which of the following?
    (A) The origin of bioluminescence in plankton predators
    (B) The disadvantages of bioluminescence in microorganisms
    (C) The varieties of marine bioluminescent life forms
    (D) Symbiotic relationships between predators and their prey
    (E) Hypotheses on the causes of bioluminescence in plankton

17. The author mentions the activities of fisheries in order to provide an example of
    (A) how ubiquitous the phenomenon of bioluminescence is coastally
    (B) how predators do make use of bioluminescence in locating their prey
    (C) how human intervention imperils bioluminescent microorganisms
    (D) how nocturnal fishing expeditions are becoming more and more widespread
    (E) how limited bioluminescence is as a source of light for human use

18. The passage provides an answer to which of the following questions?
    (A) What is the explanation for the phenomenon of bioluminescence in marine life?
    (B) Does the phenomenon of plankton bioluminescence have any practical applications?
    (C) Why do only certain specimens of marine life exhibit the phenomenon of bioluminescence?
    (D) How does underwater bioluminescence differ from atmospheric bioluminescence?
    (E) What are the steps that take place as an individual microorganism becomes bioluminescent?

1   1

Antonyms

19. INCONGRUOUS:

    (A) external
    (B) prudent
    (C) legitimate
    (D) harmonious
    (E) efficacious

20. APOSTATE:

    (A) laggard
    (B) loyalist
    (C) martinet
    (D) predecessor
    (E) skeptic

Analogies

21. SEXTANT : NAUTICAL ::

    (A) octet : musical
    (B) therapy : physical
    (C) forceps : surgical
    (D) comet : astronomical
    (E) blueprint : mechanical

22. REFRACTORY : MANAGE ::

    (A) redoubtable : impress
    (B) lethargic : stimulate
    (C) pedantic : convince
    (D) officious : arrange
    (E) aggrieved : distress

Antonyms

23. ENSUE:

    (A) litigate
    (B) precede
    (C) arbitrate
    (D) accentuate
    (E) delay

Sentence Completion

24. While the disease is in _____ state it is
    almost impossible to determine its existence by
    _____.

    (A) a dormant...postulate
    (B) a critical...examination
    (C) an acute...analysis
    (D) a suspended...estimate
    (E) a latent...observation

25. Virginia Woolf _____ conventional notions
    of truth: in her words, one cannot receive from any
    lecture "a nugget of pure truth" to wrap up between

the pages of one's notebook and keep on the
mantelpiece forever.

    (A) anticipates
    (B) articulates
    (C) neglects
    (D) mocks
    (E) rationalizes

Reading Comprehension

The curtain rises; the Cardinal and Daniel de
Bosola enter from the right. In appearance, the
Cardinal is something between an El Greco cardi-
Line nal and a Van Dyke noble lord. He has the tall,
(5) spare form—the elongated hands and features—
of the former; the trim pointed beard, the imperial
repose, the commanding authority of the latter.
But the El Greco features are not really those of
asceticism or inner mystic spirituality. They are
(10) the index to a cold, refined but ruthless cruelty in
a highly civilized controlled form. Neither is the
imperial repose an aloof mood of proud detachment. It is a refined expression of satanic pride of
place and talent.
(15)   To a degree, the Cardinal's coldness is artificially cultivated. He has defined himself against
his younger brother Duke Ferdinand and is the
opposite to the overwrought emotionality of the
latter. But the Cardinal's aloof mood is not one of
(20) bland detachment. It is the deliberate detachment
of a methodical man who collects his thoughts
and emotions into the most compact and formidable shape—that when he strikes, he may strike
with the more efficient and devastating force. His
(25) easy movements are those of the slowly circling
eagle just before the swift descent with the
exposed talons. Above all else, he is a man who
never for a moment doubts his destined authority
as a governor. He derisively and sharply rebukes
(30) his brother the Duke as easily and readily as he
mocks his mistress Julia. If he has betrayed his
hireling Bosola, he uses his brother as the tool to
win back his "familiar." His court dress is a long
brilliant scarlet cardinal's gown with white cuffs
(35) and a white collar turned back over the red, both
collar and cuffs being elaborately scalloped and
embroidered. He wears a small cape, reaching
only to the elbows. His cassock is buttoned to the
ground, giving a heightened effect to his already
(40) tall presence. Richelieu would have adored his
neatly trimmed beard. A richly jeweled and
oranamented cross lies on his breast, suspended
from his neck by a gold chain.

1   1

26. In lines 24–27 the author most likely compares the movements of the Cardinal to those of a circling eagle in order to emphasize his

   (A) flightiness
   (B) love of freedom
   (C) eminence
   (D) sense of spirituality
   (E) mercilessness

27. Which of the following best characterizes the author's attitude toward the Cardinal?

   (A) He deprecates his inability to sustain warm familial relationships.
   (B) He esteems him for his spiritual and emotional control.
   (C) He admires his grace in movement and sure sense of personal authority.
   (D) He finds him formidable both as an opponent and as a dramatic character.
   (E) He is perturbed by his inconsistencies in behavior.

Analogies

28. AUSTERE : STYLE ::

   (A) controlled : movement
   (B) affluent : wealth
   (C) subservient : demeanor
   (D) inspirational : faith
   (E) pragmatic : speech

Antonyms

29. RETROSPECTION:

   (A) introversion
   (B) deliberation
   (C) anticipation
   (D) gregariousness
   (E) equivocation

30. TOPICAL:

   (A) general
   (B) disinterested
   (C) chronological
   (D) fallacious
   (E) imperceptible

2

2

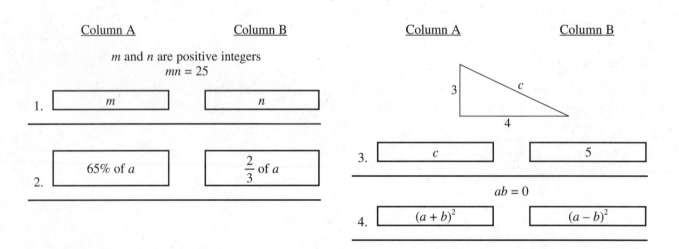

Column A   Column B   Column A   Column B

m and n are positive integers
$mn = 25$

1. m n

2. 65% of a $\dfrac{2}{3}$ of a

3. c 5

$ab = 0$

4. $(a + b)^2$ $(a - b)^2$

Directions: In the following questions, choose the best answer from the five choices listed.

5. The Center City Little League is divided into d divisions. Each division has t teams, and each team has p players. How many players are there in the entire league?

(A) $d + t + p$ (B) dtp (C) $\dfrac{pt}{d}$ (D) $\dfrac{dt}{p}$ (E) $\dfrac{d}{pt}$

6. A number x is chosen at random from the set of positive integers less than 10. What is the probability that $\dfrac{9}{x} > x$?

(A) $\dfrac{1}{5}$ (B) $\dfrac{2}{9}$ (C) $\dfrac{1}{3}$ (D) $\dfrac{2}{3}$ (E) $\dfrac{7}{9}$

7. If $\dfrac{1}{a} + \dfrac{1}{a} + \dfrac{1}{a} = 12$, then $a =$

(A) $\dfrac{1}{12}$ (B) $\dfrac{1}{4}$ (C) $\dfrac{1}{3}$ (D) 3   (E) 4

2   2

Column A	Column B

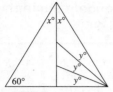

8. | y | 20 |

$$a + b = 24$$
$$a - b = 25$$

9. | b | 0 |

---

10. In 1980, the cost of p pounds of potatoes was d dollars. In 1990, the cost of $2p$ pounds of potatoes was $\frac{1}{2}d$ dollars. By what percent did the price of potatoes decrease from 1980 to 1990?

(A) 25%   (B) 50%   (C) 75%   (D) 100%
(E) 400%

Column A	Column B

$$a + 2b = 6d$$
$$c - b = 5d$$

11. | The average (arithmetic mean) of a, b, c, and d | $3d$ |

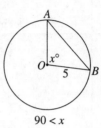

$$90 < x$$

12. | The length of AB | 7 |

$$x^5 = \frac{13}{17}$$

13. | x | $\left(\dfrac{13}{17}\right)^5$ |

2

Average expected family contribution (EFC) for dependent students, by family income: Academic year 1995–96

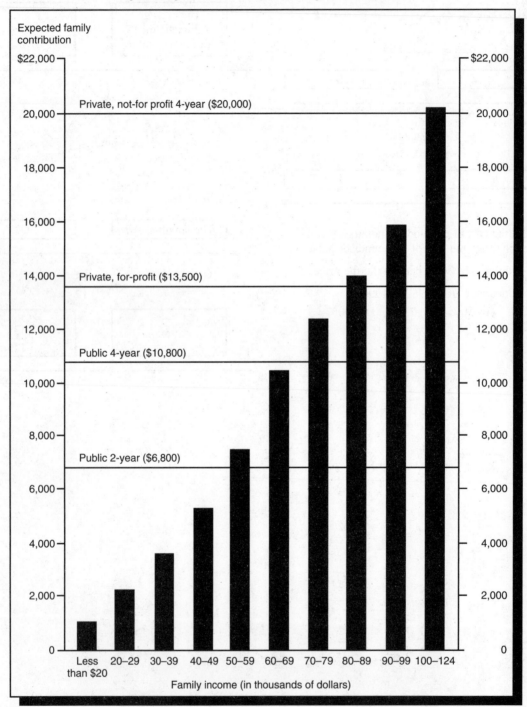

NOTE: The horizontal lines on the figure represent the average student budgets for full-time, full-year students at the indicated type of institution.

SOURCE: U.S. Department of Education.

2   **2**

14. A family's *unmet need* (which must be covered by a financial aid package) is defined to be the total cost of attending an institution of higher education minus the expected family contribution. What is the unmet need of a family whose income is $55,000 and who has a child attending a 4-year public university?

    (A) $700   (B) $3300   (C) $6800
    (D) $7500   (E) $12,500

15. If family A has an income of $95,000 per year, and family B has an income of $35,000 per year, and each has a child attending a 4-year public university, to the nearest $1000, how much more would family A be expected to pay than family B?

    (A) $4000   (B) $7000   (C) $10,000
    (D) $12,000   (E) $15,000

Column A	Column B
$\dfrac{\sqrt{24}}{2}$	$\dfrac{6}{\sqrt{6}}$

16.

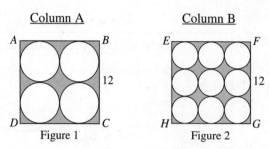

Column A   Column B

Figure 1   Figure 2

ABCD and *EFGH* are squares, and all the circles are tangent to one another and to the sides of the squares.

The area of the shaded region in Figure 1	The area of the shaded region in Figure 2

17.

18. A bag contains 3 red, 4 white, and 5 blue marbles. Jason begins removing marbles from the bag at random, one at a time. What is the least number of marbles he must remove to be sure that he has at least one of each color?

    (A) 3   (B) 6   (C) 8   (D) 10   (E) 12

19. Jordan has taken 5 math tests so far this semester. If he gets a 70 on his next test, it will lower the average (arithmetic mean) of his test scores by 4 points. What is his average now?

    (A) 74   (B) 85   (C) 86   (D) 90   (E) 94

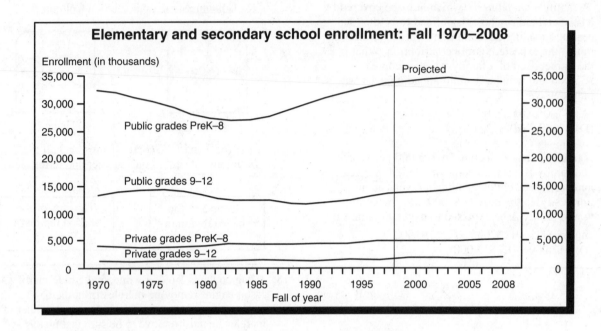

Elementary and secondary school enrollment: Fall 1970–2008

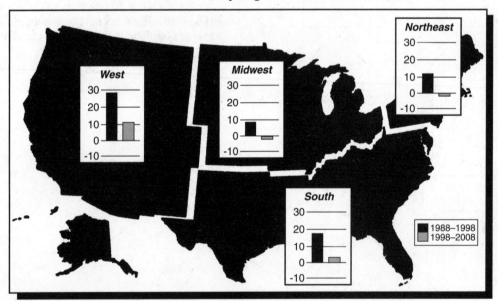

Projected percentage change in public elementary and secondary school enrollment, by region: Fall 1988 to 2008

SOURCE: U.S. Department of Education, National Center for Education Statistics.

2   **2**

20. To the nearest million, how many more students
    were enrolled in school—both public and private,
    preK–12—in 1970 than in 1988?

    (A) 3,000,000   (B) 6,000,000   (C) 10,000,000
    (D) 44,000,000   (E) 51,000,000

21. In 1988 there were 40,000,000 public school stu-
    dents in the United States, of whom 22% lived in
    the West. Approximately, how many public school
    students are projected to be living in the West in
    2008?

    (A) 9,000,000   (B) 12,000,000   (C) 15,000,000
    (D) 24,000,000   (E) 66,000,000

22. If a and b are the lengths of the legs of a right tri-
    angle whose hypotenuse is 10 and whose area is
    20, what is the value of $(a + b)^2$?

    (A) 100   (B) 120   (C) 140   (D) 180   (E) 200

Column A	Column B

The circumference of a circle is $a\pi$ inches.
The area of the same circle is $b\pi$ square inches.

23. | a | | b |

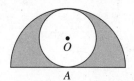

A

The circle with center O is inscribed in the
semicircle with center A.

24. | The area of the shaded region | The area of the white region |

A school group charters three identical buses
and occupies $\frac{4}{5}$ of the seats. After $\frac{1}{4}$ of the
passengers leave, the remaining passengers use
only two of the buses.

25. | The fraction of the seats on the two buses that are now occupied | $\frac{9}{10}$ |

---

26. What is the average (arithmetic mean) of 3^{30}, 3^{60},
    and 3^{90}?

    (A) 3^{60} (B) 3^{177} (C) $3^{10} + 3^{20} + 3^{30}$
    (D) $3^{27} + 3^{57} + 3^{87}$ (E) $3^{29} + 3^{59} + 3^{89}$

27. The figure at the right consists
    of four semicircles in a large
    semicircle. If the small
    semicircles have radii of
    1, 2, 3, and 4, what is the
    perimeter of the shaded
    region?

    (A) 10π (B) 20π (C) 40π (D) 60π (E) 100π

28. If a is increased by 25% and b is decreased by
    25%, the resulting numbers will be equal. What is
    the ratio of a to b?

    (A) $\frac{3}{5}$ (B) $\frac{3}{4}$ (C) $\frac{1}{1}$ (D) $\frac{4}{3}$ (E) $\frac{5}{3}$

3

3

SECTION 3—ANALYTICAL WRITING

Time—75 Minutes
2 Writing Tasks

Task 1: Issue Exploration
45 Minutes

<u>Directions</u>: In 45 minutes, choose one of the two following topics and compose an essay on that topic. You may not write on any other topic. Write your answer on separate sheets of paper.

Each topic is presented in a one- to two-sentence quotation commenting on an issue of general concern. Your essay may support, refute, or qualify the views expressed in the quotation. Whatever you write, however, must be relevant to the issue under discussion, and you must support your viewpoint with reasons and examples derived from your studies and/or experience.

Before you choose a topic, read both topics carefully. Consider which topic would give you greater scope for writing an effective, well-argued essay.

Faculty members from various institutions will evaluate your essay, judging it on the basis of your skill in the following areas.

- Analysis of the quotation's implications
- Organization and articulation of your ideas
- Use of relevant examples and arguments to support your case
- Handling of the mechanics of standard written English

Once you have decided which topic you prefer, click on the appropriate icon (**Topic 1** or **Topic 2**) to confirm your choice. Do not be hasty confirming your choice of topic. Once you have clicked on a topic, you will not be able to switch to the alternate choice.

Topic 1

"If rituals did not exist, we would have to invent them. We need ceremonies and rituals to help us define ourselves socially and culturally."

Topic 2

"In this electronic age, reading has inevitably taken a back seat to watching television and gleaning information from the World Wide Web. People learn far more readily from electronic media than they do from print."

3

3

**Task 2: Argument Analysis
30 Minutes**

<u>Directions</u>: In 30 minutes, prepare a critical analysis of an argument expressed in a short paragraph. You may not offer an analysis of any other argument. Write your essay on separate sheets of paper.

As you critique the argument, think about the author's underlying assumptions. Ask yourself whether any of them are questionable. Also evaluate any evidence the author brings up. Ask yourself whether it actually supports the author's conclusion.

In your analysis, you may suggest additional kinds of evidence to reinforce the author's argument. You may also suggest methods to refute the argument, or additional data that might be useful to you as you assess the soundness of the argument. *You may **not**, however, present your personal views on the topic.* Your job is to analyze the elements of an argument, not to support or contradict that argument.

Faculty members from various institutions will judge your essay, assessing it on the basis of your skill in the following areas:

• Identification and assessment of the argument's main elements
• Organization and articulation of your thoughts
• Use of relevant examples and arguments to support your case
• Handling of the mechanics of standard written English

The following appeared in a letter to the editor in the journal *Health Matters*.

Statistics gathered over the past three decades show that the death rate is higher among those who do not have jobs than among those with regular employment. Unemployment, just like heart disease and cancer, is a significant health issue. While many health care advocates promote increased government funding for medical research and public health care, it would be folly to increase government spending if doing so were to affect the nation's economy adversely and ultimately cause a rise in unemployment. A healthy economy means healthy citizens.

Answer Key

Section 1—Verbal Ability

1. A	6. E	11. D	16. E	21. C	26. E
2. B	7. E	12. B	17. B	22. B	27. D
3. D	8. C	13. D	18. B	23. B	28. A
4. A	9. D	14. A	19. D	24. E	29. C
5. D	10. D	15. D	20. B	25. D	30. A

Section 2—Quantitative Ability

NOTE: The letters in brackets following the Quantitative Ability answers refer to the sections of Chapter 14 in which you can find the information you need to answer the questions. For example, 1. C [E] means that the answer to question 1 is C, and that the solution requires information found in Section 14-E: Averages. Also, 20. A [13] means that the answer to question 20 is based on information in Chapter 13: Data Interpretation.

1. D [A]	6. B [O]	11. C [E,G]	16. C [A]	21. B [13]	26. E [A]
2. D [B,C]	7. B [B,G]	12. A [J,L]	17. C [K,L]	22. D [G,J]	27. B [L]
3. D [J]	8. D [J]	13. A [B]	18. D [O]	23. D [L]	28. A [C]
4. C [F]	9. B [G]	14. B [13]	19. E [E]	24. C [L]	
5. B [D]	10. C [C,D]	15. B [13]	20. B [13]	25. C [B]	

Section 3—Analytical Writing

There are no "correct answers" to this section.

Answer Explanations

Section 1—Verbal Ability

1. **A.** *Elated* (joyful, in high spirits) is the opposite of *crestfallen* (dejected).
   Think of "elated by her success."

2. **B.** The opposite of *reticence* (uncommunicativeness; restraint in speech) is *loquaciousness* (talkativeness).
   Think of "speaking without reticence."

3. **D.** If "you may wonder" how the expert reaches his conclusions, it appears that it is questionable to rely on teeth for guidance in interpreting fossils. Choice D, *inadequate*, creates the element of doubt that the clause tries to develop. Choice C, *specious*, also creates an element of doubt; however, nothing in the context justifies the idea that the reasoning is specious or false.
   Note that here you are dealing with an extended metaphor. Picture yourself hanging a heavy winter coat on a slim wooden peg. Wouldn't you worry that the peg might prove inadequate or flimsy?

4. **A.** Here the task is to determine the communal reaction to crime. The writer maintains that the criminal justice system of punishments allows the community to purge itself of its anger, its sense of *outrage* at the criminal's acts. Thus, it provides a *catharsis* or purgation for the community.
   Remember, in double-blank sentences, go through the answers, testing the *first* word in each choice and eliminating those that don't fit. In this case, you can readily eliminate Choices B and E: it is unlikely that an *essential* purpose of the criminal justice system would be the provision of either a *disclaimer* (denial or disavowal, as in disavowing responsibility for a legal claim) or a *document*.

5. **D.** Someone *vindictive* or vengeful is lacking in *mercy*. Someone *skeptical* or suspicious is lacking in *trustfulness*.　　(Antonym Variant)

6. **E.** To *ruffle* someone's *composure* is to disturb or trouble his self-possession. To *upset* someone's *equilibrium* is to disturb or trouble his balance.　　(Function)

7. E. The last sentence points out that Du Bois originally agreed with Washington's program.
Choice A is incorrect. Nothing in the passage suggests that Du Bois sacrificed effective strategies out of a desire to try something new.
Choice B is incorrect. Du Bois gained in influence, effectively winning away large numbers of blacks from Washington's policies.
Choice C is incorrect. Du Bois' quickness to depart from conventional black wisdom when it proved inadequate to the task of advancing the race shows him to be well able to change with the times.
Choice D is incorrect. Washington, not Du Bois, is described as seeking the good will of powerful whites.

8. C. The author does *not* portray Washington as versatile. Instead, he portrays Du Bois as versatile.
Choice A is incorrect. The author portrays Washington as submissive to the majority; he shows him teaching blacks not to protest.
Choice B is incorrect. The author portrays Washington as concerned with financial success; he shows him advocating property accumulation.
Choice D is incorrect. The author portrays Washington as traditional in preaching industry; he shows him advocating hard work.
Choice E is incorrect. The author portrays Washington as respectful of authority; he shows him deferring to powerful whites.

9. D. Although the author points out that Du Bois' methods led him into conflicts, he describes Du Bois as "often...well in advance of his contemporaries" and stresses that his motives for departing from the mainstream were admirable. Thus, his attitude can best be described as *approving*.

10. D. To *revile* (verbally abuse) something is the opposite of *praising* it.
Think of "reviled as a traitor."

11. D. The opposite of *propitious* (favorable, advantageous) is *unfavorable*.
Think of being pleased by "propitious omens."

12. B. An *offhand* remark is made without forethought or *premeditation*. An *aboveboard* (open) deed is done without trickery or *guile*.
                    (Antonym Variant)

13. D. The *larval* (immature) stage of an *insect* best corresponds to the *embryonic* stage of a *mammal*.   (Defining Characteristic)

14. A. Under certain circumstances scientists attack each other with *ad hominem* arguments (personal attacks) and shameless appeals.

When is this likely to occur? When facts are *established* or *demonstrable* or *ineluctable* (unavoidable)? Hardly. Under such circumstances they would rely on facts to establish their case. It is when facts prove *elusive* that they lose control and, in doing so, abandon their pretense of *objectivity*.

15. D. The key word here is *assailed*. Housman is attacking his rival. Thus he is in the tradition of scholarly *invective* (vehement verbal attack), criticizing his foe for turning to manuscripts merely for confirmation or *support* of old theories and not for enlightenment or illumination.
Again, note the use of figurative language, in this case the simile of the drunkard.

16. E. The author first states that the reasons for bioluminescence in underwater microorganisms is obscure and then proceeds to enumerate various hypotheses.

17. B. The author does not deny that predators make use of bioluminescence in locating their prey. Instead, he gives an example of human predators (commercial fishermen) who are drawn to their prey (the fish that prey on plankton) by the luminescence of the plankton.

18. B. As the previous answer makes clear, the phenomenon of plankton bioluminescence does have practical applications. It is a valuable tool for fisheries interested in increasing their catch of fish that prey on plankton.

19. D. The opposite of *incongruous* (inconsistent, not fitting) is *harmonious*.
Think of being startled by "incongruous behavior."

20. B. An *apostate* (renegade; person faithless to an allegiance) is the opposite of a *loyalist*.
Beware eye-catchers. Do not confuse *apostate* (renegade) with *apostle* (missionary; reformer).
Think of "a faithless apostate."

21. C. By definition, a *sextant* is a piece of equipment that is *nautical*. Similarly, a *forceps* is a piece of equipment that is *surgical*.
                    (Defining Characteristic)

22. B. Someone *refractory* (stubborn; unmanageable) by definition is hard to *manage*. Likewise, someone *lethargic* (sluggish; drowsy) by definition is hard to *stimulate*.   (Definition)

23. B. The opposite of to *ensue* (happen later, follow) is to *precede*.
Think of "the wedding that ensued."

24. E. A disease in a *latent* state has yet to manifest itself and emerge into view. Therefore it is impossible to *observe*.

Remember, in double-blank sentences, go through the answers, testing the *first* word in each choice and eliminating those that don't fit. When a disease is in a *critical* or *acute* state, its existence is obvious. Therefore, you can eliminate Choices B and C.

25. D. The second clause presents an example of literary *mockery*. The abstract idea of preserving a nugget of pure truth is appealing; the concrete example of setting it up on the mantel makes fun of the whole idea.

26. E. The eagle is poised to strike "with exposed talons." It, like the Cardinal, collects itself to strike with greater force. The imagery accentuates the Cardinal's *mercilessness*.

Choice A is incorrect. The Cardinal is not *flighty* (light-headed and irresponsible); he is cold and calculating.

Choice B is incorrect. He loves power, not freedom.

Choice C is incorrect. An eagle poised to strike with bare claws suggests violence, not *eminence* (fame and high position).

Choice D is incorrect. Nothing in the passage suggests he is spiritual.

Beware eye-catchers. "Eminence" is a title of honor applied to cardinals in the Roman Catholic church. Choice D may attract you for this reason.

27. D. The author's depiction of the Cardinal stresses his redoubtable qualities as a foe (calculation, duplicity, mercilessness) and as a challenge to an actor ("imperial repose," a commanding presence, smooth movements suggesting latent danger).

Choice A is incorrect. The author portrays the Cardinal's relations with his brother and mistress as cold, but he never apologizes for the Cardinal's lack of warmth. Indeed, the author somewhat savors it.

Choices B and C are incorrect. Neither esteem for a nonexistent spirituality nor admiration for a villainous autocracy enters into the author's depiction of the Cardinal.

Choice E is incorrect. A cause of perturbation to others, the Cardinal is never perturbed.

28. A. An *austere style* is severely simple and restrained. *Controlled movement* is restrained as well.   (Defining Characteristic)

29. C. *Retrospection* (looking backward; the act of surveying the past) is the opposite of *anticipation* (looking forward).

Word Parts Clue: *Retro-* means backward; *spect-* means look. *Retrospection* means looking backward.

Think of "an old man lost in retrospection."

30. A. *Topical* (local, temporary) is the opposite of *general*.

Remember that words may be used in several different ways. Here *topical* does not mean arranged according to topics (as in a topical index).

Think of "a topical anesthetic," one applied locally, not generally.

Section 2—Quantitative Ability

Two asterisks (**) indicate an alternative method of solving.

1. D. Use TACTIC 4, Chapter 12. Could m and n be equal? Sure, if each is 5. Eliminate Choices A and B. Must they be equal? No, not if $m = 1$ and $n = 25$. Eliminate Choice C, as well. Neither column is always greater, and the two columns are not always equal (D).

2. D. Since $\frac{2}{3} = 66\frac{2}{3}\%$, which is clearly more than 65%, it *appears* that Column B is greater. *Be careful*! That would be true if a were positive, but no restrictions are placed on a. If $a = 0$, the columns are equal; if a is negative, Column A is greater. Neither column is always greater, and the two columns are not always equal (D).
    **Use TACTIC 1, Chapter 12. Just let $a = 0$, and then let $a = 1$.

3. D. Use TACTIC 4, Chapter 12. Could the columns be equal? Could $c = 5$? Sure, if this is a 3-4-5 right triangle. Must $c = 5$? No; if the triangle is not a right triangle, c could be less than or more than 5. Neither column is *always* greater, and the columns are not *always* equal (D). (*Note*: Since the figure may not be drawn to scale, do *not* assume that the triangle has a right angle.)

4. C. Column A: $(a + b)^2 = a^2 + 2ab + b^2 = a^2 + b^2$ (since $ab = 0$).
    Column B: $(a - b)^2 = a^2 - 2ab + b^2 = a^2 + b^2$ (since $ab = 0$).
    The columns are equal (C).
    **Use TACTIC 1, Chapter 12: Pick two numbers whose product is 0; say $a = 0$ and $b = 1$. Then $(a + b)^2 = (0 + 1)^2 = 1$ and $(a - b)^2 = (0 - 1)^2 = 1$. Eliminate A and B and try other

values where either a or b is 0 (since $ab = 0$). The two expressions are always equal.

5. **B.** Since d divisions each have t teams, multiply to get dt teams; and since each team has p players, multiply the number of teams (dt) by p to get the total number of players: dtp.
 **Use TACTIC 2, Chapter 11. Pick three easy-to-use numbers for t, d, and p. Assume that there are 2 divisions, each consisting of 4 teams, so, there are $2 \times 4 = 8$ teams. Then assume that each team has 10 players, for a total of $8 \times 10 = 80$ players. Now check the choices. Which one is equal to 80 when $d = 2$, $t = 4$, and $p = 10$? Only dtp.

6. **B.** There are nine positive integers less than 10: 1, 2, ... , 9. For which of them is $\frac{9}{x} > x$? Only 1 and 2: $\frac{9}{1} > 1$ and $\frac{9}{2} > 2$. When $x = 3$, $\frac{9}{x} = x$, and for all the others $\frac{9}{x} < x$. The probability is $\frac{2}{9}$.

7. **B.** Solve the given equation:
 $$\frac{1}{a} + \frac{1}{a} + \frac{1}{a} = 12$$
 Add the fractions: $\frac{3}{a} = 12$
 Multiply both sides by a: $3 = 12a$
 Divide both sides by 12: $a = \frac{3}{12} = \frac{1}{4}$.
 **You can use TACTIC 1, Chapter 11: back-solve; try Choice C. If $a = \frac{1}{3}$, then $\frac{1}{a} = 3$, so the left-hand side equals 9. That's too small. Now, *be careful:* a fraction gets bigger when its denominator gets *smaller* [KEY FACT B4]. Eliminate Choices C, D, and E, and try a smaller value for a: $\frac{1}{4}$ works.

8. **D.** Use TACTIC 4, Chapter 12. Could $y = 20$? Yes, if the large triangle were equilateral, x would be 30 and y would be 20. Must $y = 20$? No, if $x = 45$, $y = 10$. (Note: Since the figure may not be drawn to scale, the triangle could be *any* triangle with a 60° angle.) Neither column is *always* larger, and the columns are not *always* equal (D).

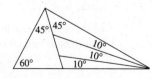

9. **B.** You don't *have* to solve for a and b. If $a - b > a + b$, then b is negative and Column B is greater.

**You *could* solve. Adding the two equations yields
 $$2a = 49 \Rightarrow a = 24.5 \Rightarrow b = -.5.$$

10. **C.** Since, in 1990, $2p$ pounds of potatoes cost $\frac{1}{2}d$ dollars, p pounds cost half as much: $\frac{1}{2}\left(\frac{1}{2}d\right)$ $= \frac{1}{4}d$. This is $\frac{1}{4}$, or 25%, as much as the cost in 1980, which represents a decrease of 75%.
 **In this type of problem it is *often* easier to use TACTIC 2, Chapter 11. Assume that 1 pound of potatoes cost $100 in 1980. Then in 1990, 2 pounds cost $50, so 1 pound cost $25. This is a decrease of $75 in the cost of 1 pound of potatoes, and

 $$\% \text{ decrease} = \frac{\text{actual decrease}}{\text{original amount}} \times 100\%$$
 $$= \frac{75}{100} \times 100\% = 75\%.$$

11. **C.** Adding the two given equations, we get $a + b + c = 11d$. Then
 $$a + b + c + d = 11d + d = 12d \Rightarrow$$
 $$\frac{a + b + c + d}{4} = \frac{12d}{4} = 3d.$$
 The columns are equal (C).

12. **A.** Since in the given figure OA and OB are radii, each is equal to 5. With no restrictions on x, AB could be any positive number less than 10; and the larger x is, the larger AB is. If x were 90, AB would be $5\sqrt{2}$, but we are told that $x > 90$, so $AB > 5\sqrt{2} > 7$.

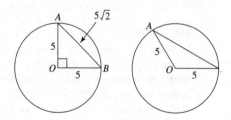

13. **A.** Column B $= \left(\frac{13}{17}\right)^5 = (x^5)^5 = x^{25}$.
 Since $0 < x < 1$, $x^{25} < x$.

14. **B.** The average expected family contribution of a family with an income between $50,000 and $59,000 is about $7,500. Since the average cost of attending a 4-year public university is $10,800, there is an unmet need of $10,800 - $7,500 = $3,300.

15. **B.** Family A would be expected to pay $10,800, the full annual cost for a 4-year public university. Family B would be expected to pay approximately $3,500. Therefore, family A would pay $10,800 - $3,500 = $7,300 more.

16. **C.** To compare two fractions, cross-multiply. Since $\sqrt{24} \times \sqrt{6} = \sqrt{144} = 12$ and $2 \times 6 = 12$, the two fractions have the same value. The columns are equal (C).

17. **C.** In Figure 1, since the radius of each circle is 3, the area of each circle is 9π, and the total area of the four circles is 36π. In Figure 2, the radius of each circle is 2, and so the area of each circle is 4π, and the total area of the nine circles is 36π. In the two figures, the white areas are equal, as are the shaded areas. The columns are equal (C).

18. **D.** If Jason were really unlucky, what could go wrong in his attempt to get one marble of each color? Well, his first nine picks *might* yield five blue marbles and four white ones. But then the tenth marble would be red, and now he would have at least one of each color. The answer is 10.

19. **E.** If a represents Jordan's average after 5 tests, then he has earned a total of $5a$ points [TACTIC E1]. A grade of 70 on the sixth test will lower his average 4 points to $a - 4$. Therefore,
$$a - 4 = \frac{5a + 70}{6} \Rightarrow 6(a - 4) = 5a + 70 \Rightarrow$$
$$6a - 24 = 5a + 70 \Rightarrow 6a = 5a + 94 \Rightarrow a = 94.$$
**Assume Jordan's average is a because he earned a on each of his first 5 tests. Since after getting a 70 on his sixth test his average will be $a - 4$, the deviation on each of the first 5 tests is 4, for a total deviation above the average of 20 points. So, the total deviation below must also be 20 [KEY FACT E3]. Therefore, 70 is 20 less than the new average of $a - 4$:
$$70 = (a - 4) - 20 \Rightarrow a = 94.$$
**Use TACTIC 1, Chapter 11: backsolve. Start with Choice C, 86. If his 5-test average was 90, he had 450 points and a 70 on the sixth test would give him a total of 520 points, and an average of $520 \div 6 = 86.666$. So, the 70 lowered his average 3.333 points. That's not enough. Eliminate Choices A, B, and C. Try Choices D or E. Choice E, 94, works.

20. **B.** Reading from the top graph, we get the following enrollment figures:

	1970	1988
Public PreK–8	33,000,000	28,000,000
Public 9–12	13,000,000	12,000,000
Private PreK–8	4,000,000	4,000,000
Private 9–12	1,000,000	1,000,000
Total	51,000,000	45,000,000

$51,000,000 - 45,000,000 = 6,000,000$.

21. **B.** In 1988, 8,800,000 (22% of 40,000,000) students lived in the West. From 1988–1998 this figure increased by 27%—for simplicity use 25%: an additional 2,200,000 students; so the total was then 11,000,000. The projected increase from 1998–2008 is about 10%, so the number will grow by 1,100,000 to 12,100,000.

22. **D.**

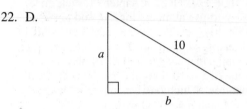

By the Pythagorean theorem,
$$a^2 + b^2 = 10^2 = 100;$$
and since the area is 20,
$$\frac{1}{2}ab = 20 \Rightarrow ab = 40.$$

Expand:
$$(a + b)^2 = a^2 + 2ab + b^2 = (a^2 + b^2) + 2ab.$$
Then
$$(a^2 + b^2) + 2ab = 100 + 2(40) = 180.$$

23. **D.** Let r, C, and A represent the radius, circumference, and area of the circle.
$$C = 2\pi r = a\pi \Rightarrow a = \frac{2\pi r}{\pi} = 2r.$$
Similarly,
$$A = \pi r^2 = b\pi \Rightarrow b = \frac{\pi r^2}{\pi} = r^2.$$
The value of Column A is $2r$, and the value of Column B is r^2. Which is greater? Dividing each by r, yields 2 in Column A and r in Column B. Since there are no restrictions, r could be greater than, less than, or equal to 2. Neither column is always greater, and the two columns are not always equal (D).
**Use TACTIC 1, Chapter 12. Let $r = 1$. Then, $C = 2\pi$ and $A = \pi$; so $a = 2$ and $b = 1$. Column B is greater: eliminate A and C. Try $r = 2$. Now, $C = 4\pi$ and $A = 4\pi$; $a = b$ and the columns are equal. Eliminate Choice B. The answer is D.

24. **C.** If r is the radius of the white circle, $2r$ is the radius of the shaded semicircle. The area of the white circle is πr^2. The area of the semicircle is $\frac{1}{2}\pi(2r)^2 = \frac{1}{2}\pi(4r^2) = 2\pi r^2$, so the area of the shaded region is $2\pi r^2 - \pi r^2 = \pi r^2$. The columns are equal (C).

**The solution is even easier if you use TACTIC 1, Chapter 12. Let the radius of the circle be 1 instead of r, and proceed as above. The area of each region is π.

25. **C.** If there are x seats on each bus, then the group is using $\frac{4}{5}(3x) = \frac{12}{5}x$ seats. After $\frac{1}{4}$ of them get off, $\frac{3}{4}$ of them, or $\frac{3}{4}\left(\frac{12}{5}x\right) = \frac{9}{5}x$ remain. What fraction of the $2x$ seats on the two buses are now being used? $\dfrac{\frac{9}{5}x}{2x} = \dfrac{\frac{9}{5}}{2} = \dfrac{9}{10}$.

**To avoid the algebra, assume there are 20 seats on each bus. At the beginning, the group is using 48 of the 60 seats on the three buses. When 12 people left, the 36 remaining people used $\dfrac{36}{40} = \dfrac{9}{10}$ of the 40 seats on two buses.

26. **E.** To find the average of three numbers, divide their sum by 3: $\dfrac{3^{30} + 3^{60} + 3^{90}}{3}$. Now use the distributive law and divide each term in the numerator by 3: $\dfrac{3^{30}}{3} + \dfrac{3^{60}}{3} + \dfrac{3^{90}}{3}$ $= 3^{29} + 3^{59} + 3^{89}$.

27. **B.** In the given figure, the diameters of the four small semicircles are 2, 4, 6, and 8, so the diameter of the large semicircle is $2 + 4 + 6 + 8 = 20$, and its radius is 10. The perimeter of the shaded region is the sum of the circumferences of all five semicircles. Since the circumference of a semicircle is π times its radius, the perimeter is $\pi + 2\pi + 3\pi + 4\pi + 10\pi = 20\pi$.

28. **A.** $a + 25\%(a) = 1.25a$, and $b - 25\%(b) = 0.75b$. So, $1.25a = .75b$, and $\dfrac{a}{b} = \dfrac{.75}{1.25} = \dfrac{3}{5}$

**If after increasing a and decreasing b the results are equal, a must be smaller than b. So, *the ratio of* a *to* b *must be less than 1.* Eliminate Choices C, D, and E. Now, either test Choices A and B or just guess. To test Choice B, pick two numbers in the ratio of 3 to 4—30 and 40, for example. Then, 30 increased by 25% is 37.5, and 40 decreased by 25% is 30. The results are not equal, so eliminate Choice B. The answer is $\dfrac{3}{5}$. (50 decreased by 25% *is* 37.5.)

Section 3—Analytical Writing

There are no "correct answers" to this section.

Answer Sheet—Model Test 3

Section 1

1. Ⓐ Ⓑ Ⓒ Ⓓ Ⓔ
2. Ⓐ Ⓑ Ⓒ Ⓓ Ⓔ
3. Ⓐ Ⓑ Ⓒ Ⓓ Ⓔ
4. Ⓐ Ⓑ Ⓒ Ⓓ Ⓔ
5. Ⓐ Ⓑ Ⓒ Ⓓ Ⓔ
6. Ⓐ Ⓑ Ⓒ Ⓓ Ⓔ
7. Ⓐ Ⓑ Ⓒ Ⓓ Ⓔ
8. Ⓐ Ⓑ Ⓒ Ⓓ Ⓔ
9. Ⓐ Ⓑ Ⓒ Ⓓ Ⓔ
10. Ⓐ Ⓑ Ⓒ Ⓓ Ⓔ

11. Ⓐ Ⓑ Ⓒ Ⓓ Ⓔ
12. Ⓐ Ⓑ Ⓒ Ⓓ Ⓔ
13. Ⓐ Ⓑ Ⓒ Ⓓ Ⓔ
14. Ⓐ Ⓑ Ⓒ Ⓓ Ⓔ
15. Ⓐ Ⓑ Ⓒ Ⓓ Ⓔ
16. Ⓐ Ⓑ Ⓒ Ⓓ Ⓔ
17. Ⓐ Ⓑ Ⓒ Ⓓ Ⓔ
18. Ⓐ Ⓑ Ⓒ Ⓓ Ⓔ
19. Ⓐ Ⓑ Ⓒ Ⓓ Ⓔ
20. Ⓐ Ⓑ Ⓒ Ⓓ Ⓔ

21. Ⓐ Ⓑ Ⓒ Ⓓ Ⓔ
22. Ⓐ Ⓑ Ⓒ Ⓓ Ⓔ
23. Ⓐ Ⓑ Ⓒ Ⓓ Ⓔ
24. Ⓐ Ⓑ Ⓒ Ⓓ Ⓔ
25. Ⓐ Ⓑ Ⓒ Ⓓ Ⓔ
26. Ⓐ Ⓑ Ⓒ Ⓓ Ⓔ
27. Ⓐ Ⓑ Ⓒ Ⓓ Ⓔ
28. Ⓐ Ⓑ Ⓒ Ⓓ Ⓔ
29. Ⓐ Ⓑ Ⓒ Ⓓ Ⓔ
30. Ⓐ Ⓑ Ⓒ Ⓓ Ⓔ

Section 2

1. Ⓐ Ⓑ Ⓒ Ⓓ Ⓔ
2. Ⓐ Ⓑ Ⓒ Ⓓ Ⓔ
3. Ⓐ Ⓑ Ⓒ Ⓓ Ⓔ
4. Ⓐ Ⓑ Ⓒ Ⓓ Ⓔ
5. Ⓐ Ⓑ Ⓒ Ⓓ Ⓔ
6. Ⓐ Ⓑ Ⓒ Ⓓ Ⓔ
7. Ⓐ Ⓑ Ⓒ Ⓓ Ⓔ
8. Ⓐ Ⓑ Ⓒ Ⓓ Ⓔ
9. Ⓐ Ⓑ Ⓒ Ⓓ Ⓔ
10. Ⓐ Ⓑ Ⓒ Ⓓ Ⓔ

11. Ⓐ Ⓑ Ⓒ Ⓓ Ⓔ
12. Ⓐ Ⓑ Ⓒ Ⓓ Ⓔ
13. Ⓐ Ⓑ Ⓒ Ⓓ Ⓔ
14. Ⓐ Ⓑ Ⓒ Ⓓ Ⓔ
15. Ⓐ Ⓑ Ⓒ Ⓓ Ⓔ
16. Ⓐ Ⓑ Ⓒ Ⓓ Ⓔ
17. Ⓐ Ⓑ Ⓒ Ⓓ Ⓔ
18. Ⓐ Ⓑ Ⓒ Ⓓ Ⓔ
19. Ⓐ Ⓑ Ⓒ Ⓓ Ⓔ
20. Ⓐ Ⓑ Ⓒ Ⓓ Ⓔ

21. Ⓐ Ⓑ Ⓒ Ⓓ Ⓔ
22. Ⓐ Ⓑ Ⓒ Ⓓ Ⓔ
23. Ⓐ Ⓑ Ⓒ Ⓓ Ⓔ
24. Ⓐ Ⓑ Ⓒ Ⓓ Ⓔ
25. Ⓐ Ⓑ Ⓒ Ⓓ Ⓔ
26. Ⓐ Ⓑ Ⓒ Ⓓ Ⓔ
27. Ⓐ Ⓑ Ⓒ Ⓓ Ⓔ
28. Ⓐ Ⓑ Ⓒ Ⓓ Ⓔ

MODEL TEST 3

SECTION 1—VERBAL ABILITY

Time—30 Minutes
30 Questions

Select the best answer to the following questions, then fill in the appropriate space on your Answer Sheet.

<u>Directions</u>: In each of the following antonym questions, a word printed in capital letters precedes five lettered words or phrases. From these five lettered words or phrases, pick the one most nearly <u>opposite</u> in meaning to the capitalized word.

---

1. PARIAH:
   (A) miser
   (B) nomad
   (C) servant
   (D) idol
   (E) renegade

2. EXACERBATE:
   (A) alleviate
   (B) bewilder
   (C) contemplate
   (D) intimidate
   (E) economize

<u>Directions</u>: Each of the following sentence completion questions contains one or two blanks. These blanks signify that a word or set of words has been left out. Below each sentence are five words or sets of words. For each blank, pick the word or set of words that <u>best</u> reflects the sentence's overall meaning.

---

3. Although he was generally considered an extremely _____ individual, his testimony at the trial revealed that he had been very _____.
   (A) intrepid...valiant
   (B) guileless...hypocritical
   (C) abstemious...temperate
   (D) meek...timorous
   (E) ingenuous...obtuse

4. The perpetual spinning of particles is much like that of a top, with one significant difference: unlike the top, the particles have no need to be wound up, for _____ is one of their _____ properties.
   (A) revolution...radical
   (B) motion...intangible
   (C) rotation...intrinsic
   (D) acceleration...lesser
   (E) collision...hypothetical

<u>Directions</u>: Each of the following analogy questions presents a related pair of words linked by a colon. Five lettered pairs of words follow the linked pair. Choose the lettered pair of words whose relationship is <u>most like</u> the relationship expressed in the original linked pair.

---

5. DEFLECT : MISSILE ::
   (A) defend : fortress
   (B) reflect : mirror
   (C) diversify : portfolio
   (D) dismantle : equipment
   (E) distract : attention

6. MULISH : PLIANCY ::
   (A) piggish : gluttony
   (B) sluggish : reluctance
   (C) kittenish : motility
   (D) apish : servility
   (E) shrewish : amiability

1   1

> Directions: Each of the following reading comprehension questions is based on the content of the following passage. Read the passage and then determine the best answer choice for each question. Base your choice on what this passage *states directly* or *implies*, not on any information you may have gained elsewhere.

How is a newborn star formed? For the answer to this question, we must look to the familiar physical concept of gravitational instability. It is a
Line simple concept, long-known to scientists, having
(5) been first recognized by Isaac Newton in the late 1600s.

Let us envision a cloud of interstellar atoms and molecules, slightly admixed with dust. This cloud of interstellar gas is static and uniform.
(10) Suddenly, something occurs to disturb the gas, causing one small area within it to condense. As this small area increases in density, becoming slightly denser than the gas around it, its gravitational field likewise increases somewhat in
(15) strength. More matter now is attracted to the area, and its gravity becomes even stronger; as a result, it starts to contract, in the process increasing in density even more. This in turn further increases its gravity, so that it accumulates still more matter
(20) and contracts further still. And so the process continues, until finally the small area of gas gives birth to a gravitationally bound object, a newborn star.

7. It can be inferred from the passage that the author views the information contained within it as

(A) controversial but irrefutable
(B) speculative and unprofitable
(C) uncomplicated and traditional
(D) original but obscure
(E) sadly lacking in elaboration

8. The author provides information that answers which of the following questions?

   I. How does the small area's increasing density affect its gravitational field?
   II. What causes the disturbance that changes the cloud from its original static state?
   III. What is the end result of the gradually increasing concentration of the small area of gas?

(A) I only
(B) II only
(C) I and II only
(D) I and III only
(E) I, II and III

Antonyms

9. CONTENTIOUS:

(A) amenable
(B) inactive
(C) dispassionate
(D) callow
(E) severe

10. DEBACLE:

(A) effort
(B) success
(C) drought
(D) transience
(E) dominance

Sentence Completion

11. Whereas off-Broadway theater over the past several seasons has clearly _____ a talent for experimentation and improvisation, one deficiency in the commercial stage of late has been its marked incapacity for _____.

(A) manifested...spontaneity
(B) lampooned...theatricality
(C) cultivated...orthodoxy
(D) disavowed...histrionics
(E) betrayed...burlesque

Analogies

12. CLOY : PALATE ::

(A) sniff : nose
(B) slit : tongue
(C) surfeit : appetite
(D) cling : touch
(E) refine : taste

13. PRATFALL : EMBARRASSMENT ::

(A) deadlock : mortification
(B) checkup : reluctance
(C) downfall : penitence
(D) diehard : grievance
(E) windfall : jubilation

1   1

Reading Comprehension

With Meredith's *The Egoist* we enter into a
critical problem that we have not yet before faced
in these studies. That is the problem offered by a
Line writer of recognizably impressive stature, whose
(5) work is informed by a muscular intelligence,
whose language has splendor, whose "view of
life" wins our respect, and yet for whom we are at
best able to feel only a passive appreciation which
amounts, practically, to indifference. We should
(10) be unjust to Meredith and to criticism if we
should, giving in to the inertia of indifference,
simply avoid dealing with him and thus avoid the
problem along with him. He does not "speak to
us," we might say; his meaning is not a "meaning
(15) for us"; he "leaves us cold." But do not the challenge and the excitement of the critical problem
as such lie in that ambivalence of attitude which
allows us to recognize the intelligence and even
the splendor of Meredith's work, while, at the
(20) same time, we experience a lack of sympathy, a
failure of any enthusiasm of response?

14. According to the passage, the work of Meredith is
noteworthy for its elements of

    (A) sensibility and artistic fervor
    (B) ambivalence and moral ambiguity   *D*
    (C) tension and sense of vitality
    (D) brilliance and linguistic grandeur
    (E) wit and whimsical frivolity.

15. All of the following can be found in the author's
discussion of Meredith EXCEPT

    (A) an indication of Meredith's customary effect
        on readers
    (B) an enumeration of the admirable qualities in
        his work
    (C) a selection of hypothetical comments at
        Meredith's expense
    (D) an analysis of the critical ramifications of
        Meredith's effect on readers
    (E) a refutation of the claim that Meredith evokes
        no sympathy

16. It can be inferred from the passage that the author
finds the prospect of appraising Meredith's work
critically to be

    (A) counterproductive
    (B) overly formidable
    (C) somewhat tolerable
    (D) markedly unpalatable
    (E) clearly invigorating

17. It can be inferred from the passage that the author
would be most likely to agree with which of the
following statements about the role of criticism?

    (A) Its prime office should be to make our enjoy-
        ment of the things that feed the mind as
        conscious as possible.
    (B) It should be a disinterested endeavor to learn
        and propagate the best that is known and
        thought in the world.
    (C) It should enable us to go beyond personal prej-
        udice to appreciate the virtues of works
        antipathetic to our own tastes.
    (D) It should dwell upon excellencies rather than
        imperfections, ignoring such deficiencies as
        irrelevant.
    (E) It should strive both to purify literature and to
        elevate the literary standards of the reading
        public.

Sentence Completion

18. Soap operas and situation comedies, though given
to distortion, are so derivative of contemporary
culture that they are inestimable _____ the
attitudes and values of our society in any particular
decade.

    (A) contraventions of
    (B) antidotes to
    (C) indices of
    (D) prerequisites for
    (E) determinants of

19. Perry's critics in the scientific world _____
that many of the observations he has made during
more than a decade of research in Costa Rica have
been reported as _____ in popular magazines
rather than as carefully documented case studies in
technical journals.

    (A) intimate...hypotheses
    (B) charge...anecdotes
    (C) applaud...rumors
    (D) claim...scholarship
    (E) apologize...fabrications

Antonyms

20. GAUCHE:

    (A) grotesque
    (B) tactful
    (C) rightful
    (D) fashionable
    (E) inane

21. HAPLESS:

    (A) fortuitous
    (B) fortunate
    (C) fortified
    (D) forbidden
    (E) forestalled

22. PROLIXITY:

    (A) proximity
    (B) disinclination
    (C) circuitousness
    (D) extremity
    (E) terseness

Analogies

23. CONTEMPORANEOUS : EVENTS ::

    (A) adjacent : objects
    (B) modern : times
    (C) temporary : measures
    (D) gradual : degrees
    (E) repetitive : steps

24. LIMERICK : POEM ::

    (A) motif : symphony
    (B) prologue : play
    (C) catch : song
    (D) sequence : sonnet
    (E) epigraph : novel

Sentence Completion

25. Slander is like counterfeit money: many people
    who would not coin it _____ it without
    qualms.

    (A) waste
    (B) denounce
    (C) circulate
    (D) withdraw
    (E) invest

Antonyms

26. DIATRIBE:

    (A) medley
    (B) dilemma
    (C) afterthought
    (D) rebuttal
    (E) praise

27. GAINSAY:

    (A) estimate
    (B) corroborate
    (C) forfeit
    (D) expend
    (E) neglect

Reading Comprehension

The Quechua world is submerged, so to speak,
in a cosmic magma that weighs heavily upon it.
It possesses the rare quality of being as it were
Line interjected into the midst of antagonistic forces,
(5) which in turn implies a whole body of social and
aesthetic structures whose innermost meaning
must be the administration of energy. This gives
rise to the social organism known as the *ayllu*, the
agrarian community that regulates the procure-
(10) ment of food. The *ayllu* formed the basic structure of the whole Inca empire.

The central idea of this organization was a
kind of closed economy, just the opposite of our
economic practices, which can be described as
(15) open. The closed economy rested on the fact that
the Inca controlled both the production and consumption of food. When one adds to this fact the
religious ideas noted in the Quechua texts cited
by the chronicler Santa Cruz Pachacuti, one
(20) comes to the conclusion that in the Andean zone
the margin of life was minimal and was made
possible only by the system of magic the Quechua
constructed through his religion. Adversities,
moreover, were numerous, for the harvest might
(25) fail at any time and bring starvation to millions.
Hence the whole purpose of the Quechua administrative and ideological system was to carry on
the arduous task of achieving *abundance* and
staving off shortages. This kind of structure pre-
(30) supposes a state of unremitting anxiety, which
could not be resolved by action. The Quechua
could not do so because his primordial response
to problems was the use of magic, that is,
recourse to the unconscious for the solution of
(35) external problems. Thus the struggle against the
world was a struggle against the dark depths of
the Quechua's own psyche, where the solution
was found. By overcoming the unconscious, the
outer world was also vanquished.
(40)   These considerations permit us to classify
Quechua culture as absolutely static or, more
accurately, as the expression of a mere state of
being. Only in this way can we understand the
refuge that it took in the germinative center of the
(45) cosmic *mandala* as revealed by Quechua art. The
Quechua empire was nothing more than a *mandala*, for it was divided into four zones, with
Cuzco in the center. Here the Quechua ensconced
himself to contemplate the decline of the world as
(50) though it were caused by an alien and
autonomous force.

1   1

28. The term "mandala" as used in the last paragraph most likely means

(A) an agrarian community
(B) a kind of superstition
(C) a closed economic pattern
(D) a philosophy or way of regarding the world
(E) a figure composed of four divisions

29. The author implies that the Quechua world was

(A) uncivilized
(B) highly introspective
(C) vitally energetic
(D) free of major worries
(E) well organized

30. With which of the following statements would the author most likely agree?

(A) Only psychological solutions can remedy economic ills.
(B) The Quechua were renowned for equanimity and unconcern.
(C) The Quechua limited themselves to realizable goals.
(D) Much of Quechua existence was harsh and frustrating.
(E) Modern Western society should adopt some Quechua economic ideas.

2   2

SECTION **2**—QUANTITATIVE ABILITY

Time—45 Minutes
28 Questions

In this section use scrap paper to solve each problem. Then decide which is the best of the choices given and fill in the corresponding oval on the Answer Sheet.

<u>Directions</u>: In the following type of question, two quantities appear, one in Column A and one in Column B. You must compare them. The correct answer to the question is

A if the quantity in Column A is greater
B if the quantity in Column B is greater
C if the two quantities are equal
D if it is impossible to determine which quantity is greater

<u>Notes</u>: Sometimes information about one or both of the quantities is centered above the two columns. If the same symbol appears in both columns, it represents the same thing each time.

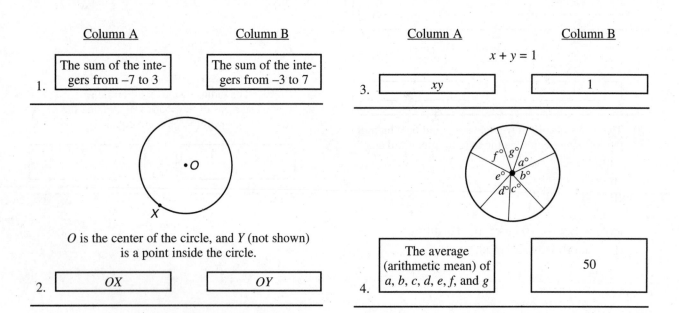

	Column A	Column B
1.	The sum of the integers from −7 to 3	The sum of the integers from −3 to 7

O is the center of the circle, and Y (not shown) is a point inside the circle.

	Column A	Column B
2.	OX	OY

Column A   Column B

$$x + y = 1$$

	Column A	Column B
3.	xy	1

	Column A	Column B
4.	The average (arithmetic mean) of $a, b, c, d, e, f,$ and g	50

<u>Directions</u>: In the following questions, choose the best answer from the five choices listed.

---

5. If 80% of the adult population of a village is registered to vote, and 60% of those registered actually voted in a particular election, what percent of the adults in the village did NOT vote in that election?

   (A) 20   (B) 40   (C) 48   (D) 50   (E) 52

6. If $\frac{3}{4}$ of a number is 7 more than $\frac{1}{6}$ of the number, what is $\frac{5}{3}$ of the number?

   (A) 12   (B) 15   (C) 18   (D) 20   (E) 24

7. An operation, ✱, is defined as follows: for any positive numbers a and b, $a ✱ b = \sqrt{a} + \sqrt{b}$. Which of the following is an integer?

   (A) 11 ✱ 5   (B) 4 ✱ 9   (C) 4 ✱ 16
   (D) 7 ✱ 4   (E) 9 ✱ 9

2   2

Column A	Column B

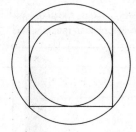

In the above figure, the small circle is inscribed in the square, which is inscribed in the large circle.

8.

The ratio of the area of the large circle to the area of the small circle	2:1

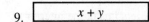

x and y are positive integers
$xy = 21$

9. | $x + y$ | 15 |

10. Two sides of a right triangle are 5 and 6. Which of the following could be the length of the third side?

   I. $\sqrt{11}$
   II. $\sqrt{31}$
   III. $\sqrt{61}$

(A) I only   (B) III only   (C) I and II only
(D) I and III only   (E) I, II, and III

Column A	Column B

$x < y$

11. | The average (arithmetic mean) of x and y | The average (arithmetic mean) of x, y, and y |

12. | The sum of the areas of two equilateral triangles whose sides are 10 | The area of one equilateral triangle whose sides are 20 |

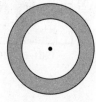

The radius of the large circle is R.
The radius of the small circle is r.
The areas of the shaded region and the white region are equal.

13. | $\dfrac{R}{r}$ | 1.5 |

2   2

Political Campaign Receipts

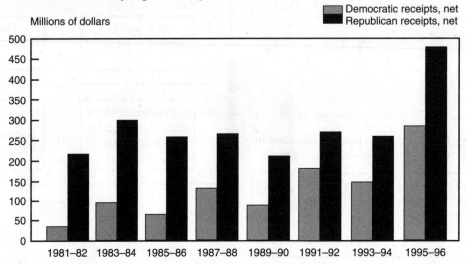

SOURCE: U.S. Bureau of the Census.

14. In which of the following pairs of years were the ratios of Republican receipts to Democratic receipts most nearly equal?

(A) 1981–82 and 1985–86
(B) 1983–84 and 1995–96
(C) 1987–88 and 1989–90
(D) 1987–88 and 1995–96
(E) 1991–92 and 1993–94

15. Between which two consecutive two-year periods was there the greatest percent increase in the Democratic receipts?

(A) 1981–82 to 1983–84
(B) 1985–86 to 1987–88
(C) 1989–90 to 1991–92
(D) 1991–92 to 1993–94
(E) 1993–94 to 1995–96

	Column A	Column B

$0 < a < 1$

16.

The area of a square whose side is a	The area of a circle whose diameter is a

The distance between Ali's house and her college is exactly 135 miles. She drove $\frac{2}{3}$ of the distance in 135 minutes.

17.

Her average speed, in miles per hour	45

18. Which of the following points lies in the interior of the circle whose radius is 10 and whose center is at the origin?

(A) (–9, 4)   (B) (5, –9)   (C) (0, –10)
(D) (10, –1)   (E) (–6, 8)

19. For any numbers a, b, and c,

$$\overset{a}{\underset{b \quad c}{\triangle}} = abc - (a + b + c).$$

For which of the following equations is it true that there is exactly one positive integer that satisfies it?

I. $\overset{a}{\underset{0 \quad a}{\triangle}} = 0$

II. $\overset{a}{\underset{a \quad a}{\triangle}} = 0$

III. $\overset{a}{\underset{2a \quad 3a}{\triangle}} = 0$

(A) none   (B) I only   (C) III only
(D) I and III only   (E) I, II, and III

2   2

Lottery Ticket Sales—Types of Game and Use of Proceeds: 1997
Type of Game

Total ticket sales: $35.5 billion

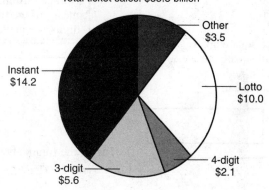

Proceeds
Total: $12.0 billion

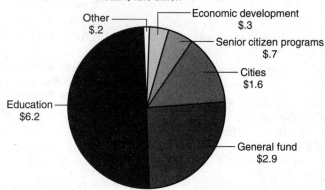

SOURCE: U.S. Bureau of the Census.

20. The revenue from lottery ticket sales is divided between prize money and the various uses shown in the graph labeled "Proceeds." In 1997, what percent of the money spent on tickets was returned to the purchasers in the form of prize money?

(A) 23.5%   (B) 50%   (C) 60%   (D) 66%
(E) 74%

21. Approximately what percent of the proceeds that went to the states' General fund would have to be given to the senior citizen programs so that the proceeds for the senior citizen programs and the Cities would be equal?

(A) 0.9%   (B) 9%   (C) 31%   (D) 48%
(E) 69%

22. If $x + y = a$, $y + z = b$, and $x + z = c$, what is the average (arithmetic mean) of x, y, and z?

(A) $\dfrac{a + b + c}{2}$ (B) $\dfrac{a + b + c}{3}$ (C) $\dfrac{a + b + c}{4}$

(D) $\dfrac{a + b + c}{6}$ (E) $a + b + c$

2   2

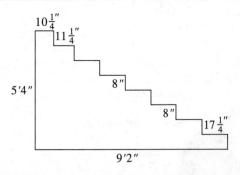

The sides of the large square are *S*.
The sides of the small square are *s*.
The areas of the shaded region and
white region are equal.

23.
$\dfrac{S}{s}$	1.5

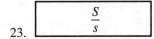

In the stair unit in the figure above, all the
angles are right angles. The left side is
5 feet 4 inches, and the bottom is 9 feet 2 inches.
Each vertical riser is 8 inches. The top step is
$10^{1}/_{4}$ inches, and each step below it is 1 inch
more than the preceding step.

24.
The perimeter in inches of the figure above	300

25.
The number of positive three-digit numbers for which the average (arithmetic mean) of the three digits is equal to 2	20

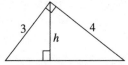

26. In the figure above, what is the value of *h*?

   (A) 2   (B) 2.2   (C) 2.4   (D) 2.6   (E) 2.8

27. Let *P* and *Q* be points which are two inches apart,
   and let *A* be the area, in square inches, of a circle
   which passes through *P* and *Q*. Which of the following is the set of all possible values for *A*?

   (A) $0 < A$ (B) $0 < A \le \pi$ (C) $A = \pi$
   (D) $A > \pi$ (E) $A \ge \pi$

28. In 1950 Roberto was four times as old as Juan. In
   1955 Roberto was three times as old as Juan. How
   old was Roberto when Juan was born?

   (A) 5   (B) 10   (C) 20   (D) 30   (E) 40

3   3

3

SECTION 3—ANALYTICAL WRITING

Time—75 Minutes
2 Writing Tasks

Task 1: Issue Exploration
45 Minutes

<u>Directions</u>: In 45 minutes, choose one of the two following topics and compose an essay on that topic. You may not write on any other topic. Write your essay on separate sheets of paper.

Each topic is presented in a one- to two-sentence quotation commenting on an issue of general concern. Your essay may support, refute, or qualify the views expressed in the quotation. Whatever you write, however, must be relevant to the issue under discussion, and you must support your viewpoint with reasons and examples derived from your studies and/or experience.

Before you choose a topic, read both topics carefully. Consider which topic would give you greater scope for writing an effective, well-argued essay.

Faculty members from various institutions will evaluate your essay, judging it on the basis of your skill in the following areas.

- Analysis of the quotation's implications
- Organization and articulation of your ideas
- Use of relevant examples and arguments to support your case
- Handling of the mechanics of standard written English

Once you have decided which topic you prefer, click on the appropriate icon (**Topic 1** or **Topic 2**) to confirm your choice. Do not be hasty confirming your choice of topic. Once you have clicked on a topic, you will not be able to switch to the alternate choice.

Topic 1

"A true university education encompasses far more than the narrow, specialized study of a single discipline. Only through exploring the broad spectrum of liberal arts courses can students become truly learned."

Topic 2

"Complete publicity makes it absolutely impossible to govern." (Kierkegaard)

3   3

Task 2: Argument Analysis
30 Minutes

Directions: In 30 minutes, prepare a critical analysis of an argument expressed in a short paragraph. You may not offer an analysis of any other argument. Write your essay on separate sheets of paper.

As you critique the argument, think about the author's underlying assumptions. Ask yourself whether any of them are questionable. Also evaluate any evidence the author brings up. Ask yourself whether it actually supports the author's conclusion.

In your analysis, you may suggest additional kinds of evidence to reinforce the author's argument. You may also suggest methods to refute the argument, or additional data that might be useful to you as you assess the soundness of the argument. *You may **not**, however, present your personal views on the topic*. Your job is to analyze the elements of an argument, not to support or contradict that argument.

Faculty members from various institutions will judge your essay, assessing it on the basis of your skill in the following areas:

- Identification and assessment of the argument's main elements
- Organization and articulation of your thoughts
- Use of relevant examples and arguments to support your case
- Handling of the mechanics of standard written English

The following passage is excerpted from a brochure promoting the sale of Cold Cone Creamery franchises in California.

Open your own Cold Cone Creamery franchise and start down the road to financial independence. Are you tired of working long hours at low pay? Join the ranks of successful business owners who have opened Cold Cone Creameries. Due to its sunny weather, California is the number-one ice cream state in the nation, with more ice cream parlors per capita than any other state. Work for yourself, set your own hours, and keep the profits, as the owner of your own successful business.

Answer Key

Section 1—Verbal Ability

1. D	6. E	11. A	16. E	21. B	26. E
2. A	7. C	12. C	17. C	22. E	27. B
3. B	8. D	13. E	18. C	23. A	28. E
4. C	9. A	14. D	19. B	24. C	29. B
5. E	10. B	15. E	20. B	25. C	30. D

Section 2—Quantitative Ability

NOTE: The letters in brackets following the Quantitative Ability answers refer to the sections of Chapter 14 in which you can find the information you need to answer the questions. For example, 1. C [E] means that the answer to question 1 is C, and that the solution requires information found in Section 14-E: Averages. Also, 20. A [13] means that the answer to question 20 is based on information in Chapter 13: Data Interpretation.

1. B [A]	6. D [B]	11. B [E]	16. A [K,L]	21. C [13]	26. C [J]
2. A [L]	7. D [A]	12. B [J,K]	17. B [H]	22. D [E,G]	27. E [L]
3. B [A]	8. C [K,L]	13. B [L]	18. A [N]	23. B [K]	28. D [H]
4. A [E,I]	9. D [A]	14. C [13]	19. C [G]	24. A [A]	
5. E [C]	10. D [J]	15. A [13]	20. D [13]	25. A [E]	

Section 3—Analytical Writing

There are no "correct answers" to this section.

Answer Explanations

Section 1—Verbal Ability

1. D. The opposite of a *pariah* or person rejected by society is an *idol* or person greatly loved by society.
Think of being "shunned as a pariah."

2. A. The opposite of to *exacerbate* (to worsen or make more harsh) is to *alleviate* or lighten.
Think of "exacerbating a quarrel."

3. B. In reputation he was a *guileless* or undeceitful person; in real life he showed himself to have been *hypocritical* or deceptive.
Note the use of *although* to signal the contrast.

4. C. Particles have no need to be wound up because the property of spinning (*rotation*) is built into their makeup: it is *intrinsic*.

5. E. By definition, a *missile* is *deflected* when it turns aside from its original direction. Likewise, someone's *attention* is *distracted* when it turns aside from its original direction.
(Definition)

6. E. Someone *mulish* (stubborn) is not characterized by *pliancy* (readiness to yield). Someone *shrewish* (ill-tempered) is not characterized by *amiability*.   (Antonym Variant)

7. C. To the author the concept is both simple and traditional, dating as it does from Newton's time.

8. D. You can answer this question by the process of elimination.
Question I is answerable on the basis of the passage. As the area's density increases, its gravitational field increases in strength. Therefore, you can eliminate Choice B.
Question II is not answerable on the basis of the passage. The passage nowhere states what disturbs the gas. Therefore, you can eliminate Choices C and E.
Question III is answerable on the basis of the passage. The end result of the process is the formation of a gravitationally bound object, a newborn star. Therefore, you can eliminate Choice A.
Only Choice D is left. It is the correct answer.

9. A. The opposite of *contentious* (quarrelsome, belligerent) is *amenable* (readily brought to yield, tractable).
Note that *contentious* derives from the verb to *contend* (to struggle or argue), not the adjective *content*.
Think of "a particularly contentious argument."

10. B. The opposite of a *debacle* (downfall; failure; collapse) is a *success*.
Think of "the Wall Street debacle of 1987."

11. A. The off-Broadway and Broadway theaters are contrasted here. The former has *manifested* or shown a talent for improvisation, extemporaneous or spontaneous performance. The latter has manifested no such talent for *spontaneity*.
Note the use of *whereas* to establish the contrast.

12. C. By definition, an excess of once-pleasing flavors *cloys* or sates the *palate* (seat of the sense of taste). An excess of once-tempting foodstuffs *surfeits* or sates the *appetite*.
(Definition)

13. E. A *pratfall* is a humiliating mishap that causes you to feel *embarrassment*. A *windfall* is an unexpected piece of good fortune that causes you to feel *jubilation*.   (Cause and Effect)

14. D. The author cites Meredith's intelligence (*brilliance*) and his splendor of language (*linguistic grandeur*).

15. E. Rather than refuting the claim, the author clearly acknowledges Meredith's inability to evoke the reader's sympathy.
Choice A is incorrect. From the start the author points out how Meredith leaves readers cold.
Choice B is incorrect. The author reiterates Meredith's virtues, citing muscular intelligence and literary merit.
Choice C is incorrect. The author quotes several such imagined criticisms.
Choice D is incorrect. The author indicates that if readers choose to avoid dealing with Meredith, they shall be doing a disservice to the cause of criticism.
Only Choice E remains. It is the correct answer.

16. E. Speaking of the "challenge and excitement of the critical problem as such," the author clearly finds the prospect of appraising Meredith critically to be stirring and *invigorating*.

17. C. The author wishes us to be able to recognize the good qualities of Meredith's work while at the same time we continue to find it personally unsympathetic. Thus, she would agree that criticism should enable us to appreciate the virtues of works we dislike.
Choices A, B, and E are unsupported by the passage.
Choice D is incorrect. While the author wishes the reader to be aware of Meredith's excellences, she does not suggest that the reader should ignore those qualities in Meredith that make his work unsympathetic. Rather, she wishes the reader to come to appreciate the very ambivalence of his critical response.

18. C. Soap operas and situation comedies are derivative of contemporary culture: they take their elements from that culture. Therefore, they serve as *indices* (signs or indications) of what is going on in that culture; they both point to and point up the social attitudes and values they portray.
Note that the soap operas and comedies here cannot be *determinants* of our society's attitudes and values: they derive from these attitudes and values; they do not determine them.

19. B. The critics *charge* (make the accusation) that Perry has published only *anecdotes* of his observations and not detailed analyses.
Note that *critics* would be unlikely to *applaud* the publication of *rumors* or *apologize* for Perry's publication of *fabrications* or lies. Thus, you can eliminate Choices C and E. Similarly, *popular magazines* would be unlikely to publish scientific *hypotheses* or examples of *scholarship*. You therefore can rule out Choices A and D as well.

20. B. The opposite of *gauche* (awkward; lacking in social grace or tact) is *tactful*.
Think of being embarrassed by "a gauche remark."

21. B. The opposite of *hapless* (unlucky) is *fortunate*.
Think of "hapless unfortunates."

22. E. The opposite of *prolixity* (wordiness) is *terseness* or brevity.
Think of "long-winded prolixity."

23. A. *Events* that are *contemporaneous* (occurring within the same time frame) exist in temporal reference to one another. *Objects* that are *adjacent* exist in spatial reference to one another.   (Defining Characteristic)

24. C. A *limerick* is a kind of *poem*. A *catch* is a kind of song.
Note how simple the relationship of the original pair of words is. Analogy questions

seldom are this easy. This should alert you to be on the lookout for something particularly deceptive among the answer choices. In this case, *catch* is used in an uncommon manner.
(Class and Member)

25. C. Whatever word you choose here must apply equally well both to slander and to counterfeit money. People who would not make up a slanderous statement *circulate* slander by passing it on. So too people who would not coin or make counterfeit money *circulate* counterfeit money by passing it on.
Note how the extended metaphor here influences the writer's choice of words.

26. E. The opposite of a *diatribe* (abusive criticism) is *praise*.
Think of "a bitter diatribe."

27. B. The opposite of to *gainsay* or contradict is to *corroborate* or support.
Beware eye-catchers. To gainsay derives from to say *against*, not from to gain.
Think of "gainsaying an assertion."

28. E. The passage compare the Quechua empire to a *mandala* because "it was divided into four parts." Thus, a *mandala* is most likely a *figure composed of four divisions.*

29. B. The author refers to the Quechua as existing in "a state of unremitting anxiety, which could not be resolved by action" and which the Quechua could only deal with by looking into himself and struggling with the depths of his own psyche. This suggests that the Quechua world was *highly introspective.*

30. D. Both the unremitting anxiety of Quechua life and the recurring harvest failures that brought starvation to millions illustrate the *harshness and frustration* of Quechua existence.

Section 2—Quantitative Ability

Two asterisks (**) indicate an alternative method of solving.

1. B. In each column, the sum includes the numbers from –3 to 3. Since all the other numbers in Column A are negative and those in Column B are positive, Column B is greater. (Note that we didn't have to calculate either sum. We just used TACTIC 5, Chapter 12 and compared the columns.)

2. A. Since Y is inside the circle it is closer to the center than X, which is on the circle. Column A is greater.

3. B. Since $x + y = 1$, at least one of the numbers is positive. If either x or y is 0, the product

$xy = 0$; and if either one is negative, then xy is negative. In each case, xy is less than 1. If both x and y are positive, then each is less than 1, and so is their product. Column B is greater.

4. A. There is not enough information provided to determine the values of a, b, c, d, e, f, and g, but they are irrelevant. Since the sum of the measures of the seven angles is 360°, their average is $360° \div 7 \approx 51.4°$. Column A is greater.

5. E. If there are x adults in the village, then $.8x$ of them are registered and $.6(.8x) = .48x$ voted. Therefore, $x - .48x = .52x$ or 52% of the adults did not vote.
**You can avoid the algebra by assuming there are 100 adults. Then 80 of them are registered and 60% of 80 = 48 of them voted.
So 52 did not vote, and $\frac{52}{100} = 52\%$.

6. D. Let the number be x, and write the equation:
$$\frac{3}{4}x = 7 + \frac{1}{6}x.$$
Multiply both sides by 12:
$$9x = 84 + 2x$$
Subtract $2x$ from each side and divide by 7:
$$7x = 84$$
$$x = 12$$
Be careful: 12 is *not* the answer. You were asked for $\frac{5}{3}$ of the number: $\frac{5}{3}(\cancel{12})^{4} = 20$.

7. D. There's nothing to do except check each choice until you find one that works. In questions such as this, it is often faster to start with E and work towards A.
E: $9 * 9 = \sqrt{9} + \sqrt{9} = \sqrt{9 + 3} = \sqrt{12}$, which is not an integer.
D: $7 * 4 = \sqrt{7} + \sqrt{4} = \sqrt{7 + 2} = \sqrt{9} = 3$, an integer.
Once you find the answer, do not waste any time trying the other choices—they won't work.

8. C. Let r and R be the radii of the two circles. From the figure, you can see that $\triangle OAB$ is a 45-45-90 right triangle, and so $R = r\sqrt{2}$ (KEY FACT J8). Therefore,

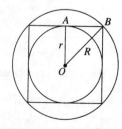

$$\frac{\text{area of large circle}}{\text{area of small circle}} = \frac{\pi R^2}{\pi r^2} = \frac{\pi \left(r\sqrt{2}\right)^2}{\pi r^2} =$$

$\dfrac{2\pi r^2}{\pi r^2} = 2$. The ratio is 2:1.

**Do exactly the same thing except use
TACTIC 2, Chapter 11. Let $r = 1$; then $R =$

$\sqrt{2}$, and the ratio is $\dfrac{\pi \left(\sqrt{2}\right)^2}{\pi (1)^2} = \dfrac{2\pi}{\pi} = 2{:}1$.

9. D.   If $x = 3$ and $y = 7$ (or vice versa), then
$x + y = 10$, and Column B is greater.
Eliminate Choices A and C. If $x = 1$ and
$y = 21$ (or vice versa), then $x + y = 22$. This
time, Column A is greater. Eliminate Choice
B. Neither column is *always* greater, and the
two columns are not *always* equal.

10. D.   Either (i) 5 and 6 are the lengths of the two
legs, or (ii) 5 is the length of a leg, and 6 is
the hypotenuse. In either case use the
Pythagorean theorem:
(i) $5^2 + 6^2 = c^2 \Rightarrow c^2 = 61 \Rightarrow c = \sqrt{61}$;
or
(ii) $a^2 + 5^2 = 6^2 \Rightarrow a^2 = 36 - 25 = 11 \Rightarrow a = \sqrt{11}$.

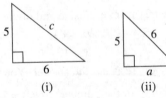

(i)   (ii)

Statements I and II only are true.

11. B.   The average of x and y is less than y, so hav-
ing another y raises the average [KEY FACT
E4]. Column B is greater.
**Use TACTIC 1, Chapter 12. Plug in numbers.
Column A: the average of 2 and 4 is 3.
Column B: the average of 2, 4, and 4 is more
than 3, because the extra 4 raises the average
(it's 3.333). The answer is B.

12. B.   If you draw a diagram, it is immediately clear
that the area of the large triangle is *more than*
twice the area of the small one. In fact, it is
4 times as great. Column B is larger.

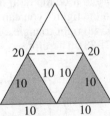

**Use the formula for the area of an equilateral
triangle of side s:

$A = \dfrac{s^2\sqrt{3}}{4}$ (KEY FACT J15).

Column A $= 2 \times \dfrac{10^2\sqrt{3}}{4} = \dfrac{200\sqrt{3}}{4}$.

Column B $= \dfrac{20^2\sqrt{3}}{4} = \dfrac{400\sqrt{3}}{4}$.

Column B is larger.

13. B.   The area of the large circle is πR^2 and the area
of the small circle is πr^2, so the area of the
shaded region is $\pi R^2 - \pi r^2 = \pi(R^2 - r^2)$. Since
the shaded region and the white region have
the same area,
$\pi(R^2 - r^2) = \pi r^2 \Rightarrow R^2 - r^2 = r^2 \Rightarrow$
$R^2 = 2r^2 \Rightarrow \dfrac{R^2}{r^2} = 2 \Rightarrow \dfrac{R}{r} = \sqrt{2}$,

which is *less* than 1.5. Column B is greater.

14. C.   For each of the pairs of years in question,
use the graph to approximate the ratio of
Republican to Democratic receipts. For example, in 1981–82, Republican receipts were
slightly over \$200 million and Democratic
receipts were about \$40 million, a ratio of 5:1.
The only two pairs of years in which the ratio
was very close were 1987–88 and 1989–90; in
both of those pairs of years the ratio was very
nearly 2:1.

15. A.   In 1981–82 the Democratic receipts were
about \$40 million and in 1983–84 they had
increased to about \$100 million, an increase of
150%. From 1991–92 to 1993–94 (Choice D),
receipts decreased. During the periods covered
by Choices B, C, and E, receipts increased,
but by less than 150%.

16. A.   Column A: the area of a square of side a is a^2.
Column B: since the diameter of the circle is
a, the radius is $\dfrac{1}{2}a$, and so the area of the
circle is $\pi\left(\dfrac{1}{2}a\right) = \dfrac{\pi}{4}a^2$, which is less than a^2,
since $\dfrac{\pi}{4} < 1$. Column A is greater.

17. B.   To find the average speed, in miles per hour,
divide the distance, in miles, by the time, in
hours. Ali drove 90 miles $\left(\dfrac{2}{3}\text{ of }135\right)$ in
2.25 hours (135 minutes = 2 hours and
15 minutes = $2\dfrac{1}{4}$ hours). $90 \div 2.25 = 40$.
Column B is greater.

18. A.   Find the distance from each point to (0,0), the
center of the circle. We're looking for a point
that is *less than* 10 units from the center.
The distance from (a,b) to (0,0) equals
$\sqrt{(a-0)^2 + (b-0)^2} = \sqrt{a^2 + b^2}$. Check each
point. A: $(-9,4)$ $\sqrt{(-9)^2 + 4^2} = \sqrt{81 + 16} =$
$\sqrt{97} < 10$ (KEY FACT N2).

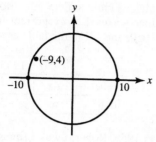

**Clearly, (0,–10) is 10 units from the origin, and so is *on* the circle. Also, since (10,0) is on the circle, (10,–1) is *outside*. The others are too close to call without knowing the formula or using the Pythagorean theorem, so if you're not sure, guess.

19. **C.** Check each choice to see which equation has *exactly one positive integer solution*.

    I. For *every* number a: $(0)(a)(-a) = 0$ and $0 + a + (-a) = 0$, so for *every* positive integer a,
    $$\triangle_{0\ -a}^{a} = 0 - 0 = 0. \text{ (I is false.)}$$

    II. $\triangle_{a\ \ a}^{a} = 0 \Rightarrow a^3 - 3a = 0 \Rightarrow a^3 = 3a.$ We're looking for *positive* solutions, so assume $a \ne 0$, and divide by a: $a^2 = 3 \Rightarrow a = \pm\sqrt{3}$. But $\sqrt{3}$ is not an integer. (II is false.)

    III. $\triangle_{2a\ 3a}^{a} = 0 \Rightarrow 6a^3 - 6a = 0 \Rightarrow 6a^3 = 6a \Rightarrow a^2 = 1.$ This equation has *one* positive integer solution, $a = 1$. (III is true.)

    Statement III only is true.

20. **D.** The difference between the total ticket sales ($35.5 billion) and the total distribution of the proceeds ($12.0 billion) was the amount returned to the purchasers of lottery tickets in the form of prize money: $35.5 billion – $12.0 billion = $23.5 billion. Divide 23.5 by 35.5 (or approximate, by dividing 24 by 36) to see that 66% of the ticket sales was allocated to prize money.

21. **C.** In order for the amount received by senior citizens programs to be the same as the amount received by the Cities, an additional $0.9 billion would have to be allocated to the senior citizens programs: $0.9 billion is approximately 31% of the $2.9 billion currently going to the General fund.

22. **D.** Whenever you have three equations, add them.

    $$\begin{aligned} x + y &= a \\ y + z &= b \\ + \quad x + z &= c \\ \hline 2x + 2y + 2z &= a + b + c \end{aligned}$$

    Divide by 2: $\quad x + y + z = \dfrac{a + b + c}{2}$

    Divide by 3: $\quad \dfrac{x + y + z}{3} = \dfrac{a + b + c}{6}$

    **Use TACTIC 2, Chapter 11: substitute for the variables. Let $x = 1$, $y = 2$, and $z = 3$. Then the average of x, y, and z is 2. When $a = 1 + 2 = 3$, $b = 2 + 3 = 5$, and $c = 1 + 3 = 4$, which of the choices equals 2? Only $\dfrac{a + b + c}{6}$.

23. **B.** The area of the large square is S^2, and the area of the small square is s^2, so the area of the shaded region is $S^2 - s^2$. Since the shaded region and the unshaded region have the same area,

    $$S^2 - s^2 = s^2 \Rightarrow S^2 = 2s^2 \Rightarrow \frac{S^2}{s^2} = 2 \Rightarrow \frac{S}{s} = \sqrt{2},$$

    which is *less* than 1.5 Column B is greater.

24. **A.** You do not need to add the lengths of the steps. Together, all the horizontal steps are equal to the bottom, and all the vertical risers are equal to the left side. The sum of the left side, 5 feet 4 inches, or 64 inches, and the bottom, 9 feet 2 inches, or 110 inches, is half the perimeter. The perimeter is $2(64 + 110) = 2(174) = 348$ inches. Column A is greater.

25. **A.** If the average of the three digits is 2, the sum of the digits is 6. The simplest thing is to list them. If there are only a few, list them all; if it seems that there will be too many to list, look for a pattern. The list starts this way: 105, 114, 123, 132, 141, 150, so there are 6 of them in the 100s. Continue: 204, 213, 222, 231, 240. There are 5 in the 200s. You can conclude, correctly, that there are 4 in the 300s, 3 in the 400s, 2 in the 500s, and 1 in the 600s. So, the total is $6 + 5 + 4 + 3 + 2 + 1 = 21$. If you don't spot the pattern, just continue the list: 303, 312, ... , 501, 510, 600.

26. **C.** Since the area of a right triangle is $\dfrac{1}{2}$ the product of its legs, the area is $\dfrac{1}{2}(3)(4) = 6$. But the area can also be calculated as $\dfrac{1}{2}bh$. Since this is a 3-4-5 triangle, the base is 5. So, $6 = \dfrac{1}{2}(5)h \Rightarrow 5h = 12 \Rightarrow h = \dfrac{12}{5}$ or 2.4.

27. **E.** If PQ is a diameter of the circle, then the radius is 1 and A, the area, is π. This is the smallest possible value of A, but A can be any number larger than π if the radius is made sufficiently large, as shown by the figures below.

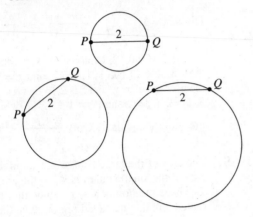

The answer is $A \geq \pi$.

28. **D.** Make a table to determine Roberto's and Juan's ages. Let x represent Juan's age in 1950, and fill in the table as shown.

	1950	1955
Roberto	$4x$	$4x + 5$
Juan	x	$x + 5$

In 1955, Roberto was 3 times as old as Juan, so

$$4x + 5 = 3(x + 5) = 3x + 15 \Rightarrow x = 10.$$

Therefore, in 1950, Juan was 10 and Roberto was 40. Because Roberto is 30 years older than Juan, Roberto was 30 when Juan was born.

Section 3—Analytical Writing

There are no "correct answers" to this section.

Answer Sheet—Model Test 4

Section 1

1. Ⓐ Ⓑ Ⓒ Ⓓ Ⓔ
2. Ⓐ Ⓑ Ⓒ Ⓓ Ⓔ
3. Ⓐ Ⓑ Ⓒ Ⓓ Ⓔ
4. Ⓐ Ⓑ Ⓒ Ⓓ Ⓔ
5. Ⓐ Ⓑ Ⓒ Ⓓ Ⓔ
6. Ⓐ Ⓑ Ⓒ Ⓓ Ⓔ
7. Ⓐ Ⓑ Ⓒ Ⓓ Ⓔ
8. Ⓐ Ⓑ Ⓒ Ⓓ Ⓔ
9. Ⓐ Ⓑ Ⓒ Ⓓ Ⓔ
10. Ⓐ Ⓑ Ⓒ Ⓓ Ⓔ

11. Ⓐ Ⓑ Ⓒ Ⓓ Ⓔ
12. Ⓐ Ⓑ Ⓒ Ⓓ Ⓔ
13. Ⓐ Ⓑ Ⓒ Ⓓ Ⓔ
14. Ⓐ Ⓑ Ⓒ Ⓓ Ⓔ
15. Ⓐ Ⓑ Ⓒ Ⓓ Ⓔ
16. Ⓐ Ⓑ Ⓒ Ⓓ Ⓔ
17. Ⓐ Ⓑ Ⓒ Ⓓ Ⓔ
18. Ⓐ Ⓑ Ⓒ Ⓓ Ⓔ
19. Ⓐ Ⓑ Ⓒ Ⓓ Ⓔ
20. Ⓐ Ⓑ Ⓒ Ⓓ Ⓔ

21. Ⓐ Ⓑ Ⓒ Ⓓ Ⓔ
22. Ⓐ Ⓑ Ⓒ Ⓓ Ⓔ
23. Ⓐ Ⓑ Ⓒ Ⓓ Ⓔ
24. Ⓐ Ⓑ Ⓒ Ⓓ Ⓔ
25. Ⓐ Ⓑ Ⓒ Ⓓ Ⓔ
26. Ⓐ Ⓑ Ⓒ Ⓓ Ⓔ
27. Ⓐ Ⓑ Ⓒ Ⓓ Ⓔ
28. Ⓐ Ⓑ Ⓒ Ⓓ Ⓔ
29. Ⓐ Ⓑ Ⓒ Ⓓ Ⓔ
30. Ⓐ Ⓑ Ⓒ Ⓓ Ⓔ

Section 2

1. Ⓐ Ⓑ Ⓒ Ⓓ Ⓔ
2. Ⓐ Ⓑ Ⓒ Ⓓ Ⓔ
3. Ⓐ Ⓑ Ⓒ Ⓓ Ⓔ
4. Ⓐ Ⓑ Ⓒ Ⓓ Ⓔ
5. Ⓐ Ⓑ Ⓒ Ⓓ Ⓔ
6. Ⓐ Ⓑ Ⓒ Ⓓ Ⓔ
7. Ⓐ Ⓑ Ⓒ Ⓓ Ⓔ
8. Ⓐ Ⓑ Ⓒ Ⓓ Ⓔ
9. Ⓐ Ⓑ Ⓒ Ⓓ Ⓔ
10. Ⓐ Ⓑ Ⓒ Ⓓ Ⓔ

11. Ⓐ Ⓑ Ⓒ Ⓓ Ⓔ
12. Ⓐ Ⓑ Ⓒ Ⓓ Ⓔ
13. Ⓐ Ⓑ Ⓒ Ⓓ Ⓔ
14. Ⓐ Ⓑ Ⓒ Ⓓ Ⓔ
15. Ⓐ Ⓑ Ⓒ Ⓓ Ⓔ
16. Ⓐ Ⓑ Ⓒ Ⓓ Ⓔ
17. Ⓐ Ⓑ Ⓒ Ⓓ Ⓔ
18. Ⓐ Ⓑ Ⓒ Ⓓ Ⓔ
19. Ⓐ Ⓑ Ⓒ Ⓓ Ⓔ
20. Ⓐ Ⓑ Ⓒ Ⓓ Ⓔ

21. Ⓐ Ⓑ Ⓒ Ⓓ Ⓔ
22. Ⓐ Ⓑ Ⓒ Ⓓ Ⓔ
23. Ⓐ Ⓑ Ⓒ Ⓓ Ⓔ
24. Ⓐ Ⓑ Ⓒ Ⓓ Ⓔ
25. Ⓐ Ⓑ Ⓒ Ⓓ Ⓔ
26. Ⓐ Ⓑ Ⓒ Ⓓ Ⓔ
27. Ⓐ Ⓑ Ⓒ Ⓓ Ⓔ
28. Ⓐ Ⓑ Ⓒ Ⓓ Ⓔ

MODEL TEST 4

SECTION 1—VERBAL ABILITY

Time—30 Minutes
30 Questions

Select the best answer to the following questions, then fill in the appropriate space on your Answer Sheet.

Directions: In each of the following antonym questions, a word printed in capital letters precedes five lettered words or phrases. From these five lettered words or phrases, pick the one most nearly opposite in meaning to the capitalized word.

1. INSIPIDNESS:

   (A) wisdom
   (B) cowardice
   (C) lividity
   (D) savoriness
   (E) tentativeness

2. SEQUESTER:

   (A) precede in sequence
   (B) permit to mingle
   (C) alter in composition
   (D) free from doubt
   (E) attempt to better

Directions: Each of the following sentence completion questions contains one or two blanks. These blanks signify that a word or set of words has been left out. Below each sentence are five words or sets of words. For each blank, pick the word or set of words that best reflects the sentence's overall meaning.

3. Book publishing has long been _____ profession, partly because, for younger editors, the best way to win a raise or a promotion was to move on to another publishing house.

   (A) an innovative
   (B) a prestigious
   (C) an itinerant
   (D) a rewarding
   (E) an insular

4. For centuries, physicists have had good reason to believe in the principle of equivalence propounded by Galileo: it has _____ many rigorous tests that _____ its accuracy to extraordinary precision.

   (A) endured...compromised
   (B) passed...presupposed
   (C) borne...postulated
   (D) survived...proved
   (E) inspired...equated

Directions: Each of the following analogy questions presents a related pair of words linked by a colon. Five lettered pairs of words follow the linked pair. Choose the lettered pair of words whose relationship is most like the relationship expressed in the original linked pair.

5. AGITATOR : FIREBRAND ::

   (A) miser : spendthrift
   (B) renegade : turncoat
   (C) anarchist : backslider
   (D) maverick : scapegoat
   (E) reprobate : hothead

6. DISPASSIONATE : PARTISANSHIP ::

   (A) enthusiastic : zealousness
   (B) disconsolate : sorrow
   (C) intemperate : moderation
   (D) volatile : immobility
   (E) ardent : involvement

<u>Directions</u>: Each of the following reading comprehension questions is based on the content of the following passage. Read the passage and then determine the best answer choice for each question. Base your choice on what this passage *states* directly or *implies,* not on any information you may have gained elsewhere.

Mary Shelley herself was the first to point to her fortuitous immersion in the literary and scientific revolutions of her day as the source of her
Line novel *Frankenstein.* Her extreme youth, as well as
(5) her sex, have contributed to the generally held opinion that she was not so much an author in her own right as a transparent medium through which passed the ideas of those around her. "All Mrs. Shelley did," writes Mario Praz, "was to provide
(10) a passive reflection of some of the wild fantasies which were living in the air about her."

Passive reflections, however, do not produce original works of literature, and *Frankenstein,* if not a great novel, was unquestionably an original
(15) one. The major Romantic and minor Gothic tradition to which it *should* have belonged was to the literature of the overreacher: the superman who breaks through normal human limitations to defy the rules of society and infringe upon the realm of
(20) God. In the Faust story, hypertrophy of the individual will is symbolized by a pact with the devil. Byron's and Balzac's heroes; the Wandering Jew; the chained and unchained Prometheus: all are overreachers, all are punished by their own
(25) excesses—by a surfeit of sensation, of experience, of knowledge and, most typically, by the doom of eternal life.

But Mary Shelley's overreacher is different. Frankenstein's exploration of the forbidden
(30) boundaries of human science does not cause the prolongation and extension of his own life, but the creation of a new one. He defies mortality not by living forever, but by giving birth.

7. The author quotes Mario Praz primarily in order to

(A) support her own perception of Mary Shelley's uniqueness
(B) illustrate recent changes in scholarly opinions of Shelley
(C) demonstrate Praz's unfamiliarity with Shelley's *Frankenstein*
(D) provide an example of the predominant critical view of Shelley
(E) contrast Praz's statement about Shelley with Shelley's own self-appraisal

8. The author of the passage concedes which of the following about Mary Shelley as an author?

(A) She was unaware of the literary and mythological traditions of the overreacher.
(B) She intentionally parodied the scientific and literary discoveries of her time.
(C) She was exposed to radical artistic and scientific concepts that influenced her work.
(D) She lacked the maturity to create a literary work of absolute originality.
(E) She was not so much an author in her own right as an imitator of the literary works of others.

9. According to the author, Frankenstein parts from the traditional figure of the overreacher in

(A) his exaggerated will
(B) his atypical purpose
(C) the excesses of his method
(D) the inevitability of his failure
(E) his defiance of the deity

Antonyms

10. FLEDGLING:

(A) experienced
(B) shy
(C) cautious
(D) pedestrian
(E) fleeting

11. EQUANIMITY:

(A) clamor
(B) disparity
(C) agitation
(D) propensity
(E) indivisibility

12. ANATHEMATIZE:

(A) appraise
(B) reciprocate
(C) patronize
(D) insinuate
(E) bless

1

1

Analogies

13. INOCULATION : IMMUNITY ::
    (A) talisman : charm
    (B) serum : antidote
    (C) exposure : weathering
    (D) indoctrination : disloyalty
    (E) invasion : fortification

14. CALLOW : MATURITY ::
    (A) incipient : fruition
    (B) eager : anxiety
    (C) youthful : senility
    (D) apathetic : disinterest
    (E) pallid : purity

Sentence Completion

15. Although he did not consider himself _____, he felt that the inconsistencies in her story _____ a certain degree of incredulity on his part.
    (A) an apostate...justified
    (B) an optimist...intimated
    (C) a hypocrite...demonstrated
    (D) a charlatan...dignified
    (E) a skeptic...warranted

16. Among contemporary writers of fiction, Virginia Woolf is _____ figure, in some ways as radical as James Joyce, in others no more modern than Jane Austen.
    (A) a doctrinaire
    (B) an introspective
    (C) a peripheral
    (D) a disinterested
    (E) an anomalous

Reading Comprehension
(This passage was written prior to 1950)

The coastlines on the two sides of the Atlantic Ocean present a notable parallelism: the eastern-most region of Brazil, in Pernambuco, has a con-
Line vexity that corresponds almost perfectly with the
(5) concavity of the African Gulf of Guinea, while the contours of the African coastline between Rio de Oro and Liberia would, by the same approximation, match those of the Caribbean Sea.

Similar correspondences are also observed in
(10) many other regions of the Earth. This observation began to awaken scientific interest about sixty years ago, when Alfred Wegener, a professor at the University of Hamburg, used it as a basis for formulating a revolutionary theory in geological

(15) science. According to Wegener, there was origi- nally only one continent or land mass, which he called Pangea. Inasmuch as continental masses are lighter than the base on which they rest, he reasoned, they must float on the substratum of
(20) igneous rock, known as sima, as ice floes float on the sea. Then why, he asked, might continents not be subject to drifting? The rotation of the globe and other forces, he thought, had caused the cracking and, finally, the breaking apart of the
(25) original Pangea, along an extensive line repre- sented today by the longitudinal submerged mountain range in the center of the Atlantic. While Africa seems to have remained static, the Americas apparently drifted toward the west until
(30) they reached their present position after more than 100 million years. Although the phenomenon seems fantastic, accustomed as we are to the con- cept of the rigidity and immobility of the conti- nents, on the basis of the distance that separates
(35) them it is possible to calculate that the continental drift would have been no greater than two inches per year.

17. The primary purpose of the passage is to
    (A) describe the relative speed of continental movement
    (B) predict the future configuration of the continents
    (C) refute a radical theory postulating continental movement
    (D) describe the reasoning behind a geological theory
    (E) explain how to calculate the continental drift per year

18. It can be inferred from the passage that evidence for continental drift has been provided by the
    (A) correspondences between coastal contours
    (B) proof of an original solitary land mass
    (C) level of sima underlying the continents
    (D) immobility of the African continent
    (E) relative heaviness of the continental masses

19. The passage presents information that would answer which of the following questions?

(A) In what ways do the coastlines of Africa and South America differ from one another?

(B) How much lighter than the substratum of igneous rock below them are the continental masses?

(C) Is the rotation of the globe affecting the stability of the present-day continental masses?

(D) According to Wegener's theory, in what direction have the Americas tended to move?

(E) How does Wegener's theory account for the apparent immobility of the African continent?

Antonyms

20. REPUDIATE:

(A) mislead
(B) minimize
(C) ascertain
(D) isolate
(E) accept

21. ALOOFNESS:

(A) exaggeration
(B) simplicity
(C) concern
(D) complacency
(E) disingenuousness

22. OBFUSCATE:

(A) insinuate
(B) exacerbate
(C) protract
(D) clarify
(E) placate

Sentence Completion

23. The epiphyte plants of the rain forest use trees for physical support but do not, like _____, sap nutrients from their hosts.

(A) fauna
(B) predators
(C) parasites
(D) insectivores
(E) stumps

24. To the embittered ex-philanthropist, all the former recipients of his charity were _____, as stingy with their thanks as they were wasteful of his largesse.

(A) louts
(B) misers
(C) ingrates
(D) prigs
(E) renegades

Analogies

25. DAMPEN : ENTHUSIASM ::

(A) moisten : throat
(B) test : commitment
(C) distract : attention
(D) reverse : direction
(E) mute : sound

26. BURST : SOUND ::

(A) ebb : tide
(B) tinder : fire
(C) blast : wind
(D) glimmer : light
(E) shard : pottery

Reading Comprehension

During the 1930s National Association for the Advancement of Colored People (NAACP) attorneys Charles H. Houston, William Hastie, James
Line M. Nabrit, Leon Ransom, and Thurgood Marshall
(5) charted a legal strategy designed to end segregation in education. They developed a series of legal cases challenging segregation in graduate and professional schools. Houston believed that the battle against segregation had to begin at the
(10) highest academic level in order to mitigate fear of race mixing that could create even greater hostility and reluctance on the part of white judges. After establishing a series of favorable legal precedents in higher education, NAACP attorneys
(15) planned to launch an all-out attack on the separate-but-equal doctrine in primary and secondary schools. The strategy proved successful. In four major United States Supreme Court decisions precedents were established that would enable the
(20) NAACP to construct a solid legal foundation upon which the *Brown* case could rest: *Missouri ex rel. Gaines* v. *Canada, Registrar of the University of Missouri* (1938); *Sipuel* v. *Board of*

Regents of the University of Oklahoma (1948);
(25) *McLaurin* v. *Oklahoma State Regents for Higher Education* (1950); and *Sweatt* v. *Painter* (1950).

In the Oklahoma case, the Supreme Court held that the plaintiff was entitled to enroll in the University. The Oklahoma Regents responded by
(30) separating black and white students in cafeterias and classrooms. The 1950 *McLaurin* decision ruled that such internal separation was unconstitutional. In the *Sweatt* ruling, delivered on the same day, the Supreme Court held that the maintenance
(35) of separate law schools for whites and blacks was unconstitutional. A year after Herman Sweatt entered the University of Texas law school, desegregation cases were filed in the states of Kansas, South Carolina, Virginia, and Delaware,
(40) and in the District of Columbia asking the courts to apply the qualitative test of the *Sweatt* case to the elementary and secondary schools and to declare the separate-but-equal doctrine invalid in the area of public education.
(45) The 1954 *Brown* v. *Board of Education* decision declared that a classification based solely on race violated the 14th Amendment to the United States Constitution. The decision reversed the 1896 *Plessy* v. *Ferguson* ruling which had estab-
(50) lished the separate-but-equal doctrine. The *Brown* decision more than any other case launched the "equalitarian revolution" in American jurisprudence and signalled the emerging primacy of equality as a guide to constitutional decisions;
(55) nevertheless, the decision did not end state-sanctioned segregation. Indeed, the second *Brown* decision, known as *Brown II* and delivered a year later, played a decisive role in limiting the effectiveness and impact of the 1954 case by providing
(60) southern states with the opportunity to delay the implementation of desegregation.

27. According to the passage, Houston aimed his legislative challenge at the graduate and professional school level on the basis of the assumption that

   (A) the greatest inequities existed at the highest academic and professional levels
   (B) the separate-but-equal doctrine applied solely to the highest academic levels
   (C) there were clear precedents for reform in existence at the graduate school level
   (D) the judiciary would feel less apprehension at desegregation on the graduate level
   (E) the consequences of desegregation would become immediately apparent at the graduate school level

28. Which of the following best describes the relationship between the *McLaurin* decision and the 1954 *Brown* v. *Board of Education* decision?

   (A) The *McLaurin* decision superseded the *Brown* decision.
   (B) The *Brown* decision provided a precedent for the *McLaurin* decision.
   (C) The *Brown* decision reversed the *McLaurin* decision.
   (D) The *McLaurin* decision limited the application of the *Brown* decision.
   (E) The *McLaurin* decision provided legal authority for the *Brown* decision.

29. Which of the following statements is most compatible with the principles embodied in *Plessy* v. *Ferguson* as described in the passage?

   (A) Internal separation of whites and blacks within a given school is unconstitutional.
   (B) Whites and blacks may be educated in separate schools so long as they offer comparable facilities.
   (C) The maintenance of separate professional schools for blacks and whites is unconstitutional.
   (D) The separate-but-equal doctrine is inapplicable to the realm of private education.
   (E) Blacks may be educated in schools with whites whenever the blacks and whites have equal institutions.

30. The aspect of Houston's work most extensively discussed in the passage is its

   (A) psychological canniness
   (B) judicial complexity
   (C) fundamental efficiency
   (D) radical intellectualism
   (E) exaggerated idealism

2   2

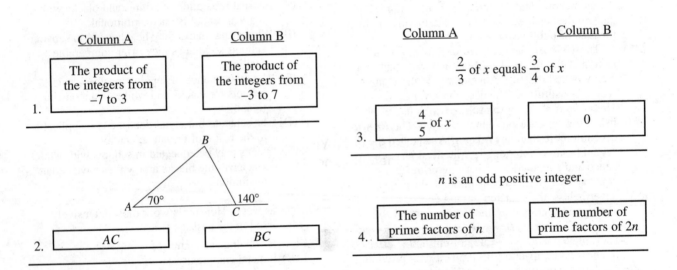

Column A

Column B

1. The product of
the integers from
−7 to 3

The product of
the integers from
−3 to 7

2. AC BC

Column A

Column B

$\frac{2}{3}$ of x equals $\frac{3}{4}$ of x

3. $\frac{4}{5}$ of x 0

n is an odd positive integer.

4. The number of
prime factors of n The number of
prime factors of $2n$

Directions: In the following questions, choose the best answer from the five choices listed.

5. Camille's average on her 6 math tests this marking
period is 75. Fortunately for Camille, her teacher
drops each student's lowest grade, and this raises
her average to 85. What was her lowest grade?

(A) 20   (B) 25   (C) 30   (D) 40   (E) 50

6. What is the surface area in square inches of a cube
whose volume is 216 cubic inches?

(A) 36   (B) 54   (C) 216   (D) 324   (E) 1296

7. Last year Leo bought two paintings. This year he
sold them for $2000 each. On one, he made a 25%
profit, and on the other he had a 25% loss. What
was his net loss or profit?

(A) He broke even.
(B) He lost less than $100.

(C) He lost more than $100.
(D) He earned less than $100.
(E) He earned more than $100.

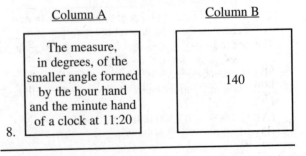

Column A

Column B

8. The measure,
in degrees, of the
smaller angle formed
by the hour hand
and the minute hand
of a clock at 11:20   140

2

2

Column A   Column B

$$x^2 - 2x - 7 = 0$$

9. | $x^2 - 7$ | | $2x$ |

10. What is the area of a circle whose radius is the diagonal of a square whose area is 4?

(A) 2π (B) $2\pi\sqrt{2}$ (C) 4π (D) 8π (E) 16π

Column A   Column B

The first term of a sequence is 1. Starting with the second term, each term is 1 less than 3 times the previous term.

11. | The smallest number greater than 100 in the sequence | | 120 |

Column A   Column B

The average (arithmetic mean) of the measures of two angles of a quadrilateral is 60°.

12. | The average of the measures of the other two angles | | 120° |

Anne drove 198 kilometers between 10:00 A.M. and 1:40 P.M.

13. | Anne's average speed, in kilometers per hour | | 55 |

Unemployed Persons 20 Years Old and Over, by Reason of Unemployment: 1997

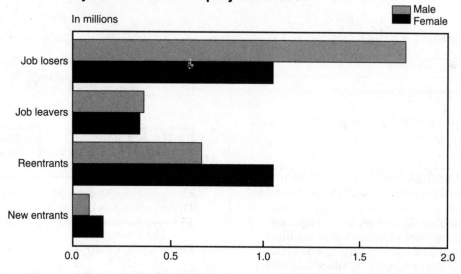

SOURCE: U.S. Bureau of the Census.

14. Of people 20 years of age or older, approximately how many more males than females were unemployed in 1997?

(A) 150,000 (B) 300,000 (C) 750,000
(D) 1,200,00 (E) 2,600,000

15. In 1997, of the unemployed males 20 years of age or older, what percent were unemployed because they had lost their jobs?

(A) 35% (B) 50% (C) 60% (D) 75%
(E) 90%

2   2

Column A   Column B

The average (arithmetic mean) amount of savings
of ten students is $60. Three of the students have
no savings at all, and each of the others has at least
$25, including John, who has exactly $130.

16.
| The largest amount, in dollars, that any one student could have | 300 |

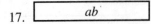
$$1 < a < b < 2$$

17.
| ab | $a + b$ |

18.
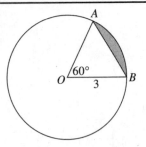

In the figure above, the radius of circle O is 3, and
m$\angle AOB = 60$. What is the perimeter of the shaded
region?

(A) $3 + \dfrac{\pi}{2}$ (B) $\sqrt{3} + \pi$ (C) $3 + \pi$

(D) $2\sqrt{3} + \pi$ (E) $6 + \pi$

19. If $m^2 = 17$, then what is the value of
$(m + 1)(m - 1)$?
(A) $\sqrt{17} - 1$ (B) $\sqrt{17} + 1$ (C) 16
(D) 18   (E) 288

Questions 20 and 21: See the diagram on the following page for information to answer the questions.

20. In the period from 1979–1989, on average, how
much longer, in years, could a 45-year old Black
man with a family income in excess of $25,000
expect to live than a 45-year old Black man with a
family income of less than $10,000?

(A) 4   (B) 6   (C) 8   (D) 10   (E) 12

21. For which of the following groups did family
income have the least significance in affecting life
expectancy?

(A) Black men at age 65
(B) Black women at age 65
(C) White men at age 45
(D) White women at age 45
(E) White women at age 65

22. At Tyler High School, there are twice as many girls
as boys on the yearbook staff. At one staff meeting,
the percentage of girls attending was twice the percentage of boys. What percent of those attending
the meeting were boys?

(A) 20   (B) 25   (C) 30   (D) 33   (E) 50

Column A   Column B

From 1970–1980 the population of Mayberry
decreased 20%.
From 1980–1990 the population of Mayberry
decreased 20%.
From 1990–2000 the population of Mayberry
decreased 20%.

23.
| The population of Mayberry in 2000 | One-half the population of Mayberry in 1970 |

The figure below consists of four circles
with the same center.
The radii of the four circles are 1, 2, 3, and 4.

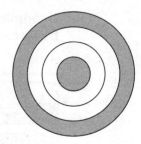

24.
| The area of the shaded region | The area of the white region |

$$30 < a < 35 < b < 40$$

25.
| The average (arithmetic mean) of a and b | 33 |

26. Paul drove m miles in h hours; Michelle drove the
same distance in $\dfrac{1}{2}$ an hour less. How fast, in

miles per hour, did Michelle drive?

(A) $\dfrac{m}{2h}$ (B) $\dfrac{2m+h}{2h}$ (C) $\dfrac{2m-h}{2h}$

(D) $\dfrac{2m}{2h+1}$ (E) $\dfrac{2m}{2h-1}$

2   2

Life expectancy among adults 45 and 65 years of age by family income, sex, and race: United States, average annual 1979–89

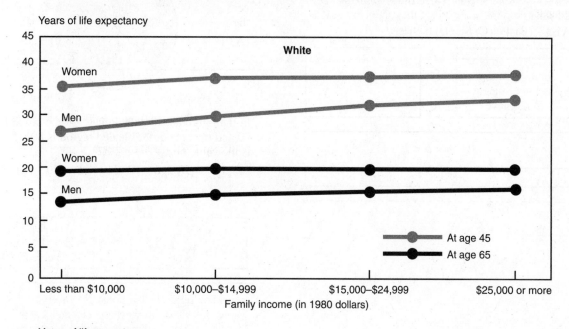

Years of life expectancy

White

Women

Men

Women

Men

At age 45
At age 65

Less than $10,000 $10,000–$14,999 $15,000–$24,999 $25,000 or more

Family income (in 1980 dollars)

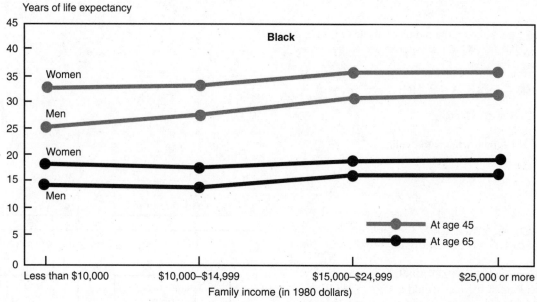

Years of life expectancy

Black

Women

Men

Women

Men

At age 45
At age 65

Less than $10,000 $10,000–$14,999 $15,000–$24,999 $25,000 or more

Family income (in 1980 dollars)

SOURCE: U.S. Bureau of the Census and National Institutes of Health.

2

2

27. A sequence of numbers begins 1, 1, 1, 2, 2, 3 and then repeats this pattern forever. What is the sum of the 135th, 136th, and 137th numbers in the sequence?

(A) 3   (B) 4   (C) 5   (D) 6   (E) 7

28.

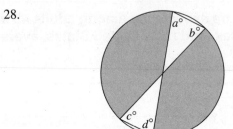

In the figure above, the diameter of the circle is 20 and the area of the shaded region is 80π. What is the value of $a + b + c + d$?

(A) 144   (B) 216   (C) 240   (D) 270   (E) 288

3

3

3

SECTION 3—ANALYTICAL WRITING

Time—75 Minutes
2 Writing Tasks

Task 1: Issue Exploration
45 Minutes

<u>Directions</u>: In 45 minutes, choose one of the two following topics and compose an essay on that topic. You may not write on any other topic. Write your essay on separate sheets of paper.

Each topic is presented in a one- to two-sentence quotation commenting on an issue of general concern. Your essay may support, refute, or qualify the views expressed in the quotation. Whatever you write, however, must be relevant to the issue under discussion, and you must support your viewpoint with reasons and examples derived from your studies and/or experience.

Before you choose a topic, read both topics carefully. Consider which topic would give you greater scope for writing an effective, well-argued essay.

Faculty members from various institutions will evaluate your essay, judging it on the basis of your skill in the following areas.

- Analysis of the quotation's implications
- Organization and articulation of your ideas
- Use of relevant examples and arguments to support your case
- Handling of the mechanics of standard written English

Once you have decided which topic you prefer, click on the appropriate icon (**Topic 1** or **Topic 2**) to confirm your choice. Do not be hasty confirming your choice of topic. Once you have clicked on a topic, you will not be able to switch to the alternate choice.

Topic 1

" 'It takes a village to raise a child.' The education of our children is the task of the community as a whole, not merely the province of teachers and local school administrators."

Topic 2

"The simple absence of data has never been enough to stop fools from inventing theories."

3

3

Task 2: Argument Analysis
30 Minutes

<u>Directions</u>: In 30 minutes, prepare a critical analysis of an argument expressed in a short paragraph. You may not offer an analysis of any other argument. Write your answer on separate sheets of paper.

As you critique the argument, think about the author's underlying assumptions. Ask yourself whether any of them are questionable. Also evaluate any evidence the author brings up. Ask yourself whether it actually supports the author's conclusion.

In your analysis, you may suggest additional kinds of evidence to reinforce the author's argument. You may also suggest methods to refute the argument, or additional data that might be useful to you as you assess the soundness of the argument. *You may **not**, however, present your personal views on the topic.* Your job is to analyze the elements of an argument, not to support or contradict that argument.

Faculty members from various institutions will judge your essay, assessing it on the basis of your skill in the following areas:

- Identification and assessment of the argument's main elements
- Organization and articulation of your thoughts
- Use of relevant examples and arguments to support your case
- Handling of the mechanics of standard written English

The following was part of an editorial in *American View*, a monthly political journal.

Welfare reform has been a success. Today, there are fewer people on the welfare rolls, and more people holding jobs, than there were before the welfare reform policies adopted under President Clinton. Former welfare recipients are better off today because they are able to support themselves. The success of maximum time limits for collecting welfare benefits demonstrates that one need not be jobless for life.

Answer Key

Section 1—Verbal Ability

1. **D**	6. **C**	11. **C**	16. **E**	21. **C**	26. **C**
2. **B**	7. **D**	12. **E**	17. **D**	22. **D**	27. **D**
3. **C**	8. **C**	13. **C**	18. **A**	23. **C**	28. **E**
4. **D**	9. **B**	14. **A**	19. **D**	24. **C**	29. **B**
5. **B**	10. **A**	15. **E**	20. **E**	25. **E**	30. **A**

Section 2—Quantitative Ability

NOTE: The letters in brackets following the Quantitative Ability answers refer to the sections of Chapter 14 in which you can find the information you need to answer the questions. For example, 1. C [E] means that the answer to question 1 is C, and that the solution requires information found in Section 14-E: Averages. Also, 20. A [13] means that the answer to question 20 is based on information in Chapter 13: Data Interpretation.

1. **C [A]**	6. **C [M]**	11. **A [A]**	16. **A [E]**	21. **E [13]**	26. **E [D]**
2. **C [J]**	7. **C [C]**	12. **C [E,K]**	17. **B [A]**	22. **A [C]**	27. **C [A]**
3. **C [G]**	8. **C [I]**	13. **B [H]**	18. **C [J,L]**	23. **A [C]**	28. **E [J,L]**
4. **B [A]**	9. **C [F]**	14. **B [13]**	19. **C [F]**	24. **C [L]**	
5. **B [E]**	10. **D [K,L]**	15. **C [13]**	20. **C [13]**	25. **D [E]**	

Section 3—Analytical Writing

There are no "correct answers" to this section.

Answer Explanations

Section 1—Verbal Ability

1. **D.** The opposite of *insipidness* or lack of flavor is *savoriness*, the quality of being flavorsome. Think of the "insipidness of overcooked boiled cabbage."

2. **B.** The opposite of to *sequester* or segregate is to *permit* to *mingle*.
   Word Parts Clue: *Se-* means apart. To *sequester* someone means to set him apart. Think of "sequestered jurors."

3. **C.** The key phrase here is "move on." If editors have to travel from firm to firm to succeed in their field, then publishing can be classified as an *itinerant* profession, a profession marked by traveling.

4. **D.** The physicists have had good reason to believe in the principle because it has *survived* rigorous or strict tests. These tests have *proved* that the principle is accurate.

Note how the second clause supports the first, explaining why the physicists have had reason to be confident in the principle.

5. **B.** *Agitator* (troublemaker) is a synonym for *firebrand. Renegade* (traitor) is a synonym for *turncoat.*   (Synonym)

6. **C.** Someone *dispassionate* or temperate in judgment is lacking in *partisanship* or bias. Someone *intemperate* or immoderate is lacking in *moderation.*   (Antonym Variant)

7. **D.** Immediately before quoting Praz, the author states that the general view of Shelley depicts her as "a transparent medium through which passed the ideas of those around her." The quotation from Praz provides an excellent example of this particular point of view.
   To answer this question correctly, you do not need to read the passage in its entirety. Quickly scroll through the passage, scanning for the name Praz; read only the context in which it appears.

8. C.   The opening sentence points out that Shelley herself acknowledged the influence of her unplanned immersion in the scientific and literary revolutions of her time. Clearly, the author of the passage concedes this as true of Shelley.

9. B.   The concluding paragraph distinguishes Frankenstein from the other overreachers in his desire not to extend his own life but to impart life to another (by creating his monster). Thus, his purpose is *atypical* of the traditional overreacher.
   To say that someone *parts from* the traditional figure of the overreacher is to say that he *differs* from it. Thus, to answer this question quickly, scan the passage looking for *overreacher* and *different* (or their synonyms).

10. A.   The opposite of *fledgling* or untried is *experienced*. The image is of a young bird just capable of leaving the nest.
   Think of "fledgling pilots trying their wings."

11. C.   The opposite of *equanimity* (emotional balance or composure) is *agitation*.
   Word Parts Clue: *Equ-* means even. *Anim-* means mind or spirit. *Equanimity* is an evenness of mind; composure.
   Think of "something shattering one's equanimity."

12. E.   The opposite of to *anathematize* or curse is to *bless*.
   Think of "anathematizing one's foes."

13. C.   *Inoculation* (introduction of a serum or vaccine into a living creature) results in *immunity*. *Exposure* to the elements results in *weathering*.   (Cause and Effect)

14. A.   Someone *callow* is immature and will not reach full development till *maturity*. Something *incipient* is beginning to become apparent and will not reach full development till *fruition*.   (Antonym Variant)

15. E.   Inconsistencies in a story would *warrant* or justify disbelief or incredulity on anyone's part, whether or not he considered himself a *skeptic* (doubter).

16. E.   If Virginia Woolf combines both radical and nonradical elements in her fictions, then she presents an *anomalous* or contradictory image.

17. D.   The author takes the reader through Wegener's reasoning step by step, describing what led Wegener to reach his conclusions.

18. A.   Since the existence of the correspondences between the various coastal contours was used by Wegener as a basis for formulating his theory of continental drift, it can be inferred that the correspondences provide evidence for the theory.
   Choice B is incorrect. The passage does not indicate that Pangea's existence has been proved.
   Choice C is incorrect. It is the relative heaviness of sima, not the level or depth of sima, that suggested the possibility of the lighter continents drifting.
   Choice D is incorrect. Mobility rather than immobility would provide evidence for continental drift.
   Choice E is incorrect. The continents are lighter than the underlying sima.

19. D.   Choice D is answerable on the basis of the passage. The next-to-the-last sentence of the second paragraph states that the Americas "apparently drifted toward the west."

20. E.   The opposite of to *repudiate* (disown; refuse to acknowledge) is to *accept*.
   Think of "repudiating a debt."

21. C.   The opposite of *aloofness* (remoteness, indifference) is *concern*.
   Think of "haughty aloofness."

22. D.   The opposite of to *obfuscate* or confuse is to *clarify*.
   Word Parts Clue: *Ob-* means completely; *fusc-* means dark; *-ate* means to make. To *obfuscate* is to becloud or make completely dark.
   Think of "obfuscating the issue."

23. C.   By definition, *parasites* sap or drain nutrients from their hosts.

24. C.   The embittered benefactor thinks of them as *ingrates* (ungrateful persons) because they do not thank him sufficiently for his generosity. He does not think of them as *misers* (hoarders of wealth): although they are stingy in expressing thanks, they are extravagant in spending money. He certainly does not think of them as *louts* (clumsy oafs), *prigs* (self-righteous fussbudgets), or *renegades* (traitors): the specific attribute he resents in them is ingratitude, not cloddishness, self-satisfaction, or perfidy.

25. E.   To *dampen enthusiasm* is to diminish it. To *mute* (muffle) *sound* is to diminish it.
   Note that Choice C is incorrect: to *distract attention* is not to diminish it but to divert it in a new direction.   (Defining Characteristic)

26. **C.** A *burst* is a sudden violent outbreak of *sound*. A *blast* is a sudden violent outbreak (heavy gust) of *wind*.

    Beware eye-catchers. Choice D is incorrect. A *glimmer* is a feeble or intermittent *light*, not a sudden violent flare or blast of light.

    (Degree of Intensity)

27. **D.** Houston believed that the battle had to begin at the graduate level "to mitigate fear" (relieve *apprehension*) of race mixing and miscegenation that might otherwise have caused the judges to rule against the NAACP-sponsored complaints.

28. **E.** The 1950 *McLaurin* decision was one of the decisions that provided legal precedents for the 1954 *Brown* decision.

    Choice A is incorrect. *McLaurin* preceded *Brown I*. Therefore, it could not have superseded a decision that had yet to be made.

    Choice B is incorrect. *Brown I* followed *McLaurin*. Therefore, it could not have set a precedent for *McLaurin*.

    Choice C is incorrect. *Brown I* reversed *Plessy* v. *Ferguson*. It built on *McLaurin*.

    Choice D is incorrect. *McLaurin* preceded *Brown I*. Therefore, it could not have limited the application of a decision that had yet to be made.

29. **B.** The separate-but-equal doctrine established by *Plessy* v. *Ferguson* allows the existence of racially-segregated schools.

30. **A.** In assessing the possible effects on judges of race mixing in the lower grades, Houston was *psychologically canny*, shrewd in seeing potential dangers and in figuring strategies to avoid these dangers.

Section 2—Quantitative Ability

Two asterisks (**) indicate an alternative method of solving.

1. **C.** Each column is the product of 11 integers, one of which is 0. Since 0 times any number is 0, each column is 0. The columns are equal (C).

2. **C.** Since by KEY FACT J2 the measure of an exterior angle of a triangle is equal to the sum of the measures of the two opposite interior angles,

    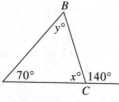

    $140 = 70 + y$, and so $y = 70$. Therefore, angles A and B are equal, and by KEY FACT J3 so are the sides opposite them: $AC = BC$. The columns are equal (C).

    **If you don't know the theorem about the exterior angle, first find x: $x + 140 = 180 \Rightarrow$

$x = 40$. Then, since the sum of the measures of the three angles of a triangle is 180, $y = 70$.

3. **C.** If $a \ne b$ and $ax = bx$, then x must be 0.
   So $\frac{2}{3}x = \frac{3}{4}x \Rightarrow x = 0 \Rightarrow \frac{4}{5}x = 0.$

4. **B.** Every factor of n is a factor of $2n$, but 2 is a prime factor of $2n$, which is not a factor of n (since n is odd). So, $2n$ has more prime factors than n. Column B is greater.

5. **B.** On six tests combined, Camille earned a total of $6 \times 75 = 450$ points [TACTIC E1]. The total of her five best grades is $5 \times 85 = 425$ points, so her lowest grade was $450 - 425 = 25$.

   **Assume that Camille's five best grades were each 85. Then each one has a deviation of 10 points above the average of 75, and the total deviation above 75 is $5 \times 10 = 50$ points. Therefore, her one bad grade must have been 50 points below 75.

6. **C.** Since the volume of the cube is 216 cubic inches, we have $e^3 = 216 \Rightarrow e = 6$. The area of each face is $e^2 = 36$ square inches, and since there are six faces, the total surface area is $6 \times 36 = 216$ square inches.

7. **C.** On the first painting, Leo made a 25% profit, so if he bought it for x, he sold it for
$$x + .25x = 1.25x = 2000 \Rightarrow$$
$$x = 2000 \div 1.25 = 1600.$$
   His profit was $400. On the second painting, Leo lost 25%, so if he bought it for y, he sold it for
$$y - .25y = .75y = 2000 \Rightarrow$$
$$y = 2000 \div .75 = 2666.67.$$
   His loss was $666.67. In all, he *lost* $266.67, which is *more than* $100.

   **In these types of problems you *never* break even. Eliminate A. When you make a profit, your purchase price is less than your selling price, and when you incur a loss, your purchase price is greater than your selling price. So the first painting cost less than $2000 and the second cost more than $2000. So Leo earned 25% of a small amount and lost 25% of a large amount. He surely lost money. Eliminate D and E. If you can't solve as above, guess between B and C.

8. **C.** Draw a diagram.

   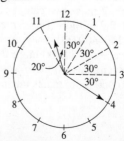

The minute hand, of course, is pointing right at 4. The hour hand, however, is *not* pointing at 11. It was pointing at 11 at 11:00, 20 minutes, or $\frac{1}{3}$ hour, ago. The hour hand is now one-third of the way between 11 and 12, so there are 20 degrees between the hour hand and 12 and another 120 degrees to 4, a total of 140 degrees. The columns are equal (C).

9. **C.**   This one is easier than it looks. Don't try to factor. Don't solve. Just add $2x$ to both sides of the given equation to get that $x^2 - 7 = x$. The columns are equal (C).

10. **D.**   If the area of the square is 4, each side is 2, and the length of a diagonal is $2\sqrt{2}$. The area of a circle whose radius is $2\sqrt{2}$ is $\pi(2\sqrt{2})^2 = 8\pi$.

11. **A.**   Write out the first few terms being careful to follow the directions. The first term is 1. The second term is 1 less than 3 times the first term: $3(1) - 1 = 2$. The third term is 1 less than 3 times the second term: $3(2) - 1 = 5$. Continue: $3(5) - 1 = 14$; $3(14) - 1 = 41$; $3(41) - 1 = 122$. The smallest number greater than 100 is 122. Column A is greater.

12. **C.**   The sum of the measures of the four angles in any quadrilateral is 360° [KEY FACT K1]. If the average of two of them is 60°, then their sum is 120° [TACTIC E1], leaving 240° for the other two angles, so their average is 120°. The columns are equal (C).

13. **B.**   To find Anne's average speed, in kilometers per hour, we must divide the distance she went, in kilometers (198), by the time it took, in hours. Anne drove for 3 hours and 40 minutes, which is $3\frac{2}{3}$ hours. So her average speed was

$$198 \div 3\frac{2}{3} = 198 \div \frac{11}{3} = 198 \times \frac{3}{11} = 54.$$

Column B is greater.

14. **B.**   The difference between the number of male and female job leavers was insignificant, so ignore them. Among the males, there were about 1.8 million job losers and 0.7 million reentrants, a total of 2.5 million. Among the females, there were about 1.05–1.1 million in each of those two categories, a total of 2.1–2.2 million. This represents a difference of 300–400,000—say, 350,000. Finally, there were about 50,000 more female than male new entrants, so there were approximately 300,000 more males unemployed than

females. Note that your figures might be slightly different, but the answer choices are so far apart, that you should definitely choose B.

15. **C.**   Adding up the number of males in each category, we see that there were appoximately 3 million unemployed males of whom 1.8 million were job losers, which is 60%.

16. **A.**   Since the average savings of the 10 students is $60, the total amount they have saved is $600 [TACTIC E1]. John has $130 and 3 students have none at all. If 5 other students have a total of $125 ($25 each, the least possible), then the tenth student will have $600 – $130 – $125 = $345. Column A is greater.

17. **B.**   Column A: since $b < 2$, $ab < 2a$.
Column B: since $b > a$, $b + a > a + a = 2a$.
Column B is greater.
**Use TACTIC 1, Chapter 12. Plug in numbers that satisfy the condition.
Column A: $(1.1)(1.8) = 1.98$.
Column B: $1.1 + 1.8 = 2.9$.
This time, Column B is greater. Eliminate Choices A and C, and try other numbers. Each time Column B will be greater. Choose B.

18. **C.**   Since each radius is 3, $OA = OB$, and by KEY FACT J3 m$\angle A$ = m$\angle B$.

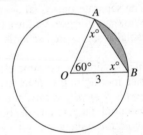

Then, $60 + x + x = 180 \Rightarrow x = 60$. Therefore $\triangle AOB$ is equilateral, and $AB = 3$. The length of arc AB is $\frac{60}{360} = \frac{1}{6}$ of the circumference. $C = 2\pi(3) = 6\pi$, so the length of arc $AB = \pi$. The perimeter of the region, then, is $3 + \pi$.
**Use TACTIC 2, Chapter 10: trust the diagram. AB looks about the same as OB, so assume it is 3, and arc AB is clearly slightly bigger. Hence, the perimeter is a little more than 6. Choices A and B are both less than 5, which is definitely too small. Between C and D *guess*. C, $3 + \pi$, is the better guess, because AB *might be* exactly 3.

19. **C.** $(m + 1)(m - 1) = m^2 - 1 = 17 - 1 = 16$.
**Since $m^2 = 17$, m is slightly more than 4, and $(m + 1)(m - 1)$ is the product of a number a little greater than 5 and a number a little greater than 3. The only reasonable choice is 16.

20. C. From the lower graph, we can see that the life expectancy at age 45 for Black men with family incomes below $10,000 was 25, whereas for those whose family income was $25,000 or more, their life expectancy was 33 years: a difference of 8 years.

21. E. The line segments constituting the graph of life expectancy for White women at age 65 are virtually horizontal. At all incomes, these women have a life expectancy of about 20 years. For none of the other categories does family income have as small an impact on life expectancy.

22. A. Even if you can do the algebra, this type of problem is easier if you use TACTIC 2, Chapter 11. Find some easy-to-use numbers. Assume that there are 100 girls and 50 boys on staff and that 20% of the girls and 10% of the boys attended the meeting. Then, 20 girls and 5 boys were there, and 5 is 20% of 25, the total number attending.
**Of course, you *can* do this algebraically. If x represents the number of boys on staff, then $2x$ is the number of girls. If y% of the boys attended the meeting, then $2y$% of the girls did. So, the number of boys attending was $x\left(\dfrac{y}{100}\right) = \dfrac{xy}{100}$, whereas the number of girls attending was $2x\left(\dfrac{2y}{100}\right) = \dfrac{4xy}{100}$. Therefore, there were 4 times as many girls in attendance as boys: $\dfrac{4}{5}$ of those at the meeting were girls and $\dfrac{1}{5}$ or 20% were boys.

23. A. Note that, when a number is decreased by 20%, what remains is 80% of the original: 80% of 80% of 80% = .8 × .8 × .8 = .512 = 51.2%, which is greater than 50%. Column A is greater.
** Use TACTIC 2, Chapter 12. *Assume* that in 1970 the population of Mayberry was 100. Then, in 1980 it was 80, in 1990 it was 64 (80% of 80), and in 2000 it was 51.2, which is greater than 50, one-half of the 1970 population.

24. C. Since the entire region is a circle of radius 4, its area is $\pi(4)^2 = 16\pi$. The white region is a circle of radius 3 minus the small shaded circle of radius 1, so its area is $9\pi - \pi = 8\pi$. Thus, the area of the white region is one-half of the total area, and the area of the shaded region is the other half. The columns are equal (C).

25. D. Use TACTIC 4, Chapter 12. Could the average of a and b equal 33? Only if the sum of a and b were 66. Is that possible? Yes, if $a = 30.5$ and $b = 35.5$. Must $a + b = 66$? Of course not. Neither column is *always* greater, and the two columns are not *always* equal (D).

26. E. Michelle drove m miles in $h - \dfrac{1}{2}$ hours. Since $r = \dfrac{d}{t}$, to find her rate, we divide the distance, m, by the time, $\left(h - \dfrac{1}{2}\right)$:

$$\frac{m}{h - \dfrac{1}{2}} = \frac{2m}{2h - 1}$$

**Use TACTIC 2, Chapter 11. If Paul drove 20 miles in 2 hours, Michelle drove 20 miles in $1\dfrac{1}{2} = \dfrac{3}{2}$ hours. So Michelle drove at $20 \div \dfrac{3}{2} = 20 \times \dfrac{2}{3} = \dfrac{40}{3}$ miles per hour.

Only $\dfrac{2m}{2h-1} = \dfrac{40}{3}$ when $m = 20$ and $h = 2$.

27. C. Since the pattern has six digits, divide 135 by 6. The quotient is 22 and the remainder is 3. Since 22 × 6 = 132, the 132nd number completes the pattern for the 22nd time. So the 133rd, 134th, and 135th numbers are 1s, and the 136th and 137th are 2s; and their sum is 1 + 2 + 2 = 5.

28. E. Since the diameter of the circle is 20, the radius is 10 and the area is 100π. Since the area of the shaded region is 80π, it is $\dfrac{80}{100} = \dfrac{4}{5}$ of the circle, and the white area is $\dfrac{1}{5}$ of the circle. So the sum of the measures of the two white central angles is $\dfrac{1}{5}$ of 360°, or 72°. The sum of the measures of all six angles in the triangles is 360°, so $a + b + c + d = 360 - 72 = 288$.

Section 3—Analytical Writing

There are no "correct answers" to this section.

Answer Sheet—Model Test 5

Section 1

1. Ⓐ Ⓑ Ⓒ Ⓓ Ⓔ
2. Ⓐ Ⓑ Ⓒ Ⓓ Ⓔ
3. Ⓐ Ⓑ Ⓒ Ⓓ Ⓔ
4. Ⓐ Ⓑ Ⓒ Ⓓ Ⓔ
5. Ⓐ Ⓑ Ⓒ Ⓓ Ⓔ
6. Ⓐ Ⓑ Ⓒ Ⓓ Ⓔ
7. Ⓐ Ⓑ Ⓒ Ⓓ Ⓔ
8. Ⓐ Ⓑ Ⓒ Ⓓ Ⓔ
9. Ⓐ Ⓑ Ⓒ Ⓓ Ⓔ
10. Ⓐ Ⓑ Ⓒ Ⓓ Ⓔ

11. Ⓐ Ⓑ Ⓒ Ⓓ Ⓔ
12. Ⓐ Ⓑ Ⓒ Ⓓ Ⓔ
13. Ⓐ Ⓑ Ⓒ Ⓓ Ⓔ
14. Ⓐ Ⓑ Ⓒ Ⓓ Ⓔ
15. Ⓐ Ⓑ Ⓒ Ⓓ Ⓔ
16. Ⓐ Ⓑ Ⓒ Ⓓ Ⓔ
17. Ⓐ Ⓑ Ⓒ Ⓓ Ⓔ
18. Ⓐ Ⓑ Ⓒ Ⓓ Ⓔ
19. Ⓐ Ⓑ Ⓒ Ⓓ Ⓔ
20. Ⓐ Ⓑ Ⓒ Ⓓ Ⓔ

21. Ⓐ Ⓑ Ⓒ Ⓓ Ⓔ
22. Ⓐ Ⓑ Ⓒ Ⓓ Ⓔ
23. Ⓐ Ⓑ Ⓒ Ⓓ Ⓔ
24. Ⓐ Ⓑ Ⓒ Ⓓ Ⓔ
25. Ⓐ Ⓑ Ⓒ Ⓓ Ⓔ
26. Ⓐ Ⓑ Ⓒ Ⓓ Ⓔ
27. Ⓐ Ⓑ Ⓒ Ⓓ Ⓔ
28. Ⓐ Ⓑ Ⓒ Ⓓ Ⓔ
29. Ⓐ Ⓑ Ⓒ Ⓓ Ⓔ
30. Ⓐ Ⓑ Ⓒ Ⓓ Ⓔ

Section 2

1. Ⓐ Ⓑ Ⓒ Ⓓ Ⓔ
2. Ⓐ Ⓑ Ⓒ Ⓓ Ⓔ
3. Ⓐ Ⓑ Ⓒ Ⓓ Ⓔ
4. Ⓐ Ⓑ Ⓒ Ⓓ Ⓔ
5. Ⓐ Ⓑ Ⓒ Ⓓ Ⓔ
6. Ⓐ Ⓑ Ⓒ Ⓓ Ⓔ
7. Ⓐ Ⓑ Ⓒ Ⓓ Ⓔ
8. Ⓐ Ⓑ Ⓒ Ⓓ Ⓔ
9. Ⓐ Ⓑ Ⓒ Ⓓ Ⓔ
10. Ⓐ Ⓑ Ⓒ Ⓓ Ⓔ

11. Ⓐ Ⓑ Ⓒ Ⓓ Ⓔ
12. Ⓐ Ⓑ Ⓒ Ⓓ Ⓔ
13. Ⓐ Ⓑ Ⓒ Ⓓ Ⓔ
14. Ⓐ Ⓑ Ⓒ Ⓓ Ⓔ
15. Ⓐ Ⓑ Ⓒ Ⓓ Ⓔ
16. Ⓐ Ⓑ Ⓒ Ⓓ Ⓔ
17. Ⓐ Ⓑ Ⓒ Ⓓ Ⓔ
18. Ⓐ Ⓑ Ⓒ Ⓓ Ⓔ
19. Ⓐ Ⓑ Ⓒ Ⓓ Ⓔ
20. Ⓐ Ⓑ Ⓒ Ⓓ Ⓔ

21. Ⓐ Ⓑ Ⓒ Ⓓ Ⓔ
22. Ⓐ Ⓑ Ⓒ Ⓓ Ⓔ
23. Ⓐ Ⓑ Ⓒ Ⓓ Ⓔ
24. Ⓐ Ⓑ Ⓒ Ⓓ Ⓔ
25. Ⓐ Ⓑ Ⓒ Ⓓ Ⓔ
26. Ⓐ Ⓑ Ⓒ Ⓓ Ⓔ
27. Ⓐ Ⓑ Ⓒ Ⓓ Ⓔ
28. Ⓐ Ⓑ Ⓒ Ⓓ Ⓔ

MODEL TEST 5

SECTION 1—VERBAL ABILITY

Time—30 Minutes
30 Questions

Select the best answer to the following questions, then fill in the appropriate space on your Answer Sheet.

Directions: In each of the following antonym questions, a word printed in capital letters precedes five lettered words or phrases. From these five lettered words or phrases, pick the one most nearly opposite in meaning to the capitalized word.

---

1. PANDEMONIUM:
   (A) amusement
   (B) indolence
   (C) deceleration
   (D) tranquillity
   (E) tolerance

2. ENERVATE:
   (A) aggravate
   (B) stimulate
   (C) edify
   (D) applaud
   (E) disregard

Directions: Each of the following sentence completion questions contains one or two blanks. These blanks signify that a word or set of words has been left out. Below each sentence are five words or sets of words. For each blank, pick the word or set of words that best reflects the sentence's overall meaning.

---

3. Surprisingly to those who view the ocean floor as a uniformly _____ waste, each vent in the floor, where seawater is heated by the earth's interior magma, has been found to be an island-like _____ with its own distinctive fauna.
   (A) teeming...habitat
   (B) lifeless...enclave
   (C) barren...oasis
   (D) sunken...grotto
   (E) hazardous...environment

4. Rather than allowing these dramatic exchanges between her characters to develop fully, Ms. Norman unfortunately tends to _____ the discussions involving the two women.
   (A) exacerbate
   (B) protract
   (C) augment
   (D) truncate
   (E) elaborate

Directions: Each of the following analogy questions presents a related pair of words linked by a colon. Five lettered pairs of words follow the linked pair. Choose the lettered pair of words whose relationship is most like the relationship expressed in the original linked pair.

---

5. GLINT : LIGHT ::
   (A) blare : sound
   (B) whiff : scent
   (C) shade : color
   (D) glut : food
   (E) wave : tide

6. DOGGEREL : POET ::
   (A) symphony : composer
   (B) easel : painter
   (C) caption : cartoonist
   (D) soliloquy : playwright
   (E) potboiler : novelist

1   1

Directions: Each of the following reading comprehension questions is based on the content of the following passage. Read the passage and then determine the best answer choice for each question. Base your choice on what this passage *states directly* or *implies*, not on any information you may have gained elsewhere.

Unlike the carefully weighted and planned compositions of Dante, Goethe's writings have always the sense of immediacy and enthusiasm.
Line He was a constant experimenter with life, with
(5) ideas, and with forms of writing. For the same reason, his works seldom have the qualities of finish or formal beauty which distinguish the masterpieces of Dante and Virgil. He came to love the beauties of classicism but these were
(10) never an essential part of his make-up. Instead, the urgency of the moment, the spirit of the thing, guided his pen. As a result, nearly all his works have serious flaws of structure, of inconsistencies, of excesses and redundancies and extraneities.
(15)   In the large sense, Goethe represents the fullest development of the romanticist. It has been argued that he should not be so designated because he so clearly matured and outgrew the kind of romanticism exhibited by Wordsworth,
(20) Shelley, and Keats. Shelley and Keats died young; Wordsworth lived narrowly and abandoned his early attitudes. In contrast, Goethe lived abundantly and developed his faith in the spirit, his understanding of nature and human nature,
(25) and his reliance on feelings as man's essential motivating force. The result was an all-encompassing vision of reality and a philosophy of life broader and deeper than the partial visions and attitudes of other romanticists. Yet the spirit
(30) of youthfulness, the impatience with close reasoning or "logic-chopping," and the continued faith in nature remained his to the end, together with an occasional waywardness and impulsiveness and a disregard of artistic or logical propriety
(35) which savor strongly of romantic individualism. Since so many twentieth-century thoughts and attitudes are similarly based on the stimulus of the Romantic Movement, Goethe stands as particularly the poet of modern times as Dante stood for
(40) medieval times and as Shakespeare for the Renaissance.

7. A characteristic of romanticism NOT mentioned in this passage is its

(A) elevation of nature
(B) preference for spontaneity
(C) modernity of ideas
(D) unconcern for artistic decorum
(E) simplicity of language

8. It can be inferred from the passage that classicism has which of the following characteristics?

I. Sensitivity toward emotional promptings
II. Emphasis on formal aesthetic criteria
III. Meticulous planning of artistic works

(A) II only
(B) III only
(C) I and II
(D) II and III
(E) I, II, and III

9. The author's attitude toward Goethe's writings is best described as

(A) unqualified endorsement
(B) lofty indifference
(C) reluctant tolerance
(D) measured admiration
(E) undisguised contempt

Antonyms

10. NEBULOUS:

(A) hypothetical
(B) querulous
(C) lamentable
(D) piquant
(E) distinct

11. DECORUM:

(A) lucidity
(B) flexibility
(C) impropriety
(D) duplicity
(E) severity

12. DENIGRATE:

(A) emancipate
(B) examine
(C) desecrate
(D) mollify
(E) extol

1   1

Sentence Completion

13. Neutron stars are believed to be the highly com-
    pressed remnants of exploding stars (supernovas)
    and thus _____ of one of the most
    _____ processes in nature.

    (A) causes...cataclysmic
    (B) products...violent
    (C) examples...equivocal
    (D) justifications...harsh
    (E) precursors...dynamic

14. The shortcomings of Mr. Brooks' analysis are
    _____ his _____ in explaining finan-
    cial complexity and the sheer importance of his
    text.

    (A) alleviated by...ineptitude
    (B) offset by...clarity
    (C) magnified by...precision
    (D) demonstrated by...adroitness
    (E) mitigated by...incompetence

Analogies

15. ERUDITE : SCHOLAR ::

    (A) remote : hermit
    (B) pliant : beggar
    (C) meandering : traveler
    (D) mendacious : liar
    (E) vindictive : conqueror

16. FERAL : DOMESTICATION ::

    (A) arable : cultivation
    (B) viral : infection
    (C) crude : refinement
    (D) frugal : economy
    (E) pliable : molding

Reading Comprehension

Given the context of social change in the early
1960s, Negro history was now the object of
unprecedented attention among wide segments of
Line the American population, black and white. In
(5) academe nothing demonstrated this growing
legitimacy of black history better than the way in
which certain scholars of both races, who had
previously been ambivalent about being identified
as specialists in the field, now reversed
(10) themselves.
Thus Frenise Logan, returning to an academic
career, decided to attempt to publish his doctoral
dissertation on blacks in late nineteenth-century
North Carolina. A 1960 award encouraged him to
(15) do further research, and his expanded *The Negro*

in North Carolina, 1876–1894 appeared in 1964.
It is true that as late as 1963 a white professor
advised John W. Blassingame to avoid black history if he wanted to have "a future in the histori-
(20) cal profession." Yet more indicative of how
things were going was that 1964–65 marked a
turning point for two of Kenneth Stampp's former
students—Nathan Huggins and Leon Litwack.
The changing intellectual milieu seems to have
(25) permitted Huggins, whose original intention of
specializing in African and Afro-American history had been overruled by practical concerns, to
move into what became his long-range commitment to the field. By 1965 when his interest in
(30) intellectual history found expression in the idea of
doing a book on the Harlem Renaissance, the factors that earlier would have discouraged him from
such a study had dissipated. For Litwack the
return to Negro history was an especially vivid
(35) experience, and he recalls the day he spoke at the
University of Rochester, lecturing on Jacksonian
democracy. Some students in the audience, sens-
ing that his heart was just not in that topic, urged
him to undertake research once again in the field
(40) to which he had already contributed so significantly. He settled on the study that became *Been
in the Storm So Long* (1979). In short, both
Huggins and Litwack now felt able to dismiss the
professional considerations that had loomed so
(45) large in their earlier decision to work in other spe-
cialties and to identify themselves with what had
hitherto been a marginal field of inquiry.

17. The author cites Logan, Huggins, and Litwack for
    their

    (A) work on curriculum reform in the public
        schools
    (B) participation in the Freedom Summer in
        Mississippi
    (C) return to the field of Afro-American history
    (D) research on blacks in nineteenth-century North
        Carolina
    (E) identification with nonviolent direct action

18. The passage suggests that Bennett's work was similar to Logan's work in which of the following ways?

I. Both Bennett's and Logan's books recorded a then relatively unfamiliar aspect of Afro-American history.
II. Both Bennett's and Logan's work were designed to appeal to a primarily academic audience.
III. Both Bennett's and Logan's work were published in a variety of formats.

(A) I only
(B) III only
(C) I and II only
(D) I and III only
(E) II and III only

19. It can be inferred that prior to 1950, for a historian to choose to specialize in black history

(A) was encouraged by the academic establishment
(B) established his academic conventionality
(C) afforded him special opportunities for publication
(D) was detrimental to his professional career
(E) enhanced his contact with his colleagues

Antonyms

20. DESTITUTION:
(A) civilization
(B) recompense
(C) affluence
(D) reformation
(E) parsimony

21. COGNIZANCE:
(A) ignobility
(B) disbelief
(C) impotence
(D) illegality
(E) unawareness

Reading Comprehension
(This passage was written prior to 1950)

We now know that what constitutes practically all of matter is empty space; relatively enormous voids in which revolve with lightning velocity
Line infinitesimal particles so utterly small that they
(5) have never been seen or photographed. The existence of these particles has been demonstrated by mathematical physicists and their operations determined by ingenious laboratory experiments. It was not until 1911 that experiments by Sir
(10) Ernest Rutherford revealed the architecture of the mysterious atom. Moseley, Bohr, Fermi, Millikan, Compton, Urey, and others have also worked on the problem.

Matter is composed of molecules whose aver-
(15) age diameter is about 1/125 millionth of an inch. Molecules are composed of atoms so small that about 5 million could be placed in a row on the period at the end of this sentence. Long thought to be the ultimate, indivisible constituent of mat-
(20) ter, the atom has been found to consist roughly of a proton, the positive electrical element in the atomic nucleus, surrounded by electrons, the negative electric elements swirling about the proton.

22. According to the passage, all of the following were true of the center of the atom EXCEPT that it

(A) had not yet been seen by the naked eye
(B) contained elements that were positively charged
(C) was very little larger than a molecule
(D) followed experimentally determinable processes
(E) was smaller than 1/125 millionth of an inch

23. By referring to the period at the end of the sentence (lines 16–18), the author intends to point up the atom's

(A) density
(B) mystery
(C) velocity
(D) consistency
(E) minuteness

24. Which of the following relationships most closely parallels the relationship between the proton and the electrons described in the passage?

(A) A hawk to its prey
(B) A blueprint to a framework
(C) A planet to its satellites
(D) A magnet to iron filings
(E) A compound to its elements

Analogies

25. GIBBER : SENSE ::
(A) jabber : noise
(B) toddle : mobility
(C) dawdle : deference
(D) vacillate : resolution
(E) disobey : order

1

1

26. UPROARIOUS : AMUSING ::
    (A) treacherous : steadfast
    (B) tumultuous : windy
    (C) menacing : aghast
    (D) repugnant : disagreeable
    (E) devious : clever

Sentence Completion

27. To a person _____ natural history, his country or seaside stroll is a walk through a gallery filled with wonderful works of art, nine-tenths of which have their faces turned to the wall.

    (A) enamored of
    (B) uninstructed in
    (C) responsive to
    (D) disillusioned with
    (E) dependent on

28. A _____ of recent cases of scientific fraud in which gross errors of fact and logic have slipped past the review panels that scrutinize submissions to journals suggests that the review system is seriously _____.

    (A) plethora...intended
    (B) lack...strained
    (C) dearth...compromised
    (D) spate...taxed
    (E) preponderance...substantiated

Antonyms

29. PRECIPITATE:
    (A) intricate
    (B) devious
    (C) posthumous
    (D) dilatory
    (E) contradictory

30. TORTUOUS:
    (A) merciful
    (B) direct
    (C) dangerous
    (D) legal
    (E) tawdry

2   2

Column A	Column B

$$a = -2$$

1. $a^4 - a^3 + a^2 - a$ $a - a^2 + a^3 - a^4$

---

a and b are primes
$a + b = 12$

2. b 8

Column A	Column B

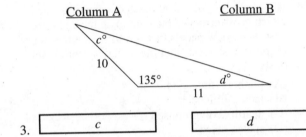

3. c d

On a test $\dfrac{4}{7}$ of the boys and $\dfrac{7}{11}$ of the girls earned over 90.

4. The number of students receiving grades over 90   The number of students receiving grades of 90 or less

---

Directions: In the following questions, choose the best answer from the five choices listed.

5. What is the measure of the angle formed by the minute and hour hands of a clock at 1:50?

(A) 90°   (B) 95°   (C) 105°   (D) 115°   (E) 120°

6. Which of the following CANNOT be expressed as the sum of three consecutive integers?

(A) 18   (B) 24   (C) 28   (D) 33   (E) 36

7. Sandrine is now 5 times as old as Nicholas, but 7 years from now, she will be 3 times as old as he will be then. How old is Sandrine now?

(A) 15   (B) 20   (C) 21   (D) 25   (E) 35

2   **2**

Column A	Column B

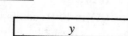

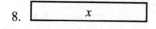

8. | x | y |

$ab = 48$

9. | $a + b$ | 50 |

---

10. If $3^a = b$ and $3^c = d$, then $bd =$
(A) 3^{ac} (B) 3^{a+c} (C) 6^{a+c} (D) 9^{ac} (E) 9^{a+c}

Column A	Column B

At XYZ Corp. the ratio of the number of male employees to the number of female employees is 3:2.
20% of the male and 30% of the females employees attended the company picnic.

11. | The number of males at the picnic | The number of females at the picnic |

At Central High School 50 girls play intramural basketball, 40 girls play intramural volleyball, and 10 girls play both sports.

12. | The ratio of the number of girls who play only basketball to the number who play only volleyball | $\dfrac{4}{3}$ |

$ab \neq 0$

13. | $(a + b)^2$ | $(a - b)^2$ |

Questions 14–15 refer to the following graph.

Percentage of students who reported using a computer

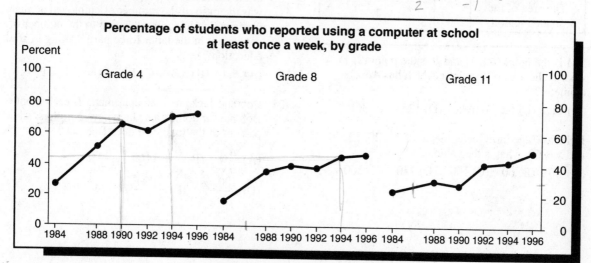

SOURCE: U.S. Department of Education.

14. If every student who was in the eleventh grade in 1996 and who used a computer in school at least once a week used a computer at least once a week in 1997, and if 20% of those students who were in the eleventh grade in 1996 and who did *not* use a computer in school at least once a week, did use a computer in school once a week in 1997, then what percent of twelfth-graders in 1997 used a computer in school at least once a week?
(A) 40%   (B) 50%   (C) 60%   (D) 70%
(E) 80%

15. Assume that in 1990 there were 3,000,000 fourth-graders in the United States. How many fewer of those 3,000,000 students used a computer in school at least once a week in 1994 than in 1990?

(A) 100,000   (B) 250,000   (C) 500,000
(D) 600,000   (E) 750,000

Column A   Column B

The measures of the angles in $\triangle$I are in the ratio of 1:2:3
The measures of the angles in $\triangle$II are in the ratio of 2:7:9

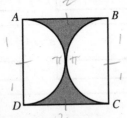

The measure of the largest angle of $\triangle$I	The measure of the largest angle of $\triangle$II

16.

The shaded region above is bounded by two semicircles and two sides of square $ABCD$. The perimeter of the shaded region is $4 + 2\pi$.

The area of the shaded region	1

17.

18. If A is the point $(-4, 1)$ and B is the point $(2, 1)$, what is the area of the circle which has AB as a diameter?

(A) 3π (B) 6π (C) 9π (D) 12π (E) 36π

19. If the average (arithmetic mean) of 10, 20, 30, 40, and x is 60, what is the value of x?

(A) 50   (B) 60   (C) 100   (D) 150   (E) 200

Questions 20 and 21: See the graphs on the following page for information to answer the questions.

20. Each of the following is a valid conclusion from the graphs and the fact that the population of the United States was greater in 1995 than in 1991 EXCEPT

(A) In 1991, adults whose highest degree was at least a bachelor's degree were more than twice as likely to participate in adult education than those whose highest educational attainment was a high school diploma or GED (high school equivalency diploma).
(B) On a percentage basis, from 1991 to 1995, the greatest increase in the adult education participation rate was among those adults whose highest educational attainment was grades 9–12, without earning a high school diploma.
(C) In 1995, more people participated in adult education programs than in 1991.
(D) From 1991 to 1995 the rate of participation in adult education among the groups represented in the graphs increased the least for those who had attained at least a bachelor's degree.
(E) In 1995, more adults with at least a bachelor's degree participated in adult education than did adults who attended some college but did not earn a college degree.

21. If in the United States in 1995, there were 50 million employed adults and 20 million adults not in the the labor force, then approximately what was the ratio of the number of employed adults participating in adult education to the number of people not in the labor force participating in adult education?

(A) 5:4   (B) 5:2   (C) 10:3   (D) 5:1   (E) 6:1

22. Bob and Jack share an apartment. If each month Bob pays a dollars and Jack pays b dollars, what percent of the total cost does Bob pay?

(A) $\dfrac{a}{b}\%$ (B) $\dfrac{b}{a}\%$ (C) $\dfrac{a}{a+b}\%$
(D) $\dfrac{100a}{b}\%$ (E) $\dfrac{100a}{a+b}\%$

2   2

Adult education participation rates in the past 12 months: 1991 and 1995

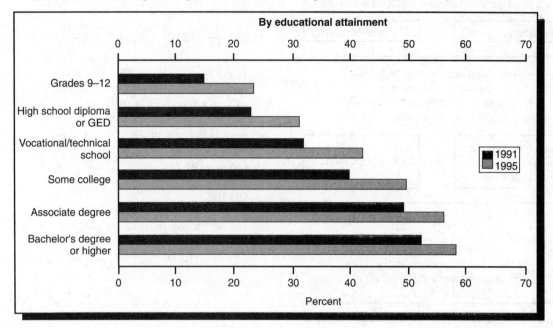

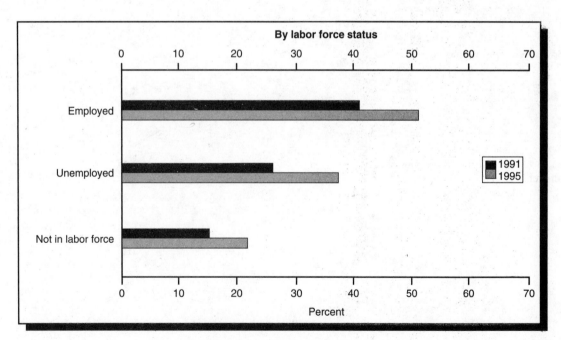

SOURCE: U.S. Department of Education.

2

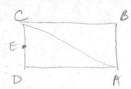

2

Column A	Column B

E is a point on line *CD*, and *ABCD* is a rectangle.

23. The area of △ABC | The area of △ABE

A wooden cube whose edges are
3 inches is painted red.
The cube is then cut into 27 cubes whose
edges are 1 inch.

24. The total surface
area of all of the
unpainted faces | 100 square inches

$$AB$$
$$+CD$$
$$\overline{AAA}$$

In the addtion problem above, each
letter represents a different digit.

25. A + C | B + D

26. If *a* is increased by 10% and *b* is decreased by
10%, the resulting numbers will be equal. What is
the ratio of *a* to *b*?

(A) $\dfrac{9}{11}$ (B) $\dfrac{9}{10}$ (C) $\dfrac{1}{1}$ (D) $\dfrac{10}{9}$ (E) $\dfrac{11}{9}$

27. In the figure at the right,
the legs of right triangle
ACB are diameters of the
two semicircles. If *AB* = 4,
what is the sum of the
areas of the semicircles?

(A) π   (B) 2π
(C) 4π   (D) 8π
(E) 16π

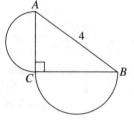

28. For how many positive integers *m* ≤ 100 is
(*m* − 5)(*m* − 45) positive?

(A) 45   (B) 50   (C) 58   (D) 59   (E) 60

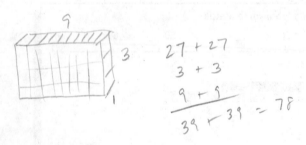

27 + 27
3 + 3
9 + 9
_____
39 + 39 = 78

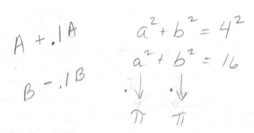

A + .1A $a^2 + b^2 = 4^2$

B − .1B $a^2 + b^2 = 16$

.↓   .↓

π   π

A + .1A = B − .1B

9   11

$A = \pi r^2$

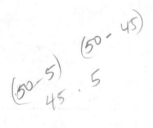

(50−5) (50−45)

45 . 5

3

3

Time—75 Minutes
2 Writing Tasks

Task 1: Issue Exploration
45 Minutes

<u>Directions</u>: In 45 minutes, choose one of the two following topics and compose an essay on that topic. You may not write on any other topic. Write your essay on separate sheets of paper.

Each topic is presented in a one- to two-sentence quotation commenting on an issue of general concern. Your essay may support, refute, or qualify the views expressed in the quotation. Whatever you write, however, must be relevant to the issue under discussion, and you must support your viewpoint with reasons and examples derived from your studies and/or experience.

Before you choose a topic, read both topics carefully. Consider which topic would give you greater scope for writing an effective, well-argued essay.

Faculty members from various institutions will evaluate your essay, judging it on the basis of your skill in the following areas.

- Analysis of the quotation's implications
- Organization and articulation of your ideas
- Use of relevant examples and arguments to support your case
- Handling of the mechanics of standard written English

Once you have decided which topic you prefer, click on the appropriate icon (**Topic 1** or **Topic 2**) to confirm your choice. Do not be hasty confirming your choice of topic. Once you have clicked on a topic, you will not be able to switch to the alternate choice.

Topic 1

"Originality does not consist in saying what no one has ever said before but in saying exactly what you think yourself." (James Stephen)

Topic 2

"We laugh at the naiveté of celebrities who complain about the public's fascination with the intimate details of their lives. Movie and television stars, pop singers, politicians—public figures all—should necessarily understand that the inevitable price of becoming a public figure is the loss of privacy."

Task 2: Argument Analysis
30 Minutes

<u>Directions</u>: In 30 minutes, prepare a critical analysis of an argument expressed in a short paragraph. You may not offer an analysis of any other argument. Write your answer on separate sheets of paper.

As you critique the argument, think about the author's underlying assumptions. Ask yourself whether any of them are questionable. Also evaluate any evidence the author brings up. Ask yourself whether it actually supports the author's conclusion.

In your analysis, you may suggest additional kinds of evidence to reinforce the author's argument. You may also suggest methods to refute the argument, or additional data that might be useful to you as you assess the soundness of the argument. *You may **not**, however, present your personal views on the topic.* Your job is to analyze the elements of an argument, not to support or contradict that argument.

Faculty members from various institutions will judge your essay, assessing it on the basis of your skill in the following areas:

- Identification and assessment of the argument's main elements
- Organization and articulation of your thoughts
- Use of relevant examples and arguments to support your case
- Handling of the mechanics of standard written English

The following advice, written by a childbirth instructor, appeared in an informational brochure for parents-to-be.

Statistics demonstrate that Caesarean births are dangerous for women. Women are three times more likely to suffer fatal complications when giving birth by Caesarean section than they are when giving birth naturally, without painkillers and labor-promoting drugs. When choosing a hospital, it is important that parents select one that does not encourage unnecessary Caesarean deliveries. Locally, I recommend Samaritan Hospital, because its rate of Caesarean delivery is less than two-thirds that of County General, which specializes in emergencies and high-risk cases.

Answer Key

Section 1—Verbal Ability

1. **D**	6. **E**	11. **C**	16. **C**	21. **E**	26. **D**
2. **B**	7. **E**	12. **E**	17. **C**	22. **C**	27. **B**
3. **C**	8. **D**	13. **B**	18. **D**	23. **E**	28. **D**
4. **D**	9. **D**	14. **B**	19. **D**	24. **C**	29. **D**
5. **B**	10. **E**	15. **D**	20. **C**	25. **D**	30. **B**

Section 2—Quantitative Ability

NOTE: The letters in brackets following the Quantitative Ability answers refer to the sections of Chapter 14 in which you can find the information you need to answer the questions. For example, 1. C [E] means that the answer to question 1 is C, and that the solution requires information found in Section 14-E: Averages. Also, 20. A [13] means that the answer to question 20 is based on information in Chapter 13: Data Interpretation.

1. **A [A]**	6. **C [A]**	11. **C [C,D]**	16. **C [D,J]**	21. **E [13]**	26. **A [C,D]**
2. **B [A]**	7. **E [H]**	12. **C [D]**	17. **B [K,L]**	22. **E [C]**	27. **B [J,L]**
3. **A [J]**	8. **D [J]**	13. **D [F]**	18. **C [L,N]**	23. **C [J,K]**	28. **D [O]**
4. **A [B]**	9. **D [A]**	14. **C [13]**	19. **E [E]**	24. **A [M]**	
5. **D [I]**	10. **B [A]**	15. **E [13]**	20. **E [13]**	25. **B [A]**	

Section 3—Analytical Writing

There are no "correct answers" to this section.

Answer Explanations

Section 1—Verbal Ability

1. **D.** The opposite of *pandemonium* or tumultuous uproar is *tranquillity* or calm.
   Word Parts Clue: *Pan-* means all; *demon-* means evil spirit. Hell or *Pandemonium*, the place where all the evil spirits dwell, is a place of noise and uproar.
   Think of "pandemonium breaking loose."

2. **B.** To *enervate* (weaken or enfeeble) is the opposite of to *stimulate* or energize.
   Think of being "enervated by the heat."

3. **C.** Rather than being *barren* or devoid of life, the vent regions are like *oases* that support life.
   Choice A is incorrect. A *waste* by definition is not *teeming* but *barren*.
   Choice B is incorrect. The vent region would not be described as an *enclave* (tract enclosed within a foreign territory).

Choice D is incorrect. A *grotto* would not be described as island-like.
Choice E is incorrect. Nothing in the sentence justifies the use of the term *hazardous*.

4. **D.** Instead of allowing the exchanges to develop fully, the playwright cuts short or *truncates* them.

5. **B.** A *glint* is a small gleam of *light*. A *whiff* is a slight puff of *scent*.   (Degree of Intensity)

6. **E.** *Doggerel* is trivial or inferior verse produced by a *poet*. A *potboiler* is a trivial or inferior literary work produced by a *novelist*.
                (Defining Characteristic)

7. **E.** The author never mentions *simplicity of language* as a characteristic of romanticism.
   Choice A is incorrect. The passage refers to a "continued faith in nature" as one aspect of Goethe's romanticism.
   Choice B is incorrect. The passage refers to impulsiveness or *spontaneity* as savoring strongly of romantic individualism.

Choice C is incorrect. Since romanticism has *formed* so many modern attitudes, one finds in romanticism ideas that seem noteworthy for their modernity.
Choice D is incorrect. The passage refers to "a disregard of artistic or logical propriety" as characteristic of romanticism.

8. **D.** You can arrive at the correct answer by the process of elimination.
Sensitivity towards emotional promptings is characteristic of romanticism; it is an unlikely characteristic of classicism. Therefore, you can eliminate Choices C and E.
Emphasis on formal aesthetic criteria is a likely characteristic of classicism. The passage talks of the formal beauty that distinguishes the classical works of Dante and Virgil. Therefore, you can eliminate Choice B.
Meticulous planning of artistic works is a likely characteristic of classicism. The passage talks of the carefully planned compositions of the classicist Dante; it also tells of the structurally flawed compositions of the romantic Goethe. Therefore, you can eliminate Choice A.
Only Choice D is left. It is the correct answer.

9. **D.** The author both admires Goethe's writings and notes their flaws; his attitude is one of *measured admiration*.

10. **E.** The opposite of *nebulous* (vague, cloudy) is *distinct*.
Think of "a nebulous memory."

11. **C.** The opposite of *decorum* (correctness, good taste) is *impropriety* or unseemliness.
Think of "dignity and decorum."

12. **E.** The opposite of to *denigrate* (belittle or defame) is to *extol* or praise.
Think of "denigrating someone's efforts."

13. **B.** If neutron stars are the remnants or remaining traces of exploding stars, then they are the *products* or results of *violent* natural processes.
Choice A is incorrect. The neutron stars did not cause the explosions; they were *caused by* the explosions.
Choice C is incorrect. There is nothing *equivocal* or inconclusive about the explosion of a star.
Choice D is incorrect. Nothing in the statement suggests that the creation of neutron stars *justifies* or vindicates the explosion of a star. In addition, *harsh* is far too weak a word to describe a stellar explosion.
Choice E is incorrect. Neutron stars come into existence after a supernova explodes. Thus, they are not *precursors* or forerunners of the explosion.

14. **B.** *Clarity* in explaining complicated financial matters would do a great deal to *offset* or compensate for shortcomings in a text.
Note the use of *and* linking the positive phrase "sheer importance of his text" with the second blank. This indicates that the second missing word must be a positive term.

15. **D.** A *scholar* is by definition *erudite* or learned. A *liar* is by definition *mendacious* or dishonest. Beware answer pairs that are loosely linked. While *travelers* may *meander* (stroll or wander aimlessly), they may equally as well proceed directly to their destination.
(Defining Characteristic)

16. **C.** Something *feral* or wild lacks *domestication* or taming. Something *crude* or rough lacks *refinement* or polish.   (Antonym Variant)

17. **C.** The three men are cited as examples of scholars who were encouraged to resume their earlier researches in black history.
Choices A, B, and E are incorrect. None of the three men were identified in the passage with these concerns.
Choice D is incorrect. Only Logan is identified with research on blacks in nineteenth-century North Carolina.

18. **D.** You can arrive at the correct answer by the process of elimination.
Statement I is supported by the passage. At the time Bennett and Logan wrote, both the pre-*Mayflower* period of black history and the nineteenth-century life of blacks in North Carolina were relatively unexplored. Therefore, you can eliminate Choices B and E.
Statement II is unsupported by the passage. Bennett's work was a popularization intended for a wide general audience. It was not aimed at academics. Therefore, you can eliminate Choice C.
Statement III is supported by the passage. Bennett's work appeared first as a series of magazine articles, then as a book. Logan's work first appeared as a doctoral thesis, then (with revisions) as a book. Therefore, you can eliminate Choice A.
Only Choice D is left. It is the correct answer.

19. **D.** According to the passage, prior to the early 1960s Negro history was not an object of particularly great renown in academe. In the 1950s, the advice given to Blassingame to avoid black history if he desired "a future in the historical profession" seemed wise— graduate students of the caliber of Huggins and Litwack felt an ambivalence about entering the field because of "practical concerns." What these concerns boiled down to was the sense that to choose black history as one's

specialization would be *detrimental* or harmful to one's career.

20. **C.** The opposite of *destitution* (privation; lack of life's necessities) is *affluence* or wealth.
Think of "the poor living in destitution."

21. **E.** The opposite of *cognizance* (conscious knowledge, awareness) is *unawareness*.
Word Parts Clue: *Cogn-* means know. *Cognizance* means knowledge.
Context Clue: "He had no cognizance of the crime."

22. **C.** The passage states that molecules are made of atoms; logically, therefore, an atom is smaller, not larger, than the molecule to which it belongs.
Choice A is incorrect. Line 5 states that atoms "have never been seen or photographed."
Choice B is incorrect. Lines 21–22 mention the presence of positive electric elements.
Choice D is incorrect. Lines 5–8 note the ingenious laboratory experiments that determine its operations or processes.
Choice E is incorrect. Lines 14–15 mention the average diameter of a molecule is 1/125 millionth of an inch. Atoms are smaller yet.

23. **E.** The comparison emphasizes the smallness or *minuteness* of atoms.

24. **C.** The satellites *circle* the planet. The electrons *swirl around* the proton. As depicted, the relationships are comparable.
Choice A is incorrect. A hawk *swoops down* upon its prey. The proton does not swoop down upon the electrons.
Choice B is incorrect. A blueprint is an outline or plan. A framework is a skeletal structure, possibly constructed in accordance with a blueprint. The relationships are not comparable.
Choice D is incorrect. Iron filings are *drawn or attracted* to a magnet. Electrons *swirl around* a proton.
Choice E is incorrect. A compound is *made up* of elements. A proton is not made up of electrons.

25. **D.** To *gibber* (chatter foolishly) is to speak without *sense*. To *vacillate* (waver) is to act without *resolution* (firmness of resolve).
(Antonym Variant)

26. **D.** Something *uproarious* is by definition extremely *amusing*. Something *repugnant* is by definition extremely *disagreeable*.
(Degree of Intensity)

27. **B.** If nine-tenths of the works of art in the gallery have their faces turned to the wall, then the visitor to the gallery has no clue whatsoever to what wonders they contain. Similarly, a person *uninstructed in* natural history wanders through the world with no clue whatsoever to nine-tenths of the natural wonders that surround him.

28. **D.** A *spate* or flood of examples of fraud suggests that the review system intended to catch such frauds is severely *taxed* or burdened.

29. **D.** The opposite of *precipitate* or hasty is *dilatory* or tardy.
Think of "a precipitate departure."

30. **B.** The opposite of *tortuous* or winding is *direct*. Beware eye-catchers. *Tortuous* has nothing to do with *torture*.
Think of "a tortuous mountain road."

Section 2—Quantitative Ability

Two asterisks (**) indicate an alternative method of solving.

1. **A.** Evaluate each column. Column A = 30 and Column B = −30. Column A is greater.

2. **B.** The only primes whose sum is 12 are 5 and 7, both of which are less than 8. Note that 1 + 11 = 12, but 1 is not a prime [KEY FACT A27]. Column B is greater.

3. **A.** In any triangle, if one side is longer than a second side, the angle opposite the longer side is greater than the angle opposite the shorter side [KEY FACT J3], so $c > d$. Column A is greater. (It is irrelevant that the third angle is 135°.)

4. **A.** It makes no difference how many students took the test nor how many were boys and how many were girls. More than half the boys *and* more than half the girls scored over 90, so more than half of all the grades were over 90. Column A is greater.
**Use TACTIC 2, Chapter 12. Assume 7 boys and 11 girls took the exam. Then 11 students (4 boys and 7 girls) got over 90 and the other 7 got 90 or less.

5. **D.** For problems such as this, always draw a diagram.

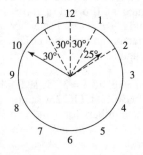

The measure of each of the 12 central angles from one number to the next on the clock is

30°. At 1:50 the minute hand is pointing at 10, and the hour hand has gone $\frac{50}{60} = \frac{5}{6}$ of the way from 1 to 2. Then, from 10 to 1 on the clock is 90°, and from 1 to the hour hand is $\frac{5}{6}(30°) = 25°$, for a total of $90° + 25° = 115°$.

6. **C.** The sum of three consecutive integers can be expressed as

$$n + (n + 1) + (n + 2) = 3n + 3 = 3(n + 1),$$

and so must be a multiple of 3. Only 28, Choice C, is *not* a multiple of 3.
**Quickly add up sets of three consecutive integers: $4 + 5 + 6 = 15$, $5 + 6 + 7 = 18$, $6 + 7 + 8 = 21$, and so on, and see the pattern (they're all multiples of 3); or cross off the choices as you come to them.

7. **E.** Set up a table.

Time	Nicholas	Sandrine
Now	x	$5x$
In 7 years	$x + 7$	$5x + 7$

Then
$5x + 7 = 3(x + 7) \Rightarrow 5x + 7 = 3x + 21 \Rightarrow 2x = 14 \Rightarrow x = 7$.
Sandrine, therefore, is 35.
**Use TACTIC 1, Chapter 11, but since Sandrine is 5 times as old as Nicholas, avoid Choice C, the only answer that is not a multiple of 5. Try Choice B, 20. Then Nicholas is 4. In 7 years, he'll be 11 and Sandrine will be 27, which is less than 3 times as old. Try a larger number: 25 or 35.

8. **D.** Use TACTIC 4, Chapter 12. Could x and y be equal? Yes; the two small triangles could be right triangles, and x and y could each be 40. Must they be equal? No; see the figure at the right, in which x < y. Neither column is *always* greater, and the columns are not *always* equal (D).

9. **D.** If a and b had to be integers, the greatest $a + b$ could is is 49 (when the numbers are 1 and 48). However, the variables do not have to be integers. If $a = .1$, and $b = 480$, then $ab = 48$, and $a + b = 480.1$. Neither column is always greater, and the two columns are not always equal (D).

10. **B.** $bd = (3^a)(3^c) = 3^{a + c}$. [KEY FACT A16]
**Use TACTIC 2, Chapter 11. Pick easy-to-use numbers for a and c; $a = 1$ and $c = 2$, for

example. Then, $b = 3^1 = 3$ and $d = 3^2 = 9$, so $bd = 27$. Check the choices. Only $3^{a + c}$ works.

11. **C.** Let the number of male and female employees be $3x$ and $2x$, respectively. Then Column A $= 20\%(3x) = .6x$ and Column B $= 30\%(2x) = .6x$. The columns are equal.
**Do the same thing, except use a number. Assume there are 300 men and 200 women and calculate.

12. **C.** Mentally, or by using a Venn diagram,

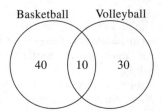

determine the number of girls who play only one sport. 40 play only basketball and 30 play only volleyball. The ratio is $40:30 = \frac{4}{3}$. The columns are equal (C).

13. **D.** Since $ab \neq 0$, neither a nor b is 0 [KEY FACT A3]. If a and b are each 1, then Column A = 4, and Column B = 0; if, however, $a = 1$ and $b = -1$, then Column A = 0 and Column B = 4. Neither column is always greater, and the two columns are not always equal (D).
**Column A $= a^2 + 2ab + b^2$.
Column B $= a^2 - 2ab + b^2$.
After subtracting $a^2 + b^2$ from each column, we have to compare $2ab$ and $-2ab$: either one could be positive and the other negative.

14. **C.** In 1996, 50% of eleventh-graders used computers in school at least once a week, and 50% did not. Of the 50% that did not use computers in school at least once a week, 20% of them did use them the following year: 20% of 50% $= .20 \times .50 = .10 = 10\%$. So, in 1997, 60% (50% + 10%) of the twelfth-graders used computers in school at least once a week.

15. **E.** Of the 3,000,000 fourth-graders in 1990, approximately 70%, or 2,100,000, of them used a computer in school at least once a week. Four years later, in 1994, those 3,000,000 were eighth-graders, and 45%, or 1,350,000, of them used a computer in school at least once a week. This is a difference of $2,100,000 - 1,350,000 = 750,000$.

16. **C.** In each triangle the largest angle is the sum of the two smaller ones ($3 = 1 + 2$ and $9 = 2 + 7$), so each is a 90° angle. The columns are equal (C).
    Use TACTIC D2: In ratio problems, write x after each number and solve.
    Column A: $x + 2x + 3x = 180 \Rightarrow 6x = 180 \Rightarrow x = 30 \Rightarrow 3x = 90$.
    Column B: $2x + 7x + 9x = 180 \Rightarrow 18x = 180 \Rightarrow x = 10 \Rightarrow 9x = 90$.

17. **B.** The perimeter of the shaded region is given as $4 + 2\pi$. You can easily prove that the lengths of the curved parts of the region are 2π and that the straight edges have a total length of 4, but you should just assume these values. Then each side of the square is 2, and its area is 4. From that subtract π, the area of a circle (two semicircles) of radius 1.

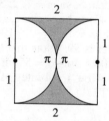

    Since π is slightly greater than 3, then $4 - \pi$ is less than 1. Column B is greater.

18. **C.** Use TACTIC 1, Chapter 10. Draw a diagram. Since the distance between $(-4,1)$ and $(2,1)$ is 6, the diameter of the circle is 6 and the radius is 3. Then the area is $\pi(3)^2 = 9\pi$.

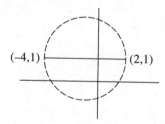

19. **E.** By TACTIC E1, if the average of 5 numbers is 60, their sum is $5 \times 60 = 300$. The 4 given numbers add up to 100 ($10 + 20 + 30 + 40$), so the fifth one, x, is 200 ($300 - 100$).
    Use TACTIC 1, Chapter 11. Test the choices, starting with 100. The average of 10, 20, 30, 40, and 100 is 40. That's too small. Eliminate Choices A, B, and C, and try a larger number—150 or 200: 200 works.

20. **A.** Each of the given statements is true except Choice A.
    (A) In 1991, more than 50% of the adults whose highest degree was at least a bachelor's degree participated in adult education, whereas among those whose highest educational attainment was a high school diploma or GED (high school equivalency diploma) fewer than 25% participated.

(B) From 1991 to 1995, among those adults whose highest educational attainment was grades 9–12, without earning a high school diploma, the rate of participation in adult education increased from about 15% to 23%, an increase of about 50%. None of the other groups had nearly that great an increase.
(C) Since the population of the country grew between 1991 and 1995, and the rate of participation in adult education programs increased in every category, the total number of people participating had to increase.
(D) From 1991 to 1995 the rate of participation in adult education for those who had attained at least a bachelor's degree increased from about 52% to 58%, the least increase of any group on *both* an absolute and percent basis.
(E) Without knowing how many adults have earned a college degree and how many have attended some college without earning a college degree, it is impossible to make this conclusion. For example, 50% of 100,000,000 is much more than 58% of 50,000,000.

21. **E.** 50% of $50,000,000 = 25,000,000$;
    20% of $20,000,000 = 4,000,000$.
    $25,000,000:4,000,000 = 25:4 = 6.25:1$.

22. **E.** The total rent is $a + b$, so Bob's fractional share is $\dfrac{a}{a + b}$. To convert to a percent, simply multiply by 100%: $\dfrac{100a}{a + b}\%$.
    Use TACTIC 2, Chapter 11. Pick two easy-to-use numbers. If Bob pays \$1 and Jack pays \$2, then Bob pays $\dfrac{1}{3}$ or $33\dfrac{1}{3}\%$ of the rent.
    Only $\dfrac{100a}{a + b}\%$ is equal to $33\dfrac{1}{3}\%$ when $a = 1$ and $b = 2$.

23. **C.** Draw diagrams. The triangles in the two columns have the same base, AB, and the same height, BC, the distance between the two parallel sides. The areas of $\triangle ABC$ and $\triangle ABE$ are equal. The columns are equal (C).

24. **A.** The area of each face of the large red cube is $(3)^2 = 9$. Therefore, the total surface area is $6 \times 9 = 54$. The surface area of each small cube is $6(1)^2 = 6$. So, the total surface area of the 27 small cubes is $27 \times 6 = 162$. Of the 162 small faces, 54 are painted red and $162 - 54 = 108$ are unpainted. Column A is greater.

25. **B.**   Since the sum of two two-digit numbers must be less than 200, A has to be 1, and the sum is 111. Therefore, $B + D$, the quantity in column B, is 11, whereas $A + C$, the quantity in Column A, is 10 (which when added to the 1 that was carried from the units digit gives 11). Column B is greater.

26. **A.** $a + 10\%(a) = a + .1a = 1.1a$. Also, $b - 10\%(b) = b - .1b = .9b$. Then, $1.1a = .9b$, and $\dfrac{a}{b} = \dfrac{.9}{1.1} = \dfrac{9}{11}$

   **If after increasing a and decreasing b the results are equal, a must be smaller than b. So, *the ratio of a to b must be less than 1.* Eliminate Choices C, D, and E. Now, either test Choices A and B or just guess. To test B, pick 2 numbers in the ratio of 9 to 10—90 and 100, for example: 90 increased by 10% is 99. 100 decreased by 10% is 90. They're not equal. Eliminate Choice B. The answer is Choice A. (110 decreased by 10% *is* 99.)

27. **B.**   Let x and y be the radii of the two semicircles.

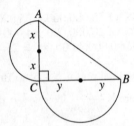

Then the legs of right triangle ACB are $2x$ and $2y$, and by the Pythagorean theorem $(2x)^2 + (2y)^2 = 4^2$. Then $4x^2 + 4y^2 = 16$, and $x^2 + y^2 = 4$. Since the area of a semicircle of radius r is $\dfrac{1}{2}\pi r^2$, the sum of the areas of the semicircles is

$$\frac{1}{2}\pi x^2 + \frac{1}{2}\pi y^2 = \frac{1}{2}\pi(x^2 + y^2) = \frac{1}{2}\pi(4) = 2\pi.$$

   **Use TACTIC 2, Chapter 11. Pick numbers a and b for the legs of the triangle. For example, if a is 2, then by the Pythagorean theorem $2^2 + b^2 = 4^2$.

28. **D.**   For $(m - 5)(m - 45)$ to be positive, either both factors are positive or both factors are negative. For $(m - 5)$ to be negative, m must be less than 5, so $m = 1, 2, 3,$ or 4 (4 values). For $(m - 45)$ to be positive, m must greater than 45, so $m = 46, 47, \ldots, 100$ (55 values). The answer is **59**. [Note that from 46 to 100 there are $100 - 46 + 1 = 55$ integers, just as there are $4 - 1 + 1 = 4$ integers from 1 to 4 (KEY FACT O1).]

Section 3—Analytical Writing

There are no "correct answers" to this section.

Index

Notes

Notes

Notes

Notes

Notes

Notes

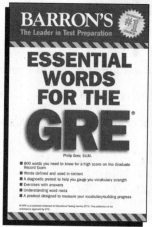

The following documentation applies if you purchased
GRE, 17th Edition book with CD-ROM.
Please disregard this information if your version does not contain the CD-ROM.

Documentation

MINIMUM HARDWARD REQUIREMENTS

The program will run on a PC with
1. Pentium II or higher recommended
2. 128 MB or more of installed RAM
3. Windows 98, ME, NT4, 2000, XP, Vista
4. SVGA (256 Colors) Monitor
5. 8X CD-ROM drive
6. Keyboard, Mouse

The program will run on a Macintosh with
1. Power Macintosh Power PC processor
   (G3 or higher recommended)
2. 128 MB or more of installed RAM
3. Mac OS® 8.6 to Mac OS® X 10.4
   (Intel Macs run via Rosetta)
4. SVGA (256 Colors) Monitor
5. 8X CD-ROM drive
6. Keyboard, Mouse

Barron's GRE CD-ROM includes an "autorun" feature that automatically launches the application when the CD is inserted into the CD drive. In the unlikely event that the autorun features are disabled, alternate launching instructions are provided below.

Windows 98/NT/2000:

1. Put the Barron's GRE CD-ROM into the CD-ROM drive.
2. Click on the Start button and choose Run.
3. Type D:\GRE.EXE (assuming the CD is in drive D), then click OK.

Macintosh:

1. Put the Barron's GRE CD-ROM into the CD-ROM drive.
2. Double-click the GRE Installer icon.
3. Follow the onscreen instructions.